P9-CQI-244

LINCOLN CHRISTIAN COLLEGE AND SEMINARY

THE PREACHER'S
COMPLETE HOMILETIC
COMMENTARY
ON THE BOOKS OF THE BIBLE

WITH CRITICAL AND EXPLANATORY NOTES,
INDEXES, ETC., BY VARIOUS AUTHORS

The Preacher's Complete Homiletic

COMMENTARY

ON THE EPISTLE OF ST. PAUL THE APOSTLE TO THE

Romans

By the REV. W. BURROWS, M.A.
Author of the Commentary on Esther

BAKER BOOK HOUSE
Grand Rapids, Michigan

Reprinted 1980 by
Baker Book House

ISBN: 0-8010-6962-9
(Thirty-one Volume Set)

PHOTOLITHOPRINTED BY CUSHING - MALLOY, INC.
ANN ARBOR, MICHIGAN, UNITED STATES OF AMERICA

THE
PREACHER'S HOMILETICAL COMMENTARY

ROMANS

—◆—

INTRODUCTION

We are asked, What! another commentary on the Epistle to the Romans?
and we reply, Yes; for there may be more light and truth to break forth from
this portion of God's word; and the commentary of this series is on different
lines from any that have been previously attempted. But our greatest opponent
is M. Renan. As we read the following extract we wonder how such a character
as St. Paul has dominated religious thought to so large an extent : "What was
Paul ? He was not a saint. The dominating feature of his character is not goodness. He was proud, unbending, unsociable ; he defends himself—self-assertive
(as we say to-day) ; he uses harsh words ; he believes himself right ; he holds to
his opinions ; he quarrels with various people. He was not a scholar ; one can
even say that he has injured science by his paradoxical contempt of reason, by
his eulogy of apparent folly, by his apotheosis of transcendental absurdity.
Neither was he a poet. His writings, works of the highest originality, are
without charm ; the form is harsh and almost devoid of grace." We do not
know what Renan's conception of goodness may be, but he says "the ideal type
of moral perfection, according to Paul, is a man gentle, honest, chaste, sober,
charitable, unfettered by riches" ; and Paul was a living exemplification of his
own ideal. As we read of Paul's zeal for the salvation of souls, of his love for
humanity, of his self-sacrifice in the promotion of every good cause, we should
say that goodness was the dominating feature of his character. In fact, we
always consider Paul as coming nearest to the divine model. But Renan

1

7888

confuses. In the passage just quoted, for instance, we are told that "Paul's writings are without charm"; while in another place we read, " Paul then wrote this admirable passage, the only one in all Christian literature which can be compared to the discourses of Jesus." How Renan can read the striking episode on love (charity) and declare that Paul was not a poet we fail to understand. But he becomes even more startling when he declares that " it is necessary to put Paul on a lower plane than Francis Assisi and the author of *The Imitation.* . . . After having been for three hundred * years the Christian doctor in an eminent degree, Paul seems nowadays near the end of his reign; Jesus, on the contrary, is more living than ever. It is no more the Epistle to the Romans which is the recapitulation of Christianity; it is the Sermon on the Mount. True Christianity, which will last eternally, comes from the gospels, not from the epistles of St. Paul. The writings of Paul have been a danger and a stumbling-block, the cause of the chief faults of Christian theology. Paul is the father of the subtle Augustine, of the arid Thomas Aquinas, of the sober Calvinist, of the bitter Jansenist, of the ferocious theology which condemns and predestinates to damnation. Jesus is the father of all those who seek in dreams of the ideal the repose of their souls." This last sentence brings before our minds the fact that Renan begins and ends by saying that no man was ever so magnificent a saint as Jesus Christ; and yet almost in the same breath he calls Him a vile impostor, and brings charges against Him of a tendency at least to immorality for which there is not the slightest foundation. Surely Renan's absurdity cannot shake the faith of centuries. Calvinism in modern days is rejected; but we must not forget that wisest men have been its adherents. It is no disgrace to be the father of Augustine, Aquinas, and Jonathan Edwards—the greatest of modern philosophical divines. And having still faith in the Epistle to the Romans, we may prosecute our work. Our adhesion to St. Paul and his epistle is warranted by the views of noblest men. Longinus, one of the most celebrated critics of heathen Rome, ranks Paul with the first orators of ancient times. We may pass to more modern times. Meyer says: "Amidst the circumstances of his (Paul's) apostolic work he developed a force and play of spirit, a cogency of thought, a purity and firmness of purpose, an intensity of feeling, a holy audacity of effort, a wisdom of deportment, a precision and delicacy of practical skill, a strength and liberty of faith, a fire and mastery of eloquence, a heroism in danger, a love and self-forgetfulness, which have secured for this chosen implement of Christ the reverence of all time." Dr. McCleod affirms: " Never did there live a nobler spirit than St. Paul. He has made the world grander by his very existence in it. He is one of our greatest kings, ruling the hearts of men; one of our greatest teachers; one of our high priests, who has offered unto God the sacrifice of a holy life and of a thankful spirit of prayer and praise." Monod writes as follows: " Imagine the world without St. Paul: it would mean the detention of the gospel, perhaps for centuries, on the borders of Asia, far from this Europe of ours, which Paul (after Jesus Christ) has made the centre of the conversion and civilisation of the world. Imagine the Bible without St. Paul: it would mean Christian truth one half

---

* We suppose Renan to refer to the Reformation, when Paul's doctrine of justification began to influence the Church.

revealed, Christian life only half understood, Christian charity only half known, Christian faith only half victorious." Coleridge once described this Epistle to the Romans as the profoundest book in existence; and a Frenchman of our time, looking at its massiveness and majesty on the one hand and at the finish and beauty of its details on the other, speaks of it as the cathedral of the Christian faith.

The Epistle to the Romans was written by St. Paul, either at the end of the year 57 or at the beginning of the year 58. It may be safe to assign the date to the spring of the latter year. It was written after some of the other epistles, but has in our Bible the position of precedence. However, the epistles are not arranged according to the order of the time in which they were written. Their order has been determined by the importance of the societies or persons to whom they were addressed. The arrangement was of rapid growth, and arose, as some assert, out of the intuitive feeling of the early Church. Let us, however, not rest satisfied with the suggestion of intuitive feeling. The arrangement is confessedly excellent, and speaks of the wisdom of the fathers of the Church who were directed by divine wisdom. If we desire a proof of the inspiration of the New Testament, we may point to the admirable order and wise systematic arrangement of the books of which it is composed. It is fitting that this epistle should stand in the forefront of St. Paul's compositions, since it was addressed to the Church situated in the metropolis of the then known world. There were collected different nationalities. From this centre of martial power and intellectual light and leading radiated many different influences. Surely not without satisfactory reason was this epistle—written on the relation of Jew and Gentile, unfolding the true doctrine of justification by faith, vindicating the ways of God with man, and enforcing lessons of wise tolerance for all time—placed in the forefront of all the sacred epistles.

The epistle may be divided into four main parts, with many subdivisions which need not now be enumerated:—Part I., the INTRODUCTION, contained in the first fifteen verses of the first chapter; Part II., the DOCTRINAL PART of the epistle, concerning JUSTIFICATION, continues thence to the end of chap. xi.; Part III. comprises the HORTATORY OR PRACTICAL PART of the epistle; Part IV. the CONCLUSION. The epistle was evidently written, not under pressure of anxiety, but in calm deliberation. It was apparently composed in the house of a Corinthian Christian, who is known to us only by the name Gaius or Caius. It was dictated by St. Paul to the amanuensis Tertius. Surely the pen of the writer would be arrested in its course as the mind was caught up by the glowing periods of the eighth chapter. What a light, what a far-away look, would be on the speaker's face as he thought on fate, free will, foreknowledge absolute! The precious letter was carried by Phœbe to Rome. A woman carried the greatest document of time. It was safe in her hands, for she was in the hands of Omnipotence. It is safe still. St. Paul has had many critics, but no compeers. In what roll of fame is Evanson's name now chronicled? Where shall we look for his monument? We ask the publisher for the work of him who assailed the genuineness of the Epistle

3

to the Romans, and very likely the publisher has not heard the name.   Time has sadly overcome the fame of Evanson, while JUST TIME has gladly increased the fame of our apostle.   He still lives as an influential power.   One St. Paul is sufficient to glorify a race.   One Epistle to the Romans is adequate to ennoble all literature.   We may approach the work in trembling, and earnestly pray for divine light and guidance as we attempt a homiletical treatment of the immortal treatise.   Our work is well-nigh done, and it is an attempt, after all; still, we unwillingly lay down the pen, and remain deeper and firmer in our admiration of St. Paul, and stronger in our conception of the depth of the riches of the knowledge, wisdom, and mercy of God.   It will be a joy if any study is cheered by rays of heaven's light, if the voice of the pulpit is clearer and fuller, if the Church is enriched, by the contribution we make to the well-being of humanity.

CHAPTER I.

CRITICAL NOTES.

Ver. 1. **Paul.**—In Latin Paulus, and equals little. Chosen, perhaps, for humility. Name of illustrious Roman family. Saul among Jews. Afterwards Paul. Very common for Jews to accept a second name of Greek origin bearing resemblance in sound. So Σαῦλος, Παῦλος. **Servant.**—Common word of slaves. Bondmen, in contrast to freemen. Paul claims to be heard as δοῦλος, bondman of Jesus Christ.

Ver. 3. **To the flesh.**—σάρξ denotes a living being in distinction from the dead, which is κρέας. It denotes also body as distinguished from mind (Stuart). **Our Lord.**—Supreme Ruler of the Church.

Ver. 4. **Declared to be the Son of God, etc.**—Endowed with power by sending the Spirit after His resurrection and exaltation.

Ver. 6. **Called of Jesus.**—κλητός refers to the external and internal call. Partakers of Christ by the call.

Ver. 7. **Grace to you and peace, etc.**— εἰρήνη, happiness of every kind; peace with God and man. God first Christ's Father and then ours. Grace and peace are cause and effect.

Ver. 8. **Your faith is spoken of, etc.**—Rome frequented by strangers, and so the faith of the Church easily made known. κόσμω, the beautiful order of the visible world.

Ver. 10. **Making request, if by any means, etc.**—Grotius happily renders: "Si forte Dei voluntas felicitatem mihi indulgeat ad nos remindi." Making request is δεόμενος—a special word for prayer, and implies a sense of need. Lightfoot says "precatio" points to the frame of mind and "rogatio" to the act of solicitation.

Ver. 12.—The apostle here uses wise gentleness without any dissimulation.

Ver. 13. **Some fruit.**—Not personal profit, as Koppe, but spiritual fruit—καρπός—fruit from spiritual seed, fruit from my apostolical labours.

Ver. 16. **The power of God unto salvation.**—In and by the gospel God shows and exerts moral power. The best equivalent for "unto" is "for." It signifies direction. The Greek word used for mental and carnal direction. Gospel, from the old Gothic *guth*, good, and *spillon*, to announce. Either "good spell" or "God's spell."

Ver. 17. **The righteousness of God.**—The justification which God bestows, or that of which He is the author. The state of pardon and acceptance as the result of the mediatorial scheme. δικαιοσύνη, man's perfect moral condition; conformity of conduct in the divine law. It was said, Great is faith, for as the reward of it the shechinah rested on Israel. The **just shall live by faith** was spoken by Habakkuk to encourage the Jews when fainting under the oppression of the Chaldeans.

Ver. 18. **The wrath of God.**—ὀργὴ Θεοῦ, God's displeasure. The phrase is plainly anthropopathic. May express a particular instance of displeasure.

Ver. 19. **That which may be known of God.**—That concerning God which is knowable. St. Basil called the natural world a school of the knowledge of God. God is knowable though still unknowable.

Ver. 20. **The invisible things of Him from the creation.**—Cyril said that the eternity of God is proved from the corruptible nature of the visible world. God's divinity, invisible attributes, manifest from creation. Manifested by the first creation and by consequent processes. Eternal power and supremacy written on nature's works. The word "creation" appears to refer to the act of creation and also to the results of that act.

Ver. 21. **Vain in their imaginations.**—διαλογισμοῖς. Thoughts, reasonings, disputations. The heart in this passage plainly refers to the mind. ἀσύνετος, wanting in foresight.

Vers. 22, 23.—Here begins a dark picture of heathenism, but fully verified from the writings of what has been called the most brilliant age of the most intellectual nations of the world. St. Paul traces man's downward progress. Evolution, but in the wrong direction.

According to the Jewish rabbis, one sin made to follow as the punishment of another. τὴν δόξαν, spoken of God, refers to the divine majesty and glory.

Ver. 25. **Who is blessed for ever.**—These doxologies common in Paul's writings. Jewish rabbis use them. Mohammedans have honoured the custom. Tholuck mentions one Arabic manuscript in the Berlin Library where the expression " God be exalted " is often used.

Ver. 28.—The apostle here states that the heathen voluntarily rejected the knowledge of the true God, which they must have gathered from the book of nature (Olshausen).

Ver. 29.—Inveteracy of all evil and pernicious habits. Finding pleasure in causing and seeing suffering.

Ver. 30. **Backbiters, haters of God.**—ὑβριστάς, ὑπερηφάνους, ἀλαζόνας. Insolent and injurious in acts, proud in thoughts, and boastful in words. Evil speakers in general. Planning more sins.

Ver. 31.—ἀσυνθέτους. Covenant breakers, treacherous. Impious as neglecting the true wisdom, and continuing in sin, heathenism (Robinson).

Ver. 32.—Sentence of God immutably written on the conscience. Approval of and delight in sin in ourselves and others, the highest pitch of wickedness.

MAIN HOMILETICS OF THE PARAGRAPH.—Verse 1.

A glorious inscription.—It is not perhaps too much to say that the most glorious time of the Church's history was the first three hundred years of its existence. Much of the romance and chivalry of Christianity disappeared when the fires of persecution were extinguished, when the stake and the faggot were displaced by the sceptre of authority, when riches instead of poverty became the reward of the Christian profession and it became the pathway to positions of worldly influence. Stirring times were those, and in them appeared the mightiest of the race. A bright galaxy of great men—great in intellect as well as in spiritual power—flourished in the first days of the Christian era. Those were the days of Peter, John, Paul, Barnabas, Ignatius, Polycarp, Irenæus, and many others of whom the world was not worthy,—men who were driven from earth and found a home in heaven ; who were dishonoured in their own time and glorified in after time ; whose writings, sayings, histories, and characters have been both the study and the admiration of the men of profoundest intellect and widest erudition who have followed. Rising high above all these great men, as King Saul, physically, above his fellows, as the mountain peak above adjacent high-lying lands, is the great apostle of the Gentiles. Paul was not great physically ; but he was better, being great both intellectually and spiritually. The greatest merely human hero of Christianity, the noblest man of all time, was "Paul, a servant of Jesus Christ, called to be an apostle, separated unto the gospel of God." Let us consider the inscription and the description which he gives of his own claim to speak with authority.

I. **The human name is changeable, while the spiritual relationship is abiding.**—Many guesses are given as to the reason why the name was changed in this instance. Dr. Wordsworth assigns no less than eight reasons for the change of " Saul" into " Paul." We need not here give them; and some are rather fanciful. We cannot presume to decide where learned men differ. Surely it is a matter of small importance. Authentic history simply records the change of the name. In our days we have had names changed. Some have cast off their surnames and have taken fresh ones in order to increase their worldly goods, or to heighten their worldly position. What will become of earthly names in the spirit world? Are our names left behind on the tombstone where they are inscribed? Is it possible to have distinguishing names amongst the multitude which no man can number? Surely the individuality of the redeemed is not dependent upon the denoting power of a name. The names of Abraham and of Lazarus are mentioned in the parable of the rich man. But this is necessary to the carrying out of the parabolic picture. There must be in

heaven many Abrahams, and many Pauls, and many Peters, by this time.
Perhaps the human names will pass away like other things of earth. Names
change as time advances. Names die because the things or persons denoted
have passed into oblivion; but the spiritual relationship is abiding. Greater
and more permanent than the name "Paul" is the title "servant of Jesus Christ."
A servant,—yea, a slave of Jesus Christ. The bondman of Him who came to
give the highest freedom. A bondman whose price was not silver or gold, but
the precious blood of Christ. A bondman who wears the easy yoke of love
and carries the light burden of devoted service. The slave of Jesus Christ is
free and restful as the child in a mother's arms. This slave will not take any
discharge. He serves on earth, and he serves as a king and a priest in heaven.
It is a spiritual relationship, firm and lasting as the throne of God.

II. **The human name separates, while the spiritual title unites.**—Human
names separate. They are given for this very purpose. The human name Paul
not only denotes a certain physical form, a small stature, sparkling eyes, and
aquiline nose, with Jewish and Grecian type of features; but to us it also
connotes certain mental and moral features. It makes us think of a different
man from St. Peter or St. John. The name Paul so sets off and separates the
apostle of the Gentiles that if any other Paul is mentioned there must be
appended some other name. Our earth names are separating attributes, while
the title "a servant of Jesus Christ" is a uniting term. "A servant of Jesus
Christ"—and thus a brother to all the Lord's followers. We may not be great
either socially or intellectually, but we march in the same noble company with
St. Paul and the other great ones of time, for we are all servants of Jesus Christ.
One touch of nature makes the whole world kin. There is a sweet touch of
spiritual nature which makes the whole family of Christ one. How beautifully
and yet how incidentally St. Paul refers to the uniting force! He seems to say,
I speak not merely as Paul, but as your brother, your fellow-servant to Jesus
Christ.

III. **The human name is an outward mark, while the divine call sets an
inward seal.**—The name brings before us the mental and moral characteristics
of the man simply by reason of the working of the law of association. The
name does not make the manhood. It is the manhood which makes the name.
In itself the name Milton is a mere outward sign and mark. It has no creative
force, and does not work inwardly. It is by what it suggests that we think of
Milton the blind poet, and are led to wonder at the sublimity of his imagination.
The name is an outward mark, while the divine call sets an inward seal. This
call is: 1. *Discriminating.* God had need of Paul, of his learning and his
wisdom, and He called him into His service. 2. *Changing.* Saul and Paul are
the same, and yet so changed by the divine call as to be different. Saul the
persecutor had the same intellect as Paul the writer of this epistle, and yet so
changed that Paul rises above Saul by infinite degrees. God's spiritual changes
amount to new creations. 3. *Elevating.* It was an upward movement when
Saul was called to be an apostle. Elevation of the moral nature is the enlargement and improvement of the mental nature. We are told that the great artist
must be pure in nature and in aim. Only the good man can be the truly
successful orator. Saul would have taken a good place amongst his fellows, but
he would never have risen to the heights of Paul. We cannot be apostles, but
by God's help we can be good, and thus in our measure great.

IV. **A noble life-purpose alone immortalises a human name.**—The men of
one idea are the rulers of the race. Paul was a man of one idea. It was—For
the gospel of God. He believed it with all his heart as the good news from
heaven. He was separated to it as good news for his own soul—good news for a
fallen race. In these days some speak of the gospel as an old-fashioned word,

but such words are the most influential. The old gospel is ever new. Paul would have gloried in the gospel had he lived to the end of time, and would have laboured more abundantly than all for its spread. His noble purpose, resolutely followed, has written his name in undying characters on the annals of time. Being the lover of Christ and His gospel, he became the true lover of his fellows,—Paul the greatest philanthropist of all men. Our names may die, but our noble purposes, resolutely achieved, cannot die. The record is in heaven. We shall be known by our purposes and by our efforts to give them fulfilment. Let us seek the immortality of goodness. Let us pray for God's grace to separate us to His gospel.

SUGGESTIVE COMMENTS ON VERSE 1.

The meaning of " apostle."—The name " apostle," which properly means a person sent, is sometimes applied in Scripture generally to any of those messengers who were sent by the Almighty to declare His will. Hence our blessed Saviour is called the " Apostle and High Priest of our profession." But in its most common use in the New Testament it is limited to the twelve who were chosen by our Lord to be the witnesses of His life, and, after His ascension into heaven, to publish His religion to the world. St. Paul was not indeed of this number, but he was invested with the full authority belonging to the apostolical office, being called by the special nomination of Christ to be an apostle. This remark he introduces to show how completely he was distinguished from the Judaising teachers who were not called to the office which they had undertaken, but assumed it of themselves, and without any authority. He was also separated unto the gospel of God, chosen from among the rest of mankind, and devoted to the service of the gospel, that he might spread the knowledge of it in the world.— *D. Ritchie, D.D.*

Called to be an apostle.—Let the disciples of Christ remember that they are all His servants; and, what department soever of that service they are called to fill, whether more public or more private, let them cherish the same spirit with Paul, counting it their honour, and feeling it their pleasure,

to serve such a Master. The more highly we think of the Master whom we serve (and in the present instance the more highly the more justly, the glorious reality ever remaining far above all our loftiest conceptions of it), the more honourable shall we deem His service; and the deeper our sense of obligation for His kindness and grace, the more ardent will be our delight in the doing of His will, and the more active and unremitting our zeal in the advancement of His glory. But Paul served Christ in a special capacity. He subjoins to his general designation his more appropriate one : " called to be an apostle, separated unto the gospel of God." The office of an apostle was the highest among the offices of the Christian Church. In every enumeration of them this stands first : " When He ascended up on high, He led captivity captive, and gave gifts unto men. And He gave some, apostles ; and some, prophets ; and some, evangelists; and some, pastors and teachers " (Eph. iv. 8, 11). And His thus " giving " them implies His bestowing upon them whatever qualifications were necessary for the due discharge of their respective functions. This the connection intimates. " Unto every one of us," the apostle had just said, " is given grace, according to the measure of the gift of Christ." He, by the endowments, ordinary and extraordinary, of the Holy Spirit, fitted each class of these spiritual functionaries for the execution of their respective trusts. In a larger enumeration, given elsewhere, apostles still hold the first place: "God hath set some in the Church, first apostles, secondarily prophets, thirdly teachers, after that miracles, then gifts of healings, helps, governments, diversities of tongues" (1 Cor. xii. 28).—*Wardlaw.*

Paul.—A little man, it should seem by his name, such as was James the Less: but as the Church of Philadelphia, though she had but a little strength, yet had a great door set open; and as Bethlehem was the least, and yet not the least, among the princes of Judah; so was this apostle the last (and perhaps the least in stature), as one born out of due time. But God (who loves to be *maximus in minimus*) had designed him to great services, and gifted him accordingly, so that he was no whit behind the very chiefest of the apostles; and for painstaking he laboured more abundantly than they all. Hence Chrysostom calleth him *insatiabilem Dei cultorem*, an insatiable servant of Christ. And himself seems as insatiable an encomiast of this apostle (the apostle he commonly nameth him "by an excellency"), for he hath written eight homilies in his commendation. And if any think he hath said too much, it is because either they have not read him or cannot judge of his worth. *Qui tricubitalis cœlos transcendit* (as the same Father saith): little though he were, yet he got above the heavens. "*A servant of Jesus Christ.*"—This is a higher title than monarch of the world, as Numa, second king of Rome, could say. Constantinus, Valentinus, and Theodosius, three emperors, called themselves *Vasallos Christi*, the vassals of Christ, as Socrates reporteth.—*Trapp.*

Change of names.—It was common among the Jews and other Oriental nations to change the names of individuals on the occurrence of any remarkable event in their lives, as in the case of Abraham and Jacob. This was especially the case when the individual was advanced to some new office or dignity. Hence a new name is sometimes equivalent to a new dignity. As Paul seems to have received this name shortly after he entered on his duties as an apostle, it is often supposed, and not improbably, that it was on account of this call that his name was changed. Thus, Simon, when chosen to be an apostle, was called Cephas or Peter. Since, however, it was very common for those Jews who associated much with foreigners to have two names, one Jewish and the other Greek or Roman (sometimes entirely distinct, as Hillel and Pollio; sometimes nearly related, as Silas and Silvanus), it is perhaps more probable that the apostle was called Saul among the Jews and Paul among the heathen. As he was the apostle of the Gentiles, and all his epistles, except that to the Hebrews, were addressed to Churches founded among the heathen, it is not wonderful that he constantly called himself Paul instead of Saul.—*Hodge.*

Slave.—The original word, δοῦλος, properly signifies a slave. Here it is a name of honour. For, in the East, the chief ministers of kings were called δοῦλοι, slaves. In this sense Moses is called δοῦλον Θεοῦ, the slave or servant of God. This honourable name, therefore, denotes the high authority which Paul possessed in the kingdom of Christ as one of His chief ministers.

MAIN HOMILETICS OF THE PARAGRAPH.—*Verse 2.*

The gospel long promised.—A scheme long in preparation, the carrying out of which seems long delayed, may be expected to be of great value and importance. The scheme of the gospel was long in preparation to human seeming. The prophetic utterances extend over thousands of years—long to human estimates. Long and short may only be known to the divine mind in

9

condescension to human weakness. How great must be the scheme of divine love and mercy which the prophets made the burden of their message! No wonder Paul felt himself empowered to write with authority, as he grasped the great idea that he was separated to the gospel of God which was proclaimed by the prophets as they walked with beautiful feet upon the mountains of early time. His one idea to stir the soul with noblest enthusiasm. Preachers of this gospel may well be calm, though the moderns may say, Oh, what an old, effete, worn-out system! Old, of course—older than the sun, older than creation; but as fresh as the verdant landscape touched into beauty by the magic hand of summer. Creation keeps unfolding new wonders to the scientist; and so the old gospel has yet more wonders to reveal.

I. **What God promises He will fulfil.**—Did He promise a gospel in Eden, then in due time—which is God's and not man's time—the promise will be accomplished. The winter has in it the promise of summer, and that season must come, though the winter blasts howl and the east winds tarry long. The winter of the race carried in it the promise of a gospel summer, and that must come, though the darkness grew denser, and though devout souls were weary waiting. For God to be untrue to His promise would be for God to be untrue to Himself, and that He can never be. Sweet the thought that God's promises cannot fail. He who gave the gospel, in His own good time will give with it every promise He has made for our good. How much the gospel carries with it to devout hearts!

II. **What God promises through a series of faithful men must be good.**—The guarantee for the goodness of this scheme is the wisdom, power, love, and mercy of the infinite and all-loving Father. Men may scoff; but let scoffing men produce their better systems. Men may jeer; but what are men in the presence of that which is the product of unerring wisdom, unfailing power, and abiding love? Is God mindful of our weakness? Does He appear to say, Look at My confidence in the goodness of this great remedial scheme, since I empower My prophets to announce it to the world in plainest terms? The mere fact that such men as Isaiah and Jeremiah have foretold this gospel shows that it must be good. Isaiah is one of the greatest of all bards, and his fancy did not so overrule his judgment as to lead him to be guilty of the folly of foretelling a worthless device. The prophets believed in this gospel as good; the apostles received it as such; the martyrs esteemed it as a good better far than the good of earthly life. It is our good, and by it we will stand. Its pleasures we will enjoy. Its delicious fruits we will taste. In its sublime banquets we will revel.

III. **What God promises through a series of faithful men conveyed through holy writings must be binding.**—That is, the gospel comes to us with highest sanctions, and we ought gladly to accept the good news. The Jews ought to accept this gospel, for it is the burden of the message of those writings for which they had great reverence. The Gentiles ought to accept it, for the holy writings are incomparably superior in their moral tone, and in many of their literary aspects, to all other writings. Let all receive the good news from heaven with thankful hearts.

IV. **What God has promised through four thousand years cannot have grown old in two thousand.**—The tree, the germ of which was planted in Eden and was developed in Palestine, has not lost its power of bearing fruit for the healing of the nations. It still bears all manner of wondrous fruit, and brings forth its fruit for every changing month. It had its fruit for the month of dire persecution, for the month of the dark ages—fruit for the month of the revival of literature; and it has fruit still for the month that may feel the sirocco breath of modern scepticism, modern luxury, and modern indifference. Grown old indeed! God's works cannot grow old till their task is done. Sometimes we think the earth is growing old; but her landscapes are as beautiful as when Adam trod the green carpet of the newly laid planet, and the stars gem the midnight sky with brilliancy as great as when Isaac went forth at eventide to meditate. Some people say the gospel has grown old. The wish may be the father of the saying, because the fool's heart is darkened. Ask the last convert to Christianity, who has really been enriched by its treasures, if it has grown old, and he will reply, It has to me about it all the freshness of youth. It has given me "the oil of joy for mourning, the garment of praise for the spirit of heaviness." It has made me and for me all things new.

SUGGESTIVE COMMENTS ON VERSE 2.

The Old Testament not a final revelation.—Paul has told us his name, and has claimed our attention by calling himself a servant of Jesus Christ—a servant of the first rank, one whose whole life is spent in proclaiming good news from God. He now further claims our attention by showing the importance of the gospel for which he is set apart. "Which He promised before": God foretold through the prophets, not only good things to come, but the announcement of the good things—*i.e.*, that salvation would be preceded by glad tidings of salvation. In one sense God actually proclaimed beforehand the good news to Abraham, but only as something far off and indistinct (Gal. iii. 8). The good news promised, but not proclaimed, by Isaiah was good news of present deliverance. "Prophet" (xii. 6): Notice that the prophet was but the mouth through (see ver. 5) which God spoke the promise (Heb. i. 1). The following words prove that the prophets referred to were those whose writings have come down to us. "Scripture": something written, sacred or profane. "Holy": that which belongs to God, of whose activity and tendency God is the one end and aim. Paul here applies to certain writings the solemn word "holy," and thus classes them with other holy objects—the Sabbath, temple, sacrifices, priesthood. Therefore whatever solemnity belongs to these belongs to the writings. In Paul's view these books, in a special sense, were God's; they were written, and everything within them tends, to work out His purposes. The promise of good news passed *through* the prophets' lips; it abides and speaks *in* the sacred writings. This verse claims attention for the gospel. That for which the way was prepared during centuries, and to proclaim the advent of which men like Isaiah and Ezekiel were sent, must indeed be great. To many of Paul's readers the prophets were almost superhuman, and to them the Old Testament was separated from all other books as holy—*i.e.*, as a book of which every word spoke from God and for God. This holy book and these prophets of God declared that in days to come good news from God would be announced. Therefore, by his readers' reverence for the book and for the men, he claims their attention. Again, by appealing to the prophets and Scriptures, Paul pays honour to the old covenant. That the ancient prophets and Scriptures foretold the gospel increases our respect for them as well as for it. Paul thus guards in this verse against the error both of those who deny that the Old Testament came from God and of those who take it to be a final revelation. We shall find that it was because the thoughts here expressed lay near to the apostle's heart that they sprang to his lips at the first mention of the gospel.—*Beet.*

Paul's doctrine not new.—It was peculiarly pertinent to the apostle's object to state that the gospel which he taught was not a new doctrine, much less inconsistent with writings which his readers knew to be of divine authority. This idea he therefore frequently repeats in reference to the method of salvation.—*Hodge.*

MAIN HOMILETICS OF THE PARAGRAPH.—Verses 3—6.

A short biography.—Some of our modern biographies are prolix, and are not warranted by either the nature of the persons whose lives are depicted or the calls made upon readers in the present day. Solomon must have said prophetically, " Of making of books there is no end." Who reads right through the ponderous volumes which assume to describe the life-course of a man whose name will not be handed down to a distant future ? It is true that the man made a stir in his sphere, but almost before the extended biography is completed the commotion has subsided. The divine Man had a short biography. How much is told and compressed in the four gospels ? The extended lives of Christ written in modern days are great tributes to the intellect and industry of their authors, as well as to the influence that the Christ still wields after the lapse of eighteen centuries ; but they do not make us speak, walk, and dwell with the living Christ in the land of Palestine, as do the graphic narratives of Matthew, Mark, Luke, and John. The shortest biography is that given by St. Paul in these four verses. How much we here learn of the Saviour's greatness !

I. **Christ was great in lineage.**—Man was made in the image and likeness of God, and has thus a noble origin. But Christ is noblest of the sons of men. He was begotten of God before all worlds, being the brightness of the Father's glory and the express image of His person. As to the origin of His human nature He was great, for, though "according to the flesh," He was not brought into this world by the ordinary processes of generation. Jesus was born in a stable and laid in a manger, but the place of birth will not either demean the noble or exalt the ignoble. Jesus as to His human nature possessed a noble origin, for kings were His noble ancestors, and kings the best that Israel could boast. He was of the seed of David. Patriarchs gave splendour to the ancestral train. The riches of time and the splendours of eternity combine to give dignity to the compound nature of the God-man.

II. **Christ was great in person.**—*Declared to be the Son of God with power.* There is here set forth an unknowable Christ. If we study the personality of the Saviour as here set forth, as well as in the four gospels, we must come to the conclusion that He is more than human, and this must be admitted by the deniers of His divinity. Here then we get something more than human ; and what is that something ? For our part we cannot rest satisfied with a something which has no definition. He must be to us either supernatural, and therefore divine, or else be rejected. The divinity of Jesus Christ is both an article of our creed and commends itself to our reason. He rises far above the littleness of our nature, and we can believe in an unknowable Christ. Why, even going no higher than that of regarding Jesus as a superior human being He is unknowable, for He is allowed to be something more than human, and therefore is lifted out of the sphere of our knowledge. The vastness of His love, the extent of His self-sacrifice, and His all-consuming zeal for the glory of God are beyond the measures of our experience. His love passeth knowledge, and thus He is unknowable. So that whether we accept a human or divine Christ, if we accept the Christ of Paul, if we accept the Christ of the four gospels, we have to do with an unknowable Saviour. And such a Saviour is the one to command our adoration. A knowable Christ is a Christ reduced to our level and robbed of His greatness. We believe in the essential divinity of Jesus Christ, and accept without reserve the statement that He was declared to be the Son of God with power.

III. **Christ was great in titles.**—Boast we of titles of honour, of marks of distinction ? The carpenter's Son from the village of Nazareth, who had not where to lay His weary head, and was obliged to beg for a little water to quench

12

His thirst, has titles which overtop the proudest names worn by the sons of man. The Son of God. How much does that imply? God has many sons. All are His sons by creation; some by adoption. Patriarchs are the eldest sons of God in time; the prophets are God's sons, whose bright pathway glows with divine visions; the apostles are God's sons, heralding forth with clarion peals the good time coming for a sin-stricken race; the martyrs are God's sons, staining the earth with their seminal blood, enriching humanity, and reaching forth to grasp the martyr's crown. Towering above all is the sonship of Jesus. He is the Son of God as no other was or could be. The very name Jesus is attractive. Do we ever tire as we sing, " How sweet the name of Jesus sounds "? Jesus, for He shall save His people from their sins. Christ, the anointed. One man is anointed to be a prophet, another to be a priest, another a king. Jesus is anointed to combine in His one person the threefold offices. Man is anointed by his fellow. This Man of Nazareth was anointed by God. Is that a mere picture? If so, Matthew was gifted with the creative faculty in the highest degree : " And Jesus went up straightway out of the water; and, lo, the heavens were opened unto Him, and He saw the Spirit of God descending like a dove, and lighting upon Him : and lo a voice from heaven, saying, This is My beloved Son, in whom I am well pleased." His Son Jesus Christ our Lord, our ruler, the ruler of all things in heaven and in earth. He has the keys of Hades and of death.

> " He everywhere hath sway,
> All things serve His might ;
> His every act pure blessing is,
> His path unsullied light."

IV. **Christ was great in character.**—The spirit of holiness infused the divine nature into the human and raised the human from the dead. The spirit of holiness dwelling in Christ speaks of the immaculate purity of His nature. He was completely good. When we speak of ordinary men and say they are good, the word is not positive but comparative. But Jesus was positively good. Here is no need for comparison. He alone was good—so good that He alone could pay the price of sin. He was good in thought, in word, and in deed. Those who moved near Jesus in private found Him good. His friends adored His goodness ; His enemies were forced to declare, I find no fault in Him. His goodness declared Him the Son of God.

V. **Christ was great in death.**—Other men see corruption, but He of whom David spoke and of whom Paul wrote saw no corruption. Whatever beauty attaches to an ordinary man in his life is removed by the touch of death. There is no beauty in the tomb :

> "Youth and hope and beauty's bloom
> Are blossoms gathered for the tomb."

Jesus Christ saw no corruption. His body rose from the new tomb just as it had been laid there by Joseph of Arimathæa. By divine power the resurrection was accomplished. Jesus led captivity captive. By death He conquered death. The resurrection of Christ is a fact of history. The very story put into the mouth of the Roman soldiers was self-defeating and strongest evidence of the truth of the Resurrection. Was Paul a fool? Some moderns seem to think he was. Honest estimates of Paul surely cannot fall so low as to believe that he would calmly write to people about an event as having recently taken place which was only a cunningly devised fable.

VI. **Christ was great in ability.**—We here refer not to His power of working miracles, but to the power flowing out of Himself by which men received grace and apostleship. What grace in such men as St. Paul ! Grace still from Christ for all receptive natures. From His fulness men and women receive grace upon

13

grace. Let us believe not in a dead but a living Christ. He has gifts of grace still to bestow. We too may receive grace. This grace rightly received will make us obedient to the faith. Obedience is the best test. This ability *creates a large number of followers.* The obedient ones to the faith are to be found among all nations. Already in the centre of the world's greatness, in the heart of corruption, are found many called of Jesus Christ. All nations are not yet obedient to the faith. The movement is slow but sure. The nations must come. All roads lead to Rome. All modern movements, all the march and play of present events, lead to Jesus Christ; for in Him shall all the nations of the earth be blessed. God has blessed Him for ever, that He may for ever rain blessings upon mankind. Sometimes it is said " for ever " is a long word, but it is not too long to express the enduring nature of the Saviour's blessedness. Let us love the Saviour as Paul did, and our love will by its creative force call into existence other loves, and the bright light of a universally pervading love will finally dispel all the gloom, all the darkness, all the discords of humanity.

Vers. 3, 4. *Christ's divinity proved by His resurrection.*—Where the construction of the text lies so that we cannot otherwise reach the full sense of it without making our way through doubts and ambiguities, philosophical discourses are necessary in dispensing the word. The present exercise, therefore, consists of two parts:—

I. **An explication of the words.**—For the scheme of the Greek carries a very different face from our translation, which difference renders the sense of them very disputable. The explication is comprised in the resolution of these four inquiries: 1. Whether the translation rightly renders it that Christ was "declared to be the Son of God," since the original admits of a different signification; 2. What is imported by the term "with power"; 3. What is intended by the following words—"according to the spirit of holiness "; 4. How those words, " by the resurrection from the dead," are to be understood.

II. **An accommodation of the words to the present occasion**, which is in showing: 1. *How Christ's resurrection may be a proper argument to prove His divinity and eternal sonship;* 2. *That it is the greatest and principal of all others.* For this we may observe, that it is not only true but more clear and evident than the other arguments for the proof of the truth of Christ's doctrine, when we consider them as they are generally reducible to these three: (1) *the nature of the thing taught by Him;* (2) *the fulfilling of prophecies in His person;* (3) *the miracles and wonderful works which He did in the time of His life.* And though these were undoubtedly high proofs of Christ's doctrine, yet His resurrection had a vast pre-eminence over them upon two accounts: 1. *That all the miracles He did*, supposing His resurrection had not followed, would not have had sufficient efficacy to have proved Him to be the Messias. But His resurrection alone, without relation to His preceding miracles, had been a full proof of the truth of His doctrine, which appears upon these two accounts: (1) *that, considered absolutely in inself*, it did outweigh all the rest of His works put together; (2) that it had a more *intimate and near connection with His* doctrine than any of the rest. 2. Because of the *general opinion and judgment that the world had of both.*

The Jews and unbelievers never attempted to assign any causes of the Resurrection besides the power of God, so as by that means to destroy the miraculousness of it; though they constantly took exceptions to Christ's other miracles, still resolving them into some cause short of a divine power, which exceptions may be reduced to these two heads: 1. *The great difficulty of discerning when an action is really a miracle;* 2. *Supposing an action is known to be a miracle, it is as difficult to know whether it proves the truth of the doctrine of that person that does it or not.* But neither of these exceptions takes place against the Resurrection; for (1) though we cannot assign the determinate point where the power of nature ends, yet there are some actions that at first appearance so vastly transcend it that there can be no suspicion that they proceed from any power but a divine; (2) should God suffer a miracle to be done by an impostor, yet there was no necessity hence to gather that God did it to confirm the words of that impostor, for God may do a miracle when and where He pleases.—*South.*

SUGGESTIVE COMMENTS ON VERSES 4, 6.

"Declared" the right word.—That the word rendered "declared" has in this case that meaning may be argued: 1. From its etymology. It comes from a word signifying "limit" or "boundary," and literally means "to set limits to," "to define"; and such in usage is its frequent signification. "To define" is nearly related both to "appointing" and to "warning," "declaring," "exhibiting a person or thing in its true nature." In the New Testament, indeed, the word, as in common Greek, is used generally to express the former idea—namely, that of constituting or appointing; but the sense which our version gives it is in many cases involved in the other. 2. The Greek commentators Chrysostom and Theodoret both so explain the word. So does the Syriac Version. 3. This explanation supposes the word to be used in a popular and general sense, but does not assign to it a new meaning. 4. Reference may be made to that familiar biblical usage according to which words are used declaratively. Thus to make guilty is to pronounce to be guilty, to make just is to pronounce to be just, to make unclean is to declare to be unclean. Hence, admitting that the words literally mean "*made* the Son of God by the resurrection from the dead," they may, with the strictest regard to usage, be interpreted "exhibited as made," "declared to be." 5. The *necessity of the place* requires this interpretation, because it is not true that Christ was made the Son of God by His resurrection, since He was such before that event. 6. The passage, unless thus explained, is inconsistent with other declarations of the sacred writers, which speak of Christ's

resurrection as the evidence of what He was, but not as making Him either Son or King. The words "with power" may either be connected adjectively with the preceding phrase and the meaning be "the powerful Son of God," or, which is preferable, adverbially with the word "declared"—"He was powerfully," that is, "clearly declared to be the Son of God." As when the sun shines out in his power he is seen and felt in all his glory, so Christ, when He arose from the dead, was recognised at once as the Son of God.—*Hodge.*

Christ's resurrection a sign of power.—But you will here naturally reply, How can this be a proper proof of that? How can His resurrection, which supposes Him to have been dead, prove Him to be such a one as existed from all eternity, and so could not die? Is the grave a medium to demonstrate a person incorruptible? or death to enforce that he is immortal? I answer that this argumentation is so far very right, and that the resurrection, considered only in a bare relation to the person rising from the dead, proves Him only to be a wonderful man, but is so far from proving Him the eternal Son of God that it rather proves the contrary. But then, if we consider it with the relation to the doctrine of that person affirming Himself to be thus the Son of God, and as the seal set to the truth of that doctrine by an omnipotent hand and an unfailing veracity, why thus it is an infallible argument to prove the real being of all those things that were asserted by that person. Christ's resurrection therefore proved Him to be the eternal Son of God, consequentially—that is, as it was an irrefragable confirmation of the truth of that doctrine which had declared Him to be so.

It is much disputed whether Christ's resurrection is to be referred to His own power raising Himself from the dead or only to the power of the Father. Those who deny His eternal divinity allow only this latter, stiffly opposing the former. To give countenance to this their opposition they seem to make challenge to any one to produce but one place of Scripture where Christ is said to have raised Himself from the dead and they will yield the cause. To which I answer, Though this is nowhere affirmed in these very terms, representing it *in prœterito*, as done, yet if Christ spoke the same thing in words importing the future the result is undoubtedly the same. And for this I desire to know what they will answer to that place where Christ, speaking of His body, says, " Destroy this temple, and in three days I will raise it up." Does not Christ personally appropriate the action to Himself and to His own power ? Wherefore that exception is a vapour and a cavil, unbecoming a rational opponent. But I add that, as to the proof of the divinity of Christ's person, it is not material whether His resurrection be stated upon His own power or the power of His Father, for both equally prove the same

thing, though in a different manner. If Christ raised Himself, it directly proves that He was God, and so had a divine nature besides His human ; for if He raised that, being dead, it must needs follow that He did it by virtue of a power inherent in another nature, which was some divine spirit. But, on the other hand, if the Father raised Him, yet still it proves Him to have been God, forasmuch as He always avouched Himself to be so, and the Father would not have exerted an infinite power to have confirmed a lie or verified the words of an impostor.

That all the miracles Christ did, supposing that His resurrection had not followed, would not have had sufficient efficacy to have proved Him to be the Messias. But His resurrection alone, taking it singly and by itself and without any relation to His precedent miracles, had been a full and undeniable proof of the truth of His doctrine and the divinity of His person. The former part of the assertion is clear from that of St. Paul : "If Christ be not risen, then is our preaching vain, and your faith is also vain ; " "Ye are yet in your sins." Now before Christ's death all His miracles were actually done, and yet, notwithstanding all these, the apostle lays this supposition—that in case, then, He had not risen from the dead, the whole proof of the gospel had fallen to the ground and been buried with Him in the same grave.—*South.*

MAIN HOMILETICS OF THE PARAGRAPH.—*Verse* 7.

A graceful salutation.—The universality of this address has led some commentators to maintain that the epistle was meant for the heathens of Rome as well as for the Christians. But this cannot be admitted. Most certainly we should say that it cannot. Imagine a letter addressed to all that be in Rome by the adherent of a new sect everywhere spoken against. Claudius sought comfort and recreation in literary pursuits ; but surely it would be a long time before he would be induced to forsake his Homer and his Virgil to find out that there was after all some literary power in the letter of a Jew who had turned Christian. Homer and Virgil still live, and schoolboys try with great pains and much reluctance to put their sentences into bad English ; while the obscure letter of the insignificant Jew is being expounded from thousands of pulpits, read by millions, and translated into a vast number of the tongues of earth. Imagine a new sect, called the Brotherhood of Love, originated amongst one of

16

the tribes of Africa, about the shores of Tanganyika. Some of the converts make their way to London and establish a brotherhood. There rises up in Africa a convert of great zeal and energy. He addresses a letter to the brotherhood in London, beginning, To all that be in London. Who would ever suppose that it was meant for the whole of London? What newspapers would print it? What Christian readers, though taught large toleration by their great chapter on charity in the First Epistle to the Corinthians, would condescend to examine this tractate? Outside the circle of the brotherhood the only likely readers would be writers on heterodox London and novelists seeking for some new sensation. Strangest fact of all, the letter from Africa to all that be in London becomes in after time one of the great epistles of all civilised peoples, and engages the attention of greatest scholars. The letter sent to Rome by the hands of Phœbe was a precious document—more precious than the law suit on which she was engaged. Rome commanded the world. Paul's Romans has commanded a larger world and wielded a wider influence than ever Rome knew or possessed. It is well worth studying. The very inscription is attractive. It gives a comprehensive view of the dealings of God with His people. It shows their high privilege, exalted relationship, and precious bestowals. It may be made to speak to us of:—

I. **The outward aspect of Christian development.**—By the words "outward aspect" we mean outward as regards the work of grace in the soul. Whatever may be our views of predestination and election, we must admit antecedent purposes in the divine mind. All schools of religious thought will subscribe to the simple creed—By grace are ye saved. If grace mean the favour and kindness of God, then that grace is antecedent to all its subjects. God and grace are inseparable words. God existed before all creatures; therefore grace must have been in essence, if not in operation, before the existence of gracious subjects and the manifestation of gracious methods. Christianity was a development along the divine line carried through all pre-Christian dispensations. The individual Christian is a development in the divine idea. Here is the glorious plan: 1. *Beloved of God*; 2. *Called*; 3. *Saints*. "Beloved of God" speaks to us of antecedent emotion. "Called" declares the emotion formulating itself into gracious action. "Saints" describes the result of emotion and action. Shall we presume to say that "beloved of God" is a consequent and not an antecedent? Shall we say that the prodigal was beloved of the father because the son turned repentantly from his journey to the father's house? Shall we not rather say that "beloved of the father" went before the prodigal's thoughts of repentance and moved him back, though he knew it not, to sweet thoughts of home, of love, of father, and of rich content?

II. **The inward aspect of Christian development.**—"Grace to you and peace." This cannot mean converting grace—this cannot refer to that peace which results to the soul of man from the realisation of the benefits conferred by justification: for these people are already Christians; they are subjects of divine grace; they have peace with God through believing in Jesus Christ. We take the salutation to mean "grace and peace be multiplied,"—perfecting grace; ever developing peace; grace for all seasons; needed grace for needy times; grace when we do not feel our need—at such times it often is that we have greatest need of grace to watch our own welfare, and keep us still moving upward and onward. As grace ripens, peace increases. Peace may be at first as the little rivulet, flowing, like the waters of Siloam, softly and sweetly from the pleasant heights of infinite love into the soul. At first peace struggles along like the mountain torrent over rugged rocks. It meets with obstructions in human nature, though renewed. By-and-by it flows in the broader land of the disciplined nature. Then peace flows a river deep, broad, refreshing,

17

fertilising.   How much happiness is implied in the wish for the increase of grace and peace !

III. **The source and channel of Christian development.**—"God our Father, and the Lord Jesus Christ." Modern developments are developments from nothing, a theory which *we* cannot understand.   The law of evolution without an evolver is to us a mystery.   It may be true, but its processes are not plain to us at least.   Organic life has developed from simpler to more complex forms in obedience to universal natural law.   Very good of the organic life !   In what school has it learnt lessons of obedience ?   Does natural law exist without a law-giver ?   Does organic life move by virtue of its own inherent force ?   Whence the life ?   Did the organic substance give itself life before it had being ?   We think that we tread more satisfactory ground as we trace all developments to God our Father.   More emphatically we thus trace Christian developments. God our Father.   Jesus Christ our Saviour.   The grace flows from God the source through Christ the channel, and refreshes the thirsty soul.   Peace comes from and by Him who is the author of our peace by virtue of His mediatorial work.   What sublimity the Christian conception unfolds !   It makes earth radiant with the light of heaven.   It lifts man to the mount of transfiguration, where all things glow with beautiful colours that transcend the poet's highest fancy or the painter's keenest skill.

Ver. 7.   *God's beloved saints.*—The apostle Paul had never been in Rome, and he knew very little about the religious nature of the converts there; but he has no hesitation in declaring that they are all "beloved of God" and "saints."   Let us look at these two points—the universal privilege, and the universal obligation of the Christian life.

I. **The universal privilege of the Christian life.**—"Beloved of God."   We are so familiar with the juxtaposition of the two ideas, "love" and "God," that we cease to feel the wonderfulness of their union.   But until Jesus had done His work no man believed that the two thoughts could be brought together. Think of the facts of life, think of the facts of nature, and let us feel how true the great saying is, that

> "Nature, red in tooth and claw,
> With rapine, shrieks against the creed"

that God is love.   Think of what the world has worshipped, and of all the varieties of monstrosity before which men have bowed—cruel, lustful, rapacious, selfish, the different deities they have adored; and then, "God hath established, proved His love to us, in that while we were yet sinners Christ died for us." Brethren, do not let us kick down the ladder by which we have climbed; nor, in the name of a loving God, put away the Christian teaching which has begotten the conception in humanity of a God that loves.   There are men to-day who now turn round upon the very gospel which has given them the conception of this truth, and accuse it of narrow and hard thoughts of the love of God.   One of the Scripture truths against which the assailant often turns his sharpest weapons is that which is involved in my text, the answer to the other question, Does not God love all ?   Yes, yes, a thousand times, yes! But there is another question: Does the love of God to all make His special designation of Christian men as His beloved the least unlikely ?   Surely special affection is not, in its nature, inconsistent with universal beneficence and benevolence.   Surely you are not honouring God when you say, It is all the same to Him whether a man loves and serves Him, or lifts himself up in rebellion against Him, and makes himself his own centre and earth his aim and his all.   "God so loved the world."   There are manifestations of His loving heart which any man can receive; and each man gets as much

18

of the love of God as it is possible to pour upon him. But a granite wall does not drink in the dew as a flower does; and the nature of the man on whom God's love falls determines how much and what manner of its manifestations shall pass into his true possession, and what shall remain without. So, on the whole, we have to answer the questions, Does God love any? does not God love all? does God specially love some? with the one monosyllable, Yes! Myths tell us that the light which, at the beginning, had been diffused through a nebulous mass, was next gathered into a sun. So the universal love of God is concentrated in Jesus Christ; and if we have Him, we have it; and if we have faith, we have Him.

II. **The universal obligation of the Christian life.**—"Called to be saints," or "the called saints." The word "called" means summoned by God. It is their vocation, not their designation. I need not remind you that "saint" and "holy" carry precisely the same idea. We notice that the true idea of this universal holiness, which *ipso facto* belongs to all Christian people, is consecration to God. The next thing is purity. Purity will follow consecration, and would not be much without it, even if it were possible to be attained. Next, this consecration is to be applied all through a man's nature. There are two ways of living in the world; and I venture to say there are only two. Either God is my centre, and that is holiness; or self is my centre, and that is sin. This consecration is only possible when we have drunk in the blessed thought, "beloved of God." You cannot argue a man into loving God, any more than you can hammer a rosebud open. But He can love us into loving Him, and the sunshine, falling on the closed flower, will expand it. There is no faith which does not lead to surrender. There is no aristocracy in the Christian Church who deserve to have the family name given expressly to them, for this honour and obligation of being saints belongs equally to all that love Jesus Christ. But consecration may be cultivated, and must be cultivated and increased. The apostle Paul's letter, addressed to the "beloved of God," the "called saints" that are in Rome, found its way to the people for whom it was meant. If a letter so addressed were dropped in our street, do you think anybody would bring it to you?—*A. Maclaren, D.D.*

SUGGESTIVE COMMENTS ON VERSE 7.

Reason for the universal address.— The universality of this address has led some commentators to maintain that the epistle was meant for the heathens of Rome as well as for the Christians. But this cannot be admitted; for the description given of the persons addressed as "beloved of God" and "called to be saints" could have no application whatever to the heathen inhabitants of Rome. The reason of the universality of the address appears to be this: The apostle is about to show that the Jewish and the Gentile converts to Christianity are precisely on a footing in regard to their religious state, and therefore he makes no distinction between them, but addresses them all, whether Jewish or Gentile converts, as equally entitled to the same honourable appellation. The expression "called to be saints" is equivalent to "called to be Christians," the members of the Christian Church being often denominated in the New Testament "the saints." The additional phrase "beloved of God" is also applied to them as Christians, and with great propriety. For since God had so far manifested His favour to them as to enable them to know and embrace the gospel, they may justly be called "beloved of God" when compared with the rest of mankind, to whom no such favour had been extended. It must not, however, be supposed that these distinguished titles are intended by the apostle to be descriptive of every individual of the Church addressed. They are given merely in reference to their outward privileges as members of the Church of Christ. As in the Old Testament the collective body of the Israelites are often called " a holy people " because they were chosen to preserve the worship of the true God, so in the New Testament particular Christian Churches are called "the saints" because they also are constituted the Church and people of God. But in neither case is any allusion intended to the personal holiness of individuals ; the reference is merely to the general privileges of the collective body.—*D. Ritchie, D.D.*

Paul's course of thought often interrupted. — All that intervenes is not properly a parenthesis, but an accumulation of clauses, one growing out of the other, and preventing the apostle finishing the sentence with which he commenced. This is very characteristic of Paul's manner, and is peculiarly obvious in his two epistles to the Ephesians and Colossians. His teeming mind protruded its rich thoughts and glowing sentiments so rapidly that his course was often impeded, and the original object for a time entirely lost sight of.—*Hodge.*

Living saints.—Those, then, that are called are saints whilst alive, and not only those that are canonised by the Pope after they are dead *in numerum Deorum ab Ecclesia Romana relati,* as Bembus profanely speaketh of their St. Francis—a sorry man, of whom (as once of Becket forty-eight years after his death) it may be disputed whether he were damned or saved. Pope Calixtus III. sainted some such in his time, as to whom Cardinal Bessarion, knowing them for naught, said, " These new saints make me doubt much of the old." —*Trapp.*

Christians to be holy.—The duty of Christians, and that is to be holy, for hereunto are they called—" called to be saints," called to salvation through sanctification. Saints, and only saints, are beloved of God with a special and peculiar love. " Called saints," saints in profession; it were well if all that are

20

called saints were saints indeed. Those that are called saints should labour to answer to the name, otherwise, though it is an honour and a privilege, yet it will be of little avail at the great day to have been called saints if we be not really so.—*Henry.*

The name Christian must be written on the conscience.—If thy name be written Christian in the book of thy conscience, this is a special argument of thy registering in heaven. For if our heart condemn us not, we have boldness and confidence towards God. If the good spoken of us be not found in our conscience, that glory is our shame. If the evil spoken of us be not found in our conscience, that shame is our glory. Therefore, as Seneca says, look to thy conscience more than to thy credit ; fame may be often deceived, conscience never. The beams that play upon the waters are shot from the sun in heaven. The peace and joy that danceth in that conscience comes from the Sun of righteousness, the Lord Jesus. If a hearty laughter dimple the cheek, there is a smooth and quiet mind within. Upon the wall there is a writing. A man sitting with his back to that wall, how should he read it ? But let a looking-glass be set before him, it will reflect it to his eyes; he should read it by the reflection. The writing our names in heaven is hid, yet in the glass of a good conscience it is presented to our eye of faith, and the soul reads it. For it is impossible to have a good conscience on earth except a man's name be written in heaven.—*Adams.*

The Christians are saints—*i.e.,* separated from the world and consecrated to the service of God—holy in principle, and destined to become more and more holy and perfect in their whole life and conduct. The redeeming grace of God in Christ the foundation of peace with God and ourselves. First grace, then peace—no grace without peace, no peace without grace. The co-ordination of Christ with God the Father in the epistolary inscriptions an indirect proof of the deity of Christ.—*Schaff.*

MAIN HOMILETICS OF THE PARAGRAPH.—Verses 8—14.

A beautiful letter.—In these days of postcards the art of letter-writing is not likely to be cultivated to any great extent. Addison's *Spectator* is placed on our shelves, but not studied. *Greyson's Letters* had a good circulation in their day, and yet, though only a few short years have passed since Henry Rogers wrote them, how seldom are they seen. Some of our novelists write in their books good letters; still, it is to be feared that the readers skim over them lightly. It is satisfactory to find that the letters of St. Paul are not dead letters. They are not read as much as we could wish, still they are read; and further, they are felt far more than they are read. In these verses we have a letter within a letter. We are not now to deal with the whole of the letter to the Romans, but with that portion which is contained in these seven verses.

I. **This is a letter with a joyful commencement.**—The postman's knock sends a thrill through the house. The greater part of his messages are appeals for help, tales of suffering, records of distress. Shall we go back to the times when letters were franked? Shall we envy those who lived in remote regions, and whose letters might lie for .weeks in the wayside post-house? In Paul's letter there is no appeal for help. He does not begin with a mournful phrase. He makes us read as he writes, " I thank my God." If we could say *my* God as we say *my* house, *my* business, or *my* estate, then we should the oftener say, I thank my God. Paul thanks God for a good report—faith spoken of throughout the whole world. How startling to modern notions to make religion the prominent topic in our letters! When writing to friends we are thankful for their health, for their safe investments, for their introduction into higher society, and so on. How far does the report of our faith reach? Is there a Church in England to-day the report of whose faith would reach as far as from Rome to Corinth? Could any modern Paul with any just metaphorical licence say with reference to any English Church, Scotch Church, American Church, or any other, " I thank my God that your faith is spoken of throughout the whole world"?

II. **This is a letter with a necessary personal reference.**—Some letters are disfigured by the presence of too many capital I's. Our letters are sometimes the record of our own doings, which may be of more interest to the writers than the readers. Paul's personal reference has an intimate connection with the welfare of others. Here is (*a*) a solemn oath ; (*b*) the true method of Christian service—with the spirit in the gospel ; (*c*) intercessory prayer.

III. **Thus this is a letter with an altruistic purpose.**—Altruism was taught before the appearance of Comte. The Comtist doctrine inculcates the sacrifice of self for the good of others. Paul's practice anticipates Comtist doctrine. Shall we say that Paul practised as well as preached, while Comtists only preach? We only know in part, so we must be forgiven as we affirm that we have never heard of Monsieur Comte's self-denying labours and sacrifices for the good of humanity. Paul desired a prosperous journey—what we all desire—a prosperous journey that we may reap some καρπόν, some earthly advantage or emolument or some mere excitement. Paul desired a prosperous journey that he might *impart*. The καρπόν he looked for was that souls might be saved as the result of his preaching. He desired a prosperous journey that he might sow spiritual seed, and in due season reap the καρπόν of a spiritual harvest.

IV. **This letter refers to the mystery of the divine " let."**—It is a mystery that there should be a let to the benevolent purpose of St. Paul. The divine lets are scattered thickly through and before all human doings and purposes. Where is the love in the let? Why does God permit the scheme to be thwarted? Why are noble purposes broken off? Why have we to sing in mournful

21

measures, How are the mighty fallen in the midst of the battle and before the conquest was gained? Why was Stephen stoned? God's love is not a mere soft sentiment, the emotion of an amiable nature. God's love is guided by wisdom. Paul was let, but God is wise; and Paul acknowledges divine wisdom. Stephen was let from further life-work by stones. But we may say with Augustine that the Church owes Paul to the prayer of Stephen. Let us see to it that the lets of life are not of our making. If the let is divine, we may be sure all is well. When God says stand still, it is that He may make a brighter revelation of His power and wisdom.

V. **This letter acknowledges a debt.**—Our letters are often claims. The creditor writes for payment. The debtor does not often voluntarily write to express his indebtedness. Paul writes, "I am debtor." The poor tentmaker might well be a debtor. Trade is bad. Tentmaking is not remunerative. Will Paul be able to pull through? His creditors are very numerous. Will they be merciful, and accept a very small composition? His creditors are Greeks and Barbarians, wise and unwise. Ah, Paul was a debtor to divine love and gracious calling! He was a debtor without any human creditors. Right royally he discharges the claim. If ever a minister were free from the blood of man, that minister was St. Paul. *We are all debtors to God*—debtors to our fellows on account of what we have received. How is the debt being discharged? Are we faithful? are we loving? are we living for others?

Ver. 11. *Genuine philanthropy.*—In these words we have a sketch of genuine philanthropy.

I. **Its distinguishing power.**—It is a power to "impart some spiritual gift, to the end ye may be established" or confirmed. There is a philanthropy that has power to impart certain material and mental gifts, but is unable to impart the spiritual. 1. All men require spiritual gifts; 2. Most men have them not; 3. None but those who have them can impart them.

II. **Its distinguishing inspiration.**—"I long." It is my deep craving, my burning desire. To enrich men spiritually is to enrich them completely and for ever. And this is evermore the supreme desire of genuine philanthropy. "Brethren, my heart's desire and prayer to God for Israel is, that they might be saved."—*Homilist.*

Vers. 11, 12. *The benefits of Christian communion.*—There was a mutual desire on the part of the apostle and the Roman Christians to see each other. Paul's special reasons were: 1. To bestow comfort on the members who had laboured under extraordinary difficulties; 2. Paul in great need of comfort himself. For years Paul had been struggling, beating out new tracks, disputing with error, perpetually striving. Long among strangers, he yearned to be with friends. This suggests:—

I. **That there is between Christians a bond of sympathy.**—A spiritual free-masonry. The fact that there is so little of it to-day is sadly suggestive. Downright Christianity compels us to a gracious consideration for other people.

II. **The benefits of Christian communion.**—1. Special help for the forlorn, gracious upliftings for the lowly, rest for the weary, counsel for the perplexed. There are times when solitude is demanded—*e.g.*, for heart-searching. Yet too much isolation not good. Brooding over our troubles makes them appear insurmountable. 2. In a *real* Christian communion there is no caste. There ought not to be. Calvin says: "In Christ's Church no one is so poor as not to be able to confer on us some important benefit; but our pride, alas! hinders us from reaping mutual advantages. The early Christians knew no caste. Mistress and maid knelt together before the Lord." There is room for more of this to-day. 3. The old saying applies: "In the multitude of counsellors," etc.

III. **The reciprocity of Christian communion.**—By mutual intercourse we are gainers. By mutual consideration of the gospel message souls are refreshed and invigorated. "The liberal soul shall be made fat, and he that watereth shall be watered also himself." Neither veteran in the Christian ranks nor young Christian can afford to ignore Christian communion. It will never lower one's dignity to listen to the advice of those who have fought more battles, seen more dangers, travelled greater distances in the heavenly way. The warnings of our fathers in the Church are like letters of gold.—*Albert Lee.*

Paul the debtor.—Paul has many names for himself—none of them lofty, all of them lowly; the highest, simply "an apostle." Sometimes it is Paul "the servant of Jesus Christ"; sometimes Paul "the aged"; sometimes Paul "the prisoner"; sometimes it is "less than the least of all saints"; sometimes "the chief of sinners." Here it is another—"a debtor." It is then of Paul the debtor we are to speak.

I. **To whom is he a debtor?**—Not to self; not to the flesh; not to the law. He owes nothing to these. We might say he is debtor to God, to Christ, to the cross. But these are not now in his mind. It is to Greek and Jew, wise and unwise, men of all nations; the whole fallen world, that he feels himself a debtor. They have done nothing for him indeed: they have persecuted, condemned, reviled him; yet that does not alter his position or cancel his debt. His debt to them is founded on something which all this ill-usage, this malice, cannot alter. Yes, a Christian is debtor to the world—not to his family only, or his nation, but to the whole world. Let this thought dwell in us and work in us, expanding and enlarging us, elevating our vision. We speak of the world being debtor to the Church: let us never forget that, according to Paul's way of thinking, and to the mind of the Holy Spirit, the Church is debtor to the world.

II. **When and how he became a debtor.**—Even as a Jew he was a debtor, for he possessed something which the world did not. It was when Paul became possessed of the unsearchable riches of Christ that he felt himself a debtor to the world. He had found a treasure, and he could not conceal it: he must speak out; he must tell abroad what he felt. He was surrounded by needy fellow-men, in a poor, empty world. Should he keep the treasure to himself? No. As the lepers of Samaria felt themselves debtors to the starving city, so did Paul to a famishing world. His debt *directly* is to God; but then, indirectly, it is to the world. Thus the Christian man feels his debt—his obligation to the world because of his obligation to God. But then a man must *know* that he has the treasure himself before he can be quickened into a feeling of his responsibility to others.

III. **How he pays the debt.**—By carrying to them that gospel which he had received. He goes to Corinth—doing what? Paying there a part of his infinite debt. He goes to Athens, to Thessalonica, to Rome—doing what? Paying in each place part of the infinite debt which he owes to God. He is a rich man, and can afford to give. We pay our debt: 1. *By making known the gospel to others*; 2. *By prayer for others*; 3. *By our givings*; 4. *By our consistent life.* Yes, you are debtors to all. Show that you feel this. Be constrained by a loving sense of your infinite obligations and responsibilities to Him who loved you.—*H. Bonar.*

SUGGESTIVE COMMENTS ON VERSES 8—13.

Rome is now changed.—The faith of the Roman Christians came to be thus talked of, not only because it was excelling in itself, but because it was eminent and observable in its circumstances. Rome was a city upon a hill; every one took notice of what was done there. Thus those who have many eyes upon them have need to walk circumspectly, for what they do, good or bad, will be spoken of. The Church of Rome was then a flourishing Church; but since that time how is the gold become dim! how is the most fine gold changed! Rome is not what it was. She was then espoused a *chaste virgin to Christ*, and excelled in beauty; but she has since *degenerated, dealt treacherously, and embraced the bosom of a stranger*, so that (as that good old book the *Practice of Piety* makes appear in no less than twenty-six instances) even *the Epistle to the Romans* is now an epistle *against* the Romans. Little reason has she therefore to boast of her former credit.—*Henry.*

Faith of the Romans had good results. —In the beginning of his epistles Paul generally subjoined to the apostolic benediction a solemn thanksgiving for the faith, charity, patience, and other virtues of the brethren to whom he wrote, to make them sensible of their happy state, and to lead them to a right improvement of the advantages which they enjoyed as Christians. The faith of the Romans which occasioned so much discourse was their turning from idols. An event of this kind could not fail to be spoken of with wonder through the whole empire, as there were multitudes of strangers continually coming to Rome from the provinces who on their return home would report what they had seen. For this the apostle thanked God, because the conversion of the Romans encouraged the inhabitants of other cities to forsake the established idolatry. Besides, Rome being the metropolis of the world, the conversion of so many of its inhabitants brought no small credit to the evidences of the gospel.— *Macknight.*

Light increased by shining.—"That is, that being with you, we may be comforted together." This is an epanorthosis in which he at the same time both corrects and explains the two proximate ends of his desire, and intimates that he desires to be with them— that whatever comfort God might bestow on them through him, he might be a partaker of the same along with them, so that teacher and taught might be encouraged in common, and the faith of each increased to their mutual advantage. By this the apostle teaches us that the brightest lights in the Church shone by communicating light, were instructed by teaching others, and by ministering to the faith of others were more and more confirmed in their own belief.—*Ferme.*

Natural that Paul should desire to see Rome.—At this time Paul had not seen Rome. But how natural was it in a man of his taste and intelligence to wish to see it! Nothing had made such a figure in history as this imperial city. From a kind of village it extended in a course of years till it became the mistress of the nations and the metropolis of the world. How powerfully must curiosity have been awakened by its extent, its majesty, its edifices, its institutions, its laws and customs! Paul was also a citizen; and while some, with a great ransom, purchased this privilege, he was freeborn. Yet his longing to see it was not to indulge the man and the Roman, but the Christian and the apostle. He longed to impart to the beloved and called of God there some "spiritual benefit." But see the order of divine grace. Before he was useful to them, they imparted some spiritual benefit to him and established his wavering confidence. For when he had landed at Puteoli and advanced towards Rome, the brethren came to meet him as far as the Appii Forum and the Three Taverns, "whom when Paul saw, he thanked God, and took courage." Here we see that the most eminent servants of God may be depressed and desponding, and that it is possible for them to derive assistance and comfort from those who are much inferior to them in office, condition, abilities, and grace. There is no such thing as independence. Let none be proud; let none despair. The Christian Church is a body, and the body is not one member, but many. "If the foot shall say, Because I am not the hand, I am not of the body; is it therefore not of the body? . . . The eye cannot say to the hand, I have no need of thee; nor the head to the feet, I have no need of you." But how was this prosperous journey according to the will of God, for which he made so many requests, to be accomplished? How little did he imagine the way in which he was to visit this famous city! He enters it, indeed; but in the character of a prisoner, driven thither by persecution, and after being shipwrecked upon a certain island. So high are God's thoughts above our thoughts, and His ways above our ways. So little do we know what we pray for. So often by strange and sometimes by terrible things in righteousness does He answer us as the God of our salvation. So fulfils He the promise, "I will bring the blind by a way that they knew not; I will lead them in paths that they have not known: I will make darkness light before them, and crooked things straight. These things will I do unto them, and not forsake them."—*W. Jay.*

MAIN HOMILETICS OF THE PARAGRAPH.—*Verses* 15—17.

The brave confession of a bold preacher.—The gospel of seeming weakness the apostle was ready to preach to the lovers of imperialistic ideas. The gospel of apparent defeat he was ready to proclaim among those who delighted to go forth conquering and to conquer. And why? Because the seeming is not the real. The gospel is not weakness, but power.

I. **Consider the gospel as a power.**—1. One may infer power from the fact of *simple existence.* The lowest forms of either vegetable or animal life testify to the presence of power. There are growth and development. The gospel is still derided as weakness, but by its existence it confronts us to-day as a power in the midst of the great powers of our modern life. Its moral force is not abated through the lapse of time. 2. Power may be inferred from *the capacity to survive attacks.* There is power in the oak to gather strength from the storm, and to gain an increase of beauty from the onslaught of winter's blasts—power in the nation which, in spite of external attacks and internal feuds, moves on in the pathway of progress. Tried by this test, what a power is the gospel! The Christian religion, from the time of its rise, has been one long trial of its power to survive attacks, and it has vindicated the apostle's confidence. 3. Power may be *concluded from ability to influence.* Influence is in itself a power. What a being is man who can project from himself a force that shall go on operating when his voice is hushed in the silence of the tomb! Now Christianity, which is the gospel in action, is the great formative force in the noblest of modern civilisations. Its influence has been felt where its divine authority has not been acknowledged. Banish the gospel from civilised society, and there would be a collapse. Eliminate the Christian element from our literature, and it would become often a Babel. The Christian religion is not yet an inert institution. It has exerted a glorious influence, and its power must still increase.

II. **Consider the gospel as a supreme power.**—As Joseph's sheaf among the sheaves of his brethren, so the gospel power amid the powers of earth. It is the sphere in which the power of God manifests its sublime energies and exemplifies its grandeur. It is as if all preceding ages had been concentrating themselves upon the production of this great work of power—as if the Almighty Himself, through a past eternity, had been preparing for this revelation of moral might. 1. There was *power in creation.* The world not self-evolved. We have been told that power is the source of elements, wisdom of affinities—power might create a chaos, wisdom must fabricate a world. Surely power has to do both

25

with elements and combinations. Power must produce atoms and bring them into cohesion. Wisdom must devise, power must execute. The wisdom of the architect and the power of the builder must be combined to erect a temple. The gospel a display of divine wisdom and power. It is the one system which reveals the mightiest moral energy of the divine Being. 2. *Power in the Old Testament economy.* Wonderful the history of the Jewish race. Glorious the rites and ceremonies of the Levitical dispensation. The ministration of the law was glorious, but the ministration of the gospel transcends in glory. Here in the gospel of God are seen : (1) *The power of wisdom to devise.* The wisdom of this world seen in cumbrous plans with inadequate results. The wisdom of God seen in simple plans and sublime results. Man plans, but power of execution fails. There is no hiatus between God's plan and God's finished work—that is, no hiatus of incompetency, though there may be the hiatus of time according to human reckoning. (2) *The power of justice.* Therein is the righteousness of God revealed. The eternal righteousness of the infinitely holy God is displayed in the gospel. What other religion can show a scheme wherein any attempt is made to vindicate the righteousness of the deity worshipped? God's condescension is seen in revealing His righteousness. (3) *The power of infinite love.* "God commendeth His love," etc. On Calvary's solemn heights mercy and truth meet together, righteousness and peace kiss each other. Infinite love as well as incarnate love, the love of the Father as well as the love of the Son, seem to speak to us in the sweat-drops that bead the brow of the sublime crucified One.

III. **Consider this supreme power in its saving efficacy.**—This is the essential glory of the gospel, that it is a power unto salvation. This is a feature never before attempted by any philosophical theories, ethical systems, or religious schemes. Philosophy, with all its boasted power, could not have accomplished the work, had it been bold enough to make the attempt. Philosophy could but film the ulcerous sore, while the rank corruption mined within. The gospel sets itself to cure the festering moral sores of a diseased humanity, and that which it set itself to do it has shown itself in millions of instances well able to accomplish. Roman power was destructive and selfish; it only concerned itself with the increase of Roman greatness. Dreary ruins marked the pathway of its triumphant progress. Christ seeks to conquer the kingdoms of this world, and every kingdom thus conquered is made more glorious. Christ seeks to subdue the individual, and every individual thus subjugated is really enfranchised and enriched with immortal treasures. This divine power saved from (a) *the guilt of sin*; (b) *the pollution of sin*; (c) *the misery of sin*; (d) *the weakness engendered by sin*; (e) *the perversity of the moral judgment produced by sin.* The reception of the gospel is the starting-point for noble endeavour, sublime deeds, heroic feats of moral daring. This salvation is to peace, to joy, to highest priesthood, noblest kingship, and the bright glories of heaven.

IV. **Consider this scheme of salvation in its comprehensiveness.**—Christianity is cosmopolitan. Among all the religions of a race bewildered by the number of its strange pantheons, Christianity is the one comprehensive religion. In this passage let us take the Jew as central and the Greek as circumferential. The circumference is to embrace the whole of humanity. This power must finally subdue all other powers. Ultimately it shall conquer the stubbornness of the Jew, overturn the power of Rome, confute the wisdom of the Greek, undermine the subtleties of the Hindoo, overthrow the inveterate prejudices of the Chinese, remove the darkness from African jungles, and demolish everywhere the strongholds of sin on this fair earth.

V. **This comprehensive scheme has its wise condition.**—It is the power of God unto salvation to every one that believeth. Faith is the apprehending and appropriating organ, and thus the moral condition is on the same plane as the

material condition. Food and medicine must be taken in order to save and
strengthen. Faith is acceptance. God by the condition honours our moral and
mental nature. Without faith sacraments and good works avail nothing. But
true saving faith is of course a living faith, including knowledge of the truth,
assent to the truth, and trust or confidence in Christ. It submits to all the
ordinances of God, and necessarily produces good works. Accept God's promise
through Jesus Christ, and salvation is yours. *If the apostle was saved, the
vilest sinners may hope.* This gospel saved Saul, the persecutor and blasphemer; the dying thief; the Philippian jailor; John Newton, the swearing
slave captain; John Bunyan, the wild tinker boy; and its efficacy is far
from being exhausted. It has a hopeful message to sinners of deepest dye.
If Paul was not ashamed of this gospel, why should we be? Some moderns seem
to make light of Paul. Even one Christian preacher is reported to have said,
"If we are not wiser than the apostles, we are great fools." Where is your
modern preacher who can preach like Paul? Where is your writer who can
equal him in argumentative skill, rhetorical power, and sublimity of imagination? Where is your philanthropist who can be compared to him in works of
benevolence, in a life of self-denial? Surely, then, I may count myself a fool if I
am ashamed of that in which the apostle gloried.

> "Ashamed of Jesus! sooner far
> May evening blush to own a star;
> Ashamed of Jesus! just as soon
> May midnight blush to think of noon;
> Ashamed of Jesus, that dear Friend
> On whom my hopes of heaven depend!
> No! when I blush be this my shame,
> That I no more revere His name.
> Ashamed of Jesus! yes, I may,
> When I've no crimes to wash away,
> No tears to wipe, no joys to crave,
> No fears to quell, no soul to save:
> Till then—nor is the boasting vain—
> Till then I boast a Saviour slain.
> And oh, may this my glory be,
> That Christ is not ashamed of me!"

Vers. 16, 17. *St. Paul's confidence in the gospel.*—Our text expresses St. Paul's
readiness "to preach the gospel at Rome also," as he had done in so many other
cities—a readiness which sprang from his confidence in the truth. We propose
to show briefly the grounds of this confidence.

I. **The certainty of his own call from heaven to be a teacher of that
religion which he had once persecuted.**

II. **His thorough conviction of the divinity of the Author of the gospel
of which he was made a minister.**—He could not hesitate to put it into comparison with any religious system which Rome could exhibit as its competitor.
He knew that it was from its author, God, and that God, the author, was always
with it. "Christ is God." What a glory is thus given to His gospel! There
are those who reject this truth; but how different is their gospel from ours!
Their Christ is man; ours, God made man. The affection of their Christ is
the benevolence of a creature; of ours, the love of God, only measured by His
condescension to stoop from heaven to earth. To them Christ is gone, and they
are left orphans; to us He is ever present.

III. **The effects produced by Christianity at Rome.**—What he has seen in
other places resulting from the gospel he had heard of at Rome. Religion is a
practical thing, and its effects when received are a true test.

IV. **Another ground of confidence is stated in the text.**—"For it is the
power of God unto salvation to every one that believeth; to the Jew first, and

also to the Greek." He thus silently contrasts the gospel with every religion known among men. This is power, they are weakness; this saves, they leave man in sin and danger still. In the gospel the power of God is employed to illuminate, to quicken, to comfort, to regenerate, and to sustain. Its power is glorifying. It raises the body from the ruins of its mortality to the glory of a deathless life.

V. Another ground of confidence on which the apostle rested is not the least.—" For therein is the righteousness of God revealed from faith to faith." It is so because it contains a revelation of the terms on which God forgives sin, or justifies men by pardon who are actually guilty. The principle of the divine government is righteousness. A righteous government is the result of necessity. God may be merciful, but He must be just. The only way in which He could be at once just and merciful must be by the provision of an adequate atonement, so that all the ends of a righteous government, the character of which is to uphold authority by the punishment of offence, might be answered. No other system had the true atonement, and it was this which exalted Christianity above them all. This gospel claims from us the most devout acknowledgment. How ought this mercy, which crowns every other, and without which every other were in vain showered upon us, to excite our gratitude! "Thanks be unto God for His unspeakable gift." The gospel claims an unshrinking avowal. "I am not ashamed of the gospel of Christ," says the apostle; and he was ready to assert its divine claims in every place. Such ought to be the spirit with which we are influenced—modest and humble, but decided and yielding. The gospel claims our grateful and practical acceptance. Salvation is the great end of the gospel. Nothing less than this can be supposed to be an adequate final cause for so wonderful an interposition as the incarnation and sufferings of the Son of God. Not to set up new forms of worship did He undergo His humiliations, but to save us from the curse of the law, the dominion of sin, and the wrath of God.— *R. Watson.*

Vers. 14-17. *The Grecian and the Roman.*—We live surrounded by Christian institutions, breathe an atmosphere saturated by Christianity. It is exceedingly difficult even to imagine another state of things. And to know what we have from Christianity, it is well to cast the eyes sometimes over the darkness from which the advent of Christ redeemed us. The apostle felt that the gospel was the power of God unto salvation to the Greeks, the Romans, the Barbarians, and the Jews.

Restlessness.—Polytheism divided the contemplation over many objects; and as the outward objects were manifold, so was there a want of unity in the inward life. The Grecian mind was distracted by variety. He was to obtain wisdom from one deity, eloquence from that Mercurius for whom Paul was taken, purity from Diana for whom Ephesus was zealous, protection for his family or country from the respective tutelary deities, success by a prayer to Fortune. Hence dissipation of mind, that fickleness for which the Greeks were famous, and the restless love of novelty which made Athens a place of literary and social gossip: "Some new thing." All stability of character rests on the contemplation of changeless unity. Christianity proclaimed, "One God, and one Mediator between God and men, the man Christ Jesus." St. Paul's view of the gospel contemplated it as an eternal divine purpose. He contemplated the changeless "yea" of God. Truth is one—error manifold—many opinions, yet there can be but one faith.

Worldliness.—There are men and nations to whom this world seems given as their province, as if they had no aspiration above it. If ever there were a nation who understood the science of living, it was the Grecians. The results were threefold : 1. *Disappointment.* Lying on the infinite bosom of nature, the Greek was yet unsatisfied. And there is an unsatiable desire above all external forms and objects in man—all men—which they can never satisfy. Hence his cravings too, like all others, were from time to time, " Who will show us any god ? " 2. *Degradation.* Religion aims at an ideal life above this actual one— to found a divine polity, a kingdom of God, a Church of the best. And the life of worldliness pronounces this world to be all. This is to be adorned and beautified. 3. *Disbelief in immortality.* The more the Greek attached himself to this world, the more the world unseen became a dim world of shades. The earlier traditions of the deep-thinking Orientals, which his forefathers brought from Asia, died slowly away ; and any one who reminded him of them was received as one would now be who were to speak of purgatory. The cultivated Athenians were for the most part sceptics in the time of Christ. Accordingly, when Paul preached at Athens the resurrection of the dead, they " mocked." And these men were startled by seeing a new sect rise up to whom death was nothing, who almost courted it.

The worship of the beautiful.—The Greek saw this world almost only on its side of beauty. His name for it was kosmos, divine order or regularity. He looked at actions in the same way. One and the same adjective expressed the noble and the beautiful. If he wanted to express a perfect man, he called him a musical or harmonious man. The cross tells us that it is the true beautiful which is divine—an inward, not an outward, beauty, which rejects and turns sternly away from the meretricious forms of the outward world, which have a corrupting or debilitating tendency.

The worship of humanity.—The Greek had strong human feelings and sympathies. He projected his own self on nature ; humanised it ; gave a human feeling to clouds, forests, rivers, seas. His effort therefore was, in his conception of his god, to realise a beautiful human being. Christ is deity under the limitations of humanity. But there is presented in Christ for worship, not power nor beauty nor physical life, but the moral image of God's perfections. Through the heart and mind and character of Jesus it was that the divinest streamed. Divine *character*, that was given in Christ to worship. In all this system one thing was wanting—the sense of sin. Christ came to convince the world of sin. For this Greece had no remedy. The universe has no remedy but one. There is no prescription for the sickness of the heart but that which is written in the Redeemer's blood. The nation which we contemplate to-day was a noble one—humanly, one of the noblest that the world has seen ; next to the Jewish, the very highest. We may judge from the fact of St. Paul's twice claiming his Roman citizenship and feeling the indignation of a Roman citizen at the indignity of chastisement.

The public life of Rome.—First, I notice the spirit of its religion. The very word shows what that was. " Religion," a Roman word, means "obligation, a binding power." Very different from the corresponding Greek expression, which implies worship by a sensuous ceremonial (θρησκεία). The Roman began, like the Jew, from law. He started from the idea of duty. But there was an important difference. The Jew was taught duty or obedience to the law of a personal, holy God. The Roman obeyed, as his Etruscan ancestors taught him, a fate or will ; and with very different results. But at present we only observe the lofty character of the early religion which resulted from such a starting-point. Different nations seem, consciously or unconsciously, destined by God to achieve different missions. The Jew had the highest—to reveal to the world holiness. The Oriental stands as a witness to the reality of the invisible above the visible. The Greek reminded the world of eternal beauty ; and the destiny of the Roman seems to have been to stamp upon the minds of mankind the ideas of law, government, order. The Roman seems almost to have existed to exhibit on earth a copy of the divine order of the universe, the law of the heavenly hierarchies.

Private life.—We observe the sanctity of the domestic ties. Very touching are all the well-known anecdotes—that, for instance, of the noble Roman matron who felt, all spotless as she was, life-dishonoured, and died by her own hand. The sacredness of home was expressed strongly by the idea of two guardian deities (Lares and Penates) who watched over it. A Roman's own fireside and hearthstone were almost the most sacred spots on earth. There was no battle-cry that came so near to his heart as that "For the altar and the hearth!" How firmly this was rooted in the nation's heart is plain from the tradition that for a hundred and seventy years no separation took place by law between those who had been once united in wedlock. There is deep importance in this remark; for it was to this that Rome owed her greatness. Moral decay in the family is the invariable prelude to public corruption. We will bless God for our English homes, partly the result of our religion—partly the result of the climate which God has given us, according to the law of compensation by which physical evil is repaid by moral blessing; so that, its gloom and darkness making life more necessarily spent withindoors than it is among Continental nations, our life is domestic and theirs is social. We find manly courage. This too is preserved in a word. "Virtue" is a Roman word—manhood, courage; for courage, manhood, virtue, were one word. Deep as Roman greatness was rooted in the courage of her men, it was rooted deeper still in the honour of her women. Personal purity is the divinest thing in man and woman. It is the most sacred truth which the Church of Christ is commissioned to exhibit and proclaim.

The decline of Roman life.—First came corruption of the moral character. The soul of the Roman, bent on this world's affairs, became secularised, then animalised, and so at last pleasure became his aim. Scepticism and superstition went hand in hand. An example of the former we have in Pilate's question, "What is truth?" Faith, not superstition, is the remedy. In Rome religion degenerated into allegiance to the State. "Sacrament" perhaps is the highest word of symbolical life in both. In Rome it meant an oath of allegiance to the Senate and Roman people. In the Christian Church it is also the oath of highest fidelity, but its import there is this: "Here we offer and present unto Thee, O Lord, ourselves, our souls and bodies, to be a lively sacrifice." The last step we notice is the decline of religion into expediency. Therefore it was necessary that One should come who should be true; the truest of all that are woman-born; whose life was truth, who from everlasting had been the truth. The penalty of that true life was the sacrifice which is the world's atonement. Men saw the mortal die. But others saw the immortal rise to take His place at the right hand of Power; and the Spirit which has been streaming out ever since from that life and death is the world's present light, and shall be its everlasting life. —*F. W. Robertson.*

Ver. 16. *The gospel a divine and saving power.*—Christ and His disciples were spoken of with derision; the early Christians were described as "a sect everywhere spoken against." Yet St. Paul was anxious to visit Rome that he might preach the gospel there. At this time Rome was mistress of the world. But, notwithstanding all the things which distinguished the city of the Cæsars, the apostle says, "I am ready to preach the gospel to you that are at Rome also. For I am not ashamed," etc. His reason for thus boasting in the gospel is found in the gospel itself. He was not ashamed of the gospel:—

I. **Because it is a power.**—The ambition of the Romans was for power. So

30

the apostle says that the gospel is a strong thing, a "power." Power is of different kinds. There is *material* force. The powers of nature are of this order. There is *muscular* force, which is common both to brutes and men. It is higher than mere material energy, inasmuch as its exercise involves life and volition. There is *mental* force, the power of ideas, the might of reason. Who can conceive the greatness of this power? By its exercise man makes the forces of nature his servants. How mighty has been the influence of some books! There is *spiritual* force, a thing which it is difficult to analyse or define. "The wind bloweth where it listeth," etc. Power to arouse the conscience, to bring the will into activity and give direction to it, to inspire devotion and reverence, and to kindle affection—this is the very highest power. Now the gospel is a mental and spiritual power. It is rational in the highest degree. It appeals to the conscience, summons the will into right exercises, and presents such a revelation of God as is fitted to awaken profoundest reverence and holiest love. The gospel is a power sublime and great.

II. **Because it is the power of God.**—In its sublime and perfect fitness to accomplish its design we have evidence of its divine source. God inspired and sent forth men to prepare the world for it, and then sent His Son to make it known. It is not simply *a* power of God, but "*the* power of God." It is the grandest display of the divine power. It is a greater thing to convert a soul from sin unto holiness than to create a world; we have in it a completer manifestation of "the fulness of the Godhead." The gospel is "the highest and holiest vehicle of the divine power." Behind all its forces God is.

III. **Because it is the power of God to save.**—Some great forces are destructive. The earthquake and avalanche carry ruin and death with them. Some great minds have been abused by being exercised so as to injure and destroy. The licentious poem spreads a more terrible ruin than any pestilence. So also the book which aims at shaking men's faith. To destroy is an easy thing. To destroy the good and beautiful is diabolic. But to create, to heal, to save, is a divine and, humanly speaking, difficult work. In it the power of God is exerted to put away human sin, heal human sorrows, transform man into the divine image.

IV. **Because it is the power of God to save man without distinction of nation or class.**—"To the Jew first, and also to the Greek." "Jews and Greeks" was a Jewish expression for all mankind. The corresponding expression amongst the Greeks was "Greeks and Barbarians." The gospel is for all men, but it was proclaimed first to the Jews. Our Lord came to them, and they are called "His own." "He came unto His own," etc. And the apostle, writing of them, said, "Of whom as concerning the flesh Christ came." The apostles were commanded to preach the gospel in all the world and to every creature, "beginning at Jerusalem." The gospel is the power of God to save man as man, without any distinctions, social or national. Its provisions are *suited* to all, *offered* to all, *free for all*.

V. **Because it is the power of God to save all men on the simplest conditions.**—"To every one that believeth." The condition of salvation is faith in the Lord Jesus Christ. This is the simplest condition. Faith is possible to all. The little child can exercise it; so can the philosopher. In many things we believe too readily. Believe in Christ, and be saved. Faith in Him as the condition of salvation is sublimely reasonable. The gospel is unalterable. Believe, and be saved.—*William Jones.*

Why Paul was not ashamed of the gospel.—It is of great moment to know the proper value of a thing before we either praise or disparise it. Let us beware of either overrating or underrating anything of which we are called to speak.

31

Of the gospel the apostle speaks as one who knew its value. The apostle so knew it as to be able to say, I am not ashamed of it. We are apt to be ashamed of it. It looks weak, foolish, unintellectual, unphilosophical. It lags behind the age. It is beginning to be supplanted by learning and eloquence. There were some places in which the apostle might have been specially tempted to be ashamed of the gospel or afraid of preaching it,—at Jerusalem, for there the whole strength of Jewish ritualism rose against it; at Athens, for there it was confronted by the power of Grecian wisdom; at Ephesus, for there the dazzling subtleties of heathen magic rose against it; at Corinth, for there the torrent of human lust and pleasure rushed against it; at Rome, for there was the concentrated energy of earthly idolatry. Yet none of these things moved him. We are tempted in our day to be ashamed of the gospel. If any might have been ashamed of it, Paul much more. His education, his life, his teachers, his companions, were all such as to make him turn aside from a thing so plain. But why was the apostle not ashamed of it? It was mighty—mightier than philosophy or argument or eloquence. It was "power." Many "apologists" for the gospel have, in their defence of it, assumed somewhat different ground from that of the apostle here. They defend it because it is noble, philosophical, reasonable, benevolent. It is all this, and more. Yet such are not Paul's reasons for glorifying in it. He has fathomed man's infinite need and misery; he has, with divinely opened eyes, looked into man's present condition and his prospects. He sees in that gospel that which meets man's great necessity as a lost being; and it is this glorious suitableness that makes him prize it so much. Had it been less than this, however intellectual and philosophical, he would have been ashamed of it. In thus listening to Paul's reasons for not being ashamed of the gospel, let us learn what he thinks of that gospel and what he understands it to be.

I. It is God's power unto salvation.—Men were lost. Nothing but a great salvation could deliver—*a salvation which embodied omnipotence.* We may say it is a gospel preceded by omnipotence, succeeded by omnipotence, accompanied by omnipotence, containing omnipotence. God's power was needed. Where has God placed it? In the gospel. The power that is needed for the salvation of a sinner is that which is contained in the gospel. The gospel alone contains this saving power. Who, then, are saved by it? Only they who believe. It is in believing this gospel that we are saved—saved at once, freely, completely, for ever. This gospel is wide as the world. It embraces all kindreds and nations and tongues. There is salvation for thee; not by working, or waiting, or praying, or reforming, but simply by *believing.* He who *believes* is saved, whoever or whatever he may be.

II. It is the revelation of God's righteousness.—This mighty gospel saves in a righteous way. Its power unto salvation consists in its being a revelation of the righteousness of God. This righteousness is not that which we call the attribute of God. It is a righteousness planned by God, provided and prepared by God, exhibited and unfolded by God to the sinner. 1. *It is a righteousness revealed.* No longer concealed, or but darkly unfolded; but fully and brightly displayed by God in Christ. 2. *It is a divine righteousness*—the righteousness of Him who was both God and man. 3. *It is a righteousness by faith.* This is the meaning of the words. "Therein is that righteousness of God, which comes to us by believing, revealed to be believed." 4. *It is righteousness presented to us to be believed.* Believe what God says to you concerning it, and straightway it is yours. 5. *It is the same righteousness which was possessed by the Old Testament saints.* "The just shall live by faith." The patriarchs "lived" by believing in Him who was to come; we "live" by believing in Him who has come. But it is one Saviour, one salvation, one cross. God's testimony to this righteousness is very full and explicit. He tells us what kind of righteousness it is, whose it is, and how we get it. It is divine, perfect, glorious, suitable—begun, carried out, completed by Christ during His life and death below : " For as by one man's disobedience many were made sinners, so by the obedience of One shall many be made righteous." The power of the gospel is wholly saving ; it is armed with power—*just in order to save.* There is nothing else in our world that can save but this.—*H. Bonar.*

The gospel the saving power of God.—One of the bravest utterances of one of the bravest of men. He had counted the cost, and knew the adverse influences he would have to cope with at Rome. His entry was the dearest wish of his heart. Though a prisoner in bonds, he was in truth the mightiest conqueror that ever graced the streets of the metropolis. He wielded a power mightier far than the armies of the empire. All forces opposed to him must go down. In the result of the contest he had not the shadow of a doubt. Why then need he be ashamed ?

I. **Divine power.**—" The power of God." This was the first reason why the apostle was not ashamed of the gospel. 1. *It is power.* The history of Christianity proves its claim to power. Wherever it goes it conquers. It proved more than a match for the iron despotism of Rome. It is the most potent force the world has ever known. False religions fall before it, and it changes the face of society. 2. *God's power.* The secret of its triumphs is that God is in it. The gospel was not the product of the world's wisdom. It came from above, and it is the highest and holiest means whereby God works on the race. A force was introduced unknown before, and it is impossible to account for it apart from God.

II. **Saving power.**—" Unto salvation." All power is not saving power. The power manifested in creation and providence is truly divine, but not necessarily saving. The power that resides in the gospel is meant to save men. 1. *It comes with a message of forgiveness.* " Who can forgive sins but God alone ? " To free from just condemnation is a mightier attribute than to rule a kingdom, and God alone supplies the remedy in the forgiveness of sins. The gospel struck at the root of the evil when every other system failed. " Who shall lay anything to the charge of God's elect ? It is God that justifieth." 2. *It is a power for the renewal of man's nature.* " Who can bring a clean thing out of an unclean ? " This is a task beyond unaided human resources. The design of Christ's mission was to save men from the dominion of sin as well as from condemnation. And for this we need a power not our own. Salvation is not the result of a combination of divine grace and human effort. It is grace all through, from first to last. The new creation is the work of the Spirit dwelling in the heart. Thus provision is made in the gospel, not only for the justification of man, but for his restoration to the divine image.

III. **Universal power.**—" To every one that believeth ; to the Jew first, and also to the Greek." This was a third reason why the apostle was not ashamed of the gospel. He was sure it would be its own witness, and work marvels in the imperial city, as it had done elsewhere. In the centre of the most solid of empires it would exert its power. It suits the needs of man everywhere. It owns no party ; it favours no sect. Its home is everywhere. It extends a helping hand to all, without respect to nation or social standing. It knows no distinction between the classes and the masses. " To the Jew first, and also to the Greek." The Jews despised it and fell, but their fall was the riches of the world. Rejection by this one or that will not prevent its universal spread. No cause therefore for being ashamed of the gospel. The words of a crucified Man are to-day more influential than the edicts of the Cæsars. For three hundred years the battle raged between Christianity and Roman paganism, till one of the most hostile emperors was compelled to exclaim with his dying breath, "Thou hast conquered, O Galilean." And the day will come sooner or later when all the world over it will be acknowledged that the Galilean King has won the day. "Whosoever shall be ashamed of Me," etc.—*D. Merson, B.D.*

Ver. 17. *Justified by faith.*—Note the change in the Revised Version. The term "just" is eliminated : the "righteous" shall live by faith. The text is used as the groundwork of the doctrine of justification by faith.

I. **What is justification by faith?**—If we apply the term "justification" to any one, we imply that he is just—*i.e.*, righteous, honest, exact, upright, proper, accurate in all his doings. But more than that : he is held to be innocent. Justification is that which declares a man blameless, innocent. When God justifies a man, this is how He looks upon him : He considers him a blameless, innocent man, not under the penalty of sin. That does not say that the man has been blameless, for every man has been, or is, a sinner ; but God is so gracious towards him, that He looks over the sin and treats the man as though he had no sin.

II. **The conditions of justification.**—"By faith"—*i.e.*, by faith in Christ Jesus. We must believe in Christ as our Saviour, as dying to make peace for us with God. This is an emphatic condition for pardon. But go further. If we take up another verse, which really belongs to the principle here discussed, we have a clearer idea. The just shall live by faith ; but "by grace are ye saved through faith"—*i.e.*, God pardons us, and holds us guiltless, if we have faith ; but not simply because we have faith, but because He loves us—loves us when we have no claim to His love.

III. **Definition of terms.**—1. *The "just"* = the "righteous" = the upright, the honest, those who are careful in all their doings, and, in these Christian days, sincere and earnest followers of Christ. 2. *"Shall live."* Pre-eminently this means "justified," held guiltless in God's sight, with sins all pardoned, and thus eligible for the life of the righteous and their reward. The righteous shall live *here*—*i.e.*, shall be happy, comforted, sustained, shall feel safe, and in time of temptation shall be succoured. The righteous also live the eternal life with God in "the many mansions." 3. *What is faith ?* A. *Negative aspect.* (1) Not bare belief. The heathen had some indistinct idea which constituted faith—*e.g.*, that there is a God mighty, etc. (2) "The devils believe." They know more of God than men do. (3) Not a bare assent to doctrine. Admit the Apostles' Creed ; but that, for any person, is intellectual concession, bare assent to the fundamental principles of the Christian religion. B. *Positive aspect.* (1) We have to accept all just mentioned—and more. When Paul said to the jailor, "Believe on the Lord Jesus Christ," etc., he surely did not mean "believe that there was such a man," but more, "believe in His power, and *trust* in it." Confidence ! But more still : taking God at His word, and coming to claim the promise, such as pardon. The old Puritans called this Christian faith a lying upon Christ, a leaning upon Him, a resting upon Him—just as the tottering man would lean on the arm of the strong one. (2) It must not be fitful, but continued, confidence. Is it "once saved always saved"? No. Though pardoned, you need *continued* faith to watch that "no man take your crown." Note in this connection that the three ideas of the text are interwoven : we *live* by faith ; we live by our *reliance* on Christ ; but it is the *just only* who so live. Those only who have sought and found pardon can enter into the rest that remaineth for the people of God.

IV. **The need for this text to-day.**—Because, with passing years, there is the fact

34

of a growing trust in external religion—a danger that faith would grow to mean, not trust and confidence in God and in Christ's merits, but trust in good works. The history of the Church points to the tendency to depart from the line of faith, and take up works as man's passport into heaven. Luther's heaviest blows were against justification by works. This had brought the Romish Church into great scandal. The Romish authorities had taught that good works cleanse men from all actual sin and reconcile us to God—a deliberate violation of the fundamental truth which declares that Christ, and not works, such as penance, fasting, etc., is the medium of our salvation.

V. **The effect of a life of faith.**—1. It makes a man a better citizen. The Christian must not sit aside, and say, I must not defile myself with earthly affairs. He may well be an active citizen, a loyal subject, patriotic to the backbone. 2. It makes a man a better neighbour. 3. Not a single duty of life but it is ennobled by Christianity. 4. The life of faith revolutionises a man—all his acts and purposes. 5. His life has a splendid effect on his surroundings. "The light of the world"; "the salt of the earth." If the *heart* be right with God, the works that a man shall do must be God-pleasing.—*Albert Lee.*

Ver. 16. *Ashamed of the gospel.*—Paul had the orator's very natural desire to refrain from saying anything calculated to shock the prejudices of his audience. When he addressed the men at Athens, he commenced by complimenting them on their devotion to religion. It had been a sufficiently difficult and delicate task to preach the gospel to Athenians, but now Paul contemplates preaching to Romans. He announces his intention in the course of a letter to the Church at Rome. He is fully conscious of the daring nature of his venture. If there were in the world one place where the gospel might be deemed more superfluous than another, surely it was Rome. Certainly the Romans would not be likely to be conscious of any need of the gospel. With Paul's experience to guide us, let us inquire why it is that so many persons are ashamed of the gospel.

I. **Because of social pride.**—The astonishing thing is that a man with Paul's abilities, heritage, and prospects of advancement should have cared to associate with such disreputable people as the early Christians were esteemed to be. Paul knew it, for he says: "Not many wise after the flesh, not many mighty, not many noble are called: but God chose the foolish things of the world, . . . the weak things, . . . and the base things, . . . and the things that are despised." If a person wanted to find suitable associates, he must go to the heathen temple. Everybody who was anybody went there. Nobody in his senses would think of attending the upper room where Christians met for such a purpose. The first Christian Churches were composed of members of the lower ranks of society. Slaves constituted the majority. Poverty was almost universal. In later days a good deal of pomp and circumstance gathered about the worship of the Christian Church. Rites and ceremonies were introduced of which the apostles knew nothing. As persons of higher rank joined the community there became less occasion for shame. When at last the emperor Constantine became a convert, all the shame arising out of social prejudice became a thing of the past. Those who followed the fashion followed the emperor and joined the Christian Church in thousands.

II. **Because of intellectual pride.**—It seemed a foolish tale that the first Christians had to tell. It was the constant sport of heathen writers that Christians worshipped a dead man of Palestine as God and as the Son of God. Paul knew that if his message excited attention in Rome, it would be attacked by men of keen intellect. His gospel would be riddled through and through with the polished shafts of sarcasm and ridicule. The majority of Romans had ceased to believe in any religion. Even the soothsayers dared not look each other in the face when performing their functions, lest they should be overcome with laughter. They had found out the emptiness of the most respected religions, and were not likely to believe such an improbable story as the Christians had to tell. When the gospel could be no longer ignored, Christians were treated with a contemptuous sneer, as those who believed the most palpable of falsehoods. Among educated young people to-day one often finds a disposition to look upon all religion as superstition. There is also a sort of empty conceit which knows no other way of indicating the possession of brains than by pretending that it is too cool and intellectual to be " taken in " by the story so often told from the pulpit.

III. **Because of moral pride.**—The greatest obstacle Paul had to overcome was his moral pride. His manner of life had been exemplary. " Ye have heard of my manner of life," he could say fearlessly. He had left a highly reputable religion, in which he had obtained distinction, for one which in many ways gave its enemies occasion to blaspheme. Paul was writing his epistle from Corinth, and much had happened in the Christian community there of which he was heartily ashamed. Unbelief, strife, and licentiousness had made the gospel a byword amongst them, and yet Paul was not ashamed of it. I have heard it said of our own Churches that their religious tone is such that one cannot with a clear conscience urge young folks to become members of them. Worse cannot be said of our Churches than was said of the Corinthian Church, and we may fearlessly take Paul's position, and with the clearest conscience urge you to join in fellowship with them. The remark is mostly a prejudiced slander ; but even if it were true, it would constitute no ground for being ashamed of the gospel. We freely enough admit that often the holiness of Church members is very low, and at times brotherly love has not been all it should be, and love to Christ has grown cold. Sometimes it has been with the Churches as it is in domestic affairs—when poverty has come in at the door, love has flown out of the window. The struggle against adverse circumstances has told heavily upon temper.—*Rev. R. C. Ford, M.A.*

SUGGESTIVE COMMENTS ON VERSES 15—17.

Paul's heroism.—Suppose a new moral system originated in some obscure village in the principality of Wales, suppose the originator of that system to have suffered the extreme penalty of the law as a malefactor, and that such a death was the essential part of that moral system, what would be thought of the heroism of the man who should go to London, and say, I am not ashamed of that system? Would any of the great preachers in London, remembering the origin of their own religion, condescend to examine the man's claims? For after all this is something like the position of our apostle. Palestine in its physical aspect insignificant? a tract of land running along the shores of the Mediterranean, one hundred and forty miles in length, forty miles in average breadth, about the size of Wales.

Nazareth an obscure village or town. "Can any good thing come out of Nazareth?" was a proverbial saying. Jesus Christ the Nazarene suffered a death equivalent to that which is now inflicted on the murderer. Such a death was and is a vital part of the gospel economy. We cannot understand a gospel which either ignores or stultifies the sacrificial nature of the Saviour's death. Thus let us try to picture the heroism of the apostle, who declares that he was ready to preach the gospel at Rome, the proud mistress of the world, the central seat of pomp, pride, and culture, with all its associations of idolatry and worldly power.

The power of God is such a force as to elevate man from sin to righteousness, from death to life, from hell to heaven, from the kingdom of Satan to the kingdom of God, and gives him eternal salvation.—*Luther.*

No reason to be ashamed.—The gospel had been proclaimed to all classes with the same results. It had won converts from them all. Over all alike it had achieved its triumphs. A greater difference in character, in habits, and in the institutions could hardly be met with than existed amongst those to whom the gospel had already found its way, and everywhere the effect was the same. There are many who can endure toil and physical suffering without shrinking, but who feel keenly contempt and ridicule. These things unman them; they recoil from them as from the most exquisite torture. All these the apostle bore with unfailing fortitude. The shame of the cross did not dismay him. The more men scorned it the more he gloried in it. To these stings he was not insensible—no generous nature can be. But the cross vanquished them all. With Christ in his eye the world might hurl what obloquy it pleased upon him. He gloried in that which men esteemed his reproach. With these facts before you, try to conceive the fulness of meaning there is in the statement, "I am not ashamed of the gospel." What a generous appreciation of the highest manifestation of the wisdom and love of God! The degree in which the spirit which animated Paul is possessed by us will measure our fitness for Christ's service and the likelihood of the success of our efforts to diffuse His gospel. None of us indeed can occupy the position which he did. His office was extraordinary. None of us is ever likely to be favoured with visions and revelations as he was. Still, let us never forget that unless our estimate of the gospel is similar to his and we are influenced by something of the same spirit, any hope of extensive usefulness is vain. What he was, not as an apostle, but as a Christian man, is what in our measure every one of us ought to be. Can we say, with something of the same meaning attached to the language, "I am not ashamed of the gospel of Christ"? Indeed, any sufferings we may be called upon to endure for the gospel, or any sacrifices we may have it in our power to make for it, are a perfect trifle in comparison with what we find verified in Paul's case. Do we so esteem the gospel that we withhold nothing. that is meet to promote its success? Has it ever cost us the sacrifice of a convenience or an indulgence to advance its interests? We hear often of the necessities of Christ's cause. How much have we spared to meet these necessities? Is it not often too true that the Master has reason to be ashamed of us, and that if men were to judge of our interest in the gospel by what we do for it, the question might well arise whether we understood it at all? Are there not many professing Christians whose prayers for the extension of Christ's kingdom are cold and few, out of all proportion to their own admission of the magnitude of its claims? Does not what they contribute to this object present a singular contrast to the amount they squander on their own personal gratifications? Let us strive to wipe off the reproach of such inconsistency. Blessings on our own soul and the smile of God on all our work will be sure to follow.—*J. Kelly.*

MAIN HOMILETICS OF THE PARAGRAPH.—Verses 18—21.

God manifest in His works.—In these days we often give undue prominence to the truth that "God is love." We seem to forget that this is compatible with God's holy and just indignation against sin. We do not question the love of the wise earthly father when he punishes the child. God is love, and as a wise God His wrath is revealed against ungodliness and unrighteousness of men. Most surely the wrath is revealed, though we cannot always read the revelation. The prosperity of the wicked in this life may be more in seeming than in reality, and the end will surely come. "The way of transgressors is hard." God's love is not a mere vapid sentiment, and cannot be allowed to override the eternal righteousness. Now St. Paul here shows that ungodly men are not excused because God has made Himself known in the frame of human nature and in the frame of the world. He anticipates modern objections, and classes those amongst the ungodly and unrighteous who tell us that by an intellectual necessity they have crossed the boundary of experience and discerned in matter the promise and potency of all terrestrial life. We fail to grasp the meaning of the expression "crossed the boundary of experience." Is that the ascertained result of a series of trials and experiments? If so, are we to be told that the ascertained result of a series of trials and experiments is *nil,* and that in matter are found the promise and potency of all terrestrial life? Is it an intellectual necessity? Is it not rather a moral obliquity which forces to the conclusion that matter is self-creating, and that God as creator is to be banished from His own creation? However, we still believe that God exists, and that His attributes are manifest in the frames both of man and of the world.

I. **Creative energy is clearly seen in the world.**—That there has been and is a Creator our faith is yet sufficiently strong to accept, though we have read books assailing its reasonableness. All that the scientists so far have done is to attempt to shake the authority of the Bible. They have not yet given us anything axiomatic. Their guesses, inferences, and so-called signs of evolutionary processes, of the eternal generation, of matter, do not amount to a demonstration. Certainly they do not formulate a creed. The scientists are not yet sufficiently agreed as to meet in general council, and to formulate a creed as to the world's origin which should supplant the Apostles' Creed. And meanwhile "through faith we understand that the worlds were framed by the word of God, so that the things which are seen were not made of things which do appear." Faith first embraces the doctrine, and observation declares that the faith is not unreasoning, is not unreasonable. We cannot lift the creature into the high position of being his or its own creator. A creator always *is.* A creature must at one period be represented by the words *is not,* if there be meaning in words, and if we still admit the word "creature" into our vocabulary. So that the creature *is,* and yet is not. He or it is both negative and positive at one and the same time. That which has been created creates itself. That which was once without life and motion gives life and motion to itself. The beautiful form, the graceful structure, the physical organism, are the products of evolution, and they have evolved themselves. They had power before they had being. They had qualities before there were material substances in which those qualities could inhere. Man is a production, and before his creation he produced himself. The producer and the product are identical, which is ridiculous. And the argument is not invalidated if we push our inquiries further back, and say that the potency of matter generated other potencies. Is there then such latent potency in one piece of matter that it can go on producing other pieces of matter far transcending the original in size, in grace, and in beauty? The primeval pieces of matter would be vastly astonished if they could see their wondrous progeny. Less than the famous dragon's tooth has brought forth multitudinous life—physical, intellectual, and moral. Can it be that matter has produced mind? Can it be that coarse matter has so mixed and fused and purified and etherealised its creations that there has been produced the intellect of man? Unutterably grand was the potency of the first germ-force which has produced immortal mind, which has sent floating through God's universe the mystic strains of music, of poetry, of eloquence, and of philosophy.

Matter is the mother of mind? Yea, mind is only matter, and the careful mother has done immensely well to her child. Let us reverence matter, for she has in her family group the human intellect, with its powers of memory, perception, acquisition, and retention. Can we believe the strange doctrine? Can we fancy the soul growing out of matter and embracing in its loves and yearning the great unknown? But why should matter be more potent in energy in past ages than in these days, when it has the advantage of being helped by some modern scientists? Why does she not produce other worlds? If this be deemed unnecessary, why does she not renovate our planet so that all defects may be removed, and a sphere given which should meet the scientist's idea of "the best possible world"? Through unknown æons, let us say, matter has remained in much the same condition, and nature shows no development of creative energy all along her mighty pathway; she does not even give a sign, show a trace, of the glory of once having been a creator. Man is a temple in ruins, but the glory has not all departed, for he is majestic in his ruins, and there are traces of great moral glory. But where are the signs on this world temple that it was once a creator? On the temple of the material universe we find no traces of an inscription to the effect that it once possessed creative energy and built itself. The world is a looking-glass into which we look and see there reflected as the creator neither matter nor human mind, neither evolution nor protoplasm, but God the Father and God the Son, a glorious unity. The evidences of design and order in the universe are sufficient for all practical purposes and adequate to establish the belief in unsophisticated minds that there has been an intelligent creator.

II. **Eternal power and wisdom are clearly seen in the world.**—The atheist can give no true account of the multitude, elegance, variety, order, and beauty that may be traced in the green earth with its ever-varying charms, and in the widespread heavens adorned with myriads of worlds. "The heavens declare the glory of God, and the firmament showeth His handiwork." "No," says M. Comte; "at the present time, for minds properly familiarised with true astronomical philosophy, the heavens display no other glory than that of Hipparchus, of Kepler, of Newton, and of all who have helped to establish these laws." "No persons," says Dr. M'Cosh, "were more willing to admit than the parties here named that the laws which they discovered must have existed before they could discover them—that the glory belongs to Him who established these laws, and *to them* but the reflected glory of having first interpreted them to mankind." We are told that the undevout astronomer is mad. What strange madness has seized the atheistical astronomer? How can one gaze at the stars without thinking of Him who alone spreadeth out the heavens, and treadeth upon the waves of the sea, "which maketh Arcturus, Orion, and Pleiades, and the chambers of the south"! Who can behold this "brave o'erhanging firmament, this most excellent canopy, the air, the majestical roof fretted with golden fire"—these spangled wonders, these lucid orbs— and not be filled with admiration of the wisdom and power there displayed! We say and feel that a God skilful in design, infinite in resource, and omnipotent in execution must have produced those spangled heavens. Here we have a comprehensive statement—eternal power. The scientist tells us that there is a latent potency in matter. How does he know if it is latent? Did he find it out with his microscope? Did he pursue the potency and discover it in the hiding-place? However that may be, there is a power antecedent to all time powers. The eternal power is beyond our comprehension, and is therefore unknowable. Eternity we know as a word, but we cannot know what it is as a condition. If it be possible for us to know eternity, then it is grasped by a finite nature and loses its infinity. It becomes a bounded eternity, which is a contradiction. Eternity we only know in part. We can simply know it as a mysterious something stretching before and after time. And yet we do not say that there is no such thing as the infinite because the finite cannot contain the infinite, and thus because it transcends our knowledge. We know the infinite in part, and believe in the unknowable. So let us not deny the eternal power because it is to us in all its vastness unknowable. Let us rise from the known to the unknown, from the powers of earth to the vast unknowable eternal power.

III. **The true divinity is clearly seen.**—The divine nature is made known both by the frame of man and of the world. A superhuman power is revealed as needful to the production of all things. If humanity could not project itself into life before it had life, then we are shut up to the conclusion of an antecedent agency giving to humanity its potencies and its energies. Divinity precedes humanity. We would not exclude the idea of divinity, for humanity is exalted by the connection. Atheists try to exalt themselves by seeking to confute the notion of a God; but in this instance it is strikingly true " he that exalteth himself shall be abased." How sadly abased is humanity when divinity is banished from its conceptions ! A superhuman agent is above the human race, a supernatural force is above and before all natural forces and powers; and that supernatural agent and force is the God, is the divinity, is the creator of the heavens and the earth.

IV. **The mental vision is obscured.**—The scientist laughs and says, All this may seem right to you, but it is all wrong to me. I have no need of your hypothesis of a divine being; matter is all-powerful, self-generating. Do you question my honesty ? Are not my intellectual powers above the average ? Does not the literary world accept with eagerness and pay liberally for my contributions ? The apostle would reply, The foolish heart is darkened, and thus the mental vision is obscured. Some of our modern scientists of a sceptical turn are praiseworthy in many respects; but there must be in them a fault somewhere, even if they are not open to Cowper's charge :—

> " Faults in the life breed errors in the brain,
> And then reciprocally those again."

Let us, however, not commit the common sin which is involved in the words, " The landscape has its praise, but not its author."

⁎ *My acknowledgment is due to the Sabbath Observance Society for permission to make use of my sermon on the Divine Unity, to which the adjudicators awarded a prize.*

Ver. 18. *God's truth and man's treatment of it.* — Two interpretations have been given to these words, either of which yields perfectly good sense. One is that the words simply mean that a man may be of unrighteous life, and yet have a knowledge of the truth. He holds the truth he possesses a certain knowledge of, but he holds it in *unrighteousness*—he is unrighteous in spite of it, and this is his condemnation. But there is another meaning of the word which is here rendered "hold." It sometimes signifies "to hold back," "to restrain," "to hinder." This sense of the word is adopted by many as that which we ought to attach to it in the passage before us ; and then it would read, "Who keep down the truth by their unrighteousness." Taking this to be the meaning of the text, let us look at it from this point of view. And notice man's conduct in reference to "the truth." "Who hold the truth in unrighteousness"—that is, as I have explained, who keep it down by their unrighteousness. It is checked and hindered, held back in its design to bless, by reason of unrighteousness. In what way ? Notice :—

I. **That sin extinguishes the love of and desire for the truth.**—It does not do so in regard to *secular* truth. The man of science pushes his inquiries into the domain of nature—the astronomer in his observatory, the chemist in his laboratory, the geologist among the rocks, each in his own way seeking the truth and desiring it. Sin does not perceptibly repress their enthusiasm nor lessen their desire for truth in science. And so likewise in other branches of inquiry. But it is very different in regard to the truth as it comes to us in God's word and sounds in the conscience. Why ? 1. *Because it does not offer itself as mere abstract truth to excite speculative interest.* It comes with great demands ; it is truth which claims *obedience*; and it is not so easy always to *obey* the truth as to talk about it and admire it. It prescribes, not simply the way in which we should believe, but also the way in which we should *walk*; and to walk rightly is a little harder than to believe rightly. God's truth addresses us in the imperative mood, and men shrink from its demands. 2. *The truth is a rebuke to a life of sin.* Every page of God's truth goes dead against sin ; and he who loves sin, who has no wish to give it up, but is bent upon keeping it, does not care to read his rebuke and to see himself written down " condemned." 3. *The truth again reveals to man the peril to which a life of sin exposes him.* It denounces judgment against sin, reveals the wrath of God against ungodliness and unrighteousness of men. Sin extinguishes all love and desire for the truth, because the truth claims obedience, rebukes and condemns sin, and declares its certain punishment.

II. **Sin destroys the soul's sensitiveness to the truth.**—It weakens the soul's power of moral perceptions. If we cultivate the habit of obeying the truth and following its lead, we shall proportionally increase our sensitiveness to its teachings. Our visions shall become clearer, and we shall have larger and distincter views of it. Obey divine truth. When you hear it speak to you, follow its indications of conduct and duty, and you will become more and more sensitive to it, you will recognise the truth with growing facility. But disobey what you know to be the truth, let it be a habit with you to disobey, and soon the voice of truth will be quenched and you will cease to hear it. You know how soon conscience may lose its sensitiveness, and gradually that which at one time you looked upon as *sin*, and were right in looking upon as sin, has come to be regarded as innocent, as something quite allowable even in a Christian man. Beware of trifling with the truth ! It is to your interest that it should come into a position of power in your nature, that it may bless you with its freedom. Beware, therefore, of letting some cherished sin hold it back and prevent it from rising within you. That sin is destroying the soul's sensitiveness. Even in the best of us the truth is kept down. It would bless us far more than it does ; but some sin checks it, and the truth is crippled in its power of usefulness to us.— *Alex. Bell, B.A.*

Ver. 21. *Gratitude.*

I. **The obligation.**—It is the duty of all men to cherish a spirit of gratitude towards God. This is evident when we consider the number, variety, magnitude, and ceaseless flow of the benefits which we enjoy. 1. The works of creation furnish us with ground for thankfulness, in that they afford pleasure to the senses, support to our life, and are an evidence of the goodness of God. 2. The structure of our bodies and the endowments of the mind are a ground for thankfulness : health and reason are inestimable blessings. 3. The position in which God has placed us is a ground for thankfulness,—the pleasures of society ; the facilities we enjoy for mental and moral improvement. 4. God's providential care is a ground for thankfulness : we have been guided, guarded, and sustained. 5. The spiritual blessings that are so freely bestowed are a ground for thankfulness,—the gift of Christ and the offer of pardon and peace to all who believe on Him ; the gift of the Spirit, with all the benefits which He confers ; the

41

promises of God and the hope that is set before us; the joy that is unspeakable and full of glory. There is no means of measuring or weighing these gifts, and their cordial acceptance is the condition of receiving many more.

II. **The consequences of neglecting this obligation.**—1. The loss of much real enjoyment; 2. The loss of man's respect; 3. The hardening of the heart; 4. The withdrawal of the blessings slighted; 5. The cursing of the blessings, though they remain; 6. The infliction of future punishment. How may gratitude be expressed? 1. By giving to God our heart's best love; 2. By working for Him among our fellow-men.—*Preacher's Assistant.*

SUGGESTIVE COMMENTS ON VERSES 18—22.

Man unaided cannot attain righteousness.—By some of those to whom the apostle addressed himself it might be thought that this method of justification was unnecessary, for that if men fulfilled the duties incumbent on them nothing more could be required to render them objects of divine favour. And no doubt, if they fulfilled their duty completely, this would be the fact. On this supposition the revelation of a new species of righteousness as the means of their acceptance with God would be wholly superfluous; for if men's own perfect obedience and freedom from sin entitle them to be justified, the necessity of any other method of justification would be entirely taken away. But the apostle goes on to show that all claim to justification on this ground is utterly hopeless, since nothing can be further from the actual condition of mankind than such an unsinning obedience as this mode of justification would require. This point he proceeds to establish by describing the moral condition of mankind; and in order to show the conclusiveness of his proof he begins by laying down this maxim, that "the wrath of God is revealed from heaven against all ungodliness and unrighteousness." If this then be the case, as it cannot be denied, and if men be ungodly and unrighteous, as is also unquestionable, it follows that justification cannot be attained by their own obedience, and therefore that it must be sought by the righteousness of faith revealed in the gospel. It cannot be doubted that God has manifested with sufficient clearness to mankind in general His wrath against

sin; nor can it be doubted that the knowledge of this displeasure implies that sin deserves punishment, and that it will actually receive the punishment which it deserves. These are truths which may be understood by all who will give due consideration to the subject; and if, notwithstanding this knowledge, they still continue to act impiously and unrighteously, they can have no claim to be justified on the footing of their own works, seeing their works are such as to subject them to inevitable condemnation. It has been maintained, indeed, that unaided reason is wholly incompetent to discover the being and perfections of God—that our minds are so darkened and debased by sin that, had not the knowledge of God been communicated and preserved by a divine revelation, it must have been finally lost in the world. This opinion has been brought forward to support the doctrine of the utter corruption of human nature by sin. But it is an opinion neither warranted by experience—for, without denying all history, we cannot deny that these doctrines were known at least to some of the ancient philosophers—nor authorised by Scripture; for here St. Paul acknowledges that what "may be known of God was manifest" to the philosophers and legislators to whom he alludes. No doubt the effects of sin in debasing the human mind are great and deplorable, but its operation is chiefly on our moral nature; for if we take the apostle as our guide, we shall own that it has not so completely deranged our intellectual powers as to disqualify us for discovering that there is a God whom we are bound to worship and obey. This knowledge the heathen actually possessed, "for God hath showed it unto them." There is, indeed, no department of nature which we have the means of observing but which may lead the contemplative mind to infer the being and perfections of God; for in all the objects that lie open to our inspection we find such manifest proofs of wise contrivance adapting the means employed to the ends to be accomplished, as cannot be explained on any possible supposition unless on admitting that they proceed from the appointment of an all-wise creator. They "became vain in their imaginations." To become vain, according to the Scripture use of that phrase, often means to become addicted to idolatry; as in 2 Kings xvii. 15, 16: "They followed vanity, and became vain, and went after the heathen, . . . and made to themselves molten images, . . . and worshipped all the host of heaven." It seems to be in this sense that the word is employed here; and the meaning of the passage appears to be, that all their notions or reasonings on the subject tended to vanity, that is to idolatry, and led them to the folly of worshipping idols rather than the living and true God.—*D. Ritchie, D.D.*

The beauty of nature should make us feel God.—Surely vain are all men by nature, who are ignorant of God, and could not out of the good things that are seen know Him that is: neither by considering the works did they acknowledge the work-master; but deemed either fire, or wind, or the swift air, or the circle of the stars, or the violent water, or the lights of heaven, to be the gods which govern the world. With whose beauty if they being delighted took them to be gods, let them know how much the Lord of them is: for the first author of beauty hath created them. But if they were astonished at their power and virtue, let them understand by them, how much mightier He is that made them. For by the greatness and beauty of the creatures proportionably the maker of them is seen. But yet for this they are the less to be blamed: for they peradventure err, seeking God, and desirous to find Him. For being conversant in His works, they search Him diligently, and believe their sight: because the things are beautiful that are seen.—*The Wisdom of Solomon.*

A mill without a miller is as absurd as a world without God.—If man thinks it a great thing to have invented telegraphy and the telephone and other modern wonders, and if in connection therewith he talks of the march of intellect and of the advance of science, why should he deem it unneedful or unmanly to believe that infinite wisdom was engaged in and displayed by the invention and formation of the human body? But further, the brain, as the seat of thought, as being now generally regarded as the mysterious sphere of intellectual operations, declares both man's greatness and man's divine origin. Yes, man is great—man is God-fashioned because he thinks. And the wonderfulness of man's nature is still more declared by the fact that his thinking machine cannot explain the process which itself performs. Some of the noblest intellects have spent time and energy in trying to solve this difficult problem, but it still remains one of the quesita. Theories have been broached, only to be nullified by succeeding theories, and the only true theory at present in existence is that it is a baffling mystery. Here a question naturally arises: If man made himself, if man evolved himself out of concomitant and concurrent chaotic atoms, why can he not more easily understand himself? The inventor and maker of a machine can understand and explain all its parts. The painter knows how his effects were produced. The poet can dissolve into their parts and explain his own rhythmical measures. And yet man, too proud to own a God, must be humble enough to confess that he

43

cannot understand himself. Let man perfect that in his physical frame which he considers imperfect, and then we shall have more patience to watch and listen as he struts with lordly airs and contemns in abhorrent language the master-work of infinite wisdom and power. We think, but cannot tell what we do when we are said to think. We cannot explain how we think. We cannot name, by any term less meaningless than the ego or self, that mysterious person which is said to think. Was then this thinking power or faculty self-evolved? Surely it is by no means satisfactory to declare that thought is a mere mixing or moving or shaking up of nervous fluid or phosphorescent particles in the brain. Are ideas merely phosphorescent gleams? In a certain sense it is true, just as we might say, No brain, no thought; no man, no thought. Nerve fibres require a living agent. Phosphorus is not self-acting. Who brings the phosphorus into action, and consents to spread over the universe its sweet intellectual light? Does the match strike fire by a process of spontaneous combustion without the aid of an active agent? Surely his power of thought lifts man above mere materialism, and is the noblest of endowments? It should speak to us of the divine origin of our nature. We come forth from and are sustained by God. The mind stamps the man with unspeakable greatness. Thoughts can penetrate and subdue where implements of husbandry and weapons of war are ineffectual. The grandeur of man's intellectual nature in its highest forms must strike us with solemn awe. How sublime this power of thought! How gloriously noble to be able beautifully to delineate on canvas either some stirring incident of external life or soul-moving conception from the internal; to trace in marble rare forms of beauty; to make the granite live and speak in our presence; to embody in poetry fancy's rich visions; to give with pen, ink, and paper living, lasting embodiment to the aerial, unsubstantial results of intellectual processes; to control the fiercest animals and the very elements of nature; to speak, and the winds are hushed, the storm is stilled, the angry waves are calmed, the ancient rocks are rent, and forth there comes the living stream sparkling in heaven's sunlight; to think, and the material world is touched to its very centre; to remember, and all the past is summed up, and moves before me in stately procession, forming groups, now solemn and now joyful; to love, and I am linked to the whole universe and the whole universe is linked to me—earth and heaven, man and God, are joined in blessed union! Well may we take up the old refrain: What a piece of work is man! How noble in reason! how infinite in faculties! In form and moving how express and admirable! in action how like an angel! in apprehension how like a god! The beauty of the world! the paragon of animals! The great Shakespeare would consent as we add: the masterpiece of the Creator's works! Man is great even in the ruin entailed by the Fall. The very magnificence of the ruins declares at the same time his greatness and the fact that he was made in the image of God—made by the Creator, and made to bear the Creator's likeness and to be His vicegerent in this lower world.

The provisions of nature speak for God.—It may be assumed for a principle, which common experience suggests to us, that matter of itself does not run into any order, etc. If not now, then not yesterday, nor from eternity; it must therefore by some counsel be digested. There is not indeed any kind of natural effect which, either singly taken or as it stands related to the public, may not reasonably be supposed to contain some argument of this truth. We do not indeed discern the use and tendency of each particular effect, but of many they are so plain and palpable that we have reason to suppose them of the rest: even as of a person whom we do plainly perceive frequently to act very wisely, at other times, when we cannot discern the drift of his proceeding, we cannot but suppose that he hath some latent reason, some reach of policy, that we are not aware of ; or as in an engine, consisting of many parts curiously compacted together, whereof we do perceive the general use, and apprehend how some parts conduce thereto, we have reason to think they all are subservient to the artist's designs. Such an agent is God ; such an engine is this visible world. We can often discover marks of God's wisdom ; some general uses of the world are discernible, and how that many parts thereof do contribute to them we may easily observe ; and seeing the whole is compacted in a constant order, we have reason to deem the like of the rest. Our incapacity to discover all does not argue defect, but excess of the Maker's wisdom—not too little in itself, but too great perfection in the work in respect of our capacity. The most to us observable piece of the universe is the earth upon which we dwell; which that it was designed for the accommodation of living creatures that are upon it, and principally of man, we cannot be ignorant or doubtful, if we be not so negligent as to let pass unobserved those many signs that show it. If we look upon the frame of the animals themselves, what a number of contrivances in each of them do appear, suitable to the kind and station of each ! If we look about them, what variety and abundance of convenient provisions offer themselves even to a careless view, answerable to all their needs ! Wholesome and pleasant food to maintain their life, yea, to gratify all their senses ; fit shelter from offence, and safe refuge from dangers: all these things provided in sufficient plenty for such a vast number of creatures ; not the least, most silly, weak, or contemptible creature but we may see some care hath been had for its nourishment and comfort. What wonderful instincts are they endued with for procuring their food, for guarding themselves and their young from danger ! But for man especially

a most liberal provision hath been made to supply all his needs, to please all his appetites, to exercise with profit and satisfaction all his faculties, to content his utmost curiosity. All things about him do minister to his preservation, ease, and delight. The bowels of the earth yield him treasures of metals and minerals, quarries of stone, and coal serviceable to him for various uses. The commonest stones he treadeth upon are not unprofitable. The surface of the earth, what variety of delicate fruits, herbs, and grains doth it afford to nourish our bodies, and cheer our spirits, and please our tastes, and remedy our diseases ! How many fragrant flowers for the comfort of our smell and delight of our eyes ! Neither can our ears complain, since every wood hath a choir of natural musicians to entertain them with their sprightful melody. Every wood, did I say ? Yes, too, the woods adorned with stately trees yield pleasant spectacles to our sight. Even the barren mountains send us down fresh streams of water. Even the wide seas themselves serve us many ways : they are commodious for our commerce ; they supply the bottles of heaven with water to refresh the earth; they are inexhaustible cisterns, from whence our springs and rivers are derived ; they yield stores of good fish and other convenience of life. The very rude and disorderly winds do us no little service in cleansing the air for our health, in driving forward. our ships, in scattering and spreading about the clouds, those clouds which drop fatness upon our grounds. As for our subjects the animals, it is not possible to reckon the manifold utilities we receive from them—how many ways they supply our needs with pleasant food and convenient clothing, how they ease our labour, and how they promote even our sport and recreation. And are we not, not only very stupid, but very ungrateful, if we do not discern abundance of wisdom and goodness in the contrivance and ordering of all these things, so as thus to conspire for our good ?—*Barrow.*

Forasmuch as by all things created is made known the "eternal power and Godhead," and the dependency of all limited beings infers an infinite and independent essence; whereas all things are for some end, and all their operations directed to it, although they cannot apprehend that end for which they are, and in prosecution of which they work, and therefore must be guided by some universal and over-ruling wisdom; being this collection is so evident that all the nations of the earth have made it; being God hath not only written Himself in the lively characters of His creatures, but hath also made frequent patefactions of His deity by most infallible predictions and supernatural operations,—therefore I fully assent unto, freely acknowledge, and clearly profess this truth, that *there is a God.—Pearson.*

Mental vision needful.—These things, Paul says, are seen, though invisible, by their manifestation in the external world. This manifestation is perpetual and universal. It is "from the creation of the world." These words may indeed be rendered "by the creation," etc., but not consistently with the latter part of the verse; nor do they, when thus rendered, give so pertinent a sense. These invisible things are seen, "being understood "—that is, it is a mental vision of which Paul speaks. The eye of the sense sees nothing but the external object; the mind sees mind—and mind possessed, not of human power and perfections, but of eternal power and divinity. The word rendered "divinity" means the "divine majesty and excellence," and therefore includes all the perfections of God. These perfections are manifested "by the things which are made ": so the word here used properly

means (see Eph. ii. 10); but it may also mean "works" generally. Being understood by His "works" would then include the dispensations of His providence as well as the products of His hands. The common version, however, is more natural and appropriate.—*Hodge.*

A wise agent revealed in the world.—Is it not a folly to deny the being of a wise agent who sparkles in the beauty and motions of the heavens, rides upon the wings of the wind, and is writ upon the flowers and fruits of plants? As the cause is known by the effects, so the wisdom of the cause is known by the elegance of the work, the proportion of the parts to one another. Who can imagine the world could be rashly made, and without consultation, which in every part of it is so artificially framed? No work of art springs up of its own accord. The world is framed by an excellent art, and therefore made by some skilful artist. As we hear not a melodious instrument, but we conclude there is a musician that touches it, as well as some skilful hand that framed and disposed it for these lessons; and no man that hears the pleasant sound of a lute but will fix his thoughts, not upon the instrument itself, but upon the skill of the artist that made it, and the art of the musician that strikes it, though he should not see the first when he saw the lute, nor see the other when he hears the harmony,—so a rational creature confines not his thoughts to his sense when he sees the sun in its glory and the moon walking in its brightness, but rises up in a contemplation and admiration of that infinite spirit that composed and filled them with such sweetness.—*Charnock.*

MAIN HOMILETICS OF THE PARAGRAPH.—*Verses 22—33.*

Polytheism and atheism.—In these concluding verses we have a dark but true record of the deplorable results of polytheism. The most degrading vices that can afflict and ruin humanity run rife in the polytheistic world. The rejection of the true God, the rejection of all true good, of every preservative influence—the rejection of God is not only the rejection of every preservative influence, but the stirring up against the rejecters of every destructive force. God gave them over to a reprobate mind to do those things which are not convenient. This is alike the teaching both of nature and of revelation. The rejection of good is the provocation of evil. The downward course is easy. Beware of first steps in sin, the provocation of evil, because by the rejection of the good evil is incited, as it were, to do us further harm and bring upon us destruction. Death is the final penalty of those who take pleasure in polytheistic and atheistic theories. Polytheism is scarcely the danger of civilised societies. The only idols we are likely to worship are idols of the mind. Our pantheons are the temples of mammon, the halls of philosophy falsely so called, the shrines of fashion, the haunts of refined but insidious and harmful pleasures. Our danger is practical atheism, and it is creeping into our places of religious worship. What is it but practical atheism which limits God to the church or chapel ? What is it but practical atheism which allows men to do in secret that which they would not do before the sight of their fellow-men ? Polytheism and atheism are nearly allied. They both conspire to rob God of His glory. The former substitutes images of corruptible men, birds, four-footed beasts, and creeping things for the glory of the incorruptible God ; the latter substitutes, rather leaves, an awful void for the repose which those enjoy who recognise, worship, and serve the Creator : the former, as we here see, generates deplorable vices, and would soon make the world both a moral and a material ruin ; the latter, likewise, would leave nations without any true safeguard. In speaking of atheistic tendencies we are not to consider the refined and moral advocates of atheism only, who may be influenced by the Christian forces about them ; but we must follow them in their tortuous windings until we come to the dire and dark ocean where humanity would be finally immersed. In the endeavour to make our paraphrase on these gloomy verses of the epistle practical and suitable to our times, let us offer a few reflections on atheism in general. We here make no blind attack upon particular men, and do not forget that men are sometimes better than their creeds ; for atheists, theists, and scientists all have their creeds, though they do not recite them in churches. Even the agnostic, who denies that we can know the absolute and infinite God, may have a creed, which may be professing himself to be wise.

I. **Atheism suits the depraved wishes.**—The head is not convinced ; but the heart, the seat of affections, is set upon this declaration, that there is no God. It is well known that the wish is the father of the thought ; and the fool has the strong wish that there may be after all no God. It would be a great relief if he could be firmly persuaded that there were no moral governor, and that man were an irresponsible creature. Responsibility is a heavy burden on the back of him who is sinful and foolish in conduct. Man finds himself trammelled not only by outward laws, but by an inward feeling that he ought to be subject to and obey those laws, and he cannot rid himself of this feeling, he cannot shake himself free from the trammels. The words " ought " and " ought not " are as fearful phantoms that torture his soul. He longs to be free, and yet cannot attain freedom. His wishes go out towards a goal which he can never reach. He keeps saying in his heart there is no God, and yet he gets no nearer to the establishment of this desired atheistic doctrine in his nature.

II. **Atheism accords with false doctrine.**—It is both the cause and the effect of false doctrine. Action and reaction work here as in other realms, only that reaction is a great productive power in this sphere. Atheism is the result of false doctrine ; and when the creed, the " no God " creed, is received, it works powerfully to the production of still greater falseness and more debasing views of life and of morals. There can be no guarantee for morals if the idea of a moral governor be banished, if indeed it can be completely banished, from the world of thought. Theism is the foundation of right religion, and right religion cannot be divorced from a correct moral code. Ethical systems are but a rope of sand if they do not begin in the idea of a moral governor. Atheism is the cause and effect of false doctrine in the heart. These produce both the professed and the practical atheist. And this in turn fosters erroneous opinions; they grow to greater potency, and become tyrannical.

III. Atheism agrees with and fosters corrupt practice.—We are far from charging all atheists with being corrupt in practice as well as erroneous in doctrine. It may be that some atheists are as pure in life as some theists. Certainly it will not do to denounce a creed because of the immorality of its adherents. It is an old and a favourite method to damage the cause by vilifying the persons. Still, when atheism has been tried, if it can ever be tried, to a large extent like the Christian religion, then will be the time to speak of its practical results. The nearest approach to such a trial was in France, when God was dethroned and reason was worshipped. This monarch soon had the sceptre of authority wrested from its grasp. Reason soon became unreason. The vilest passions were let loose. Judgment was taken away from the line. Righteousness was no longer the guide of the reins. Misrule was the confusing, disturbing, and wasting order of the day. Practical atheism had been tried, and was found wanting. When atheists live pure lives, it follows either from the unconscious influence of Christianity, or from the force of an enlightened public opinion, or from remaining respect for virtue which atheism has not destroyed. Men are naturally depraved, and practise the evil while they approve of the good. It seems ridiculous to extol the goodness of human nature in the light of history, and of that history which is being enacted daily before our eyes, and which is being recorded in our daily papers. Let atheism prevail, and the floodgates of iniquity would be thrown open, and the pestilential waters would flow with destructive and ominous sweep over our planet. Our blessings brighten as they fly and disappear. We tell the force of an element or of a principle by withdrawing it from its proper connection. Tom Paine's *Age of Reason* was printed in America, and before publishing the book he submitted the manuscript to Benjamin Franklin, who said, " Burn it; do not loose a tiger: if men are so wicked with religion, what would they be without it?" The withdrawal of religion would be the withdrawal of a great restraining force from society, and human nature would lose one important check to the outlet of its depravity. A belief in a God is a blessing which we do not fully appreciate. If it were withdrawn from the world, we should find out how great a preservative and conservative force it has been amongst mankind. Virtue, as its own reward, would not lead men to follow virtue for its own sake. The greatest happiness of the greatest number would mean the greatest happiness of the greatest number one; for selfishness would override a spirit of universal philanthropy. Utilitarianism would mean, How can I make others useful to the promotion of my individual interests? Materialism would swallow up moralism, and, like Pharaoh's lean kine, would not be bettered by the process. Moral restraints would be not only loosened, but destroyed. Passions of the vilest kind would be let loose, like so many fierce and hungry wolves. Debasing lusts would speedily quench the fires of divinity still shining in human nature. The question of existence would become a question of physical power; the weakest physically considered would have to go to the wall. The time would soon come when only Samson and the Philistines were left, and he would make a last effort by which he and his oppressors would be involved in one common and hideous ruin. And our planet would soon be destitute of intelligent inhabitants. Before this sad event the race would be indeed properly described by the graphic words, " They are corrupt: they have done abominable works; there is none that doeth good."

IV. **Atheism is an endeavour to delude conscience.**—Strange are the tricks which men play with their own nature. They endeavour to deceive their own selves, and too often succeed for a time in the art of self-deception. They strive to delude conscience by saying that there is no Creator, and therefore no moral governor. Then the voice of conscience is to be regarded as uttering a meaningless sound. In Paris they drink a mixture which they call "absinthe," which brings the mind into a delightful state. Under its influence the soul appears to rise above the clouds, and is filled with pleasant visions. But by-and-by this pleasant effect passes away, convulsions and fearful headache follow, the hair falls from the head, and the deluded victim of over-indulgence is brought either to the madhouse or to an early grave. These short-lived visions of pleasure are bought at a fearful price. Thus the atheistic fool may for a time delude conscience. Pleasant visions of freedom from moral bondage may delight; but alas! too soon the pleasant effect will vanish. The atheistic absinthe will lose its power to charm and to delude, even if it does delude for the time being—a question which may very well be asked as we consider the constituents of conscience. Let us seek then: 1. *To retain the idea of the true God in our knowledge*; 2. *To cling to the theistic truth as taught by right reason, by nature, and by revelation*; 3. *To worship and serve the Creator with heart and with head—in fact, with all our powers*; 4. *So to work, live, and pray that neither we nor our descendants may be reduced to the lowest depth of evil.* "Without understanding, covenant-breakers; without natural affection, implacable, unmerciful." Christianity develops the understanding, teaches men to feel themselves bound by their contracts, nurtures the natural affections, ameliorates and ultimately removes the implacable nature, and informs the poet to raise the song in praise of mercy. Shakespeare's "quality of mercy" is one of the sublimest strains ever chanted by mortal tongue, and it received its inspiration from the lips of the Great Teacher.

Lie.—I. **An idol a lie.**—1. As professing to be what it is not; 2. As deceiving him who trusts in it.

II. **Everything opposed to God a lie.**

III. **Everything a lie which**—1. Disappoints man's hopes; 2. Fails to satisfy the cravings of his immortal soul.

IV. **That life a lie which is not**—1. According to God's will; 2. Directed to His glory; 3. The realisation of His enjoyment.—*Rev. T. Robinson.*

Man's forgetfulness.—God has well remembered man—remembers him every day. God might easily forget man; he is so insignificant, worthless, unlovable. But He does not. God desires to be remembered by man. He has taken unspeakable pains to keep Himself before His creatures, so as to make forgetfulness on their part the greatest of all impossibilities. In everything that God has set before our eyes or ears He says, Remember Me. In every star, every flower, every mountain, every stream—in every joy, every comfort, every blessing of daily life—God says, Remember Me. It is not, however, merely a "deity," a divine being, that is to be remembered. It is the one living and true God. Every departure from this is idolatry and dishonour. This true God wishes to be remembered. 1. *Reverently.* He is great and glorious, to be had in reverence of all creaturehood. 2. *Confidingly.* His character is such that He deserves to be trusted. 3. *Joyfully.* Not by constraint, or through terror or hope of profit, but with the full and happy heart. 4. *Lovingly.* We love Him because He first loved us. 5. *Steadfastly.* Not by fits and starts, at certain "devotional seasons," but always. This God, whose name is Jehovah, is worthy to be remembered, He is so infinitely glorious, and good, and great, and lovable. The wonder is, how One so great should ever for a moment be forgotten. Yet man forgets God! He hears of Him, and then forgets Him. He sees His works, and then forgets Him. He acknowledges deliverances, and then forgets Him.

Israel is frequently charged with such things as these: 1. *They forgat His words.* 2. *They forgat His works.* Miracle on miracle of the most stupendous kind did He for Israel in Egypt and in the desert. They sang His praise, and then forgat His works. 3. *They forgat Himself.* Yes, Himself—their God, their Redeemer, their Rock, their Strength! They thrust Him out of their thoughts and memories. God lays great stress upon remembering Him and His works. Often did He use that word to Israel, " Remember." " Remember the way that the Lord led thee." " Remember the commandments of the Lord." " Remember the Sabbath day, to keep it holy." ": Remember thy Creator." In the New Testament the words of the Lord Himself must occur to every one, " This do in remembrance of Me "; and the response of the Church, " We will remember Thy love more than wine." Forget not, O man, the God that made thee. He has given thee no cause to forget Him.—*H. Bonar.*

SUGGESTIVE COMMENTS ON VERSES 23—32.

Paul includes all transgressors.— Though the apostle begins his delineation of the ungodliness and unrighteousness against which wrath is revealed by specifying the grievous misconduct of the philosophers and legislators among the heathen, it must not be supposed that he means to limit his description to those who possessed extensive knowledge and high intellectual attainments. He plainly includes all who transgressed any known duty. His allusion to the wise and eminent seems intended to suggest this important consideration, that if the wrath of God be revealed against the transgressions even of these high and honoured characters, how much more must it fall on the great body of offenders who have no such shining qualities to- counterbalance their sins? Nor must it be supposed, because the first thing specified in this dark catalogue of transgressions is the concealment of what was known concerning God, and transferring the glory which belongs only to the incorruptible God to imaginary objects of worship, that is the only or even the chief offence against which wrath is revealed. This is the only fruitful source from which the gross practical wickedness of the heathen arose, and by which it was encouraged. But according to the

principle before laid down, wrath is revealed, not only against this particular sin, but against every transgression whatever.—*Ritchie.*

Nature leaves without excuse.— " *Not as God,*" etc. The revelation in nature of God's greatness and bounty ought to have produced in their hearts admiration and gratitude. It produced neither. But it left them without excuse. And for this end it was given—i.e., to make them conscious of the guilt of their ungodliness and ingratitude. Notice that their first fault was negative. All else was the result of not using the light which God gave. " *But they became vain,*" etc. Result of not giving honour and thanks to God. Their minds were at work, but to no purpose. Their reasonings were in vain. The facts of idolatry here asserted need, unfortunately, no confirmation. The writings and relics of antiquity prove the charge. Statues of men were worshipped by the Greeks; and the mummies of birds and reptiles from the temples of Egypt fill our museums. And, as far as I know, when Paul wrote this epistle, no serious voice had been raised in heathendom against this folly. *Paul's view of natural theology.* With him creation plays a part in the moral

50

training of the Gentiles similar to that of the law in the training of the Jews. A striking coincidence is found in the only two recorded discourses addressed by Paul to heathens, each of which he begins by appealing to the works of creation. With the Jews he begins by quoting the Old Testament. In each case he appeals to an earlier revelation given to prepare the way for the gospel, and thus seeks to call forth that consciousness of guilt without which the need of the gospel is not felt. God's revelation of Himself in nature would probably bear its chief fruit in those Gentiles who heard the gospel. While listening to it they would condemn themselves, not for rejecting Christ, of whom they had never heard, but for disregarding a revelation which had been before their eyes from childhood. And just as the law retains its value even for those who have accepted the gospel, so the worth of the nature-revelation remains to those who behold the glory of God in the face of Jesus. That God reveals Himself in nature, raises natural science to a sacred study, and gives to it its noblest aim. We learn that, by the just judgment of God, godlessness, folly, and shame go together. Are not those men guilty of incredible folly who prefer to direct their highest thought and effort to the perishing objects around, rather than to those which will never pass away? Human nature is the same. The principles here asserted attest themselves before our eyes and in our hearts. The inevitable connection of godlessness, folly, and sin proclaims in words we cannot misunderstand that God is angry with those who forget Him. Heathens have observed this. Socrates, in Xenophon's *Memoir*, says that the fact that certain sins produce their own punishment proves that the law which forbids them is from God. *The true nature of sin.* It is not a mere act, but is an adverse power against which man, unaided by God,

is powerless. It has allies in our own hearts. The deep shame of the heathen is with Paul fully accounted for by the fact that God gave them up to sin. Of this all else is the necessary result.—*Beet.*

Conscience the best argument.—Our conscience is the best argument in the world to prove there is a God, for conscience is God's deputy; and the inferior must suppose a superior, and God and our conscience are alike relative terms, it not being imaginable why some persons in some cases should be amazed and troubled in their minds for their having done a secret turpitude or cruelty, but that conscience is present with a message from God, and the men feel inward causes of fear when they are secure from without—that is, they are forced to fear God when they are safe from men. And it is impossible that any man should be an atheist if he have any conscience; and for this reason it is there have been so few atheists in the world, because it is so hard for men to lose their conscience wholly.—*Ductor Dubitantium.*

Corruption of the heathen.—Greater folly than this exchange of the living and glorious God for the mere image of birds, beasts, and reptiles the world has never seen. That the heathen really worshipped such objects is well known. Philo says that the whole land of Egypt was covered with temples and groves dedicated to dogs, wolves, lions, land and water animals, crocodiles, birds, etc. With regard to the vast majority of the people, the homage terminated on the animal or the idol; and the case was little better with the pantheistical refiners and defenders of this system, who professed to worship the great and universal divine principle in these particular manifestations. Why should the higher manifestation of God in the human soul do homage to the lower development of the universal principle in a reptile? We never find the sacred writers making any account of this common subterfuge and apology for idolatry. All who bowed down to a stock or stone they denounced as worshipping gods which their own hands had made, which had eyes but saw not, ears but heard not, and hands that could not save. This corruption of morals was confined to no one class or sex. Paul first refers to the degradation of females among the heathen, because they are always the last to be affected in the decay of morals; and therefore when they are abandoned the very fountains of purity are corrupted. It is unnecessary to say more than that virtue has lost its hold on the female sex, in any community, to produce the conviction that it has already reached the lowest point of degradation.—*Hodge.*

God not the author of sin.—God may make one sin the punishment of another, though it still is to be remembered that it is one thing for God to *give a man over to sin,* and quite another to cause him to sin: the former importing it in no more than God's providential ordering of a man's circumstances, so that he shall find no check or hindrance in the course of his sin; but the latter implying also a positive efficiency toward the commission or production of a sinful act; which God never does, nor can do; but the other He both may and in a judicial way very often does. . . . In all which God is not at all the author of sin, but only pursues the great work and righteous ends of His providence in disposing of things or objects, in themselves good or indifferent, toward the compassing of the same. Howbeit, through the poison of men's vicious affections, they are turned into the opportunities and fuel of sin, and made the occasion of their final destruction.—*Dr. South.*

Holy voice of nature.—Cast your eyes over all the nations of the world. Amid so many inhuman and absurd superstitions, amid that prodigious diversity of manners and characters, you will find everywhere the same principles and distinctions of moral good and evil. The paganism of the ancient world produced indeed abominable gods, who on earth would have been shunned or punished as monsters, and who offered as a picture of supreme happiness only crimes to commit and passions to satiate. But vice armed with this sacred authority descended in vain from the eternal abode; she found in the heart of man a moral instinct to repel her. The continence of Xenocrates was admired by those who celebrated the debaucheries of Jupiter. The chaste Lucretia adored the unchaste Venus. The most intrepid Roman sacrificed to fear. He invoked the god who dethroned his father, and he died without a murmur by the hand of his own. The most contemptible divinities were served by the greatest men. The holy voice of nature, stronger than that of the gods, made itself heard and respected and obeyed on earth, and seemed to banish as it were to the confinement of heaven guilt and the guilty.—*Rousseau.*

[We are not to forget that Rousseau's holy voice of nature is infidelity, and that it is folly to talk of vice descending from an eternal abode and finding a repelling force in the heart of man. We give the extract as a graphic confirmation of St. Paul's description.]

Infidelity barren of good results.— The system of infidelity is a soil as barren of great and sublime virtues as it is prolific in crimes. By great and sublime virtues are meant those which are called into action on great and trying occasions, which demand the sacrifice of the dearest interests and prospects of human life, and sometimes of life itself—the virtues, in a word, which by their rarity and splendour draw admiration, and have rendered illustrious the character of patriots, martyrs, and confessors. It requires but little reflection to perceive that whatever veils a future world and contracts the limits of existence within the present life must tend in a proportionable degree to diminish the grandeur and narrow the sphere of human agency. As well might you expect exalted sentiments of justice from a professed gamester, as look for noble principles in the man whose hopes and fears are all suspended on the present moment, and who stakes the whole happiness of his being on the events of this vain and fleeting life. If he be ever impelled to the performance of great achievements in a good cause, it must be solely by the hope of fame : a motive which, besides that it makes virtue the servant of opinion, usually grows weaker at the approach of death ; and which, however it may surmount the love of existence in the heat of battle or in the moment of public observation, can seldom be expected to operate with much force on the retired duties of a private station. In affirming that infidelity is unfavourable to the higher class of virtues, we are supported as well by facts as by reasoning. We should be sorry to load our adversaries with unmerited reproach ; but to what history, to what record, will they appeal for the traits of moral greatness exhibited by their disciples ? Where shall we look for the trophies of infidel magnanimity or atheistical virtue ? Not that we mean to accuse them of inactivity : they have recently filled the world with the fame of their exploits—exploits of a different kind indeed, but of imperishable memory and disastrous lustre. The exclusion of a supreme Being and of a superintending Providence tends directly to the destruction of moral taste. It robs the universe of all finished and consummate excellence, even in idea. The admiration of perfect wisdom and goodness for which we are formed, and which kindles such unspeakable raptures in the soul, finding in the regions of scepticism nothing to which it corresponds, droops and languishes. In a world which presents a fair spectacle of order and beauty, of a vast family nourished and supported by an almighty Parent—in a world which leads the devout mind, step by

step, to the contemplation of the first fair and the first good, the sceptic is encompassed with nothing but obscurity, meanness, and disorder. Modern infidelity not only tends to corrupt the moral taste, it also promotes the growth of those vices which are the most hostile to social happiness. Of all the vices incident to human nature, the most destructive to society are vanity, ferocity, and unbridled sensuality ; and these are precisely the vices which infidelity is calculated to cherish.—*Robert Hall.*

Origin of idolatry.—Here then—in the alienation of the heart from God, the unsuitableness of His character to the depraved propensities of fallen creatures, and the consequent desire to have a God " who will approve their sin "—is the origin of idolatry. This view of the case accords well with the character of the " gods many and lords many of the heathen world," and with the nature of the worship with which they were, and still are, honoured. Where, among all the objects of their worship, shall we find one whose attributes indicate the operation, in the mind that has imagined it, of anything like a principle either of holiness or of love ? Where one whom its worshippers have invested with the qualities either of purity or of mercy ? All their deities appear to be the product of a strange and an affecting combination of depraved passions and guilty fears. The principal gods of the Pantheon are raised above human kind chiefly by the superior enormity of their crimes, their greater power only enabling them to be the greater adepts both in folly and in wickedness. They are the patrons and the examples of all that is vile and of all that is cruel—of intemperance, and lust, and knavery, and jealousy, and revenge. Thus men love to sin ; and they make their gods *sinners*, that they may practise evil under their sanction and patronage. The *worship* of their gods is such as might be anticipated from their *characters*. Well are their superstitions

denominated " abominable idolatries."
They consist, not merely of the most
senseless fooleries and extravagances,
but of the most disgusting impurities,
the most licentious acts of intemperance, and the most iron-hearted
cruelties. It may be remarked that
the very same tendency of human
nature to depart from Jehovah and
follow after idols evinced itself when a
fresh experiment was tried in the case
of the Jews. They alone of all nations
were put in possession of the knowledge
of the true God; and they showed a
constant inclination, for many ages of
their history, to change—to go astray
from Jehovah, and to serve " strange
gods, the gods of the heathen that were
round about them." Is it not most wonderful that the only people who were
in the right discovered so strong a
propensity to change the right for the
wrong, while those who were in the
wrong adhered pertinaciously to their
errors and were obstinately averse to
embrace what was right ? How spirited
the expostulation of Jehovah by the
prophet Jeremiah !—" Pass over the
isles of Chittim, and see ; and send
unto Kedar, and consider diligently,
and see if there be such a thing. Hath
a nation changed their gods, which are
yet no gods ? but My people hath
changed their glory for that which
doth not profit. Be astonished, O ye
heavens, at this, and be horribly afraid ;
be ye very desolate, saith the Lord."—
Wardlaw.

ILLUSTRATIONS TO CHAPTER I.

Ver. 2. *The experience of conviction.*—
When M. Monod attended the University of
Geneva, there was a professor of divinity
who confined himself to lecturing on the
immortality of the soul, the existence of
God, and similar topics. As to the Trinity
he did not believe. Instead of the Bible he
gave us quotations from Seneca and Plato.
St. Seneca and St. Plato were the two saints
whose writings he held up to admiration.
But the Lord sent one of His servants to
Geneva; and I well remember the visit of
Robert Haldane. I heard of him first as
an English or Scotch gentleman who spoke
much about the Bible, which seemed a very
strange thing to me and the other students,
to whom it was a shut book. I afterwards
met Mr. Haldane at a private house, along
with some other friends, and heard him read
from an English Bible a chapter from
Romans about the natural corruption of
man, a doctrine of which I had never heard
before—in fact, I was quite astonished to
hear of men being corrupt by nature. I
remember saying to Mr. Haldane : " Now I
see that doctrine in the Bible." " Yes," he
replied ; " but do you see it in your heart ? "
*That was a simple question, but it came home
to my conscience.* It was the sword of the
Spirit ; and from that time I saw that my
heart was corrupt, and knew from the word
of God that I could be saved by grace alone.
—*D'Aubigne.*

Vers. 3-6. *The beauty of Christ shown to
the faithful student and devout follower.*—A
sculptor once took a pupil to a statue on
which much artistic skill had been bestowed,
and said to him, " Look ! Do you see symmetry and expression and beauty there ?

Do you see accuracy of outline, delicacy of
detail, harmony of design, and perfection
of execution ? Do you see all this ? If
not, look until you do, for all is there." So
we may say : Do you see in Christ all the
glory and beauty which are described by
the four evangelists and the apostles ? Do
you see a perfect humanity and a perfect
divinity there ? Do you see incarnate love ?
Do you see earth's noble man, the God-man,
heaven's choicest treasure ? If not, look till
you do, for they are all there. Look by
prayerfully reading the sacred books. Examine by the way of experience. Oh, taste
and see that the Christ is gracious !

Vers. 3-6. *Love to Christ desired.* — A
Welsh clergyman, the late Rev. William
Howells, minister of Long Acre Episcopal
Church, once said in his pulpit that a simple-
hearted, earnest Christian girl from his own
country had preached Christ to him as he
feared he never preached *Him* to his congregation. For to his question, " My dear
child, do you love Christ ? " she replied,
" Love Christ ? Yes, sir ; my soul clings to
Him as the limpet to the rock."

" May we all enjoy this feeling ;
  In all need to Jesus go ;
Prove His wounds each day more healing,
  And Himself more fully know ! "

Ver. 4. *Strong Son of God.*—St. Paul says
that Jesus was " the Son of God with power."
The expression is significant and appropriate,
for strength was characteristic of the world's
Christ. And yet while we view the character drawn in the gospels, we must be struck
with the fact that He was strong in love.

Omnipotence was restrained; omniscience was kept in abeyance; but love never slept. He was strong in love as well when He denounced the Pharisees as when He wept at the graveside of a friend. He was indeed the incarnation of immortal love.

"Strong Son of God, immortal love."

Ver. 15. *The doing architect.*—All the Lord's people should be preachers, not with eloquent sermons, but with pure lives—not in pulpits, but in farm, and shop, and mart, and lane, and street. Two architects were once candidates for the building of a certain temple at Athens. The first harangued the crowd very learnedly upon the different orders of architecture, and showed them in what manner the temple should be built. The other, who got up after him, only observed that what his brother had spoken he could do; and thus he at once gained the cause. The man who can do the gospel may be mightier than the man who can speak the gospel. Let us be ready to preach the gospel, not at Rome, not in London, not in a costly marble pulpit, but in the home, in the business, in the lowest sphere.

Ver. 16. *The power of God.*—The Thracians had a very significant emblem of the almighty power of God. It was a sun with three beams—one shining upon a sea of ice and dissolving it, another upon a rock and melting it, and a third upon a dead man and putting life into him. What a striking illustration of the power of God in the gospel! It melts the hardest heart and raises to a life of righteousness those who were "dead in trespasses and sin." *The power of the gospel.*—A little girl, one Sabbath morning, was much affected under the sermon, and on her return home earnestly entreated her mother would accompany her to church in the evening to hear how delightfully the minister talked about Jesus Christ. The child was so intent on this object that she made the request with tears, and the mother at last consented to accompany her importunate girl to the place of worship. The preacher chose for his text Rom. i. 16. The woman was seriously and effectually impressed by the word of God, was led earnestly to seek salvation, and obtained mercy by faith in Christ Jesus. The wife now naturally became anxious for the salvation of her husband, and persuaded him also to attend the chapel. He also submitted to the influence of the truth; and both the parents became grateful to God for the child whose importunity led them to hear the gospel of salvation.—*Cheever.*

Ver. 16. *John Frith.*—"Do ye think," said John Frith, martyr, to the archbishop's men that would have let him go, "that I am afraid to declare mine opinion unto the bishops of England in a manifest truth? If you should both leave me here, and go tell the bishops that you had lost Frith, I would surely follow as fast after as I might, and bring them news that I had found and brought Frith again."—*Trapp.*

Ver. 16. *The captive whose faith saved him.* —A captive was brought before an Asiatic prince; the scimitar was already raised over the captive's head to destroy, when, pressed by intolerable thirst, he asked for water. A cup was handed him; he held it in his hand as if apprehensive lest the scimitar should fall while he was in the act of drinking. "Take courage," said the prince, "you shall be spared till you drink this water." The captive instantly dashed the cup of water to the ground. The good faith of the barbarian saved him. The word had passed, it was enough, and the captive went on his way rejoicing. God's word has passed. Believe, and be saved.

Ver. 16. *Tholuck's conviction of the truth of Christianity.*—"I am not ashamed of the gospel of Christ." In early boyhood infidelity had forced its way into my heart, and at the age of twelve I was wont to scoff at Christianity and its truths. And hard indeed has been the struggle through which I have passed, before attaining to that assurance of faith with which I am now blessed. But I acknowledge it with praise to the Almighty that the longer I live the more does serious study, combined with the experiences of life, help me to recognise in the Christian doctrine an inexhaustible fountain of true knowledge, and serve to strengthen the blessed conviction that all the wisdom of this world is but folly when compared with the glorious gospel of Jesus Christ.

Ver. 20. *God manifest in creation.*— Nature forces on our heart a Creator, history a Providence.—*Jean Paul.*

God's way of making worlds is to make them make themselves.—*Drummond.*

Manufacture is intelligible but trivial; creation is great and cannot be understood. —*T. Carlyle.*

I say the acknowledgment of God in Christ
Accepted by thy reason solves for thee
All questions on our earth and out of it.
Browning.

My own dim life shall teach me this,
That life shall rise for evermore,
Else faith is darkness at the core,
And dust and ashes all that is.—*Tennyson.*

I have gone the whole round of creation; I
    saw and I spoke;
I, a work of God's hand for that purpose,
    received in my brain
And pronounced on the rest of His handiwork
    —returned Him again
His creation's approval or censure; I spoke
    as I saw;
I report, as a man may of God's work—all's
    love, yet all's law.—*Browning.*

Ver. 20. *The mirror in Arcadia.*—I stand
before an attractive picture. The design,
the colouring, and the general effect declare
that it is the production of a master-mind
directing skilful fingers. It is not surprising
to read at the bottom of the painting the
name of a great artist placed before the
word "pinxit." No such thing, I say to
the admiring materialist, that painting was
its own pinxit. It is a self-evolved picture.
It produced itself before it was in existence.
He laughs at my folly, and scoffs at my
ridiculous scepticism. Has nature no picture
galleries? Are there no fine artistic effects?
Am I to be told that nature's own hand
painted these pictures before there was
such a hand in existence? It is not
more ridiculous to say that the picture
painted itself than to say that the world
created itself. There is a mirror reported to
be in the temple of Arcadia which represented to the spectator, not his own face,
but the image of that deity which he
worshipped. The world is a looking-glass,
and yet it does not reflect to us the image
of itself as a creator. We look into that
glass, and see neither matter nor human
mind, neither protoplasm, a fortuitous con-
course of atoms, development, nor evolution,
but God reflected as the Creator.

Ver. 20. *The harmony and order of
creation.*—The famous astronomer Athana-
sius Kircher having an acquaintance who
denied the existence of the Supreme Being,
took the following method to convince him
of his error upon his own principles. Expecting him upon a visit, he procured a very
handsome globe of the starry heavens, which
being placed in a corner of a room in which
it could not escape his friend's observation,
the latter seized the first occasion to ask
from whence it came and to whom it
belonged. "Not to me," said Kircher, "nor
was it *ever made by any person*, but came
here by *mere chance*." "That," replied his
sceptical friend, "is absolutely impossible;
you surely jest." Kircher, however, seriously
persisted in his assertion, took occasion to
reason with his friend upon his own atheistical principles. "You will not," said he,
"believe that this small body originated in
mere chance; and yet you will contend that
those heavenly bodies of which it is only a
faint and diminutive resemblance came into
existence without order and design." Pursuing this chain of reasoning, his friend was
at first confounded, in the next place convinced, and ultimately joined in a cordial
acknowledgment of the absurdity of denying
the existence of God.

Ver. 22. *The fate of a boaster.*—Simon
Tournay affords a memorable and affecting
proof of the truth of that scripture, "Professing themselves to be wise, they became
fools." In 1201, after he had excelled all
Oxford in learning, and had become so
eminent at Paris as to be made chief doctor
of the Sorbonne, he was so puffed up with
foolish pride as to hold Aristotle superior to
Moses and Christ, and yet but equal to
himself. In his latter days, however, he
grew such an idiot as not to know one letter
in a book, or to remember one thing he had
ever done.

Ver. 24. *The Goddess of Reason.*—In the
Paris papers of August 1st, 1817, we find
among the obituaries the following announcement: "Died, within these few days, in
the hospital of pauper lunatics of Salpêtrière,
where she had lived unpitied and unknown
for many years, the famous Theroigne de
Mericourt (the Goddess of Reason), the most
remarkable of the heroines of the Revolution."
This female (nearly in a state of nudity) was
seated on a throne by Fouché and Carnot in
the Champ de Mars, and hailed alternately
as the Goddess of Reason and Liberty. There
was something remarkable in the history of
the latter days of this poor creature, and her
life is not without its moral. She who was
taught publicly to blaspheme her Creator
and dishonour her sex was for the last
twenty years of her miserable life subject
to the greatest of human calamities—the
deprivation of her reason. She repented
severely of her horrible crimes, and her few
lucid intervals were filled up by the most
heartrending lamentations. She died at the
age of fifty-seven.

CHAPTER II.

CRITICAL NOTES.

Ver. 1. **Therefore thou art inexcusable, O man.**—διό, because the above description of the wickedness of mankind is true (in its main features) universally. **O man.**—A general designation. Jews classed with Gentiles. Josephus says that there was not a nation under heaven more wicked than the Jewish nation. Jews judged the Gentiles. Heathen philosophers often guilty of what they condemned in others. κρίμα, the result of judgment—the sentence.

Ver. 2.—It is not to be understood that every individual is chargeable with each and every vice named.

Ver. 3.—The Jews thought to escape judgment, for in their rabbinical creed it is written, "All Israel have a portion in the world to come, except heretics and deriders of the wise men."

Ver. 4. **Or despisest thou the riches of His goodness?**—χρηστότης, goodness in general. ἀνοχή, its exercise in postponing punishment. μακροθυμία again signifies continued ἀνοχή. καταφρονέω, to treat with contempt by word or deed. **Leading to repentance.**—Moral improvement of soul, turning from unbelief to faith. πλοῦτος sets forth the fact that God abounds in mercy and grace.

Ver. 5.—Thou art hoping to escape the judgment of God, but instead art heaping up treasure of wrath. It is not God who treasures up, but thy destruction is from thyself.

Ver. 6.—Account will be taken of the aim which has governed the moral action.

Ver. 7. **To them who by patient continuance in well-doing seek for glory and honour and immortality,** [to such] **eternal life.**—Future glory is contrasted with present shame.

Ver. 8.—ἐριθείαν denotes the spirit which seeks the victory of the party which one has espoused from self-interest in contrast to the spirit which seeks the possession of truth.

Ver. 9. **Affliction and distress.**—Metaphor from a wrestler, who finds breathing difficult.

Ver. 12.—Sin brings retribution both to those without law and to those under the law; but sentence will vary according to divine justice and mercy.

Ver. 13. **Not the hearers of the law.**—Jewish writers held that no circumcised person goes to hell. St. Paul confutes all vain opinions. The literal meaning of δικαιοῦν is to make righteous. In this epistle it is used to mean acquittal.

Ver. 14.—φύσει, by nature, as distinct from θέσει or written law.

Ver. 15.—The evidence that what the law of God requires is inscribed on the minds of the heathen is the testimony of their conscience to such moral precepts. συνείδησις, the conscience, from the word meaning to know with or within oneself. In this passage understanding rather than affection is the predominant thought. Reasonings of a man's mind upon his own actions, habits, and motives.

Ver. 18.—κατηχούμενος, being orally instructed.

Ver. 21.—This verse may be illustrated out of the Jewish writings, for they say, "He who teacheth others what he doth not himself is like a blind man who hath a candle in his hand to give light to others, whilst he himself doth walk in darkness." And again, "How can a man say in the congregation, Do not steal, when he steals?"

Ver. 22.—A crime among the Jews. Talmud accuses some of the most celebrated Rabbis of the vice of sacrilege.

Ver. 27.—φύσεως plainly means here what we call a state of nature, in distinction from a state in which a revelation is enjoyed.

Ver. 29.—Olshausen says that Ruchert is right in understanding πνεῦμα of the New γράμμα of the Old Testament, for the spirit in the Old Testament is just the New Testament in its πλήρωσις: consisting in spirit, not in letter; spiritual, not literal; a new dispensation, not of letter, but of spirit—not consisting of a written code of enactments, but conveying a new spirit—a spirit made new by the Holy Ghost.

MAIN HOMILETICS OF THE PARAGRAPH.—Verses 1—4.

The judgments of man and of God.—The inhabitant of a shell has no idea of the vastness of the external world; the rustic who has never passed beyond the bounds of his own village green is not likely to possess the most liberal views; the man who never comes into true contact with his fellows is apt to have exaggerated views of his own importance. To know yourself you must go out of yourself, as well as look into yourself. The selfishness of the Pharisee produces a narrowness of vision which results in an intolerable dogmatism and self-conceit; but the soul of the publican commands a wider range—he gazes upon the solemn heights of the infinite purity and the divine requirements, and is penetrated with a sense of his own shortcomings. The man who looks at himself in every aspect, who measures himself, not by himself, but by all that is grand and noble in the natural world, in divine revelation, and in the divine nature, will be forced to the conclusion that he is left without excuse, that he is a sinner, and must fly for refuge to the sinner's Friend and Saviour. "Therefore thou art inexcusable, O man." Let thy harsh temperament and thy severe judgments be tempered with a sense of thy own failings.

I. **The judgments of men are fallible.**—We cannot suppose the apostle to mean that the critical faculty is to be stifled. We must compare ideas. We pass judgment on scenery, on pictures, on works of art, on books, and on persons. How are we to prosecute the journey of life with anything like satisfaction, if we are not to judge? In the complexities of modern life we are compelled to judge. If we entertain without reserve our modern strangers, we should not find many of them turn out to be angels. If they are, they will be angels unawares. But our judgments must be as rules of guidance, and not as sentences of condemnation, upon our fellows. However, in all judgments, were it not well to bear in mind that we are erring creatures? Perhaps some of our judges would have escaped mistakes had they kept before them the fact that all human judgment is fallible. The critics, both literary and moral, would not have exposed themselves to shame had they been mindful of the erring nature of all human judgments.

II. **The judgments of men are often self-condemning.**—Self-preservation is one of the great instinctive laws of nature; and guided by this low motive of instinctive prompting, we ought to restrain ourselves from all harsh judgments. No pleasant task to be a judge if every sentence which is being pronounced prompts the inquiry, What is there in my past or present conduct which brings me into close relationship with the man upon whom I am now sitting in judgment? What tenderness should pervade the mind of the preacher as he finds in himself the sins, either in germ or in fuller development, which he denounces in others! Alas! our neighbours' sins we place before our eyes, while our own sins we place behind where we can scarcely see them.

III. **The judgments of men are often self-apologetic.**—In literary circles we are sometimes told that the critics are the failures, and the severest critics are those who have failed most miserably. In the moral sphere the critics are the failures; the greatest sinners too often pass the harshest judgments. And why is this? Because in excusing others they vainly think that they are excusing themselves. Vain man! thy *apologia suæ vitæ* is a miserable failure. The book thou hast written tells thy weakness, and pronounces thy condemnation. Self-apologetics are hideous failures. The Pharisee's self-apologetics in the parable have made him the opprobrium of all time. The publican's "God be merciful to me a sinner" has lifted him high in the scale of being.

In opposition let us bear in mind that:—

I. **The judgments of God are infallible.**—God is all-wise, and therefore cannot err. They are according to truth. The judgments of God are not according to men's *views* of truth, but according to truth. The judgments of God are not shaped by human shibboleths. "Our little systems have their day," but truth abides eternally. Truth is from everlasting. It existed in the mind and heart of the Infinite before the world was; the light of divine mornings shone out of the primal darkness of a newly made planet long before our modern wise ones preached to the world the truth which they pretend to have fashioned. Men may err; God cannot.

II. **The judgments of God are tempered by mercy, and in their execution delayed.**—While we read of God's wrath, we must not forget God's mercy,—

" The attribute of God Himself;
And earthly power doth then show likest God's
When mercy seasons justice."

We do pray for mercy. We all instinctively feel that there is mercy with God, and that we need mercy; but how seldom doth that same prayer teach us to render the deeds of mercy, and to exercise that judgment which is tempered by mercy. We seek to get our own debts forgiven, and then we straightway go away with the speech upon our lips, "Pay me that thou owest." There is forgiving mercy in Jesus Christ. The execution of judgment is delayed. Opportunity for repentance is afforded. But—solemn thought! dread-inspiring reflection!—

III. **The judgments of God, though tempered by mercy, and delayed in their execution, are not therefore a nullity.**—The mills of God may grind slowly, but they grind surely and exactly. Men may harden themselves in their crimes by saying, All things continue as they were from the creation—yea, all things continue as they have been through the past æons of geologic records. Know, O vain man, that hardened sinners cannot escape the judgments of God. What a call to reflection in the apostle's earnest remonstrance, "And thinkest thou this, O man?" Let thy thought move upward in the line of the divine thought; and, oh! seek to escape the judgment, the condemnation, of God by hearty repentance, and by sincere faith in God's blessed Son, and by a life of holiness.

Human judgments rebuked ; divine judgments exalted.

I. **Human judgment is pronounced by inconsistent men.**—The men who judge, often those who judge most sternly, are themselves guilty. David and Nathan. The accusers and the woman taken in adultery. In the light of the Sermon on the Mount we are all inconsistent.

II. **Divine judgment is pronounced by a perfectly righteous being.**—We notice: 1. The standard by which God judges—*truth*; 2. The spirit in which God judges—His judgment is (1) *longsuffering*; (2) *impartial*; (3) *thorough*. The character of the divine Judge is (*a*) *an inspiration* to those who seek well-doing; (*b*) *a terror* to those who obey unrighteousness.—*Homilist.*

Ver. 4. *God's government of us ; its ground and its end.*—Goodness, when it is seen in the deeds of Him who went about doing good, loses none of its awfulness; it stands out in more direct contrast to all wickedness; but we know that it is not abstract, that it is individualising, yet that it is without limitation. When we hear of God's forbearance, we ask the ancient, ever-recurring question, whether He can care enough for our doings to feel anything like that " provocation " which the Bible speaks of—whether such words must not be merely figurative, or must not detract from His holiness and majesty. When we seek to know the Father through the Son clothed in our nature, we see how purity and sympathy must be provoked every day by impurity and hardness of heart; the perfection must be diminished, if it were incapable of pain and sorrow for evil. The longsuffering becomes intelligible, like the forbearance, when we view it through this mirror. Till we so see it, we may ask ourselves whether there is not some boundary to it which we are obliged to conceive, though we cannot fix it. The cross of Calvary drives our reason from this vain and ambitious attempt. Now if this *goodness, forbearance, longsuffering*, belong to the very name and character of Him in whom we are living and moving and having our being, they constitute a wealth upon

59

which we may always draw. The more we call them to mind, the more we believe in them, the more truly and actively they become ours. We may become moulded into their likeness; we may show them forth. This is that kingly inheritance which the Scriptures and the sacrament make known to us. But here comes in the great excuse for shame and for gloom. We have not taken the events that have befallen us as if they bore this signification; the wealth has been ours, and it has been squandered. We have *despised* the riches of His goodness, forbearance, and longsuffering. But this thought has been left out of our calculation. We have "not known that the goodness of God is leading us to repentance." Events are not leading us to it, sad or joyful, sudden or successive. Our own hearts, left to themselves, will not lead us to it. The experience of our own powerlessness to change our minds, to turn them round to the Light, may be an entirely true experience. But that goodness of God, which is with us, is not merely something which we may recollect, by which we may profit: it is an active, vital power. It is the one power which can act upon spirit. It is He who convinces us of sin, because we have believed in Him in whom is not sin, and who is always with us to deliver us from sin; of righteousness, because He has gone to the Father, as the righteous Head of our race, to justify us; of judgment, because the prince of this world is judged, and because each year is hastening on the time when he shall finally be cast out.—*Maurice.*

SUGGESTIVE COMMENTS ON VERSES 1—4.

God's attributes enhance His goodness. —The apostle speaks of "the riches of His goodness." These riches appear in numberless displays. But he adds, "and forbearance and longsuffering," to induce us to consider the latter as the proof of the former. To see then the riches of His goodness, let us contemplate His forbearance and longsuffering. Everything in God enhances His patience.

I. **His greatness enhances it.**—We are more affected with an affront from an equal than from a superior, and more from an inferior than from an equal. How does the master resent an offence from his slave? or a king from a subject? All comparison fails between God and us. He is the maker of all things; and all nations before Him are as nothing. This is the Being insulted. And who is the offender? A grovelling worm upon a dunghill. And yet He bears with us.

II. **His wisdom enhances it.**—We cannot be affected with affronts of which we are ignorant. How would some be enraged if they knew only what is *said* of them by some of their

"friends"! None of our offences are secret from God. He bears all, sees all, and knows perfectly every imagination of the thoughts of our heart. And yet He bears with us.

III. **His holiness enhances it.**—If we do not think and feel a thing to be an affront, there is no virtue, for there is no difficulty in enduring it. The trial is when it touches us to the quick in some valued interest. Sin is exceedingly sinful. By nothing does God deem Himself so dishonoured. He is of purer eyes than to behold iniquity. It is the abominable thing which His soul hates. And yet He bears with us.

IV. **His power enhances it.**—Why do we put up with a thousand wrongs? We know and feel them, but we reluctantly submit because we have no way to punish them. Why are not sinners destroyed? Moses, when he had provoked the Egyptians, saved himself by flight. But whither can we go from God's presence or flee from His Spirit? Some, when they have provoked resentment, have defied it, and successfully too. But who ever hardened himself against God and prospered? His look is death. And yet He bears with us.

V. His bounty enhances it.—We complain peculiarly of an injury or an insult from one who is much indebted to us. From another, we say, we could have borne it; but he is viler than the brute, for "the ox knoweth his owner, and the ass his master's crib." We are under infinite obligations to the God we provoke. In Him we have lived, and moved, and had our being. His table has fed us; His wardrobe has clothed us; His sun has warmed us. And this is not all: His kindness continues, notwithstanding all our ingratitude. And He not only spares us, but in every way indulges us. He waits to be gracious, and is exalted to have mercy upon us. Yet are these riches of His goodness "despised." 1. *Despised by inconsideration.* We treat them as unworthy of our notice. They do not occupy our thoughts or our words. 2. *Despised by disobedience.* We resist their design, which is to lead us to repentance. God calls, but we will not answer; He knocks, but we refuse to open—who is the Lord that we should obey His voice? 3. *Despised by perversion.* We turn them into instruments of rebellion, and make them the very means of increasing our impenitency. If we thought God would destroy us the next sin we committed, it would not be committed; but since He is too kind to do this, we are induced to offend Him. We are evil, because He is good. How *unreasonable* is this contempt! If an individual were to behave towards a fellow-creature as men are continually acting towards the blessed God, no one could notice him but with astonishment and contempt. Yet we talk of the dignity of human nature, or contend that it is but slightly injured by the Fall!—*W. Jay.*

The justice of God.—Slow goes the hand of justice, like the shadow on the sun-dial—ever moving, yet creeping slowly on, with a motion all but imperceptible. Still stand in awe. The hand of justice has not stopped. Although imperceptible, it steadily advances; by-and-by it reaches the tenth, eleventh, and twelfth hour. And now the bell strikes. Then, unless you have fled to Christ, the blow, which was so slow to fall, shall descend over the head of impenitence with accumulated force. *Human standards of judgment.*—We measure from ourselves; and as things are for our use and purpose, so we approve them. Bring a pear to the table that is rotten, we cry it down—'tis naught; but bring a medlar that is rotten, and 'tis a fine thing; and yet I'll warrant you the pear thinks as well of itself as the medlar does.—*Trapp.*

By judging we condemn ourselves.—"Wherefore thou art inexcusable, O man, whosoever thou art, that judgest others." The first argument in support of his proposition is deduced from the foregone conclusion, by which the apostle has concluded that the Gentiles in general, knowing the judgment of God, yet did things contrary thereto; and therefore that proposition is enunciated illatively, and as a sort of secondary conclusion—"*Wherefore* thou art inexcusable," etc.; "for in the act of judging another thou condemnest thyself." The argument runs thus: Whosoever condemns himself in the act of judging another is inexcusable: "[But] thou, O man," says the apostle, addressing the Gentile philosophers individually, "in the act of judging another condemnest thyself"; "therefore thou art inexcusable." The proposition is a-wanting; but the other two parts of the syllogism are given in the verse, only that the assumption, by hysterosis, is placed after the conclusion, "Thou that judgest another doest the same things." He proves the assumption by an argument drawn from the effects of him who thus judged another, which effects are set forth under a comparison of equality—he who does the same things for which he judges another, in the act of judging another condemns himself. " But thou," says the apostle to each of the Gentile philosophers, " that judgest another doest the same things for which thou judgest another; therefore in the act of judging another thou condemnest thyself." The assumption is expressed in the words just quoted, which form the last clause of this verse; but, by hysterosis, the proposition, with its proof, is given in the two following verses—the proof in the second, and the proposition itself therefrom deduced in the third.—*Ferme.*

Privilege will not save. — Having shown that the Gentiles could not entertain the least hope of salvation according to the tenor of the law of nature, it was next to be considered whether the law of Moses gave the Jews any better hope. This inquiry the apostle managed with great address. Well knowing that, on reading his description of the manners of the Greeks, the Jews would pronounce them worthy of damnation, he suddenly turned his discourse to the Jews, telling them that they who passed such a judgment on the Gentiles were inexcusable in hoping to be saved through the law of Moses, because by condemning he Gentiles they virtually condemned themselves, who, being guilty of the very same crimes, were thereby under the curse of Moses' law (ver. 1). And to enforce this argument the apostle observed that God's sentence of condemnation passed in the curse of the law upon them who commit such things is known by all to be according to truth (ver. 2). But although every Jew was condemned by the curse of the law of Moses, they all expected salvation on account of their being Abraham's children and of their enjoying the benefit of revelation. Wherefore, to show them the vanity of that hope, the apostle proposed the following question: Dost thou, who condemnest the Gentiles for their crimes, and yet committest the same thyself, think that thou shalt escape the righteous sentence of God declared in the curse of the law of Moses, merely because thou art a son of Abraham and a member of God's visible Church? (ver. 3.) By entertaining such a notion thou judgest amiss of thy privileges, which are bestowed on thee, not to make sinning more safe to thee than to others, but to lead to repentance (ver. 4). These privileges therefore, instead of making thy salvation sure, if abused by thy obdurate and impenitent heart, will make thy punishment greater *in the day of wrath and revelation of the righteous judgment of God.—Macknight.*

" *Thinkest thou.*"—This is preaching to the conscience, to the quick. Our exhortations should be as forked arrows to stick in men's hearts, and not wound only, as other arrows. A poor hermit came to our Richard I., A.D. 1195, and, preaching to him the words of eternal life, bade him be mindful of the subversion of Sodom and to abstain from things unlawful; otherwise, said he, the deserved vengeance of God will come upon thee. The hermit being gone, the king neglected his words. But afterwards falling sick, he more seriously bethought himself, and waxing sound in soul as well as in body, he grew more devout and charitable to the poor.—*Trapp.*

Repentance you must have. — The consciousness and confession of one's self as a sinner is the inevitable first step in all true repentance. When one says, Oh yes, I know that we are all sinners, he merely inculpates others to lighten his own guilt, he makes no true confession of sin. When one charges himself with wrong expecting others to palliate his misdeed, it may be thinking that even God will not regard it as severely as he has stated it, he but adds insincerity to his other sins. Sometimes men boastfully declare that they have done some evil deed; this is " to make a mock at sin." It is when one, like Job, cries to God, " I have sinned," not excusing himself, not vainly hoping that God will look leniently upon his guilt, but rather himself trying to see more clearly the enormity of his iniquity, that he truly makes confession of sin. But there is no merit even in this. He confesses not for reward, but for pardon. So when he asks, "What shall I do unto Thee, O Thou Preserver of men?"

it is not with the thought of propitiating God or of winning His favour; it is with the desire to show his repentance and gratitude in present and continued obedience. So repentance stops not at sorrowing for sin; it turns away from sin and unto God.— *Robert Wesley Peach.*

MAIN HOMILETICS OF THE PARAGRAPH.—*Verses* 5—12.

Good and evil workers.—Many distinctions obtain in human societies. It is sometimes amazing to see how men and women separate themselves from one another. The man with a banking account, though it be only small, does not feel himself called upon to associate with one who has to live on his daily wages. The professional man stands aloof from the tradesman. Poets in their rhymes smile at the claims of long descent, and sing, "Kind hearts are more than coronets." But let a kind heart, enshrined in a physical form, covered with shabby clothes, present itself at the poet's door, and will it receive a hearty welcome? Kind hearts are nice when they beat in breasts covered with pearls. Still, as of old, Lazarus lies at the gate desiring the crumbs, while the coroneted sit inside the palace at the banquet. We ask, Is the man respectable? Does the woman move in good society? There is no respect of persons with God. Can the same be said of those who profess to be His children? God looks at the internal, and not the external. Character, not reputation, is what God estimates. All classes of society, all races of men, Jews and Gentiles, are reduced to the two general classes—the workers of good and the workers of evil. To which do we belong?

I. **Good workers.**—*Draw a contrast* between the good workers and the evil workers. 1. *The former have a noble aim.* Here reference is made, not to the act of aiming, but rather to the object aimed at. And what is that? It is immortal glory and honour. I paint for eternity, says the painter. His eternity is a few years of time. What is the good of his glory and honour when death has stripped his supple fingers of their power to handle the brush, and has robbed the brain of its ability to conceive beautiful combinations? The Christian's glory and honour are not bounded by the eclipsing darkness of death, for they are immortal—not subject either to oblivion or disappointment. We get our earthly glories and honours; and we find how true are the words, "Uneasy lies the head that wears a crown." There are crowns in all walks of life, and heavy, aching heads are the lots of the prize-winners. Disappointments strew the pathway of earth's glories as thickly as the leaves in Valombrosa. A few years hence oblivion will sit serenely smiling, ironically musing over the scene where our triumphs were gained. Truly "he aims too low who aims beneath the sky." The noble aim for all is immortal glory and honour. 2. *High endeavour.* They place before themselves a great object, and strive with a great spirit— they endeavour. They do not say man is the creature of circumstances, and sink down in despair. In spite of opposing circumstances, through calm and storm they seek immortal honour and glory; the flag waves on the summit; and though the ground shakes with the thunder of the cannon, they pursue their upward course of high endeavour. 3. *Patient continuance.* Endurance is the crowning quality, and patience is all the passion of great hearts. The patience of human workers is sometimes wonderful; but the patience of God's true saints is ever marvellous. Here is sublime heroism. What do I see in my vision ? A long crowd of witnesses pressing through the highways of life, whose patience is crowned by the inheritance of the promises. 4. *Obtain satisfactory results.* Glory, honour, and peace will be awarded in the final day. Who obtains these results ? Who follows in the train of characters with such lofty motives and wondrous endeavours ? Can earthborn spirits contend ? Are their souls equal to the mighty emprise ? The answer is, " Ye must be born again." Only spirits ennobled and renewed by the Holy Spirit can keep company with this sublime army.

II. **Evil workers are**: 1. *Without settled aim,* for they are contentious. They may have a material aim—riches, fame, power, pleasure—but they have no true moral aim. They set before themselves no high standard of duty. 2. *Have no high endeavour.* They obey unrighteousness. They never seek to rise above the leadings of a lower nature. Instead of leading, they are led. 3. *Have impenitent continuance.* This is their great crime. With hard and impenitent hearts they are storing up to themselves wrath against the day of wrath. There is no heroism about such continuance. The hard and impenitent heart goes on petrifying itself with great ease. The impenitent heart obeys unrighteousness and ignores the truth. 4. *Come to a sad ending.* The structure they have been building falls upon their own heads with crushing force. They have been storing up in themselves wrath against God. Thus they have been storing up against themselves wrath from God. All God's worlds have moving through them the same divine laws and methods of operation. We sow wheat, we reap wheat—tares, tares. We sow wrath, we reap wrath ; and fearful will the harvest be. In these days we ignore both the wrath and the righteousness of God. We say, God is merciful, and will be compassionate, and all will come right. Certainly all will come right, according to the will of the divine righteousness. "The gods be good unto us," cried Sicinius, when misfortune, born of folly, was hard at hand. "No," replied Menenius; "in such a case the gods will not be good unto us." Shall we cry, God be good unto us, when wrath, generated by the hard and impenitent heart, is at hand ? Ah ! let us learn from the old heathen. Let us fly the wrath to come. Whatever the day of God's wrath may mean, let us not venture to approach that day without due preparation. Let us feel that only he can abide the great day of His wrath in whom Christ dwells, the hope of glory. Turn to Christ ; seek for His grace, power, and presence.

The fairness of the divine administration.—" For there is no respect of persons with God." This cannot mean that God makes no difference between man and man. He does make a difference ; and not one, but many. Our world is a world of differences. Heights, depths, colours—mountain, valley, rock—sea, forest, stream—sun, moon, and stars,—these are some of the material or physical differences that make our world what it is. Then in man there is race, nation, colour ; gifts of body and mind ; riches and poverty. Nor can this mean that He treats men at random, without reason or plan, irrespective of character. Nor does it mean that He has no fixed plan, but takes every man as he comes, allowing each to do as he pleases. These are the things on which the unbelief of the present day lays great stress, resolving every difficulty as to truth and righteousness and judgment to come by the reiteration of the text, " God is love."

But let us consider what the apostle means by saying that God is no respecter of persons. It means two things : —

I. **That God has no respect to the outward appearance or circumstances of a man in dealing with him.**—God takes him for what *he is*, not for what he *seems.*

II. **That in regard to justice and grace God does not follow man's estimates**

at all, either outward or inward.—God has His own standard, His own way, of procedure in treating the sinner, whether for condemnation or acceptance. The usual elements which decide man's judgment have no place in God's. 1. God's estimate or rule in regard to *justice* is that the doers of the law, the whole law, the unmodified law, shall live by it. 2. God's estimate or rule in regard to *grace* is that any man, whoever he be, who will consent to be indebted to the Son of God and His work for acceptance shall be accepted. This is the way in which grace shows itself to be no respecter of persons.

The apostle's object is to declare these three things : 1. *God's purpose of dealing with the sons of men.* He is not going to let them alone, nor to allow them to have their own way. 2. *God's plan of dealing with them.* He does so as God, sovereign and righteous, yet gracious. 3. *His willingness to receive any.*—*H. Bonar.*

Patient continuance.

I. **A seeker.**—All men are seekers more or less, for the reason that no good thing is to be obtained *without* seeking. Wealth must be obtained by the exercise of patience and labour. Little by little must one penny be added to another. Patience must be the reward of content, honour the end of probity. And so eternal things must be the result of toil, of search, of self-denial, a constant journey to the end. We have—

II. **The method of seeking.**—" Who by patient continuance." The Christian life is not an isolated or a spasmodic effort, not an individual act. A life alternating between fervour and languor will lead nowhere. Steady, unremitted work *pays* best both in worldly and spiritual matters.

III. **The reward to be attained.**—" Eternal life." At first sight these words seem disappointing. They represent something less than was sought. Men have sought eternal " honour " and eternal " glory." But we are not told here that this search will be realised. The honour and glory are left out, and " eternal life " alone is mentioned as the gift of God.

The fact teaches—1. *That we are not to limit our desires in spiritual things.* Aim high, hope for the most glorious idealities of life ; they will all fall short of what is in store for them that love God. But it teaches—2. *That after all eternal life includes all things.* The glorious gift of the Son of God shall itself possess all that is worth having. Eternal life ! Shall not the most ambitious be satisfied with his immortality—with the eternal absence of all harm, and all sin, and all evil ? Surely we should in our wildest dreams desire nothing more than eternal life at the footstool of God's throne—" And it doth not yet appear." We do not know what that eternal life shall include. And if God has given us the pledge of that, we may surely rest content.—*Homilist.*

SUGGESTIVE COMMENTS ON VERSES 5—12.

What is law ?—The little word " law " must not be understood here after a human fashion—that it teaches which works are to be done and which are to be left undone, as is the case with the laws of men, which can be obeyed by works without the feeling of the heart. God judges according to the intent of the heart, and will not be satisfied by words, but all the more punishes as hypocrisy and lying those works which are done without the feeling of the heart. Therefore Paul says that no-

body is a doer of the law by the works of the law.—*Luther.*

Meritorious and gratuitous. — Paul distinguishes between meritorious and gratuitous justification, the former being that which is unattainable by works of the law, the latter that which is attainable, as James says, not by faith only, but by works also (ver. 15). That there is a natural revelation made to the heathen is proved by Paul by three arguments : 1. By many virtuous acts performed by the heathen; 2. By the natural operation of their consciences; 3. By their reasonings with one another, by which they excused or accused one another.—*Macknight.*

The best for him who does the best.— These suppositions agree both with Scripture and reason: 1. All men can do all that God requires of them; 2. All who do the best they can derive help from God as far as is needful; 3. They all have Christ as their Redeemer,

though He was never revealed to them. Who knows whether the lot of the savage be not better than that of the philosopher, and the lot of the slave than that of the king? But this much we know, that every one ought to be contented with that state in which his wise and good Creator has placed him, and to conclude that it will be the best for him if he makes the best use of it. Upon this supposition the divine impartiality stands fully justified.— *Jortin.*

MAIN HOMILETICS OF THE PARAGRAPH.—*Verses* 13—16.

The Gentile conscience.—The law as well as the existence of the Creator is written on the heart of man, and he cannot get away from that law. He may make mistakes, but he can get to know the general tenor of that law. He may not have skill to frame a correct ethical system, but he can mark the great broad outlines, and so frame his moral course. The Gentile heart is not a mere blank page—it shows divine handwriting. In its deepest degradation there are obscured traces and marks of moral glory.

I. **The Gentiles show the work of the law written in their hearts by their superiority to their gods.**—The God of the Bible is the one perfect God—perfect in His natural and moral attributes. He is a conception of divinity which declares it is not an unaided conception of humanity. We cannot read of any god fashioned after the same perfect moral order as the God of the Bible. Whether we look at the God of the Old Testament or of the New, we must feel that this is a divinity which the highest human reason has not attained. Notwithstanding all that may be said against the biblical God, we affirm that there never has been and is not any other deity unto whom we may liken Him. In the wide world's Parthenon, in the long muster-roll of deities, there is none to be compared with the Christian's God. The highest ideals are but human conceptions and imperfect: the best of them are but one-sided personifications, and represent one cardinal grace or virtue; the worst of them are personifications of some degrading lust. And this gives us a striking view of the divinity working in heathendom, that the worshipper is often superior to the deity adored. Conscience asserts its power, and the devotee rises above the deity before whom he prostrates in devotion. The written law has stronger force than the personified lust or passion. The gods of the heathen worked towards moral destruction; and the legal writing on human hearts was that saving force which interrupted the process and prevented complete moral ruin.

II. **The Gentiles show the works of the law written in their hearts by the strivings of the many.**—Moral darkness has covered the earth; but through that darkness we catch gleams of moral light, and those gleams are the strivings of many of our race after nobler things. If there had not been such strivings, we should have beheld the race sinking deeper and deeper into moral corruption, and bringing upon our planet a catastrophe which the waters of a deluge would not have repaired. We may suppose that the world's lowest moral state was at the time of the Deluge; but even then a Noah appeared who was not only found striving after righteousness, but had attained to righteousness and was a preacher of the same all his days. Our planet has presented no such miserable moral spectacle, either before or since the period of the Deluge. Men, in spite of lust, passion, pride, and ambition, are found in all countries reaching up above their surroundings towards the pure realm of infinite moralities. The feverish restlessness of humanity speaks to us of a written law in the heart and the workings of a divine conscience. There is an infinite discontent and dissatisfaction in the soul of man which is full of moral significance. It points both inward and upward—inward to the divinely constituted nature of man, and upward to the divine Being whose claims must be met and in whose Son must be realised spiritual repose. Men hear within themselves the voice of conscience, but do not give sufficient attention so as carefully to catch the words that are spoken.

III. **The Gentiles show the work of the law in their hearts by the attainments of the few.**—It could not be argued from the achievements of a Shakespeare that all men might become great poets and dramatists, from the mathematical grasp of a Newton that all might become mathematicians; but surely it is legitimate to infer from the lofty achievements of one master-mind the large possibilities of other minds. The wide expansion of one mind tells of the possibility of development of others. In the heathen world, as also in the Christian world, the men have been comparatively few who have given practical expression to the belief that in the world there is nothing great but man, in man there is nothing great but mind, and in mind there is nothing great but the moral. Still, there have been such men. It will not do for us to lay the flattering unction to our souls that there is no goodness outside the Christian religion. While we believe that Christianity has raised the morality of the world to a higher tone and given the highest example of spiritual perfection in the person of its Founder, we must not lose sight of the noble names of Socrates, Solon, Plato, and Aristotle. Defective, no doubt, they were in many aspects of their characters and their conduct ; but they were in advance of their times, and speak of a divine law written in human hearts. It is indeed wonderful how glimpses of moral truth are given by heathen writers ; and we can only account for them on the supposition that the divine hand has been writing and that conscience has been working. The Orphic mysteries seem to have contained the assertion of two deep ideas—the immortality of the soul, and impurity of sin, which required expiation. Historical evidence goes to show that the broad distinctions between crime and virtue have always been marked. Homer is not without morality, though it is uninfluenced by a future life. It is noteworthy that Hesiod contains the same figure to represent virtue and vice which was afterwards consecrated in the mouth of Christ : "The road to vice may easily be travelled by crowds, for it is smooth, and she dwells close at hand. But the path of virtue is steep and difficult, and the gods have ordained that only by toil can she be reached." It is the steep and difficult pathway of virtue which repels the many from the effort to gain the glorious summit.

IV. **The Gentiles show the work of the law written in their hearts by their reception of the divine interpretation and exposition.**—When the preacher of the divine law goes to the heathen, he finds in their nature a response to his message, and this response may act in different directions. Some of the heathen accept the message because it is the interpretation of the law written in their hearts ; or others reject the message, not because the revealed law does not harmonise with the law written in the heart, but because a lower nature asserts an ascendency, and then, either to justify rejection or to fortify in a wrong course, they persecute the messenger and seek to obliterate traces of the revealed law. The very wrath of the adherents of false doctrine, when the truth is proclaimed, declares in most cases that the true doctrine is that which correctly interprets the symbolic writing on their hearts. If we hold the truth and are confident that we have the truth, why should rage possess our natures when a messenger comes to upset our beliefs? Our confidence in the truth may cause us to look complacently at the efforts of those who come to change our beliefs.

V. The Gentiles show the work of the law written in their hearts by the witness of conscience.—A man differs from a machine in this : that the one has a law in itself—is moved, as Aristotle would say, κατὰ λόγον; the other is moved μετὰ λόγον, has a law both in and for himself. Now conscience, which is more than mere consciousness, testifies to the presence of that law, interprets, and gives it force. Conscience bears witness to the *right*, gives emphasis to the *ought*, and leaves without excuse. Conscience existed before philosophies of right and wrong, taught moral lessons, and led to some strivings after propriety of conduct. The pre-existence of conscience is supposed by the post-existence of moral philosophies. Instinctive acts of nobleness arise from the instinctive promptings of conscience. Plato's sentence cannot be upheld, that " without philosophy there is no morality." The presence and practice of morality declare a philosophic spirit and temperament ; but Enoch, Noah, and Abraham, who were highly moral, would not be classed as belonging to any philosophical school. They would not be referred to as authorities on the questions which disturb the schools—as to the nature of the concrete and the abstract, as to nature or the non-existent, as to whether there can be either not-being or being. Morality arises, not from the scholastic philosophies, but from the deeper philosophy of conscience bearing witness to the work of the law written in the heart. Conscience bears witness to the divine writing in human nature. If the Gentiles had no witnessing conscience, then apostles and missionaries have no ground of appeal.

VI. The Gentiles show the work of the law written in their hearts by their moral reasonings.—These reasonings are not exemplifications of any logical method. Their thoughts, their moral reflections, are at one time accusing and at another time excusing. Shall we suppose them engaged in the intricate process of distinguishing between right and wrong ? Shall we not rather picture the Gentile nature as a court where moral questions are being discussed ? The conscience is both witness and judge. The thoughts are as so many advocates, some pleading for and others pleading against, either accusing or excusing. Shall we not still rather consider that the thoughts of the Gentiles accuse when wrong has been done, and excuse when right has been either attempted or performed ? There is such a process going on in human nature. In some the process is carried on with clearness, and in others with a certain vagueness. How sad that accusing voices should have reason most constantly to be heard ! Yet sadder still if self-righteousness prevents the accusing voices from being properly heard, and excusing voices, in the sense perhaps not meant by the apostle, only are allowed to make themselves heard !

1. *Let us beware lest the heathen rise up in judgment against us.* How little was their light ! How great is ours ! 2. *Let us not tamper with conscience,* for God knows, and will judge the secrets of men. 3. *Let the upbraidings of conscience drive us by repentance and faith unto Jesus Christ.* 4. *The doers of the law are justified before God.* We cannot be justified by the law of the carnal commandment ; let us find refuge in the higher law of love. 5. *If we fear the approach of the day when God shall judge, let us seek for that perfect love in and by Christ which casteth out all fear.* 6. *The voice of the law speaks trouble to the conscience.* The voice of " *my* gospel," of " the gospel of God," speaks peace by Jesus Christ to every believing soul ; therefore let us cleave above all things to the gospel.

SUGGESTIVE COMMENTS ON VERSES 13—16.

Law written on the heart. — The Greek poet Sophocles speaks of " the unwritten and indelible laws of the gods" in the hearts of men ; and the Platonic philosopher Plutarch speaks of " a law which is not outwardly written in books, but implanted in the heart of man."

Conversion does not impart new faculties.—Bishop Sanderson says that Paul teaches in this verse that "*every man*, however unholy, has a conscience, though depraved; and that at the fall of man conscience itself was not lost, but its rectitude and integrity were impaired; and that, when we are born again in baptism, we do not receive the infusion of *another* conscience, but our conscience, which was before unclean, is washed by the blood of Christ, and is cleansed by faith and is enlightened by the Holy Spirit, in order that it may please God." In regeneration the man does not receive the infusion of any new qualities. After conversion men possess the same characteristics as they did before the spiritual change had taken place. They obtain new affections, likes, and desires; but they do not receive a power of loving, liking, and desiring which they did not before possess. After conversion they both will and perform the thing which is good: but before conversion the power of volition was present, and also in a degree the power of performance; but it was weak—so weak that it could not overcome the counteracting forces. If a man had by some spiritual process to be remade before he could become a Christian, then how could it be possible, in justice, for him to be accounted a responsible agent? The unconverted heathen have a written law and a witnessing conscience and moral reasonings, and they must act up to their light, and by these must they be judged. And what will be their condition in the future it is not for us to determine. The great question is, not what will become of the heathen, but what will become of us—are we acting according to our increased light and enlarged opportunities? The Gentiles "show the work of the law written in their hearts." This expression may be taken from the fact that the law of the ten commandments was written on tables of stone. It is a proper expression to represent the impression made by the Creator upon the moral nature of the creature. A thing written is impressed. The hand of God writes upon the heart of man as He writes upon the material creation. The writing is symbolical, but its meaning is plain enough for all practical purposes.

An accusing conscience.—An accusing conscience tells us for what we were designed, that we were made morally in the image and likeness of God, from what we have fallen, and to what depths of depravity we have sunk. Thus it declares our littleness, as we consider our noble resolves, our lofty purposes, our high-born ambitions; and yet our weak performances—our miserable failures to reach the goal to which our virtuous longings point. How sadly often when we would do good evil is present with us! We fall to the doing of iniquity with fatal propensity. Thus conscience indicates our greatness as we contemplate the strife between good and evil which is being waged in the arena of a man's soul. We are very far from believing the doctrine that the greatest battles are unseen, the mightiest conquests unbloody, and that moral victors are the greatest heroes. Historians make no account of the battle-fields where moral conflicts are waged; but long after the historian's busy pen has ceased its wizardry, his powerful brain is blended with the common dust, his thrilling pages have perished as the shrivelled parchment scroll, and his Marathons, Thermopylæ, and other scenes of warlike glory have been swept into oblivion, the victories achieved by moral heroes will endure. Soul conflicts are the mightiest, as often they are the severest. Spiritual warfare is the most wonderful, as it is the most mysterious. What a world is that unseen realm where good and evil are engaged in fierce encounter! An accusing conscience is the inward trumpeter that summons the nobler powers to the battle. Alas that oft-times the trumpet blast falls as it were upon the ears of dead men, and the forces in the town of Mansoul do not muster to the defence ! How blessed is it when the trumpet voice is heard and obeyed ! Sometimes the believer is depressed as he feels within himself the agony caused by the strife between the good and the evil. He may ask, How is it that there is all this strife, agony, and conflict if my citizenship is in heaven? But strife speaks of life. Dead men do not fight. Dead powers in the soul do not engage in battle. It is as the powers of the soul are awake to the love of the beautiful and the good, and are desirous of being clothed with virtuous qualities, that they contend for the mastery over evil. The more spiritual life there is in the soul, the more feeling will there be in the conscience. The prickings of conscience are painful, but they tell of a living soul. A condemning heart sends agony through the frame, but it declares vitality. A man may even take courage when conscience accuses. All sin brings its punishment in its measure. The wages of sin is death, but not death to the conscience. Sometimes it seems as if the greater the death of the spiritual nature, the greater the life of conscience. Oh, how it darts its awful pangs ! How wonderful its constitution ! We speak of burying the past ; but conscience will not allow the past to be buried. It seems to have lain dormant for years, and then it speaks, and we cannot account for the utterance. No outward circumstances, no laws of association, appear to account for the fact that conscience has spoken to our condemnation. A guilty conscience who can endure ? " The spirit of a man will sustain his infirmity ; but a wounded spirit who can bear ? " The Good Physician alone has balm with which to heal the wounded spirit.

" O conscience ! into what abyss of fears
  And horrors hast thou driven me ; out of which
I find no way, from deep to deeper plunged !"
                                        Milton.

Darwin himself admits that, of all the differences between man and the lower animals, the moral sense or conscience is by far the most important.

Self-conscious personality of man.— The bearing of this upon conscience is clear. The Scripture doctrine of man first of all affirms that view of his physical and ethical nature which we have been endeavouring to show is the only one borne out by facts. The self-conscious and self-determining personality of man is an essential part of the divine nature in man. As Dr. Pope says, this element is " essential and indestructible," while there is a sense in which the image of God in its moral lineaments was " accidental and amissible," lost in the Fall, and not utterly lost only because redemption intervened. Such a being, however, it is clear, possesses moral capacity, being raised above the circle of nature, and moving in the region of self-consciousness and self-government, and he is prepared by the very constitution of his nature to " know good and evil," not only after the tempter's way, through disobedience and yielding to evil, but after God's way, through free choice of the good. In this brief but significant description of man's original nature lies the germ of the whole Scripture doctrine of conscience.—*W. T. Davidson.*

In the Gentile heart a real judgment hall.—How can one help admiring here, on the one hand, the subtle analysis whereby the apostle discloses in the Gentile heart a real judgment hall where witnesses are heard for and against, then the sentence of the judge ; and, on the other hand, that largeness of heart with which, after drawing so revolting a picture of the moral deformities of Gentile life, he brings into view in as striking a way the indestructible moral elements, the evidences of which are sometimes irresistibly presented here by this so deeply sunken life !—*Godet.*

Two principles of justification.— Here we are assured that the " doers of the law shall be justified " ; and yet, in the subsequent part of the epistle, it is proved in the most convincing manner that " by the deeds of the law there shall no flesh be justified." It is obvious that these different passages must refer to different things, otherwise the one would be contradictory of the other. And that they refer to two different principles of justification—the one held by the Jews and heathen, the other laid down in the gospel—cannot be doubted by any person who considers the argument. In the passage before us the apostle speaks of men being justified on the Christian principle, not by a perfect obedience, entitling them to it as matter of justice, but by the righteousness of faith, which God will of His own free mercy accept, and in virtue of the atoning death of Christ follow with everlasting life. When he says that by the deeds of the law " there shall no flesh be justified," he speaks of the principle of justification implied in the law of nature and relied on by all who rejected the gospel—a justification depending entirely on men's own actions, requiring an unvarying obedience to the whole law without the least failure, and thus entitling a man to be justified as a matter of right, the conditions being fulfilled on which the attainment of it was originally made to depend. It is this species of justification which he tells us no flesh living can attain—

a truth which no person who considers the matter can doubt. These passages, therefore, are entirely compatible with one another; but they relate to different things, and each of them states with perfect correctness the truth in relation to the subject to which it applies. This passage teaches us, first, that in the great day of the Lord our most secret thoughts and actions will be judged by Him who is appointed Judge of the quick and dead. And if we should be afraid or ashamed to have some passages of our life laid open, let this incite us to watch with more circumspection over our dispositions and conduct. It teaches us further that they are not the hearers but the doers of the law who shall be justified. Now we enjoy the knowledge of the divine law in as perfect a degree as it can be enjoyed by man. Does our conduct correspond with our knowledge? This is the important and trying question which it becomes all of us to investigate with the most rigid impartiality. And if we find, as unquestionably will be the case, that our conduct has been in many respects unsuitable to our knowledge, let the discovery incite us to redouble our diligence in the work of the Lord, that so being justified by faith we may have peace with God and the hope of obtaining eternal life.—*Ritchie.*

MAIN HOMILETICS OF THE PARAGRAPH.—*Verses* 17—24.

The vain boaster.—The Jews are nationally a separate people. It is astonishing how they have preserved their nationality through all the centuries. Though scattered through all lands, they have never assimilated. But the Jews are human, and the faults of humanity they often exemplify. Jews and Christians are brought together by their failings. Jews boasted of their titles, and were often indifferent to their characters. So it often is with Christians. The name and not the thing, the profession and not the practice, is the stumbling-block of the Christian as of the Jew. Therefore, when the Christian reads of the faults of the Jews, let him ask, Is not the record written of myself? am I resting in a mere name? Notice for our instruction, for our warning, and for our direction :—

I. **The claims of the boaster.**—What is man that he should boast? A drop in the ocean of being! One atom in the mass of matter! An ant on the molehills of time! The sport of the winds! Swept like a feather by the tempest! Crushed like a moth by the hand of nature's forces! A creature of an hour to boast! An ephemeron to glory! A man whose light, knowledge, and services have all been bestowed to boast! It seems useless to heap up epithets, for the boaster is not easily killed. The Jew boasts: 1. *Of God.* David sings, " My soul

71

shall make her boast in the Lord." And this boasting was to be of such a character that the humble should hear thereof and be glad. Notice the difference —*of God* and *in God* : the proud boast *of* God, the humble *in* God. Let him that glorieth not glory of God as if He were an inferior, but glory in God as the superior. 2. *Of superior knowledge.* A man of light and of leading—a man of light and sweetness in his own esteem. We have men of light and of leading, whose leadership is found in the word "go," and not in the word "come." Doctors do not take their own medicines; preachers do not practise their own doctrine. This Jew has penetrated the inner mysteries, and knows the divine will. How many followers among Christians! With what repellent dogmatism many will speak and write of divine plans and purposes! This Jew approves of the things that are more excellent. He has fine tastes, and an elevated moral nature. Are not some of our Christians too fastidious? They soar in the region of abstractions, where the excellent things of their own fancies dwell, but neglect the common duties. They are instructed out of the law and competent to be teachers. The pulpit has lost its day and its power, is the modern cry. We are all taught, and want no prosy sermons. 3. *Of wondrous gifts.* He is a worker of miracles. He is not only a guide to the blind, but a restorer of sight. How great his pretensions—a light of them which are in darkness! Such recuperative power is in this light that, falling upon the sightless eyeballs, it will restore the power of vision. Wonderful Jew! We need thee in our blind moral world. Oh, believe it not! Christ, the Good Physician, can alone touch with restoring power the visual organ, and on the sightless eyeballs pour the gracious light of heaven. The Holy Spirit must work if the sons of darkness are to become the children of light. This Jew is not merely a teacher of babes, but boasts formative power. He develops the moral nature. He eliminates the evil and fosters the good. He might not be elected as a teacher in a board school, but if his abilities were equal to his pretensions he would be priceless as a modern educator. In our times we need instructors of the foolish as well as teachers of babes. We want the fourth "R" of religion added to the three "R's." Oh, if the Jew could do as well as he can boast, we would not join in persecuting and maligning and banishing him from our land!

II. **The disparagement of the boaster.**—The Jew has suffered from the hands of Shakespeare. The Jew does not appear to advantage on the modern stage. But has the Jew ever had reason to complain more bitterly of the treatment he has received from men of other nationalities than he has of the treatment received from one of his own nation? What sublime irony, what biting sarcasm, what withering epithets are hurled against the Jew by the Jewish Paul! He shows the Jew the estimate he forms of himself, and then places in contrast the just estimate. Here is the great moral teacher and reformer, the son of light and of sweetness, the favourite of heaven, accused of things condemned both by God's moral laws and man's civil codes, where man has any pretension to advanced civilisation. The accusation is not without some foundation, according to the testimony of history. The Jews were given to robbery. Are the modern Jews free? What about exorbitant usury? Are modern Christians free? What about the rage for gambling? What about our sweating system? What about our cotton corners, our commercial and literary syndicates? These men, if not preachers, are sometimes the great supporters of modern preachers. They occupy the chief seats at ecclesiastical feasts, not to speak of civil banquets, Lord Mayors' banquets, etc. The sin of adultery had been increasing amongst the Jews just before Paul's days. Are we not mourning nowaday that in Christian England the race is not rising in purity? The Jews were given to sacrilege. They robbed temples. They kept back tithes and offerings. Sacrilege is a word banished from some ecclesiastical dictionaries. Some there are who ruthlessly touch sacred things with unholy hands. Thou that abhorrest idols, thou that teachest a man should not steal, thou that dost advocate the sacred rights of property, thou that dost hold hard by thine own investments, dost thou commit sacrilege, dost thou seek the spoliation of any Church, dost thou lend a helping hand to the reduction of the material power of any part of Christ's kingdom? The question should be seriously pondered by us all, to whatever part of the Church of Christ we belong; so that, while we make our boast of the law, we may not through breaking the law dishonour God and cause His name to be blasphemed.

III. **Learn that high profession and low practice is harmful.**—We know not how far-reaching is the evil influence of our inconsistency. We may exhort men to judge by principles, and not by persons. Still, one bad example may do more harm than a number of good sermons will confer spiritual benefit. How is the name of God blasphemed both at home and abroad! Let us pray and work that we may be able to live as we teach. Oh for the eloquent sermon of pure lives!

SUGGESTIVE COMMENTS ON VERSES 17—24.

Self-exaltation of the Jew.—A second flight of steps in the self-exaltation of the Jew. Having attained the position described in ver. 18, he confidently aspires to something higher. While he can see all things clearly in the light of the law others are in darkness. And he is fully persuaded that he is a " guide " of those who wish to walk in the path of morality, but have not eyes to see the way. He can give the " blind men " not only guidance but sight. For he is " a light of those in darkness." He will undertake the moral training of those who have not the wisdom which he has received from the law. He looks upon them as "babes," and offers to be their " teacher," for he has " the law," in which " knowledge " and " truth " are presented in tangible shape to the mind of man. " Instructor " differs from " teacher" by including whatever belongs to moral training and direction. The " form " of an object differs from its essence as the outside from the inside. It is the sum-total of that by means of which the inward character presents itself to our senses, and thus makes itself known to us. It is that by which we distinguish one object from another. Whatever we can see, feel, or hear is the form of a material object. Whatever we can conceive is the form of a mental object. The revealed will of God is " truth," because it exactly corresponds

with an eternal reality; it is " knowledge " when grasped by the mind of man. It is pre-eminently " the truth," for it sets forth the one great reality. It is when received into the mind pre-eminently " the knowledge," for it claims to be the one chief object-matter of man's intelligence. " Truth " and " knowledge " represent the contents of " the law " in their relation to the great reality and to the mind of man. This man claims to be a " teacher " because by his acquaintance with the sacred books his mind grasps that which is the chief object-matter of intellectual effort and a correct delineation of the eternal realities. The same eternal reality and the same true matter of human knowledge has in a still higher degree assumed form and presented itself to the mind in the gospel.—*Beet.*

Jewish depravity leads to Gentile degeneracy.—The absurdity of his position is evident to all. With solemn earnestness Paul paints a still darker picture, the direct result of the man's inconsistency. Though the possession of the law fills you with exultation you trample it under your feet, and thus bring contempt on Him who gave it. By choosing your nation to be His people God made you the guardians of His name and honour. That glorious and fearful name, which to know and to honour is life eternal, you have moved the heathen to mention with derision. They have seen and ridiculed the contrast of the words and works of their own teachers. (See Lucian, lxix. 19.) They see the same contrast in you. From your bold profession they suppose that you possess the favour of the God of Israel; and they treat with contempt a deity who as they think smiles on you. By your deep depravity, as your fathers by their far-off bondage, you have led the Gentiles to blaspheme. Observe that Paul's argument strikes with equal force against all conduct of Jews or Christians which is inconsistent with profession, and which thus brings dishonour to God.—*Beet.*

The universality of the law.—The natural law under which we are placed, according to the apostle's view of it, is a knowledge and feeling of right and wrong, resulting from that reasonable nature which our Creator has given us. It is independent of any special revelation, and essentially inherent in the soul of man; and in as far as it goes it coincides, when duly enlightened, with the moral dictates of the revealed law of God. It may be and often is sadly perverted, so as to sanction actions of the deepest immorality; but when enlightened and duly applied, it enforces the duties of piety, justice, and benevolence, and many of the other virtues commanded in divine revelation—though, generally speaking, it enforces them only feebly and ineffectually, as appears by its imperfect influence on the conduct. Its authority extends to all nations, and it places those who have no more perfect rule, and who listen to and obey its impartial dictates, on the same footing, in respect of divine favour, with those who show the same respect and obedience to a divine revelation; for it proceeds from the same source with the written revelation of God's will. It is intended by its Author to answer the same end to those who have no more precise rule; and consequently it would appear plainly incompatible with the absolute

impartiality of the sovereign Judge if it had not the same effect in recommending to His favour those who conscientiously seek to obey its dictates. The reality and also the universal extent of this law are shown by the apostle from the heathen, who have no other law, doing under its guidance the things contained in the revealed will of God, from the sense of right and wrong written in their heart, and the testimony borne by their conscience to the obligation of doing good and abstaining from evil, and from their mutual reasonings when they either accuse one another of transgressing this law, or approve of those things that are in conformity to it—all of which plainly imply the existence and obligation of this natural law. Nothing can be conceived more pointed than the apostle's questions, or more unavoidable than the conclusion to which they lead; for how could the Jews believe that the law, which binds all other men to avoid sin, lays no such obligation on them, or flatter themselves that they might commit with safety those transgressions which they owned will subject all others who are guilty of them to the displeasure of God? Of this almost incredible self-delusion the folly is still further exposed in the twenty-third verse: "Thou that makest thy boast of the law, through breaking the law dishonourest thou God?" This seems to be a general inference from the preceding interrogations. By acting in this manner thou who makest thy boast of the law, as a proof of God's favour towards thee, dishonourest God by violating that law in which thou gloriest. Men may be said to dishonour God when they misapply the privileges which He has given them. Yet we do not think that the essential glory of the all-perfect Jehovah depends in any degree on men's conduct. But, according to our usual mode of conceiving human actions, it appears to reflect some dishonour on a man when he bestows favour on those who are altogether unworthy, and who, of consequence, make a wrong use of them. And this analogy we are apt, as in a multitude of other cases, to extend to the dispensations of the supreme Ruler.—*Ritchie.*

"*Behold, thou art surnamed a Jew.*" —After the returning of the Israelites from the Babylonish captivity they were all called *Judæi*, Jews, because Judah was the principal and almost the only tribe then existing, and because to that tribe the others joined themselves. And as the Jews differed from all nations in point of religion, the name "Jew" and "Israelite" at length signified the "profession of a religion." When therefore it is said, "Behold, thou art surnamed a Jew," the meaning is, "Thou art a worshipper of the true God, and enjoyest the benefit of a revelation of His will." In this and the following verses, if I mistake not, the apostle addressed the men of rank and learning among the Jews. It is no objection to that supposition that probably there were no doctors of the law nor Jewish scribes and priests at Rome when this letter was written; for as the apostle was reasoning against the whole body of the nation, his argument required that he should address the teachers of every denomination to whom the things written in this and the following verses best agree. Besides, as he had addressed the heathen legislators, philosophers, and priests in the first chapter for the purpose of showing them the bad improvement they had made of the knowledge they derived from the works of creation, it was natural for him in this to address the Jewish scribes, priests, and doctors, to show them how little they had profited by the knowledge which they had derived from revelation. Of the Jewish common people the apostle speaks (iii. 20), where he proves that they also were extremely vicious.—*Macknight.*

"*Thou that gloriest in the law through transgression of the law, dishonourest thou God?*"—He next replies to the second prerogative, and shows their boasting in God and in the law vain from their own conduct—viz., their transgression of the third commandment; for by transgressing the whole law they brought disgrace upon the law and upon God—that is, "exposed at the same time both God and His law to be blasphemed by others," which was tantamount to blaspheming the name of God and violating the third commandment themselves. Hence the apostle supplies us with two notable things for the right understanding of the third commandment: first, that he who gives occasion to others to blaspheme is guilty of blasphemy himself; and secondly, that an occasion is given to the ungodly to blaspheme by the transgression of any one of the commandments, and consequently, whatever be the commandment transgressed, that the transgression of it is also a violation of the third commandment (see 2 Sam. xii. 14).— *Ferme and Melville.*

Responsibility for light.—The heathen have abused but one talent, "the light of nature," but we thousands— even as many thousands as we have slighted the tenders of offered grace. What a fearful aggravation it puts upon our sin and misery! We must certainly be accountable to God at the great day, not only for all the light we have had, but for all we might have had in the gospel day, and especially for the light we have sinned under and rebelled against.—*Burkitt.*

MAIN HOMILETICS OF THE PARAGRAPH.—*Verses 25—29.*

False religion.—Reference is not here intended to the false religions which have cursed the earth, but to the false religion which is inside the true, which may be founded upon and be a perversion of the true. It may be noted that false religions are perversions or distortions of the true. The Jewish religion was true for the time then present. It originated in the divine mind, and was promulgated by divine agents; and yet from it sprang, or perhaps we may say in connection with it rose up, those who were further from the light and the truth than the unenlightened but virtuous heathen. Circumcision was a profitable ordinance; but it became a curse under the handling of degenerate natures. The sacraments are profitable; but sacramental efficacy and sacerdotalism, its progenitor and concomitant, have been fraught with great moral damage. The extremes of truth become falsehoods. One-sided aspects of truth lead to moral ruin. Let us look at the whole truth; let us keep before the eyes of our minds the whole of its comely form, and thus become enamoured of its beautiful and harmonious proportions.

I. **False religion is a mere system.**—This both to the community and the individual. An arranged scheme, with more or less of order, sometimes very disorderly, so that the word " system " becomes a misnomer. It is a mere vain scaffolding, which does not serve to build up any moral structure. The scaffolding will fall with hideous ruin; the religious house built on the sand by system-mongers will be swept away by the tempest of divine wrath. The false religionist is a system-worshipper; he believes in schemes. How many system-makers to-day in our Christian England! They are building but only castles in the air.

II. **False religion is thus in outward seeming.**—The further we get away from the truth, the more anxious we become to make a fair and beautiful outside. We dress and adorn the dead that it may wear the semblance of life; but memories can never show the brightness and beauty of life. The sparkling eye dancing and beaming above a poor peasant's dress is more beautiful than all the pearls and jewels with which the dead or the sickly may be adorned. There are power and beauty in a soul possessed and moved by spiritual life which cannot be imitated by the greatest zealot of outward forms and ceremonies.

III. **False religion parades itself.**—It glories in circumcision; it multiplies the number of its sacraments: its genuflections are numerous. All, however, is done to be seen of men. The false religionist does not care for moral drill except on review days. We have observed, we think, that the showy religious system, which has often in it more of the false than the true, is only possible where wealth accumulates and men and women gather. Have we ever seen an elaborate ritual in the remote hamlet; and yet is there no religion there? Can the Pharisees be religious if placed individually, like Robinson Crusoe, on desert islands? If they can, will their religion sing to their souls sweet songs to charm away the sense of loneliness? If they can, will their religion put joy and strength and solace into their hearts, making them sing for very gladness, as it did for Paul and Silas when in prison? We want a religion for battle days as well as review days; and such a religion is possessed by him whose circumcision is of the heart, in the spirit and not in the letter, whose praise is not of men, but of God.

IV. **False religion thus is impressive.**—Of course it is impressive—glare and tinsel are impressive. A glittering image would be seized by a child—a nugget of gold would be neglected. Most men and women are children in moral things. Nebuchadnezzar's golden image has become dim, yea, has altogether disappeared; but the God of the Hebrews has still a place in some hearts. The tinsel of false religion shall be destroyed; the fine gold of true religion shall not find any consuming fire—this gold will enrich for eternity.

V. **The false religion judged by the no-religion.**—Will there be the class of no-religionists in heaven? Rabbis taught that no circumcised person goes into hell, and that all Israel, except heretics and apostates, have their portion in the world to come. Circumcision opens the gates of heaven; the uncircumcised go there too, if they fulfil the law. Startling if !—if they fulfil the law. Let us not say religion is no use; let us not declare sacraments are empty forms. Let us look to our hearts, so that the man of no religion may not rise in judgment; let us fulfil the high laws of love to God, to Jesus Christ, and our neighbour. Let us obey the gospel commandment, that we should believe on the name of His Son Jesus Christ, and love one another, as He gave us commandment.

True religion.—Outward ordinances and actions are necessary in our religious life, but they are not in themselves true religion. True religion is essentially an inward state—a vital principle or power in a man's heart and spirit, without which all outward acts are worthless. This truth, so important, but so easily forgotten, is strikingly enforced in these verses—showing us, as they do, that even in the Jewish dispensation the divinely appointed ordinance which sets an indispensable mark upon every Israelite is declared to be vain and worthless if unaccompanied by a true circumcision of the heart. Still *more forcibly* then will such remarks apply to the Christian's life and profession, for ours is especially a dispensation of *the Spirit.* And as all baptised persons are called Christians, we may take up these words of St. Paul, and say, " He is not a Christian who is one outwardly, neither is that baptism which is outward in the flesh," etc. This Scripture thus personally applied to ourselves may suggest to us *two great truths* :—

I. **The value and importance of Christian ordinances.**

II. **Our religion must be something more than such outward observances,** however sacred, and must be a divine life and power in the heart, without which all religious acts are only a delusion and a sham.

I. **The value of Christian ordinances seen:** 1. *From their necessity,* owing to the very nature of man—a creature with a body and a spirit. (1) *Necessary even for individual Christians*—e.g., in hearing, reading, praying. (2) *Still more necessary for Christian congregations.* They could not act together without some outward forms and acts. 2. *From the honour put upon them by our Lord Jesus Christ.* (1) *Christ Himself appointed them.* Specially those which we call sacraments. Prayer, even a form of prayer, called by us after His name. Preaching. (2) *The blessings attached to them in the New Testament baptism:* made disciples by it (Matt. xxviii. 19); sins washed away by it (Acts xxii. 16); saved by it (1 Peter iii. 21). *The Lord's Supper:* with its visible symbols of His body and blood (Luke xxii. 19, 20); the communion of or participation in the Lord's death thereby obtained (1 Cor. x. 16). *Prayer:* all-powerful (Matt. vii. 7); Christ Himself present where two or three worshippers meet. *Preaching:* believers saved by it (1 Cor. i. 21); preaching saves men (1 Tim. iv. 16).

II. **Outward acts and ordinances worth nothing if they are all our religion.** —Jesus Christ is the only Saviour; the Holy Spirit is the only power which brings Christ and His salvation to each individual soul. 1. Hence all outward ordinances are valuable, only as they draw us near to Christ; only in their spiritual use; only as they produce or strengthen in us repentance, faith, hope, and love; only as they are blessed by the Spirit in our hearts. 2. *Hence also, if not thus used,* they may be even *more* than useless. They may be even a form of godliness without any of its power; they may shut out Christ, and hide Him from our eyes; they may delude the worshipper with an *appearance* of religion, while he has in reality *none.*

III. **Let us be on our guard against the temptation to be satisfied with an outward religion.**—Let us watch well the nature of our profession (2 Cor. xiii. 5). Let us ever look to Jesus as the centre and very soul of our religion; a true Christian life is a life from God, with God, to God, in the power of the Spirit.— *Dr. Jacob.*

Ver. 29. *Inward religion.*—Man's obligations to worship God and obey His laws are generally acknowledged. Did we not know human nature the inference would be that man is a very religious being, and that his heart must be powerfully influenced by the truths he acknowledges and the prayers he offers up. The contrary, however, is the fact. How are we to account for it? Whilst the obligations of religion are acknowledged, and its services, under some form or other, observed, yet is man the slave of sin, and his principles and practices have therefore been thus at variance with the conviction of his understanding. We cannot doubt from these facts but that man has the dreadful power of deceiving himself; that there is scarcely any error into which he falls more easily than into religious delusion—into the habit of thinking that he does God service, even while he disobeys the plainest commands; and that by outward religious performances he atones for the disregard of moral obligations. Inward religion is found in the state of the understanding. If we are Christians inwardly, then our understanding will be so enlightened as that all the truths of God essential for us to know shall be so clearly discerned as to exercise their proper influence upon us—an influence as powerful as their importance demands. We must look for inward religion in the state of the judgment—that is, to those conclusions to which we come as to the truths proposed in this book and apprehended by the understanding. What is faith in fact, intellectually considered, but an expression of our judgment on divine truth? What is the faith of credit but the expression of our judgment on the credibility of that which we believe? And what is the faith of truth and reliance, entering into the very essence of that particular faith in Christ which justifies, but the expression of our judgment that the great truths of Christianity are not merely worthy of being believed but of being admitted into the spirit and acted upon? We must look for inward religion in the state of the will. When this is right, it will be clearly manifested in submission and acquiescence. There is submission to the divine authority. There is a full acknowledgment of this great and humbling principle to which no man comes but by the grace of God: that we are under the government of God—that we belong to Jesus Christ, and have no right to ourselves. When this is fully recognised, then our will submits. And hence arises that right direction of our choice which may be said both to constitute and mark the rectitude of our will. The man may be conscious of an inward struggle—he may feel that he comes short of that state of rectitude to which his will shall be brought when, by the blessing of God, Christianity has effected all its purposes in him. But still grace gives him the victory. He is persuaded that the will of God is right, however dark and painful its appointments may at present appear; and therefore he says, "The will of God be done." We are to look for inward religion in the state of our principles. If our principles be right, they are produced by the reception of some of those original but universal truths revealed in the word of God. These, when properly received, become principles of action and conduct laid up in the heart. All men are men of principle some way or other. It is only he who is a Christian inwardly that has a principle capable of universal reference, and thus of uniform operation. Right actions show that we are under the influence of right principles. We must look for inward religion in the state of the feelings. We are to contend for the important truth that Christianity takes hold of the whole mind and is intended thoroughly to sanctify the whole man. There are some who deny that feeling forms any essential part of religion. I have no hesitation in saying that wherever Christianity is it must produce deep and strong and constant emotion.—*R. Watson.*

SUGGESTIVE COMMENTS ON VERSES 25—29.

Necessity of repentance.—*Shemoth Rabba,* f. 138, 13, declares: "Let no heretics and apostates and impious ones of Israel say, Because we are circumcised we do not descend into hell. What does the holy and blessed God?

He sends an angel and makes them uncircumcised, that they may descend into hell." We have further and melancholy confirmation of the same in the applicability of the reasoning of this chapter to many Christians, not only in the dark ages, but in our own day and in the most enlightened Churches. Many who do what they know to be wrong rely for salvation, perhaps unconsciously, upon their knowledge by means of the gospel of the way of salvation, of which knowledge the only result in their case is that they are ready to teach or to condemn others less instructed or less orthodox than themselves; or upon their outward connection with the people of God or their attention to religious ordinances. By teaching that God looks at the heart and judges all men according to their works, Paul pronounces sentence upon all such. This may be seen by reading "Christian" instead of "Jew" in this chapter. The substitution only increases the force of the argument. The difference between the words and works of some who bear the name of Christ brings practical dishonour to that name—the name of Him who died for them—and hinders the work He died to accomplish. God, who of old required the circumcision of the heart, requires to-day that men worship Him in spirit and in truth. The existence among ourselves of the deadly errors here referred to gives to this chapter an abiding and incalculable worth. From this chapter we learn the absolute necessity of repentance. Since God is angry with all sin, none but those who turn from sin can enjoy His favour. And therefore none can intelligently seek His favour but those who sincerely purpose to avoid all sin, and none but those who actually conquer sin can intelligently believe that they possess the favour of God. Not only does Paul thus prove man's absolute need of repentance, but by proclaiming God's anger against all sinners he does as much as words can do to lead men to it.

A safeguard against the perversion of justification.—This chapter is a safeguard against a common perversion of the great doctrine of chap. iii.—justification through faith. Through the failure of some teachers to give prominence to the truths of this chapter the doctrine of justification through faith has been frequently and seriously perverted. The teaching of chap. ii. occupies a place in relation to the rest of the epistle similar to that of the epistle of James in relation to the epistles of Paul, of the first gospel in relation to the remainder of the New Testament, and especially similar to that of the teaching of John the Baptist in relation to the teaching of Christ. The resemblance is seen in the modes of thought and even in the words of this chapter. It is therefore of great value as a means of harmonising these very different, and at first sight apparently contradictory, portions of the New Testament. The chapter from the study of which we now rise receives its entire value from the chapters which follow. It can do good only by preparing us for the more glorious truths of chap. iii. It is a "voice crying in the wilderness, Prepare ye the way of the Lord." Like the greatness of the prophets, it points to that which is greater than itself. We may sum up the whole and its bearing on chap. i. in the words of the Master, "Except ye repent, ye shall all likewise perish." —*Beet.*

Decline of religion shown by outward observances.—When true religion declines, the disposition to lay undue stress on external rites is increased. The Jews when they lost their spirituality supposed that circumcision had power to save. St. Paul does not deny but asserts the value of circumcision. So likewise the Christian sacraments, baptism and the Lord's supper, are of the utmost importance, and to neglect or reject them is a great sin. It is a mark of genuine piety to be disposed always to justify God and to condemn ourselves. On the other hand, a disposition to self-justification and the examination of our sins, however secret, is an indication of the want of a proper sense of our own unworthiness and of the divine excellence. There is no better evidence against the truth of any doctrine than that its tendency is immoral. Speculative and moral truths which are self-evident to the mind should be regarded as authoritative and as fixed points in all reasonings.— *Hodge.*

The way to end boastings.—If all men were willing to sacrifice their opinions when they appeared to impinge on the veracity of God, if they started back with instinctive shuddering at the very supposition of such a want of fidelity in Him, how soon would an end be put to the boastings of error, to the pride of philosophy, to lofty dictation in religion! No man with this feeling could be a universalist for a moment, and none could be an infidel.—*Barnes.*

Outward observance must be heart-prompted.—External ecclesiasticism and confession has value only when it leads to religion of the heart and life, otherwise it is only the same as heathenism. The great difference between outward and inward Christianity is internal. The true worshipper of God is inward, is concealed from the world, and is known only to God. The worth and merit of the pious person are exalted above all opinion of the world: 1. Because true piety by no means passes in the world for the highest good, but only that which is profitable and shines. 2. Because men cannot discern this inner, pure condition of heart, neither can they credit it to others. 3. Because the world cannot reward this piety. God's word is committed to us. Use it aright, support it, propagate it. In many cases it has disappeared through the fault of men—in Asia, in Africa. God's honour cannot be touched. Nothing can be charged against God; it would be blasphemy to charge Him with blame of any kind.—*Heubner.*

Outside and inside.—Many have clean hands, but unclean hearts. They wash the outside of the cup and platter when all is filthy within. Now the former without the latter profits a man no more than it profited Pilate, who condemned Christ, to wash his hands in the presence of the people. He washed his hands of the blood of Christ, and yet had a hand in the death of Christ. The Egyptian temples were beautiful on the outside, but within you shall find nothing but some serpent or crocodile. " He is not a Jew which is one outwardly." Judas was a saint without, but a sinner within; openly a disciple, but secretly a devil.

A questionable silence.—For a time I feared he (Judge Hale) was wanting in experimental religion, as he seldom spake of his own spiritual views and feelings; but upon better acquaintance I found that I was mistaken. He had heard from many in his time so much of hypocrisy and fanaticism that he was urged towards the extreme silence.

ILLUSTRATIONS TO CHAPTER II.

Ver. 1. *The poet Nash.*—We measure the excellency of other men by some excellency we conceive to be in ourselves. Nash, a poet, poor enough (as poets used to be), seeing an alderman with his gold chain upon his great horse, by way of scorn said to one of his companions, " Do you see yon fellow, how big he looks? Why, that fellow cannot make a blank verse!" Nay, we measure the goodness of God from ourselves: we measure His goodness, His justice, His wisdom, by something we call just, good, or wise in ourselves; and in so doing we judge proportionally to the country-fellow in the play, who said, if he were a king, he would live like a lord, and have peas and bacon every day, and a whip that cried " slash."

Ver. 1. *Prejudice in judgment.*—Nero thought no person chaste, because he was so unchaste himself—such as one troubled with the jaundice sees all things yellow. Those who are most religious are least censorious. Who art thou that judgest another man's servant? Those who are fellow-creatures with men should not be fellow-judges with God.

Ver. 1. *Judge gently.*—If we thoroughly looked into and understood ourselves, we should surely be more charitable in our judgments of others. And yet it is strange that the more the sinner, the more severe the critic. Perhaps our condemnation of others is supposed to be a condoning of our own misdoings. But we have to take home the exhortation, "For wherein thou judgest another, thou condemnest thyself; especially if thou doest the same thing thyself."

"Then gently scan your brother man,
  Still gentler sister woman;
Though they may gang a-kennin' wrang
  To step aside is human."

Burns.

Ver. 1. *Fault-finding.*—It is the painful necessity of people in certain positions in life that they have to find fault; but to do this with any useful result requires much tact and sympathy. When we are rebuked in this spirit, we do not resent it, but are rather obliged for the interest that is taken in us. Thomas Ken, Bishop of Bath and Wells, author of the Morning and Evening Hymns and of the Doxology, had acquired this art of profitable fault-finding. He was chaplain to Charles II., and spoke plainly to the king, who, however, was never angry at his faithfulness. "I must go," he used to say, "and hear little Ken tell me of my faults."

Ver. 2. *Clearchus on oaths.*—Clearchus says to Tissaphernes, "The oaths which we have sworn by the gods forbid us to be enemies to each other, and I should never consider him to be envied who is conscious of having disregarded such obligations; for from the vengeance of the gods I know not to what speed any one could flee so as to escape, or into what darkness he could steal away, or how he could retreat into any stronghold, since all things in all places are subject to the gods, and they have power over all everywhere alike." We have here one heathen appealing to another, to a stranger in race and religion, on the ground of a moral truth admitted by all. "According to truth." God's sentence corresponds with the reality of the case, on man's actual conduct. All judges aim at this; God attains it.

Ver. 5. *Burke and Pitt.*—"I have no fear for England," said Pitt; "she will stand till the day of judgment." "What I fear," replied Burke, "is the day of *no* judgment." So it is with us. It is the lack of judgment which makes the day of judgment so great a terror. The forgetting of the great life beyond the grave, and the consequent living as if this life were all, is due to lack of insight and shallow thinking. Eternity is disregarded because time is wasted, and so the judgment day, when all is to be accounted for, is a terrible day to think about.

Ver. 12. *The judgment day.*—A clergyman once heard an infidel jestingly say, "I always spend Sunday settling my accounts." The minister turned round and said, in accents of solemnity never to be forgotten, "You may find, sir, that the day of judgment will be spent in exactly the same manner."

Ver. 12. *Afraid of the Bible.*—A celebrated infidel once said, "There is one thing which mars all the pleasure of my life." "Indeed," replied his friend, "what is that?" "I am afraid the Bible is true," was the answer. "If I could know for certain that death is an eternal sleep, I should be happy—my joy would be complete. But here is the thorn that stings me—this is the sword that pierces my very soul: if the Bible is true, I am lost for ever." This is the Bible upon the truths of which many have lived, and in the belief of which many have died. Oh, how terribly afraid would they have been if any one had been able to show that it was untrue! For upon its truths all their hopes are built. An untrue Bible would mean an untrue Christ; and a Christless death would be a death of doom to them.

Ver. 12. *The great hereafter.*—During the enlistment of soldiers for the army, a young man, though strongly urged to join the volunteers, hesitated, and finally declined. He was able-bodied and patriotic. He had always been regarded as brave. The suggestion that personal cowardice might be the reason called forth from him this frank confession: "No; it is not *dying* that troubles me; I could stand up and be shot for my country,—*it is the hereafter.*"

Ver. 13. *Caracci, the famous artist.*—Caracci, the famous artist, while discoursing on the splendours of the ancient sculptures, and especially of the Laocoon, reproached his brother because he did not appear to be paying the slightest attention. When he had finished his description, his brother took a piece of charcoal and drew the statue as if it had been before him. Caracci in astonishment confessed that his brother had taken the most effectual way to show the beauties of the famous sculpture. "Poets paint with words, and the painter with works," was the reply. The Christian must be a doer as well as hearer of the word.

Ver. 13. *Ariosto and his house.*—Ariosto built himself a small house, and on being asked by a friend how he, who had described palaces in *Orlando*, could be content with so humble a dwelling, replied, "Words are cheaper than stones." God does not want fictitious words, but living stones, holy deeds.

81

Ver. 13. *The conscience ring.*—How beautifully was the office of conscience set forth in the ring which, according to an Eastern tale, a great magician presented to his prince! The gift was of inestimable value, not for the diamonds and rubies and pearls that gemmed it, but for a rare and mystic property in the metal. It sat easily enough in ordinary circumstances, but so soon as its wearer formed a bad thought or wish, designed or concocted a bad action, the ring became a monitor. Suddenly contracting, it pressed painfully on the finger, warning him of sin. The ring of that fable is just that conscience which is the voice of God within us, which is His law written on the fleshly tablets of the heart. We all know that the word "conscience" comes from *con* and *scie*; but what does that *con* intend? "Conscience" is not merely that which I know, but that which I know *with some other*; for this prefix cannot, as I think, be esteemed superfluous, or taken to imply merely that which I know *with* or to myself. That other knower whom the word implies is God.

Vers. 14, 15. *Conscience the oracle of God.* —Joseph Cook says that "conscience is the compass of the unknown." Epigrams are apt to be misleading. Can it be said that conscience is the compass of God? Does He require a method of measurement? May it not rather be said that conscience is our compass, if it be enlightened by the Holy Spirit and the word of God. The Gentiles have a conscience, but it is not always a properly regulated instrument of measurement. It points out a wrong and a right, but does not always say correctly which is wrong and which is right. It is the voice of God, but requires tuning.

"Yet still there whispers the small voice
    within,
Heard through God's silences, and o'er
    glory's din:
Whatever creed be taught, or land be trod,
Man's conscience is the oracle of God."
                                    Byron.

Ver. 24. *Christians injurious to Christianity.*—It is a melancholy fact that Christians—at least, professing Christians—are themselves the greatest obstacle to the spread of the gospel and the power of the gospel of Christ. Some time ago commissioners were sent over here from Japan to report on the condition of things here —for the Japanese were anxious to progress, and to adopt whatever was good in this country—and what was their report and advice? Adopt this and that in English trade and politics, but not the English religion. Ah! it was just this: the fruits of the professed religion were not such as to commend the religion itself. At least, the "supposed" fruits; for what the Japanese saw were not the fruits of the Christian religion at all. A Brahmin recently said to a Christian, "I have found you out. You are not as good as your book. If you Christians were as good as your book, you would in five years conquer India for Christ." No wonder if the Chinese when they see us forcing opium upon them, and the Africans when they see us deluging them with rum, do not want the religion of the men who do this. Alas! in our own small spheres, how often have we been hinderers of the doctrine of our book? Have we not hindered it in our neighbourhood and family, and amongst those with whom we mingle in daily life? God give us more consistency for the future, and make the man and the book harmonise better together. People often say, "Well, if I'm not altogether what I ought to be, I am no one's enemy except my own. I may not be good, but at least I do no harm." No man, however, either liveth or dieth to himself. No sin was ever committed whose consequences rested on the head of the sinner alone. What would be thought of a passenger who should cut a hole in the ship's side underneath his berth, and say, when expostulated with, that he was only his own enemy, and that he was injuring no one but himself?—*Quiver*, "'*Short Arrows.*"

Vers. 25-27. *Moral maxims not enough.*— Some men tie themselves with all manner of moral maxims, and so full oft influenced by worldly wisdom and worldly motives, pass sin by. There is such a thing as honesty being the best policy, and nothing more than policy. This is shown in the words of a well-known modern writer, where one of his characters says, "You don't think he could do anything mean or dishonourable?" "I think," was the reply, "his own good opinion of himself would guard against that; self-esteem, and not any very high notion of morality, keeps many a man from picking a pocket." What all this means is simply this, that men may seem to lead great and good lives, and yet be all wrong within; they are quite willing to follow the invitations of sin, but the cords of fear and what is called decency restrain them. The heart is all aglow with hidden lusts, and the only reason why there is no open flinging of life into the arms of beautiful sins is that the dread of social ostracism binds them and holds them in check. This is not enough, and Christianity, coming with her sweet song, so fills the soul that sin's most sorcerous chants are powerless. Sin loses its power of enticing when Jesus sings the "sweet story of old." There is no need for chains and fetters—the soul of its own free-will goes past temptation; and this is liberty in Christ Jesus.

Vers. 25-27.—*The girl in the workroom.*—A girl had been mixed with others in a workroom in the city; weeks passed on, nothing was ever said about religion, until one of the girls said to her: "I want to ask you something. I have been thinking you are a Christian. Do you mind telling me if it is so?" The one asked said, "I am sorry, Leslie, I did not show it so plainly that there could be no doubt in your mind." "Oh," said the other, "I knew from the first that you were different to the others, and now I know why." Again, a friend had passed through a trial, and one was speaking who had never owned herself religious: "I know why you got through. You had Jesu's Spirit to help."

Vers. 27-29. *John Wesley's dream.*—John Wesley once, in the visions of the night, found himself, as he thought, at the gates of hell. He knocked and asked who were within. "Are there any Roman Catholics here?" he asked. "Yes," was the answer, "a great many." "Any Church of England men?" "Yes, a great many." "Any Presbyterians?" "Yes, a great many." "Any Independents?" "Yes, a great many." "Any Baptists?" "Yes, a great many." "Any Wesleyans here?" "Yes, a great many." Disappointed and dismayed, especially at the last reply, he turned his steps upward, and found himself at the gates of Paradise, and here he repeated the same questions. "Any Wesleyans here?" "No." "Any Presbyterians?" "No." "Any Church of England men?" "No." "Any Roman Catholics?" "No." "Any Baptists?" "No." "Any Independents?" "No." "Whom have you here, then?" he asked, in astonishment. "We know nothing here," was the reply, "of any of those names you have mentioned. The only name of which we know anything here is 'Christian.' We all are Christians here; and of these we have a great multitude which no man can number, of all nations, and kindreds, and peoples, and tongues." How many there are whose only Christianity is their name, who look for their salvation from the fact that they are good members of this communion or that—often from the fact that they are red-hot and unchristian partisans! One is of Paul, and one of Apollos, and another of Cephas; and comparatively few really of Christ. Oh that we may go deep down below all names and sects and Church memberships to the foundation rock—Jesus Christ; and, viewing all differences, which are not fundamental ones, in the light of eternity and heaven, find in the fact that we are "Christians" a bond of fellowship and brotherhood while we are here!—*Quiver,* "*Short Arrows.*"

Ver. 29. *The king's son in the harp.*—An old Norse legend tells how a certain harper played as never man played—his music instinct with such power and pathos that all must listen. The secret of his power was, that concealed in the harp foot was a little child, the son of the exiled king, whose plaintive cries, mingling with the bard's story, gave it a new power. May we not say, at this time, the passionate, loving cries of our King's Son are the strength and power of all our melodies and songs?

CHAPTER III.

CRITICAL NOTES.

Ver. 1. **What advantage then hath the Jew?**—Pre-eminence. Passage brings out the idea of surplus (Wordsworth).

Ver. 3.—πίστιν τοῦ Θεοῦ—the faith of God—may perhaps be best explained by the assertion, God is faithful.

Ver. 4. **God forbid: yea, let God be true, etc.**—More proper is it that men should impute unfaithfulness to themselves than to God. **God forbid**—*i.e.*, far be it. An idiomatic exclamation. The sense in which David used the Hebrew word "tsadak," and in which his LXX. translators used δικαιῶν and δικαιοῦσθαι, is the sense in which Paul uses them. **And mightest overcome.**—Mayest prevail judicially in thy cause.

Ver. 5. **If our unrighteousness commend.**—Sets off to advantage, makes conspicuous. I speak *more humano*, in such a manner as is intelligible to men.

Ver. 7.—The truth of God, not objectively, but subjectively. Why should I suffer punishment on account of that which contributes to the glory of God?

Ver. 8.—Whose judgment is in harmony with right.

Ver. 9.—Do we bring pleas forward on behalf of ourselves—*i.e.*, in fear of a sentence of condemnation against ourselves? (Stuart.)

Ver. 10.—The apostle having mentioned that he had impeached both Jews and Gentiles of being under sin, adduces documentary evidence of the legitimacy of his impeachment (Wordsworth).

Ver. 19.—By the "law" here expositors understand the written revelation as a whole. **That every mouth may be stopped.**—Phraseology borrowed from the custom of gagging criminals.

Ver. 22. **By faith of Jesus Christ unto all and upon all them that believe.**—Faith apprehends and appropriates a personal mediator. **The righteousness of God.**—Our participation by faith in Christ as being the only righteousness that God approves, and thus is here called "the righteousness of God through faith."

Ver. 23. **The glory of God**—viz., the divine approbation.

Ver. 24.—The English, or rather Latin, word "redemption" is not a perfect synonym of the term employed by the apostle (ἀπολύτρωσις). It means a ransoming off—deliverance on the ground of ransom.

Ver. 25.—God has openly exhibited Christ to the world as a propitiatory offering for sin, unto all who believe in Him, in order that He might fully exhibit His pardoning mercy (His δικαιοσύνη) in respect to the forgiveness of sins under the past and present dispensations (Stuart).

Ver. 26.—Righteousness as distinguished from truthfulness and goodness on the one hand, and from mere justice on the other. Because of the pretermission of the former sins.

Ver. 27.—Where is then the glorying? Such is the most literal and most correct rendering of the clause. Almost tantamount to the expression, Where is then their glorying?

Vers. 30, 31.—The gospel establishes the law, because it is the most sublime manifestation of the holiness and strictness of God. Sin never appears more fearful than at Golgotha, where, on account of it, "God spared not His own Son" (Olshausen).

MAIN HOMILETICS OF THE PARAGRAPH.—*Verses* 1–8.

The surplus to the Jew.—The poor Jew has been persecuted, harassed, stripped, and robbed; and yet for the most part he has come forth with a respectable material advantage. The material surplus has been to the Jew. The money-lenders of the nations have been and are still the Jews. They value this surplus. In this respect they are like Christians. The latter profess to despise the former, but there is perhaps more envy than contempt in the feeling. The material surplus is valued more highly than the moral. The bond which we hold for money due is too oft more precious than the bond of God's oracles, which tells of our indebtedness to the divine Being. Here we have :—

I. **A great blessing conferred.**—The blessing of being God's chosen people, and this affirmed and declared to mankind by the seal of circumcision. The natural Israel a type of the spiritual Israel. How thankful we ought to be for God's distinguishing favours to the Anglo-Saxon race! The most prosperous race on the face of the earth, because God-enlightened. Let us cherish our privileges. True religion our best and only safeguard. Our *Victorias* may be submerged; our nearly four hundred gallant men may find a watery grave. He that sails in the ark of Christianity sails in an ark that is secure in all deluges and cannot be overturned by any colliding force. The chief blessing which St. Paul alludes to is that unto the Jew were entrusted the oracles of God. Wonderful that a country which has no literary greatness should have produced the noblest literary volume of all time! No; Palestine did not produce the Old Testament. It came from "the better country—that is, the heavenly." The oracles are not of man, but of God. The bards that sing in these oracles were not taught in the schools of Greece; they learnt the lore of heaven—they speak, but their utterances are in their moral aspect the speakings of God. These oracles are a greater treasure to the Jew than all his material wealth. What honour we render the Jew to-day arises from the fact, not that he is a great money power, but that he has been a great custodian and dispenser of immortal truth. And as we read the New Testament, let us not forget our indebtedness to the Jew. As we study our grand but very difficult epistle, we remember that St. Paul was a Jew. Let us try to realise the fact that unto us have been entrusted the oracles of God. Do we value the truth?

Do we put out to usury by scattering the word of God?—for we enrich ourselves by striving to enrich others.

II. **A great blessing not diminished by rejection.**—What if some did not believe. The oracles of God are no less true because hypercritics point out discrepancies. The sun is no less a sun because spots are shown on its surface; the eyes are no less useful for seeing because the modern optician pronounces them very imperfect organs of vision. What if some do not believe? I devoutly thank God for my eyesight; I prefer it vastly to the aids of modern opticians. I read gladly the oracles, for I find in them a power to heal, to bless, and to guide which no other oracles afford. I sail in the ark Christ Jesus amid all deluges. The sceptics strive to upset this ark as the *Victoria* was upset in the Mediterranean, but they have not yet built any water-tight moral vessel.

III. **This rejection is the result and proof of unrighteousness.**—The rejecter of the Bible contends for his moral rectitude, and says that will not allow him to accept what is contrary to reason and to history. He may think himself right; but perhaps he does not know himself as well as he thinks he does. Our metaphysicians examine mind in general, and leave their own mental and moral natures unexplored. A moral twist may turn the intellectual powers in a wrong direction. A rivet may let a bridge fall and destroy many lives. A moral rivet loosely made and set may cause damage. We want, not more intellectual light, but less moral darkness.

IV. **The unrighteousness of the rejecter sets forth the eternal rectitude.**—Out of chaos comes beautiful order, out of seeming evil good, in the wonderful working of divine proceedings. The rejecters of the oracles have led to the discovery of fresh confirmations of their authenticity. The rejecters have been unwittingly builders. So the unrighteousness of man sets forth the righteousness of God. It shines forth all the more brilliantly by the contrast. *The rectitude of God is not capable of swerving from the right line.* Jesuitical men may say, Let us do evil that good may come. The righteous God says, Forsake evil, and thereby good will come. If at any time the proceedings of God appear to diverge from the straight line of moral rectitude, let us be sure that the fancied divergence is only in appearance. Whatever befalls let this be our noble creed, that God must be true, though this assertion makes all men liars. *The rectitude of God is not disproved by strokes of vengeance.* A man revenges himself because he is stirred by passion, by envy, by hatred. A God takes vengeance because it is required in the interests of a moral government. The modern God is the amicable guest who winks at the sins of the host. Paul's God is a moral governor as well as an *all-father. The rectitude of God constitutes the basis of final judgment.* All must come right, for God is right. But all cannot come right to the man who is all wrong, and continues in hardness and impenitence to walk in the wrong. All will come right, and on this we calmly rest our souls. We are not troubled, for all must come right, since God is righteous. All will be well, for God is righteous. Whatever condemnation takes place in the future will be just, for a righteous God is an arbiter of all destinies. Our moralists have their ethical systems, and yet how little they know about what is wrong and what is right! God's rectitude is the eternal standard of true ethics, and that will be vindicated in the final account. The truth of God will abound, even through human falsehoods, to His glory. The truth of God's rectitude, and, blessed thought! the truth of God's love and mercy, will abound to His eternal glory. Let us embrace the mercy, and the rectitude need not cause alarm, if we embrace the mercy as revealed in the crucified *One.*

Vers. 1, 2. *The oracles of God.*—Our religious privileges are not to be thought of trifling importance because they do not produce their full effect. They cannot be a substitute for personal holiness; but man's ingratitude does not cancel his obligations, nor does the abuse of privileges destroy their value. Much, O ye Jews, as ye have abused the divine goodness, it has flowed to you in a special manner; and if you ask what advantage you have had, I reply, Much every way, because unto you were committed the oracles of God.

I. **The leading characters of the oracles of God.**—1. *Absolute truth and wisdom.* Being from God, the question of their wisdom and truth is settled. We cannot admit that there is a Being of infinite perfection without admitting His perfect wisdom and holiness. 2. *The subjects of these oracles are of infinite importance.* The oracle always speaks on those questions which are vital to our peace and safety, and on those which are curious rather than useful the oracle is silent. Yet knowledge is not prohibited—only delayed: "What thou knowest not now thou shalt know hereafter." It is sufficient for us now to know how we may be delivered from sin, and from its penalty, eternal death, and how we may daily walk so as to please Him. 3. *We have an interesting character given us of the oracles when they are called "lively" oracles.* It is this which constitutes the peculiarity of the word of God. It is a word with which the Spirit of God wonderfully works, and which He renders living. No other book has this peculiarity. Show me one which the wicked fear, which lays a secret dread upon the boldest, which cuts deep into the conscience, which comforts and supports, which deprives death of its sting—show me such a one, and you show me the Bible. Nothing explains this but the life which the Spirit imparts. With the oracles of God the author is present, whether you read or hear. You cannot avoid this power. It will make the word either "a savour of life unto life, or a savour of death unto death." 4. *The oracles of God not only speak, but make all His other oracles vocal.* God has three other oracles—nature, general providence, and personal providence. Nature has its solemn voice: "There is not a speech nor language where their voice is not heard." This is connected with the spread of the gospel. The voice of nature is not heard where the gospel is not. In heathen countries the heavens are turned into idols, and God is excluded from the thoughts of men. But when the living oracles come, then star and mountain and river proclaim their glorious Maker, and the voice of the oracle falls distinct upon every ear. There is the general providence of God exercised in the government of nations. All its arrangements display the wisdom, power, and truth of God. Yet it is all unknown to those destitute of the divine oracles. The personal providence of God confers upon us all our blessings, appoints us our station in life, and assigns to us our sorrows. Many lessons this providence teaches us. But till the living oracle speaks all is silence, and we derive no lessons of true wisdom from the events of life. 5. *The oracles of God present a peculiar character in their form;* and in this we perceive an instance of the condescension of the almighty God, who intended thus to attract and fix our attention on what to us is vitally interesting. 6. *The last character is the fulness of truth conveyed in the oracles of God.* Who can exhaust the doctrines of Holy Scripture—doctrines specially relating to God and Christ, and the depth of all redeeming love? The Bible will be the oracles of God to the Church above. Every part of that holy book will be written upon the memory of each glorified human heart, and be always receiving illustration to the glory of its great Author.

II. **These oracles are committed or entrusted to you.**—1. *They are entrusted to be read or understood;* 2. *To interpret honestly;* 3. *To make them known to others;* 4. *To apply to practical purposes.*—*R. Watson.*

Ver. 4. "*Let God be true.*"—But cannot God be true and man be true also? Does the veracity of the one infer the falsehood of the other? Not absolutely, but in particular instances. There may be, and there often is, an opposition between their testimony; and when this is the case we are not to hesitate a moment by whose claims we shall be decided. If the whole world were on one side and He on the other, let God be true, but every man a liar. And, comparatively, the credibility of the one must always be nothing to that of the other. If we receive the witness of men, the witness of God is greater. And this will appear undeniable from four admissions:—

I. **The first regards the ignorance of man and the wisdom of God.**— Man is fallible. He not only may err, but he is likely to err. He may be deceived by outward appearances, by the reports of others, by his own reasonings; for his powers are limited. Let not the wise man glory in his wisdom. How much of it is mere opinion and conjecture! With what follies have the greatest minds been charged! But God knows all things, and cannot be mistaken.

II. **The second regards the mutability of man and the unchangeableness of God.**—Creatures, from their very being, are mutable. Many of the angels kept not their first estate. Adam fell from his original condition. Who needs to be told that man never continues in one stay? New views engender new feelings, and these new pursuits. What pleases to-day may offend to-morrow. But God changes not. What He thinks now He always thought, for with Him there is "no variableness, neither shadow of turning."

III. **The third regards the weakness of man and the all-sufficiency of God.**— Man may threaten in fury, but be unable to execute—he may promise sincerely, but *cannot* fulfil. In this respect he is not always to be judged of by his conduct. But God is almighty. He who made and upholds all things by the word of His power speaks everything in the Scriptures.

IV. **The fourth regards the depravity of man and the rectitude of God.**—Man goes astray. He often knowingly deceives. Even men who are influenced by religious principles may be overcome of evil, and occasion our saying, "Lord, what is man?" How far from truth was the sentiment of Jonah: "I do well to be angry, even unto death"! How lamentable was the falsehood of Abraham! How dreadful was the perjury of Peter! But God is holiness itself. He is incapable of a wrong bias—He cannot be tempted to deceive. The use to which this fact should be applied is to reduce our confidence in man and increase our confidence in God. And yet the reverse of this is our practice. We yield where we should be cautious, and we hesitate where it is impossible for us to err. We turn from the Rock of Ages, and lean on the broken reed. What is the consequence? "Cursed be the man that trusteth in man, and maketh flesh his arm, and whose heart departeth from the Lord." Let us cease, then, from man. Not that we are to become universally suspicious and suppose that there is no sincerity in the world. It was David's error to say in his haste, "All men are liars." And when the Scripture says, "There is no faithfulness in them; men of low degree are vanity, and men of high degree are a lie," it must be taken with a qualification. Yet instances of inflexible integrity are not abundant. And we should not implicitly rely upon any one, especially in divine things. Let us respect great and good men, but not be enslaved by them; let us suffer no man to have dominion over our conscience, always searching the Scriptures to see whether these things are so in the word of truth; for God is entitled to our absolute confidence. "God' is not a man, that He should lie; neither the son of man, that He should repent: hath He said, and shall He not do it? or hath He spoken, and shall He not make it good?" Let us trust Him as He deserves. Let us always place a ready and an unshaken reliance on His word. "*Yea, let God be true, but every man a liar.*"—*W. Jay.*

Ver. 5. *God's justice not to be ignored.*—Sinful men, in their eagerness to exculpate themselves, are given to think and say such a horrid thing as this: If a sinner's sin cause God's justice and truth to shine forth more clearly, God has no right to punish the man for that very action by which God Himself, so to speak, has profited. If the Eternal reap good out of my evil, then I deserve no longer blame, at His hands at all events, but rather thanks. This is the perverted logic of evil which is expressed twice over in these words of our text: If our unrighteousness commend (or, set forth in greater clearness) God's righteousness, what shall we say? That God in inflicting vengeance upon us does an unjust thing? For example: If through a lie of mine the truth of God is made to appear more admirable, to His greater glory, why am I to be still judged as a sinner for it? Every pious heart must sympathise with the indignant rejection by the apostle of so hateful an inference as this. But the arguments by which he rebuts it are very instructive. They are two: neither of them speculative, nor professing to explain the deep mysteries of this tremendous subject—I mean of the relation of God to that sin which He permits and punishes; but both of them simply exposing the practical results which would follow from such a position. It would prove fatal, he argues, both to religion and to morality. In the first place, if God could not justly punish any sin which He is able to overrule for good, then there could be no judgment of the world at all. Obviously it would always be open to a transgressor to plead in bar of judgment that God's justice was to be somehow made more conspicuous by that very sin; and if this made it unjust in God to punish, how is God to judge the world? Now the final judgment of God is of all religious truths the most fundamental and the most certain. Any doctrine accordingly which should thus paralyse the hand of the final Judge of men or drive Him from His judgment seat is by that very fact shown to be absurd and incredible. Secondly, this blasphemous inference is as fatal to morals as it is to faith. It cuts through the distinction betwixt good and evil. If an act is no longer to be called bad or to be punished out of which some good comes, then you may do any evil you like for the sake of a good result. Of course this is on the face of it to confound moral right and wrong, and by withdrawing all practical restraint on immorality to open a perfect flood-gate of evil. Any doctrine which sanctions such a conclusion is by that very fact, not absurd only, but atrocious. Yet this immoral maxim had actually been imputed to St. Paul by certain of his contemporaries. As he comes in sight of it he cannot restrain his impatient indignation at such a calumny, but breaks through the construction of his sentence to tell us that some actually charged him with teaching and (what was even worse) with practising the vile principle, Let us do evil that good may come. Who they were that said so, or what pretext for saying it they found in his teaching, we can only guess. But there is no question that the evangelical doctrine of a sinner's gratuitous justification on the ground of Christ's righteousness (which St. Paul is here preparing to prove) has often been assailed on this very charge—that it not only confers immunity upon sinners, but actually holds out to a man an inducement to continue in sin that thereby grace may abound at last to the greater glory of God. Such a charge rests indeed upon a misconception of the gospel, as appears further on in this epistle (chap. vi. 1 ff.). It is flatly oppugnant to that consuming zeal for righteousness which blazes through every portion of this epistle, and especially through the section we have been examining. Whatever Paul taught, every reader feels that he was not a man to teach anything to weaken in the slightest the paramount claims of virtue, or the guilt and hatefulness of sin, or the majesty of God's judgment, or the wholesome dread of men for a reckoning to come. On the contrary, his whole argument rests on a basis of natural justice. It assumes that God's final judgment according to human actions is the surest of all things; that it must be impartial; that no religious privilege can lessen responsibility, but must increase it; that you cannot sophisticate sin into anything else than sin; and that God is always just in punishing every soul of man that doeth evil. You feel, therefore, that Paul is speaking out of the very heart of his faith, as well as out of the inspiration of the Holy Ghost, when he flings back with all his strength this hateful calumny, protests against the gospel, any more than the Hebrew law, being made a minister to sin, and declares that every man who ventures to do evil that good may come shall meet with a condemnation which shall be just. On the whole, then, the lesson of this section is to warn us against the insidious temptation, so near to the human heart, to break down the edge of God's justice against sin, in the hope that somehow He will prove as placable in the last judgment as He is kind and patient now, or to fancy that, because He makes His own use of sin, He will not avenge it on the sinner very strictly—especially in the case of people who belong to the true religion. All this is most perilous. We who live in Christendom are the privileged class nowadays, as Jews were once. Our superiority over the heathen is enormous "in every way"; but it confers on us no immunity to sin. It makes our evil deeds not less evil, but more so, that we do them under cover of the Christian name. In our own righteousness, therefore, we dare as little meet God at last with any hope to escape His wrath as an unbaptised infidel dare. Practically we are shut up under sin—guilty before God, with no apology to plead in bar of judgment. Hope—if we have any hope—lies neither in our knowledge of the Bible, nor in our membership in the Church, nor in any fact about ourselves at all, but only in the grace of God through the redemption that is in Christ Jesus. Gratuitous justification through the righteousness of our Surety—to that we are shut up by the apostle's logic. May God shut us all up to it by what is better than logic, the constraint of His convicting and regenerating Spirit!—*Oswald Dykes, D.D.*

SUGGESTIVE COMMENTS ON VERSES 1—8.

Importance of the third chapter of this epistle.—The third chapter of the Epistle to the Romans has, from a very early period of the Christian era, been *a special study to Paul's students.* It has been regarded—and with great justice—as of very peculiar significance in relation to some of the most important doctrines of theology. As regards more particularly the vital doctrine of *justification by faith*, it is perhaps the principal *locus classicus* that is to be found in the Bible. At that part of the chapter in which we find the culminating point of the apostle's exhibition of this great and favourite theme, Luther, in a marginal note attached to his German translation, arrests the attention of the reader, saying, "*Take heed to what is here said. It is the central and most important passage of the epistle, and indeed of the entire Scripture.*" Calvin

coincided with Luther in opinion. "*There is probably,*" he remarks, "*no passage in the whole Bible of greater significance as regards the justifying righteousness of God.*" Corresponding opinions are expressed by multitudes of other theologians and critics whose judgments are entitled to consideration. It is hence the case that, if there be, in an exposition of *the third chapter of the Epistle to the Romans* anything approximating to a thorough investigation of the broader aspects as well as of the minuter elements of the apostle's teaching, there will be the realisation of theological results of no inconsiderable magnitude and moment. The mind will most probably acquire a very definite conception of that "article of a standing or a falling Church," *justification by faith without works.* Such other articles, too, as are inseparably connected with that doctrine—the articles which refer to man's need of a gratuitous method of justification, and to God's provision of propitiation as the ground or "meritorious cause" of gracious justification, will probably be apprehended, and to a certain extent even comprehended. In this *third chapter of Romans* the apostle portrays in a most elaborate manner man's need of gratuitous justification. He likewise exhibits in some most weighty and far-reaching observations the necessity of propitiation, and its relation to justification. He says something, too, of very great significance regarding *redemption* and the *pretermission*, as well as the *remission*, of sins.—*Morrison.*

Paul confutes gainsayers.—To understand the full scope and design of this passage, we are to observe that of all the apostles of the Lord St. Paul asserts everywhere in the most copious manner the extensive mercy and compassion of God in entering into a covenant of grace with sinners, and fulfilling faithfully the promises of the gospel, notwithstanding the wickedness and infidelity of mankind, who were corrupted at the heart, and in their daily practice betrayed their impiety and want of faith ; and yet so far was the sinner from vacating the evangelical promises, and making them of none effect, that his very sins contributed to God's glory, and made His truth and grace still more illustrious ; "for where sin abounded grace did much more abound." From this doctrine of the apostle, not only the sophisters and impostors took occasion to defame and undermine the authority of St. Paul, but the hypocrites and libertines of the age made use of it to countenance and give them a security in their vices. And no wonder ; for if the preaching of the apostle were true, that the sins of men redounded to the glory of God, the divine justice could not reasonably exert itself in the punishment of sinners ; there could be no encouragement for virtue or religion—

nay, men were obliged to sin more abundantly, that God might receive the more abundant glory ; and it would be their duty on all occasions to do evil that good might come. Other aspersions that were thrown upon the apostle by his enemies he confutes by proper arguments. But this he thought unworthy of an answer ; he only expostulates with indignation, and resents it as the vilest slander and as a degree of blasphemy.—*Bishop Sanderson.*

God educes good from evil.—David does not excuse his sin on the ground that in its pardon God's mercy will be glorified, although he says that this will be the result ; but he grieves over his sins, and declares that God will judge the world, and that the wicked shall be punished. God may and does exercise His wisdom and power and love in educing the greatest good from the worst evil ; but this is the effect of His own incommunicable attributes, and not of man's sins, which are not *ordinabilia ad bonam finem.* God never does evil in order to elicit good from it, nor does He permit any man to do evil in order that good may come. The intention with which a thing is done is indeed of very great importance ; but whatever is sinful is not to be done on the plea of good intention.—*St. Augustine.*

God not an infinite Jesuit. — In some of the more dogmatic commentaries, as in Willet's, for example, and in that of Pareus, the theological bearing of the jesuitical principle condemned by the apostle is discussed. Willet asks "whether God do not evil that good may come thereof in reprobating—viz., unconditionally—the vessels of wrath, to show His power." Such is his question. It is pertinent. But he certainly fails to clear, *in the light of his peculiar theology*, the character of God. He says that the action referred to is not evil: 1. "Because it is God's will, which is always just and holy."

90

2. Because "that which tendeth to God's glory cannot be evil." 3. Because "that which is lawfully done cannot be evil." "God," he adds, "in rejecting some doth that which He may do by lawful right to dispose of His own as it pleaseth Him, as no man can reprove the potter in making some vessels of honour, some of dishonour, of the same piece of clay." 4. "But," continues he, "seeing in the end God's rejecting and reprobating some—viz., such as by their sins deserved eternal death—appeareth to be most just, it must needs also be good; for that which is just is good." In the last of these reasons the critic reverses his own theory of unconditional reprobation; and in the former three he only echoingly reiterates the idea that the jesuitical principle may be to God, though not to man, a legitimate and right glorious rule of conduct. Pareus, a short time before Willet, had trodden exactly the same round of apologetic thought; and thus, so far as we can judge, Feurborn is correct when he contends that the great theologian of Heidelberg has violated the apostle's axiom. His whole reasoning seems simply to amount to this—*that God is an infinite Jesuit.—Morrison.*

All things will manifest God's glory.— If the objections were well founded, it would entirely divest God of the character of judge of the world. The reason of this is manifest, for there is no sin that any man can commit which does not exalt some perfection of God in the way of contrast. If, then, it be concluded that because unrighteousness in man illustrates the righteousness of God, God is unrighteous when He taketh vengeance, it must be further said that there is no sin that God can justly punish; whence it follows that God cannot any longer be the judge of the world. The objection, then, is such that, were it admitted, all the religion in the world would at once be annihilated. For the sin of the world, for which men will be punished, will no doubt be made to manifest God's glory. Such is the force of the apostle's reply.—*Haldane.*

For the holiness of the divinity has blazed forth, as it were, into brighter conspicuousness on the dark ground of human guilt and human turpitude.—*Chalmers.*

MAIN HOMILETICS OF THE PARAGRAPH.—*Verses 9—20.*

A great deficit to all.—There may be a surplus of privilege, and a deficit of conduct—plenty of light from heaven, and yet such depravity that, in the midst of light, we are still in darkness. The Jews a people favoured of Heaven, and this favour not without some good results; but from time to time how dark their state, how deplorable their condition ! A dark picture is by the apostle here presented to our view—a correct representation in its general aspect. How much light in England ! And yet what a dark picture must be drawn ! Notwithstanding our Christianity and our civilisation, we have often had hard work in keeping the forces of evil at bay. Let us not too easily lay the flattering unction to our souls that we are better than the Jew. We have all the light God will shed upon our race, and yet how morally dark is our condition ! We may still mournfully cry that both Jews and Gentiles, both Christians and "heathen" (we mean by the term the peoples born in a Christian country and raised under Christian influences), are all under sin. As it is written, "There is none righteous; no, not one." Here, then, is the doctrine of *universal depravity*, which shows itself by :—

I. **Practical atheism.**—"There is none that seeketh after God." "There is no fear of God before their eyes." The avowed atheist says, "There is no God"; the practical atheist acts *as if there* were no God. So that both characters come to the same practical result, and both are the outcome of a degenerate nature. In our darker moods, how often rise to our lips the words, "There is none that seeketh after God"! Where are those who seek after God as the soul's true and only good? Where are those who can legitimately use the language of the sacred poet, "My soul thirsteth for God"? We thirst for the material benefits a God may be supposed to confer. We thirst for a material God, for a God that we can presume to put to serviceable uses, and not for a God who shall put us to serviceable uses. Each man seeks for his own God, who is thus a being subject to human imperfections and limitations. In fact, the modern Christian says God is not wisely trusted when declared unintelligible. And yet can a God of perfect rectitude be fully knowable to a creature who is all imperfect? "Canst thou by searching find out God?" Canst thou find out the Almighty to perfection? Who is there that seeks after the unknowable God—unknowable in His perfections, and yet so far knowable in the manifestation made by the God-man that we may feel it is no vain search? Is not the fear of man stronger than the fear of God, so that the words have a very wide application, "There is no fear of God before their eyes"? If God were a detective dogging each man's steps, there would be a change in society. Do we fear God as a judge? Do we fear God as a father? Have we the loving fear that prompts to holy action and sweet deeds of divine charity?

II. **A depraved understanding.**—There is a depravity of morals which works depravity of intellect. In these days we pride ourselves on our intellectual greatness. Some mental philosophers affirm that mind is sublimated matter. They are materialists. They are so far correct that our modern tendencies are materialistic. Morally it may be said "there is none that understandeth." We understand science, literature, art, commerce, creeds, an outside religion. Where is the man who touches the core and heart of the spiritual sphere? "There is none that understandeth."

III. **A depraved physical nature.**—We are so far materialists that we believe the elevation of the moral is the elevation of the physical, and that the depravation of the former is the depravation of the latter. The throat becomes sepulchral. Instead of the sweet odour of gracious words flowing through the portals of the lips, there comes the death-producing miasma of profane thoughts in the vehicle of ribald language. Honeyed lips cover the secreted poison. Thought touches speech. Evil thoughts and evil speech defile the organs of utterance. These, unrestrained, terminate in the climax of brutality. "Their feet are swift to shed blood." Destruction and misery are in their ways." Thank God, there is a force of good stronger than the force of evil. As we see men restrained from extreme violence, we the more firmly believe in an overruling good force. If it were not so, the feet would run so swiftly to shed blood that soon on this bloodstained earth there would be no blood to shed—the last man, gloated in human blood, would perish a victim of his own vile doings. Wars and rumours of wars have been many. Wild beasts in human form have fought like fiends. Modern skill and science have made the shedding of human blood one of the fine arts. Adored be the great Peace-bringer that the way of peace is not unknown! Give peace in our time, O Lord—national peace, individual peace; harmony amongst the nations—harmonious adjustment and working of all the soul's powers.

IV. **The revelation of the law.**—When the law speaks in its awful majesty, the sad doom of universal guilt is pronounced. The law is a revealing force; the law condemns; the law renders speechless when its voice is properly heard and felt in the secret chambers of imagery. When the man is so oppressed with the sense of his guilt that he can frame no words of apology, and stands self-confessed a sinner in the presence of the infinite Justice, then the light of redeeming love and mercy breaks through the oppressive gloom, the clouds are scattered, the shadows flee away, the morning light glints the mountain tops, the voice of merry singing is heard in the land, the soul glows with the gladness of the upper sphere, the spirit soars to unite itself with the spirit of the Eternal, and the redeemed man wonders at the marvel of divine grace, and humbly asks himself if it be indeed true that he is a member of that race which has shown itself capable of a depravity so appalling.

Vers. 13-18. *Dignity of human nature shown from its ruins.*—A dark picture of humanity, and yet it has two aspects. In one view it is the picture of weakness and shame ; in the other it presents a fearfully great being. I propose to call your attention to :—

The dignity of man as revealed by the ruin he makes in his fall and apostasy from God.—It has been the way of many in our time to magnify humanity ; but I undertake to show the essential greatness of man from the ruin itself which he becomes. As from the ruins of ancient dynasties and cities we tell their former greatness, so it is with man. Our most veritable though saddest impressions of his greatness as a creature we shall derive from the magnificent ruin he displays. And exactly this, I conceive, is the legitimate impression of the Scripture representations of man as apostate from duty and God. Thoughtfully regarded, all exaggerations and contending theories apart, it is as if they were showing us the original dignity of man from the magnificence of the ruin in which he lies. How sublime a creature must that be, call him either man or demon, who is able to confront the Almighty and tear himself away from His throne ! So of the remarkable picture given by Paul in the first chapter of the Epistle to the Romans. In one view we are disgusted, in another shocked, doubting whether it presents a creature most foolish and vile or most sublimely impious and wicked. And the picture of the text corresponds, yielding no impression of a merely feeble and vile creature, but of a creature rather most terrible and swift—destructive, fierce, and fearless—miserable in his greatness— great as in evil. But we come to the ruin as it is, and receive the true impression for ourselves. *We look, first of all, upon the false religions of the world*— pompous and costly rites transacted before crocodiles and onions, magnificent temples built over all monkeyish and monstrous creatures carved by men's hands, children offered up by their mothers in fire or in water, kings offered on the altars by their people to propitiate a wooden image, gorgeous palaces and trappings of barbaric majesty studded all over with beetles in gold or precious stones to serve as a protection against pestilences, poisons, and accidents. I cannot fill out a picture that so nearly fills the world. The wars of the world yield a similar impression. These are men such as history in all past ages shows them to be—swift to shed blood, swifter than the tiger race, and more terrible. Cities and empires are swept by their terrible marches, and become a desolation in their path. Destruction and misery are in their ways—oh, what destruction, misery ! how deep and long ! And what shall we think of any creature of God displayed in signs like these ? Plainly enough he is a creature in ruins ; but how magnificent a creature ! Consider again the persecutions of the good. What does it mean ? Man hates with a diabolical hatred. Feeling " how awful goodness is," the sight of it rouses him to madness, and he will not stop till he has tasted blood. And what a being is this that can be stung with so great madness by the spectacle of a good and holy life ! The great characters of the world furnish another striking proof of the transcendent quality of human nature by the dignity they are able to connect even with their littleness. But we must look more directly into the contents of human nature and the internal ruin by which they are displayed. And here you may notice, first of all, the sublime vehemence of the passions. Consider again the wild mixture of thought displayed both in the waking life and the dreams of mankind. How grand! how mean! how sudden the leap from one to the other! how inscrutable the succession! how defiant of orderly control! Notice also the significance of remorse. How great a creature must that be that, looking down upon itself from some high summit, in itself withers in condemnation of itself! So again you may conceive the greatness of man by the ruin he makes if you advert to the dissonance and obstinacy of his evil will. How great a creature is it that, knowing God, can set itself off from God, and maintain a persistent rebellion even against its own convictions, fears, and aspirations. Consider once more the religious aspirations and capabilities of religious attraction that are garnered up and still live in the ruins of humanity. Regarding man, then, as immersed in evil—a spiritual intelligence in a state of ruin—we derogate nothing from his dignity. O Thou Prince of life! come in Thy great salvation. Breathe on these majestic ruins, and rouse to life again, though it be but for one hour, the forgotten sense of their eternity.—*Bushnell.*

The consciousness of evil.

I. **Law discovers the fact of sin.**—Renan has written, " It may be said, in fact, that original sin was an invention of the Jahveist." What a strange misuse of language to speak of the sacred writers as *inventing* original sin! Can we say that Jenner invented the smallpox, or that Pasteur invented the rabies, or that any of the celebrated physicians invented the maladies which are known by their names? What these famous men did was to successfully diagnose, characterise, and to treat diseases which already existed, and which proved their malignant power by carrying thousands of men and women to the grave. Did the sacred writers invent sin? Listen to a modern writer on science who has no theological sympathy whatever, but who is constrained to give a testimony to a theological tenet that is to thousands a huge offence. " Men are born with their moral natures as deformed or as imperfect as their physical ones. To the doctrine of original sin science thus has given an unexpected support." No, revelation did not invent the doctrine of original sin ; that doctrine serious men have discerned in all ages ; that doctrine the scientist finds deep down in the grounds of human nature. What revelation has done is to define the doctrine, to make clear its real nature, to express its characters, to discover its source, to bring it home to the conscience, and, thank God, to prescribe for it a sovereign remedy. The law showed the apostle that the reality of sin was in his own heart, that it lived and worked there beneath all the moral aspects of his character ; the law convinced him that his conduct—socially and ecclesiastically blameless— was nevertheless essentially false and hollow. Says George Sand : " Proprieties are the rule of the people without soul or virtue." Says Schopenhauer : " Politeness is a conventional and systematic attempt to mask the egoism of human nature. To combine politeness with pride is a masterful piece of wisdom." And, indeed, how little do many of those grand words mean which are on our lips ! What does " good form " mean—etiquette, decorum, good breeding, " the code of honour," respectability? What do justice, temperance, diligence, benevolence, and other of our virtues mean if they are severely looked into? What do reputation, fame, success, glory, often mean? What the Frenchwoman saw, what the German saw, what we all see dimly from time to time of the dimness of human virtue, the apostle in presence of the law saw and felt profoundly ; he was overwhelmed to find under all the proprieties of his life the fact and power of sin. " We all do fade as a leaf." Before the searching brightness of the eternal righteousness our proud virtues wither ; for they have no depth of earth, no sap of life. Studying the commandments of Sinai ; pondering the exposition of the law in prophet, psalmist, and apostle ; listening to the Sermon on the Mount; beholding the beauty of the Lord,—we become conscious how deeply we are wrong at heart; what a mysterious weakness, disharmony, perverseness, exists within us; spoiling our great gifts and possibilities; involving our life in constant failure; filling us with remorse. In the purgatory of the Chinese is the mirror of sin. Into this mirror departed sinners are compelled to gaze and see all the naughtiness of their own heart, after which they are dismissed to punishment. The moral law is that mirror, here and now revealing the wickedness and deceitfulness of our heart. One of our novelists writes of " the tragedy of the mirror." The mirror has its tragedies. It makes palpable to us the ravages of grief ; it pathetically discloses the lines of suffering ; but the real tragedy of the mirror is when revelation sharply frees us from all illusions, and from its infinite depths of purity flashes back upon our consciousness the image of our moral self.

II. **By the law we discover the nature of sin.**—It discloses the real character of that dark mysterious power which forbids our perfection and felicity. And what then is sin? Sin as against God is the preference of our own will to the supreme will. "I had not known sin except the law had said, Thou shalt not covet." Sin is not limitation; we act irregularly, not because we are so much less than God, but because we are contrary to God.

III. **By the law as unfolded in revelation we discover the strength of sin.**— The presence of the law brings out the virulence and wrath of the evil principle which is in our heart. "When the commandment came sin revived." "The strength of sin is the law." The presence of the lofty, the beautiful, in the first instance evokes, stirs up, draws out, the morbid humours of the soul; the fierce light stimulates the vicious germs which are in us.

IV. **By the law as unfolded in revelation we discover the guilt of sin.**—It is the ministry of condemnation ; it convinces us that our transgressions are worthy of death. With the law before us we cannot plead that sin is ignorance. Sin is the transgression of the law, but we should think mercifully of sin committed in total ignorance of the law. But the law which convicts us first enlightens us ; we clearly see our duty, and yet persist in carrying out our own desires. With the law before us we cannot plead that sin is imperfection. It is now seen that sin is not finiteness, but contradictoriness ; it is a conflict of wills. With the law before us we cannot plead that sin is misfortune. By the deepest of instincts we discern the vast difference between a misfortune and a sin. And the law brings sin and guilt home to us personally. It does not impeach and condemn a race so much as it challenges the man, the woman, the child. Those who have no proper consciousness of sin must come to the light. We must test ourselves by the standard of Sinai ; we must submit ourselves to the white light which shines upon us and into us in the perfection of Jesus Christ. The law does not give deliverance from sin. The redemption of our life is in Christ Jesus. He turns the knowledge of sin into true sorrow for sin. Its issue is eternal life. He also awakens in us the love of holiness. We have redemption in His blood, even the forgiveness of sin. How infinite our debt to Jesus Christ ! If He has banished the light laughter of Grecian joyousness, He has brought in a diviner joy. He has changed a life of petty thoughts, narrow sympathies, ignoble aims, into a life of large ideas, of emotions at once blissful and profound, of delightful fellowships, of sublime charity, and of most glorious hope.—*W. L. Watkinson.*

SUGGESTIVE COMMENTS ON VERSES 9—20.

Jews and Gentiles guilty.—Of these passages it is unnecessary to offer a particular illustration. They are selected from different parts of the inspired books, but chiefly from the poetical parts of Scripture, and sometimes the sense is expressed rather than the words of the original. They are quite sufficient to establish the wickedness of the Jews, which they are brought to prove. But the strong and amplified expressions common in Eastern poetry must not be understood according to their literal meaning in our speech. Nor is it to be presumed that all parts of the description apply to the general body of the nation, or that there were not many good men among them who did not deserve to be thus characterised. The passages describe either the general character *of the wicked* or of the people at large *in times of great degeneracy*, though no doubt with many exceptions. They are intended as the proof of what the apostle had immediately before asserted—that the Jews as well as the Gentiles are all guilty of sin, and generally also of very heinous sins, and that, consequently, they are as far from deserving to be justified by their works as the Gentiles are. Now as these quotations express the conviction of their own inspired writers, the Jews could not deny their truth. Had the apostle described their sins in his own language, they might have refused to acquiesce in his statement; but when he merely quotes their own Scriptures in which they gloried, and the inspiration of which they admitted, they could not refuse assenting to his conclusion. It may be observed, further, of these quotations, that though intended to describe the character of the wicked, or the national character generally, in times of great degeneracy, they are, however, true to a certain extent of every individual, seeing every individual may justly be charged with much sin, though not with each of the particular sins here specified. Still, however, it was possible for the Jews to flatter themselves that these descriptions were not intended to apply to themselves, but to the heathen; and to take away the possibility of this pretence, the apostle adds in the nineteenth verse: "Now we know that what things soever the law saith, it saith to them who are under the law: that every mouth may be stopped, and all the world may become guilty before God."—*Ritchie.*

Paul's mosaic of sin.—On what principle and with what precise object did Paul select these quotations? We cannot conceive that he gives here a universal or even a comparatively fair description of the nation. He has rather gathered together into one awful picture the very darkest lines of the many delineations of character contained in the Jewish Scriptures. The men before us are of the very worst kind. The opening of their mouths is the opening of a grave. They are deadly as vipers. Their language is a curse. The prospect of murder hurries them on with rapid steps. Where they have been destruction and calamity are found. How to walk so as to be at peace they know not. The delineations form one picture. Vers. 13, 14 describe their words; vers. 15-17, their actions; ver. 18 gives the cause of the whole. Paul has, in my view, put together this mosaic of sin to prove that the Old Testament teaches that Jewish privileges do not in themselves save even from the lowest depths of sin. He does not say that the objector of chap. ii. is as bad as these men. But whatever he has pleaded for himself these might have pleaded. These bad men whose names are forgotten, but in whose character is plainly written the condemnation of God, arise from oblivion to declare that outward privileges, even though they come from God, and outward connection with the covenant people, do not necessarily save.—*Beet.*

Fear of God.—"If," says Cartwright, "the prophet and apostle had laid their heads together to have found out the most forcible words, and most significative, to shut all men, born of the seed of men, from righteousness, and to shut them under sin, they could not have used more effectual speeches than these." Clause is piled upon clause to the effect that "all have sinned and come short of the glory of God." The passages which are quoted in continuation are *tacked on* to the quotation from the fourteenth Psalm, *and not as containing additional Scripture evidence of the universality of sin,* but as exhibiting in graphic touches, and distributively, as Zwinger remarks, *representative specimens of the very varied forms* into which the essential principle of sin has in its universal range developed itself. The reference more particularly is, as Melancthon observed, to breaches of the second table of the law.—*Annot.*

"It is a grand and magnificent thing," says Origen, "always to have before the eyes of the heart the fear of God." Such fear is "the beginning of wisdom," and it is not far removed from the end of it. There is a fear indeed which "hath torment"—the fear of the lash, the dread foreboding of final woe. It is well when this fear is "cast out," and supplanted by perfect confidence in the propitious favour of God. And it is ousted from the soul when the soul is filled with love; and the soul *is* filled with love when "we have known and believed the love that God hath to us." Nevertheless there is always an element of sensitive fear in man's love to God and in man's love to man. There is a fear of doing anything to offend or to wound. This fear is inseparable from a consciousness of imperfection, and it is at once a self-imposed rein to restrain and a self-appointed watch to keep guard. When it is said that "there is not the fear of God *before the eyes*," "there" is objectively ascribed to a condition which is psychologically subjective. But the subjective may become objective when it is made the mark of reflective thought. The wicked not only do not feel as a general rule "the fear of God" —they do not even think of it as a feeling which they should cherish. It is not "kept in view" by them as an object to be realised in emotion.— *Morrison.*

Corrupt in thought, abominable in deed.—"They are corrupt, they have done abominable things; there is none that doeth good." "Men," says Bernand, "because they are *corrupt* in their minds, become *abominable* in their doings — *corrupt* before God, *abominable* before men. There are three sorts of men of which none doeth good. There are those who neither understand nor seek God, and they are the dead. There are others who understand Him, but seek Him not, and they are the wicked. There are others who seek Him, but understand Him not, and they are the fools." "O God!" cries a writer of the Middle Ages, "how many are here at this day who, under the name of Christianity, worship idols, and are abominable both to Thee and to men! For every man worships that which he most loves. The proud man bows down before the idol of worldly power, the covetous man before the idol of money, the adulterer before the idol of beauty, and so of the rest." And of such saith the apostle, "They profess that they know God, but in works deny Him, being *abominable* and disobedient, and unto every work reprobate" (Titus i. 16). "*There is none that doeth good.*" Notice how Paul avails himself of this testimony of the Psalmist, among those which he heaps together in the third chapter of the Epistle to the Romans, where he is proving concerning "both Jews and Gentiles that they are all under sin." —*John Mason Neale.*

MAIN HOMILETICS OF THE PARAGRAPH.—*Verses* 21—26.

Divine justice vindicated.—Some say Christianity is played out. Perhaps the wish is father to the saying. We may seem to have taken a pessimistic view of Christianised society. Not quite. St. Paul's collection of Old Testament texts cannot be applied to England, and to that we are indebted to Christianity. Our point is that some of the essential failings of Judaism are reproduced in

97

Christianity, and we must be on our guard. We do not admit that Christianity is played out, but we allow that modern Pauls are needed to proclaim the old gospel with new power. The sinfulness of man must be declared, the righteousness of God proclaimed, and the way of salvation opened out by faith, as the result of grace, and through the redemption that is in Christ Jesus. The opponents of the mediatorial scheme give grotesque representations of a supposed conflict between justice and mercy. Nevertheless, justice is not to be eliminated from the attributes of a perfect God. He is Himself just and the justifier of him that believeth in Jesus. All the dispensations of God make for righteousness. What we know not now we shall know hereafter. The climactic and indisputable proof of God's justice is the setting forth of Jesus to be a propitiation.

I. **God justifies Himself.**—Of course not in the way of making Himself just, for that He always and essentially is; but in the way of showing His justice, and condescending to show to men that all His ways are right. Paul does not bring before us a one-sided Deity—a Being stripped of that attribute which must be the basis of an equitable moral government. Paul vindicates the righteousness of God in His former dealings with the race; and now he brings us to see in the atonement of Christ a crowning proof of justice, as well as a manifestation of love. God is just because He freely forgives men by His grace through the redemption that is in Christ Jesus. 1. *God declares His justice.* The ancient prophet speaks of a just God and a Saviour. The apostle adopts the utterance. God's justice declared by the different economies. The history of Israel a testimony. The form of divine justice has never been absent from the march of human events. All tend to the vindication of the eternal rectitude. A twofold love of the Father and the Son speaks to us from Calvary. The voice of justice also heard. The fatherhood of God must not destroy His kingship. Eli was a mild father, the type of the modern God of some, and his sons were ruined. God speaks and rules as a father-king. God is not a great, grim, and relentless justice, neither is He a pliant amiability. The Atonement declares God's justice, and sets forth the truth that men cannot be saved merely on the ground that God is love. 2. *God honours justice.* The monarch as the representative of civil government, as the person to whom is delegated the central power around which the commonwealth is to move in circles of social order, must rule in justice tempered by mercy. God is surely more perfect. Around Him must be glorious circles of moral order. The Atonement has not wrested the sceptre from His grasp. He still sits on a throne which has justice and judgment for its foundation. A tyrant may arbitrarily pardon a rebel. A just God must devise means whereby rebels may be pardoned and justice honoured. God honoured justice when He gave His Son, for the Son was willing to be offered. In His case the sweet compulsive power of love was the only constraining force. If a life on earth of pleasure, of greatness, and of renown ending in a triumphant translation to a brighter sphere had been sufficient, God's love would have demanded no more. If there was any violence in the moral transaction, it was Deity that did violence to His own loving nature in the interests of eternal justice. 3. *God harmonises justice.* The opponents make justice and mercy two abstractions. These ideal creations are seen wrestling for victory. One determines to punish; the other is equally determined to forgive. Being equally powerful, how is the contest to end? Now justice and mercy are not distinct personalities. They are attributes of the one great personality termed God. And there can be no fierce conflict, speaking after the manner of men. God in the eternal councils deliberates. God the Father and God the Son devise the wondrous method. Behold the result. Mercy and truth meet together. Righteousness and peace kiss each other when they hear the sad triumphant refrain, "It is finished." Truth springs out of the earth which has been replenished by the stream flowing from the Rock of Ages. Righteousness looks down from heaven in glad approval. All nations must finally rejoice, for the Lord has given that which is good.

II. **God justifies believers.**—When God justifies Himself, He shows His justice. When God justifies the believer, He receives him as justified. God has made men moral agents, and does not justify them, the volition refusing the benefit. All are not justified because all are not willing—*i.e.*, all who have heard. There is a condition. It is the simple one of faith, loving acceptance, the doctor's prescription, the brazen serpent. Believe and live. Look and be saved. Take and be healed. 1. *Believing involves a confession of guilt and of helplessness.* Guilt is the awakened sense of moral sickness. The extent of feeling no matter. This is the world's want—the power to feel as well as to understand. 2. *Believing implies God's right to punish.* So that the man who believes in Christ does not make void the law and the authority of God. The believer suffers in himself the pangs of remorse, feels the pains of condemnation ; but what would the judge say to or think of the criminal who should plead his pangs and his feelings as an atonement for his crimes ? 3. *Believing in Jesus Christ carries in it the declaration of human inability.* Good works cannot save. High resolves cannot redeem. Noble endeavours cannot lift out of the pit. All the tears of a Niobe, should the race be concentrated in one image, and should the tears flow from the dawn of time to its close, cannot wash away sin. There is a fountain opened for sin and uncleanness. There is a propitiatory offering. Faith in Jesus Christ is the grand starting-point for noble endeavour, for moral enterprise, and for all holy living. Here are healing for the sick, bright raiment for the naked, precious gold for the poor, satisfying bread for the hungry, peace for the troubled, joy for the sorrowful, and laughter for the weepers. 4. *Believing in Jesus Christ supposes loving consecration.* The imperfection of many professing Christians must be admitted ; but the candid soul must confess that the world's noblest heroes have been produced by Christianity. A religion which could produce a Paul has in that one fact a good deal to say in its defence. And what should be said of a religion which has produced thousands who have followed in his train, though they have failed to reach his high measure of nobility ?

The righteousness of God.—" But now the righteousness of God without the law is manifested, being witnessed by the law and the prophets." It is of sin and righteousness that the apostle speaks so fully and so minutely throughout this whole epistle.

I. **It is the righteousness of God.**—It is a divine, not a human, righteousness. That righteousness which we had lost in Adam was, after all, but a human thing, finite like him who lost it ; but that which we gain is a divine righteousness, and by being divine forms an infinite compensation for that which Adam lost for us; and we in receiving it are made partakers of a most glorious exchange. It is called the righteousness of God, because it is a righteousness provided by Him—a righteousness which was conceived by Him and carried out in every part by Him. Again, it is called the righteousness of God, because it is a righteousness made up of the *doings* of the Son of God. It is not merely with His sufferings that this righteousness has to do, but it is with His *doings* as well. These two things enter into its composition, so that without both of them it would be imperfect. Further, it is called the righteousness of God, because it provides such a compensation for human unrighteousness, that it not only takes it all away, but brings in a new and far higher and surer footing for the sinner to rest on.

II. **It is a righteousness without the law.**—He does not mean that it is in any sense an unlawful righteousness—a righteousness not based on law ; but it means a righteousness which, in so far as we are concerned, has nothing to do with law at all. It is not a righteousness which asks any doing or working to make it what it is—"the righteousness of God "; for did it require anything of this kind on our part, it would cease to be what it is here represented to be, "the righteousness of God," and would become, to a large extent at least, "the righteousness of man." This righteousness does not send us to the law in order to be justified. Let us hold fast then this truth of the gospel, this foundation truth—righteousness without law, righteousness founded in no sense upon our keeping of the law ; but wholly and absolutely upon this fact, that another has kept the law for us, and that other no less than the Son of God Himself.

III. **This righteousness has been "manifested."**— "Now," he says, "the righteousness of God is manifested "; it has been clearly brought to light, so that there can be no mistake concerning it and no mystery in it. It is not a thing hidden, wrapped up, reserved, held back, veiled from our view. It has been clearly manifested. In every way God has sought to guard it against the possibility of being mistaken by man. In every way has He taken precautions against this being hidden from view or darkened by the words of man's wisdom.

IV. **This righteousness is a righteousness "to which the law and the prophets bear witness."**—By this expression we understand the whole of the Old Testament. It is not something (he means to tell us) now come to light for the first time, not understood in the ages gone by ; it is something which has been proclaimed from the beginning hitherto. Righteousness shone down upon the pilgrimage of Old Testament worthies, and in the light of which they walked. On this righteousness they rested, in it they rejoiced. It is no new righteousness which we preach. It is no new foundation of which we tell. It is the old one, the well-proved one. It has been abundantly sufficient in past ages, and it has lost none of its efficiency now in these last days.

V. **This righteousness is a righteousness which is by the faith of Jesus Christ.**—"Even the righteousness of God which is by faith of Jesus Christ unto all and upon all them that believe : for there is no difference." He means to say by this expression that it is a righteousness which comes to us by believing in Jesus Christ. It is not our faith that is our righteousness ; it is not our act of believing that justifies. If your faith were your righteousness, then faith would be just reduced to the level of all other works, and would be itself a work. If it were our faith, our act of faith, that justified, then should we be justified by our own acts, by our own deeds. The expression, then, "the righteousness of God, which is by faith of Jesus Christ," means simply that it is a righteousness which passes over to us, and becomes available for us, by believing in Him whose righteousness it is—that is, by believing the Father's testimony concerning Jesus Christ. Or it is just as if we were saying, I have no righteousness, seeing I am wholly a sinner ; but I take this righteousness of the Son of God, and I draw near, expecting to be treated by God just as if I and not He were the righteous person. I cannot present any suffering to Him in payment of penalty ; but I take this suffering of the Son of God, and I claim to have it reckoned to me as payment of my penalty. Thus it is "Christ is the end of the law for righteousness to every one that believeth."

VI. **This righteousness is a righteousness for the unrighteous.**—It "is by faith of Jesus Christ unto all and upon all them that believe : for there is no difference : for all have sinned, and come short of the glory of God." It is not righteousness for the good, but for the evil. It is not righteousness for the worthy, but for the unworthy. How foolish, then, to say as men, when convinced of sin, or when going back into former iniquity, are sometimes found saying, I am too great a sinner to be forgiven. Why, if you were not such a sinner, you would not need such a righteousness. This righteousness for the unrighteous is said by the apostle to be "unto all." It is a righteousness which is like the sun in the heavens. It is one sun; yet it is enough for every one, it is free to every one. You open your eye and enjoy its beams without asking any questions. Again, it is a righteousness which is "*upon* all them that believe." It is "unto all"; but it is only "upon" them that believe. The moment that we believe through grace we are accepted in the Beloved, redeemed from condemnation and from wrath. Again, the apostle affirms, regarding this righteousness for the unrighteous, that "there is no difference: for all have sinned, and come short of the glory of God." There is no difference as to its fitness for the sinner, whatever his sin may be; and there is no difference as to the fitness of the sinner for the righteousness. There is this twofold fitness: the fitness of the righteousness for the sinner, and the fitness of the sinner for the righteousness. There is no question as to the kind of your unrighteousness, the length of time, the amount or degree—there is no question about that: the simple question is, Are you an unrighteous man? Then it suits your case. And it is a righteousness near to each one of you; it is not afar off; it is not in heaven above, so that you have to climb to the seat of God to obtain it; and it is not down so low that you must dig to earth's centre to find it: it is near, it is at your very side; and if you reject it, it cannot be because of its distance. God has brought it near.—*H. Bonar.*

Ver. 24. *Justification an act of God's free grace.*—Justified by *grace*—i.e., God's part; not by *blood*—i.e., Christ's part (Rom. v. 9); not even by *faith* —i.e., man's part (Rom. v. 1); still less by *works*—i.e., the proof and manifestation of all the rest (James ii. 24). Justification is contemplated from the side of God.

I. **Justification itself.**—"Being justified." Rome *versus* Geneva—the former tending to the view that justification includes the removal of *sin*, not simply the removal of *condemnation*, as held by the latter. The structure of this epistle seems to favour the latter. The apostle begins with chaps. i.-v., discussing that awful liability to punishment which rests on Jew and Gentile alike; and only when this is disposed of does he come in chaps. vi.-viii. to treat of the removal of sin and the gift of eternal life. God comes first as a judge to pardon or absolve, and His second act is that of the Spirit imparting the regenerating seed of spiritual life. Justification is a change of relations, not of nature.

II. **Modifications of the principal idea.**—1. *The source*—in the grace of God: "being justified freely by His grace." Grace is love stooping, love in action—love manifesting itself to man; but love is eternal, therefore the revealed righteousness will endure. This is the key to the apostle's confidence. 2. *The mode*— "freely." Justification not of works, therefore not of wages; but of grace, therefore *a free gift.* This fathoms at once the *sinner's helplessness*, and exhibits the *divine munificence.* The helplessness is *spiritual*—not necessarily *mental*, or even *moral.* Man may learn, know, hate, love; but he cannot *justify* himself in the sight of God. The divine munificence is twofold. The free gift is not dependent on any human return, and in itself is the pledge of all other spiritual blessings. 3. *The means*—"through the redemption that is in Christ Jesus." Redemption is another word that looks at justification from the divine side. It contains two ideas— *ransom* paid in vindication of justice and righteousness, and *liberation* effected for the guilty party. The two combined give the principle of *substitution.* The price was His "blood," therefore not "without price," not freely to *Him.* And

101

it is "*in* Christ Jesus"—in Him in that historical sense in which *in* His own body on the tree the propitiation for sin was offered; and *in* Him in this legal and substitutionary sense in which justification is ours, only as we are treated in the Saviour's place and accepted as righteous *in* Him. We are justified by grace—*i.e.*, the source; by blood—*i.e.*, the channel; by faith—*i.e.*, the reception; by works—*i.e.*, the fruit. "By their fruits ye shall know them."
—*John Adams, B.D.*

Law cannot justify.—"Therefore by the deeds of the law there shall no flesh be justified in His sight," etc. How shall man be just before God? Wherewith shall I come before the Lord? Such questions have presented themselves to men ever since sin found an entrance into this world. Such questions demand an answer now. Let us not shrink from considering them.

I. **The very essence of God's nature is holiness.**—The outcome of holiness in effect and action is righteousness; hence God, perfectly righteous Himself, requires righteousness in His rational creatures. To come before God with acceptance we must have *righteousness*; and righteousness is obeying God's law—and obeying it perfectly—for God admits of no imperfection.

II. **What then is our condition as regards the law of God.**—1. *The law condemns us*, for we have not perfectly obeyed it. Nay, our very best actions are so mixed with imperfections that they come short of what God's holiness requires. Every one who thinks with any seriousness of God and of himself—God in His holiness, I in my sins—must necessarily ask, What must I do? how can I escape condemnation? how can I be righteous? 2. *Shall we then turn again to God's law*—try to keep it more perfectly, leave off sinning, seek righteousness by our own doings? Vain efforts! The more we try, the more plainly we shall see our failures. By the law is the knowledge of sin, but no righteousness for man. Man, left to deal with God's law with his own efforts alone, either falls into spiritual blindness and deadness of heart, or betakes him to some vain superstition to bring peace to his conscience before God, which they never can bestow.

III. **The gospel of Jesus Christ proclaims the way in which man can be justified.**—Accounted righteous before God. 1. *This is not by the law.* God cannot forgo the claims of His law, cannot clear the guilty. 2. *But the gospel does for us what the law cannot do.* 3. *The Lord Jesus, made man for us*, standing in our place, bearing our sins, rendering a perfect obedience to the law as man, has redeemed us from the just condemnation of the law. 4. *He is declared in the language of prophecy to be "Jehovah our righteousness"* (Jer. xxiii. 6). All that believe in Him are justified—they have a righteousness given to them by God. They are even said to "be made the righteousness of God" in Christ (2 Cor. v. 21).

IV. **By this marvellous work of God, wrought out for us in and by the Lord Jesus, the most blessed results ensue.**—1. *All God's glorious attributes shine forth.* His holiness is vindicated, His justice satisfied, His law honoured, His love triumphant. The glorious contradiction of Exod. xxxiv. 6 finds its blessed solution: "Forgiving iniquity and transgression and sin, and that will by no means clear the guilty." Christ taking the place of the guilty—the believer's sins forgiven. 2. *Hence God can be just, and yet justify the ungodly.* Hence He is not only merciful, but "*faithful* and *just* to forgive us our sins" (1 John i. 9).

V. **This great gospel truth of justification by faith in Christ,** almost lost in the visible Church in the times of mediæval darkness, but recovered and proclaimed anew in the Reformation, is now in the opened Scriptures set full in view for us. Let us receive it, hold it fast, rejoice in it, and let us prove in our own life that it is a doctrine according to godliness.—*Dr. Jacob.*

SUGGESTIVE COMMENTS ON VERSES 21—26.

Salvation undeserved. — Here we have an answer to the most important of all inquiries, " How shall man be just with God?" To be justified is to be acquitted from the charge brought against us, and absolved from the condemnation with which we were threatened. With regard to us the condemnation was deserved and the charge was true. This renders the case so difficult and peculiar, and calls for the apostle's development. But, in exposing the source of the privilege, he seems to use a tautology : " Being justified freely by His grace." If it be done freely, it must be of grace ; and if it be gracious, it must be free. Yet this is not saying too much. Paul knew that men were proud and vain, and that as Simon Magus thought of purchasing the Holy Ghost with money, so they, in dealing with God about their souls, wish to be merchants rather than suppliants, and would seem to buy while they are compelled to beg. But surely, if it be saying too much, it is saying enough. Surely, after this, the freeness and graciousness of the thing cannot be questioned; it is not only free and gracious as opposed to constraint, but as opposed to worthiness. Merit in a sinner is impossible —*his* desert lies all on the other side. There he is worthy of death. A man who asks a favour may have no claim upon you; but you may also have no demand upon him, and therefore, though you may justly refuse him, yet you have no right to apprehend and punish him. But God had a right to punish us, and it is of His mercies that we are not consumed. It is also free and gracious as opposed to desire. This is undeniable with regard to the constitution and accomplishment of the plan itself, for these long preceded even our being; but is it true with regard to the application of it? The publican prayed, " God be merciful to me a sinner," and went down to his house justified. And you sought and found. But what induced you to seek? A sense of your want of the blessing. But how came you to feel this after being so long insensible of it? Hearing such a preacher. But who made this preacher, and sent him, and placed him in your way, and applied what he said to your heart? And the same may be asked with regard to any other instrumentality. Go as far back as you please, when you arrive you will find Him there before you, with all His preparations and excitements, and will hear Him say as you approach, "Come, for all things are now ready."—*W. Jay.*

Mistaken view of cause.—A commentator on this chapter gives six causes of justification.

I. **The principal cause.**—The love of God the Father.

II. **The meritorious cause.**—The active and passive obedience of the Son.

III. **The efficient cause.**—The operation of the Holy Ghost.

IV. **The instrumental cause.**—The ministry of the word and the sacraments.

V. **The instrumental cause for the reception on our part.**—Faith in Christ's blood.

VI.—**The final cause.**—Eternal life by virtue and holiness.

Now with all due deference this appears to be a strange jumbling of causes, and even the schoolmen could not have gone any further. John Stuart Mill was not a theologian, perhaps a sceptic, but he was an able logician, and he teaches us to distinguish between the cause and the antecedent; and in the case of these six causes we should say that a distinction should be observed between the cause and both the antecedent and the consequent. Some of these so-called causes are no causes. They are not even antecedents, but consequents. How can the final cause be an antecedent of justification? Virtue and holiness come after justification. They

103

are its blessed results, the effects of that sanctifying process which is being carried on in the justified. If the ministry of the word and the sacraments be the instrumental cause of justification, then the Saviour's mediatorial work is not complete. The Twenty-fifth Article of the Church of England does not make the sacraments into a cause of justification : "Sacraments ordained of Christ be not only badges or tokens of Christian men's profession, but rather they be certain sure witnesses, and effectual signs of grace, and God's good will toward us, by the which He doth work invisibly in us, and doth not only quicken but also strengthen and confirm our faith in Him." The Christian man is surely a justified man, and the sacraments are tokens of his profession. If the sacraments are a cause of justification, then the article on justification by faith must be altered, for it says, "We are accounted righteous before God, only for the merit of our Lord and Saviour Jesus Christ by faith, and not for our own works or deservings."

The propitiation.—" Freely." The word " excludes merit," says Hemming —" not Christ's indeed, but ours." " It excludes," says Aquinas, " the merit of preceding works." " It excludes more," says Berga ; " it excludes the works that come after faith, as well as the works that go before it." If the justification be gratuitous on the part of God, it must be to man " without money and without price." It would no longer be a gift to believers if they purchased or deserved it by their merit. Luther translates the word " without merit " (*ohne Verdienst*). So does Sharpe. Bellarmin explains it admirably, so far as its theology is concerned, " out of His mere liberality." Limborch explains it happily, so far as its philology is concerned, as meaning *donatitie.* So far, then, as we can learn anything from the New Testament usage of the compound term employed by the apostle, we have reason to come to the conclu-

sion that, in the passage before us, it will not denote, barely and abstractly, simply " deliverance." It will, indeed, denote " deliverance," but the " deliverance " referred to will be deliverance " on the ground of something that meets all rightful claims." It will be, in some legitimate sense, " a purchased deliverance." It will be, in short, deliverance " on the ground of a ransom." " There is perhaps," says Dr. Chalmers, " no single passage in the book of inspiration which reveals, in a way so formal and authoritative as the one before us, the path of transition by which a sinner passes from a state of wrath to a state of acceptance. There is no passage—to which, if we would only bring the docility and the compliance of childhood—that is more fitted to guide and to turn an inquiring sinner into the way of peace." " These six verses," says C. P. Shepherd, " which contain the first enunciation of the doctrine of justification in this epistle—the first overflow, so to speak, of that matter of which the apostle's heart and mind were full—contain also in a short compass the completest expression of the Christian doctrine." If Christ Jesus be set forth as " propitiatory," then it must be true that He was set forth as a " propitiator," and set forth as a " propitiation," and set forth as a " propitiatory sacrifice," and set forth too as the " antitypical fulfilment of all the symbols of propitiation " that " were divinely instituted under preceding dispensations." It was Christ Himself, in His theanthropic personality, that was thus " propitiatory." He was, in His intermingled " satisfactio " and " satispassio," the meritorious cause of God's relation of propitiousness to the human family. It is in consideration of His propitiation that God, as the moral governor of the universe, is willing and is ready to forgive and to justify all such of the " ungodly " as will be induced to take up, by means of faith in the propitiator, that one mental position that will insure their voluntary reception of such divine influences as are needed to renew the heart and assimilate the characters to the archetypal character of God.—*Dr. Morrison.*

Justice and mercy.—The following passage taken in connection with others of a similar character naturally excites a little surprise: "High above all they imagine a great, grim, and relentless justice ever ready to sweep down and crush men out of existence. Long ago this would have happened, men would have been destroyed, the whole universe would have been consumed in wrath, were it not that this great and terrible Judge was pled with, restrained, forcibly held back by the struggling form of an equally powerful mercy. At last Christ appeared; He brings with Him a grand expedient, appeases justice, reconciles it to mercy, and mercy, freed from the conflict and no longer alarmed for men, goes forth and takes up its mission to save. It is not in the writings of the apostle, nor in the writings of any of the sacred penmen, that ideas like these are to be found. They are to be found, not there, but in the books and pictures of mediæval and modern theologians." We also affirm that such ideas as these are not to be found in the books of modern theologians. If they are, the books are not much read, and therefore it is scarcely worth while to quote them for the sake of refutation. The book would be regarded as a curiosity which contained such teaching. At first sight we are disposed to look with compassion upon the "struggling form" of pleading mercy; but our compassion is turned into wonder when we find that mercy is "equally powerful" with justice. Surely any person capable of writing a book on theology would see that there could be no end to the conflict between two infinitely powerful persons or attributes such as justice and mercy—the one determined to punish and the other to pardon. Equally powerful, the contest would be equal; and on what principle Christ could appear with His "grand expedient" to the settlement of this awful struggle we cannot understand. The appropriateness of the adjectives "grim" and "relentless" when applied to justice may be fairly questioned. The breakers of law, the hardened and impenitent despisers of authority, may be expected to look upon justice as grim; but shall we expect law expounders and enforcers to take this view? It certainly does not seem to us fitting that justice and mercy should be represented as two beings in deadly conflict, as descriptive of the divine procedure; for there can be no violent opposition among the attributes of the Godhead. All work together in harmony. We cannot see anything grotesque in the proceeding when God's mercy is inclined to save, and when God sees it proper to have regard to the interests of His moral government, and devises a method whereby He may be just and the justifier of him which believeth in Jesus.

MAIN HOMILETICS OF THE PARAGRAPH.—Verses 27—31.

The triumphant conclusion.—St. Paul concludes the chapter with a triumphant assertion of the principles he has been establishing. He has reached a point in the course of his reasoning where it is necessary to summarise and impress upon the minds of his readers the main questions at issue. In doing this he seems to place before us a general unity.

I. **One God.**—The monotheistic idea was peculiar to the Jew in the early world. He stood alone as the worshipper of the one living and true God. It was not therefore a new doctrine which Paul proclaimed—it was an old doctrine with a new application. The Jew seemed to believe in a Jewish God. One God for the Jew; another God for the Gentile. Paul preaches one God, an all-God, a universal God. If Paul had lived in these days, would the mention of one God have started him on a line of defènce against atheism? However, he did not, but appears to take the existence of God as an axiomatic truth, a self-evident proposition.   He does not argue, but makes assertions and quotations from heathen poets when speaking to the men of Athens.   With Paul and the men of those days to doubt the existence of God is synonymous with doubting their own existence.   One God for all, and yet the unit not lost in the whole number, the atom not absorbed in the wide ocean of being.

II. **One divine law.**—One God, one mind.   In the Trinity there is a blessed unity, one glorious personality, one mighty intellect, which is light, which has neither variableness nor shadow of turning, which knows neither the eclipse of uncertainty nor the obscuration of passing from one phase of truth to another, or from old positions which have to be abandoned to new positions which in course of advancing revelations may also have to be resigned.   One God, one mind, one law.   Superior to all laws is the law of faith.   Our scientists may ignore it as having no power in the material realm.   The thought world is higher than the material world.   Moral forces are mighty.   The law of faith reaches further than is dreamt of in our materialistic philosophies. One law for Jew and Gentile, one law of faith stretching out through all dispensations.

III. **One method of justification.**—One method for the Justifier, and one method for the justified.   God justifies freely by His grace all those who believe in Jesus.   The man is justified by faith, receives the position and the blessing of justification by faith.   Whether by or through, it is of faith, not the deeds of the law.   The man by sinfulness has placed himself outside the law.   Justification rises to a higher plane.   The law condemns.   Grace justifies.   The works of the law perplex the true heart that is seeking the true good.   The act of faith in the propitiatory offering of Jesus removes trouble from the soul, and peace reigns in the soul kingdom, and all its powers move to harmonious measures.

IV. **One attitude of mind.**—Boasting is excluded, and the attitude is one of humble thankfulness.   There is one attitude for the circumcised and the uncircumcised, for the educated and the uneducated, for those who have been good from their birth and for those who have never been brought up, scarcely dragged up, in any moral school.   The complacent, self-satisfied mind of some does not appear to say that from them boasting is excluded.   If boasting were excluded, would there be so much patronage?   Some conduct themselves as if they were lords over God's heritage, and even over God Himself.

V. **One sublime plan of life.**—To establish the honour and dignity and supremacy of the law of love, which will prompt to good works.   The law of faith generates the law of love.   He that keeps the law of love keeps all laws. He is raised above law because it has no power to condemn.   Law is not a dread, but a delight.   Law is not a hard taskmaster, but a gracious guide. Law is not an executioner, but an invigorating rule of action.   The moralist has to spell his way through difficult lessons while the schoolmaster holds the rod.   He who is learned in the law of love finds the schoolmaster a pleasant companion, who can even beguile the tediousness of the way with merry song.

SUGGESTIVE COMMENTS ON VERSES 27—31.

How faith works.—To the importance of Christ's death for the remission of sins we teach faith alone to be necessary, whereby it is not our meaning to separate thereby faith from any other quality or duty which God requireth to be matched therewith, but from faith to seclude, in justification, the fellowship of worth through precedent works, as St. Paul doth. Nor doth any faith justify but *that* therewith there is joined both hope and love; yet justified we are by faith alone, because there is no man whose works, in whole or in particular, can make him righteous in God's sight. As St. Paul doth dispute for faith without works, so St. James is urgent for works with faith. To be justified, so far as remission of sins, it sufficeth to believe what another hath wrought for us. But whosoever will see God face to face, let him show his faith by his works; for in this sense Abraham was justified — that is to say, his life was sanctified.— *Hooker.*

Faith doth not shut out repentance, love, and the fear of God, to be joined with faith in any man that is justified; but it shutteth them out from the office of justifying.—*Homily on Salvation.*

The word "faith" is used to signify the theological virtue, or gracious habit, whereby we embrace with our minds and affections the Lord Jesus Christ as the only begotten Son of God, and alone Saviour of the world, casting ourselves wholly upon the mercy of God, through His merits, for remission and everlasting salvation. It is that which is commonly called "justifying faith" whereunto are ascribed in Holy Writ many gracious effects, not as to their primary cause, but as to the instrument whereby we apprehend and apply Christ, whose merits and spirit are the true causes of all those blessed effects.—*Bishop Sanderson.*

Boasting excluded.—The change from condemnation to justification is very great. Must awaken many new feelings in one's breast—gratitude, hope, joy. One feeling which it will not awaken—pride. It cuts the tap-root of pride. It leaves no room for boast-ing. For God is everything here, and man is nothing.

I. **Boasting is excluded by the knowledge of the condition of the persons justified.**—All who are saved have sinned (ver. 23). Some flagrantly. All more than enough to bring condemnation. Certainly failed to keep the commandment, "Thou shalt love the Lord with all thy heart." All have sinned to such a degree as that they come short of the glory of God. Cannot secure His approbation, for He will not be satisfied with obedience less than perfect. Some come further short than others. A plank needed to bridge over a chasm. One two feet short, another six inches. The larger one as useless as the shorter for the purpose. The best of men cannot cross the gulf which separates a sinner from the righteous God.

II. **Boasting excluded because all are justified freely.**—"Justified" means "pronounced righteous." "Justified" in ver. 20 opposed to "pronounced guilty" in ver. 19. Justification the act of a judge. When God justifies, He sits in judgment and pronounces a verdict. Every sinner condemned already. If not justified, the sentence is hanging over him, waiting the expiry of day of grace. Yet God is saying, "Come, and let us reason together," etc. If we ask Him, He is ready. If we agree to His terms, the sentence is at once removed. Not only pardoned, but accepted. Sentence of death cancelled, and receive a title to the kingdom of heaven. He justifies freely—gratis—in the way of a gift. Thus the case of all met. Bibles are cheap, yet some too poor to buy one. None too poor to receive freely. But boasting goes.

III. **Boasting excluded because the moving cause of justification is His own grace.**—Finds in Himself the reason. Comes out of the goodness of His own heart. This disposes of all pretexts for delay, for God not more gracious to-day than He will be to-morrow. But it takes away all ground for boasting.

107

IV. **Boasting excluded in view of the means by which grace operates:** viz., the *propitiatory redemption in Christ Jesus.*—Justification is part, not all, of the redemptive work of the Lord Jesus Christ. No justification without the payment of His life as the ransom. It is the result of an obedience already given, and to which we can add nothing. This ought to remove the thought that God may be unwilling to justify. If any unwillingness on His part, it would have manifested itself before His Son humbled to death. He cannot be unwilling to see the results produced for which He gave up His Son. This gives another knock-down blow to boasting.

V. **Boasting excluded when we know the way in which we receive an interest in that redemption:** viz., *by simply believing God's word.*—Through faith the propitiatory offering is ours. An Israelite brought a lamb for sacrifice, believing that through its blood being shed his sin would be forgiven. God says, Look at My Lamb as offered for you, and believe that His blood cleanses from all sins. God justifies the man who trusts in Jesus (ver. 26). All that is Christ's becomes ours; His obedience, His sacrifice, is as efficacious as if we had obeyed and suffered. There is no more condemnation. Our trial is just, and we cannot be condemned until He is condemned. The reason of this may not be clear to us. The way of works seems perfectly intelligible. The law of works we can fully understand. But there is a law of faith also, which is as manifestly from God as is the law of works for the sinless. And by it sinners are justified freely. It is a glorious salvation, for which there ought to be much praise to God, but no boasting as regards ourselves.—*G. Wallace, D.D.*

Many of the fathers were accustomed to use the expression "by faith only" when discoursing on justification. For example, Ambrosiaster, in commenting on Rom. iv. 5, uses the expression twice over. Such were some of the pleas that were put in, and appropriately and powerfully urged, in defence of Luther. Bengel stands true to the German *Megalander*, and fell on an ingenious method of vindicating the "only." He applies arithmetic to the case. Two things only are referred to:

Faith and works 2
Works are excluded . . . 1
Faith remains alone . . . 1

One being subtracted from *two*, there remains *but one.* "It is," says Bengel, "an *arithmetical demonstration.*" Tholuck says that Erasmus remarks, "*Vox* SOLA, *tot clamoribus lapidata hoc seculo in Luthero, reverenter in patribus auditur*"—"The word 'alone,' which has been received with such a shower of stones when uttered in our times by Luther, is yet reverently listened to when spoken by the fathers." Hodge repeats the quotation and the reference. We do not know where Tholuck picked it up. But while the observation seems to bespeak, by its peculiar felicity and piquancy, an Erasmian origin, it is certainly not to be found in that great repository of felicities, and wisdom, and wit, and semi-garrulities—the *Liber Concionandi.* Now his doctrine of *justification by faith in the propitiation of Christ* not only meets the wants of men in the direction of pardon for the past—it also meets their wants in the direction of purity for the future. It involves provision for the establishment of the moral influence of moral law. Into whatever soul it finds an entrance, in that soul it raises up, as from the dust, the prostrate law, and *makes it stand.* It *sets-up* that which was *up-set* by sin. It establishes, in the sphere of the soul's inner and outer activities, an ethical influence, which is really, when we let down our line into the depths of the subject, nothing more, nor less, nor else than the native moral influence of the moral law. There is a point of unity whence both propitiation and legislation respectively start, and whither they return.—*Dr. Morrison.*

"*Do we then make void the law through faith? God forbid: yea, we establish the law.*"

I. Justification by faith without the works of the law is distinctly proclaimed in the former part of this chapter.—1. *This is a wholesome doctrine, and very full of comfort* (Art. XI.): full of comfort to the believer in Christ, wholesome in its influence on the believer's own life. 2. *This great gospel truth has been opposed* by the enemy of man, for it upsets his kingdom; *rejected* by man's pride, for it destroys his self-righteousness (Rom. x. 3); *perverted* by man's licentiousness, and made even a minister of sin (Gal. ii. 17; Jude 4). 3. *If this doctrine did make void the law*, it would not be of God; for God's law must stand and be magnified. Christ came not to destroy the law, but to fulfil it (Matt. v. 17). 4. *This doctrine establishes the law.* (1) The law is established, confirmed, honoured, when it is perfectly obeyed. (2) The law is established, confirmed, honoured, when the transgression of it is visited with God's just condemnation.

II. The law is thus established in Jesus Christ.—The believer in Jesus rests on Him as his surety, his substitute, who has perfectly obeyed the law and obtained a perfect righteousness for him, who has paid the penalty of the broken law for him by His death. How wonderfully has the law of God been magnified and honoured in the life and death of Jesus! 1. *Thus the believer in Jesus has an answer* (1) for the accuser who takes up the law against him; (2) for his own conscience, which speaks with the voice of the law. There is no condemnation to them that are in Christ Jesus (Rom. viii. 1). 2. *Thus again he has confidence and boldness towards God.* God is not only *merciful*, but *faithful* and *just* to forgive. What

an encouragement to believers! All God's perfections are on their side. 3. *Perversions and excuses.* However good and true this doctrine is, it is not liked by men until they are taught by the Holy Spirit. Men *naturally* want to be saved by their own goodness, their own righteousness. Hence (1) attempts are made to bring down God's law to the level of man's sinful nature; (2) outward observances are rested on and made much of; (3) resolutions and endeavours put for true obedience.

III. The law is also established in the believer's heart and life.—The law of God reaches to the thoughts of the heart, and requires a *loving obedience.* The believer in Christ is led by the Holy Spirit of God, given to him, abiding in him. The love of God is shed abroad in his heart. He loves God's law. He is enabled to obey it by the power of the Spirit dwelling in him. True, his obedience is not perfect. He may at times "be sore let and hindered in the Christian race." But he desires and aims at nothing short of perfect obedience. He consciously walks after the Spirit, and not according to his own natural, selfish, sinful desires. Hence St. Paul declares that the very purpose of our justification by faith is that the righteousness of the law may be fulfilled in us (Rom. viii. 4). And St. James reminds us that a faith without works is *dead*, and that a believer's life must testify before men the reality of his faith in Christ and the righteousness which that faith receives. Let us never forget (1) that by grace we have been saved through faith; (2) and that we are created in Christ Jesus unto good works, which God hath before ordained that we should walk in them (Eph. ii. 8-10). —*Dr. Jacob.*

ILLUSTRATIONS TO CHAPTER III.

Vers. 13-18. *Littleness of great men.*—On a small island of the southern Atlantic is shut up a remarkable prisoner, wearing himself out there in a feeble mixture of peevishness and jealousy, solaced by no great thoughts and no heroic spirit, a kind of dotard before the time, killing and consuming himself by the intense littleness into which he has shrunk. And this is the great conqueror of the modern world, the man whose name is the greatest of modern names, or, some will say, of all names the human world has pronounced—a man, nevertheless, who carried his greatest victories and told his meanest lies in close proximity—a character as destitute of private magnanimity as he was remarkable for the stupendous powers of his understanding and the more stupendous and imperial leadership of his will. How great a being must it be that makes a point of so great dignity before the world, despite of so much that is really little and contemptible! But he is not alone. The immortal Kepler, piloting science into the skies and comprehending the vastness of heaven for the first time in the fixed embrace of definite thought, only proves the magnificence of man as a ruin, when you discover the strange ferment of irritability and "superstition wild" in which his great thoughts are brewed and his mighty life dissolved. So also Bacon proves the amazing wealth and grandeur of the human soul only the more sublimely that, living in an element of cunning, servility, and ingratitude, and dying under the shame of a convict, he is yet able to dignify disgrace by the stupendous majesty of his genius, and commands the reverence even of the world as to one of its sublimest benefactors. And the poet's stinging line,

" The greatest, wisest, meanest of mankind,"

pictures only with a small excess of satire the magnificence of ruin comprehended in the man. Probably no one of mankind has raised himself to a higher pitch of renown by the superlative attributes of genius displayed in his writing than the great English dramatist—flowering out, nevertheless, into such eminence of glory on a compost of fustian, buffoonery, and other vile stuff, which he so magnificently covers with splendour and irradiates with beauty that disgust itself is lost in the vehemence of praise. And so we shall find, almost universally, that the greatness of the world's great men is proved by the inborn qualities that tower above the ruins of weakness and shame in which they appear, and out of which pillars and dismantled temples they rise.

Ver. 18. *Restraining grace.*—The rev. and pious Dr. Ives, whose house was on Oxford Road, and by which the criminals were carried weekly in carts to Tyburn, used to stand at his window and say to any young friends who might be near him, pointing out any of the most notorious malefactors, " There goes *Dr. Ives!* " If an explanation were asked, he took occasion to expound the innate corruption of the heart, and appealed to the *experience* of his auditors whether they had not often felt the movements of those very passions, errors, prejudices, lusts, revenge, covetousness, etc., whose direct tendency was to produce the crimes for

which these offenders satisfied the claims of public justice, and which were solely prevented from carrying them to the same dreadful fate by the restraining grace of God.

Ver. 23. *Pharisaism.*—When the late Rev. George Burder, of London, was preaching at Warwick, he was called to attend the execution of three men, one a coiner, and the other two housebreakers. " One circumstance," says Mr. B., "affected me very deeply. All the men were on ladders, then the mode of execution, with the ropes about their necks, about to be turned off, when the coiner, endeavouring to fortify his mind in this awful situation, uttered words to this purpose, which I distinctly heard, being at a short distance, ' I never killed anybody ; I never hurt anybody : I hope the Lord will have mercy upon me.' This poor creature seemed nearly to die in the spirit of the Pharisee, ' I thank God I am not as other men are, or as this publican,' for I thought he alluded to the two thieves suffering with him. I was so deeply affected that I could scarcely refrain from crying out to the man, ' Do not trust in your own righteousness : look to Christ.' This has often occurred to me as one of the most glaring instances of a self-righteous spirit that I ever knew."

Ver. 25. *Propitiation.*—Cowper, the poet, speaking of his religious experience, says, " But the happy period which was to shake off my fetters and afford me a clear opening of the free mercy of God in Christ Jesus was now arrived. I flung myself into a chair near the window, and seeing a Bible there, ventured once more to apply to it for comfort and instruction. The first verse I saw was the twenty-fifth of the third of Romans : ' Whom God hath set forth to be a propitiation through faith in His blood, to declare His righteousness for the remission of sins that are past, through the forbearance of God.' Immediately I received strength to believe, and the full beams of the Sun of righteousness shone upon me. I saw the sufficiency of the atonement He had made, my pardon sealed in His blood, and all the fulness and completeness of His justification. In a moment I believed, and received the gospel. Whatever my friend Madan had said to me so long before revived in all its clearness, with demonstration of the Spirit, and with power."

Ver. 26. *One man loses blood to save another.*—The other day a man allowed two ounces of blood to be extracted for the purpose of being infused into an invalid. The loss of blood was more than he could bear. The man died as a consequence of the sacrifice. The offering, if not the death, was voluntary. He was not compelled to the suffering. And so Jesus freely offered

Himself. He could have paralysed the arm of the Roman soldier that was raised to pierce His sacred side. Even after the wound was made He could have spoken the word of healing; but then the stream would not have flowed for the healing of the nations. Yea, after He had freely undertaken the work of our redemption, He might have stopped short and secured to Himself a glorious body-guard of more than twelve legions of angels. But His love both to God and to man sustained Him in the mighty conflict.

Ver. 26. *Eli believes the sad tidings.*—The power which resides in a word, or which operates through a word, requires one (and no more than one) condition for its operation —it must be believed. Old Eli, bowed with the weight of years, sat in the city gate of Shiloh, when a message came to him which had in it a power of death. But if Eli had not believed the fatal tidings of that Benjamite who professed to report the disastrous issue of the day's engagement, Eli would not have fallen dead in a fit by the side of the gate. The message which another Benjamite spoke at midnight to the Roman jailor had in it, on the contrary, a power of spiritual life. But if that jailor had not received Paul's record of God concerning His Son, no life could have visited his rude, dark, heathen soul. Faith is no exceptional demand on the gospel's part. It is the condition of all power which comes by word, whether it be a word that teaches or a word that commands. Though the power of God, operating through His gospel, is an exceptional power, since it is the direct energy of the Holy Ghost which quickens dead souls, yet God has chosen this particular vehicle of speech for His life-giving, saving, spiritual energy, and having chosen it, He respects its ordinary laws. Salvation must come by faith, because faith comes by hearing, and hearing by the word of God.—*Dykes.*

Ver. 26. *Zaleucus.*—Zaleucus, the ancient legislator, shared the punishment with his son, and submitted to lose one eye so that his son might not be rendered totally blind, which was the legal penalty for his transgression. Zaleucus, being both legislator and father, devised the method and endured the suffering, so that law might not be dishonoured and that fatherly love might be expressed. It would be an easy task to describe, after the manner of some writers, the contest between the grim, relentless king and the loving father. We might draw a picture that the heroic Zaleucus would not be able to recognise. He did not become three by the transaction. The ego did not stand by as a calm spectator, while the legislator and the father fought out the affair on the fertile plains of the Locri. The stern legislator and the loving father made up the one Zaleucus. The feeling of love and the sense of justice are not separate from but form a part of my personality. Justice, love, and mercy are not personalities standing away from, though still surrounding, the divine Being. They are the essential attributes of a perfect and full-orbed Deity, and are in subjection to the deliberative faculty. Above them is the great divine consciousness speaking after the manner of men. There can be no fierce conflict among the divine attributes. There never was the represented struggle. All work together in blessed harmony. A man may consult with himself; but he does not get into fierce conflict with himself, as he might if consulting with his fellows. And so even God may consult with Himself. We fail to see anything grotesque in the proceeding when God's mercy is inclined to save, and God, deeming it proper to have regard to the interests of His moral government, devises a method whereby He may be just and yet the justifier of him that believeth in Jesus.

CHAPTER IV.

CRITICAL NOTES.

Ver. 1.—Alford, following Meyer, says κατὰ σάρκα is in contrast to κατὰ πνεῦμα, and refers. to that part of our being from which spring works in contrast with that which is the exercise of faith. κατὰ σάρκα in respect to efforts by one's own natural powers, or efforts made in one's own strength.

Ver. 2. ἐξ ἔργων.—Talmud maintains that Abraham was justified by works.

Ver. 3.—Jewish Rabbis viewed Abraham's faith as so much merit. " As the reward of his faith our father Abraham inherited both this world and that which is to come, as it is said, ' Abraham believed God, and it was counted,' etc."

Ver. 4. **But of debt.**—ὀφείλημα, what one owes—a debt, a due, duty, obligation.

Ver. 7. **Blessed are they,** etc.—Paul refers them to the example of Abraham and the beatitudes of David. Another proof that he does not disparage the law (Wordsworth). ἀφίεναι.—New Testament side of forgiveness—real removal of sin. ἐπικαλύπτειν.—Old Testament side—sin only covered till atonement should be made for it.

Ver. 9.—λέγομεν γάρ supposes an affirmative to the preceding questions—viz., " The privilege belongs also to the uncircumcised." Proved by the quotation from David.

Ver. 11.—The term σημεῖον, sign, relates to the material thing; the term σφραγίς, seal, to its religious import. Seal of the covenant of grace.

Ver. 12.—Refers to believers of Jewish origin who formed the other half of Abraham's spiritual family.

Ver. 13.—Abraham was justified before the institution of circumcision and the delivery of the law, therefore by faith in Christ to come.

Ver. 15.—παράβασις, transgression, from παραβαίνειν, to trespass. A barrier cannot be crossed except in so far as it exists; so without law there is no sin in the form of transgression.

Ver. 17.—καλεῖν is the creature call of the Almighty, by which He, according to the analogy of the first act of creation, calls forth the concrete formations out of the general stream of life (Olshausen). Abraham the father of all the faithful, however far removed. In God's sight Abraham still lives; in God's sight we were already in existence when He spake to Abraham.

Ver. 18.—Against hope as man; but upon hope in God (Severian).

Ver. 19.—In this passage Abraham is represented as placed between two opposite forces— that of sight and that of faith. The look of faith fixed on the promises prevented every look cast on the external circumstances.

Ver. 24. **If we believe on Him,** etc.—Implies purpose, certainty, and continuance.

Ver. 25.—Christians assured by Christ's resurrection of the removal of their guilt. In the same way that the death and resurrection of Christ form an intimate unity, so also in man the death of the old and the rising up of the new cannot be conceived as existing without each other (Olshausen).

MAIN HOMILETICS OF THE PARAGRAPH.—*Verses* 1—17.

The father of the faithful.—The divinity of the Bible shown in this, that it confers immortality upon its heroes which no other book possesses. Abraham's trials, faith, and final victory are familiar facts to-day. He lives both in Bible story and in tradition's lore. It is a fact to be noticed that the fame of Bible heroes has spread beyond the book in which it is related. "The memory of the just is blessed;" and Abraham's memory is blessed and green because he was justified by faith and is the father of the faithful. Consider the negative and the positive aspect of Abraham's descendants.

I. **Negatively.**—His descendants: 1. *Are not the moralists.* Ethical systems cannot be a ground of justification before the unchangeable God. They run from Socrates down to Victor Cousin or Mr. Herbert Spencer. How am I to know by which ethical system I am to be saved? How am I to ascertain which is *relatively* right and which is *absolutely* right? Amid hypothetical imperatives, categorical imperatives, and apodeictical principles, what am I to do? Abraham's descendants would be few if they were confined to the ethical philosophers and their scholars.

2. *Are not the legalists.* The law maketh wrath and brings condemnation. For all are guilty of infractions of the law, both natural and revealed. Without the written law men will be judged by the natural law written on their hearts. Conscience is a witness to guilt. When it has not been killed, it doth make us all criminals. Can the criminal claim reward as a debt? Punishment is his due. 3. *Are not the ceremonialists.* We must coin the word so as to avoid a word which has become descriptive of a certain party. Forms and ceremonies have their place, but we must observe the rule, "A place for everything and everything in its place." Clothes have their use; but what use are they to the dead? First life, then clothes and food. Abraham had the righteousness of faith, being uncircumcised.

II. **Positively.**—His descendants are: 1. *Those who exercise faith.* This is the source from the human side of justification, and is the root force which generates the leaves, flowers, and fruits of the Christian character. 2. *Those who are forgiven.* The doctrine of the forgiveness of sins too often ignored. The blessing to be realised. Faith rightly exercised brings into the soul the consciousness of the divine pardon. 3. *Those who are the subjects of grace.* "By grace are ye saved." The method of grace is one for Abraham and for all God's people, from the dawn of time to its close. 4. *Those to whom belong the sure promises.* They are sure, resting upon the solid foundation of God's grace. This is a rock. All other foundations are as shifting sand. Our moods change; our ethical systems have their days; our volitions vary; our efforts, if strong to-day, are weak the next day, and they always fall far short of our noblest volitions. God's grace is immutable; His promises are firm:

> "Engraven as in eternal brass
> The mighty promise shines."

5. *Those who stand a gracious army before Him, even God, who quickeneth the dead, and calleth those things that be not as though they were.* Review the muster-roll of faith's sons and daughters, and it will be found that, though sometimes lightly esteemed, they are indeed the precious sons and daughters of Zion, comparable unto fine gold. They stand in the presence of the infinite Purity, and are ennobled by the gracious influence. (1) *Let us seek for that faith which justifies and leads on to purity.* (2) *Let us strive to walk in the steps of that faith which has been exercised by the noblest,*—these are the steps leading to spiritual greatness and happiness. (3) *Let us believe the promises sure because they are of grace.* (4) *Let us glory, not in ourselves, not in works, but in our sublime heirships.*

Ver. 3. "*What saith the Scripture?*"—In the third chapter St. Paul had brought this truth plainly forward—that all men before God are sinners. Those to whom the apostle was referring thought they had such special privileges connected with themselves that they at least ought to be exempted from this general statement. But the apostle says, No such thing; and he falls back therefore upon the question; "What saith the Scripture?" Now before I attempt to lead you to the answer which ought to be given to this question, it will be necessary that I dwell briefly upon one or two introductory points.

I. **What is meant by the Scripture?**—When St. Paul used these words he certainly referred simply to the Old Testament Scriptures; but we are never for a moment to suppose that the Old Testament and the New Testament are different; and therefore if a man ask me, "What saith the Scripture?" I am quite as ready to give him an answer out of the Old Testament as I should be to give him one out of the New, and just as ready to answer him out of the New as I should be out of the Old. But when a man asks me a question about his soul, when he is asking me how a man may get to heaven, I should like to answer him out of both Testaments, because when they are put together the one seems to explain the other, enabling a man to say, " Thus saith the Scripture."

II. **What is the authority of Scripture?**—If you ask me what there is in this book different from what there is in the best kind of other books, I have but one plain answer. It is because this book was written, not by man, but by God; it is because, though "holy men of old" wrote the book, they wrote it "as they were moved by the Holy Ghost." We speak of "the Gospel according to St. Matthew," " the Gospel according to St. Luke," or "the Gospel according to St. John"; but we say it is "the gospel of the grace of God," and we acknowledge that from first to last the book was written as God Himself put it into the hearts and minds of the different writers. So then we acknowledge in this book the authority of God Himself. No wonder therefore St. Paul should fall back upon the question of the text. I would only further remark in connection with this part of my subject that we are not to think that the Scripture was intended for men of another age or another country, as if it did not bear upon ourselves; neither must you, when you look at the Scriptures and consider them as the word of God, expect to find them without their difficulties. Even infidels who have disbelieved the Bible have testified to its morality. They have said that if they wanted to bring up their children well there was no morality like that which was to be found in the Bible. To the truth of what the Bible contains the researches of the last few years have testified.

III. " **What saith the Scripture,**" 1. *For my head?* It unfolds to me many difficulties. That great doctrine of there being three Persons—Father, Son, and Holy Ghost—but one living and true God. But the Scripture unfolds to me another great subject, and that is the plan of salvation. The apostle had been showing that all men were sinners—if sinners, they could not save themselves, and that therefore a plan must be devised by which they could be saved. Here is the plan. You and I could do nothing for ourselves. When we were condemned as sinners Christ died in our place, bore our punishment, endured the shame, suffered on the cross, and has now set us free. 2. *But " what saith the Scripture" for my heart?* I have known the Scripture turn many a bad man into a good man and make him happy, but I have never known it make a single person unhappy. To each individual I say, You have no hope; but you may have a full hope, a good hope through Christ. 3. *But " what saith the Scripture" for our life*—I mean our way of living? It tells us the impossibility of a double service: " Ye cannot serve God and mammon." Therefore if the man who loves his sin would only read, " What saith the Scripture?" he would find that he must leave off sinning if he would have peace, for "there is no peace, saith my God, to the wicked." But "what saith the Scripture" still for our life? It bids us ask ourselves, in the midst of the busy world, in the midst of all our occupations, when we rise early and late take rest—it bids us ask ourselves, " What shall it profit a man if he gain the whole world and lose his own soul?"

IV. **But how are we to know these Scriptures?**—We must search those Scriptures; and if we were asked how and when, I should say the *how* must be prayerfully and the *when* must be daily. I would say to all that if you will only follow that advice there is not one but may be mighty in the Scriptures—if you will only search them and pray over them, and that daily. There is an awful responsibility that rests upon every one who does not study that book, who does not read the Bible, who does not consider what the Scripture saith. It is just as if you were walking in a dark place, not knowing the road, and some one were to offer you a light, and you were to say, I do not require it, and refuse to take it. If a man suffered injury under such circumstances, who would marvel?— *Dr. Villiers, Bishop of Carlisle.*

How did Abraham get his righteousness ?—Justification by faith is a very old doctrine—one of the oldest *dogmas* on record. It is as old as Abraham, as old as Abel.

I. **Who justifies ?**—"It is God that justifieth." The Judge, the Lawgiver, is the Justifier. Self-justification is as useless as it is impossible.

II. **What sort of justification does He give ?**—His justification is: 1. *Righteous.* The adjustment of the question between us and God is a righteous adjustment. Nothing but this would satisfy God or ourselves, or make us feel safe in accepting it in our dealings with a holy God. This righteousness is secured by the full payment of the penalty by a surety or substitute. 2. *Complete.* It extends to our whole persons, to our whole lives, to every sin committed by us. The whole man is justified; it is no half pardon. 3. *Irreversible.* No second verdict can alter our legal position. "Who shall lay anything to the charge of God's elect ?" 4. *Divine.* It is a justification worthy of God; a justification which shall place the justified on a far higher level than the first Adam stood upon.

III. **For whom is it ?**—For the *ungodly.* Yes; for such alone. Righteousness for the unrighteous is that which the righteous One came to bring. In this matter of pardon and acceptance, the principle is not, to him that hath shall more be given, but to him that *hath nothing* shall *all* be given.

IV. **How we get it.**—By believing. In accepting God's testimony to this righteousness, in crediting His word concerning this justification, we are justified at once. The righteousness becomes ours; and God treats us henceforth as men who are righteous, as men who, on account of the righteousness which has thus become theirs, are entitled to be dealt with as righteous out and out. Of Abraham it is said, "His faith was counted for righteousness"—that is, God counted this believing man as one who had done all righteousness, just because he was a *believing* man. Not that his *act* or *acts* of faith were substituted as equivalent to work, but his *believing* brought him into the possession of all that *working* could have done. Thus, in believing, we get the righteousness. Our believing accomplishes for us all that our working could have done.—*H. Bonar.*

Ver. 3. *Belief in God.*—Belief in God is the foundation of all religion, both natural and revealed. Now as without belief in God there can be no religion, so where there is such belief in God the Scripture always of course supposes it accompanied with every other part of true religion. As the foundation of religion in general is believing in God, so the foundation of Christianity in particular is the belief of that great act of God, the raising His Son from the dead, in order to judge the world in righteousness.

I. **Now the account which the Scripture gives us of the faith of Abraham is this:** 1. *It consisted in his believing the true God,* the Maker and Governor of the universe, the Lord of heaven and earth. The nations among whom he sojourned were all idolaters, worshippers of dead men, worshippers of the kings who had reigned over them in their lifetime ; for that was the original of all the heathen idolatry. Every city or territory had its own prince, and the world was divided into small kingdoms. These kings were honoured by their flatterers with honours during their lives too nearly divine, and after their deaths they were by their ignorant people worshipped as gods. The worship paid to such gods of their own making was accordingly superstitious; and the corruption of their manners was answerable to the absurdity of their religion. From these Abraham separated himself and believed in the true God, the Maker of all things ; and for the sake of that belief forsook his native country. 2. *As Abraham's faith consisted in general in believing the true God,* so in particular it manifested itself in such acts of dependence upon Him as became a person who had just and worthy notions of the true God, whom he served ; and for this "it was counted unto him for righteousness." 3. *The faith of Abraham was not a speculation or mere credulity,* but a principle of obedience and true holiness. 4. *The faith of Abraham is opposed in Scripture, just as the faith of Christians is, not to the works of virtue, but to the rites and ceremonies of the law of Moses.* "They that are of faith," saith St. Paul (Gal. iii. 7)—that is, th·y who, believing in Christ, expect salvation through the real holiness of the gospel, and not by such outward forms and ceremonies as the Jews observed—"the same," saith he, "are the children of Abraham"; "even as Abraham believed God, and it was accounted to him for righteousness" (ver. 6).

II. **The second thing I proposed to speak of is, what it is that is particularly required of us when we likewise are in Scripture commanded to "believe in God."** —And this evidently implies : 1. Believing His being—that is, not only in a speculative manner believing that there is an infinitely perfect Being in the notional way wherein philosophers describe Him, which may easily be separate from any religious affection, but it is having upon our minds a constant sense of His being in the moral sense the supreme Governor and righteous Judge of the world. This belief of the being of God is that only which, because it will certainly produce the fruits of virtue, shall therefore certainly be "accounted unto us for righteousness." 2. The duty of believing in God implies not only our believing His being, and His being governor and judge of the world, but also that we have worthy and honourable apprehensions of His nature and attributes ; for when any man thinks he believes in God, without attending at the same time to those perfections and excellences which constitute the true and real notion of God, he deceives himself with that empty fallacy of putting words for things, and, instead of placing his religion in obeying the commands of the true Governor of the universe by the practice of all holiness, righteousness, and virtue, he will be apt to content himself with worshipping he knows not what, and he knows not how, with a blind superstition, without understanding, and without any real improvement in goodness. This is naturally the effect of ascribing absurdities to God, as those of the Church of Rome do in the matter of transubstantiation ; or of teaching things concerning Him contrary to the common and obvious notions of righteousness and goodness, as those have done who contend for the doctrine of absolute and unconditional predestination. The religion of such men usually consists more in a useless amazement of mind than in any real practise of virtue, than which nothing can be more dishonourable to God or more injurious to religion. 3. Believing in God signifies believing His revelations also, as well as what nature teaches concerning Him. The obligati·ns of revealed religion are founded upon the same ground as the obligations of natural religion, and they mutually strengthen and confirm each other. By the dictates of nature it was reasonable to expect that God would vouchsafe to make more clear to men His will by revelation ; and in all true revelation is contained a fuller enforcement and more strong confirmation of the law of nature. Men, therefore, who in Christian countries, where the gospel is preached, pretend to believe in the God of nature, and yet at the same time reject the revelation of the gospel, which is so agreeable to and perfective of the law of nature, do, generally speaking, in pretence only, and not in reality, show any more regard to natural than to revealed religion, falling for the most part into absolute atheism. Whereas they who seriously believe and practise the duties of natural religion are generally disposed to embrace also consequently the revelation of the gospel. 4. As believing in God signifies believing His revelations as well as His nature and attributes, so it always includes obedience to Him likewise, when it means that faith which shall be "counted to us for righteousness." "Abraham's faith," saith St. James, "wrought with his works, and by

116

works was his faith made perfect." And concerning ours in like manner St. Paul declares, "With the heart man believeth unto righteousness, and with the mouth confession is made unto salvation" (Rom. x. 10).—*Clarke.*

Ver. 7. *An uncommon conception.*—St. Paul throws a new light on Old Testament utterances, a spiritual interpretation not received by the Jews. He likewise gives a conception of happiness not generally accepted. Let us examine it.

I. **In order to taste joy we must feel sorrow.**—Thus in a general way sorrow has its blessed uses. The sorrow of pain tastes the joy of release. Sorrow for sin prepares the way for the joy of its removal. No wonder men make light of sin when they do not feel the sorrow it inflicts. The sorrowful pathway of the sin-stricken soul leads to the blessedness of forgiveness.

II. **In order to enjoy ease we must bear the burden.**—The burden-bearers of time may seem to have a hard lot, but they can taste a rich enjoyment when the burden is removed which is unknown to the indolent. The burden of sin is a heavy load; but what joy when the Saviour's invitation is accepted, the burden is removed, and the weary soul obtains infinite repose!

III. **In order to welcome forgiveness we must realise our helplessness.**—If a man fancies he is rich and increased in goods, he will be possessed of pride. Fancy plays fantastic tricks. Men fancy that they are morally rich. Why should they crave forgiveness? The sense of soul poverty must be antecedent to the reception of infinite riches. A man condemned will welcome the remission of sentence. Helpless, we rejoice in forgiveness.

IV. **In order to rejoice in buried sins we must feel their loathsomeness.**—We feel in no hurry to carry to the grave the beautiful child that sweetly sleeps in death. The sins that are not frowned upon by society, the sins that make us popular, we are in no haste to cover. But the sin which exposes us to the contempt of our fellows we would gladly bury many fathoms deep. All sin is hateful to God. He loves man, and yet man's sin turns divine complacency into abhorrence. All sin is loathsome. Let us haste to have it covered. It can be covered beneath the propitiation. Let us pray for the divine Spirit to show us the evil of sin, to reveal to us our own sin, and then are we likely to know the high felicity of those whose sins are forgiven.

Ver. 13. *A vast heirship.*—Is any single man heir of the world? He possesses only a part. One man possesses property, another fame, another power. Each man has his own dominion. Even of that he is not complete master. We possess in part as well as know in part. Abraham's material world was small as compared with the world of the present, but he looked beyond and above the material to the moral sphere, to the wide expanding future. Abraham's spiritual seed is heir of the world; and why? Because:—

I. **It is a dominating force.**—We may try to exalt the material, but we are being constantly confronted with the fact that the moral is mighty. Moral wisdom is mightier than weapons of war. Spiritual forces are more dominating than either material, social, or political forces. The spiritual seed is sovereign in time, as time's advance will manifest.

II. **It is a formative agency.**—The spiritual seed is working silently, almost secretly, and yet surely. The great formative agency in the highest of modern civilisations is the spiritual seed. Christ and the Christ-like—the true Abrahamic seed—are permeating all nationalities. The seed is germinating through the centuries; and when the harvest time of humanity and of God's purpose has come, the golden grain will beautify the planet.

III. **It works by means of an eternal principle.**—The righteousness of faith is the principle of the Abrahamic seed.   It is not a Pauline doctrine ; it is a divine creed.   Righteousness is eternal.   God and righteousness are synonymous. Faith in God implies faith in righteousness—faith in righteousness as a divine attribute, as a divine bestowal to the human unrighteous one.

IV.—**It conquers self, and thus conquers all.**—The tendency of the earth seed is to obtain heirship by way of merit.   The spiritual seed represses this erroneous tendency.   Not by the works of the law, but through the righteousness of faith. The seed that masters its own false tendencies must master.   True, individually, that he who conquers self conquers all.   World slaves seek possession through works.   World masters obtain possession through the righteousness of faith.

V. **It marches in harmony with the divine order.**—We may find fault with nature ; but the man who moves in harmony with those laws by which nature is governed is most likely to prove nature's master, and certainly most likely to secure the greatest good—if not to himself, to the race.   The moral and the material order are connected.   The seed that marches in harmony with the moral order will have the largest dominion.   Man's immorality has well-nigh made God's kosmos into a chaos.   Man's morality, through the righteousness of faith, will turn back the chaos into a kosmos.

VI. **It delights in the divine beauty.**—Delight in moral and spiritual beauty should promote delight in material beauty.   He is heir of the world who can delight in all things good, true, and beautiful.   Possession is not by legal enactments, but by the imperial and absorbing soul.   The peasant may possess more than the peer.   How poor an heir is that peer who spends his days in a room of the tower, where he paces up and down like a caged lion mourning over his incapacity !   How rich an heir is that peasant who can walk God's earth singing, All things are ours !

VII. **It moves to universal renovation.**—The spiritual seed is not as the material seed.   The latter seeks heirship for self-aggrandisement.   Too often it heeds not that destruction and misery are in its ways, if by that destruction it can obtain spoils of enrichment.   The former seeks heirship for universal enrichment, and thus it moves on to universal renovation.   Let us seek the true heirship of the world.   Let us pursue the right method.   Let us contemplate ultimate results.   Let us have faith in final triumph.

SUGGESTIVE COMMENTS ON VERSES 1—17.

Abraham's greatness.—The name of Abraham, as we shall afterwards see more fully, is not confined to the sacred history.   Over and above the book of Genesis there are two main sources of information.   We have the fragments preserved to us by Josephus and Eusebius from Greek or Asiatic writers.   We have also the Jewish and Mussulman traditions, as represented chiefly in the Talmud and the Koran.   It is in the former class— those presented to us by the pagan historians — that the migration of Abraham assumes its most purely secular aspect.   They describe him as a great man of the East well read in the stars, or as a conquering prince

who swept all before him on his way to Palestine.   These characteristics, remote as they are from our common view, have nevertheless their point of contact with the biblical account, which, simple as it is, implies more than it states.   He was, in practice, the friend of God, in the noblest of all senses of the word—the friend who stood fast when others fell away.   He was the first distinct historical witness, at least for his own race and country, to theism, to monotheism, to the unity of the Lord and Ruler of all against the primeval idolatries, the *natural* religion of the ancient world. In him was most distinctly manifested the gift of " faith."   In him long, long before Luther, long before Paul, was it proclaimed, in a sense far more universal and clear than the "paradox" of the reformer, not less clear and universal than the preaching of the apostle, that "man is justified by faith." "*Abraham believed in the Lord, and He counted it to him for righteousness.*" Powerful as is the effect of these words when we read them in their first untarnished freshness, they gain immensely in their original language, to which neither Greek nor German, much less Latin or English, can furnish any full equivalent. "He supported himself, he built himself up, he reposed as a child in his mother's arms," in the strength of God—in God whom he did not see, more than in the giant empires of earth, and the bright lights of heaven, or the claims of tribe and kindred, which were always before him. It was counted to him for "righteousness." This universality of Abraham's faith—this elevation, this multitudinousness of the patriarchal, paternal character, which his name involves—has also found a response in those later traditions and feelings of which I have before spoken. When Mahomet attacks the idolatry of the Arabs, he justifies himself by arguing, almost in the language of St. Paul, that the faith which he proclaimed in one supreme God was no new belief, but was identical with the ancient religion of their first father, Abraham. When the emperor Alexander Severus placed in the chapel of his palace the statues of the choice spirits of all times, Abraham, rather than Moses, was selected as the centre doubtless of a more extended circle of sacred associations. When the author of *Liberty of Prophesying* ventured, before any other English divine, to lift up his voice in behalf of universal religious toleration, he was glad to shelter himself under the authority of the ancient Jewish or Persian apologue, of doubtful origin, but of most instructive wisdom, of almost scriptural simplicity, which may well be repeated here as an expression of the world-wide sympathies which attach to the father of the faithful.—*Stanley.*

Sins hid.—"Blessed is he whose transgression is forgiven, whose sin is covered." Get your sins hid. There is a covering of sin which proves *a curse.* "He that covereth his sins shall not prosper"; there is a *covering* it by not confessing it, or, which is worse, by denying it. Gehazi's covering—a covering of sin by a lie; and there is also a covering of sin by justifying ourselves in it. I have not done this thing, or I did no evil in it. All these are evil coverings: he that thus covereth his sin shall not prosper. But there is a *blessed* covering of sin: forgiveness of sin is the hiding it out of sight, and that is the blessedness.—*Richard Alleine.*

"*Whose transgression is forgiven.*"—We may lull the soul asleep with carnal delights, but the virtue of that opium will be soon spent. All those joys are but stolen waters, and bread eaten in secret—a poor, sorry peace that dares not come to the light and endure the trial—a sorry peace that is soon disturbed by a few serious and sober thoughts of God and the world to come; but when once sin is pardoned, then you have true joy indeed. "Be of good cheer; thy sins be forgiven thee."—*Thomas Manton.*

"*Sin is covered.*"—Every man that must be happy must have something to hide and cover his sins from God's eyes, and nothing in the world can do it but Christ and His righteousness, typified in the ark of the covenant, whose cover was of gold, and called a propitiatory, that as it covered the tables that were within the ark, so God covers our sins against those tables. So the cloud covering the Israelites in the wilderness signified God's covering us from the danger of our sins.—*Thomas Taylor.*

Sin covered by Christ.—This *covering* hath relation to some nakedness and filthiness which should be covered—even sin, which defileth us and maketh us naked. Why, saith Moses to Aaron, hast thou made the people naked? The garments of our merits are too short and cannot cover us; we have need therefore to borrow of Christ Jesus His merits and the mantle of His righteousness, that it may be unto us as a garment, and as those breeches of leather which God made unto Adam and Eve after their fall. Garments are ordained to cover our nakedness, defend us from the injury of the weather, and to adorn us. So the mediation of our Saviour serveth to cover our nakedness, that the wrath of God seize not upon us. He is that " white raiment " wherewith we should be clothed that our filthy nakedness may not appear—to defend us against Satan. He is " mighty to save," etc., and to be an ornament to decorate us, for He is that " *wedding garment.*" " Put ye on the Lord Jesus Christ."—*Archibald Symson.*

Sweet is pardon. — The object of pardon, about which it is conversant, is set forth under divers expressions— " iniquity," " transgression," and " sin." As in law, many words of like import and signification are heaped up and put together to make the deed and legal instrument more comprehensive and effectual. I observe it the rather, because when God proclaims His name the same words are used— " Taking away iniquity, transgression, and sin." Well, we have seen the meaning of the expression. Why doth the holy man of God use such vigour and vehemency of inculcation, " *Blessed is the man* "? and again, " *Blessed is the man* "? Partly with respect to his own case. David knew how sweet it was to have sin pardoned; he had felt the bitterness of sin in his own soul to the drying up of his blood, and therefore he doth express his sense of pardon in the most lively terms. And then partly, too, with respect to those for whose use this instruction was written, that they might not look upon it as a light and trivial thing, but be

thoroughly apprehensive of the worth of so great a privilege. Blessed, happy, thrice happy, they who have obtained pardon of their sins, and justification by Jesus Christ.—*Thomas Manton.*

Sin not reckoned.—" Unto whom the Lord imputeth not iniquity." Aben-Ezra paraphrases it, *of whose sins God does not think,* does not regard them, so as to bring them into judgment, reckoning them as if they were not; οὐ μὴ λογίζεται, *does not count or calculate them,* does not require for them the debt of punishment. To us the remission is entirely free, our Sponsor having taken upon Him the whole business of paying the ransom. His suffering is our impunity, His bond our freedom, and His chastisement our peace; and therefore the prophet says, " The chastisement of our peace was upon Him, and by His stripes we are healed."—*Robert Leighton.*

Legality.—He to whom thou wast sent for ease, being by name Legality, is the son of the bond-woman which now is, and is in bondage with her children, and is, in a mystery, this Mount Sinai, which thou hast feared will fall on thy head. Now, if she with her children are in bondage, how canst thou expect by them to be made free? This Legality, therefore, is not able to set thee free from thy burden. No man was as yet ever rid of his burden by him; no, nor ever is like to be. Ye cannot be justified by the works of the law; for by the deeds of the law no man living can be rid of his burden. Therefore Mr. Worldly-Wiseman is an alien, and Mr. Legality is a cheat; and for his son Civility, notwithstanding his simpering looks, he is but a hypocrite, and cannot help thee. Believe me, there is nothing in all this noise that thou hast heard of these sottish men, but a design to beguile thee of thy salvation, by turning thee from the way in which I had set thee. By laws and ordinances you will not be saved, since you came not

120

in by the door. And as for this coat that is on my back, it was given me by the lord of the place whither I go; and that, as you say, to cover my nakedness with. And I take it as a token of his kindness to me; for I had nothing but rags before. And besides, thus I comfort myself as I go: Surely, think I, when I come to the gate of the city, the Lord thereof will know me for good, since I have His coat on my back, a coat that He gave me freely in the day that He stripped me of my rags. I have, moreover, a mark on my forehead, of which, perhaps, you have taken no notice, which one of my Lord's most intimate associates fixed there in the day that my burden fell off my shoulders. I will tell you, moreover, that I had then given me a roll, sealed, to comfort me by reading as I go on the way. I was also bid to give it in at the celestial gate, in token of my certain going in after it; all which things, I doubt, you want, and want them because you came not in at the gate.—*Bunyan.*

Reason and will joined in faith.— The prerogative of God extendeth as well to the reason as to the will of man; so that we are to obey His law, though we find a reluctation in our will —we are to believe His word, though we find a reluctation in our reason. For if we believe only what is agreeable to our sense, we give consent to the matter and not to the author. But that faith which was accounted unto Abraham for righteousness was of such a point as whereat Sarah laughed, who therein was an image of natural reason.—*Lord Bacon.*

Abraham's constant trust.—Though this be the only instance mentioned in Scripture of the patriarch's faith being counted to him for righteousness, yet we know that this unhesitating trust in God was the habitual temper of his mind, as it must be that of every man who would imitate the example of the father of the faithful. The Lord had communed with him previous to this

period, accompanied with the same implicit reliance on the part of the patriarch. It is this immutable trust in God which communicates its whole value to the act of obeying the divine commands; for were the command obeyed without any reference to God or any reliance on Him, this would not be an act of moral obedience, as not proceeding from the proper motive. And this implicit reliance, without any external act of obedience, was counted to Abraham for righteousness. The event on which Moses remarks that Abraham's faith was counted to him for righteousness took place when the patriarch must have been under eighty-six years of age. He received the seal of the covenant by which he and his family were constituted the Church of God when he was ninety-nine years old. Hence the reckoning of his faith for righteousness took place at least thirteen years before he and his descendants were constituted the Church of God. Now if Abraham's faith was counted for righteousness when he was not a member of the outward community of God's Church, why may not the same mark of divine favour be extended to others who, like him, place their confidence in God, and study to obey His law, though they too belong not to the visible Church of God? With all who admitted the inspiration of the Jewish Scriptures, the apostle's argument must have appeared absolutely conclusive; for when Abraham had his faith reckoned to him for righteousness he was in the situation of the pious Gentiles of every age who have lived and died out of God's visible Church. No person, then, can be entitled to maintain that the pious heathen may not, in virtue of the redemption that is in Christ, have their faith counted to them for righteousness, when we have the example of the father of the faithful himself obtaining justification while precisely in this situation. The term "father" is applied to Abraham in this passage metaphorically, to signify that he was constituted the type or

121

example to all mankind of obtaining justification. This method of justification was revealed to him, not as a special instance of divine favour to himself as an individual, but as a pattern or example of the manner in which all men may obtain this blessing, an instance of the principle on which alone any of the fallen race of mankind can be justified. In the first instance the covenant, as the divine promise is often called, was made with Abraham. But it having been declared in the covenant itself that Abraham in this transaction was the father or type of all believers, the promise extends to all men, and is as immutably certain to every human creature who walks in the steps of Abraham's faith as it was to the patriarch himself. "Now this promise," says the apostle, "was not given to Abraham and to his seed through the law, but through the righteousness of faith." The expression "the law" is apt to suggest the law of Moses. But this cannot be the meaning, for the law of Moses did not then exist. Therefore by "the law" the apostle means generally "the law of God," both moral and ceremonial, whether made known by revelation or written on the heart; and the force of his observation is, that the reward was not promised to Abraham and his seed in consequence of their meriting it by obedience to the divine law, but because God of His own free will was pleased to count their faith to them as righteousness, or to accept the imperfect righteousness of faith as if it were an unsinning fulfilment of His law.—*Ritchie.*

Canaan typical.—We know that the earthly Canaan was, in express terms, promised to Abraham and his seed. And that the promise of the heavenly Canaan was couched under this is scarcely less plain, from the two following simple considerations. First : Abraham himself, and the other believing patriarchs, so understood it; for, on the footing of this promise, they looked for the heavenly country—"for the city which hath foundations, whose builder and maker is God" (see Heb. xi. 8-10, 13-16). This country was the object of their hope, as being the subject of divine promise. But no promise of it is to be found, unless it was couched under that of the earthly Canaan, as a type; connected with the declaration, "I will be thy God, and the God of thy seed"; which also includes the promise of eternal inheritance; and, indeed, considered as the glorious sum of the promises made in the Abrahamic covenant. The whole of the gospel revelation was then, and for many ages afterwards, under the veil of figurative language, and of typical rites, objects, and events. To have given, in clear and explicit terms, the full promise of the eternal inheritance, would not have been consistent with the divine scheme of gradual development, nor with the fact of "life and immortality being brought to light" by Jesus Christ. But that the promise *was given* is manifest from the apostle's manner of expressing himself in the passages above alluded to, and from his saying of the patriarchs, who had gone to the "better country," that "through faith and patience they *inherited the promises*" (Heb. vi. 12). Secondly : This is still further evident, from believers in all ages and countries being called heirs, *according to the promise of inheritance given to Abraham.* So they are spoken of in Gal. iii. 18, 29. "If ye be Christ's," says the apostle in ver. 29, "then are ye Abraham's seed, and *heirs according to the promise*"—*i.e.*, the promise of the *inheritance* mentioned in ver. 18: "If the *inheritance* be of the law, it is no more of *promise* : but God gave it to Abraham by *promise.*" So also, in Heb. vi. 17-20, "the *heirs of promise*," who derive "strong consolation" from the word and oath of God to Abraham, are those "who have fled for refuge to lay hold on the hope set before them : which hope . . . *entereth within the veil*; whither the forerunner is entered, even Jesus." But as the word here rendered *world* is one which usually, if not uniformly, when it occurs without any restrictive noun, is used to denote the whole inhabited earth, I cannot help thinking that there is here a reference to *the whole earth* becoming the possession of Abraham's seed, of which the possession of Canaan was but a small prelude. There is an obvious difference between a *right* and *actual possession*. The whole earth may be, by the gift or promise of God, the property of this seed, although they are not yet, and may not be for a good while to come, invested with the actual possession of it. When promises are made to a seed which is to come into existence in the successive ages of the world, it is not necessary to their fulfilment that they should be enjoyed in the same manner and in the same degree, by all, from the first period to the last; for with this, in the present instance, facts do not accord. We certainly possess the blessings contained in the divine promises in a more eminent degree than the saints of old: " God having

provided better things for us, that they without us should not be made perfect " (Heb. xi. 40). Both temporal and spiritual blessings will be possessed, in a much higher degree of perfection than even now, during the period of the millennial glory of the Church. And as to these who shall be alive on the earth at the coming of Christ, they shall escape the sentence of mortality. But such differences in the enjoyment of the promises, at different periods, do not render them void of effect to any. All the seed have " the promise of the life that now is, and of that which is to come." All being finally put in possession of the " heavenly country " may be said then to *inherit the promises* in their full extent—this being their grand sum, their glorious completion. Moses and Aaron " inherited the promises," although, as a judgment for failing to sanctify the name of the Lord at the waters of Meribah, they were sentenced to finish their course short of the earthly Canaan.—*Wardlaw.*

MAIN HOMILETICS OF THE PARAGRAPH.—*Verses* 18—25.

Not for his sake alone.—It is a glorious sight, a good man struggling with adversity and endeavouring to bear patiently the ills of life—more glorious still a good man rejoicing in adversity and making difficulties minister to highest delights. Travel back many centuries to the olden time. See a good man believing, hoping, rejoicing, though the sphere of sense did not furnish ground for such mighty faith. Abraham was not a materialist. Matter, with sceptical materialism for our guide, crushes faith. Matter is mighty, but mind is mightier. We know not the omnipotent energy of the infinite Mind. Abraham did not believe that man is a mere creature of circumstances except in so far as they are directed by God. Man divinely strengthened is superior to circumstances. Abraham defied time. What are a hundred years to Him whose existence is not measured on human dial-plates ! Abraham believed in a knowable God—one whose promise was equalled by His performance. Promise and performance are coequal with God. If they were not, God would be untrue to His nature, and that He can never be. Abraham had a noble ambition. He believed in hope to the intent that he might become the father of many nations. Spiritual fatherhood is the highest and the noblest. The patriarch looked forward to a glorious and ever-increasing family. His sons and daughters are numerous. Abraham lived, believed, hoped, and prayed not for himself alone : he lived in his God and in the thought of our ennobled race. " Not for his sake alone " is inscribed on his monumental pillar. How beautifully Abraham seeks to settle the dispute between his herdmen and Lot's ! Abraham's kindly considerateness shows that he spoke not for his sake alone. Abraham the intercessor for the

123

Cities of the Plain showed himself one living for the welfare of others. Not for his sake alone is the short biography written. We are the heirs of the ages. Adown the stream of time come argosies laden with mental and spiritual wealth. We stand on the moral delta which is enriched by the alluvial deposits from the noblest men and times. We are rich, or ought to be, in the moral spoils of time. And yet how weak in faith, how puny in works ! We shake in the presence of modern pretenders like reeds before the wind. If a woman writes a book against our religion, we pile up against her magazine articles and send forth Christian evidence lecturers, as if she could hurl the Omnipotent from His throne. Why is our faith weak ? Because : 1. *We look only at the things which are seen.* Our vision is bounded by the things of sense. We must look at the things which are unseen. We believe in the unseen and unseeable things of this world—if we may use the word—on the testimony of observant men. Why not believe in the unseen things of the spiritual realm on the testimony of God and of His servants ? The things unseen are the realities—the certain and abiding realities. Let faith thus exercise itself, and it will grow. 2. *We dwell on the seeming.* Our morbid fancy leads us astray. We first fancy, and then we believe that the creation of our fancy is a child of fact. Let us seek to be, like Abraham, strong in faith. In spite of all appearances, in spite of all seeming impossibilities, let us believe in God. Can it be that Abraham in the dawn of time by his might shames our weakness ? By this weakness of faith we shut ourselves up in the gloomy castle of doubt, we lead miserable lives. Our harps are hung on the willows. Our swords rust in the sheaths. We impede true progress, and we dishonour God. We might be strong if we could look above and beyond our surroundings to the God who promises, and remember that with Him nothing is impossible. Delay there may be to human seeming, and yet that may be accomplishment in the divine purpose. Faith grows like all other powers and graces. Abraham by believing was strengthened in his faith. How wide the promise " To him that hath shall be given " ! Faith is an increasing grace. In order to increase there must be growth ; in order to growth there must be food and exercise. Faith is fed by the promise. Faith is exercised by the period of waiting. The very obstacles which would stagger the faith of a doubting soul will be made by the believing man into the means whereby his faith is strengthened. *Let us not shame our noble father.* A strong faith-soul he walks the upper plains. Does he look down on us as sickly members of his great family ? Oh to be strengthened in faith ! and then we should give glory to God by the fuller recognition of His power and faithfulness, we should be the better able to perform our duties, our lives would be filled with joy, and God's blessing would rest upon us. *Let us live for the sake of others.* The inheritance which Abraham has handed down to us let us impart to our fellows and transmit unimpaired to our descendants.

Ver. 20. *The unwavering man gathers strength.*—Physical and intellectual strength may be developed up to a certain limit, and then it declines. Physical strength, sooner or later, will be shorn of the locks wherein it lies. Intellectual strength will fade into the imbecility of age. But moral strength has no limit. It will grow through the longest life. It will develop in eternal cycles. How shall we grow in strength ? By wavering not at the promises of God.

I. **The unwavering man has a single eye.**—He looks to the promise, and not to the improbability. He treads the plank of the divine promise, looking forward to the goal of fulfilment, and thus he is not disturbed by the surging waters of scepticism.

II. **The unwavering man has a clear vision.**—The divine promise reveals to his soul the divine Promiser. He is able to perform. He must be faithful. For God to break His promise, would be for God to be untrue to His covenant, to be untrue to His own nature, and that He can never be. How strong a man must grow who clearly sees the divine attributes behind the promise !

III. **The unwavering man provides soul growth.**—He feeds on the promise. It provides a banqueting table at which the unwavering man feeds. God provides by furnishing the food. Man provides by making use of the food. We put on moral strength as we feed on the promises. We increase in strength.

IV. **The unwavering man reaches sublime heights.**—He develops in faith, giving glory to God. The Infinite condescends to the finite, and seeks to raise man out of his human finiteness into the larger spaces of divine possibilities. We give glory to God, not by our weakness, but by striving to get out of our weakness and by putting on strength. Dispute not the faithfulness of the divine Promiser. Be firm in faith, and thou shalt stand even amid the shifting sands of scepticism. Have the spiritual knowableness of faith, and thou shalt not feel the touch of agnosticism. Feed on the promise, and thou wilt become stronger and stronger.

Vers. 20, 21. *Religious faith rational.*—It is not at all true that faith itself, *i.e.* trust, is a strange principle of action ; and to say that it is irrational is even an absurdity. I mean such a faith as that of Abraham mentioned in the text, which led him to believe God's word when opposed to his own experience. It is obvious that we trust to our memory. We trust the general soundness of our reasoning powers. From knowing one thing we think we can be sure about another, even though we do not see it. We continually trust our memory and our reasoning powers, though they often deceive us. This is worth observing, because it is sometimes said that we cannot be certain that our faith in religion is not a mistake. When we come to examine the subject, it will be found that, strictly speaking, we know little more than that we exist, and that there is an unseen Power whom we are bound to obey. Beyond this we must trust ; and first our senses, memory, reasoning powers—then other authorities ; so that, in fact, almost all we do, every day of our lives, is on trust, *i.e.* faith. Scripture, then, only bids us act in respect to a future life as we are every day acting at present. We are from our birth dependent creatures, utterly dependent—dependent immediately on man ; and that visible dependence reminds us forcibly of our truer and fuller dependence upon God. It is a mistake to suppose that our obedience to God's will is merely founded on our belief in the word of such persons as tell us Scripture came from God. We obey God primarily because we actually feel His presence in our consciences bidding us obey Him. And this, I say, confutes these objectors on their own ground, because the very reason they give for their belief is that they trust their own sight and reason, because their own, more than the words of God's ministers. Now let me ask, if they trust their senses and their reason, why do they not trust their conscience also ? Is not conscience their own ? Their conscience is as much a part of themselves as their reason is ; and it is placed within them by almighty God in order to balance the influence of sight and reason, and yet they will not attend to it. For a plain reason : they love sin ; they love to be their own masters, and therefore they will not attend to that secret whisper of their hearts which tells them they are not their own masters and that sin is hateful and ruinous. For ourselves, let us but obey God's voice in our hearts, and I will venture to say we shall have no doubts practically formidable about the truth of Scripture. Find out the man who strictly obeys the law within him, and yet is an unbeliever as regards the Bible, and then it will be time enough to consider all that variety of proof by which the truth of the Bible is confirmed to us. This is no practical inquiry for us. Our doubts, if we have any, will be found to arise after disobedience. It is bad company or corrupt books which lead to unbelief. It is sin which quenches the

Holy Spirit.   If we but obey God strictly, in time, through His blessing, faith will become like sight; we shall have no more difficulty in finding what will please God than in moving our limbs or in understanding the conversation of our familiar friends.   This is the blessedness of confirmed obedience.   Let us aim at attaining it; and in whatever proportion we now enjoy it, praise and bless God for His unspeakable gift.—*Newman.*

Ver. 25.   *The possibility of a resurrection.*—The presumptions against the possibility of a resurrection operate so strongly in the minds of some that they think it needless to inquire what evidence there is for it, being persuaded that the thing itself is not capable of being supported by any evidence.   This prejudice was a very early one, for the apostle expostulates this case with King Agrippa: "Why should it be thought a thing incredible with you that God should raise the dead?"   Let us consider the force of this expostulation, and see whether it is strong enough to encounter the prejudice.   Now nothing can be said to be incredible if there is a power in any person able to effect it; for if there is such a power, that power may bring into existence that very thing which you doubt of; and it cannot be incredible that a thing should exist which may possibly really exist.   If we consider only the strength of children, it is incredible that they should build castles; but if we consider the strength and ability of men, it would be ridiculous to doubt whether they could or no.   So that the credibility or incredibility of anything depends on knowing whether there is or is not a power adequate to the undertaking.   The resurrection of the dead is in truth a very stupendous work; but neither you nor I am to undertake it: if it depended on us, it would be incredible indeed.   It is the work of God, and of Him only; and surely I have named one of credit and power sufficient to be trusted in this great affair.   And this is St. Paul's argument, "Why should it be thought incredible that God should raise the dead?"   Whoever, therefore, affirms that a resurrection is in itself a thing incredible must affirm that it is incredible that God has power to raise the dead.   And now consider who it is that can, consistently with the common and allowed principles of reason and nature, deny this power to God.   No one certainly who admits that God made the world can entertain this doubt; for if God has given us the life we now enjoy, what should hinder Him from restoring life again after this is lost?   Can there be more difficulty in giving life the second time than there was at first?   If there be any contradiction therefore in the notion of a resurrection, there must be the very same in the notion of creation.   And therefore natural religion is just as much concerned in this point as revelation; for though the belief of the fact that the dead shall be raised depends on revelation, yet our belief that God has power to raise the dead depends, not on revelation, but on the clear dictates of reason—of that reason by which we discover Him to be our creator.   And if you doubt even of this, His power of creation, you must bid adieu to all religion at once; for if God created not the world, how are you at all related to Him?   If He did not make us, what right has He to govern us? or what pretence to our obedience?   Neither you from nature nor we from revelation can ever be satisfied.   The power of God being admitted to be equal to this work, the question of the resurrection of Christ comes to be a question of fact.   And though I propose not to enter into the evidence of the fact, yet it may be proper to observe that a resurrection considered as a fact is a fact as capable of evidence as any whatever; it is an object of sense, of every sense by which we judge of the reality of things without us.   We are told that "Christ died and rose again."   Of His death, I suppose, there is no great doubt—die He certainly did.   And surely there could be no more difficulty to see and know that He was dead than in knowing when others were dead, from Adam to this day.   One would think, therefore, that those about

126

Him, who saw Him crucified and buried, might be trusted when they report that He died. But He came to life again. Very true; and it was very easy for those who conversed with Him to know whether He was alive or no. There was no more difficulty in judging of His being alive than of judging in any other case whether those we converse with are alive or no. His having been dead and buried could not possibly alter the case, or create any difficulty in judging whether He was really alive or no. So that the Resurrection, considered as a fact, was in every part of it an object of sense, and as capable of being well attested as any other object of sense whatever. Lay these things together—the romise of God to give us eternal life, His power to make good His word, the confirmation He has given us of our hope by the resurrection of Christ—and what is wanting to make the belief of this article a rational act of faith? The promises of God have never borrowed help from moral probabilities. The promises to Abraham were not of this kind; so far otherwise, that it is said of him that "against hope he believed in hope"—that is, he hoped where, humanly speaking, there was no ground for hope. There was no probability that his seed who was a stranger and pilgrim on earth should inherit the land of Canaan, possessed by great and powerful nations. Compare now this case with the case of Christians. We have great promises made to us by God in Christ Jesus, the promises of a resurrection to life. Inquire of the world; they know of no such thing—the ages past have afforded no instance of this kind; and, as far as they can see and judge, daily experience is a witness against this hope. Under these difficulties, whither shall we go for refuge and support? Whither but to the promises of God, and to this full persuasion, *that what He has promised He is able to perform?* If we hold fast this persuasion and stagger not through unbelief, then shall we indeed be the children of the faith of Abraham, whose "faith was imputed to him for righteousness."—*Sherlock.*

SUGGESTIVE COMMENTS ON VERSES 18—25.

These things are written not for Abraham's sake alone.—These things were not written for Abraham's sake alone; they were written for ours. Abraham trusted in God to quicken his unborn son—by-and-by to raise him (if need were) from the dead. We trust Him who did quicken in the flesh and raise from the dead His own supernatural Son Jesus. The gospel facts, the gospel promises, and the blessings of the new covenant in Christ are to us what the birth of Isaac was to Abraham: things all of them beyond the reach of experience or against it—things past or future or absent or spiritual—things in one way or another undiscerned by sense and to reason improbable; resting for their evidence solely on the word of the living God. To that man they are very real things—more real than anything else—who believes in God before all others. To other men they are quite unreal, shadowy, phantom-like, unbelievable. Such a faith in God is reckoned for righteousness to every man who has it, just as it was to Abraham, the father of all believers.—*Dykes.*

Christ died not as a mere teacher.—St. Paul first declares that Christ was "delivered for our offences." Now, if the single service which Christ has rendered to mankind be, as the Socinian tells us, in the character of a teacher of religion; and if, by the discovery which our Lord has made of the different conditions of the righteous and the wicked in a future life, every man, once brought to a belief of the doctrine, might be reclaimed in such a degree as to merit, by his future conduct, not only a free pardon of his past offences, but also a share of those good things which "God hath prepared for them that love Him"; if our Lord's doctrine might of itself, in this way, be a remedy for the sins of men, and if His sufferings and death were necessary only for the confirmation of His doctrine,—then might we admit it to be only in an indirect and a figurative sense that the sins of men are spoken of in this clause as having been the occasion of His death. For His doctrine would in that case be the means of their reformation, and His death would only be the means of establishing His doctrine. But if nothing future can undo the past; if we have incurred guilt without so much as the ability of meriting reward; if it is only through the power of divine grace that we can think or do anything which is right; and if, after all that divine grace has done for him, the life of the believer still consists in a perpetual conflict with appetites which are never totally subdued, and in an endeavour after perfection which never is attained; if the case really be that "if we say we have no sin we deceive ourselves, and the truth is not in us"; if, nevertheless, we are expressly assured that, on "confessing our sins, God is faithful and just to forgive us our sins, and to cleanse us from all unrighteousness"; and if, as the beloved disciple assures us, it is the "blood of Jesus Christ" which "cleanseth us from all sin,"—then must it plainly follow that the Redeemer's death was available to the expiation of the sins of men, far otherwise than merely as a solemn confirmation of the truth of the Christian religion; then must it plainly follow that Christ died to make an atonement for the sins of men, and that His blood has a direct and proper efficacy to expiate our guilt.—*Bishop Horsley.*

Faith against improbability.—For "against hope"—contrary to all natural reason for hope—"he believed in hope." He trusted with the most immovable expectation that he should become the father of many nations, according to that which was spoken,

"So shall thy seed be." This was the promise on the fulfilment of which he so confidently relied. It was given many years before the birth of Isaac to which it relates. But though every year of delay increased the natural improbability of the event, it in no degree weakened the patriarch's faith. He did not suspect that the circumstances on which its improbability depended rendered the promise unlikely to be fulfilled. He looked to nothing but the faithfulness of God, who quickeneth the dead and calleth things which be not as though they were. He knew that whatever the Almighty promised He was able to fulfil, and would fulfil. "He staggered not therefore at the promise through unbelief." He did not deliberate on the improbability of the event, the possibility of his being deceived as to the divine authority of the communication, or the unlikelihood of the supernatural event taking place in order to raise up a family to him. The expression "He was delivered" means He was given up to death, as is plain from the immediately subsequent reference to His resurrection. He was given up to death in order to atone for our offences, and as a sacrifice in virtue of which it might be just in God to forgive our sins, and raised again for our justification. These words are not intended to imply that to particular parts of our Lord's ministry particular parts of our salvation must be referred—the pardon of sin being the consequence of His death, and justification the effect of His resurrection. His whole ministry forms one connected series; and from the whole series of our Lord's obedience, and death, and resurrection, and ascension into heaven, and intercession at the Father's right hand, our salvation, and every particular part of it, are derived. By being "raised again for our justification" may be understood that His resurrection from the dead is a sure proof that His death is a full and an accepted atonement for sin, and that in virtue of it we may obtain justification by faith in His name.—*Ritchie.*

Faith rests on the nature of God and work of Christ.—Our judgment declares that God will keep His word—*i.e.*, that He will not punish for their sins those who believe the gospel. By an act of the will our entire being accepts this verdict of our judgment, and there follows at once within us, by the laws of mind fixed by God, a confident expectation that we ourselves will escape from punishment. Such is justifying faith. The faith which sanctifies is a belief of the promises. It is a sure expectation that in consequence of God's eternal purpose, by union with Christ, and through the agency of the Holy Spirit, we shall actually be, from this moment, dead to sin and living only for God. In each case according to our faith it is done to us. Again, it is because God raised Christ from the dead that we accept the teaching of Jesus as the word and promise of God. Consequently our assurance of escape from punishment, and our expectation that all the promises will be fulfilled, rest upon the historical fact of the resurrection of Christ. Our faith is therefore a leaning "on Him who raised Jesus from the dead." In the death of Christ God's infinite love is revealed to us as the firm ground of our confidence. We are sure that He who spared not His own Son will give us all things. Hence the love of God manifested on the cross of Christ is the immovable foundation on which rests our expectation of the fulfilment of each gospel promise. We may therefore describe faith in God as an assurance that God's words will come true, an assurance resting upon the nature of God as made known in the death and resurrection of Christ. From the foregoing it will be evident that faith in God, so far from being contrary to reason,.is itself the noblest kind of reasoning. For our hope we have the best reason, one which our intelligence fully approves—viz., the word and character of God. Owing to the comparative uncertainty of all human testimony, the word "believe" frequently denotes in common life an assurance mingled more or less with doubt. But the faith which God requires is the very opposite of doubt. It is therefore a full assurance that God's word will come true.—*Beet.*

ILLUSTRATIONS TO CHAPTER IV.

Ver. 3. *A lantern refused.*—If, then, we have a light for our souls, and we will not use it, who can wonder if we suffer injury? This reminds me that something of this kind actually happened. It was not so long ago that I happened to be visiting in a great castle situated on the top of a hill, near which there was a very steep cliff and a rapid river running at the bottom. A person, anxious to get home from the castle, late one night, in the midst of a violent thunderstorm, when it was blackness itself, was asked to stop till the storm was over. She declined. She was begged to take a lantern, that she might be kept in the road; but she said she could very well do without it. She left, and, perhaps frightened by the storm, she wandered from the road, and got upon the top of the cliff; she tumbled, and the next day the lifeless body of that foolish woman was found washed ashore from the swollen stream. How many such foolish ones are there, who, when the light is offered, and they have only to say, "What saith the Scripture?" are prepared to say, "I have no need of that book; I know right from wrong; I am not afraid; I fear not the end!" Oh, how many souls will be found in the last day who have tumbled over the cliff in the darkness of ignorance and unbelief, and who have perished because they have refused the light of God's truth, which would have guided them on the road to heaven!

Ver. 3. *Influence of the Bible.*—It is hazarding nothing to say that, other things being equal, the political power and promise of nations is in direct ratio with their fidelity to the word of God. When a pagan ambassador asked Queen Victoria the secret of England's national greatness she gave him a Bible, and said, "That is the secret of the greatness of England." In the Centennial letter which the President of the United States addressed to the American Sunday Schools, he said

" To the influence of the Bible we are indebted for all the progress made in true civilisation." Froude says, in his essay on Calvinism, " All that we call modern civilisation, in a sense which deserves the name, is the visible expression of the transforming power of the gospel."

Ver. 3. *Boy would not part with his Bible.* —Let me just mention a story. I remember once hearing of a little lad in a town in Lancashire, where I first began my work of preaching. He lay upon the steps of a door, in the middle of the night, in the great town of Warrington, and the policeman, or rather watchman, coming up to him, said, " What are you doing here? " The boy replied, " I am without father and mother; I have travelled thus far, and I have no food, no money, no place to lie down in." There was something in the boy's jacket which attracted the watchman's eye, and when he touched it he thought he had found a thief. " What have you here? " he asked. The boy then put his hand into his pocket, and brought out a small pocket Bible. " Well," said the watchman, " if you are so badly off, I will give you a few pence for your Bible ; I will take it home to my children, and you will be able to get your bed and food for the night." But the lad, young as he was, knew that the Bible was true; he had an experimental knowledge of the Bible, and he was ready at once with his reply. " Thank you, sir," he said, " but I won't give it up." " Why, you are starving," said the watchman. " Yes; but this is the word of God, and it tells me, ' When my father and my mother forsake me, then the Lord will take me up.' " Here was the experimental knowledge of the power of the promises. The watchman showed his humanity, his kindness, and gentleness towards the fatherless boy. He took him home and fed him, and God prospered that boy who relied on the promises. And, believe me, that is just the experience of hundreds and thousands who have found their extremity to be God's opportunity— who had found when they were very low that God could extend to them His everlasting arms, could lift them up, and bless them and preserve them.

Ver. 3. *There is no fear now.* — Lord Shaftesbury, speaking on behalf of the South American Missionary Society, said, " I remember a missionary from Fiji telling me an anecdote. You have all heard how the Fijians were raised in the scale of social life when Christianity had been introduced among them. Well, a missionary told me that this came under his observation. A ship having been wrecked off one of the islands of Fiji, a boat's crew that had got ashore from the wreck were in the greatest possible terror lest they should be devoured by the Fijians. On reaching land they

130

dispersed in different directions. Two of them found a hut, and crept into it ; and as they lay there wondering what would become of them, one suddenly called out to his companion, ' All right, Jack, there is a Bible on this chair; there's no fear now.' This poor, despised book, which this man would probably have scorned to look at, and which he didn't believe could do any one any good, he was glad enough now to hail as a proof that his life was safe. He was sure that those who cared to have and to read a Bible would not wish to eat him. I remember reading a somewhat similar story of a traveller who came to a rough hut which was owned by a very rough-looking man. The owner of the hut gave him a meal, and prepared such a bed for him as he could, but the traveller's only idea of spending the night was to keep his eyes open and his pistol near. But when the rough owner of the hut took down a Bible from its resting-place, and read a chapter, and then offered a short prayer, and then went to bed himself, the traveller knew that no danger was to be apprehended there, and quietly went to sleep."

Ver. 4. *Gentleness of Charles V.*—We are told that on one occasion a swallow having built its nest on the tent of Charles V., he generously commanded that the tent should not be taken down until the young birds were ready to fly. Truly, if he, a rough soldier, could have such gentleness in his heart towards a little bird, how much more will the Lord have it to all those who flee to Him for shelter in loving trustfulness. " He that builds his nest upon a divine promise," says one, " shall find it abide and remain until he shall fly away to the land where promises are lost in fulfilments." Believers should be the more emboldened to do this from the fact that what God has already done for them is designed to be a sure and blessed earnest of all the grander things to be done for them in the future. He never lifts any from the pit only to cast them in again. Men may do such a thing, but the Lord never does.

Ver. 4. *Mr. Hewitson's advice to Dr. Macdonald.*—In one of his prized letters his friend Mr. Hewitson once said to Robert Macdonald, D.D., " Have faith in God. Faith will be staggered by loose stones in the way if we look manward ; if we look Godward faith will not be staggered even by seemingly inaccessible mountains stretching across and obstructing our progress. ' Go forward ! ' is the voice from heaven ; and faith, obeying, finds the mountains before it flat as plains."

Ver. 9. *Christian happiness.* — In this verse there is a declaration of the Christian's blessedness. The New Testament use of the word μακάριος throws light upon

Christian happiness, and will help us to understand such songs of trust as that which closes thus :—

" There are briars besetting every path
    That call for patient care ;
There is a cross in every lot,
    And an earnest need for prayer.
But a lowly heart that leans on Thee
    Is happy everywhere."

Vers. 16, 17. *Brave negro lad.*—Courage is not confined to race or colour. A negro lad of nineteen will be remembered as the hero of the Washington disaster a short time ago. When the floors of the Government offices fell in, burying some hundreds of clerks in the ruins, this brave youth climbed to the top of a lofty telegraph pole which stood near. He drew up a ladder, one end of which he lashed to the pole, and holding the other end to the third-story window of the tottering building, saved the lives of fifteen young men. Certainly faith is not confined to race or colour. Members of Abraham's family are found everywhere. The colour of the skin is no barrier to faith. The inward spirit triumphs over the mere external.

Ver. 18. *Comfort in a cloud.*—" A friend of mine," says Paxton Hood, " told me of a visit he had paid to a poor woman overwhelmed with trouble in her little room, but she was always cheerful ; she knew the Rock. ' Why,' said he, ' Mary, you must have very dark days ; they must overwhelm you with clouds sometimes.' ' Yes,' she answered ; ' but then I often find that there is comfort in a cloud.' ' Comfort in a cloud, Mary ? ' ' Yes,' she said ; ' when I am very low and dark I go to the window, and if I see a heavy cloud I think of those precious words, " A cloud received Him out of their sight," and I look up and see the cloud sure enough, and then I think, " Well, that may be the cloud that hides Him " ; and so you see there is comfort in a cloud.' There was strong faith. She gave glory to God by believing in hope against human appearances, and God rewarded her faith by putting cheerfulness into her soul. A simple faith can do more than sublime philosophy. Against hope Abraham believed in hope."

Ver. 20. *Lord to the fore.*—" The Lord's aye to the fore," said a good Scotchwoman in her day of trial, and by this faith she was supported. God is ever in the forefront of His trusting people. He is still at the helm of human affairs. " The best of all is, God is with us," said John Wesley as he was dying, and by this trust he was supported as he passed within the veil. Yea, by this trust he was supported as he passed from scene to scene in his laborious life of surpassing energy and glorious endeavours for the benefit of his fellow-creatures and for the extension of the Saviour's kingdom.

Ver. 21. *God's promise to Abraham.*—Among the curiosities of the Bank of England may be seen some cinders, the remains of some bank-notes that were burned in the great fire of Chicago. After the fire they were found, and carefully put between boards and brought to the bank. After applying chemical tests, the numbers and values were ascertained, and the Bank of England paid the money value to the owners. If a human promise can be worth so much, how much more so is the promise of God ? Nothing can ever destroy the promise divine. " I will be their God."—*Home Words.*

Ver. 22.—*Imputed righteousness.*—Bishop Asbury being asked his thoughts on imputed righteousness, observed, " Were I disposed to boast, my boasting would be found true. I obtained religion near the age of thirteen. At the age of sixteen I began to preach, and travelled some time in Europe. At twenty-six I left my native land and bid adieu to my weeping parents, and crossed the boisterous ocean to spend the balance of my days in a strange land, partly settled by savages. I have travelled through heat and cold for forty-five years. In thirty years I have crossed the Alleghany Mountains fifty-eight times. I have often slept in the woods without necessary food or raiment. In the Southern States I have waded swamps and led my horse for miles, where I took cold that brought on the diseases which are now preying on my system and must soon terminate in death. But my mind is still the same—that it is through the merits of Christ I am to be saved."

Vers. 24, 25. *The roll-call.*—In a hospital at Scutari during the Crimean war a soldier lay dying ; he had lain there, watched by his nurses for many a long hour, apparently unconscious. On a sudden he rose up in his bed, and with a voice which startled them all —so strong it was—he shouted, " Yes, I am here ! " They laid him back upon his bed exhausted and breathless with the effort, gently soothed him, and asked him what he was doing. " Oh ! " he said, " I heard the roll-call of my regiment after the battle, and I was answering to my name." Jesus Christ was delivered for our offences and raised again for our justification. His resurrection is the pledge of that of all believers. The great roll-call will be given at the final day. The redeemed will pass to the home of endless rest and peace.

CHAPTER V.

CRITICAL NOTES.

Ver. 1.—We have peace, for Christ is our peace. Several manuscripts translate, " Let us have peace," adopted by the R.V. Justification here spoken of as an act already done—*i.e.*, when we laid hold of Christ by faith. Faith is the key of knowledge, and makes us children of God (Clem. Rom.).

Ver. 2.—Implies dignity, firmness to resist, preparation for further walk and work. δόξης τοῦ Θεοῦ—the expression denotes the heavenly existence of God, to share which is the highest good of the creature.

Ver. 4.—Patience equals patient endurance. Not so much experience as proof; affliction is our touchstone.

Ver. 5.—The love of God has been poured forth as in a stream (Wordsworth).

Ver. 6.—ἀσθεν indicates man's necessity, ἀσεβ his unworthiness.

Ver. 7. **Righteous and good.**—That is, the one righteous; the other good, merciful, benevolent.

Ver. 8.—Christ's death a vicarious death, but not necessarily expressed by the preposition here used. Divine love compared with human. The latter infinitely below the former.

Ver. 10. **When we were enemies.**—Indicates relation to God rather than conduct. But Flatt says, " Resisting God's will, and so liable to punishment."

Ver. 11.—The at-one-ment. Article points out only one way of salvation, through faith in Christ.

Ver. 12.—Adam the head of a race whose transgressions lead on to condemnation. Christ the ancestor of a seed whose faith and obedience culminate in eternal life. Rabbis spoke of a double death of the soul and of the body, and thought that but for Adam's sin man would not have died, but only expired, the spirit being dismissed by the kiss of peace. The sin of all men was wrapped up in the one act of Adam's sin, and developed afterwards in individual cases. Adam's descendants not accountable for his sins.

Ver. 13.—The law made sin more manifest. The sin of those who lived between Adam and Moses could not be sin against that law of Moses, which was not promulgated. It must have some other explanation.

Ver. 14.—Cabbalists spoke of Adam as the later or lower Adam, in contrast with the ancient Adam, the Messiah existing before the Creation.

Ver. 15.—Mankind generally included in the Fall. In the Redemption is universal provision, though not universal acceptance.

Ver. 16.—One sin, many sinners; many sins, one Saviour.

Ver. 21.—In ver. 14 death is a monarch, while here sin is the monarch. Death is the sphere where sin shows its power, for "the sting of death is sin." ἐν indicates death as the terminus of sin; εἰς points to life as the end and reward of righteousness. **But where sin abounded, grace did superabound**—*i.e.*, the pardoning mercy of the gospel has triumphed even over the sins of the Jews, which were greatly aggravated by reason of the light they enjoyed (Stuart).

MAIN HOMILETICS OF THE PARAGRAPH.—Verses 1—4.

Happy fruits.—There are luscious fruits which grow on the spiritual tree which God has planted in the wilderness of this world—planted for the benefit of His believing children ; and yet how much of their lives is passed in a state of spiritual leanness. The fruits cannot ripen and fall to the ground in a state of decay, for nothing can be lost in God's material or moral world—lost to us for the time, not lost in the greatness and goodness of the divine purposes. Why should they be lost ? Why should the golden fruit ripen and not refresh our parched natures ? Why should we not go in faith and gather the rich grapes of the spiritual Eschol, and sweeten the bitterness and lessen the feverish heat of our wearisome earth-lives ? What advantage is there in being justified if we do not enjoy peace ? Let us seek to realise the full extent of our Christian privileges. The criminal is acquitted—let him not move through life as if he were afraid of the policeman ; the dead has been brought to life—let him not wear the cerements of the tomb ; the spiritual marriage has been consummated—let the bride deck herself with jewels. The eternal Father has welcomed the returned son—let him wear the best robe, and feast on the rich viands which paternal love has provided. What are the happy fruits of justification? They are:—

I. **Peace.**—This is the fruit in the divine intention and purpose, but too often only partially realised in the human experience, therefore may the apostle exhort, "Let us have peace." May we thus amplify the apostolic injunction. 1. *Let us possess ourselves in peace.* If God be reconciled, why should we live and move as if He were unreconciled? We too often act as if the method of reconciliation had been forced from God, and as if He would relent and take back the offers of pardon and of peace. God relent? It was God's loving heart that moved towards the children of sin and of misery. We lose much of peace by losing sight of the gracious thought that God's love anticipated man's sin, and provided the remedy. Let us have peace by taking large views of the love of God. Let us have peace by fully believing that the method of justification by faith is perfectly answerable to the divine requirements, and is fully harmonious with the divine nature. 2. *Let us develop peace.* We sing, "Peace, perfect peace, in this dark world of sin?" Perhaps the words are idealistic. Perfect peace, in a nature racked, torn asunder, distorted, disfigured, by sin? Perfect peace, where chaos, dark confusion, and discords have dwelt? Perfect peace, where every power and faculty of the nature have been so long working in a contrary direction that they look as if any kind of peace were an impossibility? Happy soul that can by an act of faith enter into perfect peace! But we believe it to be a goal, perhaps never reached till we come to the land of perfect peace. Peace must grow; it can be developed. 3. *Let us value peace.* Let us have peace, not as a possession from which we would gladly part, but as a possession in which we rejoice, and which we hold dearer than material life. Who does not value peace? Let us show our high estimate by making sacrifices for its development. Let us assiduously train and practise the powers and faculties of our natures so that not one sound may be heard out of tune, and all may in glad union set forth the sublime anthem of peace. 4. *Let us move joyfully through life as the children of peace,*—peace the calm mother; joy the pleasant daughter: our joyfulness not of a boisterous character—a peaceful joy—a calm, unruffled happiness.

II. **Gracious boldness.**—Jesus Christ, our elder brother, takes us by the hand and conducts us into the glorious temple of peace, where we stand in the presence of the Holy of Holies, and see it illuminated and glorified with the sweet light of the divine favour. By the sin of the first Adam we are estranged from God. By the mediatorial work of the Second Adam we are brought into a state of friendship with God, and may have holy boldness, constant access into the divine presence. Access to God! How great the thought! How vast the privilege! Sinful men are raised high as the unsinning angels.

> "The sons of ignorance and night
> May dwell in the eternal light,
> Through the eternal Love."

III. **Joyful expectation.**—The believer is one who exercises foresight and forethought. He looks before and behind. He looks behind at his sins, and gratitude rises in his soul, as he sees them cast into the depths of the sea. He stands, a forgiven, a peaceful soul, between the behind and the before. And he looks forward with joyful hope to the glory of God. Glory will consummate and crown what grace has begun. Sublime hope!—the glory of God. Joyful expectation! To behold the glory of the All-glorious is a wonderfully entrancing idea; but, oh! can it be that the inglorious, the base, shall share in that glory?

We shrink from the thought of final extinction when we consider that there may be the sweet prospect of rising to the high abode of the eternal light. Well may the apostle sing, " We rejoice in hope of the glory of God"! Dry logic could not restrain the ardour of his impassioned nature ; and on the wings of rhetoric he rises to taste the outcoming influences of the upper paradise. In hope of the glory of God he trod the pathway of human suffering with heroic endurance. He counted all things but dross. Perils manifold, trials many, tribulations sore, were of no account to a spirit braced and inspired by the hope of the glory of God. Oh for this hope to be a practical force in our prosaic lives ! Oh for this sweet light to pierce and dispel the murky clouds that too oft darken our lives ! Why live in gloom when bright skies stretch ever our heads ? Why dwell in a dungeon when we can escape and walk the glorious terraces whence we may behold the splendid outstretching landscapes of infinite love and glory.

IV. **The sorrow which promotes joy.**—We still hear the sound of the rollers in the early Church, and they rolled out in noble form patience, experience, hope. Sometimes we think that there is no golden grain equal to that which was thrashed out by the process of tribulation which was carried on by persecution. Perhaps another Paul may come, with keen vision, to find out the nobility, the heroism, of suffering souls in modern times. How few of us can say we glory in tribulations ! Well, even the apostle did not say that. He gloried in tribulations as a means to an end ; he welcomed sorrow, not in and of itself, but as the promoter of joy—the joy which hope ever inspires. What a glorious ascending scale—tribulation, patience, experience, hope ! The sorrow of the world works despair and destruction ; the sorrow of the heroic nature works hope and eternal glory. Sorrow has its important mission in the spiritual economies. Heart throbs may be beating out sweetest music. Tears may not be shed in vain. Ah, there will be no more pain, no more tribulations, in heaven ! But may there not be the chastened yet joyful remembrance of the glorious moral work which pain and tribulation have done in time ? The tears of time may become glistening pearls in the eternal crown. There are tears which are like petrifying streams, hardening the nature from which they flow. There are tears which are like the dewdrops collected from the surrounding atmosphere by the flower to its enrichment. The troubles of earth may be the root forces out of which grow the unfading flowers of the better paradise. Certainly we read " tribulation worketh patience ; patience, experience ; and experience, hope." In the vale of sorrow let us gather the seeds of undying joy. Let us constantly enter the divine presence chamber, and in that sacred enclosure try to learn and understand the wide significance of all that happens in us and about us, and as the understanding grows and the sacred light increases we shall more and more rejoice in hope of the glory of God.

Connection between faith and peace—1. If there be one doctrine of more primary importance than another, it is that which relates to the question of our justification before God. Disguise it as he will, there is not a rational man who feels himself on terms of solid confidence with the Being who made and who sustains him. There is not one of them who can look God fully and fearlessly in the face, and say of Him, He is my friend. There is a lurking suspicion about him, in virtue of which the creature shrinks from the Creator, and flies away from the thought of Him, to such perishable vanities as may grant him temporary relief or occupation. Conceive his intercourse with the visible world to be in some way suspended, and the invisible God to draw near by some convincing manifestation, and he would not feel at ease or comfort in His presence. Let the feeling be as deep and inexplicable as it may, still is terror at God the real and the powerful and the constant feeling of nature. There is the consciousness of guilt. In these circumstances a restoration to the divine favour must be a question as big with interest to man as the question of a passage from death unto life. It stands identified with the main object of his existence. If it remain unsettled, all theology is superfluous and but the mockery of a heartless speculation. Let us, in the first place, *explain the meaning of the term "justify"*; in the second place, *show how it is that we are justified by faith*; in the third place, *how it is that by this faith we have peace with God*; and lastly, *point your attention more particularly to Jesus Christ* as the medium of conveyance through which we obtain so inestimable a blessing. We may then conclude with a few such observations as the whole topic is fitted to suggest. To justify a man, in the evangelical sense of the term, we cannot possibly make out a plea grounded on the fact of his own personal innocence; but still a plea is found, in virtue of which justice requires that he should be treated as an innocent person. God not only forbears to treat him as a subject of condemnation, but He treats him as a subject for the positive distribution of His favours. The man from an object of wrath becomes an object of fatherly affection. Let us now, in the second place, endeavour to explain how it is that we are justified by faith. He who is justified is in possession of a discharge from the penalties of a broken law and of a right to the rewards of an honoured and of a fulfilled law. But faith did not work out this discharge: faith barely imports these privileges from the quarter in which they are framed, and thus brings them into contact with the person of the believer. Christ reared the foundation—man leans upon it. Faith, though neither the procuring cause nor the meritorious ground of justification, is indispensable to it; and just as much so as the striking out of a window is to the lighting of an apartment. It is the medium of conveyance through which God hath ordained that all the blessings, purchased and wrought for us by the Saviour of sinners, shall come into contact and appropriation with the sinner's soul. Faith is no faith at all if it embrace not the whole testimony of God. But the benefits annexed to faith are various. There is forgiveness promised to it; there is the plea and the reward of righteousness promised to it; there is strength for holy obedience promised to it But there is not merely a connection between the faith of the sinner and the cessation of God's enmity against him, which is the first sense that we have given to the term of peace; there is also a connection between the faith of the sinner and a sensation of peace, which thereupon enters into the sinner's bosom. He, obtains peace and joy in believing. Such are the truths of the Christian revelation, that, in the single act of looking outwardly upon them, there is a peace which enters into the looker's mind along with his faith. There is a peace in the bare exercise of believing. The truths themselves are fitted to convey peace into the heart at the very moment that they are recognised to be truths.—*Dr. Chalmers.*

Vers. 1, 2. *The believer's blessings.*—Having clearly put before us the great Christian doctrine of justification by faith in Jesus Christ, St. Paul here dwells upon the happy results which follow a hearty reception of it.

I. **A brief but comprehensive view of the blessings secured to the true believer.**—Blessings throughout his whole existence—past, present, future. 1. *The past.* He may look back upon his years gone by and see them stained by many sins, but they are all forgiven. They have been laid upon the Lamb of God (1 Peter ii. 24), atoned for by the all-sufficient sacrifice, blotted out from the divine remembrance. He has peace—peace with God, "the peace of God, which passeth all understanding." 2. *The present.* He may consider his present position and see that, weak as he is in himself, and without anything of his own upon which he can rely, in the covenant of grace he has

135

a present and abiding security. The upholding power of the Father (1 Peter i. 5); the Son's all-prevailing intercession (Rom. viii. 34); the indwelling of the Holy Spirit (Rom. viii. 15); the sure promises of God's word,—all, all testify to the security of the foundation on which he stands. 3. *The future.* He may look forward into the unknown days of his future life—yes, even into the countless ages of eternity, though much is unknown and dark to his mortal eyes. The light of hope shines brightly on his course,—a hope that will never deceive (Rom. v. 5); a hope that is an anchor of the soul sure and steadfast (Heb. vi. 19); a hope that fastens on the heavenly inheritance. He rejoices in the hope of the glory of God.

II. Let us mark well that all these blessings are obtained for us by the Lord Jesus Christ, and secured to us in Him—in Him alone.—To possess them we must believe in Him (John vi. 35, etc.), receive Him (John i. 12), have Him (1 John v. 12), be found in Him (Phil. iii. 9), abide in Him (John xv. 5). If our faith justifies us, it is because it is the hand which lays hold on Jesus, the Lord our righteousness. If we have peace with God, the Lord Jesus Christ Himself is our peace (Eph. ii. 14); if we are standing safe in the covenant of grace, it is by Jesus that we have access into it; if we are rejoicing in hope of the glory of God, it is the same almighty Saviour Himself who is our hope (1 Tim. i. 1).—*Dr. Jacob.*

Justification by faith.—Man stands condemned at the bar of God. Can God be just and yet acquit the guilty? The gospel says, "Yes; man may be acquitted, or justified."

I. **Justification by faith.**—What is it, and how effected? Justification just means getting put right with God; and we can be put right with God only by faith in the work of God's Son for us. It is a gratuitous act. Christ says to the guilty, "You are unable to save yourself, yet your salvation is possible." How? Not by propitiating offended deity or patching up a broken fellowship. Not by works; the law condemns. The ground of acquittal from the condemnation of the law is the imputed righteousness of Christ. It is received by faith, and faith itself is God's gift; hence boasting is excluded. The guilty are acquitted in a way that humbles pride. Self-righteous efforts are of no help, but rather a hindrance. When they cease, the bitterness of death is past, and a new life opens up. The ultimate privileges are many and far-reaching, but the immediate consequence is reconciliation, or—

II. **Peace with God.**—The justified man, having received a new standing before God, feels himself no longer a culprit at the bar. The knowledge that God is at peace with him calms his guilty fears and raises him above the dread of condemnation. 1. *His peace rests on a firm foundation.* Confidence in the finished work of Christ and conscious reconciliation with God. That God is no longer angry is the pledge of forgiven sin, assurance that the danger is past and the soul is in safe keeping. 2. *Peace that satisfies the soul.* There are many refuges of lies, but there is no deception here. Conscience approves. "*My* peace I give unto you," says Christ. How different from the world's peace! "Lord, lift on us the light of Thy countenance, and give us peace"—*Thy* peace. This alone will satisfy the heart, the intellect, and the conscience. 3. *This peace is progressive in its nature.* It deepens and widens as we grow in grace and in the knowledge of God. Not like a mountain tarn, but like a brimming river, at first a tiny brook gathering as it goes, till on the plains it is strong and calm, broad and deep. "Oh that thou hadst hearkened to My commandments! then had thy peace been as a river, and thy righteousness as the waves of the sea." 4. *The peace of the justified is a permanent possession.* Adversity may deprive you of earthly wealth and death of friends, but what comes as the result of union with Christ will outlive time, and pass with us beyond death. Oh for such a blessing as this : " Come unto Me, all ye that labour and are heavy laden, and I will give you rest " !—*D. Merson, B.D.*

Ver. 1. *Justification by faith.*—The doctrine of justification by faith accepted by the Church gives strength and purity. " It was," says a man of learning and good sense, writing of the Reformation, " the growth and expansion of one positive dogma, justification by faith, that broke down and crushed successively the various doctrines of the Romish Church " (Hallam's *History of Literature*). Accepted by any soul, it gives life and peace. Consider : I. Justification ; II. Its instrument—faith ; III. Its result—peace.

I. Justification.—To justify, in Scripture, signifies always to count just or declare righteous. God is justified when He is declared righteous or shown to be just. The justification of God is not the infusion of righteousness into Him, but the manifestation or acknowledgment of His righteousness. The justification of man by God is His counting man as righteous. Rom. viii. 33 contrasts justification with condemnation, not purification : " It is God that justifieth ; who is he that condemneth ? " In all other places the word has the same or a similar meaning (acknowledged by Dr. Newman in his *Lectures on Justification*). 1. Justification includes (1) freedom from guilt, and (2) divine acceptance. Not freedom from guilt alone, for the irrational animals who are incapable of moral good or evil are free from guilt. 2. Justification by the just Judge is always grounded on obedience to law. Justice and judgment are the pillars of God's throne. 3. Justification rests either on the ground of personal obedience or righteousness, or on the ground of the accepted obedience of another in our place. In either case the obedience to law must be absolute and perfect in doing or suffering its penalty. (1) Personal obedience justifies the unfallen angels. It cannot justify sinful men. " By the deeds of the law there shall no flesh be justified in God's sight, for by the law is the knowledge of sin " (Rom. iii. 20). (2) The obedience and suffering of our Lord Jesus Christ, accepted in our place, justifies sinners. No created being had the right to place a substitute for himself before the throne of justice.

II. The instrument of justification—faith.—Faith is trust in Jesus as the Son of God and Saviour of the world.

II. The result—peace with God.—Peace with man desirable, more so peace with God. 1. State before justification is either one of indifference through the sleep of a benumbed conscience, or of unhappiness through an unsatisfied heart and diseased conscience. 2. Reconciliation with God, when the law is seen to be honoured, justice satisfied, and God " just and the justifier of him which believeth in Jesus," satisfies conscience, removes the dread of vengeance, and awakens loving, happy gratitude. 3. Lasting peace is to be found in no other way. Gratuitous pardon, without atonement, not able to give peace. To this ultimate question, in which conscience in full action impels sinners like Judas Iscariot to seek punishment even as a relief and " antedating their own misery, seek for that they would loathe to find," nothing but pardon through satisfaction of justice can give relief. Endeavours, tears, sorrows, are vain. Nothing can satisfy the sense of justice in that state of mind to which every man's conscience is aiming but trust in the justice-satisfying Saviour. That gives peace and joy.

" My heart for gladness springs,
        It cannot more be sad ;
For every joy it laughs and sings,
        Sees nought but sunshine glad.
    The sun that glads mine eyes
    Is Christ the Lord I love ;
I sing for joy of that which lies
    Stored up for me above."

J. C. J.

The grace, the joy, and the glory.

I. **The grace.**—It is here called "*this* grace,"—a well-known, most suitable, and sufficient grace, or *free love*; the free love of Father, Son, and Holy Ghost. This is "the true grace of God"; free love in the heart of God to the ungodly, to the unloving and unlovable.

II. **The access, or introduction.**—We do not create or awaken this free love by any goodness or qualification of our own. It exists independent of these. Nor did Christ, by His coming and death, create that love. This love existed before; it was this that sent Christ. "God so loved the world, that He gave His only begotten Son." Yet, without Christ, this love could never have reached us. He brings it to us, and us to it. He gives access and entrance and introduction; for the word implies all these, and is used elsewhere to signify the bringing or introducing one person to another (Luke ix. 41; Acts xvi. 20); and is employed not simply in reference to the grace of God, but to God Himself (1 Peter iii. 18; Eph. ii. 18, iii. 12). Our outward or objective introducer and introduction is Christ Himself; our inward or subjective introduction and introducer is faith.

III. **The standing, or abiding.**—In this grace, or free love, we have stood since we were introduced into it; and in it we are standing, and shall stand. "We stand in it!" This is a believing man's true position. This free love is to him—1. Abiding peace; 2. Abiding strength; 3. Abiding security. This free love is to him—1. Sunshine; 2. Rain; 3. Food; 4. Water; 5. Medicine; 6. Wine. At this well he stands and drinks, in this sun he basks, to this storehouse he comes for everything. Have we used this free love as we ought? Are we using it constantly? O free love of God, what a fountain of life and strength thou art to the weary, helpless sinner!

IV. **The rejoicing.**—This grace is not merely stability for us, but joy and hope and glory. Standing in this grace, we are filled with joy. This joy comes not merely from the past and present, but from the future; not merely from the knowledge that we are beloved of God, but from the knowledge of what that love is to do for us hereafter. We rejoice because our future is filled with hope —the hope of the glory of God. Hence the apostle's prayer, "The God of (the) hope fill you with all joy and peace in believing."

Take these lessons: 1. *Be strong in the grace that is in Christ Jesus.* 2. *Rejoice in the Lord.* 3. *Abound in hope.* 4. *Realise the glory.* Keep the eye steadfastly fixed upon it, till its brightness fills our whole being.—*H. Bonar.*

SUGGESTIVE COMMENTS ON VERSES 1—4.

The state of grace.—What is this state? and what is this standing? The state is a state of *grace*, and means the privileged condition in which all Christians are found, though they were by nature the children of wrath. It is expressed by our apostle in the preceding words: "Being justified by faith, we have peace with God, through our Lord Jesus Christ; by whom also we have access by faith into *this* grace." It may well be called "this grace," for it only flows from, and only proclaims, the exceeding riches of His grace in His kindness towards us, by Christ Jesus. But we may be recon-ciled to one another so as to be forgiven, and not be admitted into the intimacies of friendship. After Absalom was, through the intercession of Joab, allowed to return to Jerusalem, two years elapsed before he was allowed to see the king's face. But God favours us with the most familiar intercourse and communion. We come boldly to the throne of grace. In everything, by prayer and supplication, we make known our requests. We walk with God; He honours us with His confidence, and trusts us with His secrets. This grace means also approbation and complacency. He takes pleasure in them that fear Him ; He rests in his love; He joys over them with singing ; they are His children, His bride, His jewels, His glory. Hence follows sympathy and compassion. What is done to them He resents as a personal injury ; for he that toucheth them toucheth the apple of His eye. In all their affliction He is afflicted ; though He corrects them, it is for their profit. In *this* grace they *stand.* Standing here intends " firmness," " stability," " permanence." It is sometimes opposed to " condemnation " : " If Thou, Lord, shouldest mark iniquity, O Lord, who shall *stand?* " Sometimes it is also opposed to " defeat." " Take to you the whole armour of God, that ye may *stand* in the evil day ; and having done all, may *stand."* And of this they may be assured ; for whatever disproportion there is between them and their enemies, the *worm* Jacob shall thresh the *mountains.* Some warriors have barely overcome—such another victory as they gained would have almost ruined them ; but a Christian, having vanquished all his adversaries, stands with his feet on their necks, and is ready to engage as many more. " Yea, in all these things we are more than conquerors through Him that loved us." The more privileged any condition is, the more anxieties does it awaken. It is easy, therefore, to imagine what a Christian must feel if he apprehends any uncertainty as to the state he is in. But that state is as safe as it is blessed.—*W. Jay.*

The benefit of tribulation. — There are two benefits specified in this verse. The first, our present introduction into a state of favour and free access to God ; and the second, the joyful " hope of the glory of God "—that is, the glory of which God is the author. The word " glory " is often used in reference to future blessedness, to show that the happiness to be enjoyed hereafter is connected with the exaltation of all our powers and of our sphere of activity. " And not only so, but we glory in tribulations also." Not only

have we this introduction into the divine favour and this hope of future glory " but we glory in tribulations also." Since our relation to God is changed, the relation of all things to us is changed. Afflictions, which before were the expressions of God's displeasure, are now the benevolent manifestations of His love. And instead of being inconsistent with our filial relation to Him, they serve to prove that He regards us as His children. Tribulations, therefore, although for the present they are not joyous but grievous, become to the believer matter of joy and thankfulness. The way in which afflictions become thus useful, and consequently the ground of rejoicing, the apostle immediately explains. They give occasion for the exercise of the Christian graces, and these from their nature produce hope, which is sustained and authenticated by the witness of the Holy Spirit. " Tribulation worketh patience." The word rendered " patience " signifies also " constancy," " perseverance." Tribulation gives occasion to exercise and manifest a patient and persevering adherence to truth and duty under trials. " And patience, experience ; and experience, hope." The word translated " experience " means properly : 1. " Trial " or " experiment." " Great trial of affliction " (2 Cor. viii. 2)—that is, trial made by application. 2. It means the result of such trial, " evidence," " experience." 3. By another remove, " that which has been tested " and " approved." As one or the other of these significations is adopted, the clause is variously interpreted. It may mean, " The endurance of afflictions leads to the trying or testing of one's own heart " ; or, " it occasions the experience of the divine goodness, or of gracious exercises " ; or, " it produces a state of mind which is the object of approbation " ; or, " it produces evidence, namely, of a gracious state." This last seems most consistent with Paul's use of the word. See 2 Cor. ii. 9, " That I might know the proof [evidence] of you, whether ye be obedient," etc. ;

Phil. ii. 2, "Ye know the proof of him," etc. This sense suits the context also: "Tribulation calls forth the exercise of patience; and the exercise of this patience or constancy affords evidence of our being in favour of God, and therefore produces hope."

"*Let us have peace*" *the proper rendering.*—"Let us have peace" was read probably by Tertullian, and is found in all, or very nearly all, the Latin manuscripts which were used throughout the Western Church. The same reading is repeatedly quoted and commented upon by Origen and by Chrysostom, who lived at Antioch and Constantinople A.D. 347—407. Neither of these writers seems to have known the other reading. The same reading is found in all existing Greek manuscripts earlier than the ninth century, and in some of the best cursives; also in the oldest Syriac Version used in the far East, and in the three other oldest versions. The earliest trace of the reading "we have peace" is found in the Sinai manuscript, in a correction of the other reading made perhaps in the fourth century. In the Vatican manuscript a similar correction was made, perhaps in the sixth century. Three of the later uncials and a majority of the cursive Greek manuscript give this reading. It is found in the existing copies of the writings of three fathers of the fourth and fifth centuries. But the point in question does not affect their arguments; and as the writings exist only in a few manuscripts written after this reading had become common, we cannot be sure that it was actually adopted by these fathers. No early version has it except the later Syriac, which exists here, I believe, only in one copy. The only difficulty is that Paul assumes in vers. 2, 9, 10, that his readers already stand in the favour of God, and are now justified and reconciled. To this difficulty a key is found in iv. 24, "Us to whom it will be reckoned." Throughout this epistle Paul writes from an ideal and rapidly changing

standpoint. He identifies himself with that which he describes. In ii. 1, iii. 9, he leaves out of sight those saved from sin by Christ, and speaks as though all men were still actually committing sin, and therefore at war with God. He writes as though he had never heard of the gospel. In iii. 21 we hear the proclamation of peace. In chap. iv. he discusses the terms of peace. As he reads the old record of Abraham's faith and justification, he declares that it was written to confirm beforehand the good news to be afterwards brought by Christ. And as he stands by the author of Genesis he looks forward to the day when faith "will be reckoned" for righteousness to all who believe the gospel. A prospect of peace with God opens before him. While he contemplates it the gospel day dawns upon him. In this verse he calls us to wake up to the brightness of its rising. What he bids us do he realises to be actually taking place in himself and his readers. In the next verse the sun has risen, and we stand in the sunshine of God's favour. As a witness that this change of standpoint is in full accord with the genius of Hebrew thought, I may quote Driver, *Hebrew Tenses*, p. 6: "One such peculiarity is the singular ease and rapidity with which a writer *changes his standpoint*—at one moment speaking of a scene as though still in the remote future, at another moment describing it as though present to his gaze." That the very able commentators Meyer and Godet prefer the utterly unsupported reading, "We have peace," rather than attempt to expound the common rendering of the reading adopted by all recent critical editors, and the evident dissatisfaction of Fritysche and Alford with their own expositions, embolden me to suggest the rendering and exposition given above. The objection that an exhortation would be out of place in a calm exposition of doctrine vanishes when we notice that in this verse Paul passes from abstract and general doctrine to actual and individual spiritual life. He marks the transition by urging his readers to join him in claiming the blessing whose glorious results he is about to unfold. —*Beet.*

Different views of the opening verses. —" The apostle begins to demonstrate what he has affirmed of justification by *its effects.*" Tholuck entitles this passage " the beneficent pathologico-religious influence of this means of salvation." Olshausen, " of the fruits of faith," adding at the same time that the apostle could of course only sketch these consequences of faith here, but that he will develop them afterwards. Philippi, " the beneficent consequences of justification." Reuss says, " the piece describes the effect of justification on the man who is its object." Lange and Schaff, " the fruit of justification." Hodge, " the consequences of justification : (1) faith, (2) free access to God, (3) our afflictions auxiliary to hope, (4) the certainty of final salvation." Renan says, " the fruit of justification is peace with God, hope, and consequently patience." Hofmann sums up thus : " Let us enter into this relation of peace with God, in which we have the hope of glory, consolation in trials, love to God, and the certainty of deliverance from final wrath." Bossuet, " the happy fruits of justification by faith." Meyer better, " Paul now expounds *the blessed certainty of salvation for the present and future.*" Holsten has some expressions which approach this point of view. Schott entitles it, " the certainty of the believer's preservation in salvation, and of the final consummation of this salvation."—*Godet.*

Fruits of justification stated in a popular manner. — But perhaps we may obtain a simpler view of the meaning by considering the expression before us merely as the general conclusion from the whole argument as stated in the preceding part of the epistle. The apostle has proved that justification in the day of judgment can be obtained only by " the righteousness of faith " ; and he has proved

further " that justification in the present life is freely bestowed on faith alone." And in the passage before us he states, in a general and popular manner, the result of the whole reasoning,—knowing that, in order to obtain justification, we are not required to fulfil any law, moral or ceremonial, but that God of His own free grace bestows it on us, through Christ, in consideration of our faith, we have peace with God. This view corresponds with the whole preceding reasonings, and forms their proper conclusion. It is liable to none of the difficulties which are implied in other explanations, and therefore it may perhaps be thought to deserve the preference. It is of importance to bear in mind the different senses in which the word " justification " is used ; for the principle on which it depends in one of its senses is not that on which it depends in another. When it denotes privileges merely external, it requires only a confession of faith in Christ ; when it denotes the forgiveness of sin on earth and accounting us as righteous, its principle is a true and saving faith ; but when it denotes the sentence of the sovereign Judge, accounting us as righteous in the day of judgment, it depends on faith producing the fruits of righteousness.—*Ritchie.*

Encouragement to believers.—To comfort the Roman brethren under the evils which the profession of the gospel brought upon them, the apostle in the beginning of this chapter enumerated the privileges which belong to believers in general. And from his account it appears that the privileges of Abraham's seed by faith are far greater than the privileges which belonged to his seed by natural descent, and which are described in Rom. ii. 17-20. The first privilege of the spiritual seed is— That being justified by faith they have peace with God through Jesus Christ. This, to the Gentiles, must have appeared an unspeakable blessing, in regard that they had been taught by the Jews to consider themselves as

141

"children of wrath" and "enemies" of God. Their second privilege is—By the command of Christ they are admitted through faith into the covenant made with Abraham and into the Christian Church. Thirdly, they boast in the hope of beholding the glory of God in heaven—a privilege far superior to that of beholding the glory of God in the tabernacle and in the temple on earth, of which the natural seed boasted, for it is the hope of living eternally with God in heaven. Their fourth privilege is—They boast in afflictions, especially those which befall them for the name of Christ, because afflictions improve their graces and render their hope of eternal life sure. But many, even of the believing Jews, denied that the Gentiles had any reason to hope for eternal life while they did not obey Moses. Wherefore, to show that they are heirs of that and of all the blessings promised in the covenant to the seed of Abraham by faith equally with the Jews, the apostle appealed to God's shedding down the Holy Ghost upon them, even as on the Jews, and to Christ's dying for them in their ungodly state, and told them, since they were already "justified" (that is, "delivered from their heathenish ignorance and wickedness") and "reconciled" (that is, "put into a state of salvation by the blood of Christ"), they might well expect to be "saved" in due time from wrath by His life in the human nature, since in that nature He exercises the offices of Lord and Judge of the world for their benefit. The *last* privilege belonging to the spiritual seed mentioned by the apostle is, that being reconciled they can boast in the true God as their God equally with the natural seed, whose relation to God was established by the law of Moses only. And this privilege he told them they had obtained like all the rest—through Jesus Christ, by whom they had received "the reconciliation." "We even boast of afflictions." The apostle mentions "afflictions" as "matter of boasting to the spiritual seed, because their virtues were improved by afflictions." This boasting, therefore, was much better founded than the boasting of the natural seed, who, by applying the promises of national prosperity and the threatenings of national adversity contained in the law to individuals, had taught themselves to consider prosperity as a mark of the favour of God, and affliction as a token of His displeasure. A remarkable instance of rejoicing in afflictions we have in Acts v. 41: "They departed from the face of the council, rejoicing that they were counted worthy to suffer shame for His name." "Knowing that affliction worketh out patience." This effect affliction produceth by affording to the afflicted an opportunity of exercising patience, and by suggesting considerations which naturally lead the mind to that virtue.—*Macknight.*

MAIN HOMILETICS OF THE PARAGRAPH.—*Verse* 5.

A hope without shame.—The Christian never finds this world to be his rest. But he has a hope full of immortality. This enlightens his darkness and alleviates his sorrow. Like a helmet, it guards in the day of battle; like an anchor, it secures in the storms of adversity; like a pleasing companion, it travels with him through all the tediousness of the world, and reminds him of the rest that remains for the people of God. Let us consider the excellency and the evidence of this hope. Let us I. Show how it preserves from shame; and II. Ascertain its connection with the love of God.

I. **We may take three views of this hope,** and oppose it to the hope of the worldling, of the Pharisee, and of the antinomian. Hope causes shame by the insufficiency of its object—and this is the hope of the worldling; by the weakness of its foundation—and this is the hope of the Pharisee; by the falseness of its warrant—and this is the hope of the antinomian. The hope of the Christian has the noblest object, the surest foundation, the clearest warrant; and thus it maketh not ashamed. 1. *Hope may cause shame by the insufficiency of its object.* Ofttimes men of the world never reach the mark; and when they do, they are disappointed. What they gain does not indemnify for the sacrifices they have made.

> " In vain we seek a heaven below the sky :
> The world has false but flattering charms ;
> Its distant joys show big in our esteem,
> But lessen still as they draw near the eye ;
> In our embrace the visions die ;
> And when we grasp the airy forms,
> We lose the pleasing dream."

Look forward and ask, What does the worldling think as he lays down all his honours, all his riches, on this side of the grave? What does Alexander now think of his bloody trophies? What does Herod now think of killing James and condemning Peter because "it pleased the people"? What does Judas think of his thirty pieces of silver? The crowned votaries of the world seem to be happy, and are envied; but it is only by the foolish and ignorant who know them not. Sometimes they say, We are not happy, and it is not in the power of these things to satisfy our desires. On this dark ground we bring forward the Christian to advantage. The object of his hope is the greatest good a creature can possess. When we propose this hope we exclude every evil we feel or fear. Think of "the house not made with hands," etc., and the "innumerable company of angels" as the objects of his hope—the blessed hope of being like Christ and dwelling with Him evermore. The Christian need not shrink from a comparison with philosophers, princes, heroes. He leads a sublime life, and takes a grander aim. If shame could enter heaven, he would be ashamed to think that the objects of this hope engrossed so little of his attention. 2. *Hope may cause shame by the weakness of its foundation.* The Pharisee places dependence on his own works or his own worthiness. He derives his encouragement from negative qualities, from comparison of himself with others, from the number of his performances. Parable of the Pharisee. If his works were spiritual and holy, they need not afford a ground of dependence, being only a part of the building, and not the foundation. They may furnish evidence, but cannot give a title. The indulgence of such a hope is offensive to God. The man who seeks salvation by the works of the law, and not by faith of Jesus Christ, reflects upon God's wisdom as having been employed in a needless trifle. The Pharisee frustrates the grace of God and makes Jesus Christ to be dead in vain. Thus the Pharisee's hope will be found like a spider's web, curiously wrought, but easily destroyed. The basis being too weak, the superstructure falls and crushes the offender. The humbled sinner asks, How shall a man be just before God? The Bible answers, "The Son of man is come to seek and to save that which was lost." "He is the end of the law of righteousness to every one that believeth." This attracts. He says, Christ is the door, by Him I will enter; Christ is the foundation, on this I will build : I desire no other. This hope is as firm as the truth of God and the all-sufficiency of the Saviour can make it. See the Christian advancing to the throne of God. "Who is he that condemneth? It is Christ that died." The Christian is marked with the blood of sprinkling. 3. *Hope may cause shame by the falseness of its warrant.* Any hope which does not purify is false. Every expectation of heaven which those entertain who are leading immoral lives, whatever be their knowledge or their creed, is a mere fancy. A man, with all his ignorance, may as well persuade himself that he is the greatest philosopher; or, with all his indigence, may as rationally conclude that he is possessed of all the wealth of the Indies, as a man may imagine that he is on the way to heaven while he is a stranger to "newness of life"; for "without holiness no man shall see the Lord." Indeed, such a man, if he were in heaven, would not be in a beatific state. What warrant have you that heaven is your home? What reason are you able to give of the hope that is in you? The only satisfactory one is that given by the apostle. Therefore consider:—

II. **"Because the love of God is shed abroad in our hearts by the Holy Ghost, which is given unto us."**—1. *This love is the proof of the divine regard, for the affection is mutual.* "We love Him because He first loved us." And what can we desire more than to know that we are beloved of God? 2. *This love marks the characters for whom this happiness is reserved.* Who are authorised to claim the promise of eternal life? Those who seek to please and serve God. "We know that all things work together for good to them that love God." 3. *This love qualifies for the glory which shall be revealed.* The happiness of the future state is derived from the presence of God. What, then, can prepare for it but the love of God? Love must make us delight in each other's company. By loving God we are prepared for a happiness which is found only in Him. 4. *This love is the foretaste of future happiness.* We take the likeness of the excellency we contemplate, and are exalted into the perfection we adore. If our love be fixed on God, we shall become divine and heavenly. Oh the comforts of this love! They are heaven come down to earth. Heaven is the sphere of love. The heaven of love must be in us before we are in heaven. We attain the full assurance of hope neither by dreams, nor visions, nor sudden suggestions, nor by an inexplicable consciousness, but by keeping ourselves in the love of God, and abounding therein more and more.—*W. Jay.*

SUGGESTIVE COMMENTS ON VERSE 5.

"*And hope maketh not ashamed.*"— The hope which true believers entertain, founded on the very nature of pious exercises, shall never disappoint them (Psalm xxii. 5). The ground of this assurance, however, is not the strength of our purpose or confidence in our goodness, but the love of God. The latter clause of the verse assigns the reason why the Christian's hope shall not be found delusive: it is because "the love of God is shed abroad in our hearts by the Holy Ghost which is given unto us." The love of God is His love to us, and not ours to Him, as appears from the following verses, in which the apostle illustrates the greatness and freeness of this love by a reference to the unworthiness of its objects. To "shed abroad" is to communicate abundantly, and hence to evince clearly (Acts ii. 17, x. 45; Titus iii. 6). This manifestation of divine love is not any external revelation of it in the works of providence, or even in re-

demption, but it is "in our hearts." And this inward persuasion that we are the objects of the love of God is not the mere result of the examination of evidence, nor is it a vain illusion, but it is produced by the Holy Ghost: "The Spirit itself beareth witness with our spirit, that we are the children of God" (Rom. viii. 16; 2 Cor. i. 21, 22; Eph. i. 13, 14). As, however, the Spirit never contradicts Himself, He never bears witness that "the children of the devil" are the children of God— that is, that the unholy, the disobedient, the proud, or the malicious are the objects of the divine favour. Any reference, therefore, by the immoral to the witness of the Spirit in their favour must be vain and delusive.—*Hodge.*

God's love in the heart.—These words stand at the end of a list of blessings which come to the Christian simply by his faith. See context, vers. 1-5. "The love of God" spoken of in the

text is God's love to us, not our love to
God. In chap. viii. 39 it is called "the
love of God in Jesus Christ." Similarly
is it described in the context (vers. 6-8).
This love the text declares is "shed
abroad" in the believer's heart "by
the Holy Ghost which is given unto"
him. Inquire how or in what particu-
lars this is so.

I. **Because the Holy Ghost is given
to believers on the exercise of their
faith to work this work within them.**
—For Christ, by His atoning work,
procured the Holy Spirit for men.

II. **It is the work of the Holy Ghost
thus given to open to us the love of
God.**—Nothing but the Holy Ghost
can disclose to us the love of God at
the first. Nothing else does. Hence
so many read and hear of the love of
God, and yet do not apprehend it.
But the Holy Spirit coming to the
believer as described, "takes of the
things of Christ," and therein shows
to him the love of the Father (see
John xvi. 13, 14). The Holy Spirit
shows thus the *wonderfulness*, the
extent, heights, depths, lengths, breadths,
of the love of God in Christ, and its *unchangeableness* (see context, vers. 6-8,
and chap. viii. 35-39).

III. **The Holy Ghost thus given
carries the love of God beyond our
mere intellect into our inmost nature.**
—We are more than intellect. In our
best nature we are "heart." To this
the Holy Spirit can penetrate—no
other power like it—and can pervade
and fill and possess the whole with
the wonderful infinite love of God in
Christ. Every faculty and power of
holy emotion in the soul can thus be

moved and stirred, and fresh faculty
and power of holy emotion can thus
be given. Thus the love of God is
"shed abroad" or poureth forth "in
our hearts." So oil poured into a
vessel, whatever the character of the
vessel, finds its way into every part,
and even permeates through the vessel
itself. So incense shed forth in a room
fills every part of it with its fragrance,
which often extends beyond. So the
breath we breathe from the fresh
morning air penetrates in its effects to
our very flesh and blood and bones, and
is seen in the glow of our health, in
the lightness of our step, and in the
flash and brightness of the eye. Do
we know the love of God? and is it
"shed abroad in our hearts"? If so,
then *to what extent* do we know it?—
John Bennett.

Hope as a consoler.—Hope is the
sweetest friend that ever kept a distressed soul company; it beguiles the
tediousness of the way, all the miseries
of our pilgrimage.

" Jam mala finissem letho ; sed credula vitam
   Spes fovet, et melius cras fore semper ait."

Therefore, *Dum spiro spero*, said the
heathen; but *Dum exspiro spero*, says
the Christian. The one, Whilst I live
I hope; the other also, When I die I
hope. So Job, "I will hope in Thee,
though Thou killest me." It tells the
soul such sweet stories of the succeeding
joys; what comforts there be in heaven;
what peace, what joy, what triumphs,
marriage songs, and hallelujahs there
are in that country whither she is
travelling, that she goes merrily away
with her present burden.—*Adams.*

MAIN HOMILETICS OF THE PARAGRAPH.—*Verse* 6.

The fourfold aspect of Christ's work.—Death is always a solemn event,
and casts its dark shadows over the spirit. A silent dread holds the soul in
check when one enters the chamber where the good man meets his fate. The
solemn importance of all deaths is surpassed by the solemn importance of the
death of the Son of God. When Jesus died the earth was clothed in darkness
and the heavens in mourning stood.

" He dies! the Friend of sinners dies ;
   Lo! Salem's daughters weep around ;
   A solemn darkness veils the skies,
   A sudden trembling shakes the ground."

It must have been an awe-inspiring event, for we read, "Now when the centurion saw what was done, he glorified God, saying, Certainly this was a righteous man. And all the people that came together to that sight, beholding the things which were done, smote their breasts and mourned." The death of Christ opens up a large view of divine purposes. It was the climax of the Saviour's earthly mission, and this was the culminating crisis of eternal counsels and of time's preceding movements. And this sixth verse appears to open up a fourfold aspect of the Saviour's work and mission.

I. Out of the powerless comes power.—From the weak and powerless stock of humanity came Jesus, travailing in the greatness of His strength, mighty to save. The first Adam went from strength to weakness; the Second Adam went from the weakness of humanity to the might of saving grace. How was this? It was because divine strength incarnated itself in human weakness. When we were without strength, unable either to serve God aright or to save ourselves, Jesus Christ appeared to our rescue and our salvation. From Adam to Christ was a descending scale; from Christ to the close of time shall be an ascending scale. If men are to be developed out of their weakness and into noble creatures, it must be along the Christ line. The true and only satisfactory evolutionary force of humanity's upward rising is the Christ of gospel history. Christ by His death inspired healing strength into a race weakened by moral sickness.

II. Into the darkness comes light.—In due time, in the God-appointed time, in the world's needy time, when its moral darkness was dense and thick, the Sun of righteousness arose with healing in His wings. Men of light and of sweetness had been allowed plenty of scope. Philosophy and culture had no reason to complain of overhaste in the divine interposition. All had tried, and failure was the result. Light merged into darkness; sweetness became bitterness. The culture of the Greeks was no bulwark against the inroads of moral corruption. The power of the Romans could not withstand the conquering and desolating force of moral evil. Few were the stars that glimmered in the midnight sky. Are our modern men of light and sweetness mightier than the Platos and Senecas of the past? Into the darkness the light shone, and no wonder that a darkness so dense could not comprehend the light. But soon it began to feel the benign influence, and the foul forms of darkness cowered and fled swiftly away as the divine light increased.

III. Out of death comes life.—The law of nature and the law of grace. The seed dies. The golden harvest waves over the plain. Life springs out of death throughout all God's world. Calvary is the epitome of the universe, with this difference—that from Calvary's death scene there came spiritual life. All life promoted by Christ's death. This is to be judged by its tendency and purpose. This is to promote and preserve : 1. *New physical life,* and this should be more largely realised in the future than in the past. Modern science feels the impulse of the beneficent influence of Christianity, and modern science is making towards the prolongation of human existence. Modern science has worked to the incentive of deadly instruments of war, but Christianity shall work till no gunboats shall sail on earth's broad rivers and seas. 2. *Intellectual life.* Since Christ's death there has been a general increase of intellectual life, and this has been specially noticeable in countries where a pure Christianity has prevailed. There have been dark ages, but out of the darkness arose greater light—a backward flow, but the ocean of intellectual life has been moving forward, and the gracious ozone has benefited mankind. 3. *Spiritual life.* This has been the special outcome of Christ's death. Science and philosophy can scarcely be said to have attempted the enterprise. The pleasures of art and the charms of music may produce spasmodic resemblances, but only the death of Christ can generate the mysterious and blessed force we call spiritual life. Out of Christ's death has come, and is coming, the life of the redeemed—multitudinous life from this one Man's death. Will the vast plains of a renovated world be sufficiently ample to receive that great multitude who enjoy spiritual life? God's spacious heavens with their many mansions must be provided. Death shall die. Tombs shall cease. Life must be finally victorious. The death of Christ shall be universally triumphant, for out of it spiritual life shall everywhere flourish, and its pulsations will make the universe throb with joy unspeakable.

IV. **Out of and into the impious comes holiness.**—"If any man be in Christ, he is a new creation : old things have passed away; behold, all things have become new." We are in Christ as we are crucified with Him. In His death we share by faith, and through it we become new creations. Righteousness is both imputed and imparted to the believer. Opposing men may talk as they please, but it is a certain fact that the Christian religion, both in its true and false forms, has produced a purer morality, a higher tone of life, than any other religious system the world has seen. Notwithstanding all drawbacks, our England to-day is better and nobler than ever. Is not crime diminishing? Is not education spreading? Is there not consideration for the poor, the outcast, for the sick, and even for animals, which has never been before witnessed, and which is the glory of our times? The awful loss of the *Victoria* in Mediterranean waters has this compensation—that it teaches the spirit of chivalry is not dead. Let infidelity and agnosticism roll back the sweet waters of Christianity, and we shall soon have to weep and lament over a country where dire desolation would sweep with destructive force. Christ's death begins in darkness and brightens out into glorious light. Darkness covers the earth when He dies. Light irradiates the earth when by His death He conquers death. Angels in white are sitting on earth's tombs, and they are changed into palaces of beauty and of delights. Spiritual life abounds. No more need the cypress tree be planted. Angelic rapture was increased when it was seen that out of Christ's death spiritual life would arise. Fresh anthems of praise rolled along the golden streets. Louder notes of thanksgiving rose up to the splendid vaults of heaven's many mansions. Christ died for the ungodly, and angels then looked to this world and saw it lit up with the glow of divine love and blessedness; they saw its deserts rejoice and blossom as the rose, and its wildernesses made exceeding glad. Christ died for the ungodly, and angels saw dead men come forth from their many tombs, cast on one side the graveclothes, and assume the garments of the living and the blessed. Angels and good men have most splendid expectations. Christ died for the ungodly. Blessed thought! None need be excluded. Christ by His death delivers mankind from the power and thraldom of sin. Let us evermore rejoice in this fact—that "when we were without strength, in due time Christ died for the ungodly."

SUGGESTIVE COMMENTS ON VERSE 6.

The certainty of the believer's final redemption.—There is nothing so great as to be entirely independent, nothing so small as not to be of some service. The sweetest promises of God are ours in times of sadness. These Christians at Rome stood in need of encouragement to continue steadfast in their devotedness to the Saviour. It was natural for them to give way to doubts, and almost to think they could never be expected to reach heaven at last, much less to become " more than conquerors," when they gazed upon the worldly pomp of their persecutors and remembered the power with which they seemed to be invested. But the apostle bids them remember what God had already done for them. " For when we were without strength, . . . much more then being justified," etc. And the apostle establishes this point by means of two reasons :—

I. The great love which God has already bestowed on man.—It is interesting to observe how the apostle illustrates this. He refers : 1. *To the unworthiness of man as the object of it.* In all positions he appears utterly undeserving of the benign influence of God. (1) *"Without strength."* In this expression the apostle is probably accommodating himself to the natural disposition of the Romans. Their highest notion of goodness, as the word "virtue" indicates, was power or strength. Hence the apostle represents the gospel to these people as "the power of God." Nothing was so detestable in their eyes as weakness. And what a weak, helpless man was in the estimation of the Romans, that man, universal man, was in the sight of God—"without strength." (2) *"Ungodly."* This designation presents man in another aspect. True, man in every age had been searching after God; but if the virtue of any act or desire lies in the motive which prompts it, then man's quest in search of God was not pure and right. Man's character as presented by the word "ungodly" shows him to be unworthy of the divine complacency. (3) *"Sinner."* This presents man in another aspect. When God is banished from the thought as suggested by the word "ungodly," His place is usurped by unworthy rivals. The higher principles of the soul are made subordinate to the lower. (4) *"Enemy."* With this word the apostle reaches the climax of his reasoning. Man's enmity to God lies at the root of all his wickedness, and in

this man is a sad exception to everything else which God has made. Everything else in nature yields implicit obedience to God. But man disobeys his Maker. The very power which was given him to hate sin is so perverted that it is used against God Himself. 2. *The greatness of God's love to man is shown also by the sacrifice which He made to redeem him.* "Christ died for the ungodly." With reverence we would say that to redeem man was not easy even to God. As one great author remarks, "This [sin] is great in the sight of God. The whole creation is counted as but a very little thing, but the evil of sin is great. It required an infinite sacrifice to remove the curse connected with it." "While we were yet sinners Christ died for us." Oh, wondrous love !

II. The certainty of the believer's final redemption is argued also from what Christ's life in heaven is doing contrasted with what His death has done.—However important we may regard the death of Christ, we must not consider his life—we mean His life in heaven — of secondary moment. Apart from this life His death would not avail us. But the apostle asserts that the death of Christ affected our reconciliation to God. This mighty change was wrought by the death of Christ. And shall we doubt the power of His life ? Besides, the nature of Christ's work in heaven is a pledge for the final safety of the believer. Christ's intercession bears the same relation to His death as Providence does to creation. God created, and now sustains ; Christ died, and now intercedes. — *Hugh Hughes.*

MAIN HOMILETICS OF THE PARAGRAPH.—Verses 7, 8.

Incomparable love.—Of one of the daughters of our Queen it was said that she shed sunshine wherever she went. Divine love sheds sunshine in its passage through this cold world. It was thought and said that love incarnate would at once command the admiration of mankind. Divine love was incarnated, and the incarnation was treated with contempt. Divine love has been conspicuously set forth, and yet how many are blind to its excellence ! Strange word, "commendeth." We should as soon expect that the flowers would have need to commend their beauty, the birds their songs, the pearls their chastened lustre, the sun his brightness, the moon her clearness, the stars their brilliance, as God to commend His love. The word means "gives proof of," "establishes" His love; and yet how suitable the other word when we think how slow men are to appreciate the incomparable love of God! He makes His love glorious above all human love—above and beyond our furthest reach and highest conception of love. The love of God is incomparable:—

I. **On account of the greatness of the divine nature.**—Love often stretches out towards something higher than itself. Love finds, or thinks it finds, the complement of its nature in the excellence of the person loved. When we love beneath us, it is because we think there is below us a pearl of excellence by which we should be enriched. Love stretches out its tendrils to clasp the tree which has some kind of fruit which we deem needful to our welfare. Love aspires. Whereunto shall the love of God aspire? How shall the infinitely great stretch itself out to something higher and nobler and vaster? Above God there is none, and He alone is great. Below God is none who possesses any greatness which cannot be found in the divine being. Incomparable love, because not drawn out by any superior worth.

II. **On account of the self-sufficiency of the divine nature.**—How selfish at the best is human love! How often our love for others is but another aspect of self-love! Surely God is for Himself all-sufficient. If indeed He created the world that love might find a fresh channel for its overflow, it could not be that He felt any void. It must have been on account of the exuberance of His benevolence. The vastness of divine love overflowed. Unfallen natures were refreshed by its streams; and though men have sinned, it still flows on with divine fulness and life-giving influences. Incomparable love, because not moved by any inward necessity.

III. **On account of the holiness of the divine nature.**—We sometimes talk about loving the sinner and hating his sin; but it oft requires something like superhuman power to separate the sinner from his sin. "The Pharisee stood and prayed thus with himself." How graphic the touch! The mere word "solidarity" has not yet killed out of society the Pharisees who stand by themselves. Sinners who go beyond respectable sins shut themselves out of respectable society. The word "respectable" is a strong word in certain circles. Respectable sinners we may love; disreputable sinners we shun. And yet we are all sinners. If we could stand on the high plane of the infinite purity, we should see how infinitesimal the difference. The holy God loves the unholy. Sin is the one abominable thing which God hates. "He is not a God that hath pleasure in wickedness; neither shall evil dwell with Him." Incomparable love, because uninfluenced by moral worth in the objects.

IV. **On account of the completeness of the divine relationship.**—Mysterious words "God the Father and God the Son." Two, and yet not separate. Speaking after the manner of men, we say that perfect love subsisted between God the Father and God the Son; and yet the eternal Father gave proof of the incomparable nature of His love by giving His Son. Incomparable love, because it spared not the choicest gift.

V. **On account of the extent of the divine sacrifice.**—If God had given His Son to walk for thirty-three years with unfallen Adams and sinless Eves in a paradise of perfect beauty, it would have been a demonstration of love—such a demonstration as is received among men with gratitude. The love of a monarch to some distant part of the empire is shown by sending a son, and his sojourn is made a triumphal passage—everything ministers to his delight. God sends His Son, not to a glorious paradise, not to palaces of pleasure, but to a disordered planet, to haunts of sin and of sorrow. We are sometimes told that Jesus came into this world to be a teacher of moral truth. If that were so—which is not here allowed—it would have been a demonstration of divine love. What a task to teach truth to unreceptive natures! To incur the obloquy which is the portion of every moral reformer! If God had thus given His Son for a few years to teach the ignorant sons of men, and had then translated Him back again to His preincarnate condition, it would have been a demonstration of love. But He gave Him up to death. This was purposed in the eternal councils; this was prefigured in the old economy, foretold by the prophets, and kept in view by Jesus Himself as the great object of His mission. What a word is "death"! We do not understand its full significance. Hardened scientists tell us that death is but the taking down of the human house. Does the house think and feel? Is it capable of infinite longings and yearnings? Does it soar beyond the material? Can it dwell in the eternal? Surely death is not a mere material shock, a repulsion of united molecules of matter. Considering the death of the eternal Son, we are lifted out of materialism—at least, ought to be, for too many dwell upon its mere physical aspect. The sublime Sufferer teaches us that death has far more in it than the anatomist's scalpel can unfold. The death of Jesus, with its infinite anguish, with its intense soul darkness, with its awful sense of a desolate forsaking, is a mournful demonstration of God's love; for we may be allowed to think of God the Father making a sacrifice in allowing His Son to enter such a gloomy vale. 1. *If God has thus shown His love, let us admire*; 2. *If God thus loves, why should we fear?* 3. *If God has thus shown His love, let us show our gratitude*; 4. *If God has thus made love conspicuous, let it be conspicuous in our lives*; 5. *If love died that love might be pre-eminent, let us not shrink from the sacrifices which love may demand.*

God's commendation of His love.

I. **God commends His love to our attention.**—To speak of love always secures attention. Proved by the popularity of the modern novel. Word carries thoughts to family circle and its earliest associations—to spots where words are spoken and embraces given and received. Noble deeds of love recorded in ancient and modern story. Is there any love like this? 1. *Consider its choice of objects.* We choose for excellences real or fancied—fair face, happy temperament, great mind, warm heart. God chooses the unworthy, loves the unlovely. The objects of His love are the "ungodly" (ver. 6), the impious, who have no love of Him, no reverence for Him, who try to get rid of the thought of Him. He does not wait till we give signs of coming to a better state of mind; He loves us when "without strength" (ver. 6), unable to leave our miserable condition—loves us in our misery. If the Queen were to visit small-pox patients in London garrets, the whole country would be loud in her praise. How much more wonderful the King of kings visiting those stricken down by sin! He has loved "sinners," active in wickedness. A pure girl thrown into the company of foul-mouthed, brawling drunkards. He has loved "enemies" (ver. 10), who hate God so much that they try to get Him out of their thoughts, and reject with proud disdain His offered gift of salvation. 2. *Consider what love chooses to do for us.* In pity we say, Give money to the miserable wretch, wash his filthy face, and move him to a cleaner house. The love of God goes to the root of the evil. Boy bitten by mad dog—no use putting piece of sticking-plaster on wound. He has saved from "wrath" (ver. 9). The word opens before us a dark abyss, which becomes blacker the longer we gaze. God alone knows the depth of that abyss, the contents of that awful blackness. He knew what needed to bring out of the horrible pit. Only one who could go down low enough to meet men at their lowest point of need—His own Son. In love He gave His Son, the Christ, to die for us. No need to perplex ourselves with the theological question how His death removes our penalty. The same

God who has so loved us as to give His Son assures us that the death is for all who will take the benefit of it.

II. **God commends His love for our approval.**—Difference between our relation to other deeds of love and to this. Personal interest—present interest. Efficacy of Christ's death as fresh to-day as eighteen centuries ago. Eternal fate depends on our approval or disapproval of this deed of love. 1. Do we approve of the interference of His love—that all the glory of salvation belongs to Him? 2. Do we approve of the course taken by love? Some think less might have sufficed than that the Son of God should take our place before the law and meet all its demands. Am I willing that Christ should take my place and bear my wrath—willing that if there is any praise for salvation He shall have it all? (Rev. i. 5, 6.) 3. Do we approve of the place given to us in that deed of love—to receive justification as a free gift of God? God demands present response to His appeal. He says, Behold the Substitute. Do I accept of Him? Willing that my sins be laid on Him—to be justified by His blood? For that God is waiting—holding back the fires of wrath, because not willing that any should perish. Jesus Christ is delaying His return, though the Church is pleading "Come quickly," that sinners may come unto Him and find peace and life through His death for them. —*G. Wallace, D.D.*

The best thing.
I. **The best thing commended.**—"The love of God to man." Not His wisdom, power, holiness, or wealth, but His love, unsolicited, unmerited, free, unparalleled, towards us, the most undeserving of His creatures.

II. **The best thing commended by the best Judge.**—"God commendeth His love." "God only knows the love of God." A man may know the love of man, an angel may know the love of an angel; but only the Infinite can gauge the infinite.

III. **The best thing commended by the best Judge in the best possible way.**—"In that, while we were yet sinners, Christ died for us." While we were at the worst He did the best for us. "He died for the ungodly." "He tasted death for every man." "He came to seek and to save that which was lost."

IV. **The best thing commended by the best Judge in the best possible way, and for the best purpose.**—That we might be "justified by His blood," "saved from wrath," reconciled to God by the death of His Son," and "saved by His life"—yea, "joy in God through our Lord Jesus Christ"; in a word, have everlasting life.—*D. Brotchie.*

Redemption to the right and the secure.—Here are two subjects for useful thought.
I. **The moral wrongness and danger of mankind.**—The text contains the words "sinners," representing "men that are in the wrong," "transgressors of the divine law." It contains also the word "wrath," implying "danger" and "danger in consequence of the wrong." Wrath in God is not an angry passion, but a benevolent antagonism against wrong. It is a benevolent principle, not a malign passion. The opposition of love is for many reasons a more terrible thing than the opposition of anger. Men as sinners oppose God, and God as the all-loving One opposes them, and His opposition is called "wrath," and wrath because "it is a terrible thing." The other subject for thought in the text is:—
II. **The moral deliverance and rectification of mankind.**—There are two words in the text that express these two things, "justified" and "saved." I take the word "justified" not in a forensic but in a *moral* sense—the sense

151

of being made right. The word "saved" I take in a spiritual and not in a legal or material sense. It means "the restoration of the soul to lost intelligence, lost purity, lost liberty, lost love, lost friendship, with God." Now mark how moral rectification and spiritual salvation come: 1. They *flow from God's love*. "God commendeth His love [or, as some read, His own love] towards us." His love is the ultimate cause, the primal font. 2. They come from God's love *through the love of Christ*. Christ is at once the demonstration, the emblem, and the medium of God's love. Christ demonstrates the reality and strength of this divine love by His death. "While we were yet sinners, Christ died for us." His death therefore becomes that mighty, moral force to make the wrong right, the lost safe.—*D. Thomas.*

Divine love for sinners.—We infer :—

I. **That God has love.**—He is not sheer intellect; He has heart, and His heart is not malign, but benevolent. He has love, not merely an attribute, but in essence. Love is not a mere element in His nature—it is His *nature*; He is love. The moral code by which He governs the universe is but love speaking in the imperative mood. His wrath is but love uprooting and consuming whatever obstructs the happiness of His creation.

> " O Love ! the one sun,
> O Love ! the one sea,
> No life has begun
> That breathes not in Thee ;
> Thy rays have no limit,
> Thy waves have no shore,
> Thou giv'st, without merit,
> To worlds evermore."

Yes, love is the one sea. All created existences are but waves rising out of that sea, and breaking on the shores of eternity.

II. **That God has love for sinners.**—"While we were yet sinners." 1. This is not a love *that is revealed in nature*. Not on one page in the mighty book of nature is it written that God has love for sinners. Nature was written before sinners had existence. It is exclusively the doctrine of the Bible, and the central and cardinal doctrine. "God so loved the world," etc. 2. This is not the love of *moral esteem*. The holy One cannot love the corrupt character; it is the love of compassion—compassion deep, tender, boundless.

III. **That God's love for sinners is demonstrated in the death of Christ.**—"Christ died for us." 1. This demonstration is the *mightiest*. The strength of love is proved by the sacrifice it makes. "God so loved the world that He gave His *only* begotten Son." "He delivered Him up for us all." 2. This demonstration is the most *indispensable*. The only way to consume in me any enmity that I may have for a man is to carry into my soul the conviction that he whom I have hated loves me, and has always loved me. This conviction will turn my enmity into love. God knows the human soul, knows how to break its corrupt heart; hence He has given the demonstration of His love in the death of Christ. —*D. Thomas, D.D.*

SUGGESTIVE COMMENTS ON VERSES 7, 8.

The design of Christ's death.—All those who have paid their lives to the injured laws of the country have died for us ; and if we derive not improvement from it the fault is our own. But are we going to rank the death of Christ with such deaths as these ? We would rather class it with the death of an apostle. "If I be offered," says Paul to the Philippians, " upon the sacrifice and service of your faith, I joy and rejoice with you." This was noble. But was Paul crucified for us? No. "It is Christ that died"—His death is peculiarly pre-eminent. This was indicated by the prodigies that attended it. The question is, What was the design of Christ's death? Some tell us that it was to confirm the truth of His doctrine by the testimony of His blood, and to suffer, leaving us an example that we should follow His steps. And this is true, and we believe it as truly as those who will go no further. But is that the whole or the principal part of the design? We appeal to the Scriptures. There we learn that He died for us as an expiation of our guilt, and to make reconciliation for the sins of the people. He died to redeem us from the curse. Exclude this, and the language of the Bible becomes perfectly embarrassing and unintelligible. Exclude this, and what becomes of the legal sacrifices? They were shadows without a substance. For there is no relation between them and His death, as He was a martyr and an example; but there is a full conformity between them and His death, as He was an atonement. Exclude this, and with what can we meet the conscience burdened with guilt? with what can we answer the inquiry, How shall I come before the Lord? with what can we wipe away the tear of godly grief? But we have boldness to enter into the holiest by the blood of Jesus. "Surely He hath borne our griefs and carried our sorrows." His death was an offering and a sacrifice to God for a sweet-smelling savour. The all-sufficiency and acceptableness were evinced by His discharge from the grave and His being received up into glory. There within the veil our soul finds anchorage. Yet even this is not all the design. Christ died for us, not only to reconcile us, but to renovate; not only to justify us, but to sanctify. The one is as necessary to our recovery as the other, and both equally flow from the cross. "For He gave Himself for us, that He might redeem us from all iniquity, and purify unto Himself a peculiar people zealous of good works."—*W. Jay.*

Greatness of divine love. — "For scarcely for a righteous man will one die : yet peradventure for a good man some would even dare to die." The greatness and freeness of the love of God are illustrated in this and the following verse by making still more prominent the unworthiness of its objects. It is hardly to be expected that any one would die in the place of a merely righteous man, though for a good man this self-denial might possibly be exercised ; but we, so far from being good, were not even righteous ; we were sinners, ungodly, and enemies. The difference between the words "righteous" and "good," as here used, is that which in common usage is made between "just" and "kind." The former is applied to a man who does all that the law or justice can demand of him, the latter to him who is governed by love. The just man commands respect ; the good man calls forth affection. Respect being a cold and feeble principle compared to love, the sacrifices to which it leads are comparatively slight.—*Hodge.*

Singular goodness in Christ.—The apostle goes on to show the singular goodness of our Saviour in submitting to death in place of the ungodly. Ver. 7 : "For scarcely for a righteous man will one die : yet peradventure for a good man some would even dare to die." By a righteous or just man appears to be meant a man of virtue and integrity, who does no injury ; and it is certainly true that a man would not lay down his life to save from death a person who merely adheres strictly to the path of righteousness. "Though peradventure for a good man," as it is in the original, "some would even dare to die." By the good man appears to be meant a man of eminent virtue, a public benefactor, who does much good in society ; and to preserve the life of such a man some might even venture to die. This is so true that there have not been wanting instances of persons saving the life of such a man at the expense of their own.—*Ritchie.*

" *God commendeth His love toward us.*"—We should observe the commendation of God's love towards us : He "commendeth His love." The word συνίστησι signifies God's interposing, to make us know and be assured of that which otherwise we knew not, and which is exceedingly strange and incredible to us. There is another such word used for the very same purpose (Heb. vi. 17) : " God, willing more abundantly to show unto the heirs of promise the immutability of His counsel, confirmed it by an oath." The original is, He "interposed Himself," as it is in the margin, or came in between by an oath, in order to show the unchangeableness of His counsel of love to the heirs of promise. So it is here. God would make known, would make plain and incontestable, His love towards sinners, so that they should have no room left to question it. Well, and what way does He take for the purpose ? Does He give them His word for it, and interpose Himself by an oath to confirm that word ? No; both these He had done before. He comes in between, therefore, with the incarnation of His only begotten Son, and causes Him, while we were yet sinners, to die for us. As if He should have said, I will have you know the love which I bear towards you ; and because I know how hard it is for you to believe any such thing, lo ! I will cause you to be satisfied of it without dispute. I set forth My Son in the midst of you, and give Him to die for you before your eyes. Look on that, and acknowledge My love towards you. Now, brethren, is not this speaking love ? Does not this declare the love of God in terms which cannot be mistaken ? Who can think of this and charge his ruin on a want of goodwill in God ?—*S. Walker.*

The great love of Christ.—Christ has obliged us with two of the highest instances of His love to us imaginable :—

I. That He died for us.—The love of life is naturally the greatest, and therefore that love that so far masters this as to induce a man to lay it down must needs be transcendent and supernatural. For life is the first thing that nature desires, and the last that it is willing to part with. But how poor and low and in what a pitiful shallow channel does the love of the world commonly run ! Let us come and desire such a one to speak a favourable word or two for us to a potent friend, and how much of coyness and excuse and shyness shall we find. The man is unwilling to spend his breath in speaking, much less in dying, for his friend. Come to another, and ask him upon the stock of a long acquaintance and a professed kindness to borrow but a little money of him, and how quickly does he fly to his shifts, pleading poverty, debts, and great occasions, and anything rather than open his own bowels to refresh those of his poor neighbour ! The man will not bleed in his purse, much less otherwise, to rescue his friend from prison, from disgrace, and perhaps a greater disaster. But now how incomparably full and strong must the love of Christ needs have been that could make Him sacrifice even life itself for the good of mankind, and not only die, but die with all the heightening circumstances of pain and ignominy— that is, in such a manner that death was the least part of the suffering ! Let us but fix our thoughts upon Christ, hanging, bleeding, and at length dying upon the cross, and we shall read His love to man there in larger and more visible characters than the superscription that the Jews put over His head in so many languages— all which and many more were not sufficient to have fully expressed and set forth so incredibly great an affection. Every thorn was a pencil to represent and every groan a trumpet to proclaim how great a love He was then showing to mankind. And now surely our love must needs be very cold if all the blood that ran in our Saviour's veins cannot warm it; for all that was shed for us, and shed for that very purpose that it might prevent the shedding of ours. Our obnoxiousness to the curse of the law for sin had exposed us to all the extremity of misery, and made death as due to us as wages to the workman. And the divine justice, we may be sure, would never have been behindhand to pay us our due. The dreadful retribution was certain and unavoidable; and therefore since Christ could not prevent, He was pleased at last to divert the blow and to turn it upon Himself, to take the cup of God's fury out of our hands and to drink off the very dregs of it. The greatest love that men usually bear one another is but show and ceremony, compliment, and a mere appearance in comparison of this. This was such a love as Solomon says is "strong as death," and to express it yet higher, such a one as was stronger than the very desires of life.

II. The other transcendent instance of Christ's love to mankind was that He did not only die for us, **but that He died for us while we were enemies,** and, in the phrase of Scripture, enmity itself against Him. It is possible indeed that some natures of a nobler mould and make than the generality of the world may arise to such an heroic degree of love as to induce one friend to die for another. For the apostle says that "for a good man one would even dare to die." And we may read in heathen story of the noble contention of two friends, which of them should have the pleasure and honour of dying in the other's stead, and writing the inward love of his heart in the dearest blood that did enliven it. Yet still the love of Christ to mankind runs in another and a higher strain; for admit that one man had died for another, yet still it has been for his friend—that is, for something, if not of equal, yet at least of next esteem to life itself in the common judg-

ment of all. Human love will indeed sometimes act highly and generously, but still it is upon a suitable object, upon something that is amiable; and if there be either no fuel or that which is unsuitable, the flame will certainly go out. But the love of Christ does not find but makes us lovely. It "saw us in our blood" (as the prophet speaks), wallowing in all the filth and impurities of our natural corruption, and then it said unto us, Live. Christ then laid down His life for us, when we had forfeited our own to Him. Which strange action was as if a prince should give himself a ransom for that traitor that would have murdered him, and sovereignty itself lie down upon the block to rescue the neck of a rebel from the stroke of justice. This was the method and way that Christ took in what He suffered for us—a method that reason might at first persuade us to be against nature, and that religion assures us to be above it.—*South.*

A peculiar contrast.—The δέ, "but," indicates this contrast. What man hardly does for what is most worthy of admiration and love, God has done for that which merited only His indignation and abhorrence. On the verb συνιστάναι : here it is the act whereby God *establishes* beyond question the reality of His love. The apostle says τὴν ἑαυτοῦ ἀγάπην : His *own* love, or the love that is peculiar to *Him.* The expression contrasts God's manner of loving with ours. God cannot look above Him to devote Himself, as we may, to a being of more worth than Himself. His love turns to that which is beneath Him, and takes even the character of sacrifice in behalf of that which is altogether unworthy of Him. Ὅτι, "in that," is here *the fact* by which God has proved His peculiar way of loving. In the word ἁμαρτωλός, "sinner," the termination ωλος signifies "abundance." It was by this term the Jews habitually designated the Gentiles. The ἔτι, "yet," implies this idea : that there was not *yet* in humanity the least progress toward the

155

good which would have been fitted to merit for it such a love ; it was *yet* plunged in evil. The words "Christ died for us" in such a context imply the close relation of essence which unites Christ and God in the judgment of the apostle. With man sacrificing himself Paul compares God sacrificing Christ. This parallel has no meaning except as the sacrifice of Christ is to God the sacrifice of Himself. Other-

wise the sacrifice of God would be inferior to that of man, whereas it must be infinitely exalted above it. Finally, it should be observed how Paul places the subject Θεός, "God," at the end of the principal proposition, to bring it beside the word ἁμαρτωλῶν, "sinners," and so brings out the contrast between our defilement and the delicate sensibility of divine holiness.— *Godet.*

MAIN HOMILETICS OF THE PARAGRAPH.—*Verses* 9—11.

Christian assurance.—The Roman Christians would require all the helps which could be furnished. The apostle seeks to surround them with all safeguards, and to bring forth every argument and every consideration to strengthen them in the faith and prepare them for all trials. There are for us also peculiar trials, and we must seek to strengthen and encourage ourselves by the consideration of our privileges. Let us strengthen ourselves in the faith by taking account of the grounds of our assurance.

I. **Confidence from the initial process.**—"When we were enemies, we were reconciled to God." If the divine Being considered us kindly and compassionately in a state of enmity, surely He will not forsake when the alienation has been removed and a state of friendship has been established.

II. **Confidence from the further development.**—Being justified, delivered by the blood of Christ, we shall finally be saved from wrath through Him. If grace has begun, surely grace will consummate. Can there be unfinished works in the divine pathways? Can it be said of God that, having begun to build, He was not either able or willing to finish? Let us have confidence in God's goodwill. Let us believe in His omnipotence and in His ever-enduring mercy.

III. **Confidence from the unseen.**—Reconciled by the death of God's Son, saved by His life—saved by His earth life as a stimulating example, as an elevating and sanctifying influence. From the death of Christ we go backward and forward—backward to the earth life, forward to the heavenly life. Saved by His earth life as our example—saved by His heavenly life as our intercessor, as our appropriator, as our guide and protector. He ever lives to intercede. We have a great High Priest. Let us have holy boldness. He appropriates not to Himself but to believers the benefits of His mediatorial work. Sacred and benign influences come to us from the mediatorial throne. He is our guide and protector. He is the Good Shepherd guiding the sheep to the sweet pastures, where the verdant glades are ever green and refreshing streams are ever flowing. Let us follow where He leads, being assured that He will lead aright. Our times are in His hands. He is watching over our welfare.

IV. **Confidence from the inward.**—The emotional is to be watched, but not to be ignored. Our own thoughts, feelings, and experiences are to be reckoned. Some there are who make light of inward experiences; but here St. Paul seems to make the inward the climax of his argument. Not only so, but we joy in God, we exult in God, through our Lord Jesus Christ, by whom we have received the at-one-ment, the reconciliation.

V. **Christian joy is well founded, springing from the atoning work of Jesus Christ.**—Glory in self-righteousness, in fancied goodness, in good works, is vain. Not thus can we rightly joy in God. Such joy is like the chaff of the summer threshing floor which the wind will soon drive away. Let our joy spring from the finished work of the Saviour. He that exulteth, let him exult not in himself, but in that good God who gave His only begotten Son. Christian joy should be raised above the storms and tempests of time. The greater the outer darkness, the clearer shall be the inner light of Christian joy; the fiercer the outward heart, the more cheerily shall the inner joy glow and refresh.

VI. **Christian joy is abiding.**—God cannot change. Jesus is the same yesterday, to-day, and for ever. How soon our earth joys fade! How often we have joy in anticipation and sorrow in realisation! Heaven's joys do not fade. The believer joys in God as a present possession. He joys in anticipation of eternal union, and the realisation of that bliss will be bliss indeed. " I will see you again; I will remain with you: and your heart shall rejoice, and your joy no man taketh from you." Soul joy is abiding and eternal. Surely we ought to have strong confidence who have fled for refuge to lay hold on the hope set before us in the gospel.

> " Let sickness blast and death devour,
> If heaven but recompense our pains;
> Perish the grass and fade the flower,
> If firm the word of God remains."

The dead and living Christ.—" For if, when we were enemies." There are four distinct facts or events given us here, on which the argument of the passage builds itself. Two of these have reference to the history of the sinner, and two of them to the history of the sinner's Deliverer. The first two are, man's enmity and man's reconciliation; the last two are, the Saviour's death and the Saviour's life. " Herein is love, not that we loved God, but that He loved us, and sent His Son to be the propitiation for our sins." There having been in His infinite bosom this exceeding love before He gave His Son, it is wholly incredible that He should be less gracious now, less willing to bestow all needed gifts. For 1. That gift did not *exhaust* His love. It did not empty the heart of God, nor dry up the fountain of His grace. 2. That gift has not thrown any hindrance in the way of God's love. It is not now a more difficult thing for God to love us; nay, if we can say so, it is easier than ever. All hindrances have now melted away. Having thus briefly noticed this important truth, we now pass on to consider the three special heads of argument.

I. **If God did so much for us when enemies, what will He do, or rather, what will He not do, for us now that we are friends?**—Our enmity, great as it was, did not hinder His bestowing such an unspeakable gift: what is there, then, within the whole circle of the universe, which we may not count upon, now that that enmity has been removed, and we have entered into eternal friendship with Him? There may be said to be three stages in this love, at each of which it rises and increases: 1. He loved us when enemies; 2. He loves us more when friends, even in this imperfect state of still-remaining sin; 3. He will love us yet more when imperfection has been shaken off, and we are presented without spot, or wrinkle, or any such thing. Here, then, is love in which we may assuredly triumph. It was love which expressed itself by an infinite gift. He is loving us and blessing us here; oh! will He not love us and bless us in the day when we take possession of the provided inheritance?

II. **If Christ's death did so much for us, what will not His life do?**—If a *dying* Saviour did so much for us, what will not a *living* Saviour be able to do? The expression " saved " used here denotes the whole blessing which God has in store for us—complete deliverance in every sense of that word—a complete undoing of our lost estate. Its consummation is, when Jesus comes the second time without sin unto salvation. The apostle's argument rests on the fact of the existence of these two opposite states of being—the two opposite extremities of being, death and life. Death is the lowest pitch of helplessness, lower even than

157

the feebleness of infancy. It is the extremity of weakness. It is the utter cessation of all strength. Life is the opposite of this. It is the full possession of being, with all its faculties and powers. It is the guarantee for the forth-putting of all the vigour and strength which belong to the individual in whom it dwells. And it is thus that the apostle reasons : If Christ in His lowest state of weakness accomplished such marvels for us, what will He not be able to do for us now that He is in the full exercise of His almighty strength ?

III. **If Christ's death did so much for us when enemies, what will not His life do for us when friends ?**—In other words, if a dying Saviour did so much for us when enemies, what will not a living Saviour do for us when friends ? If a father, in the midst of poverty and weakness, will do much for a prodigal child, what will he not, in the day of his riches and power and honour, do for a recon-ciled son ? Hear how Scripture speaks of His *life*. " When He who is our life shall appear, then shall we also appear with Him in glory." His appearing as our life shall bring with it all that blessedness and glory which pertain to Him as the living One—as *our* life. " Because I live, ye shall live also." He cannot die ; He liveth for ever. He is the resurrection and the life ; therefore life, and all that life comprises, shall be ours. " He ever liveth to make intercession for us." Of what, then, is it that this *life* of Christ gives us the assurance ? Of salvation, says the apostle : " We shall be saved by His life." Reconciliation is the result of His death ; salvation, of His life !—*H. Bonar.*

SUGGESTIVE COMMENTS ON VERSES 9—11.

Ground of confidence.—" Much more then, being now justified by His blood, we shall be saved from wrath through Him." This and the following verse draw the obvious inference from the freeness and greatness of the love of God, as just exhibited, that believers shall be ultimately saved. It is an argument *à fortiori*. If the greater benefit has been bestowed, the less will not be withheld. If Christ has died for His enemies, He will surely save His friends. "Being justified." To be justified is more than to be pardoned ; it includes the idea of reconciliation or restoration to the favour of God, and the participation of the consequent blessings. This idea is prominently pres nted in the following verse. We are justified " by His blood." This ex-pression, as remarked above, exhibits the true ground of our acceptance with God. It is not our works, nor our faith, nor our new obedience, nor the work of Christ in us, but what He has done for us. Having by the death of Christ been brought into the relation of peace with God, being now regarded for His sake as righteous, " we shall be saved from wrath through Him." He will not leave His work unfinished ; whom He justifies, them He also glorifies. The word " wrath " of course means the effects of wrath or punishment, those sufferings with which the divine displeasure visits sin. Not only is our justification to be ascribed to Christ, but our salvation is "through" Him. Salvation, in a general sense, includes justification ; but when distinguished from it, as in this case, it means the consummation of that work of which justification is the commence-ment. It is a preservation from all the causes of destruction, a deliverance from the evils which surround us here or threaten us hereafter, and an introduction into the blessedness of heaven. Christ thus saves us by His providence and Spirit, and by His constant intercession. There is there-fore most abundant ground for con-fidence for the final blessedness of believers, not only in the amazing love of God, by which, though sinners and enemies, they have been justified and reconciled by the death of His Son, but also in the consideration that this same Saviour that died for them still lives, and ever lives to sanctify, protect, and save them.—*Hodge.*

"Justify" here means "deliver from." —"Much more then, being now justified by His blood, we shall be saved from wrath through Him." The word "justified" is here used to denote "delivered," as may be inferred from the connection of the argument. Christ died for us, saith the apostle, and thus "justified," that is "delivered," us from death, which was our due. And if we are already delivered from death by the shedding of His blood, much more shall we be saved from wrath, that is from future punishment, through Him. Such is the argument. But if we should suppose the word "justified" to have its most usual meaning, namely, "accounted righteous," there would be no room for the further effect here mentioned, of delivering us from future punishment. For justification denotes both delivering from wrath and also holding us entitled to the reward of righteousness. The apostle's assertion therefore is, that being delivered by the death of Christ from the dominion of sin and from that death which was due to us, we shall through Him also be saved from the wrath to come. The expression "much more shall we be saved from wrath" implies that Christ's dying to save us from the death due to us as sinners was the most important part of the plan of salvation; and this essential part of the dispensation being already accomplished, there can be no doubt that the natural effect of this part of it, namely, saving us from future punishment, will in due time take place also.—*Ritchie.*

The word "atonement" may be used.— The word here translated "the atonement" is twice, in the preceding verse, rendered by the word to "reconcile"; and it would have expressed the meaning more exactly had the passage been rendered "by whom we have received the reconciliation." For, according to common use of language, an atonement is a sacrifice offered for

sin; and it is received or accepted by Him whose law has been violated, and whom it is intended to propitiate. Strictly speaking, therefore, we do not receive atonement. It is both offered to God and accepted by Him. At the same time, the use of the word "atonement" instead of "reconciliation" makes no change in the meaning. For reconciliation is altogether the effect of the Atonement. It is this which removes the displeasure of God which lies on mankind as sinners, and renders Him willing to receive them into His favour. And we may without impropriety be said to receive the Atonement when we accept of these fruits of it, as they are offered in the gospel.—*Ritchie.*

Jesus reveals the love of God by deeds.—Francis Turretin says the doctrine of the Atonement is the chief part of our salvation, the anchor of faith, the refuge of hope, the rule of charity, the true foundation of the Christian religion, and the richest treasure of the Christian Church. When prophets and apostles have given us their message, their work is done. But it is different with Christ Jesus. Far more of God is revealed in what Jesus was, in what He did, and in what He suffered, than in what He taught. He revealed the mercy and tenderness of God more by His deeds than His words. Others had spoken of the beautiful, but none lived so beautifully. The evangelists give lengthened accounts of His death: the Saviour Himself ever kept it before Him, because it was of a sacrificial character. Jesus viewed death with terror, while the martyrs viewed it with delight. Surely this terror was not caused by the prospect of crucifixion, though painful. The only explanation of His death is His own: "He gave His life a ransom for many"; "His blood was shed for the remission of sins." The cross, the symbol of dishonour and weakness, is the mightiest power in the universe. Peter, in his early discourse, refers to the death of Christ as a crime on the part of the Jews in order to lead them to repentance. It is significant that Peter's whole thought should be concentrated on the cross and resurrection. How was it that Peter referred so much to His death? Christ suffered for us. It is not said that Christ taught or worked miracles for us.

St. John strongly sets forth Christ's death as a propitiation, and St. Paul maintained that Christ died for our sins. The history of the doctrine is a proof that the idea of an objective atonement was not invented by theologians.—*Abstracted from "The Atonement," by R. W. Dale.*

MAIN HOMILETICS OF THE PARAGRAPH.—Verses 12—21.

The two opposing sovereignties. — St. Peter regarded his beloved brother Paul as having written epistles in which are some things hard to be understood ; but there are some who seem to speak as if St. Peter were a weakling. They treat St. Paul in deferential style, as if they would challenge him to come forth from the unseen world and propound more difficulties for them to solve. But we follow in the footsteps of St. Peter, and feel, especially in the Epistle to the Romans, that these are things hard to be understood—things which for their explanation will require the revealing light of eternity. We cannot explain all. We do not make the vain attempt. Sufficient if some help is given to earnest seekers of the truth. In previous chapters we have found things hard to be understood, and we enter now on ground that is thickly sown with difficulties. Mystery is everywhere. It begins in the garden of Eden. Its course is the pathway of the human race. We bow in the presence of the mystery, and find sweet refuge in the arms of all-embracing mercy.

I. **The two opposing sovereigns.**—Sin and grace are the two opposing sovereigns placed before us by St. Paul as ruling in the moral sphere, and with their sceptre touching even the material world. St. Paul does not sever the moral from the material. There are forces working above, beyond, and through all material forces. Sin touches the physical. A soul act taints the race. Sin, the dread sovereign, has brought in death, trouble, moral inability. 1. *Death.* Solemn word ! What does it mean? Our understanding or misunderstanding of biblical expressions and terms has been formed very much by Milton,—of that forbidden tree whose mortal taste brought death into the world and all our woe. We read and speak as if death were unknown before Adam's fall. Pelagius anticipated modern geologists, for he affirmed that death is not a consequence of sin and that Adam would have died even if he had not sinned. The modern scientist tells us that there is ample proof in the geological remains that physical death has been the lot of the lower animals from all time. All the animals are in one chain of progressive development, and are all related. The lower animals were all subject to death ; and the highest animal, man, is by implication and analogy subject now and always in the past to physical death. Let scientists, if they please, reduce themselves to mere animals. *Well,* there is *death* and *death,*—death as the king of terrors ; death as a gentle nurse putting the child to sleep, from which it is to awake in the sweet morn of eternity's day. Death is no death to unfallen Adam, who walks his earthly course of hundreds of years, and then in the eventide, with the sweet balm of the breeze blowing about his frame, with the rich music of the birds and the rippling waters, with a gently falling sound soothing his tired nature, seeks repose upon his bed of flowers, and his spirit passes to commune with the spirit of the Eternal. Surely that apostle who could form the beautiful ideal expression to set forth the transition of Christians, "And some have fallen asleep," is not to be unthinkingly charged with the idea that mere physical dissolution is of recent introduction to our planet. Death as a terror was brought in by sin. Death in its repulsive aspect was brought in by the dreadful act of the first murderer. Death came in by sin; and the blood of the slaughtered Abel gives emphasis to the utterance, "Death has reigned, for sin has entered." Earth's gory battle-fields tell what an awful power is sin. 2. *Trouble.* Sin brings trouble. Here no elaborate arguments are required. We do not stand on debatable ground. Experience, and history which is recorded experience, declare that sin entails sorrow; and trouble, in the sense of an absence of peace, the presence of unrest. 3. *Moral inability.* Disobedience. No need to enter upon the discussion of disputed questions. We may dispute until doomsday about the freedom of the will and cognate topics; but man everywhere shows the signs of a fallen nature. Education may do something to restain the outbreak of human depravity, the restraining force of society may check; but on all hands we have marks of man's sinfulness. Divine grace is needful, and is the only adequate remedy. The one sovereign is baneful, but the other is blessed. Grace, the benign sovereign, has brought in life, peace, and moral ability. 1. *Life.* In Christ Jesus there is life eternal. And this life eternal is not a future but a present possession. It is life here and now for the believer. In the midst of the groans and pains and tears which accompany and precede death, we may enjoy the blessing of eternal life. 2. *Peace.* Sin brings trouble and unrest. Grace brings peace and sweet soul-rest. How infinitely blessed the repose which is enjoyed by the children of peace! 3. *Moral ability.* Obedience. We do not know how far grace reigns and influences. The restraining power of grace may extend to regions and persons far beyond our thought. Grace abounds unto many. Let us not in our thoughts ever turn the apostle's many into a few. The abundance of grace reigns, and though its sovereign influence many royal persons are walking through the universe of God.

II. **The seeming weakness of one sovereign and the apparent strength of the other.**—Sin still reigns. Even in our optimistic moods we must confess that sin reigns, and spreads death in all its forms and pains and unutterable agonies. Grace as a sovereign is apparently weak. Grace has been reigning for a long period, and yet, after all, how ungracious is the greater part of humanity! How far does the apostle's grace reach? Can it touch and bless the millions upon millions that are as yet outside the pale of Christianity? Oh, our faith sometimes seems ready to fail when we think that grace is still a sovereign, with, apparently at least, a very small portion of the race as its subjects.

III. **But the seemingly weak must finally overcome the apparently strong.**— Grace, after all, may not be so weak as it may appear to the superficial vision. "In due time Christ died." The due time was marked a long way on time's great dial-plate. The due time for the triumphant vindication of grace's all-abounding force and all-pervading sovereignty may yet be some distance off, if it is to be measured by the due time of the Saviour's advent. In the past by weak things God has conquered. Base things have overturned the mighty. Seeming folly has confounded wisdom. And grace, though seemingly weak, shall in due time conquer and subdue and destroy sin. "Grace shall reign through righteousness unto eternal life." Many questions trouble the anxious soul when studying such passages as the one before us. But let us not ask, Why sin, why moral evil, why a taint upon the whole race, from one man's disobedience? Let us rather say, Here is the sin, here is the undoubted fact of a depraved moral tendency; and thus in the mediatorial work of Jesus is the sovereign remedy. Seek, my soul, for the divine healing. The sick does not ask, Whence and why the pestilence? but seeks after a remedy. The wise Israelite bitten by the serpent did not ask, Whence the serpents, why the infliction, how is the virus infused? but he looked to the brazen serpent, and was healed. Thank God, we may be healed through

Jesus Christ our Lord. Let us seek that grace may reign in our hearts through righteousness unto eternal life—eternal life with all its amplitude of bliss. What eternal life means will require an eternal life to unfold. It will be ever developing into divine possibilities through eternity.

Ver. 19. *Adam and Christ.*—Up to this point Paul has been discussing condemnation and justification. " Wrath is on all, even on the *Jews*," and " the righteousness of faith is for all, even for the *Gentiles.*" In chaps. vi.-viii. he is about to consider the theme of sanctification. " Shall we continue in sin, that grace may abound? God forbid." He is passing from the one to the other. But before he does so he inserts these three concluding verses of chap. v.,· in which he tersely sums up the former subject, and consciously prepares the way for the latter. Ver. 19 is the summary.

I. **The apostle's favourite conception of two representative men.**—Adam and Christ. They are the federal heads of the human race. They are not regarded as individual units. No man ever is. He is bound by ties to his fellows that he dare not disregard. You cannot uproot even so much as a tare without uprooting along with it some of the precious wheat. " Whenever one member suffers, all the members suffer with it; or one member be honoured, all the members rejoice with it." And yet the whole tendency of modern preaching is towards *individualism.* True religion is represented as a certain definite dealing between the individual soul and Jesus Christ. That indeed is a great truth. Individual salvation is one truth; but representative responsibility is another. The statesman in the commonwealth, the minister in the congregation, the parent in the home, and the teacher in the class are all representative men.

II. **The conduct of these two men as under law to Jehovah:** Adam disobeyed, Christ obeyed.—The Greek word indicates that the first step in Adam's fall was simply *carelessness*—the neglect or refusal *to hear.* But how much may be involved in that! Carelessness or remissness on the part of the guards, that is the first step in the capture of a city or the wreck of a train. Carlessness is always culpable and blameworthy. In the case before us it was " the moral act which provoked the sentence of condemnation." It was the sin that opened the floodgates of evil upon a world. The plea of carelessness or thoughtlessness is no plea. All minimising of evil is a corrupting of the mind from the simplicity that is in Christ, " as the serpent beguiled Eve through his subtlety." But Jesus *obeyed.* He did not neglect to hear, as Adam did, through listening to the siren voices of evil. His obedience was both *voluntary* and *obediential* (cf. ver. 6 with ver. 19). A voluntary sacrifice, and yet in strictest obedience to law. The two aspects are not incompatible. They are reduced to harmony by the moving element of *love.* When we do anything in love, that does not exclude the feeling and the fact that it is also a thing of *duty.* Adam's disobedience was one act, but not so Christ's obedience. It was " the entire work of Christ in its obediential character." The Passover lamb had not merely to be slain; it must be " without blemish."

III. **The fruit or outcome of their conduct.**—" The many were made sinners " and " the many shall be made righteous." Here we meet the great Pauline doctrine of *imputation.* It is confessedly one of great difficulty. But if there be mystery in it there is also mercy. For read 2 Cor. v. 21. There are three imputations—Adam's sin imputed to us, our sins imputed to Christ, and Christ's righteousness imputed to us. These three must stand or fall together. If the principle of imputation be unjust, it is equally unjust for all the three cases. But when we speak of *Adam's* sin as being imputed to us, we are only stating a half-truth. It was *our* sin—that is, the other half: " As through one man sin entered into the world, and death through sin: and so death passed unto all

162

men, for that all *sinned*,"—not "have sinned" (A.V.), a fact which no one doubted; but "sinned" (R.V.)—sinned at a special point in time, sinned in the one man. It is all mystery, we say. Well, perhaps so it is; but the *fruit* need not be so. We are sinners through our connection with Adam; we may be made righteous through our connection with Christ,—only the one connection is that of *birth*, the other that of *faith.—John Adams.*

Ver. 21. *Grace abounding.*—Two facts are here worthy of attention and suggested by the passage :—

I. **That "sin" and "grace" are in the world as ruling powers.**—"Sin" and "grace" are two small words, but they represent mighty things. "Sin" here stands for the principle of evil, the root of all wrong; "grace," the principle of all goodness, the root of all that is virtuous and holy in the universe. In the chapter Paul speaks of these two forces as coming into the world—one through *Adam*, the other through *Christ.* These principles are the moral monarchs of the race, and monarchs always in fierce fighting. All the battlings in the world are but the results of their mutual antagonism.

II. **That the rule of the one issues in death, of the other in everlasting life.**— "As sin hath reigned unto [or, in] death." It is not necessary to regard death here as meaning the dissolution of the body, for this would have taken place had sin never been introduced into the universe; nor the extinction of our being. But it means the destruction of all that can make life worth having. "Sin, when it is finished, bringeth forth death." What is the death of a spirit but the life of wickedness? This is sin. But whilst sin leads to death, grace leads to everlasting life. What is everlasting life? Not mere life without end, but life without evil. Everlasting life is everlasting goodness.

Conclusion.—The great question is, Which is our moral monarch, "sin" or "grace"? In all hearts one must be subordinate to the other, one must reign over the other.—*Homilist.*

SUGGESTIVE COMMENTS ON VERSES 12—21.

Death by Adam; life by Christ.— "And so death passed on all men"— that is, thus it is, or so it happened, that death passed on all men. As death is the penalty of sin, and as by one man all became sinners, thus it was by one man that death passed on all men. The force of the words "and so" have been much disputed; many understand them as answering to the word "as" at the beginning of the verse: "As Adam sinned and died, *so also* do all men." But, in the first place, the words do not admit of this interpretation; Paul does not say "so also," but "and so," "thus it was." Besides, according to the view of the passage, this verse does not contain the first part of a comparison between Adam and Christ, but merely a comparison between Adam and

his posterity. It is *by one man* that men became sinners; and thus it was *by one man* that death passed upon all men. The scope of the passage is to illustrate the doctrine of justification on the ground of the righteousness of Christ, by a reference to the condemnation of men for the sin of Adam. The analogy is destroyed, and the point of the comparison falls, if everything in us be assumed as the ground of the infliction of the penal evils of which the apostle is here speaking. Not only does the scope of the passage demand this interpretation, but also the whole course of the argument. We die on account of Adam's sin: this is true, because on no other ground can the universality of death be accounted for. But if we all die on Adam's

163

account, how much more shall we live on account of Christ? The doctrine which the verse thus explained teaches is one of the plainest truths of all the Scriptures and of experience. Is it not a revealed fact, above all contradiction, and sustained by the whole history of the world, that the sin of Adam altered the relation in which our race stood to God? Did we not fall when Adam fell? If these questions are answered in the affirmative, the doctrine contained in the interpretation of ver. 12, given above, is admitted. The doctrine of the imputation of Adam's sin, or that on account of that sin all men are regarded and treated as sinners, was a common Jewish doctrine at the time of the apostle as well as at a later period. He employs the same method of expression on the subject which the Jews were accustomed to use. They could not have failed, therefore, to understand him as meaning to convey by these expressions the ideas usually connected with them. Whatever obscurity, therefore, rests upon this passage arises from taking the word " death " in the narrow sense in which it is commonly used among men : if taken in its scriptural sense, the whole argument is plain and conclusive. Let " penal evil" be substituted for the word " death," and the argument will stand thus : All men are subject to penal evils on account of one man. The simple doctrine and argument of the apostle is, that it was by the offence of one man that judgment came on all men to condemnation.— *Hodge.*

Man might have been translated.— Long before the creation of man the existence of death is proved in the domain of animal life. Now the body of man belongs to the great sum-total of animal organisation, of which he is the crown ; and therefore the law of death must already have extended to man, independently of sin. Paul's words in the First Epistle to the Corinthians, as well as those of Genesis, the sense

of which he reproduces, prove beyond doubt the natural *possibility* of death, but not its necessity. If man had remained united to God, his body, naturally subject to dissolution, might have been gloriously transformed without passing through death and dissolution. The notion of the *tree of life*, as usually explained, means nothing else. This privilege of an immediate transformation will belong to the believers who shall be alive at the time of our Lord's return (1 Cor. xv. 51, 52), and it was probably this kind of transformation that was on the point of taking effect in the person of the Lord Himself at the time of His transfiguration. This privilege, intended for holy man, was withdrawn from guilty man : such was the *sentence* which gave him over to dissolution. It is stated in the words, " Thou art dust [that is to say, thou *canst* die], and to dust shalt thou return [that is to say, thou *shalt* in fact *die*]." The reign of death over the animals likewise proves only this : that it was in the *natural* condition of man to terminate in dissolution. Remaining on the level of animalism by the preference given by him to inclination over moral obligation, man continued subject to this law. But had he risen by an act of moral liberty above the animal, he would not have had to share its lot (see also on viii. 19-22).—*Godet.*

Christ paid more than we owe.—Far more than what we owed was paid by Christ, as much more as the immeasurable ocean exceeds a drop. Doubt not, therefore, O man, when beholding such a treasure of blessings ; nor ask how the old spark of death and of sin has been extinguished, seeing that such a sea of the gifts of grace has been poured upon it.—*Chrysostom.*

Calvin as an interpreter.—Mark the language of Calvin on these words : " The free gift came upon all men unto justification of life." " Communem omnium gratiam facit, quia omnibus exposita est, non quod ad omnes extendatur re ipsâ. Nam etsi passus est Christus pro peccatis totius mundi, atque omnibus indifferenter Dei benignitate offertur ; non tamen omnes apprehendunt." "This *free gift* of God," says Calvin in the above passage, "is here declared to be common to all, because it is open to all, not because it actually extends to all. For although Christ suffered for *the sins of the whole world*, and, by the mercy of God, is offered to *all without distinction*, yet all do not lay hold of Him." In this passage Calvin speaks as an interpreter of Scripture, in the *Institutes* as the advocate of a system. His *Institutes*, moreover, were written in his earlier days; but his commentaries on Scripture were the labours of his maturer days. It is the observation of Witsius that Calvin uses one language in controversy and another when tranquilly explaining Scripture : "Tantum sæpe interest, utrum quis cum adversario contendat, an libero animo commentetur."

Words signifying sin. — The first, translated "offence" or "trespass," means "the falling from a position"; the second, by the general word "sin," implies the "missing of a mark"; while in ver. 19 we have the "disobedience" of Adam, which signifies the "neglect" or "refusal" to hear, and in ver. 14 the term "transgression," or the "overstepping" of a positive law. What is the precise significance of the statement that the "law entered that the *offence* might abound"? What is this "offence"? The majority of commentators answer, "the first sin of Adam." But in what sense is it this? In the previous steps of his argument the apostle has asserted that sin reigned from Adam to Moses. *That* sin, how-

ever, could not be a "transgression" of positive law, for as Paul asserts in chap. iv. 15, "where no law is, there is no transgression." It was rather an "offence"—a wider term, embracing definite acts of sin, whether committed *without* law or under it. Wittingly or unwittingly, it was the actual repetition of the "disobedience" of Adam. Death reigned from Adam to Moses because "sin" reigned ; and one object, at least, which was served by the law was to prove that this was indeed the case—was to prove that every "offence" was practically a real "transgression," and that both were the expression or manifestation of the "disobedience" of Adam. Thus the first way in which the law makes the "offence" to abound is by bringing the "knowledge of sin" —by putting the already existing offence in its true light. But it does so, in the second place, by being a "provocation to sin." "I was alive without the law once; but when the commandment came, sin revived, and I died." The principle contained in the law is opposed to the principle of sin. There is an exasperating antithesis between the two. So that when the light of the law is flashed upon the principle of sin in man, it arouses into intense action the slumbering volcano within, until it rushes forth in molten streams of intensified and multiplied transgressions. The office of the law is therefore to show that all the differences in the terms do not alter the real nature of the thing. And the apostle consequently returns to the general term for "sin" ($\dot{\alpha}\mu\alpha\rho\tau\dot{\iota}\alpha$), which he has held in abeyance since the beginning of the paragraph, and writes, "But where *sin* abounded, grace did much more abound."—*John Adams, B.D.*

ILLUSTRATIONS TO CHAPTER V.

Ver. 1. *A Romish student and the Bible.*— When Thomas Bilney was a Romish student in Trinity College, he carried a burdened mind in a body emaciated by penance which brought no relief. Hearing his friends one day talking about Erasmus's Testament, he felt a strong desire to possess it; but as it was a forbidden book, he did not dare to touch it. Hoping, however, that something might be found in it to ease his troubled mind, he purchased a copy, and shut himself in his room to read it. With a trembling heart he opened it, and read with astonishment, "This is a faithful saying, and worthy of all acceptation, that Christ Jesus came into the world to save sinners; of whom I am chief." Then laying it down, he exclaimed, "What! Paul the chief of sinners? yet Paul sure of being saved!" He read it again and again, and broke out into an ecstasy of joy, "At last I have heard of Jesus—Jesus Christ. Yes, Jesus Christ saves." And falling down on his knees, he prayed, "O Thou who art the truth, give me strength that I may teach it, and convert the ungodly by means of one who has been himself ungodly." Bilney being justified by faith in and through Jesus Christ, possessed peace.

Ver. 2. *Philosopher and king's son.*—Without faith it is impossible to please God. Let us not otherwise dare to come into His presence. There is nothing but wrath in Him for sin in us. Joseph charged his brethren that they should come no more in his sight unless they brought Benjamin with them. We come at our peril into God's presence if we leave His beloved Benjamin, our dear Jesus, behind us. When the philosopher heard of the enraged emperor's menace, that the next time he saw him he would kill him, he took up the emperor's little son in his arms, and saluted him with a *potesne*, "Thou canst not now strike me." God is angry with every man for his sins. Happy is he that can catch up His Son Jesus; for in whose arms soever the Lord sees His Son He will spare him. The men of Tyre were fain to intercede to Herod by Blastus (Acts xii. 20). Our intercession to God is made by a higher and surer way: not by His servant—by His Son.

Ver. 3. *The ministry of sorrow.*—The ministry of sorrow and disappointment is to test the soul and to temper it to nobler issues, as the oak is tempered and beautified by the winter's storms. Some great agony may be as a cup in which is a draught of moral strength. When we have drunk the repellent mixture, when we have felt the after-benefit, then shall we know that often apparent failure in life is in reality a success.

"Then welcome each rebuff
That turns earth's smoothness rough,
Each sting that bids nor sit nor stand, but go!
Be our joys three-parts pain!
Strive, and hold cheap the strain;
Learn, nor account the pang, daring,
Never grudge the throe."
Browning.

Ver. 5. *Dying of weariness.*—As life goes on most people begin to feel that the word "happy" has no light meaning. Sick of herself through very selfishness, the wife of the Grand Monarque, Louis XIV., thus spoke in her hour of death: "Do you not see that I am dying of weariness amidst a fortune that can scarcely be imagined? I have been young and pretty; I have tasted pleasure; I have been everywhere loved. In an age more advanced I have passed some years in the commerce of the mind; and I protest to you that all conditions leave a frightful void. I can endure no more; I wish only to die." Here surely is an illustration of the words, "Whosoever will save his life shall lose it."

Ver. 5. *"Don't you find it dull?"*—A little street waif was once taken to the house of a great lady, and the childish eyes that had to look so sharply after daily bread were dazzled by signs of splendour on every hand. "Can you get everything you want?" the child asked the mistress of the mansion. "Yes, I think so," was the reply. "Can you buy anything you'd like to have?" The lady answered, "Yes"; and the child, who was of a meditative turn of mind, looked at her half pityingly, and said wonderingly, "Don't you find it dull?" To the little keen mind, accustomed to live bird-like from day to day, and to rejoice over a better supply with the delight born of rarity, the aspect of continual plenty, and desires all gratified by possession, contained an idea of monotony that seemed almost wearisome. Many an owner of a well-filled purse has found life "dull," and pronounced, in the midst of luxury, that all things are vanity.

Ver. 6. *Kazainak, the robber chieftain.*—Kazainak was a robber chieftain inhabiting the mountains of Greenland. He came to a hut where the missionary was translating the Gospel of St. John. He wanted to know what he was doing; and when the missionary told him how the marks he was making were words, and how the book could speak, he wished to hear what it said. The missionary then read the story of Christ's suffering and death, when the chieftain immediately asked, "What has this man done? Has He robbed anybody? Has He murdered anybody?" "No," was the reply; "He has robbed no one, murdered no one; He has done nothing wrong." "Then why does He suffer? Why does He die?" "Listen," said the missionary; "this man has done nothing wrong, but Kazainak has done wrong. This man has not robbed any one, but Kazainak has robbed many. This man has murdered none, but Kazainak has murdered his brother, Kazainak has murdered his child. This man suffered that Kazainak might not suffer; He died that Kazainak might not die." "Tell me the story again," said the astonished chieftain; and the hard-hearted murderer was brought to the foot of the cross.

Ver. 6. *Debt prevents work.*—Once there was an artisan who laboured in the service of a rich Eastern master. Imprudently the man had got into immense debt with an unmerciful creditor, who told him that unless he settled accounts before the close of the year he and his family would be sold as slaves. It was impossible to pay the debt. Meanwhile his master noticed that his work was falling off every week. It was not so cleverly done as before. The weekly account of labour which he produced was lessened. One day he spoke about this to the steward. "Why, sir," the steward replied, "that poor fellow cannot possibly make good work. He cannot manage his tools, for his hands tremble. Nor can he see well what he is doing, for his eyes are filled with tears. A heavy debt is pressing upon him, and until it is paid he will not be able to do one good piece of work." "Tell him that I have paid his debt," said the generous master. The steward went and delivered the message. From that moment fresh vigour was put into the man. His hands trembled no more, nor were his eyes dim with tears. He swung the hammer with a will, and his little dwelling rang with merry songs, and he did his work better and quicker than formerly. A parable of our state. Sin paralyses our moral energies. We are weak. The debt is heavy. We cannot pay; but Christ discharges the debt. We are set at liberty and placed on a new vantage ground. We may run the heavenly course without fainting, and walk without weariness.

Ver. 6. *A father dies for his son.*—In the French revolution a young man was condemned to the guillotine and shut up in one of the prisons. He was greatly loved by many, but there was one who loved him more than all put together. How know we this? It was his own father; and the love he bore his son was proved in this way: When the lists were called, the father, whose name was exactly the same as the son's, answered to the name, and the father rode in the gloomy tumbril out to the place of execution, and his head rolled beneath the axe instead of his son's, a victim to mighty love. See here an image of the love of Christ to sinners; for thus Jesus died for the ungodly.—*Spurgeon.*

Vers. 6-8. " *None of them died for me.*"— Interest in the lepers, those special objects of the Saviour's help, has been greatly revived of late, and attention is justly drawn to the noble deeds wrought by Protestant missionaries in India. The Rev. Dr. Bowman, of the Church Missionary Society, was enabled to erect a place of worship in connection with the Calcutta Leper Asylum, and an aged woman, over eighty-two years old, was there led by the preacher to the divine Healer. A sceptic asked her if the many gods and goddesses of her own religion would not suffice; but she had an answer ready for him: "None of them died for me."—*Henry Proudfoot.*

Christ's sacrifice for sinners. — In the early ages of the Christian Church many slaves were carried prisoners out of Italy into Africa. Paulinus, Bishop of Nola, redeemed many of them, until at last his fortune was exhausted. One day a poor widow came and besought him to recover an only son who had been carried away captive. Being unable to ransom him with money, Paulinus sailed for Africa and induced the prince whose slave the young man was to set him free and take himself in exchange. The bishop performed the duties of slave so faithfully that the prince grew attached to him, and on learning his rank gave him not only his own liberty, but that of his fellow-countrymen who were in bondage.—*W. H. Hatch.*

CHAPTER VI.

CRITICAL NOTES.

Ver. 2.—Necessary connection between faith in Christ's death and abhorrence of sin. Heathen writers speak of the wise and good as dead to sensualities and animal pleasures (Wordsworth).

Ver. 3. **Baptised into His death.**—In relation to His death—*i.e.*, faith in it, acceptation, appropriation, and imitation of it. The relation symbolised by baptism is in its own nature moral and spiritual.

Ver. 4.—Baptism by immersion—and where that cannot be conveniently done, by effusion—represents death and burial, as the emerging again figures a new life (Dean Stanhope).

Ver. 5.—For if we become connate with Him by the likeness of His death, surely we shall also become by the likeness of His resurrection (Wordsworth).

Ver. 6.—Sin is here personified. The body of sin is our own body so far as it is the seat and the slave of sin.

Ver. 7.—The maxim in its physical sense proverbial among the Jews. Thus in the Talmud it is said, " When a man dies, he is freed from the commands."

Ver. 10.— **Died unto sin once.**—Made sin for the Church—a sin offering.

Ver. 11.—To both, our oneness with Him being the ground of our dying to sin, etc. To fulfil God's will, live to Him alone.

Ver. 12.—Sin works bodily desires as the utterances of itself, obedience to which gives it its domain in the body (Wordsworth). Sin personified as a sort of rival sovereign or deity.

Ver. 13.—Do not wield arms for sin. Be as one who has come out of the world of the dead into that of the living, and whose present life has nothing in common with the former.

Ver. 14. **Under grace.**—Both justifying and renewing. In the evangelical state in which grace is offered and bestowed the law is fulfilled and sin overcome. It is from the law as inadequate to effect the sanctification and secure the obedience of sinners that the apostle here declares us to be free.

Ver. 15.—Christ has freed believers from the curse of the law as a covenant, but not from obedience to the law as a rule. We are now translated from the covenant of the law to the covenant of grace (Bishop Sanderson).

Ver. 16.—Whoever wishes to be free, let him neither wish nor show any of those things which depend upon others, otherwise he must be a slave.

Ver. 17. **That form of doctrine.**—τύπον διδαχῆς. Metaphor suggested by the city where the epistle was written. Corinth famous for casting statues in bronze.

Ver. 18.—Emancipated, as a slave receiving his liberty.

Ver. 19.—Meyer renders εἰς ἁγιασμόν, in order to attain holiness, to be ἅγιος in mind and walk. Meyer lays it down that in the New Testament ἁγιασμός is always "holiness," not "sanctification"; Godet also prefers " holiness." On the other hand, Dr. Clifford gives "unto sanctification," and says that ἁγ includes the sanctifying act or process as well as result. Mr. Moule also gives "unto sanctification," and says that the word indicates rather a process than a principle or a condition—a steady course of self-denial, watchfulness. diligence. Dean Vaughan says that ἁγ indicates an act rather than quality. Bishop Westcott says it may be most simply described as the preparation for the presence of God.

Ver. 20.—Had neither learned to revere nor obey the commands.

Ver. 21.— In those things ye had your fruit of which now ye are ashamed. What fruit? None, worse than none; "for," etc.

Ver. 23.—Eternal life is not like wages due for service to God, as death is wages due for service to sin. Eternal life is a donative or free gift of God.

MAIN HOMILETICS OF THE PARAGRAPH.—Verses 1—11.

Buried, but living.—An evil propensity was generated by the first Adam. A good propensity was generated by the Second Adam. The carnal Adamites moved along a descending scale, while the spiritual Adamites move along an ascending scale. Death brooded over the race—a death that had in it no compensating qualities. Christ undertook death that He might educe life. He died unto sin once, that He and the race might live unto God. Christ's death was a death for sin and to sin. On Calvary sin received its deathblow.

It is true that sin still works, but it works as a maimed force, and finally it must be for ever destroyed. He that is dead is freed from sin's power, and must walk henceforth in newness of life. Grace does not lead to licentiousness, but to holiness of heart and of life. This is confirmed by a consideration of :—

I. The spiritual facts.—The great spiritual, central, and foundation fact of Christian life is that the old man is crucified with Christ. 1. *Crucifixion was a process of suffering.* How true is the symbolical teaching! What suffering is sometimes endured while the old man is being crucified! There are gentle natures, good creatures, that seem to be good from their birth and give a negation to the doctrine of original sin, who do not understand the suffering entailed by the moral process called the crucifixion of the old man. But even they sympathetically suffer as they enter into the sufferings of the crucified Saviour. Even they may feel that there is in them an old man that must be crucified. However, there is in other natures—perhaps the natures of the noblest—great suffering as the old man is being crucified. The noblest heroes have strong passions and fierce conflicts. The greatest battles are fought and the sublimest victories won not on earth's gory battle-fields, but in soul spheres. 2. *Crucifixion was a lingering death.* It was a surprise to find that Christ was dead already. In some the old man of sin is long in dying. We think he is dead. We rejoice in our freedom ; and the moment of rejoicing is the moment of disaster. The old man shakes the bonds, loosens the nails, and gives immense trouble. Perhaps the fault with some is that the crucifixion is not complete. A partial crucifixion is a mistake. Crucified with Christ, we must be crucified entirely. The old man in every limb must be slain if there is to be complete victory. 3. *Crucifixion was a sure death at last.* There could be no ultimate escape. The old man may seem to assert himself, but he has been nailed to the tree, and must die. If we have been crucified with Christ, then we cannot live in sin with pleasure.

II. The moral teaching.—For if we have been planted together in the likeness of His death, we shall be also in the likeness of His resurrection. This is a moral likeness. Christ's death is lifted out of the mere material aspect. We do not sufficiently consider the death of Christ in its moral and spiritual relations. Socinianism derives some of its false force from our materialism. Morally we are assimilated with Christ in His death, and so are we in His resurrection. And resurrection is not a resurrection of skin, nerves, bones, and muscles, but a resurrection of soul power. Christ rose to be the dispenser of blessings, to live a crowned life. The believer rises to live a crowned life—the life of peace, of joy, and of holiness. The believer rises to be in his sphere the dispenser of blessings. The believer is a king and a priest—royal being master and king over himself, sacred being dedicated to God and to the promotion of the universal sanctities. He walks in newness of life. If there can be anything new to Jesus, then we may say that He walks in newness of life amid the bright sons of life and of glory,—newness of life to the Unchangeable—newness of life, for He is now the mediator and intercessor. Being assimilated with Christ, we walk in the spirit world. Life is ever new. Fresh breezes blow over earth's dreary plains. Heaven's zephyrs fan the brows of the new immortals.

III. The public profession.—The early Christians were baptised into Jesus Christ, into the name of Jesus Christ, into the death of Jesus Christ. . There was first the change and then the profession. Public profession is against open sin. Some say that the doctrines of grace promote sin, and these objectors would not be the last to point the finger of scorn against the professor who leads an unholy life. The man who professes to be a Christian should be Christ-like. We profess in baptism by our sponsors. How few earnestly take up the obligation! Some few profess too much. A vast number practise too little.

IV. The inward account.—This reckoning should be constantly carried on. "Reckon ye also yourselves to be dead indeed unto sin, but alive unto God through Jesus Christ our Lord." This moral arithmetic is ennobling. Dead to sin. Alive to God,—alive to the Source of the highest life; alive to the infinite goodness; alive to the enriching outcome of the divine nature; alive to all the stirring motives to nobility of character which come from the eternal throne. The outcast from God becomes the friend of God, being alive to and by God. The soul of man is ever reaching upwards when it is reckoning itself to be alive unto God. It is opening itself out to be kissed into moral beauty and sweetness and fragrance by the refreshing beams that flow from the eternal Light.

Ver. 4. *Newness of life.*—If Christ died for our sins, He rose for us too—He rose for our justification. If He is our model in His death, He is also our model in His resurrection from the dead. We have been "buried with Him by baptism into death," says the apostle, "that like as Christ was raised from the dead by the glory of the Father, even so we also should walk in newness of life." The great apostle cannot be understood to ascribe Christ's resurrection to the Father in such sense as to exclude the agency of the Son or of the Spirit. St. Paul's point is, that the Resurrection is the work of God, and as such it occupies a common ground with the new birth or conversion of the soul; for, indeed, no truth is so clearly revealed to us as this—that spiritual life, whether given us at the first in our new birth to Christ, or renewed after repentance in later years, is the free, fresh gift of the Father of our spirits. Nature can no more give us newness of life than a corpse can rise from the dead by its unassisted power. "That which is born of the flesh is flesh." A sense of prudence, advancing years, the love of society around us, family influences, may remodel the surface form of our daily habits; but divine grace alone can turn the inmost being to God—can raise it from the death of sin to the life of righteousness—can clothe it in that "new man which, after God, is created in righteousness and true holiness." There are three characteristics of the risen life of our Lord which especially challenge attention. The first is its reality. The resurrection of Jesus Christ was a real resurrection of a really dead body. The piercing of our Saviour's side, to say nothing of the express language of the evangelists, implied the literal truth of His death; and being thus truly dead, He really rose from the dead. As St. Luke says, epitomising a history in a single expression, "He showed Himself alive after His passion by many infallible proofs." The nearer men came to the risen Jesus, the more satisfied they were that He had risen indeed. So it is with the soul. Its newness of life must be, before everything else, real. What avails it to be risen in the imagination and good opinion of other people, if, in fact, we still live in the tomb of sin? Were it not better for us if we were dead than that men should think and speak of us as being what we are? Even if our new life be not purely an imagination on the part of others, what is the value of a mere ghost of a moral renewal, of prayers without heart in them, of actions without any religious principle, of religious language far in advance of our true convictions and feelings? The first lesson which the risen Christ teaches the Christian is reality, genuineness. A second characteristic of Christ's risen life—it lasts. Jesus did not rise that, like Lazarus, He might die again. "I am He that liveth and was dead; and, behold, I am alive for evermore, and have the keys of hell and of death." So should it be with the Christian. His, too, should be a resurrection once for all. It *should* be. God's grace does not put any sort of force upon us, and what it does in us and for us depends on ourselves. The Christian must reckon himself to be dead indeed unto sin, but alive unto God through Jesus Christ. A last note of Christ's risen life. Most of it was hidden from the eyes of men. They saw enough to be satisfied of its reality; but of the eleven recorded appearances five took place on a single day, and there is accordingly no record of any appearance on thirty-five days out of forty which preceded the Ascension. His visible presence after the Resurrection is the exception rather than the rule. Here is a lesson for the true Christian life. Of every such life the most important side is hidden from the eyes of man. It is a matter of the very first necessity to set aside some time in each day for secret communion with God. In these three respects the true Christian's life is modelled upon the Resurrection. It is sincere and real. It is not a passing caprice or taste, for it lasts. It has a reserved side apart from the eyes of men, in which its true force is nourished and made the most of.—*Canon Liddon.*

Life in Christ here and hereafter.—The death and resurrection of Christ constitute the substance of the gospel, and our concern with them as doctrinal truths includes more than our admitting them into our creed. They must become internal principles, and produce in us corresponding effects. He died, and we must be dead,—dead to the law, not as a rule of life, but as a covenant of works; dead to the world, not as the scene of God's wonderful works, nor as a sphere of duty, nor as a field of usefulness, but as the enemy of God and our portion; dead to sin—this includes nothing less than our avoiding it; but it intends much more : we may be alive to it even while we forsake it; but we must no longer love or relish it, and thus no longer live in it. " How shall we that are dead to sin live any longer therein ? " We must be dead with Him. *We are dead with Him virtually;* for He is the head and representative of His Church, and therefore what He did for His people is considered as done by them. We are dead with Him efficiently; for there is an influence derived from His cross which mortifies us to sin ; and this influence is not moral only, consisting in the force of argument and motive—though this is true, and nothing shows the evil of sin or the love of the Saviour like Calvary—but it is spiritual also. He died to purify as well as to redeem; and He not only made reconciliation for the sins of His people, but received gifts for men, and secured the agency of the Holy Spirit. There is no real holiness to separate from the grace of the cross. There He draws all men unto Him. *We are dead with Him as to resemblance.* We are planted together in the likeness of His death, and therefore our death is called, as well as His, a crucifixion. " Knowing this, that our old man is crucified with Him, that the body of sin might be destroyed, that henceforth we should not serve sin." I am, says the apostle, not only dead, but crucified, with Christ. Because Christ lives, we shall live also. For we are quickened together with Christ, and are raised up and made to sit together in heavenly places—that is, in His company. " Where I am, there shall also My servant be." We have much in heaven to endear it. We may live with another, but not live like him; we may be with another, and behold his estate, but not share it. But " when He who is our life shall appear we shall also appear with Him in glory." " I appoint unto you," says He to His disciples, " a kingdom, as My Father hath appointed unto Me; that ye may eat and drink at My table in My kingdom, and sit on thrones judging the twelve tribes of Israel." Even our vile body shall be fashioned like His own glorious body. And the same duration attaches to His blessedness and ours. " I am alive," says He, " for evermore"; and our end is everlasting life. Finally, *Paul believed all this. And let us do the same ;* but let us believe it as he did—that is, let us believe that we shall live with Him if we be with Him. Some believe it without this. Their faith is only presumption. Whatever they rely upon, whether their knowledge, or orthodoxy, or talking, or profession, they are only preparing for themselves the most bitter disappointment —if they are not dead unto sin and delivered from the present evil world; for

171

if any man have not the Spirit of Christ, he is none of His." But let us also believe that "if we be dead with Him we shall also live with Him." The inclusion is as sure as the exclusion, and takes in every diversity and degree of grace. Whatever be their apprehensions of themselves, none of them all shall come short of this glory. It is as certain as the promise and oath and covenant of God, and the death and intercession of the Saviour, and the pledges and earnests of immortality, can render it. Therefore " be not faithless, but believing." It was used by Christians to animate and encourage each other in the apostle's days, as a common and familiar aphorism; and they gave it full credit: "It is a faithful saying: for if we be dead with Him, we shall also live with Him." —*W. Jay.*

Ver. 1. *Was the Sabbath abrogated ?*—The apostle wrote thus because certain men had perverted a gracious doctrine into an excuse for continued indulgence in wickedness. They heard of the grace of God, and then concluded that, since the presence of sin in the world gave God a splendid opportunity for exhibiting His grace, it were well to sin so that the grace of God might never cease to be manifested. Paul refutes this in this chapter. Bearing this in mind, we may pass on to the question, If we say that we may continue in sin so that grace may abound, may we not take *any* of God's laws, and say, " I will break this, and thus afford God greater scope for the exercise of His grace"? If we answered affirmatively, we should clear the way for a violation of *all* the moral laws. To arrive at a conclusion as to whether God's commandments *are* binding on Christians, we will take the fourth. *Was the Sabbath abrogated?* If not, then argue that the *whole* law stands good to-day. Arguments advanced to prove that the Sabbath is of universal and perpetual obligation :—

I. **The historic aspect of the question proves that the Sabbath was not an exclusively Jewish institution, and therefore the advent of Christianity did not annul it.**—1. Evidence coming from times before the Christian era. 2. Evidence from history of other nations. Uniformity of a septenary division of time throughout the Eastern world. The ancients—Homer, Hesiod, Callimachus, and others—indicate the seventh day as sacred. 3. Evidence from the doings of Christians. A change of day, but not a change of principle.

II. **Which of the laws was abrogated by the advent of Christianity?**— [Note.—There were three separate deliverances of the law—the civil, the ceremonial, and the moral.] Christ did not come to destroy the moral law; but His advent did away with the necessity for the civil and ceremonial.

III. **Notice the relation of the fourth commandment to the other portions of the Decalogue.**—Objectors say it differentiates from the other nine; but no reason for declaring it ceremonial and the others moral, and that Christ therefore sifted the law and eliminated that which referred to the Sabbath.

IV. **Christ did not repudiate the Sabbath.**—1. Would He expose the whole race to the disabilities Jehovah designed to save the Jews from ? If men were to be free in the one point, why restrict them in nine other directions ? 2. In dealing with Pharisees, etc., not a word did Christ speak which tended to degrade the Sabbath. He set the Sabbath right; Jews had deified it, and degraded man. 3. While admitting that Jesus modified Jewish notions regarding the Sabbath, modification is not abrogation.

V. **The New Testament does not countenance any contention for the abolition of the Sabbath.**—1. Some say Rom. xiv. 5 implies a revocation of the divine institution at the dawn of Christianity (see following outline). 2. They also rely on Gal. iv. 10. 3. The Colossian Christians thought good works a necessary security of salvation (Col. ii. 16-23).

VI. **The presumption is against the abrogation of the moral law, and there-**

fore against the abrogation of the Sabbath.—1. Suppose the abrogation of the seventh commandment. What terrible results might be anticipated, considering the awful wickedness of the pagan world when Christ lived! 2. Suppose the abrogation of the first commandment. Think of the idolatry of the Greek and Roman worlds in Christ's time, and the character of the idol-worship was so bad. 3. Suppose the abrogation of the sixth commandment. The world, in Christ's time, reeked with blood—*e.g.*, the arena. Could it be supposed Christ would abrogate any of these laws? Surely there was no slackening in any of them, and why suggest a slackening in the fourth?

VII. **The Sabbath is a " sine quâ non " of human life.**—Hence abrogation, in the light of our knowledge of God's feeling for man, is impossible. 1. Man has always required a day of rest. 2. Never more so than now. 3. The growth of secularising tendencies rendered a Sabbath necessary, to afford opportunity for spiritual growth and worship. So long as human nature holds sway, so long will men require safeguards in things moral and social. The spirit of the age is such that men need such safeguards; hence God will not remove those which He has established. The foregoing arguments having established the continued necessity for the Sabbath, so it is argued that all the other commandments remain in force to-day. All God's commandments are binding on Christians, who have no right to ignore any of His laws under the plea that they do not belong to the present dispensation.—*Albert Lee.*

I. **Sabbath not a Jewish institution.**—The Sabbath not an exclusively Jewish institution. 1. Evidence coming from times before the Christian era— *e.g.*, the periodical worship of Cain and Abel. Also, the Sabbath mentioned as a well-known solemnity before the promulgation of the law. It is expressly taken notice of at the fall of manna; and the incidental manner in which it is then mentioned is convincing proof that the Israelites were no strangers to the institution. 2. Evidence from history of other nations leads us to believe that the Israelites were not alone in their observance of a week of seven days—*e.g.*, the Assyrians and Babylonians in the native account of the Creation speak of Anu having put the finishing touches to the work, and " on the seventh day a holy day appointing, and commanding on that day a cessation from all business." Uniformity of septenary division of time throughout all the Eastern world— Israel, Assyria, Egypt, India, Arabia, Persia, etc. Homer, Hesiod, Callimachus, and others constantly indicate the seventh day as sacred to their countrymen. No one would venture to suggest that this idea was borrowed from Moses; for Linus, *e.g.*, who flourished before Moses, speaks of the seventh day as observed by pious persons. 3. Evidence culled from the doings of Christians. There was a change of day, but not a change of principle.

II. **Moral law now in force.**—It must be remembered that there were three separate deliverances of the law to the Jews—the civil, the ceremonial, and the moral. We admit that there was a repeal in the case of the first two; but nowhere do we find a particle of evidence to sustain the contention that the moral law was abrogated. Those who contend that this was the case forget to clear their minds of local considerations. They need to be reminded that the civil law, rehearsed in the wilderness, was set forth only for the Jews, for their especial guidance, under the peculiar circumstances of their residence, both in the wilderness and Canaan. When we consider the typical or ceremonial law, then, inasmuch as that law was a "type of Christ and good things to come," we are fully prepared to see it pass away when Christ appears upon the scene. To declare that the Sabbath, together with the whole law, had its fulfilment in Christ is a strange idea to spring upon the Church. Christ certainly did not annul the moral law, whatever action He may have taken in regard to the civil and ceremonial. He distinctly rehearsed the moral law in a comprehensive sentence or two: "Thou shalt love," etc. It is true that the Sabbath receives a large share of attention in the civil and ceremonial laws; but it is equally true that it is brought into prominence in the moral law. Since Christ did not come to destroy this last, and actually insisted upon its observance, who shall say that He eliminated the Sabbath portion, but left the others undisturbed?

III. **Review of disputed passages.**—Passages presented by anti-Sabbatarians. 1. Rom. xiv. 5. It is contended by them that this passage implies a revocation of the divine institution at the dawn of Christianity. (1) But the discussion had reference only to the peculiar customs of the Jews, to the rites and practices which they would attempt to impose on the Gentiles, and not to any questions which might arise among Christians as *Christians.* (2) Alford, predisposed to argue the abolition of the Sabbath, says that Paul's language is so sweeping as to do away with the divine obligation of keeping the Sabbath. And yet the apostle says, "Let every man be fully persuaded in his own mind." Could such a vital question as that of Sabbath observance be left to men to interpret, according to every crotchet, especially of the ignorant and godless? It is a question whether there was any allusion to the Sabbath; and even if so, it would not be a question of observing the Sabbath, but rather one of observing the seventh day rather than the first, as Christians were beginning to do. (3) One of the most able comments on this passage runs thus: "It will not do to take it for granted that the Sabbath was merely one of the Jewish festival days, simply because it was observed under the Mosaic economy. If the Lawgiver Himself said of it, when on earth, 'The Son of man is Lord even of the Sabbath day,' it will be hard to show that the apostle must have meant it to be ranked amongst those banished Jewish festival days which only 'weakness' could imagine to be still in force, a weakness which those who had more light ought, out of love, merely to bear with." 2. Gal. iv. 10. Objectors use this to prove that the observance of the Sabbath is a matter of indifference. Note that in the passage the terms "Sabbath" or "Lord's day" are not here mentioned; but assuming that they are implied, we must convict Paul of instability, and shall have reason to doubt his authority if he should allow the Romans to take one course and the Galatians another. Paul, as Olshausen observed, wished to assure the Galatians that the solemnisation in itself of certain ceremonies is not blamed (the old Church, too, had already its festivals), but what was superstitious in it—*i.e.,* the opinion that it was necessary to salvation. Men were not to rest their hopes upon the false assumption that if they observed days and months and times and years superstitiously, they had done all that was necessary to salvation. Findlay, in his work on the Galatians, explains the attitude of the Christians in Galatia. They had already fallen in with the directions of the Jewish teachers. These had made the keeping of holy days a prominent and obligatory part of Christianity, and, as the Romish Church has done, multiplied them superstitiously beyond all reason. Paul called such things "beggarly elements," and meant, doubtless, to convince the Galatians that they were falling into the mischievous tendency to regard the observance of certain days as meritorious. There is not a particle of evidence to prove that Christians were freed from the observance of the Sabbath day. 3. Col. ii. 16-23. In the Colossian Church there was the idea that good works were a security of salvation. This would tend to divert Christians from relying solely on the complete work of Jesus. This explanation is applicable to Col. ii. 16-23. They had trusted to philosophy, and vain traditions, and worshipping of angels, and to legal ceremonies, whereas all these things had ended in Christ. Some might be disposed to think themselves under obligation to keep the last day of the week, *and* the first. If so, they were not to judge those who kept the Lord's day only. Dr. Maclaren points out that Paul does not say, Therefore let no man observe any of these distinctions of meat, feast, and Sabbaths any more; but takes up the much more modest ground, Let no man *judge* you about them.—*Albert Lee.*

Ver. 9. *One victorious life.*—Two things we are said to know in connection with the death of Christ. The one is the resurrection of Christ as an historical fact. We have no reason to suppose that sacred history is less reliable than secular history. The former more reliable than the latter, for it has been assailed, and yet its testimony is unshaken. The witnesses of the Resurrection are numerous and unimpeachable. We too often lose sight of the fact that our Lord was seen after His resurrection by the large number of five hundred brethren. St. Paul could not have mentioned this number to the Corinthian Church if it were not a well-authenticated fact. The other is a revealed truth that Christ dieth no more, and arises as a natural consequence—perhaps rather a moral consequence—from the Resurrection. If He rose from the dead—and certainly He did rise—then there is no need for a second encounter with death. Let us look at the :—

I. **One death.**—What a vast multitude is that of the dead! It seems almost impossible for us to grasp the number of the living that tread this thickly peopled planet! When a man who has led a lonely life in the country goes to London, he is astonished and bewildered as he gazes at the seething mass of humanity. What would be our feelings if from some eminence we could look at the race collected together on an extensive plain? But what is the army of the living when compared with the army of the dead? We see, as we look at the living, one or two generations; while, as we consider the dead, we have to consider generation after generation, through thousands of years, that have passed into the dark and silent shades. Now of all the multitude of deaths which have occurred from the time of Adam to the present day, the death of Christ is pre-eminent and conspicuous; so that we speak of it as the one death to which the ages before Christ's coming look forward, and to which the ages after His resurrection look backward—the one death in its solemn grandeur, in its sublime portents, in its moral and spiritual significance.

II. **One conquest.**—Christ died once, but, being raised from the dead, He dieth no more. And why? 1. *Because the conquest is complete and final.* We fight our battles, both natural and moral, over and over again. One nation conquers another, but the conquered nation recovers strength, recruits its exhausted resources, and then returns to the attack. Individually we conquer our vices, and suppose them dead, when they astonish us by a return, and the conflict is renewed. Christ, by His one death, conquered death and sin—so conquered that they cannot appear as formidable opponents. They may skirmish and do immense damage, but we must believe that their ancient power has departed. Death and sin still work, but surely not as regnant forces in Christ's redeemed world. They move about in chains, and can only do as He permits who has the keys of Hades and of death. 2. *Because the conquest has served the designed moral purpose.* The death of Christ is the one death, for it answered to the movings and designs of infinite love. The death of Christ is the darkest mystery of our humanity if there be no demand for it in the moral government of the infinitely just, holy, and merciful. It is said, Why should Jesus suffer because a vindictive God so demanded? It may be asked, Why should Jesus suffer if He only died the death of a martyr? Let us remember that His sufferings were more than physical. He suffered in soul. He suffered as no martyr ever did or ever could suffer, for He suffered as sin's victim. The sharp iron of suffering entered into His holy and sensitive soul; the burden of the world's sinful load bowed His sacred head, and made the bead-like drops of sweat stand on His immaculate brow. Grief broke His heart of infinite love. The gloomy desolateness of the fatherly love being withdrawn crept over His darkened spirit. Why this intense sorrow? We are not here to satisfy the critical minds who do not earnestly desire satisfaction, but we feel that the only consistent explanation of Christ's death is the old one of evangelical teachers. And if Christ died as a sacrifice, and His death was accepted, then there is no need that He should die any more. 3. *Because the death has evidenced the divine love.* · If men will not believe in the love of God as shown in the mediatorial scheme, neither would they be persuaded though Christ should come again from the invisible world and go through the same career that He enacted in the land of Palestine. We may say it with all due reverence, that the infinite God exhausted His resources when He spared not His Son to convince men of His vast love. Christ once died at love's call. He dieth no more to convince unconvinceable creatures. A second death could not accomplish that which the first death has failed to procure. O Love divine, touch unloving hearts, and lead them to see and feel Thy infinite love!

III. **One victorious life.**—Death hath no more dominion over the risen and glorified Christ. On His sacred head are many crowns—the brightest is the crown of redemption—and He will never be any more as an uncrowned being. The sceptre of life will never again be wrested from His grasp. Strange that the Prince of life should be subject unto death; but the marvel is lessened as we think of the moral purpose, as we consider the infinite love, as we contemplate the victorious life. He sees of the unimagined travail of His soul, and is abundantly satisfied. Can there be new joys, fresh emotions, to an infinite nature? In some way or other there must be fresh emotions stirred in the soul of Jesus, for He, when on earth, looked to the joy before, and now He delights in the newly gained pleasure. He sits enthroned the Prince of life in the kingdom of life and blessedness. He dieth no more.

IV. **One blessed consequence.**—All true believers live with Him—live with Him in a larger sense than would have been before or otherwise possible. Life is enlarged and glorified by the risen life of the once crucified Saviour. Christ dieth no more: then we have an ever-living intercessor. Christ dieth no more: then we have an abiding helper. Christ dieth no more: then we need no other sacrifice and no other priest. Christ dieth no more: then we need not fear, for the Good Shepherd will ever watch over His sheep, and lead them in pastures of delight.

Ver. 9. *Christ risen, dieth no more.*—In these words we have two points which are at the bottom of all true Easter joy: 1. The reality of the Resurrection, "Christ being raised from the dead." 2. The perpetuity of Christ's risen life, "Christ being raised, dieth no more." The Resurrection is not merely an article of the Creed, it is a fact in the history of mankind. If the testimony which can be proved for the Resurrection concerned only a political occurrence or a fact of natural history witnessed some eighteen hundred years ago, nobody would think of denying its cogency. Those who do reject the truth of the Resurrection, quarrel, not with the proof that the Resurrection has occurred, but with the prior idea that such a thing could happen under any circumstances. No proof would satisfy this class of minds, because they have made up their minds that the thing cannot be. We Christians may well say it is the first of miracles, and as such it must be unwelcome to those who make their limited personal experience of the world of nature the measure of all spiritual as well as all physical truth. This is the joy, the happiness, which is brought to many a human soul by such a fact as the resurrection of Christ. It tells us that matter is not the governing principle of this universe. It assures us that matter is controlled; that there is a Being, that there is a will, to which matter can offer no effective resistance; that He is not bound by the laws of the universe ; that He, in fact, controls them. The Resurrection was not an isolated miracle, done, and then over, leaving things much as they had been before. The risen Christ is not, like Lazarus, marked off from every other man as one who had visited the realms of death, but knowing that He must again be a tenant of the grave. " Christ being risen, dieth no more." His risen body is made up of flesh, bone, and all things pertaining to the perfection of man's nature, but it has superadded qualities. It is so spíritual that it can pass through closed doors without collision or disturbance. It is beyond the reach of those causes which slowly or swiftly bring down our bodies to the dust. Being raised from the dead, it dies no more. The perpetuity of the life of the risen Jesus is the guarantee of the perpetuity of the Church. Alone among all forms of society, the Church of Christ is ensured against complete dissolution. Christ, risen from death, dying no more, is the model of our new life in grace. I do not mean that absolute sinlessness is attainable by any Christian here. " If we say we have no sin, we deceive ourselves." But faithfulness in our intentions, avoidance of known sources of danger, escape from presumptuous sins—these are possible and necessary. Those lives which are made up of alternating recovery and relapse—recovery, perhaps, during Lent, followed by relapse after Easter—or even lives lived with one foot in the grave, without anything like a strong vitality, with their feeble prayers, half-indulged inclinations, with weaknesses which may be physical, but which a regenerate will should do at once away with—men risen from the dead, yet without any seeming promise of endurance in life,—what would St. Paul say to these ? " Christ being . . . no more." Just as He left His tomb this Easter morning once for all, so should the soul once risen be dead to sin. The risen life of Jesus tells us what our own new life should be. Not that God, having raised us by His grace from spiritual death, forces us, whether we will or not, to live on continuously. But how, you ask, how can we rejoice in our risen Lord if we are so capable in our weakness of being untrue to His example ? I answer, Because what resurrection life is the strength of our own as well as its model. Pray then in the spirit of this text that at least if you have risen you may persevere. Perseverance is a grace, just as much as faith, hope, charity, contrition. The secret strength of perseverance is a share in the risen life of Jesus. Perseverance may be won by earnest prayer for union with our risen Lord.—*Canon Liddon.*

SUGGESTIVE COMMENTS ON VERSES 1—11.

Christians dead to sin.—The words, according to their most obvious meaning, seem to refer merely to the engagement to avoid sin, which is implied in the act of becoming Christians. God forbid ! exclaims the apostle, that any person should so grievously pervert the doctrine of Christ as to think that it encourages continuance in sin in order to afford the more ample scope for the exercise of divine grace, for by the very act of becoming Christians we became dead to sin. This strong expression means simply that we professed ourselves ready to die unto sin, to resist all its temptations, and through the aid of divine grace to overcome them ; and how then can we continue in the practice of that which we have so solemnly renounced? This would be contradicting, in our conduct, the profession which we have made, and showing that our profession is insincere and hypocritical, and that we have no title to the sacred character of Christians to which we lay claim. No true Christian can act on a principle so

177

directly incompatible with the engagements implied in assuming the Christian character.—*Ritchie.*

Christ died a sin offering.—" For in that He died, He died unto sin once ; but in that He liveth, He liveth unto God." To die unto sin, by the common Scripture use of the words, means to cease to commit sin. But this cannot be affirmed of any but those who have lived in the practice of it, and therefore it is wholly inapplicable to our blessed Saviour, who did no sin. No doubt the words may be so paraphrased as to make them applicable to Him without any paraphrase : " For in that He died, He died *by sin* once"— that is, died on account of it ; sin was the cause of His dying. Or perhaps still more appositely, He died for sin— that is, for a sin offering. The expression He died for " sin once " indicates that this once offering up of Himself was sufficient, and that therefore no further sacrifice was necessary. " But in that He liveth, He liveth unto God." This clause admits of being rendered like the former : " He liveth by God "—that is, by the power of God ; the allusion being to what is said in the fourth verse, that Jesus was raised from the dead by the glorious power of the Father. But the more obvious and natural idea suggested by the words is that He liveth to the praise of God—He lives to promote the glory of God by carrying the plan of providence founded on the mediatorial dispensation forward to its appointed issue, and thus accomplishing the holy and gracious purposes which the Almighty hath determined to bring to pass. The verse might therefore be paraphrased : " For in that He died, He died once for all as a sacrifice for sin ; but in that He liveth, He liveth for ever to promote the glory of God." These words convey the important and consoling doctrine, so often quoted in Scripture, that the death of Christ is a sacrifice for sin, all perfect in its nature and sufficient to reconcile us to God, and that therefore He needed

not repeat it, the once offering of Himself being sufficient " to perfect for ever them that are sanctified." And they convey the further encouraging truth that Christ, being raised from the dead, is now vested with all power as mediator of the new covenant, and " able to save them to the uttermost 'that come unto God by Him."—*Ritchie.*

Believer's death to sin gradual.—We conclude by saying that death to sin is not an absolute cessation of sin at any moment whatever, but an absolute breaking of the will with it, with its instincts and aspirations, and that simply under the control of faith in Christ's death *for* sin. The practical application of the apostle's doctrine regarding this mysterious death, which is at the foundation of Christian sanctification, seems to me to be this : The Christian's breaking with sin is undoubtedly gradual in its realisation, but absolute and conclusive in its principle. As in order to break really with an old friend whose evil influence is felt half measures are insufficient, and the only efficacious means is a frank explanation, followed by a complete rupture which remains like a barrier raised beforehand against every new solicitation ; so to break with sin there is needed a decisive and radical act, a divine deed taking possession of the soul, and interposing henceforth between the will of the believer and sin (Gal. vi. 14). This divine deed necessarily works through the action of faith in the sacrifice of Christ.— *Godet.*

Purpose of our death in Christ.— Christ once lived under the curse of sin and in a body over which death ruled. He died, and arose from the dead. By dying once He escaped for ever from the curse of sin, and from death, the result of sin. He now lives a life of which God is the only aim. In former days we did the bidding of sin, and were thus exposed to the anger of God. To make it consistent with

His justice to save us, God gave Christ to die, and raised Him from the dead. His purpose is to unite us to Christ, so that we may share Christ's life and moral nature. For this end we were formally united to Christ in baptism. We were thus joined to One who was by death set free from death, and was raised by God into a deathless life. Therefore if the purpose of God be realised in us, we are practically dead with Christ. And if so, all law proclaims us free. We therefore infer that the purpose of our death with Christ is to free us from the service of sin.

And if so, we also infer that our union with Christ is more than union with His death. For we see Christ not only free from sin, but living a life devoted to God; and we know that such devotion to Himself is what God requires from us. Therefore we are sure that God designs us to be united to Christ, both in His freedom from sin and in His active devotion to God. Consequently to live in sin is to resist God's purpose for us, and to renounce the new life to which baptism was designed to lead us.—*Beet.*

MAIN HOMILETICS OF THE PARAGRAPH.—Verses 12—21.

Two services contrasted.—Sin and righteousness are the two claimants for the moral service of man. They are the two forces battling, one for the destruction and the other for the salvation of the race. Sin finds an ally in the fallen nature of man; righteousness appeals to the nobler nature, is supported by the better instincts, and is on the side of the divine order and fitness of things. Nevertheless sin reigns in a very extensive sphere; and every effort is required, and every argument and consideration must be adduced in order that sin may not reign in the mortal body of the believer. Contrast, then, the two services :—

I. **The service of sin.**—1. *The pleasure of this service is short-lived.* Whatever view may be taken of the expression "mortal body," we shall do no violence to the phrase by making it set forth the short-lived pleasure of sin. The greater part of sin's pleasure arises from the lusts of the flesh. When the body is worn out, when the physical powers are decaying, sin has no fascinating baits to allure. The old sinner may curse the service in which he has engaged. Why, indeed, should a Christian be under any temptation to let sin reign in his mortal body? 2. *The effect of this service is degrading and weakening.* Said the old heathen, "I am nobler and born to nobler things than that I should make the soul the servant of the body." Surely the Christian is born by his spiritual birth to nobler things than the man can be by natural birth, and far be it from him to obey the lusts of the carnal nature. Let him understand the greatness of his moral manhood; let him feel the dignity which grace confers; let him realise the teaching that the service of sin is both degrading and weakening. It is a service of uncleanness. It moves downward from iniquity to iniquity. No chance of promotion in this service—no high ambitions to stir the soul to deeds of lofty emprise. Whatever beauty the soul possesses is destroyed by sin's handiwork. 3. *The fruit of this service is shame and death.* This is a kind of fruit which the sinner is compelled to gather, and gather it even in this world. It is an awfully bad sign when shame does not attend and follow the sinner's course. Indeed, he is dead while he lives. Souls alive to the beauty and glory of goodness feel bitter shame and remorse when they have fallen under the power of evil passions. Why should the man who has tasted the delights of freedom go back to slavery? Why should the man who has trod the mountain heights where God's pure breezes blow descend to the dungeons where foul miasma swelters? Why should the man who has been entranced by the comely form of righteousness embrace the loathsome carcass of sin?

II. The service of righteousness.—1. *The pleasure of this service is eternal.* It is the service rendered by the moral nature, and that is immortal. Righteousness is eternal, and the pleasure which it imparts to its adherents is ever abiding. Soul pleasure is the highest good. 2. *The effect of this service is ennobling and strengthening.* Man is a temple in ruins. The image has been defaced, the glory has departed. Ichabod is written on the desolation, and the temple is to be rebuilt and the glory regained by yielding ourselves unto God, as those that are alive from the dead, and our members as instruments of righteousness unto God. The noblest heroes have been the men of righteousness. God crowned men, the glory of the race. The bright gems of humanity have been the truth-lovers and the truth-servers. The practice of righteousness is strengthening. To do good is the way to be good, to be morally strong. It is always strengthening to follow lofty ideals, and striving continually to realise. Obedience to a form of noble teaching is glorious and enriching. The molten metal run into the form becomes strong and beautiful. The ductile heart run into the form of sound doctrine becomes strong and beautiful. 3. *The fruit of this service is lustre and life.* "The path of the just is as the shining light." A bright lustre marks the pathway which they tread. In dark days of the world's history the sons of righteousness have shone out like lustrous stars from a dark sky. True honour is the crown of goodness. Life in all its fulness is the heritage here and hereafter of those who make for, and zealously pursue after, and perseveringly practise righteousness. We ought then to resist all the efforts made by sin to reign in our mortal bodies. We ought to wage incessant war against sin ; and we are encouraged to be brave and bold in the conflict by the reflection that sin cannot gain the mastery except from our own fault. "For sin shall not have dominion over you : for ye are not under the law, but under grace." Let not the members of our bodies become the arms or weapons of unrighteousness which sin may use to our undoing. Remember that the moral and material are connected, that body and soul are united. Body and soul, all the members of the body, all the powers and faculties of the soul, all from the lowest to the highest, must be yielded unto God as instruments of righteousness.

Ver. 21. *The future state of the heathen.*—In contemplating the future state and prospects of the heathen, it is proposed to show :—
I. That the heathen are sinners against God.
II. That, being sinners, they are justly exposed to the penalty of the divine law.
III. That from this penalty they cannot be delivered without repentance and reformation.
IV. That the heathen in general exhibit no satisfactory evidence of repentance, but the contrary ; and
V. The Scriptures teach directly, and not by mere inference, that the end of heathenism is eternal death.
I. I am to show that the heathen are sinners against God. We might infer as much as this from the fact that, like us, they are the children of a fallen father and belong to a depraved and corrupted race. Are not the heathen human beings ? Do they not belong to the "one blood" of which God hath made "all men for to dwell on the face of the whole earth" ? Are they not the posterity of Adam ? If so, then undoubtedly they are depraved and sinful, for this is true of all Adam's posterity. "By the offence of one the many were made sinners." "By one man sin entered into the world, and death by sin, and so death hath passed upon all men, for that all have sinned." The Scriptures assert frequently and positively that the heathen are sinners. Thus Paul says to the converted heathen in verses already quoted, "Ye were the servants of

sin." " Ye have yielded your members servants to uncleanness, and to iniquity unto iniquity." That the heathen of our times, like those of whom Paul speaks, are "all under sin" is proved by the testimony of missionaries and of other competent and impartial witnesses. Every command of the Decalogue, every precept, whether of natural or revealed religion, is openly and shamelessly violated among them. They are, almost without an exception, idolaters. They are, to a shameful extent, the profaners even of their own sacred things. Instead of honouring and protecting their aged parents, they in some instances abandon them to perish with hunger, in others they burn them or bury them alive, and in others slaughter and devour them. Their murders are frequent and of the most horrible description. " Their lewdness," says one who had long resided among them, " is such as can never be described by a Christian writer." Their sacred books rather encourage than prohibit theft. In some places they even " pray that they may become expert in it, boast of it when successfully accomplished, and expect to be rewarded for it in the future world." " Among the common people of India," says a veteran missionary, " lying is deemed absolutely necessary, and perjury is so common that no reliance whatever can be placed upon the testimony of heathen witnesses. For a piece of money not larger than a fourpenny-piece they can be hired to swear to anything which their employer requires." The same missionary adds, " The characters of the heathen have not at all improved since the days of the apostle Paul."

II. But if the heathen have broken the law of God, then they have justly incurred its penalty. This is my second proposition. The law of God, like every other good law, has a just penalty annexed to it. Nor are we left in ignorance as to what the penalty of the divine law is. It is called in the Scriptures death—the second death. Now this penalty the heathen, by transgressing the law of God, have justly incurred. Accordingly Paul says, referring especially to the case of the heathen, " As many as have sinned without law "—that is, a written law— " shall also perish without law." Of course the guilt and the future punishment of the heathen will be in proportion to the light they have resisted. It will be far less in degree than though they had slighted the Bible and rejected a freely offered Saviour.

III. But this brings me to my third proposition, in which I am to show that the terrible penalty of the divine law, which the heathen have justly incurred by sin, cannot be remitted to them, or to any other sinners, without repentance and reformation. In the Scripture God makes repentance not only the condition but the indispensable condition of forgiveness. He not only says, " Repent, and ye shall be forgiven," but " Except ye repent, ye shall all perish." Of what avail would it be to impenitent sinners were God to pardon them? Retaining their hard and unsanctified hearts, they would instantly and continually repeat their transgressions, and fall again and again under the sentence which had been remitted. And were God to pardon them finally and receive them up to heaven, it would be no heaven to them. They would have no meetness for such a heaven.

IV. And now we come to the question under our fourth proposition—a question on the decision of which the future condition of the heathen most essentially depends. Do they, in their heathen state, repent of their sins? Do they furnish any satisfactory evidence of repentance? Most gladly would we accept such evidence if it were furnished. But where shall we look for it? Is it to be found? Did Paul find the heathen among whom he went publishing the gospel of the grace of God penitently prepared to welcome the truth? Do our missionaries find the same? I would not say that there never was a pious heathen. I hope there may have been some of this character. And as to the final salvation of pious heathen, I do not entertain a doubt. They will be forgiven as soon as they repent. They will be saved through Christ, though they may not have heard of Him in the present life. But do the heathen, in frequent instances, repent? Do they give satisfactory evidence of repentance? These questions I am constrained to answer in the negative. With such facts as these standing out before us and staring us in the face, how can we resist the conclusion that the heathen in general are impenitent, hard-hearted, not only ignorant but perverse, in love with sin, and resolved to persist in it to the bitter end? Such certainly is the conclusion to which our modern missionaries have come. They have the best possible opportunities for forming a judgment in the case, and their deliberate judgment is such as I have stated.

V. I only add that this painful conclusion is sustained by the current representations of Scripture. " The wicked shall be turned into hell, with all the nations that forget God." I know that plausible objections are urged against this scriptural conclusion ; but they are all based on false assumptions, and of course vanish as soon as they are brought into the light of truth. It is said, for example, that the heathen are in a state of invincible ignorance, that they do as well as they know. It is not true that the heathen do as well as they know or as well as they can. They know a great deal better than they do, and might do better if they would. They are criminal, culpable in the sight of God. They feel and know that they are. They know that they are deserving of punishment, and hence the various expedients to which they resort to pacify conscience and appease the anger of their gods. The heathen do not deserve so great punishment indeed as though they had resisted greater light ; but they are guilty of resisting and abusing the light they have, and unless they repent and are forgiven must receive a just punishment at the hands of God. Show me that the sinner in the other life, whether Christian or heathen, will ever relent and be humble and begin to feel after God, and I will admit that there may be hope in his case. But the truth is, he will never do this. Let us contemplate that not less than six hundred millions of the present inhabitants of our globe are heathens. Each one of these is an immortal creature, destined to live for ever. Now they have a season of probation. In a mighty stream they are pouring over the boundaries of time ; and when once they have leaped those boundaries, where do they fall? They fall to rise no more. There is a remedy for all this evil, and this we have in our own hands. It is the gospel. This offers peace and pardon to those who are guilty and ready to perish. Let the gospel be universally diffused and embraced, and the broad road to ruin is no longer frequented.—*Enoch Pond, D.D.*

SUGGESTIVE COMMENTS ON VERSES 12—21.

What is the meaning of "mortal"?— The epithet θνητῷ, " mortal," must bear a logical relation to the idea of the passage. The object of this term has been understood very variously. Calvin regards it as expressive of contempt, as if Paul meant to say that man's whole bodily nature hastens to death, and ought not consequently to be pampered. Philippi thinks that the epithet refers rather to the fact of sin having *killed* the body, and having thus manifested its *malignant* character. Flatt thinks that Paul

alludes to the *transient* character of bodily pleasures. Chrysostom and Grotius find in the word the idea of the *brevity of the toils* which weigh on the Christian here below. According to Tholuck, Paul means to indicate how evil lusts are inseparable from the present state of the body, which is destined by-and-by to be glorified. According to Lange and Schaff, the sanctification of the mortal body here below is mentioned as serving to prepare for its glorification above. It seems to us that this epithet may be

182

explained more naturally: it is not the part *destined to die* which should rule the believer's personality; the higher life awakened in him should penetrate him wholly, and rule that body even which is to change its nature. The apostle does not say now, "*that* grace may abound," words which could only come from a heart yet a stranger to the experiences of faith; but he says here, "*because* we are under grace." The snare is less gross in this form. Vinet one day said to the writer of these lines, "There is a subtle poison which insinuates itself into the .heart even of the best Christian; it is the temptation to say, Let us sin, not *that* grace may abound, but *because* it abounds." Here there is no longer an odious calculation, but a convenient let alone. Where would be the need of holding that the apostle, to explain this question, has in view an objection raised by legal Judeo-Christianity? The question arises of itself as soon as the gospel comes in contact with the heart of man. What proves clearly that the apostle is not thinking here of a Jewish-Christian scruple is the fact that in his reply he does not make the least allusion to man's former subjection to the law, but solely to the yoke which sin laid upon him from the beginning. And the literal translation of our verse is not, "For ye are no more under .the law," but "For ye are no more *under law*, but *under grace*." It is understood, of course, that when he speaks of *law* he is thinking of the Mosaic dispensation, just as, when speaking of grace, he is thinking of the revelation of the gospel. But he does not mention the institutions as such; he designates them only by their moral *character*. —*Godet.*

Bold metaphors.—The metaphors in this chapter are extremely bold; yet being taken from matters well known, they were used with great advantage. For the influence of sinful passions, in constraining wicked men to commit evil actions, could not be better repre-

sented to those who were acquainted with the condition of slaves, and with the customs by which their lives and services were regulated, than by the power which a tyrannical lord exercised over his slaves. Neither could anything more affecting be devised to show the miserable condition of a person habitually governed.—*Macknight.*

Paul speaks after the manner of men. —" I speak after the manner of men, because of the weakness of your flesh." This is an epanorthosis, in which he corrects the phraseology which he has just made use of, in saying that those who are "under grace are made over unto righteousness," since, on the contrary, they are set at liberty to serve God; and he lays the blame of this catachresis on their weakness as the occasion of it. For as they would not understand him expressing heavenly things in the language of heaven, he is compelled, in teaching them, to employ these similitudes of servitude and liberty borrowed from the intercourse of men : " For as ye have yielded your members servants to uncleanness, and iniquity unto iniquity, even so now yield your members servants to righteousness unto holiness." In these words we have the conclusion of the syllogism—viz., that those who are under grace should not sin—illustrated by a comparison of similarity with their previous conduct, both the protasis and apodosis of which are illustrated by their end.—*Ferme.*

Sin as a king.—Sin, as a raging and commanding king, has the sinner's heart for its throne; the members of the body for its service; the world, the flesh, and the devil for its grand council; lusts and temptations for its weapons and armoury; and its fortifications are ignorance, sensuality, and fleshly reasonings. Death, as the punishment of sin, is the end of the work, though not the end of the worker. —*Burkitt.*

" *Let not sin therefore.*"—As if the apostle should say, We preach purity, and not liberty, as the adversary

183

suggesteth (ver. 1 of this chapter with chap. iii. 8). Let not sin reign; rebel it well; but do not actively ob y and embrace the commands of sin, as subjects to your king. Let sin be dejected from its regency, though not utterly ejected from its residency. Give it such a deadly wound that it may be sure to die within a year and a day. Sprunt it may, and flutter as a bird when the neck is broken; but live it must not.

"*That form of doctrine.*" — Gr., "That type or mould"; the doctrine is the mould, hearers the metal, which takes impression from it in one part as well as another. And as the metal hath been sufficiently in the furnace, when it is not only purged from the dross, but willingly receiveth the form and figure of that which it is cast and poured into, so here.—*Trapp.*

Christians by grace throw off sin.— "Christians are placed in a condition of which *grace* is the prominent feature : grace to sanctify as well as grace to renew the heart ; grace to purify the evil affections ; grace to forgive offences, though often repeated, and thus to save from despair, and to excite to new efforts of obedience. Viewed in this light, there is abundant reason for asserting that Christians, under a system of grace, will much more effectually throw off the dominion of sin than they would do if under a mere law dispensation." Yet if there be one point where there is most obscurity in the minds of the majority of professing Christians, it is here. That it has largely arisen from an obscuration of the doctrine of sanctification by grace, or rather the unwise sundering of justification and sanctification in discussing this epistle, is painfully true.—*Stuart and Lange.*

The sense of sin and guilt the foundation of all religion.

I. That the shame and rem rse which attend upon sin and guilt arise from the natural impressions on the mind of man.—It is certain from experience that we can no more direct by our choice the sensations of our mind than we can those of the body. We are taught by the sense of pain to avoid things hurtful or destructive to the body; and the torments and anxiety of mind which follow so close and so constantly at the heels of sin and guilt are placed as guardians to our innocence, as sentinels to give early notice of the approach of evil which threatens the p ace and comfort of our lives. If we are perfect masters of the sensations of our mind, if reflection be so much under command, that when we say "Come," it cometh, when we say "Go," it goeth, how is it that so many suffer so much from the uneasy thoughts and suggestions of their own hearts, when they need only speak the word and be whole? Whence the self-conviction, the self-condemnation of sinners, whence the foreboding thoughts of judgment to come, the sad expectations of divine vengeance, and the dread of future misery, if the sinner has it in his power to bid these melancholy thoughts retire, and can when he pleases sit down enjoying his iniquities in peace and tranquillity? These considerations make it evident that the pain and grief of mind which we suffer from a sense of having done ill flow from the very constitution of our nature, as we are rational agents. Nor can we conceive a greater argument of God's utter irreconcilableness to sin than that He has given us such a nature that we can never be reconciled to it ourselves. We never like it in others where we have no interest in the iniquity, nor long approve of it in ourselv s when we have The hours of cool reflection are the sinner's mortification, for vice can never be happy in the company of reason, which is the true cause why profligate sinners fly to any excess that may help them to forget themselves and hide them from the light of reason, which, whenever it ceases to be the glory of man, will necessarily become his shame and reproach. No vice is the

184

better for being found in the company of intemperance, but becomes more odious in the sight of God and man. And yet how often does vice fly to intemperance for refuge?—which shows what miserable company sinners are to themselves, when they can be content to expose themselves to the contempt of all about them, merely for the sake of being free from their own censure for a season. Were it in the power of men to find any expedient to reconcile their reason to their vices, they would not submit to the hard terms of parting with their reason for the sake of being at ease with their vices. But there is no remedy: as long as we have the power of thinking, so long must we think ill of ourselves when we do ill. The only cure for this uneasiness is to live without thought; for we can never enjoy the happiness of a brute till we have sunk ourselves into the same degree of understanding.

II. **That the expectation of punishment for sin is the result of the reason given unto us. The end of those things is death.**—There are no certain principles from which we can infer the nature and sort of punishment designed by God for sinners; and as reason has left us in the dark in this particular, so neither has revelation clearly discovered this secret of providence. The representations of Scripture upon this head are metaphorical: the images are strong and lively, full of horror and dread, and lead us to this certain conclusion, that endless misery will be the lot of the unrighteous. But they do not lead us to a solution of all the inquiries which an inquisitive mind may raise upon this occasion. We read of the *fire that never goes out*, of *the worm that never dies*, both prepared to prey upon the wicked to all eternity. But what this fire is, what this worm is, that shall for ever torture, and never destroy the wicked, we are nowhere informed. Among the ancient heathens we find variety of opinions, or, to speak more properly, of imaginations, upon this

subject; and though none of them can make any proof in their own behalf, yet they all prove the common ground upon which they stand, the natural expectation of punishment for iniquity. The atheistical writers of antiquity entertain themselves with exposing the vulgar opinions of their time; and the unbelievers of our time have trodden in their steps, and pleased themselves mightily with dressing up the various and uncertain imaginations of men upon this subject. But what is this to the great point? If nature has rightly instructed us in teaching us to expect punishment for our sins, what signifies it how far men have been mistaken in determining the kinds of punishment that are in reserve for sinners? Let the learning of the Egyptians pass for superstition, and the wisdom of the Greeks for folly; yet what has the sense of nature to do with them, which teaches us to expect punishment for sin from the hand that made us? And when once the time comes in which that hand shall exert itself, this we may be sure of, that the sinner will find no further subject for laughter and diversion. Men think they gain a great point by bringing plausible reasons against the common notions of future punishment; but suppose these notions to be indeed mistakes, yet if it remains certain from the light of reason, as well as of revelation, that God will punish sin, what does the cause gain by this argument? Will you suppose that God intends to punish wickedness, and yet that He has no possible way to do it? Where lies the defect? Is it want of wisdom to contrive proper means for the punishment of sin, or is it want of power to put them in execution? If he wants neither the one nor the other, we have nothing to inquire after in this case but what His will is; and of that He has given us such evidence that we can never lose sight of it as long as we continue to be reasonable creatures. The power of conscience which every man feels in himself, the fear that pursues every sin, that haunts the most secret and most successful offenders, are great evidences of the common expectation of a judgment to come.

III. **That these common notions are the foundation of all religion, and therefore must be supposed and admitted in revealed religion, and cannot be contradicted by it.**—Some there have been who, finding no hopes for impunity to sinners under the light of reason and nature, have taken shelter in revelation; not desiring to correct and reform their vices, but to enjoy them, and yet to hide them from the wrath to come. These are great extollers of the mercy and goodness of God displayed in the gospel, great assertors of the extensive and unbounded merits of the blood of Christ, so far as to think it a reproach to their Saviour for any one to teach that the hopes of Christians may be destroyed for sin, since Christ has died to make an atonement for it. Such as these are much pleased with the thought that they do great honour to God by opening to the world the inexhaustible treasures of His mercy, the attribute in which He delights; and think they have some merit and service to plead on account of such pious labour. They imagine they pay great regard to our Redeemer, and are the only true believers in the efficacy of His death, the virtue of which was so great as to draw out the sting of sin, and leave all the pleasures of it behind to be enjoyed by the world. But would these men consider, they would find that they are offering up to God the sacrifice of fools, whilst they divest Him of wisdom and justice, and all other moral attributes, in compliment to His mercy, and represent Him to the world as a good-natured, indolent, inactive Being, unconcerned

at what passes among His creatures, and prepared to receive to equal degrees of favour the righteous and the sinner. It is beside my present purpose to show how inconsistent these notions are with the true doctrine of the gospel; and yet I cannot satisfy myself without observing that all the precepts, all the representations of Scripture, all the hopes and fears proposed to Christians, teach us another lesson, and confirm to us this great article of all religion: "*that God hath appointed a day in which He will judge the world in righteousness.*" This is the gospel doctrine; nor can a true revelation possibly teach otherwise; for God cannot contradict Himself, nor gainsay by His prophets that common light of reason which He has planted in men to be their guide and director. Natural religion is the foundation and support of revelation, which may supply the defects of nature, but can never overthrow the established principles of it; which may cast new light upon the dictates of reason, but can never contradict them. I cannot listen to revelation but in consequence of the natural notion I have of God, of His being, His wisdom, power, and goodness: destroy, then, the principles of reason, and there is no room left for revelation. I see and feel the difference between good and evil, virtue and vice: what spirit must that be which teaches me that there is no such difference? Shall I believe it to be a spirit come from God, when I know that the Spirit He has placed within me speaks the contrary? In which case there is only this choice: either to disown God for my creator, or to reject the spirit which contradicts the law of my creation and the light of reason which God has placed in the minds of men.—*Sherlock.*

MAIN HOMILETICS OF THE PARAGRAPH.—Verses 22, 23.

Four stages in the Christian's life.—The essentials of the Christian's course are marked out for us in this short passage. We here get, as it were, a bird's-eye view of all that is needful from the time of conversion to the period of entrance upon the blessing of everlasting life. We begin with the great deliverance, we pass on to the great change, we see the Christian growing in meetness for the inheritance of the saints in light, and then when the earthly trials and conflicts are over we see him passing a disciplined soul across the narrow stream of death into the unfading beauties of that life which is everlasting. The soul that passes through the experiences here laid down has nothing to fear, and is blessed indeed. Let us seek to understand its teaching. Four points claim our attention: the gracious deliverance, the glorious change, the blessed result, the happy termination.

I. **The gracious deliverance.**—It was a gracious deliverance when Noah and his sons were saved by means of the ark. Lot was rescued from the burning cities; the children of Israel were brought forth from the land of Egyptian bondage; the man-slayer found asylum in the city of refuge from the avenger of blood; David escaped the javelin thrown by the frenzied Saul; Daniel came forth from the lions' den uninjured; and the three Hebrew children marched in triumph from the furnace without having upon them so much as the smell of fire. But still more gracious is that deliverance when the soul is made free from sin. *It is a deliverance from the accusation of sin.* When we sin we depart knowingly from the rule of duty, and that departure becomes a voice of reproof and of accusation. Every sin which a man commits becomes to that man an accuser, unless he has become hardened, and then hereafter those stifled voices of his sins will speak in trumpet tones to the unutterable dismay of his spirit. Terrible is it for the man with a tender conscience and a sensitive nature to hear within the accusing voice of his past sins. And great rejoicing is heard in every house and in every street of the town of Mansoul when the man is set free from sin. *It is a deliverance from the penalty of sin.* "The wages of sin is death." "The soul that sinneth it shall die." Death physical, intellectual, and moral is the penalty of sin. Sin has a killing power. It touches, withers, and destroys the nobler parts of man's nature, so that the man by sin is dead while he lives. Gracious deliverance it is to be set free from sin's penalty, to be raised from death to life. *It is a deliverance from the tyranny of sin.* Sin is a tyrant that grips and holds his victims with an iron hand, and keeps them grinding with remorseless cruelty at the wheel of oppression. Many of sin's victims see the tyranny and long to be set free. They see the awful ruin to which they are being led, but cannot escape. They cannot escape except by the power of divine grace. It is thus alone that they can be set free from sin. It is a gracious deliverance, for it had a gracious origin. "By grace are ye saved." For it is by a gracious Author,—the gracious method of the gospel plan of salvation. It is by the name of Jesus Christ of Nazareth. "Neither is there salvation in any other; for there is none other name under heaven given among men whereby we must be saved." Oh that men would believe in Jesus Christ !

II. **A glorious change.**—It was a glorious change when Joseph passed from the prison cell to be the second ruler in Egypt. David passed from the sheepcote to the splendour of Israel's throne; Mordecai was taken to the king's gate, and placed on the king's horse, and clothed in royal apparel, and the proclamation was heard, "Thus shall it be done unto the man whom the king delighteth to honour." But not so glorious as when the slaves of sin become the servants of God. *It is a noble service.* By what rules shall we measure the nobility of a service? Shall we speak of the greatness of the being who is served, the extent of his dominions, and the number and exalted character of his servants? Thus this service transcends, eclipses, any other form of service. We cannot grasp the greatness of this Being, and must content ourselves with the proceeding of the French preacher who, when called upon to preach on the occasion of the monarch's death, exclaimed amid breathless silence, "God alone is great." Vast are the numbers of His servants. The winds and the waves obey His will. The wild beasts of the forest, the cattle on the thousand hills, the myriad songsters of earth's groves, the birds of beautiful plumage, are His servants. But higher still, for men and angels are His servants; and men the noblest and sublimest earth can boast. Men of giant intellect, of heroic natures, of wondrous spirituality, are God's servants. We see them passing the great highway of time, and as the goodly procession passes along our souls are thrilled with conflicting emotions of gladness and of intense admiration, and we ask, Is it possible that we are to be permitted to follow in this glorious train? We may here claim all men and all women as the servants of God; but remember that He has three kinds of servants—some are slaves, and serve on the principle of fear; others are hirelings, and serve for the sake of the wages; but the best are sons, and serve under the influence of love. It is the loving service that is the noblest, that is the most satisfactory, and that is the most abiding. What is the service you render? The service of love is the only one which God will graciously accept. May God baptise with the spirit of love !

III. **The blessed result.**—" Ye have your fruit unto holiness "; or, " Ye have your fruit unto sanctification." God places trees in His garden not for mere ornament but for use. God does not despise the ornamental; but God's ornamental things are useful things as well. God is a painter the wondrous combination of whose colours no human painter has ever faintly shadowed forth, an architect whose mighty structures dwarf the proudest temples and palaces of earth, a musician whose lofty strains make the loftiest of human harmonies seem poor and feeble. If we desire to see beauty, let us go, not to the art galleries of men, but to the art galleries of God—not art galleries, but nature galleries, for God's rich nature is transcendent in beauty. A Christian should be an ornamental tree and a fruit-bearing tree. Are not the most fruitful trees the most beautiful? What can equal the delicate tinting and the rich colouring of the spring blossoming of the fruitful tree? What beauty is there in the Christian who bears fruit unto sanctification ! We take it that a truly sanctified man is both a beautiful man and a useful man. The children of this world may scoff at the saint; but there is, after all, a deep inward respect for those who live godly, righteous, and sober lives. The sanctified ones are the salt of the earth. The sanctified ones are the truly useful and the truly ornamental ones of the world. A Church all of whose members bring forth fruit unto sanctification is a Church which will attract by its loveliness. A kingdom the greater part of whose subjects bring forth fruit unto sanctification is a kingdom whose foundations are strong and whose perpetual glory is secured. Bring forth fruit unto sanctification; begin it in the way of duty, and by-and-by duty will become a pleasure. Learning to read is unpleasant to the child; but in after-time the reading of good books becomes not only the necessity but the pleasure of intellectual existence. In the beginning of the divine life we are but as children learning to read; but in after-time we find the greatest delight in keeping the commandments of God. Bring forth fruit unto your own sanctification, for your own good as well as for the glory of God.

IV. **The happy termination.**—"The end everlasting life." We are permitted and enjoined by the example of the word of God to keep the end in view. And what an end ! It is an end without an end, paradoxical as the statement appears. This end is the beginning of everlasting life, the beginning of the noblest life without termination. Perfect life is the adaptation of the being to its surroundings, and the adaptation of those surroundings to the being; and such is everlasting life. We shall be fitted for celestial surroundings, and those surroundings we shall find prepared to conduce to our highest felicity. Life here is imperfect, inadequate, and incomplete; life yonder will be perfect, adequate, and complete. Let us take the term " everlasting " not merely as referring to the perpetuity of our future existence, but to the completeness of that existence in all its aspects. No life here is everlasting, because it is incomplete and imperfect. But life beyond is everlasting in the broadest sense of that word. Let us keep the end in view, in order to inspire with hope and patience in the present. Let us persevere in the noble pathway of bringing forth "fruit unto sanctification."

Ver. 22. *Tenses of Christian life.*—That twenty-second verse is the conclusion —the real conclusion—of this chapter. The twenty-third verse is merely explanatory. The twenty-second verse brings visibly before us the conclusion of that struggle that Paul has been tracing more or less throughout this sixth chapter : the two services—the old service and the new—the transition from the old to the new, the outcome of that change of masters, and the outlook that we now have. These are all embodied in this twenty-second verse—an exchange in the past, present experience, and a blessed outlook. You have here the three tenses of a Christian man's life—the past, the present, and the future : something he looks back to is past and gone, something that he now has as present experience, and something he looks forward to as final result.

I. **The exchange of masters.**—We have, then, in this past tense a blessed change, an exchange of masters, a transition from one service to another. But when I speak of the old service as a *service*, I feel that I do not express it strongly enough ; for that old service was a bondage. And yet I am almost afraid to describe the new service by that term, because we connect with the word " bondage " sentiments that are not at all agreeable. Yet the words used in this chapter of that old service and of the new one are precisely the same. We were the slaves of sin ; and we are—the same word is applied—the slaves of God. There is a freedom that is slavery. My text makes it perfectly plain that every Christian man whose experience is here described has passed from a bondage, " being made free from sin." We must have passed from bondage into freedom—passed from the bondage of sin into the freedom that grace gives. The first thing in our freedom, then, was deliverance from our sin and guilt ; but that would not have been enough for you and me. When God speaks of freedom, He does it completely. He removes the guilt, but He breaks also its power ; He takes away the love of sin, and He gives you the grace to enable you to struggle with the sin—not merely to struggle with it, but to overcome it.

II. **The new service.**—But, then, by that very freedom He has bound you. He has led you into what I should call, perhaps, a new " bondage " ; only, as I said before, that word has an evil association ; and yet it is true. By His grace and deliverance He has made me eternally His bondsman. He has set me free from the power of sin, restored my freedom, that I might serve Him. Having been made free from sin, I entered God's service ; I gave up my own supremacy, and yielded to the supremacy of God.

III. **Fruit, a test of character.**—" Ye have your fruit unto holiness." Having had this deliverance from sin, having entered into this new service, what is the present outcome of it ? It is fruit, and it is fruit that you *have*, and it is a fruit that looks forward to a particular result. Great many of us are tempted to look upon the Christian life as made up of negations. It is a positive life— something you can actually lay your hand upon and say, Now here is that which I have got through my connection with Christ, through what He has done for me, through my service rendered to Him. Here I can see what I have as a definite, clear, distinct result something that can be shown. A Christian man's life must result in a real, positive character. " Ye have your fruit unto holiness." It does not say that you are holy ; it does not say you have already attained, or that you are already perfect. It does not say that the fruit is complete, that it is ripe, that it is ready to be plucked.   No; but it is fruit growing and growing—to what?   Unto sanctification, unto holiness.   The present tense of the Christian life, then, is a consecrated life—a life of devotion to Christ, of determination to be His and His only.

IV. **Eternal growth and development.**—And now for the future tense : "the end everlasting life." It is something that is far away, something that is to come by-and-by ; but for the present we may contemplate it, and make it a power to guide us in our journey. I think of it as bringing deliverance from all that hinders. I sometimes think of it positively. Here we have but a limited amount of physical strength, but that other world will introduce us to a life where there are no checks or limitations or hindrances, but a perpetual growth of power to serve God, of faculty to be used for Him. Eternal life, everlasting life,—not a life of luxurious ease, not a life of mere enjoyment or pleasure or psalm-singing ; but a life of active, devoted service—service which God is teaching us to render here, and which I believe He will teach us in yet fuller measure to render on the other side.—*Prof. Robertson, D.D.*

Ver. 23. *A high conception of manhood.*—The nature of the gift which a man confers on his fellow may be taken as the estimate which the former entertains of the recipient's character. In a gift there should be fitness. The gift should be suitable both to the circumstances of the giver and to the character and position of the recipient. Who would think of discoursing sweet music to the deaf? Should we give a choice painting to the blind? Would it be suitable to present a work on philosophy to one who can only read with difficulty? Here is a gift which transcends all others. Next in importance and in value to the unspeakable gift is the grant of eternal life. How vast the boon our contracted minds cannot fully comprehend. The value, preciousness, and vastness of the gift of eternal life will require an eternal life to unfold and completely to understand. Most feel the value of life, and are ready to subscribe to the truth of the old remark, "Skin for skin; yea, all that a man hath will he give for his life." Some value intellectual life. What a boon if the balance of reason could be restored to the insane ! What a gift if the mental power of a Plato or a Paul could be conferred on the man who yearns to tread the high pathway of genius ! Above all gifts, if we could only rightly appreciate it, is the blessing of eternal life, which begins in the present state and is being developed in the illimitable future. The greatness and preciousness of this gift speak to us of the greatness and benevolence of the Giver. Surely the gift speaks to us likewise of the greatness of man. In one sense man is little and insignificant, but in another sense he is made only a little lower than the angels. Surely the creature is not to be belittled and despised on whom the Eternal bestows the blessing of eternal life. The possible inheritor of so great a blessing is noble and kingly. Yes, the Bible ennobles manhood. It is the one book, the one vital agency, for the elevation of the race. Man is made, not for the fleeting hour, but for the coming eternity. Man is great because God regards him as capable of the gift of eternal life.

I. **Man is great, for this gift implies a moral nature.**—As we read of the gift of eternal life we are lifted out of the marshy and sterile plain of materialism. We cannot understand the philosophers of the materialistic school. Why should a man pretend to be a lover of wisdom, to dwell in the realm of refined ideas, who is only a perishable mass of materialism? Man is little if he is only an animal, though he may be an animal that thinks—a philosopher. Man is great if he is a creature endowed with a nature that yearns after the Infinite, that soars upward to the Eternal, that loves and worships. The gift of eternal life would be both useless and impossible to a creature who is only one step raised above the beast that never thinks and never loves. The gift of eternal life can only be profitable and delightful to the creature whose nature is lightened up and glorified by a spark of divine fire. A moral nature is needful where a spiritual boon is to be received and appreciated.

II. **Man is great, for this gift implies an enduring nature.**—Men have felt the preciousness of the blessing of spiritual life even as a gift for the present phase of existence. If there were to be no hereafter, many men and women would still ask for the sustaining and cheering influences of the gift of eternal life. But if in this life we only have hope, then our God-given blessing is stripped of its transcendent charm. Yes, we look to the future. We have the confident expectation of infinite blessedness in the bright and beautiful beyond. We rise above our sorrows, we laugh at our calamities, we even sing in prison, and have transports of joy when bound to the stake, because we feed on the outcoming joys of a completed eternal life. Certainly the phantasm of some felicity which a man is to inherit hereafter as the reward of his services here can give no rest and comfort to a man toiling and suffering. A phantasm cannot sustain, but a certainty can support. We look forward in hope, in confident expectation. We are paid on the way. We have joys in the earth pilgrimage; but oh what joys await when the pilgrim's journey is over and he passes inside the pearly gates!

III. **Man is great, for this gift implies an abiding personality.**—Individualism is the doctrine of the Bible. Can the gift of eternal life be conferred on a community? It is said that corporations have no souls. In this sense a community has no soul. A mob cannot receive the blessing of eternal life. It is a spiritual blessing, and in its reception the individual soul must be engaged. The moral personality must receive the blessing—must enjoy it, and develop it, and put it to wise and holy uses in the present sphere. In the future the blessing must be perpetuated and enjoyed by the individual recipient of the boon. So that the personality of the man is an abiding and a permanent quality. He aspires after rest, but it is a personal and an abiding repose in the presence of the infinite light and goodness. Here, then, we have not the creed of the Nirvana. While we long for the sweet composure of the being which may be realised in a brighter and calmer sphere, we shrink from the Buddhist doctrine of the absorption of the individual in the unity of being. Love will delight in the diffusion of happiness, in the wide expansion of blessings; but will the destruction of personalities, the concretion of souls into one great whole, contribute to greater happiness? Each soul glowing with the love light will contribute to the general splendour. The redeemed will be a glorious unity, but a glorious plurality. There will be many harpers. Each will rejoice in his own instrument, but he will rejoice to contribute to the general harmony. The music of heaven would not be rendered more perfect by all the harpers being absorbed in the unity of one harper, however skilful the performer.

IV. **Man is great, for this gift implies incompleteness.**—Man is great by reason of what he wants as well as by reason of what he possesses. What does man want? The poet sings :—

> "Man wants but little here below,
> Nor wants that little long."

But the poet may only sing of material wants; for man wants that which alone can render his nature complete. How great is man who cannot rest until he finds repose in the arms of infinite love! How great is man whose lower life is not adequate, and who can only find satisfaction in the blessing of eternal life! Men crave for rest, and this divine yearning declares man's vastness. Man longs and yearns; ofttimes he cannot interpret these dark soul movings. Deep calleth unto the deep in the dark and wondrous ocean of his moral nature, and he cannot translate the sound nor give speech to the confused utterance. He wants, he needs, eternal life. The loving Eternal sees man's need, and graciously offers the boon in a proffered Christ.

V. Man is great, for this gift supposes a large nature.—A cargo must be proportioned to the size of the vessel. A teacher should deal with his scholar according to the scholar's capacity. A gift must be suitable to the receiver. How wondrously constituted is that being who can receive and enjoy the blessing of eternal life! In some high moments of spirit rapture the soul experiences a great strain, which is not felt on account of the greatness of the joy. When the vision has passed, when the trance has gone, the soul is exhausted. But the soul will be ever expanding; and the more of heavenly delight it receives, the more it will be capable of receiving. Wondrous thought! that man can receive a divine Guest, can walk divine heights of blessedness, delight in the presence of the eternal Light, and finally taste the bliss of the glorified. But shall we speak of the greatness of man and have no word to exalt the greatness of the divine benevolence? "The gift of God is eternal life through Jesus Christ our Lord." Almost every word proclaims the greatness of the divine benevolence. This is seen by: 1. *The fact of a gift.* The hardness and depravity of human nature are evidenced by the circumstance that divine blessings are received as things taken for granted. We soon complain if anything is wanted. We are slow to raise the song of praise when blessings are bestowed. Here is a gift undeserved and unsought, a gift originating in the divine love; and yet how small is our appreciation of the divine benevolence! 2. *The nature of the gift.* Alas! we are so materialistic that we cannot receive with any great degree of rapture the moral; we are so earthly and so earthbound that we do not heartily welcome the heavenly; and yet, if we only knew it, the gift of eternal life is every way adapted to our natures. The gift of eternal life in its full realisation means the gift of abiding peace, of ever-flowing and uninterrupted joy—of sweet fellowship in the infinite goodness, of high converse with the noblest and purest spirits. This in a measure on our wilderness pilgrimage. This without measure and in indescribable fulness and delight when we have laid aside the pilgrim's staff, have washed our earth-stained and weary feet, are clothed in the clean raiment of the glorified, and sit down at the banqueting table of infinite Love. 3. *The originating possibility of the gift.* "Through Jesus Christ our Lord." He originated the possibility of this gift in harmony with the purposes and laws of God's moral government. "The wages of sin is death." The penalty had been incurred. God's benevolence purposed a gift. But how was that purpose to be accomplished? How was the design to be rendered a possibility? Jesus Christ originated the possibility. God the Father had a mental, an emotional origination of the plan of human salvation. Jesus Christ had a practical origination. He was the self-sacrificing originator of the possibility of the great gift of eternal life to the human race. And shall we say that God's love was less than Christ's love? Is the emotional of less account than the practical? Do we not undervalue the emotional in the Saviour's earthly life? Were not His sufferings greater from the emotional than from the physical side of His nature? God's love was great; and while we speak let us remember that the emotional gave rise to the practical. The love of God gave His only begotten Son. Let us then adore the love of God in Christ Jesus our Lord. Let us magnify the divine benevolence. Let us try to understand what God does when He makes the glorious offer of the gift of eternal life to the criminals over whom hangs the sentence of death. He shows the gift shining with many lights, and they reveal vaster glories beyond. He proffers the gift; and while He proffers there gleams upon the soul the pure light of the gems of heaven. He invites to accept; and while the loving voice woos and entreats the white-robed harpers raise a chorus of welcome. Can we refuse? Is it possible that we do not appreciate the gift? Angels look down in vast astonishment; their hearts are moved with infinite pity as they behold criminals passing away from offered pardon to the place of execution. Death and eternal life. Which is it to be? What is the resolve of the noble creature man? But how ignoble by the Fall! Great in divine intention, great in possibility; but little, low, and mean by degeneracy. Let us accept the gift and realise the greatness of which we are capable.

God's great gift.—The tendency of the gospel is to exalt God and to humble man. It points to everlasting misery as the prison-house to which man's depravity and sin would lead him. And it is only by the grace of our heavenly Father that we can reach the celestial world. "The wages"—the due recompense—"of sin is death," but eternal life is the *gift* of God through our Lord Jesus Christ. In speaking of this gift, notice:—

I. **Its nature.**—1. *It will afford immunity from all the sufferings and dangers of the present life.* Suffering belongs to every station here. Uninterrupted prosperity and enjoyment would be inconsistent with a state of trial. But sufferings can have no place in the life of the redeemed in heaven. All tears shall be wiped away. 2. *It will afford pre-eminent intellectual enjoyment.* Here we know in part; then we shall know in full. Knowledge will there be unmixed with error. 3. *It will afford entire social enjoyment.* Here society is often a source of annoyance, disagreements, and pain. In heaven it will possess unmixed knowledge, be full of benevolence, will be holy and wise, and there will be no separation. 4. *It will afford unspotted holiness.* All who possess it will be holy before they are allowed to enter heaven. But there they will attain to the glory of holiness of which man can form no conception. All will be light—the image of God will be reflected from every human spirit; the Lord Jesus Christ will reign over the minds and hearts of all His people. 5. *It will afford incessant activity and endless improvement.* Although heaven is represented as a place of rest, it is likewise a state of unceasing activity. The angels are active.

II. **Its freeness.**—"The gift of God." 1. *It was not wrung from Him by importunity.* It is a life which cannot be purchased. 2. *It is not the reward of merit.* Though sometimes called a reward, it is the reward of grace, not of merit. Man may merit hell, but he cannot merit heaven. Everything leading to this eternal life is also the gift of God: the promises of the Bible; the great change by which he has become entitled to it and qualified for its enjoyment; the Lord Jesus, by whose merit eternal life was purchased,—all these are the gifts of God.

III. **Its medium.**—"Through Jesus Christ." To Him we are indebted for the hopes that animate, for the enjoyments we experience. For this end the Redeemer was given—to put men in possession of eternal life; for this purpose He laboured; and for this He suffered. 1. *By His death Christ made atonement, and procured pardon—i.e.,* salvation from spiritual death. 2. *Through Him men are delivered from moral death, and receive the principle of spiritual life.* 3. *Through Him we are adopted into the family of His Father.* 4. *Through Him, through His resurrection, we conquer material death, and obtain material bodily life.*—*Homilist.*

Ver. 23. *Eternal life a priceless gift.*—The gift of God is eternal life "in Jesus Christ our Lord." *This* is the better gift which contains that wherein all others are defective,—the gift of a well of water, not lying outside of the man, at which he may slake his thirst now and then, but springing up *in* him; the gift, not of a refreshing influence, but of a Person from whom the influence comes, and in whom he may find that perpetually which only visits him occasionally ; the gift of One who delivers the spirit from its own proper burden, who speaks to those that are heavy laden with their own selfishness, and bids them rest in Him the meek and lowly ; the gift of One who does not exact joy and sympathy and love, but kindles them and bestows them. Here is the eternal life—the only eternal life of which St. Paul knows anything. The phantasm of some felicity which a man is to inherit hereafter as the reward of his services here could give no rest or comfort to a man toiling and suffering as he was. He wanted One upon whom he could cast his sorrows, fears, sins, every hour ; One from whom he could always draw a strength and nourishment to sustain him against the continual sentence and pressure of death. If there was such a One with him then, he could believe that He would be with him always—that neither height nor depth, nor life nor death, nor things present, nor things to come, would separate him from His love. His life must be eternal life : it could not be a changeable, inconstant treasure, here to-day and gone to-morrow ; but it must be a gift fresh every day—not a property which he could claim as having been made over once for all to *him*. It must be a gift of God, which he would enjoy while he trusted in God, which he lost whenever he fancied that he had earned it. It must be a gift, therefore, for all as well as for himself—one of which he could preach to all, one of which he could say to them, You have it, however little you may know that you have it. As surely as you carry sin within you, so surely is He within you who is the enemy of sin ; as surely as you have death with you, so surely have you life with you ; as surely as you may possess the one for wages, so surely may you accept the other for the gift of God.—*Maurice.*

Ver. 23. *Death and life.*—By a striking ceremonial on Gerizim and Ebal (see Deut. xxvii. and Josh. viii. 30-35) Joshua set before the Israelites life and death, the blessing and the curse. Similar contrast in text. Composed of two antithetical clauses : three words in the one contrasted with three in the other—sin and God, death and life, wages and gift.

I. **Sin and God.**—Both are masters engaging servants. The two occupy the whole domain of moral action. Only two masters and two kinds of service. 1. *Sin as a master.* One of the smallest words in the English language, but what it names is not little. Sin often regarded as a theological term, an abstraction, dark as a thunder-cloud, but as far away. Here not an ideal abstraction, but an actual master. Sinners are servants of sin, though not certain of making any engagement. Every born Briton bound to serve his country as long as in it. So every one who continues in sin tacitly engages to serve sin (see ver. 16). Though not a person, it has the power of a master. Proof of this : they believe in it, take pleasure in it, labour for it. Though they fancy themselves their own masters, they are being drawn or driven, sometimes against their better wishes, in a course opposite to God. 2. *God the other master.* His service a perfect contrast to the other. On the one hand all that is noble and pure, on the other all that is base and defiling : here a little tribulation, a little self-denial, and then everlasting felicity ; there present pleasure and future misery, short-lived delight and everlasting sorrow : here eternal life ; there eternal death.

II. **Death and life.**—Cause of death separation from God—sentence on first parents. As branch broken from the tree dies, so they cut off from the God of life died. 1. Spiritually. Proof from Scripture (Rom. viii. 6 ; 1 Tim. v. 6). 2. Death of the body another part of the death (Rom. v. 12). 3. Here death contrasted with *eternal* life. Hence infer that eternal death especially meant ;

elsewhere described as "the second death" and "everlasting destruction from the presence of the Lord." Eternal life, in contrast with eternal death, like half of sky clear while the other half filled with thunder-clouds. True life animated by high purpose, ennobled by true goodness, brimful of joy—a life that lifts clean away from the power of vexations and cares. Such life in fellowship with Christ: "Christ in you, the hope of glory" (see Rev. iii. 20). Such life not touched by death (John xi. 25, xiv. 19; Col. iii. 3, 4).

III. Contrast: wages and gift.—1. Death the wages of sin: due reward of deeds—not imposed by an arbitrary appointment of God: the law of the universe. Just that sinner be paid for his work, whether wages please him or not. 2. Eternal life a gift. The word means the *free* gift of God. Given to all in offer (John iv. 10; 1 John v. 11); given not for service rendered, but before one has begun to serve. No need to wait for; no need to prepare. Only condition is willingness to receive. But since it is life, it means a new beginning; since it is eternal life, it must overmaster all other lives; since it is life to be enjoyed in the service of God, we must quit the service of sin (ver. 13).— *G. Wallace, D.D.*

ILLUSTRATIONS TO CHAPTER VI.

Ver. 4. *A converted Bechuana.*—The missionary Casilis told us that he was one day questioning a converted Bechuana as to the meaning of a passage analogous to that before us (Col. iii. 3). The latter said to him: "Soon I shall be dead, and they will bury me in my field. My flocks will come to pasture above me. But I shall no longer hear them, and I shall not come forth from my tomb to take them and carry them with me to the sepulchre. They will be strange to me, as I to them. Such is the image of my life in the midst of the world since I believed in Christ."

Vers. 5-7. *Carthage must be destroyed.*—It is reported of Cato that he never spake in the Senate upon public business, but he ended his speech by inculcating the necessity of destroying Carthage; his well-known maxim was, "Delenda est Carthago." The believer's motto is, "The old man must be crucified." *Destruction of sin.* — Five persons were studying what were the best means to mortify sin: one said, to meditate on death; the second, to meditate on judgment; the third, to meditate on the joys of heaven; the fourth, to meditate on the torments of hell; the fifth, to meditate on the blood and sufferings of Jesus Christ; and certainly the last is the choicest and strongest motive of all. If ever we would cast off our despairing thoughts, we must dwell and muse much upon and apply this precious blood to our own souls; so shall sorrow and mourning flee away.—*Mr. Brooks.*

Ver. 13. *Yield your members unto God.*—

Take my hands, and let them move
At the impulse of Thy love;
Take my feet, and let them be
Swift and beautiful for Thee.

Take my voice, and let me sing
Always, only for my King;
Take my lips, and let them be
Filled with messages from Thee.

Take my will, and make it Thine—
It shall be no longer mine;
Take my intellect, and use
Every power as Thou shalt choose,—

So that all my powers combine
To adore Thy grace divine,
Heart and soul a living flame
Glorifying Thy great name.
F. R. Havergal.

Ver. 21. What profit?—"What fruit had ye then?" (Rom. vi. 21). Walking in the country (says a correspondent) I went into a barn, where I found a thresher at his work. I addressed him in the words of Solomon: "My friend, 'in all labour there is profit.'" But what was my surprise when, leaning upon his flail, he answered, and with much energy, "No, sir; that is the truth, but there is one exception to it: I long laboured in the service of sin, but I got no profit from my labour." Then answered I, "You know something of the apostle's meaning, when he asked, 'What fruit had ye then in those things whereof ye are now ashamed?'" "Thank God," he replied, "I do; and I also know that now, being freed from sin, and having become a servant unto righteousness, I have my fruit unto holiness; and the end, everlasting life."

Ver. 22. *Frederick the Great and Count Schmettau.*—During the Seven Years' War Frederick the Great accompanied his soldiers on a mountain march. Count Schmettau was his lieutenant, and a very religious man. The king, impatient over the tedious route of the artillery on foot up the narrow mountain pass, indulged in jesting to drive away *ennui*—he liked a little to tease Schmettau. He knew of a confessor in Berlin whom the count would visit, and allowed a stream of jokes and derision to flow freely. "Your majesty is more witty and much more learned than I," answered Schmettau, at last finding utterance. "More than this, you are my king. The spiritual contest is in every respect unequal ; nevertheless, you cannot take away from me my faith, and as it now goes you would certainly injure me immeasurably, at the same time not make yourself insignificant." The king remained standing in front of Schmettau ; a flash of indignation came from his majesty's eye. "What does that mean, monsieur ? I injure you by taking your faith ! What does that mean ?" With immovable tranquillity answered the general, "Your majesty believes that in me you have a good officer, and I hope you are not mistaken. But could you take from me my faith, you would have in me a pitiful thing —a reed in the wind, not of the least account in council or in war." The king was silent for a time, and after reflection, called out in a friendly manner, "Schmettau, what is your belief ?" "I believe," said Schmettau, "in a divine Providence, that the hairs of my head are all numbered, in a salvation from all my sins, and everlasting life after death." "This you truly believe ?" said the king ; "this you believe is right with full assurance ?" "Yes, truly, your majesty." The king, moved, seized his hand, pressed it strongly, and said, "You are a happy man." And never from that hour did he deride Schmettau's religious opinions.

Ver. 23. *The wages of sin.*—Mr. Marshall, author of the *Gospel Mystery of Sanctification*, having been for several years under distress of mind, consulted Dr. Goodwin, an eminent divine, giving him an account of the state of his soul, and particularising his sins, which lay heavy on his conscience. In reply he told him he had forgot to mention the greatest sin of all, the sin of unbelief, in not believing on the Lord Jesus Christ for the remission of his sins and sanctifying his nature. On this he set himself to the studying and preaching of Christ, and attained to eminent holiness, great peace of conscience, and joy in the Holy Ghost. Mr. Marshall's dying words were these : "The wages of sin is death ; but the gift of God is eternal life through Jesus Christ our Lord."

CHAPTER VII.

CRITICAL NOTES.

Ver. 1.—The law is lord over the man. There is nothing shocking in the assertion that we are no longer under the law. You all know that the power of the law over a man ceases at death ; and we are dead.

Ver. 2.—The soul first married to sin, then to Christ.

Ver. 3.—Adultery considered infamous among the Romans.

Ver. 4.—Freed from the power of the law as a covenant, having endured its curse ; that the fruit of our union may be sanctified to God (Wordsworth).

Ver. 5.—The apostle does not disparage the law, and so give countenance to the Manichæan heresy. "Ab sit hoc ab animo qualiscunque Christiani" (Augustine).

Ver. 6.—The law, indeed, is still our rule, our guide, our governor, but it ceases to be a tyrant over us, a tormentor of us (Dr. Barrow). "The law," says Calvin, "puts a check upon our external actions, but does not restrain our concupiscence." "No Christian man whatsoever," says the Church of England, "is free from the obedience of the commandments which are called moral." Delivered from the law, not as regards its moral precepts, but its carnal, external performances.

Ver. 7.—I had not known the specific character and peculiar nature of lust. The law of God proclaims to man *non concupisces*, and thus he learns that concupiscence is sin. The meaning must be that he would not have known sin in any such manner and measure as he then actually did had it not been for the law.

Ver. 8.—ἀφορμήν (ἀπό and ὁρμη, to excite) ; ὁρμή, first stirring in the soul—instinct, wish, resolve ; ἀφορμή, the place from which one goes out, the outgoing itself, material, occasion.

Ver. 9.—Conscience not disturbed because ignorant of the disease. Was wretched, and lost my own proper being. Fell under the sentence of sin (Wordsworth).

Ver. 10.—ἀπέκτεινεν, slew all my self-righteous hopes, and brought me into deeper condemnation. "He who follows the law for its own sake (and not for the sake of reward) is not slain by the evil principle."

Ver. 11.—As a rapidly flowing stream rolls calmly on so long as no object checks it, but foams and roars so soon as any hindrance stops it, just as calmly does the sinful element hold its course through the man so long as he does not stem it; but if he would realise the divine commandments, he begins to feel the force of the element, of whose dominion he had as yet no boding (Olshausen).

Ver. 12.—Demand only what is just and due. Whatever ground of exegesis one takes as to chap. vii. in general, the principle that Paul speaks of himself only as an example of what others are in like circumstances must of course be admitted. Compare 1 Cor. iv. 6, where he explicitly asserts such a principle. Even Reiche, who represents the ἐγὼ σαρκικός as the commonwealth of the Jews under the law, and the *better I* as the ideal Jew without sin, is still obliged to concede that Paul appropriates to himself what belongs to others, or represents them in his own person.

Ver. 13.—καθ' ὑπερβολὴν ἁμαρτωλός, made manifest as exceeding sinful, be recognised in its entire abominableness. Is then the law of God chargeable with my condemnation? Not so. It would be a conclusion as unjust as irreverent. It is not the law. It is sin which wrought the ruin—sin, that it might be displayed in its true light as sin, as a thing so malignant that it can even use that which is good as an instrument of destruction.

Ver. 14.—Rabbins: "The law, because of its spirituality, will dwell only in the soul that is free from dross."

Ver. 15.—I am blinded, I am hurried along and tripped up, I know not how. The "I" here not the complex responsible self by whom the deed is done and the guilt incurred, but the self of the will in its higher sense, the inner man. Quotations show that in all countries there is a struggle in the breast between conscience and carnal inclination. They also show how much alike men express themselves in relation to the struggle in question. They answer still another purpose—viz., to show that language of this nature is used and is to be understood in the *popular* sense, and in this only.

Ver. 16.—οὐ θέλω, indicates, not necessity, but mere non-approbation of what is done.

Ver. 17.—Proof that sin has come upon us as a power originally foreign to us. οἰκοῦσα ἐν ἐμοί, as a stranger or guest, or as one thing in another.

Ver. 18.—More than ἐργάζεσθαι; to do the whole good I wish, and that perfectly.

Ver. 22.—Not so much the mind itself as the man choosing the mind for his principle or standpoint.

Ver. 23.—Rabbins: "We should be always stirring up the good principle against the evil one." Genitive of connection, like ὁ νομ. τ. Θεοῦ, only the latter is *without* the individual—the former is most intimately within him: in the latter God tells him what He wants; the former the man gives to himself.

Ver. 24.—The cry uttered in full consciousness of the deliverance effected by Christ.

Ver. 25.—Χάρις τοῦ Θ., "the grace of God," equal, if not preferable, as an answer to the question. The σάρξ (flesh), and, as necessarily connected with it, the ψυχή (animal soul), the whole inferior region of the life, remains still subject to the law of sin. The αὐτὸς ἐγώ is not to be construed "I myself," but *ego idem*, "I, the one and the same, have in me a twofold element." To be sure αὐτός in this signification commonly has the article, but the ἐγώ supplies it here (Olshausen).

MAIN HOMILETICS OF THE PARAGRAPH.—*Verses* 1—6.

A sorrowful and a joyful marriage.—Happy the loving wife who is married to the true husband, Jesus Christ, feels devotion to His person, accepts with loyalty His directions, and, leaning upon His arm, walks joyfully through the wilderness of this world to the revealing realm where the spirit of St. Paul will flash the brightness of his intelligence upon the mysterious utterances made in this seventh chapter, as well as in other parts of this epistle. The first six verses of the chapter present us with an allegory. We have two marriages— the one to the law and the other to Christ. The law reigns and has power while it has life; but its authority ceases when death supervenes. The law is dead as a reigning and oppressive power when Christ the liberator appears. All former bonds are destroyed when Christ comes and takes the wife wrongfully married. When this divine union is consummated, there is bliss indeed.

I. **The first marriage is:** 1. *A mere legal connection.* No true love enters into the relationship. There are no sweet dalliances between the soul and the law. We are seeking to carry out the allegory, so that it must not be inferred that we intend to advocate the dissolution of the marriage bond through mere incompatibilities of tempers, or the easy method by which the married may be set free in some countries. 2. *An irksome restraint.* The soul married to the law is bound, but longs for freedom. Notice the expressions "bound by the law" and "sweetly married to another." Bound we may be, and are, to Christ; but it is by the silver link, the silken tie, the secret sympathy, of love. 3. *A monotonous service.* During this first marriage state the soul serves in oldness of the letter; the bright spirit of love does not appear upon or in the dreary pathway of the bound wife. She perhaps pines for love, and weeps in secret; she serves in the oldness of the letter; and all freshness is being extracted from her nature. 4. *A repellent relationship.* The motions of sin, the passions of sin, work in the wife; and there are many quarrels between the soul and the law. The married life is marked by many bickerings, much disquietude; and the wife has many heart-burnings. 5. *The source of an unpleasant family.* Sometimes in earthly marriages the wife finds in her children sweet forgetfulness of the sufferings she may have endured at the hands of her husband. No blame can attach to this husband; for the law is holy, just, and good. In this case the wife's sufferings arise from the incompatibility of the relationship; and there are to her no compensations, for the fruit is unto death. None of the children wear the newness and beauty of youth. The bounding steps of young life are not heard; the joyous laughter and merry peals of healthy childhood do not enliven. Death shadows everywhere appal. A sickly group crawls through the dwelling. Who shall deliver? How long will the bondage last? "Christ hath redeemed us from the curse of the law, being made a curse for us: for it is written, Cursed is every one that hangeth on a tree." The crucified body of Christ, His whole mission, His complete mediatorial work, secures the law's death. The wife is set free. Let the joy bells be rung. A second marriage may be consummated.

II. **The second marriage is an exact contrast to the first.**—1. *It is a love connection.* When first the soul hears the voice of Christ, it is as the voice of the beloved speaking in gentlest whispers, that sound as heaven's own music, richer than any that can strike upon human ears. The Bridegroom loves the bride out of the infinite love of His own gracious nature. That love is creating; for it produces in the bride a love brighter and more enduring than any of the loves of earth. Happy marriage day when the soul is married to Him who has been raised from the dead! The sun of heaven shines through earth's gloom upon the spiritual espousals. 2. *It has joyous constraint.* Bound, but free. A slave, but unwilling to be liberated. A wife who has changed her name, merged her individuality, foregone her supposed rights, counted all her precious possessions as loss, and yet rejoices in her losses because she has found an infinite gain in the Husband who is chief among ten thousand, and altogether lovely. 3. *It is lively service.* The wife serves in newness of spirit. Where love is the spirit is ever new and ever young. The soul will serve in newness of spirit through unending cycles. When we get old, the newness of the spirit abates. But this wife never feels the decrepitude of age. The newness of the spirit is never touched by the hand of time which makes other things grow worse. Earthborn spirits will die. The glories of time will be disfigured. Our realms of beauty will be laid waste. But the Christ spirit abides for evermore. The soul wife married to Christ will joyfully serve for ever. 4. *It is the source of happy products.* We are married unto Christ that we should bring forth fruit unto God. A beautiful family blesses the divine union. Corner stones polished after the similitude of a palace adorn. Plants grown up in youthful comeliness shed their fragrance, unfold their beauty, and provide their luscious fruit. The garners are full of all

Christian graces, and afford all manner of spiritual store.   Happy the wife that is in such a case; yea, happy is that soul which is married unto the risen Saviour! Let us then not continue in bondage to the law, for it is dead; let us not try to galvanise the law into the semblance of life.   Let us seek for soul union with the immortal Christ; let us strive to serve in newness of spirit which is newness of love; for it has always upon it the dews of heaven's bright morning.

"*What does it teach?*"—A book bearing this title professes to have discovered the true interpretation of the chapter, which is said to be a description of the Jew under the Mosaic law.   Our thanks must be given to every worker who seeks to throw light on biblical difficulties.   Still we cannot feel that the question is settled.   The theory, it is said, makes the whole chapter plain, and yet the analysis of the chapter has to us the appearance of special pleading, which is like an admission of weakness.   The writer says, "It is believed that learned and pious expositors, under the influence of the strong drift of thought, have taken for granted a view of the passage which is erroneous." May not this new expositor have been led wrong under the influence of the strong drift of *his own* thought? Take his statement: "'I delight in the law of God.' This expression is distinctly Jewish, and not Christian." Why should not a Christian use συνήδομαι when speaking of the law of God? ἡδονή is evidently connected with the Hebrew עדן, "delight," "loveliness"; and why should not St. Paul use the expression, "I am pleased together with the law—what pleases the law pleases me"? This delight may not amount to highest spiritual joy, for it produces a conflict.   And again the author asks us to notice the "hopeless wail of the wretched slave" in Romans vii., and the sorrows "cheerfully borne" by the Christian as described in 2 Corinthians.   We notice and observe that St. Paul says, "We that are in the tabernacle *do groan*, being burdened." Is the groaning Christian of the Corinthians any worse than the "wretched man" of the Romans, and who at last triumphs over his wretchedness through the power of Jesus Christ? But our main objection to the writer's theory is not found in his exegesis, is not contained in his statements, but in his very strange omission.   He says St. Paul "brings in to support his assertion an illustration (*drawn, doubtless, from the recollection of his own past experience*) in which he pictures a conscientious Jew," etc.   Is the experience of Romans vii. drawn from the recollections of St. Paul as a Jew under the Mosaic law? Does the self-reproach of that chapter harmonise with the self-complacency of the Pharisee? The writer's Jew is carnal, sold under sin.   While the Saviour's Jew is described as feeling himself perfect.   He had no remorse.   He lifted a complacent brow to heaven.   His voice sounded exultingly through the temple, "God, I thank Thee," etc.   The writer's Jew says, "So then with the mind I myself serve the law of God; but with the flesh the law of sin." St. Paul's Jew—the Jew of his own pre-Christian life—says, "An Hebrew of the Hebrews: as touching the law a Pharisee; concerning zeal, persecuting the Church; touching the righteousness which is in the law, blameless." When a third edition of the book is issued, we shall be glad to hear how it comes to pass that St. Paul in chap. vii. draws a picture of the Jew so different from his own recorded state.   If a heathen became converted to Christianity, we could not suppose him describing a character which had no resemblance to his own, unless indeed he wanted to make himself better than his fellow.   Why should St. Paul in Philippians make himself a blameless keeper of the law, and in Romans make the Jew put forth feeble attempts at keeping the law.   Does any ancient or modern Jew have the strivings of Romans vii.? Jews as a class are self-righteous, and consider themselves blameless.   It is only when conviction works that the Jew begins to feel his shortcomings.   Saul had no remorse.   He persecuted the saints of God, and thought he was doing God service.   He was blameless.   When he was not blind, his soul was dark; but when darkness was over the visual orbs, his soul was getting a power of vision.   In the house of Judas sin revived.   In the days of Saul's blindness he kept crying, "O wretched man that I am! who shall deliver me from the body of this death?"   When the scales fell from his eyes, much of the despairing tone departed from his soul, and straightway he preached Christ in the synagogues, that He is the Son of God—the power of God unto salvation, the great deliverer from the curse and the tyranny of the law.   However, the theory is not so new as the words seem to imply.   Something very similar is found among the fathers of the Pietistic School and the rationalistic critics. They think that the apostle introduces himself as the personification of the legal Jew.   Godet appears to follow in the same pathway, though we cannot be quite sure as to his teaching.   Certainly he makes light of the theory that the passage applies to the regenerate man; and Godet is perhaps more ingenious in destroying other theories than in establishing one of his own.   Happy man who has never been brought into captivity to the law of sin which is in our members!   If the Christian life is a fight, a contest, a struggle, then there must be an old man of sin against which the new man in Christ Jesus makes war. Perhaps there may be a combination of experiences in the passage—the experience of the enlightened and conscientious Jew.   We obtain from the dark and more desponding parts of the description the experience of the soul under strong conviction, such as that felt by Saul in his days of blindness, to which we have referred; and the experience of the regenerate man who places before himself a lofty ideal, and feels how far short he comes of attaining the ideal.   After all, this seventh chapter must be placed among the things of St. Paul which are hard to be understood.   We do not see the necessity of straining every point, of attaching a moral meaning to every turn of a letter.   Scholarship is good, but it will not enable us to attain the unattainable; and we believe that in the present state we must be willing to confess our inability to understand everything, to solve all difficulties, and to reconcile all apparent discrepancies.

Ver. 4. *Four stages of Paul's experience.*
I. **We are to study the personal career of Paul as here sketched by himself.** —We see him at four stages.   1. *As Paul the self-satisfied* (see ver. 9).   "I was alive, apart from law, once."   This may mean one or both of two things: (1) it may indicate a state of self-unsuspectingness in distinction from one of conscious transgression; or (2) a state of self-security as opposed to one of conscious danger. Fuller autobiographic touches, as given elsewhere, throw much light upon this. Few young men are mentioned in Scripture who seem to present a more pleasant picture of the exterior bearing of their early manhood.   Paul was doubtless a model of uprightness and of conscientious religiousness.   There is every indication that he was as rigid a Churchman and as stern a moralist as could well be found; probably no young man could be found to surpass him as a model of social propriety.   Still, as he now looks back on that self-satisfied past, he owns "Apart from law, sin was dead"; it lay undisturbed in the depths of the spirit, still as death.   I was so content with my attainments that I actually came to a most charming conclusion about myself—"touching the righteousness which is in the law, *blameless!*"   That self-complacency was destined to be disturbed, 2. At a later stage we find Paul becoming *Paul the terrified.*   This transition is described between the latter part of the ninth verse and the close of the thirteenth.   "When the commandment came, sin revived"; it started up as a

reanimated body from the tomb, and the awful spectre of sin so alarmed me that "I died. And the commandment, which was ordained to life, I found to be unto death." Though it promised life, yet it promised life only to law-keepers. But I was a law-breaker; hence, there I lay, under the death sentence. Nor was this all. "Sin, taking occasion by the commandment, deceived me, and by it slew me." If there be any self-will, tell a man he must not do this or that, and he is at once provoked to wish to do it. Thus sin, through the commandment, becomes exceeding sinful. And hence, with the weight of the law which condemns heart sin pressing upon him, Paul sinks down oppressed. 3. *Paul the struggler.* He is not only convicted of sin, but he sees that the conviction is just, that the commandment is holy, just, and good. But he himself is all wrong; he wants to get right; he struggles to escape from the grasp of law. With what success he shall tell for himself in vers. 14-24. And no further than this did he get; no further could he get; no further can any one ever get who has to thread his way by the light of law alone. A rule, however excellent and perfect, will never help a man to keep it. Nor did the pure and holy law help Paul to its fulfilment. So far, and so far only, under law. But oh, happy change! 4. We have now to look at *Paul the free!* In the first verse of the eighth chapter he shows us how things stand NOW. "There is therefore NOW no condemnation," etc.—*i.e.*, from all that I have said about Christ, righteousness, grace, life, it follows that whereas I, as a guilty man, could never, under law alone, rise above a despairing struggle, yet NOW, in Christ Jesus, *I am a free man!* The condemning sentence of the law is no more. The life and power I wanted, which the law cannot give, are given me by Jesus; so that whereas, under law, I was a struggling captive, in Christ Jesus I am gloriously free. The law stirred up sin; Christ conquers. The law condemns; Christ absolves.

II. **In this personal experience Paul sets forth the peculiarity of the believer's life in Christ.**—We here learn: 1. That for a sinful man no conceivable relation to law alone can be perfectly satisfactory. Law, as such, can give neither absolution for sin nor power against it. 2. These two wants which law reveals are in Christ supplied. 3. If any believers never get beyond Paul's third stage (or the struggling one), they have their privileges in Christ yet to learn. 4. Some call the fourth stage, that of freedom, the "higher" Christian life. No; it is *the* Christian life. 5. When we thus receive Christ in all His fulness, then we shall cry, I have found it! I have found it! The secret of life, power, peace, freedom, song, is in Christ, and Christ alone. What law enjoins the Spirit of God creates; and to that holiness, when struggled after in vain when toiling alone, the spirit will soar by its own living power when Christ fills us with His glorious life.—*C. Clemance, B.A., D.D.*

Ver. 7. *Knowledge of sin by the law.*—Although the apostle aimed in this epistle to show that the law by itself was unable and unfitted to secure men's salvation, it is evident both that he honoured the law as an expression of the divine character and will, and that he considered it from a Christian point of view to fulfil a most important purpose. Especially in this verse does he set forth the law as awakening conscience to sin, and so preparing the way for the introduction of the gospel, both in the order of the divine dispensation and in the course of individual experience. His own spiritual history is represented as typical: "I had not known sin but by the law."

I. **Law is the revelation of the superior will to the subject and inferior will.** —There is a sense in which the word "law" is commonly used in the exposition of physical science. It is in such connections equivalent to uniformity of antecedence and sequence. But this, though a queer employment of the term, is secondary and figurative, part of the connotation is intentionally abandoned. The fuller meaning of law is seen when the reference is to requirements of certain modes of action, and when the requirement is made by one who has a just right to make it, a just claim upon the submission and obedience of those to whom the command is addressed. The superiority in the lawgiver does not lie simply in physical power, but in moral character and authority.

II. **Being under such law implies the possession of intelligent and voluntary nature.**—The inferior animals are not, in the proper sense of the term, under law. Nor are babes, or idiots, or any whose moral nature is undeveloped. Man as an intelligent being can apprehend law, as an active and voluntary being can obey law. Kant has put the matter in a very striking and a very just light in saying that whilst the unintelligent creation acts according to law, an intelligent being has the prerogative of acting according to the representation of law—*i.e.*, he can understand, consciously adopt, and willingly and without constraint obey the law. Freedom is the power to obey or to disobey.

III. **In proportion to the definiteness of the law is the measure of responsibility attaching to those who are subject to it.**—Confining attention to human beings possessed of thought, reason, and will, we cannot fail to detect degrees of acquaintance with the revelation which in various ways is vouchsafed to the race. There are those, as for example untutored savages and the "waifs and strays" of a civilised community, whose knowledge of the divine will is both very imperfect and very indistinct. Such in former ages was the case of the Gentiles as compared with the highly favoured Jews. Now our Saviour Himself and, following His teaching, the highly inspired apostles have plainly taught that responsibility varies with knowledge and opportunity.

IV. **On the other hand, the possession of express and verbal laws involves heightened responsibility.**—When the knowledge of duty is clear, defection and rebellion are aggravated in guilt. The sin of transgression is increased as the light sinned against is brighter. Such was the case with the Jews, who were worthy of sorer condemnation than the Gentiles where both were disobedient. Comparatively they only knew sin who knew the law by which sin is prohibited. True there is a general conscience, against which even the unenlightened transgressors are offenders, but they are the worst culprits who having the light walk not in it.

V. **Thus the law by revealing a higher standard of duty, and by making sin "exceeding sinful," prepares the way for the introduction of the divine gospel of salvation and life.**—The apostle avers that but for the law he had not known sin—*i.e.*, comparatively. If this had been all, he would have had little reason to thank the law. But in fact the law, proving the holiness and righteousness of God and the powerlessness of man to obey, served to make the introduction of a new dispensation, that of grace, doubly welcome. Men were brought to feel their need of a Saviour, and, when that Saviour came, to receive Him with alacrity and gratitude, and to use the means prescribed by which the penalties of the law may be escaped and the blessings of eternal salvation enjoyed.—*Prof. Thompson.*

SUGGESTIVE COMMENTS ON VERSES 1—6.

Christ dissolves the union.—The law is but an imperfect embodiment of the justice of God. To say that the law forbids our rescue from sin is to say that the justice of God forbids it.

But the death of Christ made it consistent with the justice of God to pardon the sinner. Therefore by the death of Christ we are released from the bondage to which the justice of

God bound us in a way which does not contradict but manifests the justice of God, and in order that we may be united to Christ, and thus live a life devoted to God (comp. Gal. iii. 13 f.). It is easy to apply this to the case of those who have broken, not only the law of Moses, but the more solemn law of Christ. As in the history of the world, so in the history of each individual, God speaks first in the form of law. Even the gospel, to those who read it first, is but an embodiment of the eternal principles of right and wrong. But these principles condemn the sinner. And many conscientious men feel that for God to pardon their sins and smile upon them would be to set aside these eternal moral principles. And because they know that God will not do this, they dare not believe His proclamation of pardon. But in this section we are reminded that the death of Christ has satisfied the eternal principles which forbade our pardon, by revealing the evitable connection of sin and death, and that, without infringing them, God may now set us free. Justification through the death of Christ, as explained in iii. 26, is plainly implied in this section. For that by Christ's death we are set free from a union with sin to which the law bound us can only mean that His death made it consistent with God's justice to set us free from the power of sin, which implies, since bondage to sin is the divinely ordained penalty of committing sin, forgiveness of our past sins. We are also plainly taught that Christ died in our place ; for He bowed for a time to the power of death, and became its victim in order to rescue us from its power.—*Beet.*

Why does Paul use the wife as a figure?—The difficult question in this verse is why Paul takes as an example a wife losing her husband and free to remarry, rather than a husband losing his wife and enjoying the same right; for the two cases equally demonstrate the truth of the maxim of ver. 1. The fact that the law bound the woman more strictly than the husband does not suffice to explain this preference. It is the application which Paul proposes to make of his example to the spiritual life which will give us the solution of the question. It shows, in point of fact, that Paul had in view, not only the breaking of the believer's soul with the law (the first husband), but also its new union to the risen Christ (the second husband). Now in this figure of the second marriage Christ could only represent the husband, and the believer, consequently, the wife. And this is what leads the apostle to take a step further, and to attribute *death* to the wife herself ; for Christ having died, the believing soul cannot espouse Him except as itself dead. The expression " to be in the flesh " is very far from being synonymous with " living in the body " (comp. Gal. ii. 20). The term " flesh," denoting literally the soft parts of the body, which are the usual seat of agreeable or painful sensations, is applied in biblical language to the whole natural man, in so far as he is yet under the dominion of the love of pleasure and the fear of pain—that is to say, of the tendency to self-satisfaction. The natural complacency of the ego with itself—such is the idea of the word " flesh " in the moral sense in which it is so often used in Scripture. —*Godet.*

Mosaic law is meant.—It has been a question to whom the apostle's argument is addressed. Many interpreters consider him as addressing himself to Christians generally, and they think that what is here established may apply to the law written on the heart as well as to the law of Moses. But if we consider that what is here established is the releasing of men from the law alluded to, that they may be made subject to another law, we shall see that no other law can be meant but the Mosaic law and the law of the gospel. For as there can be no release from the law written on the heart, the apostle's remark cannot apply to it.

203

We must therefore admit that this part of the argument is addressed to the Jewish Christians, and that it is intended to convince them that they are now at liberty, without the violation of any duty, to forsake the law of Moses and embrace the gospel. And that the apostle has in view the law of Moses may be inferred from his addressing his argument to men who "know the law," for it could hardly be said of Gentile converts that they knew the Jewish law. This illustration may seem to us to be drawn from a more familiar subject than would now be thought proper for explaining such a topic. But when we consider that in the Old Testament the relation of God to His chosen people is sometimes represented under the similitude of a marriage solemnised at Mount Sinai, and that in consequence God is represented as calling Himself their husband; and when we look back to that state of ancient manners which rendered this figurative mode of speech forcible and appropriate, we shall admit that, in speaking to the Jews, to whom this portion of the epistle is addressed, it was a very natural illustration, as well as one that explained clearly the point which the apostle meant to press on their attention. Every Jew, therefore, who carefully considered his situation merely as depending on the law must have been sensible of inordinate emotions leading him to actual sin, and he must have been aware also that for actual guilt the law made no allowance and offered no means of pardon. No doubt the Jews under the law lived in the hope of forgiveness, and no doubt those of them whose conduct was suitable to their religious privileges obtained it. But this was not derived from the strict letter of their law. It was derived from that gracious dispensation which their law prefigured, and from which alone sinners can obtain forgiveness. The law could not possibly be a principle of justification, "for when ye were under its authority," saith the apostle, "your corrupt pro-

204

pensities led you to the commission of actions which the law itself punished with death" (ver. 6). "But now," continues he, "we are delivered from the law, that being dead wherein we were held; that we should serve in newness of spirit, and not in the oldness of the letter."—*Ritchie.*

Law superseded by the gospel.—The apostle continues the subject of a complete sanctification, or, in other words, of a perfected human being after the model of Jesus. His object in this section is to show that every scrap and fragment of obligation to the law were annihilated. He addresses the Jews who were acquainted with the law, and shows them by a familiar illustration how entirely it had been superseded by the gospel, and how perfectly free they were to become Christians without any longer continuing to be Jews. It was a matter requiring great delicacy and address to maintain the divine legation of Moses and the original binding authority of his institutions, and at the same time to lead the Jews onward who had been thus educated, and every fibre of whose intellectual and moral being was inwoven in the law, and to open to their faith and admiration the greater beauties and glories of Christianity. In truth, the idea of the progressive nature of all religion, as well as of life in general, seems to be one of the. hardest lessons for man to learn, whether under the Jewish or the Christian system. He becomes fossilised in ceremonials and creeds, and hears with reluctance the ceaseless command of God's providence, Go up higher. In regard to the many questions how St. Paul's rhetoric shall be justified, and how the several limbs of his comparison shall be matched with one another, we have nothing to say while the main drift of his remarks is so apparent. Thus Beza says, " The old man is the wife, sinful desire the husband, sins the children "; and Augustine that " there are three— the soul is the woman, the passions of sin the husband, and the law the law of the husband." Origen, Chrysostom, Calvin, and others, " Men are the wife, the law the former husband, Christ the new one." If Paul were a writer who carried out his figures regularly, all such criticism would be very fine and useful; but he is not, and to attempt in every instance to set the different parts in order is not only a work of supererogation but of impossibility. To hunt needles in haymows, or to attach again the strewn leaves of the forest to the identical boughs from which they have fallen, would be as easy and as profitable as to pursue this word-criticism to its niceties, with a view of resting upon it any essential doctrine or precept. The Bible in general, and the writings of Paul in particular, lie, like great nature herself, vast, various, somewhat chaotic and disjointed, a creation in progress, and not a creation finished, but everywhere full of gleams of surpassing beauty, touches of deepest feeling, and electricities and magnetisms and fires of quickest power. The words of Professor Stuart are most true, and it would have been well if he had always " recked his own rede": " Many a time have I read the Epistle to the Romans without obtaining scarcely a glimpse of it. When I ask the reason of this, I find it in neglect to look after the *general* object and course of thought in the writer. Special interpretation stood in the way of general views; the explanation of words hindered the discerning of the course of thought."—*Livermore.*

MAIN HOMILETICS OF THE PARAGRAPH.—Verses 7—13.

A life's experiences—St. Paul divides his life into three sections: 1. When he was alive, and sin was dead; 2. When sin was alive, and he was dead; 3. When he lived again in Christ.

1. Vers. 8, 9: Before ne realises the law. He never thought of law, or sin—only of pleasure. Sin, to him, was not; law was not.

2. Vers. 9-11: Between realisation of law and conversion. He examines law; finds himself a sinner, and powerless; sin lives, he dies.

3. Chap. viii. 2: He finds Christ; asks and gains His aid; *lives* again. Righteousness is by Christ—(1) *imputed,* and (2) *imparted,* to him.

Three considerations arising from this history:—

I. **Knowledge of God's law, by itself, does not save.**—Illustrations: Chinese traveller in Europe, who comes back to China and reports that Europeans have good laws, which they do not obey, and a beautiful religion, which they do not keep. Red Indian chief, who hears a white preacher upbraiding the Indians for their sins, and says: " We know we are bad already; tell us how to get rid of our badness."

II. **What knowledge of law cannot do, knowledge of Christ can do.**—Other religions lay down laws of conduct; Christianity alone lays down law, *and gives power to keep law* (Holy Spirit).

III. **Meditation for each.**—Either I am triumphing over sin, or sin is triumphing over me—which? Christ and the evil spirit are each doing all that they can to enrol me as a follower. Which am I following? In each case, no alternatives.

Resolutions: 1. *Devotion to Christ;* 2. *Thank for law;* 3. *Ask grace to keep it.*—*Dr. Springett.*

The law's power.—St. Paul had just before declared that the true Christian is dead to the law and is delivered from it. Here he puts before us, in the form of a question, an inference which might at first sight suggest itself, that this law from which we are happily delivered is an evil thing—a thing of sin. " Is

205

the law sin?" This question is at once answered with an emphatic denial, "God forbid." Then follows a vindication of the law from such a suggestion; its operation in contact with man's fallen nature is exhibited; and the reason why, though good in itself, it brings with it condemnation and death is clearly shown.

The vindication of the law of God:—

1. *The law produces in man the knowledge of sin.*—St. Paul had previously said (iii. 20), "By the law is the knowledge of sin"; and now, referring to what he had experienced in his own case, he repeats the assertion as a personal fact, "I had not known sin but by the law." He takes the commandment, "Thou shalt not covet," as an example of the whole law, and affirms that he would not have known "lust" or "coveting" but for this prohibition—that is, he would not have known any desires or propensities in their true moral nature, would not have recognised them as sins, and the carrying out of such propensities into action would not have troubled his conscience or produced any sense of guilt. The truth of this is plainly seen in St. Paul's own life; for after his conversion, though he acknowledged that he had been "a blasphemer and persecutor and injurious," yet he could still affirm that "he had lived in all good conscience before God" (Acts xxiii. 1).

2. *Besides this the law has even the effect of stirring up and inflaming the evil propensities of man, and of adding force to the urgency of their demands.*—When anything is forbidden by God's law, there is a natural tendency in the heart of fallen man to desire all the more strongly to do it. Sin, so to speak, uses the commandment as an "occasion," a base of operations, a convenient instrument, for gaining a stronger hold upon the man and enhancing its power over him. By a mysterious perversity of the human heart an object *forbidden* engages his more lively attention; it becomes in his sight more attractive; he is deceived by its seeming desirableness; he resents the restraint imposed upon his desires; his sinfulness assumes a rebellious form. This attractiveness of forbidden objects, and the desire to do what is forbidden *because it is forbidden*, was often noticed by heathen moralists, and numerous citations to this effect have been collected from Greek and Latin authors. It seems to be inherent in the fallen nature of man.

3. *There was a time when St. Paul* (to use his own striking words) *"was alive without the law."*—He was indeed living under the Mosaic law, and well acquainted with its outward form; but he knew not its spiritual nature or the breadth of its application. He was full of confidence in himself (see Phil. iii. 4-6), and in his own righteousness he felt perfectly secure—no misgivings, no sense of sin. Sin, as far as he was concerned, was to all appearance *dead.* But when the law in all its spiritual depth and fulness was borne in upon his heart and conscience, how great a change! "Sin revived, and he died." His self-confidence was gone, the whole foundation on which he rested gave way; sin reappeared in all its evil power, and wrought all the more violently in him, until he cast himself, as it were, at the feet of that Jesus whom he had persecuted, and found peace in Him. May we not rightly judge that the spiritual conflict alluded to in this scripture was experienced by St. Paul during the three days when he lay at Damascus in bodily blindness, but with awakened conscience and the enlightenment of the Holy Spirit?

4. *So then "the law is holy, and the commandment holy, and just, and good."*—True it brings condemnation and death to man; but that is the fault, not of the *law*, but of *sin*—sin is the *cause*, the law only exhibits the *effect.* The law brings sin to light, and shows its vileness. This vileness is made the more apparent from the fact that sin is not overcome, but rather is made more rebellious, by the application of the law. Its "exceeding sinfulness" is detected and exposed by its turning the law, designed to be a

holy rule of life, into a condemnation—by its "working death in man by that which is good."

5. *We see how the law may by sin be turned from good to evil, from life to death.*—Let us learn to use it for the best and wisest purposes. "The law is good, if a man use it lawfully" (1 Tim. i. 3). Two lawful uses are available for us: (1) Let us use it to convince us of sin, and to show us that we can have no righteousness of our own, that so it may "*bring us unto Christ* to be justified by faith" in Him (Gal. iii. 26). (2) When we have found righteousness and peace in Christ, let us use it, under the guidance of the Holy Spirit, as our rule of life, seeing that we are "created in Christ Jesus unto good works," and it is the very purpose of God "that the righteousness of the law should be fulfilled in us, who walk not after the flesh, but after the spirit" (Rom. viii. 4).—*Dr. Jacob.*

SUGGESTIVE COMMENTS ON VERSES 7—13.

Law convicts.—But the expression "without the law" might also be understood as denoting "without a proper knowledge of the law." And in this sense the apostle's remark would apply to mankind universally, and might be thus paraphrased: Formerly, when I was without a proper knowledge of the divine law, I was alive—I thought myself entitled to life and all its blessings, not being aware of the sins which disqualified me for the favour of Heaven. But when the commandment came, when the divine law touched my conscience, and I became fully sensible of its extent, and found that it prohibits, not only outward transgressions, but also all inward affections which tend to produce sin, then sin revived. I became sensible that it exerted its full sway over my mind and conduct, and I died. I felt that I was exposed to death as the wages of iniquity. Such is the view which may be taken of this sentence. While we are unacquainted with the law of God, or think not of it, we are apt to entertain a favourable opinion of our moral condition; we feel no compunction for sins of which we are not properly aware. But when we come to understand and feel the extent and obligation of the law of God, we are forced to form a very different judgment of ourselves, and to acknowledge that we are actually obnoxious to that punishment from which we had formerly thought ourselves secure. It deserves the serious consideration of every man whether he may not labour under some degree of this delusion in regard to his own moral condition. "For sin, taking occasion by the commandment, deceived me, and by it slew me." This is a repetition of the sentiment expressed in the eighth verse. To see the force of it, we must bear in mind that the apostle is defending the law from the objection stated in the seventh verse, of its being calculated to promote sin; and showing how, though perfectly unexceptionable in its own nature, it had become the occasion of the fatal effects that resulted from it. In this illustration he continues to consider the sinful propensities of the mind as a living and active power continually striving to bring men under its dominion. These propensities took occasion, by means of the commandment, to deceive men. Although the law showed their evil nature, it could not restrain them; and they deceived men by means of the commandment, because, in spite of the clear knowledge of the nature of sin which the law afforded, they still seduced men into actual transgressions. The clear prohibition of the divine law rendered these transgressions more heinous; and thus the commandment was the occasion of men being guilty of more aggravated sins than they could have committed had they wanted the knowledge of the law. But there is also another sense in which our sinful propensities deceive us by the commandment—not indeed by anything in the nature of the commandment itself, but by the perversity of human nature operating by means of the commandment. For the mere circumstance of certain things being forbidden is apt to increase the desire of them, and thus lead the corrupt heart to transgress the law in order to obtain them. Sin having deceived me by means of the commandment, " it also slew me." By the sins which it tempted me to commit, it rendered me obnoxious to death.—*Ritchie.*

Belief in the law is to feel condemnation.—Unbelief in the law is as common as unbelief in the gospel. If men believe in the gospel, they soon feel the power of it. So of the law ; if they truly believe it, they will feel the power of its condemning voice. No man can be found who will deny that he has sinned. Let a man, then, only believe in reality that death eternal is, according to the law of God, annexed to his sin as a punishment, and he will be afraid—his heart will sink within him. He will have no rest, he will have fearful forebodings of wrath ; and if this be not the case, then plainly he does not believe the law. . . . To hear the law, and yet be as hopeful and merry-hearted and unconcerned as if the law were an idle tale or a mere man of straw, that shows a most miserable state of blindness and want of feeling— a state which can be accounted for only by the fact that the law is not credited, that its threatenings are not believed at all. The law not only shows us our sin, but makes us feel that we are lost—as good as dead. A man is in a room during the dark ; he sees nothing, but imagines that he is safe. At length the day breaks. Through the window of his apartment sunlight enters ; and behold, he is, though he knew not till now, in the midst of wild beasts, which, like himself, have been asleep. They awake, and put on a threatening aspect. There is a serpent uncoiling its horrid length, and there a tiger watching its opportunity for a fatal spring. The light has come, and the man now sees his danger—he is but a dead man. So when the law comes, there is seen guilt now in the past life in every part of it. There is felt now sin in the present condition of the heart. Every moment there is a discovery of sin. Everything past and present cries, as it were, for vengeance. Death everywhere stares him in the face.—*Hewitson's " Remains."*

" *Wherefore the law is holy, and the commandment holy, and just, and good."* —The conclusion from the foregoing exhibition of the effect of the law is, that it is not to be blamed for the evil which it incidentally produces. In ver. 9 Paul uses the words " law" and " commandment" as perfectly synonymous ; here they are distinguished. The law collectively, and each command separately, are alike holy, etc. The word " holy " in the first clause expresses " general excellence," " freedom from all fault " ; and contains all that is expressed by the three terms of the second clause, where " holy " means " pure," " just " means " reasonable," and " good," " benevolent " or " tending to happiness." The law is in every way excellent. " Was then that which is good made death unto me ? God forbid," etc. With a view to prevent the possibility of its being supposed that he thought disrespectfully of this holy law of God, the apostle again denies that it is directly the cause of sin, but shows that our own corruption is the real source of the evil. " Made death," agreeably to what has been said above, means " made the cause of sin and misery." The law is not this cause.—*Hodge.*

MAIN HOMILETICS OF THE PARAGRAPH.—*Verses* 14—25.

Two men in one man.—The two men in the one man are the carnal man and the inward man. As we read the history of these two men we wonder at St. Paul's power of mental analysis. He skilfully uses the pen and the discriminating power of the metaphysician. He has accurately read and studied the workings of human nature; and this result could only have been reached by the intense observation of the workings of his own nature. " Know thyself " is the old precept. Self-knowledge prepares the way for other-self knowledge. These verses, then, contain a record of the workings of St. Paul's nature. He finds in himself two men, one low and the other noble; and he mourns that the lower man so often gains the mastery over the noble man. Let us look at :—

I. **The two men.**—The one man is carnal, sold under sin. This carnal man serves the law of sin. Thus he is base in the extreme. He is of the earth earthy, and does not strive upward towards the true and the good. The other man is spiritual—at least he is so far spiritual that he loves the law which is spiritual; for this inward man delights in the law of God, and consents unto the law that is good. How opposite the characters! How striking the contrast between the two men that dwell together in the one man! There is no need for us to ask the question whether St. Paul here speaks of the regenerate or the unregenerate man. This much may be safely affirmed, that every man who is candid to himself and his fellows must confess that ofttimes he sinks so low as to be compelled to ask, Is there in me any spiritual life? I profess Christianity, but what would my uncharitable neighbours say of my religion if all the secret workings and downfalls of my lower nature were proclaimed on the housetops? How often have we lamented the beastly which has shown itself? Is it possible that I am the same man who has stood on the mount of transfiguration —I who am now desiring to be fed with the husks the swine eat? Let us, then, be merciful in our judgments.

II. **The two men in conflict.**—The fight cannot be seen; the strain on the sinews cannot be observed; the sound of the struggle cannot be heard. But these unseen conflicts are oft the most real and the most severe. The one man desires to do good; the other man strives to prevent the accomplishment of the praiseworthy desire. How true to life and to all experience! A conflict goes on in all—perhaps even in those who may appear to have altogether destroyed the divine image and completely effaced the nobler part of human nature. The poor criminal has had a struggle—light and short it may be, still a struggle— before he did the fatal act which has led to his temporal ruin at least. And oh, what a conflict when the great man—great spiritually—has fallen from his eminence and has become as other men! " Let him that thinketh he standeth take heed, lest he fall."

III. **The lower man triumphant.**—The lower man compels the spiritual man to do the thing which he hates. Is there a malicious leer on the countenance of the lower man as he forces the spiritual man to do the evil which he would not and which he abhors? Certainly he is not backward in feeling remorse. The spiritual man mourns, perhaps weeps; and the carnal man takes to himself no blame, and does not attempt to wipe away the tears. How wondrous strange that the lower man should be so often triumphant! And yet this takes place in the larger sphere of life. The wicked man spreads himself like a green bay tree; base men are exalted; the wicked are too oft in great prosperity; the carnal man rides rough-shod over the spiritual man. Sad that society should ever allow vile men to rule—sadder that the spiritual man should permit the lower to gain and keep the ascendency! But how is it to be helped? " O wretched man that I am! who shall deliver me from the body of this death?"

IV. **The inward man can only win by the help of a second man, the man Christ Jesus.**—Ethical systems cannot successfully help in this conflict. Philosophy is of no avail. Rhetorical phrases cannot nerve the nature, so as to enable us to gain moral victory. Music may inspire the soldier to deeds of daring; but what music hath charms sufficiently strong to enable the man always to perform that which is good? Reason may tell me that to follow and serve the good is a good in itself, that virtue is its own reward; but reason is soon dethroned by the power of the carnal man, vice wears an alluring mien, while virtue, with reward in its right hand, is not infrequently unattractive. Even when it is, the higher man is overridden by the lower man, if the former be not helped. The man Christ Jesus must be our helper. He allures by presenting vice in its true colours and virtue in its proper garb of attractiveness. He shows us that the higher man can be victorious by being Himself the example of unsullied holiness. He inspires with strength by the inspiration of His Holy Spirit. He removes moral weakness by cleansing us from our sins. The man forgiven is the man to fight; and though he fall beneath the adversary, yet he must in Christ's strength gain the final victory. *Let us learn not to attempt the conflict in our own strength.* The question is not, Does this description apply to the regenerate or to the unregenerate? The practical and solemn truth is that "your adversary the devil goeth about as a roaring lion seeking whom he may devour," that the spirit is willing, but the flesh is often sadly weak. *Let us not despair when we are overcome by the lower man.* Despair means ruin, while hope means salvation; and surely there is a large foundation for hope in the all-merciful High Priest, who is ready to help in every time of need. *Nil desperandum* must be the motto of the true soldier of Jesus Christ. Like brave English soldiers, he must never know when he is beaten. *Let us try to feel that the conflict is worth pursuing,* for final victory is sure in Christ Jesus, and final victory means the award of "the crown of glory that fadeth not away," an inheritance incorruptible, a place where the carnal man shall no more molest.

Vers. 14, 15. *Believer's conflict and victory.*—This last verse of the chapter not only gives us the conclusion of the argument discussed in the preceding verses, but also helps us in the interpretation of the whole passage by supplying us with an answer to the disputed question whether the conflict here described is that of a regenerate or unregenerate man. The words "I myself" in this verse must mean St. Paul *after his conversion*; and he—the same Paul—in the process of his regeneration and of the working of the Holy Spirit in him, passed through this painful conflict, and found deliverance through the Lord Jesus Christ. Though speaking of himself and recording his own experience, St. Paul here is the representative of all true Christians, who with more or less distinctness and painfulness in individual cases have to pass through a similar conflict and to rejoice in the same deliverance. This scripture therefore is most instructive to all believers in Christ who desire to be established in the faith and to live the true Christian life. And in dwelling upon it we may profitably consider: 1. The conflict engaged in; 2. The deliverance obtained; 3. The practical lessons to be learned.

I. The conflict.—This is between the enlightened mind and conscience—"the inner man" of the believer acknowledging the excellence of the law of God—and on the other hand the evil propensities of the natural man—"the carnal man," "the flesh," as it is often termed in Scripture language, refusing to obey God's law or to refrain from sin. 1. *"The law of God is spiritual" in its essential moral nature, as it emanates from the Spirit of God.* But the believer at the beginning of his regenerate life is still "carnal" (see 1 Cor. iv. 1-4)—not yet emancipated from the bondage of sin (vii. 14), which had held him under its dominion. 2. *Hence he finds himself doing what he does not in his better mind approve of.* He even hates his own sinful acts, especially after he has done them; and thus he testifies that the law is good, but sin too strong for him. Its reign is not yet overthrown. 3. *Even when his will is expressly bent upon obeying God's law he has not the power to carry out what he resolved to do.* Indwelling sin has still the mastery of him; he does what he would not. 4. *This is his unhappy state.* He "*delights in the law of God after the inward man*"; but there is another law in his body—the law of sin with its lusts and passions—bringing him under its hateful power. Something of this miserable conflict was known even to heathen men, who have recorded that they knew and approved of what was *good*, yet did what they knew was *evil*. How much more wretched must such a state of moral bondage be in a Christian who has learned to delight in God's law! Well may we assent to St. Paul's vehement exclamation, "O wretched man that I am! who shall deliver from the body of this death ?"

II. **The deliverance obtained.**—The joyful answer to the question "Who shall deliver me ?" is here very briefly expressed : "I thank God through Jesus Christ our Lord." 1. *This happy result and the manner* in which it is realised and carried out in the Christian life is explained and dwelt upon in the following chapter; but here even in this brief expression we have shown to us the source from which this blessing springs, the power by which the victory is gained. It is "Jesus Christ our Lord." 2. *The believer in Jesus Christ is not only delivered from condemnation by his Lord's atoning death* (Gal. iii. 13), *but in and through the same divine Saviour the Holy Spirit*—the very Spirit of Christ and of God—*comes and abides in him;* and as his faith grows stronger and his surrender to the Spirit's guidance becomes more complete, he is strengthened with might in the inner man. Christ dwells in his heart with His spiritual presence and power, and makes him victorious over the sin by which before he was overcome. 3. Thus the Lord Jesus, by our being united to Him, living unto Him, abiding in Him, and He in us, as our strength, our very life, is made unto us our sanctification (1 Cor. i. 30). "The life which we now live in the flesh we live by faith" in Him (Gal. ii. 20). "We can do all things through Christ which strengtheneth us" (Phil. iv. 13).

III. **The practical lessons to be learned.**—"So then with the mind I myself serve the law of God, but with the flesh the law of sin." 1. *The happy deliverance from the bondage of sin by the Spirit of Christ in the Christian has not destroyed the law of sin. It has only restrained it under the force of a superior power.* True "they that are Christ's have crucified the flesh" (Gal. v. 4), and "our old man was crucified with Christ" (Rom. vi. 6). But this "old man," this "carnal mind," the corrupt nature of fallen man, is not *dead*, nor is it improved, reformed, or changed. It is only overpowered and kept down and its evil working stopped in the true Christian life. An untamable wild animal, confined or chained by man's power, cannot exercise its savage propensities; but those propensities are still there, and ready to break out if an opportunity were given. And so the carnal mind of man—the "infection of his nature remains, yea even in the regenerate" (Art. IX.), until at last it is annihilated in the Christian's natural death. 2. *Hence the Christian through the power of the same divine Spirit which gave him his freedom from the dominion of sin must continue to assert and maintain his liberty in Christ:* "mortifying His members which are upon the earth" (Col. iii. 5), the workings and efforts of carnal mind, and keeping them in place of death. 3. *The Christian constantly led by the Holy Spirit and persistently giving himself up to His divine guidance preserves his liberty from the dominion of sin.* But any falling into unbelief, unwatchfulness, or carelessness of living will enable the law of sin in his members to rise up and reassert its power. Hence the needful admonition, "Work out your own salvation with fear and trembling" (Phil. ii. 12). Hence St. Paul says of himself, "I keep under my body, and bring it into subjection : lest that by any means, when I have preached to others, I myself should be a castaway " (1 Cor. ix. 27).　Thus the Lord Jesus is the author and finisher of our faith and of faith's whole life.　His death redeems us from the guilt of sin.　His Spirit rescues us from sin's dominion.　Abiding in Him, we are kept safe unto the end.—*Dr. Jacob.*

Vers. 14-25.　*The principle of progress through antagonism.*—The soul is awakened through the law.　This law work is a necessity of our times.　The soul is kept awake by the antagonism going on within.　For the gospel is not intended to promote at any time satisfaction with self.　So far from this, it is a plan for subordinating self to its rightful sovereign, the Saviour.　And so we are not only put out of conceit with ourselves in conviction and conversion, but kept out of self-conceit by the law of Christian progress.　In this section, as in other portions of his epistles, the apostle reveals this law as that of *antagonism.*　The imparted Spirit proves Himself a *militant* spirit.　The special tendencies in the wild heart of man are met and controlled by the Holy Spirit, and to this war within the Christian has to reconcile himself.　In fact, he is not right until this campaign of the spirit is begun.　It will help us to the proper idea to look at the law of antagonism as it obtains in the larger sphere of Christianity.　To special and undesirable tendencies on the part of men Christianity will be found to have presented such opposition as proved in due season victorious.　A few leading illustrations must suffice.　Take, for example, the case of those rude invaders who broke the power of imperial Rome to pieces.　We call them "Vandals."　Now they were wandering soldiers who loved war but hated work.　They were attached to military chiefs, and so were a constant menace to the peace of Europe.　The problem for the Christianity of that early age was how to curb this wandering and idle disposition and *settle* the nomads in Europe.　And the needful antagonism was supplied in *feudalism,* by which the soldiers were transformed into serfs and united to their chiefs by the mutual ownership of land.　And it can be shown that from this feudalism modern patriotism properly so called has sprung.　In Greece, for example, in pagan times all that passed for patriotism was love of a *city.*　No man apparently had the comprehensive love which can embrace a whole land.　They were Spartans or Athenians, but not patriots in the wider sense.　But in the wake of feudalism true patriotism came, and vast nations were formed at last who were ready to die for their fatherlands.　Thus Christianity antagonised the selfishness which was so rampant in pagan times.　But under feudalism arose *serfdom,* which proved to be only a shade better than pagan *slavery.*　How did Christianity antagonise these evils?　Now the necessity for serfs under feudalism and of slavery under paganism arose from the mischievous and mistaken idea that work is degrading.　Christianity, accordingly, in the dark ages—which were not nearly so dark as some men make them—set itself to consecrate manual labour by the example of the monks.　Devoted men in religious houses made manual labour, agriculture, and work of all kinds a holy thing, and so prepared the way for the industrial movement of later times.　Gradually it dawned upon the European mind that it is *not* a noble thing to have nothing in the world to do, that it is *not* a degrading thing to have to work, and that work may and ought to be a consecrated and noble thing.　Having thus antagonised the natural indolence of men, Christianity had next to combat his unwillingness to *think* for himself, and this was through the Reformation of the sixteenth century under Luther.　The problem of the sixteenth century was to get men, instead of leaving to others to think out the plan of salvation for them, and as priests to undertake their salvation, to think the question out for themselves, and to have as their advocate and mediator the one great high priest, Christ Jesus.　Luther, in his stirring treatise on the freedom of a Christian man, brought out in his admirable way that every believing Christian is himself a priest; and so he enfranchised human minds and gave dignity to the race. Now this law of antagonism which we have seen on the larger scale in Christianity will be found in individual experience. This is evidently the idea of the present section of the epistle. And here let us notice :—

I. **The law of God proving delightful to the converted soul.**—God's law is seen to enter into the very secrets of the renewed soul, to discern the desires and motives of the heart, and to furnish the perfect standard. It supplies the ideal.

II. **The constant sense of falling short of the ideal.**—The renewed soul feels that it somehow cannot do what it would.

III. **The cause of the failure is found in the body of death.**—What we have got to do is to fight the old self in the interests of God and of that " better self " which He has given us.

IV. **In this holy war Jesus Christ is the only deliverer.**—The more progress made, the more intense the antipathy to the evil nature within. But the deliverer is found in Jesus. He comes to dwell within us and be a " better self." He dwells within us by His Holy Spirit; and this Spirit is not only militant, but victorious.—*R. M. Edgar.*

Vers. 15-25. *A disheartening discovery.*—Some of us, when we find others failing just at the point where we should think them particularly strong, can hardly be surprised if we find that we too are failing. Paul, *e.g.*, a pattern of Christian living; yet he laments the discovery of his shortcomings. And as for ourselves, we constantly regret the discovery of our weakness in face of temptation. We are not all tempted alike, but temptation of some sort is inevitable. Think of the various resolutions for good living by different men, and how they fail—the thief, drunkard, etc. The text lets in light on one of the saddest chapters in the world's experiences. Somewhere or somehow we see the fruits of our weakness; we get daily evidence that there is "none righteous." The whole thing is a matter of experience, and by no means a theological principle merely. *Why are we so powerless ?* Because our temptations assail us at our weakest points. The man who has no love of money would never be tempted to miserliness. "Every man is tempted by his own lust"—*i.e.*, by his own particular evil bent or propensity. Many examples in Bible : Solomon, drawn away by love of women; Lot, by love of strong drink; Balaam, by love of money.

Some lessons here suggested :—

I. **Our pride receives a rebuff, and we are made to feel that we are dependants on God's grace.**—But the sense of humiliation is the only way to ultimate goodness. Moreover, only by our humiliation can we enrich our own lives and the lives of others. Paul's disheartening discovery undoubtedly went far to make him the splendid man he was, and lent a throb of living life to what he said and did and wrote for men.

II. **The text points out the need for confession.**—Paul's manliness in confessing : "In me dwelleth no good thing." Could you imagine a finer specimen of Christianity than Paul?—and yet he felt his shortcomings. In general, taking our dealings with the world as a whole, we may be noble characters; but search will reveal grave offences—hastiness, pettishness, fretfulness, evil thoughts, etc.; and especially our offences against God—want of love and loyalty to Him. These offences drive us to confession that we are sinful and need forgiving grace.

III. **A call for watchfulness.**—"When I would do good," etc. Watchfulness against a thousand things that may tend to draw us away from our true connection with Christ. Drifting is such a terrible possibility. What that means

to us, and what it means to the Saviour : it is a stain on His government.
1. Christians scarcely go wrong from sheer wilfulness—rather through carelessness; therefore be watchful. 2. We must be watchful because of the judgment
the world may form of religion. The world has no high law, no certain
judgment, no pure righteousness, no favourable bias towards religion. Hence
the possibilities of evil arising from a bad example — an unworthy display
of life.

IV. **No effort after the perfect life should be in our own strength.**—The
apostle, recognising his frailty, turns to God. Reliance on God never misplaced.
" My grace is sufficient "; " As thy day " ; " I will be with thee in six troubles,"
etc.—*Albert Lee.*

Ver. 18. *Dualism in the life.*—Who that knows anything of spiritual life does
not know by experience how in every attempt one makes to worship or obey
or keep pure and holy evil is at hand, " present with us " ? How it thrusts
itself into our most sacred moments, neutralises our best intentions, surprises us
into a fault, or, overbearing our resistance, drags the reluctant Christian into
unchristian sins ? How often, when the mind seems to be bent wholly upon good,
does a casual spectacle or a remote suggestion call up images of evil ! How
often, when no cause appears, do appetites leap forth in unexpected force, as if
they rose out of some abyss of impurity within, at the bidding of some power
of darkness ! The inertia of the flesh may reduce, as Jesus hinted, the most
willing spirit to inaction. As a watchful foe strongly posted in a troublesome
position may neutralise a much stronger army which it dares not challenge on
open ground, so this disinclination of fallen nature to what is spiritual keeps the
life of the soul to some extent inoperative. The saint may long after communion
with God in holy meditation and prayer; but no sooner does he set about it in
earnest than he is made aware of an inexplicable sluggishness or positive back-
wardness to every pious exercise, which at first he hardly understands, and
which he can never entirely overcome. What is this but the power of evil
present with me ? So always. It starts up a barrier in the path. It neutralises
desire. It paralyses effort. One's most serious intentions wither sometimes
before they ripen into act, as buds never grow to fruit when spring winds are
keen. It would be putting the case far too absolutely to say that the life of
a good man is nothing but a contemptible series of barren wishes. A life
of nothing but good intentions would not be a Christian life at all. It is
not by the blossom, but by the harvest, that a man will in the end have to
vindicate his Christian profession when the harvest day arrives. Still, no man
with a Christian heart in him ever satisfies himself by the measure of his
performance. He never is as good as he desires or means to be. There is
always a gap—a disappointing and humbling gap—betwixt the ideal cherished
and yearned after and the actual behaviour. So that the most literal interpretation of Paul's passionate complaint does not seem too strong to the dissatisfied
believer : " To will is present with me ; but to do that which is good is not "
(ver. 18). While others applaud his virtue, a saint knows how far his own
aspirations outbid his poor achievements, and in his closet he lies groaning under
the grief of failure. When the soul in her purer moments is beholding the
beauty of God's face in Christ, does she not reach out vague longings after such
a spiritual temper as she hath not attained to ? Do there not come over her
visions, divinings of a moral sublimity, a serene equipoise in goodness, a restful
perfectness of will, never yet realised ? So often as the soul seeks to arise
and possess that region of pure heavenliness which seems her own, is she not
speedily aware that she is chained to a close and heavy burden of earthliness
which weighs her down ? The flesh shuts her in, and the sweet glimpse dies

away, and her feet stumble in the clay, and the things she would she cannot do. Well for any one of us if we have not cause to understand a still more humbling confession than this.—*Dr. Dykes.*

Ver. 19. *The Christian conscience.*—" The good that I would I do not : but the evil which I would not, that I do." Who are these two—the I that desires, the I that acts ? Not two persons ; for it is one and the same Paul that both desires and acts. Nor can we say that both are the simple and consistent doings of one and the same person. There is a complication. A desire to act in one way arises within : this desire is thwarted, and action is hindered. A reluctance to act in another way is felt : the reluctance is overborne, and action takes place. And this is not as when the body refuses the bidding of the will— when energy is suspended by lassitude, or the desire of quiet broken by nervous excitement. Those conflicts, those defeats, are temporary ; but this is enduring. Those are between the flesh and the will ; this is within the will itself. For in this description there are two wills. We will one way ; we act another way. But no man can be properly said to act without willing : the motion of conscious action is voluntary ; abstinence from that motion is voluntary also. So that within the man is a will saying, " I will," and protesting against the will which is carried out in action—sitting, so to speak, bound, and witnessing its own defeat. And when we come to inquire about this frustrated will, there can be no question that it is the higher of the two, though it be thus defeated. For it bears testimony for good and against evil ; whereas its victorious adversary thwarts the good and carries out the evil. So then we find ourselves in the presence of these two phenomena in man : a higher will, a nobler consciousness, testifying to good, protesting against evil, but overborne ; and a lower will, a less noble consciousness, putting aside the good, choosing the evil, and commonly prevailing. And we may observe that both these are residents in the inner man, not belonging the one to the inner, and the other to the outer. However the lower will may become entangled with and enslaved by the bodily emotions, it is yet a decision given, not in nor by the body, but in and by the mind.

But now let us go a step farther, and let us suppose that in some given case the higher will obtains the mastery, and that the word of command which the mind gives to the body to act or not to act proceeds, not from the lower will, but from the higher ; or, if necessarily from the lower, then from the lower subordinated to and absorbed into the higher. Let us suppose, in other words, a state of things which would be expressed by " the good that I would do, that do I ; and the evil which I would not do, that I do not." Manifestly this is no impossible supposition, but one which is often, though not ordinarily, realised in fact. What have we now obtained ? Why, this : that my practical will, the ruler of the acts which I do, and the non-acts which I refuse to do, lies open to two distinct influences—one drawing it upward in the direction of good and to the avoidance of evil, the other drawing it downwards in a direction which may lead to the adoption of evil and to the avoidance of good. And there can be no question that this my practical will emanates directly from and is the expression of my personality—that it is the exponent of myself. But let us advance a step farther in this preliminary examination. This practical will is the result of thought, is the issue of determination. Are thought and determination peculiar to man? Certainly not. Every kind of organised animal life, in its measure and after its kind, possesses them. The practical will may be as limited as in the oyster, or as free as in the eagle, but it is equally in obedience to it that conscious animal action takes place. In man, of all animals, its capacities are greatest ; but its nature is not distinct. In man, with all its intellectual powers and wide-reaching susceptibilities, it is but the animal soul; in the lowest organised being, with all its narrowness and dulness, it is the animal soul still.   The Greeks, in their wonderfully accurate language, expressed by the same term (ψυχή, *psychē*) the soul of man which he has to save, and the life of the reptile which man crushes under his foot.   And it would have been immensely for our profit if we had done the same.   For then we should have understood what very few now do understand—the true nature, the true place, of this our intellectual and emotional being.   We hear frequently—in fact, it is the usual and still commonly received notion—that man is compounded of two parts,—the mortal body and the immortal soul.

Man is conscious of God, not by virtue of a higher degree of that which he possesses in common with the lower tribe of animal life, but by virtue of something which he alone is endowed with.   No mere animal has a conscience.   An animal may be trained, by hope of reward and fear of punishment, to simulate the possession of a conscience—to behave nearly as if conscious of right and wrong.   An animal may be acted on by its affections—all situated in the animal soul—so as to lead it to consult, to be united to, even to anticipate, the wishes and feelings of another animal, or of a human master; but no animal ever knew wrong as wrong, or right as right—ever shrank from inflicting pain on principle, or practised self-denial except emotionally.   Conscience, the source of the will that would do the good, that would not do the evil, is entirely a function of that nobler part, the spirit, which man possesses exclusively.   How do we know this?   What has enabled us to detect, to describe, to reason upon, this higher portion of the threefold nature of man?   I answer, We know it by revelation.   Holy Scripture has revealed to us, not God only, but our own nature.   This its threefold division was not recognised, was not perceptible, by the Greek philosophers.   Wonderfully accurate and keen as were their investigations, they could not attain to this discovery, for it was altogether above them.   Neither, again, was it entirely made known in Old Testament days; nor could it be, in the gradual unfolding of God to man. and of man to himself.   It is matter of Christian revelation.   We are first let into the secrets of our own nature when the entire redemption and renewal of that nature are disclosed.   And in this disclosure the Christian Scriptures, as they stand entirely alone, so are they throughout consistent with themselves in asserting this triple nature of man.   In fact, this consistency is kept in all the anticipatory notices in the Old Testament also.   From the first description of man's creation to the latest notice of his state by redemption, the Scripture account of him is one and the same, and is found nowhere else,—the body, created by the Almighty out of the dust of the earth; the divine nature breathed into this body, already organised, by God himself; the animal soul, common to man and the brute creation, expressed by the same term in speaking of the brutes and of man, carrying his personality, being that which he was made to be—" and man became a living soul."

But we must not treat of man's conscience, even in Christian countries, as being infallible or universally enlightened.   It is clear in its testimony, it is trustworthy in its verdicts, only in proportion as men have become Christians.   In every Christian land there are a certain number of persons, greater or less according to the purity or corruption of its Christianity, who form, as it were, the focus of the bright light of the Christian conscience.   Sometimes they are banded together, and acting on the public; but this can only be where the utterance of opinion is free.   And even in such lands the men of pure and clear Christian conscience often know not one another and work not together.   They are separated by barriers of rank, or of sect, or of other circumstance; and it is not till God's providence has made utterance inevitable that it is discovered how irresistible a power was gathering in secret.   Thoughts that it would take a bold man to utter on a platform to-day may to-morrow be carried like a tide-wave over the land, and may the next day have become a confessed basis of national action. Of course in lands where utterance is not free the Christian conscience is repressed. But even there it is, in the long-run, repressed in vain. Like the up-bursting of the boiling granite from the central heat, it will find its way through the chinks of the tightest impost of artificial rule; or, if it cannot, it will end by upheaving and shattering in a moment the compacted crust of ancient and prescriptive wrong. All this I thankfully acknowledge; but I submit that these are only partial triumphs, only flashes in the midnight, compared with what ought to be the result of the spiritual life which is growing and bearing fruit among this great people. Whole realms of thought and action are as yet in utter darkness, as far as any illumination by the Christian conscience is concerned; and this with the light shining in the midst of them. Look at private life, look at public morality, and what a strange disparity appears. There is, thank God, no lack in our land of the pure, clear life of the spirit of man, led in the light of God's countenance, guided by the gentle whisper of His Spirit.—*Dean of Canterbury.*

Vers. 24, 25. *How to be delivered from the body of death.*—In discoursing upon these words I shall endeavour to explain:—

I. **What the apostle here means by this phrase**, "the body of death." The life of every living being in general, and of every rational being in particular, is the free gift of God, bestowed originally without any claim of right, continued all along by His mere good pleasure; and whensoever He pleases, who freely gave it, it may without any injustice be taken away. For God, who was under no obligation to give life to any being at all, is much less under any obligation of justice to make any creature immortal. The mere ending, therefore, of that life, which only by the free good pleasure of God ever began, is no wrong or injury to any, even the most innocent; and this would equally be so whether death were an entire ceasing to exist, or whether it be considered a translation only from one state or manner of being to another. But though death be in itself thus natural, considered barely as the bound or limit of a finite life, yet by the time or manner, and above all by the consequences of its being inflicted, it may very properly and frequently is appointed to be the just punishment of sin. Even by the laws of men, though they know it is in itself inevitable and after death they have nothing more that they can do, yet to the most capital crimes death is the punishment. Much more in the laws of God, in whose hands the consequences of death are, and who after death can continue what punishment He pleases—much more in His laws is the threatening of death justly terrible. Our first parent in paradise was in all probability created naturally, subject to mortality; yet the punishment threatened to his transgression was death. And what the consequence of this death might be in any future state was left uncertain. Since that God has now expressly threatened eternal death as the punishment of sin. To every presumptuous, to every act of known sin has God threatened this second death: how much more to those who are laden with iniquities is "the body of this death" justly terrible!

II. **Wherein consists the wretchedness of those men** who are under the unhappy circumstances of that state which the apostle here describes by the figurative expression of being subject to "the body of this death." "O wretched man that I am!" The natural apprehension of death, considered barely in itself without any additional aggravation, is to every living being necessarily uneasy. The true sting of death, that which really and only makes the thoughts of it justly insupportable, is sin. To sinners the fear of death is what the apostle calls "being all their lifetime subject to bondage." For so long as there is reasonable hope in a future state the spirit of a man will sustain his present infirmity, will bear the thoughts even of death itself with comfort; but a spirit wounded with the expectation of death being not the end but the beginning of sorrows, who can bear?

III. **Wherein consists the difficulty here represented of men recovering themselves of this unhappy state.**—"Who shall deliver me from the body of this death?" The manner of expression, "Who shall deliver me?" is such as usually denotes such a kind of difficulty as there is very little hope of overcoming. And the ground of this difficulty is twofold, partly arising from the appointment of God, and partly from the natural circumstances of the state wherein the persons themselves are involved. By the appointment of God sinners are under the just sentence of condemnation; and out of His hands no force, no fraud, no artifice, can deliver them. What expiation, what atonement, what intercession, will prevail with Him to reverse the sentence of death they cannot naturally know, and the inquiry after it is very apt to lead men into pernicious superstitions. Repentance itself is but a ground of hope and a probable motive of compassion. Without bringing forth fruit meet for repentance, the repentance is nothing; and to bring forth such fruits really and effectually is that other part of the difficulty wherein the persons here spoken of are involved. To an habitual sinner real amendment of life and manners, and acquiring the habits of the virtues contrary to the vices he has practised, is like plucking out a right eye or cutting off a right hand; it is like the Ethiopian changing his skin or the leopard his spots. This slavery to sin is with wonderful affection described through this whole chapter, of which my text is the conclusion.

IV. **Here are the means suggested by which this difficulty, though naturally very great, may yet be overcome.**—It may be done "through Jesus Christ our Lord." He has given assurance of pardon upon condition of repentance and amendment of life. He has promised the assistance of His grace and the influences of His Holy Spirit to make effectual the endeavours of those who under great trials are sincerely desirous to obey Him. He has strengthened the motives of religion by appointing a day in the which He will judge the world in righteousness, and by bringing life and immortality more clearly to light. A firm persuasion and steadfast belief of these great truths will, with the divine assistance, effectually enable men to destroy the habit and the power of sin. And when once the habit of sin is rooted out, and the law of God becomes the governing principle and the real effectual rule of light and manners, the sting of death is then consequently taken away.

V. **Here is expressed the great reason we have to be thankful to God for vouchsafing us this method of deliverance through Christ.**—"I thank God through Jesus Christ our Lord." He might very justly, and without impeachment of His goodness too, have suffered all those to perish who had wilfully and presumptuously transgressed His righteous commands, and could even "out of the stones," as it is expressed, "have raised up children unto Abraham"—*i.e.*, He could immediately have destroyed the wilful transgressors and have created others from whom He might have expected a better obedience. But when, instead of this, His compassion moved Him to grant repentance to sinners, to admit them to a further trial, and by His gracious promise in Christ to give power to as many as would embrace and obey the gospel—this is the highest possible obligation to thankfulness, and to the most diligent endeavours of future obedience.

VI. I propose in the last place to explain **how and for what reason the apostle, in his representation of this whole matter, doth himself personate the sinner he would describe,** and chooses to express the miserable state of the greatest sinner in words seemingly spoken as if it had been concerning himself.

And this deserves to be the more carefully and distinctly cleared, because upon a wrong interpretation of these words has been founded a notion most pernicious to religion, than which nothing can be more absurd. The plain and certain meaning of these words, " I myself serve with the flesh the law of sin," is not I, Paul, who wrote this epistle, but I, the sinner, I, the miserable person, all along described in this chapter. And the reason why the apostle chose to speak after this manner is because it carries with it more of tenderness and compassion, and is more moving and less offensive to express things of this kind in the first person, which is more general, than to apply them directly and more particularly to the person intended, who may usually, with better effect, be left to make the application for himself. By the same figure of speech in his discourse about the last judgment (not through any mistaken apprehension as if the world was then coming to an end, but by the same vulgar figure of speech which I am now explaining) does the apostle, speaking of those who shall be found alive at the day of judgment, say, " We shall all be changed," and " We which are alive and remain unto the coming of the Lord." No man while he lives in the habitual practice of any known vice can possibly be in a state of salvation. He is under the law of sin and death, wretched and miserable ; nor can he by any other means be delivered from the body of this death but through Jesus Christ our Lord— *i.e.*, by the gracious helps and assistances of the gospel working in him effectual amendment of life and manners, in expectation of the righteous judgment to come.—*Clarke.*

Vers. 24, 25. *Man's fallen and redeemed life.*
I. **Man's fallen life.**—There lived in the course of the last century a great satirist, unhappily a vowed minister of God, who loved to burn out the lines of the pictures which he drew of human nature, as it were, in vitriolic acid. He seemed to delight in exhibiting all the baseness, all the meanness, all the ugliness, all even of the physical repulsiveness, that there is in man. Sometimes he exhibited him under the microscope, sometimes under the magnifier, now on a liliputian scale—the word is his own—now upon a gigantic scale. Now, whatever men's theological views may be, they shrink from these representations as a libel upon human nature. They will not allow that—

> " Every heart when sifted well
> Is but a clod of warmer dust
> Mixed with cunning sparks from hell."

There is a view of human nature which is exactly at the opposite pole to this. An eminent statesman, who died not many years ago in advanced old age, surrounded by the love of friends and the gratitude of his country, is reported to have said that we are all born very good. It was an easy, sunny, genial sort of exaggeration, and most people are content to refute it with a significant smile. There is, again, an intermediate view of human nature, which has been very ingeniously illustrated by a living poet. Human nature, he tells us, is like one of those glass balls or tops which may be seen in one of our philosophical toy shops. When it is in a state of quiescence, you can easily distinguish each tint— the bright tint on the one side, and the dark tint on the other side ; but when you touch it with your finger and set it off spinning, you become completely perplexed ; the darkness is suffused by the brightness, and the brightness is shaded by the darkness, till you do not well know what colour to call it. Something in the same way, in the incessant whirl and motion of this life of ours, men perplex you as to what judgment you shall pass upon them ; there is so much goodness in those who seem worst, and so much that is bad in those who seem best. I wish you also to consider for one moment the strange and terrible possibilities of sin which unquestionably lurk in this human nature of ours. A work which was published not many years ago contains what are believed by the initiated to be the actual confessions of an unhappy man of genius. This man in the days of his youth, upon one summer evening, declared positively that he had seen suddenly the shape of a drunken man, running past him at first, then turning to him and looking at him with a terrible glance of hatred. He knelt down for one moment to peruse his features, and then he knew that the form and figure and face which he saw were his own—his own twenty years later—his own when the long lines of excess, and lust, and passion, and care, and sickness had been ploughed down into it. Oh, who can measure the possible distance between himself now and himself twenty years hence—between the innocent babe in the cradle and the haggard and outcast Magdalen under the gaslights of some great city—between the glorious youth of the poet's vision, riding on his winged steed to the castle gates, and the same man in after-life, when his animal nature is worn down to the very stump, a grey and gap-toothed old man, lean as death? Now, if we are asked to explain these terrible possibilities of sin, if we are asked to draw out a general view of human nature which shall harmonise and take up all that there is of truth in these discordant views, then we need but turn, thank God, to our own Bibles ; we need but range upon one side those texts which tell us of the image of God that still remains in man through all the ruins of the Fall, and on the other those which tell us that the heart of man is "deceitful above all things and desperately wicked," and that "out of the heart of man proceed evil thoughts, murders, adulteries, fornications, thefts, false witness, blasphemies."

II. **The redeemed life.**—The redeemed life includes something more than even the forgiveness of sin, blessed though that be. It includes an emancipated will. Man's will, as we have seen, is weak and sick. It is a universal law of our moral life that, when we go and seek for strength by trying to lay our weak will upon a stronger will, strength is almost invariably given. Nay, to seek the strength is to find it. Evermore, when the will is felt to be weakest, we go to the incarnate God by the means which He Himself has appointed ; we go to that precious, loving, sympathising Lord ; and the language of the poor soul, addressed to Him who has trodden the bitter grapes of our sins in the awful winepress, is practically just this : Thou art whiter than driven snow, immaculate Lamb of God, upon whose pure and perfect human will, upon the perfect will of whose superhuman humanity, all the shadows of temptation could no more leave an impression than the passing shadows upon the pillared alabaster—Thou art pure, and I come to Thee for strength because Thy will is perfect. I cry unto Thee from the ends of the earth, "Lead me to the Rock that is higher than I." Take this weak will of mine and lift it up, and fold it with the unfoldings of that everlasting strength of Thine. May we not read in the light of these great truths the seventh and eighth chapters of St. Paul's Epistle to the Romans? There seem to be three stages in the seventh chapter —man before the law, man under the law, man under grace ; first, moral insensibility, then moral knowledge without moral power, then the great emancipation. First unconscious ignorance ; then comes the law of God : for in the tenth commandment, "Thou shalt not covet," the whole intense holiness and spirituality of the law seem to be concentrated, and that sword of God goes on and down, cutting deeper and deeper, until He has cleft and divided into twain on the one hand the decaying, decomposing body of moral and spiritual death, on the other hand the weak and fluttering will ; and the last and lowest cry of the fallen life is, "O wretched man that I am ! who shall deliver me from the body of this death?" while the first blessed cry of the redeemed life is even this, "I thank God through Jesus Christ our Lord." It was said now many years ago by a writer who is very unjustly forgotten that history is like a pall covering dead men's bones and all uncleanness, but that it covers them gracefully. So it does. It covers them gracefully enough. How different is it with God's inspired history! If we had to frame a history which men should suppose to be God's history, what would be its character? It should be a following on of saints and martyrs to the very throne of God. And yet how different is that divine history which we actually find in the Bible from these surmises! Turn to those chapters which record first the fall of man, then the sin of the whole world. We ask why these these things are there, why they are written. For our instruction. They justify and illustrate the Fall; and they explain that redemption which could only be wrought for sinners by the life and death, by the passion and resurrection, of our incarnate God. Yes, still as we think of the corruption and the fall of man, and of the redemption wrought by Christ, let us look at it as St. Paul looks at it in the fifth chapter of the Epistle to the Romans. Have you ever remarked how St. Paul begins there the comparison between the first and Second Adam in slow and measured lines, till, as he goes on, that great spirit of his catches fire, and there are parallel lines of light and darkness, and at last the delicate line of light broadens and deepens, shining more and more unto the perfect day? Yes, Christ our Lord, Christ the Second Adam, Christ in whom there is redemption, Christ into whom we are grafted by the baptism of the Spirit, Christ in whom we live by faith—Christ is our redemption.—*W. Alexander, D.D.*

SUGGESTIVE COMMENTS ON VERSES 7—25.

Pathology of sin.—So ends one of the most profound passages which ever proceeded from the inspired pen of the great apostle. Of its general drift no one can entertain a doubt; it describes the divided unhappy state into which sinful desires bring a man. It is the pathology of sin. It lays bare the symptoms of that inward leprosy, and tells us at last the name of the one Physician that can cure it. And many have imagined that St. Paul has done this by simply describing himself; that we are reading, not a general treatise, but a clinical lecture on a single case; that we are studying the nature of sin from the workings of the apostle's own mind. The whole passage from the seventh verse thus becomes an account of what the law was meant to do for the people of God. It was to set a mark upon sin. It was to draw their attention to their own sinfulness. Holy and just and good in itself, it provoked the self-will of those that received it, and became the cause of their fall. But their fall was not meant to be final. It is no

doubt a bold figure of speech that one man should speak thus in his own person for the whole race of mankind. Now, first, the consciousness of sin is so far a universal fact of human nature that, if any one of us is without it, it is because of some disease, a defect in his own mind. We know the better way, we choose the worse, and we are ashamed of it; these are three plain facts, which contain all that we contend for. Not those who sorrow for sin are deceiving themselves, but those who deny its existence. The consciousness of sin, then, is universal. And in what does it consist? It is the consciousness of division and strife within a man. His mind is not at peace with itself. First, that the consciousness of sin is not an exceptional state, but is as universal as the knowledge of right and wrong; secondly, that it consists in the feeling of a state of discord and division in the soul, which is represented in Holy Scripture as a war between spirit and flesh, the law of the mind and the law of the members, the soul and the body, the will and the desires; and thirdly, that such a condition must be one of misery, out of which it is natural to try to escape by that door of deliverance opened to us by Christ in His gospel. And all these belong, not to the nature of sin in itself, but only to our consciousness of it. Sin is the transgression of a law. Most of the names for sin in various languages bring out this view of its nature; it is the transgression or over-leaping of a line prescribed; it is the missing of our aim or the falling short of our duty. And so far as we have gone it appears that the consciousness of sin is possible for heathens as for Christians. Conscience is there, if its reproofs are more rare and its sensitiveness less; a higher law of life is there, though far from the highest. It is Cicero, and not a Christian, who speaks these words: "There is no conceivable evil that does not beset me; yet all are lighter than the pains of sin, for that, besides being the highest, is eternal." Such words are a comment on those of St. Paul: "When the Gentiles, which have not the law, do by nature the things contained in the law, these, having not the law, are a law unto themselves." Sin is disobedience to a known law of God. Without the Bible man could never have known why it is that conscience, which often has not the power to prevent sin, still preserves its authority to reprove it. The conscience is all that remains of God in the soul of the fallen man. Man is strong with God's strength, rich with God's abundance, intelligent with God's light, and he was meant to be holy with His holiness. It is a defiance of the present God. It is the provoking to anger of One whose anger is death. And in the Bible this representation of sin overpowers all others. When we add to these passages those in which sin is spoken of as blindness, darkness, ignorance, foolishness, we see that sin is represented, not as something having a real existence, but as a privation of existence, a loss of life which the soul might have had. And a

hundred passages might easily be cited from writers of every age to show how deeply this idea has sunk into the Christian mind. "We say," to use the words of Origen, "that all those who do not live to God are dead, and that their life, being a life of sin, is, so to speak, a life of death." It whispers to itself about the claims of *my* opinion, *my* ease, *my* special talent, *my* engrossing pleasure; it inclines to appeal from the law of duty to the decision of this selfish " I," that is evermore trying to exalt itself into a god. But these selfish behests cannot be obeyed save at the cost of others, and hence we see the deep wisdom which makes our love of our neighbour a test of our condition as towards God. Every sin is an acted lie. It is a breach of an eternal law. It is a pursuit of an empty phantasm instead of real good. If our faculties are too low to know God as He is, at least we can know what He is not. He is not one that can love sin; and all that painful pilgrimage that ended in the cross was to witness to that truth. Sin is abomination to God. See what it needs to purge it away! Keep as your dearest possession the conviction of your guilt; it is the one link within your reach of a chain that hangs down from heaven. It leads you up to confession, to atonement, to reconciliation, to a new life unto righteousness, to a joy unspeakable and full of glory. The folly and restlessness and disappointment of sin are a part of that sore burden which we brought to the foot of the cross, and besought the Redeemer to bear. "Sin and grace," says a great English writer, "cannot more stand together in their strength than life and death. In remiss degrees all contraries may be lodged together under one roof. St. Paul protests that he dies daily, yet he lives: so the best man sins hourly, even while he obeys; but the powerful and overruling sway of sin is incompatible with the truth of regeneration." The pardon of sin, then, is accompanied by an inward gift; and the nature of this will be evident from what we have learnt of the nature of sin, of which it is the corrective. It was the sense of sin that sent you to the Redeemer; it is a knowledge that a relapse is possible that keeps you by His side. Fight the good fight set before you; count it all joy that you fall into divers temptations. It is your schooling in holiness. You are free from sin; you are no longer its slaves. Christ has made you free, and you shall have your fruit unto holiness, and the end everlasting life. "I had two wills," says Augustine, "an old and a new, a carnal and a spiritual, which warred against each other, and by their discord scattered my soul." "It is the soul's sickness," he says; "bowed down by evil custom, it cannot rise up whole and complete when the truth lifts it." It is indeed a wonder. The serpent nature in us, with its head crushed under the heel of the Redeemer, wriggles and defiles, and will not die at once. The corruption in which we were born was great; but the second corruption, of a soul that has known the Lord, is still more terrible. We should watch and pray against the fatal relapse.—*Archbishop Thomson.*

Vain desire to reach the ideal.—The deception which was practised by the power of the hitherto slumbering but now rampant sinful desires consisted in this, that when the law in its glory, the moral archetype, first revealed itself to the higher nature of man, he was filled with earnest desire to seize the revealed ideal; but this desire only made him more painfully sensible of the chasm which separated him from the object after which he aspired. Thus what appeared at first a blissful ideal by the guilt of death-producing sin became changed into its opposite.—*Neander.*

Christian conquest over the body. —JEREMY TAYLOR (condensed from sermon on the *Christian conquest over the body of sin*—Rom. vii. 19): The evil natures, principles, and manners of the world are the causes of our imperfect willings and weaker actings in the things of God. Let no man please himself with perpetual pious conversation or ineffective desires of serving God; he that does not practise as well as talk, and do what he desires and ought to do, confesses himself to sin greatly against his conscience; and it is a prodigious folly to think that he is a good man because, though he does sin, it was yet against his mind to do so. Every good man can watch always; running from temptation is part of our watchfulness; every good employment is a second and great part of it; and laying in provisions of reason and religion beforehand is a third part of it; and the conversation of Christians is a fourth part of it.—MATTHEW HENRY on vers. 24, 25: When, under the sense of the remaining power of sin and corruption, we shall see reason to bless God *through* Christ and *for* Christ. Through Christ's death an end will be put to all our complaints, and we shall be wafted to an eternity without sin or sigh. It is a special remedy against fears and sorrows to be much in praise.— SCOTT: A proper knowledge of the holy law of God is the two-edged sword which gives the death-wound to self-righteousness and to Antinomianism; for it is perfectly fit to be the rule of our duty, written in our hearts and obeyed in our lives.—CLARKE: We never find that true repentance takes place where the moral law is not preached and enforced. The law is the grand instrument, in the hands of a faithful minister, to alarm and awaken sinners; and he may safely show that every sinner is under the law, and consequently under the curse, who has not fled for refuge to the hope held out by the gospel.—HODGE: It is an evidence of an unrenewed heart to express or feel opposition to the law of God, as though it were too strict; or to be disposed to throw the blame of our want of conformity to the divine will from ourselves upon the law as unreasonable. The Christian's victory over sin cannot be achieved by the strength of his resolutions, nor by the plainness and force of moral motives, nor by any resources within himself. He looks to Jesus Christ, and conquers in His strength. The victory is not obtained by nature, but by grace.—*Taken from Lange.*

"*I thank God,*" etc.—As much as to say, Jesus Christ delivers me from this wretchedness and moral death. This was the logical conclusion of the whole chapter. Jesus could do what the law could not accomplish—put an end to the internal insurrection. But in exalting Christianity to the first place, we must remember that the law occupies the second place, and that it was a good schoolmaster to bring men to Christ. The chief scope of the law was conscience; the gospel came to include in its ample culture the heart, with all its boundless affections and aspirations. The last clause is but an enumeration of what had been expressed before. There are three principal forces or creators of character which at different periods have engaged the attention of mankind. They are all good, and there is need of them all to keep the whole man sound and morally healthy and growing; but the error has been that too exclusive devotion has been given to one, and the others have been neglected. These three are: wisdom, which answers to the mind; law, which refers to the conscience; and faith, which appeals to the heart. The three most eminent civilisations or refinements of human society have been based upon these three ideas: the Grecian upon wisdom, the Hebrew upon law, and the Christian upon faith; but the greatest of these is faith. —*Livermore.*

Comfort for weak Christians.—So ends this chapter, concerning which there has been much dispute. For some have contended that the apostle does not here speak of himself, but personates another. They suppose that

he refers to a Jew, under the law, but not under grace; awakened, but not renewed; convinced, but not converted. Yet can any unregenerate person with truth say, not only "I consent to the law that it is good," but "With my mind I serve the law of God"? and "I delight in the law of God after the inward man"?—an expression of godliness that characterised the very temper of the Messiah Himself. He could say nothing more than this, "I delight to do Thy will, O My God; yea, Thy law is within My heart." At first view the language of complaint may seem much too strong to apply to the experience of a real Christian. But what real Christian would find it too much to utter when placed in the same state and occupied in the same way with the apostle? This chapter has been much perverted. There is no part of the Bible that Antinomians so much delight in, or which ungodly men who turn the grace of our God into lasciviousness so often quote. Such persons wrest also the *other* scriptures to their own destruction. And are we to argue against the use of a thing from the abuse of it? What good thing is not abused? We do not refuse raiment to the naked because there are some who glory in what ought to remind us of our shame; nor food to the hungry because some make a god of their belly. And shall we refuse to sincere and humble souls mourning over the evils of their own heart the instruction and consolation here provided for them for fear the interpretation should be applied to an improper purpose? No one really taught of God will abuse it, nor *can* he be more reconciled to his corruptions or more satisfied with his deficiencies in consequence of being able to adopt the language as his own. For shall they continue in sin that grace may abound? God forbid! How can they who are dead to sin live any longer therein? We are not to make sad the hearts of God's people, but to comfort them; for the joy of the Lord is their strength. And only the last day will show how much this section of Scripture has strengthened the weak hands and confirmed the feeble knees of those who were deeming their experience peculiar, and concluding that they had no part with the Israel of God till they heard Paul bewailing and encouraging himself thus : " For to will is present with me ; but how to perform that which is good I find not. I find then a law, that, when I would do good, evil is present with me. O wretched man that I am ! who shall deliver me from the body of this death ? I thank God through Jesus Christ our Lord. So then with the mind I *myself* serve the law of God ; but with the flesh the law of sin."—*W. Jay.*

Similar language by heathen writers.—It has been objected that the language of this section is inapplicable to men not yet justified. But we find similar language on the lips of Greek and Roman pagans. Compare Seneca's *Letters*, 52 : "What is it that draws us in one direction while striving to go in another, and impels us towards that which we wish to avoid ?" Euripides, *Hippolytais*, 379 : "We understand and know the good things, but we do not work them out." Xenophon, *Cyropædia*, VI. i. 41 : "I have evidently two souls, . . . for if I had only one it would not be at the same time good and bad, nor would it desire at the same time both honourable and dishonourable works, nor would it at the same time both wish and not wish to do the same things. But it is evident that there are two souls, and that when the good one is in power the honourable things are practised, but when the bad the dishonourable things are attempted." Euripides, *Medea*, 1078 : " I know what sort of bad things I am going to do, but passion is stronger than my purposes. And this is to mortals a cause of very great evils." Ovid, *Metamorphoses*, xvii. 17 : " I desire one thing, the mind persuades another; I see and approve better things, I follow worse things." I do not say that these passages teach the

great truth to prove which Paul quotes his own experience. Nor do they mention the law of God. But they prove that in many cases men are carried along against their better judgment to do bad things. From this Paul inferred that an inward but foreign power was the real author of his actions. And these passages also prove that even in pagans there is an inward man which approves what God's law approves. Paul does not say here that the law gives him pleasure, but that what God wrote on the tables of stone He also wrote in Paul's mind.—*Beet.*

Sensible of moral delinquencies.—1. From this passage it may be remarked that those who consider the law of God only carelessly and superficially are apt to imagine that their conduct approaches so near to a conformity with it as to give them good cause to hope for divine favour ? This is a very delusive mistake ; for, unless we are properly sensible of our moral deficiency, what motive can we have to endeavour to amend our errors ? To escape from this delusion we ought to contemplate the divine law in all its extent and in all its inflexible requirements, that, seeing how unspeakably we come short of our duty, we may rest all our hope of justification on that atonement which Christ hath made for the sins of the world. 2. When we contemplate our own utter inability to yield a perfect obedience to the divine law, let us not blame the law of God as if it were too pure and perfect for such frail creatures as we are. The law is holy and just and good. It is calculated, with unerring wisdom, for promoting the best interests of man. The fault lies solely in the degeneracy of our nature, a degeneracy which we have brought upon ourselves, and for which therefore the law of God is not answerable. Surely we cannot expect, because we have debased our nature so as to be unable to act up to the purity of the divine law, that the law of God should be debased also to adapt itself to our imperfect nature. 3. When we find how very imperfect our best endeavours are to keep ourselves from sin, let us give glory to God that in His infinite mercy He hath provided an atonement by means of which sin may be forgiven ; and let it ever be our study to live as becomes those who are redeemed by the precious blood of Christ, that so we may have the reasonable hope of obtaining at last an inheritance among them that are sanctified.—*Ritchie.*

Law cannot sanctify.—But what follows from all this? Just what the writer set out to prove : viz., 1. That the law of God, which has reason and conscience on its side, is not to be accused as being the efficient cause of sin; but that the indulgence of the sinner's own evil passions is the direct cause of his guilt and misery. 2. That the law, with all its holiness and justice and goodness, and even with reason and conscience on its side, is unable to control the person who is yet under it and is destitute of the grace of the gospel. From all this follows the grand deduction which the apostle intends to make —viz., that we must be " under grace," in order to subdue our sinful passions and desires. In other words, Christ is our ἁγιασμός as well as our δικαιοσύνη. And now, at the close of this whole representation, we may well ask : What stronger proof could the apostle produce than that which he has brought forward in order to show that the law is ineffectual as the means of subduing the power of sin and of sanctifying sinners? The law, with all its terrors and strictness, even when reason and conscience are on its side, cannot deliver ἐκ τοῦ σώματος τοῦ θανάτου τούτου. On the contrary, its very restraints are the occasion of the sinner's guilt being aggravated, because his passions are excited by them to more vehement opposition. Does not all this fully and satisfactorily establish the assertion implied in ver. 5 : τὰ παθήματα τῶν ἁμαρτιῶν, τὰ διὰ τοῦ νόμου? And yet with what admirable caution and prudence is the whole of this nice and difficult discussion conducted! The law stands fully vindicated. Even the sinner himself, who abuses it to his own aggravated guilt and ruin, is obliged to concede that it is holy and just and good. But with all its excellence and glory, with all its promise and threatenings, it never did and never can redeem one soul from death, nor " hide a multitude of sins." Christ is, after all, our only and all-sufficient Saviour ; His is " the only name given under heaven among men whereby we can be saved." He is " our wisdom, our *justification*, our *sanctification*, and our redemption." What then becomes of all the vain and selfish hopes of the legalist? The apostle has scattered them to the winds, and showed that " no man can come unto the Father except by the Son." That there is, after all, adequate help for the poor perishing sinner the apostle next proceeds to show. What the law could not accomplish Christ has effected. That control over the carnal passions and desires, which no legal penalties and no remonstrances of reason and conscience would give to him, the grace of the Holy Spirit, given through the gospel, does impart. No longer does he live to the flesh; no more does sin have a habitual and supreme control over him. Such is the happy state to which the perishing sinner comes by being brought ὑπὸ χάριν ; and this, he has abundant assurance, will be a permanent state—*i.e.*, his " grace will be crowned with glory."—*Stuart.*

ILLUSTRATIONS TO CHAPTER VII.

Ver. 6. *Newness of spirit.*—The economy of the gospel is to put a man in a new condition, and then he will appear in a new character. St. Paul says, " Now we are delivered from the law, that being dead wherein we were held ; that we should serve in newness of spirit, and not in the oldness of the letter." This statement of the apostle was strikingly illustrated in the history of Israel. The law was given, not to Israel in Egypt, but to

Israel delivered out of the bondage of Egypt. God first puts Israel into a new condition—a state of liberty—before He expects Israel to appear in a new character. The fulfilling of the law was to be the test of gratitude and love for a redemption received: " And God spake all these words, saying, I am the Lord thy God, which brought thee out of the land of Egypt, out of the house of bondage. Thou shalt have no other gods before Me," etc. " If ye love Me, keep My commandments." Take an illustration of this text from daily life. We go into a mechanic's shop. The workmen leave at 6 p.m. I enter the room at 5.45. I see one man looking at the clock—sluggishly move his tools—again look up—again work. At last the clock strikes. Down go his tools ; he hastens home. I note a striking contrast in another man who seems absorbed in his work. The clock strikes, but still he works ; his eye has not noted the flight of time. I linger, but still he works, and sings as he works. I go to him, and ask, " Why do you remain at work when your fellow-workman has left the shop ? " He smiles, and says, " Oh, the other man is a hireling ; he is paid by the hour. My father owns the shop. Of course I am anxious that his work should turn out well. I have an interest in the business. He is a good father to me," etc. The hireling serves in the " oldness of the letter "; the son in the " newness of the spirit." " I will run in the way of Thy commandments," said David, " when Thou hast enlarged my heart."—*Bardsley's " Texts Illustrated."*

Vers. 22, 23. *The law of sin.*—The Rev. William Johnston, missionary in Africa, gives the following account : One woman was much distressed, and wept, and said that she had two hearts, which troubled her so much that she did not know what to do. One was the new heart, that told her all things that she had ever been doing. The same heart told her she must go to Jesus Christ and tell Him all her sins, as she had heard at church. But her old heart told her, " Never mind ; God no save black man, but white man. How know He died for black man ? New heart said, Go cry to Him and ask. Old heart tell me, Do my work first, fetch water, make fire, wash, and then go pray. When work done then me forget to pray. I don't know what I do." I read to her the seventh chapter to the Romans, and showed that the apostle Paul felt the same things, and spoke of two principles in man. When I came to the verse " O wretched man that I am ! who shall deliver me from the body of this death ? " she said, " Ah, massa, that me ; me no know what to do." I added the words of St. Paul, " I thank God through Jesus Christ," and explained to her the love of Christ—how He died for sinners like her. She burst into tears ; and has continued ever since, so far as I know, to follow her Saviour.

Ver. 23. *A wavering will.*—

Oh, how my will is hurried to and fro,
And how my unresolved resolves do vary !
I know not where to fix : sometimes I go
This way, then that, and then the quite
    contrary ;
I like, dislike ; lament for what I could not ;
I do, undo ; yet still do what I should not,
And, at the selfsame instant, will the
    thing I would not.

Thus are my weather-beaten thoughts
    opprest
With th' earth-bred winds of my prodigious
    will ;
Thus am I hourly tost from east to west
Upon the rolling streams of good and ill ;
Thus am I driven upon the slipp'ry suds
From real ills to false apparent goods :
My life's a troubled sea, composed of ebbs
    and floods.

I know the nature of my wav'ring mind ;
I know the frailty of my fleshly will ;
My passion's eagle-ey'd, my judgment blind ;
I know what's good, and yet make choice
    of ill.
When the ostrich wings of my desires shall
    be
So dull, they cannot mount the least degree,
Yet grant my sole desire, that of desiring
    Thee.—*Quarles' " Emblems."*

Ver. 23. *St. Bern., Med. IX.*—My heart is a vain heart, a vagabond and instable heart ; while it is led by its own judgment, and wanting divine counsel, cannot subsist in itself ; and whilst it divers ways seeketh rest, findeth none, but remaineth miserable through labour, and void of peace : it agreeth not with itself, it dissenteth from itself ; it altereth resolutions, changeth the judgment, frameth new thoughts, pulleth down the old, and buildeth them up again ; it willeth and willeth not, and never remaineth in the same state.

Ver. 23. *St. August., " De Verb. Apost."*—When it would, it cannot ; because when it might, it would not : therefore by an evil will man lost his good power.

Ver. 24. *The dead body and the living man.*—It is commonly supposed that here is a reference to a cruel usage sometimes practised by the tyrants of antiquity, and which is mentioned by Virgil and Cicero and Valerius Maximus. It consisted in fastening a dead carcass to a living man. Now suppose a dead body bound to your body, its hands to your hands, its face to your face, its lips to your lips ! Here is not only a burden, but an offence. You cannot separate yourself from your hated companion. You cannot breathe without inhaling a kind of pestilence, and " Oh !" you would say, " oh how slowly the parts corrupt and fall off !

Oh, how can I longer endure it? When shall I be free? O wretched man that I am! who shall deliver me from the body of this death?" This is very strong. Yet it comes not up to Paul's case. He is speaking of such a wretchedness, not without him, but within.

Ver. 25. *Victory through Christ.*—There is an affecting passage in Roman history which records the death of Manlius. At night, on the Capitol, he had expelled the Gauls and saved the city when all seemed lost. Afterwards he was accused, but the Capitol towered in sight of the Forum, where he was tried, and he pointed, weeping, to the scene of his triumph. At this the people burst into tears, and the judge could not pronounce sentence until they had removed Manlius to a low spot from which the Capitol was invisible. What the Capitol was to Manlius, the cross of Christ is to the Christian. While that is in view in vain will earth and sin seek to shake the Christian's devotion—one look at that monument of a love which interposed for our rescue when all was dark and lost, and their efforts will be baffled.— *Clerical Library.*

CHAPTER VIII.

CRITICAL NOTES.

Ver. 1. **Who walk not after the flesh, but after the Spirit.**—Wanting in oldest manuscripts. Supposed to be a mistake. A wise addition.

Ver. 2.—Acquitted, all claim of sin is at an end.

Ver. 3.—The flesh of Christ alone is sinless. "Created in the likeness of sinful flesh," that He might be in all points tempted as men are.

Ver. 4.—Might be fulfilled, be accomplished or done in us.

Ver. 5.—The state is indicated in vii. 25, when the mind can serve the law of God, and only the flesh is subject to the law of sin.

Ver. 6. **Carnally minded** ($\phi\rho\acute{o}\nu\eta\mu\alpha\ \tau\hat{\eta}s\ \sigma\alpha\rho\kappa\acute{o}s$).—Lust, a figurative expression, occasioned by what precedes.

Ver. 10. **But the spirit is life.**—Neither spiritual life nor happiness, but a physico-moral life in the fullest sense.

Ver. 11.—The Spirit the pledge of our fellowship with the risen One (Phil.).

Ver. 15.—The Chaldee and Greek words for "father" are used so as to affect both Jews and Gentiles. "Abba," like "papa," can be spoken with the mouth, and properly, therefore, characterises genuine childlike disposition and manner (Olshausen).

Ver. 18. **For I reckon.**—As the result of deliberate calculation. On the one side suffering, on the other grace and glory. **Season** sets forth the transitory character. The glory which is about to be revealed in us, towards us, with regard to us, as Alford puts it.

Ver. 19. **Expectation.**—In the original a highly figurative word. Hope stands with head erect, and with eyes fixed towards the point from which the blessing is expected to come. **Waiteth.**—To receive something from the hands of one who extends it to you from afar. **Of the creature.**—In ver. 22 "whole creation." Some eminent expositors understand all the world except mankind. But it would be remarkable if the phrase excluded man, who is surely the head of this lower creation.

Ver. 20.—The Rabbins said, "With man's fall fell also nature into a state of corruption." **For the creation was made subject to vanity.**—Pressed down by some yoke, which made it the victim of unrealised hopes (Dr. Clemance). Creation to be delivered from the bondage of corruption to glorious liberty. A renovation of this globe, but not necessarily the restoration of every individual to light and glory.

Ver. 21.—Rabbins: "Whatever God has smitten in this world, He will heal in that which is to come in the days of the Messiah."

Ver. 22.—Rabbins speak of the pangs of the Messiah, or the sufferings and birth-throes with which His kingdom is to be introduced. Nature is awaiting the footsteps of her Liberator; and when He steps on the scene her sighs will be turned to songs (Dr. Clemance).

Ver. 23.—The lower creation craves for emancipation, and man yearns for adoption. Christ is the wave-sheaf which prefigured and sanctified the universal harvest (Olshausen).

Ver. 24.—The salvation which we now enjoy is by the exercise of hope as well as faith.

Ver. 25.—The duty of waiting with patient endurance is argued from salvation being yet a matter of hope. It enables all who possess it to wait in patience.

Ver. 26. **The Spirit itself maketh intercession for us.**—The divine Spirit works in the human spirit. $\acute{e}\nu\tau\nu\gamma\chi\acute{a}\nu\omega$, to light upon, to meet with a person. Then to go to meet a person for

228

supplication. Hence to entreat, to pray; ὑπέρ, with genitive of person, to make intercession for any one.

Ver. 27.—Though the prayer be, as some interpret the words, indistinct and inarticulate groanings, yet the divine Spirit can interpret every prayer which is inspired by Him.

Ver. 28. **All things.**—Without exception—all things visible and invisible, our troubles, even our sins.

Ver. 29.—Foreknowledge communicates the strength of grace to those to whom it refers.

Ver. 30. **Called.**—The cause of it God's love, the act of calling; the effect, bestowal of blessings.

Ver. 34.—Justification opposed to accusation, defence and advocacy to condemnation.

Ver. 36. **We are being killed.**—To express the intensely present.

Ver. 37.—Are triumphantly victorious. Have superabundant strength.

Ver. 38. **For I am persuaded, etc.**—To be induced to believe, to yield to, is πείθειν (Pass. and Midd.). θάνατος, violent death, often threatened.

Ver. 39.—High and low places from which the Christians suffered.

MAIN HOMILETICS OF THE PARAGRAPH.—Verse 1.

The natural and the spiritual man.—This admirable chapter has been called the chapter beginning with no condemnation and ending with no separation. Spener is reported to have said that, if Holy Scripture were a ring, and the Epistle to the Romans its precious stone, chap. viii. would be the sparkling point of the jewel.' Almost every verse in the chapter is a sparkling point; it dazzles with beauty from the beginning to the ending. The apostle seems to have been changed from the logician to the rhetorician. He leaves behind the dry process of reasoning, and gives scope to the workings of an enlightened and a spiritual imagination. He idealises, but his ideals are the outcome of true experience. Here are no pictures that do not represent that which is true in the spiritual realm, so that we may safely follow where our apostle leads. Here in the first verse is a true picture of the believer's happy condition. It suggests the contrast between the natural and spiritual man.

I. **The natural man.**—He is: 1. *In a state of condemnation.* This is testified by the witness of nature, by the voice of conscience, and by the verdict of God's word. In studying nature we ask, Why do discordant notes obtrude themselves amid the harmony? why do noisome weeds choke the flowers? why do earthquakes yawn, avalanches sweep, thunders roll, and pestilences destroy? We can only find one consistent explanation. The words of the old record strike our ears with new emphasis: "Cursed is the ground for thy sake; in sorrow shalt thou eat of it all the days of thy life; thorns also and thistles shall it bring forth unto thee; and thou shalt eat the herb of the field; in the sweat of thy face shalt thou eat bread, till thou return unto the ground." Man's conscience testifies to the fact of man's guilt. Systems of idolatry are built upon the fact of man's sense of condemnation and need of deliverance. The baskets of the Druids, the wheels of Juggernaut, the shrines where firstborns have been slain for the sin of the soul, testify that man's conscience says that he is in a state of condemnation. Priests could not have made a successful trade of religion if man had been free from condemnation. The moral demand of man's nature for a remedial scheme created the supply of false religions; but this demand can only be truly met in the gospel of Jesus. The word of God witnesses to man's condemnation: "Now we know that whatsoever things the law saith, it saith to them that are under the law; that every mouth may be stopped, and all the world become guilty before God." Again the word says, "For that all have sinned." The sentence is that of universal condemnation. 2. *In a condition of alienation.* The natural man is estranged from God, from truth, and from goodness. "The carnal mind is enmity against God." It does not like to entertain the thought of God. The natural man may profess to be a seeker after truth and an admirer of goodness; but he only seeks for the truth that he desires, and admires that kind of goodness which is not foreign to the depraved leanings of his nature. 3. *In a position of danger.* The sentence is passed, execution is delayed; but the decree is unalterable—" The wages of sin is death." Unalterable, if sin be persistently pursued. Therefore hasten to escape from the consequences of sin by finding refuge in Jesus, sin's destroyer.

II. **The spiritual man.**—He is: 1. *Free from condemnation.* God's word has declared it, an l that word must be true. The conscience of the spiritual man echoes the sweet declaration of God's word, for it says there is peace instead of trouble, rest in the place of unrest. The bells of heaven have rung in the soul the gracious chimes that tell of sins forgiven. Angels minister heaven's viands to the ransomed soul. 2. *A state of friendship.* Freedom from condemnation is not only acquittal, but introduction to divine friendship. Abraham was the friend of God, and thus he is the father of all the forgiven ones. What a privilege!—the friend of God. 3. *A condition of safety.* What harm can happen to him who is free from condemnation, and who is the friend of God? Omniscience is the spiritual man's guide. Omnipotence is His protector. All things in heaven and in earth move to his final welfare. Let us try to enter into the broad meaning of the ancient words, " There shall no evil happen to the righteous." Seeming evil there may be, but human seeming is not always divine reality.

III. **The ground of the spiritual man's privilege.**—" There is no condemnation to them which are in Christ Jesus." A familiar expression with St. Paul: " In Christ Jesus." The spiritual man is " in Christ Jesus." 1. *As a substitute.* If I am condemned to death and another suffers my sentence, I am in that substitute virtually. My crime is atoned for, my punishment is borne. Thus we are in Christ as our substitute. " By His stripes we are healed "; " He was wounded for our transgressions." 2. *As the ark of safety.* Noah escaped condemnation and death. Might not others have entered the ark and have been saved? Surely, for God is always merciful. However, all may fly the devouring waters of condemnation, and find safety in the ark Jesus Christ. 3. *As the pacifier.* Jesus is the peace-bringer, but He only brings true peace to the soul that sails with Him in the boat that He guides. My soul has peace when it hears the soothing strains of infinite love. 4. *As the harmoniser.* There must be divine adjustments in the soul if there is to be freedom from condemnation and consequent peace. The sense of condemnation is not completely eliminated from the nature until every power is brought into harmony with divine plans and purposes. 5. *As the perfecter.* Our translators have fittingly added the words, "who walk not after the flesh, but after the Spirit." Christ must perfect and develop the upward tendencies of the renewed man. Every step taken according to the flesh leads to condemnation, but every step taken according to the motions of the life-giving Spirit tends to peace and untold blessedness.

IV. **How do we get into Christ?**—Through faith by grace. " By grace are ye saved through faith; and that not of yourselves." The act of faith may be either definite or indefinite. Some people can point to a period when there was the conscious stretching forth of the hand of faith, laying hold of the hand of Jesus Christ. Others seem to grow up in the faith. They have been trained to look to Jesus as their Saviour. They are conscious of no startling spiritual changes; but they are conscious of faith in Jesus Christ, of love to His person, of devotion to His cause. They have peace. Jesus says to the man with the withered limb, Stretch forth thy hand. He says to all, Stretch forth thy hand of faith. It is powerless; well, obey the command, and strength will be imparted, and strength will increase. Christ seeks to lay hold of you. Do you then lay hold of Christ. If you feel your weakness,—cast yourself into the arms of the powerful Saviour. Believe, and live.

SUGGESTIVE COMMENTS ON VERSE 1.

Sin not in the body.—Some philosophers have maintained that all sin has its seat in the body and originates from it, but that the soul is absolutely pure. Does the apostle mean that Christians live according to the principles of the soul, not the evil motions of the body? No; since our Lord teaches us the heart is the seat and foundation of moral evil, for out of it proceeds all that defiles the man. Therefore when exhorted to cleanse ourselves "from all filthiness of the flesh and spirit, perfecting holiness in the fear of God," it is not implied that any moral good or evil attaches to the material body, but that we ought to abstain from those sins of which the body is the instrument and subject, such as sensuality in its various forms, and from those of which the body is not necessarily the instrument, such as pride, malice, covetousness, and other sins of fiends who have no bodies. Christians live by the grace of God, not according to the flesh or their corrupt nature, but according to the spirit, or their regenerated nature. Their spiritual principles, motives, and aims give a character of spirituality to their secular as well as to their religious acts; for whether they eat or drink, or whatsoever they do, they do all to the glory of God.—*Parlane.*

MAIN HOMILETICS OF THE PARAGRAPH.—*Verse 2.*

Perfect liberty.—The apostle carries out his parallelism. One part of this passage is set over against the other, and we are not therefore to be surprised as we read, "The law of the Spirit of life in Christ Jesus." The ruling power in the natural man is "sin and death"; the ruling power in the spiritual man is "the law of the Spirit of life in Christ Jesus." The law of the Spirit is the controlling power imposing itself on the will, guiding the understanding, regenerating the affections, and elevating the nature. The freedom we contemplate is perfect, but this perfection will not be reached till by death we are set free from all the enthralling forces. The Holy Spirit is the gift of Jesus Christ, the result to man of the Saviour's mediatorial work. The Spirit is communicated to us through Christ. The gospel frees not by its own power, but by Christ. We must come to the great central truth that Jesus Christ is the true emancipator of the race. If we have any freedom it must be in, by, and through Jesus Christ. Let us seek then to follow out the wide teaching of the text, and ask in what senses Jesus Christ makes His people free.

I. Jesus Christ makes men free by discharging from prison.—It is impossible accurately to explain the precise nature of the bearing of the Redeemer's sacrifice upon God's moral government and man's spiritual relations. Theologians may fail to give full satisfaction to the curious inquirer; nevertheless we may adhere to the truth that man was and is a sinner, and that Jesus Christ died in the penitent and believing sinner's room and stead. Man had incurred a great debt by transgression, and had not wherewith to discharge the claim; for Jesus Christ teaches the prayer, "Forgive us our debts, as we forgive our debtors." Man is under a curse, for it is written, "Cursed is every one that continueth not in all things which are written in the book of the law, to do them." Men are guilty before God, for he that offends in one point is guilty of all. Guilty the man stands in the presence of almighty God, and is as a man in prison. When a man comes to feel his guilt, he longs to be set free. His cry is, O wretched man that I am! who shall deliver me from the bondage, who shall set my conscience free from the chains with which the law has bound? And the gracious answer comes: "Christ hath redeemed us from the curse of the law, being made a curse for us; for it is written, Cursed is every one that hangeth on a tree." Jesus takes

231

away man's guilt by becoming Himself as one guilty. " Jesus is laid in the borrowed tomb, indicative of the fact that He carried borrowed sins." When the debt-bound man is set at liberty, the clouds are swept away, sweet sunshine enters the soul, the time of singing birds returns, the flowers give forth their fragrance, and all things are revived. So it is when the sinner believes that Christ Jesus has discharged every claim.

II. **Christ Jesus makes men free by finding congenial employment.**—When a man has been in prison for a term of years and is set at liberty, he finds it difficult to adapt himself to his new state of life. A man had been in prison so long that his hair had grown grey through the confinement, and his old friends did not know him, and now most of them had passed away from this world ; the old familiar scenes of childhood looked strange and almost repulsive to him ; he had forgotten the employments and the amusements in which he was accustomed to engage long, long ago, in what seemed to him another life. He came back to the prison doors, and with tears in his eyes begged to be readmitted, that he might end his days in his beloved cell. Better the confinement of the prison than the liberty of the man who does not know what to do with himself and who finds no sphere for the exercise of his powers. Now Jesus Christ introduces the freed to blessed companionships, to holy employments, to scenes and engagements where their natures will find satisfaction and their love repose. Christ Jesus makes men free by renewing the nature, and then by finding employment for that changed condition.

III. **Christ Jesus makes men free by surrounding with wholesome restraints.**—There are those who imagine that restraint and freedom are opposed ; but so far from that being the case, restraint is the true conservator, the true sweetener, of liberty. Now Jesus Christ surrounds His people with wholesome restraints that conserve and promote Christian liberty, and that enable them to enjoy the blessings of divine freedom. He places them within the circle of truth and of duty, their satisfied desires have no longings to overleap the bounds of that circle, and there they enjoy highest freedom. The true law of the Christian life is liberty to do right and restraint in the direction of wrong doing. " For, brethren, ye have been called unto liberty ; only use not liberty for an occasion to the flesh, but by love serve one another." Liberty in loving service. Slavery and freedom combined. Bondage compatible with liberty. The bird flies far and wide on the wings of love to provide for her young ones ; but however large her circuit, however wide her flight, she is bound to the nest, and seeks not to loose herself from the invisible bond. The angels in heaven find loving service liberty. We shall never experience true freedom until we know how to serve in Christian love.

IV. **Christ Jesus makes men free by binding them to Himself with the cords of love.**—It is a burlesque on freedom to imagine that it consists in shaking oneself loose from all family, social, and national restraints. There is a gracious freedom in the loving heart which it alone can experience, and which it cannot explain to any other. The heart of man is full of trembling and uncertainty, till it be fixed in the beloved object, till it has returned unto God, the soul's true rest. Away from the binding influences of the Saviour's love, we may have the so-called freedom of the homeless wanderer who goes up and down the earth seeking rest and finding none, but gathered into that love we have the home feeling of those welcomed by dear ones. When the spirit is bound to God by faith and love, it soars in the highest regions ; but when it breaks those bonds, its powers are curtailed, and it lies in wretchedness. If the Son makes free by binding to Himself with love, then are men free indeed.

V. **Christ Jesus makes men free by causing them to love the pathway of**

holiness.—The pathway of holiness is the way to freedom, and is itself freedom. It emancipates the spirit from selfishness as the rule of life, from those low passions which cramp the immortal nature, and leads upwards to those heights where the spirit revels in ever-expanding liberties. Christ Jesus is the world's great liberator. Sin is the prison-house where Satan causes his victims to serve, and holiness is the bright sphere where Jesus leads His delighted followers. " But now being made free from sin, and become the servants of the living God, ye have your fruit unto holiness, and the end everlasting life." Liberated men must let the world see that sin has no mastery. It is as Christ Jesus is born in the heart that men are made free from sin. " Though Christ were born a thousand times in Bethlehem, and not in thee, thou remainest eternally a slave." If the cross of Golgotha is not erected in thy heart, it cannot deliver from the evil one. Looking upon striking pictures of the Crucifixion will not save. Wearing gold or ivory crosses will not redeem. There must be loving attachment to the Saviour's person ; there must be believing recognition of the sacrificial nature of His death.

VI. **Christ Jesus gives men a real freedom.**—" If the Son therefore shall make you free, ye shall be free indeed." These words denote the singular excellency and the certain nature of that freedom which Jesus imparts. The opponents of the reign of Jesus talk about those trammels which religion places on the persons of His followers. But the true outcome of Christ's religion is liberty, progress, improvement. Wherever Christianity has existed in its purity, there has likewise existed the greatest liberty. Christianity and liberty are as cause and effect—the former must in the long-run produce the latter. No slavery can long exist in that atmosphere which has been permeated with Christianity. Where are our statues in honour of Jesus, the world's greatest liberator ? They are widely spread. Statues not in brass or in marble. Loving hearts in many climes set free by Jesus are the monuments of His glory. Enfranchisement of thought, freedom of utterance, and the liberty of the press all testify to the influence of the Christian religion. The onward march of improvement, the flourishing of every good and noble cause, the suppression of vice, and a large public practice of and still wider public sentiment in favour of virtue, speak to the blessedness of Jesus. Before the coming of Jesus Christ truth was bound by men's blind traditions ; but He spoke the all-powerful word, and truth stood forth in its native majesty and blessed the world with its benign influence. And thus Jesus is at once the world's liberator both intellectually and spiritually. And it is as a spiritual liberator that He is now working and shall continue to work. He sets men free from sin and fear and guilt. He gives the glorious liberty of divine sonship. His people are no longer children of the bondwoman, but of the free. But the soul cannot taste the bliss of full freedom so long as it is trammelled with the body of this flesh, and it anticipates the period when it will be fully emancipated and fly away to that more perfect sphere where there will be uninterrupted freedom and unalloyed happiness.

" *The law of the Spirit of life.*"—The apostle, in the first verse, says, " There is therefore now no condemnation to them which are in Christ Jesus, who walk not after the flesh, but after the Spirit." In the seventh chapter he had given an account of his own experience, from his conviction of sin till he triumphs in the Lord Jesus. In the text he sums up the work of salvation. Consider :—

I. **The law of sin.**—Sin is not a single act, it is a principle. It takes possession of the transgressor the moment he violates the law of God. Sin is a tyrant, whom none can conquer but the Almighty. To know what sin is, and to be delivered from it, is heaven begun on earth.

II. **Consider the law of God**, and what sin does in opposition to it. The apostle Paul had learned the truth in his own heart. " Sin taking occasion of the commandment deceived me, and by it slew me." This teaches us the awful truth that sin commands in exact proportion as we discover the holiness and purity of the law of God. Sin says, " Oppose it." Its purity presents itself in new glories. Sin says, " Oppose it still, persevere against the Almighty in all the glories of His legislation ; laugh at all His curses, and sin on." Such is the monster which inhabits our own hearts. The secret of true religion is first in knowing ourselves as sinners. But this is not all that can be said of transgression. We should not be surprised that a criminal should curse the judge who consigns him to the gallows ; but we should be surprised to find a criminal, to whom the king sends a reprieve, spurning it, and cursing the sovereign. It is not in hell that we behold sin in its deformity, it is on earth. When the gospel is proclaimed, unless the Holy Spirit change the heart, the tyrant issues his edict, " Curse God, despise His commands and invitations, laugh at heaven and hell."

III. **The law of death**—that is, the punishment of sin ; the curse due to the transgressor. Sin comprises its own punishment wherever found. In the presence of a God of justice every sin will have the punishment due to it. Neither the commands nor curses of God's holy law emanate from the sovereignty of God, but from His essential holiness. The punishment of sin will be tremendous in the extreme, while the sinner will be his own executioner. Nothing is more absurd than to talk of the deliverance of devils and lost spirits, for it impeaches the law of God. Consider what the nature of sin is. It must live, not only as feelings in the bosom, but as principles. " The Lord of hosts shall be exalted in judgment, and God who is holy shall be sanctified in righteousness."

IV. **The law of the Spirit of life.**—The gospel is called the law of the Spirit for two reasons : 1. *Because God is a legislator as well as a sovereign in His mercy.* The gospel, both in the Old and New Testaments, is called a law. " His delight is in the *law* of the Lord," in the whole truth of God. " A *law* shall go forth out of Zion." The Saviour is a king ; and where is there a king without a law ? To dream of sovereign blessings and to forget the legislative glories of the King of kings is a dangerous and delusive dream. It is impossible to save a ruined soul without meeting God as a legislator as well as a sovereign. He is both ; and we are only to live as that we may die under the influence of this truth. 2. *The Holy Spirit accompanies His own truth into the human heart.* The gospel is the medium which is made use of by the Holy Spirit to make us " meet to be partakers of the inheritance of the saints in light." Some preach parts and portions of the gospel, as if God were exclusively a sovereign ; though it may be blessed to the salvation of some, yet it is pregnant with destruction to others. " The law of the Spirit of life." Here is the triumphant consolation of the believer ; he sometimes goes through painful discipline. It is a useful discipline to the believer to humble him, to drive him downward, as the cold winter does the sap. To destroy the tree ? No ; but to strengthen its roots and promote its growth under ground, where no human eye can witness it, that the sap may afterwards ascend to the branches, that they may bear not only leaves but rich fruit.

V. **The blessing.**—" Free from the law of sin and death "; free from the condemnation and dominion of sin ; free from every curse ; free from every charge ; free from the holy law of God as a covenant ; free as Messiah Himself. If this be not true, what the apostle says in the first verse could not be true. Was there any condemnation for the Saviour after He rose ? No. Is there any for him who believes in the Saviour ? No. In what consists the freedom

234

of his humanity now? In his intense and delightful obedience to the will of God. There is no true freedom to be found but in the freedom of God, in obedience to His holy will. True liberty is the freedom from the condemnation of sin, from its dominion, and from its tyranny. This freedom involves in it a state of warfare. "The flesh lusteth against the Spirit, and the Spirit against the flesh." It opposes itself to everything opposed to God, internally and externally. Are we thus free? Some are shocked when they hear any one say they are certain of being in heaven. I dare not dispute their testimony; but I would inquire, on what ground does it rest? If their religion correspond with St. Paul's, I would say, "Triumph on, begin the song of heaven on earth." True religion is freedom, and if so, a consciousness of safety must be so likewise. The liberty of true religion is the parent of every other liberty. Contrast this with the voluntary slavery of men. Man is the slave of a slave; because the slave of Satan by nature, led captive by him at his will.—*Homilist.*

SUGGESTIVE COMMENTS ON VERSE 2.

Contrast between Paul's past and present.—The contrast of Paul's past bondage and present liberty proves that he is not now condemned. He remembers the time when, in spite of his better judgment, he did the bidding of sin. He now does the bidding of the Spirit of God. He finds that he is free from the bondage of sin only as he follows the guidance of the Spirit, and therefore infers that the guidance of the Spirit has made him free. He knows that his liberation came through Christ's death, and he enjoys it to-day by resting upon Christ. His freedom is therefore God's gift, and a proof of God's forgiveness. Just so a prisoner, whose prison doors have been opened by the king's command, has in his past imprisonment and present freedom a proof of pardon. Whereas the freedom of a law-breaker who has never been apprehended is no such proof. There are thousands to-day to whom every doubt about their present salvation is banished by a remembrance of their former bondage to sin and fruitless efforts to do right. Since Paul's liberation took place in Christ, he has a right to infer that all who are in Christ have been set free, and are therefore no longer condemned. Thus the law, by making us conscious of our bondage, not only drives us to Christ, but furnishes to those who believe an abiding proof of God's favour.—*Beet.*

The gospel frees men from sin and death.—The world in general account it liberty to give loose to their passions; but such freedom is indeed the sorest bondage to sin and Satan. None possess true liberty but those who are freed by Christ. The state of the demoniacs when healed by Christ resembled theirs. Paul was made a glorious example of it to all ages. He was once under condemnation, both because he adhered to the covenant of works and was governed by his own impetuous will; he now rejoiced in a freedom from the sin that he had indulged, and from the curse to which he had subjected himself. "The law of," etc. We shall first *explain* and then *improve* the text.

I. **Explain it.**—It is not needful to state the various interpretations given of the text. We shall adopt that which seems most easy and agreeable to the context. We will begin with *explaining the terms.* "The law of the Spirit of life in Christ Jesus" is the gospel covenant as confirmed to us in Christ and revealed to us by the Spirit. "The law of sin and death" may be understood either of the covenant of works or of our indwelling corruption. We shall next *explain the proposition contained in the terms.* The proposition is, that "the gospel frees us from the curse of the law and from the dominion of sin." This proposition is to be understood as extending to all believers. The text thus explained is capable of most useful improvement.

II. **Improve it.**—It is replete with very important instruction. It shows us the wretched state of every unregenerate man. It declares to us the only method of deliverance from that state. It affords also abundant matter of *reproof.* It reproves those who despond as though there were no hope for them. It reproves also those who speak against an assurance of faith. It may administer *comfort* also to many sincere Christians.—*Simeon.*

Difference between legal and evangelical. — It has been said that the difference between legal and evangelical doctrine appears from the relative position of two words. The doctrine of the legalist is, "Do, and live"; the doctrine of the evangelist is, "Live, and do." It is surely as absurd to expect spiritual action without spiritual life as natural action without natural life. All Christians, therefore, are raised into life from death, into which they had fallen by sin, before they love and serve God. The apostle in this verse states the causes of life and death as consisting of two laws, and his emancipation from the one as being effected by the superior energy of the other.—*Parlane.*

Gospel sets believers free.—Albeit, the apostle himself (brought in here for example's cause) and all true believers in Christ be by nature under "the law of sin and death," or under the covenant of works (called "the law of sin and death" because it bindeth sin and death upon us till Christ set us free), yet the "law of the Spirit of life in Christ Jesus," or the covenant of grace (so called because it doth enable and quicken a man to a spiritual life through Christ), doth set the apostle and all true believers free from the covenant of works, or "the law of sin and death," so that every man may say with him, "the law of the Spirit of life," or the covenant of grace, hath made me free from "the law of sin and death," or covenant of works.—*Westminster Divines.*

The outward does not make a Christian. —There are two senses in which men are said to be Christians. In common speech they obtain this name when they merely belong to the outward fellowship of the Church of Christ; but in the more exact and appropriate use of the term, it denotes those who both belong to the communion of the Church and also manifest the dispositions and conduct which our Saviour requires in His followers. To the last of these is freedom from condemnation here restricted, as is expressly signified by the apostle's words. For lest it should be supposed that all members of the visible Church are exempt from condemnation, he immediately adds this further limitation, "Who walk not after the flesh, but after the Spirit." Thus there is a twofold qualification necessary in order to exempt men from condemnation. They must be "in Christ," and they must "walk not after the flesh, but after the Spirit." [Ritchie's remarks are just, though the weight of manuscripts is against this second part of the passage. It is found in ver. 4.] Strictly speaking, indeed, this last qualification did not require to be stated in order to make up the meaning; for if we understand those who are "in Christ" to mean those who are His genuine disciples, their walking "not after the flesh, but after the Spirit" is implied. Without this qualification no man can be a sincere disciple of Christ. But the repetition shows the apostle's sense of the importance of this qualification; and was probably intended to impress us with a conviction that, in order to be sincere Christians, we must not only avoid walking after the flesh, but actually walk after the Spirit—not only "cease to do evil," but also "learn to do well."—*Ritchie.*

Ver. 2. *Freedom in this life.*—In the words, and those that go a little before, there are these three main fundamental points of religion: *The misery and bondage of man; the deliverance of man; and his duty.* Here you have his *misery*: he is under "sin and death." Here is his *deliverance*: he is "free from this by Christ." And for his *duty*, you have it in the last verse of the former chapter, speaking of his deliverance: "O wretched man that I am! who shall deliver me from the body of this death?" Then it follows, "Thanks be to God through Jesus Christ our Lord." Thankfulness is due,—not verbal thankfulness only; indeed, the whole life of a Christian, after his deliverance, is a real thanksgiving. The fearfulness and odiousness of this condition, to be in prison and thraldom and bondage to all kind of sin, natural and actual, will appear further by this, that being in subjection to our base lusts, by consequence we are *under the bondage of Satan*; for he hath power over death by sin, because he draws us to sin, and then accuseth us and torments us for sin. By sin we come to be under his bondage. So that we are under the captivity of sin; for all the power that he hath over us it is by sin. He is but God's executioner for sin. This is good news indeed to hear of freedom—good news to the Israelites to hear of freedom out of Egypt, and for the Jews to hear of Cyrus's proclamation for their freedom out of Babylon. Freedom out of bondage is a sweet message. Here we have such a message of spiritual freedom from other manner of enemies than those were. The year of jubilee was a comfortable year to servants that were kept in and were much vexed with their bondage. When the year of jubilee came, they were all freed. Therefore there was great expectation of the year of jubilee. Here we have a spiritual jubilee, a manumission and freedom from the bondage we are in by nature. "The Spirit of life in Christ makes *us free* from the law of sin and death." There can be no freedom *without satisfaction to divine justice*. Satisfaction must be with the glory of His justice, as well as of His mercy. His attributes must have full content. One must not be destroyed to satisfy another. He must so be merciful in freeing us as that content must be given to His justice, that it complain not of any loss. Now reconciliation alway supposeth satisfaction. It is founded upon it. Here it is said there is life in Christ. There is life in Christ as *God-man*, as mediator. Now this life is that life which is originally from the Godhead. Indeed, it is but the Godhead's quickening and giving life to the manhood in Christ, the Spirit quickening and sanctifying the manhood. And we have no comfort by the life of God, as it is in God's life alone severed; for, alas! what communion have we with God without a mediator? But our comfort is this, that God, who is the fountain of life, He became man, and having satisfied God's justice, He conveys life to us. The Spirit of life in Christ, first of all, it did *quicken and sanctify His human nature*. And the Spirit of life that quickeneth and sanctifieth our nature in Christ did likewise *ennoble our nature*: also *enriched it with all grace* that our nature is capable of; for the nature of Christ had this double prerogative above ours: first of all, that blessed mass of flesh, it was knit to be one person with God; and then, that nature was enriched and ennobled with all graces above ours. And this the Spirit of life did to Christ Himself, to human nature that He took upon Him, that He might be a public person. A freedom in this life, in calling, in justification, in sanctification; and in the life to come a freedom of glory.—*Sibbs.*

MAIN HOMILETICS OF THE PARAGRAPH.—*Verses 3, 4.*

The method of law and the method of love.—The method of law has failed as a justifying and sanctifying force. Perhaps not failed in the divine plans; even human failure may be divine success. Law has failed "in that it was weak through the flesh." Law could not overcome the obstructive forces of human passions, of a depraved moral nature. The method of love must now be tried; and if that fail—we may say it reverently—the divine resources are exhausted.

But this method has not failed. Law cannot show one instance of success. Love can indicate many. If the method of love had triumphed in only one case, it would prove itself a success. But it can refer to multitudes. The method of love must be allowed to run the same lengthened course in human history which has been allotted to law before a verdict is pronounced; the method of love must be examined when the final roll is completed, when the vast multitude of the children of love are gathered to the home of love, and then God's wisdom and power will be vindicated. The method of love is here exemplified and illustrated by and in :—

I. **The act of sending.**—" God sending His own Son "—emphasis on the words "*His own.*" God plucked the choice treasure from His bosom of love, and sent it forth on a strange errand; God plucked the sweetest flower from the eternal garden, and sent it forth to fill another world with its fragrance. 1. *Thus the words point us to the fact of the Saviour's pre-existence.* Let us not deny the eternal existence of Christ because it is to us unknowable. Here let us rise from the known to the unknown, from a temporary to an eternal existence, and believe in that which we cannot comprehend. " In the beginning was the Word," and this beginning is before the present system of things. It answers to that declaration in the Old Testament where Wisdom, which is Christ personified, says, " The Lord possessed me in the beginning of His way, before His works of old." Here is eternal existence declared—or at least an existence which goes far beyond our powers of understanding, for it was before God's works of old. Jesus Christ in His divine nature was not then the work of God, for He existed before all the works of God; and if Jesus be merely human, then He existed before Himself, which is absurd. And again, according to Micah, Jesus came out of Bethlehem as to His human nature, but as to His divine nature His goings forth have been from the days of eternity, from the days of old—old to us who are of yesterday; neither old nor young to Him who is " the same yesterday and to-day and for ever." We are of yesterday, and had no previous existence. The doctrine of the migration of souls is futile, for it does not enrich consciousness or enlarge experience. Is there no growth in this migration? Why do not the great souls of the past show themselves with increased capacities in other human beings? Jesus Christ was before His birth. And His life shows a richness and a vastness which speak of pre-existence. Here is to be noted the coincidence between the Old Testament and the New, which reveal the divine unity of the Bible as proceeding from one God; for Jesus says, " I came forth from the Father, and am come into the world; again, I leave the world, and go unto the Father." The personified Wisdom of the Old Testament and the incarnated Wisdom of the New are one. Jesus Christ was with the Father before His works of old. He came from the Father, from everlasting. Jesus Christ had a glory with the Father before the world was, the incomprehensible glory of an eternal existence, of being when there was no created being. Jesus Christ states the doctrine distinctly when He says, " Before Abraham was, I am "; or in other words, Before Abraham was I was. My existence is prior to the existence of him who gave tithes to Melchizedek. In this sense it was understood by the Jews when they took up stones to stone Him, as making Himself greater and older than Abraham. In this sense it must be understood by every intelligent student; and thus by this fact Melchizedek is a type of Christ, having neither beginning of days nor end of life. Therefore we say with St. Paul, " He is before all things, and by Him all things consist "; the universe subsists, keeps together, is held together in its present state, by the omnipotence of Jesus Christ. He is before all things, and thus had a prior existence, and is therefore divine. He is before all created things, and therefore uncreated. Our Saviour is glorious in the incomprehensibility of His

238

eternal existence. He comes forth from eternity to save and rescue the sons of time, and with the treasures of eternity would enrich humanity. He comes forth from the sabbatic repose of eternity to the toils and anguish of time. 2. *The words point us to the loving harmony which subsisted between the Father and the Son.* It is to be observed that our Lord does not speak much of His own love to the Father, but rather lets it speak for itself, as all true love will. This agrees with His own utterance: "But that the world may know that I love the Father; and as the Father gave Me commandment, even so I do." And the world, looking at the Saviour's life, at His devotion to the Father's will, at His loving determination through all pains, agonies, and self-sacrifices to accomplish the Father's purpose, will come to the conclusion that His love to the Father was above and beyond all human comparison. Oh that our love were one of deeds as well as of words! John the Baptist gives an emphatic utterance as to the Father's love of the Son. John, in bearing witness to the glory of Christ, says, "The Father loveth the Son, and hath given all things into His hands." This is a mysterious statement, and we cannot hope fully to understand its meaning, for we only "know in part and prophesy in part," for "we now see through a glass, darkly," a smoked glass, and nothing is clear to the vision. Our ideas are indistinct, and the words we use for their conveyance are inadequate. Human language is imperfect to express the thoughts which we have of the things seen; how much more must it be imperfect for converse about the things that are unseen! When we speak of God the Father and God the Son by means of our feeble language, we must remember that our terms and figures are bounded, and cannot express all that we think, far less all that may be thought, on such a sublime theme. Not only is our language poor, but our thought is feeble. The words "the Father loveth the Son" are familiar words enough. "Father" and "son" are primal words. They are as roots to the vast tree of humanity. Out of them spring families, tribes, nations, vast dynasties. And yet what are they in that connection? In what sense is God the Father and Jesus Christ the Son? The Father, and yet not superior to the Son? The Son, and yet equal to the Father? We cannot tell. Sublime mystery, and yet blessed thought, that our human relationships are employed to set forth divine relationships. And the love which exists between the divine Father and the Son must be something beyond the power of our intellects to comprehend. All our notions of love, gathered from earthly manifestations, must be far from doing justice to the bright flame which illumines the divine nature. Mostly in this world love is not a pure flame—too often it is but "fantasies' hot fire, whose wishes soon as granted fly"; but God's love is like Himself, free from all imperfections; and to change our figure, it flows from Himself a life-giving stream, filling heaven with joy and with glory, and then shaping for itself other channels along which to send its vast overflowings. And oh, how the love-stream went out towards the Son of God! The earthly father loves the son by virtue of the subsisting relationship. A magical influence is that which binds the father to the son, and we cannot analyse this subtle emotion. It is divinely implanted, and is the reflection of God's love to the Son. That love refreshed the Son of God in a past eternity. Before time commenced its solemn march,,in a far back eternity, God loved the Son; for Jesus was ever the Father's delight, rejoicing always before Him. Through the power of this love we are to suppose them moving in harmony and dwelling together in sabbatic repose. For true love, then, there must be harmony of nature,—

> "The secret sympathy,
> The silver link, the silken tie,
> Which, heart to heart, and mind to mind,
> In body and in soul can bind."

Now it is almost impossible to secure this perfect oneness in human relationships. But between God the Father and God the Son there could be no disparity of either tastes or tendencies or years. They are one in nature, though two in person. Their perfect harmony is seen most strikingly in the scheme of human redemption. God the Father beheld human misery with divine compassion. When He was devising schemes whereby His banished ones might not be expelled from Him, God the Son said, I delight to do Thy will, O God. Here am I; send Me. I am ready to go, travelling in the greatness of My strength, mighty to save. We are not then to view the loving Father as a mere vindictive God, from whom the Son extracts salvation. The love of the Father as well as of the Son are equally manifest in the plan of redemption. There was perfect harmony in heaven, and this harmony between the Father and the Son is communicative and productive of harmony among the angelic hosts. In confirmation of this Jesus Christ says, "Therefore doth My Father love Me, because I lay down My life, that I might take it again." In loving harmony they dwell together in eternity. And as we think of this loving harmony, we are induced to reflect how much is involved in the expression, "God sending His own Son."

II. **By the manner of sending.**—"In the likeness of sinful flesh." How great is Jesus Christ, and yet how He humbled Himself and took upon Himself the form of a servant! He assumed a true human nature. He was bone of our bone and flesh of our flesh. In all things, sin excepted, He was made like unto His brethren. He was in the world identifying Himself with its deepest needs and highest interests. He had indeed infinite pity for the infinite pathos of human life. The tears of the world's Creator are the world's great boon. They crystallise themselves into jewels of undying hope for humanity. They mingle themselves with the world's tears, and these lose more than half their bitterness. The Saviour's tears flow on fields of mourning, and there spring up harvests of joy—on valleys of death, and they bloom with the sweet life of light and immortality. He did not shut Himself up in seclusion, but went about doing good. Christ was more concerned to show His divinity by the attribute of love than by the attribute of either omnipotence or omniscience. Omnipotence belonged unto Christ, but He ever kept it in check. He spake of His power, but seemed to speak of it as if to show to men how great was the restraining force of that love which could hold omnipotence in chains. Christ had power and love, and in the conflict love was allowed the victor's place. Our Lord was omniscient, but He seldom used the attribute. Omnipotence was kept in abeyance; omniscience did not often appear; love never slept.

III. **By the purpose of the sending.**—"And for sin, condemned sin in the flesh." 1. *He destroyed sin in the flesh by a holy life.* It is said that the direction which Socrates gave to philosophical inquiry was expressed in the saying that he brought "philosophy down from heaven to earth." But Jesus Christ did a greater work, for He brought goodness down from heaven to earth, embodied it in His own person, and manifested it in all His actions. Socrates dreamt philosophical visions; but Jesus worked out schemes of benevolence, showed Himself the rare and radiant vision of goodness incarnate. We by no means undervalue Socrates and his work, and yet we must feel that he stands at an immense distance behind that vision of goodness which gladdened our sphere when Jesus Christ moved, full of grace and of truth, a being too good for earth, whom earth neglected and rejected, and yet by whose presence earth has been highly blessed, and to whose action earth owes a more glorious aspect. Some are bold enough to place Jesus Christ on a level only with Socrates, and in doing this they forget the unchallenged purity of the Saviour's life, and do not bear in mind the facts brought before us in the utterances of Jeremy Taylor: "The best

and most excellent of the old lawgivers and philosophers among the Greeks had
an alloy of viciousness, and could not be exemplary all over : some were noted
for flatterers, as Plato and Aristippus ; some for incontinency, as Aristotle,
Epicurus, Zeno, Theognis, Plato, and Aristippus again ; and Socrates, whom their
oracle affirmed to be the wisest and most perfect man, yet was by Porphyry
noted for extreme intemperance of anger, both in words and actions ; and those
Romans who were offered to them for examples, although they were great in
reputation, yet they also had great vices; Brutus dipped his hand in the blood
of Cæsar, his prince, and his father by love, endearments, and adoption ; and
Cato was but a wise man all day—at night he was used to drink wine too
liberally ; and both he and Socrates did give their wives unto their friends ; the
philosopher and the censor were procurers of their wives' unchastity ; and yet
these were the best among the Gentiles." These charges were made by writers
who lived very close upon the time at which the men flourished of whom they
wrote, and yet an attempt at refutation was not made. And yet we do not
know of any attempt to convict Jesus Christ of immorality near to the time
in which He flourished. The verdict which Pilate uttered, " I find no fault
in Him," was practically unchallenged by the chief priests, scribes, Sadducees,
Pharisees, and angry Jews. It was a verdict which all felt to be just, and which
brought conviction to every mind. If there had been but one spot on this Sun of
righteousness, there were not wanting men of microscopic power to find it out.
Pilate's wife referred to Jesus as a just man. The centurion and they that were
with him said, " Truly this was the Son of God," " Certainly this was a righteous
man." The centurion had the conception of a divine-human, holy being. He
felt that Jesus was just in claiming to be the Son of God, and he confessed
further that Jesus was holy, and none were present to contradict. The suborned
blasphemers, the two false witnesses, could only declare, " This fellow said, I am
able to destroy the temple of God, and to build it in three days." Jesus Christ
stood the trying test of His own time, of the envenomed spirits that sought His
destruction, who, if there had been any discovery to make, would have succeeded
in the attempt ; but His moral glory was superior to the fangs of jealousy and
of wickedness. Thus the sanctity and holiness of Jesus were glorious in these
darknesses, "as a beauty, artificially covered with a thin cloud of cyprus,
transmits its excellency to the eye, made more greedy and apprehensive by that
imperfect and weak restraint." Thus were found confessors and admirers even
in the midst of those despites which were done Him upon the opposing designs
of malice and contradictory ambition. Eighteen hundred years have passed
away, and it has been reserved for a modern French writer to draw sensual
pictures of the lascivious dalliances of the holy Jesus with beautiful Jewish
maidens.* But the picture is a proof rather of the evil mind that gave it birth
than of any reality in the case it is supposed to represent. If there had been
anything of this kind, we may be sure that it would not have waited eighteen
hundred years for the pen of a modern romancer to reveal. The opponents of
Jesus, whether political, intellectual, or religious, must be crushed ; while the
adherents of Jesus shall live and flourish by the power of His undying life and
by virtue of His ever-increasing justice. The Sun of Righteousness sails on in
sublime tranquillity, shedding His beneficent beams in spite of telescopic glare, of
the romancer's daring, and of the sceptic's bold denunciations. Yes, of all the
great and good men who have walked this earth, dignified the race, and whose
names have adorned the pages of history, Jesus Christ is by far the noblest, not
only on account of His intellectual greatness, though here He was without rival,
but on account of His pre-eminent goodness. His life was a thrilling record of

* " Les jeunes filles qui auraient peut-être consenti à l'aimer," etc.

goodness, shining through every feature, suggesting every thought, ennobling every action, clothing every utterance with beauty, and endowing Him with superhuman influence. So that we may indeed stand before Him and say, Thou art fairer than the sons of men,—fairer not in physical form, though thus He was comely; fairer not in mental capacity, though thus He was mighty; but fairer in holiness and in purity. So fair that, if we range the fields and gardens for types, we must gather the loveliest of flowers, for He is the rose of Sharon and the lily of the valley; if we explore the mineral world, we must take the most precious, for He is the treasure hid in the field and the pearl of great price; if we ascend to the heavens and travel from star to star, we must fix upon the most brilliant, for He is the bright morning star; if we retrace our course and go back to Israel's history, we must think of Israel's noblest characters, for Moses the world's greatest lawgiver, Aaron the head of the priesthood, and David the noblest of Israel's kings and the world's richest poet, are types of David's greater Son. Earth can give but faint types of Christ's moral beauty, and He will transcend all the glories of heaven. 2. *He destroyed sin in the flesh by a painful death.* "The Son of man came not to be ministered unto, but to minister, and to give His life a ransom for many," as the climax of His self-sacrificing ministry. Jesus Christ was a man of sorrows, and yet He moved with sublime tranquillity along the highways of life, and thus He was the best helper the children of sorrows ever met as well as a welcome guest at the feast. It is true that in the final issue sorrow broke His heart. This sorrow, however, was not His sorrow as a man, but as a mediator. We can neither climb the heights nor fathom the depths of the Saviour's sorrow in the period of His crucifixion. In that one fearful cup of sorrow was compressed the world's sin. He suffered for others in a sense in which no other has suffered, and therefore the heart-breaking nature of that calamity. If He had appeared in this world but not as a mediator, sorrow would have touched and yet would not have destroyed. Love to the eternal Father and love to the race induced Jesus Christ to tread the course of the lonely sufferer. And the solitariness of Jesus brings to our view the greatness of His love most vividly. As in lonely prayer He agonises on the mountain's side, His mighty love comes beaming from His person and clothes the barren mountain with celestial beauty. When in lonely grandeur He treads the billows, they gleam with the brightness of His ineffable love. When in His solitary struggles He sweats as it were great drops of blood, His love transforms for devout souls the bead-drops of sweat into pearls radiating divine colours of attractive brilliance. When He cries, "My God, My God, why hast Thou forsaken Me?" that cry is but the sad yet gracious musical strain which indicates the wondrous force of His all-mastering passion. The heavens were darkened, the sun was eclipsed, the earth reeled in its steady course, as if in astonishment that love so vast should meet a doom so fearful. No wonder that all the people that came together to that sight, beholding the things which were done, beholding love incarnate rejected, crucified, tortured, beholding the way in which men treat the embodied perfection of virtue, smote their breasts and returned sorrowing! No wonder that the graves were opened, and many bodies of the saints which slept arose, as if to see if it were indeed true that love could find so ungrateful a return, and that none were found so enamoured of divine love's charms as to rally round the Saviour in His defence and to His protection! The Saviour's crucifixion is indeed calculated to give us an exalted view of the force of the Saviour's love; but it is also calculated to give a depressing view of the degradation of our humanity. The darkness of earth's sins and miseries and want of power to appreciate the highest goodness clouded over and eclipsed the light of heaven's goodness. Earth has no darker sin, history has no blacker page, humanity has no fouler spot, than that of the Saviour's crucifixion.

IV. By the gracious results of the sending.—Earth was darkened by the Saviour's crucifixion, but through the darkness came ever-expanding streams of light. Thus Jesus was sin's destroyer. Thus was opened up a way for the justification and sanctification of those who "walk not after the flesh, but after the Spirit." We mourn that our sins crucified the Lord of light and of glory ; but we rejoice that out of the sinless Sufferer's offering arises the moral betterment and enrichment of mankind. Let us show our true gratitude by not crucifying the Son of God afresh, by triumphing over sin, by walking after the Spirit of light and of purity.

The coming of God's own Son in the flesh.—The third verse may be read literally, and more intelligibly, by reversing the order of the clauses, thus : "*God sending His own Son in the likeness of sinful flesh, and for sin, condemned sin in the flesh—a thing which the law could not do, in that it was weak through the flesh.*" Without entering on many collateral controversies, ancient or modern, which these words may suggest, we observe that the great lesson conveyed is that there was something which the law could not do, and which the incarnation of the Son of God did. He sent "His own Son in the likeness of sinful flesh." Not in sinful flesh, but "in the likeness of it." Does this mean that Christ's nature was a mere likeness of humanity? Surely, to put this question is to answer it ; if Christ's manhood were not real, then there is no solid footing for faith, hope, and charity on this stricken earth. But let us mark the very words of Holy Writ. God sent His Son in the likeness—not of flesh, but—of sinful flesh. It was in its very essence humanity ; but it was not in essence sinful humanity. But it never was stained with sin, and He could not know the bitterness of remorse. And yet He knew that hiding of the Father's face, that darkness of desolation, which is for us the first, last, worst result of transgression. I believe that though He never sinned He was really tempted to sin ; and that therefore there must have been something in the nature of the God-man upon which the evil one could lay hold ; that the chords which bound the heart of holy Jesus to the Father's bosom were not so screened from assault, but that the devil seized and strained them till they moaned as though they would break. Yet were they not broken. How this was we cannot tell ; but I will admit all mysteries and take my stand on the Scriptures which tell us that He suffered in soul and body from the mighty tempter's power ; suffered, as the strong wrestler suffers ere he hurls his antagonist upon the ground, as the soldier suffers ere he can rest his reeking sword on the trampled sod where the dead foe is stretched. He came in the flesh, but only in the likeness of sinful flesh. His was a true, a tried, but not a sinful humanity. What, then, did this mission of God's Son accomplish that was beyond the power of the law? We answer :—

I. **It showed that human nature is not essentially or originally sinful.**—Into our world, thus explaining away its iniquity and shortcoming, Christ has brought a vivid picture of holiness in His own life, teaching us that the law of God is at once true to the nature of man and to the nature of God. For when men looked at Him as He fulfilled the law, and saw how good He was, how pure and sinless, the first thought was, "How true a man !" and the next, "How divine !" There were indeed times when the sense of His perfection was insupportable, and the cry of the stricken heart was, "Depart from me, for I am a sinful man, O Lord." Yet even this very cry led up to the confident conviction which said, "Thou art the Christ, the Son of the living God."

II. **But, further, the mission of God's Son in the flesh also enabled us to see at once the hatefulness of sin and the loveliness of holiness.**—We can now hardly realise what a change in the nature of religious profession Christ has made. We now look upon a world into which Christ's life has been infused, upon men and women who know that He is at once their model and their strength. But this is the result of a revolution. There was nothing in the world when Christ came, nothing in known history, to attract men to what we now understand by "holiness," and gentle words never heralded such a revolution as did that cry of the great Teacher, "Take up My yoke and learn of Me."

III. But, further, the mission of God's Son effected the severance of the sinner from his sin.—That, as we have already seen, was what the law could not effect. But Christ has brought it about in fact and in our consciousness. It is in this strange division between the sinner and his sin that the power of Christ's cross is seen.

IV. The mission of God's Son thus brings it to pass that "the righteousness of the law is fulfilled in us who walk not after the flesh, but after the Spirit."—Although this be the result in the blessed experience of very many, it is a fact resting on a further mystery. And some who can go along with us in what has been already said may now stop in uncertainty. The present life of Christ is imparted to me. It is not only that my sins are forgiven, but that the power of sin is taken away. It is not only that if I were like Christ I should be happy, but it is that Christ comes into me, and by His Spirit renews me day by day. Life could never come by law, and therefore righteousness could never come by law ; but now life comes to men by Christ, a new life,—a life of holy thoughts and pure desires ; a life of love, joy, patience, peace ; a life which is like Christ's life, rather which is Christ's life. What is it to you and me that Christ has come ? Is it the power of a new life ? Is your religion only in your Bible, or is it in your heart ? Is your Saviour in heaven or in you ?—*A. H. Charteris.*

SUGGESTIVE COMMENTS ON VERSES 3, 4.

The presence of the Son proclaims the death of sin.—"Condemned sin": proclaimed the doom of sin. Since sin has been represented as a ruler, its doom must be dethronement. "In the flesh." By sending His own Son in a body of flesh like that in which sin had set up its throne, and by sending Him because of sin and to save us from sin, God proclaimed in the midst of the empire of sin that that empire will be overthrown. The birth of Christ was an invasion of a province which sin had seduced into revolt and brought under its own sway. When we see the King's Son enter the revolted province without opposition, and know that He has come because of the revolt, we are sure that the King is both able and determined to overthrow the rule of the usurper. The presence of the King's Son proclaims the usurper's coming dethronement.—*Beet.*

The Son's pre-existence.—The term "sending," by itself, would not necessarily imply the pre-existence of Christ ; for it may apply to the appearance of a mere man charged with a divine mission. But the notion of pre-existence necessarily follows from the relation of this verb to the expression "His own Son," especially if we take account of the regimen : "in the likeness of sinful flesh." It is evident that, in the view of one who speaks thus, the existence of this Son preceded His human existence. The expression "His own Son," literally "the Son of Himself," forbids us to give to the title "Son" either the meaning of "eminent man," or "theocratic king," or even "Messiah." It necessarily refers to this Son's *personal* relation to God, and indicates that Him whom God sends He takes from *His own bosom.* Paul marks the contrast between the *nature* of the envoy (*the* true *Son* of God) and the manner of His appearing here below: "in the likeness of sinful flesh." This expression "sinful flesh" (strictly, "flesh of sin") has been understood by many, especially most recently by Holsten, as implying the idea that sin is inherent in the flesh—that is to say, in the bodily nature. It would follow therefrom—and this critic accepts the consequence—that Jesus Himself, according to Paul, was not exempt from the natural sin inseparable from the substance of the body. Only Holsten adds that this *objective* sin never controlled the will of Jesus, nor led Him to a positive *transgression.* The pre-existing divine Spirit of Christ constantly kept the flesh in obedience. We have already seen (vi. 6) that if the body is to the soul a cause of its fall, it is only so because the will itself is no longer in its normal state. If by union with God it were inwardly upright and firm, it would control the body completely; but being itself since the Fall controlled by selfishness, it seeks a means of satisfaction in the body, and the latter takes advantage therefrom to usurp a malignant dominion over it. Thus, and thus only, can Paul connect the notion of sin so closely with that of "body" or "flesh." Otherwise he would be obliged to make God Himself,

as the creator of the body, the author of sin. What proves in our very passage that he is not at all regarding sin as an attribute inseparable from the flesh is the expression he uses in speaking of Jesus: "in the likeness of a flesh of sin." Had he meant to express the idea ascribed to him by Holsten, why speak of likeness? Why not say simply "in a flesh of sin"—that is to say, sinful like ours. While affirming similarity of *substance* between the flesh of Jesus and ours, the very thing the apostle wishes here is to set aside the idea of likeness in *quality* (in respect of *sin*). This is done clearly by the expression which he has chosen. Thus we understand the connection between the "condemned" of ver. 3 and the "no condemnation" (ver. 1). In His life He condemned that sin which, by remaining master of ours, would have brought into it condemnation. The relation between vers. 3 and 4 becomes also very simple. The condemnation of sin in Christ's life is the *means* appointed by God to effect its destruction in ours.—*Godet.*

MAIN HOMILETICS OF THE PARAGRAPH.—*Verses* 5—13.

Depression and elevation.—In this world we reckon up the human race by many gradations. In divine revelation the race is classified under two comprehensive terms. One class mind the things of the flesh, and the other mind the things of the Spirit. The one is carnally minded, and the other is spiritually minded. Godet speaks of the aspiration of the flesh. Surely the carnal mind does not aspire. It reaches out, not towards the higher, but towards the lower. The spiritual mind alone aspires in the true sense of that word. It reaches upwards towards the infinitely pure, good, and beautiful. The work of the carnal mind is depressing, for "to be carnally minded is death." The result of the spiritual mind is elevation, for "to be spiritually minded is life and peace." Men deem it important to secure the titles and honours of this world; but the highest title and honour is to be spiritually minded Let us seek for divine grace, for the baptism of the Holy Spirit, that we may become spiritually minded, and have that more abundant life and ever-increasing peace which is the promised inheritance.

I. **Define the two characters.**—The carnally minded is not merely the glutton, the drunkard, and the sensualist. A man may be a respectable member of society, and yet be carnally minded; for his thoughts, cares, and aims are confined to this present world. The philosopher who exalts reason, the poet who revels in bright visions, the philanthropist who works from an earthly standpoint merely to ameliorate human woe, the orator who conveys thoughts that breathe in words that burn, the patriot who shows a love of fatherland, may be all carnally minded. They mind the things of the flesh, and their vision is bounded by the things of time and sense. There is no heavenward aspiration. They may be in a state of enmity against God, which is characteristic of the carnal mind. The carnal mind is enmity against the God of love and of wisdom. The creature is in a state of enmity against that Creator who has made the senses to be the avenues of pleasure, who has created a world of beauty to minister to their delight. The fallen creature is in a state of enmity against that Creator who has devised the mediatorial scheme for redemption and salvation. He may not be subject to the law of God. The carnal mind is proud, and will not bow in subjection to the Supreme. Outwardly the man may obey; inwardly he rebels. Divine subjections reach to human volitions. Human subjections are outward and material, while the divine are inward and moral. The carnal mind cannot please God. There is dissimilarity, which causes repulsion. Like attracted to like. The carnal mind cannot walk in fellowship with the spiritual mind of the Eternal. The depraved and the Holy cannot sweetly coalesce. The carnal man is in a condition of guilt. Conscience is uneasy. He cannot please, he does not attempt to please, and he is displeasing to the infinite Justice. The spiritually minded are those whose thoughts, cares, and aims are for the things of the Spirit. This is their general and prevailing characteristic. We are not thus born. The first birth introduces us carnally minded; the second birth constitutes us, in germ at least, spiritually minded. The spiritually-minded man is one whose sins are forgiven for Christ's sake, who is an heir of heaven, who seeks so to pass through time as not to lose sight of the things of eternity, who seeks to use this world so as not to abuse. The spiritually minded is one in whom dwells the Spirit of Christ. The divine Spirit animates and elevates the human spirit. The divine Spirit impels to aspiration, and satisfies the upward lorgings of the yearning human spirit. The two spirits move in blissful union. This is so complete that they are as one spirit. The Spirit of Christ, loving, peaceful, and benign, has taken possession of the human spirit; all disturbers are driven forth, and a beautiful divine kosmos rises out of the repulsive chaos. The spiritually minded are those who please God. How wondrous the suggestion that humanity can touch divinity! How elevating the conception that human doings can affect divine pleasures! Away with the depressing suggestion that man is beneath the notice of the divine! In the beloved Son God is well pleased; and shall He not be pleased, for the Son's sake and through His work, with all those in whom that Son's Spirit dwells?

II. **Depict the two results.**—"Carnally minded is death." "Spiritually minded is life and peace." The carnal mind is death, for there is: 1. *Paralysis of the powers.* Physical sensation has not ceased; the emotional nature is not in a state of complete stupor. The carnally-minded man has his better impulses. Sometimes he is touched and moved by what appear to be divine instincts. But there is a paralysis of the God-apprehending powers of his nature. His soul does not aspire to the true soul-rest. He does not attempt to climb the sublime heights where divine visions are vouchsafed. 2. *A creeping corruption.* Physical death corrupts. Sin corrupts where it touches. Where sin reigns a corrupt force creeps. Sin spoils our pleasant palaces, defiles the throne, and plucks every jewel from the crown. 3. *Cessation of the nobler affinities.* Sin separated Adam from God. Guilty Adam did not discern the strains of fatherly love in the divine voice. Love has much work to break the spell of sin and win home the prodigal. Sin sends its victims to hiding-places in dark groves, to the far countries of want and wretchedness. Sin is death to all the home feelings. The carnally minded is dead in the finer emotions, the sweeter sensibilities, the divine affinities of his nature. The spiritually minded has: 1. *A living peace.*

A state of quiescence may belong to the solid rock.   The Stoic may have killed his emotions; the Fakeer may have reduced himself to the condition of a machine —withered and senseless.   But the spiritual mind has a living peace.   It is an inward force swaying and gently guiding.   2. *A peaceful life.*   Outward, storms— inward, peace.   A lighthouse rocked by the tempest in the rude cradle of the deep; the keepers calmly tending the light which is to cheer the mariner. Paul's outward man touched and tossed by the rude tempest of persecution; the ego, the sublime personality, was calmly tending the eternal lights.   3. *An ever-expanding life.*   " To be spiritually minded is life."   All other life is poor compared with this.   This is more abundant life.   This is eternal life.   What do we know of life in this death-stricken world?   A Samson appears once in the world's history to give us some notion of physical life.   A Solomon and, nearer our own times, a Milton and a Shakespeare tell of the largeness of intellectual life.   Jesus Christ unfolds to our view the vast possibilities of the moral life. " To be spiritually minded is life."   It is a large word composed of four letters. Life from the Infinite permeating the finite.   Life divine flowing through human valleys where death shadows darken.   4. *An enlargement of view.*   He that raised up Christ from the dead shall quicken the mortal bodies of those who are spiritually minded.   There must be greater significance in Paul's words than we have hitherto comprehended.   We read them with a materalistic bias. Can it be that he who allowed his body to be buffeted and torn by persecutors should hold out as a great prize the doctrine of the resurrection of the mere material nature?   Would St. Paul rejoice that a defective body which hampered the workings of a sublime soul was to be raised from the grave?   We do not yet know all that is meant by the resurrection of the dead.   And we take refuge in the declaration that flesh and blood cannot inherit the kingdom of God; neither doth corruption inherit incorruption.   One thing is certain, that there will be a wondrous quickening.   Life will triumph over death in miraculous manner.   Life in the righteous already triumphs over death.   The clergy are good lives on the assurance tables.   A smile passes over the countenance of the sceptic.   Good living, freedom from care, are the ready explanations.   Are they the only class placed under like conditions?   They are the only class who seek as a whole, in some measure, to attain a spiritual condition, and in doing so they realise the blessing even of physical life.   But what is physical life?   How poor its sensations !   What is intellectual life?   What is spiritual life?   The realm glows in beauty where spiritual life abounds.

" *Mortifying the deeds of the body.*"—We have been sent into this world to live out our lives on the highest level, do all that lies in us towards completing our duty, and also make the most of this present world.   But the man has not yet lived who did not find it easier to go down than to rise, who did not discover that it was easier to be soiled with sin than to keep unspotted.   There is a throne in every heart ; but the heart has not yet throbbed in which there has not been a battle for the mastery—Satan striving for the throne with God.   The text points out at least one fact, that this must be exactly reversed.   Satan must have no standing-ground, and God must be king in man's living temple.   We shall find this no easy task.   There will be a sharp, painful struggle ; an agony will be felt in the soul ; and thus we speak of " mortifying the deeds of the body."

I. **What is it to "live after the flesh"?**—1. Some have delighted to call a man " a mass of corruption "—*e.g.*, the Puritan fathers.   But have not all men, in some sort or other, some redeeming quality?   Say, a splendid morality.   But, unhappily, the law of life to such men has come to them, not from the fountain-head direct, but through some vitiated, mud-filled channel.   These highly moral men perhaps are positively indifferent about God—their morality is of human conception; and that in one sense is "living after the flesh." 2. What we are of ourselves, good as it may be, does not make us what we ought to be. If we are all in all to ourselves, if we have our own guide and rule of life, if we have not called God in to our assistance, we are certain not to walk aright. Whenever we do what *we* like, we are trying to tread the pathway of the Infinite with only finite power to guide us. If that be so, we are bound to have false and inadequate conceptions of life and destiny; and such a course one might call "living after the flesh." 3. Some are led on by impulse. The flesh is more than spirit, appetite more than reason; passions are more than obligation. Their bodies get more care than their souls. *That* is "living after the flesh." In short, a man lives after the flesh who treats the body and bodily interests as everything, and minds not the things of the soul. The body is not the most important part of a man. Beauty no guarantee of goodness.

II. **Mark the inevitable struggle for supremacy.**—In man there is a continual struggle—flesh against spirit, temporal advancement as against growth in grace, a constant estimate of the value of things, temporal things laying claim to man's best energies, religious principles too often being put into the background. These are the mistakes of worldly life. Take one special tendency of modern life—the undue exaltation of intellect. The cultivation of the mind a great boon to humanity. It helps the onward sweep of civilisation, lifts men 'out of serfdom and ignorance into the liberty that becomes a man. But if intellect be placed before true religion, this is "living after the flesh." This is putting "smaller" before "larger," making "princelet" wield the sceptre over "emperor."

III. **Mark the plain duty of man.**—He must "mortify the deeds of the body." Its parallel in the Ephesians, "Be ye renewed in the spirit of your mind," etc. If we find we are not all we should be, our struggle must be to undergo a thorough change. We are to go over our lives as we should over a garden, carefully, searchingly, pulling the weeds out by the roots, leaving only the good behind. Slay the evil habits, abolish unsafe rules, snap chains that bind us as sin-captives, get out of old ruts and step boldly on the way of life, drive out devils of hypocrisy and expediency, selfish hard-heartedness, and in the spirit of true humility kneel at the cross and claim the merits of the Saviour's dying love. All that is hard, but it is a part of the mortification.

IV. **There is a wrong way of mortification.**—1. Sudden determinations, when arrived at in our strength only, leave us as unsafe as if we went into the thick of the enemy without armour—*e.g.*, a drunkard's resolution to be sober broken in a few days. 2. The aiming at suffering as a mode of producing a change of heart—*e.g.*, the monkish method of torture for penance. 3. Beecher points to those who, having strayed from virtue, never forget their error, but check every smile with "You remember," and let the gall from the old bitterness exude on every flower of pleasure. This is not God's way. He forgets our transgressions. Having repented, and honestly sought forgiveness, forget "those things which are behind," etc.

V. **The right way of mortification.**—We have too many pet methods for making peace with God. Mortification of sinful habits not accomplished solely or primarily by bodily penance, but by divine grace. The right way is to go straight to the Saviour, and leave ourselves in His hands, asking God's help in the struggle. You want peace? Seek it without delay from Him who alone is able to give it, Christ Jesus. Tell Him you have read His compassionate invitation to the labouring and heavy-laden. "Seek Christ Himself, and do not stop short of personal dealings with Him." He will help you to mortify the sins, and you will find peace.—*Albert Lee.*

248

Things of the flesh, good and bad.—"The things of the flesh" are the bodily appetites, sympathies, and propensities. These are its great forces moving its members and its organs.

I. Things of the flesh are **good when they are subordinated to the interests of the soul.** When they are controlled by a holy intelligence, they are blessed handmaids to the spirit.

II. Things of the flesh are **bad when they are allowed to hold empire over the soul.** This they do in all unrenewed natures; the curse of humanity is when the body rules the intellect and conscience too. "What shall we eat—what shall we drink?" etc.

Things of the spirit, good and bad.—The things of the spirit are its moral intuitions, rational dictates, intuitive longings, and varied powers of thought and sentiment.

I. These things of the spirit are **good when they control** the things of the flesh, when they hold the body in absolute subjection, use it as an instrument.

II. These things of the spirit are **bad when they are devoted** to the things of the flesh. They are often thus devoted; souls are everywhere prostituted to animalism.—*Homilist.*

SUGGESTIVE COMMENTS ON VERSES 5—11.

Carnal mind enmity against God. —Frequent thoughts discover rooted affections. Operations of the mind are the indexes, κριτήρια, of a regenerate or unregenerate estate. If about carnal [things], they evidence the bent of the heart to be turned that way, and that worldly objects are dearest to them. If about spiritual, they manifest spiritual objects to be the most grateful to the soul. Carnal thoughts are signs of a languishing and feeble frame, but spiritual discover a well-tempered and complexioned soul; the most refined and elevated thoughts, which have no other groundwork than nature; the highest flights of an unregenerate soul by the wings of the greatest reason. The wisdom and virtues of the heathen were enmity, therefore translated by some *sapientia carnis*, the wisdom of the flesh. A state of nature is a state of enmity against God. Man is naturally an enemy to the sovereignty and dominion of God. "Not subject to the law of God." By law I mean not here the moral law only, but the whole will and rule of God, which is chiefly discovered in His law. Every profane man is a natural man, and consequently an enemy. Wicked

words are *demonstrative*, demonstratively denials of God. "Sensual" and "having not the Spirit" are put together. Every unrenewed man, though never so richly endowed with morals, is a natural man. A ψυχικὸς ἄνθρωπος is one led by the rational dictates of his mind, and σαρκικός is a man led by his sensitive affections. Though you have not outwardly the impurity of the flesh, yet you may flow with a greater impurity of the spirit. Though the interest of particular sins may be contrary to one another, yet they all conspire in a joint league against God. *Scelera dissident.* Sins are in conflict with one another; covetousness and prodigality, covetousness and intemperance, cannot agree, but they are all in an amicable combination against the interest of God. In betraying Christ Judas was actuated by covetousness, the high priest by envy, Pilate by popularity; but they all shook hands together in the murdering of Christ. And those various iniquities were blended together to make up one lump of enmity. Here is *alienation*, which is aversion; and *enmity*, which is opposition; and both seated in the mind, though some expound alienation according to outward, enmity according to inward, estate. But the apostle declares hatred to be complete in those two, alienation and enmity, which is both in mind and works—mind as the seat, works as the issues of it. Enemies in disposition and action, principle, and execution. Sin being the *summum malum*, the greatest evil, is naturally most opposite to God, who is the *summum bonum*, the greatest good. We hate God *as a sovereign*; man cannot endure a superior; he would be uncontrollable. We hate God *as a lawgiver*, as He is *peccati prohibitor*. We hate God *as a judge*, as *autor legis* and *ultor legis*, as *peccati prohibitor* and *pœnœ executor*. Fear is often the cause of hatred. Guilt makes malefactors tremble at the report of a judge's coming. When this fear rises high, they hate *the very being* of God. This rises so high that it aims at the very essence of God, as in Spira's case, who wished that he could destroy Him. This enmity to God's law will appear in these ten things: 1. Unwillingness to know the law of God, inquire into it, or think of it. 2. Unwillingness to be determined by any law of God. 3. The violence man offers to those laws which God doth strictly enjoin and which He doth most delight in the performance of. 4. Man hates his own conscience when it puts him in mind of the law of God. 5. Man sets up another law in him in opposition to the law of God. 6. In being at greater pains and charge to break God's law than is necessary to keep it. Men would rather be sin's drudges than God's freemen. 7. In doing thàt which is just and righteous upon any other consideration rather than of obedience to God's will, when men will indent with God, and obey Him so far as may comport with their own ends: (1) out of respect to some human consideration; (2) out of affection to some base lust, some cursed end; (3) out of slavish fear. 8. In being more observant of· the laws of men than of

the law of God. The fear of man is a more powerful curb to retain men in their duty than the fear of God. 9. In man's unwillingness to have God's law observed by any. Man would not have God have a loyal subject in the world. 10. In the pleasure we take to see His laws broken by others. Enmity to the mercy of God. God is not wronged more in any attribute by devils and men than in His mercy. This enmity against Christ reflects upon God Himself. Christ tells us often He was sent by God: an affront to an ambassador is an injury to the majesty he represents. Despising the embassy of an angel is an act of enmity against God, much more the despising the embassy of His own Son. Possess your hearts with great admiration of the grace of God towards you, in wounding this enmity in your hearts and changing your state. Inflame thy love to God by all the considerations thou canst possibly muster up. Undo thy former disaffection by a greater ardency of love. Sincerely aim at His glory.—*Charnock.*

Life a satisfied existence.—" Life," in Scripture, denotes a fully satisfied existence, in which all the faculties find their full exercise and their true occupation. Man's spirit, become the abode and organ of the divine Spirit, realises this life with a growing perfection to eternal life. *Peace* is the inward feeling of tranquillity which accompanies such an existence; it shows itself particularly in the absence of all fear in regard to death and judgment (ver. 1). There is no changing the *nature* of these two states and walks (ver. 5), and no arresting the latter in its onward march (ver. 6). The way of salvation is to pass from the first to the second, and not to relapse thereafter from the second to the first.—*Godet.*

Carnal man hates God. — Consider the *object* of man's enmity—God. A good man hates evil, all evil, and is the irreconcilable enemy of sin in every form; but as regards the creature of God and his fellow-creature, he hates no man. The carnal mind, which is the characteristic of every unregenerate man, hates not only good men, but the good, holy, and all-perfect God. Indeed, his hatred to good men arises from his enmity against God, which calls forth his dislike to them—his envious revilings, and murderous hatred, as in Cain, who hated and slew his brother: "Wherefore? because his own works were evil, and his brother's righteous." Few men are willing to admit their enmity against God, however bitterly they vilify His people on account of bearing His image. "Ye shall," says Jesus, "be hated of all men for My sake." It is true that they disguise their enmity to Christ under the pretence of hatred to His people's sins, and especially their hypocrisy. "You pretend," says one, "to hate hypocrisy only; alas! what a scorn is it for profanity to hate hypocrisy." Surely it is not because it is a sin, but for the very shadow of piety which it carries. You hate the thing itself so perfectly that you cannot bear the very picture of it. Do not deceive yourselves; the true quarrel is because they do not run to the same excess of riot with you. The principle of your hostility to them is the enmity which God hath put between the two families of Christ and Satan.—*Parlane.*

Sin the animating principle of the flesh.—Since all men are by nature fallen, all human flesh is by nature the dwelling-place of sin. Through the desires common to all flesh, the spirit of evil rules all men except those whom God has rescued. We cannot distinguish the influence of the flesh from the influence exerted through the flesh by the principle of sin. Hence sin may be looked upon as the animating principle of the flesh. The presence of this one spirit of evil in the many bodies of the unsaved gives additional unity to the idea of flesh. And since the influence of the flesh is always in the same direction, we may look upon the flesh as a living person cherishing always the one purpose of death. Many of the objects desired or disliked by the flesh can be obtained or avoided only by first obtaining or avoiding other objects. Frequently all our mental and bodily powers are at work to get that which will preserve or indulge the body—*e.g.*, efforts to make money are often put forth for this end. Such efforts really arise from the body; for they are prompted by the needs, desires, and dislikes of the body. I think we shall find that all sin arises thus. Hence the "works of the flesh" include every kind of sin.—*Beet.*

MAIN HOMILETICS OF THE PARAGRAPH.—*Verses* 12, 13.

Claims of the flesh.—I shall endeavour in the first place to settle the meaning of the terms "flesh" and "spirit" employed in the context, in order to a right conception of the import of the preposition; and in the second place compare and adjust the opposite claims of the flesh and of the spirit.

I. **Flesh most properly denotes the body in contradistinction from the soul,** the matter of which the corporeal structure is formed: "There is one flesh of men." And—

II. **As all men are possessed of this, it is by an easy figure** of speech applied to denote human nature or mankind universally: "The end of all flesh is come before God."

III. **Because the fleshly or corporeal part of our nature** may be perceived by the eye, it is sometimes used to denote *that* in religion which is merely outward and ceremonial. Thus St. Paul says, "Having begun in the Spirit, are ye made perfect by the flesh?" Thus the same apostle speaks of carnal ordinances.

IV. **On account of the deep and universal corruption of human nature, and this corruption displaying itself in a peculiar manner** in producing an addictedness to the indulgence of bodily or fleshly appetites, the term "flesh" is frequently used to denote moral corruption or human nature considered as corrupt. It is manifest from the consideration of the context that this is the sense in which it is to be taken here. "That which is born of the flesh is flesh"—that is, corrupt and sinful.

Secondly, we shall examine and adjust their respective claims, that we may discern to which the preference is due, and come then fully to acquiesce in the decision of the apostle: "Therefore we are debtors; not to the flesh, to live after the flesh." There is an ellipsis in the text which must be supplied from the train of thought in the context. Let us examine the claims of the flesh or of corrupt nature. We may conceive the flesh pleading ancient possession: the pleasures and freedom from restraint attending a compliance with her dictates; the general usage and course of the world which she reminds us has been such in every age.

I. **Its claims are founded upon usurpation; they rest on no basis of equity.**— It alienates the property from its lawful possessor; it interferes with a prior claim which nothing can fairly defeat. Sin considered as a master does not enter upon a property that is derelict or abandoned by its owner. 1. *Let us consider that the Lord is our maker, and we the work of His hands.* It is "He that created the heavens, and stretched them out; He that spread forth the earth, and that which cometh out of it; He that giveth breath unto the people upon it, and spirit to them that walk therein." The noble powers by which we are so highly distinguished from the inferior parts of the creation—the powers of thought and reason and conscience—are of His production; from Him they are derived, and by Him they are sustained. His right in us is consequently more extensive than it is possible for us to conceive in any other instance, because none else ever gave existence to the smallest particle of dust in the balance; it is incomparably more than that—to which it is compared—of the potter over the clay. 2. *If we reflect on the powers with which we are endued, we cannot suppose that they are formed for no other end than the indulgence of carnal appetites, the amassing of riches, the enjoyment of sensual pleasures, or the procuring honours and distinctions from our fellow-worms.* We shall be at no loss to perceive a strange disproportion between such powers and such pursuits, and that they cannot be confined to them without descending unspeakably beneath our level without a base forgetfulness of ourselves as well as of God, and a voluntary dereliction of our rank. 3. *If God were disposed to relinquish His claim, the usurpation of another master might be yielded to with the more plausible pretence.* But this is not the case. If we believe His word, He never means to part with His right over His creatures.

II. **Let us next examine the claims of the flesh by what we have already derived from it.**—Let us see whether it is such a master as deserves to be served any longer. Of the boasted pleasures it has afforded, say Christians, what remains but a painful and humiliating remembrance? "What fruit had ye in those things of which ye are now ashamed?" Has anything accrued to you from the service of sin which you would wish to renew? Though it might flatter your imagination with the appearance of gold, did it not afterwards "bite as a serpent and sting as an adder"? You were made to fancy that true religion was melancholy, that tenderness of conscience was needless scrupulosity, and that happiness was only to be found in the pleasures and pursuits of this world. It engaged you in the chase of innumerable vanities. You "followed after your lovers, but could not overtake them"; fled from one refuge to another till, to speak in the language of the prophet, "you were wearied in the multitude of your way." In the meantime, to all pleasant and delightful intercourse with the Father of spirits, to the soothing accents of peace and pardon issuing from Christ, and to all the consolations of piety, you were utter strangers. The more we observe what passes around us with a serious mind, the more we shall be convinced how little men are indebted to the flesh. Look at that young man, the early victim of lewdness and intemperance, who, though in the bloom of life, has "his bones filled with the sins of his youth." Survey his emaciated cheek, his infirm and withered frame, and his eyes sunk and devoid of lustre; the picture of misery and dejection. Hear his complaint, how he mourns at the last, how his flesh and his body are consumed. Behold that votary of the world, successful as he has been in the pursuit of it, and stained by no flagrant crime. Yet he has lived "without God in the world"; and now his days are drawing to a close he feels himself verging to the grave, and no hope animates, no pleasing reflection cheers him. The only consolation he receives, or rather the only relief of his anguish, is in grasping the treasures he must shortly quit.

III. **We shall examine the claims of the flesh by the aspect they bear on our future interests.**—Before we engage in the service of a master, it is reasonable to inquire into the advantages he stipulates and the prospects of futurity attendant upon his service. In the ordinary concerns of life we should consider the neglect of such an inquiry chargeable with the highest imprudence. Dreadful is it in this view to reflect on the consequences inseparably annexed to the service of corruption. "If ye live after the flesh," says the apostle, "ye shall die." "The wages of sin is death." The fruits of sin, when brought to maturity, are corruption; his most finished production is death, and the materials on which he works the fabric of that manufacture, if we may be allowed so to speak, consist in the elements of damnation. To such a master we can owe nothing but a decided rejection of his offers, a perpetual abhorrence, and an awful fear of ever being deceived by his stratagems or entangled in his snares.— *Robert Hall.*

The spirit and the flesh.—These words used, as opposed to each other, in three senses—viz., 1. Flesh = material part of man; spirit = immaterial part. 2. Flesh = lower nature of man, desires that drag down to hell; spirit = higher nature of man, desires that lift him up towards heaven (*not with, without Christ's grace*). 3. Flesh = human nature in its entirety; Spirit = God's Holy Spirit and the graces inbreathed by Him.

In what senses contrasted *here*? Not in 1, but in 2 and in 3.

Their *tendency*: Encouragement of flesh = tendency to death—death *here*, death hereafter. Examples: Drunkenness, immorality, indolence.

Encouragement of spirit = tendency to life, here and hereafter. Examples: Men who have by God's grace conquered sin—John Bunyan, John Newton.

Consideration: What is good for eternal life hereafter is, as a rule, productive of life—long, successful, happy, honoured, here.—*Dr. Springett.*

SUGGESTIVE COMMENTS ON VERSES 12, 13.

The Christian has strength imparted. —We are no longer under any such subjection to the inferior propensities of our nature, as might oblige us to continue under their dominion. From any necessity of this kind we are relieved by the powerful motives to holiness and the effectual aids to ac-quiring of it which are supplied by the gospel. Had we continued under the law, with no other advantages but those which it furnishes, we must have been debtor to the flesh, as we should have wanted that moral strength which is necessary to free ourselves from its dominion—a strength which mere law cannot supply. But under the gospel this incapacity is removed. By the Spirit of Christ dwelling in us we are enabled to restrain the inordinate tendencies of our nature, and therefore we can no longer plead the weakness of our moral powers as an extenuation of our actual sins. From the Christian every pretence of this kind is taken away, and he is rendered a debtor to the Spirit. He is laid under a sacred obligation to live agreeably to the dictates of the spiritual part of his nature, and to the suggestions of the Holy Spirit, by whom he is influenced. This also he must do if he would promote his own interest either in this life or in that which is to come.—*Ritchie.*

What do we understand by "flesh"?—Some by "flesh" understand the state under the law; others, more properly, "corrupted nature." Ye shall die without hopes of a better life. But if you mortify the deeds of the body—the deeds of the body of sin, which is elsewhere called the body of death; the first motions to sin and passionate compliances with sin, which are the springs of corrupt actions (corrupt nature is called a body here, morally, not physically; it consisteth of divers vices, as a body of divers members)—"ye shall live"; ye shall live more spiritually and comfortably and eternally hereafter. In the words we may observe a threatening and a promise. In the promise there is the condition and the reward. In the condition, the act: mortify. The object: the deeds of the body. The cause: the body. The effects: the deeds. The agents: ye and the Spirit. The principal, the Spirit; the less principal, ye; both conjoined in the work: ye cannot do it without the Spirit, and the Spirit will not do it with-

out your concurrence with Him and your industry in following His motions. Sin is active in the soul of an unregenerate man. His heart is sin's territory; it is there as in its throne before the Spirit comes. Mortification supposes life before in the part mortified. Mortification must be universal; not one deed, but deeds, little and great, must fall under the edge—the brats must be dashed against the wall. Man must be an agent in this work. We have brought this rebel into our souls, and God would have us make, as it were, some recompense by endeavouring to cast it out; as in the law, the father was to fling the first stone against a blasphemous son. We must engage in the duel, but it is the strength of the Spirit only can render us victorious. The duty is ours, but the success is from God. Heaven is a place for conquerors only. The way to eternal life is through conflicts, inward with sin, outward with the world. There must be a combat before a victory, and a victory before a triumph. An unmortified frame is unsuitable to a state of glory. There must be a meetness for a state of glory before there be an entrance into it. Vessels of glory must be first seasoned with grace. Conformity to Christ is to fit us for heaven. Unmortified sin is against the whole design of the gospel and death of Christ, as though the death of Christ were intended to indulge us in sin, and not to redeem us from it. That sin should die was the end of Christ's death; rather than sin should not die, Christ would die Himself. Implore the help of the Spirit. Listen to the convictions of the Holy Spirit. Plead the death of Christ. Let us often think of divine precepts. Let us be jealous of our own hearts. —*Charnock.*

MAIN HOMILETICS OF THE PARAGRAPH.—Verse 14.

Marks of God's sons.—Led, and not driven. Led as the scholar by his teacher; the traveller by his guide, the soldier by his captain. So the Son of God is led by the Spirit of God. The Son of God is not driven by brute force, not treated as a mere machine or as a beast of burden, but as a reasonable creature. As the man is led by patriotic feelings, by devotion to truth, by force of lofty and stirring thoughts, so and much more is the Son of God led. His soul is open to and receptive of divine influence. There is the inner world of his spiritual nature acted upon and moving in harmony with the outer force of the Spirit of God. Oh what a word led us in this connection!—led out of sin's darkness and chaos into truth's light and order, just as the new-made world was led; out of the hunger and wretchedness of guilty wanderings into the fulness and happiness of the Father's house, just as the prodigal was led; out of the world's trouble and tossing fevers into the rest of the Saviour's, as Zacchæus was led; out of the darkness and blindness of self-love into the light and clear vision of Christ-love, as Saul was led,—led onwards and upwards along the pathway of ever-increasing knowledge of the love of God in Jesus,—led from the shifting scenes of earth, through the dark valley of death, to the paradise of God, as the redeemed through all ages have been and shall continue to be led to the very close of this dispensation. Oh to yield ourselves up to divine leading!

I. **God's sons have a family likeness.**—In natural families there are likenesses. There are certain resemblances by which we know that they constitute part of the same family. The form of the features, the general build, tell us of a certain similarity. So in God's great spiritual family there is a general likeness. The botanist, by a certain similarity, declares that the plant belongs to such an order. The geologist says that such a fossil belongs to a certain stratum. The physiologist declares in the same manner that such an animal belongs to such a species. And so by certain tokens we declare that the man belongs to God's family. The one general feature by which we know the sons of God is this, that they "are led by the Spirit of God." So that it is not an outward but an inward resemblance. Thus it sometimes happens in natural families. It is not always by the mere outward features, but by the inward tastes and feelings. God's sons may be and often are outwardly different. They vary in outward form, in social circumstances, in gifts, faculties, and endowments. They may appear like Joseph, the second ruler in Egypt, swaying and managing the destinies of a mighty empire, or like the poor Jew Mordecai, sitting despised at the king's gate. They may appear like Solomon arrayed in all his glory, surrounded with luxury and girded by power; or like Lazarus, clothed in rags, dying of starvation. They may appear like St. Paul, mighty in intellect, and capable of using the pen of eloquence; or like Moses, who was slow in speech. Still, through all differences there runs the common bond of likeness. They are influenced by the Holy Spirit of God. And this common likeness is only to be seen by the man of spiritual vision and spiritual enlightenment. Only the botanist can tell to what order the plant belongs. Only the man well acquainted with the family can tell when he meets a member. Only the spiritually enlightened can mark out one of God's sons. He sees that the Son of God is led, not from beneath, but from above. He marks an unseen and yet most effective force shaping the whole of the man's nature and destiny. As a strong under current may propel the vessel along the waters, so the strong current of the Holy Spirit guides the Son of God through the troubled waters of this world.

II. **God's sons have family greatness.**—Man is highest in the scale of being. He possesses more powers and faculties than any other animal, and is capable of being acted upon in a way in which no other animal can be. Man, simply considered as a creature of this world, stands at a height far removed from all other beings. His nature stretches out and touches realms unknown to any other living force. The spiritual man—the Son of God, *i.e.*—stands still higher in the scale of being. He is acted upon by a force unknown to any other. The mere physical creature lives only in a material realm. It never rises above matter. The intellectual being lives in the realm of mind. He dwells in the region of thoughts and ideas. He is touched and moved by the thoughts of others. But the Son of God is touched and moved by the thoughts of God, He is pervaded and influenced by the Spirit of God, His soul is acted upon by the Unseen in a way which others are not, and is great in the highest sense. The greatness of God's family is here brought out in another aspect. The members of God's family are not mere children, but sons noble and stalwart. There was a time in which they were mere children, and requiring to be fed with milk, loving only childish things, and following childish sports and practices. In one sense God's family on earth will always be children; requiring to be taught, corrected, guided, and disciplined like children. In the light of the eternal ideal of manhood we speak only and understand only as children. Still, in the view of the rest of humanity the members of God's family are sons, noblest and grandest of the sons of men. Jesus Christ is by pre-eminence the Son of God, begotten before all time, " being the brightness of the Father's glory, and the express image of His person." Christians are the sons of God next in order, and yet allied unto Jesus Christ the elder brother. Their greatness is plain from this connection. Sons of God, brothers of the one great Son of God. Sons of God, in whom dwells and works the Holy Spirit of God. Are we the sons of God? Do we feel and appreciate our greatness? Do we conduct ourselves as God's sons?

III. **God's sons have a family heritage.**—Great families have their possessions. There is for each one of them a heritage. They have their lands, their houses, their money, and their position. God's family is a great family, and has its possessions. There is for each one a heritage. That blessed heritage is the precious one of the Holy Spirit to lead. The Holy Spirit leads aright. Human possession leads astray to misery and to destruction. Human reason is too often a blind guide. Boasted philosophy cannot lead the soul in the right path. The Holy Spirit of God alone can lead in a pathway of safety. How are we to know that we are being led by the Holy Spirit? We know this much, that the Spirit never leads contrary to the Bible. The Spirit never influences to go against truth, honesty, candour, uprightness, and goodness. The Holy Spirit leads to peace, to plenty, to joy, to spiritual prosperity. The Holy Spirit leads to bright realms of spiritual beauty and fulness on earth, and to the brightest land of all, even to the paradise of God. The Holy Spirit's leading and indwelling is the type and pledge of our dwelling for ever in God's blessed presence in heaven.

IV. **God's sons have a family bias.**—They all incline in the same direction. Their tendency is upward and onward. The vessels at sea have the needle which points to the pole. Wherever the vessels sail, in whatever part of the world they may be, the needles all point to the pole, and centre there as it were. So the sons of God, wherever they may dwell on earth their hearts point to the city of God. The Holy Spirit within them the foretaste of heaven. Thus heaven is in them before they are in heaven. When slaves were escaping from slavery, their eyes were fixed on the north star as the guide to the land of freedom. The Holy Spirit within is better than the north star guiding to Jerusalem above, which is free, and which is the mother of us all. The hearts of God's sons turn to the spiritual Jerusalem, to the city of the living God. They seek a city out of sight, and thus declare that they are strangers and pilgrims on the earth. By this we may know that we are being led—by this we may know that we are the sons of God, that we are earnestly and prayerfully seeking heaven through Jesus Christ, who is the way, the truth, and the life.

Ver. 15. *Led by the Spirit.*—Every gift with the possibility of which man was endowed, and every noble quality which made him beautiful and good for the eyes of God to see, all came from that one and the selfsame Spirit, moving in man's soul as He had moved from all ages in the laws of nature, and was still moving their divine uniformities. For God is the essence and source of all goodness and excellence whatsoever.

I. **Degraded humanity.**—We know, alas! only too well that through misuse of the gift of freewill we have encouraged that within us which loveth darkness better than light. Whole races have become so degraded that, even in the best members of them, the patient lamp of the omnipresent Spirit could shine with but a feeble flame. Clearly do our own hearts remind us what it is to have sinned, to feel that God has hidden His face from us, and to be almost ashamed to lift up our souls in prayer.

II. **The Spirit in pagan philosophy.**—But though the poor human creature had thus miserably come short of the glory of God, and the freshness and purity of the early light which had come with him from the divine Being who was "his home" had now faded into the "light of common day," yet all the time God was not far from any of His children. Socrates said that there was a spirit in him, not himself, which guided him all the way of his life. "As many as are led by the Spirit of God, they are the sons of God." Thus did the Spirit work in the hearts and minds of men. "No man was ever great," said Cicero, "without a divine afflatus." "This I say," wrote Seneca to his friend Lucilius, "that a Holy Spirit dwelleth within us, of our good and evil works the observer and the guardian. As we treat Him, so He treateth us ; and no man is good except God be with him." Do you not see Him in every page of history, making the virtues triumph ? Do you not read Him in the general expectancy of the world at the time of the coming of the Saviour, that attitude of suspense and hope which Tacitus and Suetonius have described, of which one of Virgil's most beautiful poems is an example, and which taught the Eastern sages to watch for the dawn of that great light which led them to the cradle of Bethlehem ?

III. **Jesus the Light.**—For mankind was not to be left for ever to grope their way in the darkness for the Lord, if haply they might feel after Him and find Him. The star which led the patient Magi through the desert was the herald of a more glorious birth than when the sons of God shouted for joy on the first morning of the world. He came and returned that the Spirit of God might come in a way in which it had never been possible for Him to come before. Christ lifted up the veil, and from that time all who came unto Him were open to all the divine influences of the Holiest of holies. As soon as He came, even before the outpouring of the day of Pentecost, the Holy Spirit was given with abundant and startling effect. The kingdom of the Spirit was already begun when the Lord of life and glory was preaching and teaching.

IV. **The purpose of the Spirit.**—As Luther wrote : "He imposeth a limit and measure to the preaching of the Holy Ghost Himself : He is to preach nothing new, nothing other than Christ and His word, to the end that we might have a sure sign, a certain test, whereby to judge false spirits." Thus the Spirit is conditioned by the Son, as the Son is by the Father. The office of the Spirit was to bring to remembrance, to interpret.

V. **Transformation to Christ's image.**—The world may say it is content to be as Socrates was, that it desires not to rise above the aspirations of Plato, that it cares not to be juster than Aristides. Philosophic sceptics may pronounce that Christianity is only one of the many forms of this world's religions, and that Buddhism is older, as interesting, and accepted by a far larger number of the human race. Others may say that they are content to follow the faith of

Christ because it has achieved great things, because it is wrapped up in the history of England, because it has founded a higher morality, a nobler chivalry, a more complete virtue, than any other creed. But by such inadequate conceptions of the relation between God and the human soul they show that they see not the Spirit, neither know Him. They recognise, perhaps, that God made man in His own image and capable of partaking in His divine nature. They recognise that man, by seeking after God, brings himself nearer to Him. They do not recognise that by gazing at the glory of the only begotten Son we become transformed after His image; they have no idea that to know of the divine personality of the Holy Spirit of Christ and of the Father is to be able to address Him, to approach Him, to talk with Him as friend talks with friend. —*Ven. W. Sinclair, D.D.*

Sons of God.

I. **The condition on which we are** "**sons of God.**"—*Not mere creatureship.* The stars, the birds, the flowers, are God's creatures. *Not mere resemblance.* Even fallen men are made in the image of God, and have a potential likeness to Him. *But filial disposition.* Men are the special creation of God; may have a special resemblance to Him; may have affection, not fear; may cry, "Abba, Father."

II. **The evidence that we are** "**sons of God.**"—1. There is the *witness of God's Spirit*; 2. There is the *testimony of the spirit of man.*

III. **The results of our being** "**sons of God.**"—1. We are "heirs of God"; 2. We are "joint-heirs with Christ."—*Dr. Thomas.*

SUGGESTIVE COMMENTS ON VERSE 14.

Sonship a connection of relation and nature.—First, it is a connection of *relation.* God's Spirit dwells not in any and leads none who are not His children by faith in Jesus Christ. Their guidance by the Spirit of God therefore manifests them to be His children. By an act of divine grace, which in all its aspects and gifts is marvellous and infinite, the sinner who believes is adopted by God and numbered among His children. He is separated from the family of Satan, and joined to the sons and daughters of the Lord God Almighty. This relation to God and His family begins with his faith, continues during life, and is perpetuated during eternity. It is also a connection of *nature.* I do not mean that they are partakers of God's essence, but of the character or image of God, such as is competent to a creature. "Whereby," says the apostle Peter, "are given unto us exceeding great and precious promises, that by these ye might be partakers of the divine nature, having escaped the corruption that is in the world through lust." The connec-

tion between this new, regenerated, or divine nature, and heaven, is obvious. Without it none could enjoy heaven, though admitted to it; for it is a holy place, a holy society, and a holy inheritance. Finally, it is a connection of *love.* I speak not of your love of God, which is so weak and faint, derived from grace and dependent on grace, and accompanied with so many imperfections, further than to say that its sincerity is inseparably connected with grace and glory. But the love of God to you is the grand security of your eternal life—that love which is from everlasting, and has drawn you to Himself—that love which is to everlasting on them that fear Him—that love which is commended in giving and not in sparing His own Son for you when enemies, that you might be the children of God. Live more and more by faith on the Son of God. Follow more closely the guidance of the Spirit of God, and seek more earnestly His supplies. Thus live worthy of your name and prospects as the children of a King, as the children of God.—*Parlane.*

MAIN HOMILETICS OF THE PARAGRAPH.—*Verses* 15—18.

Vers. 16-18. *The inheritance of sonship.*—The sin of the world is *a false confidence*; the fault and sorrow and weakness of the Church is *a false diffidence.* The *true* confidence, which is faith in Christ, and the *true* diffidence, which is utter distrust of myself, are identical. "The Spirit itself beareth witness *with* our spirit." It is that there is one testimony which has a conjoint origin—the origin of the Spirit of God as true source, and the origin of my own soul as recipient and co-operant in that testimony. The substance, then, of the evidence on which a Christian has a right to conclude that he is a child of God does not bear directly on his own state or condition at all, but upon God's feelings to him and God's relation to him. Our own souls possess these emotions of love and tender desire going out unto God; our own spirits possess them, but our own spirits did not originate them. Your sense of fatherhood—that sense of fatherhood which is in the Christian's heart, and becomes his cry—comes from God's Spirit. This passage, and that in Galatians which is almost parallel, put this truth very forcibly, when taken in connection : "Ye have received," says the text before us, "the Spirit of adoption, whereby we cry, Abba, Father." The heart with its love, the head with its understanding, the conscience with its quick response to the law of duty, the will with its resolutions—these are all, as sanctified by Him, the witness of His Spirit.

This divine witness in our spirits is subject to the ordinary influences which affect our spirits.—The Spirit's witness *comes from God*—therefore it is veracious ; but the Spirit's witness from God *is in man*—therefore it may be wrongly read.

No inheritance without sonship.—In general terms, spiritual things can only be given to men who are in a certain spiritual condition. Even God cannot bestow certain blessings and gifts until there be in me a capacity or organ to receive them. No inheritance of heaven without sonship ; just because all the blessings of that future life at last come down to this, they are of a spiritual character.

No sonship without a spiritual birth.—Fatherhood involves the *communication of a life* and the reciprocity of love; it involves a divine act and a human emotion ; it involves that the Father and the child shall have kindred life. Drop that figure, and simply rest on this—the children of God, or the children of sin ; sons because born again, or slaves and "enemies by wicked works."

No spiritual birth without Christ.—He has carried in the golden urn of His humanity a new spirit and a new life which He has set down in the midst of the race ; and the urn was broken on the cross of Calvary, and the water flowed out ; and whithersover that water comes there is life, and whithersoever it comes not there is death.

No Christ without faith.—Unless we are wedded to Jesus Christ by the simple act of trust in His mercy and His power, Christ is nothing to us. Christ is everything to a man that trusts Him ; Christ is nothing but a judge and a condemnation to a man that trusts Him not.

Then sonship with Christ necessarily involves suffering with Him.—We "suffer with Him"; *not*, He suffers with us. The death of Christ is a type of the Christian's life. It is a dying to sin; it is a dying to self ; it is a dying to an old world. That crucifying of the old manhood is to be repeated by the power of faith.

"Our sufferings are *His.*" "His sufferings are *ours.*" Oneness with Christ involves a fellowship and community on both sides, of suffering. **This community of suffering is a preparation for the community of glory.** It is not the discipline that fits ; the thing that fits goes before the discipline, and the discipline only develops the fitness.

That inheritance is the necessary result of all suffering that has gone before.
—The suffering results from our union with Christ. That union must needs
culminate in glory. Trials have no meaning, unless they are means to an end.
The end is the inheritance. What must be the end of that blessedness which
is the counterpoise and consequence to the sorrow and pain of this lower world!—
Maclaren.

Ver. 16. *The witness of the Spirit.*—Take these words in whatever sense we
may, they contain a truth of unspeakable importance. The moment we hear
them we feel that we are dealing with a matter which concerns our soul's life.
And the two points requiring our attention are—first, who are the witnesses to
be inquired of? and, secondly, what is the testimony to be elicited?

I. And first, in reference to this question of our spiritual sonship, let us see
who are the witnesses who are to decide upon the matter.—There is evidently
nothing in the text to favour a notion entertained by some, who would resolve
the witness of the Spirit into some supernatural intimation from above—some
mysterious whisper to the ear of the inner man, speaking to us, and addressing
us as those who belong to the family of God. The text rather suggests to us
that we are entering upon a calm, judicial process, in which the hoped-for verdict
can be obtained only by the testimony of two distinct and agreeing witnesses—
witnesses of tried competency to speak, and of proved faithfulness to be heard—
namely, the witness of the Holy Spirit, and the consenting testimony of our own
hearts. Chiefly, however, must our confidence stand in the first of these witnesses, the testimony of our own hearts being only derived and secondary,
subscribing to that which has been given by the Spirit of God. And the importance of having this Holy Spirit as the chief witness will appear from the nature
of the facts to be witnessed to—namely, that we are the children of God, are
received into a state of adoption and grace, are at this moment reconciled to God,
and know that He is reconciled to us. Our adoption is one of the things of God,
and He must be of God, and in God, who shall bear witness of it to us. He must
know when the act of grace went forth, and when the wandering spirit turned,
and when the weak and subjugated heart surrendered, and when the signet ring
was fixed to that covenant of mercy and forgiveness which made of the outcast
rejoicing, and of the slave a friend and child. And these are things which must
be known to the Holy Spirit, because of Him, and through Him, and by Him,
are all these effects wrought.

II. **How this important testimony is to be elicited—in what language does
the Spirit speak, and in what signs does the heart make answer?**—And in the
general elucidation of this point the first ground to be taken is that the joint witness of the text, and consequently the scriptural evidence of sonship, is to be looked
for in this—namely, an impression of inward peace arising from the discovery of
certain tendencies and dispositions answerable to the state of sonship, and referred
in Scripture to the agency of the Holy Spirit of God. And it is properly called
a joint witness, because the same Spirit who forms these tendencies in us also
manifests their existence to us. We can only know that we are adopted children
when the Spirit of God reveals to our minds, with growing light and distinctness,
the existence of those moral dispositions which prompt us to act as children act,
and to feel as children feel. Do we inquire further, " How do the children of God
act and feel?" the answer is, " We find these only in the written word." But
this still makes the Spirit of God the chief witness to us, because, until the Spirit
shines upon the word, it is a sealed book to us, a dark and meaningless record,
telling us nothing of our spiritual state, because the eyes of our understanding
are not opened. But let the Spirit open our understanding, and we find that
the entrance of God's word giveth light—light to the promises, light to the

threatenings, light to the rules of duty, light to the evidences of our hope. We understand better both the rule and that to which we are to apply the rule; and it is just the agreement between these two—the Scripture calling and the heart answering, the Spirit insisting on certain commanded feelings and our own spirits testifying that we have such feelings—that constitutes our double witness, that meets the judicial demands of a twofold testimony, that enables us to say, "The Spirit itself beareth witness with our spirit, that we are the children of God."— *P. Moore.*

Ver. 16. *Concerning the witness of the Spirit.*—This passage is something difficult, and commonly not rightly understood; for the clearing of which there are four things to be done:—

I. To show what is meant by the Spirit.
II. What is meant by the children of God.
III. What is meant by the Spirit's bearing witness with our spirit.
IV. How, or in what sense, the Spirit beareth witness with our spirit that we are the children of God.

By the Spirit here is undoubtedly meant that Holy Spirit which our Lord promised He would send upon His disciples after He was ascended into heaven, and which accordingly came upon them on the day of Pentecost, and which from thenceforth was to continue with the Church to the end of the world. This Spirit is here in the text called the Spirit *itself*, to represent Him as a person, because in the verse before the apostle had used this word "spirit" in another sense—viz., for a state and dispensation.

But, secondly, What is meant by being the children of God? To this I answer, that to be a child of God, in the Scripture phrase, is to be an heir of immortality, or to be an inheritor of the kingdom of heaven—that is to say, either in actual possession of it, or in a right title to it.

But, thirdly, What is meant by this expression of the Spirit's bearing witness with our spirit? I conceive that which the apostle here meant is this: *that the Holy Spirit by the visible, sensible operations which He wrought in and amongst Christians, that God owned them for His people, and as such would glorify them with His Son Jesus at the last day.* First of all, I say, the Spirit gave an undeniable proof to Christians that they were the children of God in descending upon the apostles on the day of Pentecost. The fulness of the evidence we have for the truth of the matters of fact wrought by the Spirit in the ancient times for the confirmation of Christ's doctrine, and the new arguments that the same Spirit hath given us since; we, at this day, have as much reason to say with St. Paul, as any in those days had, "The Spirit itself beareth witness with our spirit, that we are the children of God"—that we are Christians, in contradistinction to men of all other religions, are the very people of God, and heirs of eternal life, if we do not forfeit our title to it by a loose and wicked life. It ought to be a matter of unspeakable comfort and rejoicing to us that we have such an infallible witness as the Spirit of God to bear testimony to our minds that we are in a right and sure way to eternal happiness. The Spirit's bearing witness to our minds thus effectually that we are the children of God should be an argument to us above all others that we should never depart from our Christian profession, but that we should hold it to our lives' end without wavering—nay, and be zealous for it. For where can we have eternal life but in the faith of Jesus Christ? We are always to remember that, when the Spirit gave His witness to the Christians that they were the children of God, it was to the Christians as professing the true faith of Christ. Though it be here said of all Christians in general that the Spirit bears witness to them that they are the children of God, yet it is to be remembered that no benefit will hereby accrue to any particular person that professeth Christianity if he does not lead his life according to the precepts of it. Secondly, if it be asked what this private witness of the Spirit is to the minds of particular persons, that they are the children of God, or wherein it doth consist, I answer very briefly, as far as we can gather from the apostle's discourse, both in this place and in others of his epistles, it consists in this—viz., in the Holy Ghost's dwelling in the hearts of particular Christians, and enabling them to mortify their lusts, and to lead a holy life, in all sobriety, righteousness, and godliness. Now this indwelling of the Spirit, and these fruits therefore, wherever they are found, are to those that have them a seal of the Spirit of God upon their souls, "whereby they are sealed to the day of redemption," as the apostle expresses it (Eph. iv. 30). They are *an earnest* or *a pledge* of their future happiness, as the same apostle in other places calls them (2 Cor. i. 22, v. 5; Eph. i. 13, 14). Lastly, they are a testimony or evidence to their spirits that they are the true sons of God, and shall be glorified with Jesus Christ in another world, which is the tenor of his expression in my text. Now that this is the true meaning of the Spirit's witnessing with our spirit that we are the children of God, so far as that witness concerns particular persons, will appear evidently from what goes before in this chapter. The main design that the apostle is pursuing is to encourage and animate the Christians of his time against the sufferings and persecutions they were likely to meet with in this world upon account of their religion; and this he doth chiefly from the consideration of the great rewards that were laid up for them in the other world. And to this purpose he tells them in the tenth verse, "If Christ be in you, the body is dead because of sin; but the Spirit is life because of righteousness" (Rom. viii. 10)—that is, your body is indeed obnoxious to all sorts of outward calamities, and even to death itself, which is entailed upon the sons of Adam, upon account of sin; but yet the Spirit of Christ, which He hath given to dwell in you, will procure you a glorious life in another world, upon account of that inward spiritual righteousness which He worketh in you.

And, first of all, from this account that has been given, we learn what the true marks are of a child of God, or upon what grounds any person can rationally assure himself that he is in God's favour and shall go to heaven. For as the miraculous operations of the Spirit in the days of the apostles were the public testimony of the Holy Ghost that the Christian Church in general was the people of God and designed to everlasting happiness, so the Spirit's dwelling in the souls of particular Christians is His private testimony to particular persons that they are effectually the children of God and shall be actually raised up to everlasting happiness. Since all the evidence we can give to ourselves that we in particular are the children of God is that the Holy Spirit dwelleth within us, how infinitely doth it concern us, both to endeavour that the Holy Ghost should take up His habitation in our hearts, and also, after He hath so done, to be careful that we do not by our ill treatment of Him give Him cause to depart from us! Would we invite and prevail with the Holy Spirit to come and dwell within us? The way is to forsake our sins and to devote ourselves entirely to God's service, and to solicit Him most earnestly with our daily prayers that He would purify our hearts, that they may become a temple fit for Him to dwell in, and withal to encourage and improve every good motion and every opportunity that He puts into our hands of growing in virtue and goodness. By this means we shall allure the good Spirit of God to take up His lodging in our hearts. And when once it is our happiness to have received so illustrious a guest, oh, with what zeal should we endeavour to preserve Him!—*Archbishop Sharpe.*

Ver. 17. *Sons and heirs.*—Law and gospel. There *was* a law : " This *do,* and ye shall live." It tended to keep us in *fear.*

There *is* a *covenant.* In Christ we become adopted sons. It tends to keep us in *peace.* God is our Father. " Abba " term of affection = " dear Father."

Sequence of thought. Sons ? Sons are generally heirs. Are we heirs ? To what ? With whom ?

We find that we are heirs of *salvation* (Heb. i. 14) ; *righteousness* (Heb. xi. 7) ; *a kingdom* (James ii. 5) ; *everlasting life* (Matt. xix. 29) ; *a blessing* (1 Peter iii. 9) ; *all things* (Rev. xxi. 7).

Roman law allowed equal division among sons. We are heirs *equally* with each other, and *all* with Christ. God is impartial ; He loves and gives to all alike.

The Lord's supper. When we meet as children at our Father's table, with His Son presiding, most striking reminder of our *sonship,* our *fellowship,* and our *heirship.*—*Dr. Springett.*

Vers. 15, 16. *The Spirit of adoption.*—Let us consider first the respective offices of the two witnesses here mentioned—that is, the Spirit of God and our own spirit. Let us notice, then, the subject of their testimony. It is " that we are the children of God." The Holy Spirit gives some witness to the great fact that our sins are forgiven, and that we, being reconciled to God, are now adopted into His family. The Spirit is the only witness who can give direct evidence of this. He is not only a competent witness, but the only competent witness. To this fact of our reconciliation to God, considered as a fact, our own spirits neither do nor can give testimony. Our own spirits have nothing to do with it. He alone can do this to whom it is perfectly known, and that is the Spirit of God. There are various ways, no doubt, by which the knowledge of this testimony is communicated to the soul, answering to the different modes of speech which we find in Scripture on the subject. There is the lifting up the light of the divine countenance upon the soul ; the shedding the love of God abroad in our hearts ; the crying, " Abba, Father " ; the giving testimony to our spirits that we are the children of God ; but all come from the Spirit and produce some persuasion and assurance that I am now a child of God, through His mercy in Christ. Next, we have the witness of our own spirits. Why is the testimony of our own spirit introduced and conjoined with that of the divine Spirit ? Though there can be no delusion where the Spirit of God dwells and shines, yet there may be impressions not from Him, and which we may mistake for the sacred testimony which He bears. Against a delusion of this sort you must be most carefully guarded. Where the Spirit of God dwells as the Spirit of adoption, He dwells as the great Author of regeneration, as the source of all holy principles and feelings. Our justification and our sanctification are thus inseparable.

There are a few errors connected with this doctrine which ought to be noticed. The first is that there can be no certainty of our being now in a state of salvation ; that, in fact, it is an unattainable blessing. If it be not attainable, the state of good men under the New Testament dispensation is far inferior to the state of good men under the Old. The first man of whom we have any record that he offered a sacrifice in faith obtained the testimony, the witness of his acceptance. And if ours be a dispensation much more glorious, and if we know that the Spirit of God has this particular office, we are not to conclude that we are placed in circumstances inferior, but superior to those of the saints of the Old Testament dispensation, with respect to the assurance of acceptance with God. This notion is contrary to all the words of Christ and the apostles. Here is the promise of Christ Himself, " I will give you rest " ; and that rest is vouchsafed by the Holy Ghost, the Comforter who reveals to us the mercy of God in Christ, removes from our conscience the burden of guilt, and witnesses to us that we are no longer strangers but children and heirs. We notice another error, that this assurance and persuasion of our adoption is the privilege only of some eminent Christians. This blessing is as common as pardon ; and the whole of this objection is grounded upon some secret idea of moral worth. None of these gifts are bestowed under any other character than as the purchase of the blood of Christ, and they are all parts of the great salvation held out to you, however unworthy, without money and without price. Some persons confound this assurance of present acceptance with an assurance of final salvation. The one is distinct from the other. I find no authority for the last in the Book of God. We are called upon to live in the assurance of this divine favour, and to rejoice in hope of the glory of God ; but this conveys to us no certain assurance of final salvation. We are still to walk by the same rule and to mind the same things. The faith which brings us into this state must maintain us in it. We must still watch and pray, still lay aside every weight and easily besetting sin, still fight the good fight of faith, ever feeling that only to those who are faithful unto death shall the crown of life be given.—*R. Watson.*

Vers. 12-17. *From present life to future glory.*
I. The argument starts from that practical influence of the Spirit of God upon daily conduct with which St. Paul has lately been dealing. This he describes as being "led" by the Spirit. The phrase is a short and easy one. It accurately describes, not simply the ideal of Christian life, but even in a fair degree its actual condition. For the word "led" must be admitted to suggest something more than spiritual direction as of a guide to duty who may or may not be followed. It is true enough that the Paraclete is given to shed light on the path of right conduct across the perplexing situations of life. But so outward and formal a conception fails to exhaust the functions of the indwelling Spirit. The word "led" implies that our Leader moves us along whither He would have us go, so that we yield ourselves to His reasonable and righteous impulses (ἄγονται, ver. 14). For this is His manner of leading. He is the inspirer as well as the suggester of conduct. He persuades and enables us to walk in the way, as well as points out where it lies. If we are "led" by the Spirit, that means that to some extent we are day by day amending our ways, exerting ourselves successfully to do right, and making substantial progress in virtue. Nor is it foreign even to the word itself, far less to the nature of the case, that I should speak thus of a Christian's own exertion and active progress in spiritual life. Unquestionably the word "led" describes the attitude of the believer as in some sense or to some extent a passive one. It means that he lets himself be acted upon. He submits to the operation of a superhuman force. That is true ; and without some such force from above, it is impossible to see how human beings are to be led aright. All the same the phrase hints that a man is not merely passive under the action of the Spirit. To be "led" is a state proper to a rational and self-determining creature. It is not to be pushed like a machine or driven like dumb cattle. God acts upon us as one moral agent who is mighty and the source of influence can act upon another moral agent who is feeble and open to influence—that is to say, by secretly instigating or persuading the will to choose freely what is good. No doubt, this cannot be said to exhaust the mysterious operations of the Spirit of life ; since being our Maker and Re-Maker, He has His peculiar divine sphere of action behind conscious choice, among those hidden tendencies, powers, and aptitudes which constitute human nature itself. Of this we can say little to purpose. But, so soon as the life reveals itself in consciousness, it is obvious that the Spirit's leading is so far from shutting out the man's own activity or

freedom that on the contrary it implies it. That the apostle recognised this active side of Christian experience is clear enough from the horta†ory cast into which this first paragraph is thrown at its opening. He tells the Romans how they owed it to the blessed One who stooped to be their leader that they should " mortify the deeds of the body." They were to this extent His " debtors," as he puts it. Since God has in His grace approached and entered into man to be his guide to everlasting life, it is, so to say, the least thing man can do to give himself heartily up to such celestial guidance. The practical issue in every real Christian must be, as a matter of fact, open to observation, that his conduct does move on the whole along lines which are laid down by God in His word. Explain the mechanism how you please, here at least is the ascertainable result.

II. On the basis of this simple matter of fact, St. Paul moves forward to the second point in developing his transition from " life " to " glory." It is this : wherever you find submission to divine guidance you have evidence of a divine birth. We have, in fact, no other mark of that sacred and lofty relationship, the noblest belonging to our nature, save character. With such sober, homely, and solemn teaching as this it is easy to see how the gospel erects a barrier against devout delusions such as may readily spring out of religious enthusiasm. It frequently occurs that persons persuade themselves they are the favourites or the children of God on the ground of some vivid experience they have undergone which they take to be " conversion," or because they have been the subject of a surprising vision, a bright light beheld in prayer, or a sudden calm of mind which they feel certain could only have had a heavenly origin. Nothing can well prove more perilous to character than the security which arises from such a source. For a man to turn away from the severe moral test of obedience in duty in order to build his confidence on emotions, dreams, mental impressions, or any other non-ethical evidence of piety, is to desert the safe guidance of truth and run grievous risk of spiritual shipwreck. The shores of religious experience are strewn thick with the shattered reputations of men who perished on this sunken rock. On the other hand, when a devout person is actually walking closely in the steps of Christ, being led by His Spirit to maintain a godly and watchful temper in daily behaviour, there is a certain internal witness to his divine birth from which he may legitimately take comfort. Wherever such a persuasion as this is found within the breast it is a secret possession for him who has it. No stranger may intermeddle with it. No outsider can ever be made aware of it. It justifies itself only to the soul in which it dwells. It is the witness of God within the man ; not the same thing as an inference of the judgment based on the evidence of conduct. True, it needs, as I said, to be sustained or corroborated by a most scrupulous behaviour, else what is called the " witness of the Spirit " may be nothing but a self-imposition. Still, where it is genuine, it is simply a matter of immediate personal consciousness. It is the heart of the son becoming conscious of itself and of its Father as united in one act of mutual trust and love. From a heart so near to God, so open to Him, so humbly bold in its access to Him, so reverently affectionate in its embrace of Him, why may not words of childlike familiarity well out with a happy unconsciousness of their own daring ? To its lips may there not come without blame a spontaneous cry like the " Abba ! " of Jesus Himself ?

III. If on solid grounds a believer has made sure Paul's second arch in this brief bridge which spiritual logic builds from earth to heaven, then he is prepared to go on to the third and last : " If sons, then heirs." There is no need to institute any curious inquiry here about either the Hebrew or the Roman law of inheritance, as if the apostle's argument turned upon such niceties. A lawful and beloved son shares his father's estate all the world over. He who belongs to God's family may with safety leave the question of his future inheritance in the hands of a parent who is too generous and too opulent to leave any child without a portion.—*Dr. Dykes.*

Heirs.

I. **Then the Christian is going to a rich home and a glorious future.**— Therefore he ought not to be too much elated or depressed by the pleasures or privations of the journey. An eye to the rest and glory at the end should keep him from getting weary of the way.

II. **Then the Christian should not debase himself by an undue attachment to the things of time.**—How unreasonable to see an "heir of God" so swallowed up in the world that he has neither taste nor time to pray, or make suitable efforts to get ready for his heavenly inheritance !

III. **Then no man should speak of having made sacrifices in becoming a Christian.**—Any person making such a declaration should blush to the roots of his hair, and ask God to forgive him for an utterance so untrue.

IV. **Then an heir of God should be made "meet for his inheritance."**— Without a meetness for it, the inheritance would be a burden rather than a blessing. Our business here is to cultivate the manners, to learn the language, and acquire the tempers of our future abode. May we not forget our errand !

V. **Then, in securing this meetness, the Christian may confidently expect divine aid.**—As soon doubt the rising of the sun as that God would fail to aid and bless the man who is struggling to be pure and Christlike.—*T. Kelly, D.D.*

SUGGESTIVE COMMENTS ON VERSES 15—17.

All may be heard.—This is much for their comfort, that from whomsoever and whatsoever corner of the world prayers come up to Him, they cannot want acceptance. All languages, all countries, all places, are sanctified by Jesus Christ, that whosoever calls on the name of the Lord from the ends of the earth shall be saved. And truly it is a sweet meditation to think that from the ends of the earth the cries of souls are heard, and that the end is as near heaven as the middle, and the wilderness as a paradise, and that they who understand not one another have one living and loving Father that understands all their meanings. And as the different dialects of this body make no confusion, no Babel, but meet together, the cry sent up by the Catholic Church, which is here scattered on the earth, ascends as one perfume or incense.—*Binning.*

Proof of sonship is holiness.—From these verses we may remark that the only infallible test of our being genuine disciples of Christ is our having that

mind in us which was also in Him, and that the proof of our being "sons of God" consists in our living habitually under the influence of the Holy Spirit, in studying to discharge conscientiously all the duties to which we are called, and to avoid every sin against which we are warned in the Holy Scriptures. This we are enabled to accomplish by means of the aids of the Holy Ghost ; for "as many as are led by the Spirit of God, they are the sons of God." It may be observed further that the dispositions with which the gospel calls us to worship God do not imply a slavish dread of His displeasure, but that filial reverence and confiding thankfulness with which the unspeakable mercy of the great Father of the universe ought to inspire all who are permitted to draw near to Him through the one Mediator between God and man.—*Ritchie.*

Concurrence of two witnesses.—How do the Spirit of God and your conscience bear *witness together* that you are the children of God ? I reply, first, by the *harmony of the dictates of conscience in*

266

the soul with the dictates of the Spirit in the Bible. It was enacted in the law of Moses that at the mouth of two or three witnesses every word should be established. It is evident that in the case before us a single witness would be insufficient to prove you the children of God, and that a concurrence of the two is indispensably necessary. *The concurrence of those two witnesses appears in the harmony of the dictates of conscience with the fruits or work of the Spirit in the soul.* Now as the fruits of the Spirit are His witnesses—for by His fruits ye know Him—so conscience, discerning these fruits in itself and in all the faculties and affections of the soul, bears witness with the Spirit that you "in whom these fruits appear" are the children of God. The concurrence of these two witnesses appears *in the harmony of the dictates of conscience with the dictates of the Spirit as living witnesses.* The language of the text conveys the idea of living personality in the Spirit of God as well as in our own spirit. It is not a mere indirect or passive testimony that is given by conscience, as of Abel's faith or sacrifice, "by which he being dead yet speaketh," but the direct testimony of a living witness.—*Parlane.*

Miraculous interceptions not now to be expected.—But it may be asked, Was the witness of the Spirit limited to that age? and have Christians in the present period no reason to look for it? To these questions we cannot hesitate in replying that the witness of the Spirit is common to all ages. But it must appear somewhat presumptuous to expect, in the present state of the world, those visible and miraculous communications of the gifts of the Holy Spirit which were necessary for promoting the first establishment of the Christian religion. The witness which we are now entitled to look for is therefore so far different from what it then was, that, generally speaking, it does not consist in a special revelation to individuals, intimating their adoption into the family of Christ; nor in

such sensible communications as were common in the apostolic age, and which were perfectly intelligible and obvious to others, as well as to the persons receiving them. But it consists in the inward and unseen co-operation of the divine Spirit, which manifests itself by its effects, producing the filial temper, or what, in the preceding verse, the apostle calls "the Spirit of adoption." We presume not indeed to limit the operation of the Spirit, or to maintain that this is now the only method in which His influence is imparted; but we are entitled to think that miraculous interpositions for satisfying the minds of individuals do not constitute the usual way in which God deals with mankind, and that those silent and unostentatious influences which promote the sanctification of our nature, without abridging our free agency, are the common methods by which "the Spirit now beareth witness with our spirit, that we are the children of God."—*Ritchie.*

God's sons have emanations of God's love.—The communication of God Himself, not that we shall ever acquire God's infinite attributes, or that He will cease to be God alone, but such emanations of His love and wisdom and glory will flow into our souls as to fill us with the fulness of God, or with Godlike wisdom, holiness, love, and blessedness. "What comes nearer to a communication of Himself into us or to our having a portion in the divinity than our being made like unto Him? It would look as if the circumstances of our seeing Him led, by a sort of causal or influential energy, to the circumstance of our being assimilated to Him—as if we gathered, by a sort of radiation from His glory, the reflection of a kindred glory upon our own persons—as if His excellences passed unto us when ushered into His visible presence, and became ours by sympathy, or ours by transmission. He does not part with His character; but He multiplies His character by the diffusion of it through all the members of the blest household that is above;

and they may be most significantly called heirs of God—may be most significantly said to have God for their portion, God for their inheritance, when not only admitted to the full and immediate sight of Him, but when the efficacy of that sight is to actuate and inspire them with His very affections, to cover and adorn them with His very spiritual glories."—*John Howe.*

" *For the Spirit itself beareth witness with our spirit, that we are the children of God.*"—Here the apostle shows the ground of our union and communion with Christ, because, having His Spirit, we are of necessity His. What ties and makes one things far asunder but the same Spirit of life in both? So that Spirit which is in Him, a full, running-over fountain, dropping down, and being also infused, unites us unto Him; yea, that Spirit doth tie me as fast unto Christ as any joint ties member to member, and so makes Christ dwell in mine heart. So that now by this means we are inseparably united unto Him. For, I pray you, what is it that makes a member to be a member to another? Not the nearness of joining, but the same quickening spirit and life which is in both and which causeth a like motion. By the same Spirit I know I am conveyed into Christ and united unto Him. "The testimony of our spirit" I conceive to be when a man hath taken a survey of those excellent things belonging unto justification and sanctification, when according to the substantial truths which I know in the word belonging thereunto I observe and follow as fast as I may what is there commanded. This is the groundwork of the witness of our spirit. If a man be in the faith, and do believe the word, and if in this case the Spirit come and fill the heart with joy, then all is sure and well.—*Sibbes.*

A real participation.—It is a real participation. It is not a picture, but a nature: it is divine. God doth not

busy Himself about apparitions. It is a likeness, not only in actions, but in nature. God communicates to the creature a singular participation of the divine vision and divine love: why may He not also give some excellent participation of His nature? There is a nature, for there is something whereby we are constituted the children of God. A bare affection to God doth not seem to do this. Love constitutes a man a friend, not a son and heir by generation. The apostle argues, "If children, then heirs." He could not argue in a natural way, If friends, then heirs. And the Scripture speaks of believers being the children of God by a spiritual generation as well as by adoption. So that grace, which doth constitute one a child of God, is another form whereby a divine nature is communicated. Generation is the production of one living thing by another in the likeness of its nature, not only in the likeness of love; so is regeneration. Were not a real likeness attainable, why should those exhortations be, of being holy as God is holy, pure as He is pure? The new creature receives the image of God: not as a glass receives the image of a man, which is only an appearance, no real existence, and though it be like the person, yet hath no communion with its nature; but as wax receives the image of the seal, which though it receive nothing of the substance, yet receives exactly the stamp, and answers it in every part. So the Scripture represents it: "Ye were sealed with that holy Spirit of promise" (Eph. i. 13). Something of God's perfections are in the new creature by way of quality which are in God by way of essence. In a word, it is as real a likeness to God as the creature is capable of—laid in the first draughts of it in regeneration, and completed in the highest measures in glory.—*Charnock.*

Spirit of adoption.—The Spirit received is more than the spirit of mere *freedom*: it is the spirit of " *adoption* "—the dearest, the most intimate, the most delightful of all kinds of freedom, that of a child under a kindly indulgent, a loved and loving father. This the Spirit imparts by means of the truth—making known to our minds the character of God as it appears in the gospel, as the God of love, " in Christ reconciling the world unto Himself," " delighting in mercy." It is by leading the mind into this view of the divine character and relation to the guilty that the Spirit overcomes the enmity of the carnal mind, and fills the soul with love to God, with desire after, with joy and confidence in Him. It is thus that " *by the Spirit we cry, Abba, Father* "—not merely using the words, but being inspired with the dispositions and tempers of mind that belong to the endearing relation. It is the language of affection, of liberty of conscience, of confident expectation, of filial intimacy, of happiness unfelt before. The *words* are nothing. Alas ! how many have hundreds of times used the form of address whose hearts have been strangers to the spirit which the use of it implies ! How often has the invocation of the Lord's prayer been used, " Our Father which art in heaven, hallowed be Thy name," while there has been nothing but the moving of the lips from the power of habit and of association with time and place— nothing of the heart of a loving, confiding, expecting child ! In using both the *Syro-Chaldaic* word and the *Greek* for the same relation the apostle probably meant to convey the idea of the union of Jew and Gentile under the gospel, in addressing the same God by the same endearing appellation. Or else he uses the Syriac, and simply explains it by the Greek—" We cry *Abba*[which is] *Father.*"—*Dr. Wardlaw.*

Gratitude to the divine Spirit.—We owe much, in one sense we owe everything, to the Spirit's influences. To Him we owe our regeneration. To Him we owe our perseverance in faith and holiness. To Him we owe all the present joys and all the future hopes, as they exist and are experienced in our hearts, of God's salvation. The spiritual life in its first elements, and in all its variety of subsequent exercises and enjoyments, is His work. He commences it. He maintains, and forwards, and perfects it. We are too apt to confine our gratitude to the Father and the Son, probably from two causes :—The work of Christ in assuming our nature, and suffering and dying for us, and as commissioned by the Father so to do, has in it something more external and palpable, something on which the mind can more readily realise to its conceptions, than the work of the Spirit, which, in as far as regards the personal application of that work, is inward and spiritual ; imperceptible except in its effects, and frequently undistinguishable in our consciousness from the ordinary operations of mind. This is the case with the manner in which He helps our infirmities in prayer, and with all His other operations in the soul. We see it not, we hear it not. It does not even in imagination embody itself to any of our senses ; and even when most conscious of the effect we are not sensible of the influence which produces it. And, moreover, we justly regard the Spirit as the gift of the Father and the Son, and are in danger of forgetting the personality and the perfect voluntariness of the Spirit Himself in the whole of *His* part in the work of our redemption. It is to the work of Christ we are instructed to look for a sense of pardon, for peace and hope and joy and all spiritual excitement ; and while *that* is the object of our contemplation, we are in danger of forgetting the necessity of the Spirit's influence to our deriving from it any saving benefit. The Father sent and gave the Son ; the Son came and gave Himself ; the Spirit, though sent by the Father and the Son, performs His part, as regenerator and sanctifier, with the same personal delight and satisfaction. Let us cherish gratitude to Father, Son, and Holy Ghost—ONE GOD.—*Dr. Wardlaw.*

MAIN HOMILETICS OF THE PARAGRAPH.—Verse 18.

Is life worth living?—Question much asked by present-day philosophers. What is real answer? *Prayer Book* says Yes: "We thank Thee for our creation." Does *Bible* say so? Our passage gives answer Yes or No—*depends upon belief in future life as revealed in Scripture.*

Apart from future life, no, for large majority of human beings. In most lives painful sensations predominate over pleasant. Many sufferings. Atheist poet, who knew much of world, says :—

> "Cast up the cares thy life has seen,
> Cast up the years from sorrow free,
> And know, whatever thou hast been,
> 'Twere something better not to be."

If Bible revelation be true, yes. Life is not pain, but school; not happiness, but preparation for happiness; not glory, but way to glory, if lived with Christ.

Universal rule—glory of any kind slowly, painfully gained : manhood, success, fame, conquest, even redemption of man.

We can understand men *doubting* the future life; we cannot understand their telling us that we shall be happier if we do not anticipate it. Without it we sail in unpiloted ship on shoreless ocean, over seas on which sun never shines. With it we look up and onward in spirit of our text. Thank God. —*Dr. Springett.*

SUGGESTIVE COMMENTS ON VERSE 18.

Suffering Christians have the true prosperity.—Prosperity is to be measured by the *amount of peace.* It is a better treasure than either gold or silver. What trouble there is to get wealth, and when gotten what trouble for fear we lose the hoarded treasure ! Peace is the true wealth—soul wealth, heart wealth. It is a treasure which makes happy. Call not that man happy and prosperous who with the increase of wealth has the increase of care and sorrow. Call that man happy and prosperous whose soul is kept in perfect peace amid the storms and hurricanes of time. Sweet home of refreshment and delight is the strong tower of perfect peace. Great peace have they that love and keep God's law. Prosperity *is to be measured by the amount of true happiness.* Do we call that man prosperous who sits a miserable wretch amid his treasures and asks for what can never be given, the neglected prosperity of former days? Do we call that man prosperous whose head aches with the oppressive weight of a crown and whose soul is troubled and fever-stricken with "the fierce light that beats upon a throne"? We call that man prosperous who enjoys as much happiness as is given to mortals here below. That man is prosperous who can sing in a cell, while that man is not prosperous who weeps on a throne. The question has been sceptically asked, Happiness—what is it? A word. Where found? Our reply would be that the truest happiness to be found in this world, the most solid good, is to be obtained while walking in the pathway of duty and of godliness, for religion's ways are indeed ways of pleasantness and her paths are peace. Let us look round upon modern society, and we shall find that its most prosperous and happiest members are those who wisely and joyously keep God's commandments. Prosperity is to be *considered in relation to the end.* The psalmist was troubled, like other people, at the prosperity of the wicked. It was to him a perplexing problem.

How is it consistent with the moral government of Him who is said to reign in righteousness? "Verily I have cleansed my heart in vain, and washed my hands in innocency; for the righteous are plagued and chastened, while the ungodly prosper in the world, and increase in riches." He saw no way out of the bewildering maze until he went into the sanctuary of God, and understood their end. At the last, the dreadful last, desolation seized upon them as its lawful prey. They are utterly consumed with terrors. Come not my soul into the secrets of their dying horrors. Prosperous is the man who can sing, " My flesh and my heart faileth ; but God is the strength of my heart, and my portion for ever " Paul looked forward, and saw a bright light piercing the dark cloud of sorrow. The sufferings of the present are great. The sufferings of the persecuted how great we can scarcely understand, and yet they are not worthy to be compared with the glory that shall be revealed. Amid the shame of the present look onward to the revealing glory. Bring down the light of heaven to cheer the murkiness of earth. Let the eternal sunlight scatter the thick mists of time.

MAIN HOMILETICS OF THE PARAGRAPH.—*Verses* 19—23.

Universal groaning and redemption.—A pleasant picture is that of a renovated world, one in which shall be found neither physical nor moral evil, a universe of light, of order, and of beauty. In the Zend books it is said that after the renovation of the earth there shall be no night, no cold or hot wind, no corruption, no fear of death, no evil caused by wicked spirits ; and then the fiend, the ambitious prince, shall exalt himself no more ; further, that a dignified personage named Oschandabega (the man of the world) shall appear in the last time, and adorn the world with religion and righteousness, and restore the ancient order of things, when rest and peace shall prevail, all dissensions cease, and all grievances be done away. Large-souled men look to a good time coming, to a world restored to primeval glory. *Paradise Lost* has in it sublimer strains than *Paradise Regained*, but the latter is the inspiring hope of a true humanity. No wonder if St. Paul personified nature and represented it as rising up out of its groaning and looking forward to deliverance.

I. **Universal groaning.**—When sitting in the pleasant landscape, the soul entranced with nature's glories, the ears charmed with her harmonies, the sense of smell regaled with her fragrances, and the vision gladdened with her beauties, we ask, Where is the groaning of nature? She is pleasant enough. Nature presents herself according to the receptive mind. Ah ! there is nature's laughter ; but there are nature's tears. The song of the bird is the prelude to her wail of sorrow ; the beauty of the flower makes its decay more distressing ; the splendour of the landscape is dashed by the thought of lurking dangers. Bright nature groans that her fair face should be seamed with so many scars. Nature's fairest spots are marked with darkest blots—the earthquake yawns, the volcano belches, the avalanche sweeps, the thunder peals, the fatal disease lurks amid the flowers. Nature groans. Nature's lord groans. Who could stand the wail if all the groanings of the human race were concentrated—the death groanings of the slaughtered Abels, the remorseful groanings of the slaughtering Cains, the groanings of the wounded on earth's battle-fields, the groanings of the conquerors as they look at the awful price of victory, the groanings of the oppressed and of the oppressors ? Man's inhumanity to man makes countless thousands mourn. Instruments of music play their pleasant tunes to beguile the pathway along which the great human army marches ; but the groanings are not silenced. Even good men, those who have the firstfruits of the Spirit, groan. They feel the ruin and the disorders, and sigh for deliverance. They groan over abounding sin and over prevailing sorrow. They groan that efforts to overcome seem to be so ineffectual.

II. Universal expectation.—The great soul of inanimate nature feels that she has not been fashioned for vanity, that her beauties are the prophetic intimations of all abounding beauty, that her harmonies are the minor chords which shall usher in the glorious diapason which shall celebrate nature's deliverance from every discordant sound. What poetry in the apostle's mind! Personified nature, struggling and groaning with and beneath her fetters, is looking forward to the period when all tokens of bondage shall be removed, and there shall be a glad, triumphant entrance into the glorious liberty of the children of God. Through all time great men have had their hopeful expectations. Many of them have even rejoiced in the anticipation of the day when the powerful Liberator should appear. Gladness has entered their souls, though they have only seen the day by faith in the distant future. Good men have been men of hopeful expectancies. Their expectation has been so real, so true and earnest, that they have worked and prayed to bring into joyous fulfilment their own bright visions. They have worked for spiritual redemption, believing that along this line material redemption shall be accomplished. Creation was for redemption, and redemption shall answer back, and be in its better turn for creation. Action and reaction are equal; but the reaction of redemptive processes shall surpass the action of creation's downfall, for divine wisdom and power and love are combined in the redemptive purposes. The sons of God expect a glorious redemption. Their expectation is founded on the immutable purposes of a loving God.

III. Universal redemption.—Would God's vindication of His omnipotence be complete if this planet, small as it may be among the other worlds, were left in its ruined condition, a miserable trophy of the victory achieved by the enemy of all beauty and goodness? In the final disposition of all things, will it be permitted to the evil one to point to the earth-planet, and say, I have been too strong for infinite goodness; I saw God create the world, I heard Him pronounce it "very good," and I have spoiled His workmanship; a blasted earth-planet is the proof of my malignant power, and God could only undo the work by consigning that planet to destruction? Surely no; the good must triumph over the evil, and this it will not do if evil is to work permanent damage even in material spheres. Christ's kingdom is to include all kingdoms; and shall the material kingdom, in which His mediatorial work and reign commenced, be excluded? Shall Jerusalem receive only the Saviour's tears, and not be favoured with His renovating smiles? Shall Calvary hear only His cries of anguish, and not be allowed to listen to the strains which clothe with beauty? Shall not the sepulchres of earth be turned into palaces, and angels clothed in white sit where the weepers stood and mourned? The creature itself shall be delivered from the bondage of corruption; and much more, the creature's master by divine appointment. Man shall be delivered. The universal redemption must come. All things make for the reign of righteousness. We see it not now, but we shall see it and know it hereafter. Let us wait in hope amid the discrepancies and disorders of the present. Let us not abate either heart or patience amid the discouragements that may surround, the seeming drawbacks that may be presented. Let us work and pray for the removal of all obstructions and for the advancement of the kingdom of truth and righteousness.

Ver. 21. *The redemption of the creature.*—Meaning of terms employed: " Sons of God " = human race, in so far as redeemed to God. Creation ($\kappa\tau\iota\sigma\iota\varsigma$) = rest of animate creation. A rational division = man, though marked off by stray dividing lines, only the highest link in a chain of creation. Connection of "sons" with "creation" twofold: man's sin brought suffering on "creation"; man's redemption will bring happiness to "creation."

Origin of man's connection with creation (Gen. i. 26). As being in "God's image," he had "dominion." What he does *affects* all *creatures* round him. Examples: In animal life, degradation of the ass; in vegetable life, desolation of parts of Syria, Babylon, Palestine. On other side, elevation of the dog; improvement of natural state of Britain or United States. Inference: Man degraded, degrades nature; man redeemed will redeem nature.

Points to notice—viz., 1. Our evil doing affects not only men but *all* creation around us. 2. Any anomalies in the lower world are accounted for by anomalies in man. 3. Redemption of man means the " restitution of all things," alluded to in Isa. xi. and Acts iii. 21. Jewish rabbis said, "All creation will rise again, and paradise will be restored." 4. All this through redemptive work of Christ.— *Dr. Springett.*

Vers. 19-23. *Fallen and redeemed.*—This passage has given rise to much controversy. But the general meaning is plain enough. The apostle is speaking of the future glory of believers, and what he says is that one element in that glory will be the inheritance of a renovated creation. As set over against this burden of glory, present suffering may well seem light. While spiritual deliverance will be man's noblest possession, it will be enhanced by new bodies not subject to corruption and a new earth purged from the curse of the Fall. The teaching of the passage may be expressed in two leading thoughts :—

I. **Nature was affected by the fall of man.**—In what respect and to what extent? 1. *It was subjected to an alien principle.* "The creature was made subject to vanity." The principle of corruption entered. Taking creature here to mean nature in its material sense, as including everything on earth that God has made, except the spirit of man, we are in unison with the teaching of Scripture in saying that when man rebelled a blight fell on the divine handiwork (Gen. iii. 17, 18; Isa. lv. 12, 13). Milton says: "Nature through all her works gave signs of woe that all was lost." Whether nature would have shone in perennial beauty, had man not sinned, it would be idle to speculate. Enough to know that the "ground was cursed for man's sake." The principle of death reigned universal throughout the Creator's works. 2. *It was not a willing subjection.* "Not willingly, but by reason of Him who subjected the same." Nature had no choice in the matter. The bondage was enforced. The blight was inflicted on man's account. Nature was passive, being dragged down in the ruin. When the soul of man became tainted with sin, the earthly home of man became the abode of corruption and full of wickedness. The tenant polluted the tenement. 3. *The subjection is not final.* There is " hope that the creature will be delivered from the bondage of corruption." The subjection was in accordance with the will of God, and we can only surmise the divine purpose by picturing the final goal, " the end to which the whole creation moves." The result will doubtless be a richer splendour. A cloud of mystery hangs over the subject, but we may be sure that man and nature will both emerge from the discipline in garments of white.

II. **Nature will share in the redemption of man.**—As nature was dragged down in the fall of man, it is natural to suppose that it will be benefited by the rise of man. But we are not left to supposition. 1. *It is proved by direct statement in this passage*: "The creature itself shall be delivered from the bondage of corruption into the glorious liberty of the children of God." "The earnest expectation of the creature waiteth for the manifestation of the sons of God." Nature is here personified. She feels the misery and degradation of her present condition and longs for deliverance. This longing is prophetic.

273

The fulfilment may yet be far off, but the sun gilds the mountain tops. The revelation of the sons of God is drawing on, and nature will share in the glory to be revealed. This revelation will be at the appearing of the Lord Jesus, who will subdue *all things* unto Himself (Phil. iii. 21). All God's works will be brought into harmony with the renovated moral world. The blight with which the ground was smitten will be removed, the longing of the creature fulfilled, and all things reconciled, things in heaven and things in earth. 2. *This truth is expressed in other passages of Scripture.* In Isa. lxv. 17, Rev. xxi. 1, 2 Peter iii. 13, we read of new heavens and a new earth, from which we may, without straining, infer the establishment of a new order of things after the earth has been purged of sin. In Isa. lv. 12, 13, it is said, "Ye shall go out with joy," etc. Underlying this imagery may we not discern the truth, that when men emerge from sinful bondage into the glorious liberty which God offers, nature will in some sense share in the emancipation, for the mountains shall sing and the hills clap their hands? Can this mean anything less than that Christ's redemptive forces will be felt all over the creation? We may well believe that all things, in some way unknown to us, come under the redeeming plan, that the shadow which meanwhile clouds the creature will one day be lifted. 3. *This truth is involved in the redemption of the body.* The body is indeed part of the material creation; and if one part is to be freed from sin, the redemption of the other will surely follow. The redemption of the body is a neglected tenet of the Christian faith. The believer longs for it (ver. 23) as the goal of his hopes. It comes only in one way—viz., through Christ. When He rose from the grave, He snapped the fetters that kept the "creature" under the bondage of corruption. One body having thus risen incorruptible, have we not in this the earnest of the redemption of all bodies of the saints? A portion of the material creation being thus redeemed from the curse, is there not herein a pledge that every creature or the whole creation will yet be emancipated? There is indeed a universal expectancy. The creature itself longs for it. They who have the firstfruits of the Spirit wait for it.

Conclusion.—1. Are we waiting for this glorious emancipation? 2. Will the renovated earth be the abode of redeemed man? 3. If so, what manner of persons ought we to be?—*D. Merson, B.D.*

The history of sonship.—" The manifestation of the sons of God."

I. **Their past eternity.**—They had a history ere they were born; not conscious to themselves, but truly in the eye and purpose of God (Rom. viii. 29; Eph. i. 3, 5; 2 Tim. i. 9; Rev. xvii. 8). In these passages the history of each saint and of the Church of God is traced to that eternity in which God only existed.

II. **Their unregenerate life on earth.**—They were born no better than others; shapen in iniquity; children of wrath.

III. **Their adoption.**—1. *They are begotten again* (1 Peter i. 3). They are born of the Spirit (John iii. 3), born from above. 2. *They believe* (Gal. iii. 26). They pass out of the region of unbelief into that of faith. 3. *They receive Christ* (John i. 12). 4. *They get the name of sons* (1 John iii. 1). They are now "called" sons of God. 5. *They receive the Spirit of adoption* (Gal. iv. 5, 6). 6. *They are led by the Spirit* (Rom. viii. 14). 7. *They are chastened* (Heb. xii. 7). Discipline is their lot. 8. *They are brought to glory* (Heb. ii. 10). To this are they redeemed and called. " Whom He justified, them He also glorified." 9. *They are made like Christ Himself* (Rom. viii. 29; 1 John iii. 2).

IV. **Their time of obscurity.**—For a season they are hidden; men's eyes are holden so that they do not recognise them; they are in disguise. Their life is hid with Christ in God. It doth not yet appear what they shall be.

V. The manifestation.—The obscurity does not last always—nay, not long. The day is coming when the disguise shall drop off, and their royal robes display themselves; when He who is their life shall appear, they shall appear with Him. 1. *What this manifestation is.* The word is the same as in 1 Cor. i. 7; 2 Thess. i. 7; 1 Peter i. 7, 13, iv. 13. It is revelation, or outshining, or transfiguration. They are in this conformed to their Lord. 2. *When shall the manifestation be?* In the day of Christ's appearing; not in the day of death. 3. *How long shall the manifestation be?* For ever. A whole eternity of glory. Let us walk worthy of our prospects; content with present obscurity and shame; "passing the time of our sojourning here in fear."—*H. Bonar.*

SUGGESTIVE COMMENTS ON VERSES 19—23.

Man the soul of the world.—Schelling said: "On the loveliest spring day, while nature is displaying all her charms, does not the heart, when drinking in admiration, imbibe a poison of gnawing melancholy?" There is a third point on which science seems to us to harmonise readily with St. Paul's view; I mean the close solidarity which exists between man and the whole of nature. The physiologist is forced to see in the human body the intended goal and masterpiece of animal organisation, which appears as nothing else than a long effort to reach this consummation. As the breaking of the bud renders sterile the branch which bore it, so the fall of man involved that of the world. As Schelling said in one of his admirable lectures on the philosophy of revelation: "Nature, with its melancholy charm, resembles a bride who, at the very moment when she was fully attired for marriage, saw the bridegroom to whom she was to be united die on the very day fixed for the marriage. She still stands with her fresh crown and in her bridal dress, but her eyes are full of tears." The soul of the poet-philosopher here meets that of the apostle. The ancient thinkers spoke much of a soul of the world. The idea was not a vain dream. The soul of the world is man. The whole Bible, and this important passage in particular, rests on this profound idea.—*Godet.*

Yearnings in creation.

It was not then a poet's dream,
    An idle vaunt of song,
Such as beneath the moon's soft beam
    On vacant fancies throng,

Which bids us see in heaven and earth,
    In all fair things around,
Strong yearnings for a blest new birth,
    With sinless glories crowned.—*Keble.*

If we judge by the numerous and diversified interpretations of this passage, it is one of the most difficult of solution in the Bible, and is probably included in "some things hard to be understood" which the apostle Peter says are in his beloved brother Paul's epistles. A late critic has enumerated no less than eleven different views of the word "creature," which, indeed, is the key of the whole passage. I shall not dwell on such opinions, as that it signifies angels, the souls of the planetary world, Adam and Eve, or the souls or bodies of men. It cannot mean the Gentiles, the unconverted, or the human race in general, because many of them look to eternity with fear, not *hope.* Were vers. 19-21 to be literally understood, they can apply only to Christians, or to the new nature of Christians, which is called a "new creation." But as the creation is mentioned in the twenty-second verse (although the same original word rendered "creation" there is translated "creature" in the preceding verse), the creature in the nineteenth verse means creation or nature. The most satisfactory view of the passage, or what seems attended with fewest difficulties, is that it is a bold and noble figure in which the apostle personifies nature, and represents it as longing and expecting a blessed change from its present vanity or perversion, into order, beauty, and happiness.—*Parlane.*

A bold personification.

All true, all faultless, all in tune
  Creation's wondrous choir,
Opened in mystic unison
  To last till time expire.

Man only mars the sweet accord,
  O'erpowering with "harsh din"
The music of Thy works and words,
  Ill matched with grief and sin.

Sin is with man at morning break,
  And through the livelong day
Deafens the ear that fain would wake
  To nature's simple lay.—*Keble.*

The figure of speech called pro-sopopœia, by which irrational beings are represented as persons endowed with the qualities of rational creatures, and speaking, hearing, suffering, and rejoicing like them, is common in sacred as well as in profane writings. You find in the Bible such expressions as these: "O earth, earth, earth, hear the word of the Lord!" "Hear, O heavens! and give ear, O earth!" The trees said to the olive, the fig tree, the vine, and the bramble, Reign thou over us. No one is deceived by such personification, which is designed and fitted to convey truth in a more interesting and impressive manner. What more graphically exposes the ingratitude, the obduracy, of impenitent men, who refuse to hear God, than His appeal to the material creation, "Be astonished, O ye heavens; give ear, O earth; and be ye horribly afraid: for My people have been guilty of two great evils?" Stones are represented as hearing and witnessing God's covenant with His people, and their vows, and the earth as mourning under the sin of man, and as rejoicing in his temporal and spiritual joy. "Because of swearing, the land mourneth. The little hills rejoice on every side. Sing, O ye heavens; for the Lord hath done it! Shout, ye lower parts of the earth; break forth into singing, ye mountains! O forest, and every tree therein: for the Lord hath redeemed Jacob, and glorified Himself in Israel." The passage before us, as we have seen, is a bold personification of nature. "For the creature," or creation, etc. The present

condition of nature, or visible creation, its cause, and its temporary duration, are the topics presented in the text.

Nature to be set free.—"Bondage of corruption." Nature is prevented from putting forth its powers, from manifesting its real grandeur, and from attaining its original destiny. It is therefore bound. And its bondage is caused by the necessary decay of its products. All that nature brings forth is doomed to die. And nature is compelled to slay its own offspring. The lightning flash destroys the stately oak. The winter's cold kills the songsters of the summer. Animals devour other animals to maintain life. And this universal destruction limits the achievements of nature. Instead of constant growth, nature's beauty and strength fade away. The powers of the material creation are bound by fetters of decay. "The freedom of," etc., with which the "children of God" will be made free in the day when their glory will be revealed—this freedom creation will share. The bondage of corruption was designed to last only for a time. It was imposed when man fell, and will be removed when man's redemption is complete. Paul carries on his personification by saying that when nature was made to share "the bondage" which resulted from man's sin, a *hope* was given to it of sharing the liberty which will follow man's deliverance. Ver. 22. Proof, from an admitted fact, that nature will be made free. "Groans together." The entire creation joins in one cry of sorrow and in one great anguish. Every voice in nature which reminds us of its bondage to corruption Paul conceives to be a cry of sorrow. The storm which wreaks destruction and the roar of the hungry lion tell that the original purpose of the Creator has been perverted, and that nature is not what He designed it to be. "The whole . . . until now." This cry is universal and unceasing. And Paul remembers that nature's sorrow is the result of man's sin. He therefore infers that it will not continue for ever; that the confusion and destruction around, so inconsistent with the character and purpose of the Creator, will give way to liberty and order. In other words, he can account for the present anomalous state of nature only by supposing it to be temporary, to be preparatory to something more consistent with nature's original destiny. "In travail." The agonies of nature are but the pangs, soon and suddenly to cease, at the birth of a new earth and heaven.—*Beet.*

Creature denotes the whole of the race. —The most probable interpretation of the term "creature" therefore seems to be that which considers it as denoting the whole human race. This is the view taken of the passage by many eminent interpreters. All mankind from the beginning have felt the evils of the present system of things. Many of them looked for an amelioration of the human condition in the present life, and, generally speaking, they believed in a future state, and hoped to share in its advantages. Now the earnest waiting for the manifestation of the sons of God may include both the expected improvement of the human condition on earth and the glory that shall be manifested at the resurrection. Mankind in general had indeed no knowledge of the nature of this glory. That the word "creature" as here employed denotes all mankind is rendered probable also by the use of the term in other parts of the New Testament, where it often has this meaning. "Go ye into all the world," said out blessed Saviour to His disciples immediately before His ascension into heaven, "and preach the gospel to every creature." Here "every creature" can mean nothing but all mankind. In the same sense St. Paul uses the word: "The gospel which was preached to every creature which is under heaven," meaning obviously every human creature. This therefore is the meaning of the term, which is most consistent with the use of it in other parts of the New Testament, and the meaning which enables us most easily to explain the passage, and therefore it is probable that this is the meaning which the apostle intended.—*Ritchie.*

MAIN HOMILETICS OF THE PARAGRAPH.—*Verses* 24, 25.

The sustaining grace.—The sustaining grace is hope, for we consider it in this passage subjectively and objectively. We look forward in hope to its object, which is the perfected adoption and redemption of the believer. We may be allowed to consider hope in its bearing upon the whole of the Christian character. Perhaps we may extend the apostolic idea in this passage, as we observe :—

I. **Hope appropriates the blessings purchased by Jesus Christ.**—We are saved by hope, and thus it is the instrumental cause of salvation. "Thy faith hath saved thee." It is the hand which lays hold upon the hand of Jesus, who leads out of the pit. Hope does not save apart from its object—Jesus Christ as mediator. Hope must rest on the foundation-stone laid by God in Zion. All other hope is baseless.

II. **Hope is the "helmet of salvation."**—The head the most important part of the human frame, for therein resides the brain. Man of all animals has the largest brain and a weak defence. Reason and the inventive faculty enable him to provide against attacks. The helmet is the artificial safeguard for the human brain. The Christian soldier is crowned with the best helmet, the hope of salvation. In ancient warfare a strong arm would make the sword cleave the helmet and slay the man. No arm is sufficiently strong, no sword sufficiently well-tempered, to cleave the Christian's helmet of hope. We are saved by a strong hope.

III. **Hope holds the Christian's head above water.**—Hope is like the cork to a net—the lead upon the bottom of the net would sink it, but the cork bears it up; our troubles would sink us, the testimony of our external senses would sink us, but hope sustains. Hope is the life-buoy for the mariner. The ships of earth may sink; the billows may rise mountainous; but hope enables the man to swim in roughest seas. The tempest only makes sweet music in his soul. He rides calmly like the sea-bird on the swelling and rolling waters.

IV. **Hope is the pleasant pilot.**—The pilot takes complete control of the vessel, and conducts into the harbour. He may bring pleasant news from shore. Hope guides the soul, and tells sweet stories of succeeding joys. Amid the gloom that death's shadows cast over the dying Christian hope brings gracious rays of heavenly light to cheer. Lightsome is life, less stern is death, when hope pleasantly pilots the soul.

V. **Hope is not daunted by inscrutable purposes.**—There are mysteries in life, dark providences in human proceedings. Hope brightens the dark design; hope contentedly waits for the solution of all mysteries. Dr. Payson was once asked if he saw any special reasons for some particular dispensation of providence. " No," was his reply; " but I am as well satisfied as if I saw the design." God's will is the very perfection of reason. Hope teaches satisfaction. Philosophy kicks against the unknowable, and is in a state of unrest. Hope accepts the unknowable and also the knowable divine wisdom and goodness, and is in a state of delicious repose.

VI. **Hope waits the Father's time.**—" Then do we with patience wait for it." Time is a human word. Of course all words are human, but by the expression " time is a human word" we mean that men are subject to time conditions; and in what sense the word may be applied to the divine we cannot tell. God's time is not measured by human dial-plates. The eternal clocks are made on larger scale than the clocks of time. A child measures time by fitful fancies. A man measures time by prolonged efforts. We are all children with our fitful fancies. God's time must be measured by mighty purposes which require ages for their unfolding. Hope calmly waits at the post of duty, while God's great time is moving onward to the development of His benevolent designs.

VII. **Hope sees the unseen.**—" Hope that is seen is not hope: for what a man seeth, why doth he yet hope for?" Hope ceases when its object is realised. Perfect redemption is unseen, but we live in hope. Heaven is unseen, but hope is so strong that it brings heaven down to earth. Let a man's citizenship be in heaven—let his thoughts travel amongst the holy angels—let his spirit thirst for the joys of the upper temple—let his longings be towards the presence of the Lamb, who is without blemish and without spot, and that man must rise out of a low state of manhood into a condition that shall be sublimely glorious. With such a process carried on to perfection, he will appear as one let down from the upper sphere to this lower world. Blessed hope enables sorrowing disciples to rejoice in days of darkness, and martyrs to sing in the very hour of their martyrdom. It brings rich grapes from heaven with which to refresh the parched lips, and pours healing oil into wounded hearts. It scatters the darkness of death, chases away the gloom of the grave, by throwing around it the divine light of a glorious resurrection, and opens the kingdom of heaven to all believers. Let us then no longer dissipate our lives in a series of trifles; but let us recall ourselves to-day from fugitive events, and strike a nobler aim, and seek a more enduring interest, and cast a further anticipation on the futurity which lies before us, and on that blessed hope the realisation of which will fill our souls with joy unspeakable.

SUGGESTIVE COMMENTS ON VERSES 24, 25.

How to know hope. — Thou shalt know hope by three things, whether thou hast it or not. 1. By the mother of it, which is faith : he that hopeth believeth, for faith is the ground of things hoped for. 2. By the daughter of it, which is patience : thus do we with patience wait for it. Merchants in hope of gain endure the water, martyrs in hope of recompense endure the fire ; where there is no patience there is no hope. 3. By the companion of it, which is love : he that hath this hope purifieth himself. If then thou hast a true and lively hope of salvation, remember to increase in faith, patience, and love, which is the fulfilling of the law. Thus we suppress the rising sigh, thus we bow with submission to the will of God which afflicts us, thus we show to ourselves and others that we have the firstfruits of the Spirit. But we wait for the victor's crown ; we have not actually attained or come to the realisation of that for which we hope :

that " eye hath not seen nor ear heard, nor hath it entered into the heart of man to conceive," and therefore we patiently wait until the hour of glorious liberty, the deliverance from the bondage of corruption.—*Adams.*

Hope and despair.—Despair throws over the soul an oppressive gloom, paralyses the energies, benumbs the powers, and throws the man a wasted wreck on the sands of time ; while hope fills the soul with light, braces up the man with strength, and sends him walking through God's creation, a being endowed with powers of endurance. Despair is the result of sin's working in this world, while Christian hope is the gift of God. He has given us a good hope through grace. God might have shut us up to the darkness of despair ; but in the midst of our moral darkness mercy appeared and hope spanned the world in its many colours like a rainbow of divine promise.

MAIN HOMILETICS OF THE PARAGRAPH.—*Verses* 26, 27.

The spirit temple.—We are exhorted to remember St. Chrysostom's celebrated saying with reference to the Shekinah, or ark of testimony, the visible representation of God among the Hebrews, " The true Shekinah is man " ; the essence of our being is a breath of heaven, the highest being reveals itself in man. The highest being reveals itself in the spiritual man, for the divine Spirit helps our general weakness, suggests and leads our devotions. A radiancy of glory illuminates that human temple in which the Holy Spirit dwells.

I. **Man is still a temple, but in ruins.**—On the front of the human temple might once be read the inscription, " Here God dwells." But the glory has departed ; the lamps are extinct ; the altar is overturned ; the golden candlesticks are displaced ; sweet incense is exchanged for poisonous vapour ; homely order is turned into confusion ; the house of prayer has become a den of thieves ; Ichabod may be read on the ruins. The divine Spirit must purify the courts, restore the ruins, beautify the desolate places, and make a temple where incense and a pure offering shall arise to the Lord God of hosts.

II. **Believing man is a temple restored.**—It is sad to walk among the ruins of a deserted temple. It is pleasant to see that temple being reconstructed and rising out of its ruins even more beautiful than before. A saved man is a reconstructed temple. The broken carved work is so repaired that it surpasses in beauty the primeval glory ; the altar is re-erected ; the lamps glow with divine light ; the golden candlesticks gleam with heavenly lustre ; sweet incense floats through the aisles ; gracious strains of music rise and swell to the lofty dome.

III. **The believing man is a temple glorified.**—We visit some earthly temples

279

because they enshrine the sacred dust of departed heroes. They are like chapels of the dead. The temple of a believing man enshrines the living. The Holy Spirit glorifies the human spirit by His indwelling and His co-operating agency. We are to be the living temples of a living and indwelling Spirit. The essence of the spiritual man's life is, not a mere breath from heaven, but an abiding and a life-giving influence.

IV. **The believing man is a temple supported.**—Our stone temples are supported by external buttresses. The weakness is repaired by outward appliances. The temples of spiritual humanity are supported by inward appliances. The Holy Spirit is the directing agent. Likewise the Spirit also helpeth our infirmity, helps our general weakness, and makes us divinely strong. Hope is a sustaining grace. The Holy Spirit is a sustaining influence; likewise the spirit also. The human and the divine conjoin to subserve the gracious needs of a spiritual man groaning, sighing, and waiting for the infinite good.

V. **The believing man is a temple inspired.**—We cannot breathe into temples of stone divine yearnings. The Holy Spirit breathes into the temple of the spiritual man glorious aspirations. Our sighings after the infinite good are not our own; they are produced in us by One greater than our hearts. The groanings of the divine Spirit's productions are not the groanings of a creation subject to bondage, vanity, and corruption, but the sighings of a renewed soul for a vaster and a higher life. These groanings tell of the kingdom of God within a man. The poet's song sometimes tells of saddest thought; these groanings sing the poem of God's kingdom established.

VI. **The believing man is a temple where true worship is offered.**—The earthly temple is not built and set apart to be admired as a piece of architecture. The Christian man is not set apart to be the lifeless monument of divine grace. Here true prayer is offered,—no Gregorian chants; no pealing anthems; no angel-voiced boys sweetly warbling words they do not feel; no elaborate prayers either read, extempore or memoriter, for the prayer is unformulated, unexpressed. What a strange worship! Groanings and sighings are heard in the temple— heard not by human ears, but by the divine mind. The divine Spirit in the human spirit maketh intercession. The temple is thus blessedly consecrated.

VII. **The believing man is a temple where divine interpretations are given.** —Our interpretations are often no interpretations. Misleading words are sometimes used to conceal our ignorance. The Spirit's interpretations are real. " He that searcheth the hearts knoweth what is the mind of the Spirit." He knoweth also the true mind of the yearning nature.

VIII. **The believing man is a temple where divine harmonies prevail.**— Here are harmonies not heard by human ears. The human will is made submissive to the divine will. Intercessions are going on within us and above us according to the will of God. A life according to the divine plan is a life of harmony. Temple service conducted by the Holy Spirit has not one discordant element. Let us learn the condescension of God and the true dignity of man. God by His Spirit dwells with and in men upon the earth. The true dignity of man consists in being the habitation of God by His Holy Spirit. Let the lamps of light and of love be ever trim, the one shining with heavenly brightness and the other burning with pious fervour. Let the beauties of holiness adorn the temple. In prayer let us seek to catch the tones of the still, small voice of the indwelling Spirit. Let man open the door of his heart-temple to the divine Seeker. " Behold, I stand at the door, and knock." Can man let Him wait? Behold the desolation, and behold the true Repairer. Behold the discords, and behold the true Harmoniser. Surely man will say, Come in, Thou heavenly Restorer; take full possession of my nature; let my human spirit be the temple, unworthy though it be, for the divine Spirit !

Unutterable groans.—"Groanings that cannot be uttered." It is with the Holy Spirit that we are here brought face to face, or set side by side. As Christ does the whole work *for us,* so the Holy Spirit does the whole work *in us.* He is not visible, nor audible, nor palpable ; but not on that account the less real and personal. Here, it is His way of dealing with us and our infirmities that it is particularly referred to. We are described as feeble men, bearing on our shoulders a burden too heavy to be borne ; He comes up to us, not exactly to take away the burden, nor to strengthen us under it, but to put His own almighty shoulder under it, in the room of (ἀντι) and along with (σνν) ours ; thus lightening the load, though not changing it ; and bearing the heavier part of it with His own almightiness. Thus it is that He "helpeth" (σννανπλαμβάνεται) our infirmities ; making us to feel both the *burden* and the *infirmity* all the while that He helps ; nay, giving us such a kind and mode of help as will keep us constantly sensible of both. This is especially true in regard to our prayers. Here it is that His "help" comes in so effectually and so opportunely ; so that we are made to "pray in the Holy Ghost" (Jude 20), to "pray with all prayer and supplication in the Spirit" (Eph. vi. 18). Let us, then, learn :—

I. **True prayer is from the indwelling Spirit.**—It is He that wakes up prayer in us, both as to its matter and its manner. We knew not what or how to pray.

II. **True prayer takes the form of a divine intercession.**—We have Christ in heaven on the throne, and the Spirit on earth in our hearts, interceding ; Christ pleading for us as if we were one with Him, the Spirit pleading in us as if we were one with Him and He with us.

III. **True prayer often takes the form of groans.**—The longings produced in us by the indwelling Spirit are such as cannot give vent to themselves in words. Our hearts are too full ; our voice is choked ; articulation is stifled ; we can only groan. But the groan is true prayer. Man could not interpret it ; we ourselves do not fully understand it. But God does. "He knows the meaning of the Spirit's 'groans'" (Baxter). For thus we groan with the rest of a groaning creation ; and all these groans are at length to be heard and fully answered. 1. *Put yourself into the hands of the Spirit,* for prayer and everything else. 2. *Grieve not the Spirit.* He is willing to come to you, and take up your case ; but beware of grieving Him. 3. *Pray much.* Pray in the Spirit. Delight in prayer. Cherish the Spirit's groans.—*H. Bonar.*

SUGGESTIVE COMMENTS ON VERSES 26, 27.

Prayer.—True prayer is not pestering the throne with passionate entreaties that a certain method of deliverance which seems best to us should be forthwith effected ; but is a calm utterance of need, and a patient, submissive expectance of fitting help, of which we dare not define the manner or the time. They are wisest, most trustful, and reverent who do not seek to impose their notions or wills on the clearer wisdom and deeper love to which they betake themselves, but are satisfied with leaving all to His arbitrament. True prayer is the bending of our own wills to the divine,

not the urging of ours on it. When Hezekiah received the insolent letter from the invader, he took it and "spread it before the Lord," asking God to read it, leaving all else to Him to determine, as if he had said, Behold, Lord, this boastful page. I bring it to Thee' and now it is Thine affair more than mine. The burden which we roll on God lies lightly on our own shoulders ; and if we do roll it thither, we need not trouble ourselves with the question of how He will deal with it.—*Maclaren.*

The Spirit helps in our groaning. —The Holy Spirit, by means of the gospel which explains the meaning of the death of Christ, makes us conscious of God's love; and thus gives us the confidence of children, and elicits the cry, My Father God. Since this cry is the result of the Spirit's presence in our heart, it is the cry both of our own spirit and of the Spirit of God. It is uttered amid weariness and sorrow. Our present circumstances are utterly at variance with our true dignity as revealed by the Spirit. The contrast makes the present life a burden, and compels us to look forward eagerly to the day when we shall take our proper place as the sons of God. Our dissatisfaction with present surroundings, and our yearning for something better, give rise to inward groanings which words cannot express. Since these are a result of the filial confidence with which the Spirit by His own presence fills our hearts, they are the groans both of our own spirit and of the Spirit of God. Whatever is at variance with our dignity as sons is at variance with His purpose touching us. Whatever hinders the full development of our sonship hinders His work in us. Hence our yearning is the expression of His mind concerning

us. Therefore by moving us to yearn He groans and yearns within us. By so doing He helps us in a way in which we specially need help. Left to ourselves, we should desire and long for that which is not good. But now we are sure that our longings are according to God's will, for they are wrought in us by His Spirit. Again, since our longings express the purpose of the Spirit, they plead with God for their own fulfilment. To gratify our yearnings is to accomplish the purpose of His own Spirit—*i.e.*, of Himself. Therefore by filling our hearts with His own desires and purposes concerning us the Spirit within us cries to the Father above us. This cry the Father cannot refuse to answer. That the voice is inaudible does not lessen its efficacy; for God hears the silent wish of the heart. He knows the purpose for which the Spirit has come to dwell within us—knows it to be in accordance with His own will, and to be a purpose of blessing for men whom God has made specially His own. In short, our own yearnings, resulting as they do from the presence of the Spirit, are themselves a pledge of their own realisation.—*Beet.*

MAIN HOMILETICS OF THE PARAGRAPH:—*Verse* 28.

Consoling knowledge.—St. Paul was keenly alive to suffering. He sympathised with a suffering creation. And yet, as he stands amid suffering and desolation, a divine joy lights his countenance. Confidence sustains his soul. Whence this joy and confidence? The answer is found in the text. Amid the pains and perplexities of life we must trust in the unfailing wisdom and goodness of God. We must keep alive the consoling knowledge " that all things," etc.

I. **What is man's highest good?**—What is the highest good, not for man as a physical being, as a mere resident of earth, but for man in the greatness of his nature, in the importance of his destiny? The highest good for man is to love God, to be conformed to the image of God's Son, to be beloved of God. The degree of man's perfection is the measure of his loving God. The highest good is not material, but spiritual; the highest good is being developed both in the time-life and in the eternal existence.

II. **The dispensations of God promote the highest good.**—Man must work longer and more carefully in erecting a structure which is to endure than in making one which is soon to be taken down. The highest good has reference to the future, and the work to be done in the present must have reference to that future. The mystery of death-bed repentances must be left; the greatest lives on earth have been trained in rough schools and have tasted long experiences.

282

God will harmonise the short Christian life of the dying thief on earth and the rough, long pathway of an apostle. Most have many experiences in the Christian course. Crosses and losses are not unknown. But true to their work, and work only for our good, are the cross providences of God. The temple of the human soul is to be built up to a glorious perfection, and the builders are the trials, sufferings, and afflictions with which God's children are visited. Winter's storm as well as summer's sunshine tempers the oak; the snow that means death to the unwary traveller fertilises the land; the hurricane that shatters the building scatters the noxious vapours; the ocean that entombs brave men and fair women sends its bracing ozone on to the land. Thus all things, fair and foul, smooth and rough, prosperous and adverse, joyous and painful, are working for the greater perfection of those that truly love God.

III. **The twofold guarantee.**—This is found in the words " to them that love God, to them who are the called according to His purpose." Our love to God is the outcome of His love to us. The human love is responsive to the divine love. True love to God will bring to light the good that may be concealed by the repulsive drapery of adversity. True love from God will evoke good out of seeming evil. The love of God broods over a groaning universe, and will turn the groans into hymns of praise. And surely the love of God specially watches over the beloved. God's love can pierce the prison wall, and give glad songs to the prisoners for the truth's sake. God's love can visit the chamber of suffering, and smooth the pillow for the aching head and give heaven's light in nature's darkness. Love called, and love obeyed. Love called the human soul to divine heights. Shall love, backed by wisdom and power, leave the beloved to be destroyed by the strokes of adversity? Shall unchangeable love call, and then forsake? The purpose of divine love is that the beloved walk in the realm of perfect love; and this purpose cannot fail. Heaven and earth may fail, but divine purpose must stand. This knowledge is consoling. This confidence is sweet. " We know," and by the sustaining power of that knowledge Paul showed himself the world's great hero. Not-knowledge may be the boasted creed of some. Paul's knowledge has in it divine consolations. We know, and we walk calmly and peacefully through the unknowable. We know that all things are working together for our good, and we work joyfully towards the infinite good and repose on the infinite love.

Ver. 28. *The discipline of sufferings.*—Sufferings are either the result of our own folly or such as could not have been foreseen by us.

Why does God allow latter to happen? These answers have been suggested : God ignores man's affairs (Hinduism); God only cares for a few men (Eclecticism); God is not quite almighty (Dualism). None of these can be *Christian's* answer. *His* answer is to be gathered from this passage.

Bible nowhere says that our *comfort* or our *pleasure* is God's chief care ; but it does teach that our *good* is. (Be careful not to confuse these things.) God wishes our *happiness*, our *holiness*—not comfort or pleasure.

The *good* of pain, privation, suffering, bereavement. They correct evil, prevent evil, develop character (merchant, soldier), produce sympathy, promote brotherliness, promote enterprise (severe climates have energetic people), prepare for eternity. Example : *David* is at his *best* amid *adversities*, at his *worst* amid *comforts*.

A reservation in the statement " to them that love God." Notice : No sorrow leaves us where it found us ; it drives us from God, or brings us nearer to Him. Examples : The remorse of Judas ; the remorse of Peter.

Resolution : To look on every trouble as a test and turning-point.—*Dr. Springett.*

Ver. 28. *All things working for good.*—St. Paul believes that there is a purpose, that there is an end, towards which events are tending. It looks at first sight like a faith rather than the conclusion of an argument. Reason alone might arrive at an opposite conclusion. How can we see a providential guidance, a divine plan of any kind, in the bloody game which chiefly makes up what we call history? How in those failures of great causes, in the enervation and degradation of civilised peoples, which make philosophers like Rousseau look back with fondness to the age of barbaric simplicity? It is true enough that the purpose of God in human history is traversed, that it is obscured, by causes to which the apostles of human despair may point very effectively; and yet here, as ever, we Christians dare to say that we walk by faith where sight fails us, as elsewhere, and we see enough to resist so depressing a conclusion as that before us—to know that the course of events is not thus fatal, thus desperate. We believe in a future; we believe that all moves forward, through whatever failures, through whatever entanglements, to a predestined end, and that each race, each generation, each particular class in each society, does its part, whether we can accurately estimate that part or not, towards promoting that end.

"All things work together for good." For what kind of good? The glory of the Master and Ruler of all? No doubt they do. As nothing exists without His permission, so the very forces of evil itself will have, against their own bias and bent, to do His will and secure His triumph. He would not be God if it could be otherwise. But this is not what the apostle here says, nor does he go so far as to say that all things actually work together for the good of all human beings; for clearly our experience tells us that they do not. Who would say that his wealth was for the good of the debauchee, that his power is good for the selfish despot? It may be true enough that in the original design all things, all circumstances, were strictly designed to work together for the good of all; but man must be something else to what he generally is if he is in this sense to inherit all things, if nothing that happens is to harm him, if he is to find in all around him sources of blessedness and strength. "All things work . . . that love God." Not God's glory merely, but the good of those that love Him, is the object of His providence. Surely the child is not guilty of outrageous pride when it turns to its mother with an instinctive confidence that she will nourish and protect it; and it is the childlike that is one of the highest moral instincts in us, which leads us to believe that "like as a father . . . that we are but dust." Our Lord was careful to assure His followers that in the world they would have tribulation, and to proclaim the blessedness that would attend temporal failures. What is the "good" of which the apostle speaks? It is real, absolute —it is eternal good. It is the good of the soul rather than the body, the good of the eternal world rather than the present world. Why is it that all things are said to "work . . . that love God"? Because such love, and it only, can transform all circumstances into blessings. No life is made up of such commonplaces that each cannot be made, by this love, to sparkle with the highest moral interest. No misfortunes are so great that they cannot be built into the steps of the staircase by which souls mount to heaven. The soul which loves the imperishable can never be doomed to a real disappointment. Social or political trouble may teach us unselfishness. Religious controversy or the advance of unbelief may teach us earnestness. Probably they touch some of us far less nearly than the joys and sorrows of our private lives.

Much may be done in an hour which will last for ever. "If a thousand years are as one day before the eternal God, so surely one day may be a very eternity to the soul of man. Spiritual revolutions within the soul, the deepest changes for good or for evil, have no appreciable relation to time. Intensity, not duration, is the measure of their importance." God grant us to pray with all our hearts that, as He has prepared for them that love Him such good things as pass our understanding, so He will pour into our hearts such love towards Himself that we, loving Him above all things, may obtain His promises, which exceed all that we can desire, through Jesus Christ our Lord !—*Canon Liddon.*

SUGGESTIVE COMMENTS ON VERSE 28.

All things for the best.—The first point to be spoken of is *the excellent privilege of God's children,* that all things shall work together for the best ; both good and evil shall turn to their happiness. The reason stands thus : All things shall work together for the best to them that *love God.* Therefore all afflictions, crosses, and vexations whatsoever that betide such persons shall work together for their good ; and for this cause all God's servants must learn patiently to bear and cheerfully to undergo poverty or riches, honour or dishonour, in this world. *The first sin of all,* which hath gone over whole mankind and is spread abroad in every one of us, this by God's mercy and our repentance proves to all believers a transcendent good, for the fall and sin of the first Adam caused the birth and death of the Second Adam, Christ Jesus, who, notwithstanding He was God, took upon Him the nature of man, and hath made us by His coming far more happy than if we had never fallen. Neither would God have suffered Adam to have fallen but for His own further glory in the manifestation of His justice and mercy and for the greater felicity of His servants in Christ their mediator. And it is good we should have something within us *to make us weary of the world,* else when we have run out our race we be unwilling to depart hence. Now our bondage to this natural corruption serves exceedingly to make us mourn for our sinful disposition and hunger after our God, to be joined with Him, as we see in St. Paul's example (Rom. vii. 24), where, finding the rebellion of his nature and the strife that was in him, the flesh lusting against the spirit and the spirit against the flesh, he cries out,

saying, " O wretched man that I am ! who shall deliver me from this body of death ? " and seeketh to God in Christ for mercy straight. For the evils *of body,* such as sickness and diseases of all sorts, which daily attend our houses of clay, God by means hereof acquaints His children with their frail condition, and shows them what a little time they have to provide for eternity, thereby driving them to search their evidences and to make all straight betwixt Him and them. Outward weaknesses are oft a means to restrain men from inward evils. God usually sanctifies the pains and griefs of His servants to make them better. The time of sickness is a time of purging from that defilement we gathered in our health. We should not be cast down so much for any bodily distemper as for sin that procures and envenoms the same. That is a good sickness which tends to the health of the soul. Now the causes why all things do work together for the best to them that love God are these—viz., It is God's *decree, manner of working,* and *blessed covenant.* It is the *foundation of the covenant of Christ Jesus.* The second cause why all works together for the best to believers *is the manner of God working in things,* which is by contraries. He bringeth light out of darkness, glory out of shame, and life out of death. We fell by pride to hell and destruction, and must be restored by humiliation to life and salvation. Christ humbled Himself, being God, to become man for us, and by His death restored us to life. When our sins had brought us to greatest extremities, even then were we nearest to eternal happiness. *There is nothing in the world that to God's servants is absolutely evil, because nothing is so ill but some good may be raised out of it;* not as it is an evil, but as it is governed and mastered by a supreme cause. Sin is of all evils the greatest, and yet sinful actions may produce gracious effects through God's ordering and guiding the same. *A child of God is truly happy in the midst of all misery.* —*Sibbes.*

God's sovereignty and man's freewill declared.—The "calling" here and elsewhere spoken of by the apostle is the working in men of "the everlasting purpose of God, whereby (before the foundations of the world were laid) He hath constantly decreed by His counsel secret to us, to deliver from curse and damnation those whom He hath chosen in Christ out of mankind, and to bring them by Christ to everlasting salvation" (Art. XVII. of the Church of England). To specify the various ways in which this calling has been understood would far exceed the limits of a general commentary. It may suffice to say that on the one hand Scripture bears constant testimony to the fact that all believers are chosen and called by God, their whole spiritual life in its origin, progress, and completion being *from* Him; while on the other hand its testimony is no less precise that He willeth all to be saved, and that none shall perish except by wilful rejection of the truth. So that on the one side God's sovereignty, on the other man's freewill, is plainly declared to us. *To receive, believe, and act on both these is our duty and our wisdom.* They belong, as truths, no less to *natural* than to revealed religion, and every one who believes in a God must acknowledge both. But all attempts to *bridge over the gulf between the two are futile* in the present imperfect condition of man. The very reasonings used for this purpose are clothed in language framed on the analogies of this lower world, and wholly inadequate to describe God regarded as He is in Himself. Hence arise confusion, misapprehension of God, and unbelief. I have therefore simply, in this commentary, endeavoured to enter into the full meaning of the sacred text whenever one or other of these great truths is brought forward, not explaining either of them away on account of possible difficulties arising from the recognition of the other, but recognising as fully the *elective and predestinating decree of God* where it is treated of, as I have done in other places *the freewill of man.* If there be an inconsistency in this course, it is at least one in which the nature of things, the conditions of human thought, and Scripture itself, participate, and from which no commentator that I have seen, however anxious to avoid it by extreme views one way or the other, has been able to escape.—*Alford.*

MAIN HOMILETICS OF THE PARAGRAPH.—*Verses* 29—31.

The unseen and the seen.—The believer who has fled for refuge to lay hold upon the hope set before him has strong consolation. St. Paul looks both before and behind: he looks behind to a past eternity, and before to a coming eternity, if to the word may be applied before and after and behind. Eternity and time are conjoined in the believer's welfare. He is thus a creature of large surroundings. St. Paul seeks to inspire all believers with holy confidence. This confidence is begotten by a contemplation of :—

I. **The things that are unseen.**—"Foreknow," foreordained. Accurately speaking, the words "before" and "behind" cannot be applied to Him who is from everlasting to everlasting, who dwells in one eternal now. What it is for a God to foreknow we cannot tell. Can time words and time processes be applied to eternal conditions? Thus are suggested the limitation of human thought and the inadequacy of human language. How glibly we speak and write about divine foreknowledge and foreordination; and yet with what humble reverence should we tread the sacred ground! We can only tunnel through the mountains and find ourselves in darkness. Our rushlights cannot reveal the rich treasures and glorious mysteries. Whatever the words mean, they must mean a richness of divine love and wisdom beyond our conception. Let the words thus speak to our inmost hearts and beget sweet confidence.

II. **The things that are unseen working in the seen.**—Foreknowledge and foreordination are the precedents. Calling, justification, glorification, are the consequents. The precedents are unseen, unknown; the consequents are seen, are known. With the inner eye we see the divine processes working in the human soul. We are not called upon to stand in a past eternity and read the divine decrees. Paul's wisdom is vaster than ours, and he leaves the *fores* in a sweet vagueness. Are we called? Are we justified? Are the processes of life plainly tending to our glorification? Then let us have holy confidence; let us rejoice in the mercy and leave the mystery.

III. **The revealed purpose.**—That Christ might have a position of dignity; that all God's redeemed might have outward and inward grandeur. The position of dignity the firstborn of many noble brethren. These conformed to the moral image. If with the freedom of some we applied human words to the divine, we may say that God had a lofty ideal for humanity. That ideal was the human-divine Man who for a short space glorified Palestine. In Christ's earthly life, in its moral purity and glory, we read the divine ideal set forth in the revealed purpose of God. Christ begets confidence and inspires manhood.

IV. **The revealed purpose fulfilled in part.**—The actuals have not reached the ideal; but there have been some wonderful accomplishments. How marvellously near St. Paul himself came to the perfect image of God's Son! In the modern Church how marvellously near was the sainted Fletcher of Madeley! Many Christlikenesses are walking the earth to-day, but our vision is so imperfect that we cannot see the close resemblances. Are we being transformed and conformed? Are Christlike lineaments being drawn in our moral natures? Is the evil being eliminated? Is the good getting universally prevalent? Is the divine hand shaping our moral nature? Is there the foretaste and pledge of glorification? Then the triumphant challenge, "If God be for us, who can be against us?" What a large *if*! It rises beyond the bounds of the material universe; it touches Omnipotence. "If God be for us, who can be against us?" Who can wage successful war against the Omnipotent? Who can confute Omniscience? If we did not know better, we might suppose that some moderns were the omniscients, while God was only in mental darkness. Creatures of a day presume to teach Him who inhabits eternity. The irony of the position! Do angels smile at human folly? Angelic pity checks the tendency. But why should we start and tremble for the ark of God? There should be no nervous worry about him who can sing, "If God be for us, who can be against us?"

True conformity.—By the "image" of Christ is here meant the "moral character" of Christ. And what a character was that! Goethe says, "I esteem the four gospels to be thoroughly *genuine*, for there shines forth from them the reflected splendour of a sublimity proceeding from the person of Christ, and of as divine a kind as was ever manifested upon earth." Rousseau confesses, "If again the life and death of Socrates are those of a sage, the life and death of Jesus are those of a God." And, to quote only the words of a more recent witness, who can be charged neither with intellectual deficiency nor with excess of religious sympathy—the late Mr. Mill—"Whatever else may be taken from us by rational criticism, Christ is still left a unique figure, not more unlike all His precursors than all His followers—a divine person, a standard of excellence and a model for imitation, available even to the absolute unbeliever, and can never be lost to humanity." In the entire conformity to the character of Christ there is:—

I. The complete satisfaction of the human soul.—In all moral existences there is an *ideal character*; a felt disagreement to this ideal is moral misery—agreement is alone moral satisfaction. The cause of all the moral misery in human souls is conscious discordance with this ideal. The character of Christ is this ideal. Souls can conceive of nothing higher, can desire nothing higher. They feel that if they live up to it, they shall be filled with all joy and peace. Only as men approximate to this ideal they grow in power, rise in dignity, and abound in satisfaction. Thank God that we have this ideal so exquisitely and fully wrought out in the life of Jesus Christ. He was incarnate virtue.

II. Harmony with the human race.—The human race is sadly divided; it is severed into numerous contending sections. The human house is divided against itself and cannot stand. The human body has not only its limbs amputated, but they are rattling one against another, and all against itself. It writhes with anguish. A reunion is essential to its health and peace and vigour. But what can unite men together? Universal conformity to rituals or doctrines, to political and ecclesiastical standards? Such conformity would be no union. Universal conformity to the image of Christ would unite the race. Let all men be Christlike, and all men will love one another. When all men become Christlike, and not before then, will hostile passions cease to flow, bloody wars terminate, all contentions cease, all men embrace each other as brethren and be "gathered together" in Christ as members to one body directed by one will. If you would divide men, preach doctrines and policies and ceremonies. If you would unite them, preach Christ and the moral grandeur of His character.

III. The grand purpose of the gospel.—What is the grand aim of the gospel? To give men theological knowledge and material civilisation? No; it does this, but does something infinitely grander—it gives men the character of Christ. It is to create us anew in Christ Jesus in good works. It is to inspire us with the Spirit of Christ, without which we are none of His. "Follow thou Me." This is the burden of the whole gospel. Where the gospel does not do this for man, it does nothing of any lasting value; where it does this, it does everything. Are we like Christ? This is the testing question.

IV. The supreme duty of life.—What is our supreme duty? Assimilation to Christ. This, the grandest duty, is the most practical. 1. *We are made by imitation.* 2. *Christ is the most imitable of all examples.* (1) The most admirable; (2) the most transparent; (3) the most unchanging; (4) the most intimate. He is always with us—in the lives of good men, in the writings of true books, in the records of the evangelists, in the pulsations of conscience, in the influences of Providence.—*Homilist.*

SUGGESTIVE COMMENTS ON VERSES 29—31.

God for us.—"If God be for us, who can be against us?" Here is first a ground laid, and then a comfort built upon it. The ground that is laid is, "If God be with us." When he saith, "If God be with us," he doth not put the case, but lays it as a ground. "If God be with us," as indeed He is with all His, in electing them, in calling them, in working all for their good, in glorifying them after, etc.—"if God be with us," as He is, then this comfort is built upon this ground: "Who shall or can be against us?" For the first the ground that is laid is, that *God is with His children.* Indeed, He is with the whole world—He is everywhere; but He is with His Church and children in a more peculiar manner. The soul is spread in the whole body, but it is in the brain after another manner, as it understands and reasons. God is everywhere; but He is not everywhere comforting and directing and sanctifying, nor everywhere giving a sweet and blessed issue. God gives Himself variety of names, as there are variety of our distresses. Are we in misery? God is a rock, a shield, a tower of defence, a buckler—He is all that can be said for comfort. He is with us in His attributes and sweet relations, and all sweet terms that may support our faith, that whatsoever we see comfortable in the creature we may rise more comfortably to God, and say, God is my rock and shield, and my light and defence. And then God is with us in every condition and in every place whatsoever. He is not only a God of the mountains and not of the valleys, or a God of the valleys and not of the mountains, as those foolish people thought (1 Kings xx. 28), but He is in all places and at all times with His. If they be in prison, He goes with them (Acts xvi. 22, *seq.*); he made the prison a kind of paradise, a heaven. In all our affairs whatsoever God is with us. "Fear not," Joshua; "fear not," Moses. What was the ground of their comfort? "I will be with thee." He was with St. Paul in all conditions; therefore He bids him "fear not." The ground of all is His free love in Christ. Christ was God with us first. God, that He might be with us, ordained that Christ should be God with us—" Emmanuel," that He should take our nature into unity of person with Himself. Christ being God with us, that He might satisfy the just wrath of God for our sins, and so reconcile God and us together, He hath made God and us friends. So that this, that God is with us, it is grounded upon an excellent and sound bottom—upon the incarnation of our blessed Saviour. "Who shall be against us?" It is not a question of doubting, or inquisition to learn anything, but it is a question of triumph. He doth, as it were, cast a bank, and bid defiance to all enemies whatsoever. "Who shall be against us?" Let them stand out, Satan and the world, and all Satan's supports; let them do their worst. There is a strange confidence which is seated in the hearts of God's children that they dare thus dare hell and earth and all

infernal; they set God so high in their hearts that they dare say, with a spirit of confidence, "Who shall be against us?" First of all you see, then, that the state of a Christian in this world is an impregnable state and a glorious condition. Here is glory upon glory, from this clause to the end of the chapter: "If God be with us, who shall be against us?" If God gave His Son for us, shall He not with Him give us all things else? There is another glorious speech: "Who shall lay anything to the charge of God's people?" Another glorious, triumphant speech: "Who shall separate us from the love of God" founded in Christ? He loves Christ first and us in Christ as members; and as He loves Him eternally, so He loves us eternally too. Therefore, you see, every way the state of a Christian is a glorious condition. Here is a ground likewise of all contentment in any condition in the world. What can be sufficient to him that God cannot suffice? God, all-sufficient, is with thee; thou canst want nothing that is for thy good. Thou mayest want this and that, but it is for thy good that wantest it: those that fear God shall want nothing that is good. God is fitted for us, and we for Him. He can fill up every corner of the soul; He is larger than our souls: therefore let us be content in what condition soever we are in. God is with us.— *Sibbes.*

Prescience extendeth unto all things, but causeth nothing.—Predestination to life, although it be infinitely ancienter than the actual work of creation, doth notwithstanding presuppose the purpose of creation; because, in the order of our consideration and knowledge, it must first have being that shall have a happy being. Whatsoever the purpose of creation therefore doth establish, the same by the purpose of predestination may be perfected, but in no case disannulled and taken away. Seeing, then, the natural freedom of man's will was contained in the purpose of creating man (for this freedom is a part of man's nature), grace contained under the purpose of predestinating man may *perfect* and doth, but cannot possibly *destroy*, the liberty of man's will. That which hath wounded and overthrown the liberty wherein man was created as able to do good as evil is only our original sin, which God *did not predestinate*, but He foresaw it, and predestinated *grace* to serve as a remedy. Freedom of operation we have by nature, but the ability of *virtuous* operation by grace, because through sin our nature hath taken that disease and weakness whereby of itself it inclineth only unto evil. The natural powers and faculties therefore of man's mind are, through our native corruption, so weakened, and of themselves so averse from God, that without the influence of His special grace they bring forth nothing in His sight acceptable; no, not the blossoms or least buds that tend to the fruit of eternal life. Which powers and faculties notwithstanding retain still their natural manner of operation, although their original perfection be gone; man hath still a reasonable understanding, and a will thereby framable to good things, but is not thereunto now able to frame himself. Therefore God hath ordained *grace* to countervail this our imbecility, and to serve as His hand, that thereby we, which cannot move ourselves, may be drawn, but *amiably drawn*. If the grace of God did *enforce* men to goodness, nothing would be more unpleasant unto man than virtue; whereas contrariwise there is nothing so full of joy and consolation as the conscience of well-doing.—*Hooker.*

Object of predestination.—The object of predestination is glory: I see thee believing; I will therefore that thou be glorified like My Son. Such is the meaning of the *decree.* The predestination of which Paul speaks is not a predestination *to* faith, but a predestination to glory, founded *on* the prevision of faith. Faith is in a sense the work of God; but it contains a factor, in virtue of which it reacts on God, as an object reacts on the mind which takes cognisance of it—this is the free adherence of man to the solicitation of God. Here is the element which distinguishes the act of foreknowledge from that of predestination, and because of which the former logically precedes the latter.—*Godet.*

Christ the firstborn. — God set up Christ as the great standard or standing copy, according to which all believers should be framed and wrought just like Him : " Whom He did foreknow, He also did predestinate to be conformed to the image of His Son, that He might be the firstborn among many brethren." To the image of His Son; not to the image of the most glorious man that ever was in the world. Not to Enoch, that signal walker with God; nor Noah, the only loyal preacher of righteousness in his time; nor Abraham, God's friend and the believer's father; but His own Son, who was free from all taint of sin. As His perfect purity made Him fit to be a sacrifice to take away sin (1 John iii. 5); to be an advocate to plead against sin, "Jesus Christ the righteous " (1 John ii. 1),—so also to be the idea according to which all believers should be framed. Now the weakest habitual grace is an inchoative conformity to Christ as well as the strongest, and as well as that which is perfected in heaven, and hath in its own nature all the parts of that grace which is in Christ—as an infant in his body hath the lineaments of his father, as well as the grown son.—*Charnock.*

MAIN HOMILETICS OF THE PARAGRAPH.—*Verse* 32.

Love resolving, performing, and revealing.—The argument employed by St. Paul in this verse is one from the greater to the less. It is a self-evident principle that the greater implies and includes the less. The greater gift is that of the well-beloved Son; the less is the " all things " which are included. If all things are given into the Saviour's hands, then it must be true that believers are in possession of those things which are placed in the Saviour's hands for their spiritual well-being. Christians have many fears and doubts by the way, but they are groundless, for Jesus Christ is surely the pledge of a Father's love and watchful care. Jesus Christ is the gift which proclaims that every other needful blessing will be bestowed. Yes, Jesus is the name fraught with joy and comfort to every child of God. Let us, then, no longer doubt that infinite Goodness which gave the unspeakable gift. Let us no more dream that there can be poverty in the divine bestowals, for God "spared not His own Son, but delivered Him up for us all."

I. **Love resolving.**—When did divine Love resolve not to spare the Well-beloved? Before the mighty rocks, which count their formative processes not by years but by centuries, began their solidifying methods—before time commenced its solemn march—in the vast æon of the eternal past did divine Love consider man's ruined condition, and resolve not to spare the greatest gift which either time could know or eternity could produce. Here it may not be improper to contemplate divine Love pausing between love for the Son and pity for the fallen sons of men. What a momentous pause! What a solemn hiatus! What an important crisis! When the owner of the vineyard sent servant after servant to the husbandmen, and they slighted the opportunities of regaining a forfeited position, and beat the servants, and sent them away empty, it would have been natural for the lord of the vineyard to have said to himself, What shall I do? Shall I at once destroy those wicked husbandmen, or shall I venture among them my son and heir? God saw the people in ruin and in rebellion—saw with forevision. The interests of His moral government required the sacrifice of the well-beloved Son if a way of escape were to be devised for the rebellious. God loves the race, and yet He loves the Son. Between these conflicting loves, which shall prove victorious? Will God spare the Son, and not spare the race? Will God spare the race, and not spare the Son? What a solemn pause in the considerations of infinite Love! What will divine Love resolve? The pause, if there were a pause, was not of long continuance. What marvellous love to mankind is here revealed!— a love stretching, not only over the long centuries of time, but through the æons of eternity—a love anticipating the vast need before it had arisen! Infinite Love resolves to give up the dearest object of love to promote the welfare of guilty creatures. God has many sons both on earth and in heaven. Some are God's sons by creation, and some in a higher sense by obedience to the divine commands, by submission to the righteous will of the Eternal, by the possession and manifestation of God-like qualities. The patriarchs are God's eldest sons in time, who with giant-like mien walked the green carpet of the newly made earth—holy men of old who "spake as they were moved by the Holy Ghost." Patriarchs, seers, prophets, kings, priests, apostles, reformers, and martyrs are God's noble sons; but none of the noblest born and most highly gifted of earth would be adequate to the requirements of eternal righteousness. Angels and archangels are the sons of God. We cannot tell the period of their birth. They came forth in a manner inexplicable to our finite understandings. But they reflect the glory of the Eternal, partake in the highest degree of the divine nature, are clothed in light, are all good and pure. Here surely may be found a messenger who could become incarnate and conduct the race out of sin's darkness into the dazzling light of eternal righteousness. No. All are willing, but not one is fully qualified. God resolves to give neither the noblest of earth's great sons nor the brightest seraph who dwells with unshrinking spirit and calm delight near the eternal light, but His own well-beloved Son.

II. **Love performing.**—Divine resolution is coincident with divine performance. There may be an interval, but no hesitation. There is neither time nor space to the Infinite, so that the word "coincident" has a wider and different meaning in the divine vocabulary from what it has in the human. There is cause and effect in human affairs; but can the same be predicated of divine affairs? What are the words "antecedent" and "consequent" to Him unto whom all things, past, present, and future, are present as in one group! Oh, how inadequate is human language when we discuss divine movements! We must content ourselves with the remark that with God to resolve is with Him to perform. *God delivered up His Son to become incarnate.* Divinity enshrined itself in the temple of our humanity. How great an act of love to the human race was that when God gave up His Son to become a man amongst men!—not merely a man amongst the richest, wisest, and noblest of mankind, though He was noblest of all—not a man to be fondled on the lap of luxury, to be crowned with the laurels of fame, to wield the sceptre of power, to revel in the light region of fancy where glowing visions entrance the soul, to glide sweetly down the pearly waters amid enchanting landscapes and gentle gales that waft to the senses richest music—but a man despised and rejected, "a man of sorrows and acquainted with grief." God delivered up His Son so completely that He seemed to leave Him in solitude and sickness of heart, in weariness, thirstings, and hungerings. God is the father of the clouds, and yet He permitted Him to thirst who came to remove the moral thirst of mankind; God clothes the valleys with corn and feeds the young ravens when they cry, and yet He left Him to hunger who came to be bread from heaven for starving men. How complete the deliverance we gather from that mournful scene on Calvary when Jesus cried out, "My God, My God, why hast Thou forsaken Me?" How mysterious a revelation of divine love to the race have we in the crucifixion of the Son of God! This is indeed a profound mystery that God should seem to love His people so well as to forsake His only begotten Son. There is in the mediatorial scheme a combination of loves. We see both the love of God and the love of Jesus working and uniting in the great scheme of redemption. God "spared not His Son," and how the words impress themselves on the mind! God "delivered Him up for us all," and what a deliverance we had in that solemn hour—the world's one hour amid the almost countless hours of time—when the heavens gathered blackness and the stable earth reeled in sympathy with the divine Sufferer! These words do not set before us the act of an unfeeling father, but the deed of One whose name and whose nature is love. God "spared not." What do the words import? The word "spare" in this connection acquires new and untold significance. God did not refuse to deliver up His Son. What an appalling deliverance! Is a God capable of sacrifice in our sense of the word? If so, what a sacrifice when He delivered up His Son! Is a God capable of grief? If so, a burst of grief must have disturbed the divine repose when the Saviour's cry on the cross pierced the heavens and reached the heart of infinite Love. If ever the music of heaven were hushed, if ever a cloud were brought over and darkened the joy of the celestials, if ever there were an oppressive silence around the throne of the Infinite, it was when Jesus trod alone the winepress of His last earthly suffering.

III. **Love revealing.**—It may seem strange that God, who is sovereign Lord of all, should have a feeling to spare and yet should overcome the emotion. If in this mysterious work of human redemption it may be declared that even Christ pleased not Himself, so we say with becoming reverence that God pleased not Himself in delivering up His Son, except in so far as He desired to show His great love unto rebellious men, and thus win them back from sin and uphold the interests of His moral government. Here in the passage we have the unlimited nature of divine love revealed. The gift of Jesus Christ Himself is a clear demonstration of the vastness of divine love; but we may understand

292

it more perfectly and feel it more vividly by expanding the apostle's thought that God's great gift of Jesus implies the gift of all things. How boundless are those words! Imagine, if we can, a limit to all things, and then may we hope to comprehend the overpowering vastness of divine love. Grasp, if we can, the mighty range expressed in the simple words "all things"; let us travel, if we can, where all things terminate—let us soar on eagles' wings and scale the heights, fathom the depths, and get below their influence; and then may we trust to be able to comprehend with all saints what is the breadth and length and depth and height of that love which passeth knowledge. Science has not yet found out all the things which are even in the visible creation, and which are waiting the time of their discovery; and of those things which have been already revealed it is scarcely too much to say that one human mind cannot tell them all by name; and as yet they are not all arranged in satisfactory scientific order. All the things of science, philosophy, politics, religion, nature, revelation, the past, the present, and the future—all the things in this world of ours, and all the things, if need be, of those myriad worlds which are but guessed at by the imagination of man—are for our spiritual welfare. There can be no greater charter than this. It surpasses every other charter of blessings. We can stand nowhere out of the reach of God's blessed "all things." The atmosphere appears to be an all-pervading force, and almost everywhere are we surrounded by its beneficial agency; but God's "all things" go even further, and are more enduring. Friends may depart, relatives may become indifferent, even my father and my mother may forsake, riches may take to themselves wings and fly away, a good name may be blighted, earthly prospects may be withered and dead, health may decline, sickness may shatter and death destroy, but God's "all things" abide to the Christian amid every change and in the midst of every disaster. We may fancy that sickness and trouble take us out of the sphere of God's "all things," but they are a more blessed part than we now believe of God's "all things." We may suppose that, when struggling alone in the valley of temptation, we are far from God's "all things," but let us be assured that even the feeling of desolateness which has overwhelmed and chilled may be God's way of blessing. We may imagine, when on the bed of death and the devil tries and we experience divine hidings, that God has forsaken us; but God is there in the darkness though we see Him not. God giveth all things with the gift of His Son. What shall we more say? "For all things are yours; whether Paul, or Apollos, or Cephas, or the world, or life, or death, or things present, or things to come; all are yours; and ye are Christ's; and Christ is God's." What more could we have? Who would not be a Christian, if he be a man of such large possessions as those indicated by St. Paul? "All things are yours." We are rich beyond the power of human estimation. There are no title-deeds in this world which map out such extensive possessions.

SUGGESTIVE COMMENTS ON VERSE 32.

"*How shall He not,*" etc.—Looking back at the cross, Paul triumphantly asks, If God has already bestowed the one gift, compared with which all other gifts are nothing, how can we conceive Him to withhold any other gift? The words "all things" are limited only by God's wisdom and love. Whatever God withholds He withholds for our good. And the reasons which now prompt Him to withhold some pleasant things will soon pass away. The time is coming when these words will be fulfilled in their widest sense. "Also with Him." The gift of all things is pledged by the gift of His Son; and therefore the other gifts are inseparably linked with the one gift. "Give by His grace": as in i. 11, v. 15. "All things". recalls the same

293

words in ver. 28. When we see God giving up to shame and death His Son, that we may surround that Son in everlasting glory, we are sure that God will keep back from us no good thing, and that the ills of life, which result from the withholding of things commonly supposed to be good, are really blessings in disguise.—*Beet.*

The best being given, the least will not be denied.—It was a greater act to be in Christ reconciling the world than to be in Christ giving out the mercies He hath purchased. If He hath overcome the greatest bank that stopped the tide of mercy, shall little ones hinder the current of it? Justice and the honour of the law were the great mountains which stood in the way. Since those are removed by a miraculous wisdom and grace, what pebbles can stop the flood to believing souls? If God be the author of the greatest blessings, will He not be of the least? If He hath not spared His best treasure, shall the less be denied? It is the apostle's arguing, "He that spared not His own Son, but delivered Him up for us all, how shall He not with Him also freely give us all things?" He cannot but be as free in the least as He was in the greatest; there were more arguments to dissuade Him from that than there can be to stop His hands in other things. If anything you desire be refused by God, know it is your Saviour's mind you shall not have it; for God would deny Him nothing of His purchase. Oh, how little do we live in the sense of those truths! how doth our impatience give God the lie, and tell Him He is a deadly enemy, notwithstanding His reconciling grace!—*Charnock.*

God given His best.—"What shall we then say to these things?" Having spoken of the love of God, such a sea of love came upon Him as overcame Him. And what follows? "He that spared not His own Son, but delivered Him up for us all, how shall He not with Him also freely give us all things?" Do but consider the words a little. "He spared not His Son"; the word implies that God was sensible enough what it was to give such a Son, it implies the greatest tenderness; He felt every blow, yet He gave the blows Himself. Even as when of loving parents it is said they do not spare their children, when out of the greatest tenderness they do correct them. And He is said not to "spare His own Son," who is more His own Son than our sons can be, which are differing from ourselves, but Christ of the same substance with Himself. And the truth is, none knows how to value the gift but God Himself that gave Him, and Christ Himself that was given. And He did do it freely too: the word that is used, χαρίσεται, imports it; with Him He shall graciously give us; He gives Christ, and all things else freely with Him; therefore it implies that He gave Him up freely also. Abraham gave his son, but he was commanded to do it; but God gave His Son freely, and it pleased the Lord to bruise Him. And to show that this was the greatest gift that God could give, or had to give, what follows? Now He had given us His Son, Take all things else, saith He. I do not value heaven now I have given My Son for you; therefore take that. I do not value grace, nor comfort, nor creatures: take all freely, even as you had My Son. "If He spared not His Son," saith He, "how shall He not with Him also freely give us all things?" He hath given the greatest pawn of His love, in giving us His Son, that ever was.—*Goodwin.*

MAIN HOMILETICS OF THE PARAGRAPH.—*Verses* 33, 34.

Christ's intercessory work.

Christian faith teaches: 1. Christ's ascension to God's right hand; 2. Christ's session at God's right hand. "Right hand" = place for the *nearest* to the king, place for the *dearest* to the king (1 Kings ii. 19).

What is He doing there?—1. *Ruling* His people. The Father rules *universe*; the Son rules *human race*, whom He redeemed, until, after final judgment, He resigns that rule to the Father (1 Cor. xv. 24-28). 2. *Helping* His people. Cases in point: St. Stephen (Acts vii. 55, 56); St. Paul (Acts xviii. 9-11); St. John (Rev. i. 9-17). 3. *Interceding* for His people (Heb. vii. 25). "Ever." Examples: In "stony ways" of trouble; in "tangled paths" of perplexity; in "sandy wastes" of spiritual weariness; in "flowery glades" of comfort and ease; on "steep precipices" of great temptation; on "slippery paths" of human praise. Illustrate by various stages in ascent of a Swiss mountain.

What is He doing for you now?—*E.g.*, if steadfast; if doubting; if sinning; if tempted; if sorrowful for sin.—*Dr. Springett.*

SUGGESTIVE COMMENTS ON VERSES 33, 34.

Election a prominent principle.—Let me say at once that I am not so vain as to suppose that I can clear up the mystery of this profound subject, which has exercised the ablest minds of Christendom in all ages; I can but offer some thoughts to my readers which may help to remove some difficulties in their minds, as they have in my own. Election, whatever it may mean, is a very plain doctrine of Scripture, and a very broad, clear fact in nature and in history. Let me know God's decrees, and I joyfully accept them as my standards and rules of · judgment. But I do not feel the same reverence for man's version of God's decrees. Let us consider, first, that something like election is a very prominent principle in all God's acts and ways. It looks out on us from every page of Scripture; it is the key to the order of nature and of human history. What does it mean, this election unto eternal life? It is stated distinctly in Scripture that certain of the human race are "God's elect," and are what they are in character, privilege, and destiny in virtue of this sovereign, ordaining will of God. They were elect, but not unto themselves, or for the sake of their own future; but rather for the sake of the work which their position of privilege would enable them to do for mankind: elect to a great ministry, a noble leadership—to the front rank in the field, to the high place in the strain, to all that may purge a man of narrow, partial, and selfish imaginations, and

make him understand that "God's elect" must catch the Spirit of *the elect One*, who came into this world, "not to be ministered unto, but to minister, and to give His life a ransom for many." It will readily be conceded that the question of election would present an entirely different aspect if any human being had prevailed to look into the book of the divine decrees. There are difficult and apparently conflicting statements in Scripture on this profound subject, arising from the fact that the whole sphere of it is beyond the grasp of our thought. The doctrine of a personal election must, in the very nature of things, have a mystery in the heart of it. God's foresight, foreordering of the course of human affairs, and man's freedom, conflict with each other in a way which puzzles the understanding. God had His eye on the great human mass, when He selected and separated a people, a people to be called by His name and live to His praise; and His chief interest in that elect people, we gather from prophetic scriptures, was the hope, of which they were the children, that through them the great human world would be blessed and gathered into the everlasting kingdom of the Lord. The fundamental principle—I should rather say the radical vital force—in all the higher developments of the spiritual life in man is the movement of the divine Spirit on the springs of our thought and will. The divine life in the soul is that in which the divine will and the human are one. Marriage, the marriage of souls, is the highest, the divinest ordinance of God in the sphere of this life. The elect are elect to live this life, which standeth in the knowledge of the eternal God—elect as Israel was elect to a very lofty level of life, to a high strong strain of duty, to live like Him the symbol of whose life was the cross. The apostolic epistles are full of "election." Why? Because the men to whom and of whom they were written were full of the life. Wonder not that such "saints" as these clung sternly to their election. Wonder not that it was to an elect host that the trumpet note rang from the apostle's lips. It meant for them that God was with them against a world which would else inevitably crush them—that God would uphold their lives and their ministry till the world which hated and trampled them beneath its grinding heel should break forth in praises to the Lord. These elect ones are just the front rank in the army, those in whom the divine call to the post of toil and peril has found an eager response. The election standeth in the manifestation of a life. To draw the world to Christ is the mission of the elect soul.—*Baldwin Brown.*

MAIN HOMILETICS OF THE PARAGRAPH.—*Verses* 33—39.

Christian certainties.—St. Paul observed due proportion. He could treat of high themes, and make them bear upon the practical aspects of the Christian life. His contemplation of unutterable things never leads him away from the plain way of practical duties. Such is the perversity, such the onesidedness of our nature, that we fall into error and mischief by the contemplation of certain aspects of truth. Much damage has been done by the doctrine of election, or perhaps rather by our handling of the doctrine. Let us seek rightly to divide the truth, and make life harmonious. God's elect moved in the realm of Christian certainties, and were the world's true heroes. A certain grasp of and belief in divine truth, divine love, Christ love, will support in life's trials and perplexities. The man who knows nothing, who is not certain about anything, will never possess the martyr spirit, will never be noted for his heroism. Amongst this list of St. Paul's certainties let us note :—

I. **A good answer.**—"Who shall lay anything to the charge of God's elect? It is God that justifieth." The answer is unanswerable. God, as moral governor, alone has a right to justify ; and if He justify, then all counter-charges are vain. Who shall come between God and the redeemed soul? God has not delegated the prerogatives of His moral government to any other being in any realm whatever. If the criminal be acquitted in the earthly court, the same charge cannot be repeated. If the earthly judge have justified, who can lay a charge? God has justified, and the believer is for ever acquitted.

II. **A good plea.**—"It is Christ that died," etc. The voice of Calvary hushes the voice of condemnation to the believer. If that be not sufficient, a chorus of voices silences any reproving voice. The voice of rejoicing angels as they welcome the triumphant Mediator declares that there is no condemnation to those who are justified in consequence of Christ's finished work. The voice of the eternal Father, as He commands the pearly gates to open wide so that the King of glory may enter, proclaims that there is a way of justification. The sweet voice of an interceding Mediator at the right hand of God speaks perfect peace to the heart that fully receives the divine method of justification by faith. The evil one may condemn by laying a charge. Conscience may condemn by marshalling sins in dread array. An over-sensitive nature may condemn by saying, I am too bad to be forgiven. The plea is not our goodness. We admit our badness, and plead the counteracting goodness of the Saviour. If our badness crucified Christ, should not that crucifixion remove our badness? Shall Christ die to redeem us and then leave us in slavery, if we are willing to be ransomed? The dying Christ, the risen Christ, the interceding Christ, must remove every sentence of condemnation.

III. **A good force.**—Who shall separate us from the love of Christ? Love is power. Human love is a mighty force, in many cases stronger than death. While love reigns man cannot successfully assert the mere materialism of human nature. Love is a force not generated by material molecules. Protoplasm as the root and love as the product is a growth too marvellous for our narrow creed. If human love be strong, what about Christ's love? Christ's love to the Christlike and the love of the Christlike to Christ is a good force that must prove more than conqueror, victorious in the conflict, and yet, notwithstanding the severity of the struggle, showing a large reserve of power. A good force is that which overcomes attacks in all conceivable forms. Love triumphs in the conflict; the conqueror love must be crowned with the tokens of universal empire.

IV. **A good persuasion.**—What a sweep does Paul's persuasion take! He takes an immense survey. He stands upon a pinnacle higher than that to which Satan took Jesus. And from that sublime height Paul marshals before his mind all possible opposing powers, and yet possesses the strong persuasion that they shall all be vanquished. Neither material nor moral forces, neither seen nor unseen powers, neither the enacted past nor the unenacted future, shall triumph over the love of God. Above the heights it soars. Beneath the depths it shines. In the play and march of present events it guides. All that can be imagined in the future cannot be outside the range of its controlling agency. Death with its terrors and its mysteries, life with its modern complications, with interests and obstructing forces that are beyond the conception of the far-reaching mind of a Paul, shall not be able to hinder the triumphant course and purposes of the love of God which is in Christ Jesus our Lord. There centres the love of God; and to that centre all must radiate. Kingdoms shall flourish and decay, nations rise and fall, philosophies babble and be silenced, asserting sciences succeed one another in each succeeding age, religious systems triumph and then succumb to other religious systems, but divine love will hold on its course and be the universal victor. The hope of the world is the love of God which is in Christ Jesus our Lord. This is our holy apostle's favourite refrain. So ends another glorious strain of his heavenly music; so ends that burst of eloquence that even heathens admired; so ends that mine of celestial treasure, the eighth of Romans.

Ver. 37. "*More than conquerors.*"—Christians are more than conquerors. In patiently bearing trials they are not only conquerors, but more than conquerors —that is, triumphers. Those are more than conquerors that conquer with little loss. Many conquests are dearly bought; but what do the suffering saints lose? Why, they lose that which the gold loses in the furnace, nothing but the dross. It is no great loss to lose things which are not—a body that is of the earth earthy. Those are more than conquerors that conquer with great gain. The spoils are exceedingly rich: glory, honour, and peace, a crown of righteousness that fades not away. In this the suffering saints have triumphed; not only have not been separated from the love of Christ, but have been taken into the most sensible endearments and embraces of it. As afflictions abound, consolations much more abound. There is one more than a conqueror when pressed above measure. He that embraced the stake and said, "Welcome the cross of Christ, welcome everlasting life"; he that dated his letter from the delectable orchard of the Leonine prison; he that said, "In these flames I feel no more pain than if I were upon a bed of down"; she who, a little before her martyrdom, being asked how she did, said, " Well and merry, and going to heaven "; those that have gone smiling to the stake, and stood singing in the flames,—these were more than conquerors (Matthew Henry).

I. Christians are more than conquerors of the evolutionist school.—We do not object to evolution as the mere act or process of unfolding or developing. But we must ever be against the baseless theory that generation is the separate development of a pre-existent germ—not only the separate development, but the self-development, as if the pre-existent germ were a creative agent, and produced from itself far more than itself contained. The conjurer would have us believe that his hat contained all that he brings forth to the amazement of his audience. The evolutionist conjurer makes his pre-existent germ marvellously potential and productive. The conjurer's hat requires the presence of an intelligent and manipulating agent. The modern conjurer, if he is to be abreast with the times, must let his marvellous hat work on the theory of self-development. How the hat came there and was produced is a question not yet settled. Perhaps the hatter might give us some information. How the pre-existent germ came into existence the evolutionist does not yet accurately declare. He has produced the germ from the depths of his own inner consciousness, and his imaginative faculty has invested it with more than miraculous powers. The evolutionist of this kind is a conqueror whose conquests are a very doubtful gain. We still hold that the man is a conqueror, more and better far than such conquerors, who believes in an unseen and intelligent and all-powerful Creator who produced all pre-existent germs, and who works in and through and by all developing processes. It gives to the man the power to be more than the mere earth conqueror to believe that there is a God, that there is a divine Being, not only making for righteousness, but possessing righteousness, being Himself righteous. The human son becomes divinely strong in the sweet thought and inspiration of the divine fatherhood. The believer is in so far made more than a conqueror from the fact that he can still rejoice in this world as God's world, that on every side he gladly beholds the traces of a Father's hand. How much strength is obtained when the man can consider the heavens in their beauty, the moon and the stars in their midnight glory, the green earth with its sights and sounds of sweetness, the towering mountains, solemn and silent, watching like huge sentinels, the booming ocean with its mighty tones that speak of infinite power, and can say, My Father made them all! The footsteps of an infinite Worker have left clear footprints. The voice of the greatest Creator may be everywhere heard.

II. Christians are more than conquerors of the pessimistic school.—The pessimist is a creature to be pitied, and it is difficult to suppose that he will make a conqueror of any kind. Take the life of faith and hope out of a man, and he will be soon cast a wasted wreck on the sands of time. He is a poor creature who regards the present system or constitution of things as radically bad. We are not blind to the badness of things. There is a great deal which we would desire altered ; and yet, at the same time, we must feel that there is much to please, to delight, and to encourage. In spite of the pessimist's gloomy views, notwithstanding the presence in this world of much that makes us think of a groaning creation, we can rejoice in the mere material beauty of God's world. God has not made this planet a mere working world. If He had intended this planet to be a sphere where no pleasures were to be tasted, then the flowers need not have bloomed with beauty or exhaled their fragrance—perhaps no need of flowers at all; the birds need not have been dressed in beautiful plumage, nor have trilled forth their liquid music; no need for the richness of the fig tree, the refreshing influences of the vine, the sweetness of the olive, the strength and the beauty of the cattle in the fields and the folds, or the supplies given by the flocks and the herds. God provides us with senses by which we may drink in pleasure, and He adopts outward things to minister to such pleasure. The outward world of nature and the inward world of thought and feeling declare that we are to accept with thankfulness God's material blessings, and take hopeful views. We can rejoice in the moral forces at work in God's world. We have had, and still have, our hours of gloom. The pessimist's mood is not altogether foreign to our natures. We have groaned over abounding evil, and sorrowed over the prosperity of the wicked. Still, though cast down, we are not destroyed. We see hope for humanity. The moral forces at work are travelling on towards the final goal of the emancipation of the race from all moral evil, and the elevation of the race to a true plane of righteousness—a plane where healthy breezes blow, where the celestial sunlight quivers, where stalwart natures show a divine strength and dignity, where transfigured creatures stand forth in glory and hold sublime converse, and where all things and beings glisten with the sunlight of heaven.

III. Christians are more than conquerors of the optimistic school.—By all means let us take a hopeful view of things ; but do not let us fall into the error of believing that the present system of things is the best possible or conceivable. We can conceive much that might be improved. We can travel back in thought to a world where no sin reigned, where no disorder triumphed. That man will not be a true conqueror who does not take large and correct views of the universe and of man. The beauty of the world may inspire with joy. The sorrows of the world may prevent us being intoxicated with joy. Yes, there is much to sadden—much in a materialistic aspect. The beauty of the flower will fade— its fragrance will give place to offensive odour. The enchanting song of the bird will be silenced ; the fig tree will cease to bloom ; the vine will not give its fruit ; the sweetness of the olive will fail ; the flocks will be cut off from the fold. There will be no herd in the stalls ; a silence will reign where once was heard the lowing of the oxen ; the war-horse may tread the golden grain beneath his feet ; the shattering cannon may blow to pieces our goodly structures ; fire may lick up our treasures ; floods may desolate our lands If there be no room for pessimism, there is no room for optimism with reference to the material or moral aspect of the universe. The natural outcome of the optimistic creed is to rest in things as they are, and thus he cannot make a moral conqueror. The natural outcome of a correct creed is to see things and persons as they are, and work on and pray on towards improvement. He that conquers in the moral sphere is the best conqueror.

IV. Christians are more than conquerors of the stoical school.—A man who is indifferent to either pleasure or pain cannot pretend to be a conqueror in the moral sphere, which is being more than a conqueror in the material sphere. The man who feels and yet does not succumb to his sorrowful feelings is the man to make a more than conqueror. Some people are rendered hard and callous by the wear and tear of time. But a poor fakir, reduced to an almost senseless block of slightly animated flesh and bones, is not a conqueror to command admiration or provoke emulation.

V. Christians are more than conquerors of the despairing school.—The old warrior wept as he stood amid the ruins. Alexander is said to have wept because there were no more worlds to conquer. The old saint will not weep amid the ruins, but will lift up the triumphant shout, "We are more than conquerors." It is a glorious sight to see a good man struggling with adversity, and endeavouring to bear patiently the ills of life ; but surely it is a more glorious sight to see a good man rejoicing in adversity, and making difficulties minister to highest delights and greatest perfectness. As we rise to the mountain top to obtain a more extended view of the surrounding and far-stretching beauties of the landscape, we rise by means of those old vegetable and animal forms of which that mountain is composed; so let the believer rise even by means of the wreck and ruin of his earthly good things to obtain a better view of moral and spiritual beauties. Thus may we become " more than conquerors through Him that loved us." If we are to be more than conquerors, God must be our abiding portion, Christ must be our lasting possession. Love from Christ and love to Christ must be the sustaining force. The Lord is an abiding portion for an ever-enduring soul. When the pulse has given its last throb, when the eyes have taken the last fond look, when earthly things fail to affect, then the soul may rejoice in the Lord in sweeter realms. God, in His threefold nature, is ours now, and ours when all earthly shapes are wrapped in eternal gloom—when the sun's brilliant face is hidden in the last darkness, when the stars have rushed from the vault of night, and when all things are under a collapse prefiguring the blessed change and final glorification. Oh to feel that the Lord is ours at this present time, ours by adoption and grace, ours by participation of the divine nature, ours by the sweet might of an indwelling love!

Ver. 34. " *Who is he that condemneth ?* "—These are bold words; but they are not the words of presumption or excited feeling. The apostle is arguing for the believer's eternal security, and he draws arguments from God's eternal purpose, God's unchanging love, God's omnipotent power, and from the believer's justification. The challenge is thrown down after a process of sound reasoning. And, moreover, it is backed up by four arguments based on the mediatorial work of Christ. Who can condemn? No one can, *first* because Christ has died, *second* because Christ has risen, *third* because Christ reigns, *fourth* because Christ intercedes. Four arguments why the believer cannot be condemned.

I. **Christ's death.**—Might be viewed as an act of love or a confirmation of His doctrine; but it is only as an atonement for sin that it becomes a plea for the removal of condemnation. It is the great fundamental fact of Christianity, the basis of reconciliation between God and man, the ground on which sin is remitted. But Christ, by dying, not only made satisfaction for sin and established a new relation between God and man, but He purifies His people from sin by the cleansing efficacy of His blood. Faith in the atoning sacrifice sets free from condemnation, and washing in the cleansing fountain frees the soul from the stains and pollution of sin, while the indwelling of the Spirit secures complete sanctification.

II. **Christ's resurrection.**—This is a further and even more decisive security against condemnation. " *Yea, rather.*" As if he had said, Why refer to death? It is a sign of impotence rather than strength; and if death had been the last act of Christ, the believer's prospects would have been bounded by the grave. But Christ, by rising from the grave, proves that death has no power over Him or His. He opened up a vista beyond the grave, and gave assurance of a life hereafter. His resurrection was necessary to complete the work of His redemption. If He had not risen, what hope for us? The grave would have held us; death would have been master. But now death is swallowed up in victory. There is life for the soul of man in a risen Saviour; and there is life for the body, for as surely as Christ rose, so shall we. Ours is not the gospel of a dead Christ, but of a living Saviour; and as He lives to die no more, so shall we.

III. **Christ's exaltation.**—" Who is even at the right hand of God." He is exalted to that position that He might consummate the work of redemption. All power is His, and that power He uses to promote the work He has begun. From His throne He rules in every realm, and all who take refuge beneath His throne are safe. With such an almighty Saviour the redeemed may well exclaim, Who is he that condemneth? If the King of kings be for us, who can be against us ? Why fear condemnation when an omnipotent Saviour rules the world ? "No weapon formed against thee shall prosper, and every tongue that shall rise in judgment against thee thou shalt condemn." "The eternal God is thy refuge, and underneath are the everlasting arms."

IV. **Christ's intercession.**—"Who also maketh intercession for us." The crowning security against condemnation. This part of His mediation has special reference to the sanctification of His people, and He prays that their faith fail not. In the absence of any plea founded on their own works or character, He presents to God the merits of His own finished work. This, as a plea, is all-powerful with God. No advocate ever had a stronger plea, and no advocate ever pled with more success ; for every cause He undertakes He will carry successfully through. It is a blessed thought—before the throne we have One to plead for us. Into the holiest He has entered ; but He will come forth again. Our present Intercessor will be our future Judge. Give Him your cause to plead now ; and when He comes the second time, you will lift up your head in joy, because your redemption draweth nigh. All accusers will be silent then. No condemnation. No separation. "Who is like unto thee, O people saved by the Lord ? "—*D. Merson, B.D.*

Vers. 38, 39. *Life and death as antagonists of love.*—An able and ingenious critic proposes to read the sentence thus : "I am persuaded that neither death, nor *even* life, shall be able to separate us from the love of God which is in Christ Jesus our Lord." We all admit that, in a certain sense, both life and death are antagonists of love ; but if we were asked, Which is the greater antagonist of the two ? most of us would answer, Death, not life ; whereas it is life, not death, which is the more fatal to love. Life is often the death of love ; whereas death commonly gives love new life. Indeed, our whole conception of death is in much unchristian. We do not realise that for us death means life and immortality, a nearer access to God, a clearer vision of His glory, a more perfect participation of His grace and peace. We have so little faith in God and in His wise ordering of the universe that we can hardly rise to the level of Schiller's fine saying : "Death happens to all, and cannot therefore be an evil." We persist in taking it as an evil, although we know, or might know, it to be a good. Death *is* an antagonist of love ; for it takes from us those whom we have learned to love ; it separates us from them ; we can no longer see them, and serve them, and lavish on them the tokens and proofs of our regard. But though death severs us and them, does it sever love ? does it extinguish, or even lessen, our affection for them ? Does it not rather enlarge, refine, consecrate, our love for them ? They take a special dearness and sanctity in our thoughts. We forget what was lacking or imperfect in them. We think only of their better qualities, of how good they were, how staunch, how kind. There never was a true love yet which did not conquer death, which death did not hallow and deepen and make perfect. But does *life* always elevate love and enlarge and sanctify it ? And as with human love, so with love divine. *Death* cannot detach our love from God ; for it brings us closer to Him ; it shows Him to us more nearly as He is, and thus constrains us to a more profound, a more constant and perfect love for Him. But *life*, with its anxieties and toils, its trials and temptations, is for ever calling our thoughts away from Him, moving us to forget or to distrust Him, inspiring us with motives, affections, aims, alien and opposed to His will. If we have any true spiritual life in us, is not this the very burden of our confessions and prayers, that we do not love Him as we ought and would, that we are not like Him, that while He is righteous we are unrighteous, while He is kind we are unkind ? The more we consider and know ourselves the more welcome to us grows St. Paul's persuasion, that neither death, nor even life itself, is able to separate us from the love of God—that, if our love for Him be cordial and sincere, however imperfect it may be, it will nevertheless conquer all the opposing forces of life no less than all the powers of death. And God has none of those defects of character which alienate us from men and women whom once we held dear. To love Him is to love righteousness, truth, goodness, gentleness, peace. He is at once the ideal and the incarnation of all excellence. We shall never, as we grow wiser and more experienced, discover anything in *Him* to lessen our love and reverence. Weak and inconstant as we are, we may at least *hope* that He will not suffer even life itself to separate us from Him. Our love to God depends on His love for us. If His love can be shaken, our love will not abide. And therefore we may be sure that—somewhere in the passage, perhaps throughout it—St. Paul meant to speak of God's love for us as well as of our love for Him. And of His love for us we need have no doubt, whatever becomes of ours for Him. Even at our best we may only be able to *hope* that our love will not change; but we may know beyond all question that, even if our love should change, God's will not. The dead live to Him; to Him the living die. We are the offspring of His love; for if He did not love us and design our good, why should He have made us? And those He once loves, He loves for ever. He *is* love; He cannot deny Himself. God's love cannot change, however we may change. We shall want God's love when we die and when we pass through death into the unknown region which lies beyond its farther bourn; but how can we hope to have it then and to delight in it, if we put it from us now and shrink even from thinking too much about it? If we are sensual, sordid, selfish here, how can we hope all at once to relish that which is spiritual, noble, unselfish, divine? Before we can be persuaded that nothing shall ever separate us from the love of God, and can rest and delight in that persuasion, we must be made partakers of the divine nature. If we ask, But *how* is this divine character to be attained? how are we to rise into this better self, and to mortify that in us which is base and sordid and selfish? St. Paul replies, You must have the love of God shed abroad in your hearts. Now many of these New Testament phrases about "love" have sunk into so mere a cant, that possibly St. Paul's answer is no answer to many of us, simply because it conveys no clear thought to our minds. But if we consider it for ourselves, if we shake it free from the cant that has stuck to it, we shall find it a very clear and pertinent answer. Does any other passion change and elevate and hallow character like this, and make a man a new and a better man? When it is not a mere craving of the senses, nor even a mere longing for sympathy, nor both combined— *i.e.*, when it is true, genuine love—does it not conquer the baser and selfish instincts of the soul? has it not again and again drawn men from their vices, lifted them out of the mire of self-indulgence, and infused into them a power which has transfigured their whole nature and raised them into a pure and noble life? But if love for man or woman can thus change and elevate the character, why not love for God? He is fair and kind, He is tender and true, He is wise and strong, beyond our farthest reach of thought. If we have any love of excellence, we cannot but love Him so soon as we really know Him. If we would know God and love Him, we must find Him in Christ, in that perfect Man—so strong and yet so gentle, so true, yet so tender—who moves before us in the gospels.—*S. Cox.*

SUGGESTIVE COMMENTS ON VERSES 33—39.

The Judge makes the judged righteous.—"As by the offence of one judgment came upon all men to con-demnation; even so by the righteousness of One the free gift came upon all men unto justification of life." Here,

302

most evidently, "justification" imports "a judicial clearing from the imputation of guilt," in the precise sense and degree in which "condemnation" imports "a judicial ascertaining of guilt." The same appears in Rom. viii. 33, 34 : "Who shall lay anything to the charge of God's elect? It is God that justifieth. Who is he that *condemneth* ?" Here is the idea of a judicial process, a tribunal, a person arraigned. Now if by the condemnation spoken of we may understand an act of the Judge making the accused guilty by the infusion of unrighteousness, then also by the justification spoken of we may understand an act of the Judge making the accused righteous by an infusion of righteousness, and so justifying him. But if this would be absurd in the former case, so must it be in the latter.—*M'Ilvaine.*

"Justified" means "accounted righteous."—It is evident that the Holy Ghost useth this word "justification" to signify "a man's being accounted or declared not guilty of the faults he is charged with"; but in that respect a good and righteous person, and that too before some judge, who in our case is the supreme Judge of the world. And this is plainly the sense wherein our Church also useth the word in her Articles, for the title of the Eleventh Article runs thus : "We are accounted righteous before God," etc., which clearly shows that in her sense to be "justified" is the same with being "accounted" righteous before God; which I therefore observe, that you may not be mistaken in the sense of the word as it is used by the Church and by the Holy Ghost Himself in the Holy Scriptures, like those who confound "justification" and "sanctification" together as if they were one and the same thing, although the Scriptures plainly distinguish them ; "sanctification" being "God's act in us whereby we are made righteous in ourselves," but "justification" is "God's act in Himself whereby we are accounted righteous by Him and shall be declared

so at the judgment of the great day." —*Beveridge.*

"Justify" to pronounce just.—The word "justify" doth not signify in this place to make just by *infusing* a perfect righteousness into our natures (that comes under the head of "sanctification begun here in this life," which, being finished, is "glorification in heaven"), but here the word signifieth to pronounce "just, to quit and to discharge from guilt and punishment," and so it is a judicial sentence opposed to condemnation. "Who shall lay anything," saith Paul, "to the charge of God's elect? It is God that justifieth. Who shall condemn ?" Now, as to "condemn" is not "the putting any evil into the nature of the party condemned," but "the pronouncing of his person guilty and the binding him over unto punishment," so "justifying" is "the judge's pronouncing the law to be satisfied and the man discharged and quitted from guilt and judgment." Thus God, imputing the righteousness of Christ to a sinner, doth not account his sins unto him, but interests him in a state of as full and perfect freedom and acceptance as if he had never sinned or had himself fully satisfied. For though there is a power purging the corruption of sin, which followeth upon justifi-ation, yet it is carefully to be distinguished from it, as we shall further show hereafter. *"This for the name of 'justification'; but now for the thing itself, which is the matter first of our justification."* "The matter of justification, or that righteousness whereby a sinner stands justified in God's sight, is not any righteousness inherent in his own person and performed by him, but a perfect righteousness inherent in Christ and performed for Him."— *Ussher.*

Paul's assurance of persevering.—As there is a typical resemblance between that good land which was promised to the Jews and that better country which is reserved for us in heaven, so is there a striking resemblance between those, whether Jews or Christians, who have looked forward to the accomplishment of the promises. We see Moses while he was yet on the other side of Jordan, and Joshua soon after he had arrived on the borders of Canaan, appointing the boundaries of the twelve tribes, settling everything with respect to the distribution of the land, and ordering various things to be observed, just as if they were already in full possession of the whole country without one enemy to oppose them. This appears at first sight presumptuous, but they knew that God had given them the land, and therefore, notwithstanding the battles which were yet to be fought, they doubted not in the least but that they should obtain the promised inheritance. Thus also the apostle, in the passage before us, speaks in the language of triumph on behalf of himself and of all the Christians at Rome, and *that* too even while they were surrounded with enemies and conflicting on the field of battle. It will be profitable to consider: 1. The point of which the apostle was persuaded. This confidence being so extraordinary, let us consider: 2. The grounds of his persuasion. These were twofold—*general* as relating to others, and *particular* as relating to himself; the former creating in him an assurance of faith, the latter an assurance of hope. We notice the general grounds. These are such as are revealed in the Holy Scriptures, and are common to all believers. *The stability of the covenant* which God has made with us in Christ Jesus warrants an assurance that all who are interested in it shall endure to the end. *The immutability of God* is another ground of assured faith and hope. *The offices of Christ* may also be considered as justifying an assured hope of final perseverance. For our Lord did not assume the priestly, prophetic, and kingly offices merely to put us into a capacity to save ourselves, but that His work might be effectual for the salvation of all whom the Father had given to Him; and at the last day He

will be able to say, as He did in the days of His flesh, "Of those whom Thou hast given Me, I have lost none." If He is ever living on purpose to make intercession for them, and is constituted head over all things to the Church on purpose to save them, then He will keep them; none shall ever pluck them out of His hands, nor shall anything ever separate them from the love of God. *The particular grounds.* A humble, contrite person that is living by faith on the Son of God and maintaining a suitable conversation in all his spirit and conduct, *he* may conclude himself to be in the love of God, and be persuaded firmly that nothing shall be able to separate him from it. He then stands in the very situation of the apostle as far as respects his own personal experience, and therefore may indulge the same joyful hope and persuasion that he shall endure unto the end. Nor need he be at all discouraged on account of his own weakness, since the more weak he feels himself to be the stronger he is in reality, inasmuch as he is made more dependent on his God. In a word, an assurance of *faith* respecting the accomplishment of God's promises to believers should be maintained by all, since His word can never fail; but an assurance of *hope* respecting our own personal interest in those promises should rise or fall according to the evidences we have of our own sincerity. Address those who know nothing of this joyful persuasion, and those whose persuasion accords with that of the apostle.—*Simeon.*

A double righteousness.—In the Scripture there is a *double* righteousness set down, both in the Old and in the New Testament. In the Old, and in the very first place that righteousness is named in the Bible: "Abraham believed, and it was *accounted* unto him for righteousness." A righteousness *accounted*! And again (in the very next line), it is mentioned, "Abraham will teach his house *to do righteousness*." A righteousness *done*! In the New

Testament likewise. The former in one chapter (Rom. iv.) no fewer than *eleven* times : *Reputatum est illiad justitium*—" It is accounted to him for righteousness." A *reputed* righteousness ! The latter in St. John : " He that *doeth* righteousness, is righteous." A righteousness *done* ! Of these, the latter philosophers themselves conceived and acknowledged ; the former was proper to Christians only, and altogether unknown in philosophy. The one is a quality of the party ; the other an act of the judge declaring or pronouncing righteous. The one, ours by influence or *infusion* ; the other, by *account* or imputation. *That both these there are, there is no question.— Andrewes.*

Works do not justify.—Truth it is, that our works do not justify us, to speak properly of our justification : that is to say, our works do not merit or deserve remission of our sins, and make us, unjust, just before God ; but God of His mere mercy, through the only merits and deservings of His Son Jesus Christ, doth justify us. Nevertheless, because faith doth directly send us to Christ for remission of our sins, and that by faith given us of God, we embrace the promise of God's mercy, and of the remission of our sins —which things none other of our virtues or works properly doth, therefore the Scripture useth to say, that faith without works doth justify. And forasmuch as it is all one sentence in effect to say, Faith without works, and only faith, doth justify us ; therefore the old ancient Fathers of the Church, from time to time, have uttered our justification with this speech, " Only faith justifieth us " ; meaning no other than St. Paul meant, when he said, " Faith without works justifieth us." The right and true Christian faith is, not only to believe that Holy Scripture, and all the aforesaid articles of our faith, are true, but also to have a sure

trust and confidence in God's merciful promises, to be saved from everlasting damnation by Christ ; whereof doth follow a loving heart to obey His commandments. And this true Christian faith neither any devil hath, nor yet any man, which in the outward profession of his mouth, and in his outward receiving of the Sacraments, in coming to the church, and in all other outward appearances, seemeth to be a Christian man, and yet in his living and deeds showeth the contrary.— *Homily of Salvation.*

Imputation of righteousness. — *Imputation* of righteousness hath covered the sins of every soul which believeth ; God by pardoning our sin hath taken it away: so that now although our transgressions be multiplied above the hairs of our head, yet being justified, we are as free and as clear as if there were no spot or stain of any uncleanness in us. For it is God that justifieth ; "*And who shall lay anything to the charge of God's chosen ?* " saith the apostle. Now, sin being taken away, we are made the righteousness of God in Christ ; for David, speaking of this righteousness, saith, " *Blessed is the man whose iniquities are forgiven.*" No man is blessed, but in the righteousness of God ; every man whose sin is taken away is blessed : therefore every man whose sin is covered is made the righteousness of God in Christ. This righteousness doth make us to appear most holy, most pure, most unblamable before Him. This then is the sum of that which I say : *Faith doth justify*; justification washeth away sin ; sin removed, we are clothed with the righteousness which is of God ; the righteousness of God maketh us most holy. Every one of these I have proved by the testimony of God's own mouth ; therefore I conclude, that faith is that which maketh us most holy, in consideration whereof it is called in this place *our most holy faith.—Hooker.*

ILLUSTRATIONS TO CHAPTER VIII.

Ver. 1. *Saved by the union-jack.*—When I was in Havana there was one evening a great row in the streets, and a man was killed. Every one ran away except an Englishman, who did not see why he should run off, but stopped to do what he could for the wounded man. The city was then, as it often is, under martial law, and in a few minutes a party of soldiers came up and walked the Englishman off. He was tried then and there by a sort of drum-head court-martial, and condemned to be shot the next morning at eight o'clock. He managed to get the news conveyed to the English consul, and at a quarter to eight o'clock next morning the consul appeared in his coach-and-four, uniform, cocked hat and sword, all his orders on, etc. The shooting party was drawn out, and the prisoner was there too. The consul walked up to the officer commanding the party, and demanded the life of his countryman. "Very sorry," said the officer, " but I must carry out my orders "; and he showed the warrant signed by the governor. "Well," said the consul, "at least you'll allow me to shake hands with him before he dies." "I can't refuse that," was the reply. On which the consul stepped up to the Englishman, put his hand into his breast-coat pocket, drew out a union-jack, unfolded it, threw it over the man, and then said, "There, now; fire if you dare!" The lieutenant was staggered, the matter was referred to the governor, and the Englishman was saved. The man covered with the union-jack was saved. In Christ Jesus we are free from condemnation. "Who is he that condemneth? It is Christ that died."

Ver. 6. *Dr. Carey and the merchant.*—The soul of the Christian is at anchor; and so he is freed from the cares of fame, or of fortune, or of any other interest upon earth. And with a mind engrossed by that which is spiritual, and without room in it for the anxieties of what is seen and temporal, he in as far as these anxieties are concerned is at peace. This topic may be illustrated from a recorded conversation between Dr. Carey the missionary at Serampore and a wealthy merchant in Calcutta. One of his clerks had determined to give up all the prospects and emoluments of a lucrative situation, and henceforth devote himself to the work of evangelising the heathen. His employer, to whom this looked a very odd resolution, called on Dr. Carey, and inquired from him the terms and the advantages and the preferments of this new life to which a very favourite servant, whom he was exceedingly loath to part with, was now on the eve of betaking himself; and was very startled to understand that it was altogether a life of labour, and that there was no earthly remuneration whatever, that beyond those things which are needful for the body there was not an enjoyment within the power or purchase of money which any one of them thought of aspiring after, that with hearts set on their own eternity and the eternity of their fellow-creatures they had neither time nor space for the working of this world's ambition. There is a very deep interest in such a dialogue between a devoted missionary and a busy, active, aspiring merchant; but the chief interest of it lay in the confession of the latter, who seems to have been visited with a glimpse of the secret of true happiness, and that after all he himself was not on the way to it; whose own experience told him that, prosperous as he was, there was a plague in his very prosperity that marred his enjoyment of it; that the thousand crosses and hazards and entanglements of mercantile adventure had kept him perpetually on the rack, and rifled his heart of all those substantial sweets by which alone it can be purely and permanently gladdened. And from him it was indeed an affecting testimony when, on contrasting his own life of turmoil and vexation and checkered variety with the simple but lofty aims and settled dependence and unencumbered, because wholly unambitious, hearts of these pious missionaries, he fetched a deep sigh, and said that it was indeed a most enticing cause.—*Dr. Chalmers.*

Ver. 16. *Confidence.*—The celebrated Philip de Morney, prime minister of Henry IV. of France, one of the greatest statesmen and the most exemplary Christian of his age, being asked, a little before his death, if he still retained the same assured hope of future bliss which he had so comfortably enjoyed during his illness, he made this memorable reply: "I am as confident of it, from the incontestable evidence of the Spirit of God, as I ever was of any mathematical truth from all the demonstrations of Euclid."

Vers. 24, 25. *Sir Walter Scott.*—There is pleasure in abiding amid the storm when the anchor of a good hope fastens to the immovable throne of Him in whom is everlasting strength. When Sir Walter Scott was a little boy, he was found sitting on a knoll in a great and terrific thunderstorm. He was lying on his back, listening to the thunder, looking at the lightning, clapping his hands at each successive flash, and exclaiming with glee, "Bonnie, bonnie!" When Christian hope is in lively exercise, elements of delight may be found in the very storm which causes fear.

Vers. 24, 25. *The steadfast boy.*—A gentleman in London, having some business one morning to transact at the India House, took with him his son, then only six or seven years of age. The boy was left at one of the outer doors, with instructions to wait until his father came for him. Having been detained within for some time, the father, under the pressure of his engagements, forgot his son, and left by another door. When he reached home in the evening, the first inquiry of the wife was about the missing child, and then the father recollected all. He at once returned to the India House, and found the obedient boy waiting at his post, where he had waited the livelong day. The eternal Father never forgets, but sometimes to our shortsightedness He may appear to forget, and then hope comes to our assistance and teaches us to wait in patience the Father's time. Wait through the longest day; wait through the darkest night. The shadows will flee away; the morning of perfect explanation will appear. Sorrow may endure for the night; joy will come in the morning of divine revelations.

Vers. 24, 25. Bedridden for twenty years. —A friend once told us that when visiting a woman who had been bedridden for twenty or thirty years, she said to him, "What a useless creature I am, lying here doing nothing, just a burden to others, and everybody around me actively employed! I wonder how it is that God keeps me so long in the world?" And yet the fact was, as our friend told us, that she was the wonder of all who knew her. They could not think or say enough of her patient, cheerful resignation, her self-forgetfulness, her interest in everything and every one she saw or heard of, her sweetness of temper, her heavenly, Christlike spirit. Her lowly estimate of herself added a charm to her character and life. Her beautiful exemplification of the passive virtues rendered her one of the most useful creatures in the whole parish.

Ver. 26. Gray's teleautograph.—"The Spirit itself maketh intercession for us." Through Christ the Holy Spirit communicates our desires to God and God's grace to us. He speaks our particular wants to God. Professor Gray's teleautograph enables one to transmit his own handwriting by wire to a great distance. What is written in Chicago is reproduced in facsimile in a distant city. It is especially adapted for commercial purposes and the practical work of business men. So God's Spirit reproduces our desires, words, and deeds; and we have a witness in heaven and a record on high: all is spoken in heaven.—*Benignitas.*

Ver. 28. Blessings in disguise.—In every burden of sorrow there is a blessing sent from God which we ought not to thrust away. In one of the battles of the Crimea a cannon-ball struck inside a fort, gashing the earth, and sadly marring the garden beauty of the place. But from the ugly chasm there burst forth a spring of water, which flowed on thereafter a living fountain. So the strokes of sorrow gash our hearts, leaving ofttimes wounds and scars, but they open for us fountains of rich blessing and of new life. Our pain and sorrow, endured with sweet trust and submission, leave us with life purified and enriched, and more of Christ in us. In every burden that God lays upon us there is always a blessing for us, if only we will take it.

" Then Sorrow whispered gently : Take
This burden up. Be not afraid ;
An hour is short. Thou scarce wilt wake
To consciousness that I have laid
My hand upon thee, when the hour
Shall all have passed ; and gladder then
For the brief pain's uplifting power,
Thou shalt but pity griefless men."

Ver. 28. The happiness of suffering.—Dr. Richard Rothe, the eminent German theologian, once said, "There are people who, after experiencing in their youth the happiness of joy, come in their old age to enjoy the happiness of suffering." To superficial thinkers this remark may seem perplexing. But sufficient study of it will reveal a profound meaning in it. Certainly to the Christian there is a happiness which is the outgrowth of suffering as of nothing else, and it is a very real and precious sort of happiness.—*N. F. Boakes.*

Ver. 28. Persuasions and persuasion.—There are many "persuasions" amongst men —there is but one that is of value in the sight of God. A "persuasion" amongst men, when the word is used in a religious sense, means, What denomination in the Church do you belong to?—are you a Baptist, or a Congregationalist, or a Churchman? And a man may belong to any of these, or of the many other denominations or persuasions, and yet not be connected with the great and the right persuasion after all. In terrible agony a soldier lay dying in one of the American hospitals. A visitor asked him, "What Church are you of?" "Of the Church of Christ," he replied. "I mean, of what persuasion are you?" "Persuasion?" said the dying man, as his eyes looked heavenward, beaming with love to the Saviour; "I am persuaded that neither death, nor life, nor angels, nor principalities, nor powers, nor things present, nor things to come, nor height, nor depth, nor any other creature, shall be able to separate me from the love of God, which is in Christ Jesus our Lord." Church membership may exist without Christ membership: the first may be without any life or peace; in the latter there are both.

Ver. 28. The great dome of God's providence.—In the baptistery of the cathedral at Pisa is a wonderful dome. Spacious, symmetrical, composed of the choicest marble, it is a delight to stand beneath and gaze upon its beauties. Thus I stood one sunny April day, when suddenly the air became instinct with melody. The great dome seemed full of harmony. The waves of music vibrated to and fro, loudly beating against the walls, swelling into full chords like the roll of a grand organ, and then dying away into soft, long-drawn, far-receding echoes, melting in the distance into silence. It was only my guide, who, lingering behind me a moment, had softly murmured a triple chord. But beneath that magic roof every sound resolved into a symphony. No discord can reach the summit of that dome and live. Every noise made in the building—the slamming of the seats, the tramping of feet, all the murmur and bustle of the crowd—is caught up, softened, harmonised, blended, and echoed back in music. So it seems to me that over our life hangs the great dome of God's providence. Standing as we do beneath it, no act in the divine administration towards us, no affliction, no grief, no loss which our heavenly Father sends, however hard to bear it may be, but will come back at last softened and blended into harmony, with the overarching dome of His wisdom, mercy, and power, till to our corrected sense it shall be the sweetest music of heaven.—*J. D. Steele.*

Ver. 31. *Luther's faith.*—And for the time to come let us trust in God, that God will be with us if we be with Him, and stick to

Him. Who then shall be against us? Let the devil, and Rome, and hell be all against us if God be with us. Bellarmine goes about to prove Luther a false prophet. Luther, as he was a courageous man and had a great and mighty spirit of faith and prayer, so his expressions were suitable to his spirit. What saith he? The cause that I defend is Christ's and God's cause, and all the world shall not stand against it. It shall prevail. If there be a counsel in earth, there is a counsel in heaven that will disappoint all. God laughs in heaven at His enemies; and shall we weep? And things are in a good way if we can go on and help the cause of God with our prayers and faith that God will go on, and with our cheerfulness and joy that God may delight to go on with His own cause. We may encourage ourselves; though perhaps we shall not see the issue of these things, yet posterity shall see it.

Ver. 37. *The last words of Ignatius.*—Ignatius, who was martyred A.D. 107, said: "Let fire and the cross, let wild beasts, let all the malice of the devil come upon me, only may I enjoy Jesus Christ. It is better for me to die for Christ than to reign over the ends of the earth. Stand firm," he added, "as an anvil when it is beaten upon. It is part of a brave combatant to be wounded and *yet to overcome.*" In losing life he found it.

CHAPTER IX.

CRITICAL NOTES.

Ver. 1. I speak in Christ the truth.—Not to be rendered, "I speak the truth in Christ." The apostle, not as a man merely, but as a member of Christ, in His name, as His apostle.

Ver. 2.—λύπη, ὀδύνη, sorrow and pang.

Ver. 3.—St. Paul considers personal happiness subordinate to the general salvation.

Ver. 4.—The glory, the Shekinah; the covenants frequently repeated; the service of the tabernacle and temple; the true worship of God.

Ver. 5.—" In this passage five distinct assertions concerning our Lord, His incarnation, His existence from everlasting, His supremacy, His divinity" (Dr. Wordsworth). "Although εὐλογημένος is used by Christ, εὐλογητός never is. Had Paul wished to teach in this verse that Christ is God, he might have done so, and put his meaning beyond doubt, by writing ὅς ἐστιν, as in i. 25. Consequently the word ὤν lends no support to the former exposition" (Dr. Beet).

Ver. 6.—ἐκπέπτωκεν, has been void, as לְבָל (Jos. xxi.).

Ver. 7.—κληθήσεται, be named, and obtain celebrity.

Ver. 8.—τέκνα τ. ἐπαγγελίας, for τέκνα ἐπαγγέλμενα, those to whom pertained the felicity promised to Abraham. Heirship of God's blessings derived from the realisation of special promises.

Ver. 13. **As it is written, Jacob I loved, but Esau I hated.**—There is no necessity to soften the "hated" into "loved less"; the words in Malachi proceed on the fullest meaning of ἐμίσησα (Wordsworth). The words refer to temporal conditions (Alford).

Ver. 14.—τί οὖν ἐροῦμεν. Formula used in the Jewish schools; employed by Paul as dealing with Jews.

Ver. 17.—According to Sir G. Wilkinson, the Pharaoh here meant was Thothmes III., not drowned, but overthrown in the Red Sea. Reigned twenty-five years after that event. So Jewish tradition carried on afterwards a vigorous war with the northern nations. Sculptured records of his successes still preserved in the monuments he erected. Gave encouragement to the arts of peace. Founded numerous buildings in Upper and Lower Egypt and in Ethiopia. Made extensive additions to the temples at Thebes. Improved Coptos, Memphis, and Heliopolis by his taste for architecture. From caprice and love of change made columns with reversed capitals at Karnak. The last king of the nineteenth dynasty, Si Pta Menephtha, 'the light of the sun," was not buried in his own tomb, and *may* have been this Pharaoh. Others say Thothmes II. Two astronomical notes of time on contemporary monuments of his successor, Thothmes III., or Rameses the Great, show the accession of the latter and consequent death of the former to have taken place on the Egyptian day answering to May 4-5, 1515 B.C., or, astronomically verified, the twelfth of the second spring moon, the Hebrew second month (*Stones Crying Out*).

Ver. 18.—σκληρύνει, hardens (*indurat*). Pharaoh's heart hardened by God *in fact* by His longsuffering and delay of punishment.

Ver. 23.—ἐνδείκ. applied to wrath as known before, γνωρ. to grace as yet comparatively unknown.

Ver. 25.—Refers not only to the gathering again of the Israelites rejected in the carrying away by Shalmaneser, but also of the Gentiles rejected at the building of Babel; remnants elected from both.

Ver. 27.—Only few out of the ten tribes returned to Judæa; few left by Sennacherib; few brought to Christ.

Ver. 28.—Alford seems to include both promise and threatening in λόγος, and makes the object of the citation a confirmation of "the certainty of the salvation of the remnant of Israel, seeing that now, as then, He, with whom a thousand years are as a day, will swiftly accomplish His prophetic word in righteousness."

Ver. 31.—νόμ. δικ., and not δικ. νομοῦ, because Israel and not the Gentiles had in the economy of mercy a law which taught what was right; law not making righteous, but declaring what is right.

Ver. 32.—ὡς indicates the supposition that their works were good works.

Ver. 33.—The Jews say, "The Son of David, *i.e.*, the Messias, cometh not till the two houses of the fathers of Israel shall be taken away—to wit, the Head of the captivity of Babylon, and the Prince who is in Israel, as it is said, He shall be a stone of stumbling and a rock of ruin to the two houses of Israel, and many of them shall stumble and fall and be broken." And the Chaldee Paraphrast upon the place says thus, "And if they will not obey or receive [Him], My word shall be to them for scandal and ruin to the princes of the two houses of Israel" (Dr. Whitby).

MAIN HOMILETICS OF THE PARAGRAPH.—*Verses* 1—8.

St. Paul's intensity.—St. Paul was a thorough man, and did not believe in half measures. His spirit was always raised to a high degree. If he was opposed to Christianity, he showed himself an opponent to be dreaded. He was an intense persecutor. If he was in favour of Christianity, he showed himself an ardent admirer. The Christian religion has produced no more fervent and devoted adherent. Paul's spirit manifests itself in this opening passage.

I. **The intensity of his defence.**—He declares his truthfulness as one who speaks from the Christ standpoint. The truth in Christ should be the preacher's aim—the truth from Christ, the truth as Christ's ambassador, the truth as from one who is united to the Spirit of truth. Let us get into the light of Christ, and then we shall be delivered from all falsehood, and conscience will bear a true witness. A Christ-enlightened conscience is the only reliable witness. The witness of conscience must coincide with the witness of the Holy Ghost.

II. **The intensity of his love.**—Such was his love that his soul endured the mourning of sorrow and the harrowings of a great pang. His love had the bitter as well as the sweet aspect. All true love has its intense anguish. Jesus loved and Jesus wept; Jesus loved and Jesus sighed. Paul loved, and in consequence had great heaviness and continual sorrow in his heart. Love glides on the pleasant stream. The sun shines overhead; the banks are gay with flowers; sweet fragrances delight the senses; pleasant songs gladden the heart. But love is not always a smooth passage. The wail of distress harrows the soul; storms have to be encountered. Love's earthly portion is often great heaviness and continual sorrow in the heart.

III. The intensity of his patriotism.—He loved his country and his kinsmen according to the flesh. Such was his patriotism that he could wish himself " accursed from Christ." Whatever this may mean, it shows Paul's intensity. He was willing for any sacrifice. He would fall, if by his fall his kinsmen could rise. Too many of our so-called patriots sell their patriotism at a good price. They rise by means of swelling words. They profess self-sacrifice, and live in luxury; the country is impoverished, and they are enriched. What Paul was in words he was in deeds. Self-sacrifice was his creed and his practice. He laboured for the universal good, and earthly emolument was not his reward. He was not one of your good men who manage to make "the best of both worlds." If he were not accursed from Christ, he was accursed from earth royalties. Patriotism is inspired by a sense of the country's greatness and glory. Paul had an exalted view of the privileges with which the Israelites were favoured. They were the adopted children of God. The Shekinah shed a heaven light on their pathway; the covenants sustained a connection with heaven; the service of God exalted; the promises cheered; the moral code placed them in the forefront of nations, and is to-day the backbone of highest forms of civilisation. All these glories culminated in the glory of giving to the world the divine-human Man, the representative of manhood; the one entire and perfect chrysolite. Well indeed might Paul love that nation from which as concerning the flesh Christ came.

IV. The intensity of his perception.—Long before our day Paul knew that things are not what they seem. He distinguished between the semblance and the reality; between the being and the not-being; between the phantasm of a man and the glorious reality of a man; between an Israelite who might be known by the cast of his physical features or by the cunning of his mercantile transactions, and the Israelite who might be known by the glory of his moral manhood and by showing himself the honourable and grand heir of all the ages. The children of the promise are counted for the seed—children fashioned according to the divine ideal. The children of the flesh are not the children of God. The children of the promise are the children of the Promise-giver. The children of the Spirit are the offspring of the eternal Spirit. They rise above all materialism; they move in highest realms. Are we children of the promise? Are we living the higher life? Are we seeking and serving Christ-like aims and purposes?

Vers. 1-3. *Christian zeal.*—One thing he would not part with, the love of Christ. That love he would have with him wherever he was, wherever God might place him. Who shall separate us from the love of God which is in Christ Jesus? That he could not lose, for none can lose it who part not willingly from it. But the presence of Christ, the blissful glory of His countenance, the joy of being with his Master, the entrancing, transporting vision of Him who had called him while he was persecuting Him—this, the very bliss of eternity, the blessed-making sight of God, St. Paul was ready to forgo, if so be his Redeemer might be the more glorified and the souls of his kinsmen after the flesh. They, to whom the promises appertained, might be saved and joined to the heavenly choirs who adore the Master whom he loved. St. Paul would not be separated from the love of Christ; but he could endure to think of being separated, in place, in sight, in joy, from Christ Himself. " I could wish that I myself were accursed from Christ." He willed, like the thing devoted, separated to God, and sacrificed to Him, to be cut off from all besides; yet not from God, but from the presence of God. He who had been the "off-scouring of the world " could have borne to forfeit the very sight of God, if so be God Himself might thereby be the more glorified and souls might be won

310

to Him and live to Him eternally.   Such was an apostle's fervour, such an apostle's love.   Great must be the preciousness of zeal for souls, that God put into his soul such a thought as this, that he could bear even to be separated from the sight of Him whom His soul loved, if so be greater glory might so be gained to Him and there were more to love Him.   Precious indeed in the sight of the Lord is true zeal for souls—precious indeed, because there is nothing in the whole world so precious as the soul of man redeemed by the blood of Christ. Not the whole world, sun, moon, and countless hosts of heaven, would be as the very dust in the balance weighed with one soul for which Christ died.   Great and divine you would think the office to uphold in being and direct in their courses all those heavenly lights which brighten our day and make our night serene and calm.   When Joshua bid the sun and the moon stand still, it is said, "There was no day like that, before it or after it, that the Lord hearkened unto the voice of a man."   Great was it when, at the prayers of Elijah and Elisha, St. Peter or St. Paul, death gave back its slain—when, at apostles' prayers, the blind saw, or the deaf heard, or the lame walked.   But greater far is it when one human soul is won out of the jaws of Satan to adore its Redeemer for ever. . . . It is the greatest work in which God employs man; for it is the greatest work of God Himself.   It is the end for which God the Father made all besides; for which God the Son became man; for which God the Holy Ghost pleads with, calls, sanctifies, indwells man, and unites him unto God. The salvation of man is the combined work of the holy Trinity.   They together ordained it; they in union brought it about; and in this their work they join in with themselves the work of man.   But, then, zeal which would be heard must be self-denying.   "Charity begins at home."   Wouldst thou have true zeal, be zealous with thyself.   First have pity on thine own soul, and then have zeal for the souls of others.   And so it is a blessing to thee to be asked to aid in any act of spiritual mercy.   It is a twofold blessing to thee, in that it is an offering to Him, the good Father, thy blessed Maker, thy tender Redeemer, and He will repay thee; it is a means of denying thyself, putting restraint upon thyself, giving up to God some self-indulgence which the rather hindered thee in taking up thy cross and following Christ.   It is to exchange a weight which clogs thee for wings which shall bear thee towards thy God.—*Pusey, D. ').*

SUGGESTIVE COMMENTS ON VERSES 1—8.

"*Accursed from Christ.*"—The word translated "accursed," which in the marginal reading is rendered "separated," sometimes means also "cut off" or "destroyed."   Now, if we take it in this sense, the difficulty will be in a great measure removed; for the words will mean merely that the apostle was willing to be cut off, or to suffer death, if by that means he could save his countrymen from the calamities impending over them.   But the expression "separated from Christ" is unfavourable to this view of the meaning; for these words usually imply "separated from the favour of Christ," and consequently from the hope of salvation through Him.   This difficulty, however, is at least diminished when it is borne in mind that Paul often denominates the Christian Church "the body of Christ," and that sometimes the phrase "to be in Christ" seems to mean nothing more than being "a member of the Church of Christ."   Now, if we take the words rendered "accursed from Christ," or rather "separated from Him," to mean "separated from the Church of Christ," or "cut off by a violent death from the communion of the Church," we shall have a meaning suitable to the circumstances.   For the Jews were not cut off from being the Church of God, and destined to be destroyed; and it was not unnatural

311

for the apostle to say that he would willingly submit to this fate in their stead if that could save them. This interpretation is the more probable, that the word translated "accursed," or "separated," is the common Scripture term for denoting "excommunicated," or "cut off," from the communion of the visible Church. "If any man love not the Lord Jesus, let him be *anathema*" (the word here employed)—cut off from the privileges of a Christian and the communion of the Church. It is true that cutting off from communion of the Church was, according to the opinion of the time, equivalent to cutting off from the hope of salvation. But this opinion rested on no authority; and consequently St. Paul, in saying that he was willing to submit to this fate in place of his countrymen, does not mean that he was willing to submit to eternal condemnation for them—a wish which it seems hardly possible for him to have expressed.—*Ritchie.*

Not one must perish.—Tholuck reminds us that Paul's eye falls on the mighty company of the subjects of the Old Testament theocracy, which, offering as a whole a hostile resistance to the Christian scheme of salvation, seems on that ground to deserve total rejection. Paul's conversion to Christianity did not rob him of love for his own nation. Cast out, despised of them, he does not give them up. He still hopes for their salvation.

I. **The apostle shows his wariness.** In full keeping with Christ's warning, "Be wise as serpents," etc. He has to win a prejudiced people. Hence he identifies himself with them; and it is as brother pleading with brother, a case of winning to Christ "making a difference."

II. **Paul is moved to godly sorrow at others' danger.**—As though "Woe is me if," etc. He follows out Christ's injunction, "Bless them that curse you." Shows how the forgiving spirit of Christianity works in Christ's true followers.

III. **While pleading, Paul does not spare where blame is demanded.**—He shows the Jews that if they are not received by God they have themselves to blame. Salvation is for every one. No exclusiveness, no favouritism, no respect of persons, in the scheme of redemption. To Jews, and all others, if they are lost, pride and wilfulness, and not God's exclusion, are their ruin. It is not God who shuts the door against us.

IV. **A true child of God is willing to be a cross-bearer for the sake of those in peril.**—"I could wish myself accursed." Here is Christ mirrored in His follower. Christ willing to spend and be spent, even treading the sad way of sacrifice, that men might be saved. Paul a worthy follower, imitating Christ in this full surrender of self; ready for the great extremity, if by so doing he could save some. This is true surrender of self for the good of others. This is true self-sacrifice; and self-sacrifice is a principle pre-eminently Christian.

V. **A noble ancestry does not save us from sin's penalties.**—1. The Jews were naturally proud of their descent— a chosen people, a royal priesthood. But this ancestry brought its dangers. It fostered pride, self-confidence, blinded the sense of any need of reformation or penitence. Yet our blessings are not founded on our merits, but on the free grace of God. It was so with the Jews; it is so with every one. 2. Our privileges render the guilt of rejection and forgetfulness the more manifest. Jews were of one blood with Christ; yet they set Him at defiance, denounced Him, rejected Him. Thus they rejected Him who is blessed for ever, "God over all." Little do we know, sometimes, the extremity to which our pride takes us, the terrible guilt we incur.

VI. **Does not this strong feeling on Paul's part suggest God's tenderness to the sinner?**—Saving the vilest. Paul so knew his Lord that he knew there was pardon wherever there was penitence. The old gospel story was

312

in his mind; and he was constrained to tell it, to plead with them as one who must give account. Mercy is offered even to those who challenge Heaven to bruise and crush them. Shall we not come to Christ for mercy?—*Albert Lee.*

Paul does not wish to be damned.— Paul does not teach that we should be willing to be damned for the glory of God. 1. His very language implies that such a wish would be improper. For in the ardour of his disinterested affection he does not himself entertain or express the wish, but merely says, in effect, that were it proper or possible, he would be willing to perish for the sake of his brethren. 2. If it is wrong to *do* evil that good may come, how can it be right to wish to *be* evil that good may come? 3. There seems to be a contradiction involved in the very terms of the wish. Can any one love God so much as to wish to hate Him? Can he be so good as to desire to be bad? We must be willing to give up houses and lands, parents and brethren, and our life also, for Christ and His kingdom; but we are never required to give up holiness for His sake, for this would be a contradiction.—*Hodge.*

" I wished myself accursed."—The more I consider the passage, I am the more satisfied that the first part of the third verse should be rendered in the past time, and thrown into a parenthesis — " For I myself wished to be accursed from Christ." The considerations in support of this rendering are strong :— (1) It is *literal.* The other *is not. I wished,* not *I could wish,* is the simple and direct rendering of the verb. To make it conditional it should be in another tense or have a particle of conditionality prefixed to it. If instances to the contrary, they are exceptions to the rule. (2) The sense is complete without the parenthesis. (3) It gives a natural connection to the second verse, which otherwise it wants. (4) The emphatic expression *I myself* is in this way most naturally

explained. It evidently has the sense of, I myself *as well as they*—I too, *like them,* wished to be accursed from Christ. Our translators have shown that this emphatic expression does not naturally suit the ordinary interpretation, by omitting it—" *I myself* could wish " would not be natural ; and they have therefore separated the *myself* from the *I.* (5) It affords an interesting and beautiful sense. It assigns the *reason* of his " great heaviness and sorrow of heart." The reason lies in the recollection of what he himself had been. He too had rejected Jesus, and thought he should do many things against His name.—*Dr. Wardlaw.*

" Of whom, as concerning the flesh, Christ came."—The Christ, according to the prophecies that went before, was to be the seed of Abraham and of David. It was pre-eminently in this sense that " salvation was of the Jews." They gave birth to the Saviour. In this, God put the very highest honour upon the children of Abraham, Isaac, and Jacob, by bringing from among them the human nature of IMMANUEL. The " horn of salvation for Jews and Gentiles was raised up in the house of God's servant David." The expression " as concerning the flesh," or " as far as respects the flesh," or " as to His human nature," is a phrase which prepares us to expect something more. It is a phrase which most assuredly we should never think of using respecting any mere man. It instantly suggests the question, What was He *else*?— what was He not according to the flesh? There is an obviously designed antithesis, the taking away of which divests the words of all their force and meaning, and converts them into a useless and unnatural pleonasm, which adds weakness instead of strength and propriety to the expression and the sentiment. The antithesis is fully brought out by what follows : " Who is over all, God blessed for ever." We need not wonder that the adversaries of our blessed Lord's divinity have been sadly put to it with this most

simple and explicit declaration of that all important and essential article of gospel truth. The most commonly approved gloss is that which converts the last clause of the verse into a doxology—either making the stop in the enumeration at the word "came," or at the word "all." In the former case the doxology is, "God who is over all be blessed for ever!" in the latter simply, "God be blessed for ever!"—*Dr. Wardlaw.*

MAIN HOMILETICS OF THE PARAGRAPH.—*Verses* 9—16.

St. Paul's deep things.—Augustine asks, How can man understand God, since he does not yet understand his own mind, with which he endeavours to understand Him? This question comes home to the candid and reflective nature. If we were properly penetrated with the sense of our own littleness, we should not presume to compass the infinite greatness. "Canst thou by searching find out God? Canst thou find out the Almighty to perfection?" Zophar's questions have only one answer. Neither science nor philosophy nor theological criticism can find out the Almighty to perfection. A part of the divine ways alone is known. Paul has given a glimpse of the unknown parts, and we cannot pierce the darkness which revelation has not cleared. It is our wisdom to accept the known and wait patiently for the all-revealing light of that realm where there are no clouds. In a docile and praying spirit let us study St. Paul's mysterious utterances. In this passage we have :—

I. **The word of promise.**—In this promise we find contained a divine visit and a divine gift. God has not left the world. He is ever present, and by special interventions He gives proof of that presence. He breaks in upon the laws of nature by the intervention of higher laws, and thus declares that all law emanates from His eternal mind. He is always about us, but there may be special seasons when our vision is cleared, and then He may be said to "come." He is ever giving sons, but He gave to Joseph and Mary a special Son, that the world might more fully rejoice in the love and nearness of the Father. God's special gifts are the outcome of His general gifts. The miraculous gives proof of divine agency at work in the ordinary. Sons born to the young Sarahs of time are no less God's gifts than the sons born to a Sarah when nature's powers were in decay. Let us believe in God's presence and in God's promise.

II. **A word of mystery.**—A word, many words, of mystery. "The elder shall serve the younger. Jacob have I loved, but Esau have I hated." Divine declarations coincident with historical records, with the facts of experience. The elder shall serve the younger. The older nation serves the younger. And so with individuals. Joseph commands the service of his brethren. The enterprising youth of the family goes from the homestead, and the elder members stay at home and become his subordinates. The elders of time serve the younger ones who have just risen up to appreciate the greatness of the service. Here is the mystery. Why should some elder ones be doomed to service? Why should some younger ones command service? Why should Jacob be loved and poor Esau hated? Does God put a premium on the cunning plotters who can overreach their fellows? Does infinite Wisdom love the Jacobs who know how to feather their nests, and hate the Esaus whose prudence and worldly caution are overmastered by passion? This cannot be. We hope for a world where the needful light will be thrown on divine proceedings. Even Paul may not have fathomed the depth of meaning hidden in the words, "Jacob have I loved; Esau have I hated."

III. **A word of sovereignty.**—God's mercy does not move along the channels cut by human limitations. His mercy is guided by His sovereignty. His compassion is under the control of His will; and surely that will is both compassionate, just, and intelligent. Whatever happens, whatever doctrinal views may be broached, whatever seeming partiality may appear in divine allotments, our souls must hold on to this truth, that there is no unrighteousness with God, no injustice with Him who is the perfectly just.

IV. **A word of mercy.**—All is " of God that showeth mercy." Shining above all other words is the sweet word " mercy "; crowning and giving effect to all other deeds is the glorious deed of mercy. Mercy is the darling attribute. It encircles the eternal throne; it spans the earth like a rainbow of many attractive colours. Shrinking from the awful attribute of divine sovereignty, we find refuge in the attribute of mercy as revealed in the method of our salvation by Jesus Christ.

SUGGESTIVE COMMENTS ON VERSES 9—16.

Divine sovereignty and freewill.—I must pause again here to remind the student that I purposely do not enter on the disquisitions so abundant in some commentaries on this part of Scripture by which it is endeavoured to reconcile the sovereign election of God with our freewill. *We shall find that freewill asserted strongly enough for all edifying purposes by this apostle when the time comes.* At present he is employed wholly in asserting the divine sovereignty, the glorious vision of which it ill becomes us to distract by continual downward looks on this earth. I must also protest against all endeavours to make it appear that no inference lies from this passage as to the *salvation of individuals.* It is most true that the *immediate subject is the national rejection of the Jews*; but we must consent to hold our reason in abeyance, if we do not recognise the inference that the sovereign power and free election here proved to belong to God extend to *every exercise* of His mercy—whether temporal or spiritual, whether in providence or in grace, whether national or individual. It is in parts of Scripture like this that we must be especially careful *not to fall short of what is written*, not to allow of any compromise of the plain and awful words of God's Spirit, for the sake of a caution which He Himself does not teach us.—*Alford.*

The privileges of Jews and Christians.—It is generally thought an office

of love to conceal from persons any truths the recital of which will afford them pain ; but true love will rather stimulate us to declare such truths as are necessary to be known, though it will incline us to declare them with the greatest tenderness and circumspection. An admirable pattern presents itself before us in the text. The apostle was about to enter on a subject most offensive to the Jews, but a subject that ought in no wise to be concealed from them—namely, the determination of God to cast off their nation, and to engraft the Gentiles on their stock. But as it would be thought that he was actuated only by a spirit of revenge, he declares to them in the most solemn manner, and appeals to God for the truth of it, that, so far from wishing their hurt, he was affected with the deepest sorrow on their account, and that there was nothing he would not do or suffer if it might but be the means of saving them from the impending ruin. His enumeration of the privileges which they abused and his pathetic lamentation over them may well lead us to consider :—

I. **The exalted privileges enjoyed by true Israelites.**—The Jews as a nation were favoured beyond all the nations upon earth. But their privileges were only a shadow of those enjoyed by true Israelites. But by how much the more exalted our condition under the gospel is, by so much the more may we see—

II. **The disposition we should**

manifest towards those who despise these privileges.—The expressions used by the apostle admit of different interpretations. But in whatever sense they be taken, they certainly import that we should be deeply concerned about their state, and we should account nothing too much to do or suffer for their salvation. Inference: How far are they from a Christian spirit who not only use no means for the salvation of others, but oppose and thwart them that do! How earnest should every Christian be in seeking *his own* salvation !—*Simeon.*

God does not owe favours. — He gives not as a thing due, but as a fruit of His love, which does not imply that therein He acts arbitrarily. Such a supposition is excluded precisely because the giver in question is God, who is wisdom itself, and who *thinks* nothing good except what *is* good. The principle here laid down included God's right to call the Gentiles to salvation when He should be pleased to grant them this favour. The words, " of him that *willeth,* of him that *runneth,*" have often been strangely understood. There have been found in them allusions to the *wish* of Isaac to make Esau the heir of the promise, and to Esau's *running* to bring the venison necessary for the feast of benediction. But Isaac and Esau are no longer in question, and we must remain by the example of Moses. It was neither the wish expressed in his prayer nor the faithful care which he had taken of Israel in the wilderness which could merit the favour he asked ; and as no man will ever surpass him in respect either of pious willing or holy working, it follows that the rule applied to him is universal. So it will always be. Israel, in particular, should understand thereby that it is neither their fixed theocratic necessities nor the multitude of their ceremonial or moral works which can convert salvation into a debt contracted toward them by God, and take away from Him the right of

rejecting them if He comes to think it good to do so for reasons which He alone appreciates. But if the words of God to Moses prove that God does not *owe* His favours to any one whomsoever, must it also be held that He is free to reject whom He will ? Yes. Scripture ascribes to Him even this right. Such is the truth following from another saying of God in reference to the adversary of Moses, Pharaoh.—*Godet.*

Providence and freewill.—Now these two facts, that there is a will in man, that the universe shows marks of providence and design, are so evident when taken singly, the one from the immediate witness of our own consciousness, and the other as an inference hardly avoidable from the facts which science and history bring before us, that we ought to suspect any attempt to obliterate one or the other by bringing them into collision. I speak not now of pious efforts to make them explicable together, to enable us, if I may say so, to put our finger on the point of contact between man's will and the divine power that acts upon it : such phrases as " irresistible grace," " unconditional decree," " co-operating grace," will at once serve to recall them and to suggest their difficulties. But any one who watches at all the drift of the current of modern thought will see another set of influences at work. Two thoughts occur which in leaving this subject ought not to be passed over. First, our Church, in her article on predestination, draws a distinction between the effect of the study of it on the good and on the bad, the sincere believer and the unbeliever. To the godly it is "full of sweet, pleasant, and unspeakable consolation " ; whilst it leads the carnal to " wretchedness of unclean living." Our own hearts tell us that the distinction is just. There cannot be a more perilous symptom of the moral state than where men profess to abandon the struggle with their passions because they think they have no choice but to succumb, thus clasping to their arms that loathsome body of death which they were intended to escape from through divine aid. On the other hand, it does not detract from the sweetness of self-approval to ascribe to God alone all the good that we find within us. The Lord hardened Pharaoh's heart—that is, He withdrew from it His grace, without which it must needs be hardened, because the lost king did not wish to retain it, and had hardened himself in stubborn resolution against the Lord. Sin, then, is sometimes punished with sin. If any one begins to neglect prayer, he finds it day by day easier to do so without compunction. If any one is pursuing a course of sensual vice, he feels that the protecting sense of shame grows daily weaker in him and the craving lust more imperious. And at a certain stage in his dreary, downward course the Lord hardens his heart. God is not responsible for his sin; but when he has repelled the voice of conscience and the warning of his Bible and the entreaties of friends, then grace is withdrawn from him, and sin puts on a judicial character, and it is at once sin and punishment. Oh, beware of that cumulative power of sin! Human actions admit of three degrees: where the choice is perfectly free, as it is in light and indifferent matters; where the choice is fettered with motives hardly resistible; and an intermediate condition, where motives exist to sway but not to coerce our choice. Every sin we commit adds weight to the motives that endanger our freedom. See the folly of those who allow themselves to continue in sin, believing that hereafter, as their passions cool, they will forsake their evil ways. It is a fearful danger to immerse the moral nature in uncleanness, meaning to escape from it at a future time. Every day makes repentance more difficult; and who can tell when the face of God may be wholly averted from you, so that He will harden your heart? And even if you escape this, the bitter recollection of many a past sin will cleave to you even after your repentance.—*Archbishop Thomson.*

MAIN HOMILETICS OF THE PARAGRAPH.—Verses 17—24.

Divine liberty.—There must be in all discussions about the divine nature and the divine proceedings questions which can never be satisfactorily settled, in this world at least. This is not to be considered astonishing, if God be infinitely great and men be infinitely little. We can only fringe the boundless realm of the infinite greatness. All we appear to do in the settlement of our difficulties is to push the difficulty a little further back. We explain but never answer fairly the questions: Whence sin? Why moral evil? How is it that a Pharaoh hardens himself against light and reason, and to his own undoing? Why not have humility enough to confess our ignorance, to acknowledge that there must necessarily be much in the infinitely great, in the eternally vast and complex, which must be beyond our comprehension? We at least do not presume to settle points above reason, though, when all is seen, not contrary to reason. We simply pray that some heavenly light may be shed upon our pathway.

I. **Let us then observe that divine liberty is not arbitrary.**—Not arbitrary in the sense of being despotic or capricious. The God of love is no reasonless despot; the All-wise cannot be capricious. We talk of our fellows as having their little caprices. But if we think of the unchangeable God as being capable of change in any direction, we can never rightly suppose that He changes without sufficient reason. We are not to speak of God as having mercy on whom He will have mercy, as if the divine will were the mere faculty of moving from one being to another in the way of favour without any wise reason. If God is self-determined solely by His own judgment, it is because that judgment is regulated by infinite wisdom and goodness.

II. **Divine liberty then is ruled by the great law of right.**—What is right?

Is it dependent upon the will of Deity? Is it antecedent to that will? We should say, concomitant. The will of God is coeternal with moral right and fitness. However the law of right arises, one thing is certain, that divine liberty is not opposed to the morally right. God is eternally free, but He is not free to do wrong,—free, because God never wishes to do wrong. Divine freedom is never human licentiousness. God does not will " to show His wrath,"—either to display His divine liberty or to give vent to revenge. " What if God, willing to show His wrath," etc. St. Paul does not affirm that God does show His wrath. God makes His power known in the marvellous way in which He endures so much longsuffering. Let us believe in the eternally right, the morally fit. Let us rise above all difficulties by grasping to our hearts the truth that God can do no wrong.

III. Divine liberty is guided by all-wise though inscrutable purposes.— " Even for this same purpose have I raised thee up." Even with the help of a St. Paul we cannot read the strange language of the divine purposes. The very alphabet we cannot master ; the verbs have intricate moods and tenses which we cannot follow. The Pharaohs of time are dark mysteries. The sound of the rolling waters deadens our ears, so that we cannot catch the lessons of divine movements. God's purposes are inscrutable because of their far-reaching sweep, because of the infinite wisdom according to which they are planned. Let folly bow with reverent head in the presence of all-wise purposes. One purpose is revealed that God's name may be declared throughout all the earth. God's name is written in nature. God's new name of love is written in revelation. God's name of power and of wisdom is declared in the rise and fall of nations, in the downfall of tyrannies, in the overthrow of unrighteous thrones, in the destruction of foolish and tyrannical Pharaohs. Let us move, regulate our lives, in harmony with the revealed purpose of infinite wisdom.

IV. Divine liberty is directed to gracious ends.—The divine Potter has made known the riches of His glory on the vessels of mercy which He had afore prepared unto glory. The riches of God's glory are seen in the vessels of mercy. As the human potter takes pride in the vessels that show his skill and that are raised to positions of honour in the earthly palace, so we venture to assert that the divine Potter glories in the vessels of mercy that are raised to positions of honour in the heavenly mansions. The heart of infinite love must be touched with compassion whenever a poor, blind, misguided Pharaoh is engulfed with his hosts by the resilient waters. Whatever may be our perplexities, whatever may be our creeds, let us hear this song rising clearly above every other sound, and sweetly charming away all our doubts and fears—" There is joy in the presence of the angels of God over one sinner that repenteth." This truth we may further learn, that God's power and glory cannot be declared by numerous vessels showing incompleteness, inadequacy, incompetence, on the part of the divine Potter. Imagine a human potter having his workshop well-nigh full of vessels that none would wish to purchase. Such a potter would soon be bankrupt. Are we to imagine the divine Potter, the infinite Architect of the universe, the essential Goodness, the unerring Wisdom, forming vessels that will for ever redound to His discredit ? Vessels of mercy in large numbers will brilliantly reflect infinite goodness and wisdom as they adorn, as so many monumental pillars, the boundless temple of God's gathered worshippers. Let us learn, not to find fault with divine proceedings, not to suppose that we can understand everything, not even in thought to resist the divine will, for that will is on the side of goodness and moves in mercy to man. Above all things let us heartily obey the divine call. He calls from sin to holiness, from ruin to salvation in Christ Jesus, from the spoiling agency of the satanic potter to the repairing and glorifying agency of the divine-human Potter. Oh to be monumental vessels of divine grace and mercy in the vast storehouse of divine curiosities ! Vessels of mércy ! What exquisite skill they display ! What richness of spiritual texture ! What beauty of moral tints ! How they shine in the unclouded light that radiates about the eternal throne !

Ver. 21. *The sovereign right of God.*—Some aspects of the Deity may be less pleasing to contemplate than others. The pride of man rejoices not at first in the thought of the Majesty which overawes his littleness and compels him to submission. Yet as a hard flint forcibly struck emits a bright spark, and as a rough husk often covers a sweet kernel, so these stern views of the Almighty may, if reverently faced and meditated upon, yield salutary, ennobling, and even comforting reflections.

I. **The Potter claims absolute right to deal with the clay as He thinks fit.**— His arbitrary power does not signify the absence of proper reasons for His selection. As in the calling of Israel to peculiar service and responsibility and honour, so everywhere can an election be discerned. We do not start in the race of life with exactly similar equipment, though we live in tabernacles of clay. If the physical and spiritual powers are the same in essence, like the particles of " the same lump," yet the faculties of some have been well trained from the beginning, and their natures have developed under favourable conditions. Here is *a lesson of resignation.* He is happiest who accepts the will of God as revealed in his lot, assured that God's decision has ample justification. Even the Stoic philosophy could declare that if man knew the plans of the Superintendent of the universe and saw them in their completeness, he would at once acquiesce in the determinations of the Arbiter of his destiny. This is the truth which mingles with the error of Mohammedan fatalism. We have to do all that lies within our power, and leave the result with Him who is wise and merciful. For the potter is our Father in heaven. How much of the vexation and worry of life is due to a conceit of our capacity, and perhaps to a jealousy of the position and attainments of our neighbours ! Be content to fill a lowly place; and the time is at hand when " the pots in the Lord's house shall be like bowls before the altar."

II. **The Potter has no desire for the destruction of His workmanship.**—He cares not to waste His clay, nor to employ it in a manner to secure its speedy extinction. It is a pain to God to see His gifts abused, His image degraded, His work marred. He is said in ver. 22 to endure " with much longsuffering the vessels of wrath." *A lesson of hopefulness* is here. The Most High will not break His vessels in pieces as long as they are fit for any use, for any post, though humble and insignificant. " Potter and clay endure," however the wheel of life may turn and fashion the material into altered shapes. If the light of God shines in a vacuum, no brightness is observable. An empty heaven were a dreary home for a God of love, a silent temple for Him who glories in the praises of His people and His works.

III. **The Potter prefers to construct the choicest vessels.**—The noblest ware pays Him best, and He lovingly exerts His skill on specimens of highest art. Deny not to God the delight which every artist feels in the finest productions of his genius. The most polished mirrors best reflect His glory. *A lesson of aspiration* therefore. " Covet earnestly the best gifts." God has made His clay instinct with will and energy; He takes pleasure in the improvement of the vessels, that they may be brought into His sanctuary. It will mightily assist our struggles to be sure that the Captain longs " to bring many sons unto glory."—*S. R. Aldridge.*

The parable of the potter and the clay.—Let us notice :—

I. **What it does not teach.**—Starting from a perfectly sound and correct view as to God's absolute sovereignty and His right to dispose of men as He pleases, some have thought that St. Paul brings in his reference to the potter and his clay in order to show that in the exercise of that sovereignty God makes some souls to destruction, and that those so made have no ground of complaint. Now whatever truth there may be in such a notion as this, a close examination will show that it is not "the whole truth"—still less is it "nothing but the truth." God is sovereign Lord, and He has a right to dispose of us all as He will. But that He exercises these rights in any arbitrary or cruel way, reason and Holy Scripture alike lead us to deny. "God is love." The foreordaining of any creature to everlasting misery is utterly inconsistent with love.

II. **Its origin in the sphere of manual industry.**—[For description of the potter's work, see quotation from Thomson's *The Land and the Book* on p. 323.] Sometimes it would happen that on account of defect in clay or other cause vessel would be spoiled in process of formation. Potter would crush it up and reduce it once again to shapeless mass, which he would afterwards fashion into perhaps a quite different form. The clay which appeared unfit to make one kind of vessel he would make into another.

III. **Its place in Old Testament prophetic teaching.**—St. Paul has in his mind the opening verses of Jer. xviii. (*vide* vers. 1-6). Jeremiah's parable was spoken of the Jewish nation : "O house of Israel, cannot I do with you as this potter ? saith the Lord. Behold, as the clay in the potter's hand, so are ye in Mine hand, O house of Israel." God had a right to mould them as He chose. They rebelled. The vessel was marred in His hand. Yet He strove with them again and again. At length, notwithstanding God's purposes towards them for good, they so rebelled that they were cut off. In following chap. xix. this terrible fact also foreshadowed in figure. Prophet again receives command from God— this time to take an earthen bottle which has been baked and hardened in the fire. He is to go forth into the valley of Hinnom, and there break the bottle in the sight of the ancients and priests, and in doing so to say, "Even so will I break this people and this city, as one breaketh a potter's vessel, that cannot be made whole again." God will strive with sinners again and again, but the hardened and impenitent cannot be allowed to resist His will.

IV. **Its bearing upon St. Paul's argument.**—In the opening verses of this chapter the apostle gives expression to his grief that Israel should be hardening their hearts against the gospel. God's word and promise regarding them have not failed, for all who are Jews naturally are not Jews spiritually, and are therefore not heirs of the promise. Of the seed of Abraham only one son, Isaac, was chosen; of Isaac's two sons one was utterly rejected. Is God unjust, then? asks the apostle. Impossible! he would reply; God has an absolute right to love and to hate whom He will. And he gives instances illustrating the fact that God has proclaimed pity towards some and meted out retribution to others (vers. 17-19). The question next arises, Why doth He yet find fault? If, *i.e.*, wickedness be the result of God's will, what becomes of man's responsibility? If a man be bad, can he help it? Who can resist the will of God? This question is stated by the apostle as one which a Jewish objector might and probably would urge. And he treats it as absurd. "Nay but, O man, who art thou that repliest against God? Shall the thing formed say to Him that formed it, Why hast Thou made me thus? Hath not the potter power over the clay, of the same lump to make one vessel unto honour, and another unto dishonour?" Quite true. But St. Paul shrinks back aghast from the horrible supposition that God would predestine any creature to eternal woe. And thus he will not say that God "*created* vessels of wrath" or "*prepared them* for destruction"; but he asks : "What if God, willing to show His wrath, and make His power known, *endured with much longsuffering* the vessels of wrath fitted to destruction : and that He might make known the riches of His glory on the vessels of mercy, which He had afore prepared unto glory, even us, whom He hath called, not of the Jews only, but also of the Gentiles?" The vessels of wrath were fitted, not by God, but by themselves, for destruction. Like Pharaoh, they hardened themselves in sin. Their evil character, like Jeremiah's earthen bottle, had assumed so permanent a shape that no reforming process was possible. The vessels of mercy, on the other hand, were made such by God's grace moulding and fashioning them into the form that He willed.

V. **Its meaning to ourselves.** —Clearly this: 1. *That God's purpose is to prepare unto glory all those whom He has called into His Church* (ver. 21). The potter has a design in view in connection with every lump of clay which he takes into his hand. And God too has a design, a purpose, in every life. He is shaping us into that form which He deems most fitting. Every life has not the same purpose. One is fitted for one sphere of duty, another for another, just as the potter makes vessels of innumerable shapes. And yet each life is successful if only its own particular purpose be fulfilled. A life is no failure because it is lowly and put only to lowly uses, so long as it attains the end for which God designed it. The potter takes the clay into his hand. We are taken in hand by God when made members of His Church; and His first work in us is the forming of our souls aright. The first question is, not as to what we do, but as to what we are—what shape or form our character has taken. The potter makes vessels of various shapes, sizes, tints. God is making characters of various kinds, dealing with souls, fashioning lives, and thus preparing them "unto glory." Having taken somewhat of the form which God willed, we may then be put to some further end—used for good— employed in the carrying out of some of God's purposes of grace, and thus the preparation for glory will be advanced a further stage. 2. *That we may so resist the will of God as to alter our own destiny, though we can never alter God's purpose.* The potter, when his work is marred, presses the clay back again into a shapeless lump, and makes a vessel perhaps of quite another kind. And so, when a man has failed to profit by one kind of earthly discipline, God may subject him to another. There are afflictions which crush a man for a time, soften his heart and make it liable to receive new impressions, and thus he may be led on to begin a new life and be actuated by new aims and hopes. The character which would not assume one good form may thus be made to assume another. Still, the renewed process may fail, for some vessels are "fitted" (alas! by themselves) "to destruction."

Practical lessons: 1. *Thankfulness to God for the revelation of His will towards us.* He has willed that a place of honour and usefulness in His kingdom shall be ours. That will shall be done unless we harden ourselves against it. 2. *Warning.* Beware of resisting God's Spirit. Beware of the danger of the hardening process. Even if the vessel be remade, if afflictions soften, and the soul be renewed, the process is a terrible one. The preparation for glory is not the work of an instant. 3. *Self-examination.* Are we earnestly and prayerfully acting out the terms of our baptismal covenant? By our neglect to do so His work is marred, the preparation unto glory ceases to go forward. 4. *Heartfelt prayer.* Let our petitions ever be offered that God's will may be done in us and our will conformed to His, so that, under the shaping and fashioning influence of His hand, each may at length become "a vessel unto honour, sanctified, and meet for the Master's use, and prepared unto every good work" (2 Tim. ii. 21). —*G. E. P. Reade.*

Ver. 20. *The potter and the clay.*—Two points insisted on: 1. *God's almightiness.* He can do whatever He likes. (We do not say He *does*, but He *can* do.) 2. *Man's weakness.* God allows him to sin.

Two objections made by some men: 1. *How can God make on purpose to destroy?* Answer: Nowhere stated that He does so. (1) Similitude looks other way: no potter begins to make anything on purpose to destroy it. (2) Statement that God is father looks other way. (3) Statement that all things are made for God's good pleasure (Rev. iv. 11) looks other way. 2. *Why should God blame us if we are so powerless?* How it *has been* answered: Man, though weak, not an automaton or machine: has a will; can reasonably be blamed for sin. How it *is* answered here: How can we find fault with absolute Maker, who forms all for good purpose—with absolute Father, who brings all children into the world for good? If they disobey, who can blame Him for punishing them for their good and good of others?

Power, anger (righteous), longsuffering, must be shown. These considerations must be set over against each other: *God's power, God's purpose; man's weakness, man's responsibility.—Dr. Springett.*

SUGGESTIVE COMMENTS ON VERSES 17—24.

The hardening of Pharaoh's heart.— What effect did all these signs and wonders of God's sending have upon Pharaoh and his servants? Did they make them better men or worse men? We read that they made them worse men—that they helped to harden their hearts. We read that the Lord hardened Pharaoh's heart, so that he would not let the children of Israel go. Now how did the Lord do that? He did not wish and mean to make Pharaoh more hard-hearted, more wicked—that is impossible. God, who is all goodness and love, never can wish to make any human being one atom worse than he is. He who so loved the world that He came down on earth to die for sinners and take away the sins of the world would never make any human being a greater sinner than he was before—that is impossible and horrible to think of. Therefore, when we read that the Lord hardened Pharaoh's heart, we must be certain that that was Pharaoh's own fault; and so we read it was Pharaoh's own fault. The Lord did not bring all these plagues on Egypt without giving Pharaoh fair warning. Before each plague He sent Moses to tell Pharaoh that the plague was coming. The Lord told Pharaoh that He was his Master, and the Master and Lord of the whole earth; that the children of Israel belonged to Him, and the Egyptians too; that the river, light and darkness,

the weather, the crops, the insects, and the locusts belonged to Him; that all diseases which afflict man and beast were in His power. And the Lord proved that His words were true in a way Pharaoh could not mistake, by changing the river into blood, and sending darkness and hailstones, and plagues of lice and flies, and at last by killing the firstborn of all the Egyptians. The Lord gave Pharaoh every chance. He condescended to argue with him as one man would with another, and proved His word to be true, and proved that He had a right to command Pharaoh. And therefore, I say, if Pharaoh's heart was hardened, it was his own fault, for the Lord was plainly trying to soften it, and to bring him to reason. And the Bible says distinctly that it was Pharaoh's fault; for it says that Pharaoh hardened his own heart, he and his servants, and therefore they would not let the children of Israel go. Now how could Pharaoh harden his own heart, and yet the Lord harden it at the same time? Just in the same way as too many of us are apt to make the Lord harden our hearts by hardening them ourselves, and to make, as Pharaoh did, the very things which the Lord sends to soften us the causes of our becoming more stubborn, the very things which the Lord sends to bring us to reason the means of our becoming more and more foolish. This

is no old story with which we have
nothing to do. What happened to
Pharaoh's heart may happen to yours,
or mine, or any man's. Alas! it does
happen to many a man's and woman's
heart every day; and may the Lord
have mercy on them before it be too
late! And yet how can the Lord
have mercy on those who will not
let Him have mercy on them? Suppose a man to be going on in some
sinful habit. He comes to church, and
there he hears the word of God by the
Bible or in sermons, telling him that
God commands him to give up his sin,
that God will certainly punish him if
he does not repent and amend. God
sends that message to him in love and
mercy to soften his heart by the terrors
of the law and turn him from his sin.
But what does the man feel? He feels
angry and provoked: angry with the
preacher; ay, angry with the Bible
itself, with God's words. For he
hates to hear the words which tell
him of his sin; he wishes they were
not in the Bible; he longs to stop the
preacher's mouth; and as he cannot
do that, he dislikes going to church.
He says, I cannot, and, what is
more, I will not, give up my sinful
ways, and therefore I shall not go to
church to be told of them. So he
stops away from church, and goes on
in his sins. So that man's heart is
hardened just as Pharaoh's was. Yet
the Lord has come and spoken to that
sinful man in loving warnings, though
all the effect it has had is that the
Lord's message has made him worse
than he was before—more stubborn,
more godless, more unwilling to hear
what is good. But men may fall into
a still worse state of mind. They may
determine to set the Lord at naught;
to hear Him speaking to conscience, and
know that He is right and they wrong,
and yet quietly put the good thoughts
and feelings out of their way, and go
on in the course which they know to
be the worst. How many, when they
come to church, harden their hearts,
not caring enough for God's message
to be even angry with it, and take

the preacher's warnings as they would
a shower of rain—as something unpleasant, which cannot be helped, and
which therefore they must sit out
patiently and think about as little as
possible! And thus they let the Lord's
message to them harden their hearts.—
Charles Kingsley.

The potter at work.—I have been out
on the shore again, examining a native
manufactory of pottery, and was delighted to find the whole biblical apparatus complete and in full operation.
There was the potter sitting at his
"frame" and turning the wheel with
his foot. He had a heap of the prepared
clay near him, and a pan of water by
his side. Taking a lump in his hand,
he placed it on the top of the wheel
(which revolves horizontally) and
smoothed it into a low cone, like the
upper end of a sugar-loaf; then thrust-
ing his thumb into the top of it, he
opened a hole down through the centre,
and this he constantly widened by pressing the edges of the revolving cone between his hands. As it enlarged and
became thinner he gave it whatever
shape he pleased with the utmost ease
and expedition. This, I suppose, is
the exact point of those biblical com-
parisons between the human and the
divine Potter (Jer. xviii. 6). And
the same idea is found in many other
passages. When Jeremiah was watching the potter the vessel was marred
in his hand, and "so he made it again,
another vessel, as seemed good to the
potter to make it." I had to wait a
long time for that, but it happened at
last. From some defect in the clay, or
because he had taken too little, the
potter suddenly changed his mind,
crushed his growing jar instantly into
a shapeless mass of mud, and beginning
anew, fashioned it into a totally different vessel.—*Thomson, "The Land and
the Book,"* p. 520.

God's work in shaping our lives.—
The wheel of time spins fast, but not
carrying us away, changing but not
destroying each separate individuality.

323

In providence there are wheels within wheels. We do not understand their meaning. The clay is pressed now below into a solid base, now above into a dainty rim, but it is difficult to see what the final outcome will be till all is finished. So our lives are pressed on one side and on another; something which in our eyes is indispensable is taken away, something which to us seems needless is added. But out of the dizzy whirl, the rush and confusion of life, God is steadily working out His purpose.—*W. F. Adeney, " Pulpit Commentary."*

Men harden themselves.—The sins of men are *freely committed.* They are the effects and indications of evil dispositions of heart; and they are done with the free consent and choice of their wills. No sin could expose to wrath otherwise; nay, otherwise there could be no such thing as sin at all; all sin implying, in the very idea of it, the consent of the will. The very essence of all that is sinful lies in this. If a man were used, either by God or by a fellow-sinner, as a mere physical machine, he could not be a sinner. Now, every man who sins, sins with his will. Make what you like of God's secret purposes, it is a matter of fact which there is no questioning that they do, in no way and in no degree, interfere with the perfect liberty of the agent. Every sinner is sensible that he acts from choice; that neither, on the one hand, is he *constrained to evil,* nor, on the other, *restrained from good.* To say, in regard to the latter —that which is *good*—that man *cannot will* it, is to employ terms most inconsiderate and misleading. What *hinders* him from willing? It is obvious that the word *cannot* must mean a *moral* inability. It is neither more nor less than the absence of *right dispositions.* But the *indisposition* to that which is good is just, in other words, the *want of will* to that which is good; and there being no other inability whatever in man than this moral inability—this unwillingness—to say he *cannot will*

resolves itself ultimately into he *will not will,* inasmuch as he is kept from *willing good* by nothing but his *aversion to good.* All that can properly be meant by human freedom is the absence of all *constraint* and of all *restraint.* Man is at liberty to do whatever he wills; and if he does not *will good,* what is it that prevents him but his *love of evil?* He likes evil, and dislikes good; and therefore, in practice, chooses and does the one, and rejects and refrains from doing the other. These are truths sufficiently plain and simple; and they serve to show the meaning of the expression which follows—" fitted to destruction." —*Dr. Wardlaw.*

God's long-suffering.—It is evident that the idea of " patience and long-suffering " implies the existence of a tendency in a contrary direction, arising from something in the nature or character of the Being by whom it is exercised, and that the difficulty of its exercise bears proportion to the strength of that tendency. Now, the *holiness* of God is infinitely opposed to all sin. He hates it with a hatred that is properly and absolutely infinite. " He is of purer eyes than to behold evil; neither can He look upon iniquity." And while His holiness abhors it, His justice calls for its punishment—its punishment to the full extent of its deserts. In proportion, then, to the strength of these principles of the divine character is the *difficulty* (if it be lawful so to express it) of forbearance with those by whom it is practised—the workers of iniquity. By considering the amount of evil thought and felt, and said and done, in this world of ours every successive moment, I might set the amount of the longsuffering of a holy God before your minds in many and impressive lights. But I must forbear; it would lead me too far away from my one point. Now, by this longsuffering, the great majority of men, alas! are only encouraged in evil—hardened in their unbelief and impenitence and ungodly courses: " Because sentence against an evil work is not executed speedily, therefore the heart of the sons of men is fully set in them to do evil" (Eccles. viii. 11). They thus criminally, because wilfully, and from the love of evil, abuse the divine goodness; and, by the abuse of it, " fit themselves for destruction": " Despisest thou the riches of His goodness and forbearance and longsuffering; not knowing that the goodness of God leadeth thee to repentance? But after thy hardness and impenitent heart treasurest up unto thyself wrath against the day of wrath and revelation of the righteous judgment of God" (chap. ii. 4, 5). Others, dealt with in the same " longsuffering," are at times, after very protracted and obstinate resistance of the means of grace— of the word and providence of God (His word in all its variety of appeals and motives, and His providence in all its variety of dispensations, prosperous and adverse)—subdued to repentance, " turned to God." Their hearts relent, they believe, and are saved. Toward *both* of these classes of persons there has been shown, on the part of God, " *much* longsuffering." To many a believer—especially to such as have been converted later in life than others —might I make my appeal for the truth of this. Many a heart would melt, and many an eye would glisten with the tear of shame and of humble and grateful joy, in recollecting the past and comparing it with the present, and reflecting how long they held out against a longsuffering God; ay, and to many an unbelieving sinner, now going on in his trespasses, in despite of the patience of a holy, sin-hating, but merciful God, who is still " waiting to be gracious," might I make a similar appeal—an appeal to which, whatever impression it might make or fail to make upon his *heart*, his *conscience* would secretly and faithfully, and perhaps stingingly, respond.—*Dr. Wardlaw.*

The hardening of Pharaoh's heart.— Oh, my friends, this is a fearful thought—that man can become worse by God's loving desire to make him better! But so it is. So it was with Pharaoh of old. All God's pleading with him by the message of Moses and Aaron, by the mighty plagues which God sent on Egypt, only hardened Pharaoh's heart. The Lord God spoke to him, and His message only lashed Pharaoh's proud and wicked will into greater fury and rebellion, as a vicious horse becomes the more unmanageable the more you punish it. Therefore it is said plainly in Scripture that *the Lord* hardened Pharaoh's heart—not, as some fancy, that the Lord's will was to make Pharaoh hard-hearted and wicked. God forbid! The Lord is the fountain of good only, and not He but we and the devil make evil. But the more the Lord pleaded with Pharaoh and tried to bend his will, the more self-willed he became. The more the Lord showed Pharaoh that the Lord was king, the more he hated the kingdom and will of God, the more he determined to be king himself and to obey no law but his own wicked fancies and pleasures, and asked, " Who is the Lord, that I should obey Him?"— *Charles Kingsley.*

The potter and clay.—But some may say, Is not that a gloomy and terrible notion of God that He cannot change His purpose? Is not that as much as to say that there is a dark necessity hanging over each of us; that a man must be just what God chooses, and do just what He has ordained to do, and go to everlasting happiness or misery exactly as God has foreordained from all eternity; so that there is no use trying to do right or not to do wrong? If I am to be saved, say such people, I shall be saved whether I try or not; and if I am to be damned, I shall be damned whether I try or not. I am in God's hands, like clay in the hands of the potter, and what I am like is therefore God's business and not mine. No! The very texts in the Bible which tell us that God cannot change or repent, tell us what it is that He cannot change in—in showing lovingkindness and tender mercy, longsuffering and repenting of the evil. Whatsoever else He cannot repent of, He cannot repent of repenting of the evil. It is true we are in His hand as clay in the hand of the potter. But it is a sad misreading of Scripture to make that mean that we are to sit with our hands folded, careless about our own way and conduct—still less that we are to give ourselves up to despair because we have sinned against God: for what is the very verse which follows after that? Listen: "O house of Israel, cannot I do with you as this potter? saith the Lord. Behold, as clay is in the hands of the potter, so are ye in My hand, O house of Israel. At what instant I shall speak concerning a kingdom, to pull down and destroy it; if that nation, against whom I have pronounced, turn from their evil, I will repent of the evil which I thought to do to them. And at what instant I shall speak concerning a nation, and concerning a kingdom, to build and to plant it; if it do evil in My sight, that it obey not My voice, then I will repent of the good, wherewith I said I would benefit them." So that the lesson which we are to draw from the parable of the potter's clay is just the exact opposite which some men draw. Not that God's decrees are absolute, but that they are conditional, and depend on our good or evil conduct. Not that His election and His reprobation are unalterable, but that they alter *at that instant* at which man alters. Not that His grace and will are irresistible, as the foolish man against whom St. Paul argues fancies, but that we can resist God's will, and that our destruction comes only by resisting His will: in short, that God's will is no brute, material necessity and fate, but the will of a living, loving Father.—*Charles Kingsley.*

God's sovereignty not to be arraigned by men.—There are some persons so partial to what we may call the high doctrines of the gospel that they can scarcely endure to hear anything else: they are like persons whose taste is vitiated by strong drink or highly seasoned food; they have no appetite for anything which does not savour of their favourite opinions. This is a great evil in the Church, not only as injuring the souls in whom it exists, but as tending exceedingly to strengthen the prejudices of others against the doctrines which are so abused. Those who are thus disposed towards "the deep things of God" fancy themselves *edified* merely because their corrupt taste is gratified; but their edification is not real and scriptural, for if it were it would incline them to receive with meekness and humility every word of God, whereas they treat with contempt everything which seems to savour of plain, practical religion. We regret exceedingly that such persons exist; but we must not on their account run into an opposite extreme, and keep these doctrines altogether out of sight: we must not shun to declare unto men the whole counsel of God. Whatever is revealed in the sacred records must be brought forth in its season; nor are we at liberty to "withhold from men anything that may be profitable unto them." We therefore address ourselves to every subject in its place, though on such subjects as that which is before us we would do it with fear and trembling, conscious how unable we are to do justice to it, and fearful lest by any means we should make it an occasion of offence to those who are not prepared for the investigation of it. The sovereignty of God is to the proud heart of man an unpalatable subject; but in the passage before us we are called to vindicate it against the objections of those who are disposed, like the Jew in our text, to contend against it. To place the matter in its true light, we shall consider:—

I. **The point at issue between the objector and St. Paul.**—St. Paul had intimated that the Jews were to be rejected from, and that the Gentiles were to be admitted into, the Church

—an offensive subject to the Jews. They are represented as declaring that if God exercise sovereignty in this way, the blame of man's condemnation must be transferred to God Himself, since it was impossible for a man to resist His will. To this objection we must now reply—

II. The apostle's determination of it.—St. Paul, hearing such a blasphemous objection as this, "Why doth God yet find fault? for who hath resisted His will?" replies to it in a way of just reprehension. "O man, who art thou that repliest against God?" Consider thyself as a creature; consider thyself as a sinner. In a way of sound argument two things St. Paul proceeds to substantiate against his objector—one, that God had a right to dispose of everything according to His sovereign will and pleasure, and the other was that in the way He had hitherto disposed of them and had determined still to dispose of them He was fully justified. We may conclude with suggesting—

III. The proper improvement of the subject, which offers important hints to objectors. Strange that even Christians should determine what will and what will not consist with the divine attributes! But be assured as the heavens are high above the earth, so are His thoughts and ways higher than yours. There are many who speak of the deep things of God as if they were as plain and intelligible as the simplest truth that can be mentioned. It becomes you doubtless to investigate, and as far as possible to understand, every truth of God; but in things so infinitely above the reach of human intellect it becomes you to be humble, modest, diffident. To all persons without exception, you have other things to do than to be wasting your time about unprofitable disputes —you are now under the hands of the Potter. The question that most concerns you is, For what are you preparing? In order to ascertain this you need not look into the book of God's decrees, but simply examine the state of your own hearts. Are you diligently seeking after God? Are you living by faith on the Lord Jesus Christ, washing daily in the fountain of His blood, and renewed daily by the operations of His Spirit? This will mark you vessels of honour; and the want of this is sufficient to stamp you vessels unto dishonour.—*Simeon.*

Predestination of the vessel not its fabrication. — The all-important point for the interpretation of these verses is to decide when the act of forming the vessels took place. Does this operation represent the predestination or the moral government of God in actual time? A word of ver. 23 decides this question without giving ground for the least hesitation. This word is the key of the whole passage, and, strange to say, it is omitted by Luther and by the French translations anterior to that of Lausanne. It is the word "afore" — "which He has prepared *afore* for His glory." The predestination of the vessel, then, is not its fabrication; it precedes it. Thus, then, when God is compared to a potter who fashions the clay, the question is about His actual treatment of sinners. They are before Him one identical mass, vile and shapeless. To make the one portion vessels unto dishonour, to make them promote His glory without bettering their condition, is to treat them according to their nature; to make the other portion vessels unto honour is to treat them according to His grace which has been given them in Christ before the foundation of the world. As to the vessels of wrath, God is not the author of their nature, but only of their form; He has fashioned them, but He has not "prepared" them; their form is already a merited punishment; He shows therein His wrath. Could one believe that God was irritated against those who would be such as He had wished them to be? Would He need "a grand long-suffering" to endure His own work in the state which He had Himself determined? Has He raised with one

327

hand what He has overturned with the other ? Such a doctrine ends by doing violence to that reason in the name of which it has outraged our moral sentiments. It is clear, then, that the potter's relation to the vessels of wrath is that of the fashioner of material made ready to his hand. He is not to be blamed if the coarse clay will only make a dishonoured vessel. The preparation of the clay, the contraction of its coarse character, has been anterior to the potter's disposal of it. All he can do is to determine the destination which suits the nature of the provid d clay. In the same way God is not to be held responsible for the coarse characters sinners contract in the process of their development. They have exercised their freedom in reaching the condition when, like clay, they lie before the great Potter's wheel. All that God can be held responsible for is the form as vessels of dishonour they are to take ; and if He show His deserved wrath in disposing of them as dishonoured vessels, He is acting well within His rights. It is in the disposal of incorrigible sinners, in suffering long with them, and in at last dooming them to destruction, that He displays the severe side of His character —that side without which He could not ensure our respect. As for this wrath of God, it has been very happily denominated by some of the Germans "the love-pain [*Liebesschmerz*] of God." There is in our chapter only one predestination, that of grace ; and not only that, but the words of the apostle are weighed and chosen to prevent all misapprehension : the one are *ready* or *fit* for perdition, the other are *prepared* for glory ; the first, it is not God who has made them ready—on the contrary, He endures them " with a grand longsuffering " ; the latter, it is God who has prepared them. Still more, He has prepared them afore. Were it not for the care with which the idea of reprobation is here put aside, I should never have supposed that such a dogma had presented itself to the spirit of a sacred writer. Paul makes on purpose an antithetic parallelism, as he had done (chap. vi. 23) between wages and gift, and this parallelism finds itself in all the members of the sentence. God shows His anger towards the wicked and the riches of His glory towards the saved ; but the latter, the mercy, is altogether gratuitous. If He wish to make the power known (ver. 22), it is not His power to create evil, but to punish it ; and how to punish evil if not by evil, how to show His anger towards the clay unless by making the vessels unto dishonour.— *Monsell.*

MAIN HOMILETICS OF THE PARAGRAPH.—*Verses* 25—29.

The not-beloved become beloved.—The late Mr. Spurgeon, in his sermon on " Jacob have I loved, but Esau have I hated," says : " This text means just what it says ; it does not mean nations, but it means the persons mentioned. Jacob—that is, the man whose name was Jacob—Jacob have I loved, but Esau have I hated. Take care how any of you meddle with God's word. I have heard of folks altering passages they did not like. Our only power with the word of God is simply to let it stand as it is, and to endeavour by God's grace to accommodate ourselves to that." He will not even allow us to translate " Esau have I hated " by " the meaningl ss words ' I love less.' " Fortunately we do not want. But if we are to follow the great preacher's literalism, shall we find the doctrine of eternal predestination and election before time in the twenty-fifth and twenty-sixth verses ? He says in another place, " I may be as sure of my election as if I could climb to heaven and turn over the red roll and read my name in letters of gold. The Lord has given thee a test which never did fail yet, and never will." How about those once not beloved ? Are the names of the not-beloved written in the red roll? He says that between calling and election there is an indissoluble union. Here God calls a people which were once not His people; therefore God elects those who were once not elected. As we understand the doctrine of election carried out to its extreme lengths, the elected always are and have been God's people, and the effectual calling is only giving outward expression to the divine purpose. So again the non-elect are elected—the not-people of God become His children. Our conclusion is that repellent dogmatism on abstruse subjects is to be avoided. Positive assertions cannot bury difficulties. The reason of man cannot be stifled by swelling words. Humility is a becoming attitude in the presence of the sublimest topics that can engage human attention. We learn from the passage under discussion :—

I. **Divine grace.**—Whatever may be our views of predestination and election, we must hold fast to the doctrine of divine grace. If the gospel be a remedial scheme for the benefit of universal man, then we must not hamper that scheme by narrow views. Let us believe in the largeness and freeness of the divine mind; let God's call move through the earth, giving forth its sweet measures as fully as God's myriad songsters. God makes into His people those who were once not His people. He called the Gentiles; He called the British peoples. Let us adore God's matchless grace. God calls, and all who hear and obey may become the children of the living God, the beloved of the eternal Love.

II. **God's righteousness.**—Wonderful is the pleading of Jeremiah. "Righteous art Thou, O Lord, when I plead with Thee; yet let me talk with Thee of Thy judgments : Wherefore doth the way of the wicked prosper? wherefore are all they happy that deal very treacherously." The prophet rises above seeming anomalies in the divine proceedings, and declares, "Righteous art Thou, O Lord." Whatever may appear contradictory, yet let us rest assured that God's finished work, that God's completed plan, will vindicate the eternal righteousness. Righteous is the Lord, though He call that beloved which was not beloved, and though only a remnant of the elect nation be saved.

III. **God's provision.**—A remnant is saved. A germinating force is provided. A remnant was saved from the deluged world; a remnant was saved from the destroyed cities. God has His remnants through all time, and these become the seed forces of great harvests. In darkest periods God has His sons of light. God's germinating forces are good and true men. They are productive. They die; but the wheat dies, and over its tomb waves the golden harvest.

The remnant.—R.V., "It is the remnant that shall be saved."
I. **The doctrine of the remnant.**—1. *Teaching of Old Testament prophecy.* The text is quoted from Isa. x. 22. Words there are, "A remnant of them shall return "—*i.e.*, from the captivity, and thus be saved from ruin and extinction, which awaited the majority. Referring to that remnant (chap. vi. 13), he speaks of it as a "holy seed." In his eye small minority were a "holy seed," but great majority unsound, and therefore doomed. "Drunkards and blind," as he calls them—*i.e.*, dissolute and foolish—constituting this majority, must perish; but its perishing = necessary step towards happier future. Foresees that remnant is not only to return and so be saved itself, but it is to be also a mighty power for the saving of others. A Prince of the house of David is to be born, who is to bring wondrous influences to bear upon the bad majority, and at length to reign over a state renewed, preserved, and enlarged, a great and glorious kingdom. No need to enter into question as to how soon prophet expected reign of Prince to begin. Enough to know such a Prince at length did come, and that His object was to found a kingdom not of this world. He came and accomplished His work. His followers at first a mere remnant—twelve apostles, one hundred and twenty disciples at Jerusalem—but its mission =

through that Prince to save the world. Communities wherein no good remnant left; hopelessly doomed (Isa. i. 9 ; cp. Rom. ix. 29). 2. *Teaching of the text.* At Pentecost strangers from Rome at Jerusalem. Perhaps, too, some of those *libertini* (freedmen) who heard St. Stephen may have been Romans. In any case St. Paul here addresses a Church which had been founded at Rome, chiefly Jewish, but also partly Gentile = small minority among vast population. They right; rulers of this world and vast majority of people all wrong. They = "holy seed," which was to grow and wax strong; leaven, which was to extend itself till the whole was leavened. How this was done subsequent history of Christianity shows. 3. *General statemeut.* History, both sacred and secular, exhibits frequent periods where the corruption of human nature becomes painfully apparent in general depravity and vice. But God's Spirit has never entirely forsaken the world. Except in cases where utter ruin has resulted, a reaction has in the course of time set in, and this has always begun not with the many but the few. Often when the majority have run headlong into sin and ruin, a minority have been saved—*e.g.*, Flood, call of Abraham, Caleb and Joshua, etc. "Many are called, but few are chosen." Majority very apt to be wrong on vital questions. May be sometimes right, but as a rule lack principle and persistence. To day good impulses prevail, but gone to-morrow. [Contrast Sunday cry of "Hosanna" with Friday cry of "Crucify Him"; vacillation of crowds in every age ; popularity of Savonarola with Florentines all gone in an hour, and the once powerful and attractive preacher publicly executed ; instability of popular feeling in Reformation times and since.]

II. **What saves the remnant?**—Answer of : 1. Isaiah and prophets : "To order one's conversation aright," to "cease to do evil," to "learn to do well," to "delight in the law of the Lord," to "make one's study in it all the day long." 2. Our blessed Lord : to "seek first the kingdom of God and His righteousness," to "become as little children," to "do the will of our Father in heaven." 3. St. Paul : to "have faith in Christ, the embodiment of righteousness" (vers. 30-32), and thus to have the heart and mind set upon those objects, aims, and actions of which righteousness is composed (Phil. iv. 8).

III.. **Consolation for the saved remnant.**—1. Holding fast to that whereby the remnant is saved, there arises in the soul a peace which nothing else can give (Psalm cxix. 165). God's laws of righteousness are eternal and unchangeable. We know what they are. The majority may seek to evade them ; but the godly minority have the consolation of knowing that the eternal One is not only wise and good, but also powerful to "defend the right." This thought has nerved on the saints and heroes who have often shone as lights in a corrupt age. 2. Their influence must sooner or later be felt. "Ye are the salt of the earth." Their example and efforts have a tendency to purify. There is consolation in the thought of this.

IV. **Warning from the doctrine of the remnant.**—Not to be led astray by an evil majority (Exod. xxiii. 2). An evil majority, headed by self-righteous scribes and Pharisees, lured Jerusalem to its overthrow. Massillon, preaching before the court of France in the days of Louis XIV., spoke of the last judgment—the great testing-time when the saved remnant shall be finally severed from all others besides—in terms so awfully vivid that when the climax of his discourse was reached the whole of that brilliant assemblage rose to their feet as one man, conscience-stricken, cut to the heart. But there was no real reformation. The fashion of the time was too strong. The righteous minority in France was too small, too weak, to save the nation from the crack of doom which burst in the Revolution nearly a century later. Beware of the authority which in these days it is too much the fashion to attach to mere majorities (Matt. vii. 13, 14).— *G. E. P. Reade.*

Vers. 25-33. *Paul elects the non-elect.*—"As He saith also in Osee," etc.
This avowedly difficult passage deals with the doctrine of election, suggested by
the question of the calling of the Gentiles. Paul here sets forth the groundwork
of chaps. ix. to xi. He points out that the Israelites who were lost were ruined
by pride, refusing to comply with the divine purposes. Some have built on this
section of the epistle the doctrine of election, which Wesley thus expresses:
"By virtue of an eternal, unchangeable, irresistible decree of God, one part of
mankind is infallibly saved, and the rest infallibly damned, it being impossible
that any of the former should be damned, or that any of the latter should be
saved." What is Paul's attitude towards this? The whole chapter deals fully
with the question. 1. Paul notes the unhappy fact that the Jews were rejected
by God. 2. This he remarks in order to show that neither ancestry nor a
man's works will form any claim to justification. 3. He seeks to show that
God has a free hand, is not bound down by any restriction at all. He has
absolute right to do as He pleases, and name His own conditions for salvation.
Hence He may reject the Jews who do not comply, and accept the Gentiles who
do. 4. Paul, by his concluding statements, throws open salvation to all who are
willing to accept Christ, even those whom the Jews thought were non-elect.
The text suggests that Paul practically elects the non-elect.

I. **Paul here teaches that salvation is for all who believe in Christ.**—1. Here
he is in harmony with Peter, his contemporary. Peter (Acts iii. 25, 26) declared
the blessing of redemption to be first promised to the Jews. But the very word
"first" implied that it was to be sent to the Gentiles also. Paul agrees in
Gal. iii. 8. 2. He is in harmony with the psalmists, who teach that grace is not
exclusive (Psalms lxxii. 17, cii. 15, 22, cxvii. 1). 3. He is in harmony with
the prophets, who recognise the breadth and length, the height and depth, of
the divine redemption (Isa. xlv. 22, 23; also our text, ver. 25). Is not this
pointing to the salvation of the human race? The minor prophets teach the
same (Joel ii. 28-31, iii. 12-21; Hab. ii. 13, 14; Zeph. ii. 11, iii. 8, 9; Mal. i.
11, iii. 1-3, iv. 1-3). 4. Paul is in harmony here with his other epistles, where
he develops the doctrine of salvation for all who believe with great force (*e.g.*,
Eph. i. 10; Col. i. 20). Is not this an election of the non-elect?

II. **The once-indifferent may embrace salvation.**—Ver. 30. The Jews were
first called; the Gentiles appeared to be excluded. The Jews exhibited this
thought by their utmost scorn for Gentiles. But now, if willing to come, if
accepting the conditions of salvation, they may be saved. Once they were outside the pale, because they followed not after righteousness, had no knowledge
of it, no care nor thought about it. When they heard the gospel, they
embraced it. Then its blessings were theirs. The moment of acceptance was
the moment when the barriers of exclusion were broken down. It is so now.
We are "non-elect" so long as we reject the gospel, and no longer.

III. **There are no vested interests in the matter of salvation.**—We may be
Jews, having Abraham for our father; but that will not open the kingdom of
heaven to us. Israel, the chosen people, not saved from disaster: only a
remnant saved. We may say we are among the "elect": that, if we do not
live aright, will not save us. The question of elect or non-elect does not free us
from active living faith in Christ. We must believe in Christ and live like
Him.

IV. **Outward observance of God's laws will not secure our election.**—Israel
followed after the law, observed it to the letter, but had none of the spirit of
righteousness. Jews harboured hate, secretly served other gods, etc.; and God
rejected them, even while their altar fires were burning and their feasts were
religiously observed. Why rejected? Because they sought not their salvation
by faith, but by works. There was no inward righteousness. It was all out-

ward show. "Not every one that saith," etc. It is a case of the last being first and the first last. Any who may have the form of righteousness may miss its blessings, if they have not the power of godliness. At the last there will be a sifting; the unworthy will be set aside. In this sense "a remnant" only will be saved—only those who have loved righteousness and accepted Christ as their Saviour.

V. **If any are lost, the fault is theirs.**—They can never plead the existence of a hard-and-fast law that dooms some and delivers others. The lost are not so lost because of any decree of God. It is because they reject Christ and His offers of mercy. Therefore the need that preachers should still continue to plead with men, as those for whom they must give account. And therefore, also, the need and happy opportunity for the worst to come and plead forgiveness from the Saviour of men.—*Albert Lee.*

SUGGESTIVE COMMENTS ON VERSES 24—29.

Paul's design.—In the twenty-fourth verse the apostle explains whom he means by "the vessels of mercy": "Even us, whom He hath called, not of the Jews only, but also of the Gentiles." "To call," as the word is used in Scripture, sometimes refers to the offer of salvation made by the preaching of the gospel, and sometimes to this offer rendered effectual by the co-operation of the Holy Spirit and embraced by those to whom it is proposed. Sometimes also, as in the next verse, it denotes to denominate in a particular manner—"I will call them My people"; and in this sense it often means to make them what they are called—"I will call them My people" being precisely equivalent to "I will make them My people." Here the word is used in the last of these senses, and means "whom He hath called or constituted His people"—even us believers in Christ, not of the Jews only, but also of the Gentiles, whom God hath called to the obedience of the gospel, and thus constituted His Church and people. This application of the word, which is fixed by the following quotation, is a further proof that the preparation "for glory," mentioned in the preceding verse, does not mean eternal glory, but merely the glorious distinction of being the Church and people of God. He goes on to show that the calling of the Gentiles, and the continuing of only a small portion of the Jews in the number of the people of

God, need not appear incredible, seeing it might be clearly inferred from the Old Testament Scriptures (ver. 25), "As He saith also in Osee, I will call them My people which were not My people, and her beloved which was not beloved." The quotation is taken from Hosea ii. 23; but the apostle has inverted the order of the two clauses and slightly changed the language, though without altering the meaning. It has been thought that this prophecy relates primarily to the Israelites, and only in a secondary sense to the calling of the Gentiles. But the words are certainly most appropriate when applied to the Gentiles. "I will call them My people—that is, I will make them My people—which were not My people, and I will render her beloved which was not beloved," are phrases which describe correctly receiving into the number of the people of God those who did not formerly belong to it. They do not so well describe restoring to the number of God's people those who had belonged to it formerly. And as the apostle quotes the prophecy as descriptive of the calling of the Gentiles, we are authorised to hold this to be its proper application. To these prophecies, relating to the extension of the privilege of the people of God to the Gentiles, there is added another relating to the Israelites (ver. 26): "And it shall come to pass, that in the place where it was said unto them, Ye are not My people, there shall they be called the children of the living God." This prediction relates to the displeasure of God with His people on account of their sins, and His refusing to acknowledge them as His people—a refusal, however, which would be only temporal, for they would in due time be constituted " the children of the living God." By joining these two quotations together, the apostle confirms the doctrine which he has been inculcating, that the Gentiles, as well as the Jews, were to have the offer of the gospel made to them, and to be admitted without distinction to share in the privileges of the people of God. But though the offer of salvation through Christ was to be given to Jews and Gentiles without distinction, it had been foretold that only a small number of the Jews would accept the offered mercy (ver. 27): "Esaias also crieth concerning Israel, Though the number of the children of Israel be as the sand of the sea, a remnant shall be saved." The quotation is from Isa. x. 22, where the

prophet alludes to the consequences of the destruction brought upon the ten tribes by the Assyrians. He "crieth concerning Israel," said the apostle— that is, he openly and authoritatively declares—that though their number before their dispersion be as the sand of the sea, only a remnant—or, as it is in the original, *the* remnant—shall be saved from the general calamity, or return from their dispersion. This prediction is quoted as an illustration of the divine procedure in the present circumstances of the Jewish nation. For as the ten tribes were at that time scattered among the heathen, and ceased to be the people of God on account of their sins, a very small portion of them only escaping this calamity, so in the present times the great body of the nation would suffer a similar fate on account of the heinous guilt which they had contracted, the small number which believed in Christ only being continued a part of the Church and people of God.—*Ritchie.*

MAIN HOMILETICS OF THE PARAGRAPH.—*Verses* 30—33.

Unexpected results.—One of the errors of Judaism was exclusiveness. There was no salvation outside the Judaic system. All Gentiles were excluded. And here St. Paul not only corrects the mistake, but shows that even the Jews themselves might be excluded from divine righteousness while following their own system. Let us avoid contracted views; let not our religion warp our understanding. We may vaunt our privileges, and self-confidence may prove our destruction.

I. **Opposite pursuits.**—The Gentiles as a whole were not ethical. They did not eagerly pursue after righteousness. Israel had a glorious ethical system, and in their own way the Israelites followed after the law of righteousness. The latter had a lofty aim, while the former was not stirred by the ennobling ideal. Lofty aims must surely be good. It is better to have loved and lost than never to have loved at all. Surely it is better to aim high and lose than never to rise above the common level. The shooter is wrong, not because he aimed high, but because he refused to be guided, and thus missed the mark. The man who seeks goodly pearls is following after the law of righteousness, is seeking for the true good, is yearning for soul rest. He is earnest, humble, and sincere, and finds the Pearl of great price. The seeker and the non-seeker obtain blessings in the sovereignty of divine administrations. The one gets the Pearl of great price, and the other finds the treasure hid in the field. The non-seeker is not to be applauded for his moral indolence. The seeker is not to be condemned for his moral diligence.

II. **Unexpected results.**—The Gentile finds that which he is not seeking. The Israelite misses that which he is pursuing. How true this often is to the ways of life! Results are contrary to our expectations. Like causes do not produce like effects. We follow after fame and reach wealth. We pursue pleasure and attain misery. Results are disappointing. Our purposes are broken off. Our projected castles reach no completion. Some men work hard and fail, while others without any stretching forth of effort grasp the prizes. The Gentiles and the Jews are found in all spheres and in all kingdoms.

III. **The satisfactory explanation.**—Israel failed. Wherefore? Because they sought it not by faith; they did not move according to the divine plan. We cannot pretend to give satisfactory explanations of all the unexpected results of time. Perhaps if we were endowed with far-reaching vision and a more acute understanding many a life's inexplicables would disappear. Certain it must be that the life which is projected and prosecuted according to the divine plan cannot be a failure. We work from low results, and the end is disappointing. Moving according to the divine idea, we should reap divine fruition. Surely this must be so in the moral sphere. That blessing which the Gentile obtained is possible to the Jew. He that believeth shall be saved. The "he" is not specific, but generic. Only he that believeth. Whosoever will come may come. The divine thirst will not be assuaged until it finds the living water.

IV. **The undesigned hindrance.**—The Stone laid by God in Zion becomes a stumbling-stone and rock of offence. This is not the divine design. This Stone was chosen by God out of the eternal quarry as being most fitted for the erection of a spiritual temple. The Stone was selected by infinite wisdom, prepared by divine power, and was the expression of eternal love; and though the Stone was rejected by the foolish builders, the scribes and priests of this world, it was accepted by God, crowned with glory and honour. And God never placed this Stone in Zion to be a stumbling-block to any. Men stumble because blindness hath happened unto them in part; men stumble because human pride sets itself against divine love and wisdom. Humility would save from many a fall. He that is down need fear no fall. He that is little in his own eyes will see the greatness and preciousness of this Stone, and by its greatness will become spiritually great and noble and glorious. There is a blessed life-communicating quality in this Stone, so that those who are joined to it by faith become possessors of eternal life. By faith in this beloved Stone those not beloved become by divine grace the beloved children of God.

V **The projected effect.**—Whosoever believeth on Him shall not be ashamed, shall not make haste, shall move through life with peaceful calmness, shall face death with undaunted courage, and stand unabashed in the ineffable splendours of the eternal light. They that follow after the law of righteousness in their own strength have reason to be ashamed as they see the immense distance between the endeavour and the achievement, between the mental would and the evil result. They that follow after the law of righteousness by faith in the righteous Mediator have no reason to be ashamed, for He strengthens the mental would and leads to moral accomplishment. Through Christ, when I would do good, the power to accomplish is present with me: that power comes from the strength-giving Saviour. Ashamed of my fruitless efforts, I may well be ashamed of the weakness of my faith, the dulness of my hope, and the coldness of my love. Ashamed of my connection with the Noblest of mortals and the Highest of immortals I shall surely never be. Can it be for one moment entertained that we should be ashamed of Him who has created in time the noblest heroes of the human race? Science has its votaries, philosophy its devoted adherents, literature its admirers, history grows eloquent about the pomp and circumstance of man; but rightly considered, it is highest glory to follow in the sublime train of Him who shall gather to Himself the selected spirits of all worlds. Immortal honours are the portion of the victorious Mediator, and those honours are shared by His followers.

Ver. 33. *Divine appointment, human disappointment, human satisfaction.*—Many are the disappointments of life. Happy is the old age which can look back upon life without feeling that it is full of sorrowful memories. We may have to look back upon disappointments, but we shall not be filled with sorrow if we can feel that we have done our best, and that they have come upon us in spite of our best endeavours. But is such a retrospect possible? The wise and calm reflection of age will point us to many ways where we have gone wrong. The visions of youth have gone down into blackness. We have had noble aspirations, but ignoble performances. The stones of safety have been turned into stones of stumbling; rocks of beauty, glistening in the sunlight, have become rocks of offence. Blessed is the man who with divine light and leading has built upon the Rock of eternal beauty. Let us consider and endeavour to appreciate the wisdom of the divine appointment, and then we shall not be disappointed.

I. **The divine appointment.**—"Behold, I lay in Zion." The "beholds" of God are emphatic. They invite our attention to the consideration of the divine proceedings. The "beholds" of God are written in hieroglyphics on nature. There is the inaugurating voice directing attention to some great event or catastrophe about to follow. God writes a preface to all His greatest works. Noah's ark is God's "behold," telling of the coming calamity; the intense calm of nature is a "behold," speaking to us of the coming storm. The "beholds" of God are written in type and in figure and in plain speech in His moral dispensations. The Levitical dispensation is a sublime "behold," drawing attention to the brighter dispensation beyond; the prophetical dispensation is a clearer "behold," declaring the coming Messiah, sometimes in plainest terms. Thus it is in the passages from which St. Paul quotes in this wondrous text: Behold, says God, I lay in Zion a stone. Let the universe consider; let angels and men ponder; and the wisest will declare that the divine appointment is in every way excellent. This stone-laying: 1. *Is good, for it is the work of a wise God.* Our true conception of a God carries with it and implies the conception of a Being who is all-wise. We see wisdom in nature in many of her departments. What appears to us unwisdom may on further knowledge turn out to be highest wisdom. What we know not now we may know hereafter. And we are always met by the fact that a disturbing element has been introduced into nature. After all drawbacks there is sufficient in the world to convince the candid mind that a wise God has arranged this lower universe. If there be wisdom in the material much more is there in the moral realm. The God of wisdom laid the precious Stone in Zion. Can it be for one moment supposed that God waited for thousands of years before commencing this spiritual building, and then laid a stone which the least competent of builders would reject? 2. *Safe, for it is the work of a God of power.* The powerful will not dishonour himself by putting up that which is weak and insecure, if his ability and his resources are equal. The all-powerful God would not lay a stone in Zion which would crumble beneath the superincumbent edifice. So far the Stone has done no dishonour to the divine selection. It stands to-day. Time has gnawed no erasure on its beautiful surface. Living stones in vast numbers have been piled on this precious Corner-stone, and it upholds and gives life and firmness to all. 3. *Beneficial, for it is the work of a God of love.* God laid the Stone for the promotion of human well-being. In answer to the promptings of His infinite love and wondrous pity He laid this Stone, and it could not be thus other than to serve a beneficial purpose. He laid it, not to be a stone of stumbling, but a stone of spiritual elevation, by and on which men might rise to the light and glory of the divine goodness. This Stone has been a beneficial rock to multitudes. It was laid in the dry and arid Zion, and transformed it at once into the sunny Zion which has warmed and cheered many hearts, which has lighted the otherwise dark pathway of many mortals.

The wonder is how some of the stones were quarried and brought to their places which formed part of the temple. A greater wonder appears as we look at this spiritual Stone which is at once the foundation-stone and corner-stone of God's Church-temple. 4. *Available, for it is the work of a God of mercy.* We must not localise God's moral doings. In these days we visit Palestine as if God's manifestations were only for one little tract of land. God's Palestine is everywhere. He may work in one corner of the earth, but His glory fills the wide sphere. He laid the Stone in Zion; it is a movable stone, an omnipresent stone. Wherever there are living, believing stones of humanity, there God has laid His "living Stone," to be to them a source of life and power. The Rock of shelter is in every land for all races. Let us seek to move with open eyes and receptive hearts.

II. **The human disappointment.**—Strange that a divine appointment should prove a human disappointment! Perhaps not so strange, if we remember that the human is ever fighting against the divine. The failure of the divine appointment is not in God, but in man. Is it not so that some of the best works, even those originated by human wisdom, have been to many as stones of stumbling and rocks of offence? Not only great moral but great material reformations have been opposed. Every great invention, every great improvement, has had to fight its way against the opposition of the foolish and the wicked. We are told that Christ would have done well enough if it had not been for a Paul. He has made dark that which was light, rendered difficult that which was plain. A nice and easy religion is that of the four gospels; but a repulsive and difficult religion is that of Paul. But if Paul were removed as a stone of stumbling, the next step would be to remove the Christ Himself as a stone of stumbling. We may rest assured that those who stumble at Paul would and do stumble at the Christ. Perhaps some want a Paul removed so that they may have a Christ and a religion after their own fashion. Christ was a stone of stumbling before Paul spoke or wrote a word, and Christ would still be a stone of stumbling if Paul and his epistles could be consigned to forgetfulness. Human sin, pride, and selfishness are always disappointed when they come face to face with that which seeks their overthrow. The modern notion is that we are all to be Christs, but we are a long way from the ideal. The Christlike men, the Christs of humanity, have been as stones of stumbling and rocks of offence to their fellows. A Christ of love and gentleness would be received in modern society; but how about a Christ who uses language not allowed in drawing-rooms, and calls men hypocrites and whited sepulchres? What about a Christ whose purity and unselfishness flash scorn upon our impurities, our meannesses, our hollowness, and our intense selfishness? Christ was a stone of stumbling to the Jews. They did their best to crush and destroy. If Christ were to revisit this sphere with only the origin and the credentials with which He appeared in Palestine, what would be His reception in our Christian countries? Would this Galilean Peasant be received in the palaces of peers? Would this unlettered Nazarene be allowed to preach in university pulpits? Would this Man of plain speech be allowed to shock the ears of fashionable congregations? If they will not hear sermons about Him, would they be more willing to hear Him preach when He would tell them to sell all that they had and give to the poor? A stone of stumbling and a rock of offence is the divine Stone; but, thank God, not to all, not by any means all.

III. **Human satisfaction.**—"Whosoever believeth in Him shall not be ashamed," shall not be disappointed, shall not hurry away in terror and confusion, but shall realise peace, joy, and solid satisfaction. Believers should not be disappointed; for: 1. *The entrance of Christ brings infinite content to the soul of men.* A foundation-stone must not only rest in its place, but afford a resting-place to the stones it supports. Christ the foundation-stone affords a sweet resting-place to the lively stones of redeemed humanity. He imparts gracious content. The soul full of Christ is full of divine peace and repose. The soul cannot rest sweetly on any other stone. Discontent, restlessness, pervade the nature so long as Christ is absent. The soul was made for spiritual bread, and cannot be satisfied with the husks of time. We must feed on the Bread of life sent down from heaven. 2. *Union with Christ gives proper proportion to life.* Due proportion in an edifice cannot be secured if the foundation-stones and corner-stones be unfit and inadequate. How disproportionate are our lives! What a confused and disordered mass is the result of the life-building of a vast majority! If we would build aright, if we would construct so that part may answer to part in symmetrical order, then we must build on Christ, and in Christ, and up to Christ. A life well rounded and complete is the Christ-life. No true Christian has been disappointed when he has reached life's close. Untold satisfaction will take possession of his nature when he is raised to be a monumental and ornamental pillar in the upper temple of our God. 3. *Union with Christ gives strength to life.* This Stone is a living stone. It has communicating properties. It is itself eternally and divinely strong, and imparts strength to all who are joined to it by faith. It is divinely adhesive, and makes fast to itself all believers, and sends its strength through all the lively stones of the spiritual edifice. Strong men are Christlike men—the most Christlike and the most giantlike. Even granite shall crumble and waste away; Christ-united stones will never be dissolved. 4. *Union with Christ gives beauty and grace to life.* Grace and beauty to a building are not possible if the foundation, corner, and top-stones be inadequate and incomplete. Every stone in a building seems to catch the grace and beauty of the whole structure. Every stone in God's spiritual temple catches and shares the grace and beauty of Him who was and is altogether lovely, the very ideal of moral beauty, of spiritual loveliness. What grace and beauty are there in stones rolling in the gutter! And oh, how many are as stones rolling in the gutter! They are bespattered with the mire of low purposes, selfish and sensual aims and desires. There is grace and beauty in the stones cut, carried, and polished by the divine Artificer. These are monumental stones—monumental of divine grace and love, polished after the similitude of a palace.

SUGGESTIVE COMMENTS ON VERSES 29—33.

Why the Jew failed.—As it is written, " Behold, I lay in Zion a stumbling-stone and rock of offence; and whosoever believeth on Him shall not be ashamed." By the word translated "stumbling-stone" is meant any obstacle put in a person's way, so as to make him stumble or fall, or anything that prevents him from accomplishing his design. In quoting the prophet's metaphorical language, to show why the Jews failed to attain to the true principle of justification, the apostle brings together parts of two different prophecies, both relating, however, to the same subject, and concurring to make up the view of it which he presents. The first part is taken from

Isa. viii. 14, where the Lord is said to be " for a stone of stumbling and for a rock of offence to both houses of Israel." There can be no doubt that this prediction refers to the Messiah, and that it foretells the offence which the Jews would take at Him. He was not that great temporal deliverer to whom they fondly looked forward, and therefore they refused to believe on Him. The second part of the quotation is taken from Isa. xxviii. 16, " Behold, I lay in Zion for a foundation a stone, a tried stone, a precious corner-stone, a sure foundation : he that believeth shall not make haste"; or, as the apostle quotes it, "shall not be ashamed." There can be as little doubt that this is

337

said in allusion to the Messiah ; and it shows that none who believe on Him shall have reason to be ashamed of their faith, or have their hopes disappointed. The import of the general conclusion contained in the four last verses may be thus shortly stated : The Gentiles, notwithstanding their ignorance and wickedness, have had the offer of salvation made to them, and many of them have believed in Christ, been admitted into the Christian Church, and obtained the righteousness grounded in faith. But the great body of the Jews, although they enjoy a law which is of divine authority, have not attained a true righteousness, because, trusting that they would be justified by obedience to their law, they refused, as their own prophets had foretold that they would do, to believe in the Messiah, were therefore rejected from being the Church and people of God, and destitute of that only true righteousness which has its foundation in faith, and which will be followed with salvation. This passage suggests the following important remark : The reason why the Jews failed to obtain true righteousness was their seeking it on the principle of establishing a claim to divine favour by their legal obedience. But the apostle has already proved that it is utterly impracticable to establish any claim of this kind, seeing it is wholly impossible to give that unerring obedience to the divine law which it would require. It ought, then, to be steadily kept in mind, that it is not by works of righteousness which we have done that we become entitled to salvation ; but that we must be saved by the mercy of God, extended through the Saviour, to those who possess the righteousness of faith. Faith in Christ, therefore, and reliance on Him for salvation, should lead the Christian to a uniform endeavour to obey the divine law ; that thus possessing the righteousness which is of faith, he may be saved through the redemption that is in Christ.—*Ritchie.*

ILLUSTRATIONS TO CHAPTER IX.

Ver. 3. *Ambrose and Nazianzen.*—Out of the greatest zeal to God and love to his countrymen, the apostle wisheth himself anathema—that is, not to be separated from the Spirit and grace of Christ (for so he should have sinned), but from the comforts of Christ, the happiness that comes in by Christ, as one well interpreteth it. *Charitas exuberans · optatetiam impossibilia,* saith Luther—his over-abounding charity wisheth impossibilities ; but his wish was *voluntas conditionata,* saith one. His love to the Church was like the ivy, which, if it cleave to a stone or an old wall, will rather die than forsake it. Somewhat like to this holy wish was that of Ambrose, that the fire of contentions kindled in the Churches might (if it were the will of God) be quenched with his blood. And that of Nazianzen, that (Jonahlike) he might be cast into the sea, so by it all might be calm in the public.—*Trapp.*

Ver. 13. *The mystery of God's love.*—A gentleman who thought Christianity was merely a heap of puzzling problems said to an old minister, "That is a very strange verse in the ninth chapter of the Epistle to the Romans—'Jacob have I loved, but Esau have I hated.'" "Very strange," replied the minister ; "but what is it, sir, that you see most strange about it ?" "Oh, that part, of course," said the gentleman patronisingly and with an air of surprise, "'Esau have I hated' is certainly very strange." "Well, sir," said the old minister ; "how wonderfully we are made, and how differently constituted ! The strangest part of all to me is that He could ever have loved Jacob." There is no mystery so glorious as the mystery of God's love.

Ver. 21. *Vessels of honour and dishonour.*—A certain minister, having changed his views of some parts of divine truth, was waited upon by an old acquaintance, who wished to reclaim him to his former creed. Finding he could not succeed in his object, he became warm, and told his friend in plain terms that God had given him "up to strong delusion," and that he was "a vessel of wrath fitted to destruction." "I think, brother," replied the one who was charged with the departure from the faith with great calmness—"I think, brother, that you have mistaken the sense of the passage you last referred to. Vessels are denominated according to their contents. A chemist, in conducting a stranger through his laboratory,

338

would say, 'This is a vessel of turpentine, that of vitriol,' etc., always giving to the vessel the name of the article it contains. Now when I see a man full of the holy and lovely Spirit of Christ, devoted to His service, and imitating His example, I say that man is a vessel of mercy, whom God hath afore-prepared unto glory; but when I see a man full of everything but the spirit of the Bible—opposed to the moral government of God, seeking his own things rather than those which are Christ's—and filled with malice, wrath, and *all uncharitableness*, I am compelled to consider him 'a vessel of wrath fitted to destruction.'"

Ver. 33. *The folly of rejecting the gospel.*—Now you may reject the gospel if you please;

but wherein will your condition be improved? If on a ship where some pestilence is raging, the crew and the passengers throw the doctor and the medicine-chest overboard, and keep the pestilence with them, how much better are they off? Many there are who are bent on casting Christianity overboard, on getting rid of the Church and the priest and theology, and who art bent on keeping their sin and all its multitudinous train of mischiefs and evils. If men had become pure of heart, then there might be some reason in dispensing with superfluous ministrations; but, thus far, scepticism and the rejection of Christianity are only to make darkness darker, and sickness more fatal, and distress more painful.

CHAPTER X.

CRITICAL NOTES.

Ver. 1.—That the apostle speaks not in the preceding chapter of the absolute reprobation of Israel is evident from this prayer and vehement desire. ἡ εὐδοκία.—The good-will of my heart and my prayer on Israel's behalf is for salvation, and thus he assumes the possibility of salvation for the rejected.

Ver. 2. **A zeal for God.**—Hence some were called zealots, taking the name from those who were zealous for that which is good.

Ver. 3.—They not knowing, not considering the righteousness of God. The way for man to attain unto the position of the righteous.

Ver. 4.—Refers more especially to Christ's active obedience: "The man that doeth them shall live by them." By doing men were accounted righteous under the law; while the gospel says, Believe, and live—believe, and do as the fruit of faith.

Ver. 6. **Say not in thine heart.**—Unbelief originates from self-confidence. **Who shall ascend?**—Indicating unbelief in a risen Saviour. Salvation is a completed work; do not trouble about its vastness or its difficulty.

Ver. 7.—ἄβυσσος, the place of departed spirits, supposed by the Jews to be far below the surface of the earth. The Jerusalem Targum renders the words thus: "Oh that there were one like Jonas the prophet who would descend into the depths of the great sea!" Now we know that Jonas descending into the deep was a type of Christ; "being brought again," say the LXX., "from the abyss of the earth." Philo asks, "What need is there to take long journeys or go to sea in search of virtue, we having the root of it within us?" or, as Moses saith, "In our mouth, in our heart, and in our hand."

Ver. 8.—A holy and sweet play of the Spirit on His own inspired word.

Ver. 9. **The Lord Jesus.**—Jesus as Jehovah. Paul is referring to Jer. xxiii. 6. Mouth confession important towards men, heart belief towards God. The law is works; the gospel is faith, and works following. The resurrection of Christ is a foundation fact; receive that, and we shall include all it implies.

Ver. 10.—In the heart faith is seated; with the tongue confession is made. Between these two salvation is completed.

Ver. 12.—A favourite Pauline expression declaring the exuberant grace of Christ.

Ver. 13.—Double argument for Christ's divinity. He is called Jehovah, and is invoked.

Ver. 15.—The Midrash shir Hasschium upon these words, "the voice of truth," etc., says, "This is the voice of King Messiah crying out, and saying, How beautiful upon the mountains," etc. Those Gentiles who have never heard the gospel preached cannot be condemned for want of faith in Christ.

Ver. 17.—The message of the prophets, but received as coming from God Himself.

Ver. 18.—These words being spoken literally of the preaching of the heavens to the Gentiles, touching the power, wisdom, and goodness of God, and the psalmist speaking after of God's teaching His people by the law, the apostle accommodates these words to the revelation of God's power, wisdom, and goodness in the gospel to the heathen. To all the earth:

all the Gentiles had now heard the gospel. Paul's answer to the objector—all the ends of the earth have heard, well might the Jews. By the words, " unto all the earth," the Rabbins understood the servants of Messiah.

Ver. 20.— εὑρέθην, I was found; used of God when exciting men by His benefits to seek and worship Him.

Ver. 21.—Eben Ezra informs us that Moses Hacoben said ver. 20 is to be understood of the nations of the world, as if it had been said, I am found of nations which are not called by My name, but to My people have I stretched out My hands; and so the apostle interprets and applies the words here. ἀντιλέγοντα.—The very word used by the Jews at Rome to describe the treatment received by the gospel from themselves—*i.e.*, gainsaying. Moses declares that a despised nation may become beloved.

MAIN HOMILETICS OF THE PARAGRAPH.—Verses 1—4.

Mistakes rectified.—In previous chapters St. Paul had described the sad condition of his countrymen. And now he pours forth the ardent longings of his soul : " Brethren, my heart's good pleasure and prayer to God for Israel is, that they might be saved." Here is the utterance of the Christian patriot. Spiritual salvation is the highest good for the individual and the community. This secured, other needful good will follow in its train. Earth's patriots begin at the surface and work downwards; the Christian patriot begins at the root and works upwards. Civilise, then Christianise. Spiritual salvation is the true civilising force. Salvation in every sense is the dream and the aim of every true Christian. His soul is in heaviness because of the unsaved ; he sighs over the lost ; he weeps over the guilt and the impending doom of a great city ; he prays for his kinsmen that they may be saved.

I. **The relationships of life suggest solemn thought.**—Israelites were St. Paul's kinsmen according to the flesh. Love of kin is the surest basis for love of kind. The man who does not care for his relations is not likely to care for the world beyond. St. Paul was by pre-eminence the apostle of the Gentiles ; and may we not suppose that this broader office arose out of his love to Israel ? Love is expanding. Love to Israelites feeds love to Gentiles. However this may be, we have here St. Paul's deep love for his kinsmen according to the flesh, and it suggests to him solemn thoughts. 1. *Israel is unsaved.* Brethren after the flesh, aliens after the spirit. " That they might be saved " opens out a wide domain of thought to the apostolic mind. The spiritual mind of the apostle would scarcely content itself with the idea of the salvation of Israel as a temporal power. He was anxious, not for the restoration of David's throne as an earthly monarch, but for the establishment of the supremacy of David's greater Son and Lord. " That they might be saved " is the apostle's great goal for the human race. He walked through the earth oppressed with the thought that its millions were unsaved ; but he did not give place to despair, nor lose himself in generalities. He set himself to the work near at hand. He prayed and worked for his kinsmen. 2. *Israel had a false zeal.* St. Paul could bear witness to the zeal of the Jews. He himself had been most zealous. The men without fire and glow are the men to cumber the earth ; the men with enthusiasms are the men to exalt the race. Lofty ideas stirring the nature dignify humanity. Religious ideas are the loftiest. False zeal is better than indifference. The Jews had zeal for the ceremonials. They tithed mint, anise, and cumin ; they were punctilious about the letter of the Sabbath, about postures, and the shape of garments. Their zeal was not divinely enlightened. It was not a zeal from God. It was not pure, nor full of love. 3. *Israel had a false method.* They were going about to establish their own righteousness. Many of the sons of men are still going on this fruitless pilgrimage. The little words " their own " are suggestive. How much men will do for " their own " !

What long and weary pilgrimages men will take to establish their own righteousness! They go up and down the earth, and their last state is worse than their first. Their own righteousness is flattering to pride. Submission unto the righteousness of God is possible only to Christian humility.

II. **Solemn thought prompts intercessory prayer.**—St. Paul prayed that Israel might be saved. Prayer is a relief to the solemnity of our thought; prayer throws light on the deep problems of existence. Solemn thought depresses; intercessory prayer inspires and invigorates.

·III. **Intercessory prayer moves to outward action.**—St. Paul did not pray in the monastic cell, and shut himself out and away from the sins and sorrows of a struggling humanity. He sought strength in prayer, and used that strength in action. He obtained divine light and teaching by prayer, and he used the blessings for the good of his fellows. The praying man is the best teacher. St. Paul can show the Jews the right method. "Christ is the end of the law for righteousness to every one that believeth." The moral law discloses the wounds sin has made. The ceremonial law shadows forth the remedy. The law given as a tutor to conduct us to Christ. Its authority as a covenant terminates in Christ. "He is the end of the law for righteousness to every one that believeth." The law of works is killed by the law of love. Moses laid down rules, but he did not thereby render humanity upright. Christ inbreathed a loving spirit, and the glorified nature had no need of precise enactments. He that believeth in Christ has both a justifying and a sanctifying righteousness.

IV. **Intercessory prayer conjoined with suitable action cannot fail.**—Failure in the human thought and to the human estimate there may be, but it does not follow that there is a failure in the divine plan and purpose. "Fail" is a word for human weakness and human limitations. Fail cannot be a word for Omnipotence. Soul energy cannot brook the idea of failure. Is it to be supposed that the soul energy of the Infinite can admit failure? Man may fail, but a God must be ever victorious. It might be true that Israel was not saved, and yet that Paul's prayer was answered. Divine answers do not move along human channels. Let us pray and work in faith. Prayer offered to God cannot be fruitless. Work done for God cannot come to naught.

Ver. 4. *The end of the law.*—Two questions arise: 1. What is the "end" (τέλος) of the law? 2. How is Christ that "end"?

Answer 1. The "end" of a law is to make men righteous—teach what is right, what is wrong. Law does this by plainly declaring God's will. *Yet by this merely its end not gained.* What is wanted?

Answer 2. (1) *An ideal life*—to illustrate righteousness by perfect example. (2) *A gift of power*—to keep the law. Christ *led* the life and *gives* the power. (Doctrine of sanctification.)

Mark: No other religious system supplies these two wants. Contrast Christianity with Buddhism and Mohammedanism. Neither claims (1) to exhibit *perfect* life, or (2) give sanctifying power.

The ideal life is near to us; the gift of power is near to us (vers. 6-9).—*Dr. Springett.*

Ver. 4. *Relation of the law to the gospel.*—Now this spirit of legality, as it is called, is nearly the universal spirit of humanity. It is not Judaism alone; it is nature. They are not the Israelites only who go about to establish a righteousness of their own; the very same thing may be detected among the religionists of all countries and all ages. If a man will persist, as nature strongly inclines him, in seeking to make out a title-deed to heaven by his own obedience, then that obedience must be perfect, else there is a flaw in the title-deed which is held to be irreparable. In defect of his own righteousness, which he is required to disown as having any part in his meretorious acceptance with God, he is told of an everlasting righteousness which Another has brought in, and which he is invited, nay commanded, to make mention of. It is thus that Christ becomes the end of the law for righteousness—that is, for a justifying righteousness, or for a righteousness which gives a right to him who possesses it. There appears to be the very strength and spirit of a moral essence in that doctrine which they hold, and it seems the fruit of their more adequate homage to the law that, under the feeling of their own distance and deficiency therefrom, they have laid hold upon Christ as the end of the law for righteousness. Obedience for a legal right is everywhere denounced in the New Testament as an enterprise, the prosecution of which forms the main business of every disciple, and the full achievement of which is that prize of his high calling to which he must press forward continually. Human virtue hath ceased, under the economy of grace, to be the price of heaven; for this power is lost, and lost irrevocably, by its ceasing to be perfect. But human virtue is still the indispensable preparation for heaven; and we, helped from the sanctuary above to struggle with all the imperfections of our corrupt and carnal nature below, must, by a life of prayer and painstaking and all duteous performance, make way through the frailties and temptations of our sinful state in time, to a meetness for the joys of that endless inheritance which is beyond it. First, then, know that the legal right is what you cannot work for, but that in the gospel of Jesus Christ it is freely offered for your acceptance. But, secondly, having thus secured what the apostle in one passage calls "the end of the law," count it your unceasing business to labour for what the apostle in another passage calls "the end of the commandment." Though the law has ceased as a covenant, it has not ceased as a rule of life. Oh, let us then do honour to the faith that we profess by our abounding in those fruits of righteousness which emanate therefrom, and never let gainsayers have to allege of that holy name by which we are called that it is prostituted by those who wear it into a licence for iniquity! Let the faith of the gospel approve itself in our hearts, to bring along with it the charm and the efficacy of a new moral existence.—*Dr. Chalmers.*

SUGGESTIVE COMMENTS ON VERSES 2—4.

Zeal for God.—I desire, it may be observed, that zeal of God in general—that is, a hearty and passionate concernment for religion—the apostle here finds no fault with. On the contrary, he approves it as a commendable thing; for you see he represents it as a piece of virtue in his countrymen, and speaks it to their commendation that they had a zeal of God. A man will have but small comfort, when he comes to die, to reflect that he has been zealous of the privileges and property and rights of his countrymen, but it was indifferent to him how the service of God and the affairs of religion were managed. The apostle's carriage to the unbelieving Israelites, who, though they were zealous for God, yet were in a great mistake as to their notions of the true religion. He thinks them the more pitiable and the more excusable in that this their opposition proceeded from their zeal of God, though it was misinformed, irregular zeal. Our tenderness to mistaken zealots must always be so managed as that the true religion or the public peace suffer no damage thereby. The apostle's tacit reprehension of the Jewish zeal upon this account—that it was not according to knowledge. For be our zeal of God never so great, yet if it be not a zeal according to knowledge it is not the right Christian zeal. And though we see others never so fervent and vehement in pursuing a religious cause—and that too out of conscience

—yet if this zeal of theirs be not according to knowledge it is a zeal that justly deserves to be reproved. And though both we and they may, 'for our sincerity in God's cause, expect some allowances both from God and man, yet neither they nor we can justify it either to God or man that we are thus foolish and ignorantly zealous. So that a right zeal for God implies that we do so well inform ourselves of the nature of our religion as not to pretend a religious zeal for anything that is not a part of our religion. If our zeal for God be as it should be, it must certainly express itself in matters that are good, about such objects as God hath made to be our duty. "It is good," said St. Paul, "to be always zealously affected in a good matter." But if we mistake in our cause, if we take that for good which is evil, or that for evil which is good, here our zeal is not according to knowledge. The zeal that is according to knowledge is always attended with hearty charity. It is not that bitter zeal which the apostle speaks of, which is accompanied with hatred and envy and perverse disputings. But it is kind and sociable and meek even to gainsayers. Another inseparable property of zeal according to knowledge is that it must pursue lawful ends by lawful means, must never do an ill thing for the carrying the best cause. How many unlawful acts have popish zealots used to subject all the Christian world to their Lord and Master! How many forgeries for this purpose have they been the authors of and maintained them afterwards! How many disturbances have they given to the peace of Christendom in the most unjust and unnatural ways for the advancement of the papal cause! It was out of zeal for God's service and the interest of holy Church that so many princes have been excommunicated and deposed, that so many tumults and rebellions have been raised, that so many crusades for the extirpating heretics have been sent out. By which and suchlike means it may justly be computed that as much Christian blood has been shed for the establishing popery as it now stands—nay, and a great deal more—than ever was during all the times of the heathen persecutions for the supporting of paganism. —*Archbishop Sharpe.*

False zeal.—"A zeal of God, but not according to knowledge." The faster a man rides, if he be in a wrong road, the farther he goes out of his way. Zeal is the best or worst thing in a duty. If the end be right, it is excellent; but if wrong, it is worthless. —*Gurnall's "Christian in Complete Armour,"* vol. iii., p. 479.

It is better, according to Augustine, even to halt in the road than to run with all our might out of the proper path.—*Calvin.*

MAIN HOMILETICS OF THE PARAGRAPH.—Verses 5—11.

Life on divine conditions.—God is not a Pharaoh demanding bricks without straw; God does not require a Samson's strength from an infant's weakness, a Solomon's wisdom from the unfortunate possessor of imbecility. If God's plan of salvation seem difficult, it is not because of divine conditions, but because of human perversity. Humble souls, receptive natures, find God's method of salvation an easy, unencumbered plan. Life on divine conditions is in striking contrast to life on human conditions.

I. **Notice life on human conditions.**—Sometimes we rail against the hardness and perversity of nature. Man battling for life is often worsted in the encounter. The struggle for life ends, with too many, in death. But life would not be so hard if selfishness were eliminated from humanity. Natural life is hard on human conditions. It is not God but man that makes moral life hard. The human conditions are: 1. *Life by doing.* The law done, the life secured. Grace was there in Old Testament times, but men too often ignored the grace and went about to establish their own righteousness. God had then a blessing for contrite souls. 2. *Life by fruitless search.* Who can ascend to heaven? Who can fathom the abyss? In these modern days men can explore and investigate to marvellous heights and depths; they can almost travel along the pathway which the vulture's eye hath not seen; but they do not discover the treasure of moral life. The eye of the scientist has not seen it in the depths; the far-reaching knowledge of the philosopher has not discovered it in the heights of his sublime soaring. Spiritual life eludes the search of the wise and prudent of this world, but is revealed unto babes.

II. Notice life on divine conditions.—Natural life on divine conditions is pleasant. The life of unfallen man was life on divine conditions—life in a garden where birds sang, brooks musically rippled, flowers bloomed, fruits ripened, and where there was not the offensiveness of decay and of death. If flowers decayed, they presented no unsightly aspect, they gave forth no offensive odour. If death visited, it came in comely form. Man had no monotony, no feeling of unrest. The conditions of life are changed; but even now if we got nearer to divine conditions we should live more pleasantly. One image this of spiritual life. Pleasantly flows the stream of spiritual life to those who exercise faith. Spiritual life is in: 1. *A word of nearness.* God's words are near. Day unto day uttereth divine speech. Nature is divinely vocal. Time expresses the divine thought. Providence utters the purposes of the infinite Spirit. God's words are round about us everywhere. The atmosphere is thick with the thoughts of the Eternal. But God's words are carried by a still, small voice, and our souls are not hushed so as to catch the message. "The word is nigh thee, even in thy mouth, and in thy heart"; but time words stifle the heaven word. Let us be still, and then we shall hear the near word of God. 2. *A word of faith.* A little word, and yet very large. It carries a whole heaven in its embrace. It conquers the world, the flesh, and the devil—triumphs over death, and opens the gates of paradise. The word of faith is great, and yet its greatness is not inherent, but derived. Faith must have an object, and that object is a divine Person. Faith embraces a living Saviour; faith concerns itself with a perfect life, an atoning death, an evidencing resurrection, a victorious ascension, and an intercessory existence; faith is emotional, its seat is in the heart; faith works by love. God is emotional, and so are His true children. The intellectualist may despise the emotional; and yet to stifle emotion is to do violence to the perfection of human nature. Emotions play a large part in human doings. Emotion is a strong motive force. God would have perfect men in His kingdom, and such are those who let emotion have fair play. Faith of the head will not save. Faith which accepts the axioms of mathematics, the deductions of logic, the recorded experiments of science, or the statements of history will not save. There is a faith which accepts a perfect creed, and yet is not saving. Our want is heart faith. To-day we are developing heads and minimising hearts; our brains are weighed and measured, while our hearts are dying for want of nutriment. The light of moral knowledge may play about the head while the heart is untouched; and where hearts are unaffected there can be no true moral reformation. A heart faith clinging to a loving Christ climbs the rugged steeps of time, and gains the height of moral perfectness and spiritual beauty. Heart faith resting in Christ is the greatest motive power in the universe. 3. *A word of confession.* In these days Christ-confessing is too much confined. If the heart were full of Christ, would the mouth be full of the world? Have things changed? Are the great Teacher's words untrue, "Out of the abundance of the heart the mouth speaketh"? Are they untrue? or is it sadly true that Christ-abundance is not found in modern hearts? The head and the heart, the body and the soul, must move onwards to the accomplishment of a perfected salvation. 4. *A word of divine encouragement.* "Whosoever believeth on Him shall not be ashamed." Here we have a divine universality, a divine invitation, and a divine declaration— the largeness of divine love, the regulating force of divine wisdom, the provisions of divine power. "Whosoever." Jew or Gentile, rich or poor. "Whosoever." If a word could measure the vastness of the infinite love, that word would be the word "whosoever." Finite words, however, cannot gauge infinite realities. Enough for us to know that the love is vast, and that love invites whosoever believeth to the banqueting-house where the banner of divine love is displayed.

Vers. 6-8. *The Saviour near the soul.*—By the phrase "the righteousness which is of faith" we are to understand Christianity. Therefore Christianity is the speaker. The apostle desires to answer the question of questions, How may I be saved from my sins for the service of my God? and assumes Christianity to be speaking in answer. Christianity does not say it is necessary to go to a distance for your religion, but "the word is *nigh*." In answer to the question, How may I become a Christian indeed? the gospel reply is, Look not for the marvellous, leave the speculative; listen to the Saviour : "Behold, He stands at the door, and knocks."

I. **Christianity discourages a craving for the miraculous.**—Do not occupy yourselves with any fond conceits of a manifestation of God more striking and convincing than that which you have already. Had miracles been the likeliest method of eliciting Christian faith, they would have been continued. But they did their work, and were laid aside. Though the need has passed, the craving remains. Hence the lying legends of the Church of Rome. The last thing men will acknowledge is that the blessing is already their own if they have faith to receive it. The last power they consent to trust is Christ, the power of God. Yet, needing Christ, it is the word of Christ we already have. "The word is nigh."

II. **Christianity discourages a passion for the speculative.**—Do not consider it necessary that you should have adequate notions respecting those deep subjects before you can attain to the righteousness of faith and the blessings of salvation. Do but believe. You need not then despair of receiving heavenly teaching. The wisest of men are sent back by the gospel to the simple faith of children. This is the heavenly order : first trust, then knowledge. Theology is not religion. Theologies change, but Christ changes not.

III. **Christianity recalls us, then, from the miraculous and the speculative to the evangelical and the spiritual.**—The word of faith very familiar to those who heard Paul. And the word is nigh now. The letter of the word is nigh— a free, cheap Bible. More than that, you have Christian language already in your mouth. Mark the Apostles' Creed, the Lord's Prayer, the name of Christ. In a certain sense the word is in your heart already. Every troubled heart has a witness for Him who did what the law could not do for man. Christ speaks to the heart, and in a language which the heart comprehends. He has done this in many ways—by sorrows, by consolations, by memories. And the Saviour is near to the soul at *all* times. It is a *familiar* good. It is Christ, then, not this world, that can bless us.—*J. Gage Rigg, D.D.*

Ver. 10. *Outward observances.*—Man, a being of two parts : outward, material ; inward, immaterial. Therefore two facts must be brought into play in all relationships to God and to men.

For man's religion to be thoroughgoing, heart must be in it, body must be in it. Meaning of "worship in spirit and in truth"—*not* spirit *without* body, but spirit *along with* body.

Examples : 1. Family prayer proves your belief in God in the eyes of your household. [*Note.*—No position more honourable than Christian man — like patriarchs, priest of his household, conducting family worship.] 2. Going to church, witness to belief in God in the eyes of the world. [*Note.*—A duty, therefore, even for the deaf or *blind.*] 3. Confirmation a similar ceremony, witness that when of age of discretion you put trust in God and decide for Him. 4. Kneeling in prayer, testimony of reverence before God. Story of heathen chief, who sees Charlemagne kneeling in church, and asks, Where is the greater King? I know one must have been there, for the king was kneeling. 5. Lord's supper, testimony that you have support from some one beyond yourself.

Remember, inward, if real, must be expressed by something outward. *Beware* of outward without inward.—*Dr. Springett.*

SUGGESTIVE COMMENTS ON VERSES 5—11.

The will of God made clearly known. —The obvious import of this passage is that the knowledge of the will of God had been made perfectly accessible ; no one was required to do what was impossible, neither to ascend to heaven nor to pass the *boundless* sea in order to attain it ; it was neither hidden nor afar off, but obvious and at hand. Without directly citing this passage, Paul uses nearly the same language to express the same idea. The expressions here used seem to have become proverbial among the Jews. To be "high" or "afar off" was to be "unattainable"; "to ascend to heaven" or "to go down to hell" was "to do what was impossible." As the sea was to the ancients impassable, it is easy to understand how the question, "Who can pass over the sea?" was tantamount to, Who can ascend up into heaven? Among the later Jews the same mode of expression not infrequently occurs.—*Hodge.*

The world to be regenerated by doing our nearest duty.—My object has been and is, and I trust in God ever will be, to make people see that they need not, as St. Paul says, go up into heaven or go down to the deep to find Christ ; because He, the word whom we preach, is very near them—in their hearts and on their lips—if they would but believe it ; and ready, not to set them afloat on new and untried oceans of schemes and projects, but ready to inspire them to do their duty humbly and simply where He has put them ; and, believe me, the only way to regenerate the world is to do the duty which lies nearest us, and not to hunt after grand, far-fetched ones for ourselves.—*Charles Kingsley.*

The duty of confessing with the mouth.—As believing with the heart leads to righteousness, so confessing Christ with the mouth conduces "to salvation." Confessing Christ with the mouth is at all times an important duty ; but, at the first publication of the gospel, it was peculiarly indispensable, both for promoting the diffusion of the Christian religion and for the edification of individuals. For the open avowal of Christianity by all the disciples of Christ, accompanied with that moral purity which distinguished them and which was so striking in an age of great corruption, would naturally lead other men to examine a religion which produced such remarkable effects ; and thus many might be induced to embrace the gospel who would not otherwise have given it any consideration. In like manner, by associating continually with the Church in all the services of religion, the Christian converts would gradually become better acquainted with the gospel and more strongly induced by the influence of general example to live as became the disciples of Christ. Hence our Saviour makes confessing Him before men an express condition of His confessing men before His Father who is in heaven; and adds, that whosoever shall deny Him before men, him will He deny before His Father which is in heaven.—*Ritchie.*

The true misery to be ashamed of oneself. — This is being confounded; this is shame itself; this is the intolerable, horrible, hellish shame anp torment wherein is weeping and gnashing of teeth; this is the everlasting shame and contempt to which, as Daniel prophesied, too many should awake in that day, to be found guilty in that day before God and Christ, before our neighbours and our relations, and, worst of all, before ourselves. Worst of all, I say, before ourselves. It would be dreadful enough to have all the bad things we ever did or thought told openly against us to all our neighbours and friends, and to see them turn away from us—dreadful to find out at last (what we forget all day long) that God knows them already; but more dreadful to know them all ourselves and see our sins in all their shamefulness in the light of God, as God Himself sees them—more dreadful still to see the loving God and the loving Christ turn away from us; but most dreadful of all to turn away from ourselves—to be utterly discontented with ourselves, ashamed of ourselves—to see that all our misery is our own fault, that we have been our own enemies; to despise ourselves and hate ourselves for ever; to try for ever to get rid of ourselves, and escape from ourselves as from some ugly and foul place in which we are ashamed to be seen for a moment, and yet not to be able to get rid of ourselves. Yes, that will be the true misery of a lost soul—to be ashamed of itself and hate itself. Who shall deliver a man from the body of that death?—*Charles Kingsley.*

How will proud boasters answer?— " For with the heart man believeth unto righteousness; and with the mouth confession is made unto salvation." What answer will be made to the above words of St. Paul by those proud boasters who glory in a certain imaginary faith, which is lodged, as they presume to say, in the inmost recesses of their hearts, and which is completely to supersede the confession of the mouth? Surely it is the veriest trifling to assert that fire exists where there is neither flame nor heat.— *Calvin.*

What is to confess Christ?—It is Jesus who is to be confessed. To confess Him is to accept Him as our Saviour, and to say so. It is to profess belief in Him as the Son of God, who died for us, in whom through believing we have eternal life; for all this He said of Himself. It is before men that we are to confess Him (Matt. x. 32),—before good men, that our mutual faith may be strengthened; before bad men, that their unbelief may be shaken. How confess Him? Publicly, with our lips. Men who are ever ready to say that they believe in Christ, and never ready to say it openly, in connecting themselves with some branch of His Church, would do well to question their own sincerity. Privately, with our lips. It is a shame for Christians to dwell together, or to often talk together, and never say a loving word about their Saviour. And " not only with our lips, but in our lives." When? Now and always, in word and in deed. Why just now? Because no other moment belongs to us—because the confession must be made before men; and how soon may we cease from among men!—*Robert Westly Peach.*

MAIN HOMILETICS OF THE PARAGRAPH.—Verses 12—18.

A missionary sermon.—When St. Paul quoted the prophet, the vision of a Christ-won world had not been realised. It is still one of the unfulfilled prophecies. Yet the gospel has exercised a splendid influence.

347

I. **The influence of the gospel is readily shown by contrasts.**—1. When Paul wrote this epistle, the ancient Roman virtue, the admirable simplicity, and unconquerable courage had died away. Soo, too, had the old religion. The decay and corruption of it were accelerated by the engrafting of new and dark superstitions. The change, too, in social life was startling. Vice was deified. The secret of this? The pagan world knew not God. The sound of the gospel had *not* yet gone forth. 2. But some had heard the word, and the influence upon their lives and consciences was startling. The influence was irresistible. It modified private life, individual life, social life, state life. 3. The modern testimony as shown by a glance at English life. True we have too much cause for "the bitter cry." The theory of the present day surpasses, startlingly, the reality. But a thousand evidences exist to show that England has caught the spirit of Him "who went about doing good."

II. **Much yet remains to be done.**—*E.g.*, picture rapidly the dark spots of the earth. The prophet's vision is a vision still. The task before us is a superhuman one. 1. *Look at the work in its vastness.* Even here in England there is heathenism. Abroad, roughly speaking, eight hundred millions are heathens. You try to convert a man; ten men, a hundred could not do it, but for God's help. One man! Multiply that by eight hundred millions, and verily the work is great! Looking at the matter from a human standpoint, the work is hopeless, disheartening. 2. *There are multiplying disabilities.* Were all these millions who knew not God of one nationality, the work would appear prodigious. We can measure up the magnitude of the task when already our Bible is read and taught in two hundred and sixty tongues. 3. *There is the added-on disability of the unscrupulous trader dogging the missionary's course.* The truly business man is a noble man; but we have to take account of the blacklegs of the commercial world. 4. *The work suffers from fewness of labourers and lack of funds.*

III. **The prophet's vision must be fulfilled.**—And man must lend a helping hand. God's part of the work is sure enough. But He works through men. Men are God's instruments. Through men He forced the hand of Pharaoh; through men he found a home for Israel; through men the triumphs of Christianity have often been won. What is our response? This country's wealth is fabulous. Fifteen hundred millions sterling will but barely represent the private income of England's citizens. Against that we have raised one and a half million a year—a princely sum, if we forget to compare, say, with the expenditure on our navy, army, drink bill, and so on. Yet "the earth is the Lord's, and the fulness thereof." Of course there are two sides to every question. Here I pointed out the side of obligation. What about a natural response? Or on the consideration of charity, the brotherhood side of the question? The pride of the present age should be to have a part in helping on the kingdom of our God and of His Christ, to swell the grand and noble company of men who would crown the Saviour Lord of earth and Lord of heaven!—*Albert Lee.*

Ver. 15. *Three beautiful progressive courses.*—There is a certain sense in which it is true that beauty is in the eye of the beholder. While we believe that there must be both the idea of beauty in the perceiving subject and certain attractive qualities in the perceived object capable of exciting or helping on the sensation, we must allow that the mind has the power of transferring its ideas to the outward object and investing it with beauty. The painter sees beauty in form and colour; the musician finds only beauty in certain waves of sound, in the harmonious progression of notes. A thing or a person becomes to us beautiful by the power of association. Thus it is that the feet of the messenger are beautiful, not in themselves, but because they are instrumental in bearing a joyful message. The mere personality of the messenger is lost in the glory of the message, and he becomes beautiful by reason of transferred qualities. He shines, as it were, by reason of borrowed plumes. We are thinking rather of the message and its bearing upon ourselves than of the messenger as we sing, "How beautiful are the feet of those who preach the gospel of peace, who bring glad tidings of good things!"

I. **The progressive course of the messenger is beautiful.**—In these days, as we think of the preacher, we should say, How beautiful is the mouth, how sweet are the modulated tones, how charming is the voice, of him who preaches the gospel of peace! for we are too often more concerned with the style and manner of the messenger than with the subject-matter of the message. Sometimes at concerts we listen to the singer who sings in Italian. We cannot tell the meaning of the words, but we are charmed all the same. Are not too many in our congregations careless about understanding the preacher's message? Italian would do well enough for them if it were given so as to charm the listening ear. The messenger should be beautiful, not as a well-tuned musical instrument, not as a mere attractive human machine, but as the bearer of a great divine thought. However, the feet set before us the progressive course of the messenger as well as of his message. He runs on a divine errand. He is sent by divine commission. This opens out to us: 1. *The dignity of the messenger.* A common man acquires dignity when he becomes the monarch's messenger. What dignity should attach to him who is the heaven-sent messenger of peace and good tidings to the children of men! There is a dignity which is assumed, stilted, and offensive; but there is a dignity which is transferred, natural, and becoming; and such is the quality of the dignity that characterises him whose feet are moved by a divine impulse. Preachers should feel that they are God's ambassadors, and then they will not be soon abashed. 2. *The importance of the messenger.* In some quarters this is measured by the number of the letters attached to his name, by the honours he gained at the university, by the high position he holds in the Church, by his family connections, or by some other accidental and minor considerations. Surely this was not Paul's way of reckoning. He says, "How beautiful are the feet of him that preaches the gospel of peace!" If the man have a divine message to my soul, then he is welcome and is highly esteemed. 3. *The benevolence of the messenger.* The preacher of the gospel of peace in modern times is often rewarded by great emolument. Even if ministers and clergymen are not always well paid, and might have done better in other professions, they are, upon the whole, well provided for, and are nearly always treated with respect and occupy high social positions; so that we cannot always be sure to what degree they are actuated by benevolent motives. However, benevolence is the ideal motive, and we may thankfully believe in many cases the real motive. And how beautiful are the feet of that messenger who is moved by a benevolent impulse! He pleases not himself, but seeks to please his fellow-creatures, so that he may bring them to Christ and to goodness. His feet run swiftly, for they are charged with the electric force of love. His eyes are beautiful, for they flash forth love-light. His voice, though naturally poor, is sweet, for it is tuned by love.

II. **The progressive course of the message is beautiful.**—Peace has to the apostle the full idea of the gospel salvation; the good things are the rich, displayed, saving blessings which proceed from the one salvation. The message is one of peace and good-will to the children of men. The messenger is running and working in order to establish the kingdom of God on earth. How beautiful is the progressive course of the kingdom! 1. *There is about it the beauty of growth.* There is beauty in the works of man, beauty in things that are made. But no beauty is equal to that of growth. In the spring season it is pleasant to notice the unfolding beauty of growing nature after the deathlike sleep and barrenness of winter. How beautiful to watch the valleys being clothed with corn, and the little hills rejoicing in the gradual putting forth of verdure ! We rejoice in our children as we watch their growing and unfolding minds. There is sometimes an agony of mind as a new idea is being brought forth ; but there is pleasure as that idea grows and becomes a comely creature that can be presented to the world's intellect. The kingdom of God on earth, within a man and within a society, progresses by growth—at first small as the mustard-seed grain. Then it grows ; and by-and-by it becomes a great tree, in which birds build their nests, and beneath which men may shelter. 2. *There is the beauty of development.* Divine growths are divine developments. They are the unfolding of divine plans and purposes. The New Testament dispensation is a development of the Old. The epistles are a development of the gospels. Some people complain about St. Paul that he has rendered the simple gospels difficult. In some respects this may be true ; but if there be any truth in the charge, we must also remember to his credit that he has amplified the gospels and revealed their largeness. He has unfolded more of the length and breadth, of the depth and height, of that love which passeth knowledge. Every age should increase in knowledge ; and surely we should rejoice in the increase of spiritual knowledge. 3. *There is the beauty of silent but persuasive influence.* " The kingdom of God cometh not with observation." The great Founder of Christianity applies to Himself the words of Esaias : " He shall not strive nor cry ; neither shall any man hear His voice in the streets." Such is the unobtrusive method which He will employ for the purpose of accomplishing the greatest moral revolution which time has seen. Not with the sound of drums, not with the blare of trumpets, not with the clashing of battle arms, will this mighty Conqueror pursue His career and gain His wondrous conquests. Again He places before us the method in one of His inimitable parables : " The kingdom of heaven is like unto leaven." The yeast is placed in a mass foreign to itself, and by its silent and persistent agency it assimilates each separate particle until the whole lump is leavened. The good leaven of the gospel shall assimilate the whole of our race. How beautiful is the progression of grace in the soul of men, in the heart of human societies ! Silently but surely does the kingdom of God extend. Silently and sweetly as the light wakes up the sleeping earth and calls forth things of beauty and sounds of harmony, so does the light of the gospel of peace wake up the sleeping energies of humanity, and create things of moral beauty and sounds of spiritual harmony. Silently and persistently as great ideas shape the movements of modern civilisation, so and more the great idea of salvation by faith in Christ has shaped barbarism into civilisation, and shall perfect and glorify the civilisation already accomplished. The history of the progressive course of the gospel in the earth is a beautiful and attractive record. How beautiful, too, is the course of the gospel in the heart of the individual ! To some the study of metaphysics is delightful. What shall be said about spiritual metaphysics ?

III. **The progressive course of the recipient is beautiful.**—Picture the recipients in a besieged city. Provisions are being exhausted ; means of defence are diminishing ; the situation looks dreadful ; despair is written on many countenances ; gloom prevails almost universally. On the hilltop the messenger comes that speaks of help and safety. 1. *Thus the recipients pass from despair to hope.* And this is the true result when the message of divine peace comes to the soul of man. Despair he may well feel when he finds that he cannot attain to his ideals, when he realises the painful truth that when he would do good evil is present and thwarts the high purpose, when he is baffled and overmastered as he strives to establish his own righteousness.

But despair gives place to hope as he hears that "Christ is the end of the law for righteousness to every one that believeth." How beautiful to see hope growing and flourishing out of and on the barren ground of despair! For it is when a man is in a despairing condition that he welcomes the hopes of the gospel, and joyfully exclaims, "How beautiful are the feet of them that preach the gospel of peace, and bring glad tidings of good things!" How beautiful is the growth of hope in the soul! It is pleasant to watch the growth of the flowers in our gardens. We watch them assume their perfect shape, paint their delicate colours, produce their delicious aroma. What flower in either garden or hothouse can compare with the rich flower of hope growing in the soul garden? Its perfect shape is produced by a divine hand; its delicate colours are painted with a celestial brush; the aroma is composed of the cluster of spices gathered in the garden of the upper paradise. 2. *Thus the recipients pass from danger to safety.* So long as the besieged are in a despairing condition they are in danger, for despair paralyses the powers, weakens the faculties, and produces defeat. The very sight of the messenger running swiftly down the mountains is sufficient to remove despair, and thus lift out of danger. The gospel messenger not only tells of coming help, but of present help. The word of salvation is nigh thee. This messenger tells of a more powerful deliverer than Cyrus. King Jesus can deliver from worse than Babylonian bondage. We are in danger while we are trying the works of the law; we are in safety when we submit ourselves unto the righteousness of God—the righteousness revealed and offered through Christ Jesus our Lord. 3. *Thus the recipients pass from sorrow to joy.* In this world sorrow has its work and its benefits, but we always welcome joy. St. Paul looks upon godly sorrow, not as a continuous state, but as a force working upward and onward to divine joy. And how beautiful is the passage from sorrow to joy! Sweet is the morning light breaking over the hilltops and scattering the gloom and hideous forms of night; sweet thus is it to watch the light of divine joy gradually shining in the soul and removing all traces of sin's dark night. Pleasant it is to watch the child's countenance and see the opening joy of the young soul breaking through the countenance, and chasing away all marks of displeasure; pleasant thus is it to watch the countenance of God's new-born, spiritual child, and see how the joy of heaven is chasing away all sorrow. If he have sorrow, it is because he can do so little for Him who has done so much. As, then, we look at the progressive course of the messengers, the message, and the recipients, we may indeed join with St. Paul, and say, "How beautiful are the feet of them that preach the gospel of peace, and bring glad tidings of good things!"

Ver. 15. *The gospel of peace.*—Why this special name for Christianity? Gospel = good tidings. Christian gospel has three *chief* doctrines—viz., 1. The fatherhood of God; 2. The (necessarily following) brotherhood of man; 3. The saviourhood of Christ Jesus. From 1 and 3 follows peace *with God*; from 2 follows peace *with men*.

To prove, examine condition of those who do not know gospel. Nations who do not know 1 will be found practising self-torments, devil worship, human sacrifice, slaughter of wives and slaves at death. Grasp of 1 stops all these. Nations who do not know 2 practise constant wars, *vendetta*, slavery, polygamy, degradation of women. Knowledge of 2 stops these. Nations who do not know 3 practise superstitions of priestcraft and witchcraft—*e.g.*, medicine men, witch doctors, etc. Knowledge of 3 ends the power of these. Illustrate from missionary works.

Christian cannot rest till the gospel of peace has been preached to all who need it. Heathen Indian said to American bishop, "I go out in the dark, and am afraid; you are not afraid." Gospel.of peace sheds light and ends fear.— *Dr. Springett.*

Ver. 16. *The rejected report.*—This is the third and last time we have this interrogation recorded in Holy Writ. It originally fell from the seraphic lips of Isaiah, as a *complaint* that his announcements relative to Messiah—though so full and fervid and eloquent—had fallen flat upon his countrymen's ears, and had been dismissed by them as an idle tale. It was not only a complaint, but likewise a *prediction* that the same heedlessness and scepticism should be the characteristics of Christ's personal ministry, as well as the after ministry of apostles and Christian ambassadors. Hence, the second time it occurs it is in relation to Christ's own mission (John xii. 37, 38). Since the days of Christ and Paul, thousands of holy and devoted servants of God have put the same inquiry, as they have thought of unheeded sermons and apparently fruitless labours.

I. **That the gospel is a report.**—A report divine in its origin, unique in its character, authentic in its facts, authoritative in its statements, and marvellous in its declarations. The gospel reports the most wonderful *love*. Declaration upon declaration of this love it contains; but all seem to be comprised in that one jewel utterance by St. John, "God *so* loved the world, that He gave His only begotten Son, that whosoever believeth in Him should not perish, but have everlasting life" (iii. 16). *This* is a volume in a verse, an ocean in a dewdrop, a hemisphere of light in a solitary luminary, an eternity of mystery and mercy! Eternity cannot exhaust its wealth of interest and wonderment! This *love*, then, sinner, the gospel declares, is for *you*. While God has loved all men in general, He likewise loves every man in particular. *Sin* is the only thing in creation He hates—not *you*, my brother. Disabuse your mind of the notion that He is a cruel tyrant, a despotic ruler, an arbitrary and a vindictive judge. Away with the false idea that He *hates* you. He is a tender and compassionate Father. Let me suppose that some one of you fathers and mothers have a son who was the flower of your family, the joy of your homestead, the favourite of all; so kind, genial, affectionate, and dutiful once. But, alas! by degrees he has given way to bad company, yielded to his baser propensities, and is become openly profligate, recklessly wild. What is it, I ask, that causes you so much pain, so much sorrow, so much restlessness? Is it not your *deep-rooted love* for him? You *love your child*, though you *hate* his *evil ways*. So it is with God. Your relationship to your son is His relationship to you, only infinitely closer and dearer. And your son's recklessness of conduct is your conduct in a lesser degree to your heavenly Father; and your feelings of grief and trouble are, in an inferior sense, God's feelings of grief and pain at your sin and foolishness. The gospel reports the most wonderful *life*. All life is wonderful, from that which warbles in the song of the thrush, and blushes in the beauty of the rose, to that which glows among burning ranks of seraphim. *Life* is an overmastering problem! But we refer not now to life in its abstract essence, or life in the sense of "being," but to life in human embodiment—enshrined, active, visible *livingness*, life the fact, rather than life the principle. The life of Jesus Christ which the gospel makes known has no parallel in the history of races. The mysterious conception was grandly confirmed by the mysterious career. Unique in birth, He was unique all through. If one link in the chain be faulty, then the whole chain is a failure. But every link has been found a perfect link; the whole Life wondrously consistent, complete, unrivalled. For more than eighteen centuries this *Life* has been stirring humanity to its very core and centre. The great upheavings of religious thought, and advances of religious enterprise, and strugglings in Continental countries after religious liberty, etc., which characterise this period of the nineteenth century, are the result of this wonderful Christ-life. In philosophy He is the mightiest enigma. In life He is the inimitable ideal. In the world He is the absolute ruler. In the universe He is the highest attraction! From that *wonderful Life*, as from a fountain of eternity, has flowed vital influences which have carried verdure and freshness, beauty and blessedness, wherever they have gone. The gospel reports the most wonderful *provisions*. Provisions of *mercy* and of *merit*: of mercy to avert the penal blow and cancel the enormous guilt; of merit to re-dignify the acquitted rebel, and reinstate him in the eternal favour. Provisions equal to the demands of one soul, or a world of souls—"enough for each, enough for all, enough for evermore." There is multiplied pardon, multiplied peace, multiplied joy, multiplied life, multiplied hope, multiplied riches—of grace, of goodness, of glory. In a word, there is a variety so great, a fulness so vast, a supply so magnificent and princely, that the roll of unceasing ages will fail to exhaust either the one or the other. The gospel reports the most wonderful *results*. Obedient to the imperial summons of the Master, to "go into all the world and preach the gospel to every creature," the apostles and their coadjutors—those giant sons of the cross—embarked on their sublime but hazardous enterprise, "beginning at Jerusalem." Thence they sallied forth to the "regions beyond" and "preached Jesus and the resurrection." In less than three hundred years after they started, the gospel had sounded its report all over the Roman empire, even in cottage and palace, and gathered trophies from among the hardy sons of toil and the ranks of Cæsar's household. Jehovah and all the cohorts of the eternities are behind the instrumentality, so that ultimate success is certain. God hurries not, neither does He tarry. Eternity is His work-day, so that ere noon shall arrive He will effect His purposes and complete His undertaking. Do you contemplate this gospel as a *remedy* for the world's sicknesses? It reports success where every human prescription and every method of creature quackery has failed. Success in every case it has taken absolutely in hand. Do you contemplate it as a *revelation*? It eclipses every other, and stands out with a singularity and supremacy at once unprecedented and divine; reporting as it reveals, and revealing as it reports, Jehovah's mind and will, the sympathy and benevolence of His great heart, before which multitudes have bowed in reverence and submission. View it in what light you may, as a remedy, a revelation, a message, a system, or a history, it reports results the most astounding and sublime. It also reports the most wonderful *salvation*. So *simple* that a child may understand it; so *great* that a philosopher can never comprehend it. So *cheap* that it can be had for the asking; so *precious* that millions of gold cannot buy it. So *full* that it can never be diminished; so *universal* that none is outside of its possible benedictions.

II. **That this wonderful report by men in general is unheeded and discredited.**—"Lord, who hath *believed* our report?" The inquiry, you perceive, is, not who hath *heard* our report, or who hath *admired* our report, or who hath *eulogised* our report, or who hath heaped empty compliments, or sullen complaints, or satirical sneers, or rotten critiques on our report. No, nothing of the kind; simply "Who hath *believed* [endorsed, practically embraced] our report?" Who hath turned it savingly to account, and enjoyed experimentally its consolations? If men in general theoretically believe it, in practice they despise and disbelieve it. It is not that men do not believe religion to be a good thing, a needful thing, a blessed thing, a great and glorious thing, that hinders them from believing this "report." Nay, it is that they cannot, rather will not, give up their sins, customs, pleasures, companions, habits, pride.

III. **That such practical unbelief is a source of deep grief and anxiety to the faithful minister.**—Causing him often to cry out in secret, "Lord, *who hath* believed our report?" No man fired with the love of God, inflamed with a passion for souls, to whom truth and God and Christ and eternity are vivid and vital realities, can possibly preach on and on for years without visible success in the conversion of men and women, and not be wrung at times into an agony of distress over his apparently fruitless labours. There are some of us who know what it is to "weep between the porch and the altar" over indifferent hearers, who are constrained to exclaim, like the weeping prophet, "Is there no balm in Gilead? Is there no physician there? Why, then, is not the health of the daughter of my people recovered?" Refuse! and the next report which shall fall upon your ears may be, that a true bill has been found against you by the grand jury of the eternal court, and that you be consigned to the "place prepared for the devil and his angels," until the morning of the judgment day.—*J. O. Keen, D.D.*

Ver. 17. *Faith's production and productions.*—It is not sufficient to know the Bible intellectually, or to have its records stored in the memory. Many people can say perfectly the catechism of their Church, but are destitute of true religion. Knowledge may play about the head, while the heart is unaffected and unimproved. True faith touches the heart. True faith is emotional, as well as intellectual. Faith must work by love and purify the whole nature.

I. **How is true faith produced?**—By what is heard through the blessing of the Holy Spirit. The thing heard is through and by the revelation of God. 1. *The source of true faith is the word of God.* In these days the word of God is producing unbelief in many quarters. Do we say producing? Should we not rather say that the unbelief is there, and the word of God is used maliciously for the purpose of fostering the prior unbelief? The word of God is the source of true faith to all the true-hearted. There is in connection therewith, in its external and internal evidences, sufficient to produce faith. 2. *The channel of true faith is hearing.* We must hear, not to cavil, not to be pleased, but to find profit. We must hear as the man listens to a will being read, as a man waits to hear the sentence of the judge. We must hear as for eternity. The Holy Spirit attends the word and opens the heart. Let us pray and seek for the divine Spirit, so that we may hear and live.

II. **What does true faith produce?**—1. *It produces salvation.* Faith is not salvation, but the means by which we become or realise that we are saved. Faith is not Christ, but the hand that lays hold on the Christ. Faith is not the fruit, but that by which we pluck the fruit and are refreshed. Faith is not the blessing, but that without which the blessing cannot become ours. 2. *It works obedience.* So that to say that the faith of the gospel is destructive of morality is to argue ignorance. Faith produces prompt obedience; the faithful have been the most moral and virtuous. 3. *It is the helpmeet of simple confidence in God our father.* The children of the faith are the trustful children of God. They feel God; they hear His voice in all sounds of sweetness; they trace the impress of His feet in all things and shapes of beauty; they are not afraid of a besetting God; they march through dangers with undaunted courage. 4. *It inclines them to obey and follow their Guide, and thus they come safely to their journey's end.* The man who by faith has found salvation in and by Christ will be inclined to follow Him heartily. Let us hear, believe, and live the highest and the noblest life. A life of holiness is the best test of the sincerity of faith.

SUGGESTIVE COMMENTS ON VERSES 12—18.

Lord's goodness plenteous, impartial, and wise.—Power and benevolence are rarely united in our fellow-creatures. Here is one who has abundance, but he has no disposition to do good; he turns away his ear from hearing the poor, and seems to live as if he were born for himself only. Yea, the disposition often decreases as the capacity grows; so that there are some who not only give less comparatively, but less really, than they did when they were poorer. Then it hardly seemed worth their while to be covetous and to hoard; but now they have the means, and the temptation conquers them. On the other hand, there is many a one who has bowels of mercy, but he can only pity and shed unavailing tears over victims of distress. He is compelled to say only, "Be ye warmed, and be ye filled"; for he has it not in his hand to give such things as are needful for the body—his hand is shortened that it cannot save, though his ear is not heavy that it cannot hear. But some few there are in whom the means and the mind to use them are found united. The Lord increase their number! These are little images of Himself, in whom we equally find greatness and goodness, the resources and the readiness of compassion. He is over all, and He is rich "unto all that call upon Him." Let me look at His greatness. He is over all. All beings of every rank are under His absolute control. He rules over all *material* agents; over all *animal* agents; over all *human* agents—over the best, the greatest, the worst of men; over all *invisible* agents—over devils, over angels, over departed spirits. He is Lord both of the dead and of the living. How astonishing, then, are His possessions and His dominions! A nation seems a great thing to us. But what is the greatest nation to our earth? And what is our earth to the luminaries of heaven? Many of these are discernible by the naked eye. When this fails, art assists nature; and Herschel sees innumerably more. When the telescope fails, the imagination plunges into the immensity beyond, and we exclaim, Lo! these are parts of His ways. But how small a portion is known of Him! Yet—for His mercy equals His majesty—the *same* Lord who is over all "is rich unto all that

call upon Him." His goodness has three characters. 1. *It is plenteous.* He is *rich* unto all that call upon Him. Some, if they are bountiful, are poor in bounty. And this appears not only in the smallness of their gifts, but in the mode of giving. It seems done by restraint, not willingly and of a ready mind. It does not drop from them as honey from the comb, or flow like water from a spring; it seems an unnatural effort. You feel no more respect when they give much than when they give little; everything like nobleness is destroyed by the manner; the meanness of the disposition is betrayed; and the poor-spirited mortal can no more give kindly and generously than a clown can dance gracefully. But the Lord God is a sun. He gives grace and glory; and no good thing will He withhold. He abundantly pardons; and while He gives liberally, He upbraideth not. 2. *It is impartial.* He is rich *unto all* that call upon Him. For there is no difference between Jew and Greek. And the same will apply to sex, and age, and calling, and condition, and character. The proclamations of divine grace exclude none, whatever be their circumstances; and it is well they do not. If any were excluded, awakened souls would be sure to find themselves among the exceptions. But what exceptions can any find when they read, "Preach the gospel to every creature"—"whosoever will let him take of the water of life freely"? Evangelical mercy is like Noah's ark, that took in the clean and the unclean —only with this difference in favour of the truth above the type: there all the beasts came out as they went in; whereas, "if any man be in Christ he is a new creature." He changes all He receives, and sanctifies all He saves. 3. *It is wise.* "He is rich unto all that call upon Him." This is required, and cannot be dispensed with—not only because God wills it, but because "it seemeth good in His sight." He knows that we should never praise Him for blessings which we do not value; and He knows that we never could be made happy by them. For that which gratifies is something that relieves our wants, fulfils our desire, accomplishes our hope, and crowns our endeavours. God's way, therefore, is to make us sensible of our state, and to cause us to hunger and thirst after righteousness; and then we shall be filled: "for whoso asketh, receiveth; and he that seeketh, findeth; and to him that knocketh, it shall be opened." God reveals Himself, not only for our encouragement, but imitation; and vain is our confidence in Him without conformity to Him. Therefore, says the apostle, "Be ye followers of God, as dear children." How? In what? And walk in love, as Christ also hath loved us, an offering and a sacrifice to God of a sweet-smelling savour. Men would be like God, as the greatest of beings; but we are to be like Him, as the best of beings. They would resemble Him in His natural perfections; but we are to resemble Him in His moral. They would, as He is, be over all, and gladly have everything at their own disposal: but we are to be holy, as He is holy; and true, as He is true: and patient, as He is patient; and forgiving, as He is forgiving; and tender, as He is tender; and, according to our resources, to be rich unto all that call upon us.—*W. Jay.*

Links in the soul's redemptive chain. —The first link is *prayer.* "How then shall they call on Him?" etc. Prayer is mere calling on God; which act implies: 1. Consciousness of dependence upon Him; 2. An earnest desire after Him. The second link is *faith.* "How then shall they call on Him in whom they have not believed?" There must be faith in two things: 1. Faith in His personal existence; 2. In the entreatability of His nature. The third link is *knowledge.* "How shall they believe in Him of whom they have not heard?" Whilst there is a faith lying at the basis of all knowledge, soul-redemptive faith requires knowledge—a knowledge not of the creative, sustaining God, but of the *redeeming*

God, God in Christ. The next link is *preaching.* The redeeming God has been made known to man by preaching. Enoch, Noah, Moses, the prophets, the apostles, and even the holy Christ, all preached. And the subject of all their preaching was the redeeming God. No one can preach this properly unless he be sent. "How shall they preach unless they be sent?" All true preachers have a divine commission.—*Homilist.*

"There is no difference."—This phrase appears three times in the New Testament, and each time in connection with a different truth or aspect of salvation; and the three taken together complete the sphere of truth. (Compare Rom. iii. 22, x. 12, 13, and Acts xv. 9.) It is also noticeable that in each case a double truth is presented in connection with the recurrence of the phrase "no difference." 1. *There is no difference among sinners and believers,* for all have sinned and come short of the glory of God. The righteousness of God, which is by the faith of Jesus Christ, is unto all and upon all them that believe. All are sinners; and unto all believers comes the same all-sufficient righteousness. 2. *There is no difference between Jews and Gentiles.* The same God is Lord over all. Jehovah is not the God of Jews only, but of Gentiles also—the universal sovereign. And He is rich unto all that call upon Him. All are alike in poverty and bankruptcy; whatever may be the differences in debt, all are alike hopelessly bankrupt and unable to pay. But God is infinitely *rich* as a bestower; and all that call upon Him will receive as a free gift infinite riches of saving grace. 3. *No difference in the bestowment of the Holy Spirit.* To all believers God alike bears witness, giving them the Holy Ghost, and purifying their hearts by faith. The same Spirit, received by the same faith, purifies, empowers, and perfects character. These are great truths, but they are very humbling to the natural and carnal man. It is not meant to assert that between sinners there is absolutely

no difference, else there could be no degrees either of guilt or of punishment. Christ said to Pilate, "He that delivered Me unto thee hath the *greater sin*"; and to the scribes and Pharisees He said, "He shall receive the greater *damnation*." These words settle the fact that both sin and damnation have their grades. But as to the *fact* of sin and of guilt there is no difference. All are sinners, and one sin suffices to bring death. All have come short, whether by a greater or less deficiency. We must not compare ourselves among ourselves, or measure ourselves by ourselves, but by the perfect standard of law and duty. But there is also no difference in our justification. The righteousness of God is offered unto all and bestowed upon all who believe with the same divine impartiality. If we seek illustrations of the same sovereign power and rich grace as over all that call upon Him, we shall find it in the impartial bestowment of rich grace upon Nathanael and Saul, the woman of Canaan and the woman of Samaria, the eunuch of Ethiopia and the Philippian jailor. The impartiality of purifying and witnessing grace is shown by the Pentecosts at Jerusalem, Samaria, Cæsarea, and Ephesus. If God condemns impartially, so does He justify, exercise sovereignty of mercy in answering prayer, and in purifying and annointing believers.—*Homiletic Review.*

The ignorance of Israel cause of rejection.—No invocation without faith; no faith without hearing; no hearing without preaching; no preaching without sending. A universal apostolate is therefore the necessary corollary of a free and universal salvation. Such are the contents of our two verses, which are directed, not against Judæo-Christian prejudices, but against the ignorance of Israel, the final result of which was necessarily their rejection. Paul points out to the Jews, who took offence at the wide and universal character of his apostleship, the internal necessity on which it was based, and the positive prophetical texts which justified it. We are therefore still at the development of this theme: the ignorance of Israel the cause of their rejection.—*Godet.*

MAIN HOMILETICS OF THE PARAGRAPH.—*Verses* 18—21.

Rejected Israel without excuse. — St. Paul, while establishing his own argument, throws blame upon Israel. If the new gospel be so good, and if it have been widely preached, why so little reception? Old questions which are still being asked. St. Paul shows that rejection is in harmony with prophetic utterance. Rejecters disobey to their own damage, and will be left without excuse. The word is preached, the blessed sound goes forth, but Israel rejects. The preacher must do his work, though few be saved. The preacher must hold on his course, though moderns say, Why all this preaching? We know as much as the preacher. If they know, they do not evidence their knowledge by their practice. If they know and do, let them support the preacher who carries the message of life to the not-knowing ones. If they know, let them listen to the preacher who strives to extend their knowledge, to quicken the heart. Perhaps we need more heart work in these days. Emotional preachers may have a special work in these times of increasing knowledge.

I. **Divine wooing.**—A strange reversion. God woos man, and man should woo God. The prophet represents God as standing with stretched-forth hands. The prophet is here strongly anthropomorphic. The eternal Spirit is likened unto a human father or mother stretching forth hands to a wayward child. Does not the divine Prophet teach somewhat of the same in the parable of the prodigal son? The eternal Father sends out His love to woo back the prodigals from their wretchedness. Love sends forth its messengers. As the heavens and their hosts proclaim God's existence and perfections to the whole universe, and, mute as they are, make their voices re-echo in the hearts of all men, so, says St. Paul, with a sort of enthusiasm at the memory of his own ministry, the voice of the preachers of the gospel has sounded in all countries and in all the cities of the world.

II. **Divine retaliation.**—The law of nature is the law of God. Like is returned by like. Reject the good, and the good rejects; reject the Stone of salvation, and it becomes a stone of destruction. " On whomsoever this stone shall fall," etc. " I will provoke you to jealousy." Strong expressions from the mouth of infinite Love. A foolish nation will anger an over-wise, a self-righteous, and a confident nation. How often the no-people anger the people of high looks and lofty mien ! As the wheel of time turns the nobodies become the somebodies, even in social spheres. Foolish nations become the ruling nations. God's fools will reign everlastingly. Israel rejects, and Israel is forsaken. The Church leaves its first works, and the candlestick is removed out of its place. Let modern Churches take warning. We sometimes fear that the divine candle is not burning brightly in our modern Christianity. Awful will be the doom if Anglo-Saxon Israel is provoked to jealousy by them that are no-people, and moved to anger by a foolish nation being blessed.

III. **Divine satisfaction.**—Eternal love must be satisfied. It must find a people on whom to bestow its caresses. Jesus must see of the travail of His soul. If His own people reject, He will find believers among the Gentiles. Israel knew this, and cannot complain. If Israel were blessed with the largeness of divine love, it would not seek to complain. But oh the narrowness of humanity ! The missionary spirit is of slow growth, and seldom reaches large size in our selfish human nature. How little gratification we really receive from the news that nations are being born into the spiritual kingdom ! The nearer we get to the divine, the gladder we shall be that Christ is found of them who sought Him not, that He is made manifest unto those that asked not after Him. Let us pray for largeness of love. Let us seek to be all-inclusive, world-embracing, in our spiritual desires. Light diffused is light increased. The missionary spirit has reflex blessings. Doing good to others, we do good to ourselves.

SUGGESTIVE COMMENTS ON VERSES 18—21.

God has not failed in His part.—It is not God who has failed in His part. No ; they who have not believed (the majority of Israel) cannot excuse themselves by saying that the mission, which is an essential condition of faith, was not carried out in their case. There is not a synagogue which has not been filled with it, not a Jew in the world who can justly plead ignorance on the subject. Μὴ οὐκ ἤκουσαν : " It is not, however, the case that they have not heard, is it ? " Evidently the apostle is speaking of *those who have not believed*, consequently of the Jews. How can Origen and Calvin think here of the Gentiles ? It is the case of the Jews which is being pleaded. The pronoun αὐτῶν, their (voice), refers not to the subject of the previous sentence, but to that of the sentence of the psalm quoted

358

by Paul : *the heavens.* No one certainly will think that Paul meant here to give the explanation of this passage ; it is an application of the psalmist's words, which is still freer than that made of the passage from Deuteronomy in vers. 6-8. The apostle has just advanced, and then refuted, a first excuse which might be alleged in favour of the Jews; he proposes a second, the insufficiency of which he will also demonstrate.—*Godet.*

A foolish nation and an impious nation identical.—" By a foolish nation I will anger you." This is a repetition of the same sentiment. By a "foolish" nation is to be understood an "impious" or "idolatrous" nation. The worshipping of idols being one of the grossest follies of which rational beings can be guilty, idolaters are called in Jewish Scriptures " a foolish people," and the meaning of the words is this : " By receiving into the number of any Church and people the Gentiles who have been accustomed to the worship only of idols, I will excite the anger and envy of the Jews." And that at the commencement of the Christian era this prediction was fulfilled, both by the reception of the Gentiles into the Church of God, and by the jealousy and anger which this extension of the means of salvation produced among the Jews, is amply verified by the history. Thus when Paul preached the word of God to the Gentiles of Antioch, in compliance with their earnest request, the Jews, we are told, " when they saw the multitudes that came together, were filled with envy, and spake against those things which were spoken by Paul, contradicting and blaspheming." And when they found no other means of preventing the apostles from preaching to the Gentiles, they raised a persecution against them, and expelled them out of their coasts.—*Ritchie.*

The gospel like a light shining in darkness.—When the gospel comes, it is like a light rising upon the darkness, and dispelling it : it is light unanticipated, unsought. Jehovah came to the Gentiles by the gospel, like a person paying an unlooked-for visit—an unknown stranger arriving suddenly. The whole language of God by the prophet evidently conveys the idea of previous ignorance and sudden manifestation ; and this manifestation followed by the finding, on the part of those to whom the discovery is made, of Him by whom it is made. The idea of suddenness is strongly expressed by the words, " I am found of them that sought Me not." The finding is not represented as the result of a long process of previous seeking—of " feeling after " God. The Gentiles, immersed in all the ignorance and stupid sottishness of their idolatries, received the " knowledge of the only true God and of Jesus Christ whom He has sent," as a prisoner who had been long immured in the gloom of a dungeon, without a ray of light, and to whom darkness had become so familiar that he had given up thinking of anything else, would receive the beams of heaven, on the window being suddenly opened that had been closed and fastened with bars of iron.—*Dr. Wardlaw.*

ILLUSTRATIONS TO CHAPTER X.

Ver. 1. *Cecil's child.*—" I see my child drowning," says Mr. Cecil ; " that child's education lies near my heart. But what do I think of his education now ? Bring him safe to land first. I will talk of his education afterwards. Paul's first desire is that Israel might be saved. The great concern of preachers should be neither biblical criticism, nor the refutation of heresies, nor to be thought men of intellectual power, but that the hearers may be saved."

Ver. 2. *The balance of the sanctuary.*—In the reign of King Charles I. the goldsmiths of London had a custom of weighing several sorts of their precious metals before the Privy Council. On this occasion they made use of scales poised with such exquisite nicety that the beam would turn, the master of the company affirmed, at the two hundredth part of a grain. Nay, the famous attorney-general, standing by and hearing this, replied, " I should be loath then to have all my actions weighed in these scales." " With whom I heartily agree," says the pious Hervey, " in relation to myself. And since the balance of the sanctuary, the balances in God's hands, are infinitely exact, oh, what need have we of the merit and righteousness of Christ to make us acceptable in His sight and passable in His esteem ! "

Ver. 3. *The moral magnifying glass.*—Some people carry about with them a moral magnifying glass. They are fond of using it. Through it they look intently at their own excellences. Their virtues seem so great that they fail to see their need of pardon. David Rittenhouse, of Pennsylvania, was an astronomer. He was skilful in measuring the size of planets and determining the distance of stars. But he found that, such was the distance of the stars, a silk thread stretched across the glass of his telescope would entirely cover a star. He even found that a silk fibre, however small, placed upon the same glass would cover so much of the heavens that the star, if a small one, would remain obscured several seconds. Our sun is 886,000 miles in diameter; yet, seen from a distant star, it could be hidden behind a thread that was near the eye! Is there nothing like this in the spiritual world? Alas! there is. Too often men allow a very slender, slight thread of virtue to hide from them the glorious Sun of righteousness. Paul tells us of such. "They, going about to establish their own righteousness, have not submitted themselves to the righteousness of God."

Ver. 4. *More grace wanted.*—When Lord North, during the American war, sent to the Rev. Mr. Fletcher of Madeley (who had written on that unfortunate war in a manner that had pleased the minister) to know what he wanted, he sent him word that he wanted but one thing, which it was not in his lordship's power to give him, and that was *more grace. The place to lose self.*—A person who had long practised many austerities, without finding any comfort or change of heart, was once complaining of his state to a certain bishop. "Alas!" said he, "self-will and self-righteousness follow me everywhere. Only tell me when you think I shall learn to leave self. Will it be by study, or prayer, or good works?" "I think," replied the bishop, "that the place where you lose self will be that where you find your Saviour."

Ver. 8. *Healing at her own door.*—A lady who was very ill went from place to place on the Continent, hoping to recover her health, but all in vain, for she daily grew worse. At last, in despair, she asked a physician what she must do. "Medicine," replied he, "is useless. You have one chance, and that is to drink the waters of Pit Keathley." "What?" exclaimed she; "why, those waters are in my own estate!" She went home and recovered her health. Thus salvation is near. The word is nigh thee. The Saviour stands at the door of the heart. "Behold, I stand at the door, and knock."

Ver. 13. *The inclusive "whosoever."*—John Berridge once said, after having given out these words as his text, "I would much rather it be written, 'Whosoever shall call upon the name of the Lord shall be saved,' than 'If John Berridge shall call upon the name of the Lord, he shall be saved; because," said he, "how do I know that there might not be another John Berridge in the world, to whom those words were addressed? But when I read, 'Whosoever shall call,' etc., I know I must be included."

Ver. 17. *They trusted him.*—The French Marshal Turenne was the soldier's hero. He shared all their hardships, and they entirely trusted him. When the troops were wading through a heavy morass, the younger soldiers complained. The older ones said, "Depend upon it, Turenne is more concerned than we are. At this moment he is thinking how to deliver us. He watches over us while we are asleep. He is our father, and would not have us go through such fatigue unless he had some end in view which we cannot yet make out." Let us have this simple confidence in God our father. The faith which cometh by hearing God's word will foster such simple confidence. We must know the Father through the Son; and as we trust the Son, so we shall trust the Father.—*Quiver.*

CHAPTER XI.

CRITICAL NOTES.

Ver. 1.—Μὴ ἀπώσατο ὁ Θεὸς τὸν λαὸν αὐτοῦ; Did God cast off His own people? Observe the aorist. When God accepted a universal Church from all nations in Christ, did He by so doing cast off His own people the Jews? God forbid! God did not cast off the Jewish nation when He admitted all nations to His Church, for I, who address you in the name of Christ, am a Jew (Wordsworth). There may be a general falling away seemingly, and yet a large number remain faithful. Elijah did not see and know all. We may mistake.

Ver. 4.—The reason why the Septuagint sometimes used the feminine, and why St. Paul adopts it here, appears to be because not only a heathen god but a goddess also was worshipped under the name of Baal, and because by this variety of gender the reader is reminded that there was no principle of unity in the heathen worship, and thus the vanity of the worship itself is declared (Wordsworth). ὁ χρηματισμός, a response from God, oracle.

Ver. 6.—εἰ δὲ χάριτι, by grace, thus not of works. Salvation must be either by one or the other.

Ver 7. **The election.**—The faithful remnant which has profited by the free grace given to it by God. **Were hardened.**—πώρωσις is a medical term applied to the induration of the flesh or bones so as to become like porous stones.

Ver. 8.—A spirit of stupor, numbness, insensibility; that bewilderment or stupefaction which is the result of conscience awakened too late. The Hebrew word, as well as the Greek, is often used to signify a permission of that which we can hinder.

Ver. 11.—Did they stumble in order that they should fall? They have swerved aside from the right path, but they have not fallen down utterly so as never again to rise. They have fallen aside so that the Gentiles might excite them to rise.

Ver. 12.—**Wealth of** [to] **the world**—that is, a rich mine of blessing to a whole world, by occasioning the admission of all nations into the birthright of Israel.

Ver. 15.—The apostle awaits a boundless effect of blessing on the world from the future conversion of the Jews, which will be as life from the dead.

Ver. 16.—**Firstfruit** denotes the representative offerings by which the whole mass is consecrated to God.

Ver. 25.—πλήρωμα is a word specially applied to ships. The full complement of the Gentile world shall enter the sacred vessel of the Church, the ark of salvation.

Ver. 33.—**Judgments** are God's decrees; **and His ways** are His ways of bringing them to pass. How just is Paul's reflection upon the whole of his preceding remarks! God's works in providence and grace are mysterious, and we may well exclaim, O the depth!

Ver. 36.—God is the centre of all things; they come from Him. He is the universal Worker. All works contribute to His glory.

MAIN HOMILETICS OF THE PARAGRAPH.—*Verses 1—5.*

The divine response to the human complaint.—St. Paul argues from the known to the unknown. A master of the deductive process. God has not cast away His people; for I am saved who "am an Israelite, of the seed of Abraham, of the tribe of Benjamin." Here is definiteness which precludes the idea of forgery; here is an appeal to the national instinct. God has not cast away His people, for God's act and word show that His love is unchangeable. Paul, an Israelite, is saved. Elias is comforted by the assurance that a remnant is always preserved by God.

I. **A lonely man's complaint.**—Great men stand alone. By material means we may reach to physical heights; but we cannot climb to those heights where intellectual and moral giants dwell. We cannot always understand their lofty motives and moral purposes. Elijah was a man of the wilderness; he was lonely from necessity, and this loneliness rendered him despondent. What a mournful wail comes from the depths of his stern nature! "Lord, they have killed Thy prophets," etc. 1. *Spiritual workers have their times of trial.* All workers have their difficulties; spiritual workers have their special difficulties. Elijah's life seemed to be spent in battling with difficulties. His complaint was that his moral work did not succeed. Elijah, in the sorrow of his heart, in the depression that overtook him on account of seeming failure, claims our sympathies. 2. *Spiritual workers have troubles of their own making.* Elijah had ground for complaint; but things were not so bad as they appeared. Blessed are the hopeful! But do not let popular preachers rave against the unpopular and despondent Elijahs. Our helpful sympathies should go out towards the lonely souls weeping under the juniper trees and craving for death. 3. *Spiritual workers must ask, "What saith the answer of God?"* They must look to God and away from themselves. The wise man's words are true: "He that trusteth in his own heart is a fool." We are shortsighted; we take narrow views; we think things are going wrong if they are not moving according to our notions. God's ways are above ours; His remnants are mightier and more glorious than human majorities.

II. **A merciful God's response.**—The answer of God came sweetly to Elijah in the time of his trouble. The richness and sweetness of the divine voice are noted in times of trouble ; the silence and darkness of trouble's night are cheered by the eternal music which is lost to the soul in the bright day of prosperity. God speaks to the souls of His faithful ones in their despondency. The words give peace and encouragement ; they teach right views of life. The answers of God should hush the complaints of men. The answer of God makes known : 1. *The greatness of the divine reserve force.* When God answers out of material nature, we are astonished at the greatness of the reserve force. Human blindness says not one is left : Omniscience shows seven thousand. Complainers say nature is being exhausted : God's answer is the continued richness of nature and the opening out of fresh fields of supply. Complainers say monotheism is dead : God's answer is the muster-roll of seven thousand. Complainers say Protestantism is dying, that semi-popish churches are most crowded : God's answer is—I have a reserve force ; the truth shall prevail, falsehood must work to its own unmasking, and the heart of civilisation is this day true to the eternal principles of right. Let us not wait under our juniper trees, but go forth and fight the prophets of Baal. 2. *The faithful ones are hidden.* These seven thousand men hidden from the gaze even of a good man like Elijah. God's children are often as hidden ones. Their worth as well as their number is hidden—comparable to fine gold, but esteemed as earthen pitchers. Call to remembrance the former times when God's children were hidden in deserts, in mountains, in dens and caves of the earth. Let us be thankful to God for our times ; let us use our privileges ; let us unfurl the banner of the truth ; let us maintain our spiritual freedom. 3. *The remnant which is to be considered.* Elijah has his descendants. They are good mathematicians, but poor reckoners ; they count easily ; they are good at addition, subtraction, and multiplication. They do not reckon up the remnant ; God would have us reckon up the remnant. Noah was a remnant, but from him came mighty peoples. The Jews were a remnant, but what influence they have exerted ! The followers of the Crucified were only a remnant, but they soon overtopped the world's majorities. Our reformers were only as a remnant, and yet they filled England with light. There may be a remnant still. We vote with majorities to-day ; but it might be safer to side with the remnant left according to the election of grace. Reckon the remnant ; measure its moral force ; estimate its spiritual power ; see if it is being impelled by divine ideas. Is it a remnant according to the election of grace ? We for our part are not afraid of the remnants when they are on the side of the evil : the remnants on the side of the good must be omnipotent. If the remnant have in it a Paul and a Peter, it shall outlive all the majorities of time.

The practical question : If God were to tell some modern Elijah, " Yet I have reserved unto Myself seven thousand who have not bowed the knee to the image of Baal," would God reckon us among the noble band ? Do we bow the knee to our own images ? Are we guilty of modern idolatry ? Are we bowing to the images of the nineteenth-century Baals ? Or are we bowing at the footstool of the Creator ? Do we acknowledge His guidance in the affairs of life ? Do we trust Him in all darknesses ? Can we for Him stand alone against a multitude of false prophets ?

Ver. 3. *Divine reservation.*—The Mohammedan saying quoted by Tholuck is interesting, that " God never allows the world to be without a remainder of seventy righteous people, for whose sake He preserves it." This thought is encouraging to all despondent Elijahs. We cannot see or know all. This may be a necessary discipline for our faith. Ignorance arises from our limitation, and in this state of limitation we must walk by faith and not by sight. And faith will lead us to lay hold of the wisdom, power, and love of God. Holding by these, we shall not be without light in the darkest night, not be without hope even in our moments of despondency; and in spite of despondency we shall continue in the pathway of faithful adhesion to duty. This is one of the pleasing and relieving features in Elijah's character, that though despondent and almost despairing he was not recreant to the voice of duty. He stood alone against the prophets of Baal. Alone, yet not alone, for God was with him. Alone, yet not alone, for he was unknowingly supported, as we may well believe, by the prayers and sympathies of some, if not all, of the seven thousand who had not bowed the knee to the image of Baal. We may say that it would have looked better of them if they had come forth from their hiding-places and had rallied round Elijah in the day of battle. But we do not know all, and must not be too ready to blame. Perhaps after all they helped very effectually by their secret prayers, by their silent but forceful sympathies. Ah, we know not how far these may reach! How little true faith we have in the power of prayer and in the help of sympathy! If it be at all true that the world is preserved for the sake of the righteous people, then we may rightly suppose that the influence of the righteous is far-reaching. An invisible host helped Elijah in the day of conflict. Shall we not also believe that we are compassed about with a great cloud of witnesses? Let the thought of isolation be destroyed by the thought of God's hosts in reserve. He has His purposes; let us believe that they are wise and good.

I. **God's reservations are perfect.**—The number seven is the perfect number in the sacred writings, and may here be fittingly employed to indicate the perfection of the divine reservation. God has reserved to Himself seven thousand—a perfect host to set forth the perfection of the divine plan and the divine purposes. Whether the number stated be either a literal or an allegorical assertion, we may rightly make use of its allegorical teaching. It opens out before our minds the perfection of the divine reservations. If God be perfect in wisdom, power, and goodness, then we may rest assured that perfection marks and attends all the steps of His divine and mysterious processes. It is the glory of God to conceal a thing. The glory of His perfection is made known by His reservations as well as by His revelations. In fact, there cannot be perfection without concealment and reservation. The great mind cannot reveal itself to the shallow soul; yea, the great mind cannot reveal itself to kindred souls. The mind is greater than its own revelations. It agonises with mighty thoughts which it cannot express. And so the perfect God cannot reveal Himself to the imperfect creature. God has no limit in mastering His own thought movements; but surely there is no irreverence in saying that God is limited in this particular, that His perfection cannot be communicated to our imperfection. The perfection of His nature implies and indicates the perfection of His plan. His reserve forces speak of the perfection of His restraining power. Imperfect man does not indulge himself in reserve forces. He has no self-restraint. If he have seven thousand things or people at his disposal, he wishes to show them on his parade ground. Even when self-interest tells him not to make a display of his wealth, he breaks through all considerations of a prudential character, and lets the world into his secret. The child has no secrets; its mind is too small and open. The man-child, through the imperfection and vanity of his nature, is often hurrying to display his wealth. God is great and perfect, and His revelations are only the faint indications of the infinite nature of His resources. Elijah is shown, and he was in himself a host. But Elijah speaks to us of God's seven thousand.

II. **God's reservations cannot be either seen or counted.**—For aught we know to the contrary, Elijah was keen-eyed enough—certainly he possessed the vision of the seer. He could see into some of the mysteries of the infinite movements. He was one of the characters in the olden time who were before their age, and saw what other men did not see; and yet he had no knowledge of the seven thousand hidden away in the recesses of the divine keeping. What blindness of vision! Seven thousand righteous ones in that early period of the world's history, when the population could not be very extensive, and yet Elijah had not the pleasure of their acquaintance. A man might be pardoned if he lived in London and did not know that there were seven thousand righteous amongst its teeming millions; and yet what shall be said of Elijah, who thought that he stood alone, and was ignorant of a mighty but unseen army? But we are often possessed of the Elijah-like blindness. How little we know! How blear-eyed is our vision! The microscope does not reveal to us the laws and methods by which the atom is ruled and guided. There are mysterious pathways far beyond the range of the best-constructed telescope. God's reserve forces can be neither seen nor counted. We talk very glibly of seven thousand, but we fail to grasp the meaning. The numbers of God are not recorded in human mathematical treatises, and vast beyond the mathematician's power of computation. Lo, these are part of the divine ways! How little is known of them! We see and hear the Elijahs. God's seven thousand move in solemn and wondrous silence. Elijah's name is written on the page of the world's greatest book; Elijah's fame and greatness are sounded in the world's ear. We do not know the name of one of those seven thousand; they have no earthly fame. God is so great and has so much patience that He can keep in reserve the large number of seven thousand. What are we when God can hold back so many? Let us learn our littleness and God's greatness; let us pray for divine light and help.

III. **God's reservations are for moral purposes.**—He rescues seven thousand who have not bowed the knee to the image of Baal. God *permits* the existence of the Baal worshippers; He looks after and *promotes* the existence of the righteous remnant. But how is it when the righteous are killed? How is it when the prophets of the Lord are killed by the wicked Jezebels? He has still a righteous remnant of a hundred prophets hidden away by fifty in a cave. The death of the other prophets will create mantles of greater consecration for the living prophets. God only permits a good man to die when that good man's death will be more productive than his life. The slaughtered prophets speak from their tombs of truth and righteousness. Seven thousand righteous— a sweet, saving, wholesome remnant according to the election of grace. Seven thousand good men and women as seed corn to fill the world with the golden grain of divine truth! The seven thousand are gone, and have left no name behind; but their righteous testimony is not destroyed; their saving influence floats along the stream of time. They are not dead. A good man can never die. The voice of goodness is eternal. The helpful sympathy and influence of the seven thousand have cheered and strengthened many Elijahs sorrowing over the failure of their life-work. Failure? There is no failure with God; there can be no failure in God's work. Selfishness speaks of failure. Benevolent faith says we cannot fail. God's kingdom must be established in the earth.

Ver. 6. *The remnant saved owes all to divine grace.*—The gospel is a way of salvation by free, unmerited favour, as opposed to all self-righteousness. It may be humiliating to be able to contribute nothing to our own salvation, but to have to accept it full and free from a risen Lord; yet salvation through humiliation is better, surely, than being lost. "*Grace,*" says Dr. R. W. Hamilton, " is free favour; it can be related to no *right* and contained in no *law*. It is extrajudicial: whenever bestowed, it depends upon the mere will of him who exercises it, or upon, what is the same thing, his voluntary pledge and agreement. If this latter be withdrawn, there may be a forfeiture of integrity and fidelity, but it is only so far unjust to those deprived of it that a claim arose out of it; but no injustice accrues to them, considered in their *original circumstances.* A simple test of grace is presented by the following inquiries : *Ought* it to be exercised ? Can it be *righteously withheld* ? If we affirm the one, if we deny the other, it may be obligation, debt, reason—it cannot be *grace,* for this principle never owes itself to its object ; and in not showing it, the person still is just. If there be any necessity for it, save that of demerit and its misery, it " is no more grace." By keeping the meaning of the term steadily in view, then, it will be seen that no injustice is done any who decline salvation by free grace and insist on some form of self-righteousness. For the latter is pure favouritism, and the former can alone be adopted by a God who is no respecter of persons.—*R. M. E., in " Pulpit Commentary."*

SUGGESTIVE COMMENTS ON VERSES 1—5.

The words denote merely that Paul was a descendant of Abraham.—" For I also am an Israelite, of the seed of Abraham, of the tribe of Benjamin." Interpreters have conceived various reasons for the mention of the tribe to which the apostle belonged. But there seems to be no other reason for it but that it was customary with the Jews, in stating their descent from the patriarchs, to mention the tribe through which their descent was traced. The words denote merely that the apostle was a descendant of Abraham, entitled to all the privileges of an Israelite ; and the inference which he means his countrymen to deduce from them is, that, by believing in Christ, he is a member of the Church of God as it now exists under the Christian dispensation. He is therefore an instance of the continued favour of God to all of His ancient people who believe the gospel, and an example to prove that all of them are not rejected. He then solemnly repeats his affirmation that God hath not totally rejected the Israelites. There is no reason to think that this is meant to represent the exact number of the faithful worshippers of God in Israel at that period. The number mentioned seems rather intended to denote an indefinite and very considerable number. This answer furnishes a warning against those gloomy views of human nature which lead some pious men to think that, because wickedness seems to them

to abound, there are few sincere worshippers of God ; and especially against that uncharitable spirit which leads the zealot to presume that none but those who concur in his views of religion can expect to enjoy the favour of Heaven.—*Ritchie.*

The Lord's people a chosen remnant. —It is the part both of wisdom and of love to guard our statements against misconception. We are of necessity constrained sometimes to state truth in strong and general terms ; but in all such cases it becomes us to anticipate and to remove, as much as in us lies, all occasion for misapprehension or mistake ; we should make everything so clear that the ignorant should have nothing to ask, the captious nothing to object. St. Paul was ever alive to this duty ; he foresaw and answered every objection that could be urged against the truths he maintained. He had in the preceding chapter spoken of the Gentiles as adopted into God's family, whilst the Jews, for their obstinate disobedience, were cast off. Hence it might have been supposed that God had cast off His people altogether : but he tells them that this was not the case ; for that he himself, though a Jew, was a partaker of all the blessings of salvation ; and that as in the days of Elijah there were among the Jews more faithful servants of Jehovah than was supposed, so it was at that time—" there was a remnant," and a considerable remnant too, "according to the election of grace." We will—

I. Show that God's people are a chosen remnant.—The Lord has at this day a remnant of chosen people. In every age of the world there have been some faithful worshippers of Jehovah. Even in the antediluvian world, when all flesh had so corrupted their way that God determined to destroy them utterly, there was one pious man who boldly protested against the reigning abominations, and with his family was saved from the universal deluge. Abraham, Melchizedek, and Lot were also rare instances of piety in a degenerate age, as were also Job and his little band of friends. In Israel too, even under the impious and tyrannic reign of Ahab, there was an Elijah who was a bold and faithful witness for his God. Thus at this day also there are some who serve their God with fidelity and zeal. Neither the example of the multitude nor the menaces of zealots can induce them to bow down to Baal, or to walk after the course of a corrupt world. They are not of the world, even as Christ was not of the world; nor will they conform to it in its spirit and conduct; they will have no fellowship with the unfruitful works of darkness, but they will rather reprove them. To serve, to enjoy, to glorify, the Lord Jesus Christ is all their desire; and they "cleave unto Him with full purpose of heart." They are, however, but a remnant. We are persuaded that there are many Nicodemuses and Nathanaels at present in the shade who yet in due time will come forth to light and be "burning and shining lights" in their day and generation. There may be at this day thousands in the world who in the sight of God are "faithful and beloved," though they have not at present any name or place in the Church of Christ. Yet, after all, in comparison of the careless and ungodly world, they will be found "a small remnant," "a little flock." And for their distinguished privileges they are altogether indebted to the love of God. We should not state these things in a crude and rash way. We know they are deeply mysterious; and we are most anxious to—

II. Guard this doctrine against abuse.—Much is this doctrine hated; much, too, is it abused; but however hated, or however abused, it is the truth of God, and therefore must be maintained. Let none, however, pervert it, or draw false conclusions from it. Let none say: If this doctrine be true, *no blame attaches to me.* If this doctrine be true, *I may sit still till God shall come and help me.* If this doctrine be true, *I am in no danger whatever I may do.* That no solid objection lies against this doctrine will appear whilst we—

III. Suggest the proper improvement of it.—It should encourage all to seek for mercy at God's hands, it should fill all who are the subjects of it with the deepest humility, and it should stimulate them also to universal holiness.—*Simeon.*

MAIN HOMILETICS OF THE PARAGRAPH.—*Verses* 6—12.

Human folly and divine grace.—St. Paul's clearness of thought and precision of expression are brought out in the sixth verse. Grace and works cannot be combined in human salvation. If salvation be a free gift, it cannot be earned. Here is shown St. Paul's anxiety to establish foundation principles. Having mentioned election by grace, he cannot pass on to the discussion of his main topic without striving to leave his readers under no misapprehension. Grace is eliminated if the blessing be earned; works as a ground of merit are excluded if the blessing be freely bestowed. Salvation is so precious that it is above human price. It cannot be bought with silver, neither can it be valued with the pure gold of earth. Human efforts cannot reach divine heights. Ethical systems have failed for human salvation. Moralities have no redeeming force. The grace of God that bringeth salvation has done an effective work, and is destined to work to a still larger extent. Human efforts have shown human folly.

I. **Human folly.**—1. *Goes on a bootless errand.* Israel seeks, and does not find. Seeking their own righteousness, they could not possibly find; for all human righteousness is as filthy rags. Seeking human ideas in a Divine Messiah, they could not find; for He came to reveal the divine thought, to incarnate and unfold the divine idea of love and redeeming mercy. Seeking to establish themselves as the Church and people of God, they could not find; for He would have a pure Church, a people not guided by pride and self-will. Seeking gain, they could not find; for that which they thought to be gain was bitterest loss. Human seekers are divine losers. Folly seeks, and never finds; it mistakes the true way and the right soul end. We seek for pleasure, and find pain. We seek for riches, and find soul poverty. We seek for fame, and sink into obscurity. We seek for righteousness, and cannot get away from the sense of guilt. 2. *Produces stupor.* A spirit of slumber passes over the frame of the morally insensate. How often is the Jew a remarkable example of the possibility of combining great worldly sharpness and intellectual power with moral blindness and darkness! The Jew hath eyes to see material beauty and a prospect of material gain; but it does not follow that the Jew hath eyes to see moral beauty. There are glad prospects which his vision never beholds. And the Jews have many brethren among the Gentiles—unseeing eyes behind the eyes which can see the ways of commerce, the steeps of politics, and even the beauties of nature as science can unfold—unhearing ears behind the ears that can be thrilled with the harmonies of nature, with the swelling strains of music, with the rhythmical measures of poetry. Christ the light-bringer and sight-producer must pour the light of heaven upon the visual orbs of the foolish sleepers. 3. *Turns divine blessings into curses.* The table becomes a snare, a trap, and a stumbling-block. How true of the mere sensualist! The table spread with dainties becomes a physical snare; it is a stumbling-block to physical health, and more, also a hindrance to intellectual growth, death to moral life. Human folly turns divine blessings into curses. Amid both material and moral bounties we should learn to distinguish between use and abuse.

II. **Divine grace.**—1. *Leads on a fruitful errand.* God has no vain seekers in His kingdom. God's elect always obtain. They are wounded, but never beaten. They may be faint with pursuing, but somehow they must reach the goal. They may be cast down, but can never be destroyed in the royal part of them: the essential greatness of their manhood will survive every battle-field. They obtain and possess eternally soul treasure. 2. *Endows with moral sensibility.* God's elect have eyes to see the unseen. They pierce farther than either the range of the telescope, or the ken of the philosopher, or the scrutiny of the scientist. The eyes of the faithful require no earth spectacles. They see afar off, and as they see the vision grows and brightens. They hear sounds which earth's ear-trumpets cannot catch. They hear eternal voices; the whispers of the infinite are richer to them than the loudest choruses of time. 3. *Educes salvation.* Out of the fall a gracious rise. Destruction ministers to salvation. True temporally: the fall of one nation the rise of another. True spiritually: the fall of the Jew the rise of the Gentile. How true that Christ by His fall brought salvation! He conquered when He fell.

Ver. 12. *Human falls.*—The Fall popularly used of Adam's sin and loss of happiness in Eden. Not so used in the Bible (only in margin). Used here of

Israel's loss of land and privileged position. What St. Paul says of Israel's fall here gives us teaching about man's fall from Eden.

The Fall a sad event for man. Before it no sin, no pain, no death. Yet not altogether bad for man, or God, the all-good, would never have allowed it to happen. Israel's falls sad, yet each produced good. *First,* led to stricter observance of religion afterwards. *Second,* helped towards dissemination of Christianity. So with man's fall. Banishment from Eden :- 1. Threw man on his own resources, developed energy. 2. Gave him knowledge of self, compelled him to seek God in a way he could not have done before. 3. Pain brought out sympathy. 4. Previous to Fall human race innocent, yet like a *child;* afterwards sinful, yet like a *man.* 5. More to God's glory to be worshipped by child who *fell and came back again* than by child who did not, could not fall. Our Lord says so (Matt. xviii. 12, 13). Two sorts of fall while climbing a cliff : fall *downwards* to destruction ; fall *forwards,* from which you rise bruised, but continuing ascent. Man's fall latter.

Remember this : 1. When grumbling at toil ; 2. When suffering pain.— *Dr. Springett.*

Grace and works opposed to each other as grounds of salvation.—In reference to the doctrine of grace St. Paul maintained a most watchful and " godly jealousy." On points of a less vital nature he was ready to concede as far as possible ; but on the point of *salvation by grace through faith he was firm and immovable.* He would not give way for a moment, even though all the college of apostles had opposed him, or an angel from heaven had professed to have received a commission to proclaim anything that was inconsistent with it. In the superstructure of our religion there might be errors, yea, considerable errors, as he tells, and yet our souls be saved. Injurious indeed they would be, extremely injurious, to our welfare ; but still they would not be utterly subversive of our hopes. But if the error affected the foundation of our religion, he declared it to be utterly incompatible with our final salvation. This jealousy of his is peculiarly visible in the words which we have just read. They were not necessary to the apostle's argument. In the preceding context he is showing that God has among the Jews as well as among the Gentiles a chosen remnant : but having called them " a remnant according to the election of grace," he lays hold on the opportunity to confirm his favourite position that *salvation is altogether of grace*—so entirely of grace as absolutely to exclude works altogether from having any share in meriting or procuring it. The observation thus introduced deserves the deeper attention, because it shows how near to the apostle's heart the truth was that is contained in it. Let us then, in considering this observation, attend to :—

I. **The truth of it.**—The observation is simply this, that salvation must be altogether of grace or altogether of works ; for that the two cannot possibly coalesce, since each of them excludes the other, as light and darkness. Now this observation is true in reference to every part of our salvation. The truth of the apostle's observation being established, we proceed to show—

II. **The importance of it.**—We have already called your attention to the way in which the observation is introduced, and which we conceive marks very strongly the importance of it in the apostle's mind ; and we may notice the same from the very pointed way in which the observation is made. The apostle seems determined that nobody shall misunderstand him ; and he has effectually secured his object in that particular. To show the importance of his observation, then, we say that it establishes beyond all doubt the freeness and fulness of the gospel salvation, and it secures against all invasion the honour of God. It makes clear the path of the true penitent. On the observation thus explained we ground a few words of *advice*. Accept with gratitude this free salvation, and give no occasion for the objections that are raised against it. Recommend and adorn it by a holy conversation. Show by your lives what the proper tendency and effect of grace is. We are told that "the grace of God which bringeth salvation teaches us that, denying ungodliness and worldly lusts, we should live righteously and soberly and godly in this present world." Show, then, by all your dealings with men what true righteousness is; show by your perfect self-government in all your tempers, dispositions, and habits what true sobriety is; and show by the spirituality of your minds and the heavenliness of your lives wherein true godliness consists. This will recommend the gospel more effectually than all the encomiums that can be lavished upon it, and will operate more strongly to convince men of its excellence than all the arguments that can be urged. Let it be seen, then, that whilst you magnify and extol the grace of God, you are the truest friend of good works; for that though you exclude them from your foundation, you display them in your superstructure, and in fact raise them higher and of a nobler quality than any other people in the universe.—*Simeon.*

SUGGESTIVE COMMENTS ON VERSES 6—10.

The restoration of the Jews a blessing to the Gentiles.—" The ways of God are in the great deep, and His footsteps are not known." They are utterly inscrutable to us. " As high as the heavens are above the earth, so are His ways and His thoughts above our thoughts." We cannot see the end of any one of His dispensations. Who could ever have conceived the designs of God in suffering Joseph to be sold into Egypt? Yet did God intend by that dispensation to keep the whole Egyptian nation from perishing by famine; yea, and the very persons who sold him thither. No less mysterious are His dealings with the Jews. They are cast off, they are led captive of all nations. Yet are they suffering for the good of all people amongst whom they dwell, and even for their own ultimate advantage also. This is strongly asserted in the passage before, where their fall is said to be " the riches of the Gentiles," as their recovery also will be in a far more signal manner and degree. We presume not to think that we can ever fathom this deep mystery. Yet will it be profitable for us to consider it as far as it is revealed; and therefore we shall endeavour, according to the light given us, to show you *what an interest the Gentiles have in God's dealings with the Jews*, particularly in—

I. **Their present dispersion.**—This was designed of God for the salvation of the Gentiles. The fall of the Jews has led to the salvation of the Gentiles. The present rejection of the Jews is ultimately designed also even for the good of that benighted people. But still richer benefits will flow to the world from—

II. **Their future restoration.**—That the Jews will in due time be converted to Christianity is certain, and the effect of this upon the Gentiles will be blessed in the extreme. From this subject the following reflections naturally arise: What compassion should we feel for the Jewish nation! How should we fear and tremble for ourselves! How earnestly should we labour for the conversion of the Jews! God has decreed that they shall be converted, and we have reason to believe that the period fixed for it in the divine counsels is not far distant. It is a fact that multitudes in the heathen world are expecting a change in their religion. The Mohammedans and Hindus throughout our Eastern empire are strongly impressed with this idea; and the exertions making in every possible way for the conversion of the heathen world warrant us to hope that "their fulness" will speedily commence. At all events, "we are debtors to the Jews," and should seek to discharge our debt. Though they are at this time " enemies for our sakes, they are still beloved for their fathers' sakes "; and if, notwithstanding their present enmity against Christ, they are beloved of *God* for their fathers' sakes, should they not be beloved of *us*? Think how indebted we are to their fathers, to those who, at the peril of their lives, brought the glad tidings of salvation home to *us*; and should we not labour to recompense all this in acts of love to their descendants? It is a favourite notion with many that to attempt the conversion of the Jews is a hopeless task. But what ground is there for such a desponding thought as this? Are *they* further off from God than the Gentiles were when the gospel was first published to them? or is it a harder thing to convert *them* than to convert *us*? God expressly tells us that it is a work of less difficulty. " If thou wert cut out of the olive tree which is wild by nature, and wert graffed contrary to nature into a good olive tree: *how much more* shall these, which be the natural branches, be graffed into their own olive tree?" Despair not, then, of doing them good; but exert yourselves in every possible way for their conversion to the faith of Christ. You are told that, " if they abide not still in unbelief, they shall be graffed in again." Seek, then, to convince them of the truth of Christianity, and to bring them to the knowledge and love of their Messiah. If you desire only the conversion of the *Gentile* world, you should begin with the *Jews*, because it is the fulness of the Jews that is to operate on the *Gentiles*, and to effect, as it were, among *them* " a resurrection from the dead." But it is for God's sake whose people they are, and for Christ's sake who bought them with His blood, and for your own sake who must give an account of the talents entrusted to your care, that I call upon you to be workers together with God in this great cause; and if you have any sense of God's " goodness to you," seek to avert and terminate " His severity to them."—*Simeon.*

MAIN HOMILETICS OF THE PARAGRAPH.—*Verses* 13—22.

The right method of magnifying.—St. Paul was no empty boaster. No vain words fell from his lips. He was humble, and yet his humility did not prevent him asserting rightful claims and vindicating his position. He magnified his office by deeds as well as words. He here says: I magnify my office so that the Gentiles may be encouraged and the Jews have no reason to be disheartened. St. Paul magnifies his office :—

I. **By identifying himself with his hearers.**—He speaks to the Gentiles, not as an exclusive Jew, but as one of themselves. He goes down to their position in order to raise them to his own high level. He is a Jew, and yet the apostle of the Gentiles. The preacher must identify himself with his hearers by love, by genial sympathy, by manly effort, if he is to do them good.

II. **By seeking the salvation of some.**—" And might save some." The impelling idea of apostolic ministration. One might listen to some preachers Sunday after Sunday, and never discover that the gospel was a remedial scheme for the salvation of men. One might suppose that Christ had come on a useless errand when He came to give His life a ransom for many. The salvation of some should be the consuming desire of every preacher.

III. **By entertaining a large hope.**—Despairing men cannot make the best preachers. The general without hope is on the way to defeat. A preacher without hope cannot successfully rescue the perishing. St. Paul had large hope. The casting away of the Jewish nation was a ground of hope. He does not wail amid the ruins, but rises by their means to joyful expectations. The casting of them away is the reconciling of the world. The view expands before his eager vision. The receiving of them is life from the dead. A bright era is in the happy future. The valley of apostolic vision is not a valley of dry bones. The world is not to be for ever a vast moral sepulchre. Spiritual life shall animate the race ; moral wastes shall quickly become gardens of the Lord ; spiritual deserts shall speedily rejoice and blossom as the rose. Let hope animate the preacher, and he will lead to great successes.

IV. **By investigating divine methods.**—Some preachers have only one text. Other preachers, with several texts, have only one sermon. Other preachers, with several sermons, have only one round of elementary topics. St. Paul keeps prominent the way of salvation by faith. Christ crucified is central, and other topics are circumferential. St. Paul can give milk to babes, and meat for strong men. Indeed, the men must be very strong who can assimilate St. Paul's strong meat. How skilfully he treats the subject of the breaking off the Jewish branches ? The unbelieving Jews are broken off, while the believing Gentiles are grafted in. The wild olives become fruit-bearing and glorious because the root and fatness of the eternal olive tree are imparted—a beautiful figure of the working of divine grace. Wild olives are both grafted and changed. "If any man be in Christ, he is a new creation." Successfully to graft requires skill ; but what skill is required to graft a wild olive and make it rich ! This skill is only possible to the Divine. Philosophy, education, ethical systems, cannot graft and change. The wild olive retains its wildness. Divine grace can and does both graft and change. Wild olives become part of the fruitful tree. Even hearts of stone are turned to flesh.

V. **By considering the totality of the divine nature and the divine proceedings.**—"Behold therefore the goodness and severity of God." The God of some preachers is maimed. He is fashioned according to their tastes or their peculiar theological tenets. Severity hides the goodness, or goodness is made to obliterate the severity. The modern theologian has an all-father for a God,—an all-father whose children rule the world ; an all-father who is never to be seen, and who exists merely for the happiness of His family, the word "happiness" referring mostly to present benefits. True to the perfection of the divine nature and to the reading of history and of providence, we are compelled to behold both the goodness and the severity of God.

VI. **By making deep subjects have a practical bearing upon life's morals and manners.**—Teachers of homiletics tell us that the conclusion is the proper place for application in every style of treatment. Can the earnest preacher wait for his conclusion ? Can he always restrain the swelling tides of his soul by the weak barriers of homiletical rules ? Can a St. Paul preach for an hour, if modern light and leading would allow him to speak so long on the sublimest themes, and then say, "And now a few words by way of application"? St. Paul is always applying. After a few sentences he cautions against unseemly pride : "Boast not against the branches." He proceeds a little further, and then cautions against presumption : "Be not high-minded, but fear." He may preach election and predestination ; but according to some he is not logically consistent, for he appends, "if thou continue in His goodness." Is burning love ever logically consistent ?

Ver. 22. *The goodness and severity of God.*—Man is often so perverse as to tempt God to strike, and then God must strike sternly. It seems as if we were bent on challenging God to do His utmost to try how much we can endure. Yet the goodness of God is everywhere manifest.

I. **The history of God's dealings with the Jews a great parable of mercy to man.**—Through all the ages of their history they were the children of sparing, delivering, redeeming mercy. Their national history was rooted in redemption. Every defeat, every captivity, was not unto death, but life. Paul, summing up

371

the whole history, breathes the same strain. But there is a dark side. Life is not the one thing needful. It may be the most terrible of gifts. And the Jews, spared, endured sharpest agonies. Their final overthrow is the saddest act in the tragedy of history. Mark their modern persecutions. The world's outcasts.

II. **The principle of the divine method in which the goodness and the severity are thus intertwined.**—Psalm xcix. 8 expounds it. The goodness is for us; the severity is for the sins and follies. This involves a principle little in tune with those who hold that man is homogeneous. 1. Man's nature is in an unnatural condition, lapsed, fallen under the dominion of an alien power. There is strong internal discord. "Flesh lusteth against," etc. 2. God has declared Himself man's helper in the grand enterprise of life. God is really the author of the enterprise. It is God's revelation of Himself which reveals sin (Rom. vii. 7-13). God kindles in the soul the hope of conquering it. 3. The severity is the hand of help which He brings to us in the working out of the great problem of our lives. He distinguishes between us and our sins, and He trains us to distinguish. The one He crushes, the other He saves. No light treatment of sin in the Bible. Modern philosophy says, Do not trouble too much about sin. Heaven's philosophy says, Be in anguish about sin, because God lives to trouble it; and the soul that loves it drinks to the dregs life's cup of bitterness. 4. It is with you to hail the severity and convert it to mercy, or to cling to your sin and convert it to doom. The severity not inconsistent with abounding mercy. God does not, will not, in our state of trial, recognise that our sins and ourselves are one. If deliverance from sin be the end of it, what matters the anguish of the moment? But if you continue with sin, you hate your own soul and love the gates of death.— *J. Baldwin Brown.*

SUGGESTIVE COMMENTS ON VERSES 22, *etc.*

Final perseverance not Paul's doctrine. —The above section is a complete and designed disproof of the doctrine held by Calvin and others, but not by Augustine, that all who have been justified will be saved. For after assuming (chaps. v. 9, viii. 16, 17) that his readers are already justified and adopted as sons and heirs of God, Paul here solemnly and emphatically warns them that unless they continue in faith and in the kindness of God they will be cut off. The words "broken off," used of the unbelieving Jews, evidently denote a "separation from God," which, if it continue, will end in eternal death. Hence Paul's sorrow. That the words "cut off," used as a warning to the believing Gentiles, have the same sense is proved by the comparison of Jews and Gentiles, and by the contrast of being "cut off" and continuing in the kindness of God. Dr. Hodge asserts under ver. 22, but without proof, that Paul

speaks, not of individuals, but "of the relation of communities to the Church and its various privileges." But of this Paul gives no hint whatever. And as yet he has not mentioned in any way either the Church or its privileges, but has spoken only of the relation of individuals to Christ. On the other hand, the words "some of them" (ver. 14), "some of the twigs" (ver. 17), "they that fell" (ver. 22), point us to individuals. The word "thou," which does not always refer to an individual, is proved to do so here by its contrast with "some of the twigs." Can we conceive that Paul would support this urgent and personal appeal by warning the Roman Christians that if they do not continue in faith, although they will themselves be brought back and be finally saved, the Roman Church will perish? It has been suggested that Paul speaks of that which is possible in the abstract, but which will never actually take place. But could a mere abstract possibility call forth the earnest tones of vers. 20-22? The warning would have no force to readers who believed that God had irrevocably purposed to exert upon them irresistible influences, which would secure without fail their final salvation. He tells them to "fear." But an intelligent man will not be moved by fear of that which he knows will not happen—that certain lines of conduct lead towards a certain goal will not affect us if we are sure that the goal will not be reached. We may be moved by consequences which lie on the way to the goal, but only by such as lie within the range of possibility. There are many serious considerations which, even if Calvin's doctrine were true, would prompt us to cling to faith. But to seek to deter his readers from unbelief by speaking of what both he and they knew could never come would be unworthy of an apostle. I notice that Acts xxvii. 31—a passage very different from that before us—is the only instance given by Dr. Hodge of the mode of speech which he supposes that Paul here adopts. He says that "it is very common to speak thus hypothetically." But I do not know of a similar instance in the Bible. It may be said that Paul refers to a personal and possible, but only temporary, separation from Christ, and that those who fall will be certainly restored. I admit that such a separation would be exceedingly hurtful, though not fatal, and would be worthy of Paul's warning and his readers' "fear." But we cannot accept this important limitation without plain Scripture proof; and I hope to show that no such proof exists. Moreover the contrast between this temporary fall, which on this supposition is all that could happen to the Gentiles, and that which happened to the Jews would destroy the parallel on which the argument rests, and would increase rather than lessen the high-mindedness of the Gentiles. We now ask, Has Paul said anything elsewhere which compels us to set aside what all would admit to be the plain meaning of his words if they stood alone? Hodge says that "Paul has abundantly taught in chap. viii. and elsewhere that the connection of individual believers with Christ is indissoluble." I thankfully acknowledge that chap. viii. supplements the teaching of this section and guards it from perversion. But we have seen that it does not contradict or modify in the least the plain meaning of the words before us. And I do not know of any other passage in the epistle which even seems to teach the doctrine in question. This doctrine is also contradicted by chap. xiv. 15, which assumes the possibility of the perdition of a "brother for whom Christ died."—*Beet.*

We estimate God by ourselves.—In the prosecution of this discourse we shall first endeavour to expose the partiality, and therefore the mischief, of two different views that might be taken of the Godhead; and, secondly, point your attention to the way in which these views are so united in our text as to form a more full and a consistent representation of Him. We shall then conclude with a practical application of the whole argument.

I. **One partial and therefore mischievous view of the Deity is incidental to those who bear a single respect to His one attribute of goodness.**—They look to Him as a God of tenderness, and nothing else. In their description of Him they have a relish for the imagery of domestic life, and in the employment of which they ascribe to Him the fondness rather than the authority of a father. It may be thought that surely He at whose creative touch all loveliness has arisen must Himself be placid as the scene or gentle as the zephyr that He causes to blow over it. At present we do not stop to observe that, if the divinity is to be interpreted by the aspects of nature, nature has her hurricanes and her earthquakes and her thunder, as well as those kindlier exhibitions in which the disciples of a tasteful and sentimental piety most love to dwell. Throughout all the classes of society, in fact, it is this beholding of the goodness without a beholding along with it of the severity of God that lulls the human spirit into a fatal complacency with its own state and its own prospects. Independent of all lofty speculation, and aside from the mysteries which attach to the counsels and determinations of a predestinating God, there is abroad on the spirits of men a certain practical and prevalent impression of His severity, to which we believe that most of this world's irreligion is owing. Beholding the severity alone without the goodness, you feel it more tolerable for to live in the oblivion rather than in the remembrance of Deity. There is both a goodness and a severity; and this brings us to the second head of discourse, under which we proposed to point your attention to—

II. **The way in which these two views of the Godhead were so united in the gospel of Jesus Christ as to form a more full and consistent representation of Him.**—First, then, there is a severity. There is a law that will not be trampled on; there is a Lawgiver that will not be insulted. The great delusion is that we estimate God by ourselves, His antipathy to sin by our own slight and careless imagination, of the strength of His displeasure against much evil only by the languid and nearly extinct moral sensibilities of our own heart. We bring down heaven to the standard of earth, and measure the force of the recoil from sin in the upper sanctuary by what we witness of this recoil either in our own bosom or in that of our fellow-sinners upon this lower world. Now if we measure God by ourselves, we shall have little fear indeed of vengeance or severity from His hands. But along with this severity there is a goodness that you are also called upon to behold; and if you view both aright, you will perceive that they do meet together in fullest harmony. It is this, in fact, which constitutes the leading peculiarity of

the gospel dispensation, that the expression of the divine character which is given forth by the severity of God is retained and still given forth in all its entireness in the display and exercise of His goodness. Were we asked to state what that is which impresses on the mercy of the gospel its essential characteristic, we should say of it that it is a mercy in full and visible conjunction with righteousness. The severity of God because of sin was not relaxed, but only transferred from the head of the offenders to the head of their Substitute; and in the depth of Christ's mysterious sufferings has He made as full display of the rigours of His inviolable sanctity. That severity of God, on which we have so much insisted, so far from lessening or casting a shade over His goodness, only heightens and enhances it the more.

We must now conclude with a short practical application.—And, first, such is the goodness of God, that it overpasses the guilt even of the most daring and stout-hearted offender amongst you. Let him even have grown grey in iniquity, there is still held out to him the offer of that peace-speaking blood in which there resides the specific virtue of washing it utterly away. There is none whose transgressions are so foul and so enormous as to be beyond the reach of the Saviour's atonement. But, again, in very proportion to this goodness will be the severity of God on those who shall have rejected it. There is reconciliation to all who will; but if ye will not, the heavier will be the vengeance that awaiteth you. The kindness of God is still unquenched, even by your multiplied provocations of His broken law; but quenched it most assuredly will be if to this you add the tenfold provocation of His rejected gospel. And, finally, let us warn you all, *that no one truly embraces Christ as their Saviour who does not submit to Him as their Master and their Lord.* No one has a true faith in His promises who is not faithful in the observation of His precepts. No one has rightly taken refuge in Him from the punishment of a broken law who still heedlessly and presumptuously gives himself up to the violation of that law; for then shall he be judged worthy of a severer punishment, seeing that he has trodden underfoot the Son of God, and accounted the blood of the covenant an unholy thing.—*Chalmers.*

MAIN HOMILETICS OF THE PARAGRAPH.—*Verses* 23—28.

Dual aspects.—The gifts and calling of God are without repentance, and therefore God is unchangeable. There is no change in God, though there may appear change to men. God joins, then separates, then joins again. But faith is the cementing clay by which the branches are united to the vine. Faith lost, the sap ceases to flow and the branches fall off. Divine purposes work along the lines of human faith and human obedience. God is able to graft without faith, for we must not limit His ability—if we did, we might suppose Him grafting without faith, and yet not being able to make such branches fruitful. They might be united to the good olive tree, and yet not be possessed of any spiritual fatness. The promise is to faith; the blessing is obtained by believing. Let us be afraid of continuing in unbelief. Be not high-minded, but fear. If the natural branches were cut off, how careful should we be who were once branches wild by nature !

I. **A dual method of working.**—God's ability is such that He can work both contrary to nature and in harmony with nature. God has grafted contrary to nature; how much more in accordance with nature ! Many wild oleaster branches have been grafted, and have been wondrous specimens of the power of divine grace. Some of the noblest branches of the Christian tree have been wild Gentile branches. The ecclesiastical tree, primitive, mediæval, and modern, is crowded with many glorious branches of Gentile origin that suggest the most honoured names in the roll of the Church's history. God can work contrary to nature, as nature is seen and described by short-sighted men. Miracles are contrary to nature—contrary to man's nature, not contrary to God's nature. Man's nature is a circumscribed sphere, cribbed, cabined, and confined by men's petty notions, which they call laws, and declare to be immutable and inexorable. God's nature is a boundless sphere. His footsteps tread the vast unknown. The laws of men are only inductions from a part of the divine ways. The laws of God are hidden away in the infinite abyss. The laws of God, like the ways of God, like the sublime being of God, are unknowable. Our laws of nature are limited, for they are the expressions of limited minds—the readings of nature's methods by finite intellects. For aught we know the laws of God are unlimited, being the expressions of an unlimited intellect. We do not know all the laws of God, even those expressed in nature's operations. It does not become finite man to be wise in his own conceits. He should seek to be wise in the light of divine teaching and divine revelation.

II. **A dual method of concealing and revealing.**—God has His divine arcana. We remember a preacher discoursing in order to show that it was not to the glory of God to conceal a thing. Perhaps the proverbs of Solomon contained more wisdom than the utterances of the modern popular preacher. The glory of the Infinite is concealment. How can an infinite Being reveal Himself in fulness to a finite creature ? What glory would there be about a God whom I could comprehend and reduce to my own level ? The hero-worshipper ceases his homage when the hero appears to be stripped of transcendent and almost superhuman qualities. Some ask for a knowable God—a being without any secrets, any mysteries, any hidden purposes. The reverent aspirations of my worshipping nature go out and up towards an unknowable God. The God of mystery is the God of sublime glory. The expanding and inquiring soul, even through eternal cycles, will fail to comprehend all the mysteries of the divine nature and the divine purposes. This is but to say that our littleness cannot contain God's greatness, that the finite cannot receive and possess the Infinite. But God has mysteries which He reveals and explains; and the revelation tends to unfold the greatness of God, and to impress the receptive mind with a feeling of its own littleness. The revelation of one mystery opens out a wide prospect. Part of the divine ways is known, and we consider the dark unknown with profound awe. We ascend one mountain peak. It is very high, and its immensity subdues us with the sense of our own littleness as we see vaster heights beyond, as we consider that alps of divine nature on alps arise, and that it is hopeless for us to attempt to scale the divine altitudes. "For I would not, brethren, that ye should be ignorant of this mystery, lest ye should be wise in your own conceits." The mystery of partial blindness to Israel is in a measure explained by the fact that it tends to the enlightenment of the Gentiles. The blindness is not final. The rejection of the Jews has two ends—the proximate and the final. "The proximate end was to facilitate the conversion of the Gentiles; the final end is to restore the Jews themselves by means of the converted Gentiles, and that to bring down at length on the latter the fulness of the divine blessing."

III. **A dual method of salvation.**—Salvation for the Gentiles through the Jews; salvation for the Jews through the Gentiles. There shall come out of Zion a Deliverer. A mighty Deliverer has come out of the heavenly Zion to the earthly plains. He spoke in righteousness, travelling in the greatness of His strength, for He was mighty to save. And again in manifest and more victorious manner shall the Deliverer come out of the heavenly Zion and turn away ungodliness from Jacob; and Jew and Gentile shall embrace each other beneath the banner of mediatorial love. The Deliverer came with noiseless tread, with the silent but pervasive power of nature. And it may be that in the final ingathering there will be no miraculous interventions. All things will seem to be moving as before, until one day the Church will wake up to find herself pressed on all sides with ingathering adherents. Gladsome time when Jews and Gentiles shall love and worship the world's great King—when the vast races of humanity shall bow, as one great army of the living God, beneath the spell of omnipotent and redeeming love!

IV. **A dual emotional aspect.**—"Enemies for your sakes. Beloved for the fathers' sakes." God is not a series of cold abstractions. God is emotional. Let us not be wise in our own conceits by pretending to explain the motions of hatred and love in a God. Perhaps, however, we may say divine hatred is the projection of human wrongdoing. Divine love is the projection of the divine attribute into humanity, removing human enmities, and filling the world with a new light. Let us fear lest we invoke divine enmity. Let us supplicate divine love. "Beloved for the fathers' sakes." Good fathers are a blessed heritage to their children. Here learn the greatness of man. He possesses a dual nature: one aspect stirs the divine enmity; another aspect elicits the divine love. God looks at the man and drives him from the divine presence. God looks again at the man and embraces him as beloved. Even in the expulsion there is a force of outreaching love. Is it not thus that we often appear to ourselves? We shrink with utmost loathing from one aspect, and then we taste some little comfort by the contemplation of another aspect. But oh to be beloved for the Son's sake! The fathers of the race, the elected of God, were noble and beloved; but rising above all, and nobler than all, and more beloved than all, is the only begotten Son. Beloved for the Son's sake! "He that spared not His own Son, but delivered Him up for us all, how shall He not with Him also freely give us all things!"—the needful, ofttimes more than the needful, in the present; the pleasant, the joy-inspiring, in the blessed future.

SUGGESTIVE COMMENTS ON VERSES 23—28.

Providence a school of virtue.—That the fulfilment of these prophecies is still to come, it appears pretty obvious that a great national movement towards Christianity on the part of the Jews, and their actual adoption of a faith which they have so long held in detestation, must tell with mighty and decisive effect on the rest of the world. If the very existence of the Jews as a separate people be in itself the indication of a providence, a singular event in history which demonstrates the part taken by Him who overrules all history in the affairs of men, how much more impressive will the evidence become when this same people shall describe the actual evolution which it was predicted they should do more than two thousand years ago, shall after the dispersions and the desolations of many generations reach at last the very landing-place to which the finger of prophecy has been pointing from an antiquity so high as that of the patriarchal ages! We know not if this splendid era is to be ushered in by palpable and direct miracle. But should there be no such manifestation of the divine power conjoined with this marvellous fulfilment, there will at least be such a manifestation of the divine knowledge as will incontestably prove that God has had to do with it, and so as that history shall of itself perform the office of revelation, or men will trace the finger of the Almighty in the events which are sensibly passing before their eyes. And besides we have reason to believe of these converted Jews that they will become the most zealous and successful of all missionaries; or, like Paul before them, the preachers of that faith which they persecuted in times past and once laboured to destroy. It is said of a single Christian that he may be "the light of the world." How much more will be a whole nation of Christians! Verily, like Paul, the great prototype of the Jews, they will pre-eminently be the apostles of the Gentiles; and there will be a light to lighten these Gentiles in the very glory of the people of Israel. We must look to futurity for this great accomplishment, for, most obviously, it has not yet been realised. It will be "in the last days, that the mountain of the Lord's house shall be established in the top of the mountains, and shall be exalted above the hills; and all nations shall flow unto it. And many people shall go and say, Come ye, and let us go up to the mountain of the Lord, to the house of the God of Jacob; and He will teach us of His ways, and we will walk in His paths: for out of Zion shall go forth the law, and the word of the Lord from Jerusalem." This is all yet to come, else how could it be spoken, as an immediate sequence of its fulfilment, that "He shall judge among the nations, and shall rebuke many people"? In a school of virtue one chief end were the enforcement of great moral lessons; and this perhaps were best effected by bringing out in boldest possible relief the evil of sin, and in all their beauty and brightness the characteristics of highest moral perfection, or, which is tantamount to this, the high and holy attributes of Him in whom all perfection, as well as all power, have had their everlasting dwelling-place. Now providence is pre-eminently a school of virtue; and we may therefore expect that history, and in a more especial manner sacred history, where the manifestations of providence are seen in nearest connection with the designs of grace, will abound in such lessons. And accordingly such is the manifest purpose of many revealed evolutions or passages in the history of the divine administration, of God's dealings with the world. One main end of the divine policy in the government and final destiny of men seems to be manifestation, that both heaven and earth might learn thereby the more to hate all evil, to love and admire all worth and goodness and true greatness, whether in themselves or as exemplified by Him in whom all greatness and goodness are personified. In harmony with this view we read of the Lord Jesus being *revealed* with His mighty angels on that dread occasion when the glory of His power and sacredness shall be displayed in the destruction of sinners, and the glory of His infinite love for the holy in the triumph and happiness of the saints. And so His disposal of the Church does not terminate in but has an ulterior object to itself, even "to the intent that now unto the principalities and powers in heavenly places *might be known*, by the Church, the manifold wisdom of God." —*Chalmers.*

MAIN HOMILETICS OF THE PARAGRAPH.—*Verses* 29—32.

The unchangeableness of God's attitude towards men.—It is difficult to comprehend that, while change and decay are recognised everywhere in men and in nature, these should not have any place with God. Our preconceived notions lead us to expect shifting policies. But in these points natural and spiritual law are unlike, whatever other harmony there may be. One truth is always before us concerning God—He changes not.

I. **God's intentions towards men are unchangeable.**—1. This is shown by the fact that, notwithstanding men's unfaithfulness, He does not repent of His gifts and promises. Yet some say God has repented—*e.g.*, Gen. vi. 6, where He repented that He had made man. In reality this only points out man's limitation. He cannot think of God save as a magnified man, with man's methods of thought and action. The true explanation of this is that God's visible procedure towards man was altered. From being longsuffering and merciful He was about to show Himself a God of judgment. It is easy to conceive God's grief that the mercy had so little effect and that judgment was called for. But, in point of fact, God's feelings towards men were unchanged. It was simply a change in the method of treatment, but pointing to the same gracious end. A father, *e.g.*, has the welfare of his child at heart. Kind treatment failing, he brings strong discipline to bear. So it is with a nation and the troublesome subjects. So it was with God in the treatment of man. 2. But if there be apparent change, it is in detail, not in purpose. "Changes take place above and around the fortress, but its massive buttresses still stand unmoved, and its battlements frown defiance at the strength of the foe." Such is the parallel to God's purpose concerning men. "He willeth not the death of a sinner," etc. Since mercy will not keep the sinner in the path of righteousness, another method is pursued. 3. God may choose others, and not lose His first love—*e.g.*, He turned to the Gentiles and called them; but He did not thereby lose His regard for the Jews. There was still the gracious plan for *their* redemption. Even when they passed into mischief and sorrow, and the Gentiles were invited to participate in redemption, He still was saying, "How shall I give thee up, Ephraim?" God's heart too large only to have love for a Jew or a portion. 4. Apparent cruelty was in reality kindness. "Is error to be immortal because its eradication is painful? Is the mandrake to grow because its roots shriek when they are torn out of the ground?"

II. **Only pure perversity can cause a sinner's loss.**—It is not God who changes, but the sinner who refuses. It is the grace of God which gives the Gentiles salvation, and only rebellious resistance to that grace which excludes the Jews. This suggests man's freedom of action. He is no victim of fate. He may choose his attitude towards God, and may submit and serve, or be defiant. The rejection of the Jews was the natural result of their own obstinacy

378

and hardness—not the result of a blind, hard fate against which they were powerless.

III. **In spite of man's wilfulness God has unchangeably adhered to His scheme of mercy.**—"God's gifts and calling admit of no revocation. Once given, they are given for ever." The question is, Do *we* reject them ? God's constancy to His purposes shows : 1. The amplitude of His love—mercy offered to those who by no means deserved it. 2. Man, when lost, has been his own worst enemy, by having refused the offers of mercy. 3. The vastness of our debt to Him who decreed our salvation. While sin is universal, God's love is equally unlimited ; it traverses the whole range of sin. *What is our response ?* The question may come to us, How much owest thou unto thy Lord ? The difficulty is to answer *how* much ; for the mercy we have received is so vast, so boundless, so undeserved—it is so much a gift of God's free grace, large, unmerited, and free ! We may not say less than this,—

> " Here, Lord, I yield *myself* to Thee !
> 'Tis all that I can do."

Albert Lee.

Vers. 29-32. *Temporal restoration not promised.*—There is nothing in this passage pointing to a *temporal* restoration of the Jewish nation, or to an Israelitish monarchy having its seat in Palestine. The apostle speaks only of a spiritual restoration by means of a general pardon and the outpouring of the graces which shall flow from it. Will there be a political restoration connected with this general conversion of the people ? Or will it not even precede the latter ? Will not the principle of the reconstitution of races, which in our day has produced Italian unity, German unity, and which is tending to the unity of the Slavs, also bring about Israelitish unity ? These questions do not belong to exegesis, which confines itself to establishing these two things : 1. That, according to apostolical revelation, Israel will be converted in a body ; 2. That this event will be the signal of an indescribable spiritual commotion throughout the whole Church. As Nielsen says : " Divine impartiality, after having been temporarily veiled by two opposite particularisms, shines forth in the final universalism which embraces in a common salvation all those whom these great judgments have successively humbled and abased." There is therefore no inference to be drawn from this passage in favour of a final universal salvation (De Wette, Farrar, and so many others), or even of a determinist system, in virtue of which human liberty would be nothing more in the eyes of the apostle than a form of divine action. St. Paul teaches only one thing here—that at the close of the history of mankind on this earth there will be an economy of grace in which salvation will be extended to the totality of the nations living here below, and that this magnificent result will be the effect of the humiliating dispensations through which the two halves of mankind shall have successively passed. The apostle had begun this vast exposition of salvation with the fact of universal condemnation ; he closes it with that of universal mercy. What could remain to him thereafter but to strike the hymn of adoration and praise ?—*Godet.*

Ver. 29. *Persistence of the divine gifts.*—St. Paul having shown that the rejection of Israel was only partial, he next shows that it was only temporary—that God had not done with His people yet, but that they had still a great part to play in the spiritual history of the future.

I. **The gifts of God are without repentance.**—These two words, " without repentance," are the translation of one word, and that one word occurs only twice in the New Testament,—here, and in the passage where the apostle, contrasting godly sorrow with the sorrow of the world, says that " godly sorrow

379

worketh repentance to salvation *not to be repented of*"—that is to say, such repentance is followed by no regret; no man is ever sorry that he has repented of his sins. In like manner God's gifts, once bestowed, are not lightly recalled. Freely given, they are steadily continued from age to age—they are "without repentance"; even when misused and neglected, they are made in some way to work out the gracious purpose of Heaven. This is true of His commonest gifts of all. The word translated "gifts" is one almost entirely peculiar to the apostle in the New Testament, and is used by him in the sense of *an endowment of power*. It is analogous to what we say ourselves when we speak of the gift of the poet or the musician, of the orator or the artist, meaning thereby special aptitude or faculty for doing something. In the passage before us St. Paul is speaking of a special endowment of power bestowed upon a nation; for a nation may be specially gifted as well as a man. It was theirs, by means of super-natural revelation through prophet and seer, to minister to the God-consciousness of the human soul, to deal with the conscience and the religious life. "The spiritual thirst of mankind has for ages been quenched at Hebrew fountains": the profoundest thoughts of God and of His righteousness to be found anywhere in the world, the clearest and most fruitful ideas of His nature, His moral government, and His personal relations to the souls of men, have come to us from them. In modern days, as in ancient, God's gifts have been steadily persistent, without repentance and without recall. We thank God for harvests and fruitful seasons; let us also thank Him for men who have pioneered our way to nobler realms of thought, for men who have spoken burning words of conviction to the national conscience, for men who have grappled with great social wrongs and done battle with injustice, for men who have helped to make vivid to us the spiritual world and our own personal responsibility to the God of our life. Nor must we think only of great men and great gifts. The humblest man you meet has his own proper gift of God. But we must not stop at the intellectual and practical gifts which God bestows upon men. In the spiritual region, as in the intellectual, each hath his own proper gift of that God who divides to every man severally as He will. The grasp of faith, the intensity of love, the power of sympathy, vary. This gift of the Spirit is the gift of God Himself, as an indwelling, ennobling, and sanctifying power to His creature.

II. **The words before us speak of the call of God as well as of the gifts of God; and the call, equally with the gift, is without repentance.**—God's call takes various forms. This, which is true of nations, is true also on a smaller scale of our own personal lives. There are times when God breaks up a man's surroundings and sends him forth to new scenes and circumstances, that He may make more of the man himself. The call of God may take another form—that of summoning us to special acts of service. The men who have made the noblest sacrifices and done the noblest work have been those who have heard most clearly the call of God in their souls, and have felt most surely that He gave them their work to do. When God gives us work to do, He gives power to do it; power comes upon us as we go. Finally, the call of God to some men is a call to break away from a sinful, godless life. Such calls come at times even to the worst of men. In other ways, too, the call comes. It comes sometimes in the shape of personal trouble sweeping down upon the man's life. Perhaps he has been trying to make his life complete without God, trying to make his paradise here instead of yonder. And it may be that he seemed to succeed for a while; but only for a while. For changes come. The shadow fell where the love dwelt; there was a vacant chair, and when that chair became vacant the light of the house seemed to go out, and in the silence and desolation which followed God's voice was heard calling the stricken heart to its true home and its true rest.—*John Brown, D.D.*

God's conduct in the salvation of mankind.—This is the conclusion of the argument which Paul had pursued in regard to God's conduct in the salvation of mankind. He seems to be overwhelmed with the sense of its unsearchableness. In many things do the depths of God's wisdom and knowledge in man's spiritual restoration appear. We remark five things :—

I. **The manifestation of His righteousness in the restoration of rebels.**— Human monarchs have shown their justice in crushing rebels, but God in restoring them.

II. **The destruction of the spirit of rebellion in the restoration of rebels.**— Human monarchs may deliver rebels, but they cannot destroy the spirit of rebellion. God does this.

III. **The augmentation of the force of moral government in the restoration of rebels.**—Human monarchs may weaken their government by saving rebels, but God strengthens the force of His moral administration by redeeming transgressors.

IV. **The promotion of all the rights of His subjects in the restoration of rebels.**—Human monarchs by delivering rebels endanger the rights of loyal citizens. God in the restoration of rebels promotes the rights of all. "O the depth of the riches," etc.

V. **The election of earth instead of hell as the scene for the restoration of rebels.**—*Homilist.*

MAIN HOMILETICS OF THE PARAGRAPH.—*Verses* 33—36.

A fathomless deep.—What sublime irony is contained in the two questions repeated from the Old Testament prophet ! " Who hath known the mind of the Lord ? or who hath been His counsellor ? " Imagine the savage, the child of the wigwam and the forest, whose instinct—for it can scarcely be called reason— is little keener than the instinct of the animals he seeks to entrap ; presuming to advise the president of the British Association, the savage may plead ignorance in extenuation of his presumption. What plea shall the modern savant advance as he presumes to advise and to arraign infinite Wisdom ? The best of us only know in part. Shall men of very partial knowledge and very scanty wisdom arrogate to themselves the high prerogative of being the counsellors of Him the depth of the riches of whose wisdom and knowledge is fathomless ?

I. **Here is a deep which is unfathomable.**—Modern man is a marvel. He can plumb the ocean's depths and scale the mountains' heights with surprising accuracy. Is there any height or depth, length or breadth, placed beyond the bounds of his ken ? Modern man is great at material measurements. His scales are nicely adjusted for weighing material substances. What scales has he for moral measurements ? What plumb-line can go down to the fathomless deep of infinite wisdom, knowledge, and goodness ? He fails ; and his failure is seen by his poor attempts at criticism.

II. **A deep which is inexhaustible.**—As soon think of emptying the ocean with a cockle-shell as think of exhausting the treasures of divine goodness, wisdom, and knowledge. God's material riches in this one planet are wonderfully abundant in supply. The mansions of earth are many, and are marvellously full of material riches. Her ample storehouses have been worked for centuries, and yet there is abundance. The earth is as radiant with beauty, the stars shine as brilliantly, the sun pours forth his rays as plentifully, and the clouds send down their rains as copiously as they did for the benefit of primeval man. If God's material riches are so vast, what must be the intellectual and moral riches of that Being from whom proceeds all the glorious wealth of time !

381

III. **A deep which is incomprehensible.**—The depth of the riches of God's wisdom and knowledge cannot be proclaimed.   Poets may sing, but the poet's song falls short of the lofty theme.   Pulpit orators may declaim, but too often they only darken knowledge by well-sounding words; and sometimes the more darkness which is raised by high-swelling phrases, the better pleased are the unthinking portions of the audience.   Philosophers may dream and formulate theories, but they show no right comprehension of infinite riches.   If the riches cannot be proclaimed, much less can they be comprehended.   I cannot comprehend my own mind.   How, then, can I comprehend the mind of the Infinite?   I talk about reason, memory, and perception ; but who shall tell me what it is that reasons, remembers, and perceives ?   Who shall settle the disputed point whether conscience be original or derived, whether it be a separate faculty or the resultant of several faculties ?   Whence comes inspiration ?   How is it that at some times thoughts flash and burn with lightning-like speed and brilliance, and at other times there are no visions ?   A man's own mind is incomprehensible.   What about the infinite mind ?   Can I follow the penetrating gaze of Him who seeth all the secret things of darkness ?   Can I understand the nature of that knowledge to which the words "new" and "old" cannot have a meaning in our human sense ?   Can I comprehend the plans that overarch the sweep of mighty time ?   Thank God, though we cannot know all, we may know some.   Complete knowledge is excluded ; partial knowledge is our blessed privilege.   The riches of God's goodness fill the soul with adoring thankfulness.

IV. **The human mind cannot counsel the divine mind.**—For we do not know the mind of the Lord.   What is the meaning of mind?   What is my mind?   Is it a material or an immaterial force ?   What is the mind of a God?   What is the νοῦ of the infinite Ruler ?   What are the blessed tendencies of the eternal Spirit ?   What are the purposes and dispositions of the Godhead looking, as we say, far down the stream of ages?   I cannot counsel to good purpose even an earthly statesmen in a critical state of the country's affairs.   A vast assembly of senators deliberate, but they fail to give the proper counsel.   Who, then, shall be God's counsellor ?   Of all the prime ministers of earth, who is fit to be the prime minister of the universal King ?   Gabriel himself cannot counsel.   God requires no counsellor ; He will bring all things to successful and triumphant issues.

V. **The human mind cannot enrich the divine mind.**—We only give what we have received.   God is no man's debtor.   Still, God does not spurn our gifts.   If we do what we can, God will recompense.   If we give to Him our hearts, He will give back the gifts vastly improved.

VI. **The human mind can glorify the divine mind.**—Not by making it more glorious, but by proclaiming God's glory.   Let us show forth His glory with our lives as well as our lips; let us believe that thanks-living is the true thanksgiving.   Let the adoring song arise.   For of Him, and through Him, and to Him are all things : of Him as the source ; through Him as the channel, the directing agency ; to Him as the great blissful centre of the whole system of things.   To whom be glory for ever.   Amen.

The splendour of the divine plan.—The apostle has been carrying on a very close and elaborate argument, in which, among other things, he proves that God's intentions towards men are unchangeable.   He then points out that if there appear to be any change, it is merely in detail and not in purpose; God has unchangeably adhered to His scheme of mercy for all.   Paul then pauses to consider these things, and during that pause there rolls in upon him a sense of the splendour of the divine plan which he has been setting forth.   Hence he is moved to exclaim, "O the depth," etc.   These verses suggest :—

I. **The unbounded richness of God's wisdom and knowledge.**—One can almost imagine Paul unconsciously repeating parts of the old Scriptures to himself: such as Psalm xxxvi. 5, 6—"Thy lovingkindness, O Lord," etc. ; or passages such as Job v. 9—" Which doeth great things and unsearchable," etc. ; ix. 10— " Which doeth great things past finding out," etc. ; xxxvi. 22, etc.   God's richness in wisdom seen in all departments: 1. In nature.   2. In the method of His treatment of the helpless.   3. In His care for the dependent—the sparrow, the needy human creature.   These all wait upon Him, and are not disappointed.

> " Too wise to err, too good to be unkind."

As we look around, or into experience, or into the Scriptures, it is all the same —there are indications of boundless mercy, infinite compassion, the most touching care for His creatures.   The humblest hearer has a part in this care, can come in all his poverty, temporal or spiritual, and receive a gift.   *All* can say, " O the depth," etc.

II. **On earth we shall never fully comprehend God.**—For many reasons. 1. The depths of His riches are so great.   Ten thousand mercies only take us a small way down into the sea of His goodness.   2. Our own sense of His tenderness of judgment will never be adequate to His dealings.   To man on earth, however wise and far-seeing, the ways of God are beyond discovery— " past finding out."   3. In the whole of man's history none have succeeded in finding out the full mind of God, not even God's " friends."   He reveals just enough of Himself to serve His purpose, and no more ; with that we must be content.   A Persian one said, " The face of the beloved of God is covered with a veil.   Except He Himself remove it off, nothing can tear it from Him." Another has said, " From below, out of our misery, no path leads upwards to God.   He being all-sufficient in Himself, must descend if man is to know Him."

III. **If on earth we can never fully comprehend God, we can surely never fully recompense Him.**—For: 1. We do not even know the fulness of our debt— " Now I know in part."   2. What is finite can never reckon satisfactorily with the Infinite.   In order to fully recompense we must have wealth equal to the largeness of the gift.   And how could that be when we compare ourselves with God ?   To meet unlimited demands there must be unlimited supply; and only can He who owns all things do this.

IV. **Contemplating all this, how can we suppose that we have any claim on God for His mercies ?**—Whatever comes from Him is a gift, pure and simple, without the shadow of a claim.   How great, then, the mercy that unfolded the scheme of a free salvation—that blessed the world with forgiveness in return for rebellion—that gave Christ and Christianity, with all their blessings, even to those who had turned away to follow their own wills !

V. **Praise, then, is natural when thoughts of God's goodness come.**—It is so in other matters.   The promptings of the heart are to praise when one has done us a great kindness.   Opinion seems to demand it.   If one be slow to acknowledge kindness, the world says he is ungrateful and unworthy of any further share.   And so in connection with God's gifts and kind dealings.   Some one has said, " The right contemplation of divine verities should lead to the ascription of praise.   The scheme of the gospel, coldly viewed, paves the way for doubt and cavil, while such an apostrophe as is contained in these verses strengthens our faith.   In a word, *suppressed* praise is perilous to the spiritual constitution."   " O Lord, we will praise Thee," etc.   Finally, service ought to accompany the praise: " Lord, what wilt Thou have me to do ?"— *Albert Lee.*

383

God His own last end in everything.

I. **While God is knowable, He surpasses all our conceptions in His wisdom and His ways.**—While believing in the radical error which underlies the agnostic philosophy, we must at the same time admit that God's wisdom and knowledge, His judgment and His ways, are past our comprehension. Just as a child may know, that is be acquainted with, his parent, while at the same time he is utterly unable to follow him into the regions of pure mathematics, comprehend the differential or integral calculus, or the new department of quaternions, so a Christian may know God as He reveals himself in Christ, and yet stand in awe before His unsearchable judgments. It is God's glory to conceal a thing. If we saw through the whole administration of God, if there were no mystery or perplexity in His dealings, we should be living by *reason*, and not by *faith*. It is more consonant with our finiteness in its relation to the infinite God that we should be asked to *trust* God, even when we see no reason for His action, when clouds and darkness may be round about His throne. What we have to consider, therefore, is the proper attitude of the Christian before the profundities of God. It surely should be one of humility, of reverence, and of thankful praise. Now the partiality of Paul's revelation may be profitably contrasted with the fulness of revelation as claimed by Christ. For He claimed to have *all* that the Father doeth shown to Him. Nothing was or is concealed from Jesus. God's ways were not unsearchable to Him.

II. **Men should not in consequence dictate to God or try to be beforehand with Him.**—Now when the matter is put broadly in this way, it seems shocking presumption for men to set themselves up as superior persons, capable of dictating to the Eternal. Yet is this not the meaning of a large amount of the pessimistic literature of our time? If the pessimists had only been consulted, they could have planned a much better world than God has given us. His management has been, in their view, a mistake; and the only redeeming feature in the business is that He has somehow created the pessimists with judgments and powers superior to His own. It is time, surely, that these lamentations over a system of things so very imperfectly understood as yet should cease, and that creatures so finite should humble themselves before the Infinite and acknowledge His superiority in all things.

III. **At the same time the apostle concludes that God is His own last end in everything.**—It seems a hard thing to take in, yet the more it is pondered the truer it appears. "The supreme sun of the spiritual universe, the ultimate reason of everything in the world and work of grace, is the *glory of God*. Whole systems of truth move in subordinate relation to this; this is subordinate to nothing." "There was nothing," wrote Robert Haldane to M. Chenevière of Geneva, "brought under the consideration of the students which appeared to contribute so effectually to overthrow their false system of religion founded on philosophy and vain deceit as the sublime view of the majesty of God which is presented in these concluding verses of the first part of the epistle: 'Of Him, and through Him, and to Him are all things.' Here God is described as His own last end in everything that He does. Judging of God as such a one as themselves, they were at first startled at the idea that He must love Himself supremely, infinitely more than the whole universe, and consequently must prefer His own glory to everything besides. But when they were reminded that God in reality is infinitely more amiable and more valuable than the whole creation, and that consequently, if He views things as they really are, He must regard Himself as infinitely worthy of being most valued and loved, they saw that this truth was incontrovertible. Their attention was at the same time turned to numerous passages of Scripture which assert that the manifestation of the glory of God is the great end of creation, that He has Himself chiefly in view in all His works and dispensations, and that it is a purpose in which He requires that all His intelligent creatures should acquiesce and seek to promote as their paramount duty. Passages to this effect, both in the Old and New Testament, far exceed in number what any one who has not examined the subject is at all aware of." Now if our idea of God be high enough, we shall conclude that He stands in such perfect relations to His creatures that in seeking His own glory He is at the same time seeking their highest good. Of course we have the power of resisting this claim of God, and setting ourselves in opposition to His glory; yet this will not defeat His purpose, but be overruled for His praise. It is not selfishness in the most high God to seek His own glory; He is so perfect in His love as to be incapable of selfishness. His glory conflicts with the real good of none of His creatures.—*R. M. E., in " Pulpit Commentary."*

A magnificent ascription of praise.—In this magnificent ascription of praise a long train of reasoning finds its climax. God's redeeming plan has been traced from its conception in the eternal counsels, through its course in time in the believer's call, justification, and sanctification, up to its culmination in the heavenly glory. The apostle has passed under review the relation in which both Jew and Gentile stood to the plan of salvation, arguing that there was no difference in the sight of the righteous law, that God had shut them all up into unbelief that He might have mercy on all. Then he bursts out in words of adoring wonder at the comprehensiveness and grandeur of the plan of divine mercy.

I. **The riches of the divine perfections.**—" O the depth of the riches both of the wisdom and knowledge of God." This is a favourite mode of expression with St. Paul (cf. Rom. x. 12 ; Eph. iii. 8 ; Phil. iv. 19), and is meant to impress us with the wealth of the grace of God to guilty man. God's riches are like a mine. The apostle has been digging in this mine, and when he comes to tell his fellow-men the treasures he has found, language seems to fail him, and he exclaims, " O the depth of the riches ! " Like seams of unexhausted wealth in the bowels of the earth, so in the infinite heart of God are deep springs of love, riches of mercy and wisdom and knowledge, which no spiritual surveyor has yet touched. The apostle came back from his survey with a profound sense of the vastness of the field. Each attribute might furnish material for meditation. Knowledge and wisdom are here named, the one devising the plan and the other adapting the means to the end. The redeemed to all eternity will not exhaust the wealth of these attributes. Each new discovery will stir them to new songs of wonder and praise.

II. **The unsearchableness of the divine methods.**—" How unsearchable are His judgments, and His ways past finding out ! " God's " ways " are as inscrutable as His perfections. His plans and methods of working are mysterious. The mystery of the call of the Gentiles was kept hid since the foundation of the world, but now made known in His dealings with a lost world without respect of persons, Jew and Gentile alike being included in His all-embracing mercy. Think of His " ways " towards individuals—*e.g.*, Moses, Abraham, Saul of Tarsus. And how graciously He has dealt with us personally ! He has at His disposal an infinite wealth of appliances and means of leading erring men to Himself. " Bless the Lord, O my soul, and forget not all His benefits."

III. **The independence of the divine counsels.**—" Who hath known the mind of the Lord ? or who hath been His counsellor ? " These quotations from the Old Testament show the apostle's acquaintance with Scripture and agreement in doctrine. The glory of human redemption belongs to God alone. He did not share His secrets with any created intelligence. None could have known His mind till He was pleased to divulge it, for He held counsel with none. He had no instructor. The great thoughts that are gradually taking form throughout the ages owe their conception to His sovereign mind. "With whom took He counsel, and who instructed Him?" What a lofty view does this give us of God's unaided wisdom and knowledge and sovereign will! No suggestion from man could improve or alter the divine procedure, or aid Him in working out His plans. Each generation has its little system which lives for a day and ceases to be; but God's mighty plan lives on and develops from age to age. God is supreme, sovereign, independent of human wisdom or knowledge; and when His plan is complete, He alone shall bear the glory.

IV. **The manifestation of the divine glory.**—"For of Him, and to Him, and through Him, are all things: to whom be glory for ever." The gracious purpose which runs through the ages will, when completed, show the glory of its Author. Revelation is essentially an unveiling of God, the manifesting of His perfections being the ultimate end of the scheme of grace. The glory of human redemption belongs to Him alone. This is the goal to which the whole creation moves. God will be all and in all. 1. "For *of Him* are all things." He is the first cause, the fountain-head of the stream of grace that flows through time. It originated in His eternal love and purpose. 2. "*Through Him* are all things." It is through His sole presiding agency that the purposes of His love and grace are brought about. He that began the good work will carry it on to perfection. 3. "*To Him* are all things." The redemptive forces which He launched on the world will seek their source when their work is done. The stream of grace which broke out from beneath His throne will, after refreshing generations of weary men, return to Him in circular flow, bearing on its bosom all that is worth saving from the wreck of a ruined world. And so the end and the beginning will meet in the far-off divine event. All things will be redeemed and reconciled—things in heaven and things on earth. And throughout eternity a redeemed and reconciled universe, viewing the height and depth and length and breadth of the redeeming plan, will ascribe all the glory to Him who reigns, Jehovah God alone.—*D. Merson, B.D.*

SUGGESTED COMMENTS ON VERSES 33—36.

A vast survey of the world.—Like a traveller who has reached the summit of an alpine ascent, the apostle turns and contemplates. Depths are at his feet; but waves of light illumine them, and there spreads all around an immense horizon which his eye commands. The plan of God in the government of mankind spreads out before him, and he expresses the feelings of admiration and gratitude with which the prospect fills his heart. The word "to Him" does not refer to God's personal satisfaction, an idea which might undoubtedly be supported; for, as Beck says, "the egoism of God is the life of the world." But it is more natural to apply the term "to Him" to the accomplishment of His will, in which His own glory and the happiness of His sanctified

creatures blend together as one and the same thing. It has been sometimes attempted to apply these three prepositional clauses to the three persons of the divine Trinity. Modern exegesis (Mey., Gess, Hofm.) has in general departed from this parallel, and rightly. When Paul speaks of "God," absolutely considered, it is always the "God and Father" he intends, without of course excluding His revelation through Christ and His communication by the Holy Spirit. But this distinction is not raised here, and had no place in the context. What the apostle was concerned to say in closing was that all things proceeding from the creative will of God, advancing through His wisdom and terminating in the manifestation of His holiness, must one day celebrate His glory, and His glory only. Never was survey more vast taken of the divine plan of the world's history. First, the epoch of primitive unity, in which the human family forms still only one unbroken whole; then the antagonism between the two religious portions of the race created by the special call of Abraham—the Jews continuing in the father's house, but with a legal and servile spirit, the Gentiles walking in their own ways. At the close of this period, the manifestation of Christ determining the return of the latter to the domestic hearth, but at the same time the departure of the former. Finally, the Jews, yielding to the divine solicitations and to the spectacle of salvation enjoyed by the Gentiles as children of grace; and so the final universalism in which all previous discords are resolved, restoring in an infinitely higher form the original unity, and setting before the view of the universe the family of God fully ·constituted.— *Godet.*

ILLUSTRATIONS TO CHAPTER XI.

Vers. 1-5. *Brave the perils of ridicule.*— " As the crackling of thorns under a pot, so is the laughter of a fool," and he is a poor invertebrate creature who allows himself to be laughed down when he attempts to stick to his principles and tries to do what he believes to be right. " Learn from the earliest days," says Sidney Smith, " to inure your principles against the perils of ridicule; you can no more exercise your reason if you live in the constant dread of laughter, than you can enjoy your life if you are in constant terror of death." No coward is greater than he who dares not to be wise because fools will laugh at him. Elijah bore more than ridicule : he exposed himself to death.

Vers. 4, 5. *Salvation by grace.*—Some are all their days laying the foundation, and are never able to build upon it to any comfort to themselves or usefulness to others ; and the reason is, because they will be mixing with the foundation-stones that are only fit for the building. They will be bringing their obedience, duties, mortification of sin, and the like unto the foundation. These are precious stones to build with, but unmeet to be first laid to bear upon them the whole weight of the building. The foundation is to be laid in mere grace, mercy, pardon in the blood of Christ ; this the soul is to accept of and to rest in merely as it is grace, without the consideration of anything in itself, but that it is sinful and obnoxious to ruin. This it finds a difficulty in, and would gladly have something of its own to mix with it ; it cannot tell how to fix these foundation-stones without some cement of its own endeavours and duty, and because these things will not mix they spend fruitless efforts about all their days. But if the foundation be of grace, it is not at all of works, otherwise grace is no more grace. If anything of our own be mixed with grace in this matter, it utterly destroys the nature of grace, which if it be not alone, it is not at all.—*Biblical Museum.*

Ver. 13. *Practical preaching.*—A practical preacher is one who knows what he means to say and says it in the simplest words, who hits something because he aims at something, who acts in the spirit of the Baptist's noble words about his Master, " He must increase, but I must decrease." When Demosthenes had done speaking, the Athenians said, " Let us fight Philip." When Cicero ceased, the Romans said, " What a fine orator ! " After hearing Massillon at Versailles, Louis XIV. said to him, " I have heard many great orators in this chapel, and have been highly *pleased with them* ; but for you, whenever I hear you I go away *displeased with myself*, for I see more of my own character." Preachers magnify their office when they lead their hearers to be displeased with themselves and think much of Christ.

Ver. 22. *God is love.*—Mr. Spurgeon relates that he deemed it a strange thing when he saw on a country weathercock the motto " God is love," and he asked his friend if he meant to imply that the divine love can be fickle as the wind. " No," said he ; " this is what I mean—*whichever* way the wind blows God is love ; though the cold north wind, the biting east wind, still God is love, as much as when the warm, genial breezes refresh our fields and flocks." God is love both in severity and in goodness. Whatever be the divine aspects, the divine nature is love.

Vers. 24, 25. *Beholding the deliverer.*—On the occasion of President Lincoln's visit to Richmond, as soon as his arrival became known, the coloured people whom he had delivered from bondage crowded around in wild enthusiasm. They gazed upon the wonderful man ; they shouted, they danced ; waved their handkerchiefs and hats ; they cheered enthusiastically. Some cried, "Glory, glory ! " others, " Thank you, dear Jesus, for this ! " others, " God bless you, Massa Linkum ! " others, " Bless de Lord ! " What triumphal entry into Rome ever equalled this entry into Richmond by our delivering President ? But ere long we shall all gaze on a Greater than he, with even greater satisfaction than those redeemed ones experienced.

Vers. 24, 25. *Let us pray for the restoration of Israel.*—Oh, shall we not lament the long rejection of the ancient people of God ? Their seventy years in Babylon was nothing to this ; yea, their four hundred and thirty years' bondage in Egypt was nothing to this. Alas ! how long—how long shall God's anger last against that people ? How long shall they be under the guilt of the blood of Christ, which they imprecated upon themselves and their posterity, saying, "His blood be upon us and our children " ? Oh, pray—pray for that ancient people of God ! Oh, pray that the blood of Shiloh may cleanse them from blood-guiltiness ! When they were in favour with God, the believers among them had mind of us poor Gentiles, when we were the little sister that had no breasts ; and now, when we are sucking at the breasts of gospel ordinances and sacramental solemnities, oh ! shall we not mind them when "their breasts are cut off," and we, that were of "the wild olive tree," are grafted in to partake of the root and fatness of the good olive tree ? Oh, let us not boast against the branches !—" for if thou boastest, thou bearest not the root, but the root thee." Let us not boast, but let us beg that they may

be grafted in ; "for if the casting away of them be the reconciling of the world, what shall the receiving of them be but life from the dead ? " The day of the return and conversion of the Jews will be a day of greater gathering to Shiloh, even among the Gentiles, than we have yet seen ; and it would fare better with us if we were more employed in praying for them.

Vers. 28-32. *Providence always at work.*— God's work of providence is "His most holy, wise, and powerful preserving and governing of all His creatures and all their actions." It has no Sabbath, no night suspends it, and from its labours God never rests. If, for the sake of illustration, I may compare small things with great, it is like the motion of the heart. Beating our march to the grave since the day we began to live, the heart has never ceased to beat. Our limbs grow weary ; not it. We sleep ; it never sleeps. Needing no period of repose to recruit its strength, by night and day it throbs in every pulse, and constantly supplying nourishment to the meanest as well as to the noblest organs of our frame, with measured, steady, untired stroke, it drives the blood along the bounding arteries without any exercise of will on our part, and even when the consciousness of our own existence is lost in dreamless slumber.

Ver. 33. *Mysteries not to be pried into.*— "Arriving in the city," says the Rabbi Josuah, "I met a little boy carrying a covered dish. 'What hast thou in that dish, child ? ' demanded I. 'My mother would not have covered it, master, had she wished its contents to be known,' replied the little wit, and went on."—*From the Talmud.*

CHAPTER XII.

CRITICAL NOTES.

Ver. 1.—St. Paul sums up the argument of the foregoing part of the epistle with plain rules for Christian living, and advisedly calls religion a reasonable service. Pythagoras required intelligent worship; and much more does the great Spirit demand worship in spirit. The soul stands as the priest; the body is the offering to be consecrated by the High Priest.

Ver. 2. **And be not conformed.**—Be not configured to this world, but rather as Christ was transfigured on the mount. Be not like the men of this world whose all is in the present. Live for eternity.

Ver. 3.—Those who possess special gifts must be humble and seek a sober mind.

Ver. 5.—We are knit together in Christ, as the head in the organic life.

Ver. 6.—Prophesying is both foretelling and forthtelling. Hence preaching and expounding make the prophet. We must expound according to the rule of faith. Pleasant doctrines must not have undue prominence. We must take the word of God as a whole, and thus avoid heresies.

Ver. 9. **Cleave to that which is good.**—κόλλα, glue. Keeping yourselves glued to the good. Hold firmly to the true.

Ver. 10.—Strive to anticipate each other. Set the example of honour. When a man knows that his neighbour is accustomed to salute him, let him be the first to give the salutation. φιλόστοργοι, tenderly loving, perhaps towards one's kindred, in New Testament towards Christian brethren. Word only used in this verse.

Ver. 11.—In your haste be not idle, in your business be not lazy. As to your zeal, being not indolent; fervent in spirit, taking advantage of opportunity. The Syriac, Arabic, and Ethiopic versions, and all the Greek scholiasts, read "serving the Lord." The other reading, "serving the time," mentioned by Ambrose, St. Jerome, and Ruffinus, seems to have had its rise from the abbreviation of the word in the manuscripts. Though it may have a good sense "by accommodating yourselves to present things, if tolerance be not unlawful."

Ver. 12. **Patient in tribulation.**—θλίψις, a pressing together, pressure, from θλίβω, to press. So in Mark iii. 9, "lest they should throng Him."

Ver. 13.—Partaking of your good things with the needy. You give money; they give faith in God. Hospitality essential in those times to the spread of Christianity.

Ver. 16.—Mutually mind the same thing. Let there be unity of sentiment. Do not affect the high things of this world. Let not your wisdom be the vain fancy of self-conceit.

Ver. 17.—Provide things honest, handsome, beautiful, useful, profitable, in the sight of men. Remove every reasonable ground of suspicion. Wear the white flower of a blameless life.

Ver. 18. **Live peaceably with all men.**—If commotions arise, let there be no real fault on your side. Offences will come, but see that no offence spring from unwise ordering of life.

Ver. 19. **Give place unto wrath.**—Do not interfere with the movements of God's righteous indignation. Let not your own wrath break forth. Give place to the wrath of your enemy. These interpretations are given. Instead of trying to settle the exact meaning, we may wisely seek to combine all the interpretations and work them out.

Ver. 20.—Here are figurative expressions for the general duties of benevolence.

Ver. 21.—He is conquered by evil who wishes another to sin. He has sinned himself who strives to make another sin. Love is the conqueror. We cannot always tell where it prevails. If it do not seem to succeed in this world, it shall triumph in the world to come. How the early Church triumphed! Justin Martyr says: "That we who have given our names to Jesus do not draw back our profession while we are beheaded, crucified, exposed to wild beasts, and tortured by hooks, fire, and all kinds of torture, is sufficiently manifest; and the more that such tortures are exercised upon us, so much the more do others become believers and worshippers of the true religion through the name of Jesus."

MAIN HOMILETICS OF THE PARAGRAPH.—Verse 1.

The importance of our bodies.—If a man have a true feeling of spiritual relationship, he will not be able to refrain himself. The thought of the divine connection will rise above all the seemings of the present. He will say in effect: God is my father; I must love and serve as a son. God is my creator, and I must give that which is due. God made me in every part, redeemed me in body as well as soul, crowned with continuing mercies, and I must yield every part to His service. I offer myself not in mere sentiment. I give not some vague notion called "self," but my body—the living, acting frame, the organ and instrument of the soul's working—in evidence of the fact that my design to offer is sincere.

I. **Our bodies are important.**—The shape and fashion of man's physical frame testify to its divine origin, but we here refer to its importance as enforcing the exhortation that it be presented on God's altar as a living sacrifice. The body is important as an offering, for it is: 1. *The avenue of sin.* There may be sin committed in the secret chambers of the soul, while the body seems to move in the sphere of outward moral respectability. The fallen angels had no bodies, and yet sinned. A soul free from a physical nature might sin; but a soul fettered with physical entanglements has great difficulty in preserving moral purity. Soul and body are in constant warfare. Our physical sensations are the avenues along which the tempter travels. Surely it were easier to keep from sin if there were no body; the eye would not engender lust; the ear would not enthral with siren sounds; appetite would not dethrone man's reason. And yet the soul might not be so noble. Let us ask, not to be set free from the body of this flesh, but to have grace given, so that we may present the body a living sacrifice. Let the soul do priestly work. 2. *The soul's instrument.* St. Paul indirectly draws a distinction between "you" and "your bodies." They are not the "you," though mysteriously joined. The body is the instrument by which the man works and expresses himself. You are to "present your bodies." You must stand as kings having power over your bodies. The soul finds its outlet and touches the external world by means of the body. There may be such a thing as soul touching soul—the unseen "you" coming into contact with another unseen "you"— but for the most part we influence and are influenced by the help of material organisations. Thought works by means of brain currents and by the method of language. The spiritual life force works through and in a measure by the material frame. Where there is high spiritual surrender in the soul, it will show itself in a beautified physical nature. The body is ennobled by being presented a living sacrifice. 3. *The sure signs.* Offered bodies are signs of the completeness of the offering. The soul throws open the temple of the body for the use of heaven's King, and thus gives a token that the man is willing to serve God and to promote His glory. It is the token of a full surrender. It is an ample dedication. God lays siege to us with the sweet train of His abounding mercies. We yield to the besieging force, and give our bodies as signs of the fact that we have no reserve, that all which we call ours is God's now and for evermore. 4. *The proof of a right view*, which is that the gospel has to do with man's material and moral nature. The spiritual life is a divine force shaping our thoughts and pulsating through our bodies. Soul and body must be consecrated upon God's altar; and it must be an ever-recurring dedication. We are priests standing daily and offering up our own bodies. The richest thoughts must be embalmed in material forms. The spiritual life expresses itself to others in outward actions. Goodness dwelling in the soul will irradiate the body.

II. **God's claim is important.**—God demands, but it is put in the form of entreaty. He woos the offering as lover might beg some token of love's return. God made the body, not only to toil on the farm, to grind in the mill, to be tossed on the ocean, to groan on the battle-field, to feel the rush of commercial strife, or to be pampered in the lap of luxury, but to be presented on His altar as a living sacrifice. Human bodies are of small account in the world's metropolis. London is the slaughter-house of humanity. The centre of Christendom is untrue to Christianity's great lesson that the physical nature has a noble aspect, being made by God and being claimed as an offering. Thus low views are not to be taken of man's physical nature. By our bodies we are connected with the earth, and yet even by our bodies we are connected with heaven. The body governed by the soul may minister in highest service.

III. **God's mercies are important.**—Let us not ignore the mercies of God, for they are important factors in the life of man. They are still evident to observant natures. Nature still smiles through storms and tempests. Our bodies are touched by God's mercies—charmed by sweet music, refreshed by welcome odours, nourished by many products. God's mercy shown in redemption. The Saviour's redemptive work had for its object the welfare of the body as well as of the soul. He spent more time in healing than in teaching. His miracles are more than His sermons. Rich as was the stream of mingled water and blood that flowed from the Saviour's side, richer still was the stream of mercies that flowed from heaven. Jesus gave His body an atoning sacrifice; let us give our bodies a living sacrifice. Let our bodies be responsive. As they answer to outward, so let them answer to inward influences. Let them respond to the soul's voice, to God's voice. If the soul be strong, then the body will yield. The body, through the soul, will answer to the high voice of the divine mercies. If God have poured Himself out in mercies, shall we not answer in living sacrifices?

SUGGESTIVE COMMENTS ON VERSE 1.

A servant of Christ truly reigns.— Very touching is the incident related in the Old Testament story when Joseph's brethren stood before him and he could no longer refrain himself. His brethren were before him, and they silently but effectually called forth Joseph's deeper feelings, and he could no longer feign himself the foreign despot. If a man have genuine faith, true love to God, the inward feeling of spiritual relationship, he will not be able to refrain himself. His soul will rise upward to the supreme good; he will present himself a living sacrifice. Here is noble work for the soul. Sin's power is lessened if I stand as a priest at God's altar and am there continually offering up the body a living sacrifice acceptable to God. Egerius the Roman asked of the conquered people, "Are you the ambassadors sent by the people of Collatia that you may yield up yourselves and the Collatine people?" And it was answered, "We are." And it was again asked, "Are the Collatine people in their own power?" And answered, "They are." It was further inquired, "Do you deliver up yourselves, the people of Collatia, your city, your fields your water, your

hounds, your temples, your utensils, all things that are yours, both divine and human, into mine and the people of Rome's power?" They answer, "We deliver up all." And he replies, "So I receive you." Thus when a man presents his body a living sacrifice, it is a sign, unspoken but certain, that he delivers up all unto the service of God. He treats us as free agents, for we are morally free, and asks for our gifts and our services. Seneca, the heathen philosopher, declared that to serve God is to reign; and surely we can feel this as he could not. We are told that a prince abandoned the pleasures and splendours of his own court, then retired and assumed the name of Christodulus—a servant of Christ—accounting the glory of that name did outshine, not only that of other illustrious titles, but of the imperial diadem itself. A servant of Christ is he who serves with body as well as soul. A servant of Christ is he who truly reigns. Better than all titles is the title "servant of Christ." Æschines the philosopher, out of his admiration to Socrates, when divers presented him with other gifts, made a tender to him of himself. Can man

391

have such noble thoughts of his fellow-man, and can we raise no lofty thoughts to God? Shall we not give ourselves to God? Let body as well as soul be consecrated to this divine service.

In every sacrifice a death.—It has been said there is in every sacrifice a death, and in this sacrifice a death unto sin, out of which there arises a new life of righteousness unto God. Thus the living sacrifice is that in which, though the natural life is not lost, a new life of holiness is gained.

The moral instruction the pendant of the doctrinal.—This moral instruction is therefore the pendant of the doctrinal instruction. It is its necessary complement, the two taken together from the apostle's *complete catechism.* It is because the rational relation between the different sections of this part has not been understood that it has been possible for the connection of this whole second part with the first to be so completely mistaken. The practical part which we are beginning corresponds to the second kind of sacrifice, which was the symbol of consecration after pardon had been received (the holocaust in which the victim was entirely burned), and of the communion re-established between Jehovah and the believer (the peace offering followed by a feast in the court of the temple). The sacrifice of expiation offered by God in the passion of His Son should now find its response in the believer in the sacrifice of complete consecration and intimate communion. Is it not this promise which explains the choice of the word λογικήν, "reasonable," of which undoubtedly the true meaning is this—the service which rationally corresponds to the moral premisses contained in the faith which you profess? (Godet.) The word rendered "reasonable" is variously explained. The simplest interpretation is that which takes the word in its natural sense—namely, pertaining to the mind; it is mental or spiritual service in opposition to ceremonial and external observances.—*Hodge.*

MAIN HOMILETICS OF THE PARAGRAPH.—*Verse 2.*

Nonconformity to the world.—We must be careful not to fall into the error of disparaging this world. The habit of holding many secular things in abhorrence is nonsense, bigotry. We need to look on all questions apart from prejudice, and be perfectly ready to take them on their merits. We are to repudiate the method of the devil in life, but not necessarily repudiate the world. Jesus is witness to the fact that this is wrong; for His treatment and His reception of this world, His recognition of the great and beautiful world of nature, wherein He spake of ravens, lilies, cornfields—light touches of nature, everywhere recognising beauty, shaped and glorified at the hands of God—all this is enough to answer those who are wilfully blind to what the Lord of earth and heaven was glad to see : a world on which the Creator looked and saw that it was good.

I. "This world": what is meant by it?—1. Not the beautiful world of nature, nor the social world merely, nor the world of intellect, nor the world of commerce. 2. "It is fallen human nature, acting itself out in the human family, fashioning the framework of human society in accordance with its own tendencies." It is the reign of the "carnal mind." 3. It is also everything that is in antagonism with God. A difficulty lies in the fact of the changeability of "this world." What is "world" to me is not "world" to another. A business man's temptations differ from a professional man's, and so on. Further, according to a man's constitution, so is this "world" good or bad, safe or dangerous, to him. Thus text acts as a caution.

II. Christ's estimate of the world.—1. No attempt made by Him at depreciation. He recognised political life and social claims. Notice His treatment of commerce. He castigated, not commerce as commerce, but fraudulent commerce. He sought to show that we are not to be absorbed in this world's engagements to the forgetfulness of nobler thoughts. 2. It differed from Solomon's estimate. He was a jaded worldling when he said all was "vanity and vexation." Christ rather taught men to *use* the world, but not to abuse it. Glory in it, mingle in it, work in it, rejoice and prosper in it, but do not allow it to have such a hold upon you as to master you and fashion your soul according to its will.

III. **The influence of our environment.**—" A man is known by the company he keeps." Given the character of a man's surroundings, and we can gauge the force of his temptations and difficulties. " Physically, man is moulded by climate, by food, by occupation. Mentally, he is moulded by institutions, by government, by inherited beliefs and tendencies." So, religiously, a man's environment has the same and even more forcible effect upon him. Recognising this, the key of the text is : whatever tends to wean our soul from God ; whatever tends to vitiate our moral environment, to bring us down or keep us low, preventing our uprising, that is an evil world to us, striving to fashion us in anything but Godlike shape of our Lord and Master, whose mind we must have if we would be of God.

IV. **A Christian's attitude towards the world.**—1. He must breathe the spirit of nonconformity : not here speaking of denominational differences, but of the spirit of nonconformity to anything that curtails our reverence or spoils our service Godward, or robs us of Christ's likeness. 2. There is an *inward* nonconformity : the soul lives in the world without being absorbed in its evil. 3. There is an *outward* nonconformity : it will not appear to agree with the world's evil, but will resolutely stand against it. 4. This attitude is a difficult one. Hard not to be fashioned by the world. But this nonconformity can be attained by the help of God. Any who feel a sense of weakness, let them cast their whole care on the divine Helper. He who conquered death will not let death conquer you.—*Albert Lee.*

True nonconformity.—" The word translated ' world ' here is not *cosmos*, which in the New Testament sometimes means the material world, sometimes the existing generation of men, and sometimes the unrenewed portion of humanity, but *aion*, which is used to represent the course and current of this world's affairs, especially in a bad sense (Rom. xii. 2 ; Gal. i. 4 ; Eph. ii. 2) ; all that floating mass of thoughts, opinions, maxims, speculations, hopes, impulses, aims at any time current in the world, and which it is impossible to seize and accurately define, but which constitute a most real and effective power, being the moral or immoral atmosphere which at every moment of our lives we inhale, again inevitably to exhale ; all this is included in the *aion*, which is, as Bengel expressed it, the subtle informing spirit of the *cosmos* or world of men who are living alienated and apart from God " (Bayley). Now in the text we are exhorted not " to be conformed " to this state of things, not to be shaped and figured by the prevalent immorality of a passing generation. The exhortation includes at least three things :—

I. **Be practical theists.**—The world, the existing generation of mankind, is mainly "without God." God is not in all its thoughts. If He appear in the horizon, it is only as a fleeting vision, a passing phantom. He is not the great object filling up the horizon and causing all other objects to dwindle into shadows. *Theoretical theism* is somewhat prevalent. It talks and prays and sings and preaches throughout Christendom. But practical theism is rare and unworldly. *Mere* theoretical theism is a hypocrisy, a crime, and a curse.

393

Practical theism alone is honest, virtuous, and beneficent. Practical theism is nonconformity to the world.

II. **Be practically spiritual.**—The world, the existing generation, is essentially *materialistic*; the body rules the spirit. " What shall we eat? what shall we drink? wherewithal shall we be clothed?" This is the all-pervading, all-animating aspiration. Men everywhere judge after the flesh, walk after the flesh, live after the flesh; they are of the earth earthy. Nonconformity to the world is the opposite to this. Spirit is the dominating power. Intellect governs the body; conscience governs the intellect; moral rectitude governs the conscience. The things of the spirit are everything to them: they walk after the spirit; they live to the spirit. The soul is regal.

III. **Be practically unselfish.**—The great body of existing generations is selfish. Each man lives to himself and for himself. Self is the centre and circumference of his activities. The commerce, the governments, and even the Churches of the world, are mainly conducted on selfish principles. Each man is in quest of his own interest, his own aggrandisement, his own happiness. Nonconformity to the world means the opposite of this. It means that supreme sympathy with God, that brotherly love for the race, that absorbs the ego, that buries self, that is in truth the spirit of Christ, the spirit of self-sacrificing benevolence. " Let no man," says Paul, " seek his own, but every man another's wealth."

Conclusion : **What is true nonconformity?**—Not a mere dissent from this Church or that Church, this creed or that creed, but a dissent from that spirit of moral wrong which pervades and animates the generation. This was the nonconformity which Christ exhibited and He implored on behalf of His disciples. " They are not of the world, even as I am not of the world." Let us cultivate this nonconformity, knowing that the friendship of the world is enmity with God, and that if any man love the world the love of the Father is not in him.—*W. Thomas.*

Conformity sinful compliance.—As for the conformity to the world that is here forbidden, I believe nobody thinks there is any more intended by this prohibition than only a sinful compliance with the customs of the world, a framing of our lives and manners after the impious practices and examples that we see frequently represented before us, an indulging ourselves in such bad courses as the men of the world do too often give themselves liberty in.

Taking, now, this to be the true notion of being conformed to the world, then the being transformed by the renewing of our minds, which is put in opposition to it, must denote our being actuated with more heavenly and divine principles, and framing our conversation in such a way as is suitable to the profession of Christianity which we have taken upon ourselves. It must denote such a holy disposition and frame of soul as doth effectually produce a conformity of all the outward actions to the law of the gospel, to which the law of sin and the course of the world are opposite.

There are these two inconveniences in multiplying the signs and marks of regeneration : one is, that oftentimes such marks are given of it as that a man may be a very good Christian, and, without doubt, a regenerate person, and not find them in himself. Another inconveniency is this : that such marks are likewise given that even a bad man may experience them in himself, though some good men cannot.

The truest mark is that of our Saviour: *the tree is known by its fruits.* If a man be baptised, and, heartily believing the Christian religion, doth sincerely endeavour to live up to it; if his faith in Jesus Christ be so strong that, by virtue thereof, he overcomes the world and the evil customs thereof ; if, knowing the laws of our Saviour, he so endeavours to conform himself to them that he doth not live in any known wilful transgression of them, but in the general course of his life walks honestly and piously, and endeavours, in holy conversation, to keep a good conscience both towards God and man,—such a man, however he came into this state, and with whatever infirmities it may be attended—of which infirmities yet he is deeply sensible, and fails not both to pray and strive against them—yet he is a good man, and gives a true evidence of his regeneration, though he have not all the marks and qualifications that he may meet with in books. And such a man, if he persevere in the course he is in, will without doubt at last be justified before God and find an admission into the everlasting kingdom of our Lord Jesus Christ.—*Archbishop Sharpe.*

MAIN HOMILETICS OF THE PARAGRAPH.—*Verse 3.*

Self-glorified and God-dishonoured.—*Self-help* is a very good book, well written, containing useful information, and inculcating wise lessons; but it is to be read with caution. The very title may mislead. Self-help must not be divorced from divine help. Self-dependence and self-confidence are needful if the battle of modern existence is to be successfully fought, if prizes are to be won and trophies gathered in the closely contested arena of modern days. And yet self-dependence must not override God-dependence; self-confidence must be the wholesome product of confidence in the Creator; self-confidence must not degenerate into presumption. A man must think soberly and justly of himself, and not place an undue estimate on his faculties and his achievements.

I. **An undue self-estimate is a source of atheism.**—Samosatenus is reported to have put down the hymns which were sung for the glory of God, and caused songs to be sung in the temple to his own honour. Professedly a theist, practically an atheist. We sing "Let the Creator's praise arise" with our mouths, but in our hearts we sing, Let our own praises be celebrated! While we think of the atheists who do not worship our God, let us also think of the practical atheism of which we are too often guilty. The atheist exalts the creature above the Creator, and continues the process until the Creator is supposed to be non-existent. The creature exalted is really self. Every atheist is indeed one who is given to an exaggerated self-importance. His thoughts run out pleasantly upon the track of his own perfections. The thought of his own greatness minifies the thought of any other greatness; he brings himself to such a pass that he cannot brook the idea of a superior. Self-importance leads to self-deception and to general deception, and he vainly fancies that God will cease to exist if he thinks of Him as non-existent, if he arrays shallow syllogisms to prove that there is no God.

II. **An undue self-estimate is a source of scepticism.**—The sceptic should be one who looks about; but it is to be feared that the sceptic, as we now employ the word, is one whose external looking about is dimmed by the gaze being turned inward. The vision is introspective instead of latospective, if we may coin a word, though we should be as careful of coining words as of coining money. The sceptic is too often a vain-glorious person; *latusut in Circo spatiere,* that you may stalk proudly along. He professes to examine, but prejudice and self-importance conduct and colour the examination. He is wiser in his own conceit than seven men that can render a reason. Ajax in Sophocles says: "Others think to overcome with the assistance of the gods, but I hope to gain honour without them." How many hope to gain honour by boasting of their scepticism, agnosticism, and their difficulty of believing and receiving time-worn creeds! They are wiser than the ancients, and their greater wisdom

395

is shown in their no-knowledge and no certain beliefs.   The ancients were constructive ; the moderns are destructive.   Surely the work of construction is nobler than that of destruction.   The moderns destroy, and leave only unsightly ruins to tell of their greatness and their wisdom.

III. **An undue self-estimate is a source of bigotry.**—The narrow-minded man is in all ages the bigot.   And the man must be narrow whose views are bounded by that little circle of which self is both the centre and the circumference.   The man who considers only self has no patience with the different views of other people.   His doxy is orthodoxy, and all other and different doxy is heterodoxy.   We rail against papal infallibility, but there is a pope in every man's nature.   The errors of Roman Catholicism are the outcome of the errors of humanity.   The inquisition is not destroyed.   Bigotry stalks abroad with disdainful mien and fattens on self-esteem.   The Christian bigot denounces the unchristian sceptic, and the latter in turn denounces the former.   But bigotry treads the hall of science as well as kneels in the temple of religion.   Whenever a man is found who thinks of himself more highly than he ought to think, there is the bigot either in embryo or in full development.

IV. **An undue self-estimate is a source of God-dishonouring and of Christ-degrading.**—All sin is a dishonour done to God, and an undue estimate of self is sin and is the prolific source of other sins.   Nebuchadnezzar and his Babylon are typical.   We all have our Babylons.   They are just as baneful, though they are only ideal.   The material Babylon was harmful because of the ideal Babylon.   It was the mind-building which led to the boasting king's downfall.   He was his own architect and mason, and built a house which proclaimed his folly and procured his disaster.   Self dishonours God and degrades Christ, at least strives to dishonour and degrade.   Whence the offence of the cross ?   Self is the stumbling-stone and the true rock of offence.   Self crucifies Christ afresh.   Self must be dethroned before Christ can be enthroned.   The dethronement of self is its true enthronement and enrichment.

V. **An undue self-estimate is a source of modern display.**—We too often desire to excel in order that we may be glorified.   Display is our word.   Show, pomp, and glitter are our ambitions.   Even art, science, and literature are prostituted to the desire of making a sensation.   Envy takes possession, if other selves are exalted above our own selves.   Impatience is shown if our purposes are crossed and our projects defeated.   Let self have its proper place and sphere, but let it not blot all the glory and nobility out of existence.   Think soberly and wisely, and then life will flow evenly and sweetly along like some clear stream through a charming landscape.

MAIN HOMILETICS OF THE PARAGRAPH.—Verses 4—10.

Love cements unity.—The organisation of the human body should be an example to the believer to make him perceive the necessity of limiting himself to the function assigned him.   Not only, indeed, is there a plurality of members in one body, but these members also possess special functions.   So in the Church there is not only a multiplicity of members, but also a diversity of functions, every believer having a particular gift whereby he ought to become the auxiliary of all the rest, their member.   Hence it follows that every one should remain in his function : on the one hand, that he may be able to render to the rest the help which he owes them ; on the other, that he may not disturb those in the exercise of their gifts (Godet).

I. **Love makes unity.**—Life unites together the several members of the human body.   There may be contact, but not true unity, where there is no life.   There must be love sincere in the Church if there is to be unity. Some Churches seem to have outward coherence and no inward unity. Love does not unite the whole body. We cannot be one body in Christ without love. Faith and love make us members of the mystical body.

II. **Discriminating love recognises diversity in unity.**—The human body is one; its members are many. Nature is one; its parts are various. The Bible is one; its records stretch over the centuries: there are manifest proofs of different writers. The ocean is one; its separate waves constitute its unity. The Church is divided, and yet united: diversities of gifts and of modes of operation. Love may overlook seeming discrepancies and recognise the Church as a glorious unity.

III. **Sincere love cements unity.**—1. *It removes envy.* The minister does not envy the prophet; the intellectual preacher does not spurn the emotional; while the emotional preacher does not envy the high gifts of the intellectual. He that is ruled does not treat with contempt the authority of the ruler. 2. *It makes each man seek to fit into his place.* Every man a place from God, and every man seeking to fill his place. 3. *It imparts diligence and cheerfulness.* Our teachers should be both diligent and cheerful. A cheerful voice is a blessed tonic. Amid the sad voices of a weary humanity we need the joyful voices of messengers from the land of blessedness. Songs of hope should be sung in a despairing world. Diligence and cheerfulness are specially needed in these days, when scepticism is so diligent, when the press is so diligent, when a pessimistic tone is pervading society. If one man cannot be both diligent and cheerful, let two men unite their forces. "He that ruleth, with diligence; he that showeth mercy, with cheerfulness." Pompous and hard-hearted beadles are not sent by St. Paul on errands of mercy. They are to be cheerful messengers, taking good cheer to sad hearts and homes. Giving is to be done with simplicity. Love, and not the stately banquet, not the eloquent speech, not the prospect of an advertisement, must elicit and give the subscription. The prophet and the humblest teacher, the ruler and the ruled, the giver of alms and the receiver, meet on the one blessed plane of brotherhood.

IV. **Love beautifies unity.**—1. *Love to the Church prompts to the gracious spirit of detesting that which is evil and cleaving to that which is good.* What a beautiful aspect the Church would present if each member were glued to that which is good! Modern glue is poor stuff; it fastens to the good, but the fastening is weak. The prospect of gain or fame makes the glue wither and lose its hold. Is there any modern glue to stand the heat of persecution? Ah! there may be faithful ones in modern as in ancient times. 2. *Love to the Church generates kind affections.* "Be kindly affectioned one to another." Sweetly smooth words for rough times. There may be a need for a modern enforcement. Be kindly affectioned. How about the modern cynic? How about the morose ecclesiastic? How about the dignified official? How about the purse-proud man who condescends to say, 'Ow do? These all need the lesson taught by St. Paul of being kindly affectioned one to another. 3. *Love to the Church provokes holy emulation.* "In honour preferring one another." The emulation of love is to show the brightest example of kindness; the ambition of loving Christians is to excel each other in all acts of mutual kindness and respect. What a beautiful society! Will earth ever witness such a social paradise? Is this ecclesiastical ideal the utopia of a vain dreamer? Will earth ever thus taste the bliss of heaven? Let us not despair. Diligence and cheerfulness will accomplish much. Let each seek to do his or her duty in the allotted sphere; let us live in the love of Christ; let us love, and the grace will grow by gracious and consistent exercise.

SUGGESTIVE COMMENTS ON VERSES 4—10.

Explanation of terms.—In the Epistle to Titus there occurs the expression προϊστάσθαι καλῶν ἔργων, " to be occupied with good works"; whence the term προστάσος, patroness, protectress, benefactress, used in our epistle to express what Phœbe had been to many believers, and to Paul himself. Think of the numerous works of private charity which believers then had to found and maintain! Pagan society had neither hospitals nor orphanages, free schools nor refuges, like those of our day. The Church, impelled by the instinct of Christian charity, had to introduce all these institutions into the world; hence, no doubt, in every community spontaneous gatherings of devout men and women who, like our present Christian committees, took up one or other of these needful objects, and had of course at their head directors charged with the responsibility of the work. Such are the persons certainly whom the apostle had in view in our passage. Thus is explained the position of this term between the preceding " he that giveth " and the following " he that showeth mercy." The same explanation applies to the following regimen, ἐν σπουδῇ, " with zeal." This recommendation would hardly be suitable for one presiding over an assembly. How many presidents, on the contrary, would require to have the call addressed to them, "Only no zeal"! But the recommendation is perfectly suitable to one who is directing a Christian work, and who ought to engage in it with a sort of exclusiveness, to personify it after a manner in himself. The last term ὁ ἐλεῶν, " he that showeth mercy," denotes the believer who feels called to devote himself to the visiting of the sick and afflicted. There is a gift of sympathy which particularly fits for this sort of work, and which is, as it were, the key to open the heart of the sufferer. The regimen ἐν ἱλαρότητι, literally, " with hilarity," denotes the joyful eagerness, the amiable grace, the affability going the length of

398

gaiety, which make the visitor, whether man or woman, a sunbeam penetrating into the sick-chamber and to the heart of the afflicted.—*Godet.*

Abhorrence of evil.—It is the peculiarity of the Christian religion that while its aim is to exclude all sin from the heart, it does not dismember the soul by severing from it any faculty that is natural to it. Religion is a revolution, but its effect is only to suppress and exclude evil and establish the sovereignty of God to the heart of man. Hatred is a faculty given to us by the Creator for good. It is difficult at first, perhaps, to see its place in religion, because we see in it so plainly the evidence of man's fall. Hatred in men ordinarily is hateful, because it is vile passion, impulse, or impatience of contradiction, and is directed mainly against *me*, and not evil *principles*, evil *habits*, and evil *things*. It is a faculty liable to abuse, and the Christian man requires great grace to use it well. It has its place, however, in the Christian system, and rightly used is a potent instrument in the suppression of evil. Let us consider the direction of the text.

I. **What is evil?**—Now and then " a case of conscience" may occur in which the casuist's skill is indispensable to obtain relief from perplexity, but for the most part the knowledge of good and evil is found in every human breast. There is at work in society what may be termed an educational agency, that is teaching men in various ways what is evil and what is good. The preaching of the word and teaching of the Bible and prayer as it deprecates evil; the opposition to and exposure of evil by good men; an enlightened public opinion; the administration of the law in connection with crime; the godly training of children and conscience,—these and other influences are pervading human society, so that none can plead ignorance of the vital question before us. But for the sake of clearness let us now briefly define the term "evil." Evil is twofold,—existing as a hidden power in the soul, like the poison in the berry, the deadly forked lightning hid in the thundercloud, the dagger in its sheath ; and as it assumes a concrete form in the world of men and things—evil books, institutions, principles, habits, language, etc. In other words, evil appears in *character* and *conduct*, answering to the theological terms of *guilt* and *pollution*. The sinner has a corrupt heart and guilty life. Or again, evil may be regarded as vice and crime, and its essential characteristic is lawlessness in principle and passion. " The energetic use of faculties created for God alone." Vice is personal ; crime has reference to others, to society in its organised state.

" Of every malice that wins hate in heaven
  Injury is the end ; and all such end,
  Either by force or fraud, afflicteth others."

All men are vicious, few in proportion criminal ; but vice is the root of crime, and all in whose hearts evil is to be found may become "guilty of deadly sin." " Crimes sometimes shock us too much ; vices almost always too little." " God hath concluded all under sin,"— " there is none righteous, no, not one." What an appalling fact !—evil has established itself in every soul; all are under its curse, and need deliverance.

II. **What is to "abhor" evil?**— Dislike, repugnance, abhorrence, hatred. To abhor evil is not only to cast it out of our own bosom, but also to strive against it until it is chased out of the world. To abhor is the opposite of to love. Love seeks, first of all, to possess the object loved, and then to perpetuate it ; abhorrence, on the contrary, first separates, and then seeks to destroy. This, then, is the position we take up when we are " changed from nature to grace."

" The thing my God doth hate, that I no
  more may do,
Thy creature, Lord, again create, and all
  my soul renew;
My soul shall then, like Thine, abhor the
  thing unclean,
And, sanctified by love divine, for ever
  cease from sin."

III. **The reasons why we should hate evil.**—1. This is the very "end" for which Christ died, that He might " destroy in us the works of the devil." 2. It is implied in sanctification, separation to God, and therefore separation from evil in *thought, affection, purpose,* and *practice.* 3. Your personal safety lies along that line. " Without holiness no man shall see the Lord." 4. God employs the hatred of good men to sin as an instrument for its suppression in others. You are called upon to speak against it, to frown upon it, to expose and condemn it, and thus help to drive it out of men's hearts. 5. *Again let us inquire if there is any alternative course that may be adopted.* (1) May we *compromise* evil ? But this would be to confuse and confound all moral distinctions, and would constitute you the basest of all evil characters— a hypocrite. (2) Can we *utilise* evil ? In one sense we may, if we make it a stimulus to prayer and activity, if it stir us up to watchfulness and caution, if we strive to "overcome evil with good," and so develop our spiritual strength as "not to be overcome with evil." But it belongs to God alone to overrule evil for good in the world. The lightning that blinds and terrifies, the ethereal light, can be utilised by science; but a man may as well try to harness an untamed tiger out of the jungle, to silence the thunder, and stop the roar of the ocean, as try to control his evil passions or govern his impulses unassisted by divine grace. The sinner is ever the victim of evil against his will and conscience. (3) Is it possible so to *control* evil in the soul as to be able to *silence* it at pleasure, to have it in abeyance ? No ; for *evil thoughts spring* up within us *involuntarily*, and often in spite of the strongest resolutions and the most sacred vows; *malign spirits suggest* evil in a mysterious manner to us ; *evil associations* hold many in thrall; and it is *impulse* that leads to the commission of the most violent and shocking crimes. (4) Shall we then *yield* to this power? Then you will be unhappy, impure, degraded, forsaken, and ruined for ever. A gentleman who had resided many years in Egypt once showed me a dagger of Syrian manufacture whose blade was of poisoned steel, and he assured me that it could deal a wound which never could be healed. It is evil that can destroy "both body and soul in hell," "where their worm dieth not and the fire is not quenched." "Abhor that which is evil."

IV. **Difficulties and dangers.**—This course is not easy when : 1. *Evil is associated with fine qualities.* Don Juan and *Hebrew Lyrics* bound together in the same volume. There are paintings in the first style of art which *would be best seen at midnight and without a light.* Burke once said, "Vice itself lost half its evil by losing all its grossness." But refined and cultivated evil is the same in principle with evil in its most revolting forms, and will end as wretchedly. 2. *Spurious charity.* Ignorance, weakness, may be used as a shield and pleaded as an excuse. 3. *Social connections.* 4. *Self-interest.* 5. *Temperament* is sometimes a difficulty. The violent and hasty put a plea of extenuation in the mouth of the guilty ; the easy and indolent pass over a fault ; the sympathetic and charitable are too ready to condone evil. 6. *Timidity* which shrinks from the consequences of active strife against sin. 7. Familiarity with evil. 8. *We are secretly in love with evil*, and nothing but the regenerating, sanctifying influence of the Spirit of God can remove the love of sin. There is salvation in Jesus. "His blood cleanseth from all sin." "Our Father which art in heaven . . . deliver us from evil."— *William Bell.*

MAIN HOMILETICS OF THE PARAGRAPH.—*Verse* 11.

Fervent in spirit.—As to zeal, being not indolent ; fervent in spirit ; serving the Lord, or taking advantage of opportunity. The Epistle to the Romans is a doctrinal book, and at the same time eminently practical. There is no book which contains passages more practical than those in these concluding chapters. So long as we read these practical teachings, so well adapted to all times, we are indifferent to the utterance of those who say that the Bible is a worn-out book. The Bible is no worn-out book for the true and the good. Its teachings adapted to all. Its soothing tones are welcome to the weary, worn, troubled, and distressed. Its stimulating utterances move to energy and to fervency of spirit.

I. **A work to be done.**—The work is that of serving the Lord in every department of life, and it is thus that in the best possible manner we take advantage of opportunity. It seems more reasonable to suppose that St. Paul should write "serving the Lord" than "serving the time." The former includes the latter. Serving the Lord is the best way of serving the time. The man who serves the Lord faithfully is the one to take a wise and holy advantage of every opportunity. There can be no sublimer work than that of serving the Creator. This is the work to call forth man's noblest energies. Other service calls forth only part of man's nature, but this claims every power and faculty. Other service is only for a short period, and short as is the period the service palls upon the taste; but this service is for life, and for a life beyond this life ; and it never loses its attractiveness to the spiritual man. It will ever show new beauties, expand fresh powers, and introduce varied pleasures to the soul. We are all called to this service. The command is to all, "Son, go work to-day in My vineyard."

II. **The manner in which the work is to be done.**—By "fervent in spirit" is meant the active and energetic exercise of all those powers which distinguish man as an intellectual and a moral creature. It does not imply confusion or agitation. There must not be half-heartedness in this service. Fervency of spirit is not compatible with double service. It implies unity of heart. " Unite my heart to fear Thy name, to serve the Lord." This fervency of spirit is illustrated by St. Paul himself when he says, " This one thing I do." When a man is fervent in spirit about the accomplishment of any work, he becomes a man of one idea. Have we this fervency ? Are our souls possessed of one idea ? Let us seek to serve the Lord, and thus to serve our time to the best of our ability.

III. **Fervency of spirit is enjoined upon us by :** 1. *Positive precept.*—" Hear, O Israel, The Lord our God is one Lord ; and thou shalt love the Lord thy God with all thy heart, and with all thy soul, and with all thy strength." Fervency of spirit is required from him who is to serve God by the combination of every power and faculty of the nature. " Work out your own salvation with fear and trembling ; for it is God that worketh in you both to will and to do of His good pleasure." This fear and trembling does not lead to depression and paralysis of the powers, but to energy, to fervency of spirit. The kingdom of God is a strife and a battle, and the fervent in spirit overcomes in the conflict. 2. *By implied directions.* We are enjoined to be zealous of good works—zealously affected in a good thing. The zealous man is fervent in spirit, ardent in the pursuit of an object. How ardent should the Christian be who is pressing forward to apprehend that for which he is apprehended in Christ Jesus ! The man who feels within himself the consuming force of a great principle is ardent, is fervent in spirit. The Christian should be a man on fire. The light glows within and radiates the circle he fills. Let us be more concerned about being ardent than about showing ourselves ardent. Let the ambition be, not to blaze, but to give light and heat—though the blazing man gains the world's applause, while the true light-giving man treads the obscure pathway to heaven's immortality. 3. *By illustrious examples.* We have the examples of Paul, of John, and of Peter. Consuming energy possessed their souls. In the whole range of the world's history there are not found men so wonderfully earnest and fervent. Their intense zeal was such that we declare they were superhumanly endowed. The very reading of their lives stirs to greater fervency of spirit. Jesus left us an example that in all things we should follow His steps. His earthly life was marked by fervency of spirit. It was so great that He could say, " The zeal of Thine house hath eaten Me up." Here was intense zeal in the pursuit of God's glory which became a consuming fire. The strong nature of Jesus was being eaten up by His zeal. My little nature is scarcely warmed by the feeble spark of my zeal. This was so strong in Jesus that He forgot to take necessary food. Sublime forgetfulness ! Divine memory of divine service producing consuming ardency ! 4. *By the difficulties of the course.* Vigorous plants only can survive severe winters ; vigorous Christians only can survive the rigours of time. Fervency of spirit will be a protection against the withering blasts of earth's winters. There must be fervency of spirit if we are to outlive those unfavourable influences by which we are often surrounded. 5. *By the blessings on the way and to follow.* Great are the blessings on the way, and yet there are more to follow. Bright are the Christian's privileges on the way, and yet there are brighter to follow. Gladsome are the songs which the Christian can sing on the way, and yet there are gladder to follow. Sweet are the viands which the Christian finds on the way, and yet there are sweeter to follow. Rich are the prospects on the way, and yet there are richer to follow. Dazzling crowns on the way, but a crown of unsullied and imperishable beauty to follow. The thoughts of present bestowals and of future glory should produce fervency of spirit.

The Christian spirit in business.—Christians must give themselves up to God, body and soul. To listen to doctrine is both good and necessary; but the listening is of no avail unless that doctrine and all the preaching about it lead to something practical. Men are but shabby specimens of the Christian life unless they prove experimentally how far they give themselves up to the perfect will of God. St. Paul sets forth many exhortations to godliness—*e.g.*, a Christian must have genuine humility, or rather a right estimate of himself. He must also love truly; he must also abhor evil, have it in moral detestation. Like ivy clinging to the wall, he must cleave to the good; and so on. But a Christian also must be not slothful in business. A better rendering of this is: not so much in business, but in diligence, in zeal, in earnestness, we are not to be slothful. The whole verse suggests that the Christian life has two sides—the sacred and the secular. Some men are so thoroughly one-sided that they miss the very mark at which they aim. They need to learn that the Christian life has two sides, and that Christ demands of every Christian diligence in both.

I. **Whence shall we get the true measure of a Christian's life in this world?**— From the Founder of Christianity. "The whole lesson of Christ's life, the whole burden of His teaching, was that the common concerns of this life—its buying and its selling, its gaining and its losing, its working and its rest—shall be in like manner, by the unchanging purpose of a pure Christian spirit, a true son of God, ennobled with the essential qualities that make a heaven of heaven." Public life got its guinea-stamp from Jesus. Cæsar must have his due. In all Christ's teaching it was a question of right things in right places—*e.g.*, commerce : bad in God's house; commendable in the world.

II. **The question of worldly duty.**—The most secular duties may be performed in a way that is pleasing to God. Men have often gone wrong on the question of worldly duty. Too much discrimination between godliness and worldliness. Consequently we have too narrow standards. The extreme notions that are held are hard to reconcile with Christ's words to Christians: "Ye are the salt of the earth," "the light of the world." Worldly men, on the other hand, have narrow notions of religion. It is a mistake to say that business, and all kinds of world-life and energy, have ever been pronounced as opposed to godliness.

III. **The great secret of true world-life depends on the motive that lies behind it.**—There may be business, backed by good motive, and it may be more acceptable in God's sight than a religion splendid to look upon, but having no special motive, or a very bad one. Business done on godly principles—though curtailed thereby—far better than great gains made by questionable practices. What we want is to have our lives set squarely upon a sound basis. Christ gave us the standard for daily living, and therein we find that purity of spirit is one of its leading features.

IV. **The sound basis of all worldly occupation is Christ.**—Base every method of your lives upon Him who became man, not only to go through that final agony that won the world's redemption, but also that He might show us how to live. A man who copies Him is the Lord's freeman. If we would live aright, we must seek to be in right relations or harmony with all truths, all facts, and all realities in *this* world, as well as the world to come—otherwise there is no possibility of hearing the "Well done."—*Albert Lee.*

Religion and business.—It is said of the divine Founder of our religion that He knew what was in man, and no better proof of the assertion could be furnished than is supplied by the religion itself. For it addresses itself to man as he is—that is, not as a spiritual being merely, not as a perfect being at all, nor yet as a being who has got into some wrong world, and who should be only too anxious to get out of it again ; but it rather addresses itself to him as one who has work in the world to do, and duties towards the world to discharge, and faculties, both of body, soul, and spirit, which in the world are to find their proper employment and exercise.

I. **In the command that we are to be " not slothful in business" we seem to have a recognition of the principle that a life of ardent labour is an almost universal necessity belonging to our present state.**—And it is so ; it is part of our fallen heritage. The wisdom of the appointment is seen in many ways. Continued employment keeps the soul from much evil. Active engagements give a healthy tone to the mind ; they strengthen the moral energy of the will ; they prevent a good deal of the listlessness and inconstancy and utter feebleness of character, so often found in those who, having no stated occupation, and having nothing to compel prompt action, will do and undo, resolve and alter their resolve, continually a prey to the first ascendant influence, the sport of every wind that blows.

II. **There is nothing in the business of life, as such, which is incompatible with the claim of godliness.**—There is to be no room for the charge against us of slothfulness in business, and yet it is to be rightly said of us that we are serving the Lord. Religion consists, not so much in the superaddition of certain acts of worship to the duties of common life, as in leavening the duties of common life with the spirit of religious worship. It is worship in the husbandman when he tills the ground with a thankful heart ; it is worship in the merchant when for all successes he gives God the glory ; the servant who in all good fidelity discharges the duties of his trust is offering unto God a continual sacrifice ; and to walk humbly and obediently in the calling to which He hath called us is to be " fervent in spirit, serving the Lord."

III. So far from the active duties of life presenting any barrier to our proficiency in personal religion, **they are the very field in which its highest graces are to be exercised and its noblest triumphs achieved.** The hindrance to our spiritual proficiency is not in our occupation, but in ourselves.— *D. Moore.*

SUGGESTIVE COMMENTS ON VERSE 11.

" *Secular and spiritual.*"—There is no such thing as "secular and sacred" in the whole realm of a good man's life. The "secular" is "spiritual" when a "spiritual" man touches it ; the "spiritual" is "secular" when the "secular" man seizes it. All good work well done is sacred. The counting-house ought to be as holy as the pulpit—and often is. Professor Stuart is right : "Religion is not a thing of the stars, it is a thing of the streets." —*Aked.*

Business needful.—In the light of all I know of Jesus, I am constrained to lay down this axiom, that business is a good thing. Jesus never gainsáys that. It is said of Him, that the light is too rich and clear upon the life of Christ to-day for any man to tell us that in order to be holy we must go away in dens and caves, and avoid the emporiums of the world, and not live the world's life. That is not true. "It was not the world, but its spirit, that Christ hated. He forswore not men, not markets, not commerce. No ; but the spirit which filled men as they engaged in all these. It was not the world's work, the world's ambitions, that He hated. I say it was the spirit in which these were realised that Christ utterly abjured. He did not condemn money-changing and merchandise ; but He burned with the still fires of unimpassioned anger when men did these things in His Father's house. The spirit was base, not the act ;

403

the purpose was ignoble, not the thing."

The most secular duties may be performed in a way that is pleasing to God. And by duties I mean those which radiate in all directions—Godward, manward, heavenward, earthward. Duty merges in heaven and earth. It is like the middle point of day; one knows not whether it belongs more to daybreak or to sunset. As a rule men have discriminated between heaven and earth, godliness and worldliness; but they have never caught the idea that God has joined the two, and that it is wrong to divorce them.

Dr. Parker says that he infers from Christ's treatment of the scribes and Pharisees that it is possible for men to deceive themselves on religious methods—to suppose that they are in the kingdom of God when they are thousands of miles away from it. Is it possible that any of us can have fallen under the power of that delusion? I fear it may be so! What is your Christianity? A letter, a written creed, a small placard that can be published, containing a few so-called fundamental points and lines? Is it an affair of words and phrases and sentences following one another in regulated and approved succession? If so, it is a little intellectual conceit. Christianity is life, love, nobleness,—it is *sympathy with God.—Albert Lee.*

MAIN HOMILETICS OF THE PARAGRAPH.—Verse 12.

Three needful mental conditions.—A book which is to be a guide for all must not be of such an elaborate character as to task the energies of its readers. A sailor's chart must not be a scientific, geographical, and historical work. The Bible is a book for mankind, and must be both brief and comprehensive. If a man truly desire to live right, he will have no practical difficulty. In this twelfth chapter are rules of life precise and yet sufficiently comprehensive. Here are three rules: in hope be joyful; in sufferings be steadfast; in prayer be unwearied. Here are three states in which the Christian may be found, and three conditions proper to those states. It is a wise conception to place tribulation between hope and prayer. Tribulation is calculated to depress, but hope energises and gives courage. Tribulation drives to prayer, and finds in the exercise sustaining power. The man supported in tribulation on two sides, by hope and prayer, will come off conqueror in every trial.

I. **The state of hope and the joyful mental condition.**—Hope is a great sustainer. The human mind is ever forecasting the to-morrows. Man never is but always to be blest. The darkest day, live till to-morrow, will have passed away. The schoolboy, the apprentice, the business man, all hope. A dreary world if hope were banished from hearts and homes. When old age creeps on apace, when the bright visions of time have vanished, when the backward glance is disappointing and the onward earthly look is darkening, it is sweet to look by hope to the bright sphere where all true hopes will be realised. "Christ in you the hope of glory." Faith in Christ the foundation of hope which will not disappoint. He is both the giver and sustainer of hope. It is a blessed thing to possess a good hope through grace. The man who possesses this hope can rejoice more than one who has found great spoil. He goes rejoicing all the day, and he can even sing songs in the night-time of his earthly pilgrimage. "Rejoicing in hope." He encourages great joy, for he has great expectations.

II. **The state of tribulation and the patient mental condition.**—Tribulation is a process through which the Christian must pass. We must through much tribulation enter into the kingdom of God. It is the narrow doorway and the rugged pathway to every high throne. No kingship here or hereafter without tribulation. No royalty of nature without suffering. No nobility of character without the tribulation. A straitened way, a compressed course, for the sons

moved by high ambitions. One in his parable describes the way to instruction
much in the same way as our Lord describes the way to heaven. "Do you not
see," says the old man, "a little door, and beyond the door a way which is not
much crowded, but very few are going along it, as seemingly difficult of ascent,
rough and stony?" "Yes," answers the stranger. "And does there not seem,"
continues the old man, "to be a high hill, and a road up it very narrow, with
precipices on each side? That is the way leading to true instruction." "Strait is
the gate and narrow is the way which leadeth to life, and few there be that find
it." The way to all heavens is the way of tribulation. It separates the chaff
from the wheat in character. It prepares for divine uses. It fits for noble
employments and for highest positions. Patience is the needful mental condition,
the enduring power of great souls. The patience of God's heroic saints is
marvellous. What do I see in my vision? A long cloud of witnesses pressing
through the highways of life whose patience is crowned by the inheritance of
the promises.

III. **The state of prayer and the unwearied mental condition.**—"Continuing
instant in prayer." We still repeat the old questions, What is the Almighty that
we should serve Him? and what profit shall we have if we pray unto Him?
God anticipated the modern sceptic. Is there anything new under the sun?
We question, but we continue to pray. In tribulation the soul of man rises up
above its scepticism and gives itself to prayer. How strange that prayer cannot
be banished from the world! Philosophy cannot hush the voice of prayer.
Strange, yet not strange, for prayer is the upward look of humanity, and the
human must look to the divine, as the flowers seek the sun, as the climbing
plant stretches out for support. Let us show what profit continuing instant in
prayer will produce: 1. *Continuing instant in prayer is the way to gain strength.*
If it be true that prayer is the life of the Christian, if by this exercise we gain
supplies from heaven, then it must be by prayer that we put on strength.
There is a method of invigoration at the believer's disposal. "They that wait
upon the Lord shall renew their strength; they shall mount up with wings as
eagles; they shall run, and not be weary; and they shall walk, and not faint."
The promise is definite. Though science so called tries to reason us away from
the exercise, though scepticism hurls its shafts of ridicule, and though many
hurry past to try other means of gaining strength, we will wait upon the Lord
until weakness departs and the strength of moral manhood is obtained—until
with eagles' pinions we may soar above the earth, mists, and clouds, where
undisturbed we may catch the many voices that sound their sublime anthems
across the heavenly plains—until running in the Christian course does not
weary, and we can walk with those mighty men of old who had power to walk
with God on earth, and then were translated to walk unabashed amid angels
and archangels, with cherubim and seraphim, and all those who walk in the
light ineffable. The praying man must be strong, for thus he moves into the
life-giving sunlight. "The Lord God is a sun and shield: the Lord will give
grace and glory"—the grace to overcome weakness and to grow in strength, the
glory of a mighty warrior who triumphs over every foe. We must place ourselves in the sunlight by prayer. God promises, "I will be as the dew unto
Israel." By this figure is denoted the genial influences, vigour, and strength
which God will impart unto His people. There must be certain conditions of
the plant in relation to the surrounding atmosphere if the pearly dewdrop is
to be formed on its surface and is to exert its reviving force. The certain conditions which God requires for the fulfilment of His gracious promise are a heart
open to receive, a spirit of prayer and of supplication. The man becomes strong
into whose soul God distils the dew of His reviving influences. By prayer we
must go to the Fountain of living waters, and be refreshed; by prayer and

meditation we must feed upon the Bread of life, and thus put on strength. We need the baptism of a praying spirit. We have all kinds of men—scientific, scholarly, rhetorical, oratorical, energetic. We have men of business-like capacity, men great in books and mighty in speech ; but have we a sufficient number of the men of prayer, who plead earnestly in their closets, who by intercessory prayer put the God of Jacob to the test ? Oh for prayers the expression of hearts inhabited by the eternal Spirit,—prayers that witness to an overflowing plenitude of spiritual life ; prayers manifesting themselves in nobleness of character, in kindness of nature, in benevolence of disposition, and in a cheering beneficence as its outcome ! If we had this true prayer, what spiritual vigour would pervade the Church, and how she would move on in a career of ever-expanding conquest ! 2. *Continuing instant in prayer is the way to experience its efficacy.* What would be St. Paul's answer to those who talk about the folly of supposing that the order of nature is to be disturbed by the force of prayer, that inevitable law is to give place to the cries and necessities of an insignificant creature, that the movements of worlds are to be checked by the voice of one who is but as an atom and whose removal would soon be forgotten ? His answer is continuance in prayer. Let gnostics and agnostics, let scientists and evolutionists, let sceptics and philosophers, write, reason, and refute, but we will give ourselves to prayer. The workings of natural laws may be guessed at ; but the workings of God's spiritual laws are along high pathways which no scientist knoweth and which the keenest eye has not yet seen. However, we will give ourselves to prayer, for we have felt its power and preciousness, and so felt as not to be disturbed by clever opponents. When confined to prison, prayer is our only support and comfort ; prayer only can give us songs in the night. 3. *Continuing instant in prayer is the way to surmount temptation.* Introspection is not always productive of peaceful results even when good men carry on the process. Looking inward may ofttimes fail, but looking upward and Godward should never fail. God looks to the heart, and He will not fail to help His suffering sons. Faith in God, continuing instant in prayer, will strike the good old song, "God is our refuge and strength, a very present and an ever-present help in trouble." The face of the dying Stephen was glorified because he saw a divine Helper in heaven ; the stoned was far happier than the stoners. The mighty God helped and cheered. Prayer endows with patience in tribulation, gives songs in the prison cell, turns the dreary dungeon into a palace beautiful, transforms the sluggish streams of earth into the fashion of the river of bliss that flows o'er Elysian flowers hard by the throne of God, through landscapes of perpetual beauty. Prayer paints the rainbow of hope on the tears of tribulation ; prayer brings the sunlight of heaven behind our darkest clouds, and makes them glorious with their exquisite tinting and drapery of purple and of gold ; prayer shapes the lava which the volcano of earthly disaster has sent forth in molten streams into beautiful and glorified forms. Out of the ashes of our earth fires arise eternal riches. If men be not made spiritually strong by prayer, there is no other known method by which strength can be obtained. But they have been and may be so again. Joyfulness in hope, patience in tribulation, have been the result of continuing instant in prayer. Let us still pray in faith and in constancy, and we shall find that prayer has power, that prayer has beneficial influences, that prayer has wondrous results.

Pray on, and pray fervently.—" Continuing instant in prayer." Prayer takes for granted that God is full, and we are empty. The creature is finite, alike in evil and in good. Our poverty and want must ever be a mere nothing in comparison with the fulness of Him who filleth all in all. Prayer takes for granted that there is a connection between this fulness and our emptiness.

The fulness is not inaccessible. It is not too high for us to reach, or for it to stoop. Prayer takes for granted that we are entitled to use this channel, this medium; and that, in using it, there will be a sure inflow of the fulness into us. "Every one that asketh receiveth." Prayer takes for granted *expectation* on our part. If, then, we examine our prayers, and strip them of all that is not prayer, how little remains! Let us mark such things as the following in reference to this kind of prayer: 1. *The irksomeness of non-expecting prayer.* Sometimes there may be such an amount of natural feeling as may make what is called "devotion" pleasant. But in the long run it becomes irksome, if not accompanied with expectation, sure expectation. 2. *The uselessness of non-expecting prayer.* It bears no fruit; it brings no answer; it draws down no blessing. 3. *The sinfulness of non-expecting prayer.* The utterance of petitions is nothing to God; it does not recommend the petitioner.—*H. Bonar.*

SUGGESTIVE COMMENTS ON VERSE 12.

Constant prayer.—Cornelius prayed to God alway. The stated devotions were not wanting, but the life itself was a prayer in action. He was a man seeking God not in words only, but in all that he did. And in our busy, practical times we can only hope to pray to God always in that sense. Pressing duties encroach on meditation; their urgency engenders habits foreign to meditation. Too fast for our sight flash the thousand wheels of the great social machine, on which we are whirled round as a small part. Those constrained faces knit with anxiety that haunt you in the streets, those lips whispering busily to themselves in the crowded thoroughfare—those thousand vehicles locked in confusion at the confluence of streets, with all the occupants goaded to impatience by the words "too late"—they all remind us of the impetuous age in which we live. Who can pray to God always amidst such dire confusion? Do not despair even of that. Amidst the money-changers' tables you cannot pray as in the precincts of the temple. But there is a kind of work that becomes a prayer: *Laborare est orare.* From the most active life in this great city may be daily floating up, for aught we know, to the throne of the Most High an incense of worship more pure than any that issues from the quiet chamber of the pious recluse. I do not speak of acts of mercy and almsgiving only; that there is a prayer in these all would admit. They are an imitation of, and therefore a longing after, the loving Son of God, who is our example. For amongst men, and in aiding men, or in striving with them, do we, the disciples, find our education, as our Master made the scene of His ministry in the midst of the men whom He would serve. The soul in retirement has often grown sickly with over-consciousness of itself, and invented needs and called for help against phantoms of its own creation. But the trials that surround us in our daily duties are those which God has made for us; and to Him we turn for strength to surmount them. Turn, then, to Him; make frequent approaches to His throne, at any time, in any place; ask His help for any undertaking; and if it be one which you dare not bring before Him, abandon it. Such a practice, to use the words of Bishop Taylor, "reconciles Martha's employment with Mary's devotion, charity, and religion—reconciles the necessities of our calling and the employments of devotion. For thus in the midst of business you may retire into your chapel—your heart—and converse with God by frequent addresses and returns." And the fruits of this practice will be justice and uprightness in action, forbearance towards others, kindness towards the helpless, love towards all.

407

MAIN HOMILETICS OF THE PARAGRAPH.—Verses 13—16.

Christian communism and not monastic separation.—The monastic idea might
have in it a germ of goodness; but there was in it a selfish spirit going contrary
to the divine order, and tending to the dwarfing of human nature. Monastic institutions breed corruption. However pure and well-meaning at first, they decline,
and are likely to become hotbeds of immorality. Surely man was not made to
be a monk. Alone, man perishes. If he do not perish physically, he perishes intellectually and morally. Monasteries can never produce the highest type of men.
If there have been great men in monasteries—and we must admit their presence—
the greatness arose not by virtue of the system. If the countenance be an index
of the man, then the pictures of monks do not speak favourably of the monastic
institution as a school for the development of manhood. By separation we are
belittled; by true communism we are enlarged. God has set us in families,
and there we have a communistic idea. The tribe is an enlarged family; the
Church is a divine family; the Church of the firstborn in heaven is a vast family.
In the family and in the Church there may be differences, but there should be
oneness. Sympathy, feeling together with, binds the family. This should unite
the Church; this should bless and glorify the world.

I. **Christian communism expresses itself in benevolent deeds.**—Christian
communism does not declare that there is to be no individual or separate right
in property. The Christian Church in its youthful ardour tried the principle and
proved it a failure, and did not repeat the experiment. St. Peter did not advocate
common rights. Whilst it remained, was it not their own? After it was sold,
was it not in their own power? Christian communism means, as we understand
it, that one brother is not to spend money in useless extravagance while other
brethren are dying of starvation. Can that man be called a Christian who
pampers his dogs and his horses, who creates for himself a thousand unnecessary
wants, while Lazarus, for whom Christ died, for whom a glorious heaven waits,
lies at the gate, full of sores, unfed, untended, and unhoused? The man who does
not want to do good can easily raise objections. He can say, If I distribute to the
necessity of saints, I may encourage imposture, I may pauperise and prevent
the working of self-help. Eleemosynary aid increases the number of voluntary
paupers, and is harmful to society. But the man who sincerely desires to be
helpful will not create objections. He will find out the saints and minister to
their necessities. If the saint turn out a sinner, the benevolent man may
comfort himself with the thought that the sinner helped may feel that there is
some good in the world. Sometimes we read thrilling tales of the fabulous
wealth made by beggars and impostors. Would the writers of those tales
exchange places even if the impostors' proceedings were legitimate? Is the
begging profession likely to become overcrowded? We want more practicalness,
less selfishness, and more benevolence. " Distributing to the necessities of saints,
given to hospitality," contains a lesson which modern Christianised society has
not properly learnt. In connection with the precept let us ask, Is it true that
so much as a thousand pounds has been paid for flowers for one night's entertainment at the houses of certain leaders of London society? Can it be true
that a dinner-party given by an American millionairess in London cost no less
than four thousand five hundred pounds? Can it be true that, at the same time,
thousands upon thousands in London are pinched and drag on a miserable
existence? Is it a probable story that the owner of an estate derived an annual
income of two hundred and fifty thousand pounds from the property, and had
not time to consider the claims of those who helped to make the wealth and who
sought redress? The claimants might be mistaken; their course might be wrong;
some of their proceedings excite loathing rather than compassion. But surely

there might have been consideration. In the interests of humanity we may hope that the story is a fiction. As we look upon starving women and children we may well ask, As for these poor sheep, what have they done? Surely the children are God's saints, and their necessities ought to be relieved. Recent commotions teach us one sad lesson at least, and it is that Christianity has not leavened the whole of society.

II. **Christian communism has a hard lesson for the oppressed.**—" Bless them which persecute you; bless, and curse not." These words lose their primitive significance. The religious persecutor is now harmless; so that we may be allowed to say, No need for soldiers and policemen if this precept were obeyed. No good end is served by cursing persecutors, by maiming overlookers, by burning property. The man who curses does himself and his cause great damage. If agitation be needful, the ruthless destruction of property can serve no good end. If agitation be needful, why can it not be conducted on peaceful lines? The primitive Church acted on the principle of blessing the persecutors, and it became victorious.

III. **Christian communism teaches sympathetic projection.**—" Rejoice with them that do rejoice, and weep with them that weep." The man who has true sympathy throws himself into the position of others. He projects himself, or part of himself, into the position of the other self. This state is reached by the few, for our own sorrows are greater than the sorrows of others. Tears flow freely at the graveside of *our* loved ones. How often we can talk, and even laugh, as we follow *other* loved ones to the burial! Poetry can touch us as it sings "Somebody's darling lies there"; but how callous we often are as somebody's darling, not being our darling, is being let down into the tomb! If we cannot weep with the weepers, we often find it more difficult to laugh with the laughers. "Rejoice with them that do rejoice." Rejoice that my defeat leads to the victory of somebody else. I have tried for years to produce a good painting, to write a taking book, to compose popular sermons. I have failed; and can I rejoice when I learn that my friend has a painting hung in the gallery, or that the publishers have paid him handsomely for his work, or that the crowds are listening to his eloquence every Sunday? " Rejoice with them that do rejoice." I can laugh with the laughers, if the laughter have no reflection on my failure; I can rejoice with the joyful, if there be no reason for the working of envy. Thus I often find it easier to rejoice with the joyful who live ten miles away than to rejoice with the joyful who is my next-door neighbour. Laughter is contagious. Alas that sincere rejoicing with others is not always contagious! We can only sincerely " rejoice with those that do rejoice" as we are " of the same mind one toward another." Mind-sameness is not intellectual monotony. "The same mind" does not preclude the idea of different mental proclivities. The working man, the business man, the professional man, the scientific man, may all "be of the same mind one toward another." "The same mind" refers to the emotional rather than the intellectual side of man's nature. The same mind pervading the community would produce glorious harmony; the same mind stretching through all ranks and classes of men would bind all together.

IV. **Christian communism looks downward.**—"Mind not high things, but condescend to men of low estate." The communism of the world is the opposite of this. It minds high things if they can be made subservient to its own enrichment. The man of low estate becomes a communist, a socialist, a member of the Fabian Society. Then he sets to work to level down the high things, and to level up with those high things himself, a man of low estate. If St. Paul were to rise from the dead, and were to say in a London drawing-room, where the crush is great to get in touch with the high things of modern society, " Mind not high things, but condescend to men of low estate," he would be regarded as a very objectionable character; and if he cared, would pass a very unpleasant evening, if indeed no worse fate were awarded him   "Mind not high things, but condescend to men of low estate." Humanity's high things are often enough divinity's low things. Men of low estate were the Pauls and the Peters; men of high things were the wretched Neros. Time has strange reversals; and what is great and noble in our time may be little and ignoble in some after-time. What a conclusion! "Be not wise in your own conceits." It is good to be wise; it is bad to be conceited. The truly wise will consider the position and claims of others. The self-conceited and self-opinionated see little beyond their own small spheres. These are the people to be shut up in monastic seclusion.

SUGGESTIVE COMMENTS ON VERSES 16, 17.

Our duty to equals.—Hooker's great principle may perhaps be applied to the moral as well as the ceremonial question—that the omission of a point in Scripture does not decide against it, but only throws us upon the law of reason in the matter. We cannot judge from the comparative omission of this or that class of duties in Scripture, that therefore anything is decided as to its importance. Thus the New Testament says comparatively little about duties to equals, and enlarges upon duties to inferiors. But we may not infer from this that duties to equals do not rank as high and are not as trying a class of duties as those to inferiors or to sufferers. What may be called the condescending life was comparatively a new branch of morals; it therefore demanded a prominent place. This is not a subject altogether without a special interest in the present period of our Church, during which this branch of Christian work has been so largely developed. . . . It is impossible not to see that numbers who never would have been happy in any other way have been made happy and satisfied by the habitual exercise of compassion. . . . Montaigne says there is a spice of cruelty in compassion, because it requires pain to gratify its own special nature. There being,

however, this peculiar affection in us, which was obviously of such immense practical power for dealing with this world as we find it, . . . how was it that the old world so entirely overlooked this wonderful practical instrument? . . . And we may remark how paganism has blunted and suppressed even the natural virtues. . . . Many have fled from the bitterness of active life to seek repose in the ministration to inferiors. They have fled to the realm of compassion for peace. A great man gone is contemplated in all the softening light of pity, which, as we are told, is akin to love. And yet we know if the man were to rise to life again, immediately every old jar would come back. Life would rob him at once of the refining hue; it would lower; it would vulgarise again. The condescending life is a devoted life, but it is at the same time a protected life. The hardest trial of humility must not be towards a person to whom you are superior, but towards a person with whom you are on equal footing of competition. Generosity is more tried by an equal than by an inferior. To leave the realm of compassion for that of equality is to leave the realm of peace for that of war. Compassion is a state of peace.—*Mozley.*

MAIN HOMILETICS OF THE PARAGRAPH.—*Verses* 17—19.

Peace with honour.—"Peace with honour" was the statement of one of our great statesmen at the conclusion of a certain treaty. It is a very desirable conclusion. Peace among nations, in societies, in the Church, in the individual. There may be some who are never so much at peace as when they are at war;

but most love and desire peace. With the best intentions in the world, we may produce discord when we intended peace. It cannot always be secured in this disordered world. We must do our best, and leave results with the sovereign Disposer of all events. To do our best is to do in accordance with divine precepts.

I. **Peace is not always possible.**—Jesus Christ was the great peacemaker, and yet He was the cause of much disturbance; perhaps not the cause, but the occasion for the true cause was the wickedness of human nature. St. Paul was the apostle of peace, and yet how much commotion in and around his pathway! The preachers of peace have often been the producers of disturbance. "If it be possible, live peaceably with all men." Is it possible for the pure to live peaceably with the impure? Purity is an offence to the impure; it pricks the conscience; it produces disquiet, rebellion, and sometimes anger. Is it possible to reprove and to live peaceably with the reproved? It may be so to some, but others find it impossible. Masters of tactics move along smoothly; but are men of tact always men of stern principle?

II. **The impossibility of peace must not arise from the believer.**—"As much as lieth in you." There must be examination and close watchfulness of self. "As much as lieth in you." Let purity be maintained without offensive parade; let reproof be administered in the spirit of love and of meekness; let there be love to the person, while there is intense disapproval of the false practice.

III. **The possibility of peace is increased by:** 1. *A negative course.* "Recompense to no man evil for evil": a large precept largely neglected. The evil of being duped and cheated naturally stirs the soul of the upright; it is difficult not to retaliate. Other cases may be noted; but we must obey the precept, for that will bring peace at the last—peace to the obedient at all events. 2. *A positive course.* Be preoccupied with the comely and the honourable in the sight of men. Let this preoccupation be an antidote against those sombre thoughts and hostile projects which are cherished under the influence of resentment; let noble ideals lead the spirit out of and ·above the torturing thoughts produced by actual or fancied offences. A soul moving in high realms is peaceful, though the lower sphere has in it disturbing elements. On the mountain ranges of high pursuits we often find peace and joy which the world cannot understand and of which it cannot deprive. 3. *A self-restraining course.* "Dearly beloved, avenge not yourselves, but rather give place unto wrath." A word of difficulty is prefaced by a word of sweetness. The apostle knew that to fallen nature revenge is sweet. He gives the sweetness of "dearly beloved" to induce the rejection of the sweetness of revenge. Sinful nature says, Revenge is sweet; a higher nature says, Forgiveness is divine. Do not revenge yourselves by taking the law into your own hands. Do not revenge yourselves by saying, God will punish; He can punish better and more severely than I can, so I will give room for the working of the wrath of justice, and my offenders will not escape. Leave revenge alone, and strive after the love which speaks words of blessing and lives in the atmosphere of forgiveness. 4. *A submissive course.* "For it is written" must be our check. What is written has little authority with too many in these days. What is written for amusement, for guidance to earthly success, and so on, they regard; but what is written for moral guidance they ignore. "It is written, Vengeance is Mine, I will repay, saith the Lord." He is both a just and merciful revenger; therefore let us leave all in His hands; do not let us presume to sit in the seat of the supreme Judge. Let wilful offenders tremble, "for it is written, Vengeance is Mine, I will repay." Peace with honour in this dark world of sin; if not peace with glory, with infinite joy in the bright world of unsullied light.

Ver. 19. *The proper treatment of wrath.*—Bishop Sanderson says, "I ever held it a kind of spiritual thrift where there are *two senses* given of one place, both

411

agreeable to the analogy of faith and manners, to make use of both." It is objected that the practice of this spiritual thrift may lead to spiritual wealth, but seems to tend to exegetical poverty. There is surely no need to be alarmed by the objection here raised, for spiritual wealth must be greater than exegetical richness and accuracy. We do not by any means underrate the value of the latter, but it is not needful to the salvation of the soul. If it be, then the great majority must be unsaved. Exegetical correctness can only be the possession of the learned few, while spiritual wealth may be the possession of the many, whether learned or unlearned. Masters of exegesis are not always spiritually rich. Three interpretations of the expression "Give place unto wrath" have been given by eminent expositors; and not attempting to decide which is the true interpretation, we may, for the purposes of spiritual thrift, make use of all. Let us take, first, the most doubtful of the interpretations:—

I. **Restrain your own wrath.**—In this case the personality must be overmastered. If our wrath be allowed to work and maintain the ascendency, we cannot conduct ourselves aright with reference to the outward world and with respect to the divine government of the universe. Our own personality may seem to us, and is in a sense, important, but we must ever remember that there are other personalities to be considered. There is the personality of every member of the human race, and of every member with whom we have dealings. There is the divine personality, and we must not by personal feelings venture to interfere with divine prerogatives; we must in the truest sense restrain our own wrath before we can properly and fully acknowledge the solemn truth that vengeance belongs alone unto the Lord. The judge must be raised above personal feelings and the influence of passion, prejudice, and vindictiveness. Thus our judges are placed in positions of almost undisputed authority, and are removed from the sphere of party feelings. It is wise to restrain our own wrath. We may be unjustly indignant; we know not all the bearings of the case; offence may be taken when no offence was intended. Wrath may be unjust; it must be harmful. Revenge may be sweet, but it produces and fosters bitterness of soul; its motions in the spirit are not helpful to that holy calm where divine graces flourish. The spirit of revenge and the Spirit of God cannot harmoniously dwell in the same sphere.

II. **Give place to the wrath of your enemy.**—Meyer objects that this would only be a prudential measure. What is religion but a system that enjoins and fosters prudence? The prudent man is one who is careful of consequences. We cannot ourselves follow the high pathway marked out by the moralists who tell us to follow virtue for its own sake, that virtue is its own sufficient reward, that to consider consequences is a mere selfish principle of guidance in morals. Self-love is different from selfishness, which is fallen self-love. Self-love is surely not condemned by Him who asks, "What shall it profit a man?" We are allowed, then, to consider self and the final profit and advantage of the steps we take. Let it also be remembered that the intensely selfish man is not always prudent. He does not look to the ultimate working out of the spirit of selfishness. In seeking personal happiness he may be finding personal misery. As then a mere prudential measure, on this low ground, if we deem it low, give place to the wrath of your enemy. By opposing you may make it worse, you may fan the flame to a great heat. Look at nations. What is war but the engendering of further warfare and the necessity of maintaining large numbers of armed men, armed vessels, and powerful batteries? In the present state of society war may be a necessary evil, out of which good may arise. What good can arise from war between individual men? Has the duel ever been productive of good? Give place to the wrath of your enemy. Get out of his way, if need be. Allow it time to cool down. Do not let your heat be joined to his heat, and thus avoid increasing the caloric intensity of the moral sphere.

III. **Make way for divine wrath.**—Our wrath arises too often from personal feeling. We are offended, we are injured either by word or by deed—in mind, body, or estate—and we become angry. But God's wrath cannot arise in any such way. His wrath arises from the sense of injury done to His moral government. If God's anger have in it anything of what we may call the personal, it arises from the love and sympathy of His nature. God is a supreme judge who is raised above all prejudice and all personal feelings in meting out judgment, and therefore we may safely leave vengeance in the hands of God. He will vindicate His own rightful method of government; He will show Himself the special defender of His people. Learn, then, that man's true wisdom is to remember that vengeance is only safe in the hands of a holy God—that inquisitors are not only cruel, but presumptuously wicked. They are striving to take God's place and assert divine prerogatives. We may believe that most of the victims of the foul inquisition have been in the right; but even if they were wrong, the inquisitor has no right to come between a man and his conscience. The foulest blot on what some are pleased to call the Christian religion is the accursed inquisition; and the wonder is that enlightened men can look calmly on a Church capable of such diabolical cruelty. There is no parallel between the random persecutions made by some Protestants and the systematised, heartrending tortures, cruel maiming of harmless and holy men and women by the Roman Catholic Church. At the same time, let us not be in our turn inquisitors. Make way for divine wrath. If self-wrath were restrained, surely bigotry would cease, and persecution would be banished from the earth.

MAIN HOMILETICS OF THE PARAGRAPH.—Verses 20, 21.

Remedial punishment.—In this section, which treats of Christian morals, St. Paul refers three times to the book of Proverbs—another example of his respect, in every point, for the Old Testament. In ver. 20 we find an almost verbal repetition of Solomon's advice: "If thine enemy hunger, give him bread to eat; and if he be thirsty, give him water to drink: for thou shalt heap coals of fire on his head, and the Lord will reward thee." The corrupt precept of the Jews was, "Thou shalt love thy neighbour and hate thine enemy." The Lord gave a new commandment: "But I say unto you, Love your enemies, bless them that persecute you, do good to them that hate you, and pray for them that despitefully use you, and persecute you; that ye may be the children of your Father which is in heaven." That which Jesus taught He practised.

I. **A method of punishment which is novel.**—To return good for good is human; to return evil for evil is carnal; to return evil for good is devilish; to return good for evil is divine. This last is peculiar to Christianity,—peculiar, we should say, to a small portion of Christendom; so peculiar that when it is practised it strikes the world with astonishment. Too often we try to kill our enemies with shells and grape-shot, and not with sweet loaves and refreshing drinks. Too often our highest pitch of goodness is to make an effort to be kind to our enemies. We shake hands, but the hand wants the loving grasp; we utter words, but there is in them no heart and little love.

II. **A method of punishment which is severe.**—The figure "coals of fire" is common among the Arabs and Hebrews to denote a vehement pain. If there be any sensitiveness left in the enemy, he will be severely punished by deeds of kindness. In the highest sense the enemy is not punished whose physical nature merely is tortured. The enemy is punished when the moral nature is made ashamed and sees the enormity of his hostile attacks.

413

III. A method of punishment which is remedial.—Human methods of punishment are for the most part repressive and not remedial; divine methods are intended to be remedial. Meyer observes that in the expression "coals of fire" there is no allusion whatever to the idea of softening or melting the object. Some of our commentators are very dogmatic. Dogma is good when it furnishes satisfactory reasons for its position. Surely Meyer's interpretation opens out the way for an ingenious method of revenge. Once we saw the picture of the inquisitor who killed the man by hope; here is the Christian feeding the man in order to kill him. We cannot believe that punishment without a remedial purpose is part of the divine teaching. These "coals of fire" must both punish and soften. Whether Meyer be correct or not, we are sure that this kind of punishment is likely to lead to repentance and salvation. Divine justice is preventive; divine love is remedial and reforming. The stripes of the cat-o'-nine-tails hurt and degrade; the stripes of love hurt and reform and ennoble. The coals of fire which revengeful disciples invoke would consume; the coals of fire which Christ pours forth consume the evil and develop the good.

IV. A method of punishment which has a beneficial reflex action.—The man who tries to do good, even though his effort may fail, gets good. When we seek to do harm to our enemies, we do great harm to ourselves. On earth's battle-fields, in a moral sense at least, victory is not differenced from defeat; fiendish passions rage through the embattled hosts; there is no difference. He that overcomes evil with good overcomes three enemies at once—the devil, his adversary, and himself. The self-conqueror is the noblest and mightiest. The very effort to kindle coals of fire is beneficial. All effort is beneficial which has a noble purpose. We want love's fires glowing in this frozen world—coals of fire, not from beneath, but from above. Earth's colliers may refuse coals of fire when anger is provoked, when bad passions are in the ascendant; heaven's workmen toil the harder to produce coals of fire when the world is cold, when enmity is great. Love's coals of fire blazing from every mountain top, burning in every valley, shining in every home, warming every heart, would make a world over which angels would raise their gladdest songs.

SUGGESTIVE COMMENTS ON VERSES 20, 21.

Treating an enemy kindly is beneficial.—This method of treating an enemy is prescribed, not merely because it is abstractly right in principle, but also as the best practical means of a specific beneficial result. Do him good in return for evil, for thou shalt heap coals of fire on his head. The idea of a furnace is introduced here with reference to the smelting and moulding of ore, and not to the torture of living creatures. The coals of fire suggest, not the pain of punishment to the guilty, but the benefit of getting his heart softened and the dross removed from his character. Love poured out in return for hatred will be what the burning coals are to the ore—it will melt and purify. In the smelting of metals, whether on a large or small scale, it is necessary that the burning coals should be above the ore as well as beneath it. The melting fuel and the rude stones are mingled together, and brought into contact particle by particle throughout the mass. It is thus that the resistance of the stubborn material is overcome and the precious separated from the vile. The analogy gives the expressive view both of the injurer's hardness and the power of the forgiver's love. Christians meet much obdurate evil in the world. It is not their part either peevishly to fret or proudly to plan revenge. The Lord has in this matter distinctly traced the path for His disciples, and hedged it in. It is their business to

414

render good for evil; to pile forgiveness over injuries, layer upon layer, as diligently and patiently as those swarthy labourers heave loads of coal over the iron ore within the furnace, and not merely in conformity with the abstract idea of transcendental virtue, but with the object as directly utilitarian as that which the miner pursues. The Christian's aim, like the miner's, is to melt, and so make valuable the substance which in its present state is hard in itself and hurtful to those it touches. The Americans have on this subject a tract entitled *The Man who killed his Neighbour.* It contains, in the form of a narrative, many practical suggestions on the act of overcoming evil with good. It is with kindness —modest, thoughtful, generous, unwearied kindness—that the benevolent countryman kills his churlish neighbour; and it is only the old evil man he kills, leaving a new man to lead a very different life in the same village after the dross has been purged away. If any one desire to try this work, he must bring to it at least these two qualifications—modesty and patience. If he proceed with the air of superiority and the consciousness of his own virtue, he will never make one step of progress. The subject will day by day grow harder in his hands. But even though the successive acts of kindness should be genuine, the operator must lay his account with a tedious process and with many disappointments. Many instances of good rendered for evil may seem to have been thrown away, and no symptom of penitence appear in the countenance or conduct of the evildoer; but be not weary in well-doing, for in due season you shall reap if you faint not. Although your enemy have resisted your deeds of kindness even unto seventy times seven, it does not follow that all or that any part of this has been lost. At last the enmity will suddenly give way and flow down in penitence at some single act, perhaps not greater than any of those which preceded it, but every one that preceded contributed to the great result.—*Arnot.*

The conquest of evil.—Among sacred writers St. Paul is especially remarkable for his great gift of sympathy with human nature and human thought. In the case before us he has been inculcating a long list of difficult duties as belonging to a serious Christian life. Do not the difficulties which lie in the way of them appear to such as you and I to be almost insurmountable? This is the undercurrent of our thoughts, and St. Paul meets it by his closing words, which are not, mark you, so much an additional precept as a summing up of all the precepts that have gone before by a practical appeal to a general principle: "Be not overcome of evil, but overcome evil with good." Now here are implied two things about evil—first, its aggressive strength, and, next, our capacity for not merely resisting but subduing it. Evil is the creature repudiating the law of its being by turning away its desire from Him who is the source, the centre, the end of its existence. If it be urged that God, in making a man free, must have foreseen that man would thus abuse his freedom, it must be replied that God's horizons are wider than ours, and that we may not unreasonably believe that He foresaw, in the very cure of evil, a good which would more than compensate for its existence—that, if sin abounded, grace would much more abound. If one thing be more wonderful than another amid the many mysteries which surround the presence of evil in the world of the good and gracious God, it is the enthusiasm with which it is propagated. It has at this hour in this great city its earnest missionaries and apostles. It creates and disseminates whole literatures: here reasoning, refining, in every sense presentable; there passionate, blasphemous, revolting. It makes its converts, and then in turn it adroitly enlists them in the work of conversion. It retreats—when for the moment it does retreat—only that it presently may advance the better. Everywhere it gives a thinking man the impression, not of being simply an inert obstacle to goodness, but of being the energetic, intelligent, onward movement of some personal activity. " Be not overcome of evil." It is not, then, a resistless invader ; it is not invincible, for it is not the work of an eternal being or principle. Strong as it is, it is strictly a product of created wills. If the Oriental belief in a second principle be true, we might resign ourselves to evil as inevitable ; if the pantheistic belief in the identification of God with all created activity, we might learn to regard it with complacency. As Christians we know evil to be both hateful and not invincible. It is our duty to abhor it ; yet it is also our duty and within our power to overcome it. True it often beleaguers the soul like an investing force, which, besides cutting off supplies of strength from without, has its allies too truly in our weakness and passions within, and ever and anon makes an assault which might even prove fatal. But, for all that, it is not our master. It may be conquered, not by its own weapons, but by weapons of another kind—as the apostle says, " with good." Good, like evil, is not a mere abstraction ; it is at bottom a living person. If evil be personified in Satan, good is personified in the divine Christ ; and Satan, if conquered, must be conquered by the aid of his living, personal Antagonist. Christ and His cleansing blood, Christ and the grace of His Spirit, Christ and the virtues which Christ creates in man, are more than a match for evil, whether in our own heart or in society around us. His patience is stronger than human violence, His gentleness than the brutal rudeness of man, His humility than the world's lofty scorn, His divine charity than its cruelty and hatred.—*Canon Liddon.*

ILLUSTRATIONS TO CHAPTER XII.

Ver. 1. *Indian gives himself.*—A missionary tells of an Indian chief who came to him and offered his belt of wampum that he might please God. "No," said the missionary; "Christ cannot accept such a sacrifice." The Indian departed, but soon returned, offering his rifle and the skins he had taken in hunting. "No," was the reply; "Christ cannot accept such a sacrifice." Again the Indian went away, but soon returned once more with a troubled conscience, and offered his wigwam, wife, child, everything, for peace and pardon. "No," was still the reply; " Christ cannot accept such a sacrifice." The chief seemed surprised for a moment; then lifting up tearful eyes to the face of the missionary, he feelingly cried out, " *Here, Lord, take poor Indian too.*" That present was accepted, and the chief went home full of joy.

Ver. 2. *What stopped the saw-mill.*—In one of the older States of America resided an infidel, the owner of a saw-mill, situate by the side of a highway, over which a large portion of the community passed every Sabbath to and from the church. This infidel, having no regard for the Sabbath, was as busy, and his mill was as noisy, on that holy day as any other. Before long it was observed, however, that a certain time before service the mill would stop, remain silent and appear to be deserted for a few minutes, when its noise and clatter would recommence, and continue till about the close of the service, when for a short time it again ceased. It was soon noticed that one of the deacons of the church passed the mill to the place of worship during the silent interval; and so punctual was he to the hour that the infidel knew just when to stop the mill, so that it should be silent while the deacon was passing, although he paid no regard to the passing of the others. On being asked why he paid this mark of respect to the deacon, he replied, "The deacon professes just what the rest of you do, but he *lives*, also, such a life that it makes me feel bad *here* " (putting his hand upon his heart) "to run my mill while he is passing." "Let your light so shine before men."—*Ellen Preston.*

Ver. 4. *" Members one of another."*—That is a touching story which Dickens tells of two London 'busmen, who passed each other every day for years on the same road. They never spoke, and their only recognition was a slight elevation of their whips, when they met, by way of a salute. At length one of the coachmen disappeared, and the other, upon making inquiries, heard that he was dead. The survivor began to fret, and at last became so miserable that he actually pined to death. He could not live without the silent sympathy of his friend. Is not this an illustration of the enormous power which silent sympathy has in helping fellow-travellers over the dry, dusty, and common-place stretches of life's journey? Comforting, encouraging words in times of sorrow, need, sickness, and other kinds of distress, have perhaps a greater influence than those who speak them know; but sometimes greatest of all is the influence for good of little acts of sympathy of the silent sort, the hand-pressure, the look that shows you understand, the encouraging smile. This is to give the cup of cold water of which our Lord speaks; this is the little service which shall be rewarded.—*Elsie Croydon.*

Ver. 11. *Prescott's perseverance.*—Some years ago a student in college lost one of his eyes by a missile thrown by a class-mate. His other eye became so affected by sympathy that its sight was endangered. The best oculists could not relieve him. He was sent to Europe for medical treatment and change of climate, and tarried there three years, when he returned with only part of an eye, just enough vision to serve him in travelling about, but too little for reading. His father was an eminent jurist, and designed his son for the bar, but this calamity quenched his aspirations in that direction. He resolved to devote himself to authorship in the department of historical literature. He spent *ten years* in laborious systematic study of the standard authors before he even selected his theme. Then he spent another *ten years* in searching archives, exploring masses of manuscripts, official documents and correspondence, consulting old chronicles, reading quantities of miscellaneous books, and taking notes—all through the eyes of others—before his first work was ready for the press—*Ferdinand and Isabella.* Prescott was forty years of age when he gave this remarkable history to the public. Then followed his *Mexico, Peru,* and *Philip the Second,* works that have earned for him the reputation of a profound historian on both sides of the Atlantic. Noble work for any man with two good eyes! Noble work for a man with none!

Ver. 12. *Prayer, a necessity of Christian life.*—There is a class of animals, neither fish nor sea-fowl, that inhabit the deep. It is their home; they never leave it for the shore; yet, though swimming beneath its waves and sounding its darkest depths, they have ever and anon to rise to the surface that they may breathe the air. Without that those monarchs of the deep could not live in that dense element in which they move and have their being. And something like what they do through a physical necessity the Christian has to do by a

spiritual one. It is by ever and anon ascending to God, by soaring up in prayer into a loftier, purer region for supplies of grace, that he maintains his spiritual life. Prevent these animals from rising to the surface, and they die for want of breath; prevent him from rising to God, and he dies for want of prayer.—*Dr. Guthrie.*

Ver. 12. *Spirit of prayer.*—During the blizzard a few years ago in America, many of the telegraph wires were prostrated, and messages were sent to Chicago by the way of Liverpool, England; and the answer, after a while, came round by another circuit. And so the prayer we offer may come back in a way we never imagined; and if we ask to have our faith increased, although it may come by a widely different process to that which we expected, our confidence will surely be augmented.

Ver. 20. *Revenge.*—During the American revolutionary war there was living in Pennsylvania Peter Miller, pastor of a little Baptist church. Near the church lived a man who secured an unenviable notoriety by his abuse of Miller and the Baptists. He was also guilty of treason, and was for this sentenced to death. No sooner was the sentence pronounced than Peter Miller set out on foot to visit General Washington at Philadelphia to intercede for the man's life. He was told that his prayer for his friend could not be granted. "My friend!" exclaimed Miller, "I have not a worse enemy living than that man." "What!" rejoined Washington; "you have walked sixty miles to save the life of your enemy? That in my judgment puts the matter in a different light. I will grant you his pardon." The pardon was at once made out, and Miller at once proceeded on foot to a place fifteen miles distant, where the execution was to take place on the afternoon of the same day. He arrived just as the man was being carried to the scaffold, who, seeing Miller in the crowd, remarked, "There is old Peter Miller. He has walked all the way from Ephrata to have his revenge gratified to-day by seeing me hung." These words were scarcely spoken before Miller gave him his pardon, and his life was spared.

Ver. 21. *Forgiveness.*—The Caliph Hassan, son of Hali, being at table, a slave accidentally dropped a dish of meat, which, being very hot, severely burnt him. The slave, affrighted, instantly fell on his knees before his lord, and repeated these words of the Alcoran: "Paradise is for those who restrain their anger." "*I am not angry with thee,*" replied the caliph. "And for those who forgive offences," continued the slave. "*I forgive thee,*" added the caliph. "But above all for those who return good for evil," said the slave. "*I set thee at liberty,*" rejoined the caliph, "*and give thee ten dinaras.*" Shall we say we have not seen so great charity, no, not in Christendom? We remember with satisfaction a *Cranmer* of whom it was affirmed, "Do that man an ill-turn, and you will make him your friend for ever."

Ver. 21. *Tikhon, the poor man's friend.*— We know not that we have read a finer instance of the overcoming of evil with good, and of wrath and pride with humility and love, than in the following incident related of Tikhon, bishop of Varonej, in Russia. Tikhon, a very holy man, promoted many reforms among clergy and laity. He was pre-eminently the poor man's friend, and was among the first, if not the first of all, who wrote in favour of the serfs, and who urged that emancipation of them which some time after (about sixty years after his death) was actually accomplished. "As a friend of serfs," relates Mr. Hepworth Dixon, "he one day went to the house of a prince, in the district of Varonej, to point out some wrong which they were suffering on his

estate, and to beg him, for the sake of Jesus, to be tender with the poor. The prince got angry with his guest for putting the thing so plainly into words, and in the midst of some sharp speech between them struck him in the face. Tikhon rose up and left the house; but when he had walked some time he began to see that he, no less than his host, was in the wrong. 'This man,' he said to himself, 'has done a deed of which, on cooling down, he will feel ashamed. Who has caused him to do that wrong? It was my doing,' sighed the reformer, turning on his heel and going straight back into the house. Falling at the prince's feet, Tikhon craved his pardon for having stirred him into wrath and caused him to commit a sin. The prince was so astonished that he knelt down by the good man, and, kissing his hands, implored his forgiveness and benediction. From that hour, it is said, the prince was another man, noticeable through all the province of Varonej for his kindness to the serfs." Which of us, in daily life, will do as Tikhon did, and overcome by humility?

CHAPTER XIII.

CRITICAL NOTES.

Ver. 1.—Let every one submit to the authorities that are over him. A precept made remarkable by the time in which it was written. πᾶσα ψυχή, every soul; every office-bearer as well as member of the Church. ἐξουσία is authority, distinguished from δύναμις, power or force, and may exist where there is no authority, and even in opposition to it. If any earthly authority command anything that is contrary to the will of God, the apostles have taught us to say, "We ought to obey God rather than man" (Wordsworth). Authority used for human magistrates. In Peter iii. 22 denotes rather angelic powers. Of or from God; mediately through men. By divine permission; divine appointment. Form of government left to human discretion.

Ver. 2.—Origen having cited this and the previous verse in his dissertation against Celsus, confesses it is a place capable of much disquisition, by reason of such princes as govern cruelly and tyrannically, or who, by reason of their power, fall into effeminacy and carnal pleasures. He says this is not to be understood of persecuting powers, for in such cases that of the apostle takes place, "We must obey God rather than man," but of those powers which are not a terror to good works, but to the evil. It is a contradiction to the holiness, justice, and goodness of God to say that He has given princes any power to do any injury to their subjects. Non-resistance of the Greek commentators is the non-performance of subjection and obedience to commands. We cannot be obliged from conscience towards God to be subject to them in those things which they have no authority from God to require, and for refusal of obedience to which we have God's authority.

Ver. 3. **For rulers are not a terror.**—He is speaking of what is commonly the case, of what may fairly be expected to be the case. And even the worst authority is better than mere force.

Ver. 4.—μάχαιρα is not here a dagger, but *gladius.* The Roman power is symbolised in the Apocalypse with the great sword. Symbol of magistrate's power to punish.

Ver. 5.—διὰ τὴν συνείδησιν, for conscience' sake—because of God's institution and command.

Ver. 6.—Revenues of the Roman empire consisted chiefly: 1. Of the rents of public lands farmed by the publicans, and collected by tax-gatherers employed by them—the publicans of our version; 2. Customs or taxes on goods; 3. Tithes; 4. Pasturage, etc.; 5. Poll or personal tax; 6. Property tax; 7. Army tax—φόρος paid as capitation money according to census, τέλος paid on any other account; the former paid on things immovable, the latter on things which may be conveyed.

Ver. 8.—Augustine says that "love is a debt which is multiplied by paying." Milton says, "By owing owes not, but still pays, at once indebted and discharged." The debt of love can never be fully discharged.

Ver. 9.—Love to God and love to man said by the Jews to be the great sum or heads of the law.

Ver. 11.—Because we know the time, let us fulfil the law by love. We have been in the dark, but let us awake with the light. ὕπνου, deep sleep; dreams of the present time. Physical death. Spiritual stupor. The image of death. As χρόνος is duration of time, so καιρός is definition of time. It is a portion cut out of time, a season, an opportunity. **Salvation.**—Full spiritual salvation and day of perfect redemption viewed as connected with the universal spread of Christianity. Spiritual salvation in the world of glory. All is night here, in respect of ignorance and daily ensuing troubles.

Ver. 12. **Night.**—Time of Mosaic law, previous to Christ's first coming. Time of ignorance of God. The whole of life in this world, in comparison with the kingdom of glory. Night the heathen condition of Rome. Consummated triumph over the night of evil. Armour consisting in the power and disposition of light, truth, and righteousness. Roman armour kept bright.

Ver. 13.—εὐσχήμων, beautiful and symmetrical. Banquets, drinking feasts. Noisy crowds of drunken men ran dancing and singing through the streets. Lascivious banquets.

Ver. 14. **Be clothed.**—Exhibit Him both before men and God, both outwardly and inwardly. Put Him on, so that He only may be seen in you. Care of the flesh permitted, but not its lusts. Put on, invest yourselves with, Christ in the exercise of that union with Him which is already yours in possession. Chrysostom says it was a common phrase, "Such a one hath put on such a one"—that is, he is an imitation of him; so to put on the new man is to walk as new men, in newness of life and conversation.

MAIN HOMILETICS OF THE PARAGRAPH.—Verses 1—6.

True subjection.—There are many powers in the world—material, social, intellectual, and moral. Above all powers is the supreme Power. God ordains all powers. Man must recognise his inferiority. How the infinite Spirit directs material powers we cannot tell. There must be a way, though we cannot comprehend. But as man by the greater force of his intellectual power rules the brute creation and makes vast material changes, so God by His infinitely vast nature must have a marvellous method of controlling all powers. There are men who resist the highest ordering power. They reject God or relegate Him to some remote corner of His own universe. Such shall receive to themselves condemnation. Resistance of the supreme power leads to other resistance, engenders anarchy, and produces disaster. Man's power of resistance, though often futile, speaks of man's dignity and man's great responsibility. Man's wisdom is seen in learning the lesson of subjection. Man, sooner or later, falls by rebellion. Man rises by subjection.

I. **True subjection is inward.**—The subjection of the brute is outward; he is not a consenting party. The subjection of material forces is an affair of material pressure; when that is removed or becomes weak the material force revenges the restraint by destructive leaps and bounds. The subjection of the man is inward; with his soul he places himself beneath the higher powers. The motive force of true subjection is conscience. Thus the man who has the spirit of true subjection is ennobled and not degraded by the process. Nobility is seen in recognising human limitations and working in harmony with divine order. Greatness sees its own littleness, does not parade a fancied largeness, and thus attains to highest dignity.

II. **True subjection is upward.**—Some take downward glances; their range of vision is contracted; they resist, and that resistance binds them with galling fetters. Others take upward glances; their range of vision is large. They see a divine force beyond and above human forces. They submit, and by their very submission are elevated. The humble are exalted somewhere, somehow; all the powers are moving towards the exaltation of the souls that look upward. The recognition of a higher power is the exaltation in measure and degree of the recognising being. Thus to bend low is to rise high.

III. **True subjection works outwardly from the inward.**—The earth subject is a time-server. He works through pressure. He submits to law and pays tribute; but he is subject only for wrath, so that if he can break the law without punishment he is not averse, if he can shirk the tribute or defraud he is not indisposed. The good subject works through pressure, but it is an inward pressure. He pays tribute conscientiously. The only resistance he knows is that which is induced by an enlightened conscience, and so careful is he not to go wrong that he rather suffers wrong than be found guilty of doing wrong. The citizens of heaven are the best citizens of earth. Eternal laws are the best basis for time laws. The powers that be will find it safest and wisest to recognise the supreme Power and to foster in the nation all God-fearing spirits.

IV. **True subjection is beneficial; it benefits the individual, for it scatters fear.**—The sword does not appal when goodness emboldens. Judicial pomp does not affright when good works are maintained. 1. *It secures praise.* If it do not always secure the praise of men, it must meet with the praise of God. In lowly spheres we cannot always obtain the plaudits of the higher powers. We cannot all do some great deed which may blazon our name into the ears of the world. Westminster Abbey could not find room for monuments to be erected to all faithful subjects. Most can only tread the lowly pathway to heaven's immortality. "The trivial round, the common task," is the obscure way of the majority. Better and more enduring than the praise of fallible men is the praise of God. Sweet as may be the voice of the approving power, sweeter is the voice of an approving conscience. Royalty itself has no gifts so rich as those which a conscience royally kept can bestow. Let us be true to its claims; let us see that it moves along right lines; let us be subject to the highest Power, that ordains all higher powers. 2. *It benefits the nation.* The individual is helped to the performance of his duty by regarding himself as an important factor in the nation's welfare. If we consider ourselves as parts of the national fabric, we feel our importance and rise up to the proper sense of our duty. The claims of self should be subordinated to the claims of the state in the consideration of the Christian patriot. The nation is strong as its good men are increased. When virtue is triumphant, the nation is victorious and prosperous. Let us work to the increase of good men; and to this end let each man begin to improve himself. Good men are the seed-germs out of which other good men grow. The sword may rust in the sheath when good men abound. The executors of wrath have no functions to discharge when evildoers cease from the land. Material wealth engenders selfishness, licentiousness, and corruption. Moral wealth promotes benevolence, purity, and all things that are grandly noble. The increase of material wealth is often promotive of national decline. The increase of moral wealth tends to the larger growth and the more permanent establishment of the nation.

SUGGESTIVE COMMENTS ON VERSES 1—6.

Universal necessity of government.—Human society is so constituted that the instinct of self-preservation compels men to set up a form of government—*i.e.*, to commit to some men power over the rest. Every one knows that a bad government is almost always better than none at all. The universality and the universal necessity of government prove it to be God's will that men live under rule. But God has not prescribed a definite form of rule. Consequently the universal principle of government assumes an infinite variety of forms. We also notice that nearly always opposition to the men actually in power tends to weaken and destroy the principle of government and leads towards anarchy. How frequently the murder even of a bad ruler has been followed by utter lawlessness and by infinite loss to the nation! Consequently opposition to the individuals in power is practically, with few exceptions, an opposition to the divine principle of government. Observing this, and remembering that nothing takes place without foresight and permission of God, we may say, as Paul says, that the existing rulers, by whatever steps they mounted the throne, have been put on it by God. For God created that felt necessity for government which was their real stepping-stone to power. And He did so in full view of the persons into whose hands, throughout the ages of the world, the power would fall. We notice further that all bad conduct tends to weaken and good conduct to strengthen a government. Consequently rulers are compelled, for the maintenance of their position, to favour the good and oppose the bad. We cannot doubt that this necessity comes from the Ruler of the race. Therefore God, who has laid upon mankind the necessity of appointing rulers, has laid upon rulers the necessity of rewarding the good and punishing the bad; and has done this in order to make rulers the instruments of carrying out His own purpose of kindness to the good and punishment to the wicked. Thus rulers are, perhaps unconsciously, ministers of God, doing God's work. These considerations are an abundant reason for obedience to civil authority. Since rulers are compelled by their position to favour the good and punish the bad, resistance to them generally proves that we are in the wrong, and will be followed by the punishment which they cannot but inflict on evil-doers. Hence the motive of fear should lead to obedience. And since resistance to existing rulers tends to weaken and destroy that principle of government which God has set up for the good of the race, we ought to submit to them for conscience' sake. That we feel ourselves morally bound to pay the taxes imposed without our consent or in opposition to our judgment, and that all admit the right of the ruler to enforce payment, also confirms the divine origin of his authority.—*Beet.*

How far should a Christian resist? —But for the very reason of this precept it is asked, If it is not merely the state in itself which is a thought of God, but if the very individuals who possess the power at a given time are set up by His will, what are we to do in a period of revolution when a new power is violently substituted for another? This question, which the apostle does not raise, may, according to the principles he lays down, be resolved thus: The Christian will submit to the new power as soon as the resistance of the old shall have ceased. In the actual state of matters he will recognise the manifestation of God's will, and will take no part whatever in any reactionary plot. But should the Christian support the power of the state even in its unjust measures? No; there is nothing to show that the submission required by St. Paul includes active co-operation; it may even show itself in the form of passive resistance; and it does not at all exclude protestation in word and even resistance in deed, provided that to this latter there be joined the calm acceptance of the punishment inflicted. This submissive but at the same time firm conduct is also a homage to the inviolability of authority; and experience proves that it is in this way all tyrannies have been morally broken and all true progress in the history of humanity effected.—*Godet.*

Religious feeling required in governors and governed.—He who does not bring into government, whether as governor or subject, some religious feeling, some higher motive than expediency, is likely to make but an indifferent governor or an indifferent subject : without piety there will be no good government.— *Sir Arthur Helps.*

Corruption of an institution does not disprove divine origin.—The fact that an earthly government may be corrupt and tyrannical does not disprove the divine origin of government, any more than the fact that parents may be unfaithful to their duties proves that the family is not divinely originated, or the fact that a particular Church may become corrupt proves that the Church is not divine in its source. St. Paul, however, does not teach here that any degree of tyranny whatever is to be submitted to by a Christian. If the government attempt to force him to violate a divine command—for example, to desist from preaching the gospel or to take part in pagan worship—he must resist even unto death. Most of the apostles suffered martyrdom for this principle.—*Shedd.*

The wide sway of law.—Of law there can be no less acknowledged than that her seat is the bosom of God, her voice the harmony of the world ; all things in heaven and in earth do her homage ; the very least is feeling her care, and the greatest is not exempted from her power : both angels and men and creatures of what condition soever, though each in different sort and manner, yet all with uniform consent, admiring her as the mother of their peace and joy.—*Hooker.*

God uses all nations.—For each of the nations God had " an office " ; for each He had appointed a beginning and an end. One by one, in orderly succession, those stupendous kingdoms of the East, Babylonian and Persian, Egyptian and Greek, God had required their armies ; He had His hand upon their captains ; Assyria was His hammer, Cyrus was His shepherd, Egypt was His garden, Tyre was His jewel ; everywhere He was felt ; everywhere the divine destiny directed and controlled. The shuttle of God passes in and out, weaving into its web a thousand threads of natural human life. All history is put to the uses of God's holier manifestations ; He works under the pressure laid upon Him by the wants and necessities of social and political progress.—*Canon Holland.*

" *Wilt thou then not be afraid of the power ? Do that which is good, and thou shalt have praise of the same.*"— Archbishop Ussher, in his treatise on the " Power of the Prince and the Obedience of the Subject," quotes the following admirable paraphrase, by Primasius, of the above clause : " Either thou dost justly, and the just power will praise thee ; or, thus doing justly, although the unjust power should condemn thee, the just God will crown thee."

MAIN HOMILETICS OF THE PARAGRAPH.—Verses 7—10.

Christian citizenship and Christian brotherhood.—Compare the text with the life and precepts of Jesus. They are entire harmony. He was subject unto His parents. His precept as to Christian citizenship was, " Render unto Cæsar," etc.

I. **The need for this injunction to early Christians.**—False charges levelled against them : one was disloyalty. Paul set forth the duties of Christian citizenship. There was the added injunction, Be good to neighbours, loving all men. It was necessary to publish the fact that Christians aimed, not at the overthrow of governments, but to show sincerest loyalty and brotherly kindness. In one sense appearances were against Christians. Their mysterious meetings lent colour to the charges of conspiracy—false and wicked charges; for the whole tenor of Christ's doctrine, and Christian practice too, was: tolerate no violence; live at peace; do not retaliate; be magnanimous. Of course Christianity was opposed to the way of the world, and libellous charges gave excuse for persecution.

II. **The text deals with Christian citizenship.**—It asserts the principle of submission to civil authority. Four thoughts suggested : 1. It is impossible to secure successful action apart from organisation. Union is strength, and orderly unity is strength at its best. Confusion in council leads to internal anarchy and contempt from other powers. 2. The avowed object of all government to put down the wrong and enforce the right. Crime, the citizen's enemy ; and the government deals it deadly blows. This an unanswerable argument for Christian obedience to the state. 3. It is admitted that "by means of society not only is the race preserved, but civilisation is developed." Therefore maintain government. 4. The only basis of commercial enterprise is a thoroughly substantial government. Political crises influence the trade of a country. When Philip II. of Spain pursued his suicidal policy in the Netherlands, merchants transferred their workshops to England.

III. **Here also we have the principle of Christian brotherhood.**—1. We are to render to the individual his or her due. What men's dues are is measured by the fact that Christianity has taught men to consider each man a brother. 2. The worldly usage is that the great are honoured at the expense of the more humble. This is anti-Christian. 3. The spirit of forbearance is exhibited in the text. A disgrace to professors of religion is the habit of fault-finding, the lack of a charitable spirit. If we want to be Christlike, we shall not repay people's faults and forget their excellences. "When a leaf drops and dies, it goes down to mingle with the ground. When moss falls off, it disappears. Everything in nature, as it decays, hides itself." And so it should be in human life. 4. God's attitude that of forgetfulness of our faults. Love has sat on heaven's throne rather than judgment. And so it comes to pass that "the base of this low altarstair of suffering slopes through darkness up to the everlasting heavens, and far, far within their piercing deeps love is enthroned for ever." Cannot man learn of his God? Even the dying Christ thought first of the pardon of His murderers: "Father, forgive them." Let every man strive in his human degree to traverse the divine range of sympathy. It is not so much doctrine or creed that we want, as that Christlike spirit of love that will enable us to love God and also man—the spirit that will enable us to overcome every obstacle, and, like the Master, "bear one another's burdens."—*Albert Lee.*

Ver. 7. *Legal and moral dues.*—It has been sometimes objected that preachers put too much of the gospel into their sermons, and do not speak sufficiently of the every-day duties of life. St. Paul binds himself to the gospel, and so must his followers. But we shall not understand the gospel aright if we do not bear in mind the fact that it is to teach men to be good citizens of earth as well as of heaven. Christianity leaves no part of the nature, and no portion of society untouched; it speaks to rulers and ruled, to kings and subjects, to parents and their children. The New Testament lays down general laws by which men are to be guided in the affairs of life. The best all-round man is the one who makes a sensible application of those laws in the management of his earthly affairs. We are to bring heaven down to earth, and thus make it more blessed.

I. **Christianity teaches classification.** — There is method observable in the material universe : lower and higher forms of life—vegetable life, animal life, and intellectual life. Creation culminates in man, and in the human animal there are differences—some excel in strength and others in wisdom. God has set men in societies where there are differences; He instituted the family, which is the germ and type of all true human societies. As there are differences in the family, so will there be differences in the clan, the tribe, the nation : the rich and the poor dwell together. Where the right spirit reigns all will work together so as to make the commonwealth strong, healthy, and happy : the king will be the true father of his subjects, and they will be his faithful children.

II. **Christianity inculcates discrimination.** — It differentiates between the powers. There are higher powers and lower powers, and those who have little or no power. It seems to point out that all have their dues. Tribute is the due of one power, custom of another, fear of a third, and honour of a fourth. Shall we go far wrong if we say that honour is due to all who have not rendered themselves vile, ignoble, and utterly dishonourable ? Thus there is not only the material due, the money payment, but there are intellectual or moral dues, the payment of fear and honour. Enough has not been done when the taxes are paid. There is the emotional tribute. We are not only to uphold the throne and constitution, not only to obey our country's laws, not only to respect the magistrates and judges of the land, but to give to all men their dues. Each man has his rights, which must be respected. Shall we render to *all* their dues if we rob God? The man who robs God would rob his fellow, providing a safe opportunity were presented. What is due from the creature to the Creator? Thankfulness at least is due. Cicero said that thankfulness is the mother of all virtues. Even the very heathen said that all evil is spoken in this one word—viz., "unthankfulness." Gratitude is God's due for His wisdom and power in creation, for His mercy in preservation, for His love and grace in redemption. Life is due to Him who gave His life. Love is due to Him who poured out an infinite wealth of love upon the world. Let us live our thanks. Let our lives be made fragrant and beautiful by the influence of grateful hearts.

III. **Christianity proclaims responsibility.**—Some one said, "It is a solemn thing to die," which was met by the reply, "It is a solemn thing to live." Surely a solemn thing to live, for none of us can live to ourselves. We are debtors, whether we like it or not, to our fellows. A self-contained, self-included life is impossible. The hermit in his cave, the naturalist in his hut, the monk in his cell, cannot completely shut themselves out from their fellows. And in the present complex state of society we may well be startled as we think of the responsibilities of life. How vast the debt we owe to our fellow-creatures ! How much larger the debt we owe to God and to Jesus Christ ! How much is due to Jesus Christ, who has done more to shape human destinies into divine forms, to bless the world, to beautify existence, than all the monarchs, statesmen, warriors, philosophers, and moralists of time ! Our debt to Jesus Christ is so great that had we a thousand lives to give they would not be adequate to discharge the claim. And yet He asks no more than each is able to give. He asks thy love, thy life, thy all. Give thy life to Jesus, and He will so ennoble the offering that it will be no longer poor. Give thy love to Jesus, and He will increase it so that it will become like a live coal within thee from God's altar, and thy nature will be all aglow with the celestial flame. If thus we love Jesus, we shall learn to love our fellows more, and we shall learn from Jesus to render to all their dues. How kind, gentle, and considerate He was to all men and women ! He paid to the higher powers the tax which was required. He paid to the lower orders help and sympathy. He paid the tax of tears where tears were due; He paid the tax of sorrowful lamentations where woe was impending; He paid the tax of a sacrificed life upon the altar erected by human need and divine requirement. In the light of His large life we shall learn to take a complete view of the words, "Render to all their dues." A holy life is due to infinite goodness, to human wretchedness, to God, to angels, and to men, to others and to ourselves. We should all strive so to live that others may take knowledge of us that we have been with Jesus, as some did of the early believers. Helpful is the thought that Jesus is no hard taskmaster. He notices the right intention; He approves the pure motive and the earnest purpose. Let us go forward seeking to render to all their dues.

Ver. 10. *The last analysis.*—The first golden stair is this : we ask, What is the origin of love? Christianity answers, *Love is of God.* Hatred, then, is not of God; it is of the devil. Selfishness, jealousy, envy, all that spoils the gentle and the perfect life in us—heedlessness of others, forgetfulness of the wishes and the hopes of others, the egoism which ignores others, to say nothing of the sarcastic tongue which delights to inflict pain, or the vanity which will sacrifice a reputation for a stroke of wit, or the ambition which bustles all weaker folk aside that it may reach its own coveted goal—all this is not of God. The original impress of God upon this world was an impress of love There was a time when gentleness, tenderness, considerateness, stamped the whole creation. Wherever you find these qualities still, they are of God; something saved out of the wreck of man, fair stretches of green landscape not submerged beneath the flood of evil, or else recovered from it. God is love, and love is of God. "Every one that loveth is born of God." It follows, then, that there is a second golden stair which we may climb. "Love is of God"—that is the first stair. The second is *Love in morality.* "Love," says the apostle Paul, "is the fulfilling of the law." Let us pause again, and ask, "What then is law?" Law is a series of instructions and restraints to make us like God. It begins at the very lowest level of things, and tells us not to steal, not to covet, not to lie, and not to murder. But these crimes and vices are not so much causes as effects. And you may take the commandments one by one, and apply this test to them, and you will see at once that they would not have been needed if only men had loved one another. Get love then, and you cannot help keeping the law. Get love, and you cannot help being moral. It may seem but a scanty equipment to produce perfection, and so the seven notes of music may seem to be a scanty equipment to produce the heaven-born melodies of a Handel or Beethoven. But see how they use them—of what infinite and glorious combinations are they capable! So it is with this supreme quality of love. It is capable of all but infinite combinations and interpretations; it utters the grand music of heroism and the soft lute music of courtesy; it is patriotism, altruism, martyrdom; it stoops to the smallest things of life and governs the greatest; it controls the temper and regulates the reason; it extirpates the worst qualities and refines the best. Go one step further. Love is of God; love is morality; now you find that love is religion also. "Every one that loveth is born of God." How often do we find in the communion of other Churches men who surprise us by the spirituality and the saintliness of their lives! We hold such Churches, perhaps, to be in error; but where love reigns there is morality. And then take one more golden stair. Love is of God; love is morality; love is religion; lastly, love is life, love is immortality. "Every one that loveth is born of God"—born into a larger life. We sometimes permit ourselves to debate whether life is not more than love. There are times when we are impressed with the spaciousness of this life of ours, when we suddenly realise the joys of living, and are athirst to drink a full draught of life. We want to know everything, we want to understand everything; we would fain mix in the most crowded places of life, and feel the pulsations of the tide of humanity, and move amid its swiftest currents; and in such an hour we ask ourselves, What is love? Surely it is nothing more than a mere episode in the great drama, one of the many fruits of life—perhaps the choicest, but that is all. For when that passion of mere living possesses us it eclipses all other passions, and then we turn away from love because we see that it is a yoke, because we believe it to be a renunciation of the fulness of personal life, because it is the subjugation of our nature to the exigencies and the needs of another nature. The man and woman who do this usually live to learn that love, after all, is the one thing worth living for, and they often know what it is to sit amidst the ruins of life in a friendless old age, amidst gains and gauds that have lost their charm, and to long with inexpressible yearning for one drop of that cup which they once so contemptuously rejected. For the truth is that love is life; it is the only true and eternal life; it is the birth of a man's soul into a higher state of being. There, then, as I have said, is the last analysis of Christianity, and I pray you to accept it. Like all profound things, it is really simple; it is in fact so simple that men doubt whether it can be true. Men cannot make themselves believe and understand that Christianity is merely love, that a great church is simply the temple of love, that what all this elaborate organisation of worship and preaching aims at is this—to teach men to love God, to love each other. And so I rejoice. I see a world that is not outcast, not wholly evil, and not forsaken, for love works in it still, and God is love, and love is everywhere. Like a great bell of hope, mellow, ceaseless, glorious in its music, the words of John ring across the world, "Every one that loveth is born of God, and knoweth God."—*W. G. Dawson.*

SUGGESTIVE COMMENTS ON VERSES 7—10.

Custom.—There is some difficulty about the distinctive signification of φόρος (tribute) and τέλος (custom). By some the former is regarded as a tax upon land; by others, as upon property generally, whether movable or immovable. Those critics who give to φόρος the wider signification limit τέλος to a capitation tax; and those who confine φόρος to a tax upon land give τέλος a larger meaning, as signifying a tax upon merchandise as well as upon persons. Judging from the apostle's use of the word, φόρος was the general term for all contributions, and was used in the same sense that the word "taxes" is largely used; and in its limited sense it applies to all burdens upon landed or personal property; while τέλος was the capitation tax which our Lord told Peter to pay for himself and his Lord.—*Knight.*

"*Honour to whom honour.*"—Christians are not to neglect the laws of social life, or overlook the fact that distinction of rank is highly necessary for the economy and safety of the world. This precept especially claims our thoughtful attention in an age when an increase of knowledge, prosperity, and political freedom has removed many of the material props upon which the influence of parents and masters and those placed over us formerly rested. We might, with advantage, take a useful hint from the Lacedæmonians, who laid such stress on the training of their youth to give honour to whom honour was due.—*Neil.*

Christian brotherhood.—Love will not permit us to injure, oppress, or offend our brother; it will not give us leave to neglect our betters or despise our inferiors. It will restrain every inordinate passion, and not suffer us to gratify our envy at the expense of our neighbour's credit and reputation; but it will preserve us harmless and innocent.—*Sherlock.*

MAIN HOMILETICS OF THE PARAGRAPH.—Verse 11.

The Christian's duty and encouragement.—Different views are taken of time. Some seem to regard it as a useless commodity, to be frittered away in vain trifles. Others consider it too short for the work to be accomplished. Thus some hoard and others squander time. The majority do not look beyond the bounds of time. It is not to them fraught with eternal issues. Time, however, to the Christian is important, for it is the pathway to eternity. Time impresses eternity. How solemn the thought! All time's thoughts, words, and deeds have a bearing upon the future. How seasonable the petition, " so teach us to number our days that we may apply our hearts unto wisdom "!

I. **The Christian's knowledge.**—The Christian is or should be a man who knows. Principally he should know the season, the period, in which he lives. It is difficult in these days to know the season. This is a time of great perplexity. The world has both changed and enlarged since the days of primitive Christianity. The man who knows the time in these days is a man of extensive knowledge. Still, the Christian may know the time as far more advanced than it was eighteen centuries since. He may know that great interests are at stake. He should know that increased activity is demanded, that overwhelming zeal is required. In these days, when wealth on the one side and poverty on the other are increased, when licentiousness, lawlessness, selfishness, and indifference still prevail to an alarming extent, it becomes the Christian to keep his intellect alive to the stirring events of his period.

II. **The Christian's duty.**—" To awake out of sleep." If the apostle's time demanded wakeful spirits, much more do these times. Alas, how many so-called Christians are fast asleep! The enemy is upon them, and they do not heed the approach. Their dreams are of sweet music and of pleasant services. They are not awake to the calls of duty. They become somnambulists, and walk away from the voice of God's messenger directing them to the post of duty. Such require a thunder-peal from heaven to awake them from sleep. It is consolatory to reflect that some are awake. But none are so wide awake as to be without need of the apostolic injunction which says that it is high time to awake out of sleep. We must shake off the torpor of indifference. Sleepy men are an easy prey to evil. By sleep we put on strength, but by moral sleep we induce weakness. Awake, awake, O Church of the living God, and put on immortal strength!

III. **The Christian's encouragement.**—" Now is our salvation nearer than when we believed." The period of completed salvation is fast approaching. Every beat of the minute-hand tells its advent. Salvation in prospect was accomplished when Jesus said, " It is finished." Salvation is secured when faith lays hold on the Saviour. Salvation is perfected when the redeemed spirit enters into the perfect rest of heaven; and every moment of the believer's life brings that completed salvation nearer. There are two advents to the soul: the first advent when Christ enters into that soul and is in it the hope of glory; the second advent when either Christ will come to the soul at His second coming, or when that soul shall go to be with Christ in paradise. The blest reunion is fast approaching. Here there is a union of faith; yonder there will be a union of sight. We are united with Christ by faith. We shall be reunited, perfectly united, to Christ by blissful vision. That union will be a perfect salvation from all that harasses in the present state. The prospect is stimulating. It quickens the drowsy powers; it delivers from lethargy. As the sailor draws nearer to his native land, after a prolonged absence, every sense is quickened, and he puts on fresh energy. As the runner is nearing the goal he takes quicker steps; his eyes catch a new light; he forgets the strain in his eagerness to win the prize.

What buoyancy takes possession of the inventor's spirit when after years, it may be, of experimenting he finds himself within measurable reach of the desired discovery! Shall the Christian runner lag when the prize of eternal glory is almost within reach? Shall the Christian sailor sleep, after the storms and buffetings of time, when the clear lights of heaven shine across the intervening waters? The sound of the harpers on the eternal shores greets his ears, and he can no longer slumber. From this dim cloud-land of partial knowledge he is hastening to the sphere of the complete unfolding of many mysteries, and his soul is all eagerness to enter upon the all-revealing light of eternity. It is high time to awake out of sleep, for the times are busy, for the world is pressing close, and the other world is letting down dazzling views of its surpassing glory.

Knowledge of time.—We should know time in its:—

I. **Worth.**—Estimated at the value of: 1. *Life.* Time the measure of life of a being capable of thought, endowed with conscience, gifted with immortality. 2. *What able to be done during its progress.*

II. **Responsibilities.**—Our relation to God. Knowledge of salvation. Duties in our sphere of life. Influence we exert. Ignatius when heard clock strike said, "Now I have one hour more to account for."

III. **Uncertainty.**—Commercial institutions and projects abundantly prove this, but he who counts on time presumes on probability that has even more impressively proved its questionableness (James iv. 13, 14).

IV. **Brevity.**

V. **Powerlessness.**—It cannot destroy sin or take away its guilt. It cannot act for us. It cannot destroy the soul, though it end the life.

VI. **Irrevocableness.**—*G. McMichael, B.A.*

Self-denial the test of religious earnestness.—By "sleep" in this passage St. Paul means a state of insensibility to things as they really are in God's sight. Thus, whether in private families or in the world, in all the ranks of middle life men lie under a considerable danger at this day, a more than ordinary danger, of self-deception, of being asleep while they think themselves awake. How, then, shall we try ourselves? Can any tests be named which will bring certainty to our minds on the subject? No indisputable tests can be given. We cannot know for certain. We must beware of an impatience about knowing what our real state is. We cannot, indeed, make ourselves as sure of our being in the number of God's true servants as the early Christians were; yet we may possess our degree of certainty, and by the same kind of evidence—the evidence of self-denial. This was the great evidence which the first disciples gave, and which we can give still. The self-denial which is the test of our faith must be daily. The word "daily" implies that the self-denial which is pleasing to Christ consists in little things. This is plain, for opportunity for great self-denials does not come every day. Thus to take up the cross of Christ is no great action done once for all; it consists in the continual practice of small duties which are distasteful to us. If, then, a person ask how he is to know whether he is dreaming on in the world's slumber or is really awake and alive unto God, let him first fix his mind upon some one or other of his besetting sins. It is right then almost to find out for yourself daily self-denials, and this because our Lord bids you take up your cross daily, and because it proves your earnestness, and because by so doing you strengthen your general power of self-mastery and come to have such an habitual command of yourself as will be a defence ready prepared when the season of temptation comes. Let not your words run on; force every one of them into cation as it goes; and thus cleansing yourself from all pollution of the flesh and spirit, perfect holiness in the fear of God. In dreams we sometimes move our arms to see if we are awake or not, and so are wakened. This is the way to keep your heart awake also. Try yourself daily in little deeds to prove that your faith is more than a deceit.—*Newman.*

SUGGESTIVE COMMENTS ON VERSE 11.

Christian's view of time.—What is the true measure of time? I know that the outward measures are accurate enough; and when a man says to his friend, "Another year is gone," they understand a certain space which can be precisely computed; but if acts and activity are the true measures of time for us, and not the hands on the clock, nor the changing path of the sun, then it may be well doubted whether in fact we do know at the end of a year what or how much it is that has gone away from us. A year of earnest work in the way of duty and for the cause of God, a year of amusement, a year marked by tasting first and then drinking deep of the foul cup of some new sin, a year marked by a great change of character for the better, in which he that once served sin has made up his mind, through God's help, to serve it no more—any of these may be included under the phrase, "Another year has passed." Out of the looms of time a measured portion of the web of our life has come: the measure the same for all, the texture and the tints how different! Nay, are there not even single minutes in which the scattered lights of our thoughts are gathered into one focus, and burn an indelible imprint into the soul? A man went once to Damascus, and a light from heaven struck him blind, and the Spirit of Christ, more penetrating than that light, sent deep into his conscience the unanswerable question, "Why persecutest thou Me?" The man was St. Paul, and that minute bore in it the germ of the Church of the Gentiles and of *our* knowledge of the Redeemer. A careless student was walking with his friend, when a flash of lightning struck the friend dead and awoke the student out of his worldliness. Luther was that student, and the Reformation be-

gan from that terrible instant. Minutes like these are not to be reckoned only at their value as fractional portions of a year. Time has a quality as it has a quantity. We cannot be sure that a single day or year may not carry in it the decision of our eternity. There may be no great sign or wonder to tell us so; to all around the weight of another year upon us may seem no greater than in time past. But every part of us is growing. Habits are strengthening, feelings growing calmer, the advice of others losing its influence over us, the circle of those who might have the right to advise is fast contracting. And it is surely possible that when we are only conscious that a year is gone, our whole life, so far at least as life is a state of probation admitting of change and improvement, may have passed away with it.—*Archbishop Thomson.*

"*High time to awake out of sleep.*"— These words regard Christians themselves. This is undeniable, from the motive subjoined: "For now is our salvation nearer than when we believed." Are *believers*, then, asleep? Not in the sense they once were—this would be impossible. But there are found even in *them* some remains of their former depravity. Though the good work is begun in them, it is far from being accomplished. While the bridegroom tarried, even the wise virgins slumbered and slept. Yes, Christians are often in a drowsy frame. This is sadly reproachful. Yet if the address be proper for Christians, how much more necessary is it for those who are entirely regardless of the things that belong to their peace!—if we consider how long they have been sleeping! We ought to lament that we have lost *any* of our precious hours and opportunities. However short it may have been, the time past of our life should more than suffice, wherein we have lived to the will of man. What then should those feel who have sacrificed the whole of their youth—perhaps the vigour of mature age? What should those feel who perhaps have grown grey in the service of sin and the world? The later we begin, the more zealous should we be to redeem the advantages we have lost, and to overtake those who were wise enough to set off early. High time—if we consider that the day is arrived and the sun is risen so high. "The night is far spent," etc. We can say more than the apostle. The night *is* spent; the day is *fully come.* And we are all the children of the light and the children of the day; we are not of the night, nor of darkness. *Therefore* let us not sleep as do others. "They that sleep, sleep in the night." Our obligations always increase with our advantages. To him that knoweth to do good, and doeth it not, to him it is sin. And the servant that knew his lord's will, and prepared not himself, shall be beaten with many stripes; for where much is given much will be required. High time—if we consider the business they have to do. I am doing, said Nehemiah to some who would have interrupted him; I cannot come down to you—I am

doing a great work. How much more may a Christian say this! He has an enterprise connected with the soul and God and eternity. Some things are desirable, and some are useful; but this is absolutely indispensable—

"Sufficient in itself alone;
And needful, were the world our own."

Neglect in many a concern is injurious; but here it is ruinous—ruinous of everything, and ruinous for ever. High time—if we consider the nature of the season in which this difficult and all-important work is to be accomplished. It is short, and there is but a step between us and death. It is uncertain in its continuance, and may be terminated every moment by some of those numberless dangers to which we are exposed : once gone, it can never be renewed. High time—if we consider the danger they are in. If a man were sleeping in a house and the fire were seen, who would not think it high time for him to awake and escape for his life? This is but a weak representation of the danger of sinners. They are condemned already. High time to awake out of sleep—if we consider that all besides are awake. God, glorified saints, the children of this generation, devils, and death, are awake. "It is high time to awake out of sleep."—*W. Jay.*

MAIN HOMILETICS OF THE PARAGRAPH.—*Verse 12.*

Proper equipment.—It is proper that the children of light should put on the armour of light. There is a charm about that which is suitable and proper. The painting is attractive which is in harmony with our feeling and is the expression of our unformulated thoughts. A piece of music delights when it pleasantly touches the emotions and finds its echo in our natures. Nature clothes herself in colours suitable to the varying seasons. And the children of light should be arrayed in that which is suitable to the character. They must cast off the works of darkness. Nothing dark, unholy, or degrading should appear. They must put on the armour of light, stand ready for defence, and appear as those who can grace the company of followers who shall attend the Lord Jesus.

I. **The Christian's state is one of preparation.**—The foolish virgins who had no oil in their lamps were to blame. Their sin was one of omission. They could have provided oil, and yet failed. We are exhorted to prepare ourselves, to be in a state of preparation, and we shall be without excuse if we refuse to obey. God's storehouse is open and available. In the Tower of London we look at the armour, but we are not permitted to touch. In God's tower there is a large supply of armour, and each may therefrom supply his need. If at the last day we are asked why we have not on the armour of light, we shall be speechless. As summer draws nigh nature puts on her brightest hues and gayest colours. The lightsome season of the Saviour's second advent draws nigh. Winter's chilling frosts, howling blasts, and tossing tempests are disappearing; the sun seems to show fresh power, and sails along the azure sky with renewed splendour. We must be ready and clothed with light for the lightsome season. The Bridegroom is coming; the lights are in the distance; the music is sounding. Our hearts answer to the glad summons.

II. **The Christian's state is one of development.**—All great things are gradual in their development. The tree of rapid growth does not produce valuable timber, while the tree of slow growth becomes a prize in the market. The Christian character is great, and one which is not to be rapidly formed. Like the good tree, the Christian must gather strength and beauty alike from the winter's storms and the summer's gentle gale. There are sudden conversions. St. Paul was suddenly converted, but he says, "Let us cast away the works of darkness, and put on the armour of light." Conversion is the starting-point. It sets the man forth on a new career. He then begins to cast away the works of darkness. The more rapidly it is done the better. Justification is instantaneous, while sanctification is gradual. It may be objected that the dying thief went straight to paradise, and passed through no long periods of discipline. But we cannot tell what experiences were gone through in the short interval between the thief's conversion and his entrance into paradise. Further, we are not to judge God's ordinary rules of procedure by His extraordinary. Neither in nature nor in grace does the infinite Worker proceed by leaps, bounds, and surprises. We see method and gradual processes. If there be "faults" and dislocations, they may be taken as the exceptions which prove the rule. The Christian life is not a stagnant existence, but a growth—not a leap, but a walk—not a startling bound, but a development, a gradual and secret unfolding.

III. **The Christian's state is one of glory.**—It is a mistake to suppose that all the glory of the Christian character is to be referred to the future of eternity. There is glory in the present. Is not the light glorious? Natural, intellectual, and moral light are all glorious. The glory of God is seen in the fact that He dwells in light inaccessible. The glory of Jesus Christ is set forth in the circumstance that He is the light of the world. The mountain is glorious when the sun shines full upon it, and brings out to view its grandeur and beauty. The Christian is glorious when arrayed in the armour of light which reflects the glory of the eternal Light. Doddridge well explains: "The armour of light of those Christian graces which, like burnished and beautiful armour, would be at once an ornament and a defence, that which would reflect the bright beams that were so gloriously rising upon them. The Christian army should stand like soldiers ready for the battle with all their armour brightly polished. The glory is manifest as there shines upon them the bright beams of the Sun of righteousness."

IV. **The Christian's state is one of safety.**—The Christian is safe when he is rightly armed and makes a wise use of his weapons—when his frame is strengthened, his arm nerved, and his hand directed by the Holy Spirit. The sword of the Spirit is not like the swords of this world. This sword may be successfully used by the weak and feeble, if there be strong faith and earnest prayer. The Christian is safe as he puts on the armour of light and keeps it in constant wear. He is protected behind and before. When the king of Israel went up to Ramoth Gilead to battle, a certain man drew a bow at a venture, and smote the king of Israel between the joints of the harness. The armour of light is so constructed that no arrow can pierce the joints so as to destroy. On the moral battle-plains not one of God's royal sons can be slain. The Christian soldier may fall, but he only falls to rise victorious.

V. **The Christian's state should be one of cheerfulness.**—It is a cheerful thing to dwell in the light. The Preacher says, " The light is sweet, and a pleasant thing it is for the eyes to behold the sun." Heaven's own light is sweet, and a pleasant thing it is to behold the Sun of righteousness. He is never hid by clouds, except those of our own making; He never scorches with withering beams : He ever diffuses plenty and beauty. What a pity that we cannot always be cheerful! Let us feel that we are the children of light.

> " Your harps, ye trembling saints,
>   Down from the willows take ;
> Loud to the praise of love divine
>   Bid every string awake."

Let us wear the armour of light which is the garb of joy and cheerfulness.

The armour of light.—What is that armour of light which is spoken of in the text ? The Christian, whilst on earth, is a member of the Church militant ; he must pass through successive contests, and be defended against various attacks, at once insidious and hurtful ; nor is he to be content with merely escaping unhurt ; he is to act on the offensive ; he is to carry on a warfare against his enemies, as well as defend himself against any warfare which they wage against him. " Having your loins girt about with truth." There is first the girdle, intended to give support, by which St. Paul indicates *sincerity* ; next, the " breastplate of righteousness," a word signifying holiness, " and your feet . . . peace," signifying readiness ; next, " the shield of faith," to " quench the darts of the devil " ; next, " the helmet, which is the hope of salvation " ; and finally, " the sword of the Spirit, which is the word of God." Why is it called "the armour of light " ? First, with reference to its origin, which is heavenly ; and next, because it is only found where Christianity exists and exerts its proper influence. No man is seen in the armour of light but a true Christian. Man was never seen thus armed but under its influence or under some of the corresponding and earlier dispensations of it to mankind. Thirdly, it is called " the armour of light " because it corresponds with the character of our dispensation, which is a dispensation of light. There are many persons who see and acknowledge the necessity of gaining those spiritual victories to which alone the crown of life is promised, and therefore they begin to war what in itself is the good warfare, but they do not consider what kind of weapons they use or what it is that they trust as the means of success. Some trust in their own native strength ; but how does that correspond with the religion of which it is one of the first principles that all our strength is but weakness, and when we were without strength Christ died for the ungodly? Others trust to the firmness of their own resolves, while this religion tells them that, even in the early and first stage of gracious influence itself, which has brought them to acknowledge the excellence of divine law, when they would do good evil is present with them. Others, again, trust to their increasing acquaintance with Christian doctrine, as if supposing that there is some secret charm in this knowledge which shall sanctify the heart and transform the character. What are the motives which should induce us to array ourselves in this armour ? The first motive is derived from a consideration of the degraded state of the man who is not invested with this armour—degraded at all times, but degraded more especially when the absence of all those principles which constitute the armour of light is the result of his own rejection of the truth and gospel of Christ, What is a man without sincerity as to God? He is a hypocrite whom God will by-and-by expose. What is a man without holiness but an offensive sinner in the sight of God? The second motive is the moral elevation which this armour gives to every one who is invested with it. This moral elevation is one great end of our life, and ought to be the grand object of our ambition. The ambition of being distinguished among men, of standing high in the opinion of the world, is from beneath, and not from the Father, and will always tend to the grovelling source from which it springs; but the grace of God from its first commencement in the soul kindles a noble ambition in the soul to rise higher and higher in the scale of moral attainment.—*R. Watson.*

SUGGESTIVE COMMENTS ON VERSE 12.

Our duty in view of the approaching day. — "The night is far spent, the day is at hand: let us therefore cast off the works of darkness, and let us put on the armour of light." St. Paul speaks in this chapter of great and important duties — duties devolving upon all men, and most certainly and especially on disciples of Jesus Christ. Besides the duties named, he tells us that every other duty is comprehended in that of love— the divine law of love—and says plainly, "Love is the fulfilling of the law." And it is certain that love towards God will prompt to pure devotion, sincere worship, and acceptable obedience; love towards men will refrain from injury, and restrain from all that may hurt our character, prospects, and interests. "Love worketh no ill to his neighbour." Our time on earth is short; the longest life passes swiftly away. It is therefore supremely important that we use it to the best advantage. "Knowing the time"—its uncertainty, its dangers, the obligations it brings—an injunction as to the duty of "redeeming the time," should be regarded as most weighty and urgent. We ought to "awake" to our responsibilities, and be keenly alive to the solemnities of our state; if we are believing with our hearts unto righteousness as we approach the goal, the end of our course, "our salvation is nearer" and more fully assured.

I. **The night of ignorance, doubt, and difficulty is, for the believer, rapidly passing.**—The night of mere ceremonialism, the night of ignorance,

and the darkness of evil cannot last for ever. Many of the first Christian converts were brought up in Judaism, and were not free from the prejudices which then clung to it: from these they were partially delivered. All of them were ignorant of Messiah's true claims and offices until they had heard the gospel preached; then many of the clouds were rolled away, "the darkness was past, and the true light now shined" upon them. Still it was not yet perfect day, the night was not altogether past; there had been doubts: "Can there any good come out of Nazareth?" "Art Thou He that should come, or look we for another?" Much doubt had been removed; the night was far spent. To very many of us the darkness of this earthly life is a thing of the past; difficulties innumerable have been faced, and yielded to or overcome: we have "dragged hard uphill this heavy load of death called life"; but we begin to see light streaming from the distant hills, and soon it shall fill the vales. "The night is far spent."

II. **The day of deliverance from evil, of the assurance of hope, of the enjoyment of true Christian grace and peace, nay, the day of eternal redemption in all its blessedness, is at hand.**—The believer is in the possession of much that is valuable—peace, inward and spiritual grace, freedom from guilt—but all this is but as a drop in a bucket compared with what is to come. "*Now* are we the sons of God, and it doth not yet appear what we shall be: but we know that when He

shall appear we shall be like Him."
The night of death cometh, but even
then "there shall be light"; and that
comparative darkness is to be followed
by the glory of eternal day. *Now* we
have a foretaste of the good in store—
love, joy, peace, "rest" in the grace of
Christ; but it is a promise and pledge
of more:

"So glittering *here* the drops of light;
There, the full ocean rolls how bright."

But in many senses "the day is at
hand," as the law and fact of progress
show—as the advance of knowledge,
science, arts, etc., sufficiently indicates:
"we are on the eve" of great discoveries, greater than have yet been
made, and man shall prove in the
grandest sense to be "but a little
lower than the angels."

III. There must be the absolute
and complete renunciation of sinful
desires, habits, and works, and the
assumption of holiness, inward and
outward, which St. Paul calls "the
armour of light," because righteousness
is a defence of the soul against evil
and the powers of evil. Sinful practices are called works of darkness,
because the thought of them is conceived in souls unillumined by spiritual
knowledge and divine grace. "Men
love darkness rather than light, because
their deeds are evil." As the worst
crimes are commonly committed in
darkness or in secrecy, darkness becomes quite naturally the emblem of
wrong-doing in general, and also of
wrong-thinking. Every thought of
work contrary to the spirit of Christianity is to be rejected and abhorred.
The believer assumes "the armour of
light," "the armour of righteousness"
(see Eph. vi. 11-18), when he, in repentance, fully accepts Christ and determines to live in and by His blessed
religion. There is no defence on earth
against temptation and sin equal to
that which we derive from the teaching,
example, and grace of our Lord Jesus
Christ: he who has righteousness of
heart and holiness of life is strong,—
strong in all time, however trying or
adverse; strong even in the greatest
bodily suffering; strong in the Lord.—
Dr. Burrows.

Time is short in retrospect.—"Knowing the time"—the time of this our
mortal life. How soon it will be over,
at the longest! How short the time
seems since we were young; how
quickly it has gone! How every year
as we grow older seems to go more and
more quickly, and there is less time to
do what we want, to think seriously,
to improve ourselves! So soon, and it
will be over and we shall have no time
at all, for we shall be in eternity. And
what then? What then? That depends on what now, on what we are
doing now. Are we letting our short
span of life slip away in sleep, fancying
ourselves all the while wide awake, as
we do in dreams, till we wake really,
and find that it is daylight and that
all our best dreams were nothing but
useless fancy? How many dream away
their lives!—some upon gain, some upon
pleasure, some upon petty self-interest,
petty quarrels, petty ambitions, petty
squabbles and jealousies about this
person and that, which are no more
worthy to take up a reasonable human
being's time and thoughts than so
many dreams would be. Some, too,
dream away their lives in sin, in works
of darkness which they are forced for
shame and safety to hide, lest they
should come to the light and be exposed. So people dream their lives
away, and go about their daily business
as men who walk in their sleep, wandering about with their eyes open and
yet seeing nothing of what is really
around them—seeing nothing, though
they think that they see and know
their own interest, and are shrewd
enough to find their way about this
world. But they know nothing—
nothing of the very world with which
they pride themselves they are so
thoroughly acquainted. None know
less of the world than those who pride
themselves on being men of the world;
for the true light which shines all
around them they do not see, and

therefore they do not see the truth of things by that light—if they did, then they would see that of which now they do not even dream.—*Charles Kingsley.*

God made this life; therefore good.— For is not this mortal life, compared with that life to come, as night compared with day? I do not mean to speak evil of it; God forbid that we should say impiously to Him, Why hast Thou made me thus? No; God made this mortal life, and therefore, like all things which He has made, it is very good. But there are good nights and there are bad nights, and there are happy lives and unhappy ones. But what are they at best? What is the life of the happiest man without the Holy Spirit of God? A night full of pleasant dreams. What is the life of the wisest man? A night of darkness, through which he gropes his way by lanthorn light, slowly and with many mistakes and stumbles. When we compare man's vast capabilities with his small deeds, when we think how much he might know, how little he does know in this mortal life, can we wonder that the highest spirits in every age have looked on death as a deliverance out of darkness and a dungeon? And if this is life at the best, what is life at the worst? To how many is life a night, not of peace and rest, but of tossing and weariness, pain and sickness, anxiety and misery, till they are ready to cry, When will it be over? When will kind death come and give me rest? When will the night of this life be spent and the day of God arise? "Out of the depths have I cried unto Thee, O Lord. Lord, hear my voice. . . . My soul doth wait for the Lord, more than the sick man who watches for the morning."— *Charles Kingsley.*

A double inference.—On the one hand the night deepened, on the other the day drew near. The former of these figures signifies that the time granted to the present world to continue its life without God had moved on, was shortened; the latter, that the appearing of the kingdom of Christ had approached. Hence a double inference. As the night is dissipated, there should be an end to the works of the night; and as the day begins to shine, awaking should be completed, and there should be effected what may be called the toilet worthy of the day. The works of darkness: all that dare not be done by day, and which is reserved for night. The term ὅπλα may be translated in two ways: the instruments or arms of light. The parallel (1 Thess. v. 4-11) speaks in favour of the second sense. In that case the reference would be to the breastplate, the helmet, the sandals of the Roman soldiers, arms which may be regarded as garments fitted on in the morning to replace the dress of night. But the delineation as a whole does not seem to apply to a day of battle; rather it appears that the day in question is one of peaceful labour. And for this reason we think it more natural to apply the expression here to the garments of the laborious workman who, from early morning, holds himself in readiness for the hour when his master waits to give him his task.— *Godet.*

A difference between the primitive and modern Church.—The primitive Church was more under the influence of the lust of the flesh than of the pride of life; the modern Church is more under the influence of the pride of life than of the lust of the flesh. But pride is as great a sin in the sight of God as sensuality. This should be considered in forming an estimate of the modern missionary Church.— *Shedd.*

The certainty and the uncertainty of the event beneficial.—The fact that the nearness or distance of the day of Christ's coming was unknown to the apostles in no way affects the prophetic announcements of God's Spirit by them concerning its preceding and accompanying circumstances. The day and hour formed no part of their inspiration;

435

the details of the event did. And this distinction has singularly and providentially turned out to the edification of all subsequent ages. While the prophetic declarations of the events of that time remain to instruct us, the eager expectation of that time, which they expressed in their day, has also remained a token of the true frame of mind in which each succeeding age should contemplate the ever-approaching coming of the Lord. On the certainty of the event our faith is grounded; by the uncertainty of the event our hope is stimulated and our watchfulness aroused.—*Alford.*

MAIN HOMILETICS OF THE PARAGRAPH.—*Verses* 13, 14.

A graceful walk.—It would be a gain to the cause of holy living if Christians could be led to feel and to act as if the daylight were round about them, making bare all their actions, words, and thoughts. Men and women have too great a tendency to act as if they were children of the night. They have the vain fancy that they are shrouded by the darkness, but the mistake is seen when a beam of light falls upon their pathway, and tells them that there can be no such thing as darkness in God's nature and in God's moral government. There is night to the children of men, but there is no night to God, and there should be no night to the children of eternity. They should walk as children of the day. The clear day reveals blemishes which escape notice in the murky light. We are to think of ourselves as walking in the clear day, in the revealing sunlight. When the sun shines into the room it reveals dust dancing in the atmosphere; and so when the sun of divine requirements shines into the chambers of our souls it shows our own imperfections. Let us not be afraid of the light, but let us be afraid of that which the light makes known. Let us walk honestly, gracefully, handsomely, as in the day. What are the characteristics of a graceful Christian walk? How is a Christian to bear himself handsomely?

I. **The man will walk handsomely who exercises the knowing faculty.**—This is the proud prerogative of man—that he knows—and which sets him at the head of the lower creation. The perfect flower is well shaped in form, beautiful and attractive in colour, and sweet in fragrance; but it has not the power of rejoicing in its own beauty, and of inhaling its own fragrance. The landscape is charming, and yet it does not rejoice in its own attractiveness. The nightingale chants its lays in the lonely forest, floats its sweet liquid notes on the still surface of the midnight air, but is itself unconscious of the wealth of song. The horse shows its power as it draws the heavy load, as it fleets over the greensward, and bounds with wondrous agility over the high-raised fence. Though the horse is superior to other animals, it does not know its advantages. At times it may appear to catch a glimpse of its greatness, and to make a grasp at power; but it cannot link cause and effect, it cannot be said to know. Man rises in excellency above all other creatures in the fact that he is a knowing animal. He knows what he is—what he is in part; for his ignorance is still very great. The degree in which the knowing faculty is exercised by man is the degree in which he walks handsomely. The man does not walk gracefully who walks as in the night of ignorance. When the knowing faculty is oppressed by the mist and fog and cold of the night, then the man walks dishonourably; but when the faculty is developed by the daylight of goodness, then the man walks handsomely. Knowledge is good, but knowledge handled and controlled by evil must lead to impious results; so that for the man to walk handsomely it is needful that the knowing faculty be directed in the right channel of truth and of goodness. We must know ourselves, and we must know God in and

436

through Jesus Christ; we must know how great and vast are our posse-sions, our privileges, our dignities, our glories, our honours, and our destiny. This is the first and last great step in knowledge—to know the only true God, and Jesus Christ whom He has sent. This knowledge is life eternal. This knowledge gives eternal life, and requires eternal life for its completion. Eternal life is an ever-unfolding scene, and the knowledge of God and of Jesus Christ is an ever-developing knowledge. Growth in this knowledge is growth without cessation; and the more we increase in this knowledge the more do we possess the power of walking handsomely. So that we must begin here, at the knowledge of the only true God and Jesus Christ, if we are rightly to obey the apostle's exhortation. Let us walk gracefully, handsomely, as in the day.

II. **The man will walk handsomely who keeps in view the nobility of his origin.**—The question Whence is man? is variously answered, and is the cause of discussion in some quarters; but there is no occasion for misgiving on our part, for we believe that God is the father of men. They are God's children, made in His image and likeness, and capable of rendering Him reasonable service. In this sense man has a noble origin. He is the highest of creatures, the link between earth and heaven. On one side of his nature he touches the lowest, and on the other side he reaches to heaven. He overtops the material universe, and stands amid the immensities of eternity. But the question with which we are now concerned is as to the origin of the spiritual man. On this question the New Testament alone can be our guide. The spiritual man boasts not his first but his second birth. He is born, not of corruptible seed, but of God; he need not glory in earthly ancestors, for he is united to Jesus Christ; he does not require to speak of royal blood, since by the new birth he is linked to Him who is the King of kings and Lord of lords. There is not always with noble descent the transmission of noble qualities. Sometimes as the race proceeds the quality of the stock degenerates; but in the spiritual descent there must be the transmission of noble qualities. The man is born again that he may be made a new creature in Christ Jesus; he is born from heaven, and receives heavenly qualities which he himself must develop. How gracefully the man should walk who is thus fashioned anew, who draws a new life from the very source of life, who is begotten again by the incorruptible word and power of God, who is lifted up amid the sublime hierarchy of God's redeemed and chosen children! Art thou a King's son? Then be noble in thy doings, right royal in thy actions.

III. **The man will walk handsomely who constantly regards the large extent of his sphere.**—The man is apt to get careless who feels that he has no sphere, and that there is nothing in his surroundings demanding the exercise of his powers. He has only one talent, and so he wraps it up in a napkin, and binds himself in cerecloths. The poet who had produced his great work, and felt that life was finished, passed his days in indolence, consoling himself with the thought and the expression, There is no motive. Paley's great powers were lying waste and useless until the voice of a fellow-student called him to action and opened out to him the vast possibilities of his nature. But surely there is a sphere and there is a work for all. Man may rouse himself by the thought of the philosopher who said that man is the end of all things in a semicircle—that is, all things in the world are made for him, and he is made for God. Man is not an insignificant creature shut up in a shell, covered with which he crawls about in a little space. No doubt by the body man is confined; but by the spirit he strips himself of the burden of fleshly covering and travels through infinite spaces. He lives in the mighty past, in the ever-working present, and even in the unenacted future. This time world, changing, moving, passing

437

away, is his sphere. Then the no-time world, the life unknown, unseen, immeasurable, and infinite, is also his sphere by anticipation and by expectation. The spiritual man acts not in a semicircle merely, but in a vast circle. He is the source of undying influences. The spiritual man touches on all sides wherever he moves. An atom of influence for good set in motion must affect other atoms, and the motion will continue through unknown regions. The mountains appear strong and immovable, but motion in the material world reaches to distances beyond our comprehension. And much more is this true with reference to motion in the moral world. The good man is the centre and source of vast outlying and fertilising regions of goodness. He is surely the good seed from which other good men spring. They in their turn are good seed giving birth to other noble spirits. The upper room at Jerusalem did not seem a large sphere; it had no architectural glory. Yet there met in that place twelve of the mightiest spirits of all time. There a force was being developed which was to subdue the material power of Rome, to confute the wisdom of Greece, to give laws and rules which should influence and control the mightiest forms of civilisation, and the greatest nations of all periods. A certain widow with only two mites had, to human seeming, no extensive sphere of usefulness. She had no costly offerings; and yet those mites have been of more value to the Church of Christ than the thousands of pounds she has since received. Here indeed we require to exercise the knowing faculty, and to take broad views, and to consider our sphere as much larger than might be supposed by shallow thinking. We rise in manhood; dormant faculties are called into action as we consider the vast possibilities of the meanest life. We shall no longer creep as if going a monotonous round of mean duties, but we shall walk with stalwart spirit and with hopeful mien, as men appointed to do great works which shall in one way or other be finally successful and triumphant.

IV. **The man will walk handsomely who wisely considers the glory of his final destiny.**—What a man may become will have an important bearing upon the way in which he treats himself and the way in which he is treated by his fellows. Wisely did that man conduct himself with respectful bearing in the presence of every schoolboy, for he viewed him in the light of a possibly great future. There he saw the ruling statesman, the thrilling orator, the conquering general, the stately bishop, or the world-renowned author. There is to the spiritual man a positive great future, not after the dreams of earth-bound souls, but according to the revelations and provisions of infinite love, wisdom, and power. The spiritual man is a king on earth. The kingdom over which he rules is his own inner nature, but his kingship is imperfect and oft contested. Sometimes he is ensnared and taken captive; but in God's great future he shall be a king, and his kingship will not be contested, and he shall never be brought into bondage. The sceptre of royalty will never be wrested from his grasp. The golden crown will never be taken from his head; he shall reign for ever and for ever. In this world he is often as a king in exile, but in the other world he will be a king acknowledged. In this world he is a king in poverty, but in the other world he will be a king surrounded with untold wealth. In this world he is a king in sorrow, but in the other world he will be a king in unspeakable happiness. Here he is a king in a cottage, but there he will be a king in a house of many mansions—in a city whose walls are jasper, whose streets are gold, whose gates are pearl, whose fruits and flowers are perennial, whose society is angels, archangels, patriarchs, prophets, apostles, and martyrs. What manner of person ought such a man to be who has before him such a glorious prospect? The wise heathen said he was greater and born to greater things than that his soul should be the slave of his body. Surely the wise Christian may say in far larger sense that he is greater and born to greater things than that the soul should be slave of the body. He will walk honestly, gracefully, as in the day; not in rioting and drunkenness, not in chambering and wantonness, not in strife and envy; but putting on the Lord Jesus Christ, and making provision for the enlargement and development of his nobler nature.

The life-long putting on of Christ.

I. What this is that is put on.—It is Christ Himself that we put on; not one thing merely, such as righteousness, but everything which makes us comely and acceptable to God. Christ Himself is here described as a robe. The figure is not of His *giving* us a robe, but of His *being* that robe. It is a *whole Christ* whom we put on; it is with a whole Christ that God deals in dealing with us.

II. How this putting on is done.—The link by which we become personally connected with Christ is our own believing. "Christ is the end of the law for righteousness to every one *that believeth.*" We put on Christ simply in believing. Our reception of the Father's testimony to the work and person of Christ is the "putting on." There is no other.

III. What is the effect?—There are two aspects or sides which are to be regarded in this: 1. God's side; 2. The believer's. 1. *God's side.* God looks at us and sees us as if we were His own Son. He sees not our deformity and imperfection, but His beauty and perfection. 2. *Our side.* (1) Our consciences are completely satisfied. Not only have we the blood to purge the guilt, but we have the perfection to cover all imperfection, so that we feel that God "sees no iniquity in Jacob, and no transgression in Israel." (2) Our bands are completely loosed. The certainty of possessing God's favour in such surpassing measure gives the fullest liberty. (3) Our joy overflows. Such love! such favour! such nearness! such dignity! (4) Our motives to a holy life are increased. What manner of persons ought we to be who are so regarded by God, so beloved of Him! (5) Our zeal is quickened. Loved with such a love, and treated in so divine a way, what is there that we are not willing to do for Him?—*H. Bonar.*

SUGGESTIVE COMMENTS ON VERSES 13, 14.

Pilgrims of the dawn.—The pilgrims of the dawn tolerate nothing in themselves that the light of day would rebuke. Hence it is the counterpart of this that they make no provision for the flesh; whatever provision they take for their heavenly journey, the flesh has no share in it. The sin adhering to their natures, the old man not yet dead, is an enemy whose hunger they do not feed, to whose thirst they do not administer drink, whose dying solicitations they regard not, but leave him to perish by the way. But the supreme preparation, uniting all others in one, is the putting on of the Lord Jesus Christ. In Him alone the dignity and the purity of our nature meet; transformed into His character, we need nothing more to fit us for the holiest heavens. But nothing less will suffice His expectation at His coming. He will come to be glorified in His saints—already the likeness in ten thousand reproductions of Himself; and they shall in turn be glorified in Him. Hence the great business of the pilgrims is to occupy the precious moments of the morning in weaving into their nature the character of Christ as the apparel of the eternal day. And if in faith that worketh by love—the love that fulfilleth the law—they diligently co-operate with the

Holy Spirit, it will be His blessed function to see to it that before the Bridegroom cometh His bride, and every individual soul that makes up her mystical person, shall be found clothed in His spiritual perfection as with a garment without seam, woven from the top throughout. Beyond this we cannot go. This is the close and the secret of the whole exhortation to the pilgrims of the dawn. They have come up out of the night at the sound of His awakening voice, and have left their Egyptian darkness for ever. They are wrestling with the dangers of the morning, rejoicing in its partial satisfactions. But supremely and above all they are intent upon the coming day; in their pathway there is no death, but they wait for the more abundant life; they are full of trembling, solemn expectation of all that the day will pour out of its unfathomable mysteries. But the end of all their expectation is the person of their Lord. And to prepare for Him by being like Himself is the sum of all their preparation.—*Pope's "Kingdom of Christ."*

ILLUSTRATIONS TO CHAPTER XIII.

Vers. 1, 2. *Condescension.*—The following simple story illustrates a trait in the character of our Queen which explains much of the feeling of fond regard entertained for her by all classes of her subjects. One year, when the Court was at Balmoral, her Majesty made a promise to Jenny—the daughter of a humble Balmoral neighbour, but who was an especial favourite with her Majesty—saying, "I'll bring a pretty toy for you when we come back next year." The Court went, and the promise was thought little more of—at least on one side. Her Majesty went that year to Paris to visit the emperor of the French. Amid all the pomp and style of royalty and imperiality, there was enough in the events of the year generally to drive many others besides the peasant child from the thoughts of the sovereign of Great Britain. Well, next season came, and with it the Court returned to Balmoral. The Queen, in making her rounds, soon called on her little *protégée*, and, with a "Now, I haven't forgotten you," exhibited the promised present. While Queen Victoria was in the French capital, amid all the din and distraction of French state pageantry, she found time to think of the little Highland girl on the banks of the Dee, and then and there bought an article to please and gratify the little child. *Royal courtesy.*—Frederick II., king of Prussia, made it a point to return every mark of respect or civility shown to him in the street by those who met him. He one day observed at table that whenever he rode through the streets of Berlin his hat was always in his hand. Baron Polintz, who was present, said that his Majesty had no occasion to notice the civility of every one who pulled his hat off to him in the streets. "And why not?" said the king, in a lively tone. "Are they not all human beings as well as myself?"

Vers. 5, 6. *New experiments in government.* —It is a dangerous thing to try new experiments in a government; men do not foresee the ill consequences that must happen when they go about to alter the essential parts of it upon which the whole frame depends; for all governments are artificial things, and every part of them has a dependence one upon another. And it is with them as with clocks and watches—if you should put great wheels in place of little ones, and little ones in the place of great ones, all the movement would stand still: so that we cannot alter any part of a government without prejudicing the motions of the whole.

Vers. 9, 10. *Love to God fulfils the law.*— An orphan boy of peculiar vivacity and uncommon talents, and who had been a favourite comic performer in the heathen sports, was sent by his relations to New Herrnhut, a settlement of the Moravian missionaries. His agreeable and engaging manners gained him the affection of one of the wealthiest Greenlanders, in whose family he was placed, who had no son, and whose presumptive heir he was. At the first catechetical meeting at which he was present, being asked whether he would wish to be acquainted with our Saviour and be converted, "Oh yes!" replied he gaily; "I shall soon be converted"; on which another, who had been lately baptised, gravely told him he knew little what conversion meant—that it was to yield the heart wholly to our Saviour, and to make a surrender of every evil inclination. This he found a hard saying, and would rather have thrown up his prospects among the brethren, and returned to his amusements among the heathen; till, after considerable mental conflict, he at last ceased contending with his Maker, and yielded a willing and cheerful obedience.

Ver. 10. *Doddridge's child.*—Doddridge buried a most interesting child at nine years of age. The dear little creature was a general favourite; and he tells us in his funeral sermon that when he one day asked her how it was that everybody loved her, "I know not," she said, "unless it be that I love everybody." Tell your children this. Also read to them, "The child Samuel grew on, and was in favour both with the Lord and also with men."

Ver. 10. *Five people supported on a needle's point.*—There was a student once who asked Robertson of Irvine the old scholastic quibble, whether he could tell how many souls could be supported on the point of a needle. "Oh! dear me, yes," said he; "that is easy enough. I can tell that." "How so?" said the student. "Well," said Robertson, "as I was walking home the other night along the seashore, I passed a house where a poor widow lives; her husband was drowned at sea last winter. She has five little children, and as I looked through the window I saw in the firelight two little golden heads in the bed yonder, and another little golden head in the cradle, and two other children sitting at the mother's knee. She was working away with her needle, and it was flashing in the firelight, and was going as hard as it could go. So," continued Robertson, "I know how many souls can be supported on the point of a needle—five: don't you see?" And as I look through that window I seem to look upon the whole vision of domestic life, on mothers toiling and never calling it toil, on the vision of innumerable women all the world over who give themselves away, and are not so much as thanked for it, on the silent heroisms which redeem life, and which are its unuttered poetry, its saving salt, its divine attestation. And these heroisms, which are the birth of love, are everywhere.—*Dawson.*

Ver. 11. *Cæsar wept.*—When Cæsar, in Spain, met with a statue of Alexander, he wept at the thought that this illustrious conqueror had achieved so much before *he* had even begun his career. The man who is awake will accomplish much. Every sight will stir his soul to energy. He will emulate others in good works.

Ver. 11. *Sunrise from the Righi.*—Doubtless many readers of these pages have been among the number of the thousands of travellers who each year witness the sunrise from the culm of the Righi. So anxious were you to behold the sight that you rose from your bed the moment you heard the sound of the horn which announced that the night was far spent and the day was at hand. Hastily dressing, you were soon silently and earnestly watching for the first gleam of light in the Eastern sky. It may be that some one of you turned to see whether your friend and fellow-traveller was sharing your eager anticipations, and found him wanting. You at once hastened back to the hotel and knocked loudly at his door. He, too, had been awoke by the blast of the horn, but, being weary, was half asleep. You exclaimed, "Do you know the time? It is high time to awake out of sleep, for the sight for which you have travelled so far is far nearer than when first you were roused." He, too, was soon among the silent band of watchers, and with you beheld the King of Day as he crowned each snow-capped peak with roseate hues, and lit up the lakes of Lucerne and Zug and Lowerz below, and many a distant valley, until the whole panorama was bathed in his glorious light. St. Paul, as a watchful sentinel in the Church, as one who was eagerly expecting the glorious appearing of his Lord and Master, earnestly exhorts the Christians at Rome to live in no debt but that of love (see ver. 10). He seeks to awaken them from their indifference by reminding them that the "day of the Lord," the consummation of their "salvation," was nearer than when "first they were roused from their sleep of sin." "The night is far spent, the day is at hand: let us therefore cast off the works of darkness, and let us put on the armour of light."—*Bardsley's "Illustrated Texts."*

Vers. 11, 12. *The improvement of time.*—Boyle remarks "that sand-grains are easily scattered, but skilful artificers gather, melt, and transmute them to glass, of which they make mirrors, lenses, and telescopes. Even so vigilant Christians improve parenthetic fragments of time, employing them in self-examination, acts of faith, and researches of holy truth, by which they become looking-glasses for their souls and telescopes revealing their promised heaven." Jewellers save the very sweepings of their shops because they contain particles of precious metal. Should Christians, whose every moment of time was purchased for them by the blood of Christ, be less careful of time? Surely its very minutiæ should be more treasured than grains of gold or dust of diamonds.

Ver. 14. *The story of St. Augustine's repentance.*—Sometimes mothers' and fathers' eyes are sealed in death before the one whom they gave really gives himself to God. You have all heard of the great Augustine. There are few stories more interesting, few for which the Church has had greater cause to thank God, than the story of his repentance. His mother's heart was nearly broken by his profligacy and folly. She, like Hannah, had consecrated him from birth. She had watched over him, taught him, prayed for him. But he gave no heed to her counsel.

Her patience was sorely taxed. An old bishop one day found her almost in despair. "O woman, woman!" he said, "the child of so many prayers will be saved!" And so it was. When he was on a visit at Milan, God found him. One day, sitting with a friend, "there arose a mighty storm of grief, bringing a mighty shower of tears." He left his friend, hastened to the garden, cried, "How long? how long? Why not now?" when lo! he seemed to hear a voice as of a child repeating, "Take up and read, take up and read." And he rose from the ground, opened his Bible, and read the first verse which he found. It was, "Put ye on the Lord Jesus Christ, and make not provision for the flesh." As he read darkness vanished. His mother's prayers were answered.—*Rev. J. Marshall Lang, D.D.*

CHAPTER XIV.

CRITICAL NOTES.

Ver. 1. Him that is weak in the faith.—Defective in the faith, in the general doctrine, and thus an observer of externals. Alford and De Wette refer to the weak in faith as one who wants broad and independent principles, and is in consequent bondage to prejudices. διαλογισμοί, opinions, views, thoughts. Often much disputing among the Rabbins on receiving proselytes on account of some supposed disqualification. The subject of the former chapter was submission; the subject of this is toleration.

Ver. 2.—The weak thought that he would be more tolerated by abstaining, not only from swine's flesh, but all flesh (Theoph.).

Ver. 3.—Applies to both parties; evident from their being enlightened with the knowledge of God (Calvin, Stuart).

Ver. 4. For God is able to make him stand.—Here we have both power and will, and the passage indicates God's merciful disposition.

Ver. 5.—Here the seventh day, Sabbath, is included, but not the Christian Sunday, which was of apostolic authority, and has plainly divine sanction, and is a continuation of the Adamic Sabbath. Let every man be fully persuaded, act with full persuasion, that what he does is right. Let him have conviction founded on examination. Every man is bound to obey his conscience, but let conscience be properly enlightened and prompted by love to the Lord of the Sabbath. In the words κρίνει πᾶσαν ἡμέραν, says Olshausen, is expressed the original apostolic view, which did not distinguish particular festivals, because to it the whole life of Christ had become a festival. As, however, the season of the Church's prime passed away, the necessity could not but at the same time have again made itself felt of giving prominence to points of festival light in the general current of every-day life.

Ver. 6.—Each must seek to do what he conscientiously believes to be the Lord's will.

Ver. 7.—We are not to follow our own pleasure, nor obey our own inclinations. In life and death we, Christians, are the Lord's.

Ver. 8.—Christians are Christ's property, and they must live, not to themselves, but to one another.

Ver. 9.—Christ having died and risen again to make believers His property, will He not take care of His own?

Ver. 10.—Being accountable to Christ, we cannot be accountable in the highest sense to any other.

Ver. 11.—The phrase indicates the act of those who shall worship and acknowledge God. The knee may bend and the heart not engaged. Let us praise the Lord's mercy and justice.

Ver. 13.—Rabbins said, "When I enter the school to expound the law, I pray that no occasion of stumbling may arise through me to any." Jewish Christians guilty by imposing Judaism, Gentile Christians by repelling scrupulous Jews.

Ver. 14. Nothing is unclean of itself.—Call nothing common or unclean. A thing may become evil if done against conscience, if the doing cause offence, if it make us leave some important work undone.

Ver. 15. Because of meat.—Purposely selected as something contemptible. Eternal perdition not meant here. Destroy by causing him to act against his conscience, and so commit sin.

442

Ver. 16. **Let not your good be evil spoken of.**—Let not Christian liberty be abused by offence given to the weak.

Ver. 17. **The kingdom of God.**—What commends us to God is not the outward but the inward, only the outward must be in conformity with the inward. Peace, in opposition to discord among brethren; a peaceful and gentle demeanour.

Ver. 18. **Acceptable to God.**—The things being required of Him. Approved of men, is profitable to them. Saying of the Rabbins: "He who conscientiously observes the law is acceptable to God and approved of men."

Ver. 20.—The work of God is the faith of a fellow-Christian.

Ver. 21.—Three forms of spiritual damage, corresponding with the three blessings in ver. 17, which are prejudiced by them.

Ver. 22.—κρίνω, to judge, question, doubt, condemn; and δοκιμάζω, to approve, finely express in their combination the doubting conscience.

Ver. 23. **He that doubteth is damned.**—Condemned by his conscience, his brethren, and God. We must submit undoubtingly to the recognised will of God. The man eats sinfully who eats doubtfully. Happy the man who has faith and an approving conscience.

MAIN HOMILETICS OF THE PARAGRAPH.—*Verses* 1—4.

The weak and the strong.—St. Paul's knowledge of human nature comes out from time to time in his writings. The preacher should be a man conversant with both men and things. He should have eyes behind and before, and be able to search into the hidden mysteries of human nature. Thus St. Paul is an example to the preacher. By graphic strokes of the pen Paul touches the weakness of the strong as well as the weakness of the weak. Both require words of direction; none must be neglected by the faithful minister. St. Paul looks all round, and strives to produce a well-ordered Christian community.

I. **The weak and the strong have their faults.**—Sometimes the strong are found weaker than the weak; their very strength is an occasion of stumbling. Strength may beget an overweening self-confidence, which leads to destruction ; weakness may induce carefulness, which tends to safety. The creaking gate hangs long. The weak ones linger; the strong are cut down suddenly when sickness attacks. The strong may err on the side of liberty, the weak on the side of restraint. The strong may have a contemptuous spirit and mien; he may become impatient of the weak, and treat him with disdain. The weak may have a censorious spirit, and charge the strong with being guilty of gluttony and drunkenness. The weak said of the strong Christ, "Behold a gluttonous man and a winebibber, a friend of publicans and sinners." The strong may be too tolerant except of weakness, while the weak may be intolerant. Our danger in these days is that of the ambition of being men of strength, which means men of broad views—men with no crotchets, which means too often men of no principles. Men with crotchets are strong; the strongest part of the plank is that where the knot is found.

II. **The weak and the strong are levelled.**—They are levelled, or ought to be, by the consciousness of common weaknesses. Strong men are but men at the best. A Samson may be bound captive and led blind to the scene of merriment; a Solomon may be overthrown by lust; a Peter may be frightened by a maid's thoughtless speech. How short the distance between the strong and the weak! There is but a step between us and death. That step taken, and the strong man falls. A little vessel bursts, and the strong intellect loses its power; a wrong word is spoken, and the voice of the orator is not allowed to charm; a false step is taken, and the warrior is banished; the brother of high degree is overtaken in a fault, and is brought low. How wholesome the exhortation, "Him that is weak in the faith receive ye"! In your strength consider your weakness, and let your hearts and your arms be always open to

443

welcome and to receive the weak. Strong and weak are levelled when brought within the sweep of Omnipotence. Can there be any appreciable difference between the weak who lifts a few ounces and the strong who lifts many pounds to Him who weighs the mountains in scales and holds the immense waters in the hollow of His hands? If the strong God receive the weak children of men, those who dwell in houses made of clay, shall not weak men, who call themselves strong, and who are strong by comparison, receive the children of weakness? If the strong God receive us to divine consolations, to sublime communion, shall we not receive our brethren in the same spirit, and lay aside all doubtful disputations, all harsh thoughts, all deprecating views? How strong was He who came travelling in His greatness of His strength, mighty to save! By common consent of Christians and of unbelievers Jesus Christ has been assigned the foremost place amongst the strong ones of earth's stalwart sons. And yet with tender tones of welcome, with gentle caresses of love, He received the weak. He took the children in His arms; He was the friend of publicans and sinners. We are ambitious to be Christ's for strength; let us be ambitious to be Christ's for gentleness to the weak and erring. Let us not break, but seek to mend, the bruised reeds of our maimed humanity; let us not quench, but seek to fan into a spiritual flame, the smoking flax of the expiring heaven fires in human nature.

III. **The weak and the strong are mutually needful.**—A place for every man, and every man in his place. A law both for the world and the Church; but selfishness prevents its right working. A place for every man! And yet how many men out of places! Selfishness says, The weakest must go to the wall; Christian benevolence says, The weakest must be received and nurtured into greater strength by the strongest. Christian benevolence has wiser methods than cynical selfishness. The weak as well as the strong are needful; the weak gather strength by contact with the strong, and the strong get more strength by helping the weak. We are all needful to one another. Let, then, the strong receive the weak; and let the weak gladly accept the help of the strong.

IV. **The weak and the strong are servants of the divine Master.**—God has had patriarchs, prophets, apostles, and martyrs amongst His servants. Giant-like men have done His bidding; eagle-eyed heroes have watched His purposes; stalwart men with strong and swift pinions have done His bidding. Wisdom and eloquence have been at the divine command; but weak ones have been of service. She who could only show her love by tears, and she who could only tell the wealth of her devotion by giving two mites, stood high in the estimation of the divine Master. The strong may be ready to smile at the weakness of the brother who is almost afraid to eat lest he should offend God. But surely there is a fine spirit in that over-sensitive nature, and God appreciates the exquisite tenderness. In this tolerant age, when the Church sets the lead in fashion, in creed rejects but in practice accepts the lust of the flesh, or the lust of the eye, and mostly the pride of life, we require the weak to teach us the need of a little more sensitiveness of conscience, of a greater tenderness of moral nature.

V. **The weak and the strong must be alike holden up by immortal strength.**—God is able to make the weak stand. His ability has been proved from time to time in the records of the human race. Weak women have been made to stand, and have shamed mighty men by their exhibition of unwonted courage. Those who have been so fastidious in non-essentials as to provoke the contempt of the strong by divine power have been made to stand gloriously in the day of battle. The strongest likewise must be made to stand by God's imparted strength. The encircling strength of God embraces and empowers the weak and the strong.

In ourselves we are all weak; in God's grace, by the Spirit's might, we are infinitely strong.

Ver. 1. *The strong helping the weak.*—The words very remarkable, considering that they fell from the lips of a Jew. By birth, education, and interest he was as exclusive as could be. He would naturally have the national fault of "self-exalting opinion"—the false notion that God's highest blessings were only for Jews. He had to conquer his Jewish prejudices, and fight his way through that narrow spirit of isolation that encircled him. The story of Paul's life and his teachings shows how thoroughly he did this. We have suggested here :—

I. **The remarkable effect of Christianity on men.**—It almost amounts to miracle. Examples in history numerous. Note the contrasts between pagans and Christians in the matter of the strong dealing with the weak. Paganism, *e.g.*, said that modesty in a woman was a presumption of ugliness. It is one of the strong points of Christianity. Slavery never put down except where Christianity was in force. Before Christianity makes itself felt anywhere there is an awful waste of human life—*e.g.*, in Dahomey three thousand victims when the mother of the king of Ashantee died! Christianity always insisted that human life was sacred. Each soul for whom Christ died could say, My life is precious in the sight of God. Such a fact has led to modern charities; and all due to the work of the great burden-bearer, Christ Jesus. And Christians are to imitate Him.

II. **The text indicates that Christianity is catholic.**—Broad in its sympathies and influence. Christianity is not national and exclusive, not the heritage of English-speaking people. Christianity cares nothing about nationality, but for the salvation of all men everywhere. This is unwelcome news to some. They want to be within the select circle. Paul is ruthless in dealing with such narrowness. You who are strong, he seems to say, go and help your weaker brethren; show them your light; tell them it is for them also, because for them also Christ died.

III. **The text suggests the neighbourliness of Christianity.**—This neighbourliness exactly fits in with our natural feelings. May we not look upon a recluse as a freak of nature? Men, take them in the mass, cannot separate themselves from the outward world without a pang. The old monks "mortified" themselves by going into the gloomy monastery. Loneliness is a source of misery to the average individual. Possibly in the earliest days men tried isolation, but could not stand it. Therefore they formed themselves into communities; built villages, towns, cities, that they might come into touch with each other. Where Christianity exerts its influence men will not be satisfied with mere community. The theories that hold people together have practical expression. They must help one another—the strong help the weak.

IV. **Imitation of Christ leaves no alternative but to be helpful.**—To be hard-hearted is to be unlike Christ; and he who is unlike Christ cannot be Christ's disciple. Christ was emphatically a burden-bearer. Where He saw men strong and stalwart He passed on. "They that be whole," He said, "need not," etc. To help one who is capable of helping himself is a waste of energy, and likely to encourage idleness; but to help the needy is to exercise the soul in a noble calling. "We ought to bear the weak, and carry them along with us as we go." There is a kind of unconscious Christianity—namely, the little helps as we pass on life's way.

V. **The world is poorer than it might have been for want of the spirit of helpfulness.**—Some of us who are strong have much to answer for—to answer for the pang of dismay in the weak one when a cheery word would have been so helpful. It would almost be a blessing if we had a bit of smart suffering to remind us of the value of a little help. Then we should be less critical, more considerate, less self-absorbed, especially any of us who are spiritually strong.

VI. **Helpfulness is a duty.**—" We that are strong *ought*," etc. Think of the multitude of calls for such help: the sick, the poor, the ignorant, etc. We need of course to be discriminating in our helpfulness. There is a poverty, *e.g.*, the result of vice, a laziness that leads to rags and tatters. But what of deserving poverty? There you dare not be indifferent We can all be Christians in the world. Do not pass any by, for Christ never did that to any poor soul. He bare our sorrows. If you would be Christlike, so must you be a sorrow-bearer. Do you say, Yes; but the cost? Think, then, of the cost to Jesus. "He came in flesh, in poverty, in homelessness, in tears, with shudderings of nameless agony, that He might drink up our sorrow in the vastness of His own, and that He might open springs of everlasting consolation to all the children of trouble." Should any one find that Christians forget their duty, let him go to Christ. You have but to take your trouble to Him, and He, so strong in sympathy, will give you help. It is He who says, "Come unto Me, all ye that labour," etc.—*Albert Lee.*

SUGGESTIVE COMMENTS ON VERSES 1—4.

Christian casuistry.—There is a kind of minuter casuistry which it is extremely difficult to handle from the mere want of something very distinct or tangible to hold by, and about which there is the greatest degree of indecision, and that just from the loss at which we feel to get any decisive principle of unquestioned evidence and authority to bear upon it. And so it is that even the Christian mind fluctuates thereanent, and exhibits itself upon this subject in a state both of vacillation and variety. For while one class of the professors is heard to declaim and to dogmatise and most strenuously to asseverate with all the readiness of minds that are thoroughly made up on the matters alluded to, there is another class of them who cannot assume this certainty without cause being shown, who must have something more to allege for the vindication of their peculiarities than the mere conventional shibboleth of a party, and who wait till a clear reason approve itself to their judgments ere they can utter with their mouths a clear and confident deliverance. Some may have already guessed what the questions are to which we are now adverting. They relate to the degree of our conformity with the world, and to the share which it were lawful to take in its companies and amusements. You must be aware

on this topic of a certain unsettledness of opinion; while we know of none that wakens a more anxious degree of interest and speculation among those who are honestly aspiring after the right, and are most fearfully sensitive of the wrong in all their conversation. And if to tenderness of conscience they add a certain force of intelligence, they will not be satisfied with a mere oracular response from those who seem to be somewhat, and who speak as if from the vantage ground of their long initiation into higher mysteries. They are prepared for every surrender, and are in readiness to follow fully wherever the light of Scripture or of argument may carry them; but this light is the very thing they want and are in quest of. It is their demand for the *rationale* of this matter, with the difficulty they feel in reaching it, that has thrown them into a kind of harassment about the whole affair from which they long to be extricated. And neither in the magisterial but improved dictation of one set of Christians, nor in the yet unstable practice of another set of Christians, who are hovering about the margin that separates the Church from the world, and ever tremulously veering between the sides of accommodation and nonconformity therewith. From neither of these parties in the great professing public of our day can they find repose to their spirits, because from neither they have found effectual relief to the painful ambiguity under which they are labouring. What has now drawn our attention more especially to this subject is its strong identity in regard to principle with that question of Sabbath observation which we have recently attempted to elucidate. The elements of Christian liberty and expediency and charity appear to be similarly involved in both, so as that we may avail ourselves of the same guidance as before from the manner in which the apostle hath cleared and discriminated his way through the controversy that arose in his time about meats and days and ceremonies. It is, indeed, a very possible thing that Christianity may be made to wear another aspect than that in which she smiles so benignantly upon us from the New Testament— that, instead of a religion of freedom, because her only control is that of heavenly and high-born principle wherewith she rules, and by moral ascendency alone, over her willing and delighted votaries, she may be transformed into a narrow system of bigotry, whose oppressive mandates of " touch not and taste not and handle not " bear no relation whatever to the spiritual department of our nature—only galling and subordinating the outer man, while they leave the inner man as remote, both in principle and affection, from the likeness of God or the character of godliness as before. Better surely to impregnate the man's heart, first with the taste and spirit of our religion, and then, if this should supersede the taste and affection he before had for the frivolities of life, it impresses a far nobler character of freeness and greatness on the change of habit that has taken place, when thus made to emanate from a change of heart, than when it appears in the light of a reluctant compliance with a rigid exaction of intolerance, the rationality and rightness of which are at the same time not very distinctly apprehended. Let the reformation in question, if reformation

it be, come forth upon the habit of the man in this way—as the final upshot of a process by which the heart has been reformed, as the fruit of an internal change that has taken place on the taste and on the affections, through the power of the truth that is in Jesus, and whereby all old things have passed away and all things have become new. Better thus than by a mandate on the subject issued from the chair of authority. But it is now time to have done with this long excursion among the details and the difficulties of a casuistry by which the Christian mind has oft been exercised. For let it never be forgotten that a heart with rightly set affections and desires is, after all, the best of casuists. If the heart in its various regards be as it ought, this is our securest guarantee that the history in its various manifestations will be as it ought. The best way of restoring to light and to liberty the conscience of man is to enthrone love in his bosom. — *Dr. Chalmers.*

The effects of Christianity.—Raphael Aben-Ezra, an Alexandrian cynic, was won over to Christianity by the example of a Christian Roman centurion and his children. " I have watched you," he said, " for many a day, and not in vain. When I saw you, an experienced officer, encumber your flight with wounded men, I was only surprised. But since I have seen you and your daughter, and, strangest of all, your gay Alcibiades of a son, starving yourselves to feed these poor ruffians, performing for them day and night the offices of menial slaves, comforting them as no man ever comforted me, blaming no one but yourselves, caring for every one but yourselves, sacrificing nothing but yourselves, and all this without hope of fame or reward, or dream of appeasing the wrath of any god or goddess, but simply because you thought it right, —when I saw that, sir, and more which I have seen ; and when, reading in this book here, I found most un-

447

expectedly those very grand moral rules which you were practising, seeming to spring unconsciously, as natural results, from the great thoughts, true or false, which had preceded them; then, sir, I began to suspect that the creed which could produce such deeds as I have watched within the last few days might have on its side, not merely a slight preponderance of probabilities, but what we Jews used once to call, when we believed in it—or in anything—the mighty power of God."—*Kingsley's "Hypatia."*

MAIN HOMILETICS OF THE PARAGRAPH.—*Verses* 5, 6.

Variety of opinion, unity of spirit.—There may be no direct allusion to the Christian Sunday in this passage, and there may be no pronouncement either for or against the observance of a fixed day, as there is no declaration against either eating or not eating. Why the apostle did not say it is good to keep the Christian Sunday when he said, "It is good neither to eat flesh, nor to drink wine, nor anything whereby thy brother stumbleth," we cannot tell. But we find that he lays down a principle which should lead every right mind to the religious observance of one day in seven. He allows variety of opinion; he enforces unity of spirit, and that spirit is that all is to be done unto the Lord. If anything be left undone, it is thus left because the omission will work more truly to God's glory. Can it be truly said and successfully maintained that the abrogation of Sunday observance will tend to the glory of God? Do our Sunday pleasure-takers and our Sunday business men either enter the excursion train, indulge in their pleasures, or pursue their secular avocations "unto the Lord"?

I. **The spirit of consecration asks for full persuasion.**—1. *Now full persuasion cannot be obtained without serious examination.* And that process cannot be called serious examination which comes to the consideration of the divine word with preconceived views. People who work on these lines say they are willing to be enlightened. Their willinghood is doubtful, for they never find any teachers skilful enough to enlighten. Has a man given serious examination to this passage who says, That is all right; St. Paul advocates all days alike. No rigid sabbatarianism for me. Let me have liberty of opinion? Is not this man treated ironically by St. Paul? How can a man discern *every* day? There is no longer any distinction when all are distinguished. To set apart every day as holy is no longer to sanctify any one specially. To consecrate all our substance unto the Lord, and to refuse to "render unto Cæsar the things that are Cæsar's, and unto God the things that are God's," is a plain contradiction. Would an income-tax collector allow a man to escape on the plea that all his income is consecrated to the Queen? The tribute of days as well as the tribute of money should be consecrated unto the Lord. 2. *Serious examination cannot be conducted without consideration of all the evidence.* It would not be admissible in the court of law that evidence should not be adduced, and it must not be admitted in the court of conscience. We must carefully consider the cases of those who distinguish one day in seven and those who distinguish all days, and ask which class shows more emphatically that they are ruled and actuated by the spirit of consecration unto the Lord. The inner spirit is known by the outer life. "By their fruits ye shall know them." The inner spirit of consecrating all our days is shown by the outer life of consecrating unto the Lord one day in seven. The inner spirit of love is shown by the outer deed of love. It breaks the alabaster box of ointment of spikenard very precious, and pours it on the head of the predestined victim. It might have been sold and given to the poor, says selfishness. Love says, No; it must be consecrated to this highest service. Selfishness says, The true spirit is to consecrate all days to noble endeavours. Let there be no empty

448

sentiment; let there be no waste of time according to priestly ordering. Love says, No; one day in seven must be consecrated to the service of the All-loving, that so all days may be ennobled, that so in the recurring days the loving heart may pour itself out in an unrestrained stream of devotion. The love of some men rises above their creed. They advocate all days alike, and yet they sacredly keep their Sundays.

II. **The spirit of consecration is fully persuaded of the wisdom of observing fixed days.**—Lest the sabbatarian may be said to come to the consideration of the divine word and of the divine ordinances with preconceived views, it may be needful to show that such views are not hastily formed. All the evidence which can be adduced goes to prove that Sunday is indispensable to the establishment and propagation of Christianity in the world. Let us then bring forward some of the advantages of a fixed day of rest to both the individual and the community. We doubt not that there have evils arisen from the observance of Sunday as a day of rest. But where are we to find the unmixed good? The tares and the wheat will grow together, farm we never so carefully. Shall we give up growing wheat because we cannot prevent the springing up of tares? Shall we cease the work of trying to join good men in Christian communities because hypocrites will appear? Nay, verily. The abuse of a custom does not nullify its wise use. The perversion of an institution does not abrogate its authority and its necessity. Our Sunday must abide, though it may have attendant evils; and yet the evils are few and fanciful. They are the evils of depraved human nature rather than the evils of the day of rest; while the blessings are real and manifold. 1. *A fixed day of rest and of religious observance fences humanity*, at least that part of humanity that does not break through the Sabbath hedge; and such violators place themselves in the dangerous position of being exposed to the bite of the serpents that lurk on the outside of the sacred enclosure. Still the Sunday fence is more extended than we sometimes think. It has warded off much evil even from the heads of those who flout its protective qualities. Those who make merry at the expense of the righteous, and try to show that more evil happens to the Sabbath observer than to the Sabbath breaker, should bear in mind that the latter is moving under the protecting shield of the former. In this world the wicked even are benefited by the sufferings and the virtue of the righteous. Ten righteous would have saved a cityful, but there were not ten to be found. The true Sunday observers form a small proportion of the nation, but they are its protection. The sound stones in the national fabric may be few, but they prevent a national collapse. The Sunday fence encloses and benefits even the perverse; and much more does it benefit the faithful and the obedient. The Sunday observer is fenced from the intrusion of business, from the calls of secular life, and from the attacks of so-called pleasure. 2. *A day of rest and religious observance helps human weakness.* It is a strange feature of our nature that it should be averse to religion and yet cannot get away from it. Even in regenerate men there are adverse forces at work, and when they would do good evil is present. Two opposite forces are at work in the soul, one set drawing to religion and to goodness, and the other drawing in an opposite direction. What a constant strife rages in the town of Man-soul! The world within a man, even of a good man, is not all on the side of good. And the world outside the man is not engaged to help him forward to moral victory. The powers of evil and good are continually striving for the mastery, and we often fear that the good will be worsted in the encounter; yea, we too often find that evil conquers and the man is dethroned. This being so we cannot wisely dispense with any help which may be available to render the contest successful. A fixed day of rest is a valuable help by the way which cannot be ignored. And we may regard it not as a mere secondary but as a primary help. It is the source of much precious assistance. It brings more vividly before the mind the feeling of our personal responsibility and our immortal destiny. In the secular days we are apt to be of the earth earthy; while the manifest tendency of the Sunday is to raise above the earth, and thus we are strengthened for further conflict. Ask any good man to give up his Sunday. The request would be absurd. As well ask the soldier to give up his weapons of defence in the day of battle, the sailor to abandon the life-buoy when battling with the waves. The Sunday provides invisible weapons of defence, and is a sustaining force amid life's dark billows and howling tempests. It is helpful to the weak, and the strongest require its gracious aids. 3. *A day of rest and religious worship furthers noble endeavour.* The language of the good man is, " I will endeavour." He is not either vain-glorious or insanely self-reliant. When despair rests upon the human soul, one little ray of hope piercing the darkness will do a world of good. " I will endeavour " is apostolic language, and is a suitable motto for the man struggling to the upward heights. Sunday refreshes and recruits the weary spirit of the endeavouring man. He has made many endeavours, and has failed; but Sunday teaches that what are called failures in the moral battle are not all failures if we are still found in the pathway of endeavour. It can give higher motives for perseverance, encourages to further action, and assures final victory to the faithful. 4. *A fixed day of rest and religious worship provides a blessed outlook.* It opens a large prospect which must be invigorating. The pilgrims in their journey went up the Delectable Mountains to behold the gardens and orchards, the vineyards and fountains of water. There they drank and washed themselves, and did freely eat of the vineyards. Then the shepherds had the pilgrims to the top of a high hill called Clear, from which could be seen the gates of the celestial city. Sundays are as the Delectable Mountains, where are gardens and orchards, vineyards and fountains of water. Here weary pilgrims can drink and freely eat and be refreshed. Amongst these mountains is many a hill Clear, from which, if we have the skill and the glass of faith, we may see the gates of the celestial city. Sunday is the high hill Clear towering above all other days. Even when the hands shake as the glass is held by reason of our remembrance of life's perplexities, we may see farther than on any other day. We cannot do without our hills and mountains; they impress with a sense of the sublime. Much less can we part with our Sundays, the Delectable Mountains of time; they often show us the opened gates of heaven. We look in through those pearly gates, and behold the city shines like the sun; the streets also are paved with gold; and in them walk many men with crowns on their heads, palms in their hands, and golden harps to sing praises withal.

III. **The spirit of consecration is persuaded that the Christian Sunday is the substance which glorifies the shadow.**—The shadow often consists of dim and imperfect outlines. The sketch is a rough draft of the perfect picture which is to appear, and much work, skill, and patience will be required before the production is completed. Now the Sabbath of Eden and of Sinai is regarded by some as a rude sketch; though we consider that it is something more than a mere cloudy and disproportioned shadow, we may still consider it as a shadow, and remark that the Sabbath of the Old Testament is glorified by the Christian Sunday. 1. *The substance glorifies the shadow by intensifying its beneficent aspect.* The careful reading of the fourth commandment shows what a beneficent precept it is. It enjoins benevolent considerateness for all within the range of our influence. It treats for the physical and moral welfare of the human creature, and touches the brute creature with kind and gentle hand. And the divine Founder of Christianity intensifies this beneficent aspect. Those watchwords of the sabbatic controversy, "The Sabbath was made for man," unfold the Saviour's idea. Some of the most remarkable of His miracles were performed on this day. Wherever the Christian Sunday has been properly worked it has been a beneficent force. The physical evils of modern society are still many, but the amelioration of those evils has been due to the advance of Christian principles stimulating the movements of a true science. Sunday is one of the great means of keeping those principles before the world. It is a beneficent institution which has either directly or indirectly promoted and nurtured most of our modern benevolent enterprises. 2. *The substance glorifies the shadow by giving to it a rich spiritual tone.* Some read the fourth commandment as if it were a mere regimen of physical rest for those who felt no need of and had no desire for spiritual rest. This, however, is to read the commandment superficially. The seventh day is to be kept holy, and this cannot be done by mere idleness. The true refreshing repose for body and soul is to be found in spiritual employments. The highest repose is enjoyed by the angels, and yet they rest not day nor night. Jesus Christ, by reproving the unauthorised sabbatic restrictions of the Jews, declares the spiritual nature of the Sabbath. It is a day to be observed spiritually, and was thus observed by the apostles and first founders of the Christian Church. St. John gives emphasis to this idea when he says, "I was in the Spirit on the Lord's day." This may mean a special spiritual influence, a pneumatic condition, when great disclosures were made. Nevertheless every Christian seeking to keep the Lord's day aright will in his measure come under spiritual influence and have his divine manifestations to the soul. Here it may be noted that the expressions "the Lord's day" and "the first day of the week" indicate that this first day was one of public social worship amongst Christians in the apostolic age. The appellation "Lord's day" occurs nowhere in the New Testament except in this passage. But it occurs twice in the Epistle of Ignatius, who calls it "the Lord's day—the queen and prince of days." Chrysostom says, "It was called the Lord's day because the Lord arose from the dead on that day." Eusebius in his commentary on the Psalms says: "The Word (Christ) by the new covenant translated and transferred the feast of the Sabbath to the morning light, and gave us the symbol of true rest—viz., the saving Lord's day, the first day of the light in which the Saviour obtained the victory over death. On this day, which is the first day of the light and the true sun, we assemble after an interval of six days, and celebrate holy and spiritual Sabbath ; even all nations assemble redeemed by Him throughout the world, and do those things according to the spiritual laws which were decided by the priests to do on the Sabbath. All things whatever it was the duty to do on the Jewish Sabbath we have transferred to the Lord's day, as more appropriately belonging to it, because it has a precedence and is first in rank and more honourable than the Jewish Sabbath. It is delivered to us that we should meet together on this day, and it is ordered that we should do those things announced in Psalm xcii." Dr. Whewell in his *Elements of Morality* says : "In points on which the evidence of apostolic and catholic usage is complete, a Christian or a body of Christians has no liberty to alter the mode of observance. As an example of this, it appears to be inconsistent with Christian duty for any community to alter the day of religious observance from the first to any other day of the week, as Calvin is said to have suggested to the city of Geneva to do, in order that they might show their Christian liberty in regard to ordinances. If to do this were within the limits of Christian liberty, it would likewise be so to alter the period of the recurrence of the day and to observe every fifth day or every tenth, as was appointed in France when Christianity was rejected." 3. *The substance glorifies the shadow by showing that ceremonies do not avail without spiritual life.* Here substance and shadow coincide, for Isaiah says: "The new moons and Sabbaths, the calling of assemblies, I cannot away with; it is iniquity, even the solemn meeting." And why? Because the oblations were vain, the hands spread out in prayer were full of blood. We must cease to do evil and learn to do well before we can keep acceptable feasts. We must, in fact, seek to be more spiritual. However, let us not cry, Away with forms and ceremonies! "Of what use are forms, seeing that at times they are empty? Of the same use as barrels, which at times are empty too." They must be permeated with the spirit of Christ. Now Christianity does not permeate evil with good, for it cannot turn wickedness into righteousness and transform sin into holiness. It can permeate our evil nature by driving out sin and introducing holiness. Its motive power stimulates to action; its aim is to overcome evil by good through the destruction or banishment of evil and by the supremacy of good. It desires to transfuse the peaceful and refreshing spirit of the day of rest into all other days; but this cannot be done by its practical destruction. It does not call other days evil because it makes Sunday a special day. Christianity does not attribute moral qualities to days. In this sense every day may be alike. However, moral qualities may be brought to the observance of days, and in this manner certain days may be rendered sacred. It is observable that in the book of Exodus it is said, "And God blessed the Sabbath day," not, as in our Prayer Book, the seventh day; and thus God dedicates a day of rest. Let us bless our Sabbath day by bringing to its observance our highest powers, our best spiritual endeavours, our earnest prayerful preparation, and thus it will be to us a blessing. In blessing Sunday we bless ourselves and bless our kind. In praising Sunday we praise and exalt Sunday's Lord, and angels join to swell our chorus of praise.

IV. **The spirit of consecration says that Christ is the master.**—"For none of us liveth to himself, and no man dieth to himself. For whether we live, we live unto the Lord; and whether we die, we die unto the Lord." What, then, is the force of these words? "It means," saith St. Chrysostom, "that we are not free; we have a Master who would have us live, and willeth not that we die, and to whom both of these are of more interest than to us. For by what is here said He shows that He hath a greater concern for us than we have for ourselves, and considereth more than we do, as well our life to be wealth as our death to be a loss. For we do not die to ourselves alone, but to our Master also, if we do die." Christ, the kind master, has watched over the Church, and has preserved to us the day of rest. We are not free to destroy the sacred treasure. His concern for our spiritual welfare is so great that He has made the institution of Sunday the one institution that should be strikingly prominent and should exert a miraculous influence. We are Christ's property, redeemed by His precious blood. We are under all circumstances, living or dying, eating or abstaining, observing days or not observing them, Christ's—His redeemed people. Let us joyfully keep Sunday, and seek to make it a bright and happy day, and thus cause it to be regarded with favour by all the true-hearted.

Ver. 6. *A bright and happy day.*—The sabbatarian regards the Sunday as a day unto the Lord as well as from the Lord. To make of the Lord's day a merely ecclesiastical institution is to deprive it of its highest sanction and divest it of universal and binding authority amongst a free people. The presence of the fourth commandment in the Decalogue, the recognition of the obligation to keep the Sabbath by our Lord, as well as a true conception of the relation of the law to the Christian dispensation, is against the sweeping view that the institution is only binding upon us from considerations of humanity and religious expediency, and by the rules of that branch of the Church in which Providence has placed us. We regard Sunday as from the Lord, and keep it as unto the Lord, and believe that He intended it to be a day of true peace, joy, and refreshment. Sunday, then, should be a bright and happy day ; for—

I. Gladness is contemplated in divine arrangements.—The Almighty is the God of love, and cannot therefore be the cause of sorrow. Doubtless sadness is a blessing, not in itself, but in its effects under divine guidance. The arrangements of the material world indicate that originally this earth was intended to be a pleasant dwelling-place. It is sin which has brought about the sad change. The final arrangement of the moral world is the dispensation of the gospel ; and one of its designs was to give " the oil of joy for mourning and the garment of praise for the spirit of heaviness." Neither science, nor philosophy, nor cold morality has ever healed the broken in heart ; while this has been done by the gospel. And Sunday is the glad day on which many of these good results have been effected. Only the Sabbath of eternity will unfold the blessedness to God's redeemed which has sprung from the Sabbaths of time.

II. It interrupts the monotony of life.—Life is dull to many, and Sundays come as bright and welcome interruptions. The numbers who practically do without a Sunday, and do not appreciate its high joys and solemnities, rob existence of a great boon. Sunday changes the very quality of the life stream. We drink at secular streams and thirst again, while those who drink at the sacred stream are for ever refreshed.

III. It provides a quiet resting-place.—What the country home does for the city business man each night, that and more may the Sunday do each seventh day—that is, each recurring seventh day. It should shut out business cares and toils, and secure a quiet resting-place amid wearing activities. Sunday rest may confer a benefit which is not at all times properly appreciated, because all the circumstances of the case are not duly considered. Our thoughts are turned into new channels and our energies in fresh directions. Sunday should be a recruiting period from the battle, a quiet resting-place from the struggles, of modern existence.

IV. It promotes enlargement of nature.—Humboldt has well observed that an introduction to new and grand objects of nature enlarges the human mind. Now Sunday should introduce to new and grand objects of nature and supernature. It opens out all worlds. We may study both the natural and the spiritual. Sunday is a high peak on the level landscape of time from which we may view eternal vastnesses. It enables us to rise out of our narrow sphere and look beyond our narrow surroundings. It may teach how little are the thoughts and pursuits of men, and how infinitely vast are the thoughts of God. Without its help we are dwarfed, while by its kindly processes we are enlarged. Its visions of glory and its sounds of sweetness make glad.

V. It furthers the greater compactness of society.—In these days we hear from some quarters a good deal about the solidarity of the race, by which is understood a union of interests, of sympathies, and of pursuits. Now the only lasting unions for human societies are the outcome of the working of divine institutions. Sunday is the appointment of divine benevolence, and one of its gracious purposes is the reconstruction of the human race, so as to bind it together in one family bond under the guidance and protection of one all-loving and beneficent Father. Sunday's legitimate working is not towards the destruction of distinctions in society, but towards the blending of such distinctions, so that society may move along harmoniously. As this day gives completeness to the week, so it gives compactness to society.

VI. It furnishes stated times for public religious worship.—Man is a creature made to worship, and must have a God. "Religion," says Emerson, " is as inexpugnable as the use of lamps, or of wells, or of chimneys. We must have days, and temples, and teachers." Infidelity may reign for a time ; still it cannot long hold against the instincts and cravings for worship found in human nature. So far infidelity has not gained a widespread dominion. There is a demand for religion, and the heart of man cries out for the living God. There is a demand for worship which can only be stifled by sensuality and wickedness. Where these are not allowed to gain the mastery, where there is any spiritual development, there is both a desire for and a great pleasure in public religious worship. It must be so, for man is also a social being, and this arrangement helps to satisfy the social instincts of his nature. We miss the glad design and blessing of the Sunday if we do not engage in religious worship. They that thus honour the Lord's day will be amply rewarded.

VII. **Many have found Sunday a happy day for Christian work.**—The Christian's secular work should be done in a spiritual fashion and to the glory of God ; but the Christian welcomes Sunday because it furnishes opportunities of more directly promoting the moral welfare of mankind. He is benevolent, and Sunday must be a bright and happy day because it provides channels through which the waters of benevolence can freely flow. How happy the home where the Christian Sunday cheers and where the Christian father seeks to gladden ! When sorrow darkens the home, Sunday brightness gilds the sorrow-cloud with beautiful colours formed by ray-lights from heaven.

SUGGESTIVE COMMENTS ON VERSES 5, 6.

Discrimination of days means setting apart one day.—It has been concluded from these sayings of Paul that the obligation to observe *Sunday* as a day divinely instituted was not compatible with Christian spirituality, as this was understood by St. Paul. The context does not allow us to draw such a conclusion. The believer who observes Sunday does not in the least do so under the thought of ascribing to this day a *superior holiness* to that of other days. To him all days are, as the apostle thinks, equal in holy consecration. As rest is not holier than work, no more is Sunday holier than other days. It is another form of consecration, the periodical return of which, like the alternations of sleep and waking, arises from the conditions of our physico-psychical existence. The Christian does not cease to be a man by becoming a spiritual man. And as one day of rest in seven was divinely instituted at the creation on behalf of natural humanity, one does not see why the believer should not require this periodical rest as well as the unregenerate man. "The Sabbath was made *for man.*" So long as the Christian preserves his earthly nature, this saying applies to him, and should

turn not to the detriment but to the profit of his spiritual life. The keeping of Sunday thus understood has nothing in common with the sabbatical observance which divides life into two parts, the one holy, the other profane. It is this legal distinction which Paul excludes in our verse 5 and Col. ii.—*Godet.*

Economists laud the Sunday.—Whatever may be men's theories about the Sunday, it is a remarkable fact, and to us conclusive, that those who are the purest and noblest cling tenaciously to the Sunday. The Christian's decalogue would not be complete if the fourth commandment were erased. The Christian's sky would be darkened if Sunday were eclipsed. His days would be gloomy, his passage through life as if one were going through an underground tunnel where darkness and malodours prevailed, if the sacred light of the day of rest were extinguished. The Christian has a loving interest in the preservation of Christ's great day, the Church's great day. His loving interest is not selfish, for he knows that national prosperity and greatness are identified with the English Sunday. He is not surprised to find that foreigners can see the priceless value of our Sundays. Dr. D'Aubigné says, " Order and obedience, morality and power, are all in Britain connected with the observance of the Sabbath." La Presse says, " England owes much of her energy and character to the religious keeping of Sunday." Why cannot France follow her, as the Sabbath was made for all men, and we need its blessing? He is not surprised to hear the great political economist declare that the Sabbath as a political institution is of inestimable value, independently of its claim to divine authority. Sunday is a royal day and makes its adherents kingly. We must both know and do. "If ye know these things, happy are ye if ye do them." Knowledge is good, but doing is better. Doing right is the bright pathway to truest prosperity and divine kingship.

Sunday a spiritual blessing.—Now though it be true that man was not made for the Sabbath, yet let it never be forgotten that the Sabbath was made for man. Man was not made to move in a precise orbit of times and seasons; yet times and seasons may be arranged so as to subserve his use, and be the ministers of good both to his natural and moral ceremony. Were the keeping of the Sabbath a mere servitude of the body which left the heart no better than before, it would be a frivolous ceremonial, and ought to be exploded. But if it be true that he who sanctifies the Sabbath sanctifies his own soul, then does the Sabbath assume a spiritual importance, because an expedient of spiritual cultivation. The suspension on this day of the labour or business of the world, its scrupulous retirement from the converse or the festivities of common intercourse, its solemn congregations and its evening solitudes—these singly and in themselves may not be esteemed as moralites, and yet be entitled to a high pre-eminence among them from the impulse they give to that living fountain of piety out of which the various moralities of life ever come forth in purest and most plenteous emanation. It is not that the virtue of man consists in these things, but that these things are devices of best and surest efficacy for upholding the virtue of man. Were it not for this subserviency, the Sabbath might well be swept away; but because of this subserviency, it not only takes its place among the other obligations of Christianity, but is entitled to that reverence which is due, if not to the parent, at least to the foster-mother of them all. If the Sabbath of any one of the primitive Churches obtained not this homage from the apostle, it must have been because it was a Sabbath of ceremonial drudgery and not of spiritual exercise. And you have only to compute the worth and the celestial character of all those graces which have been sheltered and fed and reared to maturity in the bosom of this institution that you may own the high bearing and dignity which belong to it. And the maxim that what may be done at any time is never done applies with peculiar emphasis to every work against which there is a strong constitutional bias, where there is a reluctance to begin it, and the pitching of a strenuous effort to overcome that reluctance, and the pleasant deception all the while that it will just do as well after a little more postponement—a deception which, as it overspreads the whole life, will lead us to put off indefinitely, and this in the vast majority of instances is tantamount to the habit of putting off irrecoverably and for ever. Now this would just be the work of religion when shorn of its Sabbath—a work to embark upon which nature has to arrest her strongest currents, and to shake her out of her lethargies, and to suspend those pursuits to which by all the desires of her existence she is led most tenaciously to cleave, and to struggle for the ascendency of faith over sight, and of a love to the unseen God whom the mind with all the aids of solitude and prayer so dimly apprehendeth, over the love of those things that are in the world, and

455

whose power and whose presence are so constantly and so importunately bearing upon us. And will any say that in these circumstances the cause of religion is not bettered by the Sabbath, that weekly visitor coming to our door, and sounding the retreat of every seventh day from the heat and the hurry and the onset of such manifold temptations?—*Dr. Chalmers.*

A cuneiform inscription.—The Lord's day, though for us, is not ours, but the Lord's. We have no right to give it away, or to look on unmoved while it is being taken away. The Sabbath is not simply a Mosaic institution; the very word is found in the oldest cuneiform inscriptions, taking us back to a time before Moses was born. Tablets are in existence which show that thus early, in Ur of the Chaldees, the rest-day of the heart, as it was termed, was kept sacred. Sabbath observance is not a duty so much as a privilege. The Epistle of Barnabas states, "We keep the eighth day for rejoicing, because it is the day on which the Lord rose from the dead." And that ancient manual *The Teaching of the Twelve Apostles* says, "On the Lord's own day we gather to break bread and give thanks, first confessing our sins, that the sacrifice may be pure." There is a difference between the rest-day, the preservation of which is the business of the State, and the Lord's day, which it is the duty of the Church of Christ to protect and to secure.—*Canon Girdlestone.*

Son of man Lord of the Sabbath day.—Jesus Christ exercised His lordship over the Sabbath day in order that love's outflow might be unchecked. Those who watched the Saviour's miracles of healing on the Sabbath day might have learnt how He took them far back to love's primeval purpose when it created a Sabbath for man. It teaches and enforces the lesson that there is liberty to do right and restraint in the direction of wrong-doing. Jesus Christ moved through

this world as love incarnate, and the Sabbath was the blessed shrine in which He made love's richest display.

I. The Sabbath was created for man, created at the very commencement of human history, and for universal man's moral and spiritual well-being.—The world was created by the Saviour for humanity's dwelling-place; and the Sabbath for humanity's temple. The Sabbath was created for man as the sun was made for man that he might enjoy light, heat, and productiveness; as the sweet interchange of day and night and the revolving seasons were ordained for man to find this earth a pleasant dwelling-place; as the Bible was given for man's improvement and enrichment; and as heaven is provided for the redeemed as a joyful eternal home after life's cares, storms, and turmoils. The Sabbath was made for man's benefit, and it is at his peril that he either trifles with the boon, or presumes to lord it over the beneficent institution. The Son of man, then, is Lord of the Sabbath day, because He is the Son of God and the Creator. Our patriotism and our philanthropy as well as our zeal for the glory of God should impel us to put forth effort for the preservation of our English Sunday.

II. The Sabbath should be honoured in the sweet sacredness of the home.—English domestic life is one of the secrets of England's greatness, and Sunday is its great upholder and promoter. The scattered members of the family are drawn and bound together by the weekly recurrence of God's day. If the austere Sabbath-keeping of the home has rendered some perverted natures averse to religion, it has had a far different effect on large numbers. Occasionally we are presented with thrilling pictures of clergymen's sons driven to courses of wickedness by the austerities of Sabbath-keeping houses, but these are the painful exceptions, and the rule is that clergymen's families thank God for the hallowed sweetness of the parsonage home. And it is to us a cause of deep regret and of grave concern that in our cities the home is only a misnomer as applied to many of the abodes where human beings herd. God's day rightly regarded and honoured in our homes would produce a most salutary change in the community. The sabbatic leaven leavening the whole man would produce an aspect of spiritual beauty which would transform earth and even gladden heaven.

III. **The Sabbath should be honoured in the devotional sacredness of the temple.**—It is one of the blessings of our land that houses for prayer are erected in our cities, towns, villages, hamlets, and in remote mountain districts where the inhabitants and the excitements are few, and where life would otherwise move along in a dull round and on a low level. Thus our people have nowhere any excuse for dishonouring Sunday by neglecting public worship. The temple of nature is grand and imposing in many parts, but nowhere can it be found to be a substitute for the religious temple. The advocates of worship in the temple of nature have too often much talk and no worship of nature's Creator. And we miss the great design and blessing of the Sunday if we do not engage in religious worship. They that thus honour the Lord's day are amply rewarded. They may be raised above the worries of life, and forget for a season their earthly anxieties. And on the Sunday we must go to the temple if we are truly to honour the day and realise its richest experiences and taste its highest blessedness.

IV. **The Sabbath is to be honoured in the wholesome sacredness of Christian activities.**—It is not our purpose to define the work and to summon the workers to the Lord's vineyard. Suffice to say that there is plenty of moral work to be done; that the command is issued to every Christian, " Son, go work to-day in My vineyard." The fields are white unto the harvest, and the cry still is for more labourers. There would not be so much moral

dyspepsia, no need to utter vain jeremiads about Sunday's wasted opportunities, if there were more moral energy. Christians should give out as well as seek to take in on Sunday, and they would receive more if they would seek to impart more. There is that giveth and yet increaseth. The law of spiritual increase is that we do as well as hear. Happy are ye if ye do these things. Thus by a pleasing variety will the Christian Sunday be spent and the Christian be improved.

Sabbath springs from the necessity of religion.—" The Jews gave a reason why man was created in the evening of the Sabbath, because he should begin his being in the worship of His Maker. As soon as ever he found himself to be a creature, his first solemn act should be a particular respect to his Creator. To fear God and keep His commandment is the whole of man, or, as it is in the Hebrew, whole man ; he is not a man, but a beast, without observance of God. Religion is as requisite as reason to complete a man. He were not reasonable if he were not religious, because by neglecting religion he neglects the chief dictates of reason. Either God framed the world with so much order, elegance, and variety to no purpose, or this was His end at least, that reasonable creatures should admire Him in it and honour Him for it. The notion of God was not stamped upon man. The shadows of God did not appear in the creatures to be the subject of an idle contemplation, but the motive of a due homage to God. He created the world for His glory, a people for Himself, that He might have the honour of His works. It was the condemnation of the heathen world that, when they knew there was a God, they did not give Him the glory due to Him." Let us give glory to Him to whom all glory belongs. Let us join the beasts who were full of eyes within, so great their intelligence, who " rest not day nor night, saying, Holy, holy, holy, Lord God Almighty,

457

which was, and is, and is to come; and the four-and-twenty elders who fell down before Him that sat on the throne, and worshipped Him that liveth for ever and ever, and cast their crowns before the throne, saying, Thou art worthy, O Lord, to receive glory and honour and power: for Thou hast created all things, and for Thy pleasure they are and were created."

Christians unanimously observed the Lord's day.—Those that thought themselves under some kind of obligation by the ceremonial law, esteemed one day above another, kept up a respect of the times of the Passover, Pentecost, New Moons, and Feast of Tabernacles, thought those days better than other days, and solemnised them accordingly with particular observances, binding themselves to some religious rest and exercise on those days; those who knew all these things were abolished and done away by Christ's coming, *every* day alike. We must understand it with an exception of the Lord's day, which all Christians unanimously observed; but they made no account, took no notice, of these antiquated festivals of the Jews.—*Hewes.*

Let each act from conviction.—" Let him be fully persuaded in his own mind."

The Jewish convert might keep his Jewish Sabbath and the Gentile Christian might keep his own Christian Sabbath, the one might keep the seventh day and the other might keep the first day of the week, and both be blameless. St. Paul still keeps to the same subject, and what he means is about this: the thing is not concerned about fundamentals, for the thing requisite is, if this person and the other are acting for God's sake, the thing requisite is, if both terminate in thanksgiving; for, indeed, both this man and that give thanks to God. If, then, both do give thanks to God, the difference is no great one. But let me draw your notice to the way in which here also he aims a blow at the Judaizers; for if the thing required be this, the giving of thanks, it is plain enough that he which eateth it is that giveth thanks, and not he which eateth not; for how should he while he still holds to the law? As, then, he told the Galatians, "As many of you as are justified by the law, are fallen from grace," so here he hints it only, but does not uphold it so much, for as yet it was not time to do so. But for the present he bears with it; but by what follows he gives it a further opening. —*St. Chrysostom.*

MAIN HOMILETICS OF THE PARAGRAPH.—*Verses 7—9.*

Life and death harmonised.—In the opinion of most life and death are antagonistic. Death is the privation of life. The one is a something to be desired and cherished, while the other is to be dreaded and shunned. Life is the sphere of activities, while death is regarded as their cessation. We mourn when the good workman dies, as if work for him were over. But St. Paul teaches a larger view. Life and death are raised to one great level; they are spheres for a noble ministry. Both life and death are for the Lord, and it is in that light that we get to understand the greater importance of life and the sweet significance of death.

I. **Christ by His life and death lifts death out of its darkness and gives a new meaning to life.**—What a meaningless, monotonous round are the life days which are lived by the majority! Their souls are moved by no great purposes; their spirits are not touched by ennobling motives. To such life is hardly worth living. Christ gives to life a new meaning, a fresh force and vigour. Christ died and rose again that He might make life noble. Christ is the light of life, illuminating with glory, lifting out of its dulness, and showing the pathway to true greatness. Death is the shadow feared by man; its very approach casts darkness over the frame. Death loses much of its darkness and its terror when we view it in the light of Christ's claim. Death introduces to new and wider spheres. Death and life belong unto Him who by death conquered death.

II. Christ by His death and risen life made both spheres His own.—He made this earthly life His own by entering into all its trials, joys, and perplexities. He made the risen life His own by rising from the tomb. Life belonged unto Christ before His incarnation. Shall we be wrong in asserting that life in fuller measure belonged unto Christ after His resurrection? The keys of all life were delivered into His hands. In Him was a largeness of life not embraced in the prophetic vision. Death in all its solemn mystery belongs unto Him who has the keys of Hades and of death. Christ is sovereign over life and over death. If life and death belong unto Christ and the Christian be joined to Christ, then the Christian's life and the Christian's death belong unto the Lord. Life with all its possibilities, death with all its mysteries, are the Lord's. Let us so act as to show that whether living or dying we are the Lord's.

III. Christ by His death and life leads His people out of death into life.— This is specially true of the period which we call conversion. The believer is at this crisis led out of the death of sin, ignorance, and guilt into the life of holiness, knowledge, forgiveness, and the peace of God which passeth understanding. But here we contemplate a still higher leading—a leading which is progressive and continuous. Christ leads His people out of the death of selfishness into the life of love. Selfishness makes self the centre of life, the object and aim of existence; love makes Christ the centre of life, the alpha and omega of existence and of that which we regard as non-existence. But there is not such a thing as non-existence in the estimation of a Christ-loving nature. Life and death are crowned and glorified by love. And Christ will lead His people through death to the life of perfect love and of undying service.

Learn: 1. *The dignity of the Christian life.* It may be passed in lowly spheres as earth spirits estimate, but it acquires dignity as it is a Christ-owned life. Ownership imparts dignity. Royalty seems to overshadow with its greatness all its surroundings. The royalty of heaven's eternal King imparts dignity to the life of him who moves as in the loving taskmaster's sight. 2. *The sublimity of the Christian service.* It is one of love. It is one for life and for death. It is one in an ever-widening sphere. Self-service is contracting; love-service is expanding. The Christian lives for God, for Christ, for the promotion of all good and true ends. 3. *The interminable nature of the Christian's view.* Death does not bound his prophetic vision. The narrow tomb does not form a barrier to his wide-looking soul. He sees the unseen. Death opens up a larger life and shows divine service. Whether living or dying he is the Lord's.

Ver. 7. *Loving self-abnegation.*—These words would come with a startling sound to the ears of the world to which St. Paul wrote. There might be a time when none were for a party and all for the state; but the time had passed, if it ever truly existed, and the decline of the nation had begun, and national decline is marked by the increase of selfishness. But the words may come to us likewise with startling emphasis. This is a so-called Christian country. Our Christian preachers and teachers are multitudinous. Christianity has had a fairly long reign and a fairly successful course in our island; and yet have we reached the ideal set forth in the words, "None of us liveth to himself"? As we look at society in some of its aspects and in certain of our moods, the words sound to us like an ironical utterance. "None of us liveth to himself." Is not the modern doctrine, "Every man for himself"? Is it not the ripe conclusion of our modern evolutionary philosophy that the weakest must go to the wall? The man with a weak will, without push and tact, without iron nerves, must be crushed, and is often

459

crushed, by his stronger fellow. Alas that we will not look facts in the face! We are closed up in selfishness, we pamper our selfish fancies, we foster our selfish likings and prejudices, and we are very much shocked if any plain preacher tells us that we are selfish. We require still to be told that the true theory of life is that we must not live to ourselves, but unto Christ, to His Church, and for the good of humanity.

I. **In the world self strives for prominence.**—This statement requires no proof; it is almost axiomatic and self-evident. The poet sings, "Love rules the camp, the court, the grove." If the poet mean self-love, he is not far from the truth. But love in the higher and diviner sense does not rule. Do the strikes of the present day speak of loving forbearance between men and masters? What does the interest of capital mean but the interest of self? What do the claim and rights of labour mean but the claim and rights of self? What do the ten thousand wrongs, anomalies, oppressions, and in too many cases cruelties of our social system declare? They proclaim that self is striving for the prominence. This strife is everywhere,—in the remote hamlet and on the crowded exchange flags; in some of our syndicates, in our cotton corners, in our many fraudulent bubble schemes, and in our lying advertisements. Ah, self! thou unholy and rapacious monster: thou dost obtrude thy ungainly form in all departments of life; thou hast been known to wear the guise of philanthropy, to assume the garb of sanctity; thou hast not scrupled to profane the priest's sacred vestments and to sully a bishop's lawn!

II. **This self-strife leads to individual dissatisfaction and to social undoing.**—This is evident to every casual observer of society. Where self is thought about more than society and the general welfare, there is sure to be social undoing. Revolutions may have been necessary, and may have done good; but some revolutions have been influenced by a selfish spirit and have been fraught with evil. All revolutions promoted by selfishness are injurious, and can only become beneficial as the great Worker educes good out of evil. Certainly most harmful to the individual is the effort to make self prominent and supreme. The more we give to self, the more it craves; the more it gets, the more it wants. Its riches may increase, but they tend only to greater poverty. The most discontented of mortals have been those who have had ample means for the pampering of self.

III. **Self-hood, however, is subjected.**—So that it becomes true in a wider sense than we sometimes think that none of us liveth to himself. In will and purpose we live to ourselves, but in tendency and effect we live for others. The idler and the pleasure-seeker may find themselves conquered in the conflict. If they do nothing better, they serve as warnings and beacon lights to the sensible. They live to themselves, but their wasted lives tell us to shun the shifting sands of folly in which they were engulfed. It is plain that the worker cannot altogether live to himself. According to the political economists he is a productive labourer, and thus while increasing his own wealth he increa. : the wealth of the nation. Society cannot allow us to live for ourselves; for ourselves are firmly bound to and with other selves. The nation is made up of individual selves, as a building is erected by means of separate stones. As stone is bound by and to its fellow-stone, so my self is bound by and to the other self. The not-self is essential to the welfare of the self; the not-self and the self are bound together and have interests in common.

I. **In the Church there is loving self-abnegation.**—The objector says that he cannot see it. We go into the Church, and find that modern Christians are essentially selfish. Of course we cannot see it; for it is not to be seen, and a man does not see that which he does not want to see, and which is outside his range of things. He does not see that self-will is dethroned and bowing in loving submission to the divine will. In the Christian self-hood rises against the Christlike spirit. Self-hood rises, but it falls conquered by the Christian manhood. The general aim, purpose, and desire of the Christian is upward to Christ. The Christlike soul dethrones selfishness and exalts the Prince of life. Christ and not self is the centre of the Christian nature. He loves himself, but he loves himself in and for Christ, the beloved of all true men. A mere observer cannot see that which is going on in the nature of another. The conquest over self is gained in secret; the battle is bloodless and without noise. Christ-love conquers self-love; but we cannot see Christ-love riding in any triumphal car or wielding any sceptre of authority. The Christian does not live to himself. There is in him a motive power which the world does not see. And this inward life works outwardly in many beneficial ways. He must be blind indeed who does not see that many Christians have shown that they live to and for Christ, and thus in the highest sense live to and for the good of their kind. Christianity has been the most beneficial agency which has found a home and a sphere in this planet.

II. **The Christian finds in self-abnegation the widest contentment.**—When self is allowed to gain the upper hand, then there is the reign of misrule, then there is dissatisfaction. But when the life stream flows with Christ treading the waters every storm is hushed, and the course of the waters produces sweetest music. Contentment in the soul is the effect of the Christ presence and supremacy.

III. **The Christian in loving consecration obtains truest riches.**—Not that which is of any account at the bankers; but shall we still esteem soul wealth as of no avail? Self works for riches, but is crushed by the weight. If he would confess it, the man is oft richer in poverty than in wealth. Love works for Christ, and obtains soul wealth—riches here and riches hereafter.

IV. **The Christian in loving consecration secures extensive productiveness.**— Life is regarded by many as the only sphere for production. We believe in annihilation to a much larger extent than may be supposed. However, there is no annihilation. We live when we are dead. Tombs have a voice. " The memory of the just is blessed." We die to the Lord, and He is the good husbandman who will not allow the dying grain to be wasted. Over the graves of His beloved He makes the golden harvest to wave. Let us seek to show that we live unto the Lord. If we have the inward life of consecration, the blessed fruits will appear. The light of love within will shine on the world's dark pathway. Let us be comforted in seeming life failure that we live unto the Lord, for He can turn the seeming failure into success. Let us not fear death, for in the dark valley we are Christ's. He will guide safely through to the tearless, deathless land of infinite love and blessedness.

Vers. 7, 8. *Living and dying unto the Lord.*—Let us investigate the principle here laid down : that both the life of the Christian and the death of the Christian have a special place and use in the divine purposes; that there is something which every man is sent into this world for, and which it were to contravene the ends of his creation if he were to leave unfulfilled.

I. **Let us consider first the negative statement of the apostle in relation to this great principle.**—" None of us liveth to himself." None of us. Who are the " us " here spoken of ? Manifestly they are the true Christians, as opposed to men of the world; those who place themselves at the disposal of Christ, as opposed to those who care only to live to their own selfish ends; in a word, those who have made a voluntary choice of the divine service and are urged onward in the path of godliness by the power of a new affection and a

461

new hope. The text, however, may be taken in the largest sense, as the expression of a general fact in the divine government, and plainly implying that, living as we do under an economy of mutually dependent ministries—man linked with man, and class bound up with class—not only none of us ought to live to himself, but none of us can live to himself if we would. I say none of us ought to live to himself; for it is clear that God has an original and antecedent claim upon the service of every one of us—upon our time, upon our substance, upon our talents, upon our affection. We are His by every consideration which could be binding on an intelligent spirit—by the right of creation, by the mercy of continued being, by the mystery of redemption, by the derivation from Him of a spiritual nature, by gifts and covenants and revelations and hopes of heaven. "What have we that we have not received?" And what have we received which in strict justice might not have been withheld? Surely we must all feel that "every good gift is from above,"—our table, if it be spread; our cup, if it be full; the medicine, if it heal our sickness; the voice of joy and health, if it be heard in our dwellings; the sweet sense of security, if there be none to make us afraid. All secondary agencies—chance, skill, judgment, friends, influence—are but the servants of the great Benefactor bringing our blessings to us. They are the bearers of the cup, not the fillers of the cup. The Lord stands by the well, giving to every man as it pleaseth Him. Hast thou riches? "The Lord thy God, it is He that giveth thee power to get wealth." Hast thou understanding and gifts? It is the Lord that "maketh thee to differ from another," and endued thee with "a wise, understanding heart." Reputation and credit had not been thine if the Lord had not "hidden thee from the scourge of tongues"; and if the tranquillities of domestic life are thine, "He maketh peace in thy borders, strengthening the bars of thy gates, and blessing thy children within thee." What, then, follows from this but that we live to Him who gives us all the means to live; that we lay upon the altar of our obedience a living and loving sacrifice—our heart's cheerfulest, our mind's noblest, our soul's best?

II. **But there is an affirmative view of our principle to be taken.**—Besides saying our life cannot be inoperative, cannot be resultless, cannot be barren both of good and evil, the text specifies a positive designation of this life to a place among great agencies, intimates that out of it God would get honours to Himself, and so teaches us that there is no man so useless and helpless in the world as not to be able to do some good if he would. "For whether we live, we live unto the Lord." This expression may be taken first as implying the possession of a principle of internal and spiritual religion—a life derived from Christ, centred in Christ, devoted to Christ. A man must live before he acts—must be in a state of reconciliation to God before he devotes himself to His service. Religion is a choice—the choice of Christ as a Saviour, of God as a portion, of the ways of wisdom as the ways of pleasantness, of the hope of heaven as our exceeding great reward. All this supposes activity, energy, devotedness—body, soul, and spirit consecrated and given up to God; and nothing dead about us but the love of the world and self and sin. "Likewise reckon ye also yourselves to be dead indeed unto sin, but alive unto God through Jesus Christ our Lord." But, again, there is in this part of the text the assertion of a great rule of duty—a declaration that our life is to be consecrated to the great ends of moral usefulness. We "live unto the Lord" when we live for the good of His people, for the honour of His cause, for the extension of His Church, for the glory of His name. And the consciousness that we are so living, and must so live, is one of the first indications of a renewed mind.

III. **But to this declaration the text adds another, that** "when he dies, he dies unto the Lord."—He who does not live to himself shall not die to himself. Christians can neither live useless lives nor die useless deaths. God has a purpose in both and a property in both; "so that, whether they live or die, they are the Lord's."—*D. Moore.*

Vers. 7, 8. *Christian devotedness.*—This sentiment is strikingly characteristic of Christianity, and marks it with features so noble and benevolent that, whilst it is a key to its design, it offers one of the greatest motives by which its discipline and influence are recommended.

I. **No man liveth to himself.**—This is not only characteristic of the true Christian, but is essentially so; for a man who liveth to himself, by the sentence of the text, is not a Christian. It indicates: 1. *That the Christian regards the great end of his being.* Human existence must have an object. God acts not in anything without design. Nature is full of this. Every star, animal, plant, has some object. That this atom of the rock is in this place rather than that is determined by some purpose. Is man, then, exempt from this law? There is an end of life, a purpose of creation and preservation, and of the still more wondrous dispensation of redemption. It becomes us to inquire what that end is, and steadily to pursue it. 2. *No Christian man liveth to himself: this indicates the respect which he habitually has to the approbation of God.* Here, again, appears the distinction between the Christian and the man who lives to himself. The man who lives to himself cultivates that principle and this passion, does this and avoids the other; but the motive is not God, but his own self. The Christian sets God at his right hand, seeks His approbation, and to Him his heart is always open. 3. *No Christian liveth to himself: this indicates the interest he feels in the cause of Christ.* To live unto the Lord by living for His cause and to live for ourselves is impossible. The extension of the work of Christ in every age goes upon the same principle. The principle of selfishness and that of usefulness are distinct and contrary. The principle of one is contraction; of the other, expansion. 4. *No Christian liveth to himself: this indicates a benevolent concern to alleviate the temporal miseries of his suffering fellow-men.* Spiritual charities are the most important, but they are not our duties exclusively. He who lives to the Lord will have His example in view; and in that he is seen going about doing good.

II. **No Christian man dieth to himself; he dieth to the Lord.**—As a reward for not living to himself, he is not suffered to die unto himself. 1. *It may be in judgment to others.* It may be in judgment to families who have refused admonition and to unfaithful Churches when a Barnabas or an Apollos or a Boanerges is called away. 2. *It may be hastened in mercy to him.* Good men are often removed to heaven before scenes of wretchedness and misery are presented. 3. *It is prolonged in mercy to others.* He is not always taken away from the evil to come. He is sometimes to endure it, and private feelings give way to public good. (Jeremiah and St. Paul.) 4. *No Christian man dieth to himself, for his death is that by which Christ may be glorified.* Let us not be extreme in our anxieties about death, let us be anxious to glorify God in our death, and He will take care of all the rest.

III. **The man who lives and dies, not to himself, but to the Lord, is the Lord's in life and death.**—To be bound to Him, but to yield ourselves to His service and His glory. The Christian is the Lord's in life. Life includes our earthly blessings; life includes our afflictions; life is the period in which we are trained for the maturity of holiness. And the Christian is the Lord's in death. The body is laid down in hope; the grave has been sanctified by the body of Christ, and the key is in His hands. 1. *It is founded on justice.* To live to ourselves is unjust. Our obligations to God are absolute. 2. *It is founded on benevolence.* God might have rendered men much less dependent on

463

others than they are. 3. *This is a principle founded on the ministerial character.* A minister living to himself is the most pitiable object on which the eye can fall. To him was committed the cause of Christ, and he has been indifferent to the general movement, if his department has been enough to grind him his daily bread. 4. *Let us see the great end of life.* It is to live to please God ; to live as Christ lived on earth—soberly, righteously, godly, benevolently. As Christians we employ talents which will be rewarded in another state. We thus prepare for death ; and in that awful moment what a heaven it will be to know that we die to Him, and that, " whether we live or die, we are the Lord's " !—*R. Watson.*

SUGGESTIVE COMMENTS ON VERSES 7—9.

Is the Lord our Lord ?—Is the Lord of dead and living in any real sense *our* Lord ? Has He that conquered the grave conquered the worldly part in me ? Are covetousness, ambition, impurity, indolence, thoroughly put down ? Questions such as these are painful to propose, and hard to answer. If we are immersed wholly in the present world, the fashion of which passeth away, if Christ be dead in vain so far as we are concerned, the thoughts that belong to this day may help to awaken us. The mountain on the horizon seems small and dim, but towards it we are travelling, and it grows daily bigger : it is the mountain of heaven that we must scale, and there is a dark and silent valley, invisible at present, through which we must pass before we reach it. Compare the great realities that we have been looking at to-day with the all-engrossing business that draws our attention off them. The subtlest tongue will be silent before long ; the most eager strife will cease ; the wisest decision will be quoted no longer at most than the kind of right it relates to shall subsist. But we must all appear before the judgment seat of Christ ; and at that bar the issue that is decided is for eternity. May He that judges us plead our cause also ! And because we shall have acknowledged from our hearts that He is the Lord of the dead and the living, may He wash out our sins with His blood, and say, " Thou hast been faithful unto death ; I will give thee a crown of life " !—*Archbishop Thomson.*

The Redeemer's dominion.—The Redeemer's dominion over men is forcibly declared to have been the end of His ministry on earth. The apostle's words are very express and emphatic. " To this end that " signifies, in language as strong as could be used to note design, that the purpose of the Passion was the attainment of universal dominion over the human race in time and in eternity. To this end, and no other ; for this purpose, and nothing short of it ; with this design, embracing and consummating all other designs. But we must view it under two aspects : it was a purpose aimed at before the death ; in the Resurrection it was a purpose reached. He *died* that He might have the dominion ; He *lived* that He might exercise. Now, of this mighty realm of the risen Christ, the dead constitute the vast majority. " What, in comparison of the uncounted hosts, numbered only by the infinite Mind, are the few hundreds of millions that any moment are called the *living* ? It is in the realm of the shades that we contemplate our great family in its vastest dimensions, as it has from the first generation been gaining on the numbers of the living and swelling onwards to the stupendous whole bound up in the federal headship of the first and second Adam." Now, in all this vast domain, there is but one rightful Lord of the *conscience* ; there may be other lords with dominion, and they may be many, but in the realm of conscience there is only one Lord, and He is the risen Saviour !—*Pope and Saurin.*

Christ our Master.—As he always exists, as a Christian, in and by his Master, so he always exists for his Master. He has, in the reality of the matter, no dissociated and independent interest. Not only in preaching and teaching, and bearing articulate witness to Jesus Christ, does he, if his life is true to its ideal and its secret, " live not unto himself "; not with aims which terminate for one moment in his own credit, for example, or his own comfort. Equally in the engagements of domestic life, of business life, of public affairs ; equally (to look towards the humbler walks of duty) in the day's work of the Christian servant or peasant or artisan ; " whether he lives, he lives unto the Master, or whether he dies, he dies unto the Master "; whether he wakes or sleeps, whether he toils or rests, whether it be the term or the vacation of life, " whether he eats or drinks, or whatsoever he does," he is the Master's property for the Master's use.

> " Teach me, my God and King,
>   In all things Thee to see ;
> And what I do in anything
>   To do it as to Thee.

> " A servant with this clause
> Makes drudgery divine ;
> Who sweeps a room as for Thy laws
> Makes that and th' action fine."
> *Moule.*

A threefold cord binds to Christ.—Christ's *death*, Christ's *resurrection*, and Christ's *intercession*—a threefold cord, which cannot be broken—bind you indissolubly in the " bundle of life " with Him. I may be faint and weary, but my God cannot. I may fluctuate and alter as to my frames and feelings, but my Redeemer is unchangeably the same. I should utterly fail and come to nothing if left to myself ; but I cannot be left to myself, for the Spirit of truth has said, " I will never leave thee nor forsake thee." He will renew my strength by enduing me with His own power. He is wise to foresee and provide for all my dangers. He is rich to relieve and succour me in all

my wants. He is faithful to perfect and perform all His promises. He is blessed and immortal to enrich my poor desponding soul with blessedness and immortality. Oh, what a great and glorious Saviour for such a mean and worthless sinner ! Oh, what a bountiful and indulgent Friend for such a base and insignificant rebel ! What, what am I, when I compare myself, and all I am myself, with what I can conceive of my God, and of what He hath kindly promised to me ? What a mystery I am to myself and to men ! A denizen of earth to become a star of heaven ! A corruptible sinner made an incorruptible saint ! A rebel made a child ! an outlaw an heir ! A deserver of hell made an inheritor of heaven ! A stronghold of the devil changed into a temple of the living God ! An enemy and a beggar exalted to a throne, united in friendship with Jehovah, made one with Christ, a possessor of His Spirit, and a sharer of all this honour, happiness, and glory for evermore ! Oh ! what manner, what matter of love is this ? Lord, take my heart, my soul, my all. I can render Thee no more ; I could render Thee no less. It is indeed a poor return. My body and my soul are but as " two mites "; and yet—glory to Thy great name !—Thou who didst esteem those of the poor widow wilt not despise these of mine. Lord, they are Thine own, and I can only give Thee what is Thine. I melt with gratitude ; and even this gratitude is Thy gift. Oh, take it, and accept both it and me in Thyself, who art all my salvation and all my desire, for ever and for ever.—*Ambrose Serle.*

Christ and the Christian.—Have I overdrawn the claims of Jesus Christ upon the Christian ? I cannot present them in all the amplitude and depth, and at the same time the minuteness and precision, with which you will find them set forth in the New Testament as a whole. There Christ is indeed all things in all His followers. There the Christian is a being whose true reason and true life is altogether and always in Jesus Christ. He is slave, and his Redeemer is absolute owner. He is branch, and his Redeemer is root. He is limb, and his Redeemer is head. He is vessel, and the great Master of the house is always to have full and free use of Him for any purposes of His own. He has no rights and can set up no claims as against his Lord: " If I will that he tarry till I come, what is that to thee ? " —*H. C. G. Moule.*

Surrender to Christ.—To surrender at discretion to Jesus Christ, who is not a code but a master, is so far forth to put your being into right relations with itself through right relations with Him. It is to gravitate at last upon your centre, and to be in gear. It is to be possessed, spiritually possessed; but by whom? By the Lord of archetypal order; by the Prince of peace; by the Prince of life; by Him in whom, according to one profound scripture, all this complex universe itself " consists," is held together, holds together. The more of His presence and dominion, the less of fret and friction. The less resistance to Him, the more genuine and glad and fruitful action—as it were a sphere-music of the moving microcosmos of the soul. —*H. C. G. Moule.*

Christ's threefold right.—Now, if we examine, we shall find that Christ has every kind of claim and right to us. He has a right derived from His creative power. If " all things were made by Him," He made us, and not we ourselves. In consequence of this He has a propriety in us, not only such as no man can have in a fellow-creature, but such as even no father has in his own children. They are his in a subordinate and limited degree; but we are the Lord's absolutely and entirely. Suppose we were to return to Him all that we received from Him, what would be left as our own? He has a right derived from His providential care. He has not only given us life

and favour, but His visitation hath preserved our spirits. Whose are we but His in whom we live, move, and have our being? How mean to enjoy the light of His sun, to breathe His air, to eat constantly at His table, to be clothed from His wardrobe, and not own and acknowledge our obligations to Him! He has a right derived from His redeeming mercy. We are not our own, but bought with a price, and He paid it. To feel the force of this claim it will be necessary for us to weigh three things : 1. The mighty evils from which He has delivered us : sin, the power of darkness, the present evil world, death, and the wrath to come. 2. The state to which He has advanced us. Even the beginnings of it here, its earnests and foretastes, are indescribable and inconceivable ; even now the joy is unspeakable and full of glory, and the peace passeth all understanding. 3. The way in which He has thus ransomed us. All comes free to us; but what did it cost Him? Owing to our slight views of the evil of sin and the holiness of God, we are too little struck with the greatness of redemption and the difficulties attending it. It was easy to destroy man ; but to restore him, in a way that should magnify the law which had been broken, and display God as the just as well as the justifier, was a work to which the Lord Jesus only was adequate ; and what does it require even of Him? Not a mere volition, not a mere exertion, as when He delivered the Jews from Egypt, and spake the world into being. He must assume flesh and blood. He dwelt among us. For thirty-three years He was " a man of sorrows and acquainted with grief." Let us go over His history ; let us survey His sufferings; let us meditate on His agony in the garden, His shame on the cross, His abasement in the lowest parts of the earth ; and all this for enemies, and all not only without our desert, but without our desire—till we feel we are drawn and bound with the cords of a man and the bands of love—a love that passeth knowledge. Hence He has a right, derived, not only from what *He* has done, but from what *we* have done—a right derived from our dedication. If Christians, we have ratified His claims, and have actually surrendered ourselves to Him, renouncing every other owner, and saying, Lord, I am Thine; save me. Other lords beside Thee have had dominion over me; but henceforth by Thee only will I make mention of Thy name. And having opened your mouth unto the Lord, you cannot go back.—*W. Jay.*

Christian citizenship.—It is scarcely surprising that men sometimes charge Christianity with having enfeebled the civic virtues. Patriotism, they tell us, and public spirit, burned with a deeper, steadier glow in ancient Athens or Rome than in any modern city. And yet there is something of paradox in the thought that such a result can be spoken of as following upon the teaching of Jesus; for the spirit of His teaching is, as some of our modern writers would phrase it, essentially altruistic: it is inherently and fundamentally social; its starting-point is self-abandonment, its root principles are love and sacrifice, and its natural fruits in every Christian character should have been social enthusiasm. While the apparatus of social life was still pagan, the Christian was of course bound to think of himself as a member of a separate community; but the thought of citizenship or membership of a community was none the less his guiding and inspiring thought, as it should be ours, if our life is to be worthy of the privileges we inherit and the hope that is set before us in Christ Jesus. In this matter, as in all else that concerns our social and religious life, we derive useful and clear guidance from the language and the spirit of St. Paul. See how his mind was filled with thoughts of citizenship. To the Philippians he writes, " Do your duty worthily as citizens of the gospel kingdom." The Ephesians are addressed by him as " fellow-citizens with the saints." In describing his own life the thought is still the same. " In all good conscience," he says, " I have lived as a good citizen unto God." Everywhere, in fact, his language implies this fundamental thought, as the inspiring purpose of his life, that no man liveth to himself, but that we are members one of another, because we are Christ's and our life is hid with Christ in God. And if we turn from his language to the plan and conduct of his life, we see in him the very type and pattern of a true Christian patriot, working at his trade, self-supporting, independent, not forgetting his position or his rights as a Roman citizen, devoted to his own people with a devotion surpassing the power of words to express, and yet never engrossed with any earthly occupation or by any earthly ambition, and absolutely free from that enervating spirit of self-indulgence which makes such havoc of all higher purposes in the life of men. It is good for us thus to think of him for a moment apart from his great name as an inspired apostle, for thus we may hope to catch the infection of his keen and fervid interest in all the relations of our common life, and to be ourselves uplifted as we see how he uplifts and purifies all he touches with the fire of his spiritual earnestness. See how he takes these phrases about citizenship, shaming by his use of them those who care nothing for the thing itself—how he takes them up and enlists them in the service of the new kingdom; thus consecrating, so to speak, and transfiguring the citizen spirit. As we linger over all this— Paul, the Roman citizen— Paul, the Jewish patriot—Paul, the apostle of a new citizenship in the New Jerusalem, where there is neither bond nor free, neither Jew nor Gentile, no national antipathies, no class antagonisms, no party bitterness, no mean and petty rivalries, where all are brethren in Christ, and called to mutual service— the question must come up in our thoughts, What do *we* make of our citizenship? We live in crowded communities. What is our life in regard to this citizen spirit? Is the spirit strong in us? or is it weak? Does it inspire and direct our life? and is it of the Pauline type? Does it save us from the canker of pride and prejudice, and the spirit of isolation? Does it destroy the root of selfishness in us? and does it make us revolt from all forms of self-indulgence, sensuality, animalism?

Or does it somehow leave these things to grow in all their strength in our community, and to propagate themselves after their kind, as if it were no concern of ours? If so, it has to be confessed that the Holy Spirit has not yet enfranchised us, and our citizenship is not such as becometh the gospel of Christ.—*J. Percival.*

MAIN HOMILETICS OF THE PARAGRAPH.—Verses 10—15.

Self-judgment the paramount duty.—There is a certain morbid state of nature which leads men and women to spend too much time in judging themselves. There is also a censorious spirit which spends too much time in judging others. Both courses of conduct may be morally injurious. Nevertheless, we must judge ourselves, and if we do so aright we shall be the more disposed to walk charitably towards those who consider this or that not lawful.

I. **We must judge ourselves, for we have our weaknesses.**—We should not be human if we had not our weaknesses. A depraved nature suggests that we may have sins as well as weaknesses. The man who properly knows himself will make large allowance for others. If the Pharisee had known himself, had seen how contemptible was his sanctimonious and sinful pride in the view of the All-holy, he would not have directed a scornful look at the publican. There may be a littleness and a weakness about the man who prides himself upon his elevation above materialism, as there is a littleness about the man who has not learnt that the material is secondary to the spiritual. Why dost thou set at naught thy brother? Brethren have a family likeness and family failings. The strong brother of the family is not far removed from the weak. The good, stay-at-home brother did not show himself nearer heaven than the broken-down, prodigal brother who returned with tears of repentance.

II. **We must judge ourselves, for we are individually responsible.**—" We shall all stand before the judgment-seat of Christ," but each one must give account of himself to God. The strong brother will not have to give an account of the weak, but of himself. Solemn thought! How hast thou used thy strength? Has it been employed rather for self-glorification than for the helping of the weak? Thou hast gloried in thy strength; and yet what small moral use has it been to humanity! Thou hast condemned thy brother's punctiliousness; and yet the weak brother may have helped to invest material things with spiritual significances.

III. **We must judge ourselves, lest we hinder others.**—A strong man is a pleasant sight; but strength is harmful if it become a stumbling-block so as to wound the weak brother, or an obstacle against which the weak brother stumbles and falls. Is it not likely to be true that more moral damage has been done to the world by the strong than by the weak? The Samsons of time have slain their thousands. Napoleons have done damage which long years only can repair. The Byrons of song have polluted the world's ears with their melodies. Strong men, in their impatience of restraints, have engendered heresies of a pestilential character.

IV. **We must judge ourselves in the light of divine teaching.**—Material things have no moral qualities. A piece of meat has no conscience, and cannot be unclean of itself. A small square of bread cannot be incorporated with spiritual vitality. Bread of itself cannot give physical life, much less spiritual life. Still, if my weak brother esteemeth the bread supernaturally endowed, then as a strong brother I must walk charitably. The strong must not produce any painful and bitter feeling in the heart of the weak by the spectacle of free and bold eating, by the aspect of seeming irreverence with reference to sacred things. However, we must take care lest, while we vaunt our charity, we are only using another name for indifference. Charity suffereth long. Divine love suffers long. God is love, and yet God hates evil. St. John was the apostle of love, and yet he could say, " Beloved, believe not every spirit, but try the spirits whether they are of God: because many false prophets are gone out into the world." Modern so-called charity would scout the exhortation, " If there come any unto you, and bring not this doctrine, receive him not into your house, neither bid him God-speed: for he that biddeth him God-speed is partaker of his evil deeds."

V. **We must judge ourselves, lest we obstruct the Saviour's purposes.**— "Destroy not him with thy meat, for whom Christ died." Let us not stay to inquire how man, weak at his best, can obstruct the purposes of the strong Christ. Let us seek to move in harmony with the merciful purpose of the loving Mediator. He came to save the weak as well as the strong. The mission of every Christ-like soul should be a mission of salvation. Divine salvation is vaster than human. The latter is too often an affair of the letter; the former is of the spirit. Faith, hope, and love are the great words of spiritual salvation—faith in Christ, hope built upon faith, love the outcome of faith and hope. Let us work so that faith may be stronger, hope brighter, and love more far-reaching.

Ver. 10. *The coming judgment.*—It is well said that he who judges arrogates to himself Christ's office; he who bears in mind that Christ will judge us all will no more condemn. What must we think of the prisoner awaiting trial who presumes to pronounce sentence upon his fellow-prisoners? It is a course of conduct we might not naturally expect; but the unexpected happens; and we know from observation that the worst sinners are not the most lenient in their judgments. It is often the case that the purer the life, the more charitable the judgment. Who was purer than Christ, and who gentler in judgment? If He were severe, it was only to the vile pretenders. He was gentleness itself to publicans and harlots. The thought of a coming judgment should lead to gentleness and forbearance in dealing with our fellow-sinners. Alas! the thought of a coming judgment seems often eliminated from modern life. Let us consider the awe-inspiring fact.

I. **There are declarations of a coming judgment.**—The declarations of the inspired word of God tell us of a judgment to come. Our blessed Lord, by striking and terrible imagery, places before the minds of men the fact of such an event taking place in the moral government of God. Our Lord had no reason to deceive. The almost universal verdict of humanity is that Christ was the essence of goodness, and He could not be that if He were capable of deception. Can we for one moment entertain the idea of deception upon such an awful and momentous topic of consideration? We may not be able either to understand or to explain all His imagery, but the plain truth abides that there will be a general judgment. He speaks with authority, not only as being absolutely pure, but as coming forth from eternity and being intimately acquainted with all the counsels and designs of the Infinite.

II. **There are premonitions of a coming judgment.**—An appeal to the Bible is with many out of date. The preacher is not now asked to quote chapter and verse. A sentence from Shakespeare or Tennyson or Ruskin is often more welcome and more thought about than a sentence from the Bible.   But we believe that in this case the declarations of the Bible are strongly supported by the premonitions of the human soul.   Why speak we of premonitions?   Why talk we of a coming judgment?   Why, when there is a judgment here and now?   Christ has His judgment-seat in the human conscience.   The process is going on day by day—the process, we mean, of moral reckoning.   The doctrine of moral accountability to the human being is not quite destroyed.   In this enlightened age men are not to be frightened into being religious, and we quite admit that the religion of terror only is a base sort of thing.   But even now men have their doubts and fears, and these are not the product of a cunning priestcraft.   They spring from the constitution of the human soul.   It is fatuous to talk of introducing the alien principle or faculty of conscience into the human creature if there be no place for it among our moral faculties—if there be no combination of faculties out of which such a faculty as conscience could be developed; that is, if we proceed on the false principle that conscience is not original, but derived.   The doubts and fears with which the mind is tossed and harassed, the writhings of a guilty conscience, are the dread premonitions of a coming judgment.   Conscience could not make us cowards if there were no moral Governor, if there were no judgment to come, if we did not fear that somewhere and somehow there would be a judgment.   There is no need to lessen the vital importance of the question by materialising the thought.   St. Paul must speak in human language.   "We must all stand before the judgment-seat of Christ" sets before us a solemn fact.   We know not where the judgment-seat will be.   We may in vain try to fancy the myriads upon myriads of our species that have lived on the earth, from the first man who saw creation's prime to the last man who sees its final collapse, standing before the judgment-seat; but we cannot get away from our own oppressive thought that somehow there will be a judgment of the just and the unjust.

III. **There are the certainties of a coming judgment.**—These certainties are founded upon the declarations of the Bible and upon the premonitions of mankind—upon the testimony of conscience, which asserts, sometimes unwillingly, the equity and necessity of a final judgment.   We speak of a religion of love and scout the idea of a religion of fear.   But, after all, fear or misgiving of some kind or another has more to do with our religion than we are at all times prepared to allow.   Vague fears are the foundation of all the religions, true or false, that have appeared.   It is all very fine for philosophers to bid us shake ourselves free from fear and break loose from the miserable trammels of old-world superstitions and traditions.   They might as well tell us to shake ourselves free from ourselves; for these fears, these premonitions, these stirrings of conscience, are woven into the very texture of our nature.   The coming judgment is not a mere probability; it is a certainty.   If it be contended that it is only a probability, we affirm that such probabilities amount to certainties.   We say it is probable that the sun will rise to-morrow because he has risen every day for so many ages.   Probable, but not certain; and yet the business man and the farmer, in fact every sensible man, proceed as if it were a certainty that the sun will rise as aforetime.   Let us for the moment admit that the judgment to come is only a probable event, then as sensible men it becomes us to proceed in life as if that probability were a certainty.   But if we look carefully into the workings of our own moral natures, if we hear the dread warnings of conscience, the dark whisperings of the Infinite, if we listen to the words of divine wisdom, we shall assent to the statement that a coming judgment is a certainty, a crisis which we must all meet.   We must all stand before the judgment-seat of Christ—all—judges and judged, conquerors and conquered, righteous Pharisees and sinful publicans, Cæsars and their subjects, czars and their serfs, philosophers and fools, bishops and their flocks, inquisitors and their victims—there is no exception : we must all stand before the judgment-seat of Christ.

IV. **There is a preparation for the coming judgment.**—Preparation for condemnation and preparation for acquittal. Preparation for condemnation there may be, though the man does not set himself in the way of fitting himself for the awful event. The man is practically preparing himself for a felon's doom who is adopting a felon's course of conduct. Condemnation is what the sinner has earned. He has prepared the way for the sentence of death to be pronounced. "The wages of sin is death." What is our life? Are we preparing for condemnation? Are we sowing to the wind that by-and-by we may reap the dire whirlwind of righteous indignation? Is there any escape? Yes; there is a way of escape. Penitent and believing sinners have a powerful advocate in the Judge Himself. The blood of Jesus Christ cleanses from sin. "There is now no condemnation to them which are in Christ Jesus." "Who is he that condemneth? It is Christ that died, yea rather, that is risen again, who is even at the right hand of God, who also maketh intercession for us."

V. **There is a twofold feeling with reference to the judgment to come.**—Not necessarily in the same individual, but in different sections of the human race. The one feeling is that of sadness, of vague fears, sometimes of positive horror; the other feeling is that of gladness, of quiet confidence, of sweet assurance. What is our state of feeling? We too often come short of the gladness as we think of the judgment. We have our moments of confidence, and then we are tossed with fears. Happy man who can look forward to the judgment and feel no terrors in connection with that great day! Blessed is the man whose sins are forgiven, who tastes the sweets of pardon; he can see the Lord coming in dreadful majesty, and feel no alarm; he can perceive the earth quaking, and experience no terror; the stars may withdraw their light, nature may wrap herself in funereal darkness, but in the soul of the true believer is a light that shines through all glooms, is a gladness which overtops all sorrows, is a confidence which overmasters all fears.

Ver. 10. *The great assize.*—Consider : 1. The chief circumstances which will precede our standing before the judgment-seat of Christ; 2. The judgment itself; 3. Circumstances which will follow it; 4. Application to the hearer.— *John Wesley.*

Ver. 12. *Individual responsibility.*—Here is a solemn truth which must, we think, have at once lifted the thoughts of the apostle's Roman readers above the little controversies in which they were engaged into a higher and a serener atmosphere. Whatever food they ate or did not eat, whatever days they did or did not privately observe, one thing was certain—they would have to give an account of this particular act or omission, as of everything else in their whole lives. "Every one shall give account of himself to God." My duty is that which, as a man, as a Christian, I have to do. My responsibility recalls the account which I must render for what I do and what I leave undone. Duty looks to the present, responsibility to the present and the future. Duty may seem at first to represent the most disinterested of the two ideas. Responsibility, human nature being what it is, is the more practically vigorous. Responsibility goes hand in hand with power—with power of choice. No man is responsible for the size of his body, or for the colour of his hair, or for the number of his sisters and brothers. His responsibility begins exactly where his power of choice begins. It varies with that power, and upon the use he makes of it will depend the kind of account which, sooner or later, he will have to give. It stands to reason that an account must be given, if given at all, to some person. Responsibility implies a person to whom responsible man is responsible. All human society is based on this law of responsibility to persons. The strongest of all the motives that can change a man's life, both within and without, for his lasting good, is the love of God. If we could love God quite sincerely for twenty-four hours we should be other men, capable, spiritually speaking, almost of anything. But if this be so, the next motive in the order of efficiency is, beyond all doubt, the remembrance of the inevitable last account which we must each of us give before the judgment-seat of Christ. St. Augustine says, " Nothing has contributed more powerfully to wean me from all that held me down to earth than the thought constantly dwelt on of death and of the last account." This resolution to give thought to the last account would prove a useful stimulus. It is like the old Jewish law—it is a schoolmaster to bring the soul to the feet of Jesus Christ; for the thought of that account does force us to think over our lives here—not once or twice, but often—not superficially, but with a determination to see ourselves as we are. To think of ourselves thus is to anticipate its result as far as we are concerned. It is to act on St. Paul's advice—that if we would judge ourselves, we should not be judged. We can do all things through Christ that strengtheneth us ; and so with His cross before our eyes, with His gracious presence and blessing within our souls, we look forward to our account with trembling joy.—*Canon Liddon.*

Joy and peace in believing.—" Now the God of hope fill you with all joy and peace in believing, that ye may abound in hope, through the power of the Holy Ghost." It will be good to take this apostolic prayer to pieces, and mark each separate part and truth.

I. **The hope.**—It is of the things hoped for that the apostle is speaking. It is not to " hope," or to " a hope," but to " *the* hope," that he is pointing. It is not that thing called " hope," as springing up in our breasts, that he would have us dwell upon; it is the glory to be revealed, the hope which is laid up for us in heaven. This is the bright star on which he fixes our eye.

II. **The God of the hope.**—Of that hope He is the beginning, the middle, and the end; the centre and the circumference; its root and stem and branches; its seed, its blossom, and its fruit. There is not one of these " things hoped for " but is to be t aced to *Him* as its sole fountain-head.

III. **Fill you with all joy and peace.**—There is *joy,* " joy unspeakable and full of glory"; but it is not of earth. It comes down from heaven. There is *peace,* the peace which passeth all understanding : but its fountain is above. It is God who gives these ; and He does so as " the God of the hope."

IV. **In believing.**—This joy and peace, though heavenly in their origin and nature, were not miraculous. They did not gush up into the soul like water springing from the sand by some supernatural touch. They found their way into the soul by a very natural, very simple, but very effectual channel—the belief of God's good news about His only begotten Son. They were not the *reward* of believing ; they were not *purchased by* believing ; nor did they come in *after* believing : they were obtained *in* believing.

V. **That we may abound in the hope.**—The hope not only fills, but *overflows,* as the word "abound " might be rendered. It comes in and lights up the soul with its heavenly brightness; but it does more. It is so glorious and so boundless that the soul cannot contain it.

VI. **Through the power of the Holy Ghost.**—He comes in and dwells in us; thus working in us from within, not from without. He comes in as the Spirit of power and love and of a sound mind. He comes in as the earnest of the inheritance until the redemption of the purchased possession. He comes in, not in feebleness, but in power, in almighty power, to work a work in us and for us which but for Him must remain unaccomplished for ever.—*H. Bonar.*

472

SUGGESTIVE COMMENTS ON VERSES 10—15.

All shall be manifest.—All the wickedness that men have brooded on and hatched in the darkest vaults of their own hearts, or acted in the obscurest secrecy, shall be then made as manifest as if they were every one of them written on their foreheads with the point of a sunbeam. Here on earth none know so much of us—neither would we that they should—as our own consciences; and yet those great secretaries, our own consciences, through ignorance or searedness, overlook many sins which we commit. But our own consciences shall not know more of us than all the world shall, for all that has been done shall be brought into public notice.—*Bishop Hopkins.*

Another's fault may be ours.—It matters not that Christ warned us to "judge not, that we be not judged" (Matt. vii. 1), for men still hold up each other's faults, real or suspected, and inspect and dissect them, and pronounce judgment, as if they fear to find a worthy man, lest their own meanness should stand out in dark contrast. There are modifying facts of which all men are ignorant concerning every action. It therefore requires much knowledge and wisdom to render right judgment. How is it, then, that we dishonour God's command, and call fellow-beings before the bar of our illegal court for rash and presumptuous sentences? Do not, then, hold the characters of others up for dissection; do not talk much about people in any way: turn your conversation into more intellectual, less dangerous, and more profitable lines. Do not judge. The fault which you detect in another, even though radical and unmistakable, is no worse than some other evil, or often the self-same evil, in yourself. Nay, look well to it that you have not weaknesses even more shameful and grievous; for the censor is often worse than his victim. *Robert Westly Peach.*

It is a true proverb, "Though two do the same thing, it is not really the same thing"; for not the form of the deed, but the sense of the doer, decides as to whether anything is unclean or holy, or contrary to faith and love (ver. 14).—*Besser.*

Dangerous to increase restrictions.—It is always dangerous to multiply restrictions and requirements beyond what is essential—because men, feeling themselves hemmed in, break the artificial barrier; but, breaking it with a sense of guilt, thereby become hardened in conscience, and prepared for transgressions against commandments which are divine and of eternal obligation. Hence it is that the criminal has so often in his confessions traced his deterioration in crime to the first step of breaking the Sabbath day; and no doubt with accurate truth. If God have judgments in store for England, it is because we are selfish men —because we prefer pleasure to duty, party to our Church, and ourselves to everything else.—*F. W. Robertson.*

MAIN HOMILETICS OF THE PARAGRAPH.—*Verses* 16—18.

A new kind of kingdom.—We cannot prevent our good being evil spoken of, for evil men will both think and speak evil. St. Paul himself did not prevent it. Jesus Christ, the best of men, was numbered among the transgressors both in His death and in His life. We cannot hope to escape slander, but we must strive so to live that the slanderous tale may be baseless. We must conduct our lives according to the laws of God's spiritual kingdom, and thus we may move in peace amid the strife of evil tongues. "Let not then your good be evil spoken of: for the kingdom of God is not meat and drink; but righteousness, and peace, and joy in the Holy Ghost." Here we have a new kind of kingdom set up in

473

the world—new, doubtless, in the apostle's day.   If not new in these times, certainly far different from the kingdoms set up by men.   Let us examine and compare the constituent elements of this kingdom.   This is a kingdom in which :—

I. **Material forces do not reckon.**—Take any kingdom of human device and material forces are placed in the ascendant.   The kingdom of the state of course depends upon material forces.   The commercial kingdom is mainly material:stic. The modern intellectual kingdom is tending in the same direction.   What about our moral kingdoms—our kingdoms for social reform ?   There is a constant appeal for funds ; there is a large number of secretaries ; there is extensive organisation.   He who said the kingdom of God is not meat and drink stood almost alone, and yet he effected the greatest moral and social reformation the world has seen.

II. **External pomp does not count.**—The modern conception of a kingdom is that of one in which there shall be effective display.   This is the day for advertisements.   A kingdom without external pomp is not our modern notion. A kingdom without its banquets !   A kingdom without either meats or drinks does not suit an earthborn and earthbound nature.   Complexity and not simplicity is too much the modern idea of a kingdom, whether commercial, social, or ecclesiastical.

III. **Vague yearnings are not sufficient.**—George Eliot says : " Justice is like the kingdom of God : it is not without us as a fact ; it is within us as a great yearning."   The reputation of George Eliot is such that to say the sentence looks to us meaningless might be to provoke the smile of contempt.   Is then justice a yearning ?   Is the just man one who has a yearning after an abstraction defined as justice ?   Suppose justice to mean rectitude in dealing—would it satisfy any one if a man pleased himself with wronging his neighbour and indulging in yearnings after justice ?   Whatever may be said of the definition of justice, we are quite sure that the definition of God's kingdom is not correct. The kingdom of God is both within us and without us.   It is within us as a sanctifying force, making us righteous, producing peace, inspiring joy ; it is without us, for it is seen in righteous conduct, in holy lives.   It is not enough to yearn after righteousness.   Vapid sentimentalism is not adequate.   We must strive after righteousness.   Christ's righteousness must be both imputed and imparted.   Great yearnings tell of the dignity of human nature ; but great yearnings, earnest desires, without corresponding efforts tell of human littleness.

IV. **The territory cannot be measured.**—" The kingdom of God is not meat and drink."   Viewed from the standpoint of the political economist, it is a non-productive realm, and the members are supposed to be non-producers, and therefore not valuable as citizens of earth.   But the members of this kingdom do always increase the material wealth of any kingdom.   They own no lands, it may be, but all lands are better for their presence.   The political economist has not the word " righteousness " in his vocabulary, but he shows how much is lost to the community by the dishonesty of men, by the need of overlookers, etc., so that the righteous man is indirectly a producer of material wealth.   The territory of this kingdom cannot be measured.   It is unseen, but extensive.

V. **The possessions cannot be either weighed or calculated.**—They are of little account at the bank ; and yet how much gold many a man would give for peace of mind, for joy in the Holy Ghost, if he only understood the priceless nature of the blessing !   The small footrules of time cannot be applied to the righteousness of God.   We can measure the great mountains on the surface of our planet, but the great mountain of God's righteousness is of infinite height.   The righteousness also of the true member of God's kingdom rises high above scales of human measurement.   The scales of time can be so adjusted as to be sensitive to the slightest air motion, but they cannot weigh righteousness, peace, and joy.

474

Blessed possessions above all price ! More to be valued than fine gold ! Better far than rubies or diamonds !

I. This is a kingdom in which all the subjects are kings.—They are kingly, not by their first but. their second birth. They are kingly, not in outward seeming always, but in inward worth and nobility of character. They are kingly, not in *knowing* earthly love, but in *knowing* the love of heaven. They are kingly, not in being *able* at state etiquette, *able* in court graces, *able* in senate or in war, but as being able in heaven's graces, in overcoming the great enemies of humanity, in loving and serving the eternal Righteousness.

II. This is an ecclesiastical kingdom in which all are priests.—No sphere for priestly ambition, for priestly assumptions, for sacerdotal claims, in this realm, for all the members of this kingdom are priests. They offer themselves living sacrifices ; they wear the splendid vestments of righteousness. There floats around them the sacred incense of peace. They walk through earth's aisles chanting hymns of praise, for the joy of the Holy Ghost inspires and gladdens their nature.

III. This is a kingdom in which all are successful.—No blanks in this kingdom ; no disappointments ; no working for honours and dying of broken hearts. For he that in these things serveth Christ is acceptable to God and approved of men. St. Paul was not approved of men—that is, not of all men : approved of men who worthily bear the name, who show the nobility of manhood. Let us then in righteousness, peace, and joy in the Holy Ghost serve Christ, and we shall meet with highest approvals. Heaven's plaudits will amply compensate for every loss, for every effort, in the cause of truth and righteousness.

SUGGESTIVE COMMENTS ON VERSES 16—18.

" *Let not then your good be evil spoken of.*"—1. We are to inquire what we are to understand the apostle to mean by *our good*. And here we may meet with different opinions : some, by *our good*, understand our religion, which is indeed every Christian's chief good ; and according to this sense of the words the apostle must be understood to exhort us to have a regard to the honour of the gospel in all our actions, to administer no occasion to the enemies of our religion either to deride or despise our holy calling. And thus the text amounts to an argument or exhortation to move us to a simplicity of manners and an inoffensive behaviour, for fear lest we bring a reproach upon our profession. But the apostle seems to aim at something further : his business here is, not to deter us from the practice of evil, but to direct us in the use and practice of that which is good, that our virtue may be without offence, and secured from calumny and reproach ; and *our good*, mentioned in the text, is not the topic from which the apostle draws an argument or exhortation, but is the subject-matter concerning which he is giving directions. According to this interpretation of the words the text may be thus paraphrased : Be not content with merely doing that which is in itself good and commendable, but look forward to the consequences which are likely to attend it, and endeavour to prevent any mischief that may grow out of it to yourself or others, that your good may be inoffensive and irreproachable. In this sense it is that I propose to consider the text, and shall now proceed : 2. To show that our good is often exposed to be evil spoken of through our own indiscretion, and consequently that it is often in our power to prevent it. This is one way by which men expose their good to be evil spoken of. Their mistake lies in not rightly distinguishing between a servile compliance with the world and a prudent behaviour towards it; and yet there is as much difference between them as between virtue and vice: one is the way which men who sacrifice honour and conscience to their interest make use of; the other is the method which wise and good men take to recommend the practice of virtue and religion. And what a wide difference is this! In the first case to comply with the world you must be like it, you must conform yourself to it; in the other you treat the world civilly, that it may the more easily become like you—that you may gain upon and instil the principles of virtue, which may be infused by gentle degrees, but cannot be obtruded by noise and violence. Sometimes men expose their good to be evil spoken of out of pure pride and haughtiness of temper: this is the case when men have such a contempt for the world as not to think it worth their while to guard against the misapprehensions of those about them. They reckon it below their dignity to render any account of what they do, and a mark of guilt to descend so low as to justify their actions. But surely, if we estimate the thing fairly, it is betraying of that which is good to reproach, and laying of stumbling-blocks in the way of the blind. 3. That as it is often in our power to prevent our good from being evil spoken of, so in many cases it is our duty. This duty may, I think, be deduced from these principles: the honour of God and of truth, the charity that is owing to our brethren, and the justice that is due to ourselves. —*Sherlock.*

MAIN HOMILETICS OF THE PARAGRAPH.—*Verses* 19—23.

Pursuit and retreat.—In Christian warfare it is well to know when to pursue and when to retreat. We must not endanger success by any rash methods. We must consider, not only our own welfare, but the well-being of the whole Christian community. We must remember that we are parts of a whole, and must consider the proper ordering of the parts, so as to promote the successful edification of the whole. Let us then inquire:—

I. **What are we to follow?**—The answer to this question is to be given not from a worldly but a Christian standpoint—that is, the standpoint of an enlightened Christian, of one who is not for self, for self's party, for self's little sect, but for the Christian state in its widest aspect. Peace is to be followed. Not peace at any price, not peace at the sacrifice of principle. The follower of the little sect says, Just so; but how often are his principles mere crotchets? Externals are not unimportant, but peace is supreme. Edification is to be pursued. The temple will not rise if the workmen spend their time and energies in quarrelling over the shape and position of the stones. Mutual edification is too often sacrificed at the bidding of self-glorification. A man gets hold of some side aspect of the truth, or rather it gets hold of him, and he pursues it to the damage of the spiritual building. Selfish workers cannot succeed in the edification of Christ's great temple.

II. **What are we to avoid?**—The answer to this question has to do, not with the Christian's relation to the moral law, to his fellow-men as citizens of earth, but to his fellow-men as members of the invisible Church, though there are many things to be avoided which even strong faith may allow, from the consideration that their adoption may do harm to the though less and inconsiderate. It may be good and expedient to abstain from intoxicating beverages, to withdraw from certain modern amusements, to refuse complicity with many modern customs and practices, so as to raise the general moral tone. It is certainly good neither to eat flesh nor to drink wine, if by doing so the Christian brother is either offended or made to stumble.

476

III. What does the strong Christian treasure in secret?—His mighty faith, which does not mean either his articles of belief or his personal hold on the things and beings invisible. It may mean his large and enlightened view. This is the day of so-called large and enlightened views, and men parade their shop windows, which are well dressed sometimes, while the shop is poor and scanty. Intolerant men make a noise about tolerance. We want more reserve on some things and more openness on other things. Hast thou faith? have it to thyself before God. Art thou above the shibboleth of parties? have it to thyself before God. Happy is he that condemneth not himself in that thing which he alloweth. This freedom from condemnation is not always rightly founded. It springs sometimes from ignorance, sometimes from indifference, and sometimes from carelessness as to the rights of others. Happy is the man who enjoys freedom from condemnation which is rightly originated.

IV. What must all Christians shun?—The one great answer is *sin*—a word of large significance. "Whatsoever is not of faith is sin." What the enlightened conscience does not approve is sin. "Whatsoever is not of faith." Grounded on convictions. But are all convictions infallible? Certainly not. Convictions must be formed in the light of divine truth. Let the converging rays of all light centres bear upon my mind, so that I may form right views. If I doubt, I must refrain from the doubtful course; if I am fully and rightly persuaded, then I must steadfastly and joyfully walk along the appointed pathway. Let us avoid the appearance of evil. Let the strong be tender towards the weak, while the weak do not carp at the strong. Let the desire for peace be strong. Let all thoughts and energies be devoted to the edification of God's great spiritual temple, which shall overtop and outlast the gorgeous temples of time.

ILLUSTRATIONS TO CHAPTER XIV.

Vers. 1-4. *Weak faith encouraged.*—How many "stretch lame hands of faith, and grope and gather dust and chaff"! To be weak is to be miserable; and how often it means to be despised! The revivalist says, "Hope will not do; we must be certain of our salvation. I am as sure of heaven as if I were there." But St. Paul says, "Him that is weak in the faith receive ye." The revivalist rejects weak faith. Christ will neither break the bruised reed nor quench the smoking flax. The former He repairs until it sings sweetly of mercy; the latter He fans until it becomes a shining flame. A weak Christian is better than a boasting Pharisee.

> " I falter where I firmly trod,
>   And falling with my weight of cares
> Upon the great world's altar stairs
> That slope through darkness up to God,
> I stretch lame hands of faith, and grope,
>   And gather dust and chaff, and call
>   To what I feel is Lord of all,
> And faintly trust the larger hope."
>   *Tennyson.*

Vers. 4, 5. *No one to be despised.*—An Englishman, a native of Yorkshire, going to reside at Kingston, in Jamaica, was reduced from a state of affluence to very great distress; so much so, that in the time of sickness he was destitute of home, money, medi-cine, food, and friends. Just in this time of need an old Christian negro offered his assistance, which being gladly accepted, this "neighbour to him" bought medicine, and administered it himself, furnished nourishment, sat up three nights, and, in short, acted the part of doctor, nurse, and host. Through the blessing of God the old negro's efforts were rendered successful in the recovery of the sick man, who then inquired what expenses he had been at, and promised remuneration as soon as possible. The generous old Christian replied, "Massa, you owe me nothing; me owe you much still." "How do you make that out?" said the restored man. "Why, massa, me never able to pay you, because you taught me to read de word of God!" This reply so affected the man that he resolved from that time to seek the Lord.

Vers. 5, 6. *Vessel anchored in a bay.*—We have seen a vessel lying at anchor in a well-sheltered harbour while the storm raged furiously in the open sea. The vessel was fenced and protected. What portion of the storm entered the little bay only served to give a gentle motion to the ship, and make mournful music as the wind swept through the cordage. Sunday should be as the fenced-in and protected harbour for the vessel of a good man's soul. There may be

477

storms without; there should be comparative peace within. The man is anchored within the Sunday bay, and nothing will tempt him to withdraw the anchor and try the ocean of secular life until he is further strengthened and refitted for the tempest by the recruiting influences of a full Sunday. Well is it if he can feel that both himself and his Sunday are fenced by the protecting arms of Him whose love is everlasting. Secular life is full of cares. All life has its deep sorrows. But Sunday should shut out our worldly cares, and fence us in with the love of God. What a consoling message the Sunday carries! It proclaims the gracious truth, He careth for you. The Infinite cares for the finite. We who dwell in houses made of clay are cared for by Him who inhabits the praises of eternity. We who are but insignificant atoms amid the vast systems of worlds have a place in the mindful regards of Him who rolls the stars along and speaks all the promises. Sunday has its sweet voices and its rich music, and within its sacred enclosure we hear the sweet voice of infinite love's mouth and the rich music of heaven. Welcome, sweet day of rest that enfolds us in its loving arms, that gives rest when we are weary, drink when we are thirsty, and healing balm for aching heads and hearts!

Vers. 5, 6. *Lord Salisbury and the Shah.*—The *Westminster Review* would destroy the sacredness of our English Sunday, but the Westminster statesman seeks to maintain that sacredness. "The Shah was grievously disappointed because Lord Salisbury would not allow a dance on Sunday night, and he entirely failed to appreciate the Anglican prejudice against Sunday diversions." All honour to Lord Salisbury; but what shall we say of him who speaks of an Anglican prejudice? Is he infected with the false notions propounded by the writer of an article named "A rational use of Sunday"? Surely the writer of this article will not commend himself or herself to an enlightened reason. For "A rational use of Sunday" ought to have no statements which might shock a rational nature. And what shall be said to this; "There is indeed a pretty general consensus of opinion among theologians that, to use their own expression, 'The Sabbath began with Moses and ended with Christ'"? We are not aware of such "a general consensus." A few names on that side might be counted on the fingers. There are many treatises written on the opposite side, while the literature on the side of the "general consensus of opinion" is scanty. If, indeed, there be such a general consensus, it is remarkable that the English Sunday maintains its divine pre-eminence.

Ver. 6. *Wait till reckoning time.*—A good old man was much annoyed by the conduct of some of his neighbours who persisted in working on Sundays. On one occasion, as he was going to church, his Sabbath-breaking neighbours called out to him sneeringly from the hayfield, "Well, father, we have cheated the Lord out of two Sundays, any way." "I don't know that," replied the old gentleman,—"I don't know. The account is not settled yet."

Ver. 6. *Good hands at an excuse.*—I have often wondered at the cleverness with which people make excuses for neglecting heavenly things. A poor woman was explaining to me why her husband did not attend church. "You see poor working folks nowadays are so holden down and wearied out that they are glad to rest a day in the house when Sabbath comes." An unopened letter was lying on the table, which she asked me to read, believing that it was from her sick mother. It was a notice to her husband that the football team, of which he was captain, was to meet on Saturday at 3 p.m., and that, like a good fellow, he must be forward in good time. And that was the man for whom my pity was asked, as being so worn out with his work that he could hardly creep up to the church! Another woman admitted to me that she never read her Bible, but pleaded that she was too busy and had too many cares. My eye caught a great bundle of journals above the clock. She confessed that these were novels, on which she spent twopence-halfpenny every Saturday, and that she read them on the Sabbath. If you wish an excuse, the smallest thing will give you stuff enough for the weaving of it.—*J. Wells.*

Ver. 6. *Six parasangs.*—Krummacher tells of an Israelite named Boin, a resident of Mesopotamia, whom the Lord called to make a pilgrimage to the land of his fathers. Taking his family, he started westward, through the wilderness. When he was weary with a journey of six parasangs, he came upon a tent by the way, and a man said to him, "Rest here." When rested the man guided him forth. At the end of six parasangs more he found another tent with refreshments; and so on to the end of his journey in the promised land. The life of man is a pilgrimage. Six parasangs are six days; the seventh is the day of rest, the tent of refreshment by the way. The fool passes by the tent, and perishes in the wilderness; but the wise man rests there, and reaches the land of promise. For a number of years a flour-mill was worked seven days in the week. In making a change of superintendents, it was ordered that the works should be stopped at eleven o'clock on Saturday night, and to start none of them till one o'clock on Monday morning. The same men, during the year, ground many thousands of bushels more than had ever been ground in a single year in that establishment; and the men, having time for rest and Sabbath duties, were more healthy, punctual, and diligent.

Ver. 7. *Erasmus and Bilney.*—Thousands of men are influenced by persons whom they never saw. The Reformation began at Cambridge University very early in the sixteenth century by Bilney, a solitary student, reading a Greek Testament with Latin translations and notes which Erasmus had published. Bilney had never seen Erasmus, but the quiet work of Erasmus was the means of bringing Bilney to the knowledge of the truth as it is in Jesus. Bilney, again, influenced Latimer, who was one of the fathers of the English Reformation, and who suffered martyrdom for the truth. Thus the Reformation in England may be largely traced to the quiet work of Erasmus as he sat at his desk, and used his vast learning and intellect to make the word of God more familiar to the people of his time. *Buchanan and Judson.*—A young American student more than seventy years ago happened to read a printed sermon which had fallen into his hands. The sermon was entitled "The Star in the East," by Dr. Claudius Buchanan, and described the progress of the gospel in India and the evidence there afforded of the divine power. That sermon, by a man whom he had never seen, fell into the young student's soul like a spark into tinder, and in six months Adoniram Judson resolved to become a missionary to the heathen. That little printed sermon, preached in England perhaps with no apparent fruit, became through God's blessing the beginning of the great work of American foreign missions. You may not be an Erasmus or a Claudius Buchanan; but God may have as great a work for you to do as He had for them. What an influence for good Christian parents may exercise upon their children with far-reaching results to the world! The faithful Sabbath-school teacher may leaven with gospel truth young minds that may yet control the destinies of a nation. Young women, by the power of their own Christian character, may change for the better the muddy current of many a godless life. The great matter is for every one of us to live near to God, to cultivate a Christlike character, and then our life is sure to be a blessing. *You must walk with God if you would have weight with men.* Personal holiness is the key to personal influence for good. —*C. H. J., in "Pulpit Commentary."*

Ver. 8. *Death in the Lord is sweet.*—Balaam exclaimed, "Let me die the death of the righteous, and let my last end be like his." Life in the Lord is the bright way to death in the Lord, and death in the Lord is the pleasant cypress avenue to eternal glory.

" So live that, when thy summons comes to join
The innumerable caravan that moves
To that mysterious realm where each shall take
His character in the silent halls of death,
Thou go not like the quarry slave at night,
Scourged to his dungeon, but, sustained and soothed
By an unfaltering trust, approach thy grave
Like one who wraps the drapery of his couch
About him and lies down to pleasant dreams."
Bryant.

Ver. 10. *Judgments, kind.*—Jesus arrived one evening at the gates of a certain city, and He sent His disciples forward to prepare supper, while He Himself, intent on doing good, walked through the streets into the market-place. And He saw at the corner of the market some people gathered together, looking at an object on the ground; and He drew near to see what it might be. It was a dead dog with a halter round its neck, by which it appeared to have been dragged through the dirt; and a viler, a more abject, a more unclean thing never met the eyes of man. "Faugh!" said one, stopping his nose; "it pollutes the air." "How long," said another, "shall this foul beast offend our sight?" "Look at its torn hide," said a third; "one could not even cut a shoe out of it." "And its ears," said a fourth, "all draggled and bleeding." "No doubt," said a fifth, "it has been hanged for thieving." And Jesus heard them, and looking down compassionately on the dead creature, He said, " Pearls are not equal to the whiteness of its teeth." Then the people turned towards Him with amazement, and said among themselves, "Who is this? This must be Jesus of Nazareth, for only He could find something to pity and approve even in a dead dog." And being ashamed, they bowed their heads before Him, and went each on his way.—*Persian Fable.*

Vers. 10-15. *The cadi and the king.*—One of the Moorish kings of Spain wished to build a pavilion on a field near his garden, and offered to purchase it of the woman to whom it belonged, but she would not consent to part with the inheritance of her fathers. The field, however, was seized, and the building was erected. The poor woman complained to a cadi, who promised to do all in his power to serve her. One day, while the king was in the field, the cadi came with an empty sack, and asked permission to fill it with the earth on which he was treading. He obtained leave, and when the sack was filled he requested the king to complete his kindness by assisting him to load his ass with it. The monarch laughed, and tried to lift it, but soon let it fall, complaining of its enormous weight. " It is, however," said the cadi, " only a small part of the ground which thou last wrested from one of thy subjects; how then wilt thou bear the weight of the whole field when thou shalt appear before the great Judge laden with this iniquity?" The king thanked him for his reproof, and not only restored the field to its owner, but gave her the building which he had erected and all the wealth which it contained.

Vers. 14, 15. *Charitable judgments.*—Those of us who have read classic history may remember an incident in the history of the Macedonian emperor. A painter was commanded to sketch the monarch. In one of his great battles he had been struck with a sword upon the forehead, and a very large scar had been left on the right temple. The painter, who was a master-hand in his art, sketched him leaning on his elbow with his finger covering the scar on his forehead; and so the likeness of the king was taken, but without the scar. Let us put the finger of charity upon the scar of the Christian as we look at him, whatever it may be—the finger of a tender and forbearing charity—and see, in spite of it and under it, the image of Christ notwithstanding.—*Dr. Cumming.*

Ver. 18. *Livingstone's answer to the charge of neglecting his work.*—When Livingstone was charged with neglecting missionary work, he boldly answered: "My views of missionary duty are not so contracted as those w ose only ideal is a man with a Bible under his arm. I have laboured in bricks and mortar, and at the forge, and at the carpenter's bench, and in medical practice as well as in preaching. I am serving Christ when I shoot a buffalo for my men, or take an astronomical observation, or write to one of His children who forgot during the little moment of penning a note that charity which is eulogised as 'thinking no evil.'"

Ver. 19. *Sir Thomas Burnet thinking of the things which make for peace.*—Sir Thomas Burnet, the third son of Bishop Burnet, led at one time a dissipated life. At last he took a serious turn, and one evening his father observing him to be very thoughtful asked what he was meditating. "A greater work," replied he, "than your lordship's *History of the Reformation.*" "Ay," said his lordship, "what is that?" "The reformation of myself," said the young man. He fulfilled his promise, and he afterwards became one of the best lawyers of his time, and in 1741 one of the judges in the Court of Common Pleas.

CHAPTER XV.

CRITICAL NOTES.

Ver. 1.—We who are strong ought to bear the infirmities of the weak, and not to be self-pleasers.

Ver. 2. Let every one of us please his neighbour.—Not for mere gratification, but for his good.

Ver. 3. The reproaches of them that reproached thee fell on me.—Quotation from the sixty-ninth psalm. We are thus taught that the prophetical psalm is applied to Christ suffering for us. If Christ did not please Himself, how much less we! How calmly should we bear even undeserved reproaches when Christ bore those designed for God!

Ver. 5.—Christ is both the example and motive of the Christian mind. God who bestows patience; just as the God of grace is the God who imparts grace.

Ver. 6.—God of the man Christ Jesus; Father of the divine Word.

Ver. 7.—The glory of God was the end of all Christ did on earth or does in heaven.

Ver. 8.—A minister of the circumcision—that is, of the Jewish nation. Christ, the Gentile Saviour, was and is the minister of the Jew. We are all brethren; one class must not despise the other.

Ver. 10.—Both Jews and Gentiles to rejoice together in God's salvation.

Ver. 12.—Christ is here compared to a standard around which the nations should assemble. Jacob's prediction is to be thus fulfilled.

Ver. 15.—Paul writes boldly, confidently, familiarly, in this part of his epistle, or to a part of the Gentiles, to refresh the memory, and because of the special gift given to him of God.

Ver. 16.—St. Paul pictures himself as the officiating priest; the Gentile world is the offering to be presented and consecrated. The whole process of sanctification is an adorning of the sacrifice which is to be consecrated to God.

480

Ver. 17.—The things of the ministry committed to Paul of God are the things in which he will glory.

Ver. 18.—St. Paul will not take any glory to himself.   There is nothing done by him which Christ did not work; to Him be all the praise.

Ver. 19.—It might have been expected that Paul would mention Damascus, the place of his spiritual birth, as the centre of his missionary operations; but he begins at Jerusalem. Christ first sent His gospel to Jerusalem sinners.   Here is a gracious centre and an ever-widening circle.   It enlarges itself westward; it comprehends Greece, Asia Minor, the Grecian islands, the country between Asia Minor and Jerusalem, Phœnicia, Syria, part of Arabia, Rome the world's metropolis, and probably Spain.

Ver. 23. **Place in these parts.**—κλίμασι, a geographical term of the ancients.   Paul wished to visit Rome as the centre of the heathen world.   Rome a great power and wide influence; essential to direct influence in a right channel.

Ver. 26. **To make a certain contribution.**—To make a contribution of some sort or other. Meyer thus explains the passage : " To bring about a participation in reference to the poor—*i.e.*, to make a collection for them.   The contributor, namely, enters into fellowship with the person aided, in so far as he κοινωνεῖ ταῖς χρείας αὐτοῦ : κοινωνία is hence the characteristic expression for almsgiving, without, however, having changed its proper sense *communio* into the active one of communication."

Ver. 27.—Gentile converts are debtors to Jerusalem, whence came spiritual blessings.

Ver. 28. **Have sealed to them this fruit.**—Sealed applied to an instrument in writing means to make it valid, sure to answer the purpose for which it was intended   καρπός, fruit, from a Hebrew word meaning " to strip."   Fruit of the earth, of the loins, of the lips. Here the spiritual effect of Paul's preaching.   (Notes compressed from Wordsworth, Stuart, and Olshausen.)

Ver. 30.—If Paul, saith Estharis, might desire the prayers of the Romans, why might not the Romans desire the prayers of Paul?   I answer, They might desire his prayers as he did theirs, by an epistle directed to him to pray for them.   He adds, If they might desire his prayers whilst living, why not when dead and reigning with Christ?   I answer, Because then they could direct no epistle to him, or any other way acquaint him with their mind. Hence Elijah, about to be taken up into heaven, speaks to Elisha thus: " Ask what I shall do for thee before I am taken away from thee?"   We do not say that such desires for the prayers of departed saints are injurious to the intercession of Christ, but that they are idolatrous, implying that creatures are omniscient, omnipresent, and have the knowledge of the heart (Dr. Whitby).

MAIN HOMILETICS OF THE PARAGRAPH.—Verses 1—3.

Christ's example teaches mutual condescension.—Baur says, " This piece contains nothing which had not been much better said before."   In the same strain M. Renan affirms, "These verses repeat and weakly sum up what precedes." But this is surely to ignore the broader aspect of the apostle's teaching.   He here passes from what we may call the particular to the general.   It is with him no longer a question of meats, but in general of the relation between Judæo-Christianity more or less legal, of which the party of the weak was a branch, and that pure spirituality which is the proper character of Paul's gospel.   There is a statement of the general principle according to which the strong ought to conduct themselves towards the weak in all times and whatever may be the character of the infirmity.   And this condescension towards the weak is taught and enforced by the example of Christ.   If it were to be admitted that these verses were a weak summing up of what precedes, we gladly welcome the repetition for the sake of that one powerful sentence, " For even Christ pleased not Himself."   In one simple sentence we have brought before the mind the broad aspect of the spirit and mission of Him who went about doing good.   The example of Christ must ever be the Christian's motive and inspiration.   In order to get away from the spirit of self-pleasing, let us direct special attention to the words, " For even Christ pleased not Himself."

I. **Christ had a right to please Himself.**—If any person may be supposed to have such a right, that person is Jesus Christ.   1. *He had a right as creator.* All the rights which creatures possess are delegated ; they are of the nature of privileges. As a creature, I have no right over myself independent of the will of the Creator. As a member of the great brotherhood of humanity, I have no right over myself inconsistent with the rights and not tending to the welfare of such brotherhood. "No man liveth to himself" is the law of a properly constituted humanity as it is a gospel precept. But Christ in one aspect of His nature was not in a subordinate position; for He was creator. If all things were created for Him, had He not the privilege of considering Himself. As the giver of the laws of right and of justice, as the authority from whom there can be no appeal as to what is fit and proper to be done, we may suppose Him having a right to please Himself. 2. *Christ had a right as being above the law of human necessity.* Even if we set ourselves to please ourselves, we find that we are limited by our natures, by our circumstances. Society hedges us round, and will not allow us to please ourselves in an unlimited degree. Our own personal welfare will not permit self-pleasing to any large extent. The sensual man cannot please himself to an unlimited extent; the ambitious man must deny himself in order to promote his projects; the student must scorn delights and live laborious days that he may reach the goal. But Christ, as divine, is raised above the law of human necessity. Even as human He stands on a higher level of humanity than all other beings, and we may suppose that He might have pleased Himself without doing violence to society. 3. *Christ had a right as being all-wise.* The wisest are liable to error. When the foolishness of the fool tends to violence, society puts him in safe keeping, and says he has no right to please himself. Wise I may be, but my wisdom is imperfect, and therefore self should not be the law of my being and the rule of my action. Why should I with dogmatism impose my creeds upon my fellow-creatures? Why should I not consider the claims of my fellow-creatures? But Christ was all-wise. As man He was delivered from those errors and littlenesses which spoil the glory of even greatest man, and therefore He might indeed have pleased Himself and others have been benefited. 4. *Christ had a right as being all-good.* Wicked men are the class to whom there must not be permitted this course of pleasing themselves. Carry out the thought, and it will be seen that no man has a right to please himself. The higher we get in the scale of humanity, the less we have of wickedness and the less are we disposed to make self-pleasing the rule of life. The noblest men walk on the tableland of self-denial. This was the glorious tableland on which the Redeemer trod, and every spot on which He trod became fruitful of immortal flowers. The very goodness of Christ constituted a claim why He should please Himself. Why should He suffer who had no sins of His own to carry? Why should He be placed in the trying school of tribulation when there was no selfishness to be ground out of His loving nature?

II. **Christ's renunciation of such right.**—But "even Christ pleased not Himself." Let emphasis be placed on the word "even," in order to bring out the voluntary nature of this renunciation and to show the vastness of His love. Even Christ, the God-man, the Creator, pleased not Himself. 1. *Christ renounced His right by making His Father's will supreme.* Christ as man says, "I came not to do Mine own will, but the will of Him that sent Me." Perfectly constituted as Christ was as to His human nature, there might yet be in Him a lower will. But He seemed to rise up in the majesty of filial affection, and place His feet upon this lower will and give to the divine will the place of supremacy. Not for a moment did He shrink from bearing the reproaches of the wicked. God's honour was so dear to His heart that the reproaches of the wicked hurled at God were received by the Son to His wounding and to the increase of His agony. The righteous soul of Lot was vexed with the filthy conversation of the wicked; but how sharply was the soul of Christ pierced by the reproaches of the wicked against God! If David could say, "I beheld the transgressors, and was grieved," what language shall fittingly describe the agonies of David's greater Son as He listened to those who reproached God? The Saviour's grief was too great for tears; this blessed outlet to sorrow was not possible. Indeed, grief broke His heart as the reproaches of them that reproached God fell upon His sensitive nature. As we study the phenomena of the Saviour's death, we find that it was no poetical flight to say that He died of a broken heart. But we shall not carry out the purpose of the apostle if we do not notice how Christ renounced His right in relation to men. We might expect Christ the Son of God by virtue of that relationship and through affection for God not to please Himself in regard to the divine will; but will His compassion for men lead Him to desist from pleasing Himself for their welfare? Yes, it will. 2. *Christ pleased not Himself by placing Himself in contact with ignorance and sinfulness.* Difficult is it for us to realise the pain which Christ must have experienced as He came in contact with the ignorant and the sinful. We may try to draw the picture of the philosopher coming down from the heights of his studies to associate with the ignorant; we may picture the pure maiden brought up in a home of Christian purity, across the crystal waters of whose soul no shadow of wrong has ever flitted, who has all along breathed the fragrant atmosphere of virtue, being suddenly taken to live where vice reigns, where the atmosphere is rendered stifling by reason of impurity; we may think of the heroism of the Moravian missionaries who shut themselves up with the lepers in order to do them spiritual good. But both fact and fancy fail to enable the ordinary mind to understand what it was when Christ became the "friend of publicans and of sinners." His pure soul was keenly sensitive. And yet. blessed benevolence! He pleased not Himself, but went down to the dark pits of ignorance, dispelling the gloom of sinfulness, driving forth the offensive odours. 3. *Christ pleased not Himself by giving to the wants of others a foremost place.* Very touching is the incident of the wearied Jesus sitting down at Jacob's well, asking drink from the Samaritan woman. He saw her thirst, and sets Himself to remove that moral thirst before she helps Him to satisfy His physical thirst. Divine and glorious self-forgetfulness! We know not that the Saviour ever drank out of that Samaritan woman's waterpot; but this we know, that she drank from the living stream that flowed from that wearied traveller. And this incident is characteristic of all His earthly conduct—thought for others before thought for Himself. At the close of the most laborious day He never pleaded that His wearied nature required repose; but, "wearied and worn as He was, He pleased not Himself, but went forth and patiently listened to all their tales of woe, tasted their several complaints, raised each suppliant from the dust, nor left them till He had absorbed their sufferings and healed them all. He went through the land like a current of vital air, an element of life, diffusing health and joy wherever He appeared." 4. *Christ pleased not Himself, for He never demanded that the recipients of His blessings should become His servants.* We do not know that any of His disciples received from Him material blessings. He called those to be His immediate followers who were not the recipients of His physical benefits. What a large following the Saviour might have secured had He charged the sick whom He healed to repay Him for the work of mercy! The only time in which Jesus seemed to reprove the healed for their ingratitude was in the case of the ten lepers. "And Jesus answering said, Were there not ten cleansed? but where are the nine? There are not found that returned to give glory to God, save this stranger." Even here He pleased not Himself. It is not glory to Me the worker of miracles, but glory to God. He caused the healing virtue to flow from Him in copious measure like water from the abundant fountain, without any thought of Himself being refreshed by the reactive influence of the streams of His beneficence. How unlike to Christ are most men !   The world's ingratitude closes up the streams of our benevolence like a keen frost in the winter.   But the world's ingratitude never for one moment stayed the rich on-flowing of the Saviour's beneficent doings.   Oh for a baptism of the spirit displayed by Him who pleased not Himself, who had a perfect self-surrender and a complete submission to the divine will, who bore our sicknesses and carried our sorrows—the spirit of that noble apostle who counted not his life dear unto himself that he might finish his course with joy and the ministry which he had received from the Lord Jesus—the spirit of those who rejoiced that they were counted worthy to suffer such things as persecution and spoliation for His name's sake—the spirit of all in every age, of the martyrs and the noble workers of all time, who have been willing to suffer for the good of humanity !   Are we prepared at the call of duty and in obedience to the voice of God not to please ourselves, but to please our neighbour for his good to edification ?

III. **Christ's impelling motive to such renunciation our example and our inspiration.**—It was the impelling motive of love that induced Christ to tread the pathway of self-denial.   All loves are centred in Christ.   He was the embodiment and highest manifestation of truest love.   Something of this love must operate in our natures if we are to be delivered from mere self-pleasing. It cannot be cast out by mere prudential considerations.   The eagle darting down from her eyrie once lighted on a burnt offering which lay upon the altar of God, and bore it away to feed her young.   But a burnt coal adhered to the flesh of the offering, and being laid upon the dry sticks of the nest, it set them on fire, and the unfledged eaglets perished in the flames.   By self-pleasing we may seek to rob God of His rights and our fellows of their rights; but to all such unlawful spoil there will adhere the red-hot coal of justice, that will destroy our manhood, our peace, our joy, our spiritual vitality.   Let us beware how we give way to the injurious spirit of self-pleasing.   However, this evil spirit can only be effectually destroyed by the entrance of Christlike love.   True love goes out of self, seeks the enlargement of opportunities, and becomes creative in its very intensity.   The loyal and patriotic subject does not strive to pare down the demands of a wise and just sovereign; the loving child does not endeavour to strip the father's word of all binding force by skilful manipulations; and the true heart does not inquire, How can I do the very least for my God and the very least for God's creatures ? but thinks that the very greatest it can either do or offer is far too little.   Oh for a love which, though it have only two mites to give, yet casts them into the treasury of Him unto whom belongeth both the gold, the silver, and the copper, and thus enriches the ages !   Oh for a love which, though it possess only the alabaster box of ointment very precious, yet breaks the box over the Saviour's head in loving consecration to His predestined offering !   Oh for a love which, though it have only tears to offer, yet pours them in plentiful measure on the Saviour's feet, and with the rich tresses of a head, full of grateful thoughts, wipes the tear-bedewed feet of Immanuel !

Looking up, and lifting up.—In the grouping of nature dissimilar things are brought together.   Mutual service is the world's great law.   In the natural grouping of human life the same rule is found.   Dissimilarity constitutes the qualification for heartfelt union among mankind.   A family is a combination of opposites.   That there are diversities of gifts is the reason why there is one Spirit.   The same principle distinguishes natural society from artificial association. The former brings together elements that are unlike; while the latter combines the like.   Old civilisations follow a law the reverse of that which we have ascribed to the providential rule.   The daily life of each is passed in the presence, not of his unequals, but of his equals. This is not entirely evil. Now the faith of Christ throws together the unlike ingredients which civilisation had sifted out from one another. Every true Church reproduces the unity which the world had dissolved. And as the arrangements by which we stand with beings above and beings below are the origin of faith, so is the practical recognition of this position the great means of feeding the perpetual fountain of the Christian life.

A great German poet and philosopher was fond of defining religion as consisting in a reverence for *inferior* beings. The definition is paradoxical; but though it does not express the *essence* of religion, it assuredly designates one of its *effects.* True there could be no reverence for lower natures, were there not, to begin with, the recognition of a supreme Mind; but the moment that recognition exists, we certainly look on all that is beneath with a different eye. It becomes an object, not of pity and protection only, but of sacred respect; and our sympathy, which had been that of a humane fellow-creature, is converted into the deferential help of a devout worker of God's will. And so *the loving service of the weak and wanting* is an essential part of the discipline of the Christian life. Some habitual association with the poor, the dependent, the sorrowful, is an indispensable source of the highest elements of character. It strips off the thick bandages of self, and bids us awake to a life of greater sensibility. Had we hurt a superior, we should have expected punishment; had we offended an equal, we should have looked for displeasure. But to have injured the weak strikes anguish into our hearts, and we expect from God the retribution which there is no more to give. The other half of Christian discipline is of a less sad and more inspiring kind. There are those who dislike the spectacle of anything that greatly moves or visibly reproaches them; who therefore shun those who know more, see deeper, aim higher than themselves. This form of selfishness may not be inconsistent with the duty of lifting up the beings beneath us; but it is the contrary of the other portion of the devout life, which consists in looking up to all that is above us. Only the fairest and sublimest natures can remain in the presence of infirm or depraved humanity without a lowering of the moral conceptions and a depression of faith and hope. Hence the anxiety of every one, in proportion to the noble earnestness in which he looks on life, that holds himself in communion with great and good minds. He knows that the upper spring of his affections must soon be dry, unless he ask the clouds to nourish them. If therefore there be any virtue, if there be any praise, whoever would complete the circle of the Christian life will think on these things—will thrust aside the worthless swarm of competitors on his attention; in his reading will retain, in his living associations will never wholly lose, his communion with the few lofty and faithful spirits that glorify our world; and, above all, will at once quench and feed his thirst for highest wisdom by trustful and reverent resort to Him in whom sanctity and sorrow, the divine and the human, mingled in ineffable combination.—*Martineau, " Endeavours after the Christian Life."*

Ver. 1. *The duty of the strong to the weak.*

I. **The strong here are the strong in faith—the enlightened.**—Those who had correct views respecting the liberty and spirituality of the gospel were to bear with the prejudices of their weaker brethren. In this aspect the words have still their force for *us.* Religious doubts and crotchets we have always with us; although, having relation to things that are comparatively new, they vary with circumstances and fashions. The words are true also in a much wider sense.

II. **We who are strong physically ought to bear the infirmities of the weak.**— The robust should help to bear what is a burden to the delicate. The healthy

485

ought to relieve the tedium and smooth the pillow of the sick. The young should help the aged. The rich should help the poor. The infirmities of the weak we are, as it were, to put on our own shoulders, and bear for those who are tottering under them.

III. **The strong in mind ought to bear the infirmities of temper of the weak.**—Some are irritable, soon made peevish, easily roused to anger. We who are differently constituted—less sensitive, who can be calm under annoyance, slight, and opposition—ought to bear with the weaknesses of those who are possessed of a less happy disposition. Do not lose patience with their touchiness. Bear from them much in kindness. Remember that they are *weak*. Loss of temper is often a sign of weakness. (One losing in a game becomes irritable, one having the worse of an argument often loses temper.) Enforced by the fact: 1. We are all constituted differently one from another. *All have infirmities;* but the infirmities of one differ from the infirmities of another. If each sought to please his neighbour, to bear his infirmities, one another's weaknesses would become bonds of union. 2. The example of our Lord : " Let every one of us please his neighbour for his good to edification, *for even Christ pleased not Himself.*" Though rich, yet for our sakes He became poor. He emptied Himself of His glory, of His strength, that He might bear our infirmities. How remarkable was His forbearance with His disciples ! This was one of His greatest trials. And bearing the infirmities of weaker brethren will be to the Christian always the most trying exercise of self-denial. But shall any one grow weary when he remembers that " Christ pleased not Himself " ?

Thou who wishest to be considered strong, show thy strength in the true, manly, Christlike way of bearing the infirmities of the weak (Josh. xvii. 15). 1. Thou art strong in muscle and sinew ; then help those who are delicate and weak. 2. Thou art strong in nerve ; then step before the trembling, and give courage to those who are shaking with fear. 3. Thou art strong in intellect ; you can smile at popular error. But it is no mark of strength to laugh at others' weakness ; show thy strength by instructing the ignorant, guiding the erring. 4. Thou art strong in faith. Help others to realise by thy strength of faith the things unseen. Whatever be the nature of your strength, you deserve to be considered strong only by helping the weak. In God's sight, the more strength you have the more you will have to answer for at the judgment day.— *D. Longwill.*

Ver. 1. *The nobler choice.*—We may be said to spend our life in choosing, and our choice is threefold : 1. Between the greater and the smaller evil (see 2 Chron. xx. 12, 13) ; 2. Between that which is positively good and that which is distinctly evil (see Deut. xxx. 19) ; 3. Between the lower and the higher good. It is to the last of these three that the text invites attention.

I. **Our right as the children of God.**—In the parable of the prodigal son the father, addressing the elder son, says, " Thou art ever with me, and all that I have is thine." These words indicate our position toward our heavenly Father. He invites us to appropriate and to partake of " all that is His." " The earth is His, and all its fulness " (Psalm xxiv. 1); and He makes us free to possess and to enjoy, withholding nothing that is not hurtful to us. Those who in God's name forbid us to accept His provision come under strong apostolic condemnation (see 1 Tim. iv. 1-3) ; their doctrine is from below, and not from above. The truth is that " every creature of God is good, and nothing to be refused." Our right is unquestionable ; we are at liberty to partake of the fruits of the earth, of the comforts of life, of the joys which spring from human relationships, so long and so far as (1) we do not injure ourselves or wrong other people, (2) we cherish and express gratitude to the divine Giver, (3) we remember the needy, and do our best to let our friends and neighbours share our inheritance. But while it is always open to us to claim our right, and while it is sometimes desirable (if not necessary) to assert it against those who would deny it, there is often left to us another and a worthier course—*to forgo it* in favour of our neighbour's need. Here enters—

II. **Our privilege as the disciples of Christ.**—There is a large use of stimulants, as also of narcotics, amongst us; they are used, not only as medicine, but also as articles of diet, as requirements of hospitality, as sources of refreshment or enjoyment. That there is a sore and grievous abuse of these things is not merely undeniable; it is a fact that is patent and palpable; it confronts us, and challenges our attention. Now there is no law of Christ which forbids the use of these things; no precept of the Master or of His apostles can be quoted to prove their impropriety. So long as a man uses them in moderation, in such measure that no injury is done to his body or his mind, he cannot be charged with inconsistency as a Christian man. He violates no law of Christ; he is within his right. But he may be appealed to *not to stand upon his right.* It is open to him to act upon another and a higher consideration: instead of claiming his right to participate, he may elect to use his privilege to forgo and to abstain. He may be strong enough to overcome temptation himself, but he may have regard to "the infirmities of the weak," instead of "pleasing himself"; by not partaking he may, by his example of abstinence, encourage those who need encouragement to preserve sobriety in the only form which is open to them. This is the nobler choice. It is so, because: 1. *It is in harmony with the teaching of our Lord.* He taught us that it was His will that His servants should deny themselves; that they should find their lives by losing them; that it is more blessed to give than to receive; that whatever we do on behalf of His "little ones"—*i.e.*, of those who are least well able to take care of themselves—is accepted by Him as done unto Himself; and, through His inspired apostles, He has taught us that we should bear one another's burdens, that by (in) love we should serve one another, that the strong should help the weak. 2. *It is in profound accord with the action of our Lord.* It may seem to be comparing a very small thing indeed with a very great one indeed, to compare so simple an action or a habit as that of abstinence with so sublime a sacrifice as that of Jesus Christ, when He made Himself of no reputation, and took on Him the form of a servant (see Phil. ii. 5-8). But the same principle may underlie or animate two actions of widely different proportions; and it is possible for us to illustrate and to repeat, in our humble sphere and on our lowly scale, the very spirit which actuated our Lord in His great condescension, and the very life He lived when He dwelt among men, and when He died to redeem us all. It is the principle that it is better and nobler to minister than to be ministered unto; it is the spirit of self-sacrificing love. And whether this be found in a divine incarnation, or whether it be manifested in a simple action at a table in a cottage or in a hall, where a man denies himself a pleasure or a good in order that he may help his brother to stand, and to keep him from falling, the one is a moral and spiritual resemblance, as it is a moral and spiritual sequence, of the other. We act as our Master acted, we "walk even as He walked," when in any humblest scene or sphere whatsoever we forgo our individual right, in order that we may use our privilege of holy service; like our Lord, we make the nobler choice. 3. *It is the intrinsically nobler thing.* We cordially admire and unreservedly praise the men who, when their rights have been assailed, have manfully and even heroically asserted them at all hazards; they have chosen an honourable course. But they who have suffered that they might save have done more nobly still. Those Moravian missionaries who sold themselves into slavery that they might preach the gospel to their fellow-slaves; those philanthropists who have been willing to breathe the foul and fetid airs of the old-time dungeon, in order that they might make the lot of the common prisoner less intolerable than it used to be; they who have stooped that they might better serve their neighbours; they who have cheerily denied themselves the comforts and enjoyments they might have claimed, in order that they might gain a leverage with which to raise the fallen, or secure a better position in which to guide and guard the innocent and unstained,—these have chosen the worthier course, and have walked along the heavenlier heights. 4. *It is the course which will best bear reflection.* Innocent enjoyment is well in its way and in its measure. But it is very transient; it affords the feeblest and faintest satisfaction in the retrospect of it. Not so with an action or a course of self-sacrificing ministry. Upon that, however distant it may be, and however simple it may have been, we look back with a keen approval and with serene and devout thankfulness. To the very end of our life we shall thank God that we had the spirit and the strength to forgo what would have pleased ourselves, that we might bear the infirmities of the weak, and thus help them to gain their victory and to win their crown.—*William Clarkson, B.A.*

Ver. 2. *On pleasing all men.*—1. This duty incumbent on all, especially on all those who are entrusted with the oracles of God. The pleasing is to every man's neighbour—*i.e.*, every child of man; but in view of the words, "If it be possible," etc., we are to please all men. Strictly speaking, this is *not* possible. 2. Observe in how admirable a manner Paul limits this direction. We are to please men *for their good;* also *for their edification*—to their spiritual and eternal good. 3. All treatises and discourses on this subject are defective, so far as Wesley has seen. One and all had some lower design in pleasing men than to save their souls; therefore they do not propose the right means for the end. 4. Some take exception to this; yet—5. *e.g.*, Chesterfield advises his son, but badly. Wesley then proceeds to show the right method of pleasing men.

I. **In removing hindrances out of the way.**—1. First avoid everything which tends to displease wise and good men of sound understanding and real piety, such as cruelty, malice, envy, hatred, revenge, ill-nature. 2. Also the assumption of arrogant, overbearing behaviour. Whoever desires to please his neighbour for his good must take care of splitting on this rock. 3. Avoid also a passionate temper and behaviour. Passionate men have seldom many friends, at least for any length of time. 4. Also put away all lying. It can never be commendable or innocent, and therefore never pleasing. 5. Is not flattery a species of lying? Yet it is pleasing. Truly it pleases *for a while*, but not when the mask drops off. 6. Not only lying, but every species of it; dissimulation, *e.g.*, is displeasing to men of understanding. So also guile, subtlety, cunning—the whole art of deceiving

II. **In using the means that directly tend to this end.**—1. Let love not visit you as a transient guest, but be the constant temper of your soul. Let there be in your tongue the law of kindness. 2. If you would please your neighbour for his good, study to be lowly in heart. "Be clothed with humility," as against the maxim of the heathen, "The more you value yourself, the more others will value you." God "resisteth the proud, and giveth grace unto the humble." 3. Labour and pray that you may also be meek; labour to be of a calm, dispassionate temper. 4. See that you are courteous toward all men, superiors or inferiors; the lowest and the worst have a claim to our courtesy. 5. Honour all men; and the Master teaches me to love all men. Join these, and what is the effect? I love them for their Redeemer's sake. 6. Take all proper opportunities of declaring to others the affection which you really feel for them. 7. Also speak to all men the very truth from your heart; be a man of veracity. 8. To sum up all in one word: if you would please men, please God! Let truth and love possess your whole soul; let all your actions be wrought in love; never let mercy and truth forsake thee. " So shalt thou find favour and good understanding in the sight of God and man."—*John Wesley.*

Vers. 2, 3. *Pleasing our neighbours.*—There is a pleasing of our neighbours which is very different from that here described,—a pleasing of him by chiming in with his prejudices; by flattering his infirmities; by complying with his sinful wishes; by laughing at his wicked jokes; by countenancing him in his evil ways; in short, by doing, or *not* doing, that which will ensure us *popularity* with our neighbour, though at the expense of principle in ourselves. What we all must learn is to seek our neighbour's well-being, so that his evil should be our burden, and his good our happiness and reward. We must learn *so* to love him, that we shall, if necessary, *dis*please him, and put him to pain, and make him perhaps angry with us for a time, if in this way only we can do him good *in the end*; just as a kind surgeon will put us to pain in order to save our lives. " Every one of us " must thus please his neighbour, because every one has some neighbour thus to please. If we first please God, by giving Him our hearts for our own good to salvation, then we cannot but choose to please our neighbour for *his* good to edification. Should any one still ask, " Who is my neighbour ? " we should refer them to the reply given by our Lord to the same question, in the parable of the good Samaritan. Few errors are more common in daily life than supposing, either that others are of no importance to us, or that we are of no importance to others. These errors stand and fall together. The moment we discover how much our state is affected by others, that moment we also discover how much the state of others is affected by our own. Our neighbour has learned this grand lesson from his Master—not to please himself, but to please us for our good; he has trampled underfoot the selfish and unchristian saying, "I keep myself to myself"; and he has put in its place one more worthy a follower of Christ—"I give myself to thee." And though this neighbour is of little importance to the big, noisy world, he is of great importance to us. He is like the candle or the food in our house,—if the one were extinguished, and the other removed, neither would be missed by the world, but they would be very greatly missed by us and by our family. Some of our neighbours have hard or indifferent thoughts of us, as we once had of the world. Go and change them. Some are saying, " We have heard of Christianity ; we should like to see a Christian." Go and show them one, by opening to them a Christian's heart and life, and not a Christian's opinions merely. And as that good neighbour made us feel he was of importance to us, so may we as good neighbours make ourselves felt to be of importance to others. We repeat it, we need nothing else than a heart which truly loves God and man—that is, the heart of a child of God—to be an unspeakable blessing and of immense importance in our present place in society. But the apostle further sets before us Jesus Christ as the great example of self-sacrificing love, when he says, " Even Christ pleased not Himself." Even Christ ! He who is the " first-born of every creature, heir of all things," " in whom dwelt the fulness of the Godhead," " who is God over all, blessed for ever," "even *He* pleased not Himself," but sacrificed Himself for His neighbour ; and we need not ask of Him who His neighbour is, who Himself not only perfectly loved the Lord His God, but His " neighbour as Himself." Christ's neighbour was every man. " Even Christ pleased not Himself." These words describe His character. For the sake of others He came into the world ; for others He lived ; for others He prayed; for others He wept ; for others He died; for others He intercedes ; and for others He will come again ! The works and words of every day He spent upon earth are a comment upon this beautiful picture—" He pleased not Himself." He ever sought to please His neighbour, but only for his good, by the sacrifice of self. Every other pleasing is but a pleasing of self by the sacrifice of good. Thus only, let us add, can Jesus please us now, or bless us, by doing us *good*. Well might the apostle say, " He pleased not Himself " ! And such is the " mind " which must be in us if we are " in Him." " We that are strong ought to bear the infirmities of the weak, and not to please ourselves. Let every one of us please his neighbour for his good to edification. For even Christ pleased not Himself." " Now the God of patience and consolation grant you to be like-minded one toward another according to [*i.e.*, after the example of] Jesus Christ." Let the enmity to the living God which is in our natural hearts be slain by faith in His love to us through Christ, and then shall all enmity to our fellow-men be slain also. Let God's love to us be shed abroad upon our hearts by the Holy Spirit, and then shall these hearts be shut no longer by wicked selfishness against our neighbour. Let us carry our Lord's cross, and then we shall carry our brother's burden.—*Dr. Macleod.*

SUGGESTIVE COMMENTS ON VERSES 1—3.

Pleasing of others to be innocent.— Not as if His undertaking our cause was against His will, or that He ever felt it to be a task and a grievance. He was voluntary in the engagement and cheerful in the execution, and could say, " I have a baptism to be baptised with, and how am I straitened till it be accomplished ! " But He never followed the indulgence of His natural inclination. He preferred the glory of God and our benefit to His own gratification. He did not consult His ease ; but denied the demands of sleep when duty required exertion. He rejected, with anger, Peter's proposal to spare Himself from suffering. He did not consult ambitious feelings ; but refused the people when they would have made Him king. He stood not upon rank and consequence, but washed His disciples' feet, and was among them as one that serveth. He was far more delighted with Mary's reception of His word than with Martha's preparation for His appetite. He was not only thirsty, but hungry, when the disciples left Him at the well to go and buy meat ; but when they returned, and said, "Master, eat," He replied, "I have meat to eat which ye know not of." In your absence I have had something above corporeal satisfaction—I have been saving a soul from death. And observe the use the apostle makes of it. Because Christ pleased not Himself,

therefore " He let the strong bear the infirmities of the weak, and not please themselves." " Let every one of us please his neighbour for his good to edification." He indeed limits the duty. We are not to humour our brother in a sinful course, but only in things innocent and lawful ; and we are to do this with a view to secure and promote his welfare, and not for any advantage of our own. But we are not to consult our own little conveniences and appetites and wishes. We are not even to follow our convictions in every disputed matter. " Let us not therefore judge one another : but judge this rather, that no man put a stumbling-block or an occasion to fall in his brother's way. I know, and am per-suaded by the Lord Jesus, that there is nothing unclean of itself : but to him that esteemeth anything to be unclean, to him it is unclean. But if thy brother be grieved with thy meat, now walkest thou not charitably. Destroy not him with thy meat, for whom Christ died." Here again the apostle calls in Jesus as a motive and an example. He denied Himself for this weak brother, and will you, says Paul, refuse to deny yourself in a trifling forbearance on his behalf ?—*W. Jay.*

Self-pleasing not Christ's motive.— "For even Christ pleased not Himself." This does not mean either that well-doing or self-denial was distasteful to Christ; it does not mean that the exercise of benevolence was something for which He had to nerve Himself up from day to day; but it means that considerations of personal ease and comfort, of mere sensual gratification, were not paramount, did not occupy the first place. As He went here and there doing good, His mind was wholly intent on the benefit to *others.* Self-pleasing, in the ordinary acceptation of the term, was not His aim; so He said, "I delight to do Thy will, O My God." Self-pleasing, as such, commonly implies selfishness, and not infrequently indolence. Self-pleasing is living for oneself to the disregard of the claims, needs, or happiness of others. The highest, noblest form of self-pleasing, which finds delights in every good work, is not meant or alluded to in the passage under consideration. When Christ took upon Himself the form of a servant, self-pleasing was not His motive. He desired to undertake and accomplish what no other man could, and that not for His own honour, but for man's benefit. When He healed the sick, gave sight to the blind, restored hearing to the deaf, cleansed the leper, and raised the dead—when He comforted Martha and Mary concerning their brother—when He healed the broken-hearted, what was His motive? Not self-pleasing, certainly. Was His last journey to Jerusalem undertaken for any profit, honour, or worldly satisfaction? Too well He knew what was before Him: the trial, the agony, the suffering, the shame. "Father, if this cup may not pass from Me except I drink it, Thy will be done," is a striking comment on the words, "Christ pleased not Himself." "We watch Him drinking the bitter cup, enduring the agony of unknown sufferings, placing Himself in the position of sinners, exhausting their punishment; and all that His Father's will might be done—not His own will, not what He would Himself as man have desired." Here we see sublime unselfishness! We may desire and seek it, but we cannot attain unto

it. Yet look at the self-sacrificing spirit of Judson, Selwyn, Patteson, and Hannington, the martyr of Equatorial Africa; it was not self-pleasing, but Christlike unselfishness. Self-seeking stands in the way of the Church's progress, and prevents the good that might else be done. It is a blight in the family; for it is the offspring of the rankest selfishness, and militates against true happiness. Peace in the family comes from affection, and a *regard* for the *feelings, rights*, and lawful *privileges* of other members of the household. Forbearance, charity, and true gentleness flourish not where there is self-seeking. Wisdom, like the love that never faileth, "seeketh not her own"—seeketh the good of others. Unobtrusive acts of kindness, anticipation of others' wishes—oh, they are gems and stars of happiness, "blessing him that gives and him that takes"! Self-forgetfulness is the opposite of self-seeking; self-love is the very antipodes of the love that Christ taught us and gave us an example of. Self-seeking looks for its own interest and glory, true charity for the good of others. The great curse of society is selfishness, with its hollow courtesies and feigned politeness: sometimes it is not even gilded with these, and makes earth resemble hell. We read of a certain king who commanded a musician to play and sing before him. It was a time of rejoicing, and many were bidden to the feast. He took his harp, tuned it, and played sweetly and sang beautifully, so that it seemed none could equal him. The company was enraptured, and listened eagerly that not a note or strain might be lost. But what was his theme? Himself; his own excellences; his great achievements. When, however, he presented himself to the king for the expected reward, it was refused. He had had his reward—all that he deserved. Christ Himself spoke of those who "did their righteousness" before men, and condemned them. "Thou, when thou prayest, enter into thy closet; and when thou hast shut thy door, pray to thy Father which is in secret; and thy Father which seeth in secret shall reward thee openly." Benevolence and not selfishness, thoughtfulness for others rather than for oneself, self-sacrifice and not self-seeking, are taught us by Him who "pleased not Himself." The worshippers of Diana were called Dianeans, and were expected to be like her; but we are called Christians, and are to be like Christ.—*Dr. Burrows.*

Christ's example to be realised.—The example of Christ is to the believer the new law to be realised (Gal. vi. 2); hence the "for also." If, as man, Christ had pleased Himself in the use of His liberty, or in the enjoyment of the rights and privileges which His own righteousness had acquired, what would have come of our salvation? But He had only one thought—to struggle for the destruction of sin, without concerning Himself about His own well-being, or sparing Himself even for an instant. In this bold and persevering struggle against our enemy, evil, He drew on Him the hatred of all God's adversaries here below, so that the lamentation of the psalmist (lxix. 9)

became, as it were, the motto of His life. In labouring thus for the glory of God and the salvation of men, He gave back, as Isaiah had prophesied, " neither before shame nor spitting." This certainly is the antipodes of *pleasing ourselves.* Psalm lxix. applies only indirectly to the Messiah (ver. 5: "*My sins* are not hid"); it describes the righteous Israelite suffering for the cause of God. But this is precisely the type of which Jesus was the supreme realisation. We need not say, with Meyer, that Paul adopts the saying of the psalmist directly into his text. It is more natural, seeing the total change of construction, like Grotius, to supply this idea: "*but he did* as is written"; comp. John xiii. 18. Paul, vers. 1, 2, had said "us"; it is difficult indeed to believe that in writing these last sayings he could avoid thinking of his own apostolic life. But divine succour is needed to enable us to follow this line of conduct unflinchingly; and this succour the believer finds only in the constant use of the Scriptures, and in the help of God which accompanies it (vers. 4-6). —*Godet.*

MAIN HOMILETICS OF THE PARAGRAPH.—*Verse* 4.

Old writings for new times.—The mercy and wisdom of God are shown in the gift of a written revelation. Nature teaches only in symbols, and her writing must be interpreted by the writing of revelation. Human reason is at best a blind guide, and must be enlightened by divine reason; thus our need of a revelation. Men receive much light from the Bible, and yet too often treat it as if it were of no account in either the intellectual or moral sphere. Perhaps they do not know how much they owe to the "god of books." The pride and ingratitude of men are seen in the fact that they are hypercritical in studying the Bible. We owe to it what is best in our modern civilisation. We cleave to these writings, for by them patience and comfort are imparted, and hope is begotten and confirmed.

I. **These writings are ancient in their origin.**—The modern cry is for new books and for something sensational. Strong men are made by strong food. Samson lost his strength in Delilah's lap; and the Delilah lap of a light modern literature may destroy intellectual and moral manhood. Plagiarism in sermons has been a well-worn topic. We may now treat of plagiarism in our intellectual magazines and our first-class novels. The truth is that ancient writings are great intellectual storehouses; and the most precious of all are the Scriptures. These writings are confessedly the most ancient, and are surrounded by evidence more various, copious, and exhaustive than that which can be adduced in support of any other ancient writings—written in the childhood of the race, and yet contain depths of wisdom unfathomed. Moses is pelted with geological

492

stones, confronted with mathematical puzzles, and attacked with evolutionary theories, and yet he still rules from Sinai and speaks from his unknown sepulchre in Nebo. David is charged with immorality; still his lyrics charm the universe, and his sublime melodies float through our ancient structures. What modern publisher would dream of giving ten thousand pounds to that old Jew, of whose race and tribe we are ignorant, for his Hebrew manuscript of Isaiah! And yet the greatest modern singers give utterance to his poetry, and the most celebrated musical composers are inspired by his lofty periods. We do not go the length of blindly accepting the old because it is old; but surely the ancient has a claim upon respectful consideration. This is wonderful, that time has not impaired the vitality of these writings. A declaration this that they came from Him who fainteth not, neither is weary. That these writings appeared in the childhood of the race, and should by majesty of thought, by purity of influence, and by sublimity of language have lifted themselves up above surrounding darkness, ignorance, and corruption, is no small evidence of their superhuman origin. These ancient writings may be compared to strong rocks, and modern criticism to feeble wavelets. They move in impotent endeavour. When they have done their worst and retired, men will be ashamed of their folly in fearing lest God's Scriptures should be swept into oblivion.

II. **These ancient writings are prophetic in their scope.**—St. Paul does not confine himself to the prophecies, his quotation being from the Psalms. The prophecies remain as evidence to the inspiration of the Bible. Beyond these the ancient writings are prophetic because they forthtell the truth for all time. The writers stood in times beginning, and looked to after-time, and wrote both for St. Paul and his compeers, and for that army who should receive the same faith and follow in the same pathway. In this sense few modern writers are prophetic; their names will perish, and their works be forgotten. Those who have made a cheap reputation by attacking Moses and the prophets, if they could rise from the dead would be surprised to find themselves forgotten, while Moses and the prophets were still influencing mankind. Modern science of infidel tendencies may let the prophets down into deep pits, but their voices still roll forth with majesty. The prophets' scrolls may be thrown into the fire, but the flames illuminate their messages. Moses, the prophets, and the apostles are time's great teachers and true prophets because they have been taught in heaven's school.

III. **These prophetic writings are spiritual in their design.**—Above all other books they have been promotive of learning from a mere intellectual point of view. Biblical students greatest scholars. Tongue cannot tell what the Bible has thus done. Young minds have been quickened by its matchless stories; the dormant intellect has been touched to energy by its magical power, and shown unexpected ability; eloquence has risen to loftiest strains when inspired by the inspired word. It has created sublimest musical melodies, and strengthened the poet's wings for highest soarings. The novelist, while attacking, will quote a sentence to conclude and grace the page; and the historian will check his narration to admire the flowers culled from this divine garden. But secular learning is dangerous if it be not accompanied by sacred. The former too often breeds impatience and discomfort, while the latter produces patience and comfort. By that study we are introduced to " quiet resting-places." We meditate upon the patience of the saints until we catch somewhat of their spirit. Reading these ancient writings is good; keeping them stored in the memory is good. But patience is the crowning quality. " Ye have heard of the patience of Job, and have seen the end of the Lord; that the Lord is very pitiful, and of tender mercy." These writings record the incomparable drama of Job's sufferings and triumphs. Patience taught by the example of the saints. Consolation imparted by the promises.

IV. **These writings are benevolent in their purpose.**—A benevolent work to produce and strengthen hope; for when a man loses hope he becomes poor indeed. How much of our modern writing is for the destruction of hope! Attempts are more largely made to destroy the foundations of our faith; and if these be destroyed, where are our hopes? These ancient writings teach us hope in the wisdom of the divine plans, in the benevolence of the divine arrangements, and in the final good to be secured by divine proceedings; they give the hope of "an inheritance incorruptible, and undefiled, and that fadeth not away, reserved in heaven for you, who are kept by the power of God through faith unto salvation." They keep hope in lively exercise. Men have tried other writings in vain. But here is found a hope which maketh not ashamed; which has enabled its possessors to resist the "temptations of the world, the flesh, and the devil"; to breast a dark sea of troubles and overcome; to raise hymns of praise in the prison-cell; to turn the dark dungeon into a palace beautiful; and to sing while the flames were scorching the poor body,—

> "There is a blessed land making most happy;
> Never thence shall rest depart, nor cause of sorrow come."

And truly glorious is the death scene of those who are rightly sustained by Christian hope. The Scriptures only can give this divine grace.

SUGGESTIVE COMMENTS ON VERSE 4.

Things written for a purpose.—"For whatsoever things were written aforetime were written for our learning, that we through patience and comfort of the Scriptures might have hope." A quotation in the preceding verse from Psalm lxix. 9 leads the writer of this epistle to speak of whatsoever things, besides this, were written in ancient times. The particular instance suggests the universal truth as to the nature and object, not of all writings, sacred and profane, but of those regarded as sacred by the Jews.

I. **The apostle we see, then, had in mind "the law and the prophets," or all the canonical books of the Old Testament.**—These are believed to *be* and to *contain* a revelation to man of duty and hope—a revelation for the development of spiritual life and moral principle and habit. And whatever theory we may adopt, verbal, substantial, or in effect, of inspiration, we must acknowledge that St. Paul taught and believed that all the Old Testament Scriptures were given for a direct purpose, not from man, though by man—given in some way

by divine authority, or they would not be a sufficient foundation for our hope —"hope that maketh not ashamed," and which we have "as an anchor of the soul." The ten commandments were claimed to have been "written with the finger of God." "Holy men of old spake as they were moved by the Holy Ghost." The Scriptures are called "lively oracles." "Thus it is written," said Christ. "As it is written," the evangelists frequently say. "In the volume of the book it is written of me," said the psalmist— words which St. Paul quotes in the Epistle to the Hebrews. The first copies of the law were probably written on papyrus; the later on parchment, which was unrolled from right to left from a staff, and rolled on another as it was read; hence the word "volume." The Jews had profound regard for the sacred writings, and their learned men knew the number of words, and even of letters, in them. It is not necessary to hold that the Holy Scriptures were *miraculously* preserved, but the reverence for them would tend to preserve them un-

494

corrupted. That the books were all written by the men whose names they bear it may be difficult to prove; but the theory of imposture is impossible under all the circumstances. We must believe that they were written—written by men, but on the authority and by the inspiration of the Holy Spirit. Much the same may be said of the books of the New Testament. They were written for a purpose. They, it is believed, were written by divine inspiration, if not by dictation. They are the spiritual law of the kingdom of Christ. In them, nay, in the whole Bible, we are furnished with all necessary instruction, guidance, reproof, and counsel. "In them ye think [are satisfied that] ye have eternal life, and they are they which testify of Christ." These books have been received from very early times by the Christian Church, guarded, taught to the people, cited, and preserved, and are plainly worthy of all acceptation.

II. **The purpose for which the Holy Scriptures were written is one plain enough and easy to be understood.**— 1. *They were written for our learning.* This has necessarily been anticipated; but too much cannot be said upon it. We need instruction as to our natural condition and sinful state, as to the means of grace and spiritual renewal, as to the need of worshipping and serving our Creator, as to the life which we have in and through Jesus Christ our Lord, and as to the way of finding life eternal, with its fulness of joy and rivers of pleasure. 2. *The Scriptures were written that we might be patient learners in the kingdom of God,* studying His word and pleasure, that we may prove "what is that good and acceptable and perfect will of God." We are to be patient students, until we become as "scribes instructed unto the kingdom of heaven." Patience in suffering, as well as in doing, is to be learned. "If we suffer with Him [*i.e.*, with Christ], we shall also reign with Him." "The trial of our faith being much

more precious than gold that perished, though it be tried with fire, may be found unto praise and honour and glory at the appearing of Jesus Christ." We are appointed both to do and to suffer; and *how* we shall act and live is taught us in Holy Scripture. 3. *The Scriptures were written that we might have hope.* Man without them is in darkness. He may reason out for himself a way of life; but it will not bring him an assured and earnest hope. But hope is to come, in great part, by *doing* the commandments of God, and patiently submitting to affliction, being "kept by His mighty power through faith unto salvation." Thus come unto us sure *comfort* and peace, and hope becomes stronger and brighter as we advance in our Christian course, and this hope reacts upon our souls, and is an incitement to purity of life, and gives satisfaction in the very article of death.—*Dr. Burrows, Ashtabula, New York.*

The things that were written aforetime. —What St. Paul said of the Old Testament we may say of the New— of the whole Christian Bible—not least of those glorious epistles which are St. Paul's own contributions to it. All of these Scriptures, New as well as Old, are written for the learning of us who live in these later ages. Our business is to make the most of the lesson. Scripture is a manual of moral or spiritual learning. It is addressed to the heart and to the will, as well as to the intellect. It is a book for the understanding; and much more, it is a book for the spirit and for the heart. There are, no doubt, many other kinds of learning to be got from the Bible. It is a great manual of Eastern antiquities. It gives us information about the ancient world which we can obtain nowhere else. It carries us back to the early dawn of history, when as yet all that we commonly mean by civilisation did not exist. It is a handbook, again, of political experience. It shows us what a nation can do, and what it may have to suffer —how it may be affected by the conduct of its rulers—how it may make its rulers like itself. Again, it is a rich collection of moral wisdom as applied to personal conduct, and a man need not believe in divine revelation in order to admire the shrewdness and penetration of the Book of Proverbs. Again, it is a mine of poetry. It contains the highest poetry which the human race possesses—poetry before which the great masters of song must bow. It is a choice field for the study of language. In its pages we trace one beautiful language, the Hebrew, from its cradle to its grave. It gives us lessons in the use of language, to describe the emotions and the moods of the human soul, which are not to be found elsewhere. Learning of this kind has its value, and some of it is necessary if we are to make the most of this precious book ; but it is *not* the learning which St. Paul says that the ancient Scriptures were meant to impart to Christians. A man may have much of this learning, and yet he may miss altogether the true lessons that Scripture has to teach him. " That we, through patience and comfort of the Scriptures, might have hope "—that is the end of the highest learning which Scripture has to give us. The Bible is the book of God, so it is the book of the future. At first sight it seems to be altogether a book of the past. The Bible helps us as no other book does or can. It stands alone as the warrant and stimulant of hope. It speaks with a divine authority ; it opens out a future which no human authority could attest. Here is consolation and hope in Scripture for those who need and who will have it. Those who will may find in Holy Scripture patience, consolation, hope. Not in its literary or historical features, but in the great truths which it reveals about God, about our incarnate Lord, about man, in the great examples it holds forth of patience and of victory, in the great promises it repeats, in the future which it unfolds to the eye of faith, is this

496

treasure to be found. A more constant, more reverent, more thorough use of Holy Scripture is surely one of the appropriate duties of a season like Advent, for " Scripture is a long letter sent to us from our heavenly country," and we who hope in time to reach its shores should learn what we can about it and about the conditions of reaching it while we may. Thus, indeed, shall we prepare for that event which surely waits us all, the future judgment, if we shall read, mark, learn, and inwardly digest those Scriptures which God has given for our learning, that by patience and comfort of this His holy word we embrace and hold fast that hope of everlasting life which He has given us in and with His adorable Son.—*Canon Liddon.*

Our duty to study things written.— "Whatsoever things were written aforetime were written for *our* learning." For our welfare Moses wrote, David sang, Solomon spoke lessons of wisdom, and the experiences of Job were recorded; Isaiah, Jeremiah, and the other prophets opened out their scrolls for our moral well-being; the great Teacher unfolded lessons of heavenly wisdom, the four evangelists observed and recorded, Paul argued, Peter laid down practical rules, John wrote his poem of love, and the sublime work of the Revelation was penned, for our learning. God's revelation has been gradual. The knowledge of God's material works has been progressively acquired, and God's word has been given to mankind in parts. The Bible, thus given in parts and at long intervals, is possessed of striking unity. All the parts converge towards one central object— Jesus Christ. God gave to mankind a perfect world, and could at once have given a complete revelation. God revealed for the learning of the men of the olden time ; and now He has blessed by giving the gathered writings of all His inspired servants. God gave one authoritative collection of writings. Men collect the wit and wisdom of Shakespeare, or gems from voluminous authors; here, in the Bible, is treasured the wisdom of the ancients. Some overlook the wisdom, and fix only upon what they call the follies; let it be ours to look to the wisdom. It is surprising that in these ancient writings we find purest types of composition, most correct and sublime thoughts, loftiest flights of poetry and eloquence, and brightest pearls of wisdom. But more than that, the writings of the Bible contain the true standard of morals. It is our duty prayerfully to study these writings. This book bears the impress of divinity. Let the objectors write psalms like David, show powers of imagination like the prophetic bards, let fall from their lips pearls of truth equal to those of the great teachers, persuade like Paul, and touch like the apostle of love, and then we may patiently listen to their diatribes. Meanwhile we will reverently attend to those Scriptures which have been given for our learning.

Things written best.—God speaks by *His Scriptures.* " Whatsoever things were written aforetime were written for our learning; that we, through patience and comfort of the Scriptures, might have hope." *Scripta sunt*—they are written. Things that go only by tale or tradition meet with such variations, augmentations, abbreviations, corruptions, false glosses, that, as in a lawyer's pleading, truth is lost in the *quære* for her. Related things we are long in getting, quick in forgetting; therefore God commanded His law should be written. *Littera scripta manet.* Thus God doth effectually speak to us. Many good, wholesome instructions have dropped from human pens, to lesson and direct man in goodness; but there is no promise given to any word to convert the soul but to God's word. Without this antiquity is novelty, novelty subtlety, subtlety death. *Theologia scholastica multis modis sophistica*—School divinity is little better than mere sophistry. *Plus argutiarum quam doctrinæ, plus doctrinæ quam usus*—It hath more quickness than soundness, more sauce than meat, more difficulty than doctrine, more doctrine than use. This Scripture is the perfect and absolute rule. Bellarmine acknowledgeth two things requirable in a perfect rule—certainty and evidence. If it be not certain, it is not rule; if it be not evident, it is no rule to us. Only the Scripture is, both in truth and evidence, a perfect rule. Other writings may have canonical verity; the Scripture only hath canonical authority. Others, like oil, may make cheerful man's countenance; but this, like bread, strengthens his heart. This is the absolute rule: " And as many as walk according to this rule, peace be on them, and mercy, and upon the Israel of God" (Gal. vi. 16). Oh that we had hearts to bless God for His mercy that the Scriptures are among us, and that not sealed up under an unknown tongue! The time was when a devout father was glad of a piece of the New Testament in English—when he took his little son into a corner, and with joy of soul heard him read a chapter, so that even children became fathers to their fathers, and begat them to Christ. Now, as if the commonness had abated the worth, our Bibles lie dusty in the windows; it is all if a Sunday handling quit them from perpetual oblivion. Few can read, fewer do read, fewest of all read as they should. God of His infinite mercy lay not to our charge this neglect!—*Adams.*

The Scriptures an arsenal.—I use the Scriptures, not as an arsenal to be resorted to only for arms and weapons, . . . but as a matchless temple, where I delight to contemplate the beauty, the symmetry, the magnificence, of the structure, and to increase my awe and excite my devotion to the Deity there preached and adored.—*Boyle.*

Every passage fruitful. — Scarcely can we fix our eyes upon a single passage in this wonderful book which has not afforded comfort or instruction to thousands, and been wet with tears of penitential sorrow or grateful joy drawn from eyes that will weep no more.—*Payson.*

This lamp, from off the everlasting throne,
Mercy took down, and in the night of
   time
Stood casting on the dark her gracious
   bow,
And evermore beseeching men with tears
And earnest sighs to hear, believe, and
   live.
                              Pollock.

Scriptures remarkable as a literary composition.—Even as a literary composition the sacred Scriptures form the most remarkable book the world has ever seen. They are of all writings the most *ancient.* They contain a record of events of the deepest *interest.* The history of their influence is the history of *civilisation* and happiness. The wisest and best of mankind have borne witness to their power as an instrument of enlightenment and of *holiness* ; and having been prepared by " men of God who spake as they were moved by the Holy Ghost " to reveal " the true God and Jesus Christ whom He has sent," they have on this ground the strongest claims upon our attentive and reverential regard.—*Angus.*

Not to be discouraged if we do not understand.—We often read the Scriptures without comprehending its full meaning ; however, let us not be discouraged. The light, in God's good time, will break out, and disperse the darkness, and we shall see the mysteries of the gospel.—*Bishop Wilson.*

The great excellency of the word.—All things which are written are written for our erudition and knowledge. All things that are written in God's book, in the Bible book, in the book of the Holy Scripture, are written to be our doctrine. Consider that the words of Paul are not to be understanded of all Scriptures, but only of those which are of God written in God's book ; and all things which are therein " are written for our

498

learning." The excellency of this word is so great, and of so high dignity, that there is no earthly thing to be compared unto it. The Author thereof is great—that is, God Himself, eternal, almighty, everlasting. The Scripture, because of Him, is also great, eternal, most mighty and holy. There is no king, emperor, magistrate, and ruler, of what state soever they be, but are bound to obey this God, and to give credence unto His holy word, in directing their steps ordinately according unto the same word. Yea, truly, they are not only bound to obey God's book, but also the minister of the same, " for the word's sake," so far as he speaketh " sitting in Moses' chair "—that is, if his doctrine be taken out of Moses' law. For in this world God hath two swords ; the one is a temporal sword, the other a spiritual. The temporal sword resteth in the hands of kings, magistrates, and rulers under Him ; whereunto all subjects, as well as the clergy as the laity, be subject, and punishable for any offence contrary to the same book. The spiritual sword is in the hands of the ministers and preachers ; whereunto all kings, magistrates, and rulers ought to be obedient, that is, to hear and follow, so long as the ministers sit in Christ's chair, that is, speaking out of Christ's book. The king correcteth transgressors with the temporal sword ; yea, and the preacher also, if he be an offender. But the preacher cannot correct the king, if he be a transgressor of God's word, with the temporal sword ; but he must correct and reprove him with the spiritual sword, fearing no man, setting God only before his eyes, under whom he is a minister to supplant and root up all vice and mischief by God's word ; whereunto all men ought to be obedient, as is mentioned in many places of Scripture, and amongst many this is one, *Quæcunque jusserint vos servare servate et facite* : " Whatsoever they bid you observe, that observe and do." Therefore let the preacher teach, improve, amend, and instruct in righteousness with the spiritual sword, fearing no man, though death should ensue. Thus Moses, fearing no man, with his sword did reprove King Pharaoh at God's commandment. All things that are written in God's book, in the Holy Bible, they were written before our time; but yet to continue from age to age, as long as the world doth stand.—*Bishop Latimer.*

MAIN HOMILETICS OF THE PARAGRAPH.—*Verses* 5—7.

A prayer that looks for results.—Oftentimes we pray, and do not expect answers. Our prayers are in a great measure purposeless. Modern scepticism creeps into the heart of the modern Christian. What profit shall we have if we pray unto Him? expresses too much the latent feeling of many natures. Let us seek to have more faith in the efficacy of prayer; let us rise up to the position of ancient saints; let us realise our privilege, and believe that God answers prayer.

I. **The prayer.**—Notice about this prayer that it is: 1. *Brief.* Most of the prayers of the New Testament are short, and yet powerful. The model prayer is short. This, however, does not preclude long and earnest wrestling in secret. The Master was much in prayer. As the Master, so the servant should be. 2. *Comprehensive.* Short prayers are sometimes the most comprehensive. How much is comprehended in the Church of England collects! Here in one verse is a collect of large comprehension. A great soul, feeling the burden of its desire, puts much thought in few words. Little thought, many words. Let our words be few, but let our thoughts be many and earnest, as we come to the God of thought. 3. *Well planned.* God is addressed as the fountain of those qualities which are needful for the desired result. Patience and consolation are needful for Christian harmony. Provocations will arise. The strong will require patience with the infirmities of the weak; while the weak will require patience with the tendency to overbearance in the strong. Mutual forbearance demands patience and consolation from the divine source. Unity of affection will be disturbed if there be not patience. Oneness of sentiment, likemindedness, sameness of heart, must be generated from God through the gracious channel and according to the glorious example of Jesus Christ.

II. **The expected result.**—In the modern Church we find too often many minds and many mouths, and some of the mouths very large, very noisy, and very difficult to close. One mind and one mouth—the one mind of love, the one mouth of praise to God. What a blessed unity! What divine harmony! Many minds blended by the one mind of love; many mouths so united as if only one mouth were expressing the various sounds. One mind absorbed in the mind of eternal love. What a picture! The many minds and many mouths of the Church militant concentred in one mind and one mouth that glorifies God, even the Father of our Lord Jesus Christ. The children of earth spring from one Father, and should have one mind of love. The primitive Church is a pattern for the modern Church. It is true that there were discords, but there was such harmony that it was said, "See how these Christians love one another." St. Paul's prayer and St. Paul's example not without blessed results. Let us each pray and act so that one mind and one mouth may be the characteristic of the modern Church.

III. **The natural exhortation.**—"Wherefore receive ye one another." The exhortation is founded on the prayer and on the expected results. "Receive ye one another, as Christ also received us to the glory of God." How graciously wide the receptions of Christ! Our "at homes" are formal receptions occurring at wide intervals; Christ was always at home to the homeless, the sad, and the weary. The King of heaven held court with publicans and sinners. His drawing-room is the wide world, where weary hearts are seeking rest. To be presented at His court, we need neither rank, nor title, nor costly apparel. He welcomes broken hearts and contrite souls; the weak He loves to tend; the bruised reed He does not break. How difficult and how far-reaching the exhortation, "Wherefore receive ye one another, as Christ," etc. ! Let our receptions be loving and hearty. The grace of love is nobler than the pompous dignity of officialism. Let us receive one another. Let Christians exemplify the true solidarity. Let them be brothers, not in name merely, but in deed and in truth.

Ver. 6. *Worship of the unknowable-yet lovable God.*—That which is perfect cannot be made more glorious. We cannot by our adoration or admiration increase the glory of the sun, the brilliancy of the stars, the majesty of the mountains, the beauty of the landscape, the loveliness of the perfect flower, the melody of the sweet-singing bird. God is perfect, and we cannot by our worship increase His glory. He was glorious before the heavens by their splendours proclaimed His glory, and He will be glorious when they have shrivelled up as a parchment scroll. He was glorious before Adam sang His praises amid the beauties of the primeval Eden, and He will be glorious when this planet in its present form has heard the last chant of praise. But as the heavens declare His glory, as the charming landscape sets forth His divine goodness, so man may "glorify God, even the Father of our Lord Jesus Christ." What a pity that man is so often the least vocal amid the many praising voices of God's world ! Let it be ours "with one mind and one mouth to glorify God."

I. **Whom must we worship?**—It is like a truism to say that we must not worship ourselves; and yet is there not a vast deal of self-worship in our public exercises of religion ? Is not the God we worship the projected ideal of our own creation ? Idolatry is supposed to be extinct in these countries, and to have been extinct for a long period. But there are idols of the mind; and if we were gifted with the power of seeing the unseen, we should be astonished at the number of idols being worshipped in the temples set apart to the worship of the one God. Are our pantheons all destroyed ? Do we worship ourselves when we ought to worship God—ourselves, by proclaiming our goodness to the world—ourselves, by setting forth our own peculiar creed—ourselves, by listening to our favourite preacher ? Let us seek more and more to worship the eternal Spirit "in spirit and in truth." We must worship: 1. *The unknowable God.* We have been told in a recent book that God is not wisely trusted when declared unintelligible. The God who cannot be wisely trusted cannot be properly worshipped. But what reason is there to shrink from the idea of a God who is unintelligible ? Surely Zophar's question is pertinent to such objections : "Canst thou by searching find out God ? Canst thou find out the Almighty to perfection ? " If God were fully intelligible, He could not command the admiration of a noble soul and the worship of an aspiring heart. The unknown is all around us. We move amid the unknowables. We ourselves are amongst the number. Take the simple question, What is life ? and who is there to answer ? What is that subtle force which the anatomist's skill cannot detect ? Does life reside in the pineal gland as on a throne and give orders over the kingdom of man ? Is it an all-pervading force ? Is it a delicate ether extracted from exquisitely compounded and distilled material substances ? Life is, with our present faculties, unknowable. Is it any wonder that the Giver of life is unknowable ? God is infinite, and is thus unknowable. We do not know what infinite duration means. The infinite is simply a mysterious something stretching beyond the finite. The moment we think of the infinite we make it finite by our thought. The infinite is unintelligible; but we believe in a duration which can only be described by an unintelligible term. The infinite power, wisdom, and love of God are unintelligible; still we believe in a wisdom that planned and a power which worked out creative designs, and a love which, working by power and wisdom, achieved our redemption. We worship a power, wisdom, and even love which we cannot fully understand. Worship is the adoration of the loving spirit—it is the upward rising of the soul; and how can the soul rise towards that Being who is on the same level? Worship is elicited, not by the little, but by the great. The old church-builders had surely this in view when they reared their grandly vast and solemn temples. We must in our true worship rise to the unknown and see the unseen. The eternal Spirit is unknown; but finite spirits are drawn to worship " in spirit and in truth." 2. *The knowable God.* God is unintelligible, but not wholly. We feel after Him and find Him, though not the whole of His divine nature. We touch and are touched by Him on every side, and yet we do but touch the fringe of His garment of inaccessible light. A child does not know his father; and yet what would be the nature of the child's feelings if told that he did not know his father and should not love him? The child does not know and yet knows his father. The children of the eternal Father do not know and yet know. We worship a knowable God, for we worship the God and Father of Jesus Christ—the God of the human nature and the Father of the divine nature. He that hath seen Christ hath seen the Father, and cannot be said to worship a God who is wholly unintelligible. Christ, by His light, reflects on the world the eternal brightness. Christ, by His superhuman excellencies manifested in this lower sphere, makes known the excellency of God. He rises infinitely above us, but He condescendingly comes forth from the infinitely vast in the person of the incarnated Son of God. He is far away beyond our comprehension, but He stoops to the world's littleness by a revelation of His greatness in the greatness of the Saviour. Many books have been written and much study has been given about and to the life of Jesus, and still He is beyond our poor knowledge; but shall the loving bride be told that she does not know the divine Bridegroom? We know Jesus, for we live in Him and He in us. We touch His thoughts; we feel the motions of His mighty mind. We know Him sweetly and lovingly, and knowing the Christ we know the God and Father. Our sense of awe is inspired by the unknowable God. Our feeling of blessed union is fostered by the knowable God. 3. *The lovable God.* God's love is unknown and yet well known to the loving nature. He comes forth from the vast unknown, and applies to Himself a well-known and familiar human term. He is the Father of Jesus Christ. God is not an unintelligible abstraction, but a father. The divine nature has in it the principle of fatherhood. From the eternal Father spring the many time fathers. He is over one vast family, and Christ Jesus is His firstborn Son. There is fatherliness in the nature and heart of the vast Unknown, and this fatherliness broods over the children of men. We worship a Father unknown as to His vastness, but known as to His love. And yet His love is unknown. Sufficient for us to know that He loves the Son, and that He loves all those who love the Son; and shall we not add that He has a love for all the earthborn? " We love Him because He first loved us." We worship, we adore, we magnify a lovable God. As the sweet sun shining through the vast spaces of the great cathedral makes its sublimity attractive and cheers the whole edifice, so the sweeter sun of the Father's love shining through the vast spaces of His profound nature renders the vastness attractive and cheers the heart of every sincere worshipper.

II. **How must we worship?**—" With one mind and one mouth." When all hearts are melted by love's sweet flame and fused into one shining unity, then all mouths will be in blessed unison. Pure and united, harmonious strains issue from a concert of well-tuned instruments; and so from the united spirits of Christian worshippers there results united worship. Love is the true musical director which can keep all the parts going harmoniously better than the baton of the best musical conductor the world has seen. The music of love is richer, vaster, and freer from discords than the music of the best earthly composers. It is difficult to get the best-trained choir to sing as with one mouth, still more difficult to secure oneness of mind ; but this can be accomplished by the magical influence of love,—one mouth, not because all the other mouths are closed by law, by custom, or by indifference, but because all mind and speak the same things, because all voices are sweetly blended.

III. **What is to be the effect of our worship?**—The first great object and effect is plainly that God may be glorified by the aspect of a united worshipping community. The ideal described by the apostle is that of the union of the entire Church, composed of Jews and Gentiles, in the adoration of the God and Father who has redeemed and sanctified it by Jesus Christ. "This union was," as Godet says, "in a sense Paul's personal work, and the prize of his apostolic labours. How his heart must have leapt, hearing already, by the anticipation of faith, the hymn of saved humanity ! It is the part of every believer, therefore, to make all the advances and all the sacrifices which love demands in order to work for so magnificent a result." Our hearts glow at the prospect ; but, alas ! the hymn of saved humanity is far from being a perfected composition. The number of the voices is not being increased, at least not at all in proportion to the increase of the population. In one of our largest towns only a little more than one sixth of the population was found in places of worship on the census Sunday. What shall be done for our modern Babylon, where three millions have no connection at all with religious services ? We are told that in a church-going part of the country the good custom is declining. Shall we despair ? By no means. But let us ask, Are our hearts right towards God ? Do we need repentance and thorough reformation, lest God remove our candlestick out of its place ? Have Christians the one mind of love to God and to one another ? Is there the one mouth speaking only to the glory of God ? Let us not seek to attract by mere outward glitter, though we are far from deprecating any attempts which may be made to render God's house and services attractive ; but let us draw by purifying the inward. Let us earnestly and believingly pray to Him whose arm is not yet shortened, and whose willingness to save is still as vast as when He gave His well-beloved Son.

SUGGESTIVE COMMENTS ON VERSES 5—7.

Paul desires harmony.—Paul desires for the Roman Christians a harmony of spirit which will fill every mouth with one song of praise and exalt God in the eyes of mankind. He knows that this cannot be unless the strong in faith deny themselves for the good of their weaker brethren. He urges this as their bounden duty, and points to the example of Christ. By the use of the word "endurance" he admits the difficulty of the task. But he reminds them that to prompt them to such endurance the ancient Scriptures were written. And knowing that even the divine word is powerless without the presence of the divine Speaker, he prays that God, who enables them to maintain their Christian confidence, will also give them the spirit of harmony. He desires this in order that the weak, instead of losing the little faith they have, may join with the strong in praise to God. —*Beet.*

The advantage of a Church.—Here and there an unchurched soul may stir the multitudes to lofty deeds ; isolated men, strong enough to preserve their souls apart from the Church, but shortsighted enough perhaps to fail to see that others cannot, may set high examples and stimulate to national reforms. But for the rank and file of us, made of such stuff as we are made of, the steady pressures of fixed institutions, the regular diets of a common worship, and the education of public Christian teaching are too obvious safeguards of spiritual culture to be set aside. Even Renan declares his conviction that, "Beyond the family and outside the State, man has need of the Church. . . . Civil society, whether it calls itself a commune, a canton, or a province, a state or fatherland, has many duties towards the improvement of the individual; but what it does is necessarily limited. The family ought to do much more, but often it is insufficient; sometimes it is wanting altogether. The association created in the name of moral principle can alone give to every man coming into this world a bond which unites him with the past, duties as to the future, examples to follow, a heritage to receive and to transmit, and a tradition of devotion to continue." Apart altogether from the quality of its contribution to society, in the mere quantity of the work it turns out it stands alone. Even for social purposes the Church is by far the greatest employment bureau in the world. And the man who, seeing where it falls short, withholds on that account his witness to its usefulness is a traitor to history and to fact.—*Drummond.*

Intellectual young England is against churchgoing.—Intellectual young England is grandly patronising, and condescendingly allows us to attend the public services of religion if we feel so disposed. Its language is, I do not oppose churchgoing, or even say that it is undesirable. My point is merely that it is not necessary. Now necessary things are those which are requisite for a purpose. And in this sense public worship is necessary; for it is requisite for the purpose of fostering religious feeling in the individual, and for the purpose of preserving re-

ligion alive in the land. The man who says that private worship is enough, and that it is a waste of time to go to church, is not inspired with the true spirit of Christianity, which is benevolent. It is not necessary to take our meals with the family, or to join the club, or to adhere to a political party; but it is requisite for social well-being and prosperity. So that in this true sense it is necessary; and so also is it necessary "with one mind and one mouth to glorify God" in the hours of prayer. But it is affirmed that the Bible does not require it. St. Paul in this passage seems to regard it as an unquestioned duty, and his point is to prepare the earlier believers for its right performance. Young England has a curious exposition of the direct command in Hebrews, where we are told not to forsake the assembling ourselves together. He says it does not apply to churchgoing at all, for the house of God spoken of in ver. 21 is clearly not a material one. Certainly not; but it is a house on the earth, for it consists of true believers, over which Christ is the High Priest. The passage relates to a present duty which is to be performed in expectation of the approaching day. Christ, as His custom was, went to the synagogue every Sabbath day. The early Church had frequent meetings for fellowship and Christian worship. Religion must decline if the public ordinances of religion are neglected. Mere external contact with the worship of God fails indeed to secure salvation, but wilful contempt of it is the way to ruin. It is a curious feature in young England that he points to the agnostic leaders as non-churchgoers and yet as good men. Doubtless good men in the sense of being moral, but not good men in the sense of being religious and spiritual. How can an agnostic, a man who professes not to know, who willingly remains ignorant, who practically denies a God, be a good man in the highest sense? Agnosticism is not our creed, but

503

Christianity, and we must follow Christ and His apostles and all the faithful. The question arises, How much of the morality of our agnostic leaders is due to the age which has been leavened with the pure leaven of the gospel? It is very sad that too many young Englanders owe themselves to religious parents and to surrounding Christian influences, and yet ungratefully spurn the institution which has done so much for our national well-being. Our love to God and to Christ, our gratitude for saving influences, our social instincts, and our patriotism should induce us "with one mind and one mouth to glorify God" in the earthly house set apart to religious services. It may be difficult to speak definitely as to the reason why a nation has declined; but one of the leading concomitants of a nation's fall is the decline in morals and manners, and these decline with the downfall of religion. When ancient Israel forsook God, then it became an easy prey to the oppressor. Ephesus was once the metropolis of proconsular Asia; not merely in a political, but also in an ecclesiastical sense. It is placed at the head of the seven Churches. It is reported that St. John was its bishop. But Ephesus fell. Young Ephesus said it was not necessary to go to church. The first love departed; both private and public worship was neglected. At the present day the only remains of this once pleasant city are some ruins and the village of Ajosoluck. If we would not see our great metropolis in ruins, if we would not have the desolating tread of foreign foes over our fair green landscapes, we must seek the favour and protection of the eternal God, we must support the public ordinances of religion, we must work and pray for the spread and the increase of noble Christian men and women.

The God of patience.—When we say God is patient, four things are implied:—

I. **Provocation.**—Where there is nothing to try the temper, annoy, or irritate, there can be no patience. Humanity provokes God. The provocation is *great, universal, constant.* Measure His patience by the provocation.

II. **Sensibility.**—Where there is no tenderness of nature, no susceptibility of feeling, there may be obduracy and stoicism, but no patience. Patience implies feeling. God is infinitely sensitive. He *feels* the provocation. "Oh, do not this abominable thing," etc.

III. **Knowledge.**—Where the provocation is not known, however great and however sensitive the being against whom it is directed, there can be no patience. God *knows* all the provocations.

IV. **Power.**—Where a being has not the power to resent an insult or to punish a provocation, though he may feel it and know it, his forbearing is not patience—it is simple *weakness.* He is bound by the infirmity of his nature to be passive. God is *all-powerful.*—*Homilist.*

The God of peace.—Whatever may be the amount of agitation in the universe, there is one Being sublimely pacific, without one ripple upon the clear and fathomless river of His nature. Three things are implied in this:—

I. **That there is nothing malign in His nature.**—Wherever there is any jealousy, wrath, or malice of any description, there can be no *peace.* Malevolence in any form or degree is soul-disturbing. In whatever mind it exists it is like a tide in the ocean, producing eternal restlessness. There is nothing malign in the infinite heart. He is love.

II. **That there is nothing remorseful in His nature.**—Wherever conscience accuses of wrong, there is no peace. All compunctions, self-accusations, are soul-disturbing. Moral self complaisance is essential to spirit peace. God is light. He has never done wrong, and His infinite conscience smiles upon Him and blesses Him with peace.

504

III. **That there is nothing apprehensive in His nature.**—Wherever there is a foreboding of evil, there is a mental disturbance. Fear is essentially an agitating principle. The Infinite has no fear. He is the absolute master of His position.—*Homilist.*

MAIN HOMILETICS OF THE PARAGRAPH.—Verses 8—12.

Praise follows prayer.—The late Matthew Arnold strives to get rid of the words " predestination," " justification," " sanctification," as having any of the meaning attached to them by theologians, which they suppose is derived from St. Paul himself. Matthew Arnold teaches us to follow the eternal law of the moral order, which is righteousness. St. Paul seems thus only to be following in the steps of the ancient moral philosophers, tinctured with a little Jewish thought. We find Paul hard to be understood ; but we find his latest interpreter harder to understand. *St. Paul and Protestantism* will not make men in " harmony with the eternal order and at peace with God "; while the epistles of St. Paul have done vastly more for the production of righteousness among men than any books which have been written. But if Matthew Arnold is to be our guide, we must reject St. Paul, for we read : " A Jew himself, he, Paul, uses the Jewish Scriptures in a Jew's arbitrary and uncritical fashion, as if they had a talismanic character, as if for a doctrine, however true in itself, their confirmation was still necessary, and as if their confirmation was to be got from their words alone, however detached from the sense of their context, and however violently allegorised or otherwise molested." The man who quotes uncritically is to be rejected on intellectual grounds. If St. Paul have one point pre-eminent, it is that he possesses and uses the critical faculty. To wrest is to turn from truth ; and the man who wrested the Jewish Scriptures is to be rejected on moral grounds. But we are not aware of any such wresting ; the four quotations made in this paragraph do not appear to us to be either used uncritically or wrested from their context. The aptness of St. Paul's quotations is self-evident, and is itself a refutation of a mere Judaistic or Oriental use of passages. It is an easy but not quite fair way of getting rid of a difficulty by using the words " Hebraise," " Orientalise." There is, however, no need to use long and unusual words in reading these four quotations. Whether we read the texts in Hebrew, in Greek, or in our English translation, they all bear the construction put upon them by St. Paul. And we think as much may be said for all the other quotations. The sense of harmony with the universal order, the desire for and the possession of righteousness, are to come, not from psychology, not from philosophy, not from either deductive or inductive methods, but from faith in that Root of Jesse in whom the Gentiles shall trust. Here is foretold universal harmony with the eternal law of divine order. Jews and Gentiles shall blend in one song of praise to the King of righteousness. The weak and the strong shall be of one mind and one mouth when they are inspired by love to the Incarnation of righteousness. Notice in this paragraph :—

I. **A twofold purpose of Christ's mission.**—To vindicate God's faithfulness and to manifest God's mercy. Jesus Christ was the minister of the circumcision ; made under the law ; a Jew confirming unto the Jews the faithfulness of God ; by His life conforming to the law in its spiritual and essential aspect ; by His death redeeming those who were under the curse of the law. Christian ministers are sometimes taunted with propagating the worship of a dead Jew. We are not abashed by the aspersion. It is said that a living dog is better than a dead lion ; but the dead Lion of the tribe of Judah has brought forth more sweetness for the refreshment of the race than any of the living assailants of Christianity from the time of its establishment to the present hour.

505

> "In the cross of Christ I glory,
>   Towering o'er the wrecks of time;
> All the light of sacred story
>   Gathers round its head sublime."

It is wonderful what the Minister of the circumcision, by His earthly life, by His sacrificial death, and by His mediatorial reign, has accomplished. There is vastly more to come; for Jews shall extol God's faithfulness, and Gentiles from all quarters shall rejoice in God's mercy. The cross of Christ shall tower over the wrecks of human theories. Christ, by His cross, by His divine efficacy, shall reign over the Gentiles all over the round globe of the earth.

II. **A blessed result of Christ's mission.**—The establishment of a kingdom amongst the Gentiles which is righteousness, peace, and joy in the Holy Ghost. A Root of Jesse shall rise to reign. God begins at the root; God's root forces are strong and ever developing. Out of the Root of Jesse has sprung the wide-spreading tree of Christianity. The Root of Jesse did not look like a regnant power when He was crucified between two thieves. The Root appeared to be killed when it was trying to send itself above the ground. But the Root gathered to itself power from the strokes of the adversaries. Jesus reigns from His sepulchre. Other men cease to reign when death hurls down the sceptre. Jesus began to reign in fuller measure when death touched the physical form. He shall rise to reign. He is rising through all time. His utmost elevation will not be reached till in Him the Gentiles trust. He is rising, though some say He is falling. He is rising, though men say that the kingdom of Christianity is a failure. In Him shall the Gentiles trust. His kingdom is founded on trust. Holy confidence is the foundation of His divine sovereignty.

III. **The united song of praise inspired by Christ's mission.**—" Sing," " rejoice," " praise," " laud," are the words employed to set forth the exuberant nature of the feelings of those who feel and seek to glorify God for His mercy. One mind of gratitude and one mouth of praise shall be characteristic of the ransomed Gentile world. A grateful mind must be the motive force of a praising mouth. The spiritual revelation of divine mercy to the inmost soul works gratitude, and this expresses itself in hymns of praise. The singing of the grateful chorister may not to critical human ears be so correct as the singing of some who are prompted by the prospect of remuneration, but the former touches the heart of true men and blends with the upper harmonies. Let us open our souls to the incoming streams of divine mercy. Let gratitude attend the spirit, and then we shall sing with lip and with life; our daily steps will beat divine music; our days will march to heavenly harmonies; our very nights will be cheered with spirit songs. Angels will hear the strains and join to swell the melody; earth and heaven will unite, and the sound will be as the sweet notes of many skilful harpers harping with their harps.

SUGGESTIVE COMMENTS ON VERSES 8—12.

Rejoice in the Lord, a privilege and a command.—There is in man by nature such an inordinate portion of self-love, that his regards are almost exclusively confined to those who coincide with him in sentiment and contribute to his comfort. The smallest difference of opinion in things either political or religious shall be sufficient to produce, not only indifference, but in many alienation and aversion. We do not much wonder at a want of mutual affection between the Jews and Gentiles, because they imbibed from their very infancy the most inveterate prejudices against each other, and had all their principles and habits as opposite as can be conceived. But, unhappily for the Christian Church, the same disposition to despise or condemn each other remained amongst them after they were incorporated in one body and united under one head, the Lord Jesus Christ. To counteract this unhallowed temper, and to promote a cordial union amongst all the members of Christ's mystical body, was the incessant labour of St. Paul. In the whole of the preceding context he insists on this subject, recommending mutual forbearance and affection from the example of Christ, who showed the same regard both to Jews and Gentiles, both to strong and weak. The ministry of our blessed Lord had respect, primarily, to the Jews. Jesus was Himself born a Jew, and He submitted to circumcision, which was the initiatory rite whereby the Jews were received into covenant with God. When He entered upon His ministerial office, He addressed Himself exclusively to those of the circumcision; when solicited to confer His blessings on a Syrophenician woman, He refused, saying that He was "sent only to the lost sheep of the house of Israel," and that "He could not take the children's bread and cast it unto dogs," though, for the encouragement of all future suppliants, of whatever nation or character, He afterwards granted her request. In all this the Lord Jesus consulted "the truth of God, and confirmed the promises made to the fathers"; which, though they comprehended *all* the spiritual seed of Abraham, had doubtless respect to those in the first place who should also be found among His lineal descendants. Ultimately, to the Gentiles also in the very promises made to Abraham, the Gentile nations were expressly included. But, to confirm this truth, St. Paul brings passages out of all the different parts of the Old Testament, "the law of Moses, the Prophets, and the Psalms," to prove his point. These testimonies unequivocally prove that, however Jesus, for the accomplishing of the promises, ministered to the circumcision chiefly, yet He did not confine His regards to them, but ordained that all, of whatever nation, should equally be admitted to His covenant and be made

partakers of His salvation. To whomsoever our Lord communicated His salvation, it was His invariable purpose that they who partook of it should "glorify God for His mercy." The manner in which this is to be done may be gathered from the passages that are cited. The duty of every member of Christ's Church is to submit to Him—Christ is "risen to reign over the Gentiles." Now, where there is government, there must be subjection; and consequently all who would belong to Christ must "take His yoke upon them." Their submission too must be willing and unreserved. To trust in Him—Christ comes, not only as a Lord, but as a Saviour, through whom we are to find deliverance from the wrath to come. Now it is said that "in Him shall the Gentiles trust." Our duty towards Him is to believe that He is equal to the task which He has undertaken, that in Him there is a fulness of wisdom to instruct the ignorant, of righteousness to justify the guilty, and of grace to sanctify the polluted. Rejoice in Him—to "rejoice in the Lord alway" is not merely permitted as a privilege, but commanded as a duty. We dishonour Him when we do not rejoice in Him; we evidently show that we have a low apprehension of His excellency, and of the benefits which He confers. What they are doing in the Church above, that we should be doing in the Church below. Our obligations are the same, and so should also our occupations be. Are the glorified saints incessantly admiring and adoring Him who is the author of all their happiness? We also should ever be contemplating the incomprehensible wonders of His love, and rejoicing in Him with joy unspeakable and glorified. Walk in His steps—this is the particular scope of the text, the intent for which all these quotations are introduced. Our blessed Saviour has shown a gracious and merciful regard for all the human race; nor has He permitted any diversity in their habits or conduct to exclude them from His kingdom, provided they repent

507

and obey His gospel. Now our hearts should be enlarged after His example. We should not suffer little circumstantial differences to alienate us from each other. While we claim a right to follow our own judgment, we should cheerfully concede the same liberty to others. A difference of conduct may be proper for different persons, or for the same persons under different circumstances. This is evident from Paul refusing to suffer Titus to receive circumcision, when he had already administered that rite to Timothy ; as also from his performing at Jerusalem the vows of a Nazarite, after he had for twenty years renounced the authority of the ceremonial law. It is therefore by no means necessary that we all conform precisely to the same rule in indifferent matters ; but it is necessary that we cultivate charity, and maintain "the unity of the Spirit in the bond of peace." If we be not perfectly agreed in sentiment respecting things that are non-essentials, we must at least agree in this, to leave every one to the exercise of his own judgment : the weak must not judge the strong, nor the strong despise the weak, but all follow after " the things which make for peace, and things wherewith one may edify another."—*Simeon.*

MAIN HOMILETICS OF THE PARAGRAPH.—*Verse* 13.

The divine antidote against despair.—It is difficult to lead a truly religious life. This arises from our proneness to evil and from the influences working to draw us away from the path of rectitude. There are great forces against us ; but, rightly considered, there are mightier forces engaged on our behalf. This text is in itself a shield of protection. An apostle prays. A God of hope encourages. The power of the Holy Ghost is engaged. The essentials of the Christian life are being developed to establish in that hope which is the crown and guarantee of safety and of ultimate triumph.

I. **The apostle prays.**—Spiritual earnestness is characteristic of all his supplications. He prays for moral advancement. Too oft we pray for worldly good, and not to be filled with joy and peace in believing. We pray thus, if prayer be the real expression of our hearts. The apostle's prayer was intercessory. We need to know more truly the blessing of intercessory prayer. It would remove our selfishness, make us possess more of the diffusive spirit of Christianity, enlist our sympathies on behalf of the erring, prevent us being so censorious, tend to make us love the brethren, and cause us to dwell together in Christian unity.

II. **A God of hope encourages.**—There are divine agents working for the expansion of Christian hope—the God of hope and the power of the Holy Ghost. How appropriate the term when we remember the apostle's object to inspire with hope ! God is not the subject but the object of hope. Hope is the faculty or grace exercised by the creature who cannot see the future. God sees the future, and has no need to overcome the cloud of the present by drawing from the future the light of hope. God, as the object of hope, is a reason for gratitude. Nature and philosophy may teach a dread abstraction, and may thus induce a desire for atheism. Revelation declares a God of hope. There is hope in the fulness of the divine promises, in the pages of the sacred record, in the cross of our Saviour, and by the power of the Holy Ghost. It is the gracious province of the divine Spirit to work in and upon the human spirit, so that it may abound in hope. There is not often a superabundance of hope ; it is too rare a possession. Abound in hope. How excellent the nature that abounds in hope !

III. **The essentials of the Christian life are being developed.**—Faith, peace, and joy are essential elements of the Christian character. These are to be increased, and then there follows the enlargement of hope. A man filled with joy and peace has no room for despair. Peace and joy constitute the favourable sphere in which hope may abound. Peace, joy, and hope do not spring from a desire, however earnest, after righteousness. A longing after the harmony with the eternal law of moral order will fill us with despair as we feel that we are incapable of satisfying the soul's infinite longings. Peace, joy, and hope come to the soul in and through believing. The truth of this cannot be tested by any scientific method, but it is affirmed by experience.

IV. **The blessed processes employed for the attainment of a great result.**— The blessed processes are both external and internal, both human and divine, and all spiritual. All intercessory prayers are external to the objects of such petitions. Paul prays; the Mediator intercedes. The divine Spirit is external to the human spirit, and works in external spheres, even when that divine Spirit has put itself into blessed union with the human spirit. The divine Spirit is filling. When the divine Spirit fills the human spirit, then it fills with joy and peace. The very presence of the Spirit is joy and peace, for the Holy Ghost is a peaceful and joyful Spirit. All are moving towards the blessed result—superabundance of hope.

V. **The result reacts beneficially on the processes.**—Abundance of hope strengthens faith, deepens peace, enlarges joy. Beneficial reactions are to be expected in Christian processes; while maleficent reactions too often occur in other spheres. Do evil, and evil rebounds. Work in material spheres, and though the work be legitimate, harm and damage may recoil. Do good, and good beyond our doing accrues. Work in moral spheres, and though the work be imperfect, there will be a beneficial reaction beyond the measure of our efforts. Seek for more faith; cultivate peace; enlarge joy. Then hope will abound. And abounding hope will sweetly nourish all graces, like the prospering sunlight of heaven. The apostle abounded in hope in darkest scenes; and why may not we? The heathen wept amid the ruins, but the apostle could sing amid the ruins of worldly hopes; and why may not we?

Ver. 13. *Religion and pleasure.*—It is a remarkable fact that St. Paul, whose record was so stormy, can rejoice. Sketch his chequered life. Yet he speaks of the joy of faith even while the chains about his wrists are clanking. He is a happy Christian, praising God in spite of his uncomfortable quarters and his perilous position. *The secret of this?* That he weighed consequences before experience: the sufferings of the present not worthy of comparison with the glory that should follow.

I. **St. Paul sought to teach men that religion is a thing of joy.**—The general notion among the worldly runs in the opposite direction. Some say of St. Paul that his exultation was due to his natural temperament, to the atmosphere of controversy and opposition, which he dearly loved. But thousands of others have believed that religion is the groundwork of the world's joy. Sceptics and others say that they have joy—deep, solemn, self-respecting, abiding—in looking into the heavens and nature as mysteries, the delight coming from the endeavour to solve them. But the fact is indisputable that their joy is marred by this—that shutting out God they shut out all hope and encouragement.

II. **The text leaves no room for the false ideal of gloomy sainthood.**—One of the greatest injustices that can be done to the Christian cause is to take as one's ideal Christian the melancholy, wasted saint who frowns on everything but the Bible or hymn-book—the grim, gloomy creatures, extreme Puritans, who frown on laughter and lightheartedness. They do not truly reflect the religion Jesus set up among men. Nothing in Christianity to refute Solomon's saying, "To everything there is a season"; but we may make one exception there—namely, no time for the gospel of gloom. Reading between the lines of religion, you come upon the philosophy of right things in right places; but everywhere in religion you find the word "cheerfulness." 1. *To be cheerful is a duty which you owe to God.* He has placed you in a beautiful world with power to enjoy it. If you go complaining and wearing a gloomy face, it is a constant denial that God has done all things to make you happy. 2. *To be cheerful is a duty you owe to your neighbour.* By being cheerful you contribute to the happiness of those around you. We are so constituted that we are always affected by our associates and associations. 3. *Cheerfulness a duty you owe to yourself.* Life is what we make it.

III. **Religion is pleasurable, notwithstanding the element of discipline.**— Discipline an absolute necessity, otherwise many would carry their pleasures into licence. Religion has its pleasure; but it draws a necessary line somewhere. It will not tolerate forgetfulness of God and duty, laxity of service, questionable fraternity with the world that opposes God.

IV. **No real pleasure apart from religion.**—Some say the world would be just as happy without Christ's religion as with it. History gives this the lie. Were the pagans a happy race? Were the Greeks with their full pantheon happy? Think of the picture of the Christless world! Suicide resorted to and praised as a means of escape from misery. It is false to impute gloom to Christianity. Rightly interpreted, it does not sanction a single doctrine or utter a precept which is meant to extinguish one happy impulse or dim one innocent delight. "What it does is to warn us against seeking and following the lowest and most shortlived pleasures as a final end." Since all that "makes life tolerable and society possible" is due to Christ's religion, it is but another step to say that it is only through that religion that there can by any possibility be any real joy and peace.

V. **The false representations have done great mischief.**—Some have held aloof, refusing the yoke of Christ, and have lost much abiding peace. The joy and peace of religion consist in an enlarged view of life, a wider conception of the duties demanded of it, a real comfort in the day of sorrow: these have been lost to many because of misrepresentation. It is something to lose companionship of a Saviour ready to meet our sinfulness and purge it—one ready to meet our feebleness, especially since we are made up of needs.—*Albert Lee.*

Ver. 13. *God has no unfulfilled desires.*—Jesus Christ exercised His ministry amongst the Jews, and chose His apostles from the same people. The far larger proportion of primitive Christians were Jews; but the full and final commission to His disciples was to "preach the gospel to every creature." It was necessary that Christ should be of *some* nation: He came unto the Jews to fulfil the prophecies concerning Him, and to establish the *new* covenant, for which the old was a preparation. The new covenant was for the benefit of all, according to the prediction of Isaiah: "There shall be a root of Jesse, which shall stand for an ensign of the people; to it shall the Gentiles seek: and His rest shall be glorious." Thus is He set forth as *the hope*, or the object of hope, for all people. His ministers are sent for this purpose—to lead men to Him, that they may be induced to *hope* in Him and through Him. There is no exception or exclusion, except that which individuals themselves unwisely make. "I, if I be lifted up from the earth," Christ said, "will draw all men unto Me." The attraction of His love produces hope. The divine Being is not called a God of hope because He has unfulfilled desires; for He is possessed of all things, and has the universe under His control. The very perfection of His nature must be a source of happiness, and excludes the hope so necessary to men, and without which energy would be dissipated and purposes made vain. Hope implies that there is some good not yet in possession, but in God are "hid all the treasures of wisdom and knowledge." But God is the giver of all that is worth having: "Every good gift and every perfect gift is from above." To Him rational beings must look, in Him must trust. On Him we are dependent, and even "the power to get wealth" is received from Him. He permits evil. Why? It is not for us to say; but often what appears so is not so absolutely. He "out of seeming evil still educeth good." He is called "the God of hope" in view of the fact that our state morally is desperate, and that no power less than His can deliver us from it and put us in a condition acceptable to Himself. His good-will towards us is so great as to be incomprehensible. For acceptance in the Beloved, for spiritual renewal, and for life eternal we are to hope in Him. He is not like the fabled deities of old, pleased to execute vengeance; He delights in mercy, "showing it to thousands of them that love Him." But He does not show mercy to penitents that they may continue in sin: "He that confesseth and *forsaketh* it shall find mercy." It is desirable and possible to *abound* in hope, even in the most troublesome events of life. Sometimes it may be dimmed or clouded through "manifold temptations," when a resort to the very Source of hope becomes especially necessary. How many have been sustained by hope in the most fearful difficulties! Take only one example. Carlyle says, "John Knox had a sore fight for existence, wrestling with principalities in defeat, contention, lifelong struggle, rowing as a galley-slave, wandering in exile. A sore fight, but he won it. 'Have you hope?' he was asked in his last moments, when he could no longer speak. He lifted his finger, pointed upward with it, and so died." The God of hope makes His servants to *abound* in hope through His gracious Spirit by filling them with the joy of forgiveness, giving them His abiding presence, and strengthening the desire to "purify themselves, even as He is pure." From Him too cometh a sweet and sacred peace, which is diffused through the whole spiritual nature—a "peace which passeth all understanding." This peace cannot exist where sin reigns, and the conscience is not sprinkled as with the blood of our Lord Jesus Christ. The peace that abideth and flourisheth comes through *believing*, not merely through consenting to certain truths, or accepting revelation as from God, but through "believing with the heart unto righteousness." "Being justified by faith, we have *peace* with God."—*Dr. Burrows, Ashtabula, New York.*

SUGGESTIVE COMMENTS ON VERSE 13.

Paul's cheerfulness in affliction. — What can be more free and buoyant, with all their variety, than his writings? Brilliant, broken, impetuous as the mountain torrent freshly filled, never smooth and calm but on the eve of some bold leap, never vehement but to fill some receptacle of dearest peace, they present everywhere the image of a vigorous joy. Beneath the forms of their theosophic reasonings, and their hints of deep philosophy, there may be heard a secret lyric strain of glorious praise, bursting at times into open utterance, and asking others to join the chorus. . . . His life was a battle from which, in intervals of the good fight, his words arose as the song of victory.—*Albert Lee.*

The world without Christ.—"Their hearts became surcharged with every element of vileness,—with impurity in its most abysmal degradations, with hatred alike in its meanest and its most virulent developments, with insolence culminating in the deliberate search for fresh forms of evil, with cruelty and falsity in their most repulsive features. And the last crime of all, beyond which crime itself could go no further, was the awfully *defiant* attitude of moral evil, which led them, while they were fully aware of

God's sentence of death pronounced on willing guilt, not only to incur it themselves, but with a devilish delight in human depravity and human ruin to take a positive pleasure in those who practise the same." The moral emptiness and desolation of the ancient world is evident to all eyes. It had no moral and spiritual purpose by which to solve the problems that are vital to the very existence of the State. The upbuilding of political life with all its earnestness and struggle and end avour was over. Many things sank into the mere shows and semblances of realities; and, in truth, this was the case with the assemblies of the people, the senate, and the high officers of religion and the State. Everything was sacrificed to appetite, enjoyment, and play. Because heathenism had no goal beyond the grave, it had no worthy purpose and aim on this side of it.—*Seidel.*

Going without religion.—I fear that when we indulge ourselves in· the amusement of going without a religion, we are not perhaps aware how much we are sustained at present by an enormous mass all about us of religious feeling and religious conviction; so that, whatever it may be safe for us to think, for us who have had great advantages and have been brought up in such a way that a certain moral direction has been given to our character, I do not know what would become of the less favoured classes of mankind if they undertook to play the same game. The worst kind of religion is no religion at all; and these men who are living in ease and luxury, indulging themselves in the "amusement of going without religion," may be thankful that they live in lands where the gospel they neglect has tamed the beastliness and ferocity of the men who but for Christianity might long ago have eaten their carcases like the South Sea islanders, or cut off their heads and tanned their hides like the monsters of the French Revolution. When the microscopic search of scepticism, which had hurled the heavens

and sounded the seas to disprove the existence of the Creator, has turned its attention to human society, and has found a place on this planet ten miles square where a decent man can live in decency, comfort, and security, supporting and educating his children, unspoiled and unpolluted—a place where age is reverenced, infancy respected, manhood respected, woman honoured, and human life held in due regard—when sceptics can find such a place ten miles square on this globe where the gospel of Christ has not gone and cleared the way, and laid the foundations, and made decency and security possible, it will then be in order for (sceptics) to move thither, and then ventilate their views. But so long as these very men are dependent upon the religion which they discard for every privilege they enjoy, they may well hesitate a little before they seek to rob the Christian of his hope, and humanity of its faith in that Saviour who alone has given to man that hope of life eternal, which makes life tolerable and society possible, and robs death of its terrors and the grave of its gloom.—*James Russell Lowell.*

The joy of believing.—Some, because religion has been shamefully misrepresented, have stood afar off, dreading to take upon themselves the yoke of Christ. They may well consider that the joy and peace of religion consist in an enlarged view of life, a wider conception of the duties demanded of it, a real comfort in the day of affliction, a real light in the hour of darkness. There is to the Christian all the joy that is worth the name. There is a Saviour ready to meet our sinfulness, ready to purge it; there ·is a God willing to meet our feebleness, helping those who are weak in faith, compassed about with difficulties and infirmities, men and women made up of needs. There is surely joy and peace in believing and realising this. But what joy for the man who will meet his own needs? Dares he to defy the help of One who is mighty, and from whom all real good proceeds ?—never once to have a whisper of encouragement, nor a word of sympathy, nor one kindly touch of help; no great Master on whom to cast the heavy burdens of care ; no one to whom to turn and say, "Thou art my glory, and the lifter-up of my head"; no God to be a refuge and strength, a present help in the dark days of trouble ! Verily, they have failing hearts who seek for pleasure at other hands than those of the crucified One !—*Albert Lee.*

MAIN HOMILETICS OF THE PARAGRAPH.—*Verses* 14—16.

A gracious man's greatness.—It is not given to every gracious man to be great as was St. Paul ; but the man who is endowed by grace is ennobled by the endowment. Each gracious man is by grace raised to a higher platform. Let each seek to be true to his gifts, study great examples, and thus in his measure he will become great. St. Paul is a pattern.

I. **The gracious man is great in gentleness.**—How gentle at times can be some of the strongest natures ! St. Paul was gentle, and he here uses an apologetic tone. He frankly recognises the good of others. Goodness, knowledge, ability, are the qualities he acknowledges. Goodness before knowledge in the apostle's mental criterion. Goodness and knowledge make a man able to admonish. Goodness must keep pace with knowledge if the man is to be a successful admonisher.

II. **The gracious man is great in boldness.**—If we note some gracious men timid and shrinking, we must take into account original temperament. Gentle women have been made courageous by grace. Some men who are afraid of putting pen to paper, lest they should give an advantage to him who wishes that his adversary had written a book, are prompted by grace to write boldly. St. Paul writes boldly through the inspiring influence of the grace of God. St. Paul writes boldly so that he may put in mind. We need to be constantly put in mind. Children at school must have wearisome repetition. In the spiritual school we are all children, and the divine lessons must be repeated. Day unto day, day after day, must moral speech be uttered.

III. **The gracious man is great in office.**—"The minister of Jesus Christ to the Gentiles." The true preacher's office is the greatest in the universe. By some the editor's office is applauded. But too often he is only the echo of public opinion. He is the cunning man who puts into words what the public has been unconsciously thinking. If the editor be inspired by grace, he may become a priestly minister, and do good work. However, we still hold that the preacher's office is the greater. Though it is sometimes scoffingly said that the greatest miracle of Christianity is that it has survived the pulpit, we believe that it is a high position—nobler than the editor's chair, mightier than a throne, that is if the pulpit be occupied by men who are full of goodness, of knowledge, and of ability to admonish. The preacher does priestly work. He offers up the gospel as his sacrifice. He stands between the immensities of time and eternity, and directs men to high thoughts.

IV. **The gracious man is great in purpose.**—His design is that the offering up of the Gentiles might be acceptable. He speaks and prays so that the Gentiles may offer themselves as sacrifices. We need more of this priestly work. He speaks and prays that *he may* be the offerer. The gracious man is benevolent. How many offer up their fellows as a sacrifice on the altar of mammon, and the sacrificed are not benefited ! But every soul offered up as an acceptable sacrifice to God is itself divinely and eternally enriched.

V. **The gracious man is great in co-operation.**—The preacher occupies a difficult and responsible position. The voices of the day are proclaiming the

decadence of the pulpit. The sneering dilettanti ask, Why these prosy sermons?
Pleasure-loving minds declare that it is time to do away with pulpit-droning
and sermonic platitudes. Even the professing soldiers of Jesus Christ say that
they want no hermitical Peters to preach the gospel crusade against the world,
the flesh, and all manner of iniquities. And the preacher seems like to stand
alone, to be as a solitary voice " of one crying in the wilderness." But not alone,
for the Holy Ghost is the companion, inspirer, and co-worker of and with every
true preacher. Sanctified by the Holy Ghost, the good work will proceed. The
persecutions of the past did not prevent its progress. The damning smiles,
courteous sneers, and polite bowing into obscurity of the present will not stay
the triumphant march of the ministry of the gospel of God. Let preachers have
faith. Let them feel the greatness of their office and the glory of its saving
purpose. Let them pray so that they themselves may be filled with all goodness,
knowledge, and ability to admonish and minister the gospel of God.

Joy should be large.—With peace is associated joy—just the natural consequence of the state which I have endeavoured to describe. Peace passes into
joy by an almost imperceptible and easy transition. Joy, indeed, may without
impropriety be regarded as peace in a higher degree. Peace is not a state of
cold and insensible tranquillity ; it is rich enjoyment. We are creatures of
sensibility and emotion, and whatever sets us right only gives to those sensibilities
a richer experience. The very same things which impart peace excite joy. To
be assured that all we had at one time reason to fear has been for ever removed,
to have the inward testimony of our consciences to our godly sincerity in the
divine service, to be conscious of a freedom from the reigning power of sin, to
know that the blessed God looks upon us with approval, and that we are so under
His guidance and care that nothing can happen to us but for our good, and to
have the hope of heaven as our final rest, is fitted in its very nature when realised
to fill us with joy unspeakable and full of glory. To have any adequate apprehension of these things, and to be assured on good grounds that they are true of
us without gladness and elation of heart, is impossible. It would argue a desti-
tution of the most ordinary sensibilities of human nature. It is possible, indeed,
and sometimes happens, that, through the pressure of unusual trials, our attention may be diverted from the consideration of what we really are as partakers
of the blessings of redemption—we may be in temporary "heaviness through
manifold temptations"; but we have only to recall and realise what by grace is
true of us to rise superior to our sorrow, and to feel the exhilarating influence of
that hidden joy which a sense of our condition as the objects of God's love is fitted
to awaken. Present distress may be more pressing, but while it may suspend,
it never can destroy the joy which naturally flows from an assurance of our
interest in these blessings. You will notice further that the object of the prayer
is that they "may be filled with all joy and peace,"—not merely that they may
have this happy state of mind in some degree, but in a high degree; not
simply that it should be their occasional state, that they may have special
seasons of divine enjoyment, but that it should be their habitual and permanent
condition. Nothing short of this can meet the energy of the apostle's language
To be filled with anything is to have as much of it as we have room to receive
It supposes completeness of quantity in possession as well as permanency of
supply. It may be asked, Is this possible? Has it ever been realised in any
degree commensurate to what the strength of the apostle's language would seem
to imply? We may reply by asking, Is there anything in the supposed state
which the fulness of the God of hope cannot furnish? We are not, indeed, to
imagine that the excited state of feeling which great joy supposes should be continuous. This the feebleness of our nature is incapable of sustaining. It would

produce injurious exhaustion. Still, the joy and the peace may be large and habitual, yielding a settled satisfaction and enjoyment, and ready for those exuberant expressions which special occasions may demand. When this is the case we have just the condition which the apostle's language expresses. That this is the possible state we can have no reason to question. Indeed, we can hardly doubt that it was verified in Paul's own experience. Trials he had, and they were both numerous and distressing. It is impossible to peruse his history without finding abundant evidence of the heavy afflictions which he endured. But we have proof just as unmistakable of the holy joy and abundant peace by which he was refreshed and sustained. He who, when smarting from the scourge and painfully confined in the stocks in a loathsome dungeon, could sing praises to God with a full heart must have been a happy man. He who, amidst disappointments and anxieties he experienced, could exclaim, "Thanks be unto God, who always causeth us to triumph in Christ," must have had a joy in God superior to all his afflictions. This is the attainment at which every one of us should aim. It is the exalted privilege which the gospel places within our reach, and which we should seek to realise. To be satisfied with a doubtful, low condition, and to regard it as all we are warranted to expect, is to do injustice to the gospel, and to inflict injury on ourselves.—*J. Kelly.*

SUGGESTIVE COMMENTS ON VERSES 14—16.

"*The offering up of the Gentiles.*"—First, then, what are we to understand by the "offering up of the Gentiles"? Generally it may be replied that this is a figure of the conversion of the world borrowed from the ritual of the Old Testament. The whole language of the text is sacrificial. Besides the allusion in the word translated "offering up," which is currently applied in the New Testament and in the Septuagint to sacrifice, there are two other allusions which in our version are disguised; for when Paul calls himself a "minister" of Jesus Christ, he means "a priestly minister"; and when he speaks of "ministering" the gospel of God, he uses a different word still, which denotes "a ministry of sacrifice." Thus there are no less than three distinct sacrificial expressions, which conspire to show with what vividness the apostle realised the conversion of the Gentiles under the emblem of a great oblation or hecatomb presented to God. This offering of the Gentiles may be looked at in two lights—as their own act, and as the act of the pre-existing Christian Church. They are their own sacrifice, and they are our sacrifice. What is implied in each of these aspects of the truth?

First, in regard to themselves, it is implied that they shall abandon their false ideas of sacrifice and act upon the Christian, so as truly to dedicate themselves to God. The whole Christian life, inspired by gratitude and love, is a sacrifice of praise offered continually. All gifts and labours are sacrifices; martyrdom is a sacrifice; and death itself is but the last offering up—the sacrificial flame ascending to its native heaven. Again, in regard to others, it is implied that the act of sacrifice shall be performed by the pre-existing Christian Church. There is a sense in which men may be not only priests to offer up themselves, but priests to offer up others. And this priesthood of conversion, if I may so call it, is a universal priesthood. This sacrificial ministry is a part of Christianity; and each of us, missionaries, ministers, and private Christians, is invested with it, and bears his share in its labours and dignities. What a majestic continuation is this of the Levitical priesthood, in the only sense in which it can be continued! We hear much in our times of the priesthood of literature; but how poor is it to the priesthood of conversion, more especially when, as in too many cases, it is a priesthood of atheism, or at best erects its altar to an unknown God! The direct causes or prerequisites of the offering up of Gentiles: The first *is the ministry of the gospel.* This Paul puts into the foreground. The Christian sacrifice depends upon the propagation of the truth. All who take the Christian name are agreed as to this final triumph of Christianity through the simple display and publication of its truth to the ends of the earth. The other direct cause of the offering of the Gentiles *is the sanctifying work of the Holy Ghost.* A Christian advocate may seem to unsay all he has said in celebration of the ministry of truth when he passes on to exalt the ministration of the Spirit. This, however, can only be the effect of mistake on his part, or of misapprehension on the part of the hearer. The Bible does not encourage speculation as to the solitary efficiency of the word or of the Spirit, but teaches us to regard their natural and normal action as made up of the union of both. If the Spirit added to the power of the word, it would be possible to analyse the two forces; but the Spirit only develops it, and does not go beyond it, so that all is one mysterious, indivisible energy. The nations yield to truth, and not to more than truth; but the truth only comes out, and has real existence to the soul as truth, when the Spirit of God applies it. This supernatural force every Christian believes to be supplied by the agency of the Holy Ghost, so that the impossible becomes possible and the action of Christian truth is exalted to a kind of omnipotence. To all misgivings within the Church, to all scepticism without, as to the final conversion of the whole world to Christ, the Christian has one reply: " I believe in the Holy Ghost." The missionary activity of the Church *must repose upon true Christian doctrine.* The Christian work, like every other, must spring from faith; and faith again is but another name for the intelligent and cordial apprehension of the truths of apostolic Christianity. The missionary

activity of the Church must be *supported by Christian example.* We may easily deduce this principle from the second great text of the Epistle to the Romans —viz., the necessity and vital importance of a Christian morality. This is the substance of the apostolic exhortations, which begin with an appeal to those who acknowledge the mercies of God to present themselves to Him as a living sacrifice. The missionary activity of the Church *must be promoted by Christian union.* The Epistle to the Romans is the text-book of Christian union not less than of Christian doctrine and morality. The subject is actually expounded by the apostle in relation to missions. How prone are we all to forget the majestic amplitude of Christianity as the religion of the human race, which is only deformed by the attempt to confine and bandage it by the particular forms and institutions which have been generated in the history of sects, and even of nations! Yet is it a fact that there is a principle in the divine breast to which mortals may minister purest satisfaction, a satisfaction of which the " sweet-smelling savour " of all ancient offering and sacrifice was but the faintest emblem! " The sacrifices of God are a broken spirit; a broken and a contrite heart, O God, Thou wilt not despise." The return of moral beings to their great Original, with the light of reviving hope and loyalty breaking through the cloud of remorse and the tears of penitence, and the gleam of a new creation of the Spirit of God emerging from the dark and stormy chaos of sin—this is the joy of the Eternal, to which that of the first creation gives place, and which may be estimated by the infinite sacrifices which He has made to purchase such an offering from His fallen creatures. Infinite blessedness must be the result of infinite bounty; and the delight of God in the saving of each sinner, when each is saved by an unspeakable gift, must be itself unspeakable.—*Dr. Cairns.*

Men need reminding of duty.—Paul, in drawing towards the close of his epistle, seems, with the characteristic delicacy which breaks forth in many other passages, to feel that he must apologise for the freedom of his exhortations. The likest thing to it in any of the other apostles is when Peter tells the disciples to whom he writes that he addresses them, not to inform, as if they were ignorant persons, but to stir up their pure minds in the way of remembrance—and this though they already knew the things of which he was reminding them, and though they were established in the present truth. And so Paul, as if to soften the effect of his dictations—and this though his manner was the furthest possible from that of a dictator—tells his converts of his persuasion that they were filled with knowledge and goodness; and that, though he took it upon him to admonish them, he was sure, nevertheless, that they were able to admonish one another. The truth is, that neither the greatest knowledge nor the greatest goodness supersedes the necessity of our being often told the same things over again. Men might thoroughly know their duty, and yet stand constantly in need to be reminded of their duty. The great use

of moral suasion is not that thereby people should be made to know, but should be led to consider. And thus our Sabbaths and other seasons of periodical instruction are of the greatest possible service, although there should be no dealing in novelties at all—though but to recall the sacred truths which are apt to be forgotten, and renew the good impressions which might else be dissipated among the urgencies of the world. Whether then an apostle should write, or a minister should substantially present the same things, it ought not to be grievous, because it is safe. He speaks but as the helper of his congregation, and not as having dominion over them. He is but an instrument in the hands of the Holy Spirit, whose office it is, not merely to teach what is new, but to recall what is old—to bring all things to remembrance. It is true that they might already have received the gospel, and that in the gospel they stand; yet they shall have believed in vain, unless they keep in memory that which has been preached unto them. In keeping with this, Paul says in the fourteenth verse that he writes not to inform but to put in mind.—*Dr. Chalmers.*

MAIN HOMILETICS OF THE PARAGRAPH.—*Verses* 17—21.

St. Paul as a missionary.—History is precept teaching by example; history is recorded experience; and this is especially so when the history is the biography of one individual. We should read the noble actions of others, so as to be stimulated to heroic deeds. Here is a piece of autobiography which has in it much instruction. Let us seek to be inspired with love to Christ and to humanity, and we shall find our missionary sphere. It lies round about us. Some people pine because they cannot reach the distant Illyricum, while they neglect the Jerusalem of home and of country.

I. **The missionary's travels.**—In St. Paul's days travelling was very difficult when it was not done by sea, for carriage roads and vehicles hardly existed. There were no luxurious first-class carriages by which to be carried from one scene of labour to another. When it is calm, the seas over which Paul sailed are delightful; but they have also suddenly their caprices—the ship may run aground in the sand, and all that one can do is to seize on a plank. There were perils everywhere. Paul, it seems, journeyed almost always on foot, existing doubtless on bread, vegetables, and fruit. What a life of privations and trials is that of the wandering devotee! The police were negligent and brutal. St. Paul was not backed up by any great scientific or missionary societies. He was not attended

517

by a number of followers armed with breech-loaders, prepared to shoot down barbarians as if they were so many rabbits. Almost alone the great traveller went from Jerusalem and round about unto Illyricum. It lay beyond Macedonia, on the north-east coast of the Adriatic Gulf. The journey was somewhere about one thousand three hundred miles in a straight line ; and when taken in all its windings, with its towns, populous districts, pleasant valleys, stern mountain ranges, and barren climes, shows his indefatigable zeal. St. Paul did not go in search of lovely scenery. Had he done so, he might have pleased his fancy as he journeyed, say, from Antioch to Seleucia, where on all sides are copses of myrtles, arbutus, laurels, green oaks, while prosperous villages are perched upon the sharply cut ridges of the mountains. To the left the plain of Orontes unfolds to view its splendid cultivation. On the south the wooded summits of the mountains of Daphne bound the horizon. Often the route is hard ; certain cantons are peculiarly rugged, barren ; still Paul in his journeys would touch certain points which were veritable paradises. St. Paul did not go to admire works of art : had he done so, he might have gratified his taste and stayed at Athens on the way to Corinth ; for Athens had then even the appearance of being ornamented with almost all her masterpieces of art. The monuments of the Acropolis were intact ; the sanctity of that immaculate temple of the beautiful was not changed. Pœcile, with its brilliant decoration, was as fresh as it was on the first day. There were the Propylæum, that *chef-d'œuvre* of grandeur ; the Parthenon, which absorbed every other grandeur save its own ; the Temple of Victory, worthy of the battles which it consecrated ; and the Erechthæum, a prodigy of elegance and finish. Needless, however, to follow St. Paul in this discussion of the negative. He went from Jerusalem round about unto the borders of Illyricum to win hearts unto Jesus Christ, the true King, the Sovereign of the universe.

II. **The missionary's work.**—His work is to preach the gospel of Christ. The missionary is to preach whether men will hear or will forbear. He is to preach the old message instinct with fresh life and feeling. The old message adapts itself to all states of society and to all conditions of men. Thank God, our missionaries are preaching still, and among great varieties of places and people, amid many forms of outer life, amid many gradations of human comforts and human resources. Some labour among the most glorious manifestations of creative might, others upon scorched and arid plains—some in the busy life of cities, others in lonely isles. In labours abundant, in perils oft, by example, by preaching, by prayers, everywhere they seek to approve themselves unto God, and serve their generation according to His will. Politicians may lecture them ; men of science may undervalue them ; time-serving editors may pour on them their scorn ; they may be called enthusiasts, or be socially despised ; but steadfast in faith, unmoved by reproach or praise, they will reply, Whether we be beside ourselves, it is to God ; or whether we be sober, it is for your cause. Our meat is to do the will of Him that sent us, and to finish His work.

III. **The missionary's originality.**—We do not mean his originality as a genius, though St. Paul was that in spite of his detractors. We do not refer to his originality as the founder of a new ethical system, though St. Paul's system was different from and superior to any system previously propagated. We allude to St. Paul's desire to be the first in order. He would not build upon another man's foundation. That is how second-rate builders work. What are we modern builders doing but placing our petty pretentious cornices on the glorious temples raised by the giants of former times ? Well, let us do our best. A cornice is not to be despised. If we can only take out a few decaying stones and put fresh material in the place, let us be thankful that we have done something for God's great cathedral.

IV. **The missionary's beneficent design.**—To make the Gentiles obedient by

word and deed. Conversion here set forth : 1. In its nature—obedience to Christ;
2. In its Author—Christ Himself working by His Spirit ; 3. In the means employed—the gospel preached and lived by men. The Church of the future in foreign
lands, properly formed, will be inspired with a lofty humanity. It shall sweep
away all the forms of cruelty and of wrong which have lowered tribes and
nations in the estimation of their fellows. Its earnest life shall be fed with
large-hearted love, which yearns to draw all men back to the Father and to bring
about perfect union between man and man. Possessing a martyr's faith, it shall
hold to purest principles with a martyr's constancy. Honest missionary agencies
have determined the broad gauge on which the great highway of the nations
shall be constructed, and have laid down in many great centres of movement
the first lines of the permanent way. Earnest workers have heard and obeyed
the divine call : Go through the gates ; cast up the highway ; lift up a standard
for the people. By their labours every valley shall be exalted, and every
mountain and hill shall be made low, the crooked shall be made straight, and
the rough places plain. All difficulties shall be overcome; all divisions and
separations between men closed for ever. Man shall be linked with man,
and there shall be no more sea. With one heart, though of many names, the
tribes of earth shall journey together to the city of God. The redeemed of the
Lord shall return, and come to Zion with songs, with everlasting joy upon
their heads ; they shall obtain joy and gladness, and sorrow and sighing shall
flee away.

SUGGESTIVE COMMENTS ON VERSES 17—21.

Gospel miracles authentic.—"Through
mighty signs and wonders, by the
power of the Spirit of God." It is not
likely that Paul would have made
mention at all of these miracles had
they not been wrought at Rome as
well as in other places along his apostolical tour where Churches had been
planted by him. At all events he, in
epistles to other Churches, does appeal
to the miracles which had been wrought
in the midst of them. For example,
in the free and fearless remonstrance
which he held with the Galatians, he
puts the question with all boldness :
"O foolish Galatians, . . . he that min-
istereth to you the Spirit, and worketh
miracles among you, doeth he it by the
works of the law, or by the hearing of
faith ? " (Gal. iii. 1, 5.) And in the
enumeration which he makes of the
powers conferred on various of the
Church office-bearers, he tells the Corinthians that to one is given by the
Spirit of God the working of miracles;
and, more specifically still, to another
the gifts of healing, and to another
divers kinds of tongues, and to another
the interpretation of tongues (1 Cor.

xii. 9, 10). And again, in another
epistle to the same people, he says,
"Truly the signs of an apostle were
wrought among you in all patience, in
signs, and wonders, and mighty deeds "
(2 Cor. xii. 12). In this respect he tells
them that they were not inferior to
other Churches ; nor is it probable that
he would have written of these miracles
to his converts at Rome had they been
in this state of inferiority to others.
There cannot then be imagined a
more satisfactory historical evidence
for these high and undoubted credentials of a divine mission, than we are
able to adduce for the miracles which
abounded in the primitive Churches,
and for those in particular which
were worked by Paul's own hands.
He indeed, in common with the other
apostles, possessed the endowment in a
degree that might be called transcendental—insomuch as, besides having
the gift of miracles, they had the power,
by the laying on of their hands, of con-
ferring this gift upon others (Acts
viii. 18, etc.). Now whatever exhibition might have been made of such
things at Rome, certain it is that for

miracles both at Corinth and in Galatia we have testimony in such a form as makes it quite irresistible. Here we have, in the custody of these two Churches from the earliest times, the epistles which they had received from Paul; the original documents have been long in their own possession, while copies of them were speedily multiplied and diffused over the whole Christian world. In these records do we find Paul, in vindication of his own apostleship, and in the course of a severe reckoning with the people whom he addresses, make a confident appeal to the miracles which had been wrought before their eyes. Had there been imposture here the members of these two Churches would not have lent their aid to uphold it. They would not have professed the faith which they did in pretensions which they knew to be false, and that for the support of a claim to divine authority now brought to bear in remonstrance and rebuke against themselves. We might multiply at pleasure our suspicions of Paul, and conjure up all sorts of imaginations against him, but no possible explanation can be found for the acquiescence of his converts in the treachery of the apostle, or rather of their becoming parties to his fabrication, if fabrication indeed it was. One can fancy an interest which he might have in a scheme of deception; but what earthly interest can we assign for the part which they took in the deception, knowing it to be so? Or on what other hypothesis than the irresistible truth of these miracles can we explain their adherence to the gospel, and that in the face of losses and persecutions, nay, even of cruel martyrdoms, but over and above all this the taunts and cutting reproaches to the bargain of the very man who could tell them of the miracles which themselves had seen as the vouchers of his embassy from God, and threatened, if necessary, to come amongst them with a rod and make demonstration in the midst of them of his authority and power? Had there been

520

deceit and jugglery in the matter, why did they not let out the secret, and rid themselves at once and for ever of this burdensome visitation? The truth is, that the overpowering evidence from without, and their own consciences within, would not let them. There is no other historical evidence which in clearness and certainty comes near to this; and whether we look to the integrity of these original witnesses, men faithful and tried, or to the abundant and continuous and closely sustained testimony which flowed downward in well-filled vehicles from the first age of the apostles, we are compelled to acknowledge a sureness and a stamp of authenticity in the miracles of the gospel, not only unsurpassed, but unequalled by any other events, the knowledge of which has been transmitted from ancient to modern times.—*Dr. Chalmers.*

Gospel to be preached as a witness.—Even where St. Paul preached with little or no success, he might be said to have no more place in that part—no more, for example, at Athens, although he left it a mass of nearly unalleviated darkness—just as our Lord's immediate apostles might well be said to have no more place in those towns that rejected their testimony, and against which they were called to shake off the dust of their feet, and then to take their departure — fleeing from the cities which either refused or persecuted them, and turning to others.. The way in fact of apostles or ministers, the outward instruments in the teaching of Christianity, is the same with the way of the Spirit, who is the real agent in this teaching, by giving to their word all its efficacy. He may visit every man, but withdraws Himself from those who resist Him—just as the missionaries of the gospel might visit every place, and have fulfilled their work even in those places where the gospel has been put to scorn, and so become the savour of death unto death to the people who live in them. Yet we must not slacken in our endeavours for the evangelisation of the whole earth, although the only effect should be that the gospel will be preached unto all nations for a witness, and the success of the enterprise will be limited by the gathering in of the elect from the four corners of heaven. It is a matter of unsettled controversy whether Paul ever was in Spain, or was able to fulfil his purpose of a free and voluntary journey to Rome, his only recorded journey there being when taken up as a prisoner in chains. At the beginning of the epistle he tells them of his prayer, and here expresses his hope of again seeing them in circumstances of prosperity, when, after a full and satisfactory enjoyment of their society, he might be helped forward by them on his way to the country beyond. Let me here notice, in passing, how accordant the movements both of Paul beyond Judæa and of our Saviour and the apostles within its limits, as described in the gospels and Acts, are with the abiding geography of towns and countries still before our eyes. It is in itself a pleasing exercise to trace this harmony of Scripture with the known bearings and distances of places still; and even serves the purpose of confirmation as a monumental evidence to the truth of Christianity.—*Dr. Chalmers.*

MAIN HOMILETICS OF THE PARAGRAPH.—*Verses* 22—24.

Thwarted purpose.—Purposes are often thwarted in this world, and the mystery is that the purposes of good men are crossed while those of bad men too frequently prosper. The complaint of the psalmist is still ours: "I have seen the wicked in great prosperity," etc. St. Paul's desires were not realised. If St. Paul failed at times, and not infrequently, why should we look for a pathway always according to our plans? Even a Paul may preach in vain in a city given over to the worship of Astarte; even a Luther cannot convert the pope; even a Gordon must perish at Khartoum. We must expect failures, but we must not by them be daunted. Failures in our social plans may prepare us to expect failures even in God's work. Failure to us, perhaps not failure to God.

I. **A purpose is thwarted.**—St. Paul is said not to have been a social man, and yet here we find him having formed the purpose of seeking Christian fellowship with the saints at Rome. He appears to mourn that he had been much hindered from going to them. The social desire of St. Paul was crossed; he could not then visit Rome. Our visits are hindered; let us learn our limitations. Human movements, even in what we call trivial affairs, are under high control.

II. **A purpose is pursued.**—If a purpose be desirable and praiseworthy, then there is no need to abandon it because we have been checked. The great man can wait. I am hindered now, but I may come at some future time. I cannot now realise my ideal, but I press onward in patient hope. A man's conduct in littles is prophetic of what he will do in greats.

III. **The purpose is subordinated.**—St. Paul had a great desire to see the Roman Christians; but he must preach the gospel until he found no more place. So long as there is occasion and opportunity for Christ's work, so long the worker must overlook personal desires. What a large lesson? Too oft we visit our friends, and let Christ's work stand on one side. The claims of religion are subordinated to our personal desires. St. Paul's personal desires were subordinated to the claims of religion.

IV. **The purpose is desirable.**—The visit here proposed is not one at the bidding of social etiquette; it is a visit for mutual spiritual enrichment. The desire is to be refreshed with the company of God's people. The communion of saints is an article of our creed; but how little practised! Communion of saints is a desirable object, a delightful contemplation; but it must not interfere with higher work. The active and passive sides of the Christian character must be developed. If these verses are not Pauline, they contain much divine instruction, and testify to the inspired wisdom of the compilers. It is justly remarked : " It may here be observed that such signs, evidently unintentional, of conflicting feelings in the letter, and such consistency between the letter and the narrative, are strong confirmation of the authenticity of both." Let us seek, then, to gather lessons of moral wisdom, and leave the critics to pursue their unsatisfactory way. Why destroy the old paths when no better new ones have been discovered ?

Ver. 23. *The observant man.*—Meyer, following Luther, makes the word τόπον mean space, scope. But the apostle's scope was conditioned by a standing place, a central point ; and here it is most natural to think of such a place. Tholuck says : "The apostles were accustomed to carry on missionary labour in the metropolitan cities, leaving the further extension of the gospel to the Churches established there, and therefore, after all, to let the pagani remain heathen." The thoroughly dynamical view which the apostles had of the world is reflected even in their thoroughly dynamical missionary method, according to which they conquered the capital and central points of the ancient world (Lange). *Having no more place in these parts,* namely, in Greece, where he then was. The whole of that country being more or less leavened with the savour of the gospel, Churches being planted in the most considerable towns, and pastors settled to carry on the work which Paul had begun, he had little more to do there. He had driven the chariot of the gospel to the sea-coast, and having thus conquered Greece, he is ready to wish there were another Greece to conquer. Paul was one that went through with his work, and yet did not think of taking his ease, but set himself to contrive more work, to devise liberal things (Matthew Henry).

I. **The observant man finds his place.**—It is sometimes said that there is a place for every man. Perhaps there may be. One thing is certain, that we cannot understand the *whole* of the divine plans and purposes with reference to our *seemingly* disordered and wrongly governed world. The men without a place to human appearance may have a place in the divine mind and purpose. So let us not too soon despair, too readily abandon hope. However, it is sad to think of the many hundreds of our fellow-countrymen at this late period of the Christian era who must feel that there is no place for them in this large-roomed planet. "A place for every man!" cries out the man with a sneer who huddles in the casual ward, or tries to catch a little sleep in the penny doss. "A place for every man!" wails out the poor hungry clerk, or starving dock labourer, or the victim of the strike, who walks day after day through the dry places of our towns and cities seeking work and finding none. But perhaps they are not without fault, and we mean by that expression a special fault which has placed them at a disadvantage in the keenly contested race of modern society. Perhaps they have not been observant men. Their intelligence has not been wide awake. They have moved through the world in a kind of mental stupor ; of course in too many cases there may have been vice—the vice of idleness, the vice of drunkenness, the vice of incapacity, brought on by their want of well-directed effort. A man who is wide awake, who is willing and obedient, must find some sort of place, even though there are always crowds of applicants for every vacant place in our thickly populated country of Great Britain—some sort of place, and in many cases and in the long run he will eat of the fat of the land. St. Paul had his difficulties. He was hunted and harried as much as the poor criminal who desires to reform is hunted by the hard-hearted policeman ; and yet St. Paul found his place—a place of work, a place as the central point of Christian influence, a place where he could fix a divine force which would produce spiritual motion in the surrounding sphere and bring forth beneficial results.

II. **The observant man sees where there is no place.**—Easy enough for us to see that there is no place when the larder is empty, when the pocket is lean, when the hungry stomach craves for food—easy enough for the political candidate to see that there is no place when the votes are given to the opponent—easy enough for the preacher to see that there is no place when the pews are empty, for to the preacher a place, however large and well-arranged, without people is no place;—not so easy to see that there is no place when things are outwardly smooth and pleasant. St. Paul had a fairly prosperous course in this Grecian missionary tour, and yet he finds out that there was for him no more place in those parts. We must observe both to find out the place and see when there is no place.

III. **The Christianly observant man is willing to remove where there is no place.**—We are told not to meddle with those who are given to change. "A double-minded man is unstable in all his ways." When a candidate presents himself for a position, the question is put, How long has he been in his last place? A frequent change of places is a blot on a man's career, and not likely to minister to success. But a man is not always to blame because he has had many changes and removals. A man is not to blame because he has not been endowed with broad acres surrounding a mansion, where he succeeds to a race thus amply provided for, so as to be under no necessity of removing; a man is not to blame because he has not been made a bishop, who can adhere to the diocese until decrepitude succumbs to death; a man is not to blame because he has not been gifted with the artifices of the popular preacher, who can keep his chapel filled, and when his power of oratory fails can live on his former reputation and the curious pertinacity of the faithful, who cleave to their beloved pastor and their favourite chapel. Changes are at times needful and very beneficial. Nature has her many changes, and by these changes the earth is ever fresh, young, and beautiful. St. Paul had his many changes, and yet he was a trustworthy man. If he had been asked, How long have you been in your last place? he might not have been able to have given an answer that would have been considered satisfactory to the modern inquirer. He moved from place to place, but every place he filled right nobly. Of his own accord he left no place until he made it the centre and source of a widespreading Christian beneficence. Christ was the centre of his soul motives. The extension of the Christian kingdom was the sublime purpose of his life. The spiritual well-being of humanity was the large place which he had to fill during his earthly career.

IV. **The Christianly observant man recognises his limitations.**—This is a hard thing to do. Repellent to flesh and blood, repellent even to the so-called Christianised nature, is it to recognise that the place which we have long held can be no longer ours. We cannot bring ourselves complacently to feel that we have had our turn, that our time is over, and others must take our place. There are limitations of time and of place. There is limitation also in the direction of desire. A great desire dwelt in the apostle's mind for many years, and yet the desire did not attain completion. A great desire, and yet not granted; a great desire for a small favour, and yet refused. An apostle may desire, an apostle may long for some good thing; but an apostle even cannot accomplish his heart's desire, cannot put himself into possession of the good thing. For he can hardly have been said to have paid the Romans an episcopal visit when he was taken to Rome as a prisoner. His desire was scarcely granted in the sense intended. When our seven bishops—noble men—were taken to the London Tower, it could not have been said that their desire to go to London to be present at some clerical convention had been granted. They went to London; but there all the analogy ceases. Our desires are not always productive of the intended results. We must recognise our limitations of time, place, and purposes.

523

Notice : 1. *An indication of man's greatness.* He is a creature capable of great desire. The affections of the mind stretch out towards the attainment of some good and grand ideal. A great desire to come to a small company of proscribed Christians is no grand thing in the world's esteem. But there are grand ideals not understood by the world's shallow philosophy. It is a great desire when a man longs to put himself in connection with the nobly faithful, and wishes to develop the goodness of the race. 2. *An indication of man's littleness.* He cannot turn "no place" into the "some place"; the "no" remains "no," if such be the divine purpose. The earth philosopher cannot turn the negative into the positive, or the positive into the negative, when the divine Logician has so arranged the premisses of His syllogism for our lives. 3. *An indication of man's wisdom.* When he confesses his littleness, when he seeks to fill nobly his little sphere, when he acknowledges the current of divine events, and moves from the part where there is no place to another where there may be gracious opportunity.

MAIN HOMILETICS OF THE PARAGRAPH.—Verses 25—29.

St. Paul as a dispenser of alms.—Renan asks, " Does not the English race in Europe and in America present to us the same contrast, so full of good sense as regards things of this world, so absurd as regards things pertaining to heaven? " What he designates the absurdity as regards heavenly things has tended to make the English race good for the things of this world. Godliness has the promise of the life that now is, other things being equal. St. Paul's good sense as regards things of this world comes out in this passage. The spiritual is with him supreme, but he is far from ignoring the material.

I. **St. Paul does not believe in doing charitable work by proxy.**—He went himself to Jerusalem, and did not waste the contributions of the Macedonian saints by needless extravagance. He was careful not to touch one particle of the sacred treasure; he bore his own expenses. If St. Paul had lived in these days, we cannot suppose him travelling third class on his own account and first class as the organiser of a public charity. He was not the man to spend ninepence out of every shilling in salaries, etc., while only threepence is dispensed in charity. The work was a ministry, a sympathetic mission. The poor saints at Jerusalem were not made to feel any degradation.

II. **St. Paul registers the kindness and indebtedness of the givers.**—" It hath pleased them of Macedonia and Achaia to make a certain contribution." Here is the true spirit of Christian philanthropy—to find pleasure in giving. The luxury of doing good is the theme of the poet, but it should be the realisation of every true man. Charitable work should be a pleasure, while it is a debt. A pleasant thing to discharge debts of this kind. A general principle is here laid down. Partakers of spiritual things should minister unto their benefactors in carnal things. Here is a kind of commodity not contemplated by the political economist. Spiritual things are never quoted on 'Change. We grudge an archbishop his £10,000 or £15,000 a year, while we make no complaint if a great singer gets her £40,000 for a short tour, or a novelist receives £4,000 or £6,000 for the novel, and so on. Spiritual things are with the apostle realities, and rise above carnal things in importance. We require more reality and less make-believe in our religion. Our estimates stand in need of alteration.

III. **St. Paul is careful faithfully to discharge his trust.**—Whatever may be the meaning of the sealing, it is certain that the whole passage indicates St. Paul's carefulness and faithfulness. He would not lay himself open to suspicion by tampering with public moneys; all must be straight. Ministers cannot be too careful about pecuniary affairs; scandals soon arise, and are very difficult to silence. The public are too ready in representing ministers as being fond of money.

IV. **St. Paul believes in material blessing, but he believes much more in spiritual blessing.**—I go to Jerusalem to minister alms, and thus confer a blessing; but I shall come to you in a fulness of blessing which does not belong to material things. This confidence he derives from his own experience as a preacher of the gospel, and from the character of those to whom he proposes a visit. If the gospel is to benefit, it must be both faithfully preached and earnestly received. St. Paul may not go to Rome as he intended, but the fulness of blessing is not thereby curtailed. God's methods are not limited by human workers; there is a fulness of blessing for every earnest seeker. Let us not depend upon human instruments, however gifted. While we wisely and thankfully use all the means placed at our disposal, let us not place upon them undue dependence.

Ver. 27. *A poor political economist.*—The cold-blooded science of political economy is the natural product of a materialistic age. No doubt there is much truth in the science and benefit to be derived from its study, but sometimes it seems as if it were truth pushed to the extreme. It does not take into account higher laws and sanctions; it reckons little or nothing of moral force, of spiritual wealth. Thus St. Paul would not take high rank in the school of modern political economy. Though we call him a poor political economist, we feel that he has done more for the wealth (weal) of mankind than those who would set him scientifically right according to their view of science. Let us consider the so-called failings of this poor political economist.

I. **He esteems the unproductive spiritual more highly than the productive material.**—The words "productive" and "unproductive" loom largely above the horizon of the political economist. He only sees wealth in the material. But we shall see his mistake and get nearer to the Pauline view, if we bear in mind that the moral element is duly considered in every well-ordered and civilised community. Our civil codes, our costly array of judicial executors, affirm that the moral is highly important. Man stripped of the moral would degenerate into the savage, and even political economists allow that the savage condition of the race is not one that is conducive to the production of material wealth. Thus the moral rises above the material, and again the spiritual above the moral; and the latter cannot attain its full growth without the fostering influences of the former. So far we have proceeded on the erroneous principle that man is a mere time creature, as if he were destitute of an immortal nature. If man possess a soul, if he be a being capable of loving and serving God, if he have vast aspirations that tell of a divine original and an eternal destiny, then material riches will not satisfy—there must be the possession of spiritual wealth. A just view of human nature must lead to the conclusion that spiritual blessings are most valuable.

II. **He makes the unproductive labourer the productive consumer.**—According to the political economist the productive labourer—that is, the producer of mere material wealth—has alone the right to be a consumer. All so-called unproductive labourers should be allowed to die of starvation. What, then, becomes of the political economist himself? He replies that he is producing by teaching how to lessen the cost of production. We may then declare that every spiritual worker is indirectly helping to the production of material wealth. No spiritual work is without its good results to the community. The governors that have not themselves been particularly religious have felt the necessity of establishing and supporting religious institutions, as being necessary to the safety and welfare of the community. The spiritual workman is worthy of material hire. Spiritual blessings went forth from Jerusalem; the Gentiles received those blessings, and thus became debtors.

III. **He acknowledges the law of supply and demand.**—The supply in this case is spiritual things, and the urgent demand on the part of the suppliers is for carnal things. Supply meets and creates a demand. The supply of spiritual things meets the indefinable but certain wants of humanity. The supply meets the need and creates a large desire for further supplies. He that asks for material wealth and gets it, obtains an inordinate craving for more and soul dissatisfaction; he who asks for spiritual wealth obtains such infinite satisfaction and repose that he prays for more. The material riches of this world are too often soul-pauperising, while spiritual gold is soul-enrichment. This supply of spiritual things on the part of the Jews does not create the demand for carnal things, but it constitutes a good argument why the rich Gentiles should be liberal. If we have it in our power, let us give largely where we have received largely.

IV. **He invests the material waster with priestly sanctions.**—The Gentiles are to minister carnal things; they are to exercise priestly functions; they offer up contributions as spiritual sacrifices. Who in these days would think of calling the man a priest simply because he gives sordid money? But it is not the mere giving of money or of alms that imparts priestly glory. It is the purpose for which and the spirit in which the money is given which make the difference. The man who has received spiritual things, feels his indebtedness, and gives of his carnal things as a small and grateful payment in discharge of the debt incurred, exercises a liturgical office sweeter and richer than he who in most melodious measures chants the sublimest ritual ever penned. Thus there may be priests without the laying on of episcopal hands. Loving hearts and grateful spirits may invest with a garb of glory that the most sumptuous priestly vestments cannot equal. Let us try to feel and understand that we may all engage in great services. We may do spiritual work, not only in the Church, but in the world temple of humanity. We may do carnal things after a spiritual fashion. Every day we may minister at divine altars; every day we may offer up spiritual sacrifice. Let us learn divine co-operation. The poor in carnal things may impart of their spiritual things, while the materially rich may gratefully respond by giving of their carnal things.

V. **The word " charity " in its modern sense is a misnomer as applied to Church contributions.**—If there were a right feeling abroad in the Christian community, there should be no need for bazaars, for musical services, for eloquent preachers with their stirring appeals to be charitable. What should we think of the creditor who should send an eloquent preacher to the debtor pleading with him in touching terms to be charitable and pay his debts? We are debtors for spiritual things; and yet when we give the least driblet to discharge the claim, we call it charity and pride ourselves on our benevolence. When will the Christian world get to feel that spiritual blessings lay us under a great debt? How much owest thou unto thy Lord? How much owest thou to Him whose love and self-sacrifice are beyond compare? How much owest thou to the gospel-enlightened world in which thou art privileged to live? Let us try to feel that we are debtors to infinite love and goodness.

Ver. 29. *Paul's desire to visit Rome.*—It had been a long-cherished wish of the apostle Paul to visit Rome; but something had always come in the way. And when at length his wish was granted, it looked as if his purpose were going to be defeated, for he went as a prisoner. Nevertheless he was an ambassador of the King of kings, though an ambassador in bonds.

I. **The apostle's object in visiting Rome.**—1. *Not to gratify a personal craving* *or wish*; not to view the magnificence of the metropolis, or sit at the feet of its philosophers, statesmen, or poets. 2. *What Rome needed was the knowledge of the gospel of Christ.* With all its greatness the Eternal City knew not God, and already the "dry rot" of decay was gnawing at the heart of the solid fabric. Nothing could save it from the inevitable "decline and fall" but a force that knew no decay. That force was the gospel with its proclamation of God's love to man, the forgiveness of sins, the purification of man and society, and the assurance of life everlasting. The only power that would have saved Rome was, not her armies, but the gospel of the crucified Nazarene. The acceptance of a thought from God would have done more to strengthen her than all the wealth of her dependencies and the devices of her statesmen. Moral decay can only be arrested by moral force. History tells us that the nations that forget God utterly perish. It was Paul's wish, then, to proclaim in this mighty city a message which would have saved its corrupt society—the message of God to those who forget Him, "the fulness of the blessings of Christ."

II. **The ground of the apostle's confidence.**—"I am sure," etc. He was not ignorant of the demoralised state of society as seen in the fearful picture he draws in the first chapter, yet he was confident that the gospel of Christ was the cure. 1. *He had the promise of Christ.* "Preach the gospel to every creature." "Lo, I am with you alway." These and suchlike promises would assure him that his labour would not be in vain. No stronghold could be so impregnable that it would not yield to the forces of God; no society so corrupt that it could not be purified by atoning blood; no darkness so dense that light from heaven would fail to penetrate it. How, then, could he doubt? He would be mighty through God. 2. *He would derive confidence from past experience.* His message had never failed elsewhere, and he would have fruit in Rome also. Systems of idolatry had been shaken, and the strongest would yet fall. 3. *He was encouraged to go to Rome by the state of his own feelings.* He regarded the wish to go to Rome as God-implanted. This was to him a divine call. In Rom. i. 9 he says: "God is my witness," etc. When Providence points in a certain direction, is it not a duty to follow? May God make our duty clear, and then we cannot fail.—*D. Merson.*

SUGGESTIVE COMMENTS ON VERSES 24, etc.

Did Paul visit Spain?—"Whensoever I take my journey into Spain, I will come to you: for I trust to see you in my journey, and to be brought on my way thitherward by you, if first I be somewhat filled with your company." "Whensoever," "As soon as"; "As soon as I take my journey," etc. Whether Paul ever accomplished his purpose of visiting Spain is a matter of doubt. There is no historical record of his having done so either in the New Testament or in the early ecclesiastical writers, though most of those writers seem to have taken it for granted. His whole plan was probably deranged by the occurrences at Jerusalem which led to his long imprisonment at Cæsarea and his being sent in bonds to Rome. "To be brought on my way"; the original word means, in the active voice, to attend any one on a journey for some distance as an expression of kindness and respect, and also to make provision for his journey. Vers. 26, 27. "For it hath pleased them of Macedonia and Achaia to make a contribution for the poor saints which are at Jerusalem." Having mentioned this fact, the apostle immediately seizes the opportunity of showing the reasonableness and duty of making these contributions. This he does in such a way as not to detract from the credit due to the Grecian Churches, while he shows that it was but a matter of justice to act as they had done. "It

527

hath pleased them," verily; "and their debtors they are"—that is, "It pleased them, *I say*; they did it voluntarily, yet it was but reasonable they should do it." The ground of this statement is immediately added: "For if the Gentiles have been made partakers of their spiritual things, their duty is also to minister unto them in carnal things." "If the Gentiles have received the greater good from the Jews, they may well be expected to contribute the lesser."—*Hodge.*

MAIN HOMILETICS OF THE PARAGRAPH.—*Verses* 30—33.

St. Paul was not self-assertive.—It has been affirmed that St. Paul was self-assertive (as we say). No proofs are attempted to establish the declaration. Our reading of this epistle has not tended to make us accept the accusation. These verses do not appear to make valid the affirmation,

I. **It is not the act of the self-assertive to beseech the prayers of others.**—Self-assertion, we are told, is the presumptuous assertion of one's self or claims. Presumptive assertion does not condescend to the language of humble entreaty. Imagine a Napoleon beseeching for the prayers of his officers and soldiers. Imagine a pope turned a suppliant to the worshipping faithful. Imagine the Pharisee beseeching the publican to strive together with him in his prayers. Prayer is a strife, not against God, but against ourselves and against the powers of evil. Intercessory prayer is a method of mutual helpfulness. This is generated and strengthened for the sake of Jesus Christ and by the love of the Spirit. The love of (belonging to) the Spirit, embracing perhaps the two ideas—(1) felt by, and (2) inspired by, the Holy Spirit.

II. **It is not the act of the self-assertive to contemplate dangers.**—Arrogance may frown on the unbeliever, and scouts the idea that its service will not be accepted. Paul contemplates dangers, and does not expect a career of uninterrupted triumph. Deliverance is to be expected, not from the might of his own genius, but from the help of the Omnipotent. While St. Paul does not go out of his way to borrow troubles from the future, he seeks defence against the coming danger which is probable. His fears not groundless. Fears do not prevent the performance of duty. He does not start back, saying there are lions in the way.

III. **It is not the act of the self-assertive to recognise a controlling will.**—This is not the language of modern presumption. "By the will of God." Does the expression rule in commerce, in politics, science, or even religion to the extent that it ought? Too oft we pray for God's help in our plans, but are not careful to inquire if they be in accordance with the divine will. Are our visits undertaken in submission to the divine will? Do we seek for joy and refreshment in accordance with the divine will? Do we thus seek even for spiritual joy and refreshment?

IV. **It is in accordance with the acts of "our" apostle to conclude with a suitable prayer.**—"Now the God of peace be with you all." "The God of peace," as: 1. *Dwelling in peace.* Let us try to think of the sublime calm in which the Infinite reposes. Throughout the unthinkable past of a vast eternity God dwelt in peace. All the parts of His divine nature moved in unison; there were no conflicting forces. A true conception of the law of right and a will to carry out that law were seen working together. The natural and moral attributes of God were in harmonious adjustment. God is to and for Himself all-sufficient, therefore ineffable peace. Godlikeness supposes a reaching-up to the possession of such a peace in our degree and measure. 2. *Imparting peace.* True peace comes not from the inward but the outward. Divine peace is from above. The worldling tries to work peace *from within*; the true-hearted seeks peace *from without*. As the God of peace dwells in His people, so peace is imparted. He gives it by the indwelling of Christ, who is the Prince of peace; by the operation of the Holy Spirit, who is the sweet dove of peace; by the rearrangement of the inner nature, which is the forerunner of peace if it is to be permanent. Human peace a reflection of the divine and the result of divine working in the soul. 3. *A guardian power.* The God of peace guards and protects, hence St. Paul's prayer. A better guard than armed men, than armour-plated vessels, than impregnable castles. Divine peace guards: (1) from the fevers of earthly strifes; (2) from the rough tossings of ambition; (3) from the cankering worry of over-anxiety; (4) from the intrusion of dread forebodings; (5) and from the onslaughts of scepticism. "A peace, which is not the peace of Christ, is often rudely disturbed; for it is but a dream and a slumber, in the midst of volcanic powers, which are employing the time in gathering up their energies for a more awful conflict." But the peace of God cannot be rudely disturbed; safely guarded are those amongst whom dwells the God of peace.

Vers. 4, 12. *A doctrine of hope.*—The two verses are so consecutive in thought that I may omit the intervening words, and take them together as giving us a doctrine of hope. It is hope not limited by the horizon of this life, but one that passes beyond it, "a hope full of immortality." We need such a doctrine. Which of us is satisfied with the world as it is, and with ourselves as we are? Certainly there is cause enough for those dissatisfactions, longings, and imaginings which are common to mankind, but which wait for some promise and some power to transmute them into hope. Is there such a promise and power? I allege the two verses of the text, which speak of God as the God of hope. The first points to the Scriptures as written "that we might have hope"; the second represents the actual creation of this hope as the effect of faith, in the power of the Holy Ghost. Our thoughts are thus turned to the Bible and to ourselves.

I. **The Bible is the book of hope.**—From Genesis to Revelation it is progress, preparation, expectation, a consecutive course in which things that *are* become conditions and pledges of things that *are to be.* There is a sound of events approaching. There are steps in the distance; they draw nearer. Some one is coming. The book is a continuous advent; it is the word of the God of hope. So He shows Himself even at the moment of the Fall. There is tenderness in the tones of judgment, and the sentence on the enemy is made a promise to our race. Already it is known that some time, some how, there shall be a reversal of the victory of evil. The cause of hope has begun. How is it carried on? I answer, By a threefold method, consisting of verbal promise, historic fact, and moral preparation. It is not through any one of these, but through the three taken together, that the Bible is the book of hope. I will note them first in the Old Testament, then in the New. 1. *In the Old Testament.* Firstly, there is the line of spoken prophecy from the first promise to the father of the faithful, of blessing to all nations, to the last word of the last prophet. Secondly, we see that this course of prophecy is interwoven with a course of history. The progressive words are heard amid progressive facts. Thirdly, the gradual elevation of hope is due to something more than verbal prophecy and historic fact. It is due to the moral and spiritual education which is all the time going on. "The hope of the promise made of God unto the fathers: to which the twelve tribes, instantly serving God day and night, hope to come" (Acts xxvi. 6, 7). So spake one who knew well what was the hope of Israel, and was then asserting that its fulfilment had begun. It had begun, and that was all. I pass 2. *To the New Testament* as presenting the second stage in the history of hope, that in which our own lives are cast. The Christ had come; but He was gone, and to all appearance had left the world as it was. The course of hope had therefore to begin again, conducted as before by promises, by facts, and by preparations of heart. (1) The words of promise are become more numerous, more ample, and more plain. They are ever on the lips of the Lord; angels utter them as He ascends; apostles proclaim them for doctrine, warning, exhortation, and comfort, and repeat them as personal anticipations of triumph and joy. (2) Then, as to the facts. If the gospel history be taken for true, for what did all this prepare? What shall be the end of a history which is thus begun and broken off abruptly at the moment of success? If there be any sequence in things, the first advent ensures the second. (3) Still stronger in the New Testament is the argument from moral and spiritual preparation. We know the moral effect proper to the gospel, which appears in the epistles, which has been realised in all ages, and is realised in countless instances at this day. It is a high education of conscience and of the sentiments which govern life. It is an elevation and refinement of a man's feeling for truth and righteousness, for purity and charity. It is something which includes these, and is more than these—a tone and temper which we call holy, not of this world, caught from the mind of Christ. It appears in a lively sense of immortality, a kindred with things eternal in aspiring to the likeness of God, in habitual converse with God, in fellowship with the Father and the Son. Now, apart from all the prophecy, is not this state of heart a prophecy itself? "If in this life only we have hope in Christ, we are of all men most pitiable." If you have lost confidence in the Scriptures as the word of God, you may propose to yourself what you will, but you have lost the title-deeds of hope. You have lost and cannot replace them. If you search the world, no other charter can be found.

II. The text directs us not to the frustration of hope, but to its fulfilment.— Speaks of powers which create hope, not of influences which destroy it. "The God of hope fill you," etc. That is a prayer for personal experience, and an account of how it is attained. Hope, it says, is the product of believing; abounding in hope of joy and peace in believing, and all through the power of the Holy Ghost. 1. Hope must be the effect of believing if it is to enter the region of the unseen. There we have nothing to go by but the word of One who knoweth all. Revelation discovers things future, and faith becomes hope in the act of looking towards them. Here faith is presented as a state of mind antecedent to hope, and out of which hope arises. But that depends on the things believed, and the manner of believing them. But what are the things believed in our case? They are a gospel—good tidings. They are the facts of the manifestation of the Son of God for man, and in their bearing on ourselves they are a revelation that He has loved us, and given Himself for us, and washed us from our sins in His own blood, and reconciled us to God, and redeemed us for His own possession, and given us a right in His merits, and a participation in His life, and a present union with Himself, wrought by the Spirit and sealed by the sacraments. 2. Certainly these are things to cause joy and peace in believing,—joy in the first apprehension, and fresh emotion of gladness in every fresh apprehension of them; and peace as the permanent habit of a mind at rest, independent of all movements of emotion. 3. Yet in all this process there is something more than the word of God and the thoughts of man—it is "through the power of the Holy Ghost." He it is who generates the faith which believes and raises it into the hope which expects. That is not to be forgotten by us who live in the dispensation of the Spirit. The recognition of it is not fulfilled by the recital of an article in the creed, or the confession of a mysterious doctrine, but by a conscious dependence, an habitual appeal which gives a new character to the inward life, and an experience of light, counsel, and comfort which come by the word, but by something more than the word, a "something far more deeply interfused," a Spirit mingling with our spirit, a communion of the Holy Ghost. If, then, these experiences are by this power, we must look for them in that way; and as God is true we may expect them according to our need.—*Canon Bernard.*

SUGGESTIVE COMMENTS ON VERSES 30—33.

The verses are authentic.—The authenticity of vers. 30-33 is acknowledged by Lucht. Volkmar admits only that of ver. 33, adding the first two verses of chap. xvi. We have seen how little weight belongs to the objections raised by Baur and those critics to the authenticity of chap. xv. in general; we have not therefore to return to them. As to the opinions formerly given out by Semler and Paulus, according to which this whole chapter is only a particular leaf intended by the apostle either for the persons saluted in chap. xvi. or for the most enlightened members of the Church of Rome, they are now abandoned. The apostle was no friend of religious aristocracies, as we have seen in chap. xii., and he would have done nothing to favour such a tendency. Besides, what is there in this chapter which could not be read with advantage by the whole Church? We have proved the intimate connection between the first part of the chapter and the subject treated in chap. xiv., as well as the connection between the second part and the epistle as a whole, more particularly the preface (chap. i. 1-15). The style and ideas are in all points in keeping with what one would expect from the pen of Paul. As Hilgenfeld says: "It is impossible in this offhand way to reject chaps. xv. and xvi.; the Epistle to the Romans cannot have closed with chap. xiv. 23, unless it remained without a conclusion." M. Reuss expresses himself to the same effect; and we have pleasure in quoting the following lines from him in closing this subject: "The lessons contained in the first half of the text (chap. xv.) are absolutely harmonious with those of the previous chapter and of the parallel passages of other epistles, and the statement of the apostle's plans is the most natural expression of his mind and antecedents, as well as the reflection of the situation of the moment. There is not the slightest trace of the aim of a forged composition, nor certainly of the possibility that the epistle closed with chap. xiv."—*Godet.*

ILLUSTRATIONS TO CHAPTER XV.

Ver. 3. *Indian chief.*—There was an Indian chief who lived in North-west America, amongst the cold and the ice and the snow. This chief had a visitor, a white man, who came and spent a night with him. In the morning the chief took his visitor outside the wigwam or hut in which he lived, and asked him a question. "How many people do you think," said the chief, "passed by this hut last night?" The visitor looked at the snow very carefully, and saw the foot-marks of one man distinctly imprinted upon it. There were no other foot-marks to be seen, so he said to the chief, "Only one man has passed by." The chief, however, told him that several hundred Indians, in fact a whole tribe, had passed his wigwam in the night. And then he explained to him that when the Indians did not want it to be known in which direction they had gone, the chief of the tribe walks first, and all the rest of the tribe follow in single file, each man placing his feet exactly in the foot-marks of the chief, so that no new foot-marks are made, and it looks as if only one man had gone by instead of hundreds. By this clever trick the enemies of the tribe are not able to find out in which way they have gone, nor to overtake them. Now Jesus Christ is our chief. He has gone first over the path of life, and He has left us His foot-marks—His example. We must place our feet where He placed His.

Ver. 3. *Narcissus and the fountain*—One day Narcissus, who had resisted all the charms of others, came to an open fountain of silvery clearness. He stooped down to drink, and saw his own image, but thought it some beautiful water-spirit living in the fountain. He gazed, and admired the eyes, the neck, the hair, and the lips. He fell in love with himself. In vain he sought embraces from the beautiful water-spirit. He talked to the charmer, but received no responses. He could not break the fascination, so he pined away and died. The moral is, Think not too much nor too highly of yourselves. However, it is not by the mere presentation of the fable, but by the consideration of the glorious fact, that we must endeavour to be delivered from the injurious spirit of self-pleasing. "For even Christ pleased not Himself." Look not to the fable of Narcissus, regard not mere prudential considerations, but consider Christ, your elder brother, who lived a life of self-denial, and who left us an example, that we should follow His steps. His affection for God the Father induced Him to take to Himself the reproaches that were cast upon God; His compassion for men induced Him to bear their sorrows and to suffer for their welfare. Let us seek to be ruled by affection for God and by compassion for our fellow-men.

Ver. 3. *Imitation of Christ.*—In Paris the weavers of the Gobelin Tapestries sit concealed *behind* the fabrics working the pattern designed by a great artist. Passing through the room, one is struck by their loveliness; the work grows thread by thread under the busy fingers. The pattern they copy from is placed *above* their heads, and they have to *look up* for direction and guidance. *We* must *look up* to Jesus as our perfect pattern while weaving the trials, experience, and daily mercies our heavenly Father has placed as threads in our hands. And no stitch can be wrong if worked by faith's steadfast gaze. " Looking unto Jesus," let us be content to stand behind our work, leaving the result to Him.—*J. K. Cowing.*

Ver. 3. *Chinese plaque.*—A gentleman had a Chinese plaque with curious raised figures upon it. One day it fell from the wall on which it was hung, and was cracked right across the middle. Soon after the gentleman sent to China for six more of these valuable plates, and, to ensure an exact match, sent his broken plate as a copy. To his intense astonishment, when six months later he received the six plates and his injured one, he found the Chinese had so faithfully followed his copy that each new one had a crack right across it. If we imitate even the best of men, we are apt to copy their imperfections; but if we follow Jesus and take Him as our example, we are quite sure of a perfect pattern. No fear of a flaw in His life; no fear of any mistake through following Him.—*Our Own Magazine.*

532

Ver. 3. *A Japanese girl's simile.*—At a meeting in Japan the subject was, " How to glorify Christ by our lives." One girl said, " It seems to me like this : One spring my mother got some flower seeds—little, ugly, black things—and planted them. They grew and blossomed beautifully. One day a neighbour, seeing the flowers, said, ' Oh, how beautiful ! Won't you, please, give me some seeds?' Now, if the neighbour had only just seen the flower seeds, she wouldn't have asked for them. It was only when she saw how beautiful was the blossom she wanted the seed. And so with Christianity. We speak to our friends of the truths of the Bible ; they seem to them hard and uninteresting. But when they see these same truths blossoming out in our lives into kindly words and good acts, then they say, ' How beautiful these lives ! ' Thus by our lives, more than by our tongues, we can preach Christ."—*E. J. B.*

Ver. 3. *The Vatican picture.*—Years ago, in a Roman palace, there hung a beautiful picture, upon which crowds went to gaze. Among them a young painter unknown to fame went daily to look upon it, until his soul was refreshed by its beauty, and a great longing came into his heart to copy it; but he was sternly refused permission. He returned repulsed, but not discouraged. Day and night its beauty haunted him. Copy it he *must.* Daily he came to the palace, coming early and leaving late, and, sitting before the picture, gazed upon it till it grew into him and became a part of himself; and one day he hurried home to his easel and began to paint. Each day he came and gazed at the picture, and then went home and reproduced, bit by bit, unweariedly, patiently, something of its beauty. Each fresh day's look corrected the last day's faults ; and as he toiled his power grew, and his hidden genius blazed out. Months after, in that humble studio, there stood such a wonderful copy of the Vatican picture that those who saw it could not rest until they had seen the beautiful original. We who have seen Jesus must represent Him ; but only as we look to Him daily, kneeling at His feet and gazing up into His face, do we gain power to reproduce His beauty. Daily " looking unto Jesus " we get power, skill, courage, and love, and are full of the one desire to be like Him.—*Our Own Magazine.*

Ver. 4. *President Webster on the Bible.*—On one occasion, when seated in the drawing-room with Mr. and Mrs. Ely, at Rochester, Mr. Webster laid his hand on a copy of the Scriptures, saying with great emphasis, "This is the Book!" This led to a conversation on the importance of the Scriptures and the too frequent neglect of the study of the Bible by gentlemen of the legal profession, their pursuits in life leading them to the almost exclusive use of works having reference to their profession. Mr. Webster said : " I have read through the entire Bible many times. I now make a practice to go through it once a year. It is the book of all others for lawyers, as well as for divines ; and I pity the man that cannot find in it a rich supply of thought and of rules for his conduct. It fits man for life ; it prepares him for death." The conversation then turned upon sudden deaths, and Mr. Webster adverted to the then recent death of his brother, who expired suddenly at Concord, N.H. " My brother," he continued, " knew the importance of Bible truths. The Bible led him to prayer, and prayer was his communion with God. On the day on which he died he was engaged in an important cause in the court then in session ; but this cause, important as it was, did not keep him from his duty to his God. He found time for prayer, for on the desk which he had just left was found a paper, written by him on that day, which for fervent piety, a devotedness to his heavenly Master, and for expressions of humility I think was never excelled."

Ver. 4. *Robin Hood before the word of God.*—I came once myself to a place, riding on a journey homeward from London, and I sent word overnight into the town that I would preach there in the morning, because it was holiday ; and methought it was a holiday's work. The church stood in my way, and I took my horse and my company and went thither. I thought I should have found a great company in the church, and when I came there the church door was fast locked. I tarried there half an hour and more. At last the key was found, and one of the parish comes to me and says, " Sir, this is a busy day with us. We cannot hear you ; it is Robin Hood's day. The parish are gone abroad to gather for Robin Hood : I pray you let them not." I was fain there to give place to Robin Hood. I thought my rochet should have been regarded, though I were not ; but it would not serve—it was fain to give place to Robin Hood's men. It is no laughing matter, my friends. It is a weeping matter, a heavy matter—a heavy matter, under the pretence of gathering for Robin Hood, a traitor and a thief, to put out a preacher, to have his office less esteemed ; to prefer Robin Hood before the ministration of God's word ; and all this hath come of unpreaching prelates. This realm hath been ill provided for, that it hath had such corrupt judgments in it, to prefer Robin Hood to God's word. If the bishops had been preachers, there should never have been any such thing ; but we have good hope of better. We have had a good beginning. I beseech God to continue it ! But I tell you, it is far wide that the people have such judgments ; the bishops they could laugh at it. What

was that to them ? They would have them to continue in their ignorance still, and themselves in unpreaching prelacy.—*Latimer.*

Vers. 5, 6. *Glorify God.*—I do not wonder that the men nowadays who do not believe the Bible are so very sad when they are in earnest. A writer in one of our reviews tells that he was studying the poems of Matthew Arnold, who believed, not in a living God, but in a something or other, which somehow or other, at sometime or other, makes for righteousness. The sad and hopeless spirit of the poet passed for the time into the reviewer, and he felt most miserable. He went out for a walk. It was a bleak, wintry day, and he was then at Brodrick, in Arran. The hills were in a winding-sheet of snow, above which arose a ghastly array of clouds. The sky was of a leaden hue, and the sea was making its melancholy moan amid the jagged, dripping rocks. The gloom without joined the gloom within, and made him very wretched. He came upon some boys shouting merrily at play. " Are you at the school ? " he asked. " Yes," was the reply. " And what are you learning ? " " I learn," said one, " what is the chief end of man." " And what is it ? " the reviewer asked. The boy replied, " Man's chief end is to glorify God and to enjoy Him for ever." He at once felt that the boy was taught a religion of grandeur and joy, while the poet's was a religion of darkness and despair.—*J. Wells.*

Ver. 11. *The cheer of praise.*—Much of our work for Christ is too barren of all joy and enthusiasm, and we need the cheer of praise. The English ploughboy sings as he drives his team ; the Scotch Highlander sings as he labours in glen or moor ; the fisherman of Naples sings as he rows ; and the vintager of Sicily has his evening hymn. When Napoleon came to a pass in the Alps where the rocks seemed impassable for the ammunition waggons, he bade the leader of the bands strike up an inspiring march, and over the rocks on a wave of enthusiasm went the heavy waggons. Earthly battle-fields have resounded with praises from bleeding Christian soldiers, and pain has been forgotten as the lips of the dying have sung, " When I can read my title clear," and " How sweet the name of Jesus sounds." Martin Luther has well said, " The devil cannot sing " ; and we know that David's harp drove the evil spirit out of King Saul.

Ver. 15. *God of all grace and Mohammed.*—He heads every surat or chapter (with the exception of one) of the Koran with the words Bismillahi, Arrahmani, Arruheemi, signifying, " In the name of the most merciful God." Or, as some prefer, " In the name of the God of all grace." Savary says, " This formula is expressly recommended in the Koran." The Mohammedans pronounce it whenever they slaughter an animal, at the commencement of their reading, and of all important actions. It is with them that which the sign of the cross is with Christians. Gidab, one of their celebrated authors, says that when these words were sent down from heaven the clouds fled on the side of the east, the winds were lulled, the sea was moved, the animals erected their ears to listen, the devils were precipitated from the celestial spheres.

Ver. 26. *Contribution for the poor.*—Van Lennep tells us that among the Nestorian

Christians dwelling in the fertile plain of Ooroomia charity assumes an almost apostolic form; for it is their yearly practice to lay by a certain portion of their crops in order to supply the wants of their brethren living among the rugged mountains of Koordistan, whose food often fails them altogether or is carried away by their more powerful enemies. Deeds of charity are highly extolled in the Koran, and the value of such acts is more particularly felt where the rulers take no interest in works of public utility.

CHAPTER XVI.

CRITICAL NOTES.

Ver. 1.—In the East women were not permitted to mix in the society of men as in the Western world they are at present. Women were kept in a secluded room, γυνὰ κεῖον. Thus it might be necessary to have deaconesses as well as deacons, that the former might look to the indigent or sick. After all, Phœbe may not have been a deaconess in an official sense. The word means a servant higher than δοῦλος; one who has charge of the alms of the Church, an overseer of the poor and sick. It is significant that this epistle was conveyed by the hands of a woman from Corinth, where woman was degraded, to Rome. How great the reformation wrought by the gospel!

Ver. 3.—Thirty persons saluted. Explained partly by the character of the city to which Paul wrote, and partly by the character of the apostle who had preached the gospel extensively. He begins with Jewish Christians, and puts Priscilla's name before her husband's, partly on account of her greater worth and partly to show that in Christ Jesus there is neither male nor female.

Ver. 5. **Epænetus.**—This and other names which follow down to ver. 15 designate persons otherwise unknown to us, but known to the apostle.

Ver. 7. **My kinsmen.**—Kindred. Perhaps in this passage the wider sense of fellow-countrymen. It is difficult to state what is the imprisonment here mentioned.

Vers. 8, 9.—Amplias and Urbanus, two of few Latin names. Aquila, Junia, Rufus, Julia, etc., are names of Greek origin, and probably for the most part of a lower class, such as freedmen and slaves (Wordsworth). Peter's name not mentioned. Conclusive against the pretensions of Rome.

Ver. 10.—Apelles is a name used by Horace in ridicule, but here ennobled by St. Paul. Origen says, "approved by suffering and great tribulation."

Ver. 11.—Narcissus, perhaps a freedman of Nero. Another Narcissus was put to death before the date of this epistle.

Ver. 14.—Everything to be consecrated by Christianity. Phœbe (the name of Diana) is a deaconess of the Church. Nereus and Hermes are Christianised. Striking is the contrast between Tryphena and Tryphosa, with their sensuous meaning and voluptuous sound, with the sterner words that follow, labouring in the Lord. Eusebius says that Hermes was the author of *The Shepherd*; but Lange says that the author of the book was the brother of Pius, bishop of Rome, and lived about the year 150. This book, pretending to give the revelation of an angel in a dream, once contended for authority with the Epistle to the Hebrews, and was held by some of the Alexandrian school in equal esteem with the Scriptures, and quoted as such; but it was never admitted into the canon.

Ver. 16.—A holy kiss given at the feast of love. Justin Martyr says, "We mutually salute each other by a kiss, and then we bring forward the bread and the cup." Tertullian calls it "the kiss of peace and the seal of prayer." Discontinued on account of scandalous reports. Still practised in the Greek and Oriental Churches. Rabbins attached much importance to a kiss. Every kiss causes that spirit cleaves to spirit.

Ver. 17.—No argument here for tradition or the inquisition. For even common people may discern true doctrine from false. We must seek for light on God's revealed word.

Ver. 20.—Here is St. Paul's own superscription, written with his own hand in all his epistles. The Author of peace is the Giver of victory. συντρίψει, selected with special regard to Gen. iii. 15.

Ver. 21.—Timothy and Sosipater with St. Paul at Corinth, where he wrote this epistle. Lucius perhaps St. Luke.

Ver. 22.—Tertius, a secretary with a Roman name to write to Romans.

Ver. 23.—Gaius, said to be the first bishop of Thessalonica; but it is a recurring name like Lucius. We need not attempt to attach it to any person, nor make it a cause of perplexity. Quartus a Roman name. Erastus the quæstor of the city, probably Corinth.

Vers. 25-27.—Editors are divided as to the position of the doxology, but its genuineness is substantiated by external and internal evidence. This concluding sentence contains the kernel of the doctrine of the whole epistle. The way for this evangelical revelation had been quietly prepared by the prophetical Scriptures. According to Bengel's comparison, there was in the Old Testament the silent movement of the hands of a clock, but it sounded forth the hour with an audible voice in the gospel. In vers. 25, 26 St. Paul speaks of a purpose hidden, now revealed and made known. Bishop Lightfoot says that the idea of secrecy or reserve disappears when μυστήριον is adopted into the Christian vocabulary by St. Paul; and the word signifies simply a truth which was once hidden, but now is revealed—a truth which, without special revelation, would have been unknown. Of the nature of the truth itself the word says nothing. It may be transcendental, mystical, incomprehensible, mysterious, in the modern sense of the term; but this idea is quite accidental, and must be gathered from the special circumstances of the case.

Ver. 27. **The only wise God.**—This, as the fathers' note, cannot exclude the divine nature of Jesus Christ, who is the wisdom of the Father, from this title, any more than those words "who only hath immortality" excludes Christ from being immortal.

MAIN HOMILETICS OF THE PARAGRAPH.—Verses 1, 2.

Phœbe as a champion.—Some women of the present day are champions of what they are pleased to call " women's rights." They would subvert divine arrangements. Eve and not Adam is now to be lord of the creation. It is true the party is small; it is also true that they do not bear in mind how much Christianity has done for the ennobling of women. To all classes we fancy Paul's words may be addressed : " I commend to you Phœbe our sister, . . . a champion of many, and of myself also."

I. **Phœbe the champion of a great cause.**—Phœbe was a servant of the Church which is at Cenchrea. A deaconess, according to some. This not necessary. The expression seems to denote the devotion of a Christian woman to the service of the poor and of the sick. Noble knight-errantry, to visit as an angel of goodness the abodes of poverty, to give bread to the hungry, and good cheer to the sick, to make the widow's heart sing for joy, to dispel the gloom of earth with the light of heaven, and to reap the blessing of those that were ready to perish. A noble ministry, in which angels rejoice and which the Saviour discharged. Many modern women are thus champions of the poor and of the sick. All hail to the Christian champions of all time !

II. **The champion of a great apostle.**—Picture a melancholy man walking beneath the pine trees that stretch from Corinth to Cenchrea. His mind is burdened with the care of the Churches; he is distressed for his unsaved countrymen ; the disorders of the Corinthian Church rend his sympathetic soul ; he almost wishes for death. But Phœbe, with buoyant nature, and with loving trust in the infinite possibilities of goodness, champions the strong man, and charms him out of his momentary weakness. Or again, overcome by his various labours and exposures, his strength gives way. Phœbe champions in sickness, and refits the tempest-tost vessel to encounter fresh seas where more spiritual treasure is to be gained. Earth's records do not tell half the tale of the championships of the Church's women.

III. **The champion of a great composition.**—If Phœbe went to Rome on legal business, she carried two important documents—her own legal document and St. Paul's letter to the Romans. The success of the former might tend to her own enrichment; the safe transmission of the latter may enrich the ages. Look well to the roll, Phœbe; for its preservation includes thy immortality and the salvation of millions. But thou hast faithfully discharged thy trust, and we thank thee in the name of the Lord. 1. *Champions may require championship.* Paul may require a Phœbe. Phœbe may need the assistance of Roman saints. Thus the greatest of us are taught our littleness. 2. *A great man confesses his obligation.* St. Paul seeks to pay his debt of gratitude by appealing to the Christian generosity of the Roman Church. 3. *Learn the oneness of the true Church.* The Church at Rome bound to the Church at Cenchrea by the Christian work done there by Phœbe. Spiritual work reaches through undreamt spheres. 4. *Let all our receptions be in the Lord as becometh saints.* As we receive one another in the Lord, so may we joyfully expect that the Lord will receive us in the great day of final triumph.

SUGGESTIVE COMMENTS ON VERSES 1, 2.

Difference between man and woman one of degree.—Now to put the truth in this way may seem to teach the inherent inferiority of woman; in reality it teaches nothing of the kind. The difference between man and woman is not a difference of degree, but of order. Woman does not and cannot emulate man in many departments of physical activity. It is not for her to lead armies, to guide fleets upon the ocean, or to stand in the more laborious ranks of toil upon the land. It *is* for her to share all the knowledge, all the wisdom, all the intellectual activities of the world. But essentially man is ever the worker and fighter, the bread-winner, the husband or band of the house, cementing its walls with the sweat of labour, and guarding it against the forces of dissolution which are without. The glory of a young man is his strength; and in so far the pagan ideal of manhood has a truth to express and enforce. On that ground woman cannot challenge or displace man.

" For woman is not undevelopt man,
  But diverse. Could we make her as the man,
  Sweet love were slain; his truest bond is this—
  Not like to like, but like in difference."

But difference does not imply inferiority. There are other qualities which go to the making of perfect human life besides strength, just as there are other qualities besides the untempered wealth of sunlight which make the springtide and the summer. Perfect human life needs sweetness as well as strength, the element of tenderness as well as of force. Life is not all lived in the arena and in the street, and behind the victories of the market-place lies the fact of the home. When a man steps out into the glare of public labour, he is already what the home has made him. It is the eternal and unalienable heritage of woman to mould man; to nurture his body into strength and his mind into soundness; to equip him for the warfare of life and inspire him for its victories; to breathe through him the wishes of her soul, and teach him how to gain the ideals which her purity reveals, her ambition craves, her love demands. The good woman by her intuitions reaches a realm of truth often denied to man in his most logical deductions, and then she becomes virtually the inspiration of man, and it is thus woman who makes the world. "The souls of little children," says one of the noblest women writers of our time, "are marvellously tender and delicate things, and keep for ever the shadow that first falls on them, and that is a mother's, or, at least, a woman's."

There never was a great man who had not a great mother; it is scarcely an exaggeration. The first six years of our life make us; all that is added later is veneer. The meanest girl who dances and dresses becomes something higher when her children look up into her face and ask her questions. It is the only education we have which they cannot take from us. It is a mistake to say that this is the only education; but, at least, is it not a great education? What higher dignity can we conceive than the dignity of shaping in silence and patience the forces that mould and guide the world? Can that sphere be called narrow from which such potent influences stream? That which woman confers on man is moral light and sweetness,

" Till at the last she sets herself to man
Like perfect music unto noble words."

There is no strife for pre-eminence between them, no superiority or inferiority. The difference is of order, not degree, and that is what St. Paul means when he says that " woman is the glory of the man." It is not enough to say that the glory of woman is that she is the helper of man. No great cause succeeds without woman. No nation can be great that does not reverence woman and does not offer the freest scope and sphere for her influence to be felt; and I confess that we, as Protestant Churches, have not yet recognised to the full the power of service that is in woman. We have left it to Catholics to form sisterhoods of merciful visitation. We, in our dread of mariolatry, have forgotten the women who ministered to Jesus and have ignored the presence of women in the Church. Not altogether, indeed; we, too, have had our Dinah Morrises in the early days of Methodism; we have to-day our Sisters of the People working in the slums of London; and here and there we have had our Protestant St. Theresas, our Florence Nightingales, our Elizabeth Frys, our Sister Doras. I do not say that every one of you should go and do likewise.

This is not the lesson or the message of Mary's life. You cannot all find your mission in the slums, in the prison, in the hospital; but I will tell you what you can do,—you can attain the private sainthood of self-denial and sympathy; you can find some sick sister to whom your visit would be sunlight, some little child to be made cheerful with your love, some obscure spot of earth to be brightened by your charity. You cannot row out against the darkness of the night, as Grace Darling did, to rescue the shipwrecked; but you may find next door to you some forlorn soul, tossed in the wild storms of life, to succour and to save. You cannot find cloistral seclusion, as the virgins of the early Church did, nor is it well you should; but you can make the nursery a cloister where the fruits of God ripen, and the store, the school, the home, a place where the fragrance of holiness may be felt. —*Dawson.*

Christianity exalts woman. — The Rev. S. Swanson, speaking some time ago at Manchester, showed that the religions of the East were powerless to regenerate the heart and purify the life, and that, however excellent some of them may appear in theory, they utterly failed in practice. Among other things he said, " I ask what adaptation have we found in these religions to meet the wants, to heal the wounds of woman, and to give her her proper and rightful position? What have they done to free her from the oppression that imprisons, degrades, and brutalises her? What has 'the light of Asia' done to brighten her lot? What ray of comfort have these religions shed into the shambles where she is bought and sold? What have they done to sweeten and purify life for her? Why, her place in the so-called paradises of some of them, in the way in which it is painted, only burns the brand of shame more deeply on her brow!"

The deaconess should be free. — " I commend unto you Phœbe our sister, which is a servant of the Church which is at Cenchrea" (Rom. xvi. 1). If the Greek word here translated "servant" had been rendered as in the sixth chapter of Acts, the third of the First Epistle to Timothy, and in many other passages of the apostolical writings, the verse would have run thus: "I commend unto you Phœbe our sister, which is a *deacon* of the Church which is at Cenchrea." Reserving, therefore, all questions as respects the functions of the persons whom the word designates, but adhering to the form which is nearest to the Greek, we may say that undeniably there is mention of female "deacons" in the New Testament. The deacon Phœbe must, moreover, have been a person of some consideration. St. Paul begins with her name the list of his personal recommendations or salutations to the Roman Church, and recommends her at greater length than any other person. "That ye receive her in the Lord, as becometh saints, and that ye assist her in whatsoever business she hath need of you : for she hath been a succourer of many, and of myself also." Evidently this "servant of the Church," this "succourer" of apostles, could have been no mere pew-opener, no filler of a purely menial office. Now there is one most subtile way of sterilising that eternal wedding. It is, without wholly debasing either sex in the other's eyes, to teach them to live apart, think apart, love apart, for the greater glory of God and of themselves, as if they were different species of one genus, the union of which could produce nothing but hybrids. Where thus marriage assumes in the eyes of the candidate for superhuman sanctity the shape of a fleshly pollution; where woman ceases to be man's earthly helpmeet—where it becomes good for man to live alone—the familiar mingling of the sexes in the active ministrations of religion, unfettered and untrammelled, is impossible. The deaconess should be free as the deacon himself to leave her home at any time for those ministrations ; she should be in constant communication with her brethren of the clergy. But place her under a vow of celibacy, every fellow-man becomes to her a tempter whom she must flee from. Hence the high walls of the nunnery, in which eventually we find her confined ; hence the vanishing away of her office itself into monachism. The details above given are sufficient, I think, to show that there is a wide difference between the Deaconesses Institute of our days and what is recorded of the early female diaconate. That was essentially individual ; and the only analogy to it lies in the "parish deaconess," who goes forth from Kaiserswerth or elsewhere to devote herself to a particular congregation ; although even she is far from holding that position as a member of the clergy (*cleros*) which is assigned to her by the records of Church history. —*J. M. Ludlow.*

MAIN HOMILETICS OF THE PARAGRAPH.—*Verses* 3—5.

Ver. 3. *The glory of Christian work.*—Prisca is the real name for this woman ; Priscilla is the diminutive according to the common mode of forming such appellations. She belonged, like Phœbe, to the women who were prominent because of the energy of their faith, and deserved the honourable position before her husband, Aquila. "The frequent sneers at Paul about his views respecting the female sex and their prerogatives might be spared us were this chapter carefully read. The order here is a sufficient answer ; the wife's name first, because she was foremost, no doubt. The standard is, after all, capacity, not sex. Both are called ' my helpers ' ; and it would seem that, as such, they were both engaged in spiritual labours, which term includes vastly more than public preaching."

   I. **Christian work is beneficial.**—All work is beneficial, so long as it is true and honest. The sleep earned by labour and the food bought and relished as the result of wholesome toil will be conjointly productive of strength. Consider, for instance, the compact and knotted lump of muscle on the blacksmith's forearm. The rower's chest is expanded by exertion. The practised wrestler firmly grips the limbs of his opponent. Even a Samson is stripped of his physical powers by lolling in the lap of a Delilah. Intellectual strength is increased by keeping the brain forces in action. There are undoubtedly differences of mental endowment; still the greatest men are indebted to work. If genius be the power of prolonged attention, of persevering plodding in one particular direction, then by the same road many more might travel until they come to the height where they might be called men of genius. If work be beneficial in the secular, much more is it in the moral and spiritual sphere. Priscilla and Aquila showed their wisdom by being co-workers in Christ Jesus. The spiritual nature is strengthened by exercise. Great is the power of habit; it is a kind of second nature, and is the resultant of repeated acts. Moral habit does not merely give to a man a second nature, but restores him to the blest nature enjoyed in paradise, when primeval and unfallen man was so strong that to do the good was delightful. Habit is bred by repeated acts, and spiritual strength is generated by activity. Priscilla may be only what is called a weak woman, but she becomes strong by being a co-worker in Christ Jesus. Divine work and human work co-operating result in the splendid product of the Priscillas and Aquilas of time, of the men and women who have overcome the wicked one, whose moral strength is a marvel—of those who are strong supporting pillars of God's Church on earth, and who become glorious, enduring, monumental pillars in the Church triumphant.

II. **Christian work is uniting.**—There is a brotherhood in work which is not found in either pleasure or idleness. Pleasure-seekers are not strong in fraternal affection. They may whirl in the dance, they may sport over the wine-cup, they may chaff and make merry at the gaming-table; but they know not brotherhood in the truest sense. Work is one way of creating and cementing the bond of brotherhood. Work makes co-workers, and produces a divine brotherhood. Men engaged in a great work cannot come down to intermeddle with the petty squabbles of mere idlers. Co-workers in Christ Jesus are brothers from the very fact. An invisible and indissoluble bond of brotherhood binds together all the workers in Christ Jesus throughout all the ages. A grand spiritual co-operative company stretches from Christ to the last earthly helper in Christ Jesus. Co-workers in Christ Jesus—men and women, and even children. Co-workers in Christ Jesus are Pauls, Priscillas, and Aquilas. The man of strength, the woman of gentleness, the man of no marked speciality, are all closely related by being co-workers in Christ Jesus; brothers and sisters in Christian work,—a noble band; a glorious company; a happy and united family, who move in the sphere of contentment because their minds, their heads, hearts, and hands are fully absorbed in Christian work.

III. **Christian work is immortalising.**—If we are ambitious for immortality, we must work. A ready wit, a sharp intellect, may enable a man to make a commotion in his day; but only the workers can produce that which shall possess an enduring life. After all, there is no real immortality about any earthly work. Our cathedrals will crumble; our paintings will shrivel up like the burnt parchment scroll; our books will pass into oblivion. The true immortality comes from Christian work and from the possession of the Christian spirit. The immortality of Priscilla and Aquila is typical of the immortality of all Christ's workers. Horace and Livy were great in their day. They still rule in school, college, and university. We read the *Odes*, and are amused by the satires of the one; we study the clear and pleasing narrative of the other. Horace and Livy are classics. Paul is no classic. Some say his compositions are defective; and yet, wonderful to relate, Horace and Livy give no such extended fame as Paul has done to his friends and acquaintances at Rome. It is not likely that another Paul will arise; it is not probable that another Epistle to the Romans will be written. But there is a greater book being written. Its records stretch from creation's prime to creation's doom. The pen is held by angel fingers; the characters glow with divine light; the pages are illuminated with wondrous colours. *There* are written the names of all Christian workers. This is the true immortality. Are we workers in Christ Jesus?

Learn: 1. *That we may all have a sphere for work.* We cannot all be Pauls; but we may be Priscillas, we may be the humbler Aquilas. We may not be Luthers; but we may be Melancthons. Let us not refuse our sphere because it does not look important. 2. *That the man who rightly fills his sphere will obtain divine commendation.* Paul, with the breath of inspiration going through his mighty mind, commended his fellow-workers. If Paul commended, much more will Jesus. The meanest worker may take courage as he remembers Him who commended two mites and a cup of cold water. 3. *That the man who rightly fills his sphere will obtain divine elevation.* It is said that the stone which is fit for the wall will not be left lying in the way. But we think (of course we may be wrong) that we have seen many fit stones lying neglected in the highways—stones with ample fitness, but without push and blatancy to proclaim their fitness. It is a pleasant doctrine, for men who have succeeded, that we all get what we are worth. Well, let us hope that the creed is correct. But there can be no lawful doubt about this creed, that the man who rightly fills his sphere as a worker for Christ Jesus, will obtain elevation. Priscilla and Aquila were raised by their works into the same plane with St. Paul. Divine commendation is itself divine elevation. The plaudit "Well done" lifts us at once amid the hosts of God's brilliant workers, where our spirits may find infinite satisfaction and our natures joyful repose.

Ver. 4. *The helpfulness of Christian purpose.*—Perhaps we do not sufficiently take into account the unseen forces of life. There are forces coming out of others which act upon us powerfully, though it may be unconsciously. Surely there must be a forceful influence about loving and noble purposes, even though we have no direct knowledge of the formation and existence of such purposes. We sometimes say, Give him credit for good intentions. We talk about giving credit; but where good intentions really exist, where noble purposes are truly formed, those who are concerned, those who are the objects contemplated, are debtors and not creditors. Let us try to understand more fully what we owe to others. Here we have:—

I. **A loving purpose.**—Paul had evidently an attractive power. He gained the love, affection, and esteem of others. He speaks of some who were ready to pluck out their eyes on his behalf, and give them unto him, if by that means they could help his weak vision. And in this fourth verse we read of two who for his life laid down their necks. The expression may be merely figurative and proverbial, but it tells of loving purpose. It may have been the product of personal attachment, but we may also suppose that it arose from the broader influence of Christian love. Personal attachment can do much, but personal attachment increased by Christian love can do more. How large the love in this case! "Greater love hath no man than this, that a man lay down his life for his friend." The love of woman is wonderful, and leads to acts of sublime heroism; but here is the love of a man also purposing the sacrifice of life. O wondrous love! O exalting power of divine grace! Priscilla and Aquila were ready to hazard their lives for a friend; but for His foes was the loving Saviour crucified.

II. **A noble purpose.**—The purposes of love are not always noble. Sometimes the love of a fond mother induces her to sacrifice existence to the claims of a wayward child. However, the purposes which are formed by Christian love should always be of a noble character. The cause and the person on behalf of which and whom Priscilla and Aquila hazarded the lives were worthy in the highest degree. The cause was the extension of Christ's kingdom among the Gentiles; the person was the apostle of the Gentiles. The cause and the person were noble in the highest degree, and to human seeming were indissolubly united. Of course, though the workman die, God can carry on His work; but it appeared to these two good, benevolent souls that Paul was a chosen instrument for the special work, and that therefore his life was sacred. They were undoubtedly right. Did not God say that Paul was a chosen vessel to bear Christ's name unto the Gentiles? It was a noble purpose to hazard their lives for the salvation of one who seemed so indispensable to the world's welfare. Let us see that the cause is noble to which we attach ourselves, that the person is worthy for whom we are about to make sacrifices; and then let us not be afraid to form great purposes on their behalf.

III. **An unfulfilled purpose.**—We do not know where and when Priscilla and Aquila "laid down their own necks." We do not hear that the sword or axe of the executioner severed the heads from the bodies of these devoted Christians; but they were ready. The intention was there, and was good; the purpose was sublime and self-sacrificing—just as praiseworthy in the eyes of infinite wisdom, in the estimation of Paul, as if the purpose had culminated in dire fulfilment. Unfulfilled purposes sometimes are sad because they speak painfully of moral weakness, of human impotence. This unfulfilled purpose was joyful. It reveals the greatness of the souls of those in whom and by whom it was formed. It declares that a saving arm had been interposed, and the lives of these two self-devoted heroes were spared to the Church for a space longer. Let us form great purposes; and if Providence see it needful to prevent them being carried out, we may be sure that the thing of good which was in our hearts will meet with divine approval and reward.

IV. **The apostolic acknowledgment of the unfulfilled purpose.**—We are all human, and God does not wish us to get away from the feelings proper to humanity. Paul likewise pays attention to the proper feelings of men and women, and gratefully records the design. He gives public thanks to Priscilla and Aquila. "Unto whom I give thanks,"—I, Paul, the greatest man of the age, next to his divine Master; I, Paul, whose name shall outlast the names of all his opponents, and shall be coeval with Christianity itself, and that shall be coeval with the human race. Perhaps the two did not know all this, for nearness blinds us to greatness; but they were doubtless happy on the reception of the commendation. Happy those commended by Paul! Happier those commended by Jesus Christ!

V. **A loving and noble purpose has a far-reaching influence.**—Priscilla and Aquila were thanked by Paul and also by all the Churches of the Gentiles. They felt their indebtedness to Paul, and were thankful to those who had watched over his career and helped his usefulness. Modern Christians, too, many of them so called, are heedless of the lives and welfare of their preachers. Let them think of the Churches of the Gentiles that thanked Priscilla and Aquila because they laid down their own necks for Paul's life. Are we sufficiently thankful for our blessings? Are we trying to do what we can? We may not be, most likely are not, able either to write or to speak like St. Paul; but are we so mean because we cannot do the higher thing we will not do the lower thing? Our influence, our prayers, our sympathy, our self-sacrificing purpose, will be all helpful, and we must not withhold them. Where duty calls let us be ready to go, and God will bless and acknowledge even good intention. Purpose and accomplishment may not be always needful, may not be always possible ; but God looks to the heart, and accepts the offering of the loving heart.

Ver. 5. *Enlargement of Christian opportunity.*—The Thirty-nine Articles of Religion are a wonderful compendium of theology. They are placed at the end of the Church of England Prayer Book, and are not sufficiently studied. The clergy assent to them in theory, but many dissent from them in practice. Taken as a whole, the articles ought to be received by every Christian. Certainly we ought to find no difficulty with Article XIX. : " The visible Church of Christ is a congregation of faithful men, in the which the pure word of God is preached, and the sacraments be duly ministered according to Christ's ordinance in all those things that of necessity are requisite to the same." If this be a correct definition of a Church, then we come fairly to the conclusion that a Church is not a structure, neither is it an invisible something stretching through the centuries, but may be found in a house, in an unconsecrated building. It is wholesome and impressive to make buildings sacred, consecrated to divine and special uses; but we must widen our view, and seek to believe that there may be a Church in the house. Let the sacredness of the larger assembly be communicated to the smaller. Let us believe that Christ is present where the family meets for divine worship. Happy the home where Christ dwells ! We think with pleasure of the sweet Bethany home where the divine Christ visited and communicated to the loving sisters the fragrance of His devout feelings and sublime thoughts. How pleasantly life would flow along in that Bethany home, like some clear stream through a charming landscape ! Every home may be blessed in even larger degree by the unseen but graciously felt presence of Him who promises to be with His believing people to the end of time. A Church in the house is enriching. Consider :—

I. **The family as a germinating force.**—From the family spring the clan, the tribe, the nation. The primeval institution is that of the family. It precedes all human institutions, and shall outlast them if we are right in speaking of the redeemed in heaven as a family, united by love, where God is the gracious Father. The family is typical, and the elements of the type may often with good effect be transferred to the antitype. The closer the resemblance of the nation to the family, the firmer and more glorious will that nation become. The Church in the house may teach many wholesome lessons to the Church in the church, in the temple, in the chapel, and perhaps in the cathedral. Have we enough family feeling in our places of worship ? Is there a sense of unity ? Is there family affection ? Do the terms " brotherhood " and " sisterhood " speak clearly of spiritual brotherhood and sisterhood ? Does the Father symbolise the fatherhood of God ? Let us begin where God begins, with the family, and have a Church in every house. Let the divine seed there germinate, and thence work out large growths.

II. **The family as consecrated.**—A beautiful picture comes to us from the far-off time. When Abraham removed his tent he renewed his altar. Every tent should have its altar. Every home, whether cottage, villa, mansion, or palace, should have its altar whereon the sacrifice of praise and prayer may be offered. The family will be blessed indeed which constitutes a Church. A pious family will be prepared to receive a congregation of Christians. Priscilla's house may have been commodious, and thus a likely place for the meeting of either Ephesian or Roman Christians for worship. It is well to have a commodious house. It is better to have a commodious heart, a spirit open to communication from the eternal Spirit. Consecrated families will make consecrated Churches, and these will always solidify and beautify the nation.

542

III. **The family as exalted.**—We are far from undervaluing the elegance of a good English home. Most English clergymen live in well-appointed and spacious houses. If in a rural district we see a good house, we shall not often make a mistake if we conclude that it is the vicarage or rectory. Now it is all very fine for those who live in mansions to dilate on the happiness and comfort of the cottage. They do not show any readiness to make an exchange. Nevertheless we maintain that the true exaltation of the home is that it be consecrated by the presence of true religion. The Church in the house exalts and dignifies. Let us seek thus to make our homes exalted, happy, and rightly blessed. Better than the gold of earth is the fine gold tried in the fire which maketh gloriously rich ; better than outer seeming is that genuine courtesy and consideration for others which the gospel teaches. Family discords are the soonest healed by the touch of the hand of divine love. This makes the family firmly cohere.

IV. **The family as influential.**—Opportunities for usefulness are not wanting where there is a family. What a large sphere for mothers ! How much depends upon their work, prayers, and influence ! It is said that where fathers and mothers can read and write the children will be able to read and write ; and so we believe that where fathers and mothers are genuinely and wisely religious the children will not go far astray. Exceptions there may seem to be ; but perhaps the exceptions could be explained if we could see and know all the circumstances. From the sacred home there goes a saving influence. Who shall say what the well-beloved Epænetus, the firstfruits of Achaia unto Christ, owed to the churchly home of Priscilla and Aquila ? Why, the home at Cenchrea was a first-rate theological college without any dons or professors or classical or mathematical tutors. What an advertisement for a modern college to be able to state that Apollos, an eloquent man and mighty in the Scriptures, was one of its alumni ! What a short life the mere eloquent man possesses ! Apollos has left no visible traces ; but if he worked well and faithfully he has his reward, and in that reward will share those who showed to him the way of God more perfectly. Let us then seek to look above and beyond our narrow surroundings. Christian influence is not confined by the walls of the home. Opportunities increase as we try to improve every opportunity which is presented, and sphere enlarges as we seek to fill it right nobly and with true loyalty to Christ. The stately homes, and even the cottage homes, of England and of all lands stand pleasantly as they are palaces of divine grace adorned with the beauties of holiness.

Ver. 5. *Piety at home.*—The influence that a man's home has on his character will never perhaps be fully measured in this world ; the last day alone will show how many a man's life was affected for eternity by what he saw and heard under the roof where he was born. No wonder that our Lord should say to a converted soul, " Go home to thy friends, and tell them " (Mark v. 19). He that can introduce religion into his home has dug a well of living water of which the blessing shall spread far and wide. Yet home is precisely the place where a Christian often finds it most difficult to speak of his Master. There is frequently a kind of reserve among relatives and friends on the highest and holiest of all subjects. There are hundreds who seem shut up and silent by their own firesides who have plenty to say for Christ out of doors. The words of our Lord are often painfully verified : " A prophet is not without honour, but in his own country, and among his own kin, and in his own house " (Mark vi. 4). But a Christian must not be stopped in the path of duty by difficulties. The habit of shrinking from things because they bring with them a cross is one which must be steadily resisted. The servant of Christ has no business to choose his own work. The work that his Father puts before him is the work to which he must put his hand, however poorly he may do it. If we refuse to face duties because they are difficult, we shall find one day that sins of omission lie very heavy on the conscience. "Lord, pardon all my sins," said dying Archbishop Ussher, "but specially my sins of omission." If it be a plain duty to show our religion at home, the true Christian at any rate must try.

I. **Home is the place where God's servants in every age have specially shown their religion.**—This may be traced in both the Old and New Testament writings.

II. **Home is the place where some of the brightest lights of the modern Church of Christ have shone most brightly.**—The homes of Martin Luther and Philip Henry were models of a Church in a house. To home influence Dr. Doddridge and John Wesley were greatly indebted for the Christian eminence they afterwards attained. The family religion of such men as Venn and Scott and Leigh Richmond and Bickersteth was even more remarkable than that high standard of Christianity which they maintained before the world. These good men never forgot to tell the Lord's doings to those of their own house.

III. **Home is the place to which we are all under the greatest natural obligation.**—Where should we be if parents had not tenderly cared for us, trained, and taught us in the days of our infancy and youth ? Let any one think what an immense amount of trouble and expense he occasioned before he came to man's estate. What a trial of temper and patience he frequently was in his childhood ! What a huge unpaid debt is standing against him under the roof where he was born ! Surely the best return he can render is a spiritual one. If the Lord Jesus have done anything for his soul, let him never rest till his family are partakers of the benefit.

IV. **Home is the place where a Christian has the greatest opportunities of doing good.**—There are seasons when doors of usefulness are opened to a relative which are completely closed to all outside the family circle. In the time of affliction and death the members of a home are drawn together ; hearts and consciences at such a crisis are often tender and willing to hear ; at an hour like that a Christian member of a family may prove an unspeakable blessing. The days of darkness in this sad world will come to the most prosperous households ; happy is the household in such days in which there is some one who can seize the occasion and tell what the Lord Jesus has done and can do for our souls.

V. **Home, finally, is the place where the Christian can do the greatest amount of harm.**—Let us suppose that he stands alone in the midst of an unconverted family ; all around him are alike asleep in trespasses and sins. Now if a Christian under such circumstances hold his peace and never says a word for his Master, he incurs a heavy responsibility. His very silence is a positive injury to souls. "To him that knoweth to do good, and doeth it not, to him it is sin" (James iv. 17). Reader, let these things sink down into your heart, and consider them well. Whatever religion you possess, whether much or little, take care that it can be seen at home. The Christianity that came down from heaven was never meant to shine only in the society of fellow-worshippers and members of the same communion ; it was meant to leaven the family circle and to sanctify all the relations of the private household. He that never feels moved to tell his friends and relatives what the Lord has done for his soul may well doubt whether he has anything to tell. Who, after all, can tell the wealth of happiness that he may confer on his own family circle if he can only bring Jesus Christ into it ? How many households at this present day are nothing but bitter wells of Marah, from the want of true religion ! How much of selfishness, ill-temper, and worldliness would be driven from many firesides if the gospel of

Christ were to come into the house with power! Let the Christian never forget that the surest way to make home happy is to obtain a place, in it for Christ. —*The Right Rev. J. C. Ryle, D.D.*

Vers. 3-5. *How the pew may help the pulpit.*—How Christian men and women may best aid the Christian ministry is a very important question. An answer to it is to be found in the example of Aquila and Priscilla. From the various notices of this devoted pair to be found in the Acts of the Apostles and Paul's epistles, we are led to conclude that they form a pattern to all Christians. The history of Aquila and Priscilla goes to show that Christian men and women, in the married relation, may continue to be increasingly useful in Christian work and to the Christian ministry. Aquila and Priscilla were worthy of the honourable title "helpers in Christ Jesus," because :—

I. **Aquila and Priscilla were "helpers in Christ Jesus" to the apostle by the sympathy of their Christian character.**—They were *both* Christians. Whether they became so before or after making Paul's acquaintance it is hard to say. The likelihood is that they were "disciples" before Paul came to Corinth and lodged and wrought with them. Paul's coming thither was the beginning of a lifelong friendship between them. He found a congenial home in the great, corrupt Corinthian city under their roof. Their own domestic life was drawn into closer bonds by the gospel, and was thus made a means of spreading the gospel. In like manner every Christian husband and wife may be helpful to their minister. The Church needs, the world needs, not families and individuals merely Christian in name, but Christian in reality. Happy the homes where there is an Aquila or a Priscilla—happier still where there are *both* ! On the prayers and sympathies of such the Christian minister can confidently depend.

II. **Aquila and Priscilla were "helpers in Christ Jesus" to the apostle by the spiritual devotion of their domestic life.**—They had "a Church in the house" (ver. 5; 1 Cor. xvi. 19). This may mean : 1. The members and dependants of the family ; or 2. In all likelihood that a little company of Christian friends and neighbours met statedly for worship under their roof. Their trade as tentmakers admitted of their having accommodation for the purpose. Note also, wherever they went in connection with their trade, they had a "Church in the house"—their home was the meeting-place of believers. This shows their Christianity to have been of no formal character. It required zeal, courage, and perseverance in those days and places to be pronounced Christians, and especially to give countenance, as Aquila and Priscilla did, to the faith and followers of "Jesus the Nazarene." In this respect they were valued aids to the apostle. By means of such Churches in the house the light and love of the Christian faith were kept from perishing amid the corruption and darkness of heathen society. All honour to this devoted pair ! There ought to be a Church in the house of every Aquila and Priscilla—*i.e., family religion* ought to be sedulously cultivated. The whole household should be bound together by the ties of a common faith and worship. The time once was when family religion was more universal than it is now. *Once* the *head* of the household was, as a natural thing, its *priest.* Is it so *now*? Is family *worship* universally practised by professing Christians ? Are there not many so-called Christian homes where the family altar is unknown, never burning with the flame of piety ? Give me a Church in every house, and you give me a more potent factor than multitudes of ministers and missionaries. There is work in abundance at home and abroad for our Pauls; but what a noble field there is for our Aquilas and Priscillas ! Soon may every home in our land become a "sanctuary," every father a "priest unto God," every mother a "helper in Christ Jesus" !

III. **Aquila and Priscilla were "helpers in Christ Jesus" to the apostle because they were intelligent and well-instructed Christians.**—They were well grounded in the truths of the Christian faith, and could "give a reason for the hope that was in them." This is very clearly implied in the fact that it was owing to their instructions that the distinguished preacher Apollos was "taught the way of God more perfectly." One hardly knows whether more to admire his *humility* or their *ability* and Christian sympathy. In consequence of their teaching his eloquent tongue found a nobler theme—a risen, an historic Christ. Here, then, we find *lay* agency, and *female* agency too, of the best kind, and directed in the best way. No wonder Paul openly thanks them in his own name and in that of the Gentile believers—thanks them for being instrumental in giving to the Church, as a fully equipped *Christian* preacher, the mighty Apollos ! Wherever this eloquent evangelist went, the Churches of Christ would have reason to thank this worthy couple. Is there no scope for *lay* help now ? Is there no need for intelligent and well-instructed Christians—men and women *able* and *willing* to speak a word for Christ to the young, the ignorant, the neglected in the home, the Sabbath school, the mission hall ? Though *unordained*, Aquila and Priscilla were noble helpers in Christian work. Think not that only *ordained* teachers and preachers are fitted or to be expected to serve Christ. Every true-hearted minister will rejoice in the increase of wisely guided *lay* effort.

IV. **Aquila and Priscilla were "helpers in Christ Jesus" to the apostle because they put themselves into danger for his sake.**—"Who have for my life laid down their own necks." We know not exactly when or where ; possibly during the riot in Corinth (Acts xviii.), or in Ephesus (Acts xix.), which latter disturbance was of so violent a character that Paul compared it to a "fighting with beasts" in the amphitheatre (1 Cor. xv. 32). On one or other of these occasions Aquila and Priscilla, with exemplary self-sacrifice, came to the apostle's help, and to all appearance encountered danger on his account. Here he renders, with characteristic mindfulness, grateful thanks for their kindness. "A friend in need is a friend indeed," and such friendship they had manifested. Thank God there is no need for this special form of self-sacrifice nowadays. Self-sacrifice, however, can be shown in other ways. Give to preachers of the word Christian *sympathy*. Stand by them when slandered or opposed. Pray for them and their work. Be self-denying enough to give of your time and means to aid in the extension of Christ's kingdom. What a noble ambition to be a "helper in Christ Jesus" ! It merited the praise of Paul ; it still merits the praise of Paul's Master. Are you a helper or a hinderer in the work and to the ministers of Christ ?—*Thomas S. Dickson, M.A.*

SUGGESTIVE COMMENTS ON VERSES 3—5.

First converts interesting.—Paul here remembers many, and speaks of them all with affection ; but he salutes Epænetus as his well-beloved. We are not bound to love all in the same manner or in the same degree. The apostle calls this convert "fruits unto Christ." If converted, sinners are the seal and reward and glory and joy of the preacher ; they are infinitely more so of the Saviour Himself. As the author of their salvation, He will enjoy their blessedness and receive their praises for ever. Epænetus is here said to be the "*first*fruits unto Christ in Achaia." Yet Paul says to the Corinthians, "Ye know the house of Stephanas, that it is the firstfruits of Achaia." The apparent difficulty is easily solved by the fact that the house of Stephanas was the first family that was converted, but that Epænetus was the first convert in the family. Christians at first were few in number, and driven together by persecution. They were therefore well known to each other and to their ministers. The conversion of a man to Christianity in a heathen place must have been peculiarly *observable*. It was the production of " a new creature," which would of course be greatly wondered at. It was displaying the " heavenly " where all was " earthly and sensual and devilish " before. And we see it was *worthy* of attention. Earthly minds are most interested by the events of this life ; but what Paul noticed in Achaia was the first man that was called there out of darkness into the kingdom of God's dear Son. He knew that the conversion of one soul far transcended in importance the deliverance of a whole kingdom from civil bondage. Kingdoms will soon be no more ; but such a soul will shine a monument of grace and glory for ever and ever. How long Epænetus in the place and in the family stood alone as a professed Christian we know not ; but it is no uncommon thing for an individual to be similarly situated. We have often seen single converts seeking and serving Christ as the firstfruits of the neighbourhood or the household wherein they lived. The way in which and the means by which these persons are brought forward before others would, if stated, be found to be very various and often remarkable. And the circumstances in which these *first* converts are placed are interesting. They are in a post of *trial*; they have to take up their cross daily, and hourly too ; and a cross too heavy to be borne without divine aid. Little do many who have been religiously brought up, and whose relations and friends, if not decidedly pious, are not hostile—little do they know what some have to endure, especially at the commencement of their religious course ; when, instead of assistance and countenance, so much needed, they meet with neglect, and opposition, and sneers, and reproach from all around them, and from all that are dear to them. They are also in a post of *duty*. They are required to be, not only harmless and blameless, but

exemplary in their conduct. The reason is that they will attract peculiar notice. Everything they do will be canvassed by a shrewdness sharpened by enmity, and ready to magnify every failing. *They* will be judged by their profession, and their religion will be judged by *them*. And they are to put gainsayers to silence, and constrain them by their good works which they behold to glorify God in the day of visitation. They are to adorn the doctrine of God our Saviour in all things, and by walking in wisdom to win those that are without. They are not to repulse by rudeness or chill by disdain ; they are never to betray a feeling that says, " Stand by thyself ; come not near to me : I am holier than thou." They are not, by stiffness and affectations in little and lawful things, to lead people to suppose that their religion is made up of oddities and perversenesses. Yet, in things of unquestionable obligation and real importance, they must be firm and immovable, always abounding in the work of the Lord ; for not only will conscience require this in the testimony they are always to bear for God, but such consistency alone will enthrone them in the convictions and esteem of others. For they are also in a post of *honour* ; they have a peculiar opportunity of showing their principles Later converts may be equally conscientious, but *these* coming after, when they have the sanction and co-operation of others, cannot so obviously appear to be on the Lord's side, nor so fully evince the purity and power of their motives, as those who come forward *alone*, and say to all others, however numerous, however influential, however endeared, Choose you this day whom you will serve; but as for me, I will serve the Lord. They have therefore the privilege of taking the lead, and of being examples instead of followers. And they may be the means of prevailing upon others. We have seldom seen an instance of failure. The effect has not always immediately appeared ; but where they have been enabled to walk worthy of God unto all pleasing, after a little while they have no longer gone *alone* to the house of God, but in company—in company even with those who once stood aloof, or before even opposed.—*W. Jay.*

A good man induces others to show zeal.—The "*good* man" is he who, while he conforms to the requirements of justice, lays himself out, at the same time, for the good of others in the active exercise of liberal, philanthropic benevolence, or of zealous disinterested patriotism—the man who seems to live for others rather than for himself, making a business of beneficence, "doing good to all as he has opportunity." For a man of this description a universal interest is excited. He has a place in the hearts of all whose affection or esteem is worth the having. Every wish of theirs respecting him is for a blessing. His life is desired, his death devoutly deprecated; and while, to preserve the life of the merely just man, it is hardly, if at all, to be expected that any one should think of laying down his own, for the life of the "good man," a life so eminently valuable, and so much endeared by the union of unsullied integrity with private benevolence and public spirit, there might be found some whom the warmth of affectionate gratitude or the ardour of patriotic zeal would induce to part with their all, and to add even their lives to the sacrifice. Aquila and Priscilla risked their lives, and in risking showed their readiness to part with them, had it been necessary, to preserve to the Churches of Christ and to the world the precious life of the apostle of the Gentiles. So imminent was their peril, so cheerful their zeal in his behalf, that he speaks of them as if they had really become martyrs for his sake: "who have for my life laid down their own necks." The history of mankind is not without similar instances of self-devotion in the room of others.—*Dr. Wardlaw.*

The source of woman's power.—Those do not discriminate sufficiently who

imagine that the source of woman's power arises principally from the beauty of her countenance. For although it may begin there, yet the charm and fascination are also manifested in a whole kingdom of gentle influences, distinguishing her from the other sex—such as the soft and graceful movement of her person, the tones of her voice, the loving moderation evinced in every action and expression, her yielding courtesy, her supreme repose, the complete suppression and concealment of her independent wishes and will where they would clash with those of others. All these and suchlike qualities inspire men with that love and admiration which we wrongly suppose to be excited alone by the more tangible charms of feature and face.—*Christian Age.*

Coincidences between historian and actor.—Cenchrea adjoined to Corinth; St. Paul, therefore, at the time of writing the letter, was in the neighbourhood of the woman whom he thus recommends. But, further, that St. Paul had before this been at Cenchrea itself appears from the eighteenth chapter of the Acts; and appears by a circumstance as incidental and as unlike design as any that can be imagined. "Paul after this tarried there (viz., at Corinth) yet a good while, and then took his leave of the brethren, and sailed thence into Syria, and with him Priscilla and Aquila; having shorn his head in Cenchrea: for he had a vow" (xviii. 18). The shaving of the head denoted the expiration of the Nazaritic vow. The historian, therefore, by the mention of this circumstance, virtually tells us that St. Paul's vow was expired before he set forward upon his voyage, having deferred probably his departure until he should be released from the restrictions under which his vow laid him. Shall we say that the author of the Acts of the Apostles feigned this anecdote of St. Paul at Cenchrea, because he had read in the Epistle to the Romans that "Phœbe, a servant of the Church of

Cenchrea, had been a succourer of many, and of him also"? or shall we say that the author of the Epistle to the Romans, out of his own imagination, created Phœbe "*a servant of the Church at Cenchrea*," because he read in the Acts of the Apostles that Paul had " shorn his head " in that place ? —*Paley.*

Coincidence of date. — Under the same head—viz., of coincidences depending upon date—I cite from the epistle the following salutation : " Greet Priscilla and Aquila, my helpers in Jesus Christ, who have for my life laid down their own necks; unto whom not only I give thanks, but also all the Churches of the Gentiles." Now what this quotation leads us to observe is the danger of scattering names and circumstances in writings like the present, how implicated they often are with dates and places, and that nothing but truth can preserve consistency. We may take notice of the terms of commendation in which St. Paul describes them, and of the agreement of that encomium with the history. " My helpers in Christ Jesus, who have for my life laid down their own necks; unto whom not only I give thanks, but also all the Churches of the Gentiles." In the eighteenth chapter of the Acts we are informed that Aquila and Priscilla were Jews; that St. Paul first met with them at Corinth ; that for some time he abode in the same house with them ; that St. Paul's contention at Corinth was with the unbelieving Jews, who at first "opposed and blasphemed, and afterwards with one accord raised an insurrection against him"; that Aquila and Priscilla adhered, we may conclude, to St. Paul throughout this whole contest, for when he left the city they went with him (Acts xviii. 18). Under these circumstances, it is highly probable that they should be involved in the dangers and persecutions which St. Paul underwent from the Jews, being themselves Jews; and, by adhering to St. Paul in this dispute, deserters, as they would be accounted, of the Jewish cause. Further, as they, though Jews, were assisting St. Paul in preaching to the Gentiles at Corinth, they had taken a decided part in the great controversy of that day, the admission of the Gentiles to a parity of religious situation with the Jews. For this conduct alone, if there was no other reason, they may too have been entitled to "thanks from the Churches of the Gentiles." They were Jews taking part with Gentiles. Yet is all this so indirectly intimated, or rather, so much of it left to inference, in the account given in the Acts, that I do not think it probable that a forger either could or would have drawn his representation from thence; and still less probable do I think it that, without having seen the Acts, he could, by mere accident, and without truth for his guide, have delivered a representation so conformable to the circumstances there recorded.—*Paley.*

MAIN HOMILETICS OF THE PARAGRAPH.—*Verses* 6—16.

St. Paul's conception of the respectable.—In modern society we do not all move among what are called the respectable classes. There are classifications. It is sometimes highly amusing to hear one of the followers of him who was the friend of slaves, prisoners, freedmen, mere nobodies, parties whom you know one cannot know, declaré that people are not respectable. In what is called Christianised society of to-day it is not the qualities but the quantities that a man possesses which command respect. The social pride of the day is odious. Some of the followers of fishermen are as proud as Lucifer. There are ecclesiastical dignitaries in every branch of the Church who need to study the kind of friends whom their great apostle saluted.

I. There is one quality possessed by all who command respect.—That quality is the one of being in Christ, in the Lord. The question with the apostle is not, Is he in our set? Is he the kind of person we ought to know? Does he attend our church? Does he speak our shibboleth? The question which absorbs all other inquiries should be, Is he in Christ? is he in the Lord?—in Christ by vital union with Him, deriving from Him spiritual life and force by active co-operation with all His loving plans and purposes.

II. **Some have a bareness of quality which does not immortalise.**—Some are saved, but so as by fire. They are Christians, and that is all which can be affirmed. There must have been many more names in the Roman Church, names known, it may be, to the apostle, in addition to those here mentioned; but their names find no place in this immortal scroll of honour. Even in this list are names with no special marks of approval; they are honourable, but do not take the foremost places. It is something, a precious something, precious beyond compare, to be numbered amongst Christ's redeemed; but it is something more to be numbered amongst Christ's valiant workers, amongst His true and stalwart soldiers. It is a noble ambition to leave behind a name which the world will not let die; but nobler to have a name which Christ will mention with approval amid the plaudits of rejoicing angels.

III. **Others have a richness of quality which commands special respect.**— We cannot be the firstfruits of our country in respect to time; but may we not be in respect to fulness, ripeness, and completeness? The richest fruits of our season—what a noble ideal! We cannot be the personally well-beloved of St. Paul, but the well-beloved of Him who knoweth all things and knows those who ardently love and serve Him. Helpers in Christ; mighty labourers in the Lord. However mean our position, however isolated our lot, we may all be helpers in Christ. He has need of all; He lays claim to the service of all. Helpers with Paul in Christ are all the faithful workers through the centuries. Faithful helpers in Christ are the world's mighty labourers. Earth's minsters do not entomb their ashes; national mausoleums do not enshrine their effigies; earth's historians do not indite eloquent panegyrics on their memories. But what are earthly glories? *Vanitas vanitatum.* Our national mausoleum now honours the names of those whom Christian England a short time ago dishonoured and illtreated. Christ's approvals do not thus change. His valuations are always correct; His awards are discriminating; His immortalities alone endure.

Immortal friendships.—There were women at Rome wearing in a single necklace of pearls a fortune of a hundred thousand pounds. Their very names have perished with their follies and vices, while Phœbe's name is resplendent for ever in Paul's gospel. Open your commentaries at this chapter, and note how often the dreary remark occurs, " Nothing is known of this person." Nothing known of Epænetus and Urbanus and Olympas? If Alexander the Great and Napoleon Bonaparte could make their choice now, have you any doubt they would gladly exchange their fame for such a divine enrolment as this in the letter of some prophet or missionary—Alexander, the beloved, and Napoleon, my fellow-worker in the Lord? Let us first endeavour to find out how these names came to be in our Bible at all, and then consider the immortal friendships they celebrate. Three or four of them appear elsewhere in sacred history, and possibly two of them in the annals of Rome; but all the rest stand alone in this postscript of the letter which more than any other contains Paul's gospel. How wide was its reach already! Most of the names are of Greek origin. Only a few years before he had come to the centre of learning and the arts with the wisdom of God unto salvation, and now Greece and her colonies furnish him with twenty-one names for his roll of honour. Rome contributes nine more. His own people, to whom the covenants and the oracles of God belonged, are represented by only

550

four Hebrew names ; and Persis is not a name, it means "the Persian woman." The Orient and all the world are laid under contribution, but these names reflect no splendours of earthly honour. Phœbe, the first to appear in this galaxy, is the feminine of Phœbus Apollo ; she was named from the fabled divinity which Virgil describes, "Semper rubet aurea Phœbe." Yes, she shines for ever. But the name which her heathen parents gave her was a decoration of idolatry. And nearly all of these names had been tarnished by the superstitions and degradations of a false religion in which faith was perishing.

The glorious obscure.—Our English Bibles only hint at the fact that the greater number of persons mentioned are not known by name to Paul : "Salute them which are of the households of Aristobulus and of Narcissus." This is not a literal translation of what was written : "Salute them who came out from the men belonging to Aristobulus and Narcissus." They are the converted slaves of these great Roman families, the poor creatures who were corralled overnight like cattle, or chained to posts around their palaces. Now they are grouped, to the number of hundreds perhaps, among the shining ones of God. Nameless men, and men of obscure and of tarnished names, make up this divine enrolment. And this is the first practical lesson it yields us : how to make our names shine ; how to remove reproaches, justly or innocently incurred, and come out of obscurity and be remembered with veneration and affection. Some good man will be writing a letter by-and-by ; you and I can get into its postscript. There is a Lamb's book of life to be written ; we can all get into that divine enrolment.

The friends of childhood.—But these names do no stand here merely because they represent good men and women. They are also pledges of immortal friendships. This is a dull chapter to many because they do not know how to translate it. The friends of my childhood, friends on both sides of the ocean, my fellow-workers in the gospel, my beloved in the Lord—these are the faces that look at me out of this chapter, like the portraits which compose the clouds in Raphael's great picture in Dresden. The Christian friendships immortalised here are only meant to bring back to you the names you love best in the fellowship of Christ.

How a friendship began.—Remember how Paul came to know Timothy at first, and then think of the special providence that has led to your most precious intimacies. Do you notice that there are no glittering generalities in this postscript ? "Remember me to all inquiring friends." No, indeed ; Paul is the inquiring friend. He remembers the very things Phœbe and Prisca and Mary and all the rest have done who have bestowed much labour on him and on the brotherhood.

Unknown heroes and heroines.—Do you remember, or did you ever know, in detail all the little things which your own brethren and sisters in this congregation have done ?

Helpful friendships.—The helpfulness of Christian friendships—this is our last and best lesson. It is helpfulness in the every-day work of life. There is no helping in church-work or in spiritual culture without taking hold of the work of making a living and of getting on in business. "Assist Phœbe in whatsoever business she hath need of you." How were they to go about that ? The word means law—business. She was engaged in a lawsuit. Immense interests were involved because it had been appealed to the Supreme Court at Rome. And there were saints at Rome in Cæsar's household. Maybe they were slaves ; but there were lawyers in those days of the servile class. They could get the ear of the court ; they could do something ; they could try to do something. This is what Paul asks : Assist her in her law business. Brethren, help one another in law business if you are ever so unfortunate as to get involved in law business, and in commercial business, and in all sorts of honest business. It may be that Philologus and Julia his wife, Nereus and his sister, and Olympas, describe three homes where a little Church used to meet in turn, and that "the brethren with them" are this Church within their houses. But who are "Asyncritus, Phlegon, Hermas, Patrobas, Hermes, and the brethren who are with them"? No wife or sister is mentioned to indicate their homes. There is nothing but their bare names. But this clause after their names speaks volumes. I believe the "brethren who are with them" are their workmen or partners in the same business. Perpetuate the Christian brotherhoods which have been sealed in the business combinations for gospel work in Rome, in convents of the deserts and in alpine passes, in soldiers' bivouacs, in sailors' forecastles, and in the frugal homes of our ancestors. Never let your warehouses get too big nor your homes too splendid and too frigid for this family life of God's dear children.

The source of immortal friendships.—And who is Tertius? He has hardly any name. There is a Secundus somewhere else, and a Quartus here. The second, the third, and the fourth—who is the third man, Tertius? Tertius is the amanuensis. He has been in the Lord as well as Paul all through this wonderful composition. Parchment, pen, ink, his own skilful hand, and the heart that is burning within him in the radiance of these sublime truths, are all in the Lord. Now we have found the true source of immortal friendships. It is Christ Himself. Two men who are in the Lord must help one another as the left hand helps the right. They are one divine life.—*Rev. Wolcott Calkins, D.D.*

SUGGESTIVE COMMENTS ON VERSES 6—16.

Usefulness of women.—Admitting that the Bible be the word of God, we might have inferred from His wisdom and goodness that no part of it can be useless. But we are expressly assured that "all Scripture *is* profitable for doctrine, for reproof, for correction, for instruction in righteousness." Therefore this long postscript, this catalogue of particular salutations, has its uses. It certainly shows us the principle that actuated the first Christians—all men were to know that they were the disciples of Christ by their loving one another. It shows also how mistaken they are who think the New Testament does not sanction private friendship. It also proves how impossible it was to forge this epistle, abounding as it does with so many specific allusions; for these not only render detection possible, but easy. Hence Paley much avails himself of this chapter in his *Horæ Paulinæ.* Neither is it improper to observe from it the error of Popery: Papists say that Peter was the bishop of Rome. But, had he been there, is it credible

for a moment that he would have been overlooked by our apostle? The probability indeed is that he never was there. There is no evidence of it in the Scripture; and we know for what purposes of delusion it has been pretended—the Roman succession of bishops from him. But who can help observing how many females are mentioned here? Phœbe, Priscilla, Mary, Junia, Tryphena, Tryphosa, Persis, the mother of Rufus, Julia, the sister of Nereus. All these, with the exception of two, are not only mentioned, but commended; and these two would not have been saluted by name unless they had been persons of religious excellence, for Paul valued no other qualities compared with this. But all the rest of these worthies have ascribed to them some attainments or service "in the Lord." Let not, therefore, females suppose that they are cut off from usefulness in the cause of Christ. The most eminent servants of God have acknowledged their obligations to them, and ascribed no little of their success to their care and kindness.

Servants have blessed God for pious mistresses. Children have been prepared for the preaching of the word and the devotion of the sanctuary by the earlier but important efforts of a mother. How much does even the religious public owe to the mothers of Newton and Cecil, and a thousand more, from whom the Churches have derived such able ministers! To Hannah we owe a Samuel; and to Lois and Eunice, his mother and grandmother, we owe a Timothy. They are at home in almsdeeds, like Dorcas, who made garments for the poor; and are peculiarly adapted to visit the sick and the afflicted. The wife may win the irreligious husband without the word, and fan his devotion and give speed to his zeal when he is in the way everlasting. Who would keep them from those public meetings where feelings are to be excited which they will be sure to carry away and improve at home? In a word, women have the finest heads, and hearts, and hands, and tongues for usefulness in the world. Who does not wish to see them always under a religious principle? Who would not have them, *appropriately*, more encouraged and employed as workers together with the servants of Christ? "Help," therefore says the apostle, "those women that laboured with me in the gospel, whose names are in the book of life."—*W. Jay.*

The influence of a good woman.— That was a strange influence which Beatrice exercised over the great poet Dante, which not only moulded and affected his actions, but which entered into the spirit of his poetry, directed his thoughts, and gave the inspiration of his genius. Beatrice became to Dante the symbol of pure and holy things. "Death itself disappeared before the mighty love that was kindled in the heart of the poet: it transformed, it purified all things." And then, when Beatrice died, his love became resigned, submissive; death sanctified it instead of converting it into remorse. The love of Dante destroyed nothing; it fertilised all, it gave a giantlike force to the sentiment of duty. The poet said: "Whenever and wherever she appeared to me, I no longer felt that I had an enemy in the world; such a flame of charity was kindled in my heart, causing me to forgive every one that had offended me." The death of Beatrice imposed fresh duties upon him. That which he felt he had then to do was to render himself more worthy of her; he resolved to keep his love for her to the last day of his life, and bestow upon her an immortality upon earth. In his love for the beautiful, in his striving after upward purity, Beatrice was the nurse of his understanding, the angel of his soul, the consoling spirit which sustained him in poverty and in exile, in a cheerless, wandering, and sorrowful existence. *La Vita Nuova*, a little book which Dante wrote probably at the age of twenty-eight, in which he relates, both in prose and verse, the emotions of his love for Beatrice, is an inimitable little book of gentleness, purity, delicacy, of sweet and sad thoughts, loving as the note of the dove, ethereal as the perfume of flowers; and that pen, which in later years resembled a sword in the hand of Dante, here delineates their aspect, as Raphael might have done with his pencil. There are pages—those, for example, where is related the dream of Beatrice—the prose of which is a finished model of language and style far beyond the best style of Boccaccio.

A picture of the primitive Church.— "Here is," says Gaussen, "a picture to the life of a primitive Church; we can see to what height the most ignorant and weak of its members can rise. . . . We wonder at the progress already made by the word of God solely through the labours of travellers, artisans, merchants, women, slaves, and freedmen, who resided in Rome." Not only did the apostle know a large number of these workers, because he had been connected with them in the East (Andronicus and Junias, Rufus and his mother, for example), or because he had converted them himself (Aquila and Priscilla); but he also received news from Rome, as is proved by the intimate details into which he entered in chap. xiv.; and he might thus know of the labours of many of those saluted, whom he did not know personally. Such is probably the case with the last persons designated, and to whose names he adds no description. The Greek origin of the most of these names constitutes no objection to the *Roman* domicile of those who bear them. What matters it to us that, as M. Renan says, after Father Garucci, the names in *Jewish* inscriptions at Rome are mostly of Latin origin? If there be any room for surprise, five or six Latin names would perhaps be more astonishing at Ephesus than fifteen or sixteen Greek names at Rome. Have we not proved over and over that this Church was recruited much more largely from Gentiles than from Jews, and that especially it was founded by missionaries who had come from Syria, Asia, and Greece? M. Reuss no doubt asks what became of all those friends of Paul, when, some years later, he wrote from Rome his Epistles to the Colossians and Philippians; and later still, the Second to Timothy. But in writing from Rome to the Churches of Colosse and Philippi, he could only send salutations from individuals who knew them. And a little before the Second to Timothy there occurred the persecution of Nero, which had for the time dispersed and almost annihilated the Church of Rome. Our conclusion, therefore, is not only that this passage of salutations may have been written to the Church of Rome, but that it could not have been addressed to any other more suitably. As at the present day Paris, or even Rome, is a sort of rendezvous for numerous foreign Christians of both sexes, who go thither to found evangelistic works, so the great pagan Rome attracted at that time the religious attention and zeal of all the Christians of the East. Let us remark, in closing, the exquisite delicacy and courtesy which guide the apostle in those distinguishing epithets with which he accompanies the names of the servants or handmaids of Christ whom he mentions. Each of those descriptive titles is as it were the rough draft of the *new name* which those persons shall bear in glory. Thus understood, this enumeration is no longer a dry nomenclature; it resembles a bouquet of newly blown flowers which diffuse refreshing odours.—*Godet.*

MAIN HOMILETICS OF THE PARAGRAPH.—*Verses* 17—19.

Mark the separatists.—It is to be borne in mind that there are separatists *and* separatists. Separation is not in itself a crime; some of the movements which have been most beneficial to mankind have been caused by separatists whose names have been cast out as evil. Jesus Christ Himself was a separatist, and was crucified as a destroyer of ancient customs; St. Paul was a separatist, and the Jewish Church regarded him with disfavour. On the separatist is thrown the *onus probandi*. If he can show worthy cause for the step he has taken, well and good; but if not, we must mark him and avoid.

I. **Mark the separatist as to:** 1. *His doctrine.* Is it contrary to, is it out of harmony with, the received doctrine? This question supposes that the doctrine which we have learned is the truth, and that is older than the hills, coequal with the divine existence. The novelty of a doctrine is rather a *primâ facie* argument against than for its truth, though unsound minds eagerly accept a doctrine simply because it is novel. Creeds are to be exploded, not because they are unsound, but because they are old-fashioned. Bread is an old-fashioned article of food, but it still holds a place amid most luxurious modern banquets. Mark the new doctrine; examine its claims; but do not be like some hosts, who always appear ready to smile upon a fresh face. 2. *His style of delivery.* In these days style is all-important. The manner in which the thing is dressed is quite as impressive as the thing. A flowing writer commands attention. What do we care about thought, if we are only charmed with glowing periods? A graceful speaker will win the modern audience, and lead captive silly souls; the man who with good words can put his own conduct in a rosy light, and by fair speeches can deceive and flatter the hearts of his hearers, will easily cause divisions and offences. We love good style, but we ask that it be the exponent of good and true doctrine. 3. *His motive force.* Is he serving the Lord Jesus Christ, or his own belly? There was not very much to be gained in the way of earthly good on either side in those early times. Perhaps there was the promise of gain on the side of ungodliness—that is, against the doctrines taught by the apostles. It is always difficult to judge motives; but if a man lose money, fame, influence, position, by his advocacy of certain doctrines, we may be persuaded that he, at all events, feels that they contain truth. So far he proves his sincerity.

II. **Resist the separatist:** 1. *By obedience.* The simple man, rough in speech and rude in manners it may be, will not be able to withstand the man of honeyed words and flattering speeches. But the obedient soul, however simple, will be made strong. Obedience is better than eloquence; the willing and the obedient shall eat the good of every land, intellectual and moral. Stand in the strong tower of obedience, and no weapon thrown by seductive besiegers shall do any damage. 2. *By wisdom towards the good.* We are asked, What is the good? We reply that the good is the morally fit and proper; the good is marked out by the noblest men of the past. What the All-good tells me is good I believe; what the Bible positively declares to be good I believe; what my enlightened conscience affirms to be good, and in the practice of which I find peace and rest, I joyfully accept. 3. *By simplicity concerning evil.* Some people are simple enough concerning evil; they are easily caught and victimised; the honey beguiles, and they are ignorant of the sting which it encloses. Notwithstanding the advance of education and of science and of a free press, the simplicity of many modern souls is most amusing. After all, it may be that the simplicity of the cheated is better than the duplicity of the cheater: the simplicity of the good may excite the laughter of the fast men, but while it may occasion some mistakes, it will in the long-run keep them in the safest pathway.

SUGGESTIVE COMMENTS ON VERSE 19.

What obedience does.—In the concluding chapter of this epistle St. Paul warns against such doctrines and practices as militate against a true and pure Christianity, which he styles "the doctrine which ye have learned," and properly characterises the teachers and promoters of false doctrines as intent on serving themselves. But to those who had given up idolatry and committed themselves fully to the service of the one true God, through the grace of Christ our Lord, he says, "Your obedience is come abroad unto all men"—*i.e.*, is generally known, for it could not be otherwise.

I. **This obedience came by hearing, as the word itself implies.**—"Faith cometh by hearing, and hearing by the word of God." Hearing, to be profitable, must be serious, attentive, and conscientious. There must be a desire to *learn*, to *profit*, and to *do* what is seen to be good and right. Obedience to the teaching of the gospel of Christ, to be acceptable, must proceed from repentance, be inspired by faith, and be animated by the love of God, through the influence of divine grace. The obedience of the early Christians prompted them to meet the most fearful trials, and in many cases to endure martyrdom itself. The case of the martyrs at Sebaste, under the emperor Licinius, A.D. 320, well illustrates this obedience of faith in the last extremity. They were condemned to stand naked on a frozen lake during a night of bitter cold, though if any were willing to renounce Christ, they might go into a tent or cottage on the shore, where they would find food, clothing, light, and fire. In the middle of the night two men perishing with cold presented themselves at the door of the hut, and found relief and refreshment at the expense of faith and duty; but the centurion himself, with a faithful companion, went out and took the place of these two, and when the sun arose the exact number of the condemned was complete, made perfect through fearful suffering, "faithful unto death." Our obedience is to be continued through "all the changes and chances of this mortal life," and is to be "a light shining in a dark place."

II. **The obedient are wise unto that which is good.**—They learn to distinguish "good" in reality from good only in name and appearance. To them nothing is good which has not its origin in right principle. Hence corrupt maxims, deceitful habits, and selfish purposes are avoided and hated. "Their eye is single, and their whole body full of light." "Their eyes look right on." They do not escape adversity, but are assured it will turn to their advantage, here or hereafter: in trial they find compensations, and in the deepest affliction the comfort of divine love. They walk on steadily, rejoicing in the presence of their Master and in the expectation of eternal blessedness. "The wisdom which is from above is theirs," and

leads them above all things to do the will of their Father in heaven. They have one aim, to keep as far as possible the words of Christ: "Be ye therefore perfect, even as your Father which is in heaven is perfect." And so, adding grace to grace, they daily approach nearer the standard they have in mind. A friend once visited the studio of Michael Angelo, and saw him engaged on one of his great statues. In a month or two he came again, and thought that the artist had made no progress; but Angelo pointed out a line here and a wrinkle smoothed out there, when the friend said, "True; but these are but trifles." When the great artist replied, "Trifles make perfection; but perfection is no trifle."

III. **The obedient are simple as concerning evil.**—Their motives are *unmixed*; for so the word translated "simple" primarily means. They are not like the animal which looks up with one eye and down with the other. They realise the impossibility of serving both God and mammon. They *are* what they *seen*. They eschew

"hypocrisy,
The only ill that stalks abroad unseen by men
     or angels;
But goodness thinks no ill where no ill
     seems."

"In simplicity of godly sincerity they have their conversation [*i.e.*, their behaviour] in the world." The plans, plots, and devices of the worldly enter not, should not enter, into their thoughts, or ever be entertained by them. "They avoid evil, turn from it, and pass away." And as they hate evil, the baleful effects of evil shall not permanently affect them, and swift-winged calamity shall turn away from them. They must, however, know something of the world in order to be safe—"wise as serpents, but harmless as doves"; but they pray and endeavour to escape evil, to be delivered from its tyranny and power, "hating even the garment spotted by the flesh." —*Dr. Burrows.*

MAIN HOMILETICS OF THE PARAGRAPH.—Verse 20.

The peace-destroyer's destruction.—From the visible enemy who threatens, the apostle's eye turns to the invisible world, where he discovers, on the one side the more formidable enemy of whom his earthly adversaries are the instruments, and on the other the all-powerful ally on whose succour the Church can reckon in this struggle. The expression "God of peace" is designedly chosen to describe God as one who, if the Church fulfil its task well in these circumstances, will take care to overthrow the designs of its adversaries and preserve harmony among the faithful. No wonder that the Christian's energies are paralysed if he only considers the smallness of his own resources and the greatness of the powers with which he has to cope; but his heart may be strengthened by the reflection that he has a powerful Friend on whom he may rely, and whose help he may successfully invoke. The Christian may be inspired by the thought that the valour of God is his defence. He may well rise superior to difficulty, remembering that victory is finally certain, for God fights on his side. The work is now going forward under the direction of God. Shortly the finishing stroke will be given. Satan will be a bruised foe under the feet of the triumphant saints.

I. **The peace-maker.**—The endearing character under which God is presented before us in this passage is that of the peace-maker. The God of peace—the author, originator, and maker of peace. Peace-maker! Delightful to be able to introduce harmony into a world of disorder, to cause a holy calm to reign in a realm which had presented the scene of wild chaos. Among the Saviour's greatest material works is that by which he calmed the troubled waters of the storm-tossed lake. If he be great who introduces harmony into the disorder of material things, what shall be affirmed of the greatness of Him who introduces order where moral discord prevailed, who gives peace to troubled natures? Jesus Himself says, "Blessed are the peace-makers." The highest type of man is the peace-maker. Christ as the peace-maker is endeared to troubled hearts. God is by pre-eminence the God of peace. He gave Christ to be a peace-maker. It was God that first made this planet beautiful by the gentle sway of peace. When sin touched with its spoiling hand the calm sea of this world's peace, it was God's mercy that floated over the troubled waters the words of hope. When the world attained its highest and darkest reach of moral confusion, it was God that brought into the world the gospel method whereby spiritual unrest was to be removed and peace flow into the hearts of mankind. The character of the peace-maker is ennobled by the thought that God is the offended being, and yet He proposes conditions of peace and makes possible a way of peace. He secures the method of peace at infinite cost. He *spared not* His Son.

II. **The peace-destroyer.**—By how much the character of the peace-maker is ennobled, in the same proportion may the character of the peace-destroyer sink in our estimation. It is Godlike to create. It is devil-like to destroy. Destructionists should always bring forward good reasons for the methods they pursue. Our natures would rise in rebellion and in wrath against the wretched and powerful being who should disturb the harmonies of the celestial spheres. But a worse catastrophe has happened. Satan with his tainting hand has touched our humanity, and lost spirits are seen wandering, through a dismal planet, from the Source of life, from the Spring of eternal strength and happiness. The devil destroyed the world's moral peace when he first entered the garden of peace, and ever since he has been working in the same direction. Satan has destroyed the peace of hearts, the peace of individuals, the peace of Churches, and the peace of nations.

557

> " There is a land of peace,
>   Good angels know it well;
>   Glad songs that never cease
>   Within its portals swell;
>   Around its glorious throne
>   Ten thousand saints adore
>   Christ, with the Father—one,
>   And Spirit evermore."

Into that land of peace no ruthless disturber can ever enter.

III. **The peace-destroyer's destruction at the hand of the peace-maker.**—In order to perpetuate harmony it is necessary to banish that, or at least to eliminate the power of that, which has been the cause of discord. To preserve the harmony of a kingdom it may be needful to banish the rebels. The peace of the family can be preserved by the exclusion of the quarrelsome member, or by its reformation. The peace of God's human family is always endangered by the presence of Satan. He appears to be beyond reform. We do not limit the power of the Infinite. But as that power did not prevent Satan's fatal meddling, so we have no reason to suppose that God's power will turn the prince of darkness into a veritable angel of light. Satan must be bruised, and so bruised as to be able to do no further moral mischief. He has been bruised in part by Christ's victorious achievements. Bruised, but not effectually rendered harmless. He is being bruised by the dispensation of the Holy Spirit and by the instrumentality of God's Church. God will finish the work in righteousness, and Satan will be effectually bruised beneath the feet of God's people. Satan will be powerless, and over his slain form the Church will ride in triumph. Let us, then, not fear for God's truth. Relying on God's promises, we are not to fear the wiles of our great adversary. We must battle and not be dismayed. We must pray and wait in hope for the period of final extinction of Satan as a harmful foe.

IV. **The peace-maker's "due time" we cannot measure.**—God's "shortly" is not to be measured by our minutes. The little child with its inadequate notions of time cannot measure the "shortly" of a wise father. How can the children of time, whose day is but as a butterfly existence, measure the day of Him who is from everlasting to everlasting? We are sometimes disposed to ask, Has the Eternal been so taken up with the consideration and the management of other and higher worlds that He has forgotten us in our low estate—forgotten that His children are well-nigh overwhelmed by the triumphant progress of sin and misery—forgotten that the world has been long groaning beneath the oppression of the evil one—forgotten that the lovers of the truth are comparatively few and their efforts seemingly uninfluential—forgotten that many anxious souls are waiting for the fulfilment of the promise that shortly God will bruise Satan under their feet? But when we get away from the contracting influences of the present world, when we breathe the enlarging atmosphere of God's broad realm of infinite thoughts, we may get to understand that our " shortly " is a word that impatience utters in moments of defeat and perplexity—that God's " shortly " may be a word uttered by a Being possessed of infinite wisdom and power, and who can wait, to use a human word, through the slow-moving centuries of time. Where is the mind sufficiently large that can sweep with rapid glance through all that space—if of space or of any notion of limitation we may speak in this connection—that must be comprehended in the "shortly" of Him who fills the boundless realm of eternity? A season must be allowed in which the efficacy of the Saviour's mediatorial mission shall be vindicated—in which the glory of the Church as a militant force must be evidenced. A great work has to be done before God's "shortly " can be consummated. We must consider God's " shortly " in the light of eternity and by the side of those comprehensive plans which must be entertained by the infinite mind.

V. Human peace-makers will share in the final triumph.—The limbs of the Church will not always be fettered ; the feet of God's saints will not always be fastened in the stocks ; the iron of oppression will not always eat into their souls. With firm and joyous tread they will victoriously walk over their crushed adversary. Under our feet for ever will be the enemy of our souls. Peaceful millennial reign ! blessed sabbatic repose ! when

> "Sin, my worst enemy before,
> Shall vex mine eyes and ears no more;
> Mine inward foes shall all be slain,
> Nor Satan break my peace again."

Ver. 20. *Satan bruised.*

I.—1. A reference to Gen. iii. 15 : apostle points to certainty of Christ's victory as guarantee of ours. 2. An echo of promise in Psalm xci. of victory over all antagonists—pestilence, terror, flying arrow, destruction. " Thou shalt tread upon the lion," on " the adder." Power to conquer sins known and hidden. 3. An echo of Luke x. 19. All these are gathered into the promise of the text. Christ's heel being on the head, we have only to keep down a little fragment of the writhing body, a little bit of vertebræ. If we try in His strength, we shall come off more than conquerors.

II. What strenuous effort is needed to keep down a snake's head, a desperate life-and-death struggle ! Incongruous epithet at first sight, " the God of *peace.*" Why not " God of *strength* " ? Our victory only possible by possessing the peace of God. The reason we fall so easily is because we lack that sense of rest in God. That peace of God, and the God who gives that peace, will help us to overcome.

III. "The peace of God " (see Phil. iv. 7) will keep us as a garrison keeps a fortress. The Christian's armour the gospel of peace (Eph. vi. 15).

IV. Ask God for His peace ; then in the fiercest struggle we shall have quiet hearts,—peace amid endless agitation ; repose in tempest ; quiet spirit in the battle.

V. All will come by communion with Christ ; His conquest our inspiration. " Shortly ? " Yes ; by simple obedience and loving fellowship swift victory comes. If not, not His fault, but ours. On eternity's dial seventy years but a moment. The longest life-struggle but a little while ; then the far-exceeding weight of glory. Thy Master conquered ; keep near Him, scorning short-lived temptations, calm in such brief struggles ; then " under our feet for ever the enemies of our souls."—*Alexander Maclaren, D.D.*

SUGGESTIVE COMMENTS ON VERSE 20.

Conquest of Satan ensured.—The conquest of Satan is ensured by this : When we are at peace with God, the devils themselves are subject to us. When God was in Christ reconciling the world, He was in Christ " destroying him that had the power of death " (Heb. ii. 14), and bringing Satan under the feet of the Mediator and the feet of His members. This was the intent of God in the first promise of a Mediator, to destroy him who had infected mankind and brought death into the world. The bruising his head was the design of Christ's mission (Gen. iii. 15), that the great incendiary who had broken the league and set afoot the rebellion might feel the greater smart of it. And ever since it is by the gospel of peace and the shield of faith that we are only able to " quench the fiery darts of the devil," and make his attempts fruitless (Eph. vi. 15, 16), by the reconciliation God hath wrought and published by the gospel. God, as a " God of peace," " shall tread him under the feet " of believers (Rom. xvi. 20). Unless He had been a God of peace, we had never been delivered from that jailor who held us by the right of God's justice. And since we are delivered, God, as a God of peace, will perfect the victory, and make him cease for ever from bruising the heel of the spiritual seed. As God hath given peace in Christ, so He will give the victory in Christ. Peace cannot be perfect till it be undisturbed by invading enemies and subtle adversaries endeavouring to raise a new enmity. Our Saviour spoiled him of his power upon the cross, and took away the right he had to detain any believer prisoner by satisfying that justice and reconciling that God who first ordered their commitment. He answers his accusations as He is an "advocate" at the right hand of God; and at the last, when death comes to be destroyed, and no more to enter into the world, the whole design of the devil for ever falls to the ground. Since we are at peace with God, while we are here the devil himself shall serve us; and the messenger of Satan shall be a means to quell the pride of a believing Paul by the sufficiency of the grace of God, while he fills the heart of an unbelieving Judas with poison and treason against his Master. —*Charnock.*

Satan not to be feared.—And as good angels shall not, so it is certain likewise that evil angels shall not; good angels will not, and bad angels shall not. Saith He, "I will build My Church upon this rock"—that is, "this faith and confession that Christ is the Son of God, and a heart and life answerable"— "and the gates of hell shall not prevail against it" (Matt. xvi. 18). They may assault it, but they shall not prevail. My brethren, this devil whom you fear, and who tempteth you, as Jesus Christ hath under His feet, so He will have him under your feet too one day; do but stay awhile, He shall tread down Satan under your feet shortly (Rom. xvi. 20) You need fear nothing, therefore, either in heaven or in earth. —*Goodwin.*

The Reconciler the Subduer.—All corrupters of divine truth and troublers of the Church's peace are no better than devils. Our Saviour thought the name Satan a title merited by Peter, when he breathed out an advice, as an axe at the root of the gospel, the death of Christ, the foundation of all gospel truth; and the apostle concludes them under the same character which hinder the superstructure, and would mix their chaff with his wheat. "Get thee behind Me, Satan" (Matt. xvi. 23). It is not, "Get thee behind Me, Simon," or, "Get thee behind Me, Peter"; but, "Get thee behind Me, Satan : thou art an offence to Me." Thou dost oppose thyself to the wisdom and grace and authority of God, to the redemption of man, and to the good of the world. 1. As the Holy Ghost is the Spirit of truth, so is Satan the spirit of falsehood; as the Holy Ghost inspires believers with truth, so doth the devil corrupt unbelievers with error. Let us cleave to the truth of the gospel, that we may not be counted by God as part of the corporation of fallen angels, and not be barely reckoned as enemies of God, but in league with the greatest enemy to His glory in the world. 2. The Reconciler of the world will be the Subduer of Satan. The God of peace sent the Prince of peace to be the restorer of His rights, and the hammer to beat in pieces the usurper of them. As a God of truth, He will make good His promise; as a God of peace, He will perfect the design His wisdom hath laid and begun to act. In the subduing Satan, He will be the conqueror of His instruments. He saith not, God shall bruise your troublers and heretics, but Satan. The fall of a general proves the rout of the army. Since God, as a God of peace, hath delivered His own, He will perfect the victory, and make them cease from bruising the heel of His spiritual seed. 3. Divine evangelical truth shall be victorious. No weapon formed against it shall prosper; the head of the wicked shall fall as low as the feet of the godly.

The devil never yet blustered in the world but he met at last with a disappointment. His fall hath been like lightning, sudden, certain, vanishing. 4. Faith must look back as far as the foundation-promise, "The God of peace shall bruise," etc. The apostle seems to allude to the first promise—a promise that hath vigour to nourish the Church in all ages of the world. It is the standing cordial; out of the womb of this promise all the rest have taken their birth. The promises of the Old Testament were designed for those under the New, and full performance of them is to be expected, and will be enjoyed by them. It is a mighty strengthening to faith to trace the footsteps of God's truth and wisdom from the threatening against the serpent in Eden to the bruise he received on Calvary and the triumph over him upon Mount Olivet. 5. We are to confide in the promise of God, but leave the season of its accomplishment to His wisdom. He will bruise Satan under your feet, therefore do not doubt it; and shortly, therefore wait for it. Shortly it will be done, that is, quickly, when you think it may be a great way off; or shortly, that is, seasonably, when Satan's rage is hottest. God is the best judge of the seasons of distributing His own mercies, and darting out His own glory. It is enough to encourage our waiting, that it will be, and that it will be shortly; but we must not measure God's *shortly* by our minutes. —*Charnock.*

MAIN HOMILETICS OF THE PARAGRAPH.—*Verses* 21—24.

St. Paul's honesty.—Ver. 20 concludes with a benediction, and ver. 24 repeats the same benediction. This is not according to the usual style of this epistle; therefore, apart from manuscript evidence, we may conclude that ver. 24 is spurious. If not, the repetition shows the intensity of St. Paul's affection and his high estimate of the need of the grace of our Lord Jesus Christ. We should recognise the need of divine grace. Theophylact says as he began so he ends with prayer. Let all our works be begun, continued, and ended in prayer, that thus we may glorify God's holy name, and finally by His mercy obtain everlasting life.

I. **St. Paul's honesty.**—Some people's conception of honesty is simply that of rendering legal dues. The man who is honest under compulsion is not honest. Opportunity makes the thief; and the man who does not steal simply because there is not an opportunity, or because he is afraid of consequent disclosures, is not honest. There are many so-called Christians whose conception of honesty is erroneous, at least the conception judged by the practice. What shall we make of the honesty of him who arrogates to himself all the glory of some religious or philanthropic enterprise, and has no meed of praise for his "workfellow"? "Timotheus my workfellow" would by many be passed over in silence. "Timotheus my workfellow!" Quite true; but what could he have done without Paul? I have the pluck and the genius! Timotheus—well, a good sort of fellow enough in his way. Sufficient honour to him that he worked under my leadership. St. Paul's honesty is to give honour to whom honour is due, to bestow praise where it is due with unsparing hand. He is honest in his fair dealing with the amanuensis. Tertius, who wrote this epistle, is allowed an honourable place. Tertius could not expect much from his writings. It was not a lucrative profession in those days. In fact, theological literature seldom pays even in these Christian times. St. Paul, who dictated the finest epistle of time, and Tertius who wrote, did not receive any emolument: their reward is on high; their treasure is in the heavens. Noble Paul! Worthy Tertius! Better to have written the Epistle to the Romans than the best-paying production of modern literature. Neither St. Paul nor Tertius would have been able to form a successful literary syndicate. They had too many brains to trade on the brains of others. Their moral purpose was too high to let them be mere intellectual sweaters. Neither Paul nor Tertius found a literary Mæcenas. The strains of Virgil and of Horace secured the recovery of lands and a fruitful farm in the Sabine country. The strains of St. Paul secured martyrdom. If Tertius had lived in the Augustine age of Roman literature, he would not have been welcomed at the Roman court. What matters it if Augustus despise, if Mæcenas ignore, if Nero persecute, if moderns scorn, so long as conscience approves. The age is benefited, and the plaudit of heaven is secured.

II. **St. Paul's acknowledgment of hospitality.**—" Gaius mine host, and of the whole Church, saluteth you." St. Paul did not think that his moral life and courteous demeanour were a sufficient compensation for the hospitality of Gaius. It is amusing how much some people take for granted. They appear to think that the world is made for them, and cannot do too much for their selfish individualism. " Gaius mine host." When they were to depart, Gaius made them (the Christian pilgrims) a feast, and they did eat and drink and were merry. Now the hour was come that they must be gone, wherefore Mr. Greatheart called for a reckoning; but Gaius told him that at his house it was not the custom for pilgrims to pay for their entertainment. He boarded them by the year, but looked for his pay from the good Samaritan, who had promised him at his return whatsoever charge he was at with them faithfully to repay him. Then said Mr. Greatheart to him : " Beloved, thou dost faithfully whatsoever thou dost to the brethren and to strangers, which have borne witness of thy charity before the Church, whom if thou yet bring forward on their journey after a godly sort, thou shalt do well." The Greatheart of St. Paul was gladdened by the hospitality of " Gaius mine host," and he has been amply repaid by the good Samaritan.

III. **St. Paul's estimate of officialism.**—Adulation is not Paul's characteristic. He is not seen running after and bowing down to the city chamberlain. The gold chains and the purple garments of a state official do not exert an irresistible influence over St. Paul's nature. Imagine St. Paul preparing a great sermon to be delivered before the mayor and corporation of Corinth ! St. Paul respectfully acknowledges Erastus as the chamberlain of the city, but he uses no flattering adjectival epithets. Erastus the chamberlain stands on the same plane as Quartus, a brother. Erastus the chamberlain does not stand so high as " the beloved Persis, which laboured much in the Lord." Erastus the chamberlain perhaps laboured much in the state, and was made a state dignitary. The Guildhall was open for his reception. But St. Paul does not enlarge on the great honour conferred on the new Christian religion by the adherence of Erastus the chamberlain. It is not Erastus who confers honour on Christianity, but Christianity confers honour on Erastus. The honour that cometh from God is the highest and only enduring. Let us seek to labour much in the Lord.

> " Work on, work on, nor doubt, nor fear,
> From age to age this voice shall cheer :
> Whate'er may die or be forgot,
> Work done for God it dieth not."

Ver. 22. *Tertius, the amanuensis.*—" One Paul, a travelling preacher, has written a treatise which will never perish " : such an assertion made in Corinth in the year 58 of our era would have provoked incredulous laughter. Even the apostle himself would have smiled at the suggestion that countless ordinary folk and many scholars in distant ages would study his writings. Although Phœbe, who carried the letter, regarded it as sacred, she knew not that she ministered to the nineteenth century. The Christian faith is enveloped in miracle. Our holy books have had fortunes almost as extraordinary as their contents, for though they were composed to meet some need that was then pressing, their interest is perennial, and they have been copied word by word and letter by letter by innumerable scribes who passed them on and on until they came into our hands. This " passing on " is characteristic of the true religion itself. And further, this gospel of universal importance—this onward marching thing—is always accompanied by illustrations of its beneficent might. There is a Tertius always at hand. Deliverance is proclaimed by freedmen : in truth the gospel is the unfolding of the experience of those who have welcomed Christ. Paul and Tertius write, and Phœbe carries, truths inscribed on the tablets of their hearts. The epistle was a life before it was a record. It is God's method to make converts by means of converts, and always to ensure that His messages concerning the Physician shall be conveyed by such as can give personal testimony to the Physician's kindliness and skill, for Christ's truth cannot be effectually disseminated apart from the presence of Christ's men. Is Tertius to be censured as intrusive for making mention of himself ? The appearance of the personal element is valuable, and sometimes it may even be conspicuous without offence to humility. As a witness, it is never impertinent. It is proper for Tertius, the scribe, to show himself, for he is an instance in point, and has something to say which is important to a right decision. He has a right to lift his head and say, " Amen ! "

I. The dwelling-place.—Tertius dwelt " in the Lord." A careless glance at a man catches only the sight of a material frame and physical relations, but looking with a little more attention you see a soul encompassed by sorrows, joys, doubts, convictions, and busied perhaps with the interests of family, church, nation. Ambitions, lusts, ideals, make many kinds of worlds. How diverse, and in some cases how small, the spheres in which men live! " Where dwellest thou ? " is a cardinal question ; where the treasure is there will the heart be also. Living in a luxurious and vicious city, it is quite likely that some six years before he sat writing at Paul's dictation Tertius may have known only the swine's world ; so that afterwards he understood very vividly those sentences read in the congregation to which he belonged—those sentences referring to revelry and devilry, which close with the congratulation, " But ye are washed, but ye are sanctified." There had been a resurrection unto Christ. I am " in the Lord." Although the statement has a mystic sound, there should be no complaint on that account, seeing that the true religion must include all noble elements, and must create conditions which need a novel dress as well as some that can be fitly clad in familiar raiment. We sit at Christ's feet, and yet we are more than pupils, for we are " in Him." He sends us on errands, and yet we " abide in Him." Yes, He drew us up into Himself—into His great life. Tertius has found refuge and home in Him who is eternal love. Individuality, instead of being absorbed and lost, becomes more definite and complicated as intellect, conscience, and heart are nourished by the Life indeed. To be in Christ is to begin to realise the significance of the union of the branches with the Vine. It is to be in safety and peace though in the world there may be tribulation. It is to be in fellowship with that compassion which cared for the poor, that wrath which scathed hypocrisy, that prayerfulness which was ever mindful of God, that truth and justice and love which once were condensed into the divine manful history which struck the true keynote for humanity's song. *Christ*—what a realm of redeeming and educating forces the capacious name suggests ! " It hath pleased the Father that in Him all fulness should dwell." Tertius, living in the vast world called Christ, dates his work from that abode. The poor man, who a short time since was a Corinthian heathen dwelling in some foul night on which God could look only with condemnation and painful pity, gives us this

563

description of his residence—"in the Lord." This honour have all the saints, for the phrase on which we dwell occurs scores of times elsewhere in connection with Christians widely apart so far as nationality, character, and knowledge were concerned. Tertius was admitted to some of Christ's aims and plans, and there ran through the convert's mind, feeling, and will a current of Christ's life.

II. **Reflect upon the service Tertius rendered.**—It might have been irksome to occupy hour after hour in putting down those separate strokes and curves, but the persons for whom we labour, and the objects to be secured, may charm drudgery into a delight. The mood is a magician. Common sounds were music on the day that love was reciprocated, and no cloud could hide the shining sun. We were fenced round from annoyances and saw good in everything. While intrinsically noble engagements are a weariness unless coloured by some affection, tasks otherwise dreary are invested with beauty when associated with persons that are dear. For Paul—beloved for his own sake and for the heaven which was opened by his gospel—it was pleasant to leave ordinary business and to write all day. In the great day there will be wonderful surprise to countless helpers of mankind who have never seen Jesus at the head of their philanthropic enterprises, and to kindly hearts that have never supposed Him to be in the hungry whom they have fed and the oppressed whom they have delivered. They will make a wondrous discovery as they hear Christ's generous commendations. Tertius writes "in the Lord," and aids an apostle to get his thoughts circulated throughout the world. The dependence of the great upon the small, how common that is, and how impressive! The artist asks the guidance of a rustic; poets, philosophers, statesmen, are indebted to lowly craftsmen for the publication of their fancies, speculations, and plans. The great admiral is rowed by a common sailor to the ship which is to lead the fleet to victory. The soul of Paul utilises the skill Tertius acquired in his pre-Christian days, a fact reminding us that the employment of common powers is almost or quite as necessary as the exercise of distinguished ability. How often it happens that men who could be public benefactors are chained by circumstances which men of a different order could easily break if they possessed public spirit! What a glorification of lower powers and persons is here exhibited! Penmanship is caught up into the service of Paul's Spirit-instructed mind: what honour for the simple acquirement! We wonder at the dignity conferred on the brain substances when they are used as the instruments of a soul that shapes far-reaching plans, and is alive with human and divine love; spirit admitting matter to partnership endows it with new virtues, gives it wider influence, and dyes the temporal thing with eternal colours; similarly a holy cause sanctifies and lifts into nobler realms of power men and talents that without it would be of poor account. Tertius becomes a clerk in God's office, and writes despatches from the heaven in which he dwells. "Did the amanuensis get any blessing in the task he performed?" is not an inquiry which will be made by you who have found God's truths to open up their preciousness to your own hearts whilst you have striven to make them known. Though he made no bargain, doubtless Tertius was blessed in his deed, for he heard the music that he played for the ears of strangers. Tertius was scarcely the same man after climbing the mountains of truth with Paul. To see those thoughts taking shape was like being present at the creation of a planet. We linger a little longer to note the *love of Tertius for men far away.* "I, Tertius, greet you." The love of God is mingled with the love of man, and God's Bible truths come rich with human sympathies. The Lord's servants are neither machines nor postmen, seeing that they bring in friendliness a divinely friendly gospel; nor can the message of the living God of love be uttered by unloving lips. Tertius puts the thread of his own love into the cord that binds man to God and man to man. We greet the children of God far away—our kin who should know our Saviour, shelter beneath His cross, and receive the gifts of the Holy Ghost. They belong to us. If they are saints, we greet them as fellow-heirs of the grace of Christ; if they are ignorant, cruel, deceived, hopeless, befouled, we greet them still, and entreat them to receive redemptive advantages. We are their debtors, and owe to them the glad tidings. If God wills to communicate with them, we will write the letter and inscribe therein the testimony of our own good-will, assured that the Father will not erase the greeting. The things of least intrinsic worth involve few incentives to brotherly beneficence, whereas those of highest value invoke all generous sympathies. God's noblest benefactions are never dumb, nor can they be selfishly entertained, for they refuse to stay with any recipient who will not ask for company in listening to their strains. If we would keep the sounds from passing to other ears, the music ceases.—*W. J. Henderson.*

Vers. 20-24. *A fortifying and enduring force.*—As we read St. Paul's not infrequent form of benediction, " The grace of our Lord Jesus Christ be with you all," we have about it a feeling of reality. If some men were to use the form, we should feel that it was inappropriate, because it did not seem to harmonise with their nature. We cannot use such expressions gracefully and fittingly, because we have not a deep, true feeling of religion. What is the religion of most but a mere surface affair? Is there any depth about it? In any practical sense does it appear to us to be the real good for life? Do we feel that to have the good-will of Christ towards us is better than to have the good-will of the great and noble of this world? How much trouble we take to obtain the good-will of those who occupy influential positions; and yet how languid is our zeal, how scanty our efforts, when the good-will of Jesus Christ is concerned?

I. **The good-will of Christ is a fortifying force.**—Surely not without good reason does St. Paul pray for the favour of Christ to be with His people at the close of his reference to the great adversary Satan, and in connection with his warning against those who wrongfully cause divisions. The grace of Christ only can successfully strengthen. Those in whom the grace of Christ effectually dwells, those who inhabit this strong tower of divine grace, are blessedly safe. Satan may hurl his missiles against the tower, but they only rebound. False teachers may try their delusive words, but gracious souls cling to the true doctrine. They are wise and strong unto that which is good, but simple, innocent, and pure concerning evil. If we would be strong, it must be in and by the grace of Jesus Christ our Lord.

II. **The grace of Christ is a uniting force.**—It is by the love and favour of Christ that we are united to Christ; and it is as we are united to Christ that we are united to one another. All the branches united to the vine constitute one plant. They are one with the vine and with one another. And so the members of Christ are members of one another. Salutations are abundantly scattered through this closing chapter. The love and favour of Paul run through every verse; but he seems to feel that this is not sufficient, and says all must be united by the grace of Christ. Shall we be surprised at the appearance of these forms so close together? Shall we say there is some error? Shall we not rather say that St. Paul strongly felt the necessity of Christ's favour? And if we are to be firmly and sweetly united, it must be by the binding power of the favour of our Lord Jesus Christ.

III. **The favour of Christ is an exalting force.**—Sometimes we seek the favour of great men, that by their influence we may be raised, in our turn, to positions of honour and influence. We play the toady, and our acting meets with neither applause nor emolument. We are something like those poor actors that are hissed from the stage ; and the sadness of it is that the hissing comes from our own disappointed hearts.   Christ's favour is life ; and life in this sense means, not mere existence, but plenitude of existence, fulness of blessing, exaltation in the largest sense.   Oh, what vastness of significance in the prayer, "The grace of our Lord Jesus Christ be with you all" !

IV. **The favour of Christ is an enduring quality.**—Does St. Paul repeat the prayer because he is afraid that the grace may be withdrawn ?   By no means. .   "Christ is the same yesterday and to day and for ever."   His grace is continuous.   We may withdraw ourselves from its benign influence.   The sweet sun of the Saviour's grace is shining through the clouds we have formed by our unbelief, or our sins envelop us in dismal darkness.   Let us abide in the sunlight.   Let us answer apostolic prayers, our own prayers, by keeping our natures open to the reception of Christ's grace.   Oh to be in the grace of Jesus Christ !   Oh to feel the fortifying, uniting, exalting, and enduring qualities of our Saviour's condescending favour !

MAIN HOMILETICS OF THE PARAGRAPH.—Verses 25—27.

" *The only wise God.*"—Plato calls God Mens.   Cleanthus used to call God Reason, and Socrates thought the title of Σοφός too magnificent to be attributed to anything else but God alone.   Wisdom is the property of God alone.   He is only wise.   It is an honour peculiar to Him.   Upon this account, that no man deserved the title of wise, but that it was a royalty belonging to God, Pythagoras would not be called Σοφός, a title given to their learned men, but Φιλόσοφος.   The name "philosopher" arose out of a respect to this transcendent perfection of God.   God is wise, but wisdom does not convey to the mind the complete conception of a God.   If wisdom be the choice of worthy ends and of the best means to accomplish them, then there must be the superadded notion of power.   Wisdom would be naked without power to act, while power would be useless without wisdom to guide.   Wisdom and power are the two essential attributes of the divine nature.   The apostle therefore rightly joins the two conceptions.   To Him that is of power—to the only wise God.

I. **God is the only wise originally.**—Human wisdom is not an original but an acquired endowment.   One man is born with more brain power than another, and yet wisdom is not a birth gift, but an after-development.   Many men with great brain power have great lack of wisdom.   Our ripest wisdom is the product of our richest experience, oftentimes the result of repeated failures.   Man is wise after the event.   Wisdom fails when looking into the future.   And yet man in his vanity presumes to arraign the wisdom of God.   The rays of the sun are not original, but derived ; and those rays upbraid the sun because he is not doing his appointed work more perfectly.   The common soldier has physical force and seldom mental power.   He could no more direct an army than the wisest general could manage the planetary system ; and yet that soldier is glib enough in saying how the general ought to have managed.   Foolish man can lay down laws and rules for the only wise God.   He is the spring of wisdom to all and in all.   The instinct of the cunning insect and the wisdom of a philosopher are derived from the wisdom of the All-wise.

II. **God is the only wise essentially.**—Wisdom is not an essential attribute of humanity.   It is an attribute too often conspicuous by its absence.   The vast majority of men possess neither knowledge nor wisdom.   Knowledge has increased in the earth, but there has not been a corresponding increase of wisdom.   Some men appear to be so weighed down and oppressed by their knowledge that there is not space and atmosphere for the growth and exercise of wisdom.   Our knowledge is the slow accumulation of years of toil, and in the process wisdom is not being evolved. God does not waste the bloom and freshness of His everlasting years in seeking to know. The divine knowledge is intuitive. There are to the divine mind no arcana. The mysteries hidden in the divine breast are not mysteries to the divine nature. He would not be a perfect God if He were not complete in knowledge, in wisdom to make the right use of knowledge, and in power to carry out the behests of wisdom.

III. **God is the only wise unchangeably.**—Change is the striking characteristic of humanity. While many men are seldom wise, no man is wise at all hours. We only wish we were. Memory is a sad book to read, as it relates the story of our many follies. The backward look of life is depressing, for the pathway is strewn with the ruins caused by our lack of wisdom. Our wisdom has been wanting when most needful, and our wise purposes have been broken off because of the lack of power. There can be no depressing backward looks to the divine mind. Wisdom never fails. The Lord possessed wisdom in the beginning of His way to the human aspect, before His works of old. Divine wisdom was set up from everlasting, from the beginning or ever the earth was. And God can never say, My purposes have been broken off for lack of power.

IV. **God is the only wise effectually.**—Abortive plans and purposes strew our pathway. Our Babel towers end in confusion. Our strutting monarchs grovel with the beasts. Broken hearts are too oft the result of our unattainable ideals. Where is the complete life that has seen sublime visions and has had power to work out the dreams effectually and successfully? God would not be omnipotent were He capable of forming a purpose and yet incapable of bringing that purpose to a successful issue. His wisdom in the conception of a planet where there should be variety, beauty, the fitness of every creature for its use, the subordination of one creature to another, and the joint concurrence of all to one common end, has been successfully worked out. A ruined planet is a magnificent testimony to the effectual wisdom of God. The splendour of the ruins speaks of the splendour of the primitive structure. God's wisdom and power are not at fault because the earth temple has been despoiled and left in a state of disrepair. The proper time was not come; the planet will not always wander through space disconsolately. God's wisdom and power will touch even material things into glorious order, beauty, and harmony. God's wisdom in the conception of a kingdom where all should be peace, joy, and righteousness has been so far successfully worked out—*so far*; for the conception has not been fully evolved. God's wisdom in the conception of a redemptive scheme whereby nations should be made obedient to the faith has been effectual. Christianity has the highest moral standard; and Christians have walked on the highest moral plane. The Christian Church, notwithstanding its many drawbacks, in spite of all its adversaries may assert, is a noble testimony for the wisdom of God.

V. **God is the only wise progressively.**—His wise plans and purposes are unfolding and evidencing more of their beauty and harmony as the ages advance. The moral light which dawned on the darkened Eden has been shining more and more through all time's dispensations; and onward the orb of light will move and unfold its radiance until the perfect day of complete divine disclosures. The gospel arcanum was published in paradise, but in such words as Adam did not fully understand; it was both discovered and clouded in the smoke of the sacrifices; it was wrapped up in a veil under the law, but not opened till the death of the Redeemer; it was then plainly said to the cities of Judah: Behold, your God comes. The revelation of the mystery is advancing; clearer light shines on the upper pathway; the completed revelation will redound to the glory of the divine wisdom.

VI. **God is the only wise gloriously.**—"To God the only wise be glory through

Jesus Christ for ever." Day unto day uttereth speech of the divine glory. Dispensation after dispensation brilliantly proclaims the divine wisdom. "Glory to God in the highest" was the strain sung at the Saviour's advent. "Glory to God in the highest" will be the strain sung in fuller measure when Jesus shall see of the full travail of His soul, and is satisfied—when all the redemptive plan of the divine wisdom is revealed in full-orbed splendour. The strains how full and sweet—full as the sound of many waters, sweet as the notes sent forth by the skilful harpers harping on well-tuned instruments—when the universal Church shall surround the throne of the eternal Wisdom—when all the angels stand round about the throne, and exhort the elders and the four beasts, and shall fall as one united throng before the throne on their faces, and shall worship God, saying : "Blessing, and glory, and wisdom, and thanksgiving, and honour, and power, and might be unto our God for ever and ever. Amen."

SUGGESTIVE COMMENTS ON VERSE 27.

Creatures without a known end demonstrate God's wisdom.—The creatures working for an end, without their own knowledge, demonstrate the wisdom of God that guides them. All things in the world work for some end; the ends are unknown to them, though many of their ends are visible to us. As there was some prime Cause which by His power inspired them with their several instincts, so there must be some supreme wisdom which moves and guides them to their end. As their being manifests His power that endowed them, so the acting, according to the rules of their nature, which they themselves understand not, manifests His wisdom in directing them; everything that acts for an end must know that end, or be directed by another to attain that end. The arrow doth not know who shoots it, or to what end it is shot, or what mark is aimed at; but the archer that puts it in and darts it out of the bow knows. A watch hath a regular motion, but neither the spring nor the wheels that move know the end of their motion; no man will judge a wisdom to be in the watch, but in the artificer that disposed the wheels and spring by a joint combination to produce such a motion for such an end. Doth either the sun that enlivens the earth, or the earth that travails with the plant, know what plant it produceth in such a soil, what temper it should be of, what fruit it should bear, and of what colour? What plant

knows its own medicinal qualities, its own beautiful flowers, and for what use they are ordained? When it strikes up its head from the earth doth it know what proportion of them there will be? Yet it produceth all these things in a state of ignorance. The sun warms the earth, concocts the humours, excites the virtue of it, and cherishes the seeds which are cast into her lap, yet all unknown to the sun or the earth. Since therefore that nature, that is the immediate cause of those things, doth not understand its own quality nor operation, nor the end of its action, that which thus directs them must be conceived to have an infinite wisdom. When things act by a rule they know not, and move for an end they understand not, and yet work harmoniously together for one end that all of them, we are sure, are ignorant of, it mounts up our minds to acknowledge the wisdom of that supreme Cause that hath ranged all these inferior causes in their order, and imprinted upon them the laws of their motions, according to the idea in His own mind, who orders the rule by which they act, and the end for which they act, and directs every motion according to their several natures, and therefore is possessed with infinite wisdom in His own nature. God is the fountain of all wisdom in the creatures, and therefore is infinitely wise Himself. As He hath a fulness of being in Himself, because the streams of being are derived to other things from Him, so He hath a fulness of wisdom, because He is the spring of wisdom to angels and men. That Being must be infinitely wise whence all other wisdom derives its original, for nothing can be in the effect which is not eminently in the cause; the cause is always more perfect than the effect. If, therefore, the creatures are wise, the Creator must be much more wise; if the Creator were destitute of wisdom, the creature would be much more perfect than the Creator. If you consider the wisdom of the spider in her web, which is both her house and net; the artifice of the bee in her comb, which is both her chamber and her granary; the provision of the pismire in her repositories for corn,—the wisdom of the Creator is illustrated by them: whatsoever excellency you see in any creature is an image of some excellency in God. The skill of the artificer is visible in the fruits of his art; a workman transcribes his spirit in the work of his hands; but the wisdom of rational creatures, as men, doth more illustrate it. All arts among men are the rays of divine wisdom shining upon them, and by a common gift of the Spirit enlightening their minds to curious inventions, as Prov. viii. 12, "I, Wisdom, find out the knowledge of witty inventions"— that is, I give a faculty to men to find them out; without my wisdom all would be buried in darkness and ignorance. Whatsoever wisdom there is in the world, it is but a shadow of the wisdom of God, a small rivulet derived from Him, a spark leaping out from uncreated wisdom: "He created the smith that bloweth the coals in the fire, and makes the instruments" (Isa. liv. 16). The skill to use those weapons in warlike enterprises is from Him: "I have created the waster to destroy." It is not meant of creating their persons, but communicating to them their art; He speaks it there to expel fear from the Church of all warlike preparations against them. He had given men the skill to form and use weapons, and could as well strip them of it and defeat their purposes. The art of husbandry is a fruit of divine teaching (Isa. xxviii. 24, 25). If those lower kinds of knowledge that are common to all nations and easily learned by all are discoveries of divine wisdom, much more the nobler sciences intellectual and political wisdom: "He gives wisdom to the wise, and knowledge to them that know understanding" (Dan. ii. 21); speaking of the more abstruse parts of knowledge, "The inspiration of the Almighty gives understanding" (Job xxxii. 8). Every man's soul is endowed more or less with those noble qualities. The soul of every man exceeds that of a brute; if the streams be so excellent, the fountain must be fuller and clearer. The first Spirit must infinitely more possess what other spirits derive from Him by creation; were the wisdom of all the angels in heaven and men on earth collected in one spirit, it must be infinitely less than that what is in the spring, for no creature can be equal to the Creator. As the highest creature already made, or that we can conceive may be made, by infinite power would be infinitely below God in the notion of a creature, so it would be infinitely below God in the notion of wise.— *Charnock.*

God's works represent Him.—As a beam of light passing through a chink in a wall, of what figure soever, always forms a circle on the place where it is reflected, and by that describes the image of its original, the sun, thus God in every one of His works represents Himself. But the union of all the parts by such strong and secret bands is a more pregnant proof of His omnipotent mind. Is it a testimony of great military skill to range an army, composed of divers nations that have great antipathies between them, in that order which renders it victorious in battle? And is it not a testimony of infinite providence to dispose all the hosts of heaven and earth so as they join successfully for the preservation of nature? . . . Sophocles was accused by his ungrateful sons, that his understanding being declined with his age, he was unfit to manage the affairs of his family; he made no other defence before the judges, but recited part of a tragedy newly composed by him, and left it to their decision whether there was a failure in his intellectual faculties, upon which he was not only absolved, but crowned with praises.—*Bates.*

Excellence of this epistle.—Ancient and divine are the gospel tidings of our salvation. Delightfully they harmonise with the types and predictions of the Old Testament. And their offers and blessings graciously extend to all nations of mankind, and by the Holy Ghost are made effectual to some of all ranks and degrees. With what faith and love ought they, then, to be received, submitted to, obeyed, and practised. And infinite is the glory that redounds to God, from this His wonderful work of our salvation.—*John Brown of Haddington.*

Thus endeth the apostle Paul's Epistle to the Romans; a writing which, for brevity and strength of expression, for regularity in its structure, but, above all, for the unspeakable importance of the discoveries which it contains, stands unrivalled by

any mere human composition; and as far exceeds the most celebrated productions of the learned Greeks and Romans, as the shining of the sun exceedeth the twinkling of the stars.—*Macknight.*

It is related of Melancthon, by his contemporary Mylius, that he was constantly engaged in explaining the Epistle to the Romans, which he was accustomed to regard as the key to the whole Scriptures. And that he might more thoroughly understand its doctrines, and more fully investigate its scope and signification, he expounded this epistle, both orally and in writing, more frequently than any other part of the New Testament. It is said, also, that in his youth he often wrote out this epistle, as Demosthenes wrote out Thucydides.—*Professor Tholuck.*

Like a wall of adamant, St. Paul's writings form a bulwark around all the Churches of the world; while he himself, as some mighty champion, stands even now in the midst, casting down every high thing that exalteth itself against the knowledge of God, and bringing into captivity every thought to the obedience of Christ.—*Chrysostom.*

ILLUSTRATIONS TO CHAPTER XVI.

Ver. 2. *A succourer of many.*—A Christian lady of ample means, large culture, fine intelligence, and, better than all, of noble heart, was watching at the bedside of her only child, who lay a-dying. What promise of future greatness lay in the well-shaped brain! What sweet castles had the loving mother built as she trained and watched her darling; and now the goodly castle was fast falling before her eyes. The bedroom was spacious and well furnished, but she had only eyes for the one treasure about to be removed. The morning sun was sweetly shining through the window, as if regardless of the mother's sorrow—or should we rather say as if desirous of scattering the gathering gloom?—but she scarcely noticed as she prayed, "O God, spare my darling child!" But, unlike too many, she prayed in submission to the divine will; and that will

was that the beautiful boy shall be taken to reach a higher manhood in the vast hereafter. With bleeding heart she followed the child to his last earthly resting-place. He was another link in the chain lifting her up to the better world, but he was also the means of enlarging her nature. She lost her child, and yet the loss was to her and to those about her a gain. She lived for others more than she had ever done before. Her ears and her heart were open to the tale of sorrow. Every home where sorrow entered was visited by her who was quickened by sorrow into the large exercises of benevolence. She was lovingly active; she was wisely benevolent; and on her tomb was this epitaph placed by the survivors:—

ERECTED TO THE MEMORY OF ONE WHO LIKE PHŒBE, WAS A SUCCOURER OF MANY.

Ver. 2. *Mutual help.*—The cobbler could not paint the picture, but he could tell Apelles that the shoe-latchet was not quite right; and the painter thought it well to take his hint. Two neighbours, one blind and the other lame, were called to a place at a great distance. What was to be done? The blind man could not see, and the lame man could not walk. Why, the blind man carried the lame one: this former assisted by his legs, the other by his eyes. Say to no one then, "I can do without you," but be ready to help those who ask your aid; and then, when it is needed, you may ask theirs.—*Smith.*

Ver. 3. *Work with God.*—Dr. Philip, in a missionary speech, alluded to a remark made by Mr. Newton: "'When I get to heaven, I shall see three wonders there. The first wonder will be to see many people there whom I did not expect to see; the second wonder will be to miss many people whom I did expect to see; and the third and greatest wonder of all will be to find myself there.' I have also found three wonders. I have seen men of great wealth and of great talent, who have had many opportunities of forwarding the cause of God, do nothing; I have seen many humble and despised individuals, but whose hearts were right with God, do wonders; but the greatest wonder of all is to find that so humble an individual as I am should have been at all useful in the work. I take nothing unto myself but shame and humility before God."

Ver. 3. *"My helpers in Christ Jesus."*—

Lord, speak to me, that I may speak
In living echoes of Thy tone;
As Thou sought, so let me seek
Thy erring children lost and lone.

O lead me, Lord, that I may lead
The wandering and the wavering feet;
O feed me, Lord, that I may feed
Thy hungering ones with manna sweet.

O strengthen me, that while I stand
Firm on the rock and strong in Thee,
I may stretch out a loving hand
To wrestlers with the troubled sea.

O teach me, Lord, that I may teach
The precious things Thou dost impart;
And wing my words, that they may reach
The hidden depths of many a heart.

O give Thine own sweet rest to me,
That I may speak with soothing power
A word in season, as from Thee,
To weary ones in needful hour.

O fill me with Thy fulness, Lord,
Until my very heart o'erflow,
In kindling thought and flowing word,
Thy love to tell, Thy praise to show.

O use me, Lord, use even me,
Just as Thou wilt, and when, and where;
Until Thy blessed face I see,
Thy rest, Thy joy, Thy glory share.
                              F. R. Havergal.

Ver. 4. *Parable of the sealing-wax.*—"How fearfully hot it is!" cried a stick of sealing-wax. "It's positively exhausting. I can't stand much more of this"; and thereupon the poor thing began to bend and twist under the heat. But it grew hotter and hotter still, as a cruel hand kept it remorselessly in the flame of a candle. Then the wax began to melt, and portions dropped off on to a sheet of paper placed to catch them. And these were moulded into shape under pressure of a signet. "Really," said the sealing-wax, "I didn't know that I could look so splendid. Just see this crest!" Adversity tends to the development of character, and especially when it is a desire to help others in adversity. Priscilla and Aquila were placed in the fire of trouble through their friendship with Paul, and they received the divine crest—"Who have for my life laid down their necks."

Ver. 4. *Piety at Home.*—St. Paul, speaking of widows, says they should first learn to show piety at home. He means, probably, that before undertaking any wider sphere of work they should be sure that home duties were not neglected. So, too, when a devil had been cast out of a man by our Lord, and the man had asked to be allowed to accompany his deliverer, he was told to go home to his friends and tell what had been done for him—tell it chiefly by his altered conduct. Even the world understands that a man ought not to show his worst self to his friends at home. In a brilliant modern comedy one of the characters is pronounced a "jolly good fellow." "Did you ever see one of these jolly good fellows at home?" another asks. How much significance underlies that simple question. Does he first show unselfishness, obedience, reverence—in a word, piety—at home?—*Quiver, "Short Arrows."*

Ver. 5. *Justin Martyr's reply to the prefect.*—Justin Martyr gives us a little insight into the gatherings of the early Christians. "Where do you assemble?" said the prefect. Justin replied: "Wherever it suits each one by preference and ability. You take for granted that we all meet in the same place; but it is not so, for the God of the Christians is not circumscribed to place, but, being invisible, fills heaven and earth, and is everywhere worshipped and glorified by the faithful." Rusticus then said: "Tell me where you meet together, or in what place you collect your disciples." Justin said: "I am staying at the house of one Martinus, and I know no other place of meeting besides

571

this, and if any one wished to come to me, I communicated to him the words of truth."

Ver. 5. *A beautiful blessing.*—A little while before she died, Oliver Cromwell's mother gave the Protector her blessing in these words : "The Lord cause His face to shine upon you, and comfort you in all your adversities, and enable you to do great things for the glory of your Most High God, and to be a relief unto His people. My dear son, I leave my heart with thee. A good night !" Mothers with low ambition wish their sons to do great things for themselves, but this mother's ambition was that her son should act only with the object of glorifying God and serving man. She bade him "good night" when dying in this dark world, but in a brighter world she would wake up to bid him "good morning."—*Quiver, "Short Arrows."*

Ver. 5. *A mother's influence.*—A stranger was once introduced to the emperor Napoleon Buonaparte as the son of a distinguished father. "Nay," said the emperor, "do not tell me who was his father, but who was his mother." The same emperor said, "She who rocks the cradle rules the world"; and declared the great want of France to be "good mothers."—*Quiver, "Short Arrows."*

Ver. 5. *The dignity of motherhood.*—Soon after Napoleon's assumption of the imperial purple, he chanced to meet his mother in the gardens of St. Cloud. He was surrounded by courtiers, and half playfully held out his hand for her to kiss. "Not so, my son," she gravely replied, at the same time presenting her hand in return ; "it is your duty to kiss the hand of her who gave you life." Parents who keep up their dignity can influence their children much more for good when they grow up. It is quite possible to play with and be companions to them without losing their respect, but it can never be right to allow children to break the Fifth Commandment.—*Quiver, "Short Arrows."*

Ver. 8. *The tomb of Amplias.*—The archæological researches in Rome of recent years have thrown much light upon the life of the early Christians in that city; but no discovery has produced such interest as that announced of the tomb of Amplias. Says Paul in Rom. xvi. 8: "Greet Amplias, my beloved in the Lord." Who was Amplias? Who were his friends ? Why was he buried in this particular place ? The answers to these questions are all furnished by the discovery of his tomb ; and a flood of light is let in upon the times of the early Roman Christians. His tomb stands in one of the catacombs excavated in the time of Domitian, on the ground then belonging to Flavia Domitilla, his niece. Roman history preserves the fact that Flavia became a Christian. Amplias, the friend of Paul, must have been a distinguished man. Because he was buried in Flavia's cemetery we judge they were personally acquainted. By Paul's greeting we imagine he was a minister of the New World. Then the tomb is of such a character that only the possessor of great wealth could have constructed so remarkable a resting-place. Was this the work of Flavia, niece of the great Domitian ? Was it erected at the cost of his family, or by the early Christians of Rome ? These questions may not be answered, for the investigations are not yet concluded. All that we know at present is that there is no tomb in the catacombs that equals it for the beauty of its adornments and the variety of pictorial illustrations. The frescoes in the Golden House of Nero, and the adornments of the house of Germanicus in the Palatine, are not to be compared, so it is reported, with the symbolic illustrations of the tomb of Amplias, the teacher of Flavia, the beloved of Paul.—*Christian Commonwealth.*

Ver. 12. *Lord Shaftesbury's tribute to a humble woman.*—Very tender was Lord Shaftesbury's reference on one occasion to the kind heart which led him to Christ. He was for a time, at an early period of his life, left solely in charge of an old Scottish nurse. This humble woman took infinite pains to teach him the story of Christ's love, and with such success that the great earl confessed, "All that I am to-day, and all that I have done, I owe, under God, to that good woman's influence."

Vers. 17, 18. *Archbishop Tait on divisions.*—Speaking at the Swansea Church Congress, Archbishop Tait said : "It is now many years since, I remember, this happened to me : I was travelling a whole day in the mail in company, as it happened, with a great historian, politician, and literary man, well known in that day, and well remembered still, who had then but recently returned from a lengthened sojourn in India. We were talking of the divisions which at that time distracted the kingdom of Scotland in religious matters ; and he said, 'When a man has lived a long time in a country in which people worship cows, he comes to think less of the divisions which separate Christians.' I presume there was a great moral lesson in this random saying. I confess it made a great impression on my heart. I have never forgotten it, and it has been the endeavour of my life to profit by it. A godly bishop said to me once of a brother as godly as himself, but much given to controversy, 'Poor man, he is always writing about the three orders of the ministry, when those to whom he is writing are doubting whether there be a God in heaven.'"

INDEX.

HOMILIES FOR SPECIAL OCCASIONS.

7888

220.7
P9226
v.26

LINCOLN CHRISTIAN COLLEGE AND SEMINARY

3 4711 00163 8412